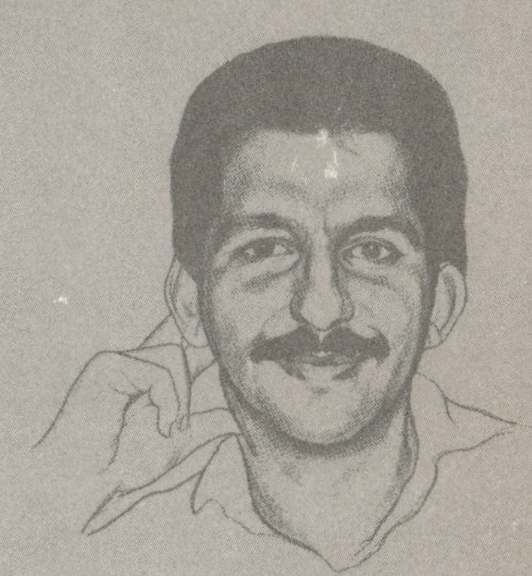

George Stavrinos
Illustrator
Page 358

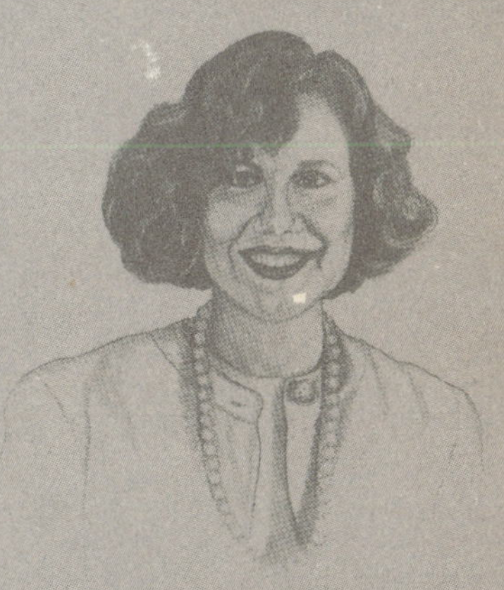

Margaret Volker-Ferrier
Fashion Illustrator
Page 272

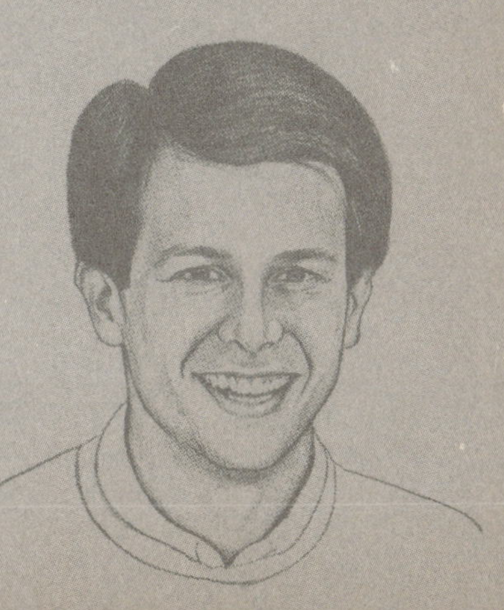

Chris Wilhoite
Art Director
Page 420

1987 Artist's Market

Acknowledgement

Each year Artist's Market *features portraits with the Close-up interviews. We were in the process of choosing an artist to do them when we received an illustration from one of our listings. One look at the sample, a pen-and-ink portrait, told us we had found our artist. In Lee Hammond, an illustrator and drawing instructor from Kansas, we found more than an artist; she proved to be a superwoman who could hurdle short deadlines and murky photographs. When a package from Lee arrived at our office, business would stop for a few minutes while everyone admired her lifelike portraits. Her artistry has immeasurably enhanced the book, and her spirit of cooperation has inspired us all.*

Distributed in Canada by Prentice-Hall of Canada Ltd., 1870 Birchmount Road, Scarborough, Ontario M1P 2J7.

Managing Editor, Market Books Department: Constance J. Achabal

International Standard Serial Number 0161-0546
International Standard Book Number 0-89879-246-0

1987
Artist's Market

Where & How to Publish
Your Graphic Art

**Edited by
Susan Conner**

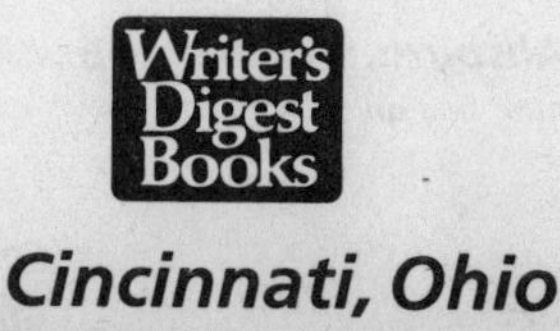

Cincinnati, Ohio

Contents

Appendix

The 1987 *Artist's Market* focuses on the artist as a salesman. An artist needs to realize that informed planning, selective marketing and sophisticated presentation are the tools of effective salesmanship—and effective salesmanship plays a crucial part in the success of an artist.

This thirteenth edition of the *Artist's Market* is your personal sales kit. It presents all the tools for selling your artwork—an instruction manual that lays the groundwork for your sales campaign, a list of markets for your wares, tips from experts and a compendium of resources for supplemental information. Whether you are a beginner or an established professional, your salesmanship will be enhanced by using the various components of this kit.

First, read the instructions. Naturally, you're anxious to present your portfolio to an art director and make a sale. However, an experienced salesman knows that his foot won't get past the proverbial door without an invitation. A successful salesman opens doors by establishing a promotional campaign to pave the way for his product presentation. By reading the upfront article, "The Art of Self-Promotion," you will possess the key to unlocking a potential goldmine of market opportunities.

That goldmine exists in the Markets section of this book. With over 2,500 markets listed, the *Artist's Market* offers more than just a directory of names and addresses. This is a sourcebook containing names of contact persons and their addresses, needs, requirements and 'inside' information. The goldmine has been enriched this year by over 630 new listings. All the new listings are marked with an asterisk (*) so you can locate them easily.

And many changes occur each year in existing freelance markets. We have updated previous market listings with 47 company name changes, 238 address/phone changes, 286 contact person changes, 271 listings whose art needs have changed and 223 changes in pay rates.

Keep up-to-date with general market trends by reading the section introductions. These are concise summaries of each market area providing helpful tips on art requirements. There you will also find the names of additional publications that provide thousands of names and addresses of art buyers (but no marketing information). These resources usually can be found in reference or business libraries; otherwise they can be purchased from the publisher or at a bookstore.

No sales kit is complete without advice from experts. Because their perceptions are so helpful, we feature an artist or an art buyer in each section of the book. Chris van Allsburg, Martin Pedersen and Jim Borgman are three of the 16 prominent artists and art directors who share their secrets and insights into the freelance world.

The last section of the book, "The Business of Freelancing," guides you through the intricacies of contracts, record keeping, mailing procedures and taxes. Turn to the Glossary for the definition of a term you may not know.

Your sales kit is complete. Now it's up to you to actualize all those dreams and countless hours of training. Equipped with creativity, enthusiam and persistence, plus the knowledge gained by reading *Artist's Market*, you will be able to reap the rewards of a successful freelance career.

—Susan Conner

Markets in this book are organized according to their professional category, such as book publishers or magazines. However, artists find that their talents apply to many categories. The following list will help you locate the markets that are seeking your specialty:

- Airbrush artists can find opportunities in advertising agencies and art/design studios as well as in magazines and book publishing.
- Animators and filmmakers should check the listings for audiovisual firms, businesses and associations.
- Audiovisual artists will find work in not only advertising and audiovisual firms but also in businesses, associations and institutions, art/design studios and record companies.
- Calligraphers should refer to advertising agencies, businesses, associations, greeting card companies, magazines, newspapers and syndicates.
- Cartoonists should look to advertising agencies, businesses, associations, greeting card companies, magazines, newspapers and syndicates.
- Chartists and map makers are needed by architectural firms, advertising agencies and art/design studios.
- Game designers are sought by businesses and greeting card firms.
- Interior designers and renderers can refer to the Architectural, Interior & Landscape Design Firms section.
- Mechanical or layout artists find opportunities in advertising agencies, architectural firms, businesses clothing manufacturers, associations and institutions, performing arts groups and record companies.
- Model makers are needed by architectural firms, art/design studios, businesses and collectibles manufacturers (listed under Businesses).
- Package designers are sought by advertising agencies, art/design studios, businesses and clothing manufacturers.
- Scientific or medical illustrators should check advertising agencies, associations and institutions, magazines and book publishers.

Fine art also has its markets.

- Posters are needed by greeting card companies, record companies, art publishers, art/design studios, collectibles manufacturers and associations.
- Paintings and prints are sought by art publishers, magazines, book publishers and interior design firms.
- Pen-and-ink renderings and watercolors are needed by greeting card companies, syndicates and clip art firms (pen-and-ink only), book publishers and art publishers.

How to read a market listing

The listings in this book are more than names and addresses. Listings include information on whom to contact, what type of work is needed, how artists are used and payment method and amount. Note the features illustrated by this sample listing:

(1)*JOVART STUDIOS, Box 2291, San Francisco CA 94126. (2)Art Director: Jorge Morales. (3) (4)Audiovisual firm. Clients: corporations.
Needs: (4)Works with 5 freelance artists/year. (6)Works on assignment only. Uses artists for design, illustration, brochures, catalog, mechanicals, logos and chart/graphs.

First Contact & Terms: (7)Send query letter with resume. (8)Samples not filed are returned by SASE. (9)Reports only if interested. (10)Write to schedule an appointment to show a portfolio, (11)which should include final reproduction/product. (12)Pays for design by the hour, $10 minimum. (13)Considers complexity of the project and client's budget when establishing payment. (14)Rights purchased vary according to project.

Tips: (15)"We cannot answer every query, but we use freelancers occasionally and resumes will be kept on file but not necessarily acknowledged."

(1)An asterisk (*) preceding a listing means it is new to this edition.

(2)Names of contact persons are given in most listings. If not, address your work to the art director or person most appropriate for that field.

(3)Dates indicating when the market was established are listed in this area of the listings only if they are 1984, 1985, 1986. This is to indicate the firm or publication is new and possibly more open to freelance artists. The risk is sometimes greater when dealing with new companies. So far as we know, all are reputable but some are unable to compete with larger, older companies. Many do survive, however, and become very successful.

(4)Editorial descriptions and client lists appear in listings to help you slant your work toward that specific business.

(5)The number or percentage of jobs assigned to freelance artists or the number of artists a market uses gives you an idea of the size of the market.

(6)Many firms work on assignment only. Do not expect them to buy the art you send as samples. When your style fills a current need, they will contact you.

(7)If a market instructs you to query, please query. Do not send samples unless that is what they want you to do.

(8)Many art directors keep samples on file for future reference. If you wish to have your samples returned, include a self-addressed, stamped envelope (SASE) in your mailing package. Be sure to include an International Reply Coupon (IRC) if you are mailing to a foreign market.

(9) Reporting times vary from market to market, and some—such as this listing—will only contact you if it is interested in your work.

(10)Markets want you to either mail portfolio materials or present them in person. Note whether to call or write for an appointment to show your portfolio.

(11)The type of samples you include in your portfolio reflect your understanding of the market; inappropriate samples signify a lack of market research. When an art director specifies, as this one does, that you should include final reproduction/product in your presentation, do so.

(12)Payment terms.

(13)Markets often negotiate payment terms. Therefore, they do not specify the amount of payment. Instead, they list the factors which they consider when establishing payment.

(14)Note what rights the market prefers to purchase. If several types of rights are listed, it usually means the firm will negotiate. But not always. Be certain you and the art buyer understand exactly what rights you are selling.

(15)Read the tips added to many of the listings. They give you handy personalized advice or a view of general market area information.

The Art of Self-Promotion

by Susan Conner

Salesmanship. To a marketing specialist, that's a nice word. It represents an ability to present a product's benefits in a convincing manner. An artist, however, often disdains the salesman, who seemingly represents what an artist doesn't want to become—a deceptive huckster. "Business is business; art is art; and never the twain shall meet," the artist snips.

The point that artists often miss is that salesmanship can also be a creative endeavor. A salesman must prove that his product provides additional, or at least the same, benefits as his competition's without the drawbacks. To do this, he analyzes what he has to offer, then adapts his basic selling approach to emphasize the product's benefits in the most effective way. Similarly, an artist organizes and manipulates the composition of his artwork so that his message gets across in a striking fashion. Both artist and salesman must plan, organize and present their material in a creative and unique way.

The ability to present yourself and your artwork effectively is more important now than ever because of the large number of freelance artists competing in the marketplace today. There are still ample opportunities for artists in every field, but the competition is keen. Each artist must employ his unique creative skills in promoting his art—in other words, being his own salesman. You must remember, being your own salesman does *not* entail a transformation into a fast-talking, slice-it/dice-it/anyway-you-like-it wheeler dealer. Effective salesmanship allows you to retain your artistic standards.

An expert in packaged goods marketing, Richard Payne suggests in his book, *Market Yourself for Success*, that freelancers should apply the same principles involved in packaging consumer products to promoting themselves in the marketplace. Pretend that you have been assigned the task of creating and executing a comprehensive program for a client, says Payne, a client who happens to bear the same name as you. Apply the same objectivity and creative zeal to your own promotional efforts that you would apply to a commissioned assignment. Payne emphasizes that a self-promotional campaign is not a mammoth undertaking. It involves setting up a realistic, practical plan for the coming year that is consistent with your long-range goals.

Setting the stage

Your promotional campaign rests on a foundation composed of certain building blocks. They are as follows: know yourself; know your market; and be a professional. Understanding these fundamentals is crucial to the preparation of your marketing plan. They are the "instructions" of your do-it-yourself kit. You're anxious to assemble the kit, but reading the directions makes the assembly so much easier.

Know yourself

A salesman must know his product's strengths and weaknesses before he can establish its position in the marketplace. It's best to take some time and examine what your artistic goals are. Is art a sideline for you? Perhaps a part-time effort is the thing for you. If art is your sole preoccupation, make it your sole occupation. If you wish to support yourself as a fulltime artist, will the persistent effort involved be draining or exhilarating? Is your best work done individually or as a team member? Do you have the discipline to work at home or would you rather work in a more structured environment? Are you a self starter? Then the ultimate question: Do you have the persistence and determination to pursue a long-range goal?

Once you have determined the perimeter of your career goals, your decisions concerning the extent of your self-promotional efforts will be easy.

Know your market

Take some time to explore your artistic aptitude. Don't be afraid to 'blue-sky' your talents by investigating different techniques and mediums. Discover what you enjoy doing the most; be comfortable with your work. As the *Art Marketing Handbook* of the North Light Art School states, "Your work is not going to appeal to all people. Each of us has individual preferences and tastes. You must strive to be at peace with your work, believe in what you're doing and feel a rightful pride about placing your talent before the public."

Once you have found your niche, strive to be the best you can be. Those who excel are usually the specialists, artists who have focused on a particular segment of a broad category, such as medical illustration or architectural delineation. By focusing on a specialty, it is easier to establish a distinctive reputation.

Once you've found your specialty, become thoroughly acquainted with the field. Read the trade magazines (most of which are available at your local library). Familiarize yourself with the business directories such as the *Standard Directory of Advertisers* or the *Magazine Industry Marketplace* because they are informational goldmines. They not only provide mailing lists but they give you an idea of the scope of your market. Comb the Yellow Pages for local contacts; establish communication with art directors in your area to get an idea of what the realities of the business are.

Consider joining a professional organization. National and local organizations provide contacts in the business, friends with similar goals, and updates on the latest business trends. They also sponsor competitions which can bolster your resume. Some of the major organizations are:

Art Directors, Club, Inc.
488 Madison Ave., New York NY 10022
American Institute of Architects
1735 New York Ave. NW, Washington DC 20006
Association of American Editorial Cartoonists
22 Mimosa Dr., Harrison AZ 72601
American Society of Landscape Architects
1733 Connecticut Ave. NW, Washington DC 20009
Center for Arts Information
625 Broadway, New York NY 10012
Graphic Artists Guild
30 East 20 St., New York NY 10003
Greeting Card Association
Suite 300, 600 Pennsylvania Ave. SE, Washington DC 20005
Society of Illustrators
28 E. 63rd St., New York NY 10021
Society of Typographic Arts
Suite 301, 233 E. Ontario, Chicago, IL 60611

A further list of agencies and organizations can be found in the *American Art Directory*.

Once you have established a certain niche in the arts, you will continually find new avenues to explore. In the beginning, it is often best to look in your own backyard for opportunities—the new public relations firm in town that needs a brochure or the music club that recently opened which needs a poster. Once you have established yourself on the local level, venture onwards to regional or state concerns, then national businesses.

Talent directories are good examples of successful promotion. Illustrators and designers advertise samples of their best work in these annual directories, buying one or two-page spreads. Some of the best-known are the *Creative Black Book*, *R.S.V.P.*, *American Showcase*, *Graphic Artists Guild Directory*, the *Art Directors' Index to Illustration*, the *Madison Avenue Handbook* and *Chicago Creative Directory*.

There should be a song for newcomers to the arts called "Breakin' In Is Hard to Do." It takes time to develop your confidence and your reputation. Jobs are likely to be low-paying at first. But with perserverance and application of your creative abilities, you will be able to succeed in the freelance market.

Be professional

Established freelance artists have learned that part of the success formula lies in being a business professional. Your freelancing venture will be successful only if you seriously apply yourself, and that means conducting yourself in a business-like way. Keep accurate records, meet appointments and return calls. Establish a filing system to keep your records in order. Project a courteous but forthright manner so that clients will accept you as a trustworthy business associate.

Always dress professionally. Forget about power clothes or optimal eye contact, but be aware that the way you dress does project a certain image. Clothes tailored in a classical style always convey a polished appearance. After all, you are one of the most important parts of your promotional package.

Your professional patina will be enhanced by secure finances. At the beginning of your freelance career, have a cash reserve or at least a part-time job to fill in the gaps between checks. Be sure to keep accurate records of transactions and agreements; many headaches will be averted when you file self-employed tax forms.

Your self-promotional package

Your artwork also needs professional styling. The manner in which your work is presented is the key to prospering as a commercial artist. You are in a visual industry, and you will be judged on your ability to set yourself apart from your competition with style and sophistication.

Assembling your self-promotional package is a creative sales problem. Apply the same artistic skills to your own presentation that you apply to someone else's product. Make your promotional campaign a creative challenge.

The contents of your promotional package can vary, but the basic components include a:

- cover letter
- résumé
- business card
- brochure or flyer
- samples
- portfolio

The main purpose of your promotional package is to provide a concise overview of your talents. That can be achieved by using only a few components if the cost of producing the entire package is prohibitive. Since you have set your goals and your budget for the near future, you will know how ambitious you can be with your package. No matter what the size, make it visually exciting. A small coordinated brochure and résumé present a much better image than a complete yet unimaginative package.

Establish a visual unity to your presentation. Each printed piece should be topped by your letterhead, which in a graphic way summarizes your specialty. Notice in the example how Barbara Gordon, noted artist representative, coordinates her mailing pieces through the use of a clever, and appropriate logo—the portfolio itself. Throughout the whole kit, remember to use the same paper stock, typeface and color scheme to unify the graphic presentation.

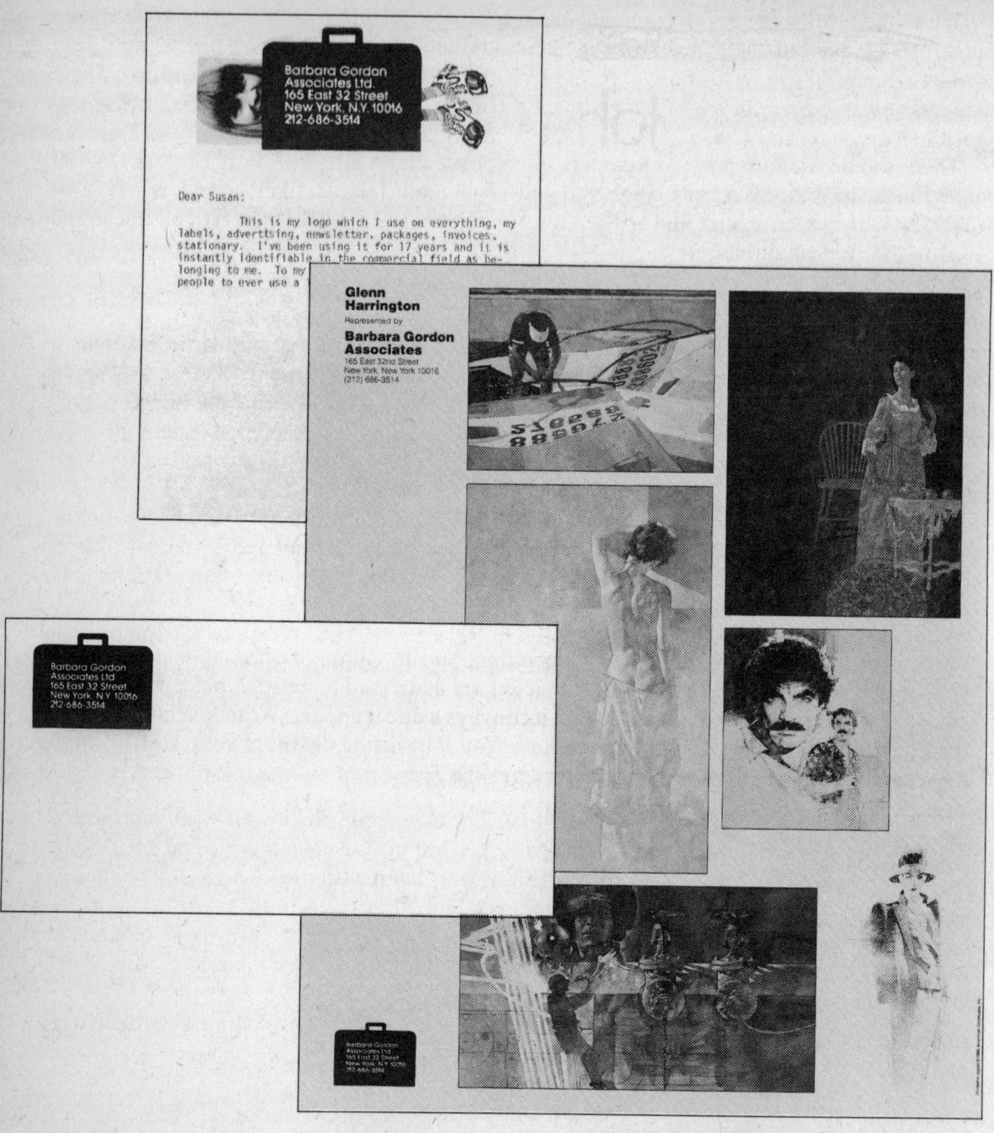

Barbara Gordon, a prominent artist and photographer representative from New York City, finds yet another use for a portfolio—as a logo. "This is my logo which I use on everything—my labels, advertising, newsletters, packages, invoices and stationery. I've been using it for 17 years, and it is instantly identifiable in the commercial field as belonging to me. To my knowledge, I was one of the first people to ever use a logo in our field (as a representative)."

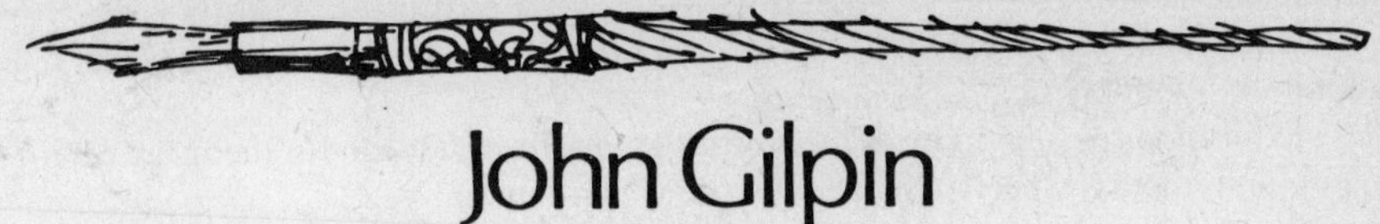

John Gilpin

553 West Marshall Street
West Chester, Pennsylvania 19380
215-692-3445

Simplicity is the key to creating an effective letterhead, according to John Gilpen, art director of the Philadelphia Inquirer. "The cleaner, the better." Gilpen is also a freelance artist whose illustrations and cartoons appear in the National Review and the New Yorker. His many pursuits are effectively represented by the pen which he uses as his logo. "I used to have a lot of funny characters in my letterhead, but that didn't work."

The cover letter

There's no way around it. You have to use your writing skills to make an opening statement. However, you're not expected to write *Remembrance of Things Past*. What an art director wants to read is a short summation saying who you are, what you do, and how your work is suited to his firm.

A cover letter personalizes your presentation; you're talking directly to someone about yourself. Make sure the envelope and the letter are addressed to a name, not a position. The letter should be individually typed so that it conveys a direct appeal. Write several versions of the letter to send to different types of markets. You'll be listing details of your work history in the résumé, so take the opportunity in the cover letter to point out the less obvious points of your experience such as your strength at portraiture or whatever quality seems applicable to the market that you are querying.

Since your cover letter is your opening statement, make it a spotlight of what's to come. Make it brief but subtly tantalizing. Be sure to include the following points:

- who you are and why you're writing
- what art style or services you're offering
- why your work is suitable for this market
- when and where to contact you.

Include a request for an appointment to review your portfolio, either in person or through the mail. State that you will be making a follow-up call, and be sure to do so.

Résumé

The dictionary defines a résumé as "a brief account of personal, educational, and professional qualifications and experience, as of an applicant for a job." For an artist, this means his art-related experience, education and achievements.

This part of your kit spotlights your best features and your most outstanding achievements. So that the important facts stand out, keep this piece one or two pages long. As with your cover letter, you may need more than one version for different markets. For example, advertising agencies are looking for product illustration, while magazines search for interpretive skills.

The elements in the résumé have to be well-organized. Remember to list education and achievements in reverse chronological order. The résumé should be printed or typed on your letterhead, which states your name, address, area code and phone number. It should be organized along these lines:

- List your professional specialties, such as medical illustration, airbrush, pen-and-ink rendering.
- Your professional experience should include freelance and staff work. State your employ-

ers' names and addresses plus job descriptions.

• Your educational background should include the degrees you have earned, the year of graduation and your major.

• While exhibitions pertain more to the fine artist, an illustrator can list them as evidence of his stature and appeal. Specify the show's title, location and year.

• You will need three or more awards and competitions to warrant a separate category. Otherwise, list them under exhibitions.

• Professional objectives give an art director an idea of your direction. Include your major skills and the freelance work you are aiming for. Recent graduates should place this category along with education, tying the two together.

If you have just graduated from art school, emphasize the quality of your education (a note of prominent professors helps) over the lack of professional experience. Established artists emphasize prestigious accounts and awards, with their educational background as a last note. In other words, state your strongest evidence in the beginning, then back it up with additional strengths.

Brochure

A brochure serves as a versatile marketing tool. It can be a multi-purpose folder, a one-page flyer, or a multi-purpose booklet. It can be mailed alone, left behind for an art director's file, handed out in place of a business card or included with other material to round out a mailing package. A brochure provides a concise overview of your skills and background while presenting printed examples of your work. It can say it all; it's a mini-package in itself.

Decide how you intend to use your brochure. If it is to be your only mailing piece, it must be comprehensive in its scope; it must supply all the necessary information about your skills and successes. Include brief captions explaining each sample of your work (note the client's name and how the piece was used). If the brochure is to be included in a promotional package, it should provide a brief synopsis of your talents, printed boldly, plus a few striking examples of your work. As a companion piece, it follows up the résumé as a visual summary of your abilities. As a follow-up to an interview or sales call, this piece should be a reminder of your qualifications.

Keep in mind these guidelines when planning your brochure:

• Use standard paper sizes. This piece should never be larger than 8½x11'' so it can fit easily into files.

• Though it can be printed in black and white, color gives you more visual impact. If your use of color is your strength, then advertise it.

• Wait a year or so to print a brochure if you are a recent art school graduate. It is an investment that might be more effective if you can list more achievements and reproduce commercial rather than student work.

Samples

We've come to the 'visual candy' of your promotional package. Samples, whether they are tear sheets, photostats or slides, are visual statements that best convey your style and technique. Select only the most appropriate and only the best. Many art directors claim they judge you by the worst piece they see.

Gear your samples to the specific needs of your market. If the firm requests color washes of race horses, then send color washes of race horses. The most frequent complaint from art directors is that freelance artists submit so many inappropriate samples. Study your market and use common sense; an architectural firm is not interested in your cartoon skills.

Submit no more than ten to twelve samples and no less than five. None should exceed 8½x11''; large works should be represented by transparencies. Label each of your samples with your contact information and copyright notice, plus a brief description of how the work was used. It is preferable to send nonreturnable samples, but if you need them returned, indicate that request in your cover letter, on a slide sleeve and on the slides; include a self-addressed stamped envelope that is large enough to return your samples.

There are five basic formats for samples, which are:

● Slides or transparencies. A transparency is a positive image "intended to be observed by light that passes through the image and base as on a viewer or by projection." Transparencies come in four sizes: 35mm, 2¼x2¼", 4x5" and 8x10". A slide is merely a 35mm transparency mounted in a cardboard frame.

● Photographs. Acceptable sizes are 8x10" and 5x7". Strive for color accuracy or a sharp contrast in black and white work.

● Photostats (also called stats). Black-and-white line drawings are best reproduced by photostats, which are themselves produced by a photographic process utilizing paper negatives. Because they can be enlarged or reduced, photostats are convenient nonreturnable samples. Look in the Yellow Pages for photographic services which will shoot photostats.

● Photocopies. While an inexpensive sample, photocopies should be used to reproduce only black-and-white work. Include crisp copies that are not blurred, lined or dotted.

● Tear sheets. These examples of your published work can bolster your professional image. Usually a client will provide the artist with tear sheets after the work is published. They should be laminated to prevent tearing and folding.

No matter what format you choose for the case, you must follow a few basic principles in presenting its contents. Choose only your best work. Quality is better than quantity. Most directors prefer to see printed samples or transparencies rather than slides. Label everything. It's a simple point to overlook, but have your samples facing the same direction. Keep your explanations simple and direct. Let your art speak for itself. If your work needs an interpreter, it's not suitable for the graphic market.

Business card

Carrying this small card confirms the fact that you're a professional. It should list your name, phone number and address plus a mention of your specialty. If your letterhead includes a logo, it should be carried through to your card. Collect samples of cards and study what elements work. Use simple, clear type, a basic design and standard dimensions (2x3½").

The business card serves many purposes. It can be a calling card, an addendum to your package, or a leave-behind after an interview. It's a convenient hand-out at club meetings or unexpected encounters with art directors.

Portfolio

You've been able to get your foot into the door with your first submission of self-promotional materials. You've called to request an appointment to show your portfolio to the art director, either in person or through the mail, and he has agreed. Now is your chance to display to him the artist that you really are.

A portfolio is like a magician's hat. It's merely a container awaiting the magic touch. You can purchase a portfolio case at an art supply store, but you still won't have a 'portfolio.' No matter how impressive the case is, it's the artwork inside that gives it meaning.

The overall appearance of the portfolio does affect your professional presentation. A neat, organized three-ring binder is going to create a better impression than a bulky, time-worn leather case. Graphic designers often like to use their imaginations in creating their portfolio, making it a sophisticated wrapper for the material inside. No matter how creative you wish to be, let the outer case serve as an indication for the important matter inside.

The size of the portfolio should be dictated by the size of your work. Include as much original work as possible, but try to keep it within manageable proportions. A good yardstick to apply is the standard desktop. If you're forced to spread your portfolio across the entire length of an art director's desk, you have an unmanageable size. Remember that the bottom line of your presentation is making it as easy as possible for the prospective buyer to view your work. The most popular sizes for cases are between 11x14'' and 18x24''.

Various types of cases offer different benefits and drawbacks. An 8½x11'' three-ring binder is durable, inexpensive and easy to handle. It keeps your work in order, with dividers adding convenient breaks. Try to use polyester or vinyl page protectors with backing in the ring binders so the sheets will not tear. Toothed binders are cumbersome; they unfold to take up an entire desktop. Also the acetate sleeves inside tend to rip. The most popular portfolios are simulated leather with puncture-proof sides that allow the use of loose samples.

No matter what format you choose for the case, you must follow a few basic principles in presenting its contents. Choose only your best work. Quality is better than quantity. Most directors prefer to see printed samples or transparencies rather than slides. Label everything. It's a simple point to overlook but have your samples facing the same direction. Keep your explanations simple and direct. Let your art speak for itself. If your work needs an interpreter, it's not suitable for the graphic market.

Since the drop-off policy is prevalent, have at least two or three portfolios at hand. One can be left when necessary, another can be used on personal calls, while the third can be sent to out-of-town prospects. Mini-portfolios are handy for simultaneous submissions. Let it be known that you will retrieve your portfolio either the next morning or the following evening. Most businesses are honorable; you don't have to worry about your case being stolen. But things do get lost so, just in case, make sure you've included only duplicates, which can be insured at a reasonable cost.

Determine what samples to include in your portfolio by the type of market you're approaching. This breakdown of market categories will help you prepare for a specific presentation.

Advertising, audiovisual and public relations firms. Since many entry-level jobs at advertising agencies require mechanical skills, present some samples which show strong layout skills and perhaps a project you have developed from rough sketches to comprehensives. Product illustration often calls for an ability to read blueprints, so include some sketches that reflect this ability. Audiovisual artists should present ten to twelve 35mm slides, and video artists should submit video disks containing examples of their work. Storyboards are essential for animators to demonstrate their method of concept development. Television stations look for graphic artists who can use color well and who can work with a 3x4'' box format.

Architecture, interior and landscape design firms. Rendering skills are needed in all aspects of this category. Architects should include photographs of model-making projects. In addition to drafting or final rendering samples, landscape architects should submit sequential photos of gardens or grounds they have designed, the photos showing the grounds in different seasons. Interior designers should demonstrate their specialty, whether it is industrial space planning or residential decoration, with before and after shots. Each sample should specify the client, your involvement in the project, the time frame of the job and your payment.

Art design studios. Show your knowledge of color and concept development plus a good design sense. Designers should include sketches to show rendering skills, roughs of graphic solutions and comprehensive layouts. Illustrators and designers generally develop a specialty, and your samples should reflect your interests. Product designers need to show photographs of the products they have designed, prototypes and drafting samples. So many projects involve a team approach that it is wise to specify what part you played in a group undertaking.

Associations and institutions. Portfolio samples for this category should reproduce well in print, exhibit low-cost design solutions and show flexibility for application to several uses. Since many markets are service-oriented, they publish many brochures, pamphlets and booklets which require freelance assistance in their preparation. Therefore show your layout abilities by presenting printed samples which you have designed and sketches that show experimental layouts. Many markets here use logos as their identifying marks and need artists who can create strong symbolic designs.

Book publishers. Include examples of black-and-white art which are suitable for both line and halftone reproduction. Some of your color work should have a limited color range, suggesting your command of preseparated art. Show a full-color jacket you have designed and another that could be preseparated. Include a sample of a book dummy, even if it is a rough. Make the samples actual size to demonstrate your knowledge of book sizes. Make sure some of your samples demonstrate your sense of sequence and continuity.

Businesses and fashion. Businesses often commission industrial pieces. Industrial designers should show samples that reflect a consistency of design, a sense of pure graphics and a knowledge of manufacturing processes. A package designer creates graphic symbols and manipulates the design of labels; his samples should show a strong color sense and a knowledge of typography. Artists should show a command of all facets of print advertising. An expertise in computer art is a plus. Examples of computer-generated art should demonstrate your command of graphs or of display solutions.

Fashion illustrators must demonstrate a facility with markers, pastels, wash, and pen-and-ink. Their portfolios should include samples of work they can readily produce to facilitate quick turnaround times and also experimental sketches to show a flair for style.

Manufacturers of collector's plates look for portraiture skills and landscape rendering; they look for good technique and creative style rather than specific subject matter. Show samples of your illustration technique; transparencies and slides capture your palette accurately and are convenient for review.

Greeting cards and paper products. In your sample package, request the company's art guidelines. These will give you specific requirements needed for your portfolio. Their requirements are as diverse as the subjects they feature. For example, Elizabeth Stanley of Maine Line Company prefers to see 8½x11'' photographs with the cover displayed on the left, the inside on the right. On the other hand, Ned Stern of Amberley Greeting Card Co. likes to review original and published work, examining the presentation, technique and style. Most companies will review slides or photographs, but many will accept tear sheets and photostats. The publisher might select one or more of your samples for a card illustration; include samples, therefore, that reduce or enlarge in proportion to the line's card sizes. If you have an idea for a line of cards, then include dummies, which are 8- to 10-inch actual-size cards.

Magazines. Magazines must have a specialty in order to be marketable. Therefore artists who are specialists, such as fantasy or wildlife artists, succeed in this arena. Samples should display your illustrative style and medium. If you have published illustrations, include tear sheets, which will bolster your professional status. Photostats and photocopies adequately represent black-and-white work, while photos or transparencies best represent color. For submission by mail, each piece should be accompanied by a brief statement listing the magazine in which the illustration appeared, the art director with which you worked and your price range.

Art directors prefer to see original roughs of cartoons. Make sure each rough is labeled with your name, address and phone number plus a cartoon reference number because individual pieces can get shuffled.

Newspapers and newsletters. Strong black-and-white work is needed here. Art directors want to see examples of line drawings; show ten to twelve examples (photosats or tear sheets) of your best work. If your work has been printed, include information on its use. Cartoons should be directed towards timely or topical events; note the political slant of the paper you're approaching to make sure your humor is appropriate. Newsletters are focused upon business or hobby pursuits; study them likewise.

Performing arts. Since so much work in this area involves the preparation of promotional materials such as programs and brochures, include examples of your layout abilities. You must also show an ability to complement print with striking illustrations which capture a character's persona. Creative directors look for a certain 'feel' for their milieu; if you took piano lessons for years, you might have a better grasp of a symphony's repertoire than of a theatre's.

Lighting or set designers need samples of drafting and model-making abilities, plus a few sketches to demonstrate an aptitude for drawing.

Record companies. Creative directors are looking for a distinctive style that packs a wallop. They frequently look to freelance artists to supply them with experimental designs and styles that are ahead of their times. Black-and-white work should be unusually bold, and colors should be particularly eye-catching. Since many companies also need publicity materials, show any samples of poster work or work used in P-O-P displays. To show your design sense, include some comprehensive sketches.

Syndicates and clip art firms. An impressive sample package often carries more weight with a syndicate than a portfolio presentation. Each syndicate receives so many submissions from both illustrators and cartoonists that they prefer in many cases to choose outstanding work from a sample package, then request further artwork to be forwarded. "We can't see everybody," said David Seidman of the Los Angeles Times Syndicate, 'so, in all fairness to everyone, we prefer to receive work through the mail." The best policy is to catch the art director's eye with outstanding black-and-white illustrations or cartoons which are both funny and well-drawn, with an interesting character as a focal point. Include several samples showing one character in several situations to demonstrate your ability to portray that character in a continuous manner. Above all, avoid clutter and intricate detail that will not reproduce well.

Art publishers. Subject matter must have a widespread appeal. Color plays a vital part in this field, since many clients of art publishers are interior decorators. Your portfolio should include illustrations of pretty people and perfect landscapes. This is an ideal outlet for the fine artist. However, do not lug original works into a publishing house. Instead, make transparencies of large works to make your portfolio transportable. Number prints and list the original size, media and price on a separate sheet, or write a short explanatory text to accompany each piece.

Once you've sent out a few mailings and have shown your portfolio, both in-person and through the mail, you'll be able to begin to evaluate your self-promotional efforts. Judge what has worked best and decide where you need to improve. Keep records of your mailings so that you can review the effectiveness of your efforts. If you have done a "blind" mailing, remember that the usual return is only one to three per cent. Keep your eyes open for attractive business cards or letterheads which might supply some creative input for your own design, and discuss with other artists their self-promotional efforts. Just as your expertise in art has grown with experience, your ability to present yourself will grow.

Keep in mind that you're in a very competitive marketplace, but there are opportunities waiting for you. You can stand out from the crowd by using your creative gifts in your own behalf. You are your own best salesman, because you know what you're offering. Let your talents work for you.

The Markets

Advertising, Audiovisual & Public Relations Firms

The power of persuasion is the common thread in artwork used in the advertising, audiovisual and public relations fields. Artwork, whether it be product illustrations, point-of-purchase designs or computer images, should evoke viewer emotion to a product. The evocative power of art has enhanced the current trend of selling "the image" along with the product.

It is the art director who establishes the tone of an advertising or public relations campaign. From the account executive he learns the wishes of a client, then determines the scope of the project. Usually art directors are faced with a short deadline and require a quick turnaround time. Thus they look for artists with flexibility, speed and a knowledge of print production. Because of the time factor, many art directors prefer to deal with local (within driving distance) artists who are at hand to make last-minute changes, though technological advances in long-distance communications now allow instantaneous exchanges.

Since this is the field of visual presentation, you must present yourself professionally— from a well-groomed appearance to a streamlined portfolio. Determine which firms use the services you provide by reading the listings in this section, then contact the art director or art buyer to make an appointment to present your portfolio. If you are mailing the portfolio, call the art director so he can expect to receive your package. Be sure to include information concerning other advertising campaigns you have participated in, noting the extent of your involvement, the client, the art director and your price range. Include roughs, thumbnails and comprehensives that demonstrate your working process from concept to finished work. Audiovisual artists should present 35mm slides, and video artists should submit disks containing examples of their work.

Don't be surprised if you don't hear immediately from an art director after an interview. Be prepared to offer 'leave-behinds'—a resume, samples, brochure or business card—so that your style, name and address remain available. He'll contact you when an assignment arises that he feels fits your style.

Names and addresses (but no marketing information) of additional firms can be obtained from the *Standard Directory of Advertisng Agencies*, the *Audio Video Market Place*, the *Literary Market Place*, *O'Dwyers Directory of Public Relations Firms* and the *Madison Avenue Handbook*. Read the weeklies *Advertising Age* and *Adweek* to keep current on the changes in the advertising field.

Alabama

J.H. LEWIS ADVERTISING AGENCY INC., Box 3202, Mobile AL 36652. (205)438-2507. Senior Vice President/Creative Director: Larry D. Norris. Ad agency. Clients: retail, manufacturers, health care and direct mail. Buys 15 illustrations/year.
Needs: Works with illustrators and designers. Uses artists for mechanicals and layout for ads, annual reports, billboards, catalogs, letterheads, packaging, P-O-P displays, posters, TV and trademarks.
First Contact & Terms: Prefers southern artists. Query. SASE. Reports in 5 days. No originals returned to artist at job's completion. Payment by hour: $40-80, layout; $30-50, mechanicals. Pays promised fee for unused assigned work.

SPOTTSWOOD VIDEO/FILM STUDIO, 2524 Old Shell Rd., Mobile AL 36607. (205)478-9387. Contact: Manning W. Spottswood. AV/film/TV producer. Clients: industry, education, government and advertising. Produces mainly public relations and industrial films and tapes.
Needs: Assigns 5-15 jobs/year. Artists "must live close by and have experience." Uses approximately 1 illustrator/month. Works on assignment only. Uses artists for illustrations, maps, charts, decorations, set design, etc.
First Contact & Terms: Send resume or arrange interview by mail. Reports only if interested. Pays for design by the hour, $25 minimum; by the project, $150 minimum. Considers complexity of project, client's budget, skill and experience of artist, geographic scope of finished project, turnaround time, rights purchased and quality of work when establishing payment.
Tips: "We are very small and go from project to project—most of them very small."

Arizona

FARNAM COMPANIES, INC., Box 34820, Phoenix AZ 85067-4820. (602)285-1660. Creative Director: Trish Spencer. Inhouse advertising agency—Charles Duff Agency—for animal health products firm. Clients which sell through distributors to feed stores, tack shops, co-ops, pet stores, horse and cattle industry.
Needs: Works with 3-10 freelance artists/year. Works on assignment only. Uses artists for illustrations for brochures, labels and ads. Especially looks for realism, skill in drawing animals and quick turnaround.
First Contact & Terms: Send query letter with resume and tear sheets to be kept on file. Prefers any type of samples "which clearly show quality and detail of work." Samples not filed are returned only if requested. Reports back only if interested. To show a portfolio, mail appropriate materials, which should include original/final art, final reproduction/product and tear sheets. Pays for illustrations by the project, $100 minimum. Considers client's budget, skill and experience of artist, and geographic scope for the finished product when establishing payment. Rights purchased vary according to project.
Tips: "Mail us samples of work. They should be of animals (horses, dogs, cats, cattle and small animals) with rates and time estimates if possible."

FILMS FOR CHRIST ASSOCIATION, 2628 W. Birchwood Circle, Mesa AZ 85202. Contact: Paul S. Taylor. Motion picture producer. Audience: educational, religious and media. Produces motion pictures and videos.
Needs: Works with 1-5 illustrators/year. Works on assignment only. Uses artists for books, catalogs, and motion pictures. Also uses artists for animation, slide illustrations and ads.
First Contact & Terms: Query with resume and samples (photocopies, slides, tear sheets or snapshots). Prefers slides as samples. Samples returned by SASE. Reports in 4 weeks. Provide brochure/flyer, resume and tear sheets to be kept on file for future assignments. No originals returned to artist at job's completion. Considers complexity of project, and skill and experience of artist when establishing payment.

GILBERT ADVERTISING, LTD., Suite 102, 3216 N. 3rd St., Box 15710, Phoenix AZ 85060. Creative Director: T.R. Gilbert. Specializes in corporate identity; newspaper and magazine ads; brochures, catalogs and catalog sheets; and direct mail programs. Clients: primarily small firms in manufacturing and commercial services.

The asterisk before a listing indicates that the listing is new in this edition. New markets are often the most receptive to freelance contributions.

Needs: Works with 10-20 freelance artists/year. Artists "must be willing to sell all rights to reproduction of artwork for established or agreed-upon fee. We do. not deal through artist's agents." Works on assignment only. Uses artists for advertising, brochures, catalogs, mechanicals, retouching, direct mail packages, charts/graphs, AV presentations, lettering and logos.

First Contact & Terms: Send query letter with brochure, resume, business card, slides, photostats, photocopies, photographic prints, and/or tear sheets to be kept on file. Do *not* send original work. Samples not kept on file are returned by SASE. Reports only if interested. Pays for design by the project, $100-500 average; for b&w illustration by the project, $50-400 average; for color illustration by the project, $200-1,500 average. Considers complexity of project and client's budget when establishing payment.

Tips: Artists should "be professional in their presentations. Show only your best quality pieces; keep materials sharp and clean. Computer-assisted artwork creation will become more and more prevalent. As a tool for artists, we expect computers to save a great deal of time and to generate new avenues for design."

PAUL S. KARR PRODUCTIONS, 2949 W. Indian School Rd., Box 11711, Phoenix AZ 85017. (602)266-4198. Contact: Paul Karr. Utah Division: 1024 N. 250 East, Box 1254, Orem UT 84057. (801)226-8209. Contact: Michael Karr. Film producer. Clients: industrial, business, educational, TV and cable.

Needs: Occasionally works with freelance filmmakers in motion picture and video projects. Works on assignment only.

First Contact & Terms: Advise of experience and abilities.

Tips: "If you know about motion pictures or are serious about breaking into the field, there are three avenues: 1) have relatives in the business; 2) be at the right place at the right time; or, 3) take upon yourself the marketing of your idea, or develop a film idea for a sponsor who will finance the project. Go to a film or video production company, such as ourself, and tell them you have a client and the money. They will be delighted to work with you on making the film. Work, and approve the various phases as it is being made. Have your name listed as the producer on the credits. With the knowledge and track record you have gained you will be able to present yourself and your abilities to others in the film business and to sponsors."

PHILLIPS-RAMSEY, 829 N. 1st Ave., Phoenix AZ 85003. (602)252-2565. Senior Art Director: Jamie Hernandez. Ad agency. Clients: savings and loan, racetrack, hotel, restaurant, high tech, public utility, consumer goods, medical, home builders. Client list provided for SASE.

Needs: Works on assignment only. Uses artists for illustration, photography and production.

First Contact & Terms: Send brochure to be kept on file. Reports only if interested. Pays by the project. Considers complexity of the project, client's budget, geographic scope for the finished product, turnaround time and rights purchased when establishing payment. Buys all rights; "our agency only works on a buy-out basis."

THE PRODUCERS, INC., 1095 E. Indian School Rd., Phoenix AZ 85014. (602)279-7767. President: Judi Victor. Ad agency and audiovisual firm. Clients: developers, financial industry, computer industry, retailers, restaurants, builders and government.

Needs: Works with 20-25 freelance artists/year. Uses artists for layout and design, illustration, photography, videography, air brush, cartooning, animation and calligraphy. "Expediency, accuracy, creativity and ability to work with type and design simultaneously are especially important."

First Contact & Terms: Send query letter with brochure and samples to be kept on file. Samples not filed are returned. Reports within 2 weeks. Write for appointment to show portfolio, which should include tear sheets, comps, photostats or actual material (brochures, etc.) Pays by the hour, $10-30 average. Considers complexity of the project, client's budget, skill and experience of artist and turnaround time when establishing payment. Buys all rights.

Tips: "Always write first, then follow up with a call for an appointment. Send samples if you feel it will help give you the edge over the many other artists we interview constantly."

JOANNE RALSTON & ASSOCIATES, INC., 3003 N. Central, Phoenix AZ 85012. (602)264-2930. Vice President: Gail Dudley. PR firm. Clients: financial institutions; real estate developers/homebuilders; industrial, electronics, manufacturing firms, hospital; resort hotels.

Needs: Works with freelance illustrators and designers. Uses artists for brochures/flyers. Selects freelancers based on needs, cost, quality and ability to meet deadlines.

First Contact & Terms: Send flyers/brochures and ads to be kept on file. No originals returned to artist at job's completion. Request an appointment to show a portfolio. Negotiates payment based on client's budget, amount of creativity required from artist, where work will appear, artist's previous experience/reputation and ability to meet deadlines.

***WFC ADVERTISING**, (formerly Winters, Franceschi & Callahan), Suite 600, 32020 N. Central Ave., Phoenix AZ 85004-1544. Creative Director: Charlie Thomas. Ad agency. Estab. 1980. Clients: construction, financial, retail and communications.
Needs: Works with 2-3 freelance illustrators/month. Uses freelancers for billboards, consumer and trade magazines, brochures/flyers, newspapers, P-O-P displays and TV storyboards and animation.
First Contact & Terms: Call for appointment to show portfolio or make contact through artist's rep. Selection based on portfolio review. Negotiates payment based on bids from artist and how often work used.
Tips: Wants to see originality and individual techniques.

Arkansas

ADI ADVERTISING/PUBLIC RELATIONS, Box 2299, Ft. Smith AR 72902. President: Asa Douglas. Ad agency/PR. Clients: retail, personal service, small manufacturing, political.
Needs: Assigns 150-200 freelance jobs/year. Regional artists only, within two-days mail time. Works on assignment only. Works with 2-3 freelance illustrators and 5-10 freelance designers/month. Uses artists for consumer and trade magazines, billboards, brochures, catalogs, newspapers, stationery, signage and posters.
First Contact & Terms: Send brochure showing art style. Samples not kept on file are returned by SASE. Reports only if interested. Write to schedule an appointment to show portfolio, which should include roughs, original/final art, final reproduction/product and photographs. Pays for design by the hour, $10-100; pays for illustration by the hour, $25-300. Considers complexity of project, client's budget, skill and experience of artist and rights purchased when establishing payment. Buys all rights.
Tips: "Creative needs are satisfied with unusual often un-known ideas then is a need for creative thinking on paper that can be added to a complete campaign. Show complete scope of your ability to work from production through design."

MANGAN RAINS GINNAVEN HOLCOMB, 911 Savers Federal Bldg., Little Rock AR 72201. Contact: Steve Mangan. Ad agency. Clients: recreation, financial, consumer, industrial, real estate.
Needs: Works with 5 designers and 5 illustrators/month. Assigns 50 jobs and buys 50 illustrations/year. Uses artists for consumer magazines, stationery design, direct mail, brochures/flyers, trade magazines and newspapers. Also uses artists for illustrations for print materials.
First Contact & Terms: Query with brochure, flyer and business card to be kept on file. SASE. Reports in 2 weeks. No originals returned to artist at job's completion. Call or write to schedule an appointment to show a portfolio, which should include final reproduction/product. Pays for design and illustration by the hour, $72.

California

***AIRLINE FILM & TV PROMOTIONS, INC., VALLEY STUDIO**, Valley Studio, 13246 Weidner St., Pacoima CA 91331. (818)899-1151. Vice President: Alf Jacobsen. Public relations firm; airline promotions and advertising. Clients: airlines, motion picture and TV studios. Client list provided for SASE.
Needs: Works with 48 freelance artists/year. Uses mostly local artists. Works on assignment only. Uses artists for design, illustrations, brochures, catalog, retouching, press releases, motion pictures, logos and advertisements.
First Contact & Terms: Send query letter with brochure showing art style or resume and tear sheets, photostats, photocopies, slides and photographs. Samples not filed are returned by SASE. Reports only if interested. To show a portfolio, mail thumbnails, roughs, original/final art, final reproduction/product, color, tear sheets, photostats, photographs and b&w. Considers complexity of project, client's budget, and skill and experience of artist when establishing payment. Rights purchased vary according to project.

***ATARI CORP.**, 1196 Borregas Ave., Sunnyvale CA 94086. Director Creative Services: M. Stevens. Computer and games manufacturer. Clients: dealers and consumers.
Needs: Works with 6 or more freelance artists/year. Local artists only. Works on assignment only. Uses freelance artists for design, illustrations, brochures, catalog, books, mechanicals, retouching, posters, press releases, motion pictures, charts/graphs and advertisements. "Artists must be talented in his or her field and must be deadline oriented."
First Contact & Terms: Send query letter with brochure showing art style and tear sheets. Samples not

filed are not returned. Reports only if interested. Considers complexity of project and client's budget when establishing payment. Buys all rights.
Tips: "We have a considerable amount of work to be done. We do not buy each project as though it were the only job—or a Picasso"

BEAR ADVERTISING, 1424 N. Highland, Hollywood CA 90028. (213)466-6464. President: Richard Bear. Clients: fast food enterprises, sporting goods firms and industrial. Assigns 50-100 jobs/year.
Needs: Works with 1-2 illustrators and 2 designers/month. Local artists only. Uses artists for illustrations for annual reports, design of direct mail brochures, mechanicals and sign design.
First Contact & Terms: Call for interview. No originals returned. Negotiates pay.

RALPH BING ADVERTISING CO., 16109 Selva Dr., San Diego CA 92128. (619)487-7444. President: Ralph S. Bing. Ad agency. Clients: industrial (metals, steel warehousing, mechanical devices, glass, packaging, stamping tags and labels), political, automotive, food and entertainment.
Needs: Local artists only. Works on assignment only. Uses artists for consumer and trade magazines, brochures, layouts, keylines, illustrations and finished art for newspapers, magazines, direct mail and TV.
First Contact & Terms: "Call first; arrange an appointment if there is an existing need; bring easy-to-present portfolio. Provide portfolio of photocopies and tear sheets, and client reference as evidence of quality and/or versatility." Reports only if interested. No original work returned to artist at job's completion. Pays by the hour, $5-50 average; by the project, $10 minimum. Considers complexity of project and client's budget when establishing payment.

***ALDEN BUTCHER PRODUCTIONS, INC.**, #700, 6331 Hollywood Blvd., Hollywood CA 90028. Art Department: Greg King. Audiovisual/video and film production firm. Clients: all varieties of corporations and industry requiring AV productions.
Needs: Local artists only; no fine artists. Works on assignment only. Uses artists for illustration, titles, layout and paste-up, mechanical illustration.
First Contact & Terms: Send query letter with resume, original art, slides or photostats to be kept on file. Reports back only if interested. Call for appointment to show portfolio. Pays by the hour, $10-35 average. Considers complexity of the project, client's budget, skill and experience of artist, and turnaround time when establishing payment. Buys all rights; "Art commissioned is usually only mechanical in nature."
Tips: "Don't bring and show everything you have ever done, including personal 'doodle' sheets. Bring your *best* work and be to the point about your skill and what you can do for us."

***CAMELLIA COLOR CORPORATION**, 2010 Alhambra Blvd., Sacramento CA 95816. (916)454-3801. Owner: Herb Shannon. Professional photo lab.
Needs: Works with 300 freelance artists/year.
First Contact & Terms: Send query letter. Reports back within 5 weeks. To show a portfolio, call to schedule an appointment. Pays for design by the hour. Considers complexity of project when establishing payment. Purchases all rights.

CUNDALL/WHITEHEAD/ADVERTISING INC., 3000 Bridgeway, Sausalito CA 94965. (415)332-3625. Contact: Alan Cundall. Ad agency.
Needs: Works with 6 designers/month. Uses artists for consumer magazines, stationery design, direct mail, slide shows, brochures/flyers, trade magazines and newspapers. Also uses artists for layout, paste-up and type spec.
First Contact & Terms: Send query letter and resume to be kept on file for future assignments. Write to schedule an appointment to show a portfolio. No originals returned to artist at job's completion. Pays for design by the hour, $35 minimum. Considers budget and complexity of project when establishing payment.
Tips: "Seek the counsel of a top agency art director as to the merits of your portfolio before seeing other agencies. Send resume and letter. We are besieged by 3-5 calls a week to see portfolios. We can't."

DIMON & ASSOCIATES, Box 6489, Burbank CA 91510. (213)849-7777. Creative Director: Jerry Michaud. Ad agency/printing firm. Serves clients in industry, finance, computers, electronics, health care and pharmaceuticals.
First Contact & Terms: Send query letter with tear sheets, original art and photocopies. SASE. Provide brochure, flyer, business card, resume and tear sheets to be kept on file for future assignments. Considers complexity of project, turnaround time, client's budget, and skill and experience of artist when establishing payment.

DJC & ASSOCIATES, 6117 Florin Rd., Sacramento CA 95823. (916)421-6310. Contact: Donna Cicogni. Ad agency. Assigns 120 jobs/year.
Needs: Works with 1 illustrator/month. Local artists only. Works on assignment only. Uses artists for consumer and trade magazines, stationery design, direct mail, TV, brochures/flyers and newspapers.
First Contact & Terms: Send query letter with brochure showing art style or resume and samples. Samples not kept on file are returned by SASE. Reports in 1 week. Call to schedule an appointment to show a portfolio which should include original/final art, final reproduction/product, etc. No originals returned to artist at job's completion. Negotiates pay.

ESTEY, HOOVER ADVERTISING AND P.R., INC., Suite 225, 3300 Irvine Ave., Newport Beach CA 92660. (714)549-8651. Creative Director: Art Silver. Clients: consumer, financial, real estate, industrial and medical.
Needs: Works on assignment only. Wants highly talented professional illustrators, but will consider serious "up and coming" talent. Uses freelance artists for ads, magazine, newspaper, TV, AV, brochures, catalogs, posters, annual reports, story boards. Likes "thinking, contributing illustration."
First Contact & Terms: Call for appointment or send "head sheet"—not originals. Reports only if interested. Prefers to see original material and published samples; will expect costs and price at time of viewing. Pays $50-5,000/project, net 30 days, or ongoing. Considers complexity of project, client's budget, skill and experience of artist, geographic scope of finished project and deadline when establishing payment.

FILM COMMUNICATORS, 11136 Weddington St., North Hollywood CA 91601. Produces educational and training motion pictures, slides, study prints, brochures, books, pamphlets, filmstrips, mailing pieces and advertisements.
Needs: Assigns 20-25 jobs/year. Prefers local artists with at least 2 years experience in putting together brochures and ads. Works with 1 illustrator and 3 designers/month. Works on assignment only. Uses freelancers for catalogs, brochures, other promotional materials, ad illustrations and forms.
First Contact & Terms: Send brochure showing art style and samples in care of advertising department. Interested in "any samples similar to the type of promotional materials we use (i.e., brochures, catalogs, etc.)." Samples returned. Reports in 2 weeks. Call or write to schedule an appointment to show portfolio which should include roughs, original/final art, final reproduction/product and photostats. Pays by the project, $50 minimum. No originals returned to artist following publication. Buys all rights.
Tips: "The business market is catching up with the consumer market in its need for clever and interesting designs. However, we still need to emphasize clear, simple designs that don't take away from the selling point. Have some knowledge of direct mail, brochures and self-mailers."

FILM GROUP, INC., Suite 179, 8033 Sunset Blvd., West Hollywood CA 90046. Vice President/Creative Director: Chip Miller. Production Director: Travis Walker. AV producer. Clients: entertainment, motion picture, music, television and cable video. Client list provided for SASE.
Needs: Assigns 10-20 freelance jobs/year. Works with 2-3 illustrators and 2-4 designers/month. Artist must have experience working with similar firms. Works on assignment only. Uses artists for trade magazines, billboards, brochures, filmstrips, movies, AV presentations and posters.
First Contact & Terms: Send query letter with brochure and resume to production director to be kept on file; contact through artist's agent. Prefers slides as samples; returned by SASE. Reports only if interested. Pays by the hour, $35-75 average. Considers complexity of project, client's budget, skill and experience of artist and turnaround time when establishing payment. Negotiates rights purchased.

FRANKLIN & ASSOC., 600 B. St., San Diego CA 92101. (619)231-6168. Art Directors: Tom Frost, Jan Rudin. Ad agency. Clients: banks, paint manufacturer, radio stations, auto dealers, real estate, dental clinics.
Needs: Works with 12-15 freelance artists/year. Uses artists for production, art direction, illustration, comp work and photography. Especially looks for good hand skills and good production knowledge.
First Contact & Terms: Experienced, available artists only. Send resume and samples to be kept on file; call for appointment to show portfolio. Prefers tear sheets or photostats as samples. Samples are filed, not returned. Reports only if interested. Pays by the hour. Considers client's budget, skill and experience of artist and turnaround time when establishing payment. Buys all rights.
Tips: "Write/call first, samples requested. Experience relevant to quality level of work we do."

***GOAL PRODUCTIONS**, 2027 N. Lake Ave., Alta Dena CA 91001. (213)797-7668. Executive Producer: Jack Oswald. Film/TV producer. Serves clients in marketing, industry and education. Produces motion pictures, videotapes, slidefilms and filmstrips.
Needs: Assigns 0-10 jobs/year. Artists "must be experienced and have reference from a first hand

associate." Uses 1 animator/month and 1 designer/year. Works on assignment only. Uses artists for "productions that our basic staff of five or six cannot handle. Usually sound or camera assistants or grips."
First Contact & Terms: Send resume or query letter and arrange interview by mail. Send samples "only on request." Samples returned by SASE if not kept on file. Reports in 1 month. Payment varies with each client's budget. Original artwork returned to artist "depending on the contract we are working on." Negotiates rights.

HANNA-BARBERA PRODUCTIONS INC., 3400 Cahuenga Blvd., Hollywood CA 90068. (213)851-5000. Publisher: Harry Love. TV/motion picture producer. Clients: TV networks. Produces animation and motion pictures.
Needs: Uses artists for animation and related artwork as needed. *Uses mostly local artists.*
First Contact & Terms: Provide resume to be kept on file for future assignments.

HUBBERT ADVERTISING AND PUBLIC RELATIONS CO., INC, 3189-A Airway Ave., Costa Mesa CA 92626. Art Director: Chris Klopp. Ad agency. Clients: real estate and miscellaneous (all product, service).
Needs: Works with 10-20 freelance artists/year. Local artists only (southern California). Uses artists for line art/paste-up, advertising collateral illustration, b&w and 4-color; and layout comps. Especially seeks professionalism (marker skills); efficiency (clean); and deadline awareness (fast turnaround).
First Contact & Terms: Send query letter with resume and samples to be kept on file. Accepts any kind of copy that is readable as samples. Samples not filed are returned by SASE. Reports back only if interested. Write for appointment to show portfolio. Pays by the hour, $10-35 average. Pays in 90 days. Considers complexity of the project, client's budget and turnaround time when establishing payment. Rights purchased vary according to project.

ED MARZOLA AND ASSOCIATES, 5555 Melrose Ave., Building B-173/300 Hollywood, CA 90038. (213)468-5497. President: Ed Marzola. Ad agency. Clients: automotive, aerospace, industrial, publishing and entertainment.
Needs: Works with 8-10 freelance artists/year. Works on assignment only. Uses artists for paste-up, photography, make-up, styling, model making and illustration. "Be cost conscious and know enough about printing process to be able to save us money when job is printed."
First Contact & Terms: "Only real requirements are that artist deliver on-time, on-budget." Send query letter with brochure, business card, photographs, slides, tear sheets, etc., to be kept on file. Samples not filed are returned by SASE. Reports within 10 days. To show a portfolio, "mail appropriate materials, or call or write to schedule an appointment." Portfolio should include thumbnails, roughs, original/final art, final reproduction/product, color, tear sheets, photostats, photographs, b&w or any suitable means of showing skills. Pays by the project, $100 minimum. Considers complexity of the project, client's budget, skill and experience of artist and turnaround time when establishing payment. Rights purchased vary according to project.
Tips: Send professionally finished, clean material. Even if it is a photocopy, we can tell the professional artists from the marginal ones. Be on time, be on budget."

WARREN MILLER PRODUCTIONS, 505 Pier Ave., Hermosa Beach CA 90254. (213)376-2494. Owner: Warren Miller. Produces sports documentaries, commercials, television format films and video cassettes for home use.
Needs: Works with 1 ad illustrator and 1 advertising designer/year. Works on assignment only. Uses artists for direct mail brochures, magazine ads and posters.
First Contact & Terms: Send query letter with samples (original sports illustration—skiing, sailing, windsurfing, etc.) or write for interview. Reports within 2 weeks. Buys nonexclusive rights. Samples returned by SASE. Provide resume to be kept on file for future assignments. "We pay by the project and since they range from brochures to full color film posters, it is impossible to give a fair range. Some of these are complicated; some already laid out and need only finished art." Considers complexity of project and skill and experience of artist when establishing payment.
Tips: There is "less 'standard' work and a trend toward contemporary, avant-garde art in our area of business. We prefer to work with artists who have done sports illustrations and recreation-oriented art, but we respond to great talent. Please send some kinds of samples and background information on assignments."

PALKO ADVERTISING, INC., Suite 207, 2075 Palos Verdes Dr. N., Lomita CA 90717. (213)530-6800. Account Services: Judy Kolosvary. Ad agency. Clients: business to business.
Needs: Uses artists for layout, illustration, paste-up, mechanicals, copywriting and P-O-P displays. Produces ads, brochures and collateral material.

First Contact & Terms: Prefers local artists. Send query letter with brochure, resume, business card and samples to be kept on file. Write for appointment to show portfolio. Accepts tear sheets, photographs, photocopies, printed material or slides as samples. Samples not filed returned only if requested. Reports back only if interested. Pay is "discussed and negotiated." Negotiates rights purchased.

PANORAMA PRODUCTIONS, 2353 De La Cruz Blvd., Santa Clara CA 95050. Graphics Manager: Debbie Moore. Audiovisual firm. Clients: industrial and commercial.
Needs: Works with a varying number of freelance artists/year. Uses artists for computer graphics, paste-up, layout, technical drawings, illustrations, medical illustrating, cartooning, storyboards, and boardwork.
First Contact & Terms: Send query letter with resume to be kept on file. Reports only if interested. Pays by the hour, $5-10 average. Considers skill and experience of artist when establishing payment. Buys all rights.
Tips: "We interview only after receiving and reviewing resumes. From the resumes we match skills and experience to the potential job requirements."

***ROUNDTABLE FILMS**, 113 N. San Vicente Blvd., Beverly Hills CA 90211. Advertising Manager: Steven Gamer. Audiovisual firm. Clients: Fortune 100 companies.
Needs: Works with 10-20 freelance artists/year. Prefers local artists. Works on assignment only. Uses artists for design, illustrations, brochures, catalog, books, magazines, newspapers, P-O-P displays, mechanicals, retouching, animation, direct mail packages, motion pictures, logos and advertisements. Artists should have "creativity, good listening skills, realistic idea of their worth in regard to what the market will bear."
First Contact & Terms: Send query letter with samples. Samples not filed are returned only if requested. Reports back within 10 days. Call or write to schedule an appointment to show portfolio which should include thumbnails, roughs, original/final art and final reproduction/product. Pays for design by the hour, $35; by the project, $100; by the day, $240. Considers complexity of project, client's budget, skill and experience of artist, how work will be used and turnaround time when establishing payment. Rights purchased vary according to project.
Tips: "Show me how you will help me succeed in my job; help the company generate sales; and do it cost efficiently. Anyone that can prove those three facts will usually go to work for me."

RICHARD SIEDLECKI DIRECT MARKETING, Box 817, El Toro CA 92630. (714)768-5830. Direct Marketing Consultant: Richard Siedlecki. Consulting agency. Clients: industrial, publishers, associations, air freight, consumer mail order firms, and financial. Client list provided for SASE.
Needs: Assigns 15 freelance jobs/year. Works with 2 freelance designers/month. Works on assignment only. Uses artists for consumer and trade magazines, direct mail packages, brochures, catalogs and newspapers.
First Contact & Terms: Artists should be "experienced in direct response marketing." Send query letter with brochure, resume and business card to be kept on file. Reports only if interested. Pays by the hour, $25 minimum; by the project, $250 minimum. Considers complexity of project and client's budget when establishing payment. "All work automatically becomes the property of our client."
Tips: Artists "must understand (and be able to apply) direct mail/direct response marketing methods to all projects: space ads, direct mail, brochures, catalogs."

***TELEVISION ASSOCIATES**, 2410 Charleston Rd., Mountain View CA 94043. (415)967-6040. Marketing Coordinator: Maria Mancini. Audiovisual firm. Clients:: corporate, industrial and music.
Needs: Works with 10 freelance artists/year. Works on assignment only. Uses artists for design, illustrations, brochures, magazines, newspapers, mechanicals, lettering, logos and advertisements. Artist should have diversity and dependability.
First Contact & Terms: Send query letter with resume and samples. Samples not filed are returned only if requested. Reports within 2 weeks. Call or write to schedule an appointment to show a portfolio, which should include original/final art and final reproduction/product. Negotiates payment. Considers complexity of project, client's budget, and skill and experience of artist when establishing payment. Buys all rights.
Tips: "Professionalism is expected."

VIDEO IMAGERY, 204 Calle De Anza, San Clemente CA 92672. (714)492-5082. Contact: Bob Fisher. Audiovisual firm. Clients: industrial and manufacturing. Client list available for SASE.
Needs: Works with 2 freelance artists/year. Seeks local artists only. Works on assignment only. Uses artists for art work for videos.
First Contact & Terms: Send brochure, photostats or tear sheets to be kept on file. Samples not filed are returned only if requested. Reports only if interested. Call for appointment to show portfolio. Pays

by the day, $100-150 average. Considers complexity of project, client's budget and rights purchased when establishing payment. Rights purchased vary according to project.

VIDEO RESOURCES, Box 18642, Irvine CA 92713. (714)261-7266. Producer: Brad Hagen. Audiovisual firm. Clients: automotive, banks, restaurants, computer, transportation and energy.
Needs: Works with 8 freelance artists/year. Southern California artists only with minimum 5 years' experience. Works on assignment only. Uses artists for graphics, package comps, animation, etc.
First Contact & Terms: Send query letter with brochure showing art style or resume, business card, photostats and tear sheets to be kept on file. Samples not filed are returned by SASE. Considers complexity of the project and client's budget when establishing payment. Buys all rights.

WANK, WILLIAMS & NEYLAN, 401 Burgess Dr., Menlo Park CA 94025. (415)323-3183. Art Director: Alvin Joe. Ad agency. Clients: restaurants, public transit, financial and industrial accounts, including electronics.
Needs: Works with 10 illustrators/month. Local artists primarily. Uses freelance artists for billboards, trade magazines, direct mail, P-O-P displays, brochures, catalogs, posters, signage, newspapers and AV presentations.
First Contact & Terms: Query with resume of credits. Works on assignment only. Payment depends on individual job.

GLORIA ZIGNER & ASSOCIATES INC., 328 N. Newport Blvd., Newport Beach CA 92663. (714)645-6300. President: Gloria Zigner. Contact: Vice President Jeff Zigner. Advertising/PR firm. Clients: hotels, insurance companies, hospitals, restaurants, financial institutions, manufacturers, electronic companies, corporate identities, builders and developers. Buys 12-24 illustrations/year.
Needs: Works with 2-3 illustrators and 2-3 designers/month. Uses artists for billboards, P-O-P displays, consumer magazines, stationery design, multimedia kits, direct mail, brochures/flyers, trade magazines and newspapers. Also uses artists for design, color separations, layout, lettering, paste-up and type spec.
First Contact & Terms: Local artists only. Write for interview. Reports only if interested. Provide brochure, flyer, business card, resume and tear sheets to be kept on file for future assignments. No originals returned at job's completion. Pays promised fee for unused assigned work.

Los Angeles

N.W. AYER, INC., 888 Figueroa, Los Angeles CA 90017. (213)621-1400. President/Creative Director: John Littlewood. Associate Creative Director: Ivan Horrath. Executive Art Director: Bob Bowen. Senior Art Director: Lionel Banks. Ad agency. List of clients provided upon request.
Needs: Uses 1-2 illustrators/month. Uses artists for billboards, P-O-P displays, filmstrips, consumer magazines, direct mail, television, slide sets, brochures/flyers, trade magazines, and newspapers.
First Contact & Terms: "People interested should research what type of clients N.W. Ayer has in such references as *Advertising Agency Register* and in the Red Book." Provide tear sheets, original art or photocopies to be kept on file for future assignments. Send portfolio to Ivan Horrath. Negotiates payment based on client's budget and amount of creativity required from artist. No originals returned at job's completion.

BANNING CO., Suite 210, 11818 Wilshire Blvd., Los Angeles CA 90025. (213)477-8517. Art Director: Bill Reynolds. Ad agency. Serves a variety of clients.
Needs: Works with 2 comp artists and 2-3 designers per month. Works on assignment only. Uses designers for P-O-P displays, consumer and trade magazines, stationery design, direct mail, brochures/flyers and newspapers.
First Contact & Terms: Call for interview. Prefers slides as samples. Samples returned by SASE. Reports within 2-3 weeks. Provide business card and brochure to be kept on file for future assignments. No originals returned at job's completion. All pay is based on job. Considers complexity of project, client's budget, turnaround time and rights purchased when establishing payment.
Tips: "This is a business first; art folks need some business skills—not just artistic ones. Have patience and confidence."

BOSUSTOW VIDEO, 2207 Colby Ave., West Los Angeles CA 90064-1504. Contact: Tee Bosustow. Video production firm. Clients: broadcast series, feature films, corporate, media promotion and home video.
Needs: Works with varying number of freelance artists depending on projects. Local artists only. Works on assignment only. Uses artists for titles, maps, graphs and other information illustrations.

First Contact & Terms: Hires per job; no staff artists. Send brochure showing art style and resume only to be kept on file. Do not send samples; required only for interview. Samples not filed are returned by SASE. Reports only if interested. Pays by the project, $50-500 average. Considers complexity of skill and experience of artist, project, client's budget and turnaround time when establishing payment. Usually buys all rights; varies according to project.

BOZELL JACOBS KENYON ECKHARDT, INC., Suite 900, 10850 Wilshire Blvd., Los Angeles CA 90024. (213)879-1800. Senior Art Director: Mike Phillips. Ad agency. Clients: consumer/industrial. Media used include billboards, consumer and trade magazines, direct mail, newspapers, radio and TV.
Needs: Works on assignment only.
First Contact & Terms: Call for personal appointment to show portfolio. Prefers photocopies, b&w/color or printed samples. Reports only if interested. Provide business card, resume and samples to be kept on file for possible future assignments. Pays by the project, $150-2,500 average. Considers complexity of project, turnaround time, client's budget, rights purchased, and skill and experience of artist when establishing payment.
Tips: Show current work.

GARIN AGENCY, #614, 6253 Hollywood Blvd., Los Angeles CA 90028. (213)465-6249. Mangager: P. Bogart. Ad agency/public relations firm. Clients: real estate, banks.
Needs: Works with 1-2 freelance artists/year. Local artists only. Works on assignment only. Uses artists for "creative work and TV commercials."
First Contact & Terms: Send query letter with photostats or tear sheets to be kept on file for one year. Samples not filed are not returned. Does not report back. Negotiates pay; by the hour. Considers client's budget and turnaround time when establishing payment. Buys all rights.
Tips: "Don't be too pushy and don't overprice yourself."

GUMPERTZ/BENTLEY/FRIED, 5900 Wilshire Blvd., Los Angeles CA 90036. (213)931-6301. Executive Art Director: Steve Hallingsworth. Ad agency. Clients: stockbrokers, banks, food companies and visitors' bureaus.
Needs: Works with 3-4 illustrators and photographers/month. Uses artists for illustration. Negotiates pay.
First Contact & Needs: Call to arrange interview to show portfolio.

***THE HALSTED ORGANIZATION**, 3519 West Sixth St., Los Angeles CA 90020. (213)386-8356. Art Director: Damon G. Shay. Ad agency, public relations and marketing firm. Clients: manufacturers, medical/dental, sporting goods and general consumer. Client list provided upon request.
Needs: Works with 15-20 freelance artists/year. Prefers local artists with own studio. Will consider all. Uses artists for design, illustrations, brochures, mechanicals, retouching, posters, direct mail package, press releases, lettering and logos. Looks for "clean work, type spec ability is rewarded, photo retouch is great."
First Contact & Terms: Send query letter with brochure showing art style or resume and tear sheets, photostats, photocopies, slides and photographs. Samples not filed are returned only if requested. Reports back within 10 days. Call to schedule an appointment to show a portfolio which should include roughs, original/final art, tear sheets and b&w. Pays for design by the hour, $12.50-50; by the project, $120-no limit; by the day, $90-no limit. Pays for illustration by the hour, $12.50-50; by the project, $100-no limit; by the day $90-no limit. Considers complexity of project, turnaround time and client's budget, rights purchased when establishing payment. Buys one-time rights or reprint rights; rights vary according to project.
Tips: "Be enthusiastic, look professional and have a concise and varied portfolio. Smile."

IMAGE STREAM, 5450 W. Washington Blvd., Los Angeles CA 90016. (213)933-9196. Art Director: Ben Peros. Design Director: Brad Hood. Producer of AV materials for various live formats, film and video. Clients: industry, government and advertising. Produces "usually the larger multi-image shows (12-18 projectors), but some smaller (3-6 projectors) are also produced."
Needs: Professional artists with 3-5 years' experience only. Assigns 10-15 jobs/year. Works with 2-6 designers/year. Works on assignment only. Uses artists for "overload situations, sometimes for presentation boards for proposals." Looking for stage designers.
First Contact & Terms: Arrange interview by phone; then send resume and slides, brochure/flyer, business card and slide sheet to be kept on file. "Don't send original art—prefer to see it in portfolio." Samples returned by SASE. Reporting time is discussed at portfolio review. Payment is negotiated. Payment varies with each client's budget. No originals returned following publication. Negotiates rights purchased.
Tips: "I look for a steady hand, clean work, good design sense and technical expertise of the graphic

arts. Working knowledge of photography is very helpful. Our work is a hybrid of design, graphics, photography and special effects, and animation. AV is a very fast growing, fairly young industry. Good qualified artists are hard to find. A technical aptitude is helpful in developing the potential in this field."

PAUL MUCHNICK CO., 5818 Venice Blvd., Los Angeles CA 90019. (213)934-7986. Art/Creative Director: Paul Muchnick. Ad agency. Serves clients in mail order, giftwares, publishing, housewares and general consumer products.
Needs: Local artists only. Uses artists for layout, paste-up, brochures/flyers and retouching for newspapers, magazines and direct mail.
First Contact & Terms: Call for interview. No originals returned to artist at job's completion.

***NATIONAL ADVERTISING AND MARKETING ENTERPRISES**, (N.A.M.E.), 1352 S. Flower St., Los Angeles CA 90015. Contact: J. A. Gatlin.
Needs: Works on assignment only. Uses artists for graphic design, letterheads and direct mail brochures.
First Contact & Terms: Send query letter with tear sheet, photostats and photographs. Samples not returned. Sometimes buys previously published work. Reports in 4 weeks. To show a portfolio mail appropriate materials. Pays by the hour, $15-40.
Tips: "Submit repros of art, not originals."

NEEDHAM, HARPER WORLDWIDE, INC., Suite 900, 11601 Wilshire Blvd., Los Angeles CA 90025. (213)208-5000. Manager, Art Services: Annie Ross. Ad agency. Serves clients in automobile, heavy equipment baking California lottery, savings and loan.
Needs: Works with about 4 freelance illustrators/month. Uses freelancers for all media.
First Contact & Terms: Contact manager of art services for appointment to show portfolio. Selection based on portfolio review. Negotiates payment.
Tips: Wants to see variety of techniques.

RAPP & COLLINS/WEST ADVERTISING, 5900 Wilshire Blvd., Los Angeles CA 90036. (213)936-9600. Vice President/Creative Director: Michael Goodwin. Ad agency. Clients: banking, food, fashion, etc. Client list provided upon request.
Needs: Works with 30-40 freelance artists/year. Uses artists for photography, illustration and art-mechanicals.
First Contact & Terms: Send photographs or tear sheets to be kept on file. Samples not filed are returned only if requested. Reports only if interested. Call for appointment to show portfolio. Considers complexity of the project, client's budget, skill and experience of artist, geographic scope for the finished product, turnaround time and rights purchased when establishing payment. Buys first rights.

***ROGERS & COWAN, INC.**, Suite 400, 10000 Santa Monica Blvd., Los Angeles CA 90067. (213)201-8800. Contact: Account Executive. PR firm. Clients: entertainment and corporate.
Needs: Works with freelance illustrators as needed. Uses freelance artists for billboards, consumer and trade magazines, direct mail, posters, newspapers, AV presentations and news releases.
First Contact & Terms: Local artists only. Phone for appointment. Works on assignment basis only. Payment "depends on the job."

***THE SCOTT AGENCY, INC.**, Suite 910, 714 W. Olympic Blvd., Los Angeles CA 90015. (213)745-6881. President: Ford Scott Rollo. Estab. 1985. Ad agency and public relations firm. Clients: automotive, financial, fashion, electrical, electronic and furniture.
Needs: Works with 50 freelance artists/year. Prefers local artists. Uses freelance artists for design, illustrations, brochures, catalog, magazines, newspapers, P-O-P displays, mechanicals, retouching, animation, billboards, posters, direct mail packages, press releases, lettering, logos, charts/graphs and advertisements. Artist should have "good life drawing if it applies. Neat, clean, accurate. Good spelling if it applies. Reliable. Flexible on budgets."
First Contact & Terms: Reports only if interested. Call to show portfolio, which should include thumbnails, roughs, original/final art, final reproduction/product, color, photographs and b&w. Pays for design by the hour, $30 minimum. Pays for illustrations by the project. Considers client's budget, turnaround time and rights purchased when establishing payment. Rights purchased vary according to project.
Tips: Artists should "show up for scheduled appointments or give sufficient advance notice why not. Be neat and dress businesslike."

SanFrancisco

ARNOLD & ASSOCIATES PRODUCTIONS, 2159 Powell St., San Francisco CA 94133. (415)989-3490. President: John Arnold. Audiovisual firm. Clients: general.
Needs: Works with 30 freelance artists/year. Prefers local artists, award-winning and experienced. "We're an established, national firm." Works on assignment only. Uses artists for multi-media, slide show and staging production.
First Contact & Terms: Send query letter with brochure, tear sheets, slides and photographs to be kept on file. Call to schedule an appointment to show a portfolio, which should include final reproductions/product, color and photographs. Pays for design by the hour, $15-50; by the day, $200-500. Pays for illustration by the hour, $35-65. Considers complexity of the project, client's budget and skill and experience of artist when establishing payment.

***CHARTMASTERS**, 201 Filbert St., San Francisco CA 94133. (415)421-6591. Art Manager: Robert Burnett. Audiovisual firm.
Needs: Works with 5-6 freelance artists/year. Artists must sign W-2 form and work on premises as temporary employee." Uses artists for designs, illustrations, mechanicals, animation and chart/graphs. Experience in 35mm slide production, presentation and multi-image shows essential.
First Contact & Terms: Send resume and slides. Samples not filed are returned. Reports back only if interested. Call or write to schedule an appointment to show a portfolio. Pays for design by the hour, $10-18. Considers complexity of project and skill and experience of artist when establishing payment. Rights purchased vary according to project.

FOOTE, CONE, & BELDING, 1255 Battery St., Box 3183, San Francisco CA 94119-3183. (415)398-5200. Executive Creative Director: Mike Koelker. Ad agency. Clients: apparel, food, utilities, household cleaner.
First Contact & Terms: Send samples of work (slides) and follow up by phone. Negotiates payment based on client's budget. No originals returned at job's completion.

FURMAN FILMS, 3466 21st St., San Francisco CA 94110. (415)824-8500. Producer: Will Furman. Audiovisual and motion picture production firm. Clients: variety of corporate clients, and agricultural co-ops.
Needs: Works with 5 freelance artists/year. Uses artists for paste-up, design, maps, illustrations, signs and type spec. Especially important are speed, accuracy, knowledge of film/video media, and flexibility in working hours.
First Contact & Terms: Works on assignment only. Send query letter with resume and business card to be kept on file; write for appointment to show portfolio. "Information is kept on file and interviews done when need arises for freelance assistance." Prefers photostats, photographs or tear sheets as samples. Samples returned by SASE. Reports only if interested. Pays by the hour, $8-20 average; pays by the project, $100-250 average. Considers complexity of the project, client's budget, skill and experience of artist, turnaround time and rights purchased when establishing payment. Buys all rights or variable rights according to project; negotiates rights purchased.

***HEAPING TEASPOON ANIMATION**, 4002 19th St., San Francisco CA 94114. (415)626-1893. Owner: Chuck Eyler. Audiovisual firm. Clients: ad agencies, other production firms and local businesses.
Needs: Works with 5 freelance artists/year. Uses artists for design, mechanicals, animation and motion pictures. "Artists should have good pencil line quality and inbetweening experience."
First Contact & Terms: Send query letter with brochure showing art style or resume, tear sheets, photocopies and renderings/designs. Samples not filed are returned by a SASE. Reports back within 3 months with SASE and only if interested. Call or write to schedule an appointment to show a portfolio, which should include thumbnails, roughs, original/final art and video reels. Pays for design by the hour, $10-90; for illustration by the hour, $8-20. Considers complexity of project, client's budget and skill and experience of artist when establishing payment. Rights purchased vary according to project.

***JOVART STUDIOS**, Box 2291, San Francisco CA 94126. Art Director: Jorge Morales. Audiovisual firm. Clients: corporations.
Needs: Works with 5 freelance artists/year. Works on assignment only. Uses artists for design, illustrations, brochures, catalog, mechanicals, logos and charts/graphs.
First Contact & Terms: Send query letter with resume. Samples not filed are returned by SASE. Reports only if interested. Write to schedule an appointment to show a portfolio, which should include final reproduction/product. Pays for design by the hour, $10 minimum. Considers complexity of project and

client's budget when establishing payment. Rights purchased vary according to project.
Tips: "We cannot answer every query, but we use freelancers occasionally and resumes will be kept on file but not necessarily acknowledged."

KETCHUM COMMUNICATIONS, 55 Union St., San Francisco CA 94111. (415)781-9480. Executive Creative Director: Kenneth Dudwick. Ad agency. Serves clients in food and medicine.
Needs: Uses freelancers for consumer and trade magazines, newspapers, print ads and TV.
First Contact & Terms: Call for appointment to show portfolio. Selection based on portfolio review, mailers from freelancers and contact by reps. Negotiates payment based on client's budget, amount of creativity required from artist and where work will appear.
Tips: Wants to see in portfolio whatever best illustrates freelancer's style. Include past work used by other ad agencies and tear sheets of published art.

***LORD & BENTLEY**, 2016 Taraval, San Francisco CA 94116. (415)564-8384. Creative Director: Allan Barsky. Ad agency.
Needs: Works with 20 freelance artists/year. Prefers experienced artists only. Works on assignment only. Uses artists for design, illustrations, brochures, catalogs, magazines, newspapers, P-O-P displays, mechanicals, retouching, billboards, posters, direct mail packages, logos and advertisements. Artists must "understand reproduction process; the job is to enhance copy strategy."
First Contact & Terms: Send 6 photocopies of published/printed work. Samples not filed are not returned. Does not report back. To show a portfolio, mail appropriate materials, only photocopies of final reproduction/product. Pays for design by the hour, $20-75. Pays for illustration by the hour, $20-100. Considers skill and experience of artist when establishing payment. Buys all rights.

LOWE MARSCHALK, (formerly Dailey & Associates), 574 Pacific, San Francisco CA 94133. (415)981-2250. Creative Director: John McDaniels. Ad agency. Clients: primarily travel, wine and food.
Needs: Works with 3-4 freelance illustrators and 2 freelance designers/month. Uses freelancers for billboards, consumer and trade magazines, direct mail, brochures/flyers, newspapers, P-O-P displays, stationery design and TV.
First Contact & Terms: Call for appointment to show portfolio. Selection based on past association and review of portfolios. Negotiates payment based on usage and where work will appear.
Tips: Wants to see features that demonstrate freelancer's originality and competency.

MERCHANDISING FACTORY, Suite 500, 3 Embarcadero Center, San Francisco CA 94111. (415)956-4990. Production Managers: Roger Takiguch and Debbie Schwamd. Ad agency. Clients: real estate, airlines, restaurants, banks, sporting goods, retail paper products, food services and grocery store products.
Needs: Works with 2 illustrators and 2 designers/month. Mostly local artists. Uses artists for filmstrips, slide sets and brochures/flyers; also for color separations, layout, lettering, paste-up, retouching and comps.
First Contact & Terms: Query with samples (tear sheets, photocopies) or arrange interview. SASE. Reports within 1 week. Provide business card and tear sheets to be kept on file for future assignments. No originals returned to artist at job's completion.

O'KEEFFE'S INC., 75 Williams Ave., San Francisco CA 94124. (415)822-4222. Marketing Manager: Abby Lipman. Manufacturer of skylights, aluminum building products and fire-rated glass door, window and wall systems for architects, contractors and builders.
Needs: Works with 1-5 freelance artists/year. Works on assignment only. Uses artists for advertising, brochure and catalog design, illustration and layout.
First Contact & Terms: Reports back only if interested. Call or write for appointment to show portfolio. Pays by the hour, $25-50 average. Considers complexity of the project, skill and experience of artist, and turnaround time when establishing payment.
Tips: "Work more on planning, not necessarily on the finished piece—that's the printer's art."

EDGAR S. SPIZEL ADVERTISING INC., 1782 Pacific Ave., San Francisco CA 94109. (415)474-5735. President: Edgar S. Spizel. AV producer. Clients: "Consumer-oriented from department stores to symphony orchestras, supermarkets, financial institutions, radio, TV stations, political organizations, hotels and real estate firms." Works a great deal with major sports stars and TV personalities.
Needs: Uses artists for posters, ad illustrations, brochures and mechanicals.
First Contact & Terms: Send query letter with tear sheets. SASE. Reports within 3 weeks. Provide material to be kept on file for future assignments. No originals returned at job's completion. Negotiates pay.

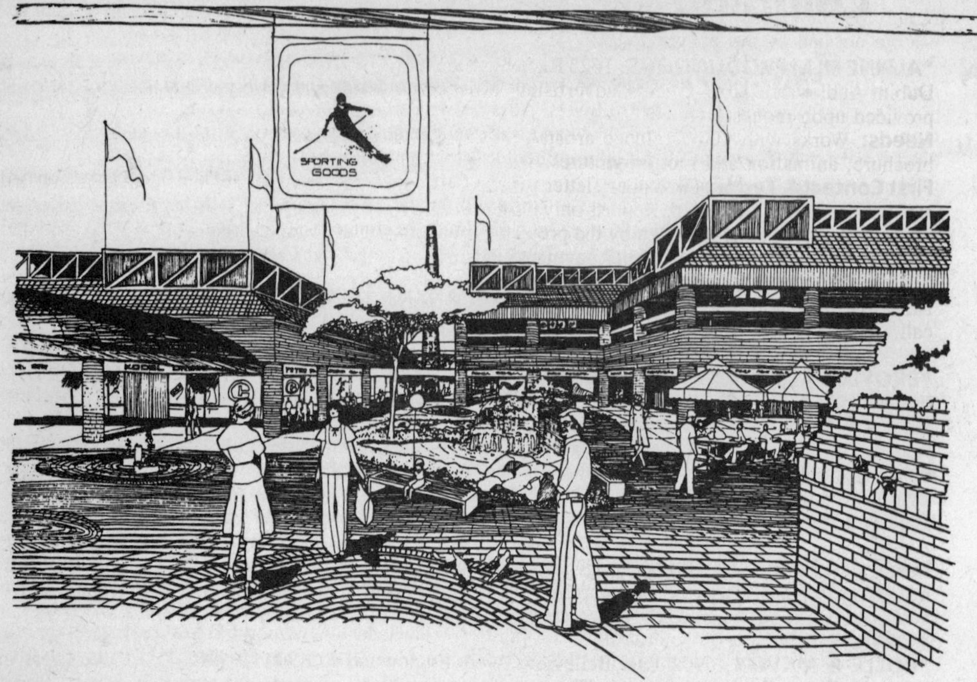

Lawrence Kramer of Corte Madera, California, received an assignment from L.A. Paul, creative director of Undercover Grahics in San Francisco, to depict a shopping mall for a brochure. The pen & ink illustration conveyed a "casual lifestyle for an upscale community," says Paul. Kramer received $400 and secured further work as a result of the piece.

***UNDERCOVER GRAPHICS**, Suite A, 1169 Howard St., San Francisco CA 94103. (415)626-0500. Creative Director: L.A. Paul. AV producer. Clients: musical groups, producers, record companies and book publishers.

Needs: Works with 2-3 illustrators and 2-3 designers/month. Uses artists for billboards, P-O-P displays, corporate identity, multimedia kits, direct mail, TV, brochures/flyers, album covers and books.

First Contact & Terms: Send query letter with brochure or resume, tear sheets, slides, photographs and/or photocopies. Samples returned by SASE. Reports in 4 weeks only if interested. To show a portfolio mail roughs, original/final art, tear sheets and photographs. Originals returned to artist at job's completion. Pays $250-5,000, comprehensive layout and production; $10-25/hour, creative services; $25-500, illustrations. Considers complexity of project, client's budget, skill and experience of artist and rights purchased when establishing payment. Pays original fee as agreed for unused assigned illustrations. Provide brochures, tear sheets, slides, business card and/or resume to be kept on file for future assignments. Originals returned to artist at job's completion. Pays $250-5,000, comprehensive layout and production; $10-25/hour, creative services; $25-500, illustrations. Considers complexity of project, client's budget, skill and experience of artist and rights purchased when establishing payment. Pays original fee as agreed for unused assigned illustrations.

Tips: Artists interested in working with us should "be creative and persistent. Be different. Set yourself apart from other artists by work that's noticeably outstanding. Don't be content with mediocrity or just 'getting by' or even the 'standards of the profession.' *Be avant-garde*."

❝People want art they can relate to. Architects need to make spaces more humane.❞

John K. Awsumb, Vickrey Orreset Awsumb Associates

Colorado

***ALPINE FILM PRODUCTIONS**, 1623 Race St., Denver CO 80206. (303)393-1189. Producer: Dee B. Dubin. Audiovisual firm. Clients: advertising firms, corporations and variety of businesses. Client list provided upon request.
Needs: Works with 100 freelance artists/year. Works on assignment only. Uses artists for design, brochure, animation and motion pictures.
First Contact & Terms: Send query letter with brochure showing art style or resume. Samples not filed are returned only if requested. Reports only if interested. To show a portfolio, mail appropriate materials plus tear sheets. Pays for design by the project. Considers client's budget, how work will be used and rights purchased when establishing payment. Rights purchased vary according to project.
Tips: "We are primarily a film production company, but we do use a lot of freelance artists (including film crew presonnel), and some graphic and design artists." Mail information and follow up with phone call.

***BROYLES ALLEBAUGH & DAVIS, INC.**, 31 Denver Technological Center, 8231 E. Prentice Ave., Englewood CO 80111. (303)770-2000. Executive Art Director: Kent Eggleston. Ad agency. Clients: industrial, hi-tech, financial, travel and consumer clients; client list provided upon request.
Needs: Works with 12 illustrators/year; occasionally uses freelance designers. Works on assignment only. Uses freelance artists for consumer and trade magazines, direct mail, P-O-P displays, brochures, catalogs, posters, newspapers, TV and AV presentations.
First Contact & Terms: Send business card, brochure/flyer, samples and tear sheets to be kept on file. Arrange interview to show portfolio or contact through artist's agent. Prefers slides or printed pieces as samples. Samples returned by SASE if requested. Reports only if interested. Negotiates payment according to project. Considers complexity of project, client's budget, skill and experience of artist, geographic scope of finished project, turnaround time and rights purchased when establishing payment.

***COLLE & MCVOY**, 6900 East Belleview Ave., Englewood CO 80111. (303)771-7700. Creative Director: Doug Gens. Ad agency. Clients: newspaper, banks, department store, ski resort, florist, hospital and amusement park.
Needs: Works with 3-4 freelance artists/year. Prefers local artists, but open to experienced "lancers" outside Denver. Very interested in Boulder. Uses artists for design, illustrations, brochures, catalog, magazines, newspapers, P-O-P displays, mechanicals, retouching, animation, billboards, posters, direct mail packages, logos, charts/graphs, advertisements and radio.
First Contact & Terms: Send query letter with brochure showing art style or resume and tear sheets, photostats, photocopies, slides, photographs and "whatever they want to show." Samples not filed are returned only if requested. Reports only if interested. Call or write to schedule an appointment to show a portfolio, which should include thumbnails, roughs, original/final art, final reproduction/product, color, tear sheets, photographs, b&w and "whatever they want to show." Negotiates payment. Rights purchased vary according to project.
Tips: "Our ratio of black-and-white to four-color is about 80:20. But we're always trying to influence our clients to do more four-color. However, we look forward to new styles and techniques for black-and-white work. We're more interested in an individual's style than what he/she has done. Also, we rely on the artist's conceptual ability, because we feel the artist must have that freedom."

KINETIC DESIGN SYSTEMS, (formerly Computer Image Productions), 8201 E. Pacific Pl., Denver CO 80231. (303)750-5000. Art Director: Cliff Ericson. Computer video animation producer. Clients: international broadcasters; advertising agencies; industrial, corporate and medical institutions; filmmakers and numerous independent clients who utilize broadcasting in their advertising.
Needs: Works with 1 illustrator and 1-2 graphic artists/year. Especially needs 1 illustrator and 1-2 graphic artists. Uses artists for storyboards, background illustration, print ads and production art. Artwork done daily.
First Contact & Terms: Send resume and samples (animated graphics on video cassette, samples of illustration, storyboards, graphic design and printed pieces). Samples not returned. Provide resume and business card to be kept on file one year for possible future assignments. Payment varies.

STARWEST PRODUCTIONS, 1391 N. Speer Blvd., Denver CO 80204. (303)623-0636. Creative Director: Steve Pettit. Ad agency/audiovisual firm. Clients list provided upon request with SASE.
Needs: Works with 2-4 freelance artists/year. Local artists only, experienced in audiovisual, print, storyboard. Works on assignment only. Uses artists for full concept to paste-up. Especially seeks paste-up skills.
First Contact & Terms: Send resume and slides, tear sheets, photostats to be kept on file. Samples not

filed are returned. Reports within 30 days. Write for appointment to show portfolio. Pays by the project, $1,000. Considers client's budget, and skill and experience of artist when establishing payment. Negotiates rights purchased.

Tips: "Always looking for someone with 'new' ideas."

Connecticut

THE BERNI CORP., Marketing Design Consultants, 666 Steamboat Rd., Greenwich CT 06830. (203)661-4747. Contact: Stuart Berni. Clients: manufacturers and retailers of consumer products. Buys 25 illustrations/year. Write or call for interview; local professionals only.

Needs: Uses artists for illustration, layout, lettering, paste-up, retouching and type spec for annual reports, catalogs, letterheads, P-O-P displays, packaging, design, production and trademarks. Pays $15-50. Pays promised fee for unused assigned work.

EAGLEVISION, INC., Box 3347, Stamford CT 06905. (203)359-8777. Principal/Creative Director: Michael Macari, Jr. Audio-video firm. Clients: corporate/industrial, music and arts and consumer home video programmer, also cable TV.

Needs: Works with 25-50 freelance artists/year. Works on assignment only. Uses artists for computer and digital graphics and animation footage, as well as scriptwriters.

First Contact & Terms: "Good quality and creativity" are especially important. Send query letter and samples to be kept on file. Prefers ¾" or ½" VHS or BETA Hi-Fi videotapes as samples. Samples not filed are returned by SASE. Reports within 1 week only if interested. Write for appointment to show portfolio. Pays by the project or by amount of material/footage. Considers complexity of project, skill and experience of artist, and rights purchased when establishing payment. Buys one-time rights, all rights or variable rights according to project.

EDUCATIONAL DIMENSIONS GROUP, Box 126, Stamford CT 06904. (203)327-4612. Visual Editors: Marguerite Mead and Greg Byrnes. AV producer. Audience: businesses, schools and libraries. Produces filmstrips, motion pictures, slide sets and videotapes.

Needs: Works with illustrators and designers. Works on assignment only. Uses designers and mechanical artists for catalogs, filmstrips, direct mail flyers and brochures, etc.

First Contact & Terms: Send query letter with resume, photocopied samples and photostats. Samples returned only if requested. Reports in 2 weeks. Provide resume to be kept on file for future assignments. Originals only returned at job's completion when return has been negotiated earlier. Pays by job for filmstrip, slide and film illustrations, charts, graphics and diagrams. "Payment depends totally on type of project."

Tips: Looks for neatness, organization, fresh ideas and versatility.

***ERIC HOLCH/ADVERTISING**, 49 Gerrish Lane, New Canaan CT 06840. President: Eric Holch. Clients: companies who advertise in trade magazines.

Needs: Works with 3 freelance artists/year. Works on assignment only. Prefers food, candy, packages, and sea scapes as themes for advertising illustrations for brochures, ads, etc. Pays $100-2,000 average.

First Contact & Terms: Send query letter with brochure showing art style or samples to be kept on file. Write to schedule an appointment to show a portfolio, which should include roughs and photocopies original/final art. Buys one-time rights, all rights or negotiates rights purchased depending on project. Considers skill and experience of artist and client's preferences when establishing payment.

THE McMANUS COMPANY, Box 446, Greens Farms CT 06436. (203)255-3301. President: John F. McManus. National advertising/marketing/PR agency. Serves clients in data processing, corporate, consumer, industrial, social agencies, automotives and other industries.

Needs: Works with 4 illustrators/month. Works on assignment only. Uses artists for art direction (TV commercials), graphic design (print ads and collateral pieces), illustration, publications, filmstrips, multimedia kits, storyboards and packaging.

First Contact & Terms: Send resume (to be kept on file for future assignments). Samples returned by SASE; reports back on future assignment possibilities. Write for interview to show portfolio. "Payment is determined on use of creative work, whether it will appear in national or regional media."

MARKETING EAST INC., 520 West Ave., Norwalk CT 06850. (203)866-2234. Contact: W. Greene. Ad agency.

Needs: Works with 2-3 freelance artists/year. Experienced artists only. Uses artists for mechanicals, etc.

First Contact & Terms: Send photostats, photographs, slides or tear sheets as samples to be kept on file. Samples not filed are returned only if requested. Reports only if interested. Call for appointment to show portfolio. Pays by the job. Buys all rights

THE MERRILL ANDERSON CO. INC., 1166 Barnum Ave., Stratford CT 06497-5402. (203)377-4996. Contact: Michael Minardo. Clients: financial.
Needs: Works with 2 illustrators/month. Uses artists for direct mail and brochures/flyers. Also uses artists for cartoons and realistic illustrations. Assigns 20 illustrations/year.
First Contact & Terms: Arrange interview to show portfolio. Prefers photographs, b&w line drawings or color art as samples. Reports in 2 weeks. Works on an assignment basis only. Provide brochure to be kept on file for future assignments. No originals returned to artist at job's completion. Pays $50/job.

STANLEY H. MURRAY ADVERTISING, Box 4876, Greenwich CT 06830. (203)869-8803. President: Stan Murray. Ad agency/PR firm. Assigns 200 jobs/year.
Needs: Works with 5-10 illustrators and 5-10 designers/month. Uses artists for billboards, P-O-P displays, filmstrips, consumer magazines, stationery design, multimedia kits, direct mail, slide sets, brochures/flyers, trade magazines and newspapers.
First Contact & Terms: Query with resume. SASE. Reports within 1 week. Provide materials to be kept on file for future assignments. No originals returned at job's completion. Pays $30/hour.

PALM, DEBOMIS, RUSSO, INC., 800 Cottage Grove Rd., Bloomfield CT 06002. (203)242-6258. Art Director: Lynn Schultz. Ad agency. Clients: consumer and industrial products and services.
Needs: Works with 2-3 illustrators/month. Works on assignment only. Uses illustrators for consumer magazines, trade magazines and technical illustration. Also uses artists for layout, illustration, technical art, paste-up, retouching, lettering and storyboards for TV, newspapers, magazines, radio, billboards, direct mail and collateral.
First Contact & Terms: Submit samples or call for interview. Prefers slides, photographs, photostats, b&w line drawings and originals as samples. Samples returned by SASE "if requested." Reports within 4 weeks. Provide business card, resume, samples and tear sheets of work to be kept on file for future assignments. No originals returned at job's completion. Pays by the project, $100-1,000 average. Considers complexity of project, client's budget, skill and experience of artist and turnaround time when establishing payment.
Tips: "Try not to submit too many styles of work—only what one is best at."

THE WESTPORT COMMUNICATIONS GROUP INC., 155 Post Rd. E., Westport CT 06880. (203)226-3525. Art Director: H. Lindsay. AV producer. Clients: educational and corporate. Produces filmstrips, multimedia kits, slide sets, sound-slide sets and booklets.
Needs: Works with 10-15 illustrators/year. Uses artists for filmstrip, slide, booklet, brochure and trade magazine illustrations.
First Contact & Terms: Send query letter and tearsheets to be kept on file. Reports within 1 month. Arrange interview to show portfolio. Pays $35/educational filmstrip frame; negotiates pay on other assignments.

Delaware

ALOYSIUS, BUTLER, & CLARK, Bancroft Mills, 30 Hill Rd., Wilmington DE 19806. (302)655-1552. Creative Director: Newton Bugbee. Ad agency. Clients: banks, industry, restaurants, real estate, hotels, small, local businesses, transit system, government offices.
Needs: Assigns "many" freelance jobs/year. Works with 3-4 freelance illustrators and 3-4 freelance designers/month. Uses artists for trade magazines, billboards, direct mail packages, brochures, newspapers, stationery, signage and posters.
First Contact & Terms: Local artists only "within reason (Philadelphia, Baltimore)." Send query letter with resume, business card and sample to be kept on file all except work that is "not worthy of consideration." Call for appointment to show portfolio. Prefers slides, photos, stats, photocopies as samples. Samples not kept on file returned only if requested. Reports only if interested. Works on assignment only. Pays by the project. Considers complexity of project, client's budget, and skill and experience of artist when establishing payment. Buys all rights.

CUSTOM CRAFT STUDIO, 310 Edgewood St., Bridgeville DE 19933. AV producer.
Needs: Works with 1 illustrator and 1 designer/month. Works with freelance artists on an assignment basis only. Uses artists for filmstrips, slide sets, trade magazine and newspapers. Also uses artists for print finishing, color negative retouching and airbrush work.

First Contact & Terms: Send query letter with slides or photographs, brochure/flyer, resume, samples and tear sheets to be kept on file. Samples returned by SASE. Reports in 2 weeks. No originals returned to artist at job's completion. Pay varies.

LYONS, INC., 715 Orange St., Wilmington DE 19801. (302)654-6146. Vice President: P. Coleman DuPont. AV/video/literature/display design producer. Clients: corporate and industrial.
Needs: Has need for storyboard artists and multi-image designers. Works on assignment only. Uses artists for multimedia presentations, collateral, literature, advertising and displays.
First Contact & Terms: Send resume. Prefers printed pieces, original art, storyboards, slides and/or video and multi-image samples—screening facilities available. Samples returned by SASE. Reports only if interested. Provide flyer or slides to be kept on file for future assignments. Pays by the hour, $6-14 average. Considers complexity of project, client's budget, and skill and experience of artist when establishing payment.

SHIPLEY ASSOCIATES INC., 1300 Pennsylvania Ave., Wilmington DE 19806. (302)652-3051. Creative Director: Jack Parry. Ad/PR firm. Serves clients in harness racing, industrial and corporate accounts, insurance, real estate and entertainment.
Needs: Works with 2 illustrators and 1 designer/month. Assigns 9 jobs/year. Works with freelance artists on assignment only. Uses artists for annual report illustrations, mechanicals, brochure and sign design.
First Contact & Terms: Query with previously published work. Prefers layouts (magazine & newspaper), mechanicals, line drawings and finished pieces as samples. Samples not returned. Reports within 2 weeks. Provide resume, samples and tear sheets to be kept on file for possible future assignments. No originals returned at job's completion. Negotiates payment.

District of Columbia

JAFFE ASSOCIATES, Suite 200, 2000 L St. NW, Washington DC 20036. (202)783-4848. Office Manager: Lora Wegman. PR and marketing firm. Clients: commercial real estate, banks, national associations, architectural and engineering, health care, law firms and accounting. Places advertising only to limited extent.
Needs: Works with several designers. Uses artists for stationery design, multimedia kits, direct mail, television, slide sets and brochures/flyers.
First Contact & Terms: Send resume and portfolio for review. "Freelancers are employed on basis of past experience, personal knowledge or special expertise." Provide brochures, flyers, business cards, resumes and tear sheets to be kept on file for future assignments. Originals returned only if prearranged. Negotiates payment based on client's budget, amount of creativity required from artist and artist's previous experience/reputation.
Tips: "Interested in samples of produced work and details regarding availability and ability to produce work on short time schedules. *Do not* deluge account executives with calls."

HENRY J. KAUFMAN & ASSOCIATES, PR Division, 2233 Wisconsin Ave., Washington DC 20007. Senior Vice President/Creative Director: Roger Vilsack. Ad agency. Clients: electronics firms, trade associations, government contracts, financial, consumer services and products.
Needs: Works with 50 illustrators and photographers/year. Uses freelance artists for billboards, consumer and trade magazines, direct mail, P-O-P displays, brochures, posters, newspapers and AV presentations.
First Contact & Terms: Send mailer or brochure. Works on assignment basis only. Payment is by the project; negotiates according to client's budget.

MANNING, SELVAGE & LEE, INC., Suite 300, 1250 Eye St. NW, Washington DC 20005. (202)682-1660. Contact: Creative Director. PR firm. Clients: pharmaceutical firms, nonprofit associations, real estate developers, corporations and high-tech firms.
Needs: Uses artists for illustration, paste-up and design.
First Contact & Terms: Send tear sheets, photostats, photocopies, slides and photographs. Call or write to schedule an appointment to show a portfolio, which should include best work. Pays for design by the hour, $20-55; by the project, $150-5,000.

SCREENSCOPE, INC., 3600 M St. NW, Washington DC 20016. President: Marilyn Weiner. Chairman: Harold M. Weiner. Audiovisual firm. Clients: large industrial corporations, PBS and trade associations.
Needs: Works with 10 freelance artists/year. Artist must have a minimum of 3 years' experience. Works on assignment only. Uses artists for graphic design, promotional materials and technical

assistance in making films. Especially important is a sense of design and promotion.
First Contact & Terms: Send query letter with brochure and photostats, photographs or slides to be kept on file for 1 year. Samples not filed are returned by SASE only if requested. Does not report back. Pays negotiable rate, but not less than $150. Considers complexity of the project when establishing payment. Buys all rights.

Florida

***JOSEPH ANTHONY ADVERTISING AGENCY, INC.**, 8300 Congress Ave., Boca Raton FL 33499. (305)994-2660. Art Director: L.J. Moscariello. In-house direct mail firm. Clients: American consumer homes.
Needs: Works with 3-4 artists/year. Artist must have direct mail experience. Works on assignment only. Uses artists for advertising design and catalog layout; brochure design.
First Contact & Terms: Send query letter with resume, copies or print. Samples not filed are returned only if requested. Reports back within 3 months. Write to schedule an appointment to show a portfolio, which should include thumbnails, roughs, original/final art and final reproduction/product. Pays for design by the hour, $8-15. Pays for mechanical paste up/keyline by the hour, $7-10. Considers complexity of project, client's budget, how work will be used, turnaround time and rights purchased when establishing payment.

COVALT ADVERTISING AGENCY, 12907 NE Seventh Ave., North Miami FL 33161. (305)891-1543. Creative Director: Fernando Vasquez. Ad agency. Clients: automotive, cosmetics, industrial banks, restaurants, financial, consumer products.
Needs: Prefers local artists; very seldom uses out of town artists. Artists must have minimum of 5 years' experience; accepts less experience only if artist is extremely talented. Works on assignment only. Uses artists for illustration (all kinds and styles), photography, mechanicals, copywriting, retouching (important), rendering and lettering.
First Contact & Terms: Send query letter with brochure, resume, business card and photostats, photographs, slides or tear sheets to be kept on file. Samples not filed not returned. Reports only if interested. Call for appointment to show portfolio. Payment varies according to assignment. Considers complexity of project, client's budget, skill and experience of artist, and turnaround time when establishing payment. Buys all rights or reprint rights.
Tips: "If at first you don't succeed, keep in touch. Eventually something will come up due to our diversity of accounts. If I have the person, I might design something with his particular skill in mind."

CREATIVE DIRECTORS INC., 1320 S. Dixie Hwy., Coral Gables FL 33146. Co-Creative Director: Thomas W. Ferguson. Ad agency. Clients: real estate builders and developers.
Needs: Works with 6 freelance artists/year. Artists must speak English. Works on assignment only. Uses artists for architectural renderings, illustrations and photo retouching.
First Contact & Terms: Send query letter with samples of style. Call to schedule an appointment to show a portfolio. Pays for illustration by the project, $150 minimum. Considers complexity of project and client's budget when establishing payment. Rights purchased vary according to project.
Tips: "We look for professional level talent and dependability. Ninety percent of the freelance we commission is for architectural renderings; mostly single-family homes, condominiums and townhouse complexes."

CREATIVE RESOURCES INC., 2000 S. Dixie Hwy., Miami FL 33133. (305)856-3474. President: Mac Seligman. Ad agency/PR firm. Clients: travel, hotels, airlines and resorts.
Needs: Works with 6 illustrators/designers/year. Local artists only. Uses artists for layout, type spec and design for brochures, ads, posters and renderings.
First Contact & Terms: Send query letter with resume and samples. No file kept on artists. Original work returned after completion of job. Call or write to schedule an appointment to show a portfolio, which should include thumbnails. Pays for design $20-40/hour or negotiates pay by job or day. Pays for illustration by the hour, $40; amount varies by the project and day. Considers complexity of project, client's budget, and skill and experience of artist when establishing payment.

> **❝ Tight airbrush rendering is coming back, and these artists are hard to find. ❞**
>
> *Sid Navratil, Sid Navratil Art Studio*

Close-up

Miles Hardiman
Illustrator
Denver, Colorado

"Drive, desire and talent," in that order, are the characteristics Miles Hardiman lists when defining a successful freelance artist. A top ad illustrator who has carved out a distinguished 32-year career, Hardiman exemplifies all three qualities.

College-educated, but basically self-taught in art, Hardiman created an illustrative edge by teaching himself to read blueprints. "A lot of the work I do is very technical in nature in that I sometimes have to build an illustration of a nonexistent product. The client gives me engineering drawings or blueprints to work from; I had to learn how to read these types of drawings" in order to complete assignments.

The technically-oriented illustrations appear primarily with Hardiman's best-known accounts, Yamaha® and Honda®, but his realistic illustrations have enhanced ads for Levi's®, Del Monte®, Coors®, Olympia® and Wonder Bread®, to name a few.

His drive to become a nationally-known illustrator led to deliberate career decisions. He's lived in Kansas City, Seattle and San Francisco in order "to be available to a certain market, to get my reputation built along certain lines." He now resides in Denver, Colorado, because it's a central market—"I can be anywhere in the United States and back in one day."

As a novice, Hardiman's self-promotional efforts consisted mainly of in-person contact and a small printed piece. "I carried my portfolio around and knocked on doors to show samples of my work; I called and made contacts." As an established illustrator, he now relies on clients seeing his printed work and his *Creative Black Book* ad with its accompanying handouts. But he believes careers move in stages and is therefore producing "a quality brochure with a mailing list to help me reach the whole market that's out there."

He believes a good promotional piece is invaluable to keep your name and work in an art director's mind, since luck and timing play as important a role in landing a job as does talent. But he cautions beginners to make sure it is well designed: "If you can't produce a beautiful handout yourself, then hire someone who can. If it looks like a piece of garbage, it's going to do you more harm than good."

Hardiman's approach to business is relaxed and flexible, an attitude honed through years of experience, concern for his clients, an understanding of his career's direction and recognition of the "real" world. If a job is obtained through one of his representatives, he lets him handle the contract considerations; if it's a direct assignment, Hardiman aims for a cooperative effort, "a sense of cohesion between me and the agency's creative people." He considers compromise a part of this business: "Don't do things that are going to drive the client away if being flexible means the client will come back to you for another job."

His career-long desire for excellence is revealed in his commentary on the professional artist. "The pro reaches a point in his career when he realizes that what he's doing isn't quite good enough and he's willing to take it further. When *you* feel a piece of work is finished and it's good, take it further. You have to push yourself."

—Sally Prince Davis

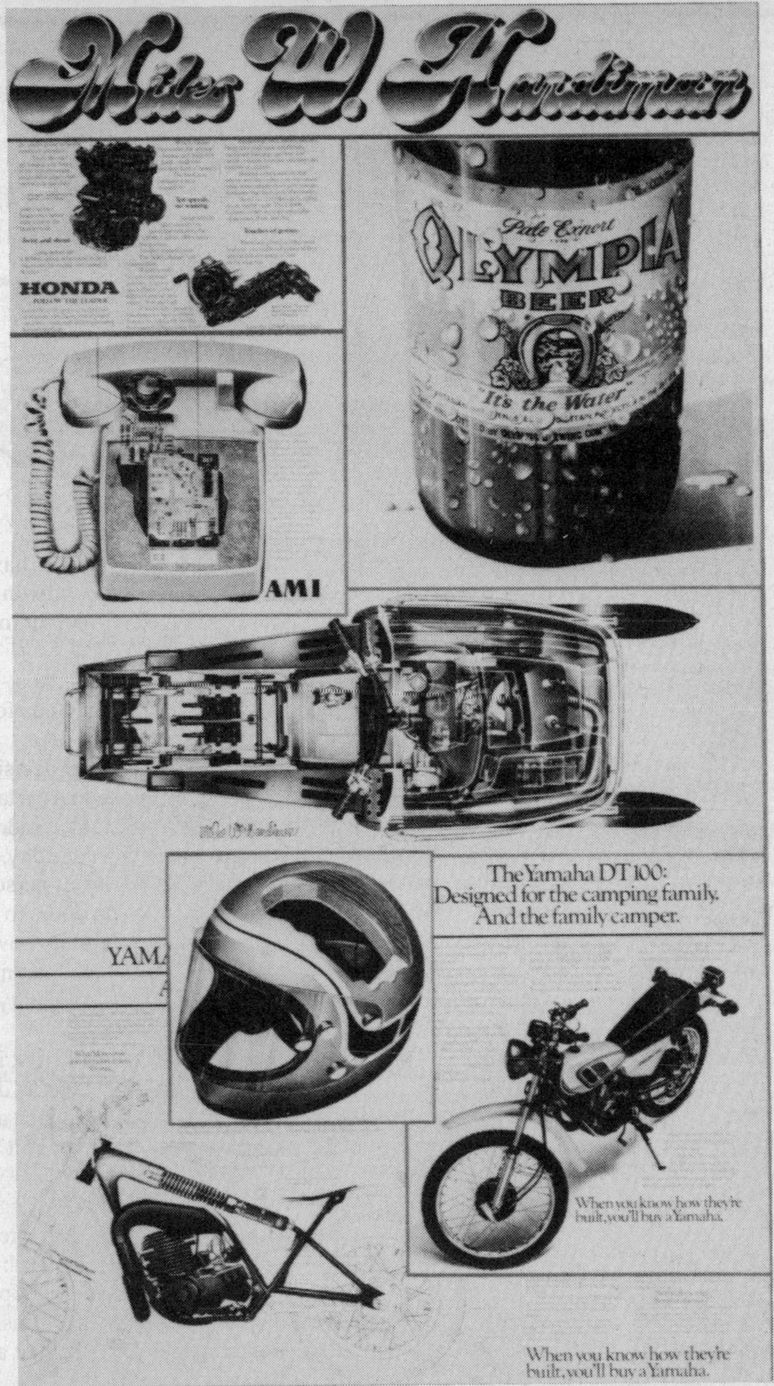

Hardiman finds that his annual ads in the Creative Black Book, *a directory of freelance artists, attract top-notch clients. Thus, the page pays for itself immediately. He also receives 2,000 tear sheets of the page for his own promotional use.*

MICHAELJAY INC., 10383 Oak St. NE, St. Petersburg FL 33702. (813)577-2993. President: Michael Anderson. Audiovisual firm. Clients: developers, medical lab equipment, insurance firms, boating industry.
Needs: Works with 4 freelance artists/year. Prefers local artists. Uses artists for mechanical art and paste-up for slides, illustrations, line art for slides. Especially important are mechanical art skills, animation of art and slide design.
First Contact & Terms: Send query letter. Set up an appointment for interview. Pays by the hour, $12.50-30 average. Considers complexity of project and turnaround time when establishing payment. Buys all rights.
Tips: "Present clean mechanical work and show skills in slide design."

MULTIVISION PRODUCTIONS, 7000 SW 59th Place, S. Miami FL 33143. (305)662-6011. President: Robert Berkowitz. AV/film producer. Serves clients in industry and advertising. Produces multi-image sound-slide materials.
Needs: Assigns 50 jobs/year. Prefers "in-camera slide art specialists." Works with 2 animators and 3 designers/month. Uses artists for multi-image, AV/film projects.
First Contact & Terms: Send samples (prefers slides) and arrange interview by mail. Samples not kept on file returned. Reports within 1 week. Portfolio should include resume, samples and business card to be kept on file. Pays by the project. Method of payment is negotiated with the individual artist. No originals returned following publication. Buys all rights.
Tips: "Forox and animation specialists are needed for slides."

PRUITT HUMPHRESS POWERS & MUNROE ADVERTISING AGENCY, INC., 516 N. Adams St., Tallahassee FL 32301. (904)222-1212. Ad agency. Clients: business to business, consumer. Media used include: billboards, consumer and trade magazines, direct mail, newspapers, P-O-P displays, radio and TV.
Needs: Uses artists for direct mail, brochures/flyers, trade magazines and newspapers. "Freelancers used in every aspect of business and given as much freedom as their skill warrants."
First Contact & Terms: Send resume. Provide materials to be kept on file for future assignments. Negotiates payment based on client's budget and amount of creativity required from artist. Pays set fee/job.
Tips: In portfolio, "submit examples of past agency work in clean, orderly, businesslike fashion including written explanations of each work. Ten illustrations or less."

GERALD SCHWARTZ AGENCY, Suite 506, 600 Alton Rd., Miami Beach FL 33139. (305)538-0385. Executive Vice President: Felice P. Schwartz. Ad/PR/fund-raising firm. Clients: banks, savings and loan associations, hospitals, universities, philanthropic agencies, political party campaigns and hospitals. Assigns 100 jobs and buys 25 illustrations/year.
Needs: Works with 2 illustrators/month. Uses artists for billboards, filmstrips, slide sets, brochures/flyers and newspapers.
First Contact & Terms: Query with samples (photocopies). SASE. Reports within 2 weeks. No file kept on artists. Originals returned at job's completion. Payment by job.

STARR PRODUCTIONS INC., 4862 SW 72nd Ave., Miami FL 33155. (305)663-3327. Production Coordinator: Tab Licea. AV producer. Clients: industry (80%) and advertising (20%). Produces "sales and marketing primarily, with some financial reporting and a little training."
Needs: Assigns approximately 100 jobs/year. Works with 2-3 illustrators and 1-2 designers/month. Works on assignment only. Uses artists for overall show design, cartoon work, paste up and board work.
First Contact & Terms: "We prefer AV experience and demand a high energy level." Send resume, then arrange interview by phone. Provide resume and business card to be kept on file for possible future assignments. No originals returned after publication. Buys all rights.

Georgia

BURST/GOSA PRODUCTIONS, INC., 1190 Euclid Ave. NE, Box 5354, Atlanta GA 30307. (404)523-8023. President: Fran Burst. Audiovisual firm. Clients: major corporations, religious organizations, nonprofit groups. Client list provided on request with SASE.
Needs: Works with 5 freelance artists/year. Uses artists for design and layout of graphics for 16mm film, slides and printed material, and some conceptual design for slide art. Artists should have a "good handle on graphic design and layout."
First Contact & Terms: Artists in Atlanta area only; minimum two years' experience. Works on

assignment only. Send query letter with resume to be kept on file. Reports only if interested. Pays by the hour or by the project. Considers client's budget, skill and experience of artist, turnaround time and rights purchased when establishing payment. Rights purchased vary according to project.

***D'ARCY-MACMANUS & MASIUS**, Suite 1901, 400 Colony Sq., Atlanta GA 30361. (404)892-8722. World-wide office in New York; agencies also in Chicago, Detroit, St. Louis and San Francisco. Contact: Executive Art Director. Ad agency. Clients: dairy products, finance, package goods, amusement parks and resort properties.
Needs: Works with 5 or more illustrators/month. Works on assignment only. Uses freelance artists for billboards, consumer and trade magazines, direct mail, P-O-P displays, brochures, catalogs, posters, signage, newspapers and AV presentations.
First Contact & Terms: Arrange interview to show portfolio; prefers to see b&w product work for newspaper reproduction. Samples returned by SASE. Reports in 2 weeks. Payment varies.
Tips: "Make it short and to the point."

DAVID W. EVANS/ATLANTA, INC., 550 Pharr Rd. NE, Atlanta GA 30305. (404)261-7000. Creative Director: Michael Jones-Kelly. Ad agency. Clients: industrial and consumer.
Needs: Works with 3 freelance illustrators/month. Uses freelancers for billboards, consumer and trade magazines, direct mail, brochures/flyers, newspapers, P-O-P displays, stationery design and TV.
First Contact & Terms: Send samples. Prefers work "that has been produced—rather than daydreams." Samples are filed and not returned. Negotiates payment based on individual needs of job.
Tips: Especially interested in realistic illustrators. "Show me work that accomplishes objectives. I'll go to museums and galleries for fine art shows."

FILMAMERICA, INC., Suite 209, 3177 Peachtree Rd. NE, Atlanta GA 30305. (404)261-3718. President: Avrum M. Fine. Audiovisual firm. Clients: corporate producers, advertising agencies.
Needs: Works with 2 freelance artists/year. Works on assignment only. Uses artists for film campaigns. Especially important are illustration and layout skills.
First Contact & Terms: Send query letter with resume and photographs or tear sheets to be kept on file. Samples not filed are returned only if requested. Reports back only if interested. Write for appointment to show portfolio. Pays by the project, $500 minimum. Considers complexity of the project and rights purchased when establishing payment. Rights purchased vary according to project.
Tips: "Be very patient!"

FLUKER & ASSOCIATES ADVERTISING AGENCY, 379 Rogers Ave., Macon GA 31204. (912)742-7551. Graphic Department Head: De Stephenson. Ad agency/AV/marketing/PR firm. Clients: commercial and industrial firms.
Needs: Assigns 40-50 freelance jobs/year. Works on assignment only. Uses artists for billboards, direct mail packages, catalogs, filmstrips, movies, signage and P-O-P displays.
First Contact & Terms: Send query letter with brochure and samples to be kept on file. Prefers slides and photographs as samples. Samples not kept on file returned only if requested. Reports only if interested. Write for appointment to show portfolio. Pays by quotations only. Considers client's budget, and skill and experience of artists when establishing payment. Buys all rights.

PAUL FRENCH AND PARTNERS, INC., Rt. 5, Box 285, LaGrange GA 30240. (404)882-5581. Contact: Ms. Gene Byrd. Audiovisual firm. Client list provided upon request.
Needs: Works with 3 freelance artists/year. Works on assignment only. Uses artists for illustration.
First Contact & Terms: Send query letter with resume and slides to be kept on file. Samples not filed are returned by SASE. Reports back only if interested. To show a portfolio, mail appropriate materials. Pays for design and illustration by the hour, $25-100 average. Considers client's budget when establishing payment. Buys all rights.
Tips: "Be organized."

GARRETT COMMUNICATIONS, Box 53, Atlanta GA 30301. (404)755-2513. President: Ruby Grant Garrett. Production and placement firm for print media. Clients: banks, organizations, products-service consumer. Client list provided for SASE.
Needs: Assigns 24 freelance jobs/year. Works with 1 freelance illustrator and 1 freelance designer/month. Experienced, talented artists only. Works on assignment only. Uses artists for billboards, brochures, signage and posters.
First Contact & Terms: Send query letter with resume and samples to be kept on file. Samples returned by SASE if not kept on file. Reports within 10 days. Write to schedule an appointment to show a portfolio which should include roughs and tear sheets. Pays for design by the hour, $35-50; by the project $100 minimum, by the day, $150 minimum. Pays for illustration by the hour, $35 minimum, by

the project, $100 minimum; by the day, $100 minimum. Considers client's budget, skill and experience of artist and turnaround time when establishing payment. Negotiates rights purchased.
Tips: Send "6-12 items that show scope of skills."

HAYNES ADVERTISING, 90 Fifth St., Macon GA 31201. (912)742-5266. Contact: Phil Haynes. Ad agency. Clients: financial, industrial, automobile, professional.
Needs: Assigns 10 freelance jobs/year. Works on assignment only. Uses artists for brochures, newspapers and AV presentations.
First Contact & Terms: Send query letter with photocopies and press proofs to be kept on file. Samples not kept on file returned by SASE. Reports only if interested. Call or write for appointment to show portfolio. Pays by the project, $50-200 average. Considers complexity of project when establishing payment. Negotiate rights purchased.

KAUFMANN ASSOCIATES, One Willow Sq., St. Simons Island GA 31522. (912)638-8678. Creative Director: S.C. Kaufmann. Ad agency. Clients: resort, food processor, bank.
Needs: Assigns "very few" freelance jobs/year. Works on assignment only. Works with 1 freelance illustrator/month. Uses artists for brochures.
First Contact & Terms: Send samples to be kept on file. Reports only if interested. Considers complexity of project, client's budget, and skill and experience of artist when establishing payment. Buys all rights.

LEWIS BROADCASTING CORP., Box 13646, Savannah GA 31406. Public Relations Director: C.A. Barbieri. TV producer.
Needs: Uses artists for direct mail brochures, billboards, posters, public service TV spots and motion picture work. Works on assignment only.
First Contact & Terms: Send query letter with resume and printed photocopied samples. Samples returned by SASE. Reports in 2 weeks. Provide business card and resume to be kept on file. Originals returned to artist at job's completion. Pay "depends on job."
Tips: "Be willing to flesh out others' ideas."

PRINGLE DIXON PRINGLE, 3340 Peachtree Rd. NE, Atlanta GA 30326. (404)688-6720. Creative Director: Perry Mitchell. Ad agency. Clients: fashion, financial, fast food and industrial firms; client list provided upon request.
Needs: Works with 2 illustrators/month. Local artists only. Works on assignment basis only. Uses freelance artists for billboards, consumer and trade magazines, direct mail, P-O-P displays, brochures, catalogs, posters, signage, newspapers and AV presentations.
First Contact & Terms: Arrange interview to show portfolio. Payment varies according to job and freelancer.

***SMITH MCNEAL ADVERTISING**, 368 Ponce De Leon, Atlanta GA 30308. (404)892-3716. Senior Art Director: Darryl Elliott. Ad agency. Clients: hotels, industry and food.
Needs: Works with very few freelance artists. Works on assignment only. Uses artists for illustrations, mechanicals and layouts. Artist should have "good layout skills, visualization, speed, accuracy."
First Contact & Terms: Send query letter with resume and samples. Samples not filed are returned by SASE. Reports only if interested. Write to schedule an appointment to show a portfolio, which should include roughs, final reproduction/product and tear sheets. Pays for design by the hour, $14-50. Pays for illustration by the project, $100-2,000. Considers complexity of project, client's budget, how work will be used and when turnaround time when establishing payment. Buys all rights.

J. WALTER THOMPSON COMPANY, 2828 Tower Pl., 3340 Peachtree Rd. NE, Atlanta GA 30326. (404)266-2828. Executive Art Director: Bill Tomassi. Creative Director: Bob Jones. Ad agency. Clients: mainly financial, industrial and consumer. This office does creative work for Atlanta and the southeastern US.
Needs: Works with freelance illustrators. Works on assignment only. Uses artists for billboards, consumer magazines, trade magazines and newspapers.
First Contact & Terms: Send slides, original work, stats. Samples returned by SASE. Reports only if interested. No originals returned at job's completion. Call for appointment to show portfolio. Pays by the hour, $20-35 average; by the project, $100-6,000 average; by the day, $150-3,500 average. Considers complexity of project, client's budget, skill and experience of artist and rights purchased when establishing payment.
Tips: Wants to see samples of work done for different clients. Likes to see work done in different mediums. Likes variety and versatility. Artists interested in working here should "be *professional* and do top grade work." Deals with artists' reps only.

TUCKER WAYNE & CO., Suite 2700, 230 Peachtree St. NW, Atlanta GA 30303. (404)521-7600. Creative Department Business Manager: Rita Morris. Ad agency. Serves a variety of clients including packaged products, food, utilities, transportation, agriculture and pesticide manufacturing.
Needs: A total of 8 art directors occasionally work with freelance illustrators. Uses freelancers for consumer and trade magazines, newspapers and TV.
First Contact & Terms: Call creative secretary for appointment. Selection based on portfolio review. Negotiates payment based on budget, where work will appear, travel expenses, etc.
Tips: Each art director has individual preference.

Hawaii

MILICI/VALENTI ADVERTISING INC., Amfac Bldg., 700 Bishop St., Honolulu HI 96813. (808)536-0881. Contact: Creative Director. Ad agency. Serves clients in food, finance, utilities, entertainment, chemicals and personal care products.
Needs: Works with 3-4 illustrators/month. Artists must be familiar with advertising demands; used to working long distance through the mail; and be familiar with Hawaii. Uses artists for illustration, retouching and lettering for newspapers, multimedia kits, magazines, radio, TV and direct mail.
First Contact & Terms: Provide brochure, flyer and tear sheets to be kept on file for future assignments. No originals returned to artist at job's completion. Pays $200-2,000.

***PACIFIC PRODUCTIONS**, Box 2881, Honolulu HI 96802. (808)531-1560. Production Manager: Biu Bennett. AV producer. Serves clients in industry, government and education. Produces almost all types of AV materials.
Needs: Assigns 2 jobs/year. Works with 3 illustrators, 2 animators and 2 designers/year. Uses artists for all types projects.
First Contact & Terms: Artists located in Hawaii only. Send query letter and samples (photostats or slides preferred). Samples returned. Provide resume to be kept on file for possible future assignments. Works on assignment only. Reports in 2 weeks. Pays by the project. Payment varies with each client's budget. No originals returned to artist following publication. Negotiates rights purchased.

Illinois

WILLIAM HART ADLER, INC., 5 Revere Dr., Northbrook IL 60062. (312)291-1730. President: Bill Adler. Ad agency. Clients: housewares, electronics/hi-fi—"wide variety" of firms.
Needs: Works with 4-5 illustrators/year. Works primarily with local freelancers. Chooses freelancers on a referral basis or phone for appointment. Works on assignment only. Uses freelance artists for billboards, consumer and trade magazines, direct mail, P-O-P displays, brochures, catalogs, posters, signage, newspapers and AV presentations.
First Contact & Terms: Negotiates payment; varies according to job and freelancer.

BRACKER COMMUNICATION, 330 W. Frontage Rd., Northfield IL 60093. (312)441-5534. President: Richard W. Bracker. Ad agency/public relations/publishing firm. Clients: construction, financial, acoustical, contractors, equipment manufacturers, trade associations, household fixtures, pest control products.
Needs: Works with 4-6 freelance artists/year. "Use only artists based in the Chicago area for the most part. We look for ability and have used recent graduates." Works on assignment only. Uses artists for graphic design/key line. Especially important are type specing, design/layout and photo handling.
First Contact & Terms: Phone or send resume to be kept on file; write for appointment to show portfolio. Reviews any type of sample. Reports within 2 weeks. Negotiates and/or accepts quotations on specific projects. Considers complexity of project, skill and experience of artist, and turnaround time when establishing payment. Buys all rights.
Tips: "Don't make assumptions about anything."

BRAGAW PUBLIC RELATIONS SERVICES, 800 E. Northwest Hwy., Palatine IL 60067. (312)934-5580. Principal: Richard S. Bragaw. PR firm. Clients: professional service firms, associations, industry.
Needs: Assigns 12 freelance jobs/year. Local artists only. Works on assignment only. Works with 1 freelance illustrator and 1 freelance designer/month. Uses artists for direct mail packages, brochures, signage, AV presentations and press releases.

First Contact & Terms: Send query letter with brochure to be kept on file. Reports only if interested. Write to schedule an appointment. Pays by the hour, $25-75 average. Considers complexity of project, skill and experience of artist and turnaround time when establishing payment. Buys all rights.
Tips: "Be honest."

CAIN AND COMPANY (ROCKFORD), 2222 E. State St., Rockford IL 61108. (815)963-1321. Manager, Graphic Services: Randall E. Klein. Ad agency/PR firm. Clients: financial, industrial, retail.
Needs: Assigns 6 freelance jobs/year. Uses artists for consumer and trade magazines, billboards, direct mail packages, brochures, catalogs, newspapers, filmstrips, movies, stationery, signage, P-O-P displays, AV presentations, posters and press releases "to some degree."
First Contact & Terms: Send query letter with brochure, resume, business card, samples and tear sheets to be kept on file. Call or write for appointment to show portfolio. Send samples that show best one medium in which work is produced. Samples not kept on file are not returned. Reports only if interested. Works on assignment only. "Rates depend on talent and speed; could be anywhere from $5 to $30 an hour." Considers skill and experience of artist and turnaround time when establishing payment. Buys all rights.
Tips: "Have a good presentation, not just graphics."

JOHN CROWE ADVERTISING AGENCY, 1104 S. 2nd St., Springfield IL 62704. (217)528-1076. Contact: John Crowe. Ad/art agency. Clients: industries, manufacturers, retailers, banks, publishers, insurance firms, packaging firms, state agencies, aviation and law enforcement agencies.
Needs: Buys 3,000 illustrations/year. Works with 4 illustrators and 3 designers/month. Works on assignment only. Uses artists for color separations, animation, lettering, paste-up and type spec for work with consumer magazines, stationery design, direct mail, slide sets, brochures/flyers, trade magazines and newspapers. Especially needs layout, camera-ready art and photo retouching.
First Contact & Terms: "Send a letter to us regarding available work at agency. Tell us about yourself. We will reply if work is needed and request samples of work." Prefers tear sheets, original art, photocopies, brochure, business card and resume to be kept on file. Samples not filed returned by SASE. Reports in 2 weeks. Pays $25/hour illustration/camera-ready art; $4-10 per sketch. No originals returned to artist at job's completion. No payment for unused assigned illustrations.
Tips: Seeks neat, organized samples or portfolio. "Disorganized sloppy work in presenting talent" is the biggest mistake artists make. Forsees a trend toward computer art.

***DYNAMIC GRAPHICS**, 6000 N. Forest Park Dr., Peoria IL 61614. Art Director: Frank Antal. Grahics firm for general graphic art user.
Needs: Works with 50 freelance artists/year. Works on assignment only. Uses artists for illustrations. Needs artists with "originality, creativity, professionalism."
First Contact & Terms: Send query letter with brochure showing art style or tear sheets and photocopies. Samples not filed are returned. Reports back within 1 month. To show a portfolio, mail appropriate materials, which should include final reproduction/product or photostats. Pays by the project; "We pay highly competitive rates but prefer not to specify." Pays for illustration by the project. Considers complexity of project, skill and experience of artist and rights purchased when establishing payment. Buys all rights.
Tips: "Submit styles that are the illustrator's strongest and can be used successfully, consistently."

FILLMAN ADVERTISING INC., 304 W. Hill St., Champaign IL 61820. (217)352-0002. Art/Creative Director: Mary Auth. Ad agency. Serves clients in industry. Assigns 60 jobs and buys 10 illustrations/year.
Needs: Works with 1-2 illustrators and 2-3 designers/month. Uses mostly local artists. Works on assignment only. Uses artists for stationery design, direct mail, brochures/flyers, trade magazines.
First Contact & Terms: Send query letter with originals, photographs, b&w line drawings, photocopies of inputs or finished printed pieces. Samples returned by SASE. Reports in 2 weeks. Send business card and resume to be kept on file for possible future assignments. No originals returned to artist at job's completion. Pays $35-600/project; by the hour, $15-25 average. Pays promised fee for unused assigned illustrations. Considers skill and experience of artist when establishing payment.

FOLEY ADVERTISING INC., 17W715 Butterfield Rd., Oakbrook Terrace IL 60181. (312)782-1791. Ad agency. President: J.E. Foley. Industrial agency. Serves clients in equipment for science and manufacturing. Assigns 200 jobs/year.
Needs: Works with 3 designers/month. Local, industrial artists only. Works on assignment only. Uses artists for layout and mechanicals.
First Contact & Terms: Send query letter with samples to be kept on file and arrange interview to show portfolio. Considers complexity of project and client's budget when establishing payment.

IMPERIAL INTERNATIONAL LEARNING CORP., Box 548, Kankakee IL 60901. (815)933-7735. President: Spencer Barnard. AV producer. Serves clients in education. Produces filmstrips, illustrated workbooks, microcomputer software, video tapes.
Needs: Assigns multiple jobs/year. Works with variety of designers/year. Works on assignment only. Uses artists for original line art, color illustrations and graphic design, computer graphics.
First Contact & Terms: Send query letter and tear sheets to be kept on file. Samples returned only if requested. Reports back only if interested. Method and amount of payment are negotiated with the individual artist. No originals returned to artist following publication. Considers skill and experience of artist when establishing payment. Buys all rights.

ELVING JOHNSON ADVERTISING INC., 7804 W. College Dr., Palos Heights IL 60463. (312)361-2850. Art/Creative Director: Michael McNicholas. Ad agency. Serves clients in industrial machinery, construction materials, material handling, finance, etc.
Needs: Works with 2 illustrators/month. Local artists only. Uses artists for direct mail, brochures/flyers, trade magazines and newspapers. Also uses artists for layout, illustration, technical art, paste-up and retouching.
First Contact & Terms: Call for interview.

LERNER SCOTT CORP., 1000 Skokie Blvd., Wilmette IL 60091. (312)251-2447. Vice President/Managing Art Director: Mark Bryzinski. Direct marketing/ad agency. Clients: insurance and communications companies, wholesale distributors, entertainment (Playboy Clubs), trade schools, nurseries and consumer products.
Needs: Works with 8 freelance artists/year. Chicago area artists only. Works on assignment only. Uses artists for advertising, brochure and catalog design, illustration and layout; P-O-P displays, and signage.
First Contact & Terms: Send query letter with business card, photocopies or tear sheets to be kept on file. Samples not filed returned only if requested. Reports only if interested. Call for appointment to show portfolio. Pays by the project. Considers complexity of project when establishing payment.

***WALTER P. LUEDKE & ASSOCIATES**, Sweden House, 4615 E. State St., Rockford IL 61108. Ad/art agency. Serves clients in: machine tool, electrical/electronics, kitchen equipment, print equipment, construction, speed reducer and retail advertising.
Needs: Works with 2 illustrators/month. Works on assignment only. Uses artists for layout, illustration, technical art, paste-up, exploded views and retouching; newspapers, TV, magazines, billboards, direct mail and P-O-P display.
First Contact & Terms: Provide brochure and business card to be kept on file for possible future assignments. No originals returned to artist at job's completion. Reports within 30 days. Pays by the job or hour, $10 minimum. Considers complexity of project, client's budget, skill and experience of artist, geographic scope of finished project, turnaround time and rights purchased when establishing payment.
Tips: Artists must "let me know they exist and where, etc. Looking for a future takeover person with customers of his own to meld into our small operation and to possibly take charge and end up owning the business (5 to 10 years)."

MARTINDALE & ASSOCIATES, 701 W. Gulf Rd., Mt. Prospect, Arlington Heights IL 60056. (312)437-6400. President: R. Martindale. Communications consultants. Clients: financial. Media used include billboards, consumer and trade magazines, direct mail, newspapers, radio and TV.
Needs: "Work load varies; usually our extra assignments (beyond what our regular staff can service efficiently) bunch up in active months such as January, May, September and October. Those extra assignments might be 5 or 6 newspaper ad layouts, 2 or 3 brochures, and perhaps a special design assignment." Works on assignment only. Uses artists for work in direct mail, brochures/flyers and newspapers.
First Contact & Terms: Write and request personal interview to show portfolio. Provide resume to be kept on file for future assignments. Reports within 10 days. Pays by the hour or by the project. Considers complexity of project, client's budget, skill and experience of artist, and turnaround time when establishing payment.
Tips: "We prefer to let the individual decide what he or she wants to show. If they can't show a strong portfolio, we can't expect them to be strong enough for our purposes." Artist should "stay within the *guidelines* of the assigned project."

ARTHUR MERIWETHER, INC., 1529 Brook Dr., Downers Grove IL 60515. (312)495-0600. Production Coordinator: Lori Ouska. Audiovisual firm, design studio and communications services. Clients: industrial corporations (electronics, chemical, etc.) plus consumer clients.
Needs: Works with 10-20 freelance artists/year. Artists should have minimum 2 years' experience. Prefers local artists, will occasionally work with out-of-state illustrators. Uses artists for

keyline/pasteup, illustration and design. Especially important are knowledge of audiovisual and print production techniques.

First Contact & Terms: Send query letter with resume, business card, slides and tear sheets. Samples returned by SASE. Reports only if interested. Payment varies per project and artist's experience. Also considers client's budget, skill of artist and turnaround time when establishing payment. Rights purchased vary according to project; usually buys all rights.

***MINDSCAPE, INC.**, 3444 Dundee Rd., Northbrook IL 60062. (312)480-7667. Art Director: Jack Nichols. Software publisher.

Needs: Works with 6-10 freelance artists/year. Minimum three years' experience. Works on assignment only. Uses artists for design, illustrations, brochures, catalog, books, mechanicals, retouching, animation and computer graphics. Artist must have design and production skills.

First Contact & Terms: Send query letter with brochure showing style or resume and samples. Samples not filed are returned by SASE. Reports only if interested. Call or write to schedule an appointment to show a portfolio, which should include roughs, original/final art, final reproduction/product, color and B&W. Pays for illustrations by the project, up to $3,000. Considers complexity of project, skill and experience of artist and turnaround time when establishing payment. Buys all rights.

TOM MORRIS INC., Suite 55, 2720 River Rd., Des Plaines IL 60018. Contact: Creative Director. AV producer/art studio/industrial advertising agency. Clients: industrial marketers. Produces print media, charts, filmstrips, motion pictures and slides.

Needs: Works with 10 freelance illustrators and 12 designers/year. Works on assignment only.

First Contact & Terms: Prefers photographs and b&w or color line drawings as samples. Samples returned by SASE. Reports in 2 weeks. Provide resume and tear sheets to be kept on file for possible future assignments. Pay depends on project. Buys all rights.

MOTIVATION MEDIA INC., 1245 Milwaukee Ave., Glenview IL 60025. (312)297-4740. Creative Graphics Manager: Perry Anderson. Clients: consumer and industrial. Producers of multi-image programs, speaker support and sound-slide programs, filmstrips, motion picture and videotape productions.

Needs: Works with 10 production artists and 5 designers/month. Assigns approx. 675 jobs/year. Works on assignment only.

First Contact & Terms: Query with resume and nonreturnable samples (photocopies, duplicates, etc.). SASE. Replies in 2 weeks if interested. Provide resume to be kept on file for future assignments. Pays $10-18/hour, multi-image, charts/graphs art direction; $10-30/hour, illustrations; also pays by the job. Considers complexity of project, client's budget, skill and experience of artist and turnaround time when establishing payment. Pays 30 days after receipt of invoice.

Tips: "Send resume and copies of work. Our schedule does not allow us extensive time for interviewing. Though I need people who know slide production, I'm interested in people who know all areas of art production. Be able to see a project through from input to completion. In your resumes, be brief and to the point; list experience. In your portfolio, specify AV or said experience."

NEW ORIENT MEDIA, Communications Building, Second and Main Sts., West Dundee IL 60118. (312)428-6000. President: Bob Sandidge. AV producer. Clients: corporate, educational and industrial. Produces filmstrips, multimedia kits, sound-slide sets and computer slides.

Needs: Assigns 200 jobs/year. Prefers Chicago area artists. Uses artists for realistic illustrations, b&w line art and paste-up.

First Contact & Terms: Query with previously used work and arrange interview to show portfolio. SASE. Reports within 1-2 weeks. Negotiates pay.

***TELEMATION PRODUCTIONS, INC.**, 3210 W. Westlake, Glenview IL. (312)729-5215. Art Director: Mitch Levin. Video production house. Clients: automotive firms, corporate clients, advertising agencies and private producers.

Needs: Works with 3-5 freelance artists/year. Computer graphics experience and art background required. Works on assignment only. Uses artists for design, illustrations, animation, logos, charts/graphics and advertisements. Artists should have "good illustration skill, a strong sense of design and be visually-oriented."

First Contact & Terms: Send query letter with resume and samples. Samples not filed are not returned. Reports only if interested. Call to schedule an appointment to show portfolio, which should include original/final art, final reproduction/product, color and slides if applicable. Pays for design by the hour, $10-15. Pays for illustration by the hour, $10-15. Considers skill and experience of artist when establishing payment. Buys all rights.

Tips: Artists should "be enthusiastic toward learning a new computer graphic system."

H. WILSON CO., 555 Taft Dr., South Holland IL 60473. (312)339-5111. Contact: Advertising Manager.
Needs: Assigns 20 jobs/year. Works with 2 illustrators and 2 designers/month. Uses artists for sales and marketing presentations, catalogs, direct mail, convention exhibits and promotion.
First Contact & Terms: Send query letter with resume and samples (ads, brochures, etc.), then arrange interview to show portfolio. SASE. Reports within 2 weeks. No originals returned at job's completion. Provide resume, business card and brochure to be kept on file for future assignments. Pays "for creative work on a job basis, final art on an hourly basis."

Chicago

N.W. AYER, INC., One Illinois Center, 111 E. Wacker Dr., Chicago IL 60601. (312)645-8800. Contact: Iris Rogers. Ad agency. "We cover a very wide range of clients."
First Contact & Terms: Call for personal appointment to show portfolio. Negotiates payment based on client's budget and the amount of creativity required from artist.
Tips: Portfolio should consist of past work used by ad agencies and commercial art.

BETZER PRODUCTIONS INC., 450 E. Ohio St., Chicago IL 60611. President: Joseph G. Betzer. Produces slide films and motion pictures.
Needs: Uses artists for motion picture animation and slide film art.
First Contact & Terms: Send query letter with resume.

CLEARVUE, INC., 5711 N. Milwaukee, Chicago IL 60646. (312)775-9433. Curriculum Product Development: Joe Vest. Audiovisual firm.
Needs: Works with 10-12 freelance artists/year. Works on assignment only. Uses artists for art for filmstrip programs.
First Contact & Terms: Send query letter to be kept on file. Prefers to review art boards or samples of actual filmstrips. Reports back within 10 days. Write for appointment to show portfolio. Pays $30-40 per frame—average program is 35-50 frames. Considers complexity of the project and budget when establishing payment. Buys all rights.
Tips: "Have some knowledge of filmstrip production requirements."

FRANK J. CORBETT, INC., 211 E. Chicago Ave., Chicago IL 60611. (312)664-5310. Associate Creative Director: Bill Reinwald. Ad agency. Serves clients in pharmaceuticals.
Needs: Works with 8-10 freelance illustrators/month. Uses freelancers "for almost everything."
First Contact & Terms: Call for appointment to show portfolio or make contact through artist's agent. Selection based on portfolio review. Negotiates payment based on client's budget.
Tips: Wants to see the best of artist's work including that used by ad agencies, and tear sheets of published art. Especially interested in good medical illustration, but also uses a wide variety of photography and illustration.

***THE CREATIVE DEPARTMENT, LTD.**,311 W. Superior, Chicago IL 60610. (312)440-9794. Vice President: Helen White. Estab. 1985. Ad agency/art studio. Clients: mostly industrial manufacturers of electronic components, railcars, T.V. components.
Needs: Works with 4 freelance artists 1 year. Prefers local artists only with minimum three years' experience. Works on assignment only. Uses artists for design, illustrations, brochures, catalog, P-O-P displays, retouching, posters, direct mail packages, lettering, logos and advertisements. Artists should have good lettering skills, marker renderings, creative ideas, knowledge of papers and inks, and varnishes.
First Contact & Terms: Send resume, tear sheets and photocopies. Samples not filed are returned by SASE only if requested. Reports back only if interested. Call to schedule an appointment to show portfolio, which should include thumbnails, roughs, original/final art, final reproduction/product, color, tear sheets photostats, photographs and b&w. Pays for design and illustration by the hour, $20 minimum. Considers complexity of project, client's budget and skill and experience of artist when establishing payment. Buys all rights.
Tips: "Don't show fashion illustrations when I'm interested in designing brochures for steel companies and faucet manufacturers!"

THE CREATIVE ESTABLISHMENT, 1421 N. Wells, Chicago IL 60610. (312)943-6700. President: Joan Beugen. Also: 115 W. 31st St., New York NY 10001. (212)563-3337, and 832 Sansome, San Francisco CA 94111. (415)982-0800. Chairman: Ira Kerns. AV/multimedia/motion picture producer. Clients: Fortune 500 and other major U.S. corporations. Audience: top level executives, managers,

John Lambert of Arlington Heights, Illinois, received this assignment from Helen White, the creative director of The Creative Department Ltd. "The artwork was designed to convey a message of safety and high manufacturing standards," says Lambert. Created by line and airbrush, the piece "opened other doors for technical illustration."

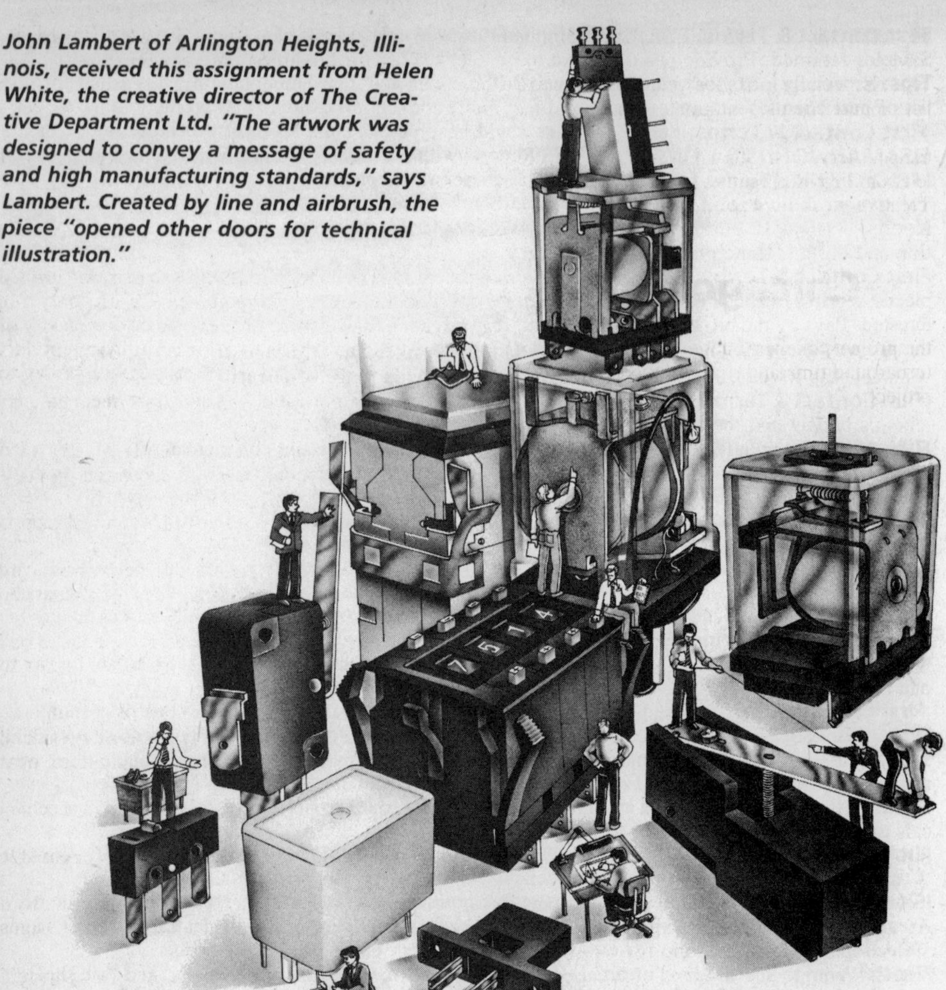

salesmen, distributors and/or suppliers of the specific client. "We produce slides, films and multimedia presentations primarily for industry. Our specialty is large sales and management meetings, using multiscreen slide projection. The slides we use range over every conceivable type and format, since we produce in the neighborhood of 30,000 slides a month."

Needs: Works with 8-10 illustrators and 1-5 designers/month. Local artists only. Works on assignment only. Uses artists for motion pictures and slides. "We use illustrators, cartoonists, designers, costume and set designers, sculptors, model-makers . . . you name it."

First Contact & Terms: "I am most interested in hearing from artists and art directors who have experience in slides as opposed to print work. However, we do use illustrators occasionally and show them how to prepare their work for reproduction into slides." Send resume, brochure/flyer, business card, tear sheets and sample slides to be kept on file. Samples not filed returned by SASE. Reports within 2 weeks. Call to schedule an appointment to show a portfolio, which should include photographs and story boards—"actual slides." Originals returned at job's completion if special arrangements are made. Pays by the hour, $15-20; by the project, $450/week. Considers client's budget and turnaround time when establishing payment.

DANIEL J. EDELMAN, INC., 211 E. Ontario, Chicago IL 60611-3219. (312)280-7000. AV Manager: Raul Perez. PR firm.

Needs: Works with 1 illustrator/month. Works on assignment basis only. Uses artists for local projects including daily newspapers and trade publications.

First Contact & Terms: Call for appointment to show portfolio. Prefers slides or photos as samples. Samples returned. Provide business card to be kept on file for possible future assignments.
Tips: Especially looks for "unique design and a variety of work that shows all of an artist's talents; also a list of past clients."

EISAMAN, JOHNS & LAWS ADVERTISING, Suite 2400, 333 N. Michigan Ave., Chicago IL 60601. (312)263-3474. Creative Director: Mike Waterkotte. Ad agency. Clients: Chicago office—automotive, TV station, radio station.
Needs: Assigns 12-20 freelance jobs/year. Works on assignment only. Uses artists for mainly illustration and design, some photography.
First Contact & Terms: Call or write for appointment to show portfolio. Prefers to review "printed pieces; reprints of Black Book ad, etc." Samples not filed returned only if requested. Reports only if interested. Pays by the project, amount depends entirely on budget for project. Considers complexity of the project, client's budget, skill and experience of artist, geographic scope for the finished product, turnaround time and rights purchased when establishing payment. Rights purchased vary according to project.

HILL AND KNOWLTON, INC., 1 Illinois Center, 111 E. Wacker Dr., Chicago IL 60601. (312)565-1200. Creative Director: Jacqueline Kohn. PR firm. Clients: corporate, financial, industrial products, medical, pharmaceutical, and public utilities.
Needs: Works with 1-2 illustrators/month. Works on assignment only. Uses artists for annual reports, brochures, employee publications and associated print and collateral.
First Contact & Terms: Call for appointment to show portfolio, which should include business card, brochure/flyer, samples and tear sheets to be kept on file. Prefers printed samples, slides or original photos and art as samples. Reports back whether to expect possible future assignments.
Tips: Has very broad needs of highest quality. Will discuss these and particular needs during initial call. Artists interested in working here should be "punctual on appointments; arrange portfolio to pertain to our needs only."

IMAGINE THAT!, Suite 4908, 405 N. Wabash Ave., Chicago IL 60611. (312)670-0234. President: John Beele. Ad agency. Clients: broadcast, insurance firm, University of Illinois sports program, pharmaceuticals, retail furniture stores, real estate and professional rodeo.
Needs: Assigns 25-50 jobs and buys 15 illustrations/year. Uses artists for layout, illustration, mechanicals and photography.
First Contact & Terms: Arrange interview to show portfolio with Sheila Dunbar. Pay is negotiable.

ISKER & ADAJIAN INC., 435 N. Michigan Ave., Chicago IL 60611. (312)222-1646. Contact: K. Bird. Ad agency/PR firm/art agency/AV producer/art studio. Clients: tourism and manufacturing. Assigns 100 jobs/year.
Needs: Works with artists on billboards, P-O-P displays, filmstrips, stationery design, multimedia kits, direct mail, TV, slide sets, brochures/flyers, trade magazines, album covers, newspapers and books. Also uses artists for layout, illustration, retouching and mechanicals. Works on assignment only and sometimes, *but rarely*, on a speculative basis.
First Contact & Terms: Query with resume, business card, brochure/flyer and samples to be kept on file or arrange interview to show portfolio. SASE. Prefers photostats, slides or original work as samples. Reports only if interested. No originals returned at job's completion. Pays "going rates." Considers client's budget, and skill and experience of artist when establishing payment.
Tips: Artists should "be very competent (or very reasonable in pricing); have samples that show originality and have samples rendered in media usually used: ink, wash, felt pens, etc. Oils are not too common. Show best work only. No more than 10-12 samples."

KEROFF & ROSENBERG ADVERTISING, 444 N. Wabash, Chicago IL 60611. (312)321-9000. Creative Supervisor: Dan Oditt. Ad and design agency. Clients: realty, financing, hotels.
Needs: Works with 10-12 freelance artists/year. Local, experienced artists only. Uses artists for advertising illustration and layout, brochure illustration, model making and signage.
First Contact & Terms: Send query letter with resume and photostats, photographs, slides or tear sheets to be kept on file. Samples not filed returned by SASE only if requested. Reports only if interested. Write for appointment to show portfolio. Considers complexity of project and turnaround time when establishing payment.
Tips: "Freelancers usually get the overflow, so it's frequently under a tight deadline. So be prepared."

***LAUREN INTERNATIONAL LTD.**, 752 W. Buena, Chicago IL 60613. Contact: Lauren Grey. Produces industrial films, filmstrips, print pieces and multimedia presentations.

Needs: Works with writers, illustrators, graphic designers, bottom lit slide artwork artists and photographers. Works on assignment only.
First Contact & Terms: Prefers slides or photos or whatever's applicable as samples. Reports back whether to expect possible future assignments. Pay depends entirely on person and job. Provide brochures/flyers and resume to be kept on file for future assignments. No originals returned to artist at job's completion.
Tips: "Professionals only, please."

MANDABACH & SIMMS, Suite 3620, 20 N. Wacker Dr., Chicago IL 60606. (312)236-5333. Creative Director: B. Bentkover. Ad agency. Clients: food services, financial, graphic arts and real estate.
Needs: Works with 5-10 freelance illustrators/month. Works on assignment only. Uses freelancers for print advertising and collateral material.
First Contact & Terms: Send business card and tear sheets to be kept on file. Samples not filed are not returned. Reports back whether to expect possible future assignments. Negotiates payment based on client's budget.
Tips: Wants to see work relating to their clients' needs. Artists interested in working here should be "creative, businesslike, and remember the objective."

MANNING, SELVAGE & LEE/MID-AMERICA, Suite 1713, 2 Illinois Center, 233 N. Michigan Ave., Chicago IL 60601. (312)565-0927. PR firm. Managing Director: James O. Ahtes. Clients: medical, industry, food, beverage and corporate.
Needs: Assigns 2-3 jobs/year. Local artists only. Uses artists for brochures/flyers, and company magazines.
First Contact & Terms: Query with samples (include prices on samples) and arrange interview to show portfolio. Wants only samples of finished work: "depending on your specialty—the best, most recent (within 2 years) work you have done for the largest clients you have." Samples returned by SASE within 2 weeks. Works on assignment only. Provide brochure/flyer to be kept on file for possible future assignments. Pays $300-5,000/project; $50-150/hour—"we ask for estimate in advance." Considers complexity of project, client's budget, skill and experience of artist, and turnaround time when establishing payment.
Tips: "Artists interested in working with us should have good selection of brochures, mailers, annual reports, as well as a list of clients. Usually we ask freelance artists to send us a background letter telling us about work done and specialty if any. If interested, we will set up an appointment to view work, ask for a card, brochure, or something to be left behind for our files. We already have a number of artists we work with, so new ones are most likely to be kept on file."

MARKETING SUPPORT INC., 303 E. Wacker Dr., Chicago IL 60601. (312)565-0044. Executive Art Director: Robert Becker. Clients: plumbing, heating/cooling equipment, chemicals, hardware, ski equipment, home appliances, crafts and window covering.
Needs: Assigns 300 jobs/year. Works with 2-3 illustrators/month. Local artists only. Works on assignment only. Uses artists for filmstrips, slide sets, brochures/flyers and trade magazines. Also uses artists for layout, illustration, lettering, type spec, paste-up and retouching for trade magazines and direct mail.
First Contact & Terms: Arrange interview to show portfolio. Samples returned by SASE. Reports back only if interested. Provide business card to be kept on file for future assignments. No originals returned to artist at job's completion. Pays $15/hour and up. Considers complexity of project, client's budget, and skill and experience of artist when establishing payment.

***NYSTROM**, division of Herff Jones, Inc., 3333 N. Elston Ave., Chicago IL 60618. Contact: Editorial Department. AV producer. Serves clients in education. Produces multimedia kits for elementary education, including filmstrips, booklets, transparencies, copymasters, picture cards and study prints.
Needs: Works with "a few" illustrators and animators and designers/year, "but most are for large assignments." Chicago area artists only. Works on assignment only. Uses artists for photos, original artwork, box design, and keylining and pasteup.
First Contact & Terms: Send resume, "samples optional," to be kept on file. Prefers "original work if convenient; otherwise photostats will do." Samples returned by SASE if not kept on file. Reports in 2 weeks. Pays by the project or by the hour, "depending on project and type of work called for." Amount of payment is negotiated with the individual artist. Payment varies with each client's budget. No originals returned to artist following publication. Buys all rights.
Tips: "We do not wish to be contacted by phone."

O.M.A.R. INC., 5525 N. Broadway, Chicago IL 60640. (312)271-2720. Creative Director: Paul Sierra. Spanish language ad agency. Clients: consumer food, telephone communication, TV station and public utilities.

Needs: Number of freelance artists used varies. Local artists only. Works on assignment only. Uses artists for consumer magazines, posters, newspapers and TV graphics.
First Contact & Terms: Send query letter with resume of credits, slides or originals (color) and photostats (b&w); follow with phone call. Samples returned by SASE. Reports within 3 weeks. Payment is by the project; negotiates according to client's budget. Buys all rights.
Tips: Three trends in this field are: "messages aimed at young audiences, bilingual TV commercials and more sophisticated Spanish language commercials." Artists interested in working here "must have sensitivity to the Hispanic culture. An artist should never sacrifice pride in his/her work for the sake of a deadline, yet must nevertheless meet the specified time of completion. Show only your best work during an interview, and don't take too much time."

POLYCOM TELEPRODUCTIONS, (formerly The Poly Com Group Inc.), 201 E. Erie, Chicago IL 60611. (312)337-6000. Executive Producer/Director: Mr. Carmen V. Trombetta. Producer: Debbie Heagy. Videotape teleproducer. Clients: 60% are major Chicago advertising and PR firms and educational/industrial enterprises and 40% are corporate enterprises. Produces filmstrips, motion pictures, multimedia kits, overhead transparencies, slide sets, sound-slide sets, videotapes and films.
Needs: Works with 2-3 illustrators/month. Works on assignment only. Assigns 150-200 jobs/year. Uses artists for motion pictures, videotape teleproduction, television copy art, storyboard animation and computer animation.
First Contact & Terms: Query with resume, business card and slides which may be kept on file. Samples not kept on file are returned by SASE. Reports in 2-3 weeks. Original art returned to artist at job's completion. Negotiates pay by project.
Tips: "Artists must be familiar with film and videotape. We need more videotape and computer graphics artists."

SIEBER & McINTYRE, INC., 625 N. Michigan Ave., Chicago IL 60611. (312)266-9200. Contact: Creative Services Manager. Ad agency. Clients: pharmaceutical and health care fields.
Needs: Work load varies. Works on assignment only. Uses freelancers for medical trade magazines, journal ads, brochures/flyers and direct mail to physicians. Especially needs sources for tight marker renderings and comp layouts.
First Contact & Terms: Send query letter with resume and samples. Call for appointment to show portfolio, which should include roughs, original/final art, final reproduction/product, color, photostats and photographs. Reports within 2 weeks. Pays by the hour, $10-50. Negotiates payment based on client's budget, where work will appear, complexity of project, skill and experience of artist and turnaround time.
Tips: "Rendering with markers very important." Prefers to see original "terrific work" rather than reproductions, but will review past work used by other ad agencies. Needs good medical illustrators but is looking for the best person—one who can accomplish executions other than anatomical. Artists should send resume or letter for files.

SOCIETY FOR VISUAL EDUCATION, INC., 1345 W. Diversey Pkwy., Chicago IL 60614. Graphic Arts Manager: Cathy Mijou. Audiovisual and microcomputer firm. No outside clients; all work done for SVE products and services. Produces filmstrips, micro software, video disks and some print materials (but not books) for education market—schools, libraries, etc.
Needs: Works with 10 or more freelance artists/year. Works on assignment only. Uses artists for keyline/paste-up, illustration, design, photography, and computer graphics for filmstrips, micro software and print materials. Artist must have demonstrated ability in these areas.
First Contact & Terms: Send query letter and photostats, tear sheets, etc. to be kept on file. Nonreturnable samples only. Reports only if interested. Payment varies according to scope and requirements of project. Considers complexity of the project, budget, skill and experience of artist, turnaround time and rights purchased when establishing payment. Buys all rights.

STONE & ADLER, INCORPORATED, division of Young & Rubicam, Inc., 1 S. Wacker Dr., Chicago IL 60606. (312)346-6100. Art Buyer: Connal Small. Ad agency/direct marketing firm. Clients: industrial, publishing, consumer.
Needs: Uses freelancers for billboards, consumer and trade magazines, brochures/flyers, newspapers, P-O-P displays, stationery design, TV and especially direct marketing.
First Contact & Terms: Call for appointment to show portfolio. Selection based on portfolio review. Negotiates payment based on client's budget and particular job.
Tips: Wants to see anything in portfolio which indicates individual's style (original and printed samples). Uses all styles of work.

Indiana

C.R.E. INC., 400 Victoria Centre, 22 E. Washington St., Indianapolis IN 46204. Senior Art Director: Roger Dobrovodsky. Ad agency. Clients: industrial, banks, agriculture and consumer.
Needs: Works with 15 freelance artists/year. Works on assignment only. Uses artists for line art, color illustrations and airbrushing.
First Contact & Terms: Send query letter with resume, and photocopies to be kept on file. Samples not filed are returned. Reports back only if interested. To show a portfolio, mail appropriate materials or call or write to schedule an appointment; portfolio should include original/final art, final reproduction/product and tear sheets. Pays by the project, $100-up. Considers complexity of the project, client's budget, skill and experience of artist and rights purchased when establishing payment. Buys all rights.
Tips: "Show samples of good creative talent."

CALDWELL-VAN RIPER, INC. ADVERTISING-PUBLIC RELATIONS, 1314 N. Meridian St., Indianapolis IN 46202. (317)632-6501. Associate Creative Director: John Bugg. Ad agency/PR firm. Clients are a "good mix of consumer (banks, furniture, food, etc.) and industrial (chemicals, real estate, insurance, heavy industry)."
Needs: Assigns 100-200 freelance jobs/year. Works with 10-15 freelance illustrators/month. Works on assignment only. Uses artists for consumer and magazine ads, billboards, direct mail packages, brochures, catalogs, newspaper ads, P-O-P displays, storyboards, AV presentations and posters.
First Contact & Terms: Send query letter with brochure, samples and tear sheets to be kept on file. Call for appointment to show portfolio. Accepts any available samples. Samples not filed are returned by SASE only if requested. Reports only if interested. Pay is negotiated. Considers complexity of project, client's budget, skill and experience of artist and rights purchased when establishing payment. Buys all rights.
Tips: "Send 5 samples of best work (copies acceptable) followed by a phone call."

HANDLEY & MILLER, INC., 1712 N. Meridian, Indianapolis IN 46202. (317)927-5545. Art Director/Vice President: Irvin Showalter. Ad agency. Clients: package goods, sales promotion, retail, direct response, institutional and financial.
Needs: Works with 2 freelance illustrators/month. Works on assignment only. Uses freelancers for consumer and trade magazines, brochures/flyers, newspapers and P-O-P displays.
First Contact & Terms: Call for appointment to show portfolio, which should include photostats, slides and original work. Selection based on portfolio review. Reports within 5 days if interested. Send business card and brochure/flyer to be kept on file. Pays standard day rate; by the hour, $30-75 average; by the project, $200-2,000 average; also by contract. Considers complexity of project, client's budget, skill and experience of artist, and turnaround time when establishing payment.
Tips: Likes to see a variety of techniques.

***KARTES VIDEO COMMUNICATIONS**, 10 E. 106th St., Indianapolis IN 46280. Senior Art Director: Susan Thomas. Video production company. and publishing facility.
Needs: Works with 20-50 freelance artists/year. Artist must have experience and samples. Works on assignment only. Uses artists for design, illustrations, books, P-O-P displays, mechanicals, retouching, direct mail packages and lettering.
First Contact & Terms: Send query letter with brochure showing art style or tear sheets. Samples not filed are returned only if requested. Reports only if interested. Call or write to schedule an appointment to show a portfolio, which should include thumbnails, roughs, original/final art, final reproduction/product, color, tear sheets, photostats, photographs, b&w and representative work in any area. Pays for illustrations by the project, $50-1,000. Considers how work will be used when establishing payment. Rights purchased vary according to project.

MARTIN A. LAVE MARKETING, 3400 W. 86th St., Indianapolis IN 46268. (317)872-0971. Art Director: Lisa Brandau. Production Managers: Amy Feldman, George Wilson. Ad agency. Clients: schools, retailers and industrials.
Needs: Works with 5-6 freelance artists/year. Local artists only. Works on assignment only. Uses artists for layout and mechanicals. Especially looks for design capability.
First Contact & Terms: Send query letter with resume and photocopies. Call or write to schedule an appointment to show a portfolio which roughs, original/final art and tear sheets. Pays by the hour, $25-60 average; by project, $50-500 average. Considers complexity of project and client's budget when establishing payment. Buys all rights.
Tips: "Trend toward more design and more four-color projects and wider range of print projects—general increase in work load and client base."

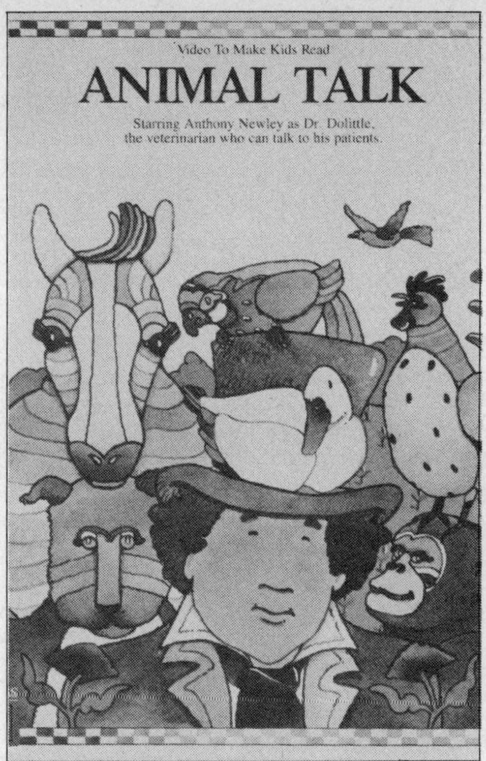

Freelance artist Andrea Eberbach of Indianapolis, Indiana, created this lively wrap-around cover for a videotape as an assignment from Kartes Video Communications, Inc. She used ink, dyes and pencil to capture the fantasy world of veterinarian Dr. Dolittle who talks to his animal patients.

OUR SUNDAY VISITOR INC., Department of Religious Education, 200 Noll Plaza, Huntington IN 46750. Religious education audience. Produces sound filmstrips and multimedia kits.
Needs: Subjects range from the miracles and parables of Jesus to modern church history, liturgy, stories and doctrine. Works on assignment only.
First Contact & Terms: Send slides, resume, tear sheets, brochures/flyers and samples to be kept on file. Prefers to keep samples but will return upon request. Reports back whether to expect possible future assignments. No originals returned to artist at job's completion.

QUINLAN KEENE PECK & McSHAY, INC., 5435 Emerson Way N., Indianapolis IN 46226. Executive Art Director: David Stahl. Ad agency. Client list provided for SASE.
Needs: Assigns 60 freelance jobs/year. Works with 4 freelance illustrators and 1-2 freelance designers/month. Uses artists for trade magazines, billboards, direct mail packages, brochures, catalogs, newspapers, filmstrips, movies, stationery, signage and posters.
First Contact & Terms: Send query letter with resume to be kept on file. Reports only if interested. Works on assignment only. Call for appointment to show portfolio. Pays by the project. Considers complexity of project, client's budget, geographic scope of finished project and turnaround time when establishing payment. Negotiates rights purchased.

❝*There are more and more smaller agencies emerging with one or two major accounts. Most of these have no creative department and freelance every project out. There are fewer I-can-do-everything people, making it easier to select freelancers to fill needs.***❞**

Gary Otteson, Travis Waley & Associates, Inc.

Iowa

EBEL ADVERTISING AGENCY, (formerly Griffith & Somers Advertising Agency), 770 Orpheum Bldg., Sioux City IA 51101. (712)277-3343. President: Elmer Ebel. Ad agency. Clients: industrial, financial, agricultural and business.
Needs: Works with 1 illustrator/month. Artist should have previous agency experience. Uses artists for illustrations, cartoons, multimedia kits, brochures, direct mail, catalogs and multipage flyers.
First Contact & Terms: Query with samples (tear sheets). Reports in 3 weeks. Provide brochure and resume to be kept on file for possible future assignments. No originals returned to artist at job's completion. Pay negotiated.

LA GRAVE KLIPFEL INC., 1707 High St., Des Moines IA 50309. (515)283-2297. Art Director: Rex Anthony. Ad agency. Clients: "wide range" of accounts—financial, industrial and retail; client list provided upon request.
Needs: Works with 3-4 illustrators or designers/month. Local artists only. Works on assignment only. Uses freelance artists for billboards, consumer and trade magazines, direct mail, P-O-P displays, brochures, catalogs, posters, signage, newspapers, TV art direction and AV presentations.
First Contact & Terms: Phone first and follow with mailed information. Negotiates payment by the project and on freelancer's previous experience.
Tips: "Present resume or self-promotion piece. Have a portfolio of no more than 20 pieces. Be neat and clean with presented pieces. Be brief and concise in talking about work; avoid speeches."

MOHAWK ADVERTISING CO., 1307 6th St. SW, Box 1608, Mason City IA 50401. (515)423-1354. Vice President/Executive Art Director: Phil Means. Senior Art Director: Steve Erikson. Ad agency. Clients: industrial, agricultural, financial, consumer.
Needs: Assigns 15-25 jobs/year. Works with 1-3 illustrators/month. Works on assignment only. Uses artists for consumer and trade magazines, billboards, brochures and posters.
First Contact & Terms: Send query letter with tear sheets, photostats, photocopies to be kept on file. Samples returned by SASE if not kept on file. Reports within 10 days. Write for appointment to show portfolio. Pays for design by the hour $20-50; for illustraion by the hour, $10-50. Considers complexity of project, client's budget, turnaround time and rights purchased when establishing payment. Buys reprint rights or all rights; negotiates rights. No originals returned at job's completion.

Kansas

LANE & LESLIE ADVERTISING AGENCY INC., Petroleum Bldg., Box 578, Wichita KS 67201. President: David W. Lane. Ad agency. Clients: banks, savings and loans, consumer products and fast food.
Needs: Works with 1 illustrator and 6 designers/month. Uses artists for storyboards, billboards, P-O-P displays, filmstrips, multimedia kits, direct mail, slide sets, brochures/flyers, trade magazines and newspapers. Also uses artists for photography and retouching.
First Contact & Terms: Send query letter with resume, tear sheets, photostats, photocopies, slides and photographs. Call or write to schedule an appointment to show a portfolio, which should include original final art, final reproduction/product, tear sheets, photostats and photographs. No originals returned to artist at job's completion. Pays by the hour and by the project; payment based on project. "We prefer to buy all rights."

MARKETAIDE, INC., Box 500, Salina KS 67402-0500. (913)825-7161. Production Manager: Cathy Ansiover. Full-service advertising/marketing/direct mail firm. Clients: financial, agricultural machinery, industrial, some educational, and fast food.
Needs: Prefers artists within one-state distance and possessing professional expertise. Works on assignment only. Uses freelance artists for illustrations, retouching, signage.
First Contact & Terms: Send query letter with resume, business card and samples to be kept on file. Accepts any kind of accurate representation as samples, depending upon medium. Samples not kept on file are returned only if requested. Reports only if interested. Write for appointment to show portfolio. Pays by the hour, $15-75 average; "since projects vary in size we are forced to estimate according to each job's parameters." Considers complexity of project, skill and experience of artist, how work will be used, turnaround time and rights purchased when establishing payment.
Tips: Artists interested in working here "should be highly-polished in technical ability, have a good eye for design and be able to meet all deadline commitments."

MARSHFILM ENTERPRISES, INC., Box 8082, Shawnee Mission KS 66208. (816)523-1059. President: Joan K. Marsh. Audiovisual firm. Clients: schools.
Needs: Works with 1-2 freelance artists/year. Works on assignment only. Uses artists for illustrating filmstrips. Artists must have experience and imagination.
First Contact & Terms: Send query letter, resume and slides or actual illustrations to be kept on file "if it is potentially the type of art we would use." Samples not filed are returned. Reports within 1 month. Write for appointment to show portfolio. Considers client's budget when establishing payment. Buys all rights.

TRAVIS-WALZ AND ASSOCIATES, INC., 8417 Santa Fe Dr., Overland Park KS 66212-2749. Contact: Gary Otteson. Ad agency. Serves clients in food, finance, broadcasting, utilities, pets, gardening and real estate.
Needs: Works with 2-4 illustrators/month. "We generally work with in-town talent because of tight deadlines." Commissioned work only. Uses illustrators for billboards, P-O-P displays, consumer magazines, direct mail, brochures/flyers, trade magazines and newspapers. Also uses artists for retouching. Does not buy design or layout. Agency has its own design staff.
First Contact & Terms: Send query letter with brochure showing art style or tear sheets, photostats and photocopies. Samples returned by SASE. Reports only if interested. Call to schedule an appointment to show portfolio, which should include final reproduction/product and tear sheets. No originals returned to artist at job's completion. Pays for design by the project, $100 and up. Pays for illustration by the project $150 and up. Considers complexity of project, client's budget and turnaround time when establishing payment.
Tips: "We must see your work to buy. The best way to sell yourself is by your samples shown in person or brochure mailed to us. We see 4 to 5 freelancers a week. Competition is extremely tough. The market has a glut of very talented people. Try to find a specialty that no one else is doing."

Kentucky

DAN BURCH ASSOCIATES, 2338 Frankfort Ave., Louisville KY 40206. (502)895-4881. Art Director: Joe Burch. Specializes in business-to-business and packaged goods advertising marketing and technical communications, brand and corporate identity, P-O-P displays, trade show exhibits, brochures, catalogs, direct mail, AV, packaging and signage. Clients: industrial, technical and consumer goods manufacturers and services.
Needs: Uses freelance artists for illustration and photo retouching on advertising and collateral materials.
First Contact & Terms: Send query letter with samples of work to be kept on file for future assignments. Negotiates payment.

DE BORD & OWEN, INC., 1027 Broadway Ave., Box 9640, Bowling Green KY 42101. (502)782-1774. Contact: Judith Owen. Ad agency/PR firm. Clients: industry, banks, hospitals and professionals.
Needs: Assigns 20-30 freelance jobs/year. Works on assignment only. Uses artists for brochures, catalogs, P-O-P displays and posters.
First Contact & Terms: Send query letter with brochure showing art style or resume and samples. Considers any type of samples. Samples not kept on file are returned only if requested. Reports only if interested. Call to schedule an appointment to show a portfolio, which should include final reproduction/product and photographs. Pays for design and illustration by the hour, $7.50-10 average. "We like for the artist to quote each job in advance if possible." Considers complexity of project, skill and experience of artist and rights purchased when establishing payment. Buys reprint rights or all rights.
Tips: "We use a lot of freelance talent for airbrushing, etc. Move toward computer graphics is a new development. We always try and take time to see an artists work, portfolio, etc."

FESSEL, SIEGFRIEDT & MOELLER ADVERTISING, 1500 Heyburn Building, Box 1031, Louisville KY 40201. (502)585-5154. Vice President/Executive Art Director: James A. Berry. Ad agency. Clients: mostly consumer firms, some industrial.
Needs: Works with 3 illustrators/year. Works primarily with local freelancers. Uses freelance artists for billboards, consumer and trade magazines, direct mail, P-O-P displays, brochures, catalogs, posters, signage, newspapers and AV presentations.
First Contact & Terms: Arrange interview to show portfolio. Works on assignment only. Payment varies according to project estimates.

McCANN-ERICKSON, LOUISVILLE, 1469 S. 4th, Louisville KY 40208. (502)636-0441. Creative Director: Todd Hoon. Ad agency. Serves clients in health care, retailing, manufacturing and quick-service food.
Needs: Freelance needs vary. Works on assignment only. Uses artists for billboards, P-O-P displays, consumer and trade magazines, direct mail, TV, brochures/flyers and newspapers; occasionally humorous or cartoon-style illustrations.
First Contact & Terms: Call for appointment to show portfolio or make contact through artist's rep. Prefers to review actual art (original) or slides. Samples returned by SASE if they are slides. Provide brochure/flyer, samples and tear sheets to be kept on file. Reports in 1 week. Negotiates pay; pays by the project, $200-3,500 average. Considers client's budget, skill and experience of artist, turnaround time and rights purchased when establishing payment.
Tips: "We have a renewed interest in use of illustration. There is a market for more sophisticated illustration interpretation—clients are more receptive to a greater degree of abstraction, even when representating product. This allows us as an art broker to make greater use of illustration. Keep us informed of your current workstyles as they evolve."

***SHEEHY & KOPF INC. ADVERTISING**, 10400 Linn Station Rd., Louisville KY 40223. Creative Director: Rosyln Hosier. Ad agency. Clients: investment companies, entertainment, health care, interior design and industrial.
Needs: Works with 10 freelance artists/year. Works on assignment only. Uses artists for illustrations, mechanicals, retouching, animation and lettering.
First Contact & Terms: Send query letter with brochure showing art style or resume and samples. Samples not filed are returned only if requested. Reports only if interested. Call or write to schedule an appointment to show a portfolio, which should include original/final art, final reproduction/product, color, tear sheets, photostats and photographs. Pays for design by the hour, $35-60. Pays for illustration by the project, $50 minimum. Considers complexity of project, client's budget, skill and experience of artist, how work will be used, turnaround time and rights purchased when establishing payment. Rights purchased vary according to project.
Tips: "Be concise. Make appointments before calling on anyone. Leave samples for reference of style and information on where to be reached including phone number. Call occasionally with updates."

Louisiana

HERBERT S. BENJAMIN ASSOCIATES, Box 2151, 2736 Florida St., Baton Rouge LA 70821. (504)387-0611. Art Director: Francelle Dietrich. Clients: food, financial, industrial, retail fashion/furniture, etc.
Needs: Works with 2-3 illustrators/month. Works with freelance artists on assignment only. Uses artists for industrial, trade and business journals; newspapers, TV, brochures/flyers, newsletters.
First Contact & Terms: Call for appointment to show portfolio. Provide resume and samples to be kept on file for possible future assignments. Especially needs good retail illustrator in advertising areas such as furniture, fashion, etc. Illustrators must conform to area rates.
Tips: When reviewing an artist's work, particularly looks for "competence in drawing and lettering and knowledge of type, originality in ideas, simplicity and strength of design, and technique."

CARTER ADVERTISING INC., 800 American Tower, Shreveport LA 71101. (318)227-1920. President: Bill Bailey Carter. Ad agency. Clients: hotels, motor vehicles and manufacturing. Assigns 500 jobs and buys 50 illustrations/year.
Needs: Works with 2-3 illustrators and 2-3 designers/month. Prefers local artists. "Must have heavy production experience." Uses artists for billboards, P-O-P displays, filmstrips, consumer magazines, stationery design, multimedia kits, direct mail, television, slide sets, brochures/flyers, trade magazines, album covers, newspapers, books and mechanicals.
First Contact & Terms: Query with resume or arrange interview to show portfolio. SASE. Reports within 2 weeks. Provide brochure, flyer, business card, resume, tear sheets, etc., to be kept on file for future assignments. No originals returned at job's completion unless otherwise agreed upon. Pay negotiated by project. Considers complexity of project, client's budget, skill and experience of artist, geographic scope of finished project, turnaround time and rights purchased when establishing payment.

CUNNINGHAM, SLY & ASSOCIATES, INC., Box 4503, Shreveport LA 71134. Creative Director: Harold J. Sly. Ad agency. Clients: industrial/financial.
Needs: Works with 6-10 freelance artists/year. Works on assignment only. Uses artists for layout/design, illustrations, photo retouching, mechanical art and airbrushing. Especially looks for mechanical skills.

First Contact & Terms: Send query letter with brochure, resume, business card and samples to be kept on file. Samples not filed are returned only by request. Reports back only if interested. Pays by the hour, $20-50 average. Considers complexity of the project, client's budget and turnaround time when establishing payment. Rights purchased vary according to project.

DUKE UNLIMITED, INC., Suite 205, 1940 I-10 Service Road, Kenner LA 70065. (504)464-1891. President: Lana Duke. Ad agency. Clients: industrial, investment, medical, restaurants, entertainment, fashion and tourism.
Needs: Assigns 50 freelance jobs/year. Works with 2 freelance illustrators and 1 freelance designer/month. Works on assignment. Uses artists for consumer and trade magazines, billboards, direct mail packages, brochures, catalogs, newspapers, filmstrips, movies, stationery, signage, P-O-P displays, AV presentations, posters and press releases.
First Contact & Terms: Send query letter with brochure, resume, business card, photostats and tear sheets to be kept on file. Contact only through artist's agent. Samples returned only if requested. Reports only if interested. Pays by the project, $150-1,000 average. The artist must provide a firm quotation in writing. Considers complexity of project, client's budget, skill and experience of artist, turnaround time and rights purchased when establishing payment. Buys all rights.
Tips: "We use more computer graphics, mixing photography and illustration, resulting in surreal effect. This has created *less* need for photo retouching and special effects, and has put greater emphasis on designer working more closely with the printer or photographer."

Maryland

ADVERTISERS' CO-OP INC., #2N, 10 Post Office Rd, Silver Springs MD 20910. (301)565-5223. President: Keith Krause. Ad agency/PR firm. Clients: various types. Clients list provided for SASE.
First Contact & Terms: Send query letter with resume and samples to be kept on file. Call for appointment to show portfolio. "Photocopy samples of work are sufficient." Reports only if interested. Works on assignment only. Pays by the hour. Considers skill and experience of artist and turnaround time when establishing payment.
Tips: Artists should "make up an 8½x11 package with short resume plus montage of work samples that show type of work they feel most comfortable doing. If an expert in technical airbrush—say so. If architectural rendering is a specialty, voice that fact."

SAMUEL R. BLATE ASSOCIATES, 10331 Watkins Mill Dr., Gaithersburg MD 20879-2935. (301)840-2248. President: Samuel R. Blate. Audiovisual and editorial services firm. Clients: business/professional, US government, some private.
Needs: Works with 5 freelance artists/year. "We prefer to work with artists in the Washington-Baltimore-Richmond metro area." Works on assignment only. Uses artists for cartoons (especially for certain types of audiovisual presentations), illustrations (graphs, etc.) for 35mm slides, pamphlet and book design. Especially important are "technical and aesthetic excellence and ability to meet deadlines."
First Contact & Terms: Send query letter with resume and tear sheets, photostats, photocopies, slides and photographs to be kept on file. "No original art, please. SASE for return." Call or write for appointment to show portfolio, which should include final reproduction/product, color, photographs and b&w. Samples are returned by SASE. Reports only if interested. Pays by the hour, $20-40. "Payment varies as a function of experience, skills needed, size of project, and anticipated competition, if any." Also considers complexity of the project, client's budget, turnaround time and rights purchased when establishing payment. Rights purchased vary according to project, "but we prefer to purchase first rights only. This is sometimes not possible due to client demand, in which case we attempt to negotiate a financial adjustment for the artist."
Tips: "The demand for technically-oriented artwork has increased. At the same time, some clients who used artists have been satisfied with computer-generated art."

COE COMMUNICATIONS, INC., Suite 2, 131 Rollins, Rockville MD 20852. (301)881-2820. Executive Vice President: Janice V. Long. Audiovisual firm. Clients: associations, corporations and nonprofits.
Needs: Works with 25-30 freelance artists/year. Works on assignment only. Uses artists for photography, artwork and editing.
First Contact & Terms: Send resume to be kept on file. Samples not filed are returned by SASE. Reports only if interested. Pays by the project, $500-15,000 average. Buys all rights.

HOLECHEK COMMUNICATIONS, Suite 305, 204 N. Liberty St., Baltimore MD 21201. (301)837-4200. Art Director: James T. Holechek. Executive Vice President: James T. Holechek. Ad agency. Clients: publishers, cosmetic, fragrance, manufacturers, clothing manufacturers, computer services, housewares manufacturers. Client list provided "only if it is applicable to the work the freelancer is doing for us."
Needs: Assigns 50-100 freelance jobs/year. Works with 2-4 freelance illustrators and 2-4 freelance designers/month. "Fast delivery time *usually* requires that the artist live in the Baltimore area, but depending on the scope of the project, we sometimes go to New York for freelancers." Works on assignment depending on the particular situation. Uses artists for consumer and trade magazines, billboards, brochures, catalogs and stationery.
First Contact & Terms: Send query letter with business card and samples to be kept on file. Write for appointment to show portfolio. "We take a large number of freelance calls, but we do request that no one call before contacting us in writing first. Photocopies are fine; we don't need an extensive presentation to determine the usefulness of a talent." Samples not kept on file are not returned. Reports if interested. Pays by the project. "Each project must be considered independent of others and prices vary accordingly." Considers complexity of project and turnaround time when establishing payment. Negotiates rights purchased.
Tips: "Walk softly but carry a good portfolio." Especially looks for a "variety of samples of talent, cost, turnaround, personality—although some of these don't come in the portfolio, they're just as important."

IMAGE DYNAMICS, INC., Suite 1400, 1101 N. Calvert St., Baltimore MD 21202. (301)539-7730. Art Director: Erin Ries. Ad agency/PR firm. Clients: wide mix, specializing in restaurants and hotels, associations, colleges, hospitals and land developers.
Needs: Local artists only. Works on assignment only. Uses artists for illustration, design and paste-up; frequently buys humorous and cartoon-style illustrations.
First Contact & Terms: Call to arrange interview to show portfolio; "please do not drop in or write. Bring lots of b&w and 2-color samples; have printed or produced work to show." Samples are returned. Reports only if interested. Provide business card and samples to be kept on file for possible future assignments. Pays flat fee or by the hour, depending on project and budget. Considers complexity of project, client's budget, skill and experience of artist and turnaround time when establishing payment.
Tips: "We are able to use freelance illustrators more towards a more creative product."

GILBERT SANDLER & ASSOCIATES, INC., 501 St. Paul Pl., Baltimore MD 21202. (301)837-7100. Senior Art Director: Loren Patten. Ad agency. Clients: institutional advertising (financial, industrial) and PR.
First Contact & Terms: Call for an appointment to show portfolio. Negotiates payment based on client's budget and particular job. "Prefers to get an estimate from the freelancer and negotiate payment based on the budget."
Tips: Wants to see a little bit of all freelancer can do in portfolio but especially specific style and best work. Uses many types of art and prefers to see artist's speciality.

SHECTER & LEVIN ADVERTISING/PUBLIC RELATIONS, 2205 N. Charles St., Baltimore MD 21218. (301)889-4464. Production Executives: Virginia Lindler. Ad agency/PR firm. Serves clients in real estate, finance, professional associations, social agencies, retailing, apartments and manufacturing.
Needs: Works with 3-4 illustrators/month. Uses designers for billboards, consumer magazines, stationery design, direct mail, television, brochures/flyers, trade magazines and newspapers. Also uses artists for layouts and mechanicals for brochures, newspaper and magazine ads.
First Contact & Terms: Write for an interview to show portfolio. No originals returned to artist at job's completion. Negotiates pay.

MARC SMITH CO., Box A, Severna Park MD 21146. (301)647-2606. Art/Creative Director: Marc Smith. Advertising agency. Clients: consumer and industrial products, sales services and public relations firms.
Needs: Works with 6 illustrators/month. Local artists only. Uses artists for layout, illustration, lettering, technical art, type spec, paste-up and retouching; illustrators and designers for direct mail, slide sets, brochures/flyers, trade magazines and newspapers; designers for billboards, P-O-P displays, film strips, consumer magazines, stationery, multimedia kits and TV; occasionally buys humorous and cartoon-style illustrations.
First Contact & Terms: Send query letter with brochure showing art style or tear sheets, photostats, photocopies, slides or photographs. Keeps file on artists; does not return original artwork to artist after completion of assignment. Call or write to schedule an appointment to show a portfolio which should

include thumbnails, roughs, original/final art, final reproduction/product, color and tear sheets. Pays by the hour, $25-150.
Tips: "More sophisticated techniques and equipment are being used in art and design. Our use of freelance material has intensified. Project honesty, clarity and patience."

VAN SANT, DUGDALE & COMPANY, INC., The World Trade Center, Baltimore MD 21202. (301)539-5400. Creative Director: Stan Paulus. Ad agency. Clients: consumer, corporate, associations, financial, and industrial.
Needs: Number of freelance artists used varies. Works on assignment basis only. Uses freelance artists for consumer and trade magazines, brochures, catalogs, newspapers and AV presentations.
First Contact & Terms: Negotiates payment according to client's budget, amount of creativity required, where work will appear and freelancer's previous experience.

WOLFF FREED GREENBERG INC., 100 E. 23rd St., Baltimore MD 21218. (301)243-1421. Creative Director: Robert Canale. Ad agency. Clients: industrial, fashion and financial firms—"from furs to petroleum, autos, savings and loans, etc."; client list provided upon request.
Needs: Works with "many, many illustrators and are in the process of building file of artists." Local artists only. Works on assignment basis only. Uses freelance artists for billboards, consumer and trade magazines, direct mail, P-O-P displays, brochures, catalogs, posters, signage and newspapers.
First Contact & Terms: Call to set up appointment for portfolio review. Negotiates payment according to client's budget.

Massachusetts

ARNOLD & COMPANY, 1111 Park Sq. Bldg., Boston MA 02116. (617)357-1900. Senior Vice President: Len Karsakov. Executive Creative Director: Wilson Siebert. Ad agency. Clients: fast food, financial and computer firms, retail.
Needs: Works with 10-12 illustrators/month. Works on assignment only. Uses freelance artists for billboards, consumer and trade magazines, direct mail, P-O-P displays, brochures, catalogs, posters, signage, newspapers, TV and AV presentations.
First Contact & Terms: Query with "good" samples. Samples returned by SASE. Reports within 1 week. Provide business card, brochure/flyer and samples to be kept on file for possible future assignments. Arrange interview to show portfolio. Pays by the project. Negotiates payment according to client's budget and where work will appear.
Tips: "Show your best work—a distinctive style and full range."

ASTRA COMMUNICATIONS, 581 Riverside Ave., Medford MA 02155. (617)391-0441. President: Charlotte B. Berman. Ad agency. Clients: computer and real estate firms, restaurants and retail women's clothing stores.
Needs: Works with 1-4 freelance artists/year. "If the artist is doing paste-up work, we would like him/her to be willing to do it at our office." Works on assignment only. Uses artists for pen & ink sketches, ad layouts and design, and pasteup of mechanicals. "We need art that will reproduce well. We also look for speed of completion; good type selection, specifying; good knowledge of how to prepare complicated mechanicals for magazines and brochures; and generic product sketching."
First Contact & Terms: Send query letter, business card, samples and prices to be kept on file. Samples not filed are returned by SASE only if requested. Reports only if interested. Pays by the hour, $7-25 average; by the project, $25 minimum. Considers complexity of the project, client's budget, skill and experience of artist and turnaround time when establishing payment. Rights purchased vary according to project. "If the artwork is something we specifically ask to have drawn and give specifics for, we consider we own the rights."
Tips: "Please keep in mind we are usually a low-budget operation. But we are willing to try new people."

ROBERT BATOR AND ASSOCIATES, 40 Marion St., Chicopee MA 01013. Art Director: Robert Bator. Ad agency. Clients: newspapers, restaurants, small businesses and recording companies.
Needs: Uses artists for illustration, lettering, record jacket design, books, brochures/flyers, album covers, fashions—women's garments, casual and bathing wear.
First Contact & Terms: Send query letter with brochure showing art style, resume, tear sheet, photographs or photostats—*no slides* to be kept on file. Samples returned only if requested. Reports within 10 days. Write to schedule an appointment to show a portfolio, which should include original/final art. No originals returned to artist at job's completion. Pays for design by the project, $550

maximum; pays for illustration by the hour, $25-500. Considers complexity of project when establishing payment.
Tips: Prefers a "clean, brilliant style."

BLACK & MUSEN, INC., Box 465, East Longmeadow MA 01028. (413)567-0361. Art Director: Merle Black. Ad agency. Clients: consumer and industrial companies.
Needs: Works with 6 freelance artists/year. Artists must live within local area for paste-up and mechanicals; within 75-mile radius for layouts and designs. Works on assignment only. Uses artists for mechanicals and paste-ups and layouts for special projects (ads and collateral material). Especially looks for accuracy and crispness for paste-up; creativity for layouts.
First Contact & Terms: Send resume to be kept on file; call for appointment to show portfolio. Prefers to review tear sheets or actual layouts. Reports back. Considers complexity of the project, client's budget, skill and experience of artist and turnaround time when establishing payment. Buys all rights.

COSMOPULOS, CROWLEY & DALY, INC., 250 Boylston St., Boston MA 02116. (617)266-5500. Chairman of the Board/Creative Director: Stavros Cosmopulos. Advertising and marketing agency. Clients: banking, restaurants, industrial, package goods, food and electronics.
Needs: Works with 6 illustrators and 1 animator/month. Works on assignment only. Uses artists for billboards, P-O-P displays, filmstrips, consumer magazines, stationery design, multimedia kits, direct mail, television, slide sets, brochures/flyers, trade magazines and newspapers.
First Contact & Terms: Send business card, photostats or slides. Samples not filed are returned by SASE. Reports only if interested. Make an appointment to show portfolio. No originals returned to artist at job's completion. Pays by the project, $50-10,000 average. Considers complexity of project, client's budget, geographic scope of finished project, turnaround time and rights purchased when establishing payment.
Tips: "Give a simple presentation of the range of work you can do including printed samples of actual jobs—but not a lot of samples."

***THE DR GROUP INC.**, 10 Post Office Sq., Boston MA 02109. Creative Director: William Allen. Direct marketing ad agency. Clients: industrial, financial, publishing firms.
Needs: Number of freelance artists used varies; has 5 art directors. Usually works with local freelancers. Works on assignment basis only. Uses freelance artists for direct mail and collateral.
First Contact & Terms: Arrange interview to show portfolio. Payment varies according to job.

FLAGLER ADVERTISING/GRAPHIC DESIGN, Box 1317, Brookline MA 02146. (617)566-6971. President/Creative Director: Sheri Flagler. Specializes in corporate identity, brochure designs, fashion and technical illustration. Clients: cable television, finance, real estate, fashion and direct mail agencies.
Needs: Works with 10-20 freelance artists/year. Works on assignment only. Uses artists for illustration, mechanicals, retouching, airbrushing, charts/graphs and lettering.
First Contact & Terms: Send resume, business card, brochures, photocopies or tear sheets to be kept on file. Call or write for appointment to show portfolio. Samples not filed are not returned. Reports back only if interested. Pays for design by the project, $100-1,500 average; for illustration by the project, $150-1,200 average. Considers complexity of project, client's budget and turnaround time when establishing payment.
Tips: "Send a range and variety of style showing clean, crisp and professional work."

HBM/CREAMER, INC., 1 Beacon St., Boston MA 02108. (617)723-7770. Art Buyer: Anne Mary Blevins. Ad agency. Clients: consumer, financial, hi-tech and fashion.
Needs: Will look at storyboard artists and illustrators, but prefers to work with illustrators who have advertising experience. Works on assignment only.
First Contact & Terms: Send samples; follow up with phone call. Payment is contingent upon work involved.

HILL HOLLIDAY CONNORS COSMOPULOS INC., John Hancock Tower, 200 Clarendon St., Boston MA 02116. (617)437-1600, ext. 3487. Art Buyer: Lowry Maclean. Ad agency. Clients: computer firm, banks, consumer products, *Globe* newspaper, lottery, etc.
Needs: Works with 750 freelance artists (illustrators, designers; photographers)/year. Works on assignment only. Uses artists for illustration and photography. Fast turn-around time is important.
First Contact & Terms: Send nonreturnable samples to be kept on file. Samples not filed are not returned. Does not report back. Write for appointment to show portfolio. Pays by the project. Considers complexity of the project, client's budget, turnaround time and rights purchased when establishing payment. Rights purchased vary according to project.

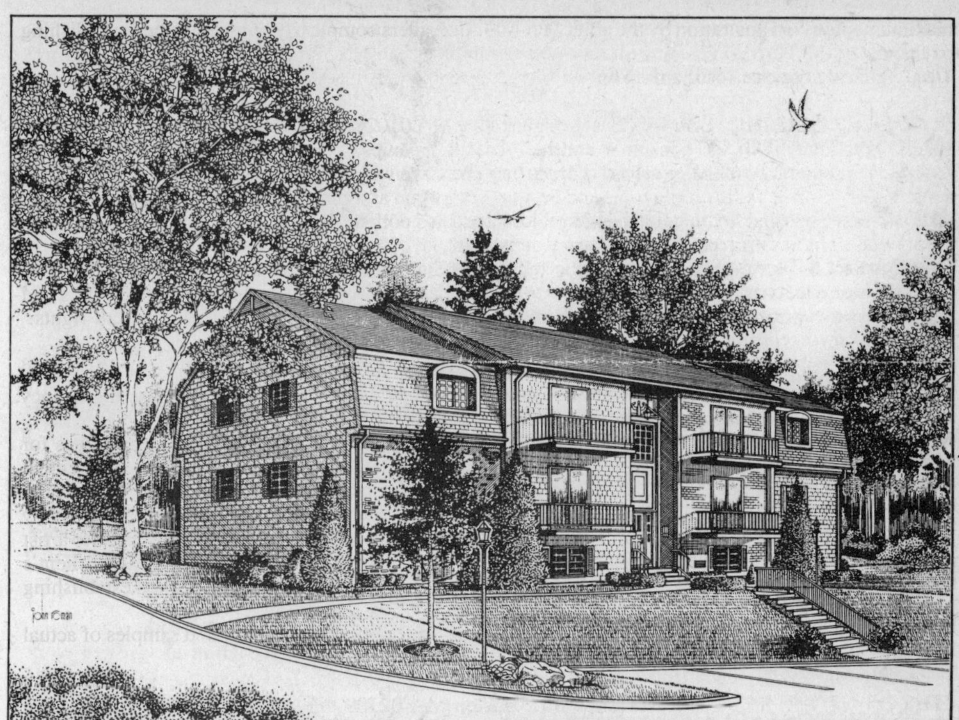

John Roman of Scituate, Massachusetts, received $1,500 from Flagler Advertising in Brookline, Massachusetts, for this pen & ink illustration. Completed for a condominium project, the illustration was used as a brochure cover and newspaper advertisements. Sheri Flagler, president/creative director of the advertising firm, says the piece conveys the feeling of "a beautiful living space in a nice area, for a very reasonable price."

LAYMAN ASSOCIATES, INC., 280 Bridge St., Dedham MA 02026. (617)329-7030. Contact: L.A. Layman. Ad agency. Clients: industrial, commercial and services, especially capital equipment manufacturers.
Needs: Works with 2 designers/month. Prefers local artists. Uses designers for direct mail, slide sets and trade magazines. Also needs artists for technical illustration, type spec, layouts, retouching, paste-up and lettering for newspapers, trade magazines, direct mail, P-O-P displays, collateral and exhibits.
First Contact & Terms: Send query letter with brochure showing art style and samples to be kept on file. No originals returned to artist at job's completion. Call or write schedule an appointment to show a portfolio, which should include original/final art and final reproduction/product. Pays for design by the hour, $25; pays for illustration by the project, $25-200.

ROB MACINTOSH COMMUNICATIONS, INC., 92 Massachusetts Ave., Boston MA 02115. (617)267-4912. President: Rob MacIntosh. Ad agency. Clients: graphic arts industry—printers, paper manufacturers and computer software.
Needs: Works with 20 freelance artists/year. Works on assignment only. Uses artists for various assignments from primary illustration to spot work. "We need a total range of skills; that's why we use freelancers."
First Contact & Terms: Send brochure, resume, business card and photostats, photographs, slides or tear sheets to be kept on file. Samples not filed are returned by SASE only if requested. Reports only if interested. Pays by the project, $200 minimum. Considers complexity of project, client's budget, skill and experience of artist and turnaround time when establishing payment. Rights purchased vary according to project.

PHOTOGRAPHERS' COLOR SERVICE, 10 Harvard St., Worcester MA 01609. (617)752-1921. President: Alice Richmond. Photographic studio. Clients: educational, industrial and business. Produces filmstrips, slide sets and color prints.

Needs: Assigns 30 jobs/year. Uses artists for slide and ad illustrations.
First Contact & Terms: Query with resume and samples. Samples returned with SASE. Reports in 2 weeks. Provide business card to be kept on file for possible future assignments. Negotiates pay by the project.

JAMIL SIMON ASSOCIATES, 20 Woodland, Arlington MA 02174. (617)491-4300. Associate Producer: Lisa Podoloff. Audiovisual firm. Clients: hotels, computer companies, government and nonprofit agencies.
Needs: Works with 5-8 freelance artists/year. Local artists only. Works on assignment only. Uses artists for drawings for slide presentations, printed materials, layouts and presentations.
First Contact & Terms; Send query letter with brochure and tear sheets to be kept on file. Samples not filed are returned only if requested. Does not report back. Pays by the project, $75-250 average. Considers complexity of the project and skill and experience of artist when establishing payment. Rights purchased vary according to project.

***SPENCER, BENNETT, NOWAK, INC.**, 380 Fall River Ave., Seekonk MA 02771. (617)336-5801. Creative Director: David P. Duncan. Ad agency. Clients: 90% industrial. Media used include trade magazines, direct mail, P-O-P displays, trade show exhibits and editorial (industrial).
Needs: Works on assignment only.
First Contact & Terms: Call for personal appointment to show portfolio, which should include tear sheets, photocopies of tear sheets of finished projects, and photocopies of rough and comprehensive layouts. Unsolicited material is returned only if accompanied by SASE. Reports in 1-2 weeks. Provide business card to be kept on file for possible future assignments. Considers complexity of project, client's budget, skill and experience of artist and turnaround time when establishing payment. Hourly fee: $20-50.
Tips: "Portfolio should be directed to 1 or 2 styles, 10 to 12 items, layout (30%), and some tear sheets." Selects artist according to concept, comprehensive layout ability and translation to finished work (presentation), and technical illustration.

TR PRODUCTIONS, 1031 Commonwealth Ave., Boston MA 02215. (617)783-0200. Production Manager: Tom Cramer. Audiovisual firm. Clients: industrial and high-tech.
Needs: Works with 5-10 freelance artists/year. Works on assignment only. Uses artists for slide graphics, layout, mechanical, computer graphics, and 2-color and 4-color collateral design. Especially important is clean, accurate board work.
First Contact & Terms: For slide work, artist must have experience in design and mechanicals for slides/multi-image. Send query letter with brochure showing art style, resume and slides to be kept on file. Samples not filed are not returned. Reports only if interested. Pays by the hour, $8-15 average. Considers complexity of project, client's budget, skill and experience of artist and turnaround time when establishing payment. Buys all audiovisual rights.

Michigan

***LEO J. BRENNAN ADVERTISING**, 2359 Livernois, Troy MI 48083-1692. (313)362-3131. Administrative Manager: Virginia Janusis. Ad agency and public relations firm. Clients: mainly industrial, automotive, banks and C.P.A.'s.
Needs: Works with 10 freelance artists/year. Artist must be well experienced. Uses artists for design, illustrations, brochures, catalog, retouching, lettering, keylining and typesetting.
First Contact & Terms: Send query letter with resume and samples. Samples not filed are returned only if requested. Reports only if interested. Call or write to schedule an appointment to show a portfolio, which should include thumbnails, roughs, original/final art, final reproduction/product, color, tear sheets, photostats, photographs and b&w. Considers complexity of project, client's budget, skill and experience of artist, and turnaround time when establishing payment. Buys all rights.

COMMON SENSE COMMUNICATIONS, INC., 225 W. Morley Dr., Saginaw MI 48605-3196. (517)755-8171. Executive Art Director: Bob Lauka. Art Director: James Kinnaman. Serves clients in machinery, automobiles, insurance, building supplies and banking.
Needs: Buys 25 full-color illustrations/year. Works on assignment only. Uses artists for illustrations, color separations, layout, lettering, paste-up, retouching and type spec for ads, annual reports, billboards, catalogs, letterheads, packaging, P-O-P displays, posters, TV and trademarks.
First Contact & Terms: Send slides, printed samples, business card, brochure/flyer, resume, tear sheets or "all the information an artist has available for analyzing assignments" to be kept on file for

possible future assignments. SASE. Reports within 4 weeks. Artist quotes his price. Considers client's budget when establishing payment. Agency pays for unused completed work ("assignments usually approved or disapproved at tissue stage").
Tips: "Have a complete portfolio of work showing how you developed a project right through the finished product. That way I can determine whether or not I need to work more closely with artists or I can feel confident that they can work on their own to achieve the result we need."

CREATIVE HOUSE ADVERTISING INC., Suite 200, 24472 Northwestern Hwy., Southfield MI 48075. (313)355-3344. Executive Vice President/Creative Director: Robert G. Washburn. Advertising/graphics/display/art firm. Clients: residential and commercial construction, land development, consumer, retail, finance and manufacturing. Assigns 20-30 jobs and buys 10-20 illustrations/year.
Needs: Works with 3 illustrators and 2 designers/month. Local artists only. Uses artists for filmstrips, consumer magazines, multimedia kits, direct mail, television, slide sets, brochures/flyers, trade magazines and newspapers. Also uses artists for illustration, design and comp layouts of ads, brochures, catalogs, annual reports and displays.
First Contact & Terms: Query with resume and business card, brochure/flyer and resume to be kept on file. Samples returned by SASE. Reports in 2 weeks. Provide review and presentation of samples. No originals returned to artist at job's completion. Arrange interview to show portfolio, which should include originals, reproduced and published pieces. Pays $50-5,000/project; $10-60/hour. Considers complexity of project, client's budget and rights purchased when establishing payment. Reproduction rights are purchased as a buy-out.
Tips: There is a trend toward "computerization to expedite research, reference and techniques. Maintain the basics of art, illustration and medium. Be flexible in pricing/budgeting."

***CRUNCH BIRD STUDIOS, INC.**, 32969 Hamilton Court, Farmington Hills MI 48018. (313)553-4747. Director: Ted Petok. Audiovisual firm. Clients: automotive and general manufacturing. Client list provided upon request.
Needs: Works with 15-20 freelance artists/year. Works on assignment only. Uses artists for design and animation.
First Contact & Terms: Send query letter with brochure showing art style. Samples not filed are returned by SASE. Reports only if interested. To show a portfolio, mail film. Pays for design by the project, $200-2,500. Considers client's budget when establishing payment. Buys all rights.

***D'ARCY MASIUS BENTON & BOWLES, (DMB&B)**, 1715 N. Woodward, Box 811, Bloomfield Hill MI 48303. (313)646-1000. Contact: Art Director (send for list of art directors). Ad agency.
Needs: Uses freelancers for consumer and trade magazines, brochures/flyers and newspapers.
First Contact & Terms: Call art coordinator or art director for appointment to show portfolio.
Tips: Each art director has individual specifications.

JACOBY & COMPANY, 828 West Chester Rd., Grosse Pointe MI 48230, (313)822-6055 or (313)499-8321. President: Albert K. Jacoby. Ad/PR agency. Clients: manufacturers, publisher, professional association, auction services, real estate and race tracks (horse).
Needs: Works with 3 illustrators and 6 designers/month. Works on assignment only. Uses artists for layout, illustration, technical art, type spec, paste-up, retouching and lettering for newspapers, magazines, TV, billboards, sales meetings, conventions and seminars.
First Contact & Terms: Send materials to be kept on file for future assignments. No originals returned to artist at job's completion. Reports only if interested. Arrange appointment or mail samples (tear sheets and photocopies). Considers complexity of project and client's budget when establishing payment.

LAMPE COMMUNICATIONS, INC., Box 5339, West Bloomsfield MI 48033. (313)332-3711. Production Manager: A.M. Lampe. PR firm. Clients: industry.
Needs: Assigns 100 freelance jobs/year. Works with 1 freelance illustrator and 2 freelance designers/month. Works on assignment only. Uses artists for trade magazine ads, brochures, stationery, signage and press releases.
First Contact & Terms: Send query letter with business card to be kept on file. Samples not kept on file are returned by SASE. Reports only if interested. Considers complexity of project, client's budget, and skill and experience of artist when establishing payment. Buys all rights.

MOLNER & CO., ADVERTISING, 21500 Greenfield Rd., Oak Park MI 48237. (313)968-2770. President: Monroe "Bob" Molner. Serves clients in a variety of industries.
Needs: Buys 100-150 illustrations/year. Local artists only. Works on assignment only. Uses artists for

print ads, TV storyboards, layouts, and fashion and furniture illustrations.
First Contact & Terms: Query. SASE. Reports in 1 week. Pays $10-50, fashion or furniture illustration; $20-30/hour, layout. Pays original fee as agreed for unused assigned illustrations. No originals returned to artist at job's completion.

PHOTO COMMUNICATION SERVICES, INC., 6410 Knapp NE, Ada MI 49301. (616)676-2429. President: Michael Jackson. Audiovisual firm. Clients: commercial and industrial; "local to international, large variety."
Needs: Works with 10 freelance artists/year. Works on assignment only. Uses artists for multi-image slide presentations, film and video. Especially important is knowledge of animation and pin registration.
First Contact & Terms: Send query letter with brochure, resume, business card, photographs or slides to be kept on file. Call or write for appointment to show portfolio. Samples not filed are returned by SASE only if requested. Reports back only if interested. Negotiates payment by project. Considers complexity of the project, client's budget, skill and experience of artist, geographic scope for the finished product, turnaround time and rights purchased when establishing payment. Negotiates rights purchased.

SYNCHRONOUS MEDIA INTERNATIONAL, 1217 Turner, Lansing MI 48906. Contact: Terry Terry. Audiovisual firm. Clients: industrial, commercial, government. Client list provided for SASE.
Needs: Works with 10-30 freelance artists/year. Works on assignment only. Uses artists for voice and camera talent, and graphics. Especially looks for communication skills and professional attitude.
First Contact & Terms: Send query letter with brochure showing art style or resume and tear sheets, photostats, photocopies, slides and photographs. Reports back only if interested. Write to schedule an appointment to show a portfolio, which should include thumbnails, roughs, original/final art, final reproduction/product, tear sheets, photostats and photographs. Pays for design and illustration by the hour, $8 minimum. Considers complexity of the project, client's budget, and skill and experience of artist when establishing payment. Rights purchased vary according to project.

***THOMPSON ADVERTISING PRODUCTIONS, INC.**, 31690 W. 12 Mice Rd., Farmington Hills MI 48018. (313)553-4566. Vice President: Clay Thompson. Ad agency. Clients: automotive, marine, industrial, high tech and health care.
Needs: Works with 20 freelance artists/year. Works on assignment only. Uses artists for design, illustrations, layout, retouching, and creative concept. Artist should have a "strong sense of design communication."
First Contact & Terms: Send query letter with resume and samples. Samples not filed are returned only if requested. Reports only if interested. Write to schedule an appointment to show a portfolio, which should include thumbnails, roughs and original/final art. Pays for design and illustration by the hour, minimum; by the project, $100 minimum. Considers complexity of project, client's budget, and skill and experience of artist. Rights purchased vary according to project.
Tips: Artist should "be prepared to show samples of layout work and demonstrated skills and be prepared to quote a price."

J. WALTER THOMPSON COMPANY, 600 Renaissance Center, Detroit MI 48243. (313)568-3800. Assistant Art Administrator: Maryann Inson. Ad agency. Clients: automotive, consumer, industrial, media related.
Needs: Usually does not use freelancers; deals primarily with established artists' representatives and art/design studios.
First Contact & Terms: Contact only through artist's agent. Assignments awarded on lowest bid. Write to schedule an appointment to show a portfolio, which should include thumbnails, roughs, original/final art, final reproduction/product, color, tear sheets, photostats and photographs. Pays for design and illustration by the project.
Tips: Agency deals with proven illustrators from an "approved vendor's list." New vendors are considered for list periodically. "Portfolio should be comprehensive but not too large. Organization of the portfolio is as important as the sample. Mainly, consult professional rep."

Minnesota

ART & COPY OVERLOAD, Suite 2, 2010 Marshall Ave., St. Paul MN 55104. (612)644-3443. Contact: John Borden. Ad agency. Clients: food, ice, medical, financial, industrial, manufacturing.
Needs: Works with 8 freelance artists/year. Requires 2 years' commercial experience, prefers local

artists. Works on assignment only. Uses artists for layout, paste-up, drawing and illustration. Especially important is an understanding of layout.
First Contact & Terms: Send brochure, resume, business card and photostats or photocopies to be kept on file up to 1 year. Samples not filed are returned by SASE. Does not report back. Call for appointment to show portfolio. Pays by the hour, $18-50 average or by the day, $40-180 average. Considers complexity of the project, client's budget, skill and experience of artist and rights purchased when establishing payment. Rights purchased vary according to project.

BATTEN, BARTON, DURSTINE, & OSBORN, INC., 900 Brotherhood Bldg., 625 4th Ave. S., Minneapolis MN 55415. (612)338-8401. Art Buyer: Pam Schmidt. Ad agency. Clients: industrial, food, financial and corporate.
Needs: Uses artists for consumer and trade magazines, newspaper, billboard, P-O-P/collateral, story boards comp work. Works on assignment only.
First Contact & Terms: Call for appointment to show portfolio, which should include slides, photographs or photostats as samples. Helpful to provide samples that can be kept on file for future reference. No originals returned at job's completion. Pays by the project; negotiates payment based on time/work involved, skill and experience of artist, occasionally where work will appear. Also requires estimates and reviews them with client's budget in mind.
Tips: "When we're considering someone for a job, its very important to be able to refer to leave-behind materials."

JOHN BORDEN & ASSOCIATES, Suite 2, 2010 Marshall Ave., St. Paul MN 55104. (612)644-3443. Contact: John Borden. Ad agency. Clients: business, industrial, financial, food and food related and advertising. Assigns 15 jobs and buys 50 illustrations/year.
Needs: Works with 4 illustrators/month. Local professionals only. Uses artists for layouts, finished art, type spec, consumer and trade magazines, stationery design, direct mail, billboards, TV, brochures/flyers and newspapers.
First Contact & Terms: Query with samples or call to arrange interview to show portfolio. Prefers photographs, photostats and b&w line drawings as samples. Especially looks for layout ability, styles of art, and calligraphy. Prefers to review 18-50 samples. Samples returned by SASE. Reports in 2 weeks. Provide brochure/flyer, photostats or reprints of samples to be kept on file for possible future assignments. Works on assignment only. Originals become client's property at job's completion. Reports in 2 weeks. Pays $18-50/hour; $300-10,000/project.
Tips: Also owns Art and Copy Overload Service supplying freelancers to other companies that need them (for annual reports, etc.).

FABER SHERVEY ADVERTISING, 160 W. 79th St., Minneapolis MN 55420. (612)881-5111. Creative Director: Paul D. Shervey. Ad agency. Clients: business to business, industrial and farm.
Needs: Works with 25 freelance artists/year. Prefers local artists. Uses artists for retouching, line art, keyline, illustration.
First Contact & Terms: Send brochure and business card. Do *not* send samples. Does not report back. Call or write for appointment to show portfolio. Pays by the hour, $20-80 average. Considers complexity of project when establishing payment. Buys all rights.

LINHOFF PRODUCTIONS, Box 24005, 4400 France Ave. S, Minneapolis MN 55424. (612)927-7333. Art Director: LuAnne Speeter-Belden. Audiovisual firm. Clients: banks, computer companies and financial services companies.
Needs: Works with 8-15 freelance artists/year. Local artists only; must work inhouse. Works on assignment only, or as vacation replacement. Uses artists for keylining, artwork and typesetting. Especially important are ruling; an eye for layout; good word skills for proofreading; copy camera capabilities; graphic arts computer; typesetting knowledge a plus (Comp-Edit 5810). Experience with audio-visual preparation preferred.
First Contact & Terms: Send query letter with resume and photocopies to be kept on file. Samples not filed are returned by SASE. Reports within 2 weeks. Call to schedule an appointment to show a portfolio, which should include color and original/final art, AV projects (slides, viewgraphs). Pays by the hour, $8 minimum. Considers skill and experience of artist when establishing payment. Buys all rights.
Tips: "Much of our art preparation is predesigned and often 'mechanical' or repetitive. This is not a forum for an artist with flamboyant design skills. Instead, we want people that can envision the final AV product and can create clean yet exciting visuals."

PEDERSON HERZOG & NEE INC., 6401 University Ave. NE, Minneapolis MN 55401. (612)333-1234. Art Director: Ann Taylor. Ad agency. Serves clients in automotive, sporting

equipment, farming equipment and industrial supplies. Assigns 12 illustrations/year.
Needs: Works with 2 illustrators and 1 designer/month. Local artists only. Uses artists for billboards, P-O-P displays, consumer magazines, television, trade magazines, newspapers and brochures.
First Contact & Terms: Query with samples to be kept on file for future assignments. No originals returned at job's completion. Pays $50-2,000/job.

RUHR/PARAGON, INC., Suite 600, 1221 Nicollet Mall, Minneapolis MN 55403. (612)332-4565. Art Director: Doug Lew. Ad agency. Clients: consumer and industrial firms; client list provided upon request.
Needs: Works with 30 illustrators/year; very seldom uses freelance designers. Works on assignment only. Uses freelance artists for billboards, consumer and trade magazines, direct mail, P-O-P displays, brochures, catalogs, posters, signage, newspapers, AV presentations and sometimes TV.
First Contact & Terms: Send samples to be kept on file. Negotiates payment according to client's budget; then the amount of creativity, where work will appear and previous experience are taken into consideration.

***VANGUARD ASSOCIATES, INC.**, Suite 485, 15 S. 9th St., Minneapolis MN 55402. (612)338-5386. Creative Director: Ralph Dorsch. Ad agency. Clients: aluminum foil manufacturer, fashion and food firms, governmental agencies; client list provided upon request.
Needs: Works with 12 illustrators/month; occasionally uses freelance designers. Works on assignment basis only. Uses freelance artists for billboards, consumer and trade magazines, direct mail, P-O-P displays, brochures, posters, newspapers, multimedia campaigns and AV presentations.
First Contact & Terms: Must see samples. Out-of-town artists query with resume and samples; local artists arrange interview to show portfolio. Payment is by the project; negotiates according to client's budget.

ROY WALLACE AND ASSOCIATES, INC., 1200 Foshay Tower, 821 Marquette Ave., Minneapolis MN 55402. (612)340-9620. Account Executive & Manager, Graphic Design and Production: Betsy Massie. PR firm. Clients: transportation companies, manufacturing companies, high technology companies, agribusiness, etc.
Needs: Number of jobs assigned to freelance artists varies. Write for appointment to show portfolio. Works on assignment only. Uses artists for brochures, AV presentations and annual reports.
First Contact & Terms: Send query letter with brochure, resume and business card to be kept on file. Reports within 30 days. Pays by the hour or by the project. Considers complexity of project, client's budget, skill and experience of artist and turnaround time when establishing payment.

Missouri

FRANK BLOCK ASSOCIATES, Chase Park Plaza, St. Louis MO 63108. (314)367-9600. Art Directors: Ray Muskopf and Dave Meinecke. Ad agency. Clients: primarily industrial firms; client list provided upon request.
Needs: Works with 6 illustrators/month. Works on assignment only. Uses freelance artists for billboards, consumer and trade magazines, direct mail, brochures, catalogs, posters, signage, newspapers, TV and AV presentations.
First Contact & Terms: Arrange interview to show portfolio. Negotiates payment by the project and on freelancer's ability.

BRYANT, LAHEY & BARNES, INC., Suite 210, 4200 Pennsylvania, Kansas City MO 64111. (913)677-3494 or 677-4711. Art Director: Terry Pritchett. Ad agency. Clients: agricultural and veterinary.
Needs: Local artists only. Uses artists for illustration and production, including keyline and paste-up, consumer and trade magazines and brochures/flyers.
First Contact & Terms: Query by phone. Send business card and resume to be kept on file for future assignments. Negotiates pay. No originals returned to artist at job's completion.

D'ARCY MASIUS BENTON & BOWLES, Gateway Tower, 1 Memorial Dr., St. Louis MO 63102. (314)342-8600. Senior Vice President/Director of Creative Services: Carl Klinghammer. Ad agency. Clients: all types including brewery.
Needs: Works with 20-30 freelance illustrators and 10 freelance designers/month. Works on assignment only. Uses freelancers for billboards, consumer and trade magazines, direct mail,

brochures/flyers, newspapers, P-O-P displays, stationery design and TV.
First Contact & Terms: Call for appointment to show portfolio. Reporting time varies. Provide brochure/flyer, resume and tear sheets to be kept on file for possible future assignments. Negotiates payment based on client's budget, amount of creativity required from artist and where work will appear.
Tips: Likes to see latest styles and techniques (anything from realism to abstract) in portfolio.

FREMERMAN, ROSENFIELD & LANE, Suite 2102, 106 W. 14th St., Kansas City MO 64105. (816)474-8120. Creative Director: Marvin Fremerman. Art Director: Leanne Zembrunner. Ad agency. Clients: retail, consumer and trade accounts; client list provided upon request.
Needs: Works with 10-15 illustrators/month. Works primarily with local artists. Uses freelance artists for billboards, consumer and trade magazines, direct mail, P-O-P displays, brochures, catalogs, posters, signage, newspapers and AV presentations.
First Contact & Terms: Arrange interview to show portfolio. Query with resume of credits and samples. Payment is by the project or by the day; negotiates according to client's budget and where work will appear.

GARDNER ADVERTISING, 10 S. Broadway, St. Louis MO 63102. (314)444-2000. Director of Creative Services: Bob Fanter. Ad agency. Clients: primarily consumer food and dog food; also industrial, financial, recreation and services.
Needs: Works with about 15 illustrators/month and occasionally uses designers for packaging. Uses artists for consumer print and TV.
First Contact & Terms: Call for appointment to show portfolio or contact through artist's rep. Negotiates pay based on budget and where work will appear, whether color or b&w, etc.

GEORGE JOHNSON, ADVERTISING, 763 New Ballas Rd. S., St. Louis MO 63141. (314)569-3440. Art Director: Dean Weiler. Ad agency. Serves clients in real estate, financial and social agencies.
Needs: Works with 1-2 illustrators/month. Local artists only. Uses artists for illustrations, animation, layout, lettering, paste-up, retouching, type spec and design for annual reports, billboards, catalogs, print ads, letterheads, packaging, P-O-P displays, posters, TV and trademarks.
First Contact & Terms: Write or call for appointment to show portfolio, which should include tear sheets, roughs and work done for other ad agencies. SASE. Reports within 1 week. Originals returned at job's completion.

KENRICK ADVERTISING INC., 7711 Carondelet, St. Louis MO 63105. (314)726-6020. Creative Director: Clancy Strock. Full service advertising firm. Serves clients in automotives, animal care products, agriculture, retail and business to business.
Needs: Uses illustrators and designers for ad design layout, direct mail brochures, signs, sets, slide shows, P-O-P displays and packages, billboards, filmstrips, letterhead, TV, newspapers, books, flipcharts, illustrative lettering and retouching.
First Contact & Terms: Query with samples (tear sheets or photocopies) and arrange interview to show portfolio. Reports within 4 weeks. Provide business card and tear sheets to be kept on file for future assignments. Returns original artwork only when "arrangements have been made prior to assignment."

***MARITZ COMMUNICATIONS CO.**, 1315 N. Highway Dr., Fenton MO 63026. (314)225-2686. General Manager: Dan King. Audiovisual firm; motion business theater. Clients: 250 of Fortune 500.
Needs: Works with 15-20 freelance artists/year. Artist must have experience in business. Uses artists for design, illustrations, P-O-P displays, mechanicals, animation, lettering and logos. "We don't buy art for art's sake. We buy to solve problems and please clients."
First Contact & Terms: Send query letter with brochure showing art styles or resume, tear sheets and photocopies. Samples not filed are not returned. Reports only if interested. Call to show a portfolio, which should include roughs, original/final art, final reproduction/product and color. Payment varies. Considers complexity of project, client's budget, skill and experience of artist, turnaround time and rights purchased when establishing payment. Buys all rights.
Tips: "Outside purchases sporadic with quick turnaround."

***NEW AVENUE STUDIO**, 10953 Olive St. Rd., Creve Coeur MO 63141. (314)997-4221. President: Matthew Wilkinson. Estab. 1985. Ad agency and product designers and manufacturers of graphics serving the souvenir market, ad agencies, t-shirt companies, poster and paper products. Client list available with SASE.
Needs: Works with 8-14 freelance artists/year. Uses artists for design, illustrations, poster, logos, advertisements and souvenir designs for many of the major U.S. cities. Eye for good use of color(s), good balance.

First Contact & Terms: Send query letter with brochure showing art style or tear sheets, photocopies and photographs. Samples not filed are returned by SASE. Reports back within 2 weeks. To show a portfolio, mail appropriate materials or write to schedule an appointment; portfolio should include roughs, original/final art, tear sheets, photostats and photographs. Pays for design and illustration by the project, $30-250. Considers complexity of project, how work will be used, turnaround time and rights purchased when establishing payment. Righs purchased vary according to payment.
Tips: "Let us know if you think you have a unique style or talent."

PREMIER FILM VIDEO & RECORDING, 3033 Locust St., St. Louis MO 63103. (314)531-3555. Secretary/Treasurer: Grace Dalzell. AV/film/animation/TV producer. Serves clients in business, religion, education and advertising. Produces videotape, motion 35mm, 16mm and Super 8mm, strip films, cassette dupes 8 tracks, TV and radio spots.
Needs: Assigns 50-60 jobs/year. Works with 8-10 illustrators, "a few" designers/month. Works on assignment only. Uses artists for strip film and slide presentations, TV commercials and motion picture productions.
First Contact & Terms: Send resume to be kept on file. "We do not accept samples; we review them during interviews only." Reporting time varies with available work. Pays by the project; method and amount of payment are negotiated with the individual artist. Pay varies with each client's budget. No originals returned to artist following publication; "copies supplied when possible." Buys all rights, but sometimes negotiates.
Tips: "In developing a brochure, begin by simply stating work capability and area of work most capable of producing, i.e., animation, cartoons, production, direction or editing—whatever you want to do for a living. Be specific."

STOLZ ADVERTISING CO., Suite 500, 7701 Forsyth Blvd., St. Louis MO 63105. (314)863-0005. Contact: Executive Creative Director. Ad agency. Clients: consumer firms.
Needs: Works with 2 illustrators/month; occasionally uses freelance designers. Uses freelance artists for billboards, consumer and trade magazines, direct mail, P-O-P displays, brochures, posters, newspapers and AV presentations.
First Contact & Terms: Arrange interview to show portfolio or query with samples. Negotiates payment according to particular job.

Montana

SAGE ADVERTISING/BILLINGS, Box 20977, Billings MT 59104. (406)652-3232. Art Director: Lori Richards-Burda. Ad agency/AV/PR firm/radio and TV; "a full service agency." Clients: financial, utilities, industry, hotel/motel, real estate.
Needs: Assigns 24 freelance jobs/year. Works with 2 freelance illustrators/month. Works on assignment only. Uses artists for filmstrips, AV presentations, photography and illustration.
First Contact & Terms: Send query letter with resume and photocopies to be kept on file. Samples not kept on file are returned only if requested. Reports within 2 weeks. Call or write to schedule an appointment to show a portfolio, which should include roughs, final reproduction/product, color, tear sheets, photostats and photographs. Pays for illustration by the project, $150. Considers complexity of project, client's budget, skill and experience of artist, geographic scope of finished project, turnaround time and rights purchased when establishing payment. Negotiates rights purchased.

Nebraska

MILLER FRIENDT LUDEMANN INC., 801 S. 48th St., Lincoln NE 68510. Senior Art Director: Patrick Osborne. Art Director: Dave Christiansen. Ad agency/PR firm. Clients: bank, industry, restaurants, tourism and retail.
Needs: Works on assignment only. Uses artists for consumer and trade magazines, billboards, direct mail packages, brochures, newspapers, stationery, signage, P-O-P displays, AV presentations, posters, press releases, trade show displays and TV graphics. "Freelancing is based on heavy workloads. Most freelancing is pasteup but secondary is illustrator for designed element."
First Contact & Terms: Send query letter with resume and slides to be kept on file. Samples not kept on file are returned by SASE. Reports within 10 days. Write for appointment to show portfolio, "if regional/national; call if local." Portfolio should include thumbnails, roughs, original/final art, final reproduction/product, color, tear sheets and photostats. Pays by the project, $100-1,500 average. Considers complexity of project, client's budget, skill and experience of artist, turnaround time and

rights purchased when establishing payment. Buys all rights.
Tips: "Be prompt, have work done on time and be able to price your project work accurately. Make quality first."

J. GREG SMITH, Suite 102, Burlington Place, 1004 Farnam St., Omaha NE 68102. (402)444-1600. Art Director: Shelly Bartek. Ad agency. Clients: financial, banking institutions, associations, agricultural, travel and tourism.
Needs: Works with 3 illustrators/year. Works on assignment only. Uses freelance artists for consumer and trade magazines, brochures, catalogs and AV presentations.
First Contact & Terms: Send query letter with brochure showing art style or photocopies. Reports only if interested. To show a portfolio, mail original/final art, final reproduction/product, color and b&w. Payment is by the project; negotiates according to client's budget.
Tips: Current trends include a certain "flexibility." Agencies are now able "to use any style or method that best fits the job."

New Jersey

SOL ABRAMS ASSOCIATES INC., 331 Webster Dr., New Milford NJ 07646. (201)262-4111. President: Sol Abrams. Public relations firm. Clients: real estate, food, fashion, beauty, entertainment, government, retailing, sports, nonprofit organizations, etc. Media used include billboards, consumer magazines, trade magazines, direct mail, newspapers, P-O-P displays, radio and TV.
Needs: Assigns 6 freelance jobs/year. "For practical purposes, we prefer using artists in New Jersey-New York area." Works on assignment only. Uses artists for consumer magazines, billboards, brochures, catalogs, newspapers, stationery, signage, AV presentations and press releases.
First Contact & Terms: Send query letter with photographs and photostats which may be kept on file. Samples not kept on file returned by SASE. Reports only if interested. Pay varies according to client and job. Considers client's budget, and skill and experience of artist when establishing payment. Buys all rights.
Tips: "As one who started his career as an artist before deciding to become a public relations consultant, I empathize with young artists. If material interests me and I cannot use it, I might develop leads or refer it to people and firms which may use it. Artists should be honest and sincere. Dedication and integrity are as important as talent."

ADLER, SCHWARTZ INC., 140 Sylvan Ave., Englewood Cliffs NJ 07632. President: Peter Adler. Ad agency. Clients: automotive, shipping and consumer product firms.
Needs: Buys 50 illustrations/year. Uses artists for billboards, P-O-P displays, consumer magazines, trade magazines, newspapers, direct mail, slide presentations, brochures/flyers. Also uses artists for layout, lettering, color separations, paste-up, retouching and type spec for brochures, annual reports, print ads, letterheads, packaging, posters and trademarks. Especially needs line drawings and washes of people, cars and interiors.
First Contact & Terms: Send query letter with business card, tearsheets and an SASE. Reports in 2 weeks. Call for an appointment to show a portfolio.

DAVID H. BLOCK ADVERTISING, INC., 33 S. Fullerton Ave., Montclair NJ 07042 (201)744-6900. Executive Art Director and Vice President: Karen Deluca. Clients: finance, industrial, consumer, real estate, bio-medical. Buys 100-200 illustrations/year.
Needs: Prefers to work with "artists with at least 3-5 years experience in paste-up and 'on premises' work for mechanicals and design." Uses artists for illustrations, layout, lettering, type spec, mechanicals and retouching for ads, annual reports, billboards, catalogs, letterheads, brochures and trademarks.
First Contact & Terms: Arrange interview. SASE. Reports in 2 weeks.
Tips: "Please send some kind of sample of work. If mechanical artist: line art printed sample. If layout artist: composition of some type and photographs or illustrations."

CABSCOTT BROADCAST PRODUCTION, INC., 517 7th Ave., Lindenwold NJ 08021. (609)346-3400. President: Larry Scott. Audiovisual firm, production company. Clients: retail, broadcasters (radio and TV), ad agencies and industrial users.
Needs: Works with 5 freelance artists/year. Prefers local artists experienced in television storyboarding. Works on assignment only. Uses artist for art, layout and storyboard creation. Especially important are freehand skills.
First Contact & Terms: Send query letter with brochure showing art style, resume and slides to be kept

on file. Prefers any type sample that gives an idea of artist's style. Samples are returned by SASE if requested. Reports only if interested. To show a portfolio, mail appropriate materials, which should include tear sheets, photostats and photographs. Negotiates payment by the project. Considers complexity of project, client's budget, skill and experience of artist and turnaround time when establishing payment. Negotiates rights purchased.

***CHAMPION ADVERTISING AGENCY**, 86 Davison Place, Englewood NJ 07631. Art/Creative Director: Jerry Hahn. Clients: jewelers, manufacturing and retail.
Needs: Assigns 100-150 jobs/year. Need for freelance illustrators varies and uses 2 design studios for needed work. Works on assignment or on speculation basis if okay. Uses freelancers for fine line art, scratchboard of jewelry products for newspaper reproductions. Uses artists for catalog design, illustrators for packaging and display concepts.
First Contact & Terms: Query in person with proofs, photostats or repros of line art, tear sheets or previously published work. Do not send original art or slides unless specifically requested. Samples returned only if requested. Reports in 1 week. Provide business card, brochure/flyer, resume, sample proofs and tear sheets to be kept on file for possible future assignments. Pays $25-65 depending on product, scratchboard or pen & ink; $100 average, full color rendering of product; $250 + , full color realistic illustration. Considers complexity of project and client's budget when establishing payment.
Tips: "My agency is a prospect for photographers, retouchers and scratchboard or line artists with jewelry or cosmetic experience, but hourly rates vary and are confidential. I look for graphic honesty . . . true product renderings in pen & ink for newspaper reproduction."

***THE CHERENSON GROUP**, 300 Regent St., Livingston NJ 07039. Contact: Senior Art Director. Clients: housing developers, financial institutions, sports facilities, real estate firms and retailers. Buys 100 illustrations/year; local artists only. Query with samples. SASE. Reports in 1 week.
Needs: Illustrations, color separations, layout, lettering, paste-up, type spec and design for annual reports, billboards, catalogs, letterheads, print ads, P-O-P displays, posters and trademarks.
First Contact & Terms: Pays $10-40/hour, design; $8-12/hour, mechanicals; $8-25/hour, illustrations. Pays promised fee for unused assigned work.

CREATIVE PRODUCTIONS, INC., 200 Main St., Orange NJ 07050. (201)676-4422. Partner: Gus J. Nichols. Audiovisual firm. Clients: pharmaceutical firms, paper manufacturers, chemical and financial firms.
Needs: Works with 30 freelance artists/year. Artists must be within 1 hour travel time to studio with 1 year's experience. Uses artists for mechanicals, paste-ups, charts and graphs. Especially important is "accuracy, neat work and the ability to take direction."
First Contact & Terms: Send resume to be kept on file. Call for appointment to show portfolio. Reports back only if interested. Pays by the hour, $8-12 average. Considers skill and experience of artist when establishing payment.
Tips: Artists "need to do mechanicals in the conventional way and also operate a graphic computer."

DAVIS, HAYS & COMPANY, 426 Hudson St., Hackensack NJ 07601. (201)641-4910. Contact: Art Director. Estab. 1984. Ad agency, public relations firm. Clients: medical, healthcare, marketing research, service industries and beauty.
Needs: Works with 3-5 freelance artists/year. Artist must have experience working with agencies. Uses artists for design, layout, mechanicals, illustration and production. "Professionalism and deadline and budget restrictions awareness are important."
First Contact & Terms: Send query letter with photostats to be kept on file. Samples not filed are returned only if requested. Reports within 1 month. Call or write to schedule an appointment to show a portfolio, which should include roughs and original/final art. Pays by the hour, $20-50 average. Considers complexity of the project, client's budget and turnaround time when establishing payment. Buys all rights.
Tips: "We are looking for positive thinkers: those who say 'we'll find a way to do it' even when there are no easy answers. Also looking for artists with knowledge of MacIntosh graphics."

DIEGNAN & ASSOCIATES, Box 298, Oldwick NJ 08858. (201)832-7951. President: Norman Diegnan. PR firm. Clients: commercial.
Needs: Assigns 25 freelance jobs/year. Works on assignment only. Uses artists for catalogs and AV presentations.
First Contact & Terms: Send brochure and resume to be kept on file. Write for appointment to show portfolio; may also send portfolio. Reports only if interested. Pays artist's rate. Considers client's budget when establishing payment. Buys all rights.

GRAPHIC WORKSHOP INC., 466 Old Hook Rd., Emerson NJ 07630. (201)967-8500. Creative Director: Al Nudelman. Sales promotion agency. Clients: AV, computer accounts, industrial tools, men's wear, ladies' wear.
Needs: Works with 10-15 freelance artists/year. Prefers local artists with a minimum of 3-5 years' experience; "retail layout and some design background helpful." Works on assignment only. Uses artists for illustration, paste-up and mechanical, design comps. Especially looks for knowledge of type and good design sense.
First Contact & Terms: Send query letter with business card and slides or "whatever shows work off the best". Samples not filed are returned only if requested. Reports back only if interested. Pays by the hour, $10-15 average; by the day, $75-100 average. Considers client's budget, complexity of the project, and skill and experience of artist when establishing payment. Buys all rights.

IMAGE INNOVATIONS, INC., 405 S. Amwell Rd., Somerset NJ 08873. President: Mark Else. Film/multi-image/video producer. Clients: school, association, corporate and governmental.
Needs: Does not work with talent outside of metropolitan New York area. Works on assignment only. Uses artists for filmstrips, motion picture, multi-image multimedia kits, storyboards, packaging, books and brochures.
First Contact & Terms: Send resume, letter of inquiry and/or flyer to be kept on file. Samples returned by SASE. To show a portfolio, a freelance artist should mail appropriate materials, which should include "whatever artist feels is representational. Pays for design and illustration by the project. Considers client's budget, amount of creativity required, where work is to appear and artist's previous experience/reputation when establishing payment.
Tips: "Learn the technology along with technique."

JANUARY PRODUCTIONS, 249 Goffle Rd., Hawthorne NJ 07507. (201)423-4666. Art Director: Susan Banta. AV producer. Serves clients in education. Produces sound filmstrips and read-along books and cassettes.
Needs: Assigns 5-10 jobs/year. Works with 5 illustrators/year. "While not a requirement, an artist living in the same geographic area is a plus." Works on assignment only, "although if someone had a project already put together, we would consider it." Uses artists for artwork for filmstrips, sketches for books and layout work.
First Contact & Terms: Send query letter with resume, tear sheets, photocopies and photographs. To show a portfolio, mail appropriate materials or call to schedule an appointment. Portfolio should include original/final art, color and tear sheets. Pays for illustration by the project, $200 minimum. No originals returned following publication. Buys all rights.

J. M. KESSLINGER & ASSOCIATES, 37 Saybrook Place, Newark NJ 07102. (201)623-0007. Art Director: J. Dietz. Advertising agency. Serves business-to-business clients.
Needs: Uses 1-2 illustrators/month for illustrations, mechanicals, direct mail, brochures, flyers, trade magazines and newspapers. Prefers local artists. Works on assignment only.
First Contact & Terms: Phone for appointment. Prefers photostats, tear sheets, slides as samples. Samples returned by SASE only if requested. Reports only if interested. Does not return original artwork to artist unless contracted otherwise. Negotiates pay. Pays by the hour, $15-50 average. Pay range depends on the type of freelance work, i.e. mechanicals vs. creative. Considers complexity of project, client's budget, skill and experience of artist, and rights purchased when establishing payment.

MORVAY ADVERTISING AGENCY, 177 Valley St., South Orange NJ 07079. (201)762-3331. Art Director: Mrs. Tobia L. Meyers. Ad agency. Clients: electronic, restaurants, clothing, caterers, luggage hardware, travel and auto rental.
Needs: Assigns about 5 jobs/year. Prefers local artists. Works on assignment only. Uses artists for catalog covers, photo retouching and paste-up.
First Contact & Terms: Send query letter with resume, tear sheets, photostats, photocopies or photographs. Samples returned by SASE. Reports in 4 weeks. Call or write to schedule an appointment to show a portfolio, which should include original/final art, final reproduction/product, tear sheets, photostats, photographs or b&w. Pays for design by the hour, $5 minimum; by the project, $10 minimum; pay "depends on job required." Considers complexity of project, client's budget, and skill and experience of artist when establishing payment.
Tips: "Call first and set up an appointment." Especially looks for clean work and sharp pen line rendering. Negatives and proper spelling (where applicable) count!"

SPOONER & CO., Box 126, Verona NJ 07044. (201)857-0053. President: William B. Spooner III. Industrial ad agency. Clients: mills, mixers, vacuum pumps, metals and ores, plastic blow molding machines and conveyor belts.

Needs: Works with 2 illustrators and 2 designers/month. Works on assignment basis only. Uses artists for stationery design, slide sets, brochures/flyers and trade magazines. Also uses artists for layout, illustration, technical art, type spec, paste-up, retouching and lettering for newspapers, trade magazines, direct mail, technical literature and trade shows.

First Contact & Terms: Call first or send letter with qualifications and experience. Provide brochure, flyer, business card and resume to be kept on file. Do not send original work. Samples returned by SASE. Reports back only if interested. Payment negotiated. Considers complexity of project, client's budget, and skill and experience of artist when establishing payment.

STARBUCK CREATIVE SERVICES, 26 Steven Tr., West Orange NJ 07052. Senior Vice President: B. Siegel. Ad agency. Clients: health care. Client list provided for SASE.

Needs: Works with 2-5 freelance artists/year. Uses artists for special projects and back-up.

First Contact & Terms: Send query letter with brochure, resume, business card and photostats, photographs, slides or tear sheets to be kept on file. Samples not filed are returned by SASE only if requested. Reports within 3 weeks. Write for appointment to show portfolio. Payment open. Considers complexity of the project, client's budget, skill and experience of artist, geographic scope for the finished product, turnaround time and rights purchased when establishing payment. Rights purchased vary according to project.

***TAA INC.**, 65 Horse Hill Rd., Cedar Knolls NJ 07927. (201)267-2670. Production Manager: Eileen Cronin. "Inhouse ad agency." Clients: pharmaceutical marketing.

Needs: Assigns 3 freelance jobs/year. Works with 1 freelance illustrator/month. Works on assignment only. Uses artists for direct mail packages, brochures and posters.

First Contact & Terms: Send query letter with brochure to be kept on file. Samples not kept on file are returned only if requested. Reports only if interested. Write to schedule an appointment to show a portfolio. Pays by the hour, $20 minimum. Considers "my own judgment on what job is worth before the work is done" when establishing payment. "If unforeseen complications arise, artist must tell me."

Tips: "Artists should know someting about the company before they come in."

WREN ASSOCIATES, INC., Communications Park, 208 Bunn Dr., Princeton NJ 08540. (609)924-8085. Production Manager: Debbie Schur. Audiovisual firm. Clients: industrial, *Fortune 500* (automotive, pharmaceutical, financial, etc.).

Needs: Works with 10-25 freelance artists/year. Artists should have minimum of 1-2 years' experience. Uses artists for mechanical preparation, photography, storyboard and design, video crew, typesetting, Forox photography, computer slide generation, project management. Especially important are design and mechanical preparation skills, slide preparation skills, multi-imge training, Forox experience, computer slide experience, rendering and storyboarding.

First Contact & Terms: Send query letter with resume and slides and videocassettes of completed shows. Letter and resume are filed; samples are returned if postage is paid by the artist. Reports back only if interested. Call for appointment to show portfolio. Pays by the hour, $8-35; by the project, $100 minimum; by the day, $100-350. Design rates vary according to skill level and project; photography rates vary according to project. Considers client's budget, and skill and experience of artist when establishing payment. Rights purchased vary according to project.

Tips: "Wren Associates is very interested in attracting experienced multimedia designers and producers. We are most interested in seeing videotapes of completed projects which include photography direction, narration, soundtrack direction and strong conceptual skills. Freelance artists who are interested in our firm but do not fulfill this experience level should be able to show their level of expertise in the production of slides, Forox photography and/or video."

ZM SQUARED, 903 Edgewood Lane, Cinnaminson NJ 08077. (609)786-0612. Executive Director: Mr. Pete Zakroff. AV producer. Clients: industry, business, education and unions. Produces slides, filmstrips, overhead transparencies and handbooks.

Needs: Assigns 8 jobs/year. Works with 2 illustrators/month. Prefers artists with previous work experience who specialize. Works on assignment only. Uses artists for cartoons, illustrations and technical art.

First Contact & Terms: Send resume and samples (slides preferred). Samples returned by SASE. Provide samples and brochure/flyer to be kept on file for possible future assignments. Reports in 3 weeks. Pays by the project. Payment varies with each client's budget. No originals returned to artist following publication. Buys all rights.

New Mexico

AIRY ADVERTISING, INC., Box 70, Albuquerque NM 87103. (505)242-1120. Art Director: Joe McDonnell. Ad agency. Clients: industrial, land developer, clip art/editorial service, bank, gospel

music network, fast food chain and home builder.
Needs: Works with 5-7 freelance artists/year. Works on assignment only. Uses artists for illustrations, mechanicals/production and layouts. Especially looks for ability to draw and for clean/precise art production. "We buy realistic pen & ink-type illustrations."
First Contact & Terms: Send resume and samples; samples are returned by SASE. Resume is filed. Call or write for appointment to show portfolio. Samples not filed are not returned. Prefers slides, tear sheets, paste-ups or photostats as samples. Reports back only if interested. Pays by the hour, $12-15 average; sometimes by the project in advance by estimate. Considers complexity of the project, client's budget, and skill and experience of artist when establishing payment. Negotiates rights purchased; vary according to project.
Tips: "Call first."

New York

ACKERMAN ADVERTISING COMMUNICATIONS INC., 55 Northern Blvd., Greenvale NY 11548. (516)484-5150. Creative Director: Skip Ackerman. Art Director: Maxine Brenner. Serves clients in food, finance and tourism.
Needs: Works with 4 illustrators and 2 designers/month. Local artists only. Uses artists for layout, paste-up, illustration and retouching for newspapers, TV, magazines, transit signage, billboards, collateral, direct mail and P-O-P displays.
First Contact & Terms: Arrange interview. No originals returned.

GENE BARTCZAK ASSOCIATES INC., Box E, North Bellmore NY 11710. (516)781-6230. Manager: Gordon Willson. PR firm. Clients: technical industrial companies and related organizations.
Needs: Buys 10-15 illustrations/year. Works with 1-2 illustrators/month. Works on assignment only. Uses artists for P-O-P displays, direct mail, brochures/flyers; and design and mechanicals for ads and catalogs.
First Contact & Terms: Send query letter with business card and resume to be kept on file. No original work returned at job's completion. Reports back whether to expect possible future assignments. Negotiates payment. Pays promised fee for unused assigned work.

***CAMPUS GROUP COMPANIES**, 24 Depot Sq., Tuckahoe NY 10707. (914)961-1900. Contact: Melanie Suskin. Audiovisual firm.
Needs: Works with 25 freelance artists/year. Works on assignment only. Uses artists for design, illustrations, brochures, catalogs, books, mechanicals, animation, posters, direct mail packages, press releases, motion pictures, logos, charts/graphs and advertisements. "Artists must have computer art skills, good design and board skills."
First Contact & Terms: Send query letter with resume and samples. Samples not filed are returned only if requested by artist. Reports within 12 weeks. Write to schedule an appointment to show a portfolio, which should include as much as is relative. Pays for design by the hour, $10-30. Pays for illustration by the hour, $10-30. Considers complexity of project, skill and experience of artist and turnaround time when establishing payment. Purchases all rights.
Tips: "Our company does not train artists; we have only skilled experienced artists."

CASTAGNE COMMUNICATIONS, 63 Adams St., Bedford Hills NY 10507. (914)241-1965. Art Director: Kirsten Smith. Ad agency. Clients: industry.
Needs: Assigns 12 freelance jobs/year. "Strongly prefer local artists." Works on assignment only. Works with 1 freelance designer/month. Uses artists for trade magazines and brochures.
First Contact & Terms: Send query letter with resume to be kept on file. Reports only if interested. Call or write for appointment to show portfolio. Pays by the project. Considers complexity of project, client's budget, and skill and experience of artist when establishing payment. Material not copyrighted.

ALAN G. EISEN CO. INC., 1188 Round Swamp Rd., Old Bethpage NY 11804. (516)752-1008. President: Alan G. Eisen. PR firm. Clients: consumer and individual product manufacturers, service organizations and financial firms.
Needs: Works with 1 illustrator/month average. Local artists only. Works on assignment only. Uses illustrators for jobs dealing with consumer magazines, direct mail, brochures/flyers, trade magazines, annual reports and newspapers.
First Contact & Terms: Send query letter with resume and photographs. Samples not returned. Reports within weeks. Provide business card, brochure/flyer and resume to be kept on file. Pays by the project. Total rights purchased.

HEALY, SCHUTTE & COMSTOCK, 1207 Delaware Ave., Buffalo NY 14209. (716)884-2120. Associate Creative Director: Dennis Domkowski. Ad agency. Clients: food service, industrial, retail department stores, consumer food, financial and health-related accounts; client list provided upon request.
Needs: Works with 5 illustrators/month. Uses freelance artists for consumer and trade magazines, direct mail, P-O-P displays, brochures, catalogs, posters, signage, newspapers and AV presentations.
First Contact & Terms: Contact is usually through representative—illustrator or design group. Payment is by the project.

HUMAN RELATIONS MEDIA, 175 Tompkins Ave., Pleasantville NY 10570. (914)769-7496. Vice President: Peter Cochran. Audiovisual firm. Clients: junior and senior high schools, colleges, hospitals, personnel departments of business organizations.
Needs: Works with 5 freelance artists/year. Prefers local artists. Uses artists for illustrations for filmstrip and slide programs and software packaging. "It is helpful if artists have skills pertaining to science-related topics."
First Contact & Terms: Send query letter with resume and samples to be kept on file. Samples not filed are returned by SASE. Reports back only if interested. Call for appointment to show portfolio, which should include slides or tear sheets. Pays for design by the project, $65-650. Pays for illustration by the project, $65-250. Considers complexity of the project, client's budget, skill and experience of artist and turnaround time when establishing payment. Rights purchased vary according to project.
Tips: "It is important that samples are seen before face-to-face interviews."

KOPF & ISAACSON, 35 Pinelawn Rd., Melville NY 11747. Art Directors: Art Zimmermann or Evelyn Rysdyk. Ad agency. Clients: technical, i.e. telephones, computer firms etc.; some consumer, i.e. clothing manufacturing, travel agencies.
Needs: Works on assignment only. Uses some illustrations and some layout/comp.
First Contact & Terms: Send query letter with resume and slides or tear sheets to be kept on file. No phone queries. Samples not filed are returned by SASE only if requested. Reports back only if interested. Write for appointment to show portfolio. Pays by the hour, $6-30 average; by the project, $150 minimum. Considers complexity of the project, client's budget, skill and experience of artist, and geographic scope for the finished product when establishing payment. Rights purchased vary according to project.

McANDREW ADVERTISING, 2125 St. Raymond Ave., Bronx NY 10462. (212)892-8660. Art/Creative Director: Robert McAndrew. Ad agency. Clients: industrial and technical firms. Assigns 200 jobs and buys 120 illustrations/year.
Needs: Works with 2 illustrators and 4 designers/month. Uses mostly local artists. Uses artists for stationery design, direct mail, brochures/flyers and trade magazines.
First Contact & Terms: Query with brochure showing art style and photocopies, business card and brochure/flyer to be kept on file. Samples not returned. Reports in 1 month. No originals returned to artist at job's completion. Call or write to schedule an appointment to show a portfolio, which should include roughs and final reproduction/product. Pays $20-40/hour and $100 by the project for annual reports, catalogs, trade magazines, letterheads, trademarks, layout and paste-up. Considers complexity of project, client's budget, and skill and experience of artist when establishing payment.

McCUE ADVERTISING & PUBLIC RELATIONS, Press Bldg., 19 Chenango St., Binghamton NY 13901. Contact: Donna McCue. Ad/PR firm. Clients: retailers, nonprofit and industrial.
Needs: Artists with at least 2 professional assignments only. Uses artists for direct mail, television, brochures/flyers, trade magazines, newspapers, mechanicals and logo design.
First Contact & Terms: Send a query letter with resume, brochure, flyer, business card and tear sheets to be kept on file. Reports in 3-4 weeks. No originals returned at job's completion. Negotiates payment.

LLOYD MANSFIELD CO. INC., Suite 900, 237 Main St., Buffalo NY 14203. (716)854-2762. Executive Art Director: Joseph Lennert. Ad/PR firm, marketing communications. Serves clients in a variety of industries.
Needs: Assigns a minimum of 3 jobs and buys 25 illustrations/year. Uses artists for illustrations, mechanicals, layout and retouching.
First Contact & Terms: Local artists primarily. Works on assignment only. Query with resume and arrange interview to show portfolio. Especially looks for "neatness and creativity of presentation." SASE. Reports in 3 weeks. Provide business card, brochure/flyer or resume to be kept on file for possible future assignments. Pays $12-50/hour.

ERIC MOWER & ASSOCIATES, INC., 101 S. Salina St., Syracuse NY 13202. (315)472-4703. Contact: Peter Kapcio or William Baylis. Ad agency/PR firm. Clients: industry, fast food, banks, agricul-

ture, insurance, wines/beverages, jewelry, clothing, sportswear and horse racing.
Needs: Works with 100-150 freelance artists/year. "We are open to any artist who is good, professional, works within the budget and is on time with due dates." Works on assignment only. Uses artists for advertising, brochure and catalog illustration, display fixture design, P-O-P displays, model making and signage.
First Contact & Terms: Send query letter with brochure, resume, business card, photostats, slides, photographs or original work and tear sheets to be kept on file. Samples not kept on file are returned by SASE only if requested by artist. Reports only if interested. Pays by the hour or by the project. Considers complexity of project, skill and experience of artist, how work will be used, turnaround time, rights purchased and client's budget when establishing payment.

RICHARD-LEWIS CORP., 455 Central Park Ave., Scarsdale NY 10583. President: R. Byer. Clients: machinery, tool, publishers, office supplies, chemical, detergent, film and printing supplies.
Needs: Local artists only. Uses artists for illustrations, retouching and some ad layout and mechanicals.
First Contact & Terms: Query with resume or arrange interview to show portfolio. SASE. Reports in 2-3 weeks. Negotiates pay.

RONAN, HOWARD, ASSOCIATES, INC., 11 Buena Vista Ave., Spring Valley NY 10977-3040. (914)356-6668. President: Muriel Brown. Ad/PR firm. Clients: still and motion picture (cine) photography products and services; video production products; lighting products; electronic components.
Needs: Works with 2-3 freelance artists/year. Uses artists for mechanicals, retouching, charts/graphs and AV presentations.
First Contact & Terms: Send query letter. "Samples and/or other material will not be returned. Please do not send unordered material with a demand for return. It is an unwarranted burden on our shipping department." SASE. Reports immediately. Pays $25 minimum for illustrations, layout, lettering, paste-up, retouching and mechanicals for newspapers, magazines, catalogs and P-O-P displays. Pays promised fee for unused assigned illustrations.

HORACE SADOWSKY & ASSOCIATES, 20 Jerusalem Ave., Hicksville, Long Island NY 11801. (516)681-6550. President/Creative Director: Horace Sadowsky. Clients: industrial, medical, electronics, housewares, giftwares, building contractors.
Needs: Local artists only. Works on assignment only. Uses designers for brochures/flyers and trade magazines. Uses artists for layout, illustration, technical art, paste-up and retouching for magazines, direct mail, brochures, annual reports and corporate promotions.
First Contact & Terms: Send query letter with resume and samples. Reports only if interested. Call to schedule an appointment to show a portfolio, which should include roughs, original/final art and photographs. Pays by the hour, $10 minimum. Considers client's budget, and skill and experience of artist when establishing payment. No originals returned to artist at job's completion.
Tips: "Call for appointment in advance. Do *not drop in*. Bring current portfolio to interview."

RIK SHAFER ASSOC. INC., 260 Main St., Northport NY 11768. (516)754-1750. President: Rik Shafer. Full service agency.
Needs: Works with 12 freelance artists/year. Prefers artists in the Northeast region. Works on assignment only. Uses artists and graphic designers for advertising and brochure design and layout, brochure illustration, and posters.
First Contact & Terms: Send query letter, brochure, resume and photostats to be kept on file. Samples not kept on file are returned. Reports back to artist. Pays by the project. Considers complexity of project, skill and experience of artist, and how work will be used when establishing payment.

SPITZ ADVERTISING AGENCY, 530 Oak St., Syracuse NY 13203. Contact: William Spitz, Nick Bibko or Chris Slater. Serves clients in plastic products, hotels, finance and electronics.
Needs: Uses artists for illustration, design, animated cartoons, technical art layout and retouching for catalogs, direct mail, graphics, trademarks, letterheads, newspapers, trade magazines, radio, TV and billboards.
First Contact & Terms: Mail samples. Payment varies with job.

***TECHNICAL EDUCATIONAL CONSULTANTS**, Suite 2010, 76 North Broadway, Hicksville NY 11801. (516)681-1773. Vice President: Arnold Kleinstein, Ph.D. Clients: all industries and schools. Client list provided for SASE.
Needs: Works with 1 freelance artist/year. Artist must have knowledge of artwork on computers. Works on assignment only. Uses artists for design and illustrations.
First Contact & Terms: Send query letter. Samples not filed are returned. Reports back within 7 days.

Call to schedule an appointment to show a portfolio. Considers turnaround time when establishing payment. Buys all rights.
Tips: Artist should "have experience in designing computer screens used in training."

WALLACK & WALLACK ADVERTISING, INC., 33 Great Neck Rd., Great Neck NY 11021. Art Director: John Napolitano. Ad agency. Clients: fashion eyewear, entertainment, computer and industrial.
Needs: Works with 10-15 artists/year. Uses artists for mechanicals, layout and design, illustration, photography and retouching. Mechanical and print production skills are important.
First Contact & Terms: Send query letter with brochure showing art style or resume, business card and photocopies to be kept on file. Samples returned only if requested. Reports only if interested. To show a portfolio mail roughs and final reproduction/product. Pays for design by the hour, $7-16; by the day $100-200. Pays for illustration by the project, $75-1,000. Considers complexity of the project, client's budget, skill and experience of artist, turnaround time, geographic scope for the finished product, and rights purchased when establishing payment. Rights purchased vary according to project.
Tips: "Only present that work at which you are most proficient. If you have made a commitment to the design profession—be professional. Develop your talents—don't demand only the high-priced, ambitious assignments. Put your best efforst into every job—especially your portfolio. Taking risks is back! Appreciating a rich history of design and art is apparent in much work."

WINTERKORN LILLIS INC., Hiram Sibley Bldg., 311 Alexander at East Ave., Rochester NY 14604. (716)454-1010. Creative Director: Wendy Nelson. Ad agency. Clients: consumer packaged goods and industrial firms; national and international level only—no regional accounts.
Needs: Works with 8-10 new illustrators/year; 6-10 new designers/year. Works on assignment only. Uses freelance artists for trade and consumer magazines, direct mail, P-O-P displays, brochures, posters, AV presentations and literature, and coverage for sales promotions and sales meetings.
First Contact & Terms: Query with samples to be kept on file. Prefers slide carousel or laminated tear sheets as samples. Samples returned only if requested. Reports only if interested. Pays by the project, $700-8,000 average. Considers complexity of project, client's budget, skill and experience of artist, turnaround time and rights purchased when establishing payment.
Tips: "Present only top professional work, 18 pieces maximum, in a very organized manner."

ZELMAN STUDIOS LTD., 623 Cortelyou Rd., Brooklyn NY 11218. (718)941-5500. General Manager: Jerry Krone. AV producer. Serves clients in industry, education, government and advertising. Produces slides, videotape and film (Super 8 and 16mm).
Needs: Assigns 30 jobs/year. Works with 3 designers/year. Local artists only (25-mile radius). Works on assignment only. Uses artists for art design and cel preparation.
First Contact & Terms: Send samples (slides preferred). Samples returned with SASE. Provide samples, brochure/flyer and tear sheets to be kept on file for possible future assignments. Reports in 2 weeks. Pays by the project. Payment varies with each client's budget. No originals returned to artist after publication. Buys all rights.

New York City

A.V. MEDIA CRAFTSMAN, INC., Room 600, 110 E. 23rd St., New York NY 10010. (212)228-6644. President: Carolyn Clark. AV firm. Clients: public relations firms, publishers, banks, security firm, ad agencies, educational publishers and internal corporate communications departments. Produces filmstrips, multiscreen slide shows, multimedia kits, overhead transparencies, cassettes, sound-slide sets and videotapes. Assigns approximately 20 jobs/year.
Needs: Works with audiovisual illustrators and designers only and mechanical artists on a project basis. "Artists must have total knowledge of graphic slide production and kodalith pin registration techniques. Others please do not apply." Local, experienced audiovisual artists only.
First Contact & Terms: Provide resume and tear sheets or a photocopy of art to be kept on file. Samples not filed are not returned. Reports only if interested. "You may be called to bid on projects. Jobs on *freelance* basis only. Educational and training budgeting on the lower side, generally."

ADELANTE ADVERTISING INC., 386 Park Ave. S, New York NY 10016. (212)696-0855. Vice President: Ted Amber. Ad agency. Clients: national consumer. Client list available.
Needs: Works with a varying number of freelance artists. Seeks experienced professionals. Sometimes works on assignment only. Uses artists for a variety of jobs.
First Contact & Terms: Send query letter, brochure, resume and samples to be kept on file. Prefers photographs, slides or tear sheets as samples. Samples not filed are not returned. Reports only if

interested. Call for appointment to show portfolio. Pays by the hour, $15 minimum. Considers complexity of the project, client's budget, skill and experience of artist, geographic scope for the finished product and turnaround time when establishing payment. Rights purchased vary according to project.

ADMASTER INC., 95 Madison Ave., New York NY 10016. (212)679-1134. Director of Visual Services: Andrew Corn. Clients: businesses. Produces slide sets, multimedia kits, multiple images, video cassettes and brochures. Assigns 300 jobs/year.
Needs: Works with 5 illustrators and 1 designer/month. Local artists only. Uses artists for slides, motion pictures and TV.
First Contact & Terms: Send query letter with resume. Reports in 1 week. Write to schedule an appointment to show a portfolio, which should include story boards, slides and video. Samples returned by SASE if not kept on file. No originals returned to artist at job's completion. Buys all rights. Pays by the project, $500 minimum. Considers skill and experience of artist when establishing payment.
Tips: Artists should have "good clean corporate samples."

AHREND ASSOCIATES INC., 80 5th Ave., New York NY 10011. (212)620-0015. Vice President/Production: Beth Lippman. Ad agency. Clients: publishers, industrial, direct response and mail order firms, financial institutions and nonprofit organizations.
Needs: Works with a few illustrators and 3-5 designers/month. Works with local illustrators and designers only. Uses designers for consumer magazines, direct mail, catalogs and brochures/flyers. Also uses artists for design, layout, lettering, paste-up and type spec.
First Contact & Terms: Send a letter with business card, resume or tear sheets to be kept on file. Reports in 1 week. No originals returned to artist at job's completion. Write for interview. "In each instance, cost is agreed upon (specifically or within a range) before work is assigned." No payment for unsatisfactory assigned work; "if because of client's change of mind, full payment."
Tips: "Should have advertising, preferably direct response, experience. Must know basic requirements for submission to printers, platemakers and others involved in production of promotional material (except for illustrations or spots which will be used as elements of a mechanical and are not the mechanicals themselves)." Especially looks for an "awareness of the product that is being sold and of the audience the product is aimed at" in samples.

AVRETT, FREE AND GINSBERG, INC., 800 3rd Ave., New York NY 10022. (212)832-3800. Art/Creative Director: Frank C. Ginsberg. Serves clients in food, publishing, drug manufacturing, toiletries and clothing.
Needs: Uses artists for storyboards and concept.
First Contact & Terms: Assigns numerous illustrations/year. Send resume, art or previously published work. SASE. Reports within 2 weeks.

JOHN BRANSBY PRODUCTIONS, LTD./EFFECTIVE COMMUNICATION ARTS, INC. (EGA), 221 W. 57th St., New York NY 10019. Vice President: W. Comcowich. Film, video, videodisc producer. Clients: "Federal government and *Fortune 500*; we concentrate in the fields of science, medicine and technology." Produces filmstrips, videotapes and interactive videodisc programs and print materials. Assigns 40 jobs/year.
Needs: Works with 2-3 illustrators and 1-2 designers/month. Works on assignment only. Uses artists for motion pictures, computer graphic design and professional monographs. Also uses artists for 16mm film animation design and graphics, 35mm slide illustration and graphics, and medical illustrations.
First Contact & Terms: Query with resume and slides, photographs and color prints (no originals). SASE. Reports in 4 weeks. Provide brochure/flyer and resume to be kept on file for future assignments. Negotiates pay by the project.
Tips: "There is greater need for medical artists and animators."

ANITA HELEN BROOKS ASSOCIATES, PUBLIC RELATIONS, 155 E. 55th St., New York NY 10022. (212)755-4498. President: Anita Helen Brooks. PR firm. Clients: fashion, "society," travel, restaurants, politics and diplomats, books. Special events; health and health campaigns.
Needs: Number of freelance jobs assigned/year varies. Works on assignment only. Uses artists for consumer magazines, newspapers and press releases. "We're currently using more abstract designs."
First Contact & Terms: Call for appointment to show portfolio. Reports only if interested. Payment determined by client's needs. Considers client's budget and skill and experience of artist when establishing payment.
Tips: Artists interested in working with us must provide "rate schedule, partial list of clients and media outlets. We look for graphic appeal when reviewing samples."

CANAAN COMMUNICATIONS INC., 310 E. 44th St., New York NY 10017. (212)682-4030. President: Lee Canaan. PR firm. Clients: restaurants, celebrities, corporate accounts, advertising agencies, political, art museums and galleries. Client list provided for SASE.
Needs: Assigns 12 freelance jobs/year. Works on assignment only. Uses artists for consumer and trade magazines, brochures, catalogs, newspapers, filmstrips and stationery.
First Contact & Terms: Send query letter with brochure, resume, business card, samples and tear sheets to be kept on file.

CANON & SHEA ASSOCIATES, INC., 875 Ave. of Americas, New York NY 10001. (212)564-8822. Art Director: Michael Smith. Ad/PR/marketing firm. Clients: business to business and final services.
Needs: Assigns 20-40 jobs and buys 50-60 illustrations/year. Mostly local artists.
First Contact & Terms: Send query letter with brochure showing art style or resume and tearsheets. To show a portfolio, mail original/final art or write to schedule an appointment. Pays by hour: $20-35, animation, annual reports, catalogs, trade and consumer magazines; $25-50, packaging; $50-250, corporate identification/graphics; $8-28, layout, lettering and paste-up.
Tips: "Artists should have industrial or consumer materials as samples and should understand the marketplace."

***CDBIII-KRISTY**, Suite 18D, 400 W. 43rd St., New York NY 10036. (212)244-6187. Artistic Director: Charles David Brooks III. Ad agency and audiovisual firm. Clients: merchants. Client list provided for SASE.
Needs: Works on assignment only. Uses artists for design, illustrations, brochures, newspapers, posters, direct mail packages, press releases and advertisements.
First Contact & Terms: Send query letter with brochure showing art style or resume and tear sheets. Samples not filed are not returned. Reports only if interested. To show a portfolio, mail tear sheets. Considers complexity of project, client's budget, and skill and experience of artist.

THE CREATIVE ESTABLISHMENT, 115 W. 31st St., New York NY 10001. (212)563-3337. Producer: Diana Davis. AV/film/multi-image producer. Serves clients in industry. Produces materials for businesss meetings, product introductions, corporate image and P-O-P.
Needs: Assigns 20 jobs/year. New York metropolitan area artists only. "Artists must have at least 3 years' experience in work applied for." Works with 5 board artists, 1 animator and 2 designers/month. Uses artists for most projects.
First Contact & Terms: Send resume and samples (12 or more slides preferred). Samples not filed are returned with SASE. Reporting time depends on current needs. Call or write to schedule an appointment to show a portfolio, which should include story boards/final slides. Pays for design by the day, $250 maximum; pays for illustration by the project, $50-200 maximum. No originals returned to artist after publication. Negotiates rights purchased.
Tips: "With more use of computer art, freelancers now need a more technical background."

CRYSTAL PICTURES INC., 1560 Broadway, New York NY 10036. (212)757-5130. Contact: S. Tager. Motion picture/TV producer/distributor. General audience.
Needs: Works with 1 illustrator/month. New York City artists only. Uses artists for film posters, press books, motion pictures, catalogs, paste-ups and mechanicals.
First Contact & Terms: Send nonreturnable samples (nonreturnable copies) and describe skills relevant to requirements. No file kept on artists. No originals returned to artist at job's completion.

RAUL DA SILVA & OTHER FILMMAKERS, 137 E. 38th St., New York NY 10016. (212)696-1657. Creative Director: Raul da Silva. TV/film/animation/AV producer and limited publishing firm. Clients: business, industrial, institutional, educational and entertainment.
Needs: Works with 3-4 illustrators and 1 designer/month. "Seeking several artists with experience in slide/multimedia production, layout and materials. Also seeking designers, plus illustrators capable of rendering sci-fi/fantasy art in the *Heavy Metal* style—see the magazine for the years '77-'79." Works on assignment only. Uses artists for filmstrips, motion pictures, record jackets, multimedia kits, storyboards and titles.
First Contact & Terms: Send resume including references with phone numbers and addresses, and electrostatic copies which will *not* be returned. Samples returned by SASE only if requested; samples "always kept on file if they merit space. Do not send any original work without obtaining our request for it." Returns only solicited work. Reports within 2 weeks only if interested. Payment for illustrations and layout "depends completely on end use." Storyboards, $15-50/frame; continuity design, $300 and up/program. Considers complexity of project, client's budget, skill and experience of artist, turnaround time and rights purchased when establishing payment.
Tips: "We are a small, highly professional studio using only committed, *skilled* professionals who

enjoy having their good work appreciated and rewarded. Hobbyists, dabblers usually do not make the grade for us."

DANCER-FITZGERALD-SAMPLE INC., 405 Lexington Ave., New York NY 10174. Director of Art Services: James Hushon. Ad agency. Serves clients in food, household products, beauty products, publishing, hosiery and automobiles.
Needs: Works with 25 illustrators and 3 designers/month. Works on assignment only. Uses artists for billboards, P-O-P displays, filmstrips, consumer and trade magazines, TV, slide sets, brochures/flyers and newspapers; cartoons and humorous and cartoon-style illustrations (4-5 each year). Also uses artists for layout, retouching and lettering.
First Contact & Terms: Send printed pieces, slides or flyers as samples. Samples returned by SASE. No originals returned to artist at job's completion. Pays $200-5,000, depending upon use and degree of difficulty. Considers complexity of project, client's budget and rights purchased when establishing payment.

DARINO FILMS, 222 Park Ave. S, New York NY 10003. (212)228-4024. Creative Director: Ed Darino. Film/animation producer. Clients: educational, some industrial, TV station and corporate.
Needs: Works with 5-8 illustrators, 2-3 animators/month, plus airbrush artists and lettering artists. Also works with freelance designers. Uses artists for motion pictures. Works on assignment only.
First Contact & Terms: "No visits and no calls." Provide business card, brochure/flyer to be kept on file for future assignments. Reports back on future assignment possibilities. Payment to illustrators by illustration or by week; animators, within union salary; background artist, per background only (union scale). 3-6 month internship program.
Tips: Especially looks for "flexible communication of the graphic message in mailed submissions."

DITTMAN INCENTIVE MARKETING, 22 W. 23rd St., New York NY 10010. (212)741-8040. Art Director: W. Whetsel. AV producer/print sales promotion agency. Serves clients in corporations. Produces multimedia motivational materials and single-projector individual selling presentations.
Needs: Assigns 18 jobs/year. Works with 4 designers/year. Works on assignment only. Uses artists for multimedia, motivational materials and single-project individual selling presentations.
First Contact & Terms: Provide resume and slides, original publications to be kept on file for possible future assignments. Reports within weeks. Pays by the project or by the hour, "depending on task." Considers complexity of project, client's budget, turnaround time and sometimes skill and experience of artist and rights purchased when establishing payment. No originals returned to artist following publication. Negotiates rights purchased.
Tips: "We maintain extremely high standards, and only those artists who feel that their work is extraordinary in creation and execution should contact us. We work only with artists who have a high level of imagination and intense pride in the finished product—supported, of course, by samples that prove it."

CHRISTOPHER DIXON, INC., 116 E. 63rd St., New York NY 10021 (212)838-9069. President: Christopher Dixon. Motion picture/television production firm. Clients: entertainment industry.
Needs: Works with 3-4 freelance artists/year. Works on assignment only. Uses artists for storyboarding, promotional materials, design title sequence, computer animation and posters.
First Contact & Terms: Send resume to be kept on file. Reports back only if interested. Call for appointment to show portfolio. Pays by the project, $200-5,000 average. Considers complexity of the project, skill and experience of artist and rights purchased when establishing payment. Buys all rights.
Tips: "Send resume, follow up with a phone call."

DOLPHIN PRODUCTIONS, 140 E. 80th St., New York NY 10021. (212)628-5930. Contact: Allan Stanley. TV producers.
Needs: Uses artists for animation and graphic design.
First Contact & Terms: Submit cassette (video). Provide resume to be kept on file for future assignments. Reports within 3 weeks. Considers complexity of project, client's budget, and skill and experience of artist when establishing payment.

JODY DONOHUE ASSOC., INC., 32 E. 57th St., New York NY 10022. (212)688-8653. Contact: Interview, Review Portfolios Department. PR firm. Clients: fashion and beauty. Media used includes direct mail and P-O-P displays.
Needs: Works with 1-5 illustrators and 1-5 designers/month. Uses artists for P-O-P displays, stationery design, multimedia kits, direct mail, slide sets and brochures/flyers.
First Contact & Terms: Send brochure to be kept on file. Call for personal appointment to show portfolio. No originals returned to artist at job's completion. Negotiates payment based on client's

budget, amount of creativity required from artist, and where work will appear.
Tips: Wants to see recent work that has been used (printed piece, etc.) and strength in an area (i.e., still life, children, etc.).

RICHARD FALK ASSOC., 1472 Broadway, New York NY 10036. (212)221-0043. PR firm. Clients: industry, entertainment and Broadway shows.
Needs: Uses 5 artists/year. Uses artists for consumer magazines, brochures/flyers and newspapers; occasionally buys cartoon-style illustrations.
First Contact & Terms: Send resume. Provide flyer and business card to be kept on file for future assignments. No originals returned to artist at job's completion. Pays for illustration by the project, $50-250.
Tips: "Don't get too complex—make it really simple."

TONI FICALORA PRODUCTIONS, 28 E. 29th St., New York NY 10016. (212)679-7700. Film/TV commercial producer. Serves clients in advertising. Produces TV commercials.
Needs: Assigns 50 jobs/year. Prefers artists who specialize. Works on assignment only. Uses artists for "elaborate sets requiring freelance stylist and prop persons."
First Contact & Terms: Send query letter with resume, no samples. Call to schedule an appointment to show a portfolio, which should include color and photographs. Reports within weeks. Pays by the project. Amount of payment is negotiated with the individual artist and varies with each client's budget. No originals returned to artist after publication. Buys all rights.

FLAX ADVERTISING, 1500 Broadway, New York NY 10036. (212)944-9797. Contact: Linda Ely. Clients: women's fashions, menswear and fabrics. Assigns 100 jobs and buys 100-200 illustrations/year.
Needs: Uses artists for mechanicals, illustrations, technical art, retouching and lettering for newspapers, magazines, fashion illustrations, P-O-P displays, some cartooning and direct mail.
First Contact & Terms: Local artists only. Arrange interview to show portfolio. Reports in 1 week. Pay varies.

ALBERT FRANK-GUENTHER LAW, 71 Broadway, New York NY 10006. (212)248-5200. Senior Art Director: D. Algieri. Ad agency. Clients: financial, general consumer.
Needs: Works with varying number of illustrators and designers/month. Uses artists for trade papers, consumer papers, and magazines.
First Contact & Terms: Contact only through artist's agent, who should send query letter with tear sheets. Call to schedule an appointment to show portfolio, which should include original/final art, final reproduction/product, color, tear sheets, photostats, photographs and b&w. Pays for design by the hour, $35 minimum; by the day, $250 minimum. Pays for illustration by the project, $150 minimum.
Tips: "Show excellent work only."

GRAPHIC MEDIA, INC., 12 W. 27th St., New York NY 10001. (212)696-0880. Creative Director: Scott Nicol. Audiovisual/visual communications firm. Clients: financial, advertising, public relations.
Needs: Works with 2-3 freelance artists/month. Works on assignment only. Uses artists to design graphic slides and print collateral and to prepare camera-ready art. Especially important are strong graphic design and color sense and meticulous neatness in art preparation.
First Contact & Terms: Send query letter with resume to be kept on file. Prefers to review slides. Reports back only if interested. Write for appointment to show portfolio. Pays by the hour, $14-25 average. Considers client's budget and artist's skill and experience when establishing payment. Rights purchased vary according to project.

GREY ADVERTISING INC., 777 3rd Ave., New York NY 10017. Print Business Manager: Gerda Henge. Needs ad illustrations.
Needs: Works on assignment only.
First Contact & Terms: Contact only through artist's agent. Call for an appointment to show a portfolio, which should include/original final art. Pays by the project, $500 minimum. Considers client's budget and rights purchased when establishing payment.
Tips: "Most of our advertising is done with photography. We use illustrations on a very limited basis."

CHARLES HANS FILM PRODUCTIONS INC., 25 W. 38th St., New York NY 10018. (212)382-1280. Art Director: Evelyn Simon. AV producer. Clients: industrial and corporate. Produces filmstrips, motion pictures, multimedia kits, overhead transparencies, slide sets, sound-slide sets, slide-a-motion and videotapes.
Needs: Works with 10-15 illustrators/year. Works on assignment only. Uses artists for "all phases of artwork," including chart work, paste-ups, mechanicals and some illustration and design as in animation or spot illustrations. The majority of the work is for slides.

First Contact & Terms: Send query letter with slides to be kept on file. SASE. Reports within 2 weeks. Call to schedule an appointment to show a portfolio, which should include original/final art. Pays for design by the hour, $15-20; payment for illustration varies.

HERMAN & ASSOCIATES INC., 488 Madison Ave., New York NY 10022. President: Paula Herman. Serves clients in insurance, retailing (cameras, carpet), travel and tourism.
Needs: Prefers local artists who have worked on at least 2-3 professional assignments previously. Works on assignment only. Uses artists for mechanicals, illustrations and retouching for newspapers, magazines and direct mail.
First Contact & Terms: Send brochure showing art style and whatever best represents artist's work as samples. Samples returned by SASE. Reporting time "depends on clients." Reports back whether to expect possible future assignments. Write to schedule an appointment to show a portfolio. Pays by the project.
Tips: "There is a trend toward more illustration. Artists interested in working with us should be persistent—keep following up."

JOCOM INTERNATIONAL, (formerly Teleconcepts International), Suite 701, 250 W. 57th St., New York NY 10019. (212)586-5544. TV producer. Serves clients in industry, education and government. Produces films, videotape, teleconferences and multi-city closed-circuit satellite telecasts.
Needs: Assigns 6-12 jobs/year. Works with 2 illustrators and 2 designers/month. Uses artists for film and videotape.
First Contact & Terms: Send query letter. Works on assignment only. Provide samples, business card and tear sheets to be kept on file for possible future assignments. Reports in 2 weeks. Method and amount of payment are negotiated with the individual artist. No originals returned to artist following publication. Negotiates rights purchased.

JIM JOHNSTON ADVERTISING INC., 551 5th Ave., New York NY 10176. (212)490-2121. Art/Creative Director: Doug Johnston. Serves clients in publishing, corporate and business-to-business.
Needs: Works with 3-4 illustrators/month. Uses artists for consumer magazines, trade magazines and newspapers.
First Contact & Terms: Query with previously published work or samples, or arrange interview. SASE. Reports in 2 weeks. Provide tear sheets to be kept on file for possible future assignments. Payment by job: $250-6,500, annual reports; $250-2,000, billboards; $125-2,500, consumer magazines; $150-5,000, packaging; $250-1,000, P-O-P displays; $150-1,500, posters; $125-600, trade magazines; $100-1,000, letterheads; $200-1,500, trademarks; $300-2,500, newspapers. Payment by hour: $20 minimum, catalogs; $5-20, paste-up. Pays 25% of promised fee for unused assigned illustrations.

JORDAN, CASE & McGRATH, 445 Park Ave., New York NY 10022. (212)906-3600. Art Director: Robin Bennett.Clients: toiletries and drugs manufacturers, food companies, food product firms, liquor and wine, hosiery, insurance and bank. Assigns 50 jobs/year.
Needs: Works with 3 illustrators/month. Uses artists for billboards, consumer magazines and TV storyboards.
First Contact & Terms: Arrange interview. Provide example of work along with name, phone number, etc. to be kept on file for future assignments. Originals returned only upon request.

CHRISTOPHER LARDAS ADVERTISING, Box 1440, Radio City Station, New York NY 10101. (212)688-5199. President: Christopher Lardas. Ad agency. Clients: paper products, safety equipment, chocolate-confectionery, real estate, writing instruments/art materials.
Needs: Works with 6 freelance artists/year. Local artists only; must have heavy experience. Works on assignment only. Uses artists for illustration, layout, mechanicals.
First Contact & Terms: Send query letter with brochure showing art style or photocopies to be kept on file. Samples not filed are returned only if requested. Reports back only if interested. Write for appointment to show portfolio, which should include roughs, original/final art, color, b&w or tear sheets. Pays by the hour, $20-30. Considers client's budget when establishing payment. Buys all rights.
Tips: Artists generally don't follow-up via mail! After artists make initial phone contact, we request a mail follow-up: e.g. photocopies of samples and business card for future reference. Few comply."

WILLIAM V. LEVINE ASSOCIATES, 31 E. 28th St., New York NY 10016. (212)683-7177. Vice President: Mark Netski. AV producer. Serves clients in industry and consumer products. Produces sales meeting modules and slides for speaker support.
Needs: Assigns 20 jobs/year. Works with 2-3 artists/month. Works on assignment only. Uses artists primarily for illustration, cartoons, etc.
First Contact & Terms: Send resume. Reports in 2 weeks. Pays by the project. No originals returned to artist after publication. Negotiates rights purchased.

MALLORY FACTOR INC., 1500 Broadway, New York NY 10036. PR firm. Clients: *Fortune* 500 companies, hotels. Client list provided for SASE.
Needs: Assigns 25 freelance jobs/year. Works with 4 freelance illustrators and 2 freelance designers/month. Artists must be local. Works on assignment only. Uses artists for brochures, stationery, posters and advertising.
First Contact & Terms: Call or write for appointment to show portfolio. Samples not kept on file are not returned. Reports only if interested. Pays for design by the hour, $15; by the project, $220. Pays for illustration by the project, $150. Consider client's budget and turnaround time when establishing payment. Buys all rights.
Tips: "Have sample of a project that was done for business and is completed."

***MANHATTAN VIDEO PRODUCTIONS, INC.**, 12 West 27th St., New York NY 10001. Video production firm serving banks, Fortune 500 companies.
Needs: Works with 3 freelance artists/year. Works on assignment only. Uses artists for brochures, mechanicals, logos and ads.
First Contact & Terms: Send query letter with brochure showing art style. Samples not filed are returned by SASE. Reports only if interested. To show a portfolio, mail appropriate materials. Pays for design by the hour, $10 minimum. Pays for illustration by the hour, $10 minimum. Considers client's budget, skill and experience of artist and turnaround time when establishing payment. Rights vary according to project.
Tips: "No phone calls."

MARTIN/ARNOLD COLOR SYSTEMS, 150 5th Ave., New York NY 10011. (212)675-7270. President: Martin Block. Vice President Marketing: A.D. Gewirtz. AV producer. Clients: industry, education, government and advertising. Produces slides, filmstrips and Vu Graphs, large blow-ups in color and b&w.
Needs: Assigns 20 jobs/year. Works with 2 illustrators and 2 designers/month. Works on assignment only.
First Contact & Terms: Send query letter with resume to be kept on file. Call or write to schedule an appointment to show a portfolio, which should include original/final art and photographs. Pays for design by the hour, $15 minimum; pays for illustration by the hour, $25 minimum. Original artwork returned to artist after publication. Negotiates rights purchased.

PETER MARTIN ASSOCIATES, INC., (formerly PM Group, Ltd.), 770 Lexington Ave., New York NY 10021. Account Group Director/Senior Vice President: Jill Shaw. PR firm/AV/ad agency. Clients: travel, wine and spirits, consumer and food.
Needs: Works on assignment only. Uses artists for posters, direct mail packages, brochures, signage, P-O-P displays and invitations.
First Contact & Terms: Send query letter with brochure, resume, business card, samples and tear sheets to be kept on file except for "those that do not interest us." Prefers photostats as samples. Samples not kept on file are returned by SASE if requested. Reports within 2 weeks. Write for appointment to show portfolio. Payment depends upon job, but conforms to artists' usual scales." Considers complexity of project, client's budget and turnaround time when establishing payment. Buys all rights.
Tips: "We seek bold, imaginative work. Show us only your best and not a lot of that either."

MEDICAL MULTIMEDIA CORP., 211 E. 43rd St., New York NY 10017. (212)986-0180. AV/motion picture/TV producer. Clients: pharmaceutical manufacturers and manufacturers of diagnostic equipment (e.g. x-ray, ultrasound, CAT scanning, nuclear imaging). Audiences: health care industry—sellers and/or users. Produces educational programs in health sciences. Buys 150-200 designs/year.
Needs: Works with 1-2 illustrators/month and infrequently with designers. New York artists only. Uses artists for album covers, books, catalogs, filmstrips and motion pictures. Also uses artists for layout, multimedia kits, paste-up, technical charts and medical illustrations.
First Contact & Terms: Send brochure/flyer, resume and tear sheets to be kept on file for future assignments. No originals returned to artist at job's completion. Call for interview to show a portfolio. Buys all rights. Pays $8-15/hour, mechanicals; $25-40/hour, design.

MUIR CORNELIUS MOORE, INC., 750 Third Ave., New York NY 10017. Creative Resources Administrator: Virginia Martin. Specializes in business to business advertising, sales promotion, corporate identity, displays, direct mail and exhibits. Clients: financial, high technology, industrial and medical accounts.
Needs: Works with 15-25 freelance artists/year. Works on assignment only. Uses artists for design, illustration, mechanicals and lettering; brochures, catalogs, books, P-O-P displays, posters, direct mail packages, charts/graphs, AV materials, logos, exhibits and advertisements.

First Contact & Terms: Send query letter with tear sheets and photographs to be kept on file. Prefers samples that do not have to be returned, but will return unfiled material by SASE. Reports only if interested. To show a portfolio, mail final reproduction/product, tear sheets, photographs and b&w or call to schedule an appointment. Pays by the project. Considers complexity of project, client's budget, skill and experience of artist, how the work will be used, turnaround time and rights purchased when establishing payment.

MULLER, JORDAN, WEISS, INC., 666 5th Ave., New York NY 10103. (212)399-2700. Contact: Art Director. Ad agency. Clients: fashion, agricultural, plastics, food firms, financial, corporate—"wide variety of accounts."
Needs: Works with 25 illustrators/year. Uses freelance artists for consumer and trade magazines, direct mail, P-O-P displays, brochures, posters, newspapers and AV presentations.
First Contact & Terms: Phone for appointment. Works on assignment basis only. Payment varies according to job.

NEWMARK'S ADVERTISING AGENCY INC., 253 W. 26th St., New York NY 10001. Art/Creative Director: Al Wasserman. Art/ad agency. Clients: manufacturing, industrial, banking, leisure activities, consumer, real estate, and construction firms.
Needs: Works with 1 designer/every 2 months. Uses artists for billboards, P-O-P displays, consumer magazines, slide sets, brochures/flyers and trade magazines. Also uses artists for figure illustration, cartoons, technical art, paste-up and retouching.
First Contact & Terms: Provide stat samples to be kept on file for future assignments. No originals returned to artist at job's completion. Pays $8-15/hour, paste-up and $75-3,000 or more/job.

NOSTRADAMUS ADVERTISING, Suite 1128-A, 250 W. 57th St., New York NY 10107. Creative Director: B.N. Sher. Specializes in annual reports, corporate identity, publications, signage, flyers, posters, advertising, logos. Clients: ad agencies, book publishers, nonprofit organizations and politicians.
Needs: Works with 5 freelance artists/year. Uses artists for advertising design, illustration and layout; brochure design, mechanicals, posters, direct mail packages, charts/graphs, logos, catalogs, books and magazines.
First Contact & Terms: Send query letter with brochure, resume, business card, samples and tear sheets to be kept on file. Do *not* send slides as samples; will accept "anything else that doesn't have to be returned." Samples not kept on file are not returned. Reports only if interested. Call for appointment to show portfolio. Pays for design, mechanicals, and illustration by the hour, $15-25 average. Considers skill and experience of artist when establishing payment.

OVATION FILMS INC., 15 W. 26th St., New York NY 10010. (212)686-4540. Contact: Art Petricone.
Needs: Works on assignment only. Uses artists for exhibit/set design and animation.
First Contact & Terms: Arrange interview. Prefers "original art where possible" as samples. Samples returned by SASE. Provide samples and tear sheets to be kept on file for possible future assignments.

PERPETUAL MOTION PICTURES, INC., 17 W. 45th St., New York NY 10036. (212)953-9110. Producer: Hal Hoffer. Animation/TV/film producer. Clients: industrial, corporate, ad agencies and TV networks.
Needs: Local artists only. Uses artists for comps and animatics, and animation design. "Use very little freelance work."
First Contact & Terms: Query with resume and samples. SASE. Reports in 2 weeks. Pays $30-100/panel or going rate by day. Pays $150 minimum.

PHOENIX FILMS INC., 468 Park Ave. S., New York NY 10016. (212)684-5910. President: Heinz Gelles. Vice President: Barbara Bryant. Clients: libraries, museums, religious institutions, U.S. government, schools, universities, film societies and businesses. Produces and distributes motion pictures and educational films. Assigns 20-30 jobs/year.
Needs: Local artists only. Uses artists for motion picture catalog sheets, direct mail brochures, posters and study guides.
First Contact & Terms: Query with samples (tear sheets and photocopies). SASE. Reports in 3 weeks. Buys all rights. Originals returned to artist at job's request. Pays on production. Free catalog.

RICHARD H. ROFFMAN ASSOCIATES, Suite 6A, 697 West End Ave., New York NY 10025. (212)749-3647. Vice President: John Bowman. PR firm. Clients: restaurants, art galleries, boutiques, hotels and cabarets, nonprofit organizations, publishers and all professional and business fields.
Needs: Assigns 24 freelance jobs/year. Works with 2 freelance illustrators and 2 freelance designers/month. Uses artists for consumer and trade magazines, brochures, newspapers, stationery, posters and press releases.

First Contact & Terms: Send query letter and resume to be kept on file; call or write for appointment to show portfolio. Prefers photographs and photostats as samples. Reports only if interested. Pays by the hour, $10-25 average; by the project, $75-250 average; by the day, $150-250 average. Considers complexity of project, client's budget, and skill and experience of artist when establishing payment. Buys first rights or one-time rights. Returns material only if SASE enclosed.
Tips: "Realize that affirmative answers cannot always be immediate—do have patience."

PETER ROTHHOLZ ASSOCIATES INC., 380 Lexington Ave., New York NY 10017. (212)687-6565. President: Peter Rothholz. PR firm. Clients: government (tourism and industrial development), publishing, pharmaceuticals (health and beauty products), business services.
Needs: Works with 2 illustrators, 2 designers/month. Works on assignment only.
First Contact & Terms: Call for appointment to show portfolio which should include resume or brochure/flyer to be kept on file. Samples returned by SASE. Reports in 2 weeks. Assignments made based on freelancer's experience, cost, style and whether he/she is local. No originals returned to artist at job's completion. Negotiates payment based on client's budget.

JASPER SAMUEL ADVERTISING, 406 W. 31st St., New York NY 10001. (212)239-9544. Art Director: Joseph Samuel. Ad agency. Clients: health centers, travel agency, hair salons, etc.
Needs: Works with 5-10 freelance artists/year. Works on assignment only. Uses artists for advertising, brochure and catalog design, illustration and layout; product design and illustration on product.
First Contact & Terms: Send query letter with brochure, resume, business card, photographs and tear sheets to be kept on file. Samples not filed are returned. Reports within 1 month. Call or write for appointment to show portfolio. Pays by the project. Considers complexity of the project and skill and experience of the artist when establishing payment.

PHOEBE T. SNOW PRODUCTIONS, INC., 240 Madison Ave., New York NY 10016. (212)679-8756. Vice President: Lisbeth Bagnold. AV production company. Serves clients in industry. Produces slides, film and video materials.
Needs: Assigns 50 jobs/year. Works on assignment only. Uses artists, designers and illustrators for slides, film and video materials.
First Contact & Terms: Send resume to the attention of Barbara Bagnold, Production Coordinator; arrange interview by phone. Reports within 1 week. Pays by the project or by the hour. No originals returned following publication. Buys all rights.

THE SOFTNESS GROUP INC., 3 E. 54th St., New York NY 10022. Executive Vice President: Carol Blades. PR firm. Clients: corporations and manufacturers.
Needs: Works with 3 illustrators, 1 designer/month. Uses artists to work with filmstrips, consumer magazines, stationery design, multimedia kits, slide sets, brochures/flyers, trade magazines and newspapers.
First Contact & Terms: Query with resume and samples. SASE. Reports in 2 weeks. Provide brochure or flyer to be kept on file for future assignments. No originals returned to artist at job's completion. Negotiates pay.

***SPACE PRODUCTIONS**, 451 West End Ave., New York NY 10024. (212)986-0857. Contact: Producer. "We work in mass communications, using all types of AV materials, film, animation and TV, but the emphasis is on TV." Serves clients in advertising, industry, government and cultural and educational institutions. Produces commercials, information and entertainment programs, sales/marketing, point of purchase and other types of properties.
Needs: Assigns 20-25 jobs/year. Uses a "dozen or more" illustrators, animators and designers/year. "No geographical restrictions, but artist-applicants should note that we are located in New York City." Uses artists for art direction, graphics, illustration, design/print and TV.
First Contact & Terms: Send resume and samples (copies, any type; subjects that suggest the individual style of an artist's work). Samples not filed are returned by SASE. Provide resume, samples, brochure/flyer, business card or tear sheets—"a small representative sampling"—to be kept on file for possible future assignments. Reports in 2 months. Pays $10-50/hour. Method and amount of payment are negotiated with the individual artist or agent. Payment depends on assignment and varies with each client's budget. Original artwork sometimes returned to artist following publication. Rights purchased vary, "depending on assignment and client."

SPINDLER PRODUCTIONS, 1501 Broadway at 44th St., New York NY 10036. (212)730-1255. Contact: Art Director. Audiovisual firm.
Needs: Works with 30-40 freelance artists/year. Uses artists for everything from board work to illustrations. "Artists should be able to interpret difficult-to-understand concepts and translate them into clear, concise graphics."

First Contact & Terms: Send samples to be kept on file. Prefers slides as samples. Samples not filed are returned by SASE only if requested. Reports only if interested. Write for appointment to show portfolio. Pays by the hour, $15 minimum. Considers skill and experience of artist when establishing payment. Buys all rights.
Tips: "Unless strictly freelance, all work is by client-dictated project. No library, style catalog, or preconceived approach is considered."

***SSC&B, INC.**, 1 Dag Hammarskjold Plaza, New York NY 10017. (212)605-8000. Senior Art Buyer: Patti Harris. Ad agency. Clients: home products, cosmetics, and food.
Needs: Works with 150 freelance artists/year. Works on assignment only. Uses photographers and illustrators for magazines, newspapers, and billboard advertisements. Artist should have "good design sense, color quality and reproduction knowledge."
First Contact & Terms: Send letter with tear sheets. Samples filed are not returned. Does not report back. Call to schedule an appointment to show a portfolio, which should include tear sheets, photographs and b&w. Negotiates payment. Considers complexity of project, client's budget, how work will be used, turnaround time and rights purchased when establishing payment. Rights purchased vary according to project.
Tips: Artist should contact art buyers "only if work is applicable to agency's accounts."

LEE EDWARD STERN ASSOCIATES, 1 Park Ave., New York NY 10016. (212)689-2376. President: Lee Stern. Communications planning/editorial services. Clients: businesses of all kinds. Client list provided for SASE.
Needs: Assigns 6-10 freelance jobs/year. Works on assignment only. Uses artists for direct mail packages, brochures, annual reports, video-cassette bridges, titles.
First Contact & Terms: Send query letter with resume and samples. Material usually kept on file. Prefers expendable printed material as samples. Samples not kept on file are returned only if requested. Reports only if interested. Write for appointment to show portfolio. Pays by the hour, $20-25 average. Considers complexity of project, client's budget, skill and experience of artist when establishing payment. Rights purchased varies.
Tips: "Few assignments here, but fun and creativity are encouraged."

SULLIVAN & BRUGNATELLI ADV., INC., 740 Broadway, New York NY 10003. (212)505-1110. Executive Art Director: John Benetos. Ad agency. Serves clients in packaged goods; consumer foods and drinks, ie., fruit juices; banking and over-the-counter drugs.
Needs: Works with 4 illustrators/year, mostly line artwork. Works on assignment only. Uses artists for consumer and trade magazines and newspapers.
First Contact & Terms: Send query letter with brochure showing art style. Prefers 8x10" chromes, original artwork if possible, tear sheets and photos as samples. Samples returned. Reports within 1 week. To show a portfolio, mail final reproduction/product and color. Pays for design by the project, $500-1,500. Pays for illustration by the project, $300-2,000.
Tips: There is a trend toward "more competition, but moving away from conventional executions can create more opportunities. I prefer to get a card in the mail, as opposed to a phone call to arrange appointments. After I've seen a sample I'll welcome a call."

TALCO PRODUCTIONS, 279 E. 44th St., New York NY 10017. (212)697-4015. President: Alan Lawrence. TV/film producer. Clients: nonprofit organizations, industry, associations and public relations firms. Produces motion pictures, videotapes and some filmstrips and sound-slide sets.
Needs: Assigns 4-10 jobs/year. Works with an average of 1 illustrator/month for filmstrips, motion pictures, animation and charts/graphs. Prefers local artists with professional experience.
First Contact & Terms: Send query letter with resume. SASE. Reports only if interested. Portfolio should include roughs, final reproduction/product, color, photostats and photographs. Pay varies according to assignment; on production. On some jobs originals returned to artist after completion. Buys all rights. Considers complexity of project, client's budget and rights purchased when establishing payment.
Tips: "Do not send anything but a resume!"

THE TARRAGANO COMPANY, 230 Park Ave., New York NY 10169. (212)972-1250. President: Morris Tarragano. Ad agency and PR firm. Clients: manufacturers of products and services of all types. Media used include consumer and trade magazine, direct mail and newspapers.
First Contact & Terms: Write for an appointment to show portfolio and/or send resume. Selection based on review of portfolio and references. Negotiates payment based on amount of creativity required from artist and previous experience/reputation.

TELEMATED MOTION PICTURES, Box 176, New York NY 10012. (212)475-8050. Producer/Director: Saul Taffet. AV/TV/film producer. Clients: industry, ad agencies, film producers and business.

Produces filmstrips, motion pictures, slide sets and sound-slide sets.
Needs: Local artists only.
First Contact & Terms: Call to arrange interview. Do not submit art. Buys all rights. Pays on production. Pays $5-10 minimum/hour for animation, charts/graphs, storyboards, lettering, illustrations, retouching and technical art.

TOGG FILMS, INC., 630 9th Ave., New York NY 10036. (212)974-9507. Producer/Director: Grania Gurievitch. AV/film producer. Serves clients in industry, education and government. Produces educational documentaries.
Needs: Experienced New York City area artists only. Works on assignment only. Uses artists for opticals and credits design.
First Contact & Terms: Send query letter. Reports only if interested. Pays by the project. Amount of payment is negotiated with the individual artist. Considers complexity of project, client's budget, skill and experience of artist, turnaround time and rights purchased when establishing payment. Original artwork not returned after publication. Buys all rights, but will negotiate.
Tips: "The chances are *very* slim that we could hire an artist!"

VAN VECHTEN & ASSOCIATES PUBLIC RELATIONS, 427 E. 74th St., New York NY 10021. (212)570-6510. President: Jay Van Vechten. PR firm. Clients: medical, tourism, industry. Client list provided for SASE.
Needs: Assigns 20+ freelance jobs/year. Works with 2 freelance illustrators and 2 freelance designers/month. Works on assignment only. Uses artists for consumer and trade magazines, brochures, newspapers, stationery, signage, AV presentations and press releases.
First Contact & Terms: Send query letter with brochure, resume, business card, photographs or photostats. Samples not kept on file are returned by SASE. Reports only if interested. Write for appointment to show portfolio. Pays by the hour, $10-15 average. Considers client's budget when establishing payment. Buys all rights.

MORTON DENNIS WAX & ASSOCIATES INC., Suite 1260, 1560 Broody, New York NY 10036. (212)247-2159. President: Morton Wax. Public relations firm. Clients: entertainment, communication arts and corporate.
Needs: Artists must have references and minimum 3 years of experience. Works on assignment only. Uses artists for trade magazine ads, brochures and other relevant artwork.
First Contact & Terms: Send query letter with resume, photostats or tear sheets to be kept on file. Samples not filed are returned by SASE. Reports only if interested. Write for appointment to show portfolio. "We select and use freelancers on a per project basis, based on specific requirements of clients. Each project is unique." Considers complexity of project, client's budget, turnaround time and rights purchased when establishing payment. Rights vary according to project.

North Carolina

CAROLINA BIOLOGICAL SUPPLY, 2700 York Rd., Burlington NC 27215. (919)584-0381. Art Director: Dr. Kenneth Perkins. AV producer. Serves clients in education. Produces filmstrips, charts and booklets, educational games.
Needs: Assigns 20 jobs/year. Works with 2 illustrators/month. Prefers artists located in the southeast who do good line work and use watercolor, acrylic or airbrush. Works on assignment only. Uses artists for illustration work, both biological and medical. "We buy some cartoons for our pamphlets, filmstrips and advertising and some cartoon-style illustrations."
First Contact & Terms: Send query letter with resume and samples (prefers photostats or slides) to be kept on file. Samples returned by SASE not filed. Reports within 1 month. Call or write to schedule an appointment to show a portfolio, which should include roughs, original/final art, final reproduction/product and tear sheets. Amount of payment is negotiated with the individual artist; by the hour, $12 minimum. Considers complexity of project, skill and experience of artist and rights purchased when establishing payment. No originals returned to artist following publication. Buys all rights.

***CLASSROOM WORLD PRODUCTIONS**, 22 Glenwood Ave., Box 28166, Raleigh NC 27603. Contact: E.E. Carter. AV producer. Clients: educational, industrial, governmental and religious. Produces filmstrips, multimedia kits and sound-slide sets.
Needs: Works with 1 designer/month. Uses artists for filmstrip animation, slide illustrations and catalog design.
First Contact & Terms: Query with resume and samples. Reports in 1-4 weeks. Provide brochures,

flyers, resume and samples to be kept on file for future assignments. Negotiates pay; sometimes pays royalties.

GARNER & ASSOCIATES, INC., Suite 350, 3721 Latrobe Dr., Charlotte NC 28211. (704)365-3455. Art Directors: Arkon Stewart, Cathy Morris. Ad agency. Clients: "wide range" of accounts; client list provided upon request.
Needs: Works with 2 illustrators/month. Works on assignment only. Uses freelance artists for billboards, consumer and trade magazines, direct mail, P-O-P displays, brochures, catalogs, posters, signage, newspapers and AV presentations.
First Contact & Terms: Send printed samples or phone for appointment. Payment is by the project; negotiates according to client's budget.

***HEGE, MIDDLETON & NEAL, INC.**, Box 9437, Greensboro NC 27408. President: J.A. Middleton, Jr. Ad agency.
Needs: Assigns 200 freelance jobs/year. Works with 5 freelance illustrators and 5 freelance designers/month. Works on assignment only. Uses artists for consumer and trade magazines, billboards, direct mail packages, brochures, catalogs, newspapers, stationery, signage, P-O-P displays and posters.
First Contact & Terms: Send query letter with brochure, resume, business card, photographs and tear sheets to be kept on file. Samples returned by SASE if requested. Reports only if interested. Write for appointment to show portfolio. Pays by the project, $20-6,000 average. Considers complexity of project, client's budget, skill and experience of artist, geographic scope of finished project, turnaround time and rights purchased when establishing payment. Buys all rights.

LEWIS ADVERTISING, INC., 2309 Sunset Ave., Rocky Mount NC 27801. (919)443-5131. Senior Art Director: Scott Brandt. Ad agency. Clients: fast food, communications, convenience stores, financials. Client list provided upon request with SASE.
Needs: Works with 20-25 freelance artists/year. Works on assignment only. Uses artists for illustration and part-time paste-up. Especially looks for "consistently excellent results, on time and on budget."
First Contact & Terms: Send query letter with resume, business card and samples to be kept on file. Call for appointment to show portfolio. Artists should show examples of previous work, price range requirements and previous employers." Samples not filed returned by SASE only if requested. Reports only if interested. Pays by project. Considers complexity of the project, client's budget, turnaround time and ability of artist when establishing payment. Buys all rights.

MORPHIS & FRIENDS, INC., Drawer 5096, 230 Oakwood Dr., Winston-Salem NC 27103. (919)723-2901. Art Director: Joe Nemoseck. Ad agency. Clients: banks, restaurants, clothing, cable, industry and furniture.
Needs: Assigns 20-30 freelance jobs/year. Works on assignment only. Works with approximately 2 freelance illustrators/month. Uses artists for consumer and trade magazines, billboards, direct mail packages, brochures and newspapers.
First Contact & Terms: Send query letter with photocopies to be kept on file. Samples not filed are returned only if requested. Reports only if interested. Call to schedule an appointment to show a portfolio, which should include roughs and final reproduction/product. Pays by the hour, $20 minimum. "Negotiate on job basis." Considers complexity of project, client's budget, skill and experience of artist, geographic scope of finished project, turnaround time and rights purchased when establishing payment. Buys all rights.
Tips: "Send a letter of introduction with a few samples to be followed up by phone call."

SSF ADVERTISING, Division of Inform Inc., Drawer 1708, Hickory NC 28603. (704)328-5618 or 322-7766. Art Director: Jeff Decker. Ad agency. Clients: association management, public relations, industrial relations and advertising.
Needs: Assigns 50 freelance jobs/year. Works with 1 freelance illustrator and 1-3 freelance designers/month. Prefers artists in the Southeast. Uses artists for consumer and trade magazines, billboards, direct mail packages, brochures, catalogs, newspapers, P-O-P displays and posters.
First Contact & Terms: Send query letter with brochure to be kept on file. Accepts any type of samples. Samples not kept on file are returned. Reports only if interested. Call or write for appointment to show portfolio. Pays by the hour or by the project. Considers complexity of project, client's budget, and skill and experience of artist when establishing payment. Buys all rights.

THOMPSON AGENCY, Suite 200, 1 Tryon Centre, 112 S. Tryon St., Charlotte NC 28284. (704)333-8821. Managing Art Director: Gordon Smith. Ad agency. Clients: banks, fast food, soft drink, TV station, resort, utility, automotive services, city convention and visitors bureau.
Needs: Assigns approximately 200 freelance jobs/year. Works with 5 freelance illustrators/month.

Works on assignment only. Uses artists for consumer and trade magazines, billboards, direct mail packages, brochures, newspapers, signage, P-O-P displays and posters.
First Contact & Terms: Send query letter with brochure showing art style or photocopies to be kept on file. Samples returned by SASE if requested. To show portfolio, mail appropriate materials or write to schedule an appointment; portfolio should include final reproduction/product. Reports only if interested. Pays for design by the project, $500-7,500; pays for illustration by the project, $350-3,000. Considers complexity of project, client's budget, skill and experience of artist, turnaround time and rights purchased when establishing payment. Buys all rights.
Tips: "In general, we see a bolder use of ideas and techniques. We try to screen all work before appointment. Work must be professional and very creative.

Ohio

***BUTLER LEARNING SYSTEMS**, 1325 W. Dorothy Ln., Dayton OH 45409. (513)298-7462. President: Don Butler. Produces training programs.
Needs: Works with 2 freelance artists/year. Local artists only. Uses artists for design, illustrations, catalog and books.
First Contact & Terms: Contact by phone. Samples not filed are returned only if requested. Reports back within 7 days. Call to schedule an appointment to show portfolio, which should include thumbnails, roughs and original/final art. Payment varies. Considers complexity of project and client's budget when establishing payment. Buys all rights.

FAHLGREN & SWINK, INC., Suite 901, 1 Seagate, Toledo OH 43604. (419)241-5201. Creative Director: Steve Drongowski. Ad agency. Serves clients in healthcare and finance.
Needs: Works with 5-6 freelance illustrators/month. Uses freelancers for consumer and trade magazines, A/V direct mail, brochures/flyers, newspapers and P-O-P displays.
First Contact & Terms: Call for appointment to show portfolio or make contact through artist's rep. Selection is usually based on reviewing portfolios through reps but will see individual freelancers. Negotiates payment based on client's budget, amount of creativity required from artist and where work will appear.
Tips: Pieces that are produced are best in portfolio. "Printed pieces have a lot more credibility."

FARRAGHER MARKETING SERVICES, 7 Court St., Canfield OH 44406. (216)533-3347. Creative Director: Linda Nicholas. Marketing service firm. Serves clients in industry and technical science. Assigns 20w jobs/year.
Needs: Works on assignment only. Uses artists for P-O-P displays, stationery design, direct mail, brochures/flyers and trade magazines. Also uses artists for annual reports, catalogs, brochures, corporate identity, newsletters and promotional materials.
First Contact & Terms: Query with resume and photographs and originals. Samples returned by SASE. Reports as soon as possible. Provide resume, brochure/flyer and business card to be kept on file. Originals returned to artist at job's completion if requested. Negotiates pay.
Tips: "Be practical and businesslike."

THE FILM HOUSE INC., 6058 Montgomery Rd., Cincinnati OH 45213. (513)631-0035. President: Ken Williamson. TV/film producer. Clients: industrial and corporate. Produces filmstrips, motion pictures, sound-slide sets and videotapes.
Needs: Assigns 30 jobs/year. Uses artists for filmstrip animation and ad illustrations. Works on assignment only.
First Contact & Terms: Send a query letter with resume and business card to be kept on file. Samples returned by SASE. Reports in 1 week. Negotiates pay; pays by the project.
Tips: "Maintain contact every 45 days."

GERBIG, SNELL/WEISHEIMER & ASSOC., Suite 600, 425 Metro Pl. N., Dublin OH 43017. (614)764-3838. Vice President, Creative Director: Christopher J. Snell. Art Director: Diane Hay. Ad agency. Clients: business to business, financial and medical.
Needs: Works with 30 freelance artists/year. Works on assignment only. Uses artists for illustration, design, keyline and photography.
First Contact & Terms: Send query letter with brochure, resume, business card and photostats, photographs, slides or tear sheets to be kept on file. Samples not filed returned only if requested. Reports only if interested. Write for appointment to show portfolio. Considers complexity of the project, client's budget, skill and experience of artist, geographic scope for the finished product and turnaround time when establishing payment. Rights purchased vary according to project.

GRISWOLD INC., 55 Public Sq., Cleveland OH 44114. (216)696-3400. Executive Art Director: Tom Gilday. Ad agency. Clients: consumer and industrial firms; client list provided upon request.
Needs: Works with 30-40 illustrators/year. Works primarily with local artists, but occasionally uses others. Uses freelance artists for billboards, consumer and trade magazines, direct mail, P-O-P displays, brochures, catalogs, posters, newspapers and AV presentations.
First Contact & Terms: Works on assignment only. Arrange interview to show portfolio. Provide materials to be kept on file for possible future assignments. Payment is by the project; negotiates according to client's budget.

HAYES PUBLISHING CO. INC., 6304 Hamilton Ave., Cincinnati OH 45224. (513)681-7559. Office Manager: Marge Lammers. AV producer/book publisher. Produces educational books, brochures and audiovisuals on human sexuality and abortion. Free catalog.
Needs: Uses artists for direct mail brochures and books.
First Contact & Terms: Send slides and photographs. Samples returned by SASE. Reports in 2 weeks. Provide business card to be kept on file for possible future assignments. Pays by job.

IMAGEMATRIX, 2 Garfield Pl., Cincinnati OH 45202. (513)381-1380. Vice President: Peter Schwartz. Total communications for business.
Needs: Works with 25 freelance artists/year. Local artists only; must have portfolio of work. Uses artists for paste-up, mechanicals, airbrushing, storyboards, photography, lab work, illustration for AV; buys cartoons 4-5 times/year. Especially important is AV knowledge, computer graphics for video and slides and animation understanding.
First Contact & Terms: Works on assignment only. Artwork buy-out. Send business card and slides to be kept on file. Samples not filed are returned by SASE. Reports within 2 months. Write for appointment to show portfolio. Pays by the hour, $9-35 average; by the project, $150 minimum. Considers complexity of the project, client's budget, skill and experience of artist and turnaround time when establishing payment. Buys all rights.
Tips: "Specialize your portfolio; show an understanding of working for a 35mm final product. We are using more design for video graphics and computer graphics."

GEORGE C. INNES & ASSOCIATES, Box 1343, 110 Middle Ave., Elyria OH 44036. (216)323-4526. President: George C. Innes. Ad/art agency. Clients: industrial and consumer. Assigns 25-50 jobs/year.
Needs: Works with 3-4 illustrators/month. Works on assignment only. Uses illustrators for filmstrips, stationery design, technical illustrations, airbrush, multimedia kits, direct mail, slide sets, brochures/flyers, trade magazines, newspapers and books. Also uses artists for layout and design for reports, catalogs, print ads, direct mail/publicity, brochures, displays, employee handbooks, exhibits, products, technical charts/illustrations, trademarks, logos and company publications.
First Contact & Terms: Send query letter with brochure showing art style or tear sheets, photostats, photocopies, slides and photographs. Samples not filed are not returned. Reports in 2 weeks. To show a portfolio, a freelance artist should mail appropriate materials. No originals returned to artist at job's completion. Pays for design by the hour, $5-15; pays for illustration by the hour, $5-15.

JONES ANASTASI CORBETT & LENNON ADVERTISING, 40 S. 3rd St., Columbus OH 43215. (614)221-2395. Creative Director: Joseph Anastasi. 4-A agency. Clients: hospitals, insurance, colleges, industries, financial institutions—"variety of accounts."
Needs: Number of freelance artists used varies. Uses freelance artists for billboards, consumer and trade magazines, brochures, posters, newspapers and AV presentations.
First Contact & Terms: Arrange interview to show portfolio; *will not see walk-ins*. Works on assignment only. Payment is by the hour, by the day, or by the project; negotiates according to client's budget.
Tips: "Do some research on clients and present portfolio in accordance."

THE JONETHIS ORGANIZATION, Suite 401, 159 S. Main St., Akron OH 44308. (216)375-5122. Project Manager: Jane Byrd. Marketing services firm. Clients: industrial, consumer and retail. Client list provided upon request.
Needs: Works with 6-8 freelance artists/year. Uses artists for design and production. Especially important are design sense, language understanding and production sense.
First Contact & Terms: Send query letter with resume to be kept on file. Call for appointment to show portfolio. Reports only if interested. Pays by the project. Considers complexity of project, client's budget, skill and experience of artist, and turnaround time when establishing payment. Buys all rights.

***LANG, FISHER & STASHOWER**, 1010 Euclid Ave., Cleveland OH 44115. (216)771-0300. Executive Art Director: Larry Pillot. Full service ad agency. Clients: consumer firms.

Needs: Works with 8 illustrators/year. Local artists primarily. Works on assignment only. Uses freelance artists for billboards, consumer and trade magazines, direct mail, P-O-P displays, brochures, catalogs, posters, signage, newspapers and AV presentations.
First Contact & Terms: Query with resume of credits and samples. Payment is by the project; negotiates according to client's budget, amount of creativity required, where work will appear and freelancer's previous experience.

LOHRE & ASSOCIATES, 1420 E. McMillan St., Cincinnati OH 45206. (513)961-1174. Art Director: Charles R. Lohre. Ad agency. Clients: industrial firms.
Needs: Works with 2 illustrators/month. Local artists only. Works on assignment only. Uses freelance artists for trade magazines, direct mail, P-O-P displays, brochures and catalogs.
First Contact & Terms: Send query letter with resume and samples. Call or write to schedule an appointment to show portfolio, which should include final reproduction/product. Especially looks for "excellent line control and realistic people or products." Pays for design by the hour, $12 minimum; pays for illustration by the hour, $6 minimum.
Tips: Looks for artists who can draw well and have experience in working with metal inks.

MCKINNEY/GREAT LAKES ADVERTISING, 1166 Hanna Bldg., Cleveland OH 44115. (216)621-0648. Art Director: Doug Pasek. Clients: mainly industrial and a few consumer accounts; client list provided upon request.
Needs: Works primarily with local freelancers but uses others. Uses freelance artists for consumer and trade magazines, direct mail, brochures, catalogs, newspapers and AV presentations.
First Contact & Terms: Arrange interview to show portfolio. Payment is by the project or by the day; negotiates according to client's budget and where work will appear.
Tips: "We primarily use photography; using more retouchers who are also illustrators."

CHARLES MAYER STUDIOS INC., 168 E. Market St., Akron OH 44308. (216)535-6121. President: C.W. Mayer, Jr. AV producer since 1934. Clients: mostly industrial. Produces film and manufactures visual aids for trade show exhibits.
Needs: Works with 1-2 illustrators/month. Uses illustrators for catalogs, filmstrips, brochures and slides. Also uses artists for brochures/layout, photo retouching and cartooning for charts/visuals.
First Contact & Terms: Send slides, photographs, photostats or b&w line drawings or arrange interview to show portfolio. Samples not kept on file are returned. Reports in 1 week. Provide resume and a sample or tear sheet to be kept on file for future assignments. Originals returned to artist at job's completion. Negotiates pay.

ART MERIMS COMMUNICATIONS, 700 Bulkley Building, Cleveland OH 44115. (216)621-6683. President: Arthur M. Merims. PR firm. Clients: industry.
Needs: Assigns 10 freelance jobs/year. Prefers local artists. Works on assignment only. Works with 1-2 freelance illustrators and 1-2 freelance designers/month. Uses artists for trade magazines, brochures, catalogs, signage and AV presentations.
First Contact & Terms: Send query letter with samples to be kept on file. Call or write for appointment to show portfolio, which should include "copies of any kind" as samples. Pays by the hour, $10-20 average or by the project. Considers complexity of project, client's budget, and skill and experience of artist when establishing payment.
Tips: When reviewing samples, looks for "creativity and reasonableness of cost."

PENNY/OHLMANN/NEIMAN INC., 1605 N. Main St., Dayton OH 45405. (513)278-0681. Creative Director: Karen Ingle. Art Directors: Jim Rupp, Jim Sichman. Ad agency.
Needs: Works with 3 illustrators and 3 designers/month. "Only pros who have had work published. Proximity is important." Uses artists for P-O-P displays, album covers, TV, renderings of building interiors, audiovisuals, billboards, calligraphy, cartoons, catalog illustrations/covers, convention exhibits, magazine editorial decorative spots, direct mail brochures, letterheads, layout, posters and trademarks.
First Contact & Terms: Call or write for interview. Prefers slides, photographs, photostats and b&w line drawings as samples. Samples not returned. Reports within 1 week. Works on assignment only. Provide a brochure and/or business card to be kept on file for future assignments. No originals returned to artist at job's completion. "Jobs paid per quota."

JEROME H. SCHMELZER & ASSOCIATES, 750 Prospect Ave., Cleveland OH 44115. (216)696-5550. Vice-President: Michael Prunty. Ad agency and public relations firm. Clients: retail, industrial, institutional. Client list provided on request.
Needs: Assigns 15-20 freelance jobs/year. Works with 1 freelance illustrator/month. Uses artists for

consumer and trade magazines, brochures, catalogs, filmstrips, P-O-P displays and AV presentations.
First Contact & Terms: Local artists only. Send query letter with resume, business card and samples to be kept on file. Write for appointment to show portfolio. Prefers photographs and photostats as samples. Samples returned only if requested. Reports only if interested. Works on assignment only. Pays by the hour and by the project. "We keep originals at completion of job." Considers complexity of project, skill and experience of artist, and turnaround time when establishing payment. Buys all rights.
Tips: "Be professional, business-like and able to handle pressure of time."

TRIAD, (Terry Robie Industrial Advertising, Inc.), 124 N. Ontario St., Toledo OH 43624. (419)241-5110. Vice President/Creative Director: Janice Robie. Ad agency/graphics/promotions. Clients: industrial, consumer, medical.
Needs: Assigns 30 freelance jobs/year. Works with 1-2 freelance illustrators/month and 2-3 freelance designers/month. Works on assignment only. Uses artists for consumer and trade magazines, brochures, catalogs, newspapers, filmstrips, stationery, signage, P-O-P displays, AV presentations, posters and illustrations (technical and/or creative).
First Contact & Terms: Send query letter with resume and slides, photographs, photostats or printed samples to be kept on file. Samples returned by SASE if not kept on file. Reports only if interested. To show a portfolio, mail appropriate materials or write to schedule an appointment; portfolio should include roughs, original/final art, final reproduction/product and tear sheets. Pays by the hour, $10-60; by the project, $25-2,500. Considers client's budget, and skill and experience of artist when establishing payment. Negotiates rights purchased.
Tips: "We are interested in knowing your specialty."

***VIDEO GENESIS, INC.**, 24000 Mercantile Rd., Beachwood OH 44122. (216)464-3635. President: Howard Schwartz. Video production/post-production. Clients: various corporations, cable companies and universisites.
Needs: Works with 3 freelance artists/year. Works on assignment only. Uses artists for lettering, logos and charts/graphs. "We do not look for specific skills in an artist. The artist should make us aware of their best abilities and if a need for those abilities arises, we will use their services."
First Contact & Terms: Send query letter with brochure showing art style. Samples not filed are returned only if requested. Reports only if interested. Write to schedule an appointment to show a portfolio, which should include whatever the artist feels is the best representation of his/her work. Considers complexity of project and client's budget when establishing payment. Rights purchased vary according to project.
Tips: Artist should "write us to request an appointment or send in the appropriate information/samples. All information sent to us is kept in a permanent file and all applicants are considered for each project."

Oklahoma

ANDERSON BAKER BEAM, Box 4114, Tulsa OK 74159. (918)587-8883. Art Director: Anne Evans. Ad agency. Clients: primarily financial institutions. Client list provided upon request with SASE.
Needs: Works with 12-15 freelance artists/year. Local artists get first consideration only because of time factors. Works on assignment only. Uses artists for everything from illustration and design to paste-up. Especially looks for the ability to translate written or verbal instructions into effective art.
First Contact & Terms: Send query letter with samples. Samples not filed returned by SASE. Reports only if interested. Pay varies. Considers complexity of project, client's budget, skill and experience of artists, geographic scope for the finished product, turnaround time and rights purchased when establishing payment. Buys all rights.
Tips: "Show us how versatile you can be. If you're good in more than one aspect of art (i.e., cartooning, airbrushing, illustration, pen & ink sketches—whatever), we'd like to know that."

***BEALS ADVERTISING, INC.**, 5005 Penn, Oklahoma City OK 73112. 848-8513. Art Director: T. Brogan. Ad agency.
Needs: Works with 12 or more freelance artists/year. Uses artists for design, illustrations, animation and lettering.
First Contact & Terms: Send query letter with tear sheets and photostats. Samples not filed are returned only if requested. Call to show a portfolio, which should include roughs and final reproduction/product. Pays for design by the project, $40 minimum. Pays for illustrations by the project, $50-3,000. Considers skill and experience of artist, and how work will be used when establishing payment. Buys all rights.

***THE ECONOMY COMPANY**, 1200 N.W. 63rd St., Oklahoma City OK 73116. (405)840-1444. Art Director: William Mathison.
Needs: Works with 100 freelance artists/year. Works on assignment only. Uses artists for illustrations in educational books. Artist "must have experience, and include several full-color samples of editorial and book illustrations in portfolio."
First Contact & Terms: Send query letter with resume and tear sheets, photocopies or slides. Samples not filed are returned only if requested. Reports only if interested. Buys all rights.

***LOWE RUNKLE COMPANY**, 6801 N. Broadway, Oklahoma City OK 73116. Senior Art Director: Dean Clark. Ad agency. Clients: banks, petroleum, food manufacturer. Client list provided for SASE.
Needs: Works with 30 freelance artists/year. Local artists preferred, but out-of-towners used for longer project work. Works on assignment only. Uses artists for design, illustrations, brochures, P-O-P displays, mechanicals, retouching, animation, billboards, posters, direct mail packages, lettering, logos, charts/graphs and advertisements.
First Contact & Terms: Send query letter with brochure showing art style or resume and slides. Samples not filed are returned by SASE. Reports back within 3 weeks. Call or write to schedule an appointment to show a portfolio, which should include thumbnails, roughs, original/final art, final reproduction/product and color. Pays for design by the hour, $35-100. Pays for illustration by the hour, $35-100. Considers complexity of project, client's budget, skill and experience of artist, and turnaround time when establishing payment. Buys all rights.
Tips: Artist should have "a varied portfolio (client-wise)."

Oregon

WILLIAM CAIN INC., 1500 SW 1st Ave., Portland OR 97201. (503)222-5940. Art Director: Jack Allen. Ad agency. Clients: industry, port authority.
Needs: Assigns 340 freelance jobs/year including photographers. Works with 2 freelance illustrators and 4 freelance designers/month. Prefers artists with "quality work, dependability and a firm understanding of price before beginning job." Works on assignment only. Uses artists for consumer and trade magazines, direct mail packages, brochures, newspapers and P-O-P displays.
First Contact & Terms: Send brochure to be kept on file. Prefers photostats or printed brochures as samples. Samples not kept on file are returned. Reports only if interested. Call or write for appointment to show portfolio. Pays by the project, $150-2,000 average. Considers complexity of project, client's budget, and skill and experience of artists when establishing payment. Buys all rights.
Tips: "Make sure your work is competitive with the top people in your field. Deliver on time. Be extremely neat in your presentation. Don't talk too much."

CREATIVE COMPANY, INC., 345 Court St. NE, Salem OR 97301. (503)363-4433. President/Owner: Jennifer Larsen. Specializes in corporate identity and packaging. Clients: local consumer-oriented clients, professionals and trade accounts on a regional and national level, all in the Salem/Valley area.
Needs: Works with 3-4 freelance artists/year. Prefers local artists. Works on assignment only. Uses artists for design, illustration, retouching, airbrushing, posters and lettering. "Clean, fresh designs!"
First Contact & Terms: Send query letter with brochure, resume, business card, photocopies and tear sheets to be kept on file. Samples returned only if requested. Reports only if interested. Call for appointment to show portfolio. "We require a portfolio review. Years of experience not important if portfolio is good. We prefer one-on-one review to discuss individual projects/time/approach. Pays for design by the hour, $24-40 average. Considers complexity of project and skill and experience of artist when establishing payment.
Tips: "Don't drop in, always call and make an appointment. Have a clean and well-organized portfolio, and a resume or something to keep on file."

GREEN/ASSOCIATES ADVERTISING, INC., Box 2565, 1176 W. 7th St., Eugene OR 97402. (503)343-2548. Art Director: Bob Smith. AV/film/animation/TV producer; full-service ad agency with marketing and PR services.
Needs: Assigns 50-150 jobs/year. Works with 1 illustrator and 1 designer/month; 10 illustrators/year. Prefers experienced local artists, "unless the talent is rare, i.e., animation." Works on assignment only. Uses animators rarely. Uses artists for "all kinds of projects. We use freelancers when our staff is overloaded."
First Contact & Terms: Send photostats, resume, samples, business card, tear sheet or other materials "if applicable and appropriate" to be kept on file. "Photostats (6) will do if they adequately show artist's works." Samples returned by SASE. Reports within weeks. "If we are talking a specific project—as we usually are—we report in a matter of days." Pays by the project. Method and amount of

payment are negotiated with the individual artist. Pay "depends totally in project and artist's capability. This small market does not pay as well as larger ones." No originals returned to artist following publication "unless agreed to in advance." Negotiates rights purchased. "We usually reserve rights for clients."

Pennsylvania

AMERICAN ADVERTISING SERVICE, 121 Chestnut, Philadelphia PA 19106. Creative Director: Joseph Ball. Ad agency.
Needs: Uses artists for advertising, billboards, package design, graphic design, commercials, cover design, exhibits and art renderings.
First Contact & Terms: Prefers personal contact, but mailed art or photocopies OK. Not responsible for art after submission.

ANIMATION ARTS ASSOCIATES INC., Lee Park, Suite 301, 1100 E. Hector St., Conshohocken PA 19428. President: Harry E. Ziegler. AV/motion picture/TV producer. Clients: government, industry, education and TV. Audience: engineers, doctors, military, general public. Produces 35/16mm films, sound/slide programs and filmstrips.
Needs: Works with designers and illustrators. Uses artists for filmstrips, motion pictures and animation.
First Contact & Terms: Call for interview. Provide resume to be kept on file for possible future assignments. No work returned at job's completion. Pays $5-10/hour, cartoon and technical animation.

BAKER PRODUCTIONS INC., 4159 Main St., Philadelphia PA 19127. (215)482-2900. President: Alan Baker. Produces TV film and videotape commercials, documentaries, industrial films, and computer graphics.
Needs: Buys approximately 100 designs/year. Uses artists for computer graphics and medical illustration. Uses very few freelancers.
First Contact & Terms: Local artists only. Prefers artists with broadcast art or ad agency experience. Write for interview. Prefers photographs as samples. Samples not returned. Reports within 1 week "if prospect is pending"; otherwise, in 3 weeks. Works on assignment only. Provide resume to be kept on file for possible future assignments. Buys all rights. Pays $9/panel, storyboards; $12/title card, titles.
Tips: Most graphics used are computer generated.

TED BARKUS CO. INC., 1512 Spruce St., Philadelphia PA 19102. President/Creative Director: Ted Barkus. Ad agency/PR firm. Serves clients in finance and in manufacturing of various products.
Needs: Works with 2 illustrators and 1 designer/month. Local artists with experience working with similar firms only. Works on assignment only. Uses designers for billboards, P-O-P displays, consumer and trade magazines, stationery design, multimedia kits, direct mail, TV, slide sets and newspapers. Uses illustrators for brochures/flyers.
First Contact & Terms: Send business card, slides, photographs and b&w line drawings to be kept on file. Samples returned by SASE. Reports in 2 weeks. No original work returned after job completed. Pays by the project or by the hour, $10-25 average. Considers complexity of project and skill and experience of artist when establishing payment.

EDUCATIONAL COMMUNICATIONS INC., 761 Fifth Ave., King of Prussia PA 19406. Contact: Art Director. Audiovisual firm. Clients: automotive, pharmaceutical.
Needs: Works with 2-3 freelance artists/year. Works on assignment only. Especially important are cartoon or technical illustration skills.
First Contact & Terms: Send query letter with resume, tear sheets, photostats, photocopies, slides and photographs to be kept on file. Samples are not returned. Does not report back. Write to schedule an appointment show a portfolio, which should include original/final art, final reproduction/product, color, tear sheets, b&w and slides. Pays by the hour, $15 minimum. Considers complexity of the project, and skill and experience of artist when establishing payment. Buys all rights.
Tips: "Work submitted must be clean, professional, and corporate in nature. Speed, ability to follow directions, and ability to think creatively are important. Ability to meet deadlines essential."

***HARDMAN EASTMAN STUDIOS, INC.**, 1400 E. Carson St., Pittsburg PA 15203. (412)481-4450. General Manager: Barbara Jost. Audiovisual firm. Clients: audiovisual and industrial.
Needs: Works with 1-2 freelance artists/year. Local artists only. Works on assignment only. Uses artists for design, illustrations, mechanicals and charts/graphs. Artists should have the "experience to design art for 35mm slide and TV crop format, also the ability to communicate with clients and translate input into what is required for end use."

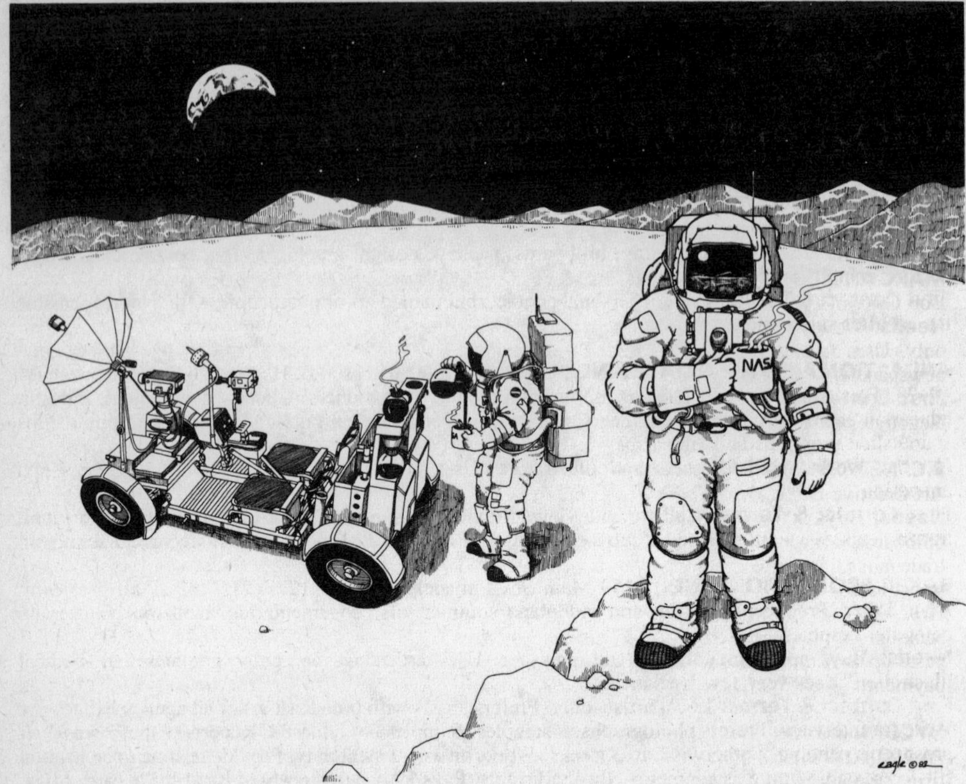

"A high-tech look for a low-tech coffee distributor" was the assignment Joseph Eagle of King of Prussia, Pennsylvania, received from Educational Communications Inc. Eagle received $100 for this pen & ink illustration, which resulted in more assignments from the same company.

First Contact & Terms: Send query letter with resume. Samples not filed are not returned. Reports only if interested. Write to schedule an appointment to show a portfolio, which should include roughs, original/final art, color and photographs. Payment varies. Considers complexity of project, client's budget, skill and experience of artist, and turnaround time when establishing payment. Buys all rights.
Tips: "Do not call. Send letter and resume!"

JERRYEND COMMUNICATIONS, INC., Rt. #2, Box 356H, Birdsboro PA 19508. (215)689-9118. Vice President: Gerald E. End, Jr. Advertising/PR Firm. Clients: industry, banks, technical services, professional societies and automotive aftermarket.
Needs: Assigns 3-5 freelance jobs/year. Works "primarily with local artists for time, convenience and accessibility." Works on assignment only. Uses 1-2 freelance illustrators/month. Uses artists for trade magazines, brochures, signage, AV presentations, posters and press releases.
First Contact & Terms: Send query letter with brochure showing art style to be on file. Samples not filed returned only if requested. Reports within 2 weeks. Call to schedule an appointment to show a portfolio, which should include roughs, final reproduction/product and tear sheets. Pays for design by the hour, $25-50 average. Considers complexity of project, client's budget, turnaround time and rights purchased when establishing payment. Buys all rights.
Tips: Have a "realistic approach to art; clients are conservative and not inclined to impressionistic or surrealistic techniques."

J.B. LIPPINCOTT CO., Media Development/Health Sciences Division, E. Washington Square, Philadelphia PA 19105. (215)238-4200. Editor-in-Chief, Media Department: H. Michael Eisler. AV producer. Audiences: nursing and medical professions. Produces self-instructional and other

educational multi-frame audiovisual presentations in the health sciences (16mm, ³/₄'' videocassettes and 35mm sound filmstrips). Free catalog.
Needs: Assigns 3 jobs/year. Artists should have previous experience with slides, filmstrips and motion pictures, also with anatomy, biology and medical illustrations for projectables. Prefers, but is not restricted to, local artists (Boston-Washington corridor). Works on assignment only. Uses artists for full-color artboards for 35mm strips; illustrations for 16mm filming with background, sized and colored for filming and projection; and line drawings for workbooks.
First Contact & Terms: Query with brochure/flyer and resume to be kept on file for future assignments. Reports in 1 month. Material copyrighted. No originals returned to artist at job's completion. Pays by the project; "payment varies depending on media format." Buys all rights.

MARC AND COMPANY, 3600 U.S. Steel Bldg., Pittsburgh PA 15219. (412)562-2000. Art Director: Bob Griffing. Ad agency. Clients: retailers, fast food, office furniture.
Needs: Works with 4-5 illustrators/month. Works primarily with local artists. Works on assignment only. Uses freelance artists for direct mail, P-O-P displays, brochures, catalogs, posters, signage, newspapers, storyboards and AV presentations.
First Contact & Terms: Query with resume first and then arrange interview to show portfolio. Negotiates payment according to client's budget.

B.C. NEWTON MARKETING & ADVERTISING, 178 N. Madison Ave., Highland Park PA 19082. Art/Creative Director: B.C. Newton. Ad agency. Clients: retail, consumer and industrial.
Needs: Buys 200 illustrations/year. Local artists only. Works on assignment only. Uses artists for billboards, consumer magazines, stationery design, direct mail, television, slide sets, brochures/flyers, trade magazines, newspapers and books; lettering, layout, paste-up and mechanicals. Especially needs storyboards, slide presentation for audiovisuals and illustration.
First Contact & Terms: Send business card, brochure/flyer, photostats and slides. SASE. Reports back only if interested. No originals returned to artist at job's completion. Pays $5-10/hour for layout, paste-up and mechanicals. Considers complexity of project and client's budget when establishing payment.

NYCOM, (formerly New York Communications, Inc.), Suite 300, 101 Bryn Mawr Ave., Bryn Mawr PA 19010. (215)352-5505. Creative Director: Paul Greeley. Motion picture/TV/marketing consulting firm. Clients: radio & TV stations.
Needs: Uses artists for motion pictures and storyboards. Works with 2 illustrators and 1 designer/month.
First Contact & Terms: Query with resume. Reports within 1 week. Works on assignment only. Provide resume, sample storyboards, business card, brochure/flyer to be kept on file for future assignments. Samples not kept on file returned by SASE. No originals returned to artist at job's completion. Considers skill and experience of artist and turnaround time when establishing payment.

PERCEPTIVE MARKETERS AGENCY LTD., Suite 903, 1920 Chestnut St., Philadelphia PA 19103. (215)665-8736. Art Director: Marci Mansfield-Fickes. Ad agency. Clients: retail furniture, contract furniture, commuter airline, lighting distribution company; several nonprofit organizations for the arts, and a publishing firm.
Needs: Works with 15-20 freelance artists/year. Uses mostly local talent. In order of priority, uses artists for mechanicals, photography, illustration, comps/layout, photo retouching and design/art direction. Concepts, ability to follow instructions/layouts and precision/accuracy are important.
First Contact & Terms: Send resume and photostats, photographs and tear sheets to be kept on file. Accepts as samples—"whatever best represents artist's work—but preferably not slides." Samples not filed are returned by SASE only. Reports only if interested. Call for appointment to show portfolio. Pays by the hour, $10 minimum; by the project, $50 minimum. Considers complexity of the project, client's budget and turnaround time when establishing payment. Buys all rights.
Tips: "Freelance artists should approach us with unique, creative and professional work. And it's especially helpful to follow-up interviews with new samples of work, (i.e., to send a month later a 'reminder' card or sample of current work to keep on file.)"

THE REICH GROUP, INC., 230 S. Broad St., Philadelphia PA 19102. (215)546-1636. Art Director: Yvonne Mucci. Ad agency. Specializes in print media and direct mail/collateral material. Clients: banks, insurance companies, business to business services, associations, religious groups.
Needs: Works with 15-20 freelance artists/year. Uses artists for advertising and brochure design and illustration, design of direct mail kits and illustrations for association magazines. Rarely uses unusual techniques; prefers primarily realistic styles. No cartoons.
First Contact & Terms: Send query letter with samples to be kept on file; write for appointment to

show portfolio. Prefers to review photocopies or other types of samples which are nonreturnable. Reports only if interested. Works on assignment only. Pays by the hour, $12-25 average; by the project, $125-400 average. Considers skill and experience of artist, turnaround time and rights purchased when establishing payment.
Tips: "Show commercial work that has been used in print. No school samples or experimentals."

E.J. STEWART, INC., 525 Mildred Ave., Primos PA 19018. (215)626-6500. Production Coordinator: Karen Brooks. TV producer. Serves clients in industry, education, government, interactive video and advertising. Produces videotape programs and commercials.
Needs: Assigns 50w jobs/year. Works with 2 illustrators and 2 designers/month. Philadelphia area artists only. Works on assignment only. Uses artists for set design and storyboards.
First Contact & Terms: Send resume, brochure/flyer and business card to be kept on file. Reports in 3 weeks. Method and amount of payment are negotitated with the individual artist. No originals returned to artists following publication. Buys all rights.
Tips: "There is more interest in computer generated animation in our field. 10% of work is cartoon-style illustrations."

THOMAS R. SUNDHEIM INC., The Benson East, Jenkintown PA 19046. Vice President/Creative Director: John F. Tucker, Jr. Serves clients in industrial and scientific products and services.
Needs: Works with 3 illustrators, 3 designers/year. Prefers local artists. Works on assignment only. Uses artists for illustration, technical art, retouching, trade magazines, direct mail and collateral; also work on P-O-P displays, stationery design and newspapers.
First Contact & Terms: Provide business card, brochure/flyer and samples to be kept on file. Prefers roughs through final as samples. Samples returned by SASE. No originals returned to artist at job's completion. Call to schedule an appointment to show a portfolio.
Tips: "Imitation is all I'm finding—and imitation of pretty bad stuff. Learn about our clients' products before coming in—don't expect me to brief you." Looks for the artist's *style* in samples or a portfolio.

Rhode Island

BUDEK FILMS & SLIDES, 73 Pelham St., Newport RI 02840. (401)846-6580. Director: Elizabeth Allen. AV producer. Serves clients in education. Produces 35mm slides of architecture, painting and sculpture.
Needs: Assigns 1-4 jobs/year. "Purchases slides of architecture, painting or sculpture, textiles, decorative arts."
First Contact & Terms: Send query letter with resume, and samples (original 35mm color slides preferred). Samples not filed returned by SASE. Reports within 3 weeks. Write to schedule an appointment to show a portfolio, which should include samples "appropriate to their work/slides." Pays for design by the project, $100 minimum. Considers complexity of project, client's budget, skill and experience of artist and rights purchased when establishing payment.
Tips: "We want only the highest quality of slides. They must be originals and come with complete copyrights."

South Carolina

BRADHAM-HAMILTON ADVERTISING, INC., Box 729, Charleston SC 29402. (803)884-6445. Art Director: Mike Schumpert. Ad agency. Clients: financial institutions, fashion, hotel, resort, mall, dairy, restaurants, fast food, contractor, manufacturer.
Needs: Assigns 100 freelance jobs/year. Works with a total of 2-3 freelance illustrators and 2-3 freelance designers. Uses artists for consumer and trade magazines, billboards, direct mail packages, brochures, newspapers, filmstrips, P-O-P displays, AV presentations and posters. Needs pen & ink, pencil, wash, acrylic and airbrush.
First Contact & Terms: Send query letter with brochure and samples to be kept on file. Call for appointment to show portfolio. Prefers photostats or tear sheets as samples. Samples not kept on file returned by SASE. Reports within 2 weeks. Works on assignment only. Pays $50-500 average. Considers complexity of project, client's budget, skill and experience of artist and turnaround time when establishing payment. All rights purchased.
Tips: "Approach us in a business-like, professional way: write a letter and follow-up with a phone call. Submit samples of specific type of work requested."

Tennessee

WARD ARCHER & ASSOCIATES, INC., 65 Union at Front, Box 3300, Memphis TN 38173-0300. (901)526-8700. Creative Director: Eddie Tucker. Ad agency/PR firm. Clients: industrial, agricultural, consumer goods. Media used include billboards, consumer magazines, trade magazines, direct mail, newspapers, P-O-P displays, radio and TV.
Needs: Works with 4 illustrators/month. May be assigned as many as 4 jobs in 1 month. Uses artists for P-O-P displays, stationery design, direct mail and brochures/flyers.
First Contact & Terms: Write with resume requesting an interview to show portfolio. Reports in 4 weeks. Works on assignment only. Provide business card and brochure/flyer to be kept on file for future assignments. "Many variables determine price."

JANUARY & ASSOCIATES, 4701 Fronsdale Dr., Nashville TN 37220. (615)834-6323. Owner/CEO: John January. Ad agency. Clients: banks, fast food restaurants, industry, hospitals, music, entertainment and retail stores.
Needs: Assigns 26 freelance jobs/year. Works with 2 freelance illustrators and 2-5 freelance designers/month. Local artists only. Works on assignment only. Uses artists for trade magazines, billboards, brochures, catalogs, newspapers and filmstrips.
First Contact & Terms: Send resume to be kept on file. Write or call for appointment to show portfolio. Prefers slides, photographs or photostats as samples. Pays by the hour or by the project. Considers complexity of project and client's budget when establishing payment. Negotiates rights purchased.

MUSICAL IMAGE DESIGNS, 1212 Ardee Ave., Nashville TN 37216. (615)226-1509. Creative Director: Stacy Slocum. Estab. 1984. Ad agency serving the music industry.
Needs: Works with an unlimited number of freelance artists/year. Uses artists for trademarks, letterheads, and T-shirts.
First Contact & Terms: Send resume and samples to be kept on file. Prefers samples showing clear b&w designs on 8½x11 paper. Samples not filed are returned by SASE. Reports within 1 month. Considers complexity of the project and skill of artist when establishing payment. Buys first rights or all rights.
Tips: "Send sample of your idea involving musical instruments, stars, etc. If we accept your ideas and designs we will send a purchase agreement. All work must be original and unpublished."

Texas

ALAMO AD CENTER INC., 217 Arden Grove, San Antonio TX 78215. (512)225-6294. Art Director: Elias San Miguel. Ad agency/PR firm. Serves clients in medical supplies, animal breeding, food, retailing (especially jewelry), real estate and manufacturing.
Needs: Works with 6 illustrators and 4 designers/month. Local artists only. Works on assignment only. Uses artists for work in consumer magazines, brochures/flyers, trade magazines, album covers and architectural renderings and "overflow work."
First Contact & Terms: Send brochure, flyer, business card, resume and tear sheets to be kept on file. SASE. Reports in 4 weeks if interested. Arrange interview to show portfolio, which should include tear sheets. No originals returned at job's completion. Pay is negotiated. Considers skill and experience of artist when establishing payment.

AVW PRODUCTIONS, 2241 Irving Blvd., Dallas TX 75207. (214)634-9060. Vice President: Bob Walker. AV/film/animation producer. Serves clients in industry and advertising. Produces multi-image materials, multiple-exposure slides, etc.
Needs: Works with 1-2 illustrators, 1-2 animators and 1-2 designers/year. Artists must work at the company's facility in Dallas. Works on assignment only. Uses artist for "any projects that the inhouse staff can't handle."
First Contact & Terms: Send resume, samples (slides preferred) and arrange interview by phone. Samples not kept on file are returned. Provide resume, samples, brochure/flyer and business card to be kept on file for possible future assignments. Reports within weeks. Pays by the project or by the hour. Method and amount of payment are negotiated with the individual artist. Payment varies with each client's budget. No originals returned to artist following publication. Negotiates rights purchased.

BOZELL JACOBS KENYON & ECKHARDT, Box 619200, Dallas-Ft. Worth Airport TX 75261-9200. (214)556-1100. Creative Director: Ron Spataro, Neil Scanlan, Artie McGibbens. Ad agency. Clients: all types.
Needs: Works with 4-5 freelance illustrators/month. Works on assignment only. Uses freelancers for billboards, newspapers, P-O-P displays, TV and trade magazines.
First Contact & Terms: Call for appointment to show portfolio. Reports within 3 weeks. Provide business card, brochure/flyer, resume and samples to be kept on file for possible future assignments. Samples not kept on file are returned. Payment is negotiated.
Tips: Wants to see a wide variety including past work used by ad agencies and tear sheets of published art.

DYKEMAN ASSOCIATES INC., 4205 Herschel Rd., Dallas TX 75219. (214)528-2991. Contact: Alice Dykeman or Carolyn Whetzel. PR firm. Clients: business, industry, sports, environmental, energy, health. Assigns 150 jobs/year.
Needs: Works with 5 illustrators/designers per month. "We prefer artists who can both design and illustrate." Local artists only. Uses artists for design of brochures, exhibits, corporate identification, signs, posters, ads, title slides, slide artwork and all design and finished artwork for graphics and printed materials.
First Contact & Terms: Arrange interview to show portfolio. Provide business card and brochures. No originals returned to artist at job's completion. Pays by the project, $40-1,500 average; "artist makes an estimate; we approve or negotiate." Considers complexity of project, client's budget, skill and experience of artist and turnaround time when establishing payment.
Tips: "Be enthusiastic. Present an organized portfolio with a variety of work. Have a price structure but be willing to negotiate per project."

EVANS WYATT ADVERTISING, Gibralter Savings Bldg., 5151 Flynn Pkwy., Corpus Christi TX 78411. (512)854-1661. Contact: Mr. E. Wyatt. Advertising/exhibit/display/director.
Needs: Assigns 400 freelance illustrations/year; uses some cartoons and humorous and cartoon-style illustrations. Works on assignment only.
First Contact & Terms: Send a query letter with resume, brochure/flyer, tear sheets and photocopies to be kept on file. "No originals, please." Samples not filed are returned. Reports in two weeks. Arrange an interview to show portfolio, which should include scrapbook, slides or stats. Pays by the project, by the day, or by the hour, $75-150, with a $500 maximum. Considers client's budget and skill and experience of artist when establishing payment. "We pay flat for all rights."
Tips: More "by the project" assignments at negotiated charge. "Send 6-12 samples or copies of general scope of work plus best specialty and price expected."

***GULF STATE ADVERTISING AGENCY**, 3410 West Dallas, Houston TX 77019-3892. (713)521-1010. Art Director: Karen Gregory. Ad agency. Clients: financial, restaurant and industrial firms; client list provided upon request.
Needs: Number of freelance artists used varies. Local artists only. Works on an assignment only. Primarily uses freelance artists for brochures and sometimes for consumer and trade magazines, and newspapers.
First Contact & Terms: Send business card and photostats to be kept on file. Samples not kept on file are returned by SASE. Reports in 1 week. Payment is by the project; negotiates according to client's budget and where work will appear.

HEPWORTH ADVERTISING CO., 3403 McKinney Ave., Dallas TX 75204. (214)525-7785. Manager: S.W. Hepworth. Ad agency. Clients: finance, food, machinery and insurance.
Needs: Works with 2 illustrators and 2 designers/month. Local artists only. Uses artists for billboards, consumer magazines, direct mail, slide sets, brochures/flyers and trade magazines.
First Contact & Terms: Send a query letter with tear sheets to be kept on file. No originals returned to artist at job's completion.
Tips: Looks for variety in samples or portfolio.

KNOX PUBLIC RELATIONS, Suite A, Guthrie Creek Park, 708 Glencrest, Longview TX 75601. (214)758-6439. President: Donna Mayo Knox. PR firm. Clients: civic, social organizations, private schools and businesses.
Needs: Works with 2 illustrators/month. Works on assignment only. Uses artists for billboards, stationery design, multimedia kits, direct mail and brochures/flyers.
First Contact & Terms: Send query letter with brochure showing art style or resume and samples. Samples returned by SASE. Reports in 3 weeks. Call or write to schedule an appointment to show a portfolio. Originals returned to artist at job's completion. Pays by the hour, $10 and up.
Tips: "Please query first."

***LEVEL FOUR COMMUNICATIONS**, Three Dallas Communications Complex LB134, Irving TX 75039-3510. (214)869-7620. President: Doris Seitz. Ad agency. Clients: corporate and banking.
Needs: Works with 5-6 freelance artists/year. Uses local artists with a minimum of three years' experience. Works on assignment only. Uses artists for design, illustrations, brochures, catalog, books, magazines, newspapers, P-O-P displays, mechanicals, retouching, billboards, posters, direct mail packages, press releases, motion pictures, lettering, logos, charts/graphs and advertisements. Looks for "first-quality, high-level corporate design capability; a clean, sophisticated style.
First Contact & Terms: Contact through agent's agent or send query letter with resume and samples. Samples not filed are not returned. Reports only if interested. To show a portfolio, mail original/final art, final reproduction/product, color, tear sheets and photographs. On a typical brochure, pays for design by the project, $200 minimum. Pays for illustrations by the project, $200 minimum. Considers client's budget, skill and experience of artist, turnaround time and rights purchased when establishing payment. Purchases all rights but can negotiate; rights purchased vary according to project.

LOWE-MARSCHALK, (formerly Metzdorf-Marschalk), 3040 Postoak, Houston TX 77056. (713)840-0491. Vice President, Creative Supervisor: Ellie Malivis. Ad agency. Clients: consumer, food, financial and some industrial firms.
Needs: Works with 12 illustrators/year. Works on assignment only. Uses freelance artists for billboards, consumer and trade magazines, direct mail, catalogs, posters, newspapers and advertising.
First Contact & Terms: Send slides, tear sheets, photostats or cards showing style used, or contact through artist representative. Reports only if interested. Usually deals with artist representative about payment for illustrators. Pays by the project, $125-4,000 average. Considers complexity of project and rights purchased when establishing payment.
Tips: "We are looking for artists with specific styles or specialties or unusual treatments to otherwise mundane subjects. Send examples of your work before attempting to make an appointment. Postcard mailings have been successful."

McCANN-ERICKSON WORLDWIDE, Briar Hollow Bldg., 520 S. Post Oak Rd., Houston TX 77027. (713)965-0303. Senior Vice President/Creative Director: Jesse Caesar. Ad agency. Clients: all types including industrial, gasoline, transportation/air, entertainment, computers and high tech.
Needs: Works with about 20 freelance illustrators/month. Uses freelancers in all media.
First Contact & Terms: Call for appointment to show portfolio. Selection based on portfolio review. Negotiates payment based on client's budget and where work will appear.
Tips: Wants to see full range of work including past work used by other ad agencies and tear sheets of published art in portfolio.

McNEE PHOTO COMMUNICATIONS INC., 9261 Kirby, Houston TX 77006. (713)796-2633. President: Jim McNee. AV/film producer. Serves clients in industry and advertising. Produces slide presentations, video tapes, brochures and films. Also a brokerage for stock photographs.
Needs: Assigns 20 jobs/year. Works with 4 illustrators/month. Prefers local artists with previous work experience. Uses artists for brochures, annual reports and artwork for slides, film and tape.
First Contact & Terms: "Will review samples by appointment only." Provide resume, brochure/flyer and business card to be kept on file for possible future assignments. Works on assignment only. Reports within 1 month. Method of payment is negotiated with the individual artist. Pays by the hour, $30-60 average. Considers client's budget when establishing payment. No originals returned after publication. Buys all rights, but will negotiate.

PHOTO-SYNTHESIS INC., Suite 190, 3160 Commonwealth, Dallas TX 75247. Producer: John Kindervag. AV producer. Clients: mostly corporate. Produces slide sets and audiovisual shows. Assigns 15 jobs/year minimum.
Needs: Local artists only. Works on assignment only. Uses artists for slide illustrations and freelance production people.
First Contact & Terms: Send a query letter with resume and photostats, slides or printed material. Reports only if interested. Arrange for an appointment to show a portfolio, which should include resume, business card, tear sheet, brochure and/or flyer to be kept on file. Pays by the project; or pays $5-30/hour. Considers skill and experience of artist when establishing payment.
Tips: There is a trend toward "expansion to all forms of business communications. Artists interested in working for us should be neat, clean and dependable."

***ROMINGER ADVERTISING AGENCY**, 3600 Commerce, Dallas TX 75226. Art Directors: Lee Dean and Nelson Greenfield. Ad agency. Clients: hotels, real estate, corporate and industrial.
Needs: Works with 2-3 illustrators/year. Local artists only. Works on assignment basis only. Uses freelance artists for billboards, consumer and trade magazines, direct mail, P-O-P displays, brochures, catalogs, posters, signage, newspapers, and AV presentations and production.

First Contact & Terms: Query with resume of credits and samples. Payment is by the day or by project.

NEAL SPELCE COMMUNICATIONS, Suite 400, 333 Guadalupe, Two Republic Plaza, Austin TX 78701. (512)476-4644. Creative Director: D. Childress. Ad agency. Serves clients in finance, hospitals, professional associations and real estate.
Needs: Works with 3 illustrators and 4 designers/month. Works on assignment only. Uses artists for consumer and trade magazines, direct mail, newspapers, P-O-P displays, brochures/flyers and TV.
First Contact & Terms: Write requesting interview to show portfolio (illustrations and printed pieces incorporating the illustrations), send resume, slides or photostats or make contact through artist's rep. Samples returned by SASE. Reports within 2 weeks. Provide resume, brochure or promotional materials showing work and/or samples to be kept on file for future assignments. Pay is negotiable.
Tips: "We tend to use illustrators, rather than designers, for freelance work."

TEXAS PACIFIC FILM VIDEO, INC., 501 N. I35, Austin TX 78702. (512)478-8585. Producer: Laura Kooris. Film/video production firm. Clients: ad agencies, music companies, etc. Client list provided for SASE.
Needs: Works with many freelance artists/year. Uses artists for set design, logos and signs, and costumes and makeup.
First Contact & Terms: Works on assignment only. Send query letter with samples to be kept on file; write for appointment to show portfolio. Prefers reels as samples. Samples not filed are returned by SASE. Reports only if interested. Pays by the project or by the day. Considers client's budget and skill and experience of artist when establishing payment. Rights purchased vary according to project.

WOMACK/CLAYPOOLE, Suite 501, 8585 N. Stemmons Fwy., Dallas TX 75247-3805. Senior Art Director: Bailey Burk. Ad agency. Clients: petroleum, aviation, financial, insurance and retail firms.
Needs: Works with 2-3 illustrators/month. Uses freelance artists for billboards, brochures, AV presentations, print and collateral pieces.
First Contact & Terms: Send query letter with brochure showing art style or tear sheets, photostats and photocopies. Write to schedule an appointment to show a portfolio, which should include original/final art and final reproduction/product. Payment is by the project, $300-1,500. Considers client's budget or where work will appear when establishing payment.
Tips: "In the field, there are more promotions to complement advertising campaigns. Also, computer graphics should be a strong medium for the last part of the twentieth century. As for approaching our firm, set reasonable prices on the total layout of artwork."

ZACHRY ASSOCIATES, INC., Box 1739, 709 N. 2nd, Abilene TX 79604. (915)677-1342. Art Director: T. Rigsby. Ad agency, audiovisual and printing firm. Clients: industrial, institutional and religious service. Client list provided for SASE.
Needs: Works with 6 freelance artists/year. Works on assignment only. Uses artists for illustration, calligraphy and mechanical preparation.
First Contact & Terms: Send query letter with samples, if available, to be kept on file. Samples not filed are returned by SASE. Call or write to schedule an appointment to show portfolio, which should include roughs, final reproduction/product or anything pertinent to talent offered. Pays for design by the hour, $10 minimum; pays for illustration by the project, $35 minimum. Considers complexity of the project, client's budget and turnaround time when establishing payment. Rights purchased vary according to project.

Utah

FRANCOM ADVERTISING, INC., Suite D 100, 5282 S. 320 West, Salt Lake City UT 84107. (801)263-3125. President: A. Sterling Francom. Ad agency. Clients: banks, car dealers, restaurants, industrial, video rental. Client list provided upon request.
Needs: Assigns 120 freelance jobs/year. Local artists only. Works on assignment only. Works with 3 freelance illustrators and 2 freelance designers/month. Uses artists for billboards, direct mail packages, brochures, catalogs, newspapers and signage.
First Contact & Terms: Send query letter with resume and tear sheets and photostats to be kept on file. Samples returned by SASE if not kept on file. Reports within 2 weeks. Call or write to schedule an appointment to show a portfolio, which should include original/final art, final reproduction/product, tear sheets and photostats. Pays by the project, $25-1,500; amount of payment negotiated with artist in advance. Considers complexity of project, client's budget and turnaround time when establishing payment. Material not copyrighted.

Tips: Artists should possess "creativity and professionalism, and full service capability from design concept to printer. Portfolio must include current commercial work similar to or complimentary to advertising agency's regular types of art work. Artwork submitted must be *commercial* art, not portraits, scenes, etc., either the original or published art of sample brochures, ads from newspapers, magazines, etc." Current trends include contemporary and computer generated design using high tech colors.

Vermont

IMAGE, 138 S. Willard St., Burlington VT 05401. (802)862-8261. President: Linda Kelliher. Ad agency. Clients: restaurants, automotive, ski resorts, banks, universities. Client list provided upon request.
Needs: Works with 3 freelance artists/year. Works on assignment only. Uses artists for illustrations and mechanical preparation when busy.
First Contact & Terms: Send query letter with resume and samples to be kept on file. Samples not filed returned only if requested. Reports within 2-3 weeks. Write for appointment to show portfolio, which should include photostats, photographs, slides or tear sheets. Considers complexity of project, client's budget, skill and experience of artist, geographic scope for the finished product, turnaround time and rights purchased when establishing payment. Rights purchased vary according to project.

Virginia

DAN ADVERTISING & PUBLIC RELATIONS, 408 W. Bute St., Norfolk VA 23510. (804)625-2518. Art Director: Ron Pohling. Ad/PR firm.
Needs: Uses artists for work in building and mechanical renderings, airbrushing, animation, TV animation, TV/film production, P-O-P displays, filmstrips, consumer magazines, multimedia kits, slide sets, brochures/flyers and finished work. Negotiates pay.
First Contact & Terms: Query with samples of previously published work. SASE. Provide brochures, flyers, resume, tearsheets, samples and 3/4" video tape when possible to be kept on file for future assignments. Originals returned at completion on some jobs.

DEADY ADVERTISING, 17 E. Cary St., Richmond VA 23236. (804)643-4011. President: Jim Deady. Specializes in corporate identity, displays and publications. Clients: tobacco and porcelain accounts, and projects.
Needs: Works with 10-15 freelance artists/year. Local or regional artists only with minimum of 2 years' experience with an agency. Works on assignment only. Uses artists for design, illustration, mechanicals, retouching and airbrushing; brochures, magazine, newspaper and advertisements.
First Contact & Terms: Send query letter with resume to be kept on file; also send samples. Call or write for appointment to show portfolio, which should include photostats. Other sample are returned. Reports back only if interested. Pays for design by the hour, $35-75 average, or by the project, $250-2,500 average; for illustration by the project, $275-1,500 average. Considers client's budget, skill and experience of artist and turnaround time when establishing payment.
Tips: "Be on time with all projects."

PAYNE ROSS & ASSOCIATES ADVERTISING, INC., (formerly Payne Ross & Devins Advertising, Inc.), 206 E. Jefferson St., Charlottesville VA 22901. (804)977-7607. Creative Director: Lisa Ross. Ad agency. Clients: resorts, thoroughbred farms, manufacturing plants, banks.
Needs: Works with 12-20 freelance artists/year. Uses artists for photography, illustration and copy-writing; occasionally for paste-up.
First Contact & Terms: Send query letter with brochure showing art style or resume and tear sheets, photostats, slides, photographs and other printed pieces. Reports back only if interested. To show portfolio, mail appropriate materials, which should include original/final art, final reproduction/product, photostats and photographs. Pays for design by the hour, $15-40; pays for illustration by the project, $200-1,500. Pay varies according to "experience, type of work, etc." Considers skill and experience of artist and turnaround time when establishing payment. Rights purchased vary according to project.
Tips: "There is more popularity in use of illustration for brochure and print advertising. Also there is more acceptance of this by client particularly photography and illustration together. We find more integration between copy and design in conceptual stage. Therefore designer, illustrator, photographer must be flexible."

WILLIAM C. PFLAUM CO. INC., Reston International Center, Reston VA 22091. (703)620-3773. Art Director: John Cuddahy. PR firm.
Needs: Works with 1-2 designers/month. Uses artists for stationery design, direct mail, brochures/flyers, trade magazines and newspapers.
First Contact & Terms: Local artists only. Query with samples. No originals returned at job's completion.

SIDDALL, MATUS AND COUGHTER, Fidelity Bldg., 9th & Main Sts., Richmond VA 23219. Art Directors: Jessica Welton, Tom Hale. Ad agency/PR firm. Clients: industrial, travel, land development, bank, chemical.
Needs: Assigns 50 freelance jobs/year. Works on assignment only. Works with 4 freelance illustrators/month. Uses artists for consumer and trade magazines, billboards, direct mail packages, brochures, newspapers and posters.
First Contact & Terms: Send query letter with samples and tear sheets to be kept on file. Call or write for appointment to show portfolio, which should include printed samples to be kept on file. Samples returned only if requested. Reports only if interested. Considers complexity of project, client's budget, skill and experience of artist, geographic scope of finished project, turnaround time and rights purchased when establishing payment. Buys all rights.

Washington

***EHRIG & ASSOCIATES**, 4th & Vine Building, Seattle WA 98121. (206)623-6666. Associate Creative Director: Greg Erickson. Full-service advertising and public relations firm serving sports teams, consumer ad and industries.
Needs: Works with 30 freelance artists/year. Works on assignment only. Uses artists for design, illustrations, brochures, catalog, P-O-P displays, mechanicals, retouching, animation, billboards, posters, direct mail packages, press releases, motion pictures, lettering, logos, charts/graphs and advertisements.
First Contact & Terms: Samples not filed are returned with SASE. Call or write to schedule an appointment to show a portfolio, which should include final reproduction/product. Pays for design and illustration by the project. Considers client's budget and skill and experience of artist when establishing payment. Negotiates rights purchased.
Tips: "Frequency and persistence are what's needed. Don't give up."

***INLAND AUDIO VISUAL COMPANY**, N. 2325 Monroe St., Spokane WA 99205. (509)328-0706. Assistant Manager: Val Ellingson. Audiovisual firm. Clients: advertising agencies and associations.
Needs: Works with 5 freelance artists/year. Works on assignment only. Uses artists for design, illustrations, retouching, animation, lettering, logos, charts/graphs and multi-image. Artist must have multi-image design skills.
First Contact & Terms: Send query letter with resume. Reports only if interested. Write to schedule an appointment to show a portfolio. Considers complexity of project, client's budget and turnaround time when establishing payment. Rights purchased vary according to project.

SODERBERG AND ASSOCIATES, INC., Suite 500, 220 W. Mercer, Seattle WA 98119. Creative Director: Stan Soderberg. Ad agency. Serves clients in entertainment, manufacturing, finance, restaurants, automobile retailing, airplane kit manufacturing and sportswear manufacturing, fashion retailing, hotels, property management, supermarket and computor services.
Needs: Works with 5-10 illustrators, 10-15 designers/month. Uses artists for layout, illustration, type spec, paste-up, retouching and lettering for newspapers, magazines, TV, billboards, P-O-P displays, filmstrips and direct mail.
First Contact & Terms: Send business card and flyer to be kept on file. Originals sometimes returned to artist at job's completion.

WATTS-SILVERSTEIN, 1921 2nd Ave., Seattle WA 98101. (206)443-4200. Contact: R. Lindberg. AV producer. Serves clients in industry and advertising. Produces multi-image slide shows and print collateral.
Needs: Assigns 25 jobs/year. Works with 2 illustrators and 2 animators/month. Works on assignment only. Uses artists for "all our slide shows."
First Contact & Terms: Send resume and samples (slides preferred). Samples returned with SASE. Provide resume, samples and business card to be kept on file for possible future assignments. Reports within 2 weeks. Method and amount of payment are negotiated with the individual artist. Original art returned after publication. Negotiates rights purchased.

West Virginia

GUTMAN ADVERTISING AGENCY, 600 Board of Trade Building, Wheeling WV 26003. (304)233-4700. President: Milton Gutman. Ad agency. Clients: finance, glass, resort, media, industrial supplies (tools, pipes) and furniture.
Needs: Works with 3-4 illustrators/month. Local artists only except for infrequent and special needs. Uses artists for billboards, stationery design, television, brochures/flyers, trade magazines and newspapers. Also uses artists for retouching work.
First Contact & Terms: Send materials to be kept on file for possible future assignments. Call for an appointment to show a portfolio. No originals returned at job's completion. Negotiates payment.

Wisconsin

BARKIN, HERMAN, SOLOCHECK & PAULSEN, INC., 777 E. Wisconsin Ave., Milwaukee WI 53202. (414)271-7434. Account Executive: Kathleen Sieja. Wisconsin's oldest PR firm. Clients: educational organization, financial, manufacturing, hospital, insurance, brewery, leisure time and real estate development.
Needs: Works with freelance illustrators and designers according to individual needs. Uses artists for all communications media.
First Contact & Terms: Call account executive for appointment to show portfolio. Negotiates payment depending on job requirements.

THE CRAMER-KRASSELT CO., 733 N. Van Buren, Milwaukee WI 53202. (414)276-3500. Associate Creative Director: Dave Hofmann. Ad agency. Clients: consumer, financial , industrial and service account.
Needs: Uses artists for consumer and trade magazines and newspapers.
First Contact & Terms: Call for names of individual art directors to contact. Sometimes shows are set up for portfolio review by all art directors and interested persons. Negotiates payment based on quotes from freelancers and available budget.

HOFFMAN YORK & COMPTON, 330 E. Kilbourne Ave., Milwaukee WI 53202. (414)289-9700. Contact: Art Director. Ad agency. Serves clients in machinery, food service.
Needs: Works with "many" illustrators/month. Needs vary. Uses freelancers and studios for all print media.
First Contact & Terms: Call for appointment to show portfolio. Negotiates payment.
Tips: Wants to see best work. Will probably use freelancer's area of specialty.

L. QUILLIN & ASSOCIATES, INC., V.I.P. Bldg., 2101 Victory St., La Crosse WI 54601. (608)788-8292. Vice President: Wayne Krause. Ad agency. Clients: manufacturing, business to business.
Needs: Works with 6-8 freelance artists/year. Especially important are skills, creativity and understanding needs. Works on assignment only.
First Contact & Terms: Send query letter with resume and samples to be kept on file. Samples not filed are returned only if requested. Reports back only if interested. Call for appointment to show portfolio. Pay varies. Considers complexity of the project, client's budget and turnaround time when establishing payment. Buys all rights.

SORGEL-STUDIOS, INC., 205 W. Highland Ave., Milwaukee WI 53203. (414)224-9600. Contact: Art Director. AV producer. Clients: business, corporate, multi-image and videotapes. Assigns 100 jobs/year.
Needs: Works with 10 illustrators/year. Uses artists for stylized illustrations, human figures and animation.
First Contact & Terms: Query with resume and samples (slides). SASE. Reports in 3 weeks. Provide resume and brochures/flyers to be kept on file for possible future assignments. No originals returned to artist at job's completion. Negotiates pay.
Tips: "Most of our artwork is now computer generated and that limits our use of freelancers."

Canada

ATKINSON FILM-ARTS LTD., 19 Fairmont Ave., Ottawa, Ontario K1Y 1X4 Canada. (613)728-3513. Personnel Manager: Cathy Morriscey. Animation production house. Produces animated motion

pictures—cartoon and technical, series, features. Clients: corporate interests, government, small business, all areas.
Needs: Works with 150 freelance artists/year. Local artists perferred. Works on assignment only. Uses artists for animation, background and layout art. Artists must have "a graduate diploma from a classical animation program or a minimum of 3 years' experience in an animation studio and a demo reel of sample materials."
First Contact & Terms: Send query letter with resume and slides, photographs and other demo reels. Samples not filed are returned only by request. Reports only if interested. Call or write to schedule an appointment to show a portfolio, which should include thumbnails, roughs, original/final art, photographs and demo reels. Pays by the footage or per piece of artwork, "competitive rates." Considers complexity of the project, client's budget, skill and experience of artist, geographic scope for the finished product, turnaround time and rights purchased when establishing payment. Buys all rights.
Tips: "Freelance artists must have experience and a complete portfolio with demo reel and/or photographs of work depending upon which area of specialty."

***CAMPBELL-EWALD (CANADA) LIMITED**, 2nd Floor, 156 Front St. W, Toronto, Ontario Canada M5J 2L6. (416)977-0875. Creative Director: Trevor F. Goodgoll. Estab. 1982. Ad agency. Clients: airlines, business machines, liquor, financing, pharmaceutical, insulation products, candy and plastics.
Needs: Assigns 25 freelance jobs/year. Works on assignment only. Uses artist for consumer and trade magazines, newspapers and some occasional brochures.
First Contact & Terms: Send resume, samples and tear sheets to be kept on file. Samples not kept on file are returned. Nonresidents include IRC. Reports within 15 days. Call or write for appointments to show portfolio. Payment is "entirely dependent on artist's skills. Illustrators are usually paid on a project basis." Considers complexity of project, client's budget, skill and experience of artist and turnaround time when establishing payment. Buys all rights.
Tips: Artists should "understand that the creative director is reponsible for a tremendous amount of day to day work and should be prepared for polite 'put-offs.' Keep trying! Artists will always receive clear briefings from us and will be given the creative freedom necessary to do their very best. Don't show or bring too much. Quality, not quantity. Be patient and keep trying for an appointment."

***NORM DREW ENTERTAINMENT FEATURES**, Suite 608 L, Laurier House, 1600 Beach Ave., Vancouver, B.C. V6G 1Y6 Canada. (604)689-1948. Contact: Norman Drew. Producer of audiovisual and print graphic art, TV commercials, slide shows, TV animated series, cartoon art-comic strips, panels, greeting cards, books for educational, advertising and entertainment use. Clients: TV networks, stations, ad agencies, corporations, government, publishers, newspapers and multi-media.
Needs: Freelance assistants for animation, comic strip, comic panels, lettering, children's books.
First Contact & Needs: Send query letter, photocopies of your best examples. "Do not send animation demo films/tapes unless requested. Unsolicited films/tapes will not be returned without adequate return postage/shipping fee included. Please include SASE with International Reply Coupon if replies to questions required. Keeps sample page/letter on file pending possible assignments." American paid by footage; graphic art by piecework. Buys all rights.

INSIGHT COMMUNICATIONS, 1850 Champlain Ave., Box 363, Whitby, Ontario L1N 5S4 Canada. (416)686-1144. Art Director: Garnet McPherson. AV firm. Clients: corporate, industry and travel industry.
Needs: Assigns 45 freelance jobs/year. Works with 2 freelance illustrators and 3 freelance designers/month. Prefers "local artists for assignment; any artist for stock art or photography." Uses artists for brochures, filmstrips, P-O-P displays, AV presentations, posters and graphics.
First Contact & Terms: Send query letter with business card and samples to be kept on file. Samples not kept on file are returned by SASE only if requested. Reports within 3 weeks. Call for appointment to show portfolio, which should include slides and tear sheets. Pays by the project, $25-2,500 average. Considers complexity of project, client's budget, skill and experience of artist and rights purchased when establishing payment. Negotiates rights purchased.
Tips: "In contacting us, artists should send query with samples, then call 2 weeks later for an appointment."

McCANN-ERICKSON ADVERTISING OF CANADA, Britannica House, 151 Bloor W, Toronto, Ontario MS5 1S8 Canada. (416)925-3231. Contact: Art Directors. Ad agency. Clients: consumer food, beverage and service industry accounts.
Needs: Local artists only. Works on assignment only. Uses freelance artists and photographers on all accounts.
First Contact & Terms: Especially looks for a "unique style" in a portfolio—also "enthusiasm and dedication." Call to schedule an appointment to show portfolio with individual art directors. Payment is

by the project; negotiates according to client's budget and freelancer's previous experience.
Tips: "Artists should be more selective in the work they show. One poor piece of work lets down the whole portfolio."

***PULLIN PRODUCTIONS, LTD.**, 822 Fifth Ave. SW, Calgary, Alberta T2P 0N3 Canada. Creative Director: Art Feinstough. Audiovisual firm.
Needs: Works with 4 freelance artists/year. Works on assignment only. Uses artists for design, illustrations, brochures, P-O-P displays, animation, motion pictures, lettering and charts/graphs.
First Contact & Terms: Send query letter with resume and samples. Samples not filed are not returned. Reports only if interested. To show a portfolio, mail appropriate materials. Pays for design by the hour, $10-50. Considers complexity of project, client's budget, skill and experience of artist, how work will be used and turnaround time when establishing payment. Buys all rights.

***WARNE MARKETING & COMMUNICATIONS**, Suite 810 111 Avenue Rd., Toronto, Ontario M5R 3M1 Canada. (416)927-0881. President: Keith Warne. Ad agency.
Needs: Works with 8 freelance artists/year. Works on assignment only. Uses artists for design, illustrations, brochures, catalog, P-O-P displays, mechanicals, retouching, billboards, posters, direct mail packages, logos, charts/graphs and advertisements. Artists should have "creative concept thinking."
First Contact & Terms: Send query letter with resume and photocopies. Samples not filed are not returned. Reports only if interested. Write to schedule an appointment to show a portfolio, which should include roughs and final reproduction/product. Pays for design by the project, $85-125. Pays for illustration by the project, $125-200. Considers complexity of project, client's budget, and skill and experience of artist when establishing payment. Buys all rights.
Tips: Artist should "send samples (photocopies) and wait for assignment. There is an increasing need for technical illustration in the field."

> **66** *Color is playing a more important part of publishing; trendy colors are more apparent. I see more new, fresh ideas more quickly than before. Everything seems to change faster with looser styles.* **99**
>
> *Marty Roelandt, Antioch Publishing Company*

Architectural, Interior & Landscape Design Firms

In architecture, a completed project is a collective product. A client's ideas are sketched by an architectural delineator; model builders then construct three-dimensional buildings, complexes or even cities. Using rough sketches, architectural drafters make detailed drawings that builders use in the preparation of blueprints. Landscape architects then move in to redesign natural settings, planning not only the placement of greenery but also traffic flow. Before the client is ready to move in, interior designers plan, supervise and coordinate the design and furnishing of the interior space.

Each facet of architectural art requires good draftsmanship, a knowledge of blueprints and building materials plus a good sense of perspective. Renderings must be technically precise so a client knows what to expect. Delineators must show a dramatic flair with watercolors, gouache or acrylics. Model-making requires a facility with wood, plastic or plaster. Landscape architects must be able to prepare site plans and construct models. The fundamentals of design, space planning and color coordination are necessities for an interior designer.

Select firms which suit your style and work habits. Some projects require on-site construction visits, while others call for renderings which can be done at home or at the office. Submit a query letter with slides or photographs of your projects. Architects should send samples of their rendering skills and photographs of model-making projects. In addition to any drafting or final rendering samples, landscape architects should submit photos of gardens or grounds they have designed; sequential photos should show the grounds in different seasons. Interior designers should demonstrate their specialty, whether it is industrial space planning or residental decoration, with before and after shots.

Magazines which provide essential information on the industry are *Architectural Digest*, *The AIA Journal*, *Architectural Record* and *Interior Design*, as well as *House & Garden*, *House Beautiful* and *Better Homes and Gardens*. Names and addresses of firms are available in *ProFile*.

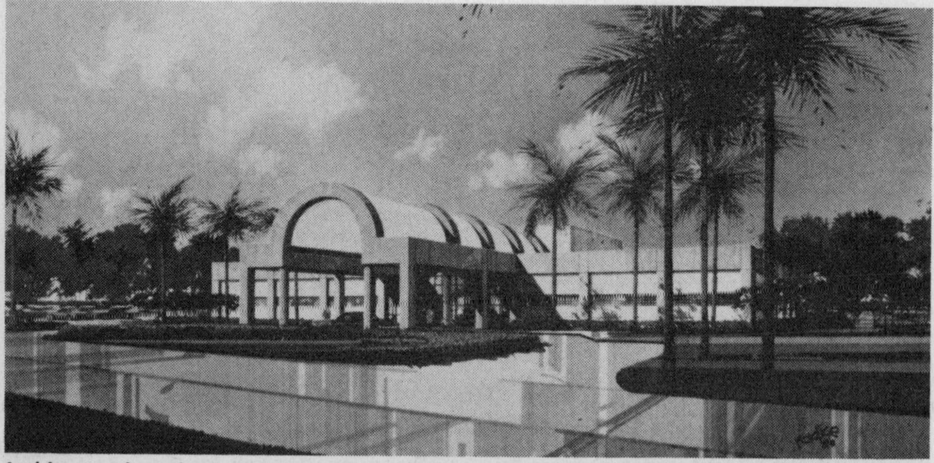

Architectural renderer Richard Radke of Chicago, Illinois, wanted to convey "how the building would fit into the existing environment" for a client of Hansen Lind & Meyer in Orlando, Florida. Radke was paid $1,800 for the rendering, completed with markers and tempera.

***A&E DESIGN, INC.**, 5644 N. Dale Mabry, Tampa FL 33614. (813)885-4605. President: Gordon Amato, A.I.A. Architectural/engineering firm. Clients: residential, commercial and institutional.
Needs: Works with 2 freelance artists/year. Works on assignment only. Uses artists for advertising design, interior, landscape and architectural renderings, and model making.
First Contact & Terms: Send query letter with brochure showing art style or resume and samples. Samples not filed are returned only if requested. Reports only if interested. To show a portfolio, mail photographs and brochure. Pays for illustrations by the project, $600-2,000. Considers complexity of project, skill and experience of artist, and turnaround time when establishing payment.

ABEND SINGLETON ASSOCIATES INC., 20 W. 9th, Kansas City MO 64105. (816)221-5011. Contact: Steve Abend. Clients: corporate, government, institutional, commercial and residential. Services: architectural, interior design, engineering, planning and landscape architecture.
Needs: Works with 8 freelance artists for architectural renderings; 1, interior design; 2, graphic design; 2, model making; 1, landscape design; and 1, stained glass.

***ALLEN & PHILIP ARCHITECTS**, Suite B-101, 2702 N. 44th St., Phoenix AZ 85008. (602)957-8466. Vice President/Interiors: Virginia Swift Taylor. Architectural/interior design firm. Clients: hotel, office, industrial and medical.
Needs: Works with 5 freelance artists/year. Uses artists for brochure and interior design and architectural renderings.
First Contact & Terms: Send query letter with resume, slides and photographs. Samples not filed are returned. Reports only if interested. Call or write to schedule an appointment to show a portfolio, which should include color and photographs. Considers client's budget and turnaround time when establishing payment.

***ARCHITECTS CHARTERED**, 210 N. Albany Ave., Atlantic City NJ 08401. (609)347-1050. Vice President: William J. Gallo. Architectural/interior design firm providing feasibility studies, deficiencies analysis, architectural planning and construction management. Clients: long term health care, educational, commercial, industrial, banking and restaurants.
Needs: Uses artists for brochure and landscape design, architectural renderings, design consulting and model making.
First Contact & Terms: Send query letter with brochure showing art style. Samples not filed are returned by SASE. Reports only if interested. Call to schedule an appointment to show a portfolio, which should include original/final art, color, tear sheets and photographs. Considers complexity of project, client's budget, skill and experience of artist, and how work will be used when establishing payment.

***ARCHITRONICS**, Suite D-44, 3 Sunset Way, Henderson NV 89015. (702)435-1150. President: David F. Welles. Architectural/interior design firm.
Needs: Works with 2 freelance artists/year. Works on assignment only. Uses artists for interior design, interior renderings and architectural renderings and model making.
First Contact & Terms: Send query letter with brochure showing art style or resume, tear sheets, photostats, photocopies, slides and photographs. Samples not filed are returned only if requested. Reports only if interested. Call or write to schedule an appointment to show a portfolio, which should include thumbnails, roughs, original/final art, final reproduction/product, color, tear sheets, photostats, photographs and b&w. Payment varies. Considers complexity of project, client's budget, skill and experience of artist, turnaround time and rights purchased when establishing payment.

MILLARD ARCHULETA/EDDY PAYNTER ASSOCIATES, 7440 N. Figueroa St., Los Angeles CA 90041. (213)254-9121. Director of Design: Frank J. Wong/AIA. Architectural firm providing original prints and limited editions. Clients: financial institutions, shopping centers, corporate office buildings.
Needs: Works with 12 freelance artists/year. Uses artists for interior and architectural renderings, landscape design, and model making.
First Contact & Terms: Contact only through artist's agent, who should send brochure, slides and photographs to be kept on file. Reports only if interested. Call for appointment to show portfolio, which should include final reproduction/product and color. Pays for illustration by the project, $500-1,000 average. Considers complexity of budget and skill and experience of artist when establishing payment.
Tips: "A very popular current trend is abstract design."

Market conditions are constantly changing! If this is 1988 or later, buy the newest edition of Artist's Market *at your favorite bookstore or order directly from* Writer's Digest Books.

ARNOLD & STACKS ARCHITECTS, Box 69, 527 W. Washington, Jonesboro AR 72403. (501)932-5530; Box 1560, 901 Central Ave., Hot Springs AR 71902. (501)624-4678. Contact: Doug Arnold. Architectural/interior and landscape/design firm providing planning, design, architecture, landscape, graphic and interior design, and construction administration. Clients: private, public residential, governmental, educational, industrial.
Needs: Works with 1-2 freelance artists/year. Uses artists for advertising design, brochure design, illustration and layout; landscape and interior design, architectural and interior renderings, design consulting and furnishings.
First Contact & Terms: Send query letter with brochure, resume, business card, slides, photographs and tear sheets to be kept on file. Reports within 2 weeks. Call for appointment to show portfolio. Pay rate "depends on work, circumstances, etc." Considers complexity of project, client's budget, skill and experience of artist and turnaround time when establishing payment.

ART-IN-ARCHITECTURE PROGRAM, U.S. General Services Administration, 18th and F Sts. NW, Washington DC 20405. (202)566-0629. Director: Donald Thalacker. Clients: federal agencies.
Needs: Works with varying number of artists for murals, wall hangings, sculpture and stained glass. Uses artists to create works as an integral part of federal architecture. Recent commissions include interior sculpture by Robert Irwin, mural by Jennifer Bartlett and plaza sculpture by Richard Serra.
First Contact & Terms: Send query with resume and slides. Reports in 4 weeks. To show a portfolio, mail resume and nonreturnable labeled 35mm color slides of existing work in plastic sheet to be kept on file. Pays $750-250,000 for original art.
Tips: "Getting exposure is usually the key to getting more exposure. Even if you're not selected for a commission, your work has at least been seen and studied. And once your work has been seen, somebody may remember it. Don't waste time and money creating a design to submit to the panel. Send quality slides of completed work. Even if your work is great, a poor slide won't sell it. Though many commissioned works have been done by big names like Louise Nevelson and George Segal, there is plenty of room for locally and regionally-known artists. Of the approximately 20 artists accepted annually from about 1,000 applications, there are as many local and regional artists as there are nationally-known people." Looks for originality and a track record of good work. There is a trend towards "collaboration among artists, architects, landscape architects, designers, etc."

***ASSOCIATED INDUSTRIAL DESIGNERS, INC.**, 32 Court St., Brooklyn Heights NY 11201. (212)624-0034. President: Dr. Robert I. Golberg. Specializes in brand and corporate identity, displays, interior design, packaging, and signage. Clients: "all major firms."
Needs: Works with "many" artists/year. Works on assignment only. Uses artists for brochure and direct mail, package illustration; P-O-P displays, mechanicals, retouching, model making, lettering and logo design.
First Contact & Terms: Send brochure/flyer, resume and photostats. Samples returned. Pays by the hour for design; by the project for illustration; also negotiates.

LEON BARMACHE DESIGN ASSOCIATES LTD., 225 East 57th St., New York NY 10022. (212)759-3840. Executive Designer: Leon Barmache F.A.S.I.D. Interior space planners and designer. Clients: private.
Needs: Needs artists to render interiors, furniture, rugs, etc., from rough sketches; b&w or color, for presentations. Also uses artists for design, illustration, displays and model making.
First Contact & Terms: Send query letter with brochure, resume and photostats, copies or tear sheets to be kept on file. Samples not filed returned by SASE only if requested. Reports within 2 weeks if interested. Call or write for appointment to show portfolio. Pays by the project, $250-500 average for design and illustration. Considers the skill and experience of artist when establishing payment.
Tips: Artist should have "a portfolio of renderings showing his drawing capabilities using the means available—pencil, ink, marker, gouache, airbrush, etc."

DWIGHT E. BENNETT & ASSOCIATES, 3929 Long Beach Blvd., Long Beach CA 90807. (213)595-1691. Contact: Dwight Bennett. Architecture firm. Clients: industrial, residential and commercial.
Needs: Assigns 6 jobs/year. Local artists only. Uses artists for architectural renderings.
First Contact & Terms: Query with brochure or samples. Reports within 1 week. Pays $400-2,500.

***BERGERON-CROFT LTD.**, 1536 Sams Ave., Harahan LA 70123. President: Raymond Bergeron. Architectural firm providing all architectural and engineering services, planning and energy consulting. Clients: residential, commercial, local public agencies.
Needs: Works with 3-6 freelance artists/year. Works on assignment only. Uses artists for advertising illustration, brochure and interior design, furnishings and model making.
First Contact & Terms: Send query letter with brochure, resume and business card to be kept on file.

Call for appointment to show portfolio. Reports within 1 week if interested. To show a portfolio, mail appropriate materials. Negotiates payment. Considers complexity of project and client's budget when establishing payment.

ALEXANDER BRAILAS ASSOCIATES, 8722 Ferris, Houston TX 77096. (713)668-2848. Architect: Alexander Brailas AIA. Architectural firm providing architecture and related services. Clients: institutional, commercial, industrial, health facilities, educational.
Needs: Works on assignment only. Uses artists for architectural renderings and model making.
First Contact & Terms: Send query letter with brochure to be kept on file. Reports only if interested. Call for appointment to show portfolio. Pays according to specific project requirements. Considers complexity of project, client's budget, skill and experience of artist, how work will be used and turnaround time when establishing payment.
Tips: Especially looks at color, composition and draftsmanship in samples or portfolio. Does not like artists "pushing trendy fads with color and composition."

BRENDLER-DOVE ASSOCIATES, INC., Suite 260, 1919 Oakwell Farm Pkwy. San Antonio TX 78218-1774. (512)829-1761. Marketing Director: William J. Dail, Jr. Architectural, interior design, landscape design and promotional service firm. Clients: developers.
Needs: Works with 30 or more freelance artists/year. Uses artists for advertising and brochure design, illustration and layout; signage, charts and model making.
First Contact & Terms: Artists are "subcontracted under BDA corporate name." Send query letter with resume, business card and samples to be kept on file. Prefers finished pieces or photographs as samples. Samples not filed not returned. Reports within 30 days. Call or write for appointment to show portfolio. Payment varies according to project. Considers complexity of project, client's budget, skill and experience of artist, how work will be used, turnaround time and rights purchased when establishing payment.

BRUEGGEMAN & CAULDER, ARCHITECTS P.A., 1510 S. Broadway, Little Rock AR 72202. (501)375-0222. Administrative Assistant: Velma Caulder. Architectural firm providing design of commercial, residential structures, hospitals, churches, schools, high rise apartments, single family housing projects.
Needs: Local artists only. Works on assignment only. Uses artists for architectural renderings.
First Contact & Terms: Send query letter with brochure, business card and original works in watercolor to be kept on file. Call or write for appointment to show portfolio. Pays for design by the project, $400 minimum. Considers client's budget, and skill and experience of artist when establishing payment.

L.M. BRUINIER & ASSOC. INC., 1304 SW Bertha Blvd., Portland OR 97219. (503)246-7412. President: Lou Bruinier. Architectural design/residential planner/publisher of plan books. Clients: contractors and individuals.
Needs: Works with 1-3 freelance artists/year. Uses artists for design and illustration, brochures, catalogs and books. Especially needs 3-dimensional perspectives (basically residential).
First Contact & Terms: Send resume and photostats or photocopies to be kept on file. Material not filed is not returned. Reports only if interested. Pays for design by the hour, $6-15 average; for illustration by project, $40-500 average. Considers the complexity of project and skill and experience of the artist when establishing payment.

***RAYMOND F. CAIN**, 606 Coral, Honolulu HI 96813. (808)521-5361. Vice President: Ray Cain. Landscape design/engineering/planning firm providing hotel and resort planning.
Needs: Works with 3-4 freelance artists/year. Uses artists for brochure design, landscape and architectural renderings.
First Contact & Terms: Send query letter with brochure showing art style or resume. Samples not filed are returned. Reports back. Write to schedule an appointment to show a portfolio. Considers skill and experience of artist when establishing payment.

***CAMBRIDGE ARCHITECTS INTERNATIONAL INC.**, 1033 Massachusetts Ave., Cambridge MA 02138. (617)661-4100. Interior Design Director: Beth Miller. Estab. 1985. Architectural/interior design/landscape design firm providing architectural, interior, and landscape design, programming, planning; construction supervision for commercial, industrial, residential and institutional clients.
Needs: Works with 1-5 freelance artists/year. Works on assignment only. Uses artists for interior, landscape and architectural renderings; model making.
First Contact & Terms: Send query letter with brochure showing art style or resume, tear sheets, photostats and photographs. Samples not filed are returned only if requested. Reports only if interested. Call or write to schedule an appointment to show a portfolio, which should include final reproduction/prod-

uct, color, photographs and b&w. Payment varies. Considers complexity of project, client's budget, skill and experience of artist, and turnaround time when establishing payment.

ALLEN R. CARNEY, A.I.A. & ASSOCIATES, 6000 Grand Central Ave., Box 5146, Vienna WV 26105. (304)295-9410. AIA, Architect: Allen R. Carney. Architectural/interior design firm offering architectural, engineering and interior design. Clients: residential, churches, banks, commercial, institutional.
Needs: Works with 2 freelance artists/year. Uses artists for brochure design, illustration and layout; interior and landscape design and renderings; architectural renderings, charts and model making.
First Contact & Terms: Prefers local artists. Works on assignment only. Send query letter with brochure, resume and business card to be kept on file. Prefers to review slides or tear sheets. Material not filed returned by SASE only if requested. Reports within 2 weeks. Pays for design by the hour, by project, or by the day. Considers complexity of the project, client's budget, skill and experience of artist, and turnaround time when establishing payment.

CBT/CHILDS BERTMAN TSECKARES & CASENDINO INC., 306 Dartmouth St., Boston MA 02116. (617)262-4354. Architectural/interior and landscape design/urban design planning firm. Clients: developers and owners of offices and multifamily housing projects; institutions (schools and universities, churches, hospitals); government (municipal, state and federal).
Needs: Works with 3 freelance artists/year. Experienced artists in the greater Boston area only. Works on assignment only. Uses artists for brochure design, illustration and layout; landscape, interior and architectural renderings; and model making.
First Contact & Terms: Send query letter with brochure, resume, business card, photostats, slides, photographs and tear sheets to be kept on file; nothing that has to be returned (2-3 samples maximum). Samples not kept on file not returned. Does not report back. Pays for design by the project, $100-1,000 average; for illustration by the project, $50-600 average. Considers complexity of project, skill and experience of artist, and turnaround time when establishing payment.

CHAMPLIN/HAUPT INC. ARCHITECTS, 424 E. 4th St., Cincinnati OH 45202. (513)241-4474. Designer: Joan Tepe. Architecture/interior design firm providing complete architectural services, planning, interior design for commercial, institutional and business clients.
Needs: Works with 2 freelance artists/year. Desires artists who can deliver work on time, have a good portfolio and references. Works on assignment only. Uses artists for interior and architectural renderings and occasionally custom artwork.
First Contact & Terms: Send query letter with brochure, photographs or good quality photocopies to be kept on file. Does not report back; "artist should follow up." Call for appointment to show portfolio. Pays for illustrations by the project, $300-500 average; pay rate depends on size and difficulty. Considers complexity of project and how work will be used when establishing payment.

CHRISMAN, MILLER, WOODFORD, INC., 326 S. Broadway, Lexington KY 40508. (606)254-6623. Contact: Karen A. Jones, ASID. Architectural, interior and landscape design and planning engineering firm. Clients: corporate (commerical, industrial); private (residential—large commissioning only); local, state and federal government agencies; and institutional (educational, health care, religious).
Needs: Works with varied number of freelance artists/year. "Artist must be able to come into our offices or to visit job site per project demands. More than 90% of our work is conducted in Kentucky." Works on assignment only. Uses artists for architectural renderings.
First Contact & Terms: Send query letter with brochure/flyer or resume; write for appointment. Samples returned by SASE. Reporting time depends on circumstances of individual projects. Reports back whether to expect possible future assignments. Provide business card, brochure, flyer, samples and tear sheets to be kept on file for possible future assignments. Amount and method of payment vary according to client's budget and contractual agreement.
Tips: "We'll work with anyone, regardless of location. Persons we work with must make themselves readily available to our clients and staff. We will appreciate good art without regard to reputation of artist, etc."

FJ CLARK INCORPORATED, 126 N. McDuffie St., Anderson SC 29621. (803)261-3902. President: Frank J. Clark, AIA. Architectural/interior/urban design firm. Clients: institutional, governmental, college and university, industrial and residential.
Needs: Works with approximately 4 freelance artists/year. Works on assignment only. Uses artists for brochure design and layout, interior and landscape design, interior and architectural renderings, and model making.
First Contact & Terms: Send query letter with brochure, resume, photographs, tear sheets or photocopies to be kept on file. Samples are not returned. Reports back only if interested. Pays by the project

for design and illustration. Considers complexity of project, skill and experience of artist and how work will be used when establishing payment.

CONNELLY ABBOTT TRULL P.A., 222 N. Pine, Magnolia AR 71753. (501)234-7008. President: T.G. Connelly. Architectural firm providing complete architectural-engineering services. Clients: residential, institutional, commercial and industrial.
Needs: Works with 4-6 freelance artists/year. Works on assignment only. Uses artists for interior, landscape and architectural renderings; interior design consulting; furnishings; and model making.
First Contact & Terms: Requires 5 + years' experience in artist's area of specialty. Send brochure and color photographs or photocopies to be kept on file. Samples not filed are returned by SASE only if requested. Reports back to artist. Write for appointment to show portfolio. Pays by the hour or by the project for design and illustration. Pay is negotiated. Considers complexity of the project, client's budget, skill and experience of artist, how work will be used, turnaround time and rights purchased when establishing payment.

***COPE LINDER ASSOCIATES**, 30 South 15th St., Philadelphia PA 19102. (215)981-0200. Contact: Lynda Cloud. Architectural/landscape design firm providing full range of architectural, landscape, urban design and planning services: consulting, planning, design, working drawings, supervision. Clients: residential, industrial, developer.
Needs: Works on assignment only. Uses artists for brochure design, illustrations and layout; interior, architectural and landscape renderings; and model making.
First Contact & Terms: Send query letter with brochure and photostats, photographs or original work to be kept on file. Call or write for appointment to show portfolio. Samples not filed are returned by SASE. Reports only if interested. Considers complexity of project, client's budget, skill and experience of artist and turnaround time when establishing payment.

MAURICE COURLAND & SON/ARCHITECTS-ENGINEERS-PLANNERS, Central Savings Bank Building, 2112 Broadway, New York NY 10023. (212)362-7018. Contact: R.H. Courland or N.M. Courland. Architecture/engineering/space planning/design firm. Clients: industrial, banks, residential, commercial, restaurants, corporate, financial institutions, government, public and semi-public, institutional and educational.
Needs: Buys 2-6 renderings of new buildings and building restoration work/year. Works on assignment only. Uses artists for architectural and interior renderings, murals/graphics and scale models occasional recognition of purchases of artwork (paintings; sculpture; etc.)
First Contact & Terms: Send query letter with brochure, resume, business card and tear sheets to be kept on file. Portfolio should include color photos. SASE. Reports within "weeks." Negotiates pay/project. Certain projects require design and execution; murals; sculpture; paintings; graphics; logos; presentation (color) renderings; exteriors and interiors. Considers complexity of project, client's budget, skill and experience of artist and how work will be used when establishing payment.

THE CRAYCROFT ARCHITECTS, INC., Suite 400, 2602 McKinney Ave., Dallas TX 75204-2520. (214)871-0401. Vice President: Don H. Price. Architectural firm providing programming, design, construction documents, project administration. Clients: multifamily housing, hotels, country club facilities, commercial office buildings, retail shopping centers.
Needs: Works with 2-3 freelance artists/year. Local artists mainly; credentials necessary. Works on assignment only. Uses artists for architectural renderings and model making; more presentation type material is needed for neighborhood opposition meetings, planning and zoning meetings, public hearings, governmental approvals, etc.
First Contact & Terms: Call for appointment to show portfolio. Pays for illustration by the project, $500-1,500. Considers complexity of project, client's budget, skill and experience of artist, how work will be used and turnaround time when establishing payment.

CREATIVE RETAILING, INC., Suite 265, 2222 Martin St., Irvine CA 92715. (714)476-8611. President: Clark Richey. Store planning and design firm. Plans, designs and installs retail speciality chain stores including space planning, fixturing, decor design, visual merchandise presentation and establishment of image.
Needs: Works on assignment only. Uses artists for advertising and brochure design and illustration, brochure layout, interior design, interior and architectural renderings, design consulting, furnishings, charts and model making.
First Contact & Terms: Send query letter with brochure showing art style or resume, tear sheets, photostats, photocopies and photographs. Reports within 30 days. Call to schedule an appointment to show a portfolio, which should include final reproduction/product, color, photostats, and photographs. Pays for design by the project, $250-4,000. Pays for illustration by the project, $250-1,500 average. "All

creative work becomes the property of Creative Retailing." Considers complexity of project, client's budget, and skill and experience of artist when establishing payment.
Tips: "Artist should have the ability to put on paper what the project designer visualizes, also a progressional presentation.

JERRY CUMMINGS ASSOCIATES INC., Suite 301, 420 Boyd St., Los Angeles CA 90013. (213)621-2756. Contact: Jerry Cummings. Landscape architecture firm. Clients: commercial and residential.
Needs: Assigns 20-30 freelance renderings/year. Works with artists for architectural and landscape renderings. Works on assignment only.
First Contact & Terms: Send query letter with brochure showing art style or resume and photographs. Reports within 2 weeks. Samples returned by SASE. Reports back on future possibilities. Call or write to schedule an appointment to show portfolio, which should include original/final art. Pays by the hour, $25 minimum. Considers complexity of project, client's budget, and skill and experience of artist when establishing payment.
Tips: "Be sure your work is appropriate for our typing office *Landscape Architect* (example Portrait & Carton)."

DAT CONSULTANTS LTD., SFA, 118 W. 16th St., New York NY 10011. (212)741-2121. Architect: S. Fernandez. Architecture and interior design firms. Clients: industrial, residential, commercial and institutional.
Needs: Assigns 10 jobs and buys 10 renderings/year. Prefers local artists. Uses artists for renderings, interior design, sculptures, graphics and scale models.
First Contact & Terms: Query with resume or arrange interview to show portfolio. Reports in 1 week. Pays $200-400/job or $15-25/hour.

JOHN LAWRENCE DAW & ASSOCIATES, 912 Baltimore Ave., Kansas City MO 64105. (816)474-9410. Architect: J.L. Daw. Architectural/interior design firm. Clients: commercial, institutional.
Needs: Uses artists for brochure design and layout, interior design, architectural renderings and model making.
First Contact & Terms: Send query letter with brochure and resume to be kept on file. Accepts "whatever artist feels is expendable" as samples. Samples not returned. Reports back to artist. Call or write for appointment to show portfolio.

***DESIGN COLLABORATIVE ARCHITECTS P.C.**, 765 Fairfield Ave., Bridgeport CT 06604. (203)576-1720. Vice President: August Sarino. Architectural/interior design firm. Services: architecture, planning, interior design, master planning. Clients: commercial, residential, corporate and industrial facilities.
Needs: Works with 10 freelance artists/year. Works on assignment only. Uses artists for advertising, brochure and interior design; advertising and interior illustrations; architectural renderings, design consulting, furnishings, charts and model making.
First Contact & Terms: Send query letter with brochure showing art style or resume, slides and photographs. Samples not filed are returned by SASE. Reports only if interested. Call or write to schedule an appointment to show a portfolio, which should include roughs, final reproduction/product color and photographs. Negotiates payment. Considers complexity of project, skill and experience of artist, and turnaround time when establishing payment.
Tips: "Quality work and timely service response to requested need."

THE DESIGNPOINT, 307 Laurel St., San Diego CA 92101. (619)234-2565. President: R. Milberg. Art Director: Kerry Summers. Interior and graphic design firm also providing space planning, corporate identity, package design. Clients: commercial.
Needs: Works with 10 freelance artists/year. Local, qualified artists only. Works on assignment only. Uses artists for brochure illustration, interior and architectural renderings, and model making.
First Contact & Terms: Send query letter with brochure showing art style or resume to be kept on file. Reports only if interested. Call for appointment to show portfolio, which should include original/final art and final reproduction/product. Pays for design and illustration by the project, $200 minimum. Considers complexity of project, client's budget, and skill and experience of artist when establishing payment.

ROBERT E. DES LAURIERS, A.I.A., ARCHITECT & ASSOCIATES, 9349 El Cajon Blvd., La Mesa CA 92041. (619)469-0135. President: Robert E. Des Lauriers, A.I.A. Architectural firm providing architectural services for churches, schools, commercial and residential interior design.
Needs: Works with 6-10 freelance artists/year. Local artists only with strong background. Works on assignment only. Uses artists for brochure illustration; interior and landscape design and renderings; archi-

tectural renderings, design consulting, furnishings and model making.
First Contact & Terms: Send query letter with brochure, resume, business card and photographs to be kept on file. Samples returned only if requested. Reports within 10 days. Write for appointment to show portfolio. Pays for design and for illustration in lump sum. Considers complexity of project, client's budget, skill and experience of artist and how work will be used when establishing payment.

WILLIAM DORSKY ASSOCIATES, 23200 Chagrin Blvd., Cleveland OH 44122. (216)464-8600. Designers: Curt Johnson. Architecture firm. Clients: commercial, residential, institutional.
Needs: Works with artists for architectural renderings, interior design, graphic design, signage design, model making, sculpture, and landscape design. Works on assignment only.
First Contact & Terms: Call for interview to show photos or transparencies. Samples returned by SASE; reports back on future assignment possibilities. Provide resume and brochure to be kept on file.
Tips: "Prepare reproducible examples of work that can be kept on file for ready reference."

***DURRANT GROUP**, One Dubuque Plaza, Dubuque IA 52001. (319)583-9131. Interior Designer: Jane Jewen-Vitale. Architectural firm. Services: architectural, interior design, engineering and construction management. Clients: commercial and some residential.
Needs: Works with 4-5 freelance artists/year. Works on assignment only. Uses artists for interior design. "Currently looking for a weaver for custom work."
First Contact & Terms: Send query letter with brochure showing art style. Samples not filed are returned only if requested. Reports only if interested. Call to show a portfolio, which should include original/final art and photographs. Negotiates payment. Considers client's budget when establishing payment.
Tips: Artist should "be organized and efficient."

THE EGGERS GROUP, P.C., 2 Park Ave., New York NY 10016. (212)725-2100. Director of Interior Design: Robert H. Welz, A.I.A. Architectural/interior design firm providing full architectural and interior design services. Clients: institutional, corporate, residential, academic.
Needs: Works with 10 freelance artists/year. Works on assignment only. Uses artists for interior and architectural renderings, and model making.
First Contact & Terms: Send query letter with resume and samples to be kept on file. Reports only if interested. Call or write for appointment to show portfolio. Prefers that artists show portfolio in person. Pay is negotiable. Considers client's budget, and skill and experience of artist when establishing payment.

***EHNI ASSOCIATES, LTD., ARCHITECTS & INTERIOR DESIGNERS**, 16 Charlotte St., Charleston SC 29403. (803)577-0410. Architectural/interior design firm providing complete services.
Needs: Works with 6-8 freelance artists/year. Works on assignment only. Uses artists for brochure illustration, interior and architectural renderings, design consulting, model making and photography.
First Contact & Terms: Send query letter with brochure, resume, photographs and tear sheets to be kept on file. Reports back to artist. Call or write for appointment to show portfolio. Pay varies according to artistic talents and project needs. Considers complexity of project, client's budget, skill and experience of artist, how work will be used, turnaround time and rights purchased when establishing payment.

FALICK/KLEIN PARTNERSHIP, INC., Suite 1900, 5847 San Felipe, Houston TX 77057-3005. (713)782-9000. Contact: David G. Puckett. Architectural/interior design firm providing full services. Clients: institutional (hospitals), developers, governmental, financial, professional office buildings.
Needs: Works with 10-30 freelance artists/year. "Experienced, innovative" artists only. Uses artists for advertising illustration and layout, brochure design; interior, landscape and architectural renderings and model making.
First Contact & Terms: Send query letter with brochure to be kept on file. Reports only if interested. Write for appointment to show portfolio.

FEICK ASSOCIATES, 224 E. Water St., Sandusky OH 44870. (419)625-2554. Architect: John A. Feick. Architectural firm providing complete architectural services. Clients: residential, commercial and industrial.
Needs: Works with 1 freelance artist/year. Works on assignment only. Uses artists for architectural renderings.
First Contact & Terms: Send query letter with brochure showing art style. Reports only if interested. Call to schedule an appointment to show a portfolio, which should include thumbnails, roughs and original/final art. Pays for design and illustration by the project, $200 minimum. Considers complexity of project and client's budget when establishing payment.
Tips: "Be brief and concise in contact."

FEREBEE, WALTERS AND ASSOCIATES, Box 2029, Charlotte NC 28211. (704)542-5586. Architectural/planning/interior and landscape design firm providing complete environmental design and planning services. Clients: residential, commercial, industrial, institutional.
Needs: Works with 2-3 freelance artists/year. Uses artists for advertising design and layout, brochure design, and interior and architectural renderings.
First Contact & Terms: Send query letter with brochure, resume and tear sheets; also send samples and business cards. Prefers to see samples that are best illustration of talent. Samples not returned. Does not report back. Considers complexity of project, client's budget, skill and experience of artist, how work will be used, turnaround time and rights purchased when establishing payment.

ROBERT P. GERSIN ASSOCIATES, 11 E. 22nd St., New York NY 10010. President: Robert P. Gersin. Industrial design firm providing interiors, architecture, graphics, packaging, products and exhibits.
Needs: Works with freelance designers/technicians for implementation assistance to permanent staff on various projects.
First Contact & Terms: Send query letter with resume, tear sheets, photostats, slides or photographs. Prefers slides as samples. Samples returned by SASE. Reports in 2-3 weeks. To show portfolio, mail thumbnails, roughs, final reproduction/ product, photographs or b&w. Negotiates payment. Considers client's budget, skill and experience of designer/technician and how work will be used when establishing payment.
Tips: "Be professional and pay attention to details. Develop skills and interest in professional work instead of focusing on money and short-term commitments."

GHOTING ASSOCIATES, (formerly Vinod M. Ghoting), 8501 Potomac Ave., College Park MD 20740. (301)474-3719. Contact: Vinod M. Ghoting, AIA. Architectural/interior design/urban design firm providing complete architectural, urban design and interior design services, from schematic design through construction documents and management. Clients: residential, institutional, medical, commercial and industrial.
Needs: Works with 1 freelance artist/year. Local artists only at this time. Works on assignment only. Uses artists for interior design and renderings.
First Contact & Terms: Send query letter with photographs and photostats to be kept on file. Reports within 15 days. To show a portfolio, mail appropriate materials, which should include photostats. Pays for design by the hour, $12-20; pays for illustration by the project, $250-500. Considers clients budget, complexity of project, skill and experience of artist when establishing payment.

***GIFFELS ASSOCIATES INC.**, 25200 Telegraph, Southfield MI 48086-5025. Administrator: D. Lewis-Thompson. Architectural firm providing architecture and engineering. Clients: residential, industrial, institutional and commercial.
Needs: Works with 3-4 freelance artists/year. Local artists only, 5 years' experience. Works on assignment only. Uses artists for advertising and brochure design and layout.
First Contact & Terms: Send query letter with brochure showing art style. Samples not filed are returned by SASE. Reports only if interested. To show a portfolio, write to schedule an appointment. Pays by the project. Considers complexity of project, skill and experience of artist, and turnaround time when establishing payment.

GREEN & ASSOCIATES, Suite C-26, 105 S. Alfred, Alexandria VA 22314. (703)548-7010. Contact: James F. Green. Interior design firm providing residential and contract interior design and space planning plus custom furniture design. Clients: residential, corporate offices and retail design.
Needs: Number of freelance artists used/year varies. Prefers local artists; "sometimes we require on-site inspections." Works on assignment only. Uses artists for interior design and interior and architectural renderings.
First Contact & Terms: Send query letter with brochure, resume and photostats or photographs, color preferred, to be kept on file. Reports only if interested. Pays for design and illustration by the project, $250 minimum. "Persons we work with must be able to make themselves available to our clients and staff. We will appreciate good art without regard to reputation of artist, etc." Considers complexity of project, client's budget and skill and experience of artist when establishing payment.

***GRESHAM, SMITH AND PARTNERS**, 504-A Brookwood Blvd, Birmingham AL 35209. (205)870-4455. Interior Architecture Administrative: Angela A. Lackey. Architectural/interior/landscape/engineering firm for corporate, commercial, healthcare and government clients.
Needs: Works with a various number of freelance artists/year. Works on assignment only. Uses artists for interior design.
First Contact & Terms: Send query letter with brochure showing art style or resume, tear sheets and photographs. Samples not filed are returned by SASE only if requested by artist. Reports back only if in-

terested. To show a portfolio, mail appropriate materials that are representative. Pays for design and illustration by the project. Considers client's budget, skill and experience of artist, how work will be used and price of artwork when establishing payment.

H.K.S. & PARTNERS, 1111 Plaza of Americas, Dallas TX 75201. (214)969-5599. President: Ron Brame. Architecture/interior design also providing artworks for architectures and interiors. Clients: corporate, commercial, institutional, residential, industrial and health care.
Needs: Works with 20-30 freelance artists/year. Uses artists for advertising and brochure design, brochure layout, interior design and renderings, architectural renderings, design consulting and model making.
First Contact & Terms: Send query letter with brochure and slides, tear sheets, photographs or original work to be kept on file. Samples not kept on file returned by SASE only if requested. Reports only if interested. Call or write for appointment to show portfolio. Pays for design and illustration by the project. Considers skill and experience of artist and turnaround time when establishing payment.

JOHN D. HAINES, ARCHITECTS AND PLANNERS, INC., Route 7, Manchester VT 05254-0403. (802)362-3776. Contact: Marian Louise. Architectural firm providing total design/planning services. Clients: commercial, governmental, residential, educational, cultural.
Needs: Works with 5-6 freelance artists/year. Works on assignment only. Uses artists for brochure illustration, landscape design and renderings, architectural renderings, furnishings and model making. Especially needs artists for renderings.
First Contact & Terms: Send resume and business card to be kept on file. Reports back only if interested. Considers complexity of the project, skill and experience of artist and turnaround time when establishing payment.

***HANSEN LIND MEYER**, 455 S. Orange Ave., Orlando FL 32801. (305)422-7061. Director of Design: Charles W. Cole, Jr. Architectural/interior design firm providing complete architecture and engineering services. Clients: commercial, healthcare, justice and government.
Needs: Works with 6 freelance artists/year. Works on assignment only. Uses artists for interior, landscape and architectural renderings, maps and model making.
First Contact & Terms: Send query letter with resume and samples. Samples not filed are returned only if requested. Reports only if interested. To show a portfolio, mail thumbnails, final reproduction/product, color and photographs. Pays for illustrations by the project, $400-3,500. Considers complexity of project, client's budget, skill and experience of artist, and turnaround time when establishing payment.

HUNTER/MILLER & ASSOCIATES, 225 N. Fairfax St., Alexandria VA 22314. (703)548-0600. President: Jeffrey Miller. Architectural/interior design/landscape design firm offering comprehensive services. Clients: commercial, institutional, government.
Needs: Works with 1-2 freelance artists/year. "Experienced, quality artists" only. Works on assignment only. Uses artists for brochure design, illustration and layout; interior design and renderings; architectural renderings, design consulting, furnishings, charts, maps and model making.
First Contact & Terms: Send query letter with brochure, resume, business card and samples to be kept on file. Reports back only if interested. Call or write to schedule an appointment to show a portfolio, which should include original/final art. Pays for design and illustration by the hour, $5-25. Considers skill and experience of artist and client's budget when establishing payment.

IDENTITA INCORPORATED, Suite 515, 1000 N. Ahsley Dr., Tampa FL 33602. (813)221-3326. Interior and graphic design firm providing consultative services to health care facilities. Clients: institutional, hospitals, courthouses and parking garages.
Needs: Works with 3 freelance artists/year. Works on assignment only. Uses artists for architectural renderings, interior and graphic design and signage.
First Contact & Terms: Send query letter. Samples returned. Reports within 2 weeks. Payment varies according to job.

THE IMAGE GROUP, 398 S. Grant Ave., Columbus OH 43215. (614)221-1016. Contact: Richard Henry Eiselt. Architecture/interior design firm. Clients: commercial.
Needs: Uses artists for restaurant design, architectural and full-color renderings, graphic and interior design, paintings, sculpture, signs and wall art.
First Contact & Terms: Mail photos or transparencies. Pay varies according to client's budget, and skill and experience of artist.

***INTERACTIVE RESOURCES, INC.**, 117 Park Place, Pt. Richmond CA 94801. (415)7435. Marketing Director: Julia Ellegood. Architecture/interior design/investigation of Construction Defects. Clients: corporations, municipal governments, attorneys and lenders.
Needs: Works with 1-3 freelance artists/year. Uses artists for architectural renderings.

Close-up

Charles W. Cole
Design Director
Hansen Lind Meyer
Orlando, Florida

Since clients are anxious to see what their buildings will look like, the architectural firm Hansen Lind Meyer commissions renderings "for virtually every job we do," according to Charles W. Cole Jr., design director for the firm's Orlando, Florida, office.

Founded in 1961, Hansen Lind Meyer specializes in governmental, judicial, commercial, and healthcare structures. From its Iowa City, Iowa, base, the firm has expanded to Chicago and Orlando, and as business has grown, so has the need for freelance renderings.

Renderings range from pen-and-ink line drawings to sophisticated airbrush paintings, he says. The stylistic complexity of a rendering is determined by the type of building and the reproduction plans for the final work, explains Cole; if a client wants to advertise a simple brick structure in the newspaper, for instance, then a pen and ink drawing would suffice. However, if the rendering is going to be reproduced in a glossy, four-color brochure, then airbrush might be preferrable.

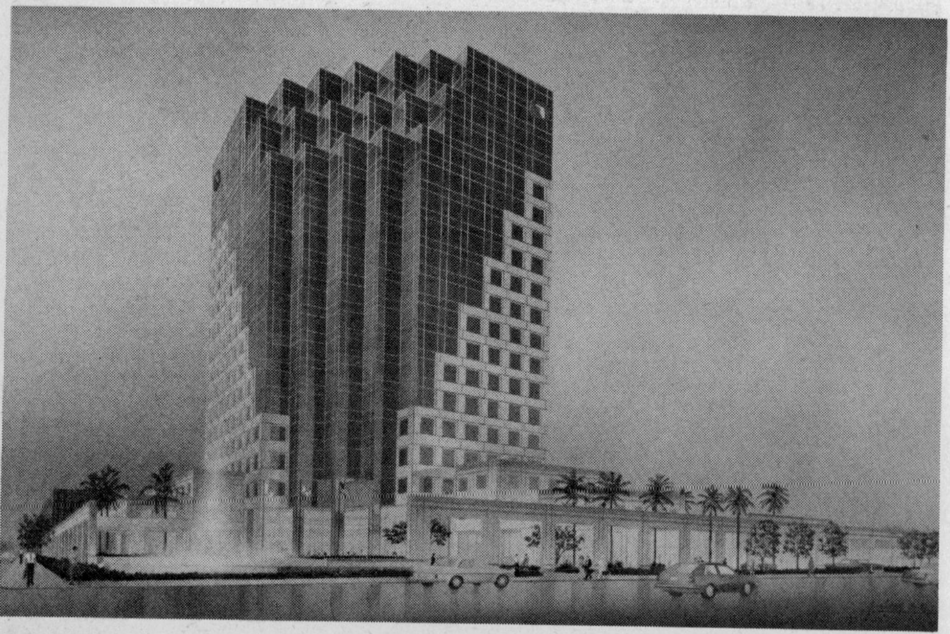

James Smith of Chicago, Illinois, wanted to convey a "surreal presence of architecture" in this rendering. The ink and pencil drawing was used by Hansen Lind Meyer as a client presentation. Smith includes this piece in his portfolio to demonstrate his sense of proportion, use of accurate detail and draftsmanship.

"Airbrush is becoming very 'in' for architectural rendering," says Cole, "because it can replicate the look of slick building materials, like marble or reflective glass. While more traditional techniques still have their place in the depiction of earthy or natural substances, airbrush is better suited to building materials architects favor today."

Cole, as do other art directors, likes freelance artists to send photographs of their work that he can keep on file. When he needs a rendering done in a certain style, he'll search this file for an appropriate artist. Turnaround time for a rendering is generally four to six weeks, during which time the artist will do one or two rough sketches that Cole approves before the final version is undertaken. Payment varies, depending upon stylistic complexity, anywhere from $400 for a pen and ink drawing to $3,500 for an airbrush painting, he says.

Most architectural renderings are the work of teams, says Cole, since few artists are skilled at both perspective and painting. "In my experience, the person who does the detailed layout sketch usually isn't the same person who does the final rendering," he says. "It seems to be a communal process."·

Successful architectural renderers know their work is "really a sales tool, not an end in itself," says Cole. When they develop a rendering, these artists think of the client's business needs, keeping in mind their work may be used to persuade a board of directors to support a project or to entice potential lessors, he explains.

Under these circumstances orange skies and purple streets won't do, says Cole. "The best renderings strike a balance between artistic statement and client needs."

—Bebe Raupe

First Contact & Terms: Send query letter with resume and samples. Samples not filed are returned only if requested. Call to schedule an appointment to show a portfolio. Considers complexity of project, client's budget and skill and experience of artist when establishing payment.
Tips: "Be direct to our needs and show me only examples of your renderings that relate to our types of projects."

***JAMES ARCHITECTS & ENGINEERS, INC.**, Box 55809, 2828 E. 45th St., Indianapolis IN 46205. (317)547-9441. Visual Arts Coordinator: Theresa Thompson. Architectural/interior design firm providing architectural, engineering, interior design, planning design and construction administration. Clients: government, corporate, institutional, criminal justice, commercial and industrial.
Needs: Works with 3-4 freelance artists/year. "Some projects/clients would prefer local artists." Works on assignment only. Uses artists for advertising design, brochure design and illustration, architectural renderings and photographs. Especially needs enivornmental sculputre and mobiles.
First Contact & Terms: Send query letter with brochure showing art style or resume, tear sheets, photostats, slides and photographs. Samples not filed returned only if requested. Reports only if interested. Call to schedule an appointment to show a portfolio, which should include roughs, final reproduction/product, color and photographs. Pays for design by the hour, $15-70. Pays for illustration by the hour, $15-70. Considers complexity of project, client's budget, skill and experience of artist, and turnaround time when establishing payment.

BEN H. JOHNSON & ASSOCIATES, Suite 123, Executive Plaza, 12835 Bellevue-Redmond Rd., Bellevue WA 98005. (206)455-5502. Principal: Ben H. Johnson, A.I.A. Architectural/interior design firm providing architecture, planning and interior design. Clients: single family and multi-family residential, retail, offices, churches, libraries; yacht and corporate aircraft interiors.
Needs: Works with 6 freelance artists/year. Artists must exhibit "a willingness to meet time and/or cost deadline (or not accept the commission)." Works on assignment only. Uses artists for brochure illustration, interior and architectural renderings, landscape design and model making.
First Contact & Terms: Send query letter with resume, business card, photostats, slides, photographs, photocopies or tear sheets. Reports within 1 week. Call for appointment to show portfolio. Pays by the hour, $8-22 average for design, $6-18 average for illustration. Considers complexity of the project, client's budget, skill and experience of artist, and rights purchased when establishing payment.

Tips: "There is a tremendous hesitancy to use artistic graphics except in the largest projects. It is only after a design and contract drawings are nearly complete that graphic art is required for sales and/or publicity presentations."

LAWRENCE KASSER ASSOCIATES, ARCHITECTS AND PLANNERS, Box 495, Bellows Falls VT 05101. (802)463-9576. President: Lawrence Kasser. Architectural/interior design/landscape design firm providing design, construction documents and promotional material. Clients: commercial, residential, institutional, developers.
Needs: Works with 3 freelance artists/year. Uses artists for brochure design, illustration and layout; interior and landscape design and renderings; architectural renderings, design consulting, furnishings, architectural photography, promotional film productions, and model making.
First Contact & Terms: New England area artists only, with 3 years' experience. Works on assignment basis. Send query letter with brochure and samples to be kept on file; write for appointment to show portfolio. Prefers slides as samples. Reports within 3 weeks. Pays for design and illustration by the hour. Considers client's budget when establishing payment.

ARLAN KAY & ASSOCIATES, 110 King St., Madison WI 53703. (608)251-7515. Architect: Arlan Kay. Architectural firm offering architecture and construction management. Clients: commercial, residential, and institutional with 70% of work in recycling/restoration of existing buildings.
Needs: Works with 1-2 freelance artists/year. Prefers local artists. Works on assignment only. Uses artists for brochure design and architectural renderings.
First Contact & Terms: Send query letter with brochure to be kept on file. Reports only if interested. Pays for illustration by the hour, $7-25 average; by the project, $100-500 average; or by the day, $50-150 average. Considers complexity of project, client's budget, and skill and experience of artist when establishing payment.

GEROLD F. KESSLER & ASSOCIATES INC., 2101 S. Clermont, Denver CO 80222. (303)756-1536. Contact: Gerold Kessler. Landscape/architecture/project planning firm providing consulting services as project planners/land planners/landscape designers. Clients: residential and industrial.
Needs: Works with 1 artist for architectural renderings; 1, graphic design; 1, model making; and 1, landscape design. Local artists only. Works on assignment only. Also uses artists for site plans and subdivision development layout.
First Contact & Terms: Send query letter with resumes. Reports within 1 week. Call or write to schedule an appointment to show a portfolio, which should include photostats and photographs. Samples returned by SASE. Pays $500-700, landscape and general site renderings; $600-1,000, subdivision land plan; $20-50/hour for design and illustration.

KIRKHAM, MICHAEL AND ASSOCIATES, 9110 W. Dodge Rd., Omaha NE 68114. (402)393-5630. Architectural designer: David Scott Nordstrom. Full service architecture, interior design, landscape design, engineering and planning firm. Clients: commercial, industrial, institutional, governmental, healthcare, housing.
Needs: Works with 5 freelance artists/year. Works on assignment only. Uses artists for advertising and brochure design, illustration and layout; landscape design, architectural renderings and design consulting.
First Contact & Terms: Send query letter with brochure, business card and photos and slides to be kept on file. Reports only if interested. Write for appointment to show portfolio. Pays according to variable contracts. Considers complexity of project, client's budget, skill and experience of artist, how work will be used, turnaround time and rights purchased when establishing payment.

KNAPP ASSOCIATES LTD., ARCHITECT-MARKET ANALYST, 2801 Fish Hatchery Rd., Madison WI 53713. (608)271-0140. President: E. John Knapp AIA. Architectural and market analysis firm providing full service architectural services, market analysis and demographic studies for site locations, nationwide. Clients: professional, retail.
Needs: Works with 3 freelance artists/year. Works on assignment only. Uses artists for architectural renderings, design consulting and model making.
First Contact & Terms: Send query letter with brochure and resume to be kept on file. Reports only if interested. Pay is negotiated by the project. Considers client's budget, and skill and experience of artist when establishing payment.

FRANCES KOO & ASSOCIATES, INC., Suite 105, 601 University Ave., Sacramento CA 95825. (916)924-1375. Chief Architect: Francis Koo. Clients: commercial, industrial, military, institutional and residential.
Needs: Assigns 20 jobs/year. Works on assignment only. Works with 3 artists for architectural render-

ings; 3, interior design; 1, graphic design; 1, advertising art; 2, signage design; 2, model making; 2, murals; 1, wall hangings; 2, landscape design; and 1, charts/graphs.
First Contact & Terms: Send query letter with resume, business card and brochure to be kept on file. SASE. Reports in 1 week. Samples returned by SASE; reports back on future assignment possibilities. To show a portfolio, mail appropriate materials or write to schedule an appointment; portfolio should include anything that indicates quality. Maximum payment: $1,600, architectural renderings; $1,500, art renderings; $3,000, graphic design; $15,000, scale models; $5,000, signs; $250,000, murals and sculpture. Pays minimum $500. Negotiates payment for paintings and wall art. Considers complexity of project, skill and experience of artist and turnaround time when establishing payment.
Tips: "We like to have a name list in different type of service artists provide, then we can contact them when we need that kind of service."

KRESSCOX ASSOCIATES, P.C., 2909 M St. NW, Washington DC 20007. Contact: Jerrily Kress. Clients: commercial and governmental.
Needs: Works with artists for architectural renderings, graphic design, signage design, model making, wall hangings, sculpture and landscape design. Works on assignment only.
First Contact & Terms: Query with resume or arrange interview. Reports in 1 week. Samples returned by SASE. Reports back on future assignment possibilities. Provide resume, brochure or flyer to be kept on file. Pays by job.

***KZF, INC.**, 111 Merchant St., Cincinnati OH 45246. (513)772-1117. Graphics Specialist: Cari C. Branden or Principle/Architectural Design: Robert W. Doran, A.I.A. Architectural/Interior Design/Engineering firm. Clients: commercial and industrial.
Needs: Works with 2-3 freelance artists/year. Local artists only. Works on assignment only. Uses artists for interior and architectural renderings, and model making.
First Contact & Terms: Send query letter with brochure showing art style or resume, tear sheets and photographs. Samples not filed are returned by SASE. Reports only if interested. To show a portfolio, mail roughs, original/final art and final reproduction/product. Considers complexity of project, client's budget, skill and experience of artist, how work will be used, turnaround time and rights purchased when establishing payment.
Tips: Artist should send "solid, consistent professional examples."

LABUNSKI ASSOCIATES ARCHITECTS, 115 W. Van Buren, Harlingen TX 78550. (512)428-4334. President: R.A. Labunski. Architectural firm providing architecture, construction, design, space planning, interiors, advertising. Clients: commercial, retail, residential, corporate, banks, hotel/motel/restaurant.
Needs: Works with 5 freelance artists/year. Works on assignment only. Uses artists for advertising design, illustration and layout; brochure design, interior and architectural renderings, design consulting, furnishings and model making.
First Contact & Terms: Desires "affordable, practical" artists with referrals/references. Send query letter with brochure, resume and business cards to be kept on file; also send samples. Samples returned by SASE. Reports within 2 weeks. Call or write for appointment to show portfolio. Pays by the project. Considers complexity of project, client's budget, and skill and experience of artist when establishing payment.

JOSEPH LADD & ASSOCIATES, P.C., 2405 Westwood Ave., Richmond VA 23230. (804)355-0849. President: Joseph N. Ladd, AIA, CCS. Architectural firm providing architecture, interior design and space planning. Clients: private sector; federal, state and local governments.
Needs: Works with 1 freelance artist/year. Artist must have work experience. Works on assignment only. Uses artists for architectural renderings, interior, landscape and graphic design, furnishings, design consulting, model making and signage.
First Contact & Terms: Send brochure/flyer, business card and resume to be kept on file. Reports in 1 week. Payment varies according to the job.
Tips: Artists "must maintain quality workmanship."

LANDOW AND LANDOW ARCHITECTS, PC, 3000 Marcus Ave., Lake Success NY 11042. (516)326-1111. President, AIA: Lloyd J. Landow. Architectural/interior design firm providing complete architectural, space planning and interior design services. Clients: corporate and institutional.
Needs: Uses artists for architectural renderings and model making. Also commissions for buildings.
First Contact & Terms: Send query letter with brochure, resume, business card, photostats, photographs and tear sheets to be kept on file. Samples returned by SASE if not kept on file. Reports only if interested. Considers complexity of project, client's budget, skill and experience of artist and turnaround time when establishing payment.

ERNEST LUTHER LANE, AIA, 2635 Noble Rd., Cleveland Heights OH 44121. (216)381-7701. Contact: Ernest Luther Lane. Architectural/construction management firm.
Needs: Currently works with 0 freelance artists. Works on assignment basis only. Uses artists for architectural renderings.
First Contact & Terms: Send query letter with brochure to be kept on file. Reports within 4 weeks. Negotiates pay per service. Considers client's budget; "prefer owner to select artist."

LANE & ASSOCIATES, ARCHITECTS, 1318 N. "B", Box 3929, Fort Smith AR 72913. (501)782-4277. Contact: John E. Lane, AIA-ASID. Architectural and interior design firm providing architecture and interiors for remodeling and new construction; also art consultant. Clients: residential, multi-family, commercial and industrial.
Needs: Works with 10-12 freelance artists/year. Uses artists occasionally for architectural renderings, charts, graphic design and advertising illustration; selects or commissions art pieces for clients; paintings, drawings, sculpture, photographs, macrame, tapestry (all mediums). Arranges art exhibits for large local bank—"would like sources of talent for various mediums, painting, sculptures, photography, drawings, etc."
First Contact & Terms: Prefers to be able to meet in person with artist. Send query letter with resume, business card, tear sheets, slides or photos of work and brochure to be kept on file. Samples returned by SASE, but "would prefer to retain." Write to schedule an appointment to show a portfolio. Payment varies. Considers complexity of project, client's budget, skill and experience of artist, how work will be used, turnaround time and rights purchased when establishing payment.

LOUISVILLE ART GLASS STUDIO, 1110 Baxter Ave., Louisville KY 40204. (502)585-5421. Specializes in art glass and design fabrication. President: Gary D. Meeker. Clients: commercial, residential, churches and related liturgical.
Needs: Works with 2 artists for interior design; 3, graphic design; 2, sculpture; and 4, stained glass. Also uses artists for leaded glass design. Prefers artists with previous glass experience. Works on assignment only.
First Contact & Terms: Query with resume and samples to be kept on file. Reports within 4 weeks. Samples not filed returned by SASE. Prefers slides or photos as samples. Pays by the job, based on square footage and size of work; or by the hour.
Tips: There are "more good freelance artists availiable now than at any other time but not enough good, qualified craftsmen to execute the work." Artists approaching this firm should have "confidence that our execution will be of the very best quality and the newest techniques."

MAHER & ASSOC. ARCHITECTS SC., 810 N. Plankinton Ave., Milwaukee WI 53203. (414)276-0811. President: J. Thomas Maher A.I.A. Architectural firm providing total architectural and interior design. Clients: industrial, commercial, hotel and medical.
Needs: Works with several freelance artists/year. Works on assignment only. Uses artists for interior and landscape design, interior and architectural renderings, design consulting, furnishings and model making.
First Contact & Terms: Send query letter with brochure showing art style or resume, photostats, photocopies, slides and photographs that can be retained. Samples not filed are returned only if requested. Reports back within 5 days. To show a portfolio, mail photographs and b&w. Pays by the project. Considers design, skill and experience of artist, complexity of project, how work will be used and turnaround time when establishing payment.
Tips: "We use greater freelance artists because we are doing a great deal more work. Contact us immediately."

MANIKTALA ASSOCIATES, P.C., 100 Metropolitan Dr., Box 4753, Syracuse NY 13221. (315)457-1210. Managing Architect: Alan D. Nock. Architectural and engineering firm providing architectural, structural, civil, electrical, mechanical, geotechnical engineering disciplines; construction inspection, interior design, construction cost estimating. Clients: industrial, commercial, municipal, governmental, private.
Needs: Works with 4 freelance artists/year. Uses artists for advertising and brochure design and illustration, and brochure layout.
First Contact & Terms: Send query letter with brochure and business card to be kept on file. Reports within 2-3 weeks. Works on assignment only. Pays by the project. Considers complexity of project, client's budget, skill and experience of artist, how work will be used, turnaround time and rights purchased when establishing payment.

MARTIN & DETHOFF REGISTERED ARCHITECTS, 422 Franklin St., Reading PA 19602. Contact: Robert S. Martin. Architectural/interior design firm providing architectural, engineering and interior design. Clients: commercial.

Needs: Works with 4 freelance artists/year. Works on assignment only. Uses artists for architectural renderings and furnishings.
First Contact & Terms: Send query letter with resume to be kept on file. Reports back only if interested. Pays by the project, $250 minimum. Considers complexity and size of project when establishing payment.

THE MATHES GROUP, 201 St. Charles Ave., 23rd Floor, New Orleans LA 70170. (504)586-9303. President: Edward C. Mathes. Architectural/interior design/landscape design firm providing all services associated with architecture, landscape architecture and interior design. Clients: commercial (90%) and residential (10%).
Needs: Works with 10 freelance artists/year. Works on assignment only. Uses artists for interior design, architectural renderings, design consulting, furnishings, model making and as sources for artwork.
First Contact & Terms: Send query letter with brochure, resume, samples and tear sheets to be kept on file unless unsuitable. Prefers slides, photographs, clear photocopies as samples. Samples not kept on file returned only if requested. Reports only if interested. Write for appointment to show portfolio. Pays by the project for design and illustration. Considers complexity of project, client's budget, and skill and experience of artist when establishing payment.

MESSINA ARCHITECTURAL GROUP, (formerly Messina Associates-Architect), Box 1125, San Carlos CA 94070. (415)364-6405. Contact: Frank Jon Messina. Architecture/interior design firm. Clients: industrial, residential and commercial. Assigns 10-12 jobs/year.
Needs: Works with 1 artist for architectural renderings; 5, interior design; 1, mural; 1, wall hangings; and 10, landscape design. Works on assignment only.
First Contact & Terms: Query with samples. Reports within 1 week. Samples returned by SASE. Reports back on future assignment possibilities. Provide business card and flyer to be kept on file for future assignments. Pays $400 minimum/job.

METCALF HAEFNER ARCHITECTS, 1052 Main St., Stevens Point WI 54481. (715)344-7205. Partner: Michael Metcalf. Achitectural firm providing building design, planning, energy design, interior design and rendering. Clients: residential, commercial, industrial, medical and religious.
Needs: Works with 3 freelance artists/year. Uses artists for advertising, interior and landscape design; landscape and architectural renderings, furnishings and model making.
First Contact & Terms: Send brochure, resume, business card and samples to be kept on file. Call or write for appointment to show portfolio. Pays by the project. Considers complexity of the project, client's budget, and skill and experience of artist when establishing payment.
Tips: "We occasionally enter national competitions in partnership with artists of our choosing."

***MEYER SCHERER AND ROCKCASTLE, LTD.**, 325 Second Ave. N., Minneapolis MN 55401. Principal: Garth Rockcastle. Architecture/interior and landscape design firm providing design, document preparation and construction supervision. Clients: residential, commercial, institutional and industrial.
Needs: Works with 5-6 freelance artists/year. Works on assignment only. Uses artists for advertising, interior and landscape design; brochure design and layout, design consulting. "We occasionally enter national competitions in partnership with artists of our choosing without reimbursement to the artist unless we are winners. Contact for details. We also collaborate with artists on special projects such as for stained glass or for building furniture."
First Contact & Terms: Send query letter with resume and slides. Samples not filed are returned by SASE. Reports only if interested. Write to schedule an appointment to show a portfolio, which should include roughs, original/final art and color. Pays for design by the hour, $15 minimum. Considers complexity of project, client's budget, skill and experience of artist, how work will be used, turnaround time and rights purchased when establishing payment.

MITCHELL & JENSEN, AIA, ARCHITECT & ENGINEER, 4247 Philadelphia Dr., Dayton OH 45405. (513)277-9338. Architect: Stan Mitchell. Architectural firm providing architectural engineering, landscape, planning, interiors and energy management design.
Needs: Works with 1-4 freelance artists/year. Uses artists for interior and architectural renderings, design consulting and furnishings.
First Contact & Terms: Send query letter to be kept on file. Prefers quality slides as samples. Samples returned only if requested. Reports back only if requested. Call for appointment to show portfolio. Pays for design by the hour, project or day; for illustration by the project, $250-1,000 average. Considers complexity of project, client's budget, skill and experience of artist and how work will be used when establishing payment.

***NICHOLS CARTER GRANT ARCHITECTS INC.**, 1784 Peachtree St. NW, Atlanta GA 30309. Partner: Alex Carter. Architectural/landscape design and planning firm providing full design services for the

construction of various building types. Clients: residential, commercial and institutional.
Needs: Works with 2 freelance artists/year. Prefers local artists. Works on assignment only. Uses artists for architectural renderings and model making. Artist "must have preliminary submittal for review."
First Contact & Terms: Send query letter with resume, slides and photographs. Samples not filed are returned accompanied by SASE. Reports only if interested. To show a portfolio, mail color and photographs. Pays for design by the hour, $50-70. Pays for illustrations by the project, $500-5,000. Considers complexity of project, client's budget and how work will be used when establishing payment.
Tips: "Must produce quality work and respond to schedule."

CHARLES E. NOLAN JR & ASSOCIATES, Box 1788, Alamogordo NM 88310. (505)437-1405. President: Charles E. Nolan Jr. Architectural firm providing architectural design, interior design, feasibility studies and master planning. Clients: commercial, institutional, educational, government.
Needs: Works with 2-3 freelance artists/year. Uses artists for architectural renderings, furnishings, murals and sculpture in building design.
First Contact & Terms: Send query letter with brochure, slides and photos (color or b&w) to be kept on file. Samples returned if not kept on file. Reports within 14 days. Pays for design by the hour, $10-40 average; by the day, $100-300 average. Pays for illustration by the hour, $10-15 average. Considers complexity of project, skill and experience of artist and how work will be used when establishing payment.

***NORTHEN AND DURHAM, INC.**, 4740 Alicia Dr., Virginia Beach VA 23462. (804)499-7018. President: Oscar Northen, Jr. Architectrual firm providing all architectural services. Clients: commercial, residential, institutional, govermental.
Needs: Works with 1 freelance artist/year. Prefers local artists. Works on assignment only. Uses artists for brochure and interior design and architectural renderings.
First Contact & Terms: Send brochure and business card to be kept on file. Reports only if interested. Pays for design and illustration by the hour, $25-50 average. Considers client's budget, skill and experience of artist and how work will be used when establishing payment.

THE OSBORNE ASSOCIATES, 161 W. Wisconsin Ave., Milwaukee WI 53203. (414)271-0123. Principal: Edward Osborne. Architectural firm offering full architectural and engineering services for any type of project. Clients: residential developers, commercial and cemetery owners (mausoleums).
Needs: Works with freelance artists 6 times/year. Works on assignment only. Uses artists for landscape design and architectural renderings.
First Contact & Terms: Send query letter with brochure and resume to be kept on file. Call for appointment to show portfolio. Accepts any type of samples. Samples not filed are returned. Reports within 10 days. Pays for illustration by the project, $300-700 average. Considers complexity of the project, and skill and experience of artist when establishing payment.
Tips: Especially looks for "accuracy, life-like quality and detail" in samples or portfolio.

***OSSIPOFF, SYNDER & ROWLAND (ARCHITECTS) INC.**, 1210 Ward Ave., Honolulu HI 96814. President: Sidney E. Snyder, Jr., AIA. Architectural/interior design firm of residents of commercial (offices), residential, and institutional buildings.
Needs: Works with 5-10 freelance artists/year. Artist should be in Hawaii for this contact. Works on assignment only. Uses artists for interior design, architectural renderings, furnishings, model making and fine arts in building projects.
First Contact & Terms: Send query letter with brochure showing art style. Reports back. Write to schedule an appointment to show a portfolio. Payment determined by job.
Tips: Interested in high quality.

PDT & COMPANY ARCHITECTS/PLANNERS, 7434 Montgomery Rd., Cincinnati OH 45236. (513)891-4605. Contact: Ray Gephart.
Needs: Works with 2 artists for architectural renderings; 5, interior design; 1, model making; and 3, landscape design. Uses artists for architectural renderings. Works on assignment only.
First Contact & Terms: Mail samples (examples of finished work). Samples returned by SASE; reports back on future possibilities. Provide business card and brochure to be kept on file. Pays by job.

QUINN ASSOCIATES INC. - ARCHITECTS AIA, 114 W. Main St., New Britain CT 06051. (203)678-1319. President: Richard W. Quinn AIA. Architectural firm providing architectural design, interior design and planning. Clients: commercial, institutional, residential.
Needs: Works with various numbers of freelance artists/year. Works on assignment only. Uses artists for brochure design, interior and architectural renderings, and furnishings.
First Contact & Terms: Send query letter with brochure, resume and samples to be kept on file. Pre-

fers slides or photographs as samples. Samples returned by SASE only if requested. Reports within 30 days. Call or write for appointment to show portfolio. Payment varies with assignment. Considers complexity of project, client's budget, and skill and experience of artist when establishing payment.

DAVID C. RACKER ASLA & ASSOCIATES, 3120 S. 950 E., Bountiful UT 84010. (801)295-5335. Contact: Dave Racker. Landscape architecture/land planning firm, providing consulting services. Clients: commercial, residential and industrial.
Needs: Assigns 20-30 jobs/year. Works with artists for renderings, graphic design and scale models.
First Contact & Terms: Send a query letter. SASE. Reports in 2 weeks. Pays for illustration by the hour, $5 minimum.

RESEARCH PLANNING ASSOCIATES, 1831 Chestnut St., Philadelphia PA 19103. (215)561-9700. Designer: Susan Klinker. Architectural and interior design firm providing architectural interior design, feasibility studies and architecture. Clients: commercial.
Needs: Works with 4-10 freelance artists/year. Uses artists for architectural renderings, interior, graphic and brochure design; interior and landscape art renderings; furnishings, design consulting, charts, mural artwork, model making and signage.
First Contact & Terms: Send query letter. Samples returned by SASE. Works on assignment only. Provide resume, business card, brochure, flyer, samples and tear sheets to be kept on file for possible future assignments. Negotiates payment. Pays for design and illustration by the hour. Considers complexity of project, client's budget, skill and experience of artist and turnaround time when establishing payment.

***RKT&B (ROTHZEID KAISERMAN THOMSON & BEE, P.C., ARCH & PLANNERS)**, 134 Charles St., New York NY 10014. Partner: Carmi Bee. Architectural firm that designs buildings (new construction, restoration, rehab., medical facilities, retail, housing, offices).
Needs: Works with 3-10 freelance artists/year. Works on assignment only. Uses artists for brochure design and architectural renderings.
First Contact & Terms: Send query letter with brochure showing art style. Samples not filed are returned by SASE. Reports only if interested. To show a portfolio, mail appropriate materials. Payment varies. Considers complexity of project, client's budget, skill and experience of artist, how work will be used, turnaround time and rights purchased when establishing payment.
Tips: "We rarely use people—we are a longshot."

ROBERT AND COMPANY, 96 Poplar St. NW, Atlanta GA 30335. (404)577-4000. Art Director: Julia Farrow. Architecture/engineering/planning firm providing marketing and support graphics for company and clients. Clients: industrial, governmental/municpal, educational, military, medical, multi-residential.
Needs: Works with 5-6 freelance artists/year. Local artists preferred. Uses artists for advertising and brochure illustration; landscape, interior and architectural renderings; charts, maps and model makings; also uses photographers.
First Contact & Terms: Send query letter with resume, samples and tear sheets to be kept on file. Prefers photostats, slides, photographs as samples; original work only necessary for interview. Samples not kept on file returned by SASE only if requested. Reports only if interested. Write for appointment to show portfolio. Pays by the project; requests artist's estimate/bid. Considers complexity of project, skill and experience of artist, and turnaround time when establishing payment.

ROE/ELISEO, INC., 576 5th Ave., New York NY 10036. (212)398-1078. Vice President: Phyllis R. Ghougasian. Architecture/interior design firm providing architectural planning, design, interior design and construction services. Clients: health, commercial, industrial, government.
Needs: Works on assignment only. Uses artists for brochure design, illustration and layout; interior and landscape design; interior, landscape and architectural renderings; model making.
First Contact & Terms: Send query letter with resume, slides, photographs or original work to be kept on file. Samples not kept on file are returned by SASE. Reports only if interested. Pays by the project; rate depends on scope of project, fee, structure, etc. Considers client's budget when establishing payment.

JEAN SEDOR DESIGNS, 305 S. Main St., Janesville, WI 53545. Interior Designer: Jean Sedor. Interior design firm. "We function as interior designers doing everything from finish schedules to supervising and contracting for entire art programs for various installations." Clients: contract, i.e., banks, insurance companies, utilites, etc.
Needs: Works with freelance artists. Works on assignment only. Uses artists for art furnishings.
First Contact & Terms: Send query letter with brochure, resume, business card, slides, photographs,

original work and tear sheets to be kept on file. Samples returned only if requested. Reports only if interested. Call or write for appointment to show portfolio. Pays for design and illustration by the project, $100-12,000 average. Considers client's budget, skill and experience of artist and how work will be used when establishing payment.

RICHARD SEIDEN INTERIORS, 238 N. Allen St., Albany NY 12206. (518)482-8600. President: Richard Seiden. Interior design firm. Provides residential and contract interior design. Clients: residential.
Needs: Works with 4 artists for graphic design; 3, signage design; 2, model making; 3, murals; 4, wall hangings; 3, landscape design; 2, charts/graphs; and 2, stained glass. Works on assignment only.
First Contact & Terms: Send query letter with resume, tear sheets and photostats. SASE. Reports in 3 weeks. Provide materials to be kept on file for future assignments. Pays $150-1,800, original wall decor; also according to project. To show a portfolio, mail roughs. Pays for design by the hour, $25 minimum. Considers complexity of project, skill and experience of artist, and client's budget when establishing payment.
Tips: Prefers to see photos rather than slides, if possible.

SFS INTERIORS, 14 W. Kirk Ave., Roanoke VA 24011. (703)345-5220. Interior Designer: Jeanne Green. Interior design firm providing specifiers, consultants, purchasing agents. Clients: contract commercial (some residential).
Needs: Works with 2-6 freelance artists/year. Uses artists for brochure and landscape design, and interior renderings.
First Contact & Terms: Send query letter with brochure and samples to be kept on file. Prefers slides, photographs as samples. Samples not kept on file are returned only if requested. Reports within 15 days. Works on assignment only. Pays for design by the hour; for illustration by the project. Considers complexity of project and client's budget when establishing payment.

ROGER SHERMAN ASSOCIATES, R.S. INTERIORS, Suite 300, 13530 Michigan Ave., Dearborn MI 48126. (313)582-8844. Contact: Jan Sellers. Interior design and contract purchasing firms providing architectural and interior design for commercial restaurants, stores, hotels and shopping centers and complete furnishing purchasing. Clients: commercial.
Needs: Artists with past work experience only, able to provide photos of work and references. Works on assignment only. Uses artists for architectural renderings, furnishings, landscape and graphic design, model making and signage; also for special decor items as focal points for commercial installations, such as paintings, wood carvings, etc.
First Contact & Terms: Send query letter with brochure/flyer or resume and samples to be kept on file. Prefers slides and examples of original work as samples. Samples not returned. Reporting time depends on scope of project. Call or write for appointment. Negotiates payment; varies according to client's budget.

SIEGEL SKLAREK DIAMOND, AIA, ARCHITECT INC., 10780 Santa Monica Blvd., Los Angeles CA 90025. (213)474-3244. Architecture firm providing planning and limited interior design services. Clients: commercial and residential. Buys 6 renderings/year.
Needs: Works with 3 artists for architectural renderings; 3, graphic design; and 2, landscape design. Local artists only. Works on assignment only.
First Contact & Terms: Query with samples and arrange interview to show portfolio; no calls. Samples returned by SASE; reports back on future assignment possibilities. Work must be reproducible in b&w, i.e. line drawing with color added. Provide resume and business card to be kept on file for future assignments. Pays by the project for design and illustration.

***SINCLAIR ASSOCIATES, INC.**, 15 N. Ellsworth Ave., San Mateo CA 94401. (415)348-6865. Principal Architect: George L. Sinclair. Estab. 1985. Architectural firm providing full architectural design services. Clients: residential, commercial, retail, public and industrial.
Needs: Works with 2-5 freelance artists/year. Works on assignment only. Uses artists for advertising and brochure design and layout; brochure illustration; interior and landscape design, and architectural renderings.
First Contact & Terms: Send query letter with brochure showing art style or resume and photocopies. Samples not filed are not returned. Reports only if interested. Call or write to schedule an appointment to show a portfolio. Considers complexity of project, client's budget, skill and experience of artist, and how work will be used when establishing payment.

***SKIDMORE OWINGS AND MERRILL**, 1 Maritime Plaza, San Francisco CA 94111. Associate Partner: W. Weber. Architectural firm.
Needs: Works with 10 freelance artists/year. Works on assignment only. Uses artists for interior, land-

scape and architectural renderings, maps and model making. Especially needs "high quality work."
First Contact & Terms: Send query letter with brochure showing art style or resume, tear sheets, photostats, photocopies and photographs. Samples not filed are not not returned. Does not report back. To show a portfolio, mail appropriate materials.
Tips: Artist should "show a few excellent examples."

SPACE DESIGN INTERNATIONAL, INC., Suite 445, 309 Vine St., Cincinnati OH 45202. (513)241-3000. Director of Communications: Cecily Hudson. Architectural interior and graphic design firm providing programming, space planning, store planning, interior and graphic design. Clients: corporate, professional, retail, institutional.
Needs: Prefers artists with experience; it helps if artists are nearby. Works on assignment only. Uses freelance artists for architectural and interior design renderings, graphic design and model making.
First Contact & Terms: Send query letter with samples and brochure/flyer or resume to be kept on file. Write for appointment to show a portfolio, which should include original work if reviewed in person; if mailed in, prefers reproductions. Samples returned by SASE. Negotiates payment by the project or by the hour; varies according to client's budget.

GEORGE STATEN & ASSOCIATES INC., ARCHITECTS & PLANNERS, Suite 101, 4849 N. Mesa, El Paso TX 79912. (915)544-7000. Contact: George Staten AIA. Architecture/interior design firm. Clients: residential, institutional, hotel, medical and commercial.
Needs: Works with 3 artists for architectural renderings; 1, interior design; 2, graphic design; 2, signage design; 1, model making; 2, sculpture; 2, landscape design; and 2, stained glass.
First Contact & Terms: Query or write for interview. SASE. Reports in 1 week. Works on assignment only. Provide resume, business card and brochure to be kept on file for future assignments. Pays $200-2,500, architectural renderings; $50-1,000, building interiors; $300-3,000, full-color renderings; $100 minimum, landscape design.

***D.J. STEPHANS, AIA, ARCHITECT**, 3560 Breckenridge Ct. A6, Madison WI 53713. (608)274-9235. Architect: Daniel Stephans. Architectural firm providing full architectural services and construction management. Clients: multi and single family housing, churches and offices.
Needs: Works with 1 freelance artist/year. Works on assignment only. Uses artists for advertising and brochure illustration, and interior, landscape and architectural renderings.
First Contact & Terms: Send query letter with brochure and photographs to be kept on file. Samples not filed are returned. Reports back only if interested. Pays for illustration by the project, $85-600 average. Considers complexity of the project, client's budget, skill and experience of artist, how work will be used and turnaround time when establishing payment.

***ROBERT J. STURTCMAN—ARCHITECT**, Box 2269, Taos NM 87571. (505)758-4933. Owner: R. Sturtcman. Architectural/interior design firm. Clients: residential, schools and office-retail.
Needs: Uses artists for advertising and brochure design; interior and architectural renderings and model making.
First Contact & Terms: Send query letter with brochure showing art style. Samples not filed are returned by SASE. Reports back within 30 days. Write to schedule an appointment to show a portfolio. Pays for design by the hour, $15 minimum. Considers client's budget when establishing payment.

***SUNDBERG, CARLSON AND ASSOCIATES, INC.**, 914 West Baraga Ave., Marquette MI 49855. (906)228-2333. Designer/Illustrator: Mike Lempinen. Architectural/interior design/engineering firm providing architectural design, interior design, graphic design, illustration architectural renderings, and model making. "We have used freelance rendering and model making services on an as needed basis in the past. We are currently testing the market for brochure, advertising and architectural rendering services, and are especially interested in beginning a file on available art services; freelance, art houses, publication firms, etc. Our firm is also interested in obtaining information on the market demand for art services."
First Contact & Terms: Send query letter with brochure showing art style or resume, tear sheets, photostats and printed pieces. Samples not filed are not returned. Reports only if interested. To show a portfolio, mail appropriate materials. Pays for design by the hour, $8-50. Pays for illustration by the hour, $10-50. Considers complexity of project, client's budget, and skill and experience of artist when establishing payment.
Tips: "Please do not send returnable pieces, slides or photos. We can not return unsolicited materials."

SUNDESIGNS ARCHITECTS, 901 Blake Ave., Glenwood Springs CO 81601. Architects: D.K. Moffatt and C.F. Brenner. Architectural/interior and landscape design/land planning firm providing commercial and residential architectural design and land planning of residential P.U.D.'s and resorts. Cli-

ents: bank buildings, office buildings, resorts and housing developers.
Needs: Works with 6 freelance artists/year. Local, experienced and innovative artists only. Uses artists for advertising illustration, brochure and interior design, landscape, interior and architectural renderings.
First Contact & Terms: Send query letter with brochure showing art style to be kept on file. Reports within 1 month. Write to schedule an appointment to show a portfolio, which should include thumbnails, roughs, final reproduction/product, color and photographs. Pays by the hour, $45 minimum; by the project, $500 minimum. Considers complexity of project, client's budget, and skill and experience of artist, how work will be used and turnaround time when establishing payment.

***SWAIN ASSOCIATES, INC.**, 222 Third St., Cambridge MA 02142. (617)661-3773. Associate: Robyn Jones. Architectural/land design firm providing architecture, urban design, land planning, landscaping design, architectural interiors/space planning for residential, commercial and institutional clients.
Needs: Works with 3 freelance artists/year. Uses artists for brochure design, architectural renderings, furnishings and model making.
First Contact & Terms: Send query letter with brochure showing art style or resume and tear sheets, photostats, photocopies, slides, photographs or "whatever best respresents work." Samples not filed are returned only if requested. Reports only if interested or if requested. To show a portfolio, mail appropriate materials or call or write to schedule an appointment; portfolio should include thumbnails, roughs, original/final art, final reproduction/product, color, tear sheets, photostats, photographs, b&w or best appropriate representation work." Payment depends *entirely* on product skills needed."

THE TARQUINI ORGANIZATION, A Professional Association of Architects and Planners, 1812 Federal St., Camden NJ 08105. (609)365-7270. Vice President: Robert Giacomelli AIA. Architectural firm. Clients: commercial, residential, municipal.
Needs: Works with 2 freelance artists/year. Uses artists for advertising, brochure and interior design; architectural renderings and model making.
First Contact & Terms: Send query letter with brochure and business card to be kept on file. Samples returned by SASE if requested by artist. Reports only if interested. To show a portfolio, mail thumbnails. Works on assignment only. Pays per job basis. Considers client's budget and how work will be used when establishing payment.

THOMAS-CAMPBELL-PRIDGEON, INC., 735 E. Main St., Box 3028, Spartanburg SC 29304. (803)583-1456. Vice President: Richard Campbell. Architectural firm offering design services with interior and landscape design. Clients: commercial, education, governmental, industrial, residential, religious.
Needs: Works with 1-2 freelance artists/year. Works on assignment only. Uses artists for brochure design and architectural renderings.
First Contact & Terms: Send query letter with brochure to be kept on file. Prefers to review photocopies. Reports only if interested. Pays for illustration by project. Considers complexity of the project, client's budget, and skill and experience of artist when establishing payment.

TUGGLE & GRAVES, INC.-ARCHITECTS, 215 Broadway, San Antonio TX 78205. (512)222-0194. Contact: Tuggle or Graves. Architectural/interior design firm offering architectural and space planning. Clients: school districts, commercial, government, industrial, residential.
Needs: Works with 3 freelance artists/year. Artists with three years' experience only. Works on assignment only. Uses artists for brochure and interior design, architectural renderings, maps and model making.
First Contact & Terms: Reports within 1 day if interested. Call or write for appointment to show portfolio. Pays for design by the project, $200-1,000 average. Considers complexity of project, client's budget, skill and experience of artist and how work will be used when establishing payment.

PHILIP TUSA DESIGN INC., Box 14, Roosevelt Island Station, New York NY 10044. (212)753-2810. President: Philip M. Tusa. Specializes in interior design. Clients: commercial firms, corporations and residential.
Needs: Works on assignment only. Uses artists for illustration, model making, interior rendering and drafting.
First Contact & Terms: Send query letter with resume, tear sheets, photostats, photocopies, slides and photographs. Reports back only if interested. Call to schedule an appointment to show a portfolio, which should include thumbnails, roughs, original/final art, final reproduction/product, color, tear sheets, photostats, photographs and b&w. Pays for illustration by the hour, $10 minimum; by the project, $100 minimum. Considers complexity of project, client's budget, skill and experience of artist,

how work will be used, turnaround time and rights purchased when establishing payment.
Tips: "The need for 'low overhead' prompts small companies to increase the use of freelance work. Keep in touch!!"

URBAN DESIGN ASSOCIATES, 258 Church St., New Haven CT 06510. (203)865-3381. Architect: George Conklin. Specializes in architectural design and solar design. Clients: commercial, residential, housing project.
Needs: Works with 3 artists for architectural renderings; 1, interior design; 1, graphic design; 1, signage design; 1, model making; and 1, landscape design. New England-New York area artists only. Works on assignment only.
First Contact & Terms: Send query letter with thumbnails. SASE. Reports in 2 weeks. No samples returned. Provide resume and brochure to be kept on file. Payment by job: $250 minimum, architectural renderings; $300 minimum, scale models; $150-350, graphic design; $100-300, signs. Considers complexity of project and client's budget when establishing payment.

VALENTOUR ENGLISH AND ASSOCIATES, Registered Architects, 470 Washington Rd., Pittsburgh PA 15228. Interior Designer: Denise L. Lostetter. Architectural firm providing architectural and interior design, working drawings, etc. Clients: primarily institutional and some commercial.
Needs: Works with 1 freelance artist/year. Local artists only. Works on assignment only. Uses artist for advertising illustration and interior renderings.
First Contact & Terms: Send resume to be kept on file. Reports within 2 weeks. Write for appointment to show portfolio. Pays for design by the project, $20 minimum. Considers complexity of project, client's budget, skill and experience of artist, how work will be used, turnaround time and rights purchased when establishing payment.

VERCESI & SCHARFSPITZ, ARCHITECTS, 353 Broad Ave., Leonia NJ 07605. Contact: Tony Vercesi. Architectural firm providing full architectural services. Clients: residential (custom homes and apartment houses); commercial (space improvements, office and industrial buildings).
Needs: Works with several freelance artists/year. Artists "must be talented and productive." Works on assignment only. Uses artists for interior design, architectural renderings, design consultation, furnishings and model making.
First Contact & Terms: Send query letter with brochure showing art style. Reports only if interested. Write to schedule an appointment to show a portfolio, which should include photographs. Pays for design by the hour, $15-25; by the day, $50-150. Pays for illustration by the hour, $15-50; by the day, $100-200. Considers complexity of project, client's budget, and skill and experience of artist when establishing payment.
Tips: "Possess the necessary credentials in the form of examples of work, etc."

VICKREY/OVRESAT/AWSUMB ASSOCIATES, INC., 500 S. Magnolia Ave., Orlando FL 32801. (305)425-2500. Senior Vice President: John K. Awsumb, AIA. Coordinator-Project Development: Sandra Moore. Architectural/Interior Design firm providing architecture, planning, interior design, space planning and construction administration services. Clients: industrial, office, residential, religious, military, hotel and restaurant, educational, medical, and recreational facilities.
Needs: Works with 1-5 freelance artists/year. Works on assignment only. Uses artists for interior and architectural renderings, and model making.
First Contact & Terms: Send query letter with brochure showing art style and slides to be kept on file. Samples not kept on file are returned only if requested. Reports back only if artist requests. Call for appointment to show portfolio, which should include original/final art and color. Pays for design by the project $1,000-25,000. Considers client's budget when establishing payment.
Tips: "Please send brochures and then follow up with a call."

LORRIN L. WARD, ARCHITECT INC., 341 W. 4th St., Chico CA 95928. (916)342-4265. President: Lorrin Ward. Architecture firm. Provides architectural design, planning, project administration. Clients: governmental, industrial and commercial. Buys 2-5 renderings/year.
Needs: Works with 2 artists for architectural renderings; 1, model making; and 1, landscape design. Prefers artists who have worked with other firms of this type.
First Contact & Terms: Query with brochure. SASE. Reports within 1-2 weeks. Provide resume, business card and brochure to be kept on file for future assignments. Pays for design by the hour, $15-35 average; by the project, $100-900 average; by the day, $120-280 average. Pays for illustration by the hour, $20-40 average; by the project, $200-900 average; by the day, $150-400 average. Considers complexity of project, skill and experience of artist, turnaround time and rights purchased when establishing payment.

HENRY P. WILHELMI, LANDSCAPE ARCHITECT/COMMUNITY PLANNER, 420 E. Genesee, Syracuse NY 13202. (315)474-7567. Contact: Henry P. Wilhelmi. Clients: government and institutions.
Needs: Works with 3-4 artists for architectural renderings; 1-2, graphic design; occasional, signage design; occasional, model making; 1-2, murals; and 1-2, sculpture. Local artists only. Works on assignment only.
First Contact & Terms: Mail photos or transparencies. Samples returned by SASE; and reports back on future possibilities. Provide resume, business card, brochure, flyer and tear sheet or any combination which will provide basic data to be kept on file for future assignments. Pays by job.

CLIFFORD N. WRIGHT ASSOC. ARCHITECTS, 4066 W. Maple, Birmingham MI 48010. (313)647-2022. President: William L. Baldner A.I.A. Vice President: William D. Shiels A.I.A. Architectural firm providing total architectural services. Clients: residential, commercial, light industrial.
Needs: Works with 10 freelance artists/year. Works on assignment only. Ues artists for landscape and interior design, interior and architectural renderings, design consulting and furnishings.
First Contact & Terms: Send brochure and resume to be kept on file. Reports only if interested. Call for appointment to show portfolio. Pays by the project for design and illustration. Considers complexity of project, client's budget, and skill and experience of artist when establishing payment.

***ZANE YOST & ASSOCIATES, INC.**, 144 Island Brook Ave., Bridgeport CT 06606. (203)384-2201. Marketing Director: Joanne Carroll. Architectural firm. Clients: residential developers (multi-family housing), banks and commercial developers.
Needs: Works with 4-6 freelance artists/year. Works on assignment only. Uses artists for advertising illustration, brochure design, architectural renderings and model making.
First Contact & Terms: Send query letter with brochure showing art style or resume, tear sheets, photocopies and slides. Samples not filed are not returned. Reports only if interested. To show a portfolio, mail appropriate materials. Pays for illustration by the hour, $40 minimum; by the project, $800-1,500. Considers complexity of project, client's budget, and skill and experience of artist when establishing payment.

> **“** *With a lot of different styles that have developed over the last few years, most illustrators can give you what you want when you need it most. There is a large number of young illustrators in the field right now who have added vitality to the business.* **”**
>
> **John Arocho, *Forum***

Rather than trying to be all things to all people, art/design studios have focused on client specialization. Within this framework of specialization, however, a diversity of services exists. Studios can run the gamut from one-man operations to a corporation, the scope of the studio determining how wide an assortment of assignments it can handle—from mechanicals and retouching to designing annual reports, packaging products and publications.

Because of the need to meet tight deadlines, many studios prefer to work with local artists. Research the talents needed by studios in your region and approach only those who request your specialities. Consult the *Yellow Pages* and the *Business to Business Directory* to locate local studios and then the *Design Directory* to learn their areas of specialization. If the studio is not listed, call to determine this information; gear your portfolio and samples to those specifications.

Since a graphic designer must be able to organize disparate elements into a pleasing unity, the portfolio should reflect good organizational skills and a graphic plan. Include only your best work, which should be well-designed and of manageable size. Comprehensives are a must for graphic designers. Product designers should include photos of manufactured products or prototypes as well as drafting and rendering samples. On projects involving the construction of models, keep a running photographic account of the project so you will have appropriate examples in your portfolio. Samples of work that have appeared in print help to establish a designer's credibility. Since so much graphic design is involved in the preparation stages of a project, an employer will be looking for artists skilled in preparing roughs and mechanicals. It is a good idea to have more than one portfolio to cover the drop-off policy and mail submissions; each piece should be marked with a brief, explanatory note.

Read the Close-ups of Martin Pedersen of Jonson Pedersen Hinrichs & Shakery and of Jeff Berman of J.H. Berman & Associates for their insights into the art/design field.

AARON, SAUTER, GAINES & ASSOCIATES/DIRECT MARKETING, Suite 1200, 3500 North Central, Phoenix AZ 85012. (602)265-1933. President: Cameron G. Sauter. Specializes in brand identity, direct marketing, direct response ads, catalogs and P-O-P displays for retail stores, banks, industrial, mail order and service companies.
Needs: Works with 5-10 freelance artists/year. Uses artists for advertising, brochure and catalog design and illustration, mechanicals, retouching and direct mail packages.
First Contact and Terms: Seeks artists with professionalism, speed and experience only. Send query letter with brochure, resume and business card to be kept on file. Prefers original work, photos or slides as samples. Samples returned by SASE if not kept on file. Reports only if interested. Works on assignment basis. Pays for design, by the hour, $15-50 average; by the project, $100-1,000 average; by the day, $50-100 average. Pays for illustration, by the hour, $25-75 average; by the project, $100-2,000 average; by the day, $100-150 average. Considers complexity of project, client's budget, skill and experience of artist and turnaround time when establishing payment. "All art is purchased with full rights and no limitations."

 *The asterisk before a listing indicates that the listing is new in this edition. New markets are often the most receptive to freelance contributions.*

ADAM, FILIPPO & MORAN DESIGN CONSULTANTS, 1206 5th Ave., Pittsburgh PA 15219. (412)261-3720. Contact: Robert Adam, Lewis Filippo, Dennis Moran. Specializes in annual reports, brand identity, corporate identity, displays, interior design, packaging, publications and signage. Clients: major corporations and facilities.
Needs: Uses artists for mechanicals, retouching and model making.
First Contact & Terms: Send query letter with brochure, resume, business card and slides to be kept on file for 6 months. Samples returned only by SASE. Reports only if interested. Call or write to schedule an appointment to show a portfolio, which should include thumbnails, roughs, original/final art, final reproduction/product, color, tear sheets, photostats and photographs. Pays for design by the hour, $12-25 average. Considers client's budget, skill and experience of artist and turnaround time when establishing payment.
Tips: Be willing to negotiate any items.

***ADLER, SCHWARTZ INC.**, 140 Sylvan Ave., Englewood Cliffs NJ 07632. (201)461-8450. Art Director: Fred Witzig. Specializes in brand identity, corporate identity, displays and direct mail. Clients: ad agencies.
Needs: Works with 100 freelance artists/year. Uses artists for design, illustrations, mechanicals and retouching.
First Contact & Terms: Send query letter with brochure showing art style or resume and samples. Samples not filed are returned only if requested. Reports only if interested. Call to schedule an appointment to show a portfolio, which should include roughs, original/final art, final reproduction/product, tear sheets and photographs. Considers complexity of project, client's budget, skill and experience of artist, how work will be used, turnaround time and rights purchased when establishing payment.

***LEONARD ALBRECHT ASSOCIATES**, 7354 Bolsa Ave., Westminster CA 92683. (714)898-0553. Owner: Leonard Albrecht. Specializes in industrial design.
Needs: Works with 2-3 freelance artists/year. Uses artists for design, illustrations, mechanicals and model making.
First Contact & Terms: Send query letter with brochure showing art style or resume. Reports within 10 days. Write to schedule an appointment to show a portfolio. Considers skill and experience of artist when establishing payment.

ANCO/BOSTON, 441 Stuart St., Boston MA 02116. (617)267-9700. Graphic Director: Julie Gallagher. Art agency. Clients: educational publishers, commercial and industrial.
Needs: Works with 10 illustrators. Local artists only. Uses artists for books, charts, graphs, technical art and paste-up. Most of the artwork required is one-color line art.
First Contact & Terms: Send query letter with resume and photocopies. All art becomes the property of Anco/Boston. To show portfolio, mail appropriate materials or call to schedule an appointment; portfolio should include original/final art, final reproduction/product, tear sheets and photostats. Pays for design by the project, $25 minimum; pays for illustration by the project, $10 minimum.
Tips: "We are interested only in b&w line art. Our work is for educational materials and is frequently of a technical nature."

ANDREN & ASSOCIATES INC., 6400 N. Keating Ave., Lincolnwood IL 60646. (312)267-8500. Contact: Kenneth E. Andren. Clients: beauty products and tool manufacturers, clothing retailers, laboratories, banks, cameras and paper products.
Needs: Assigns 6-7 jobs/month. Local artists only. Uses artists for catalogs, direct mail brochures, flyers, packages, P-O-P displays and print media advertising.
First Contact & Terms: Query with samples or arrange interview. SASE. Reports in 1-2 weeks. Pays $15 minimum/hour for animation, design, illustrations, layout, lettering, mechanicals, paste-up, retouching and type spec.

ANTISDEL IMAGE GROUP, INC., 3242 De La Cruz Blvd., Santa Clara CA 95054. (408)988-1010. President: G.C. Antisdel. Specializes in annual reports, corporate identity, displays, interior design, packaging, publications, signage and photo illustration. Clients: high technology 80%, energy 10%, and banking 10%.
Needs: Works on assignment only. Uses artists for illustration, mechanicals, retouching, airbrushing, direct mail packages, model making, charts/graphs, AV materials and lettering.
First Contact & Terms: Send query letter with resume, business card and tear sheets to be kept on file. Reports back only if interested. Call or write to schedule an appointment to show a portfolio, which should include color, tear sheets, photographs and b&w. Pays for design and illustration by the project. Considers complexity of project, client's budget, skill and experience of artist, how work will be used, turnaround time and rights purchased when establishing payment.
Tips: "Our top grade clients are not subject to 'trendy' fads."

THE ART WORKS, 4409 Maple Ave., Dallas TX 75219. (214)521-2121. Creative Director: Fred Henley. Specializes in annual reports, brand identity, corporate identity, displays, packaging, publications, signage, illustration and photography.
Needs: Works with 15-20 freelance artists/year. Uses artists for advertising, brochure, catalog and book design and illustration; advertising, brochure and catalog layout; P-O-P displays, mechanicals, retouching, posters, direct mail packages, lettering and logos.
First Contact & Terms: Send brochure, business card, slides, original work to be kept on file. Samples returned by SASE only if requested by artist. Reports within 7 days. Call or write for appointment to show portfolio. Pays for design and illustration by the project. Considers complexity of project, client's budget, skill and experience of artist and turnaround time when establishing payment.

ARTHUR RITTER, INC., 45 W. 10th St., New York NY 10011. (212)505-0241. Art Director: Valerie Ritter. Specializes in annual reports, corporate identity, brochures, catalogs and promotion for publishers, corporations, public service organizations and hospitals.
Needs: Works with 5 freelance artists/year according to firm's needs. Does not always work on assignment only; "sometimes we need a freelancer on a day-to-day basis at the studio." Uses artists for advertising design and illustration, brochure design, mechanicals, charts and graphs.
First Contact & Terms: Prefers experienced artists, although "talented 'self-starters' with design expertise/education are also considered." Send query letter with brochure, resume and samples to be kept on file. "Follow up within a week of the query letter about the possibility of arranging an appointment for a portfolio review." Prefers printed pieces as samples. Samples not filed are returned by SASE. Pays for design by the hour, $10-20 average; by the project, $100-500 average; or by the day, $65-120 average. Pays for illustration by the project, $50-500 average. Considers complexity of the project, client's budget, skill and experience of the artist and turnaround time when establishing payment.

***BAKER STREET PRODUCTIONS LTD.**,Box 3610, 502 Range St., Mankato MN 56001. (507)625-2448. Contact: Karyne Jacobsen. Specializes in publications. Clients: publishers.
Needs: Works with 2 freelance artist/year. Prefers colorful juvenile-style art. Uses artists for illustrations, catalogs and books.
First Contact & Terms: Send query letter with resume and tear sheets. Samples not filed are returned by SASE only if requested. Reports within 2 months. Write to schedule an appointment to show a portfolio, which should include roughs, tear sheets and photographs. Pays for design and illustration by the project. Considers complexity of project, client's budget and skill and experience of artist when establishing payment.

CAROL BANCROFT & FRIENDS, 185 Goodhill Rd., Weston CT 06883. (203)226-7674. President: Carol Bancroft. Specializes in art for children. Clients: publishing companies, ad agencies, studios and major corporations.
Needs: Works with 30 freelance artists/year. Uses artists for advertising, brochure, catalog and book illustration.
First Contact & Terms: Send slides, tear sheets and photos to be kept on file. Samples not kept on file are returned by SASE. To show a portfolio, mail appropriate materials, which should include final reproduction/product, color and tear sheets. Pays by the project, 70-75% of total job. Considers complexity of project, client's budget, turnaround time and rights purchased when establishing payment.
Tips: "Send a lot of good color samples we can keep on file."

BANKA-MANGO, Room 274, Merchandise Mart, Chicago IL 60654. (312)467-0059. Director of Graphic Design: Joseph R. Mango. Specializes in brand and corporate identity, displays, exhibits and shows, interior design and signage. Clients: retail stores and manufacturers of retail products.
Needs: Works with 1-2 freelance artists/year. Works on assignment only. Uses artists for packaging design and illustration, brochure design, mechanicals, retouching, poster illustration, model making, charts/graphs, lettering and logo design.
First Contact & Terms: Send query letter with brochure/flyer or resume to be kept on file. Call or write for appointment to show portfolio. Pays by the project on completion for design and illustration.
Tips: "Have good, current samples."

BARNSTORM STUDIOS, Suite 301, 2502½ W. Colorado Ave., Colorado Springs CO 80904. (303)630-7200. Art Director: Douglas D. Blough. Specializes in corporate identity, brochure design, multi-image slide presentations and publications. Clients: ad agencies, high-technology corporations.
Needs: Works with 2-4 freelance artists/year. Works with local, experienced (clean, fast and accurate) artists on assignment. Uses artists for design, illustration, brochures, mechanicals, retouching, AV materials and lettering.
First Contact & Terms: Send query letter with resume and samples to be kept on file. Prefers "good

originals or reproductions, professionally presented in any form" as samples. Samples not filed are returned by SASE. Reports only if interested. Call or write for appointment to show portfolio. Pays for design by the project, $100 minimum. Pays for illustration by the project, $50 minimum, b&w; $100, color. Considers client's budget, skill and experience of artist, and turnaround time when establishing payment.
Tips: "Trend toward New Wave design/pastel colors. Portfolios should reflect an awareness of these trends. We try to handle as much inhouse as we can, but we recognize our own limitations (particularly in illustration)."

LAWRENCE BENDER & ASSOCIATES, 512 Hamilton Ave., Palo Alto CA 94301. (415)327-3821. President: Lawrence Bender. Specializes in annual reports. Clients: electronic manufacturers.
Needs: Works with 12 freelance artists/year. Uses artists for design, illustration, mechanicals, retouching and airbrushing.
First Contact & Terms: Send query letter with resume, business card and samples to be kept on file. Samples not kept on file returned only if requested. Reports only if interested. Call or write for appointment to show portfolio. Pays for design by the hour, project or day. Pays for illustration by the project. Considers complexity of project, client's budget, skill and experience of artist and rights purchased when establishing payment.

J.H. BERMAN AND ASSOCIATES, Suite 621, 2025 I St. NW, Washington DC 20006. (202)775-0892. Senior Vice President: Jackie Deitch. Specializes in annual reports, corporate identity, publications and signage. Clients: real estate developers, architects, high-technology corporations and financial-oriented firms (banks, investment firms, etc.).
Needs: Works with 10-15 (6 consistently) freelance artists/year. Uses artists for design, illustration, brochures, magazines, books, P-O-P displays, mechanicals, retouching, airbrushing, posters, model making, AV materials, lettering and advertisements. Especially needs designers, illustrators, technical illustrators, architectural renderers and mechanical/production artists.
First Contact & Terms: "Artists should be highly professional, with at least 5 years' experience. Highest quality work required. Restricted to local artists for mechanicals only." Send query letter with brochure, resume, business card and samples to be kept on file. Call or write for appointment to show portfolio or contact through agent. "Samples should be as compact as possible; slides not suggested." Samples not kept on file returned by SASE. Reports only if interested. Pays for design by the hour, $12-50 average. Pays for illustration by the project, $200 minimum. Considers complexity of project, skill and experience of artist, how work will be used, turnaround time and rights purchased when establishing payment.
Tips: Artists should have a "totally professional approach."

JOHN BLAIR & CO., 1290 Avenue of the Americas, New York NY 10104. Vice President, Corporate Relations: Josef B. Rosenberg. Blair Television: Kenn Donnellon. Blair Radio: Dorothy Lancaster. Blair Entertainment: Leslie Lillien. Uses local artists for technical charts, annual reports, sales literature, booklets, illustrations and exhibit designs.

BOB BOEBERITZ DESIGN, 247 Charlotte St., Asheville NC 28801. (704)258-0316. Owner: Bob Boeberitz. Graphic design studio. Clients: galleries, retail outlets, restaurants, car dealers, land developers, computer software, record companies and publishers.
Needs: Works with freelance artists on occasion. Uses artists primarily for illustration; occasionally buys humorous or cartoon-style illustrations.
First Contact & Terms: Send query letter with brochure, resume, photostats, photocopies, photographs, business card, slides and tear sheets to be kept on file. "Anything too large to fit in file" is discarded. Reports only if interested. To show a portfolio, mail appropriate materials or write to schedule an appointment; portfolio should include original/final art, final reproduction/product, color and b&w. Pays for illustration by the project, $50 minimum. Considers complexity of project, client's budget, skill and experience of artist and turnaround time when establishing payment. Buys all rights.
Tips: "Be able to do a variety of styles. There are no 'specialists' in the Asheville area."

***BOOKMAKER'S INC.**, 305 N. Main, Westpoint CT 06880. (203)226-4293. President: Frank Crump. Specializes in publications. Clients: book publishers.
Needs: Works with 40 freelance artists/year. Uses artists for illustrations and books. "We are agents and book designers. We represent artists in juvenile and text books (for elementary school)."
First Contact & Terms: Send query letter with brochure showing art style or tear sheets, photostats, photocopies and slides. Samples not filed are returned. Reports within 2 weeks. To show a portfolio, mail color, tear sheet and photostats. Considers skill and experience of artist when establishing payment.

Close-up

J. H. Berman
President, J. H. Berman & Associates
Washington, D.C.

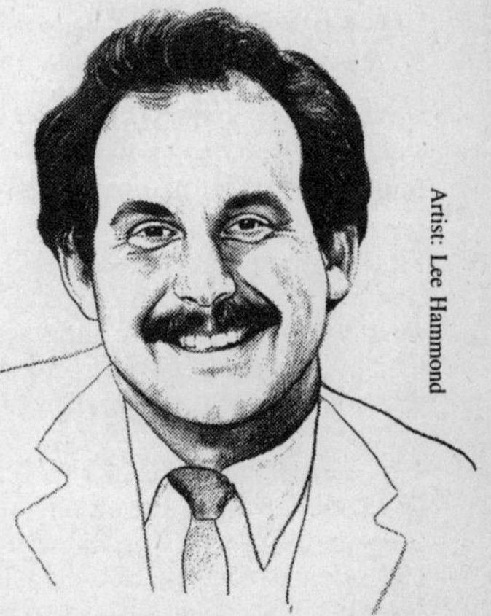

In 1975, Jeff Berman's graphic design and commercial art "studio" was a spare room in his apartment. Now, twelve years later, his business has matured into one of the most prestigious corporate design firms on the East Coast.

Keeping the business manageably small and making a total commitment to quality have been the key factors in the company's success, says Berman, owner and president of J. H. Berman & Associates.

"We currently have a staff of ten people and work with as many as 15 freelancers a year for our typical work. If a client requests something beyond our normal scope, we will subcontract it to a freelancer or firm strong in that specialty," he says. Because the company serves a specialized clientele of real estate developers, architects, high-tech firms, and financial organizations, the highest quality in concept and execution is the only standard. "Since we deal largely in creating corporate identities, or 'images,' and since most of our work comes through referrals and from established clients, everything we do must be 'top-notch.' We simply can't afford anything less."

Accordingly, no less is expected of the freelancer than of the firm's own staff artists. "Generally, we prefer freelancers to have five to six years' experience. We need people who can walk in and know what they're doing without coaching. They need to be responsive to the client, to generate good ideas, and then, to produce them according to our standards."

We use a lot of 'mechanical' artists because of the large volume of camera-ready copy that we generate," he says, adding that it's impractical to work with nonlocal 'mechanical' artists.

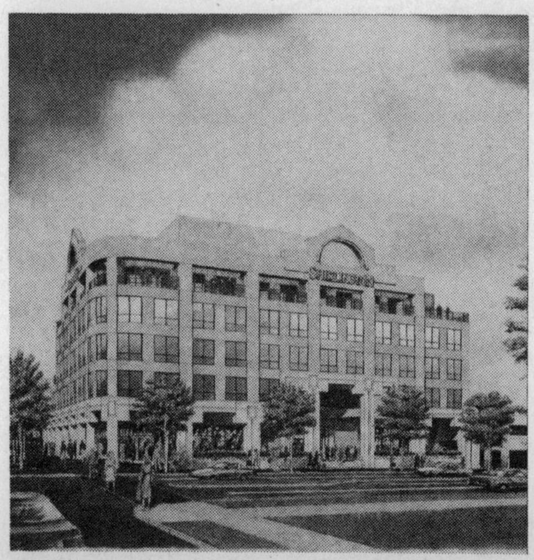

Isao Oishi of Baltimore, Maryland, created this delineation of a town center for Berman & Associates. The corporate design firm serves a specialized clientele of real estate developers, architects, high-tech firms and financial organizations. Oishi's work reflects the 'top-notch' quality of work Berman expects.

Because of its many architecture and construction clients, the firm often needs artists with drafting and rendering skills. But being so specialized also makes such artists scarce. "Architectural renderers are about the most difficult to find, so we can never find too many of them."

Another area in which there is growing need is computer-aided design and drafting, or CADD. Berman & Associates uses it most often for generating audiovisual materials and covers for annual reports, but usually subcontracts the work to firms with CADD systems. However, some of these firms now lease their systems to freelancers.

Berman says, "Certainly, every designer has to have sensitivity to copy and message. And one who can combine visual and verbal communication can be a lot more useful in the field."

—Sam A. Marshall

***THE BOOKMAKERS, INCORPORATED**, 298 East South St., Wilkes-Barre PA 18702. (717)823-9183. President: John Beck. Specializes in publications and technical illustrations. Clients: mostly book publishers.
Needs: Works with 10-20 freelance artists/year. Uses artists for illustrations, brochures, catalogs, retouching, airbrushing, posters and charts/graphs.
First Contact & Terms: Send query letter with resume, tear sheets, photostats, photocopies, slides and photographs. Samples not filed are returned by SASE. Reports only if interested. Write to schedule an appointment to show a portfolio, which should include thumbnails, roughs, original/final art, final reproduction/product, tear sheets, photostats and b&w. Pays for illustration by the project, $20-2,400. Considers complexity of project, client's budget, skill and experience of artist, how work will be used and turnaround time when establishing payment. Buys all rights.
Tips: "We are especially interested in versatility."

BOWYER ASSOCIATES, INC., Suite 401, 43 Eglinton Ave. E, Toronto, Ontario M4P 1A2 Canada. (416)484-8848. President: Robert Bowyer. Studio. Clients: retail, industrial and commercial.
Needs: Assigns approximately 150 jobs/year to freelance artists. Works with 2 freelance illustrators/month. Sometimes works on assignment. Uses artists for illustrations and finished artwork.
First Contact & Terms: Send resume to be kept on file if interested. Reports only if interested. Pays by the project. Considers complexity of project, client's budget, and skill and experience of artist when establishing payment. Buys all rights.
Tips: Especially looks for "originality, self-expression and neatness." Artists should "show only top quality work and finished artwork, anything artist thinks is good, in a range from illustration to packaging. Do not show artwork that you did in school—this lacks diversity."

BRODSKY GRAPHICS INC., 270 Madison Ave., New York NY 10016. (212)684-2600. Art Director: Ed Brodsky. Specializes in corporate identity, direct mail, promotion and packaging. Clients: ad agencies and corporations.

66Our field has become increasingly more high-tech and specialized. Knowledge of equipment and procedures is required of our management-level readerships. 99

Teri Wilhelm, Harris Communications

Needs: Works with 10 freelance artists/year. Works on assignment only. Uses artists for illustration, mechanicals, retouching, airbrushing, charts/graphs, AV materials and lettering.
First Contact & Terms: Send business card and tear sheets to be kept on file. Reports back only if interested. Considers complexity of project, client's budget, skill and experience of artist and turnaround time when establishing payment.

***BROOKS STEVENS DESIGN ASSOC.**, 1415 W. Donges Bay Rd., Mequon WI 53092. (414)241-3800. President: Kipp Stevens. Specializes in corporate identity, packaging and industrial design. Clients: manufacturing companies.
Needs: Works with 5 freelance artists/year. Uses artists for illustrations, P-O-P displays, retouching, model making and logos.
First Contact & Terms: Send query letter with resume. Samples not filed are returned only if requested. Reports only if interested. Call or write to schedule an appointment to show a portfolio, which should include roughs, original/final art, final reproduction/product and color. Pays for design by the hour, $11 minimum; by the project, $100 minimum. Pays for illustrations by the hour, $11 minimum; by the project, $100 minimum. Considers complexity of project, client's budget, skill and experience of artist, and turnaround time when establishing payment.

***CANYON DESIGN**, A 102, 20945 Devonshire St., Chatsworth CA 91311. (818)700-1173. Art Director/Owner: David O'Connell. Specializes in brand identity, corporate identity, displays, packaging and signage. Clients: manufacturers, distributors and others.
Needs: Works with 28 freelance artists/year. Uses artists for design, illustrations, P-O-P displays, retouching, AV materials and lettering. "We are looking for a media buyer or coordinator and an office manager/production manager."
First Contact & Terms: Send query letter with brochure showing art style. Samples not filed are returned by SASE. Reports only if interested. Call to schedule an appointment to show a portfolio, which should include roughs, original/final art, final reproduction/product, color and tear sheets. Pays for design by the hour, $15-25; by the project, $100 minimum; by the day $100 minimum. Pays for illustration by the hour, $15-50; by the project, $100 minimum. Considers complexity of project, client's budget, skill and experience of artist, how work will be used, turnaround time and rights purchased when establishing payment.
Tips: "Check the going rates in the area before asking for Madison Ave. fees. Location of an agency or studio has a lot to do with determining the prices charged to a client. Don't include pieces in your portfolio that you have to make excuses for. More emphasis on creative and less on copy and price in the field. Also there is a fine art or painterly approach to illustration. The L.A. market has a strong color palette—atomic and neon colors."

THE CHESTNUT HOUSE GROUP INC., 540 N. Lakeshore Dr., Chicago IL 60611. (312)222-9090. Creative Directors: Norman Baugher and Miles Zimmerman. Clients: major educational publishers. Arrange interview.
Needs: Illustration, layout and assembly. Pays by job.

A. CHRISTIE DESIGN, 207 Pontiac St., Lester PA 19113. (215)521-2569. President: Alice P. Christie. Specializes in corporate identity, interior design, publications, technical illustration, human factors and product design. Clients: corporations including industry, engineering, technical publishing, printing services and electronics.
Needs: Works with 5-10 freelance artists/year. Local artists only. Uses artists for design, illustration, brochures, mechanicals, retouching, posters, model making, charts/graphs, AV materials, lettering, logos and advertisements.
First Contact & Terms: Send query letter with samples to be kept on file. Prefers photostats, slides and tear sheets as samples. Samples not kept on file are returned by SASE. Reports back within 2 weeks. Write for appointment to show portfolio. Pays for design and illustration by the hour, $3.55 first use. "Pay higher when satisifed with performance." Considers complexity of project, client's budget, skill of artist and turnaround time when establishing payment.
Tips: "Be able to do what you claim."

> **❝ Artists must be able to work in various mediums. Their technical versatility will increase their availability by projects. ❞**
>
> *Vinod Ghoting, Ghoting & Associates*

***MARK CHRISTY ASSOCIATES, INC.**, 5135 Liberty Ave., Pittsburgh PA 15224. (412)687-5135. Office Manager: Michael McCallian. Specializes in interior design. Clients: hotels, corporations, medical institutions and residences.
Needs: Works with 3 freelance artists/year. Prefers local artists. Especially needs watercolor. Uses artists for illustrations and renderings of interior settings.
First Contact & Terms: Send query letter with resume and photographs. Samples not filed are returned only if requested. Reports only if interested. Call to show a portfolio, which should include original/final art and color. Considers complexity of project, how work will be used and turnaround time when establishing payment.
Tips: "We like to see the ability of the artist to handle a mixture of styles: traditional, contemporary, architectural and furniture-oriented. Presentation must be finished and professional looking."

***WOODY COLEMAN PRESENTS, INC.**, 490 Rockside Rd., Cleveland OH 44131. (216)661-4222. President: Woody Coleman. Artist's agent. Clients: ad agencies, PR firms and direct corporations.
Needs: Works with 25 freelance artists/year. Artists must have three years, experience. Especially needs photo realistic with figure and product. Uses artists for illustrations.
First Contact & Terms: Send query letter with brochure showing art style or tear sheets, slides and 4x5 transparencies. Samples not filed are returned by SASE. Reports only if interested. To show a portfolio, mail color and 4x5 transparencies. Pays for illustration by the project, $400-10,000. Considers complexity of project, client's budget, skill and experience of artist, how work will be used, turnaround time and rights purchased when establishing payment.
Tips: Artist should send "8 of their 10 best samples within their area of expertise."

COLLINS DESIGN, 9090 N. 51st St., Milwaukee WI 53223. (414)354-2200. President: Scott Collins. Specializes in corporate identity, displays, packaging, technical illustration, industrial design and product development. Clients: manufacturers and corporations, medium and large.
Needs: Works with 3 freelance artists/year. Artists should have "industrial design background with experience in rendering, mechanical drawing and model making." Uses artists for design, illustration, P-O-P displays, mechanicals, model making and product development and styling.
First Contact & Terms: Send query letter with resume to be kept on file. Write for appointment to show portfolio, which should include slides or flat work. Samples not kept on file are returned only if interested. Payment is "based on experience, capability and direct negotiation with artist." Considers complexity of project, client's budget and turnaround time when establishing payment.
Tips: There is the "potential for full-time employment based on performance."

CONTOURS CONSULTING DESIGN GROUP, INC., 864 Stearns Rd., Bartlett IL 60103. (312)837-4100. Director, Graphics Group: Richard Wittosch. Specializes in annual reports, brand identity, corporate identity, displays, direct mail, packaging and signage. Clients: various corporations.
Needs: Works on assignment only. Uses artists for illustration, mechanicals and retouching.
First Contact & Terms: Send query letter with tear sheets. Call to schedule an appointment to show portfolio, which should include roughs, final reproduction/product, color and b&w. Pays for design by the hour, $30-50; pays for illustration by the project, $200-800. Considers client's budget when establishing payment.
Tips: In the field, there are more copy solutions to problems than visuals. There is a limited use of art because budgets have reduced art buy outs. We are looking for strong concept solutions rather than style alternatives."

CORPORATE GRAPHICS, 1447 Lombard St., San Francisco CA 94123. (415)474-2888. President: Edward de St. Maurice. Specializes in annual reports, corporate identity, direct mail, publications and advertising. Clients: include high tech firms, banks, real estate firms; diversified clients.
Needs: Uses artists for illustration, mechanicals, charts/graphs and lettering.
First Contact & Terms: Send query letter with resume photostats, slides or tear sheets to be kept on file. Reports within 1 month. Call for an appointment to show portfolio. Considers client's budget, and skill and experience of artist when establishing payment.

CREATIVE DESIGN CENTER, INC., 23141-K La Cadena Dr., Laguna Hills CA 92653. President: Robert Greene. Vice President: Clair Samhammer. Specializes in corporate identity, displays, interior design, packaging, technical illustration and product design and development. Clients: manufacturing and marketing groups (medical, data processing/office equipment and consumer products).
Needs: Works with 15 freelance designers/year. Prefers designers with "minimum 3-5 years' experience, except in exceptional cases, and proven ability." Works on assignment only. Uses designers for design, illustration, brochures, P-O-P displays, mechanicals, model making and logos.
First Contact & Terms: Send query letter with brochure, resume, business card and samples to be kept

on file. Write for appointment to show portfolio. Samples not kept on file are returned only if requested. Pays for design and illustration by the hour, $15-25 average. Considers client's budget, skill and experience of designers and turnaround time when establishing payment.
Tips: Especially looks for "poetic, knowledgeable and intelligent solutions" as samples. Not interested in designers with "their heart on their sleeve and an ego chip on their shoulder."

CREATIVE WORKS, 300 Prosperity Farms Rd., North Palm Beach FL 33408. (305)844-8222. Interior Designer (Drafting): Suzi Addessa. Art Director (Mechanicals): Ken Roscoe. Specializes in corporate identity, displays, interior design, packaging, signage, product and sales offices. Clients: ad agencies, public relations firms, real estate developers, manufacturers and promoters.
Needs: Works with 50 freelance artists/year. Uses local (work inhouse), experienced artists. Uses artists for design, illustration, mechanicals, airbrushing, model making and drafting. Especially needs drafting/mechanical people.
First Contact & Terms: Send query letter with resume to be kept on file. Samples not kept on file are returned by SASE only if requested. Reports within 1 week. Write to schedule an appointment to show a portfolio, which should include original/final art and photographs. Pays by the hour for drafting and mechanicals. Considers complexity of project, client's budget, skill and experience of artist and turnaround time when establishing payment.
Tips: "Send resume for interest and follow by appointment."

***CREEL MORRELL INC.**, 308½ Congress Ave., Austin TX 78701. Contact: Michael Overton. Specializes in annual reports, corporate identity, displays, landscape design, interior design, technical illustrations, publications and signage.
Needs: Uses artists for illustrations, mechanicals, retouching, airbrushing, model making, copywriting and AV materials.
First Contact & Terms: Send query letter with brochure, resume, business card and whatever samples available to be kept on file. Samples not filed are returned only if requested. Reports only if interested. To show a portfolio, mail appropriate materials or call to schedule an appointment; portfolio should include final reproduction/product, color, tear sheets, photostats, photographs or slides of work. Payment depends on each situation. Considers client's budget, skill and experience of artist, how work will be used and rights purchased when establishing payment.

CSOKA/BENATO/FLEURANT INC., 134 W. 26th St., New York NY 10001. (212)242-6777. President: Robert Fleurant. Clients: insurance, national retail chains and communications.
Needs: Uses artists for record jacket covers and sales promotion projects.
First Contact & Terms: Assigns 10-20 jobs/year. Arrange interview. Pays $15-25/hour, layout; $8-15/hour, paste-up and mechanicals; $500 maximum/job, record jacket covers. Negotiates payment by job for annual reports, catalogs, packaging, posters and P-O-P displays.
Tips: Professional presentation of work is a *must*.

CWI INC., 255 Glenville Rd., Greenwich CT 06831. (202)531-0300. Contact: Geoffrey Chaite. Design studio. Specializes in annual reports, brand identity, corporate identity, point of purchase and collateral material, displays, exhibits and shows. Clients: packaged goods, foods, tools, publishing, drugs, tobacco, banks and sports.
Needs: Works with up to 10 illustrators and 2-3 designers/month. Minimum 5-8 years' experience. Uses artists for P-O-P displays, stationery design, multimedia kits, direct mail, slide sets, brochures/flyers, trade magazines, newspapers, layout, technical art, type spec, paste-up, retouching and lettering. Especially needs photography, illustration and paste-up.
First Contact & Terms: Send flyers, business card, tear sheets, b&w line drawings, roughs, previously published work, comps and mechanicals to be kept on file for future assignments. May return originals to artist at job's completion. Payment is negotiated.

***DANMARK & MICHAELS, INC.**, 378 S. Oyster Bay Rd., Hicksville NY 11801. (576)931-6500. Art Directors: Fred Haynes or Alan DeLuca. Specializes in technical illustrations. Clients: publishers of text books.
Needs: Works with several freeelance artists/year. Artist should have some experience in technical illustrations. Uses artists for illustrations, airbrushing, charts/graphs and maps. "We are always looking for good illustrators."
First Contact & Terms: Send query letter with resume and photocopies. Samples not filed are returned only if requested. Reports only if interested. Call or write to schedule an appointment to show a portfolio, which should include original/final art. Payment varies. Considers complexity of project, skill and experience of artist, and turnaround time when establishing payment.
Tips: "Artist must meet the deadlines required and have the ability to do the job."

***JOSEPH B. DEL VALLE**, Suite 1123, 41 Union Square West, New York NY 10003. Director: Joseph B. Del Valle. Specializes in annual reports, publications and book design. Clients: various publishers and museums.
Needs: Works with approximately 6 freelance artists/year. Artists must have experience and be able to work on a job to job basis. Uses artists for design, books and mechanicals.
First Contact & Terms: Send query letter with resume. Reports only if interested. Call or write to schedule an appointment to show a portfolio, which should include final reproduction/product. Pays for design by the hour, $15-25. Considers client's budget and turnaround time when establishing payment.

DESIGN & PRODUCTION INCORPORATED, 7110 Rainwater Pl., Lorton VA 22079. (703)751-5150. Design Director: Daniel Murphy. Specializes in displays, interior design, signage and exhibition design. Clients: ad agencies, PR firms, architectural firms, institutions and major corporations.
Needs: Works with 10-20 freelance artists/year. Uses artists for design, illustration, brochures, catalogs, mechanicals, model making and exhibit design.
First Contact & Terms: Prefers local artists who are established professionals. Works on assignment only. Send query letter with brochure, resume and samples to be kept on file; call for appointment to show portfolio. Prefers slides or tear sheets as samples. Samples not filed are returned by SASE. Reports within 2 weeks. Pays for design by the hour, $50-200 average; by the project, $1,000-15,000 average. Pays for illustration by the hour, $25-50 average; by the project, $1,000-3,000 average. Considers complexity of project, client's budget, and skill and experience of artist when establishing payment.
Tips: "Only expereinced freelancers need apply. Develop a style, a definite, recognizable trait that can be associated to you exclusively."

***DESIGN ASSOCIATES**, 10503 Nile Ct., Tampa FL 33615. (813)855-6129. President; Thom Hammond. Specializes in corporate identification, architectural delineation and product design and illustration.
Needs: Works with 5 freelance artists/year. Artists must have 3-5 years experience in a specific area. Uses artists for the design, illustration and layout of advertising and brochures plus product design, P-O-P displays and calligraphy.
First Contact & Terms: Send query letter with brochure showing art style or tear sheets, photostats, photocopies, slides and photographs. Samples not filed are returned if accompanied by SASE. Reports back within 10-30 days. Call to schedule an appointment to show a portfolio, which should include thumbnails, roughs, original/final art, final reproduction/product, color, tear sheets, photostats and photographs. Pays for design by the hour, $25-50. Pays for illustration by the hour, $25-50. Considers complexity of project, skill and experience of artist, how work will be used and turnaround time when establishing payment.
Tips: "The presentation or packaging of art has to be professional. A highly stylized artist is probably at a disadvantage because often times we need someone who can imitate a style our client is already accustomed to."

DESIGN COMMUNICATION, INC., Suite 1009, 1346 Connecticut Ave. NW, Washington DC 20036. (202)833-9087. Art Director: Joanne Zamore. Specializes in annual reports, corporate identity, publication, audio visual presentation and programs and communication consultation. Clients: corporations, government agencies, architects and developers, and associations.
Needs: Works with 12 freelance artists/year. Prefers local artists. Works on assignment only. Uses artists for design, illustration, brochures, magazines, mechanicals, retouching, airbrushing, charts/graphs, AV materials and logos.
First Contact & Terms: Send query letter with resume, tear sheets and photocopies to be kept on file. Samples not kept on file returned by SASE only if requested. Reports only if interested. Call for appointment to show potfolio. Pays for design by the hour, $11-20 average. Pays for illustration by the project, $300-2,500 average. Considers complexity of project, client's budget, skill and experience of artist, how work will be used, turnaround time and rights purchased when establishing payment.
Tips: "Be persistent and show enthusiasm. Budgets are getting smaller again and clients are looking for the lowest bidder."

***DESIGN MARKS CORPORATION**, 1462 W. Irving Park Rd., Chicago IL 60613-1997. (312)327-3670. President: Nathaniel Ascher Marks. Specializes in annual reports, brand identity, corporate identity, displays, direct mail, packaging, publications and signage. Clients: corporations, associations and government agencies.
Needs: Works with various freelance artists/year. Uses artists for illustrations and mechanicals.
First Contact & Terms: Send query letter with resume only. No samples. Reports only if interested. Write to schedule an appointment to show a portfolio, which should include thumbnails, roughs, original/final art, final reproduction/product, color and tear sheets. Considers complexity of project, client's

budget, skill and experience of artist, how work will be used, turnaround time and rights purchased when establishing payment.

DESIGN NORTH, INC., 8007 Douglas Ave., Racine WI 53402. (414)639-2080. Design Directors: Dennis Wolken (corporate), Jim Neill (promotional). Specializes in annual reports, brand identity, corporate identity, displays, all internal and external collateral. Clients: direct accounts—financial/medical, consumer/industrial products.
Needs: Works with 10 freelance artists/year. "Freelancer must not call directly or be in competition with us on accounts." Works on assignment only. Uses artists for illustration, photography, retouching, airbrushing and lettering.
First Contact & Terms: Send query letter with brochure and photostats, slides, photocopies and tear sheets to be kept on file. Samples not kept on file are returned in 2 weeks. Pays by the project. Considers client's budget, skill and experience of artist, and turnaround time when establishing payment.
Tips: "Show an accurate representation, be professional, honest and service-oriented."

THE DESIGN OFFICE OF STEVE NEUMANN & FRIENDS, Suite 103, 3000 Richmond Ave., Houston TX 77098. (713)629-7501. Contact: Cynthia J. Whitney. Specializes in corporate identity and signage. Clients: architects, interior designers, developers, hospitals, universities, etc.
Needs: Works with 2-4 freelance artists/year. Artists must be local with "good background." Uses artists for design, illustration, retouching, model making, drafting and signage. Especially needs full-time and/or part-time production person.
First Contact & Terms: Send query letter with brochure, resume, references, business card and slides to be kept on file. Reports back within 15 days. Write for appointment to show portfolio. Pays for design by the hour based on job contract. Considers complexity of project, client's budget, skill and experience of artist, and how work will be used when establishing payment.
Tips: "We have acquired a computer which utilizes graphics, and we have less need of freelance artists."

THE DESIGN QUARTER, 2900 4th Ave., San Diego CA 92103. (619)297-7900. Executive Vice President/Design: Brian Lovell. Specializes in annual reports, corporate identity, direct mail and publications. Clients: corporations and publishers.
Needs: Works with 6 freelance artists/year. Uses artists for catalogs, books, mechanicals, retouching, airbrushing, model making and charts/graphs.
First Contact & Terms: Send business card to be kept on file. Prefers photostats, photocopies and tear sheets as samples. Samples not kept on file are returned only if requested by SASE. Reports back only if interested. Call for appointment to show portfolio. Pays for design by the hour, $10-30 average; by the project, $25-1,800 average. Pays for illustration by the hour, $25-50 average; by the project, $100-5,000 average. Considers complexity of project, client's budget, and skill and experience of artist when establishing payment.

DESIGN TRAIN, 434 Hidden Valley Ln., Cincinnati OH 45215. (513)761-7099. Contact: Joseph Pagliaro. Specializes in brand identity, corporate identity, direct mail, packaging, publications, AV educational programs and book covers computer graphics. Clients: book publishers and industrial manufacturers.
Needs: Works with 1-2 freelance artists/year. Artists must be experienced, usually local. Works on assignment only. Uses artists for illustration.
First Contact & Terms: Send query letter with brochure showing art style or resume and tear sheets and photocopies to be kept on file. Samples are not returned. Reports back only if interested. Call or write for appointment to show portfolio. Pays for illustration by the project, $50-1,500. Considers complexity of project, client's budget, and skill and experience of artist when establishing payment.
Tips: "Computer graphics capability is opening new areas by allowing higher productivity with lower costs. We seek artists who are skilled in sound basic drawing skills and use of color."

DESIGN VECTORS, INC., A2, 408 Columbus Ave., San Francisco CA 94133. Contact: Tony Williams or Jim Tetzlaff. Specializes in brand identity, corporate identity, displays, direct mail, packaging, magazine design, publications and signage. Clients: public relation firms, banks, ad agencies and other corporations.
Needs: Works with 12 freelance artists/year. Local artists only. Uses artists for design, illustration, brochures, magazines, mechanicals, airbrushing, charts/graphs and advertisements.
First Contact & Terms: Send query letter with brochure showing art style or resume and samples to be kept on file. "Send only resume or samples that we can keep." Reports back only if interested. Pays for design and illustration by the hour, $10 minimum. Considers complexity of project, client's budget, skill and experience of artist and turnaround time when establishing payment.

DESIGN WORKS, INC., 521 W. Ormsby Ave., Louisville KY 40203. (502)636-9101. Chief Designer: Ron Patterson. Specializes in corporate identity, displays and packaging. Clients: advertisers and ad agencies.
Needs: Works with 3-5 freelance artists/year. Artist must work in-house. Works on assignment only. Uses artists for design, illustration, mechanicals and retouching.
First Contact & Terms: Call or write for appointment to show portfolio. Accepts photostats, slides, photocopies or tear sheets as samples. Samples not filed are returned only if requested. Reports back only if interested. Pays for design by the hour, $15-25 average. Considers complexity of project, client's budget, and skill and experience of artist when establishing payment.

DESIGNS FOR MEDICINE, INC., 301 Cherry St., Philadelphia PA 19106. (215)925-7100. President: Peter W. Bressler. Specializes in annual reports, corporate identity, packaging, technical illustrations, product design and graphic design. Clients: ad agencies, manufacturers and inventors.
Needs: Works with 8 freelance artists/year. "Local artists only to work in our office primarily; experience required varies." Works on assignment only. Uses artists for design, illustration, brochures, mechanicals, airbrushing, model making, lettering, logos and advertisements.
First Contact & Terms: Send query letter with brochure, resume, business card and samples to be kept on file, except for slides which will be returned to sender. Prefers slides and tear sheets as samples. Samples not filed returned. Reports within 3 weeks. Write for appointment to show portfolio. Pays for design by the hour, $5-20 average (quotation basis). Considers complexity of project, client's budget, and skill and experience of artist when establishing payment.
Tips: "Be aggressive, very talented and creative."

DESIGNWORKS, INC., 5 Bridge St., Watertown MA 02172. (617)926-6286. Art Directors: S. Bindari, J.R. Bush. Provides design for publishing industry. Specializes in educational publications. Clients: book publishers.
Needs: Works with 10 freelance artists/year. Works on assignment only. Uses artists for book illustration, charts/graphs. Prefers styles "appropriate for educational materials."
First Contact & Terms: Send query letter with brochure showing art style or resume and samples. To show a portfolio, mail appropriate materials or write to schedule an appointment. Portfolio should include final reproduction/product, tear sheets, b&w or anything showing final product. Pays for illustration by the project, $200 minimum. Considers complexity of project, client's budget, and skill and experience of artist when establishing payment.
Tips: "We like samples for our files but we do not have a lot of office time for reviewing portfolios as we are producing during work hours ourselves."

DESKEY ASSOCIATES, INC., 15 W. 39th St., New York NY 10018. Director of Graphic Operations: Emmitt B. Sears. Specializes in brand and/or corporate identity, displays, packaging, illustration and mechanical art. Clients: corporations.
Needs: Works with approximately 10 freelance artists/year. Uses artists for design, illustration, P-O-P displays, mechanicals, retouching, airbrushing, model making, charts/graphs, lettering and logos.
First Contact & Terms: "Artists should present their resume, hourly wages and make a written request to present their work." Send query letter and resume to be kept on file. Prefers to see "best samples of areas in which artist may be of help—design/mechanicals/photos of models designed and very rough conceptual sketches." Samples are not returned. Reports back within days. Write to schedule an appointment to show a portfolio, which should include thumbnails, roughs and "whatever is possible to show that will not be returned in some cases." Pays for design by the hour, $10 minimum. Pays for illustration by the project, $250 minimum. Considers complexity of project, client's budget, skill and experience of artist, and turnaround time when establishing payment.
Tips: "Too often artists present work that is a finished product—one wonders what efforts or contributions were made to develop the final product."

***GABRIEL DI FIORE ASSOC.**, 625 Stanwix St., Pittsburgh PA 15222. (412)471-0608. Owner: Gabe Di Fiore. Specializes in annual reports, corporate identity, direct mail and publication. Clients: ad agencies, PR firms and corporations.
Needs: Works with 20 freelance artists/year. Uses artists for illustrations, mechanicals, retouching, charts/graphs and lettering. Especially needs mechanicals and illustrations.
First Contact & Terms: Send query letter with brochure showing art style or resume, tear sheets and slides. Samples not filed are returned by SASE. Reports only if interested. Call or write to schedule an appointment to show a portfolio, which should include thumbnails, roughs, original/final art and tear sheets. Pays for design by the hour, $10 minimum; pays for illustration by the hour, $10 minimum. Considers complexity of project, client's budget and how work will be used when establishing payment.

DI FRANZA-WILLIAMSON INC., 1414 Avenue of the Americas, New York NY 10019. (212)832-2343. Contact: Jack Williamson. Clients: businesses and advertising agencies.
Needs: Assigns 250 jobs/year; local artists with 2-3 years minimum experience only. Uses artists for layout, comps, illustration, cartoons, lettering and retouching for catalogs, direct mail brochures, flyers, packaging, P-O-P displays and slides.
First Contact & Terms: Send query letter with resume and request interview. No work returned. Payment by hour: $12-20, design and layout; $15-50, illustrations; $15-20, mechanicals and paste-up; $15-22, type spec. Considers complexity of project, client's budget, skill and experience of artist, and how work will be used when establishing payment.
Tips: "Show me good work." There is a "need for designers who can draw. Show me roughs and layouts, not just finished pieces. Illustration is coming back."

ANTHONY DI MARCO, ADVERTISING AND DESIGN AGENCY, 2948 Grand Route St. John, New Orleans LA 70119. (504)948-3128. Creative Director: Anthony Di Marco. Specializes in brand identity, packaging, publications, and technical illustration. Clients: individuals and major corporations.
Needs: Works with 5-10 freelance artists/year. Seeks "local artists with ambition. Artists should have substantial portfolios and an understanding of business requirements." Uses artists for design, illustration, mechanicals, retouching, airbrushing, posters, model making, charts/graphs. Computer-generated graphics are a current interest.
First Contact & Terms: Send query letter with resume, business card and slides and tear sheets to be kept on file. Samples not kept on file are returned by SASE. Reports back within 1 week if interested. Call or write for appointment to show portfolio. Pays for design and illustration by the project, $50-500 average. Considers complexity of project, skill and experience of artist, turnaround time and rights purchased when establishing payment.
Tips: "Keep professionalism in mind at all times. Artists should put forth their best effort."

DIAMOND ART STUDIO LTD., 11 E. 36th St., New York NY 10016. (212)685-6622. Creative Directors: Gary and Douglas Diamond. Vice Presidents: John Taylor, Mary Nittolo, Phil Rowley. Art studio. Clients: advertising agencies, corporations, manufacturers and publishers. Assigns 500 jobs/year.
Needs: Employs 10 illustrators/month. Uses artists for comprehensive illustrations, cartoons, charts, graphs, illustrations, layout, lettering, logo design, paste-up, retouching, technical art and type spec.
First Contact & Terms: Send resume and tear sheets to be kept on file. SASE. Write for interview to show a portfolio. Pays for design by the hour. Pays for illustration by the project. Considers complexity of project, client's budget, skill and experience of artist, and turnaround time when establishing payment.
Tips: "Leave behind something memorable and well thought out."

DIMENSIONAL DESIGN, 11046 McCormick, North Hollywood CA 91601. (213)877-5694. Contact: Design Director. Specializes in brand and corporate identity, displays, exhibits and shows, packaging, publications, signage and technical illustration, direct mail marketing, movie titles and film production. Clients: multi-field corporations, manufacturers, shopping centers and advertising agencies.
Needs: Works with 20-30 freelance artists/year. Works on assignment only. Uses artists for advertising, brochure and catalog design, illustration and layout; P-O-P displays, mechanicals, retouching; poster, book and direct mail package design and illustration; model making, charts/graphs, lettering and logo design.
First Contact & Terms: Send query letter with brochure/flyer, resume and tear sheets, photostats, photocopies, slides and photographs "as one unit to us." Samples returned by SASE, "but would like to keep samples, resume/brochure, etc. on file." Reports in 2 months. Call or write for appointment. Pays for design $10-35 average/hour; pays for illustration $15-40; also negotiates.
Tips: "Become as professional as possible, not only in art, but also in art reproduction."

DONATO & BERKLEY INC., 386 Park Ave. S, New York NY 10016. (212)532-3884. Contact: Sy Berkley or Steve Sherman. Advertising art studio. Specializes in direct mail response advertising, annual reports, brand identity, corporate identity and publications. Clients: ad agencies, public relations firms, direct response advertisers and publishers.
Needs: Works with 1-2 illustrators and 1-2 designers/month. Local experienced artists only. Uses artists for consumer magazines, direct mail, brochures/flyers, newspapers, layout, technical art, type spec, paste-up, lettering and retouching. Especially needs illustrations, retouching and mechanical paste-up.
First Contact & Terms: Call for interview. Send brochure showing art style, flyers, business card, resume and tearsheet to be kept on file. No originals returned to artist at job's completion. Call to schedule an appointment to show a portfolio, which should include thumbnails, roughs, original/final art and final reproduction/product. Pays for design and illustration by the hour and by the project. Considers com-

plexity of project and client's budget when establishing payment.

Tips: "We foresee a need for direct response art directors and the mushrooming of computer graphics. Clients are much more careful as to price and quality of work."

***EDITING, DESIGN & PRODUCTION, INC.**, 4th Floor, 400 Market St., Philadelphia PA 19106. (215)592-1133. Production Manager: Jacqui Brownstein. Specializes in publications. Clients: publishers.

Needs: Works with approximately 18 freelance artists/year. Uses artists for design, illustrations, books and mechanicals. Especially needs designers of college textbook interiors and/or covers.

First Contact & Terms: Send query letter with brochure showing art style or resume, tear sheets and photocopies. Samples not filed are retuned only if requested. Reports within 2 weeks. Call to schedule an appointment to show a portfolio, which should include roughs, final reproduction/product, tear sheets and photostats. Pays for design by the project, $200-500. Pays for illustration by the project, $10-30/piece. Considers complexity of project and client's budget when establishing payment.

Tips: "Our textbooks can be very complex and we require typed specifications and tissue layouts for every element in the book."

***EHN GRAPHICS, INC.**, 244 E. 46th St., New York NY 10017. (212)661-5947. President: Jack Ehn. Specializes in annual reports, corporate identity, direct mail, publications and signage.

Needs: Works with 10-12 freelance artists/year. Uses artists for illustrations, books, mechanicals, retouching and direct mail packages.

First Contact & Terms: Send query letter with samples. Samples not filed are retuned only if requested. Reports only if interested. Call or write to schedule an appointment to show a portfolio, which should include original/final art and final reproduction/product. Considers complexity of project, client's budget, and skill and experience of artist when establishing payment.

DAVE ELLIES INDUSTRIAL DESIGN, INC., 2015 W. Fifth Ave., Columbus OH 43212. (614)488-7995. Creative Manager: Ron Bushman. Specializes in corporate identity, displays, interior design, packaging and signage.

Needs: Works with 10 freelance artists/year. Prefers regional freelance artists with 3-5 years' experience. Works on assignment only. Uses artists for design, illustration, mechanicals, model making, AV materials and logos.

First Contact & Terms: Send query letter with resume, business card and slides to be kept on file. Samples not kept on file returned by SASE. Reports within 2 weeks. Call or write for appointment to show portfolio. Considers complexity of project, client's budget, skill and experience of artist and turnaround time when establishing payment.

Tips: Especially looks for "quality not quantity, professionalism, variety and effective problem solving" in samples.

RAY ENGLE & ASSOCIATES, 626 S. Kenmore, Los Angeles CA 90005. (213)381-5001. President: Ray Engle. Specializes in annual reports, brand identity, corporate identity, displays, packaging, publications and signage. Clients: ad agencies, public relation agencies and corporations.

Needs: Works with 2-3 freelance artists/year. Local artists only. Works on assignment only. Uses artists for illustration, retouching and model making.

First Contact & Terms: Send query letter with resume, tear sheets, photostats and photocopies to be kept on file. Samples not kept on file are returned by SASE. Reports only if interested. Call or write to schedule an appointment to show a portfolio, which should include thumbnails, roughs, original/final art, final reproduction/product, color and tear sheets. Pays for design by the hour, $15-40; by the project $50 minimum; by the day, $100-300. Pays for illustration by the hour, $15-50; by the project, $50 minimum; by the day, $100-400. Considers complexity of project, client's budget, skill and experience of artist, how work will be used and turnaround time when establishing payment.

Tips: "Think of how you can be of service to us—not how we can be of service to you."

ENSIGN DESIGN INC., 201 College Ave., Salem VA 24153. (703)389-0482. President: Jim Edgell. Specializes in corporate identity, displays, packaging, publications, signage, technical illustrations, product design prototypes and models. Clients: industry, communications and consumer products.

Needs: Works with "a few" freelance artists/year. Prefers local artists and that they work on premises. Uses artists for illustration, airbrushing and model making. Especially needs a good airbrush artist.

First Contact & Terms: Send query letter with resume to be kept on file. Samples not filed are returned by SASE. Reports only if interested. To show a portfolio, mail appropriate materials, which should include roughs, original/final art and final reproduction/product. Pays by the hour, $6-20 average. Considers complexity of project, clients's budget, and skill and experience of artist when establishing payment.

Tips: "Assemble a portfolio showing broadest range of skills as those who can overlap into more than one area of design."

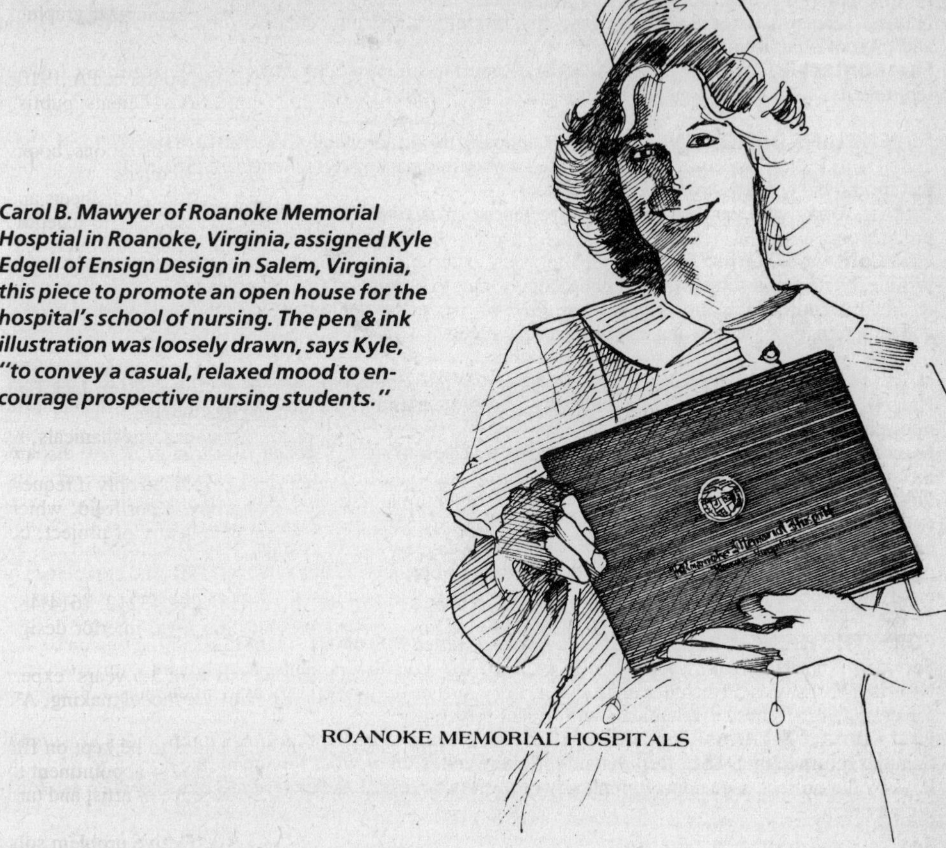

Carol B. Mawyer of Roanoke Memorial Hosptial in Roanoke, Virginia, assigned Kyle Edgell of Ensign Design in Salem, Virginia, this piece to promote an open house for the hospital's school of nursing. The pen & ink illustration was loosely drawn, says Kyle, "to convey a casual, relaxed mood to encourage prospective nursing students."

MEL ERIKSON/ART SERVICES, 31 Meadow Rd., Kings Park NY 11754-3812. (516)544-9191. Art Director: Toniann Manfredi. Specializes in publications and technical illustration. Clients: book publishers.
Needs: Works with 8-10 freelance artists/year. Local artists only. Uses artists for advertising illustration, book design and illustration, mechanicals, retouching and charts/graphs.
First Contact & Terms: Send query letter with resume and photocopies to be kept on file. Samples not kept on file are not returned. Does not report back. Call to schedule an appointment to show a portfolio, which should include final reproduction/product. Pays for design by the hour, $4.50-20; by the project, $50-1,000; by the day, $40-100. Pays for illustration by the hour, $4.50-$9; by the project, $25-$100; by the day, $40-80. Considers complexity of project and client's budget when establishing payment.
Tips: "Call first—show only work relative to my needs."

ETC COMMUNICATIONS GROUP, (formerly ETC Graphics), 61 W. 23rd St., 7th Fl., New York NY 10010. (212)645-6800. President: Edwart T. Chin. Specializes in direct mail and marketing-oriented corporate graphics. Clients: Fortune 500 corporations, ad agencies, PR firms, magazine publishers, small- and medium-size companies.
Needs: Works with 17 freelance artists/year. Minimum 2-3 years' experience. Works on assignment only. Uses artists for design, illustration, catalogs, mechanicals, retouching, airbrushing and lettering.
First Contact & Terms: Send query letter with brochure, resume, business card and tear sheets or photocopies to be kept on file. Samples not filed are returned by SASE. Reports within 2 weeks. Write for appointment to show portfolio. Pays for design by the hour, $10-20 average; for illustration by the hour, $10-20 average, or by the project, $25-300 average. Considers complexity of project, client's budget, skill and experience of artist, how work will be used, turnaround time and rights purchased when establishing payment.

FINN STUDIO LIMITED, 154 E. 64th St., New York NY 10021. (212)838-1212. Creative Director: Finn. Clients: theatres, boutiques and magazines, fashion and ad agencies.
Needs: Uses artists for T-shirt designs, illustrations, calligraphy; creative concepts in art for fashion and promotional T-shirts.
First Contact & Terms: Mail slides. SASE. Reports within 4 weeks. Pays $50-500; sometimes also offers royalty.

***5 PENGUINS DESIGN, INC.**, 1648 W. Glenoaks Blvd., Glendale CA 91201. (818)502-1556. President: Dauri Pallas. Specializes in corporate identity and packaging. Clients: advertising for the motion picture industry, television and home video.
Needs: Works with varying number of freelance artists/year. Uses artists for design, mechanicals and production.
First Contact & Terms: Artists should be "very experienced and professional." Send query letter with resume, business card, tear sheets, photocopies, etc. to be kept on file. Samples not kept on file are not returned. Reports back only if interested. Pays for design by the hour at varying rates. Considers skill and experience of artist when establishing payment.

HANS FLINK DESIGN INC., 7-11 S. Broadway, White Plains NY 10601. (914)328-0888. President: Hans D. Flink. Specializes in brand identity, corporate identity, packaging and signage. Clients: corporate, packaged products.
Needs: Works with 10-20 freelance artists/year. Uses artists for design, illustration, P-O-P displays, mechanicals, retouching, airbrushing, model making, lettering, logos and package related services.
First Contact & Terms: Send query letter with brochure and resume to be kept on file. Reports back only if interested. Call or write for appointment to show portfolio. Pays for design by the hour, $10-35 average; by the project, $500-3,000 average; by the day, $100-250 average. Pays for illustration by the project, $250-2,000 average. Considers complexity of project, client's budget, skill and experience of artist, how work will be used, turnaround time and rights purchased when establishing payment.

FORSYTHE FRENCH, INC., 108 BN. Scott Ave., Betten MO 64021. (816)322-2580. Director/Design Services: Alan Hickman. Specializes in architectural graphics. Clients: hospitals and universities.
Needs: Works with 5 freelance artists/year. Local artists only. Works on assignment only. Uses artists for design, brochures, mechanicals and model making.
First Contact & Terms: Send query letter with resume to be kept on file. Prefers slides as samples. Samples returned by SASE. Reports only if interested. Call or write for appointment to show portfolio. Pays by the project. Considers complexity of project, and skill and experience of artist when establishing payment.

FREE LANCE EXCHANGE, INC., 111 E. 85th St., New York NY 10028. (212)722-5816. Multi-service company.
Needs: Uses artists for cartoons, charts, graphs, illustrations, layout, lettering, logo design and mechanicals.
First Contact & Terms: Mail resume and photocopied samples. "Say you saw the listing in *Artist's Market*." Provide materials to be kept on file for future assignments. No originals returned to artist at job's completion.

FREEMAN DESIGN GROUP, 415 Farms Rd., Greenwich CT 06831. (203)968-0026. President: Bill Freeman. Specializes in annual reports, corporate identity, packaging, publications and signage. Clients: corporations.
Needs: Works with 5-10 freelance artists/year. New York City/Fairfield County artists only. Works on assignment only. Uses artists for illustration, mechanicals, retouching and airbrushing.
First Contact & Terms: Send query letter with brochure and business card to be kept on file. Call for appointment to show portfolio. Prefers to review slides, tear sheets or original work at time of interview *only*. Material not filed is returned by SASE only if requested. Reports back only if interested. Pays for design by the hour, $15-20 average, or by the project, $50-2,500 average; for illustration by the project, $50-1,000 average. Considers complexity of project, client's budget, how work will be used and rights purchased when establishing payment.
Tips: "Present a clean portfolio of your best work, not necessarily printed samples."

FREEMAN DESIGN INCORPORATED, 2555 M Street NW, Washington DC 20037. (202)296-7272. Creative Director/President: Sheila Freeman. Specializes in corporate identity, displays, direct mail, publications, image development, brochures (capability, selling), newsletters and AV presentations. Clients: corporations, associations and public relation firms.
Needs: Works with 20 freelance artists/year. Prefers artists with "one year experience at least, to work

in our office." Uses artists for illustration, mechanicals, retouching, airbrushing, charts/graphs and lettering.
First Contact & Terms: Send query letter with resume, business card, tear sheets and slides to be kept on file. Reports only if interested. Write for appointment to show portfolio. Pays for design by the hour, $15-20 average; pays for illustration by the project; for mechanicals, $12. Considers complexity of project, client's budget, and skill and experience of artist when establishing payment.

STEPHANIE FURNISS DESIGN, 1327 Via Sessi, San Rafael CA 94901. (415)459-4730. Contact: Stephanie Furniss. Specializes in corporate identity, architectural and environmental graphics, supergraphics, interior design, packaging, sculpture and signage.
Needs: Works with 5 freelance artists/year. Uses artists for lettering and production work.
First Contact & Terms: Send query letter with resume and business card. Call or write to schedule an appointment to show a portfolio, which should include thumbnails, roughs, original/final art, final reproduction/product, color, tear sheets, photostats, photographs and b&w. Pays for design by the hour, $8-25. Considers complexity of project, skill and experience of artist, and turnaround time when establishing payment.
Tips: "Write first. Call second for appointment. Show up for appointment promptly and with *good* portfolio (nothing just thrown together)."

GAILEN ASSOCIATES, INC., Suite 105, 800 Oak St., Winnetka IL 60093. (312)446-5003. President: Bob Gailen. Specializes in annual reports, brand identity, corporate identity, packaging, publications and signage. Clients: direct mail, ad agencies, marketing firms.
Needs: Works with 5 freelance artists/year. Works on assignment basis. Uses artists for illustration, photography, airbrushing and model making.
First Contact & Terms: Send query letter with resume and samples to be kept on file. Does not report back. Pays for design, by the hour $25 minimum; for illustration, per illustrator's quote. Considers complexity of project, client's budget, and skill and experience of artist when establishing payment.

GARRETT COMMUNICATIONS, INC., Box 53, Atlanta GA 30301. (404)755-2513. President: Ruby Grant Garrett. Specializes in brand identity, corporate identity and packaging. Clients: manufacturers, public relation firms and ad agencies.
Needs: Works with 6 freelance artists/year. Works on assignment only. Uses artists for illustration, mechanicals, retouching, airbrushing, P-O-P displays, model making and lettering. Buys 3 cartoons, 6 cartoon-style and 6 humorous illustrations/year.
First Contact & Terms: Send resume, business card and samples to be kept on file. Samples not kept on file are returned only if requested. Reports within 10 days. Call to schedule an appointment to show a portfolio, which should include thumbnails, original/final art and photostats. Pays by the hour, $35 minimum. Considers client's budget, turnaround time and rights purchased when establishing payment.
Tips: "State what you cannot do. Live with your quote and place conditions in writing."

GIOVANNI DESIGN ASSOCIATES, 137 E. 36th St., New York NY 10016. (212)725-8536. Contact: John E. Frontino. Specializes in packaging. Clients: industry and fragrance/cosmetic firms.
Needs: Works on assignment only. Uses artists for advertising, brochure and catalog design, illustration and layout; P-O-P displays, mechanicals; poster, book and direct mail package design and illustration; AV presentations, lettering and logo design "as needed."
First Contact & Terms: Send brochure/flyer, slides, resume, business card and tear sheets to be kept on file. Samples not kept on file are returned by SASE. Reports "as soon as possible." Submit portfolio for review. Negotiates payment method and payment.

ERIC GLUCKMAN COMMUNICATIONS, INC., 60 E. 42nd St., New York NY 10165. (212)697-3670. President: Eric Gluckman. Specializes in corporate identity, direct mail, publications, industrial advertising and promotion, corporate capability brochures and sales promotion (trade). "We usually deal directly with client."
Needs: Works with 20 freelance artists/year. Artists should have 3 years' experience minimum. "All rights to art and photography revert to client." Works on assignment only. Uses artists for design, illustration, brochures, mechanicals, retouching, airbrushing, direct mail packages, posters, charts/graphs, lettering, logos and advertisements.
First Contact & Terms: Send query letter with resume and samples to be kept on file. No slides as samples. Samples not kept on file returned by SASE. Reports only if interested. Call or write to Art Director: Clare Ultimo for appointment to show portfolio. Pay is negotiable. Considers complexity of project, client's budget, skill and experience of artist, and turnaround time when establishing payment. Buys all rights.
Tips: "Be professional, make deadlines."

***GOFF DESIGN GROUP**, 69 Water St., San Francisco CA 94133. (415)441-5084. Art Director: Andrea Bryck. Specializes in annual reports, corporate identity, direct mail, packaging, publications, marketing and communications planning and design. Clients: ad agencies and major corporations.
Needs: Works with 10-15 freelance artists/year. Prefers three years' experience. Uses artists for design, illustrations, mechanicals, retouching, airbrushing, model making, AV materials and lettering.
First Contact & Terms: Send query letter with resume, tear sheets, photostats, photocopies, slides and photographs. Samples not filed are returned by SASE. Reports only if interested. Call or write to schedule an appointment to show a portfolio, which should include roughs, original/final art, final reproduction/product, color, tear sheets, photostats, photographs, b&w or whatever form will best represent artist's work. Pays for design by the hour, $18 minimum. Considers complexity of project, client's budget, skill and experience of artist, how work will be used, turnaround time and rights purchased when establishing payment.

GOLDSMITH YAMASAKI SPECHT INC, Suite 510, 900 North Fanklin St., Chicago IL 60610. (312)266-8404. Industrial design-consultancy. Chairman: William M. Goldsmith. Specializes in corporate identity, packaging, product design and graphics. Clients: industrial firms, institutions, service organziations, ad agencies, government agencies, etc.
Needs: Works with 6-10 freelance artists/year. "We generally use local artists, simply for convenience." Works on assignment only. Uses artists for design (especially graphics), illustration, retouching, model making, lettering and production art.
First Contact & Terms: Send query letter with resume and samples to be kept on file. Samples not kept on file are returned only if requested. Reports only if interested. Call or write to schedule an appointment to show a portfolio, which should include roughs and final reproduction/product. Pays for design by the hour, $20 minimum; pays for illustration by the project, payment depends on project. Considers complexity of project, client's budget, skill and experience of artist, how work will be used, turnaround time and rights purchased when establishing payment.
Tips: "If we receive many inquiries, obviously our time commitment may be short, necessarily. Please understand. We use verly little outside help, but it is increasing (mostly graphic design and production art)."

ALAN GORELICK & ASSOCIATES INC., Graphic Designers, 999 Raritan Rd., Clark NJ 07066. Also at One Nichols Rd., Morristown NJ 07960. President/Creative Director: Alan Gorelick. Specializes in corporate identity, displays, direct mail, signage, technical illustration and company and product literature. Clients: health care and pharmaceutical corporations, industrial, manufacturing.
Needs: Works with 6-10 freelance artists/year. Works with "seasoned professional or extremely talented entry-level" artists only. Uses artists for design, illustration, brochures, mechanicals, retouching, airbrushing, posters, direct mail packages, charts/graphs, logos and advertisements.
First Contact & Terms: Send query letter with brochure, resume, business card, photostats, slides, photocopies and tear sheets to be kept on file. Samples not filed are returned by SASE only if requested. Reports only if interested. Write for appointment to show portfolio, which should include thumbnails, roughs, original/final art, final reproduction/product, color, tear sheets, photostats, photographs and b&w. Pays for design by the hour, $15-35 average. Pays for illustration by the hour, $15-50 average. Considers complexity of project, client's budget, and skill and experience of artist when establishing payment.
Tips: Requires "straight talk, professional work ethic and commitment to assignment."

GRAPHICUS, 11046 McCormick, North Hollywood CA 91601. (213)877-5694. President: Wayne Hallowell. Specializes in annual reports, brand and corporate identity, displays, exhibits and shows, packaging, publications, signage and technical illustration. Clients: advertising agencies, corporations, manufacturers (in all fields); "we supply all areas of corporate communications."
Needs: Works with 20 freelance artists/year. Prefers at least 5 years' experience. Works on assignment only. Uses artists for advertising, brochure and catalog design and illustration, advertising layout, P-O-P displays, mechanicals, poster, book and direct mail package design and illustration; model making, AV presentations, lettering, and logo and package design. Especially needs "good, clean, knowledgeable artists who are true professionals and know what happens to their work after it leaves the drawing boards."
First Contact & Terms: Send query letter with resume, tear sheets, photostats, slides and photographs. Samples returned by SASE "only when requested; it is far better to have samples available in our offices." Reports in 4 weeks. Reports back on whether to expect possible future assignments. Call or write to schedule an appointment to show portfolio, which should include thumbnails, roughs, original/final art, final reproduction/product, tear sheets and photographs. Pays for design by the project, $1,000-$10,000. Pays for illustration by the project, $1,000-15,000.
Tips: "An artist should know the profession, become more business-like and train as an athlete does. Be creative, be yourself, be clean."

GRAPHICUS ART STUDIO, 2025 Maryland Ave., Baltimore MD 21218. (301)727-5553. Art Director: Charles Piccirilli. Specializes in annual reports, advertising campaigns, brand and corporate identity, displays, packaging, publications and signage. Clients: recreational sport industries, fleet leasing companies, technical product manufacturers, commercial packaging corporations, direct mail advertising firms, realty companies and home heating oil companies.
Needs: Works on assignment only. Uses artist for advertising, brochure, catalog and poster illustration, retouching and AV presentations. Especially needs high quality illustration.
First Contact & Terms: Send query letter with resume, photocopies and photographs; prefers originals as samples. Samples returned by SASE. Reports on whether to expect possible future assignments. To show a portfolio, mail appropriate material or call to schedule an appointment; portfolio should include original/final art. Pays by the project.
Tips: Artists should have "flexibility."

***GROUP FOUR DESIGN**, 147 Simsbury Rd., Avon CT 06001-0717. (203)678-1570. Production Manager: Joyce Gatonska. Specializes in corporate communications, product design and packaging design. Clients: corporations dealing in consumer products and office products.
Needs: Works with 5-10 freelance artists/year. Artists must have at least two years' experience. Uses artists for illustrations, mechanicals, airbrushing and model making.
First Contact & Terms: Send query letter with resume and slides. Samples not filed are returned. Reports only if interested. To show a portfolio, mail roughs and original/final art. Pays for design by the hour, $12-20. Considers client's budget, and skill and experience of artist when establishing payment.
Tips: "We look for creativity in all artists seeking employment and expect to see that in their resume and portfolio."

HAMILTON DESIGN, INC., 2130 Stella Ct., Columbus OH 43215. (614)481-8016. Contact: Bill Hamilton or Joan Etter. Specializes in brand identity, displays, packaging, publications and direct mail—merchandising and selling ads. Clients: publications and manufacturers.
Needs: Works on assignment only. Uses artists for advertising and brochure layout; catalog design and layout, P-O-P displays, mechanicals, retouching and direct response packages.
First Contact & Terms: Send query letter with resume and slides. Samples not kept on file are returned. Reports in 2 weeks. Call for appointment to show portfolio. Pays for design and illustration by the hour, $10-70 average. Considers how work will be used and rights purchased when establishing payment.

PAIGE HARDY & ASSOCIATES, 1731 Kettner Blvd., San Diego CA 92101. (619)233-7238. Contact: Paige Hardy or Lorie Kennedy. Specializes in corporate identity, publications, technical illustration and advertising art. Clients: retail firms and publications.
Needs: Works with 25 freelance artists/year. Usually works on assignment only. Uses artists for advertising, brochure and catalog design, illustration and layout; mechanicals, retouching and logo design. Especially needs production artist/paste-up with heavy experience.
First Contact & Terms: Send query letter with resume. Samples not returned. Reports in 1 week. Call or write for appointment to submit portfolio for review. Pays by the hour and project; negotiates payment.

HARPER & ASSOCIATES, INC., 2285 116th Ave. NE, Bellevue WA 98004. (206)462-0405. Creative Director: Randi Harper. Office Manager: Kelley Wood. Specializes in brand and corporate identity. Clients: high tech, manufacturers professional services, (i.e., architects, doctors, attorneys, yacht brokers, stockbrokers, etc.), food, fashion, etc.
Needs: Works with 10-12 freelance artists/year. Works on assignment only. Uses artists for illustration and airbrush.
First Contact & Terms: Send resume and slides. Samples returned by SASE. Reports only if interested. Pays for design by the hour, $8-20; for illustration by the hour, $10-30, or by the project. Considers complexity of project, client's budget, skill and experience of artist, how work will be used, turnaround time and rights purchased when establishing payment.
Tips: "Be honest about your abilities and do not be afraid to turn down an assignment if it is not appropriate for you."

HARRINGTON-JACKSON, INC., 10 Newbury St., Boston MA 02116. (617)536-6164. Specializes in collateral materials—brochures, flyers, posters and other sales/promotional pieces. Clients: manufacturers and trade (industrial).
Needs: Works with 3-4 freelance artists/year. Local artists only with 2-3 years' experience. Works on assignment only. Uses artists for illustration, brochures, mechanicals, retouching and airbrushing. "We especially need experienced (2-3 years) mechanical artists who can work in our studio."

First Contact & Terms: Send query letter with resume to be kept on file for 6 months. Reports only if interested. Call for appointment to show portfolio. Pays for illustration by the hour, $6-10; for mechanical art, $6-10. Considers skill and experience of artist when establishing payment.
Tips: "Call 2-3 hours in advance to make sure someone is available to review portfolio."

HERBST, LAZAR, ROGERS & BELL, INC., 37 North Duke St., Lancaster PA 17602. (717)291-9042. Office Manager: Sarah Preston. Specializes in brand identity, corporate identity, displays, interior design, packaging, publications, signage, technical illustration, human factors, market placement research, product design and cost reduction. Clients: manufacturers, ad agencies and retailers.
Needs: Works with 10 freelance artists/year. Artists should be within driving distance; "prefer freelancers to work in house." Works on assignment only. Uses artists for illustration, brochures, catalogs, mechanicals, model making, charts/graphs, lettering, logos advertisements and market research.
First Contact & Terms: Send query letter with brochure, resume, business card and slides to be kept on file. Samples not kept on file are returned. Reports within 15 days. To show a portfolio, mail appropriate materials or write to schedule an appointment; portfolio should include thumbnails, roughs, final reproduction/product and photographs. Pays for design by the hour, $7-25; pays for illustration by the hour, $10-$25. Considers complexity of project, and skill and experience of artist when establishing payment.
Tips: "In the field there is much, preliminary work on market placement and product use, prior to design. Collateral materials tie in, also."

***HILLMAN CONSORTIUM**, 1021 Pearl, Boulder CO 80302. (303)443-6099. President: Jack L. Hillman. Specializes in corporate identity, displays, industrial design and packaging. Clients: manufacturers.
Needs: Works with 12 freelance artists/year. Prefers local and experienced artists. Works on assignment only. Uses artists for design, brochures, mechanicals, posters, model making, charts/graphs, AV materials, lettering and logos. Especially needs "an experienced, well-rounded industrial designer."
First Contact & Terms: Send query letter with brochure, resume, business card and samples to be kept on file. Samples "originally should be any medium appropriate to the subject. In person I like to see originals or the finished piece." Samples not filed are returned by SASE only if requested. Reports within 1 week. Pay varies. Considers client's budget and skill and experience of artist when establishing payment.
Tips: "Only the best are considered: ability to meet schedules, professionalism, neatness; organization."

***DAVID HIRSCH DESIGN GROUP, INC.**, 205 W. Wacker Dr., Chicago IL 60606. Specializes in annual reports, corporate identity, publications and promotional literature. Clients: PR, real estate and financial firms.
Needs: Works with over 12 freelance artists/year. Uses artists for design, illustrations, brochures, retouching, airbrushing, AV materials, lettering, logos and photography.
First Contact & Terms: Send query letter with brochure showing art style or samples. Samples not filed are returned by SASE. Reports only if interested. Call or write to schedule an appointment to show a portfolio, which should include roughs, final reproduction/product, tear sheets and photographs. Considers complexity of project, client's budget and how work will be used when establishing payment.
Tips: "We're always looking for talent at fair prices."

GRANT HOEKSTRA GRAPHICS, INC., 333 N. Michigan Ave., Chicago IL 60601. (312)641-6940. President: Grant Hoekstra. Specializes in publications. Clients: publishers, ad agencies and corporations.
Needs: Works with 15 freelance artists/year. Local artists with experience only. Works on assignment only. Uses artists for design, illustration, brochures, retouching and lettering. Especially needs "illustrator who understands 'fundamental Christian' market."
First Contact & Terms: Send samples and prices to be kept on file. Call for appointment to show portfolio. Prefers photocopies as samples. Pays for design by the hour, $15-50 average. Pays for illustration by the project $10-1,000 average. Considers complexity of project, client's budget and how work will be used when establishing payment.

THE HOLM GROUP, 3rd Floor, 405 Sansome, San Francisco CA 94111. (415)397-7272. Specializes in corporate identity and collateral. Clients: corporations.
Needs: Works with 5-10 freelance artists/year. Uses artists for illustration, mechanicals, retouching, airbrushing, lettering and logos.
First Contact & Terms: "Artist must send 'leave behind' first; then, we'll call to see portfolio." Send query letter with brochure, resume, business card and samples to be kept on file (except for bulky items

or items requested returned). "Photocopies of samples are fine if they demonstrate the quality of work." Samples not kept on file are returned by SASE. Reports only if interested (may be much later). Pays for design by the hour, $20-25 average; by the project, $300-900 average. Pays for illustration by the project, $350-1,000 average. Pays $15-20 in production. Considers complexity of project, client's budget and turnaround time when establishing payment.
Tips: "Put together an eye-catching resume to leave behind."

MEL HOLZSAGER/ASSOCIATES, INC., 275 Seventh Ave., New York NY 10001. (212)741-7373. President/Art Director: Mel Holzsager. Specializes in corporate identity, packaging and general graphic design. Clients: publishers and manufacturers.
Needs: Works with occasional freelance artists according to the work load. Prefers local artists. Uses artists for advertising and brochure illustration, mechanicals and retouching.
First Contact & Terms: Send brochure showing art style to be kept on file. Samples returned if requested. Call or write to schedule an appointment to show a portfolio, which should include thumbnails, roughs and original/final art. Negotiates payment.
Tips: A mistake artists make is "trying to be too versatile. Great specialization would be stronger."

***ROY HORTON STUDIOS, INC.**, 119 West 57 St., New York NY 10019. (212)246-0040. President: Roy Horton. Specializes in brand identity, corporate identity, displays, direct mail and packaging.
Needs: Works with 5-8 freelance artists/year. Artists must have ten years' experience. Especially needs mechanicals and ruling. Uses artists for P-O-P displays, mechanicals, retouching, airbrushing and lettering.
First Contact & Terms: Send query letter with brochure showing art style or resume and tear sheets. Reports only if interested. Write to show a portfolio, which should include roughs and original/final art. Pays for design by the hour, $18-20. Pays for illustration by the project, $50-200. Considers client's budget, and skill and experience of artist when establishing payment.

FRANK HOSICK DESIGN, Box H, Vashon Island WA 98070. (206)463-5454. Contact: Frank Hosick. Specializes in brand identity, corporate identity, packaging, product design and model building. Clients: manufacturers.
Needs: Works on assignment only. Uses artists for illustration, mechanicals, retouching, airbrushing and model making.
First Contact & Terms: Send query letter with brochure, resume, business card and samples to be kept on file. Samples not kept on file are returned only if requested. Reports only if interested. Call for appointment to show portfolio. Pays for design by the hour, $15-50 average; by the project, $100 minimum; or by the day, $75-350 average. Pays for illustration by the hour, $15-50 average; by the project, $100-1,500 average; or by the day, $75-350 average. Considers complexity of project, client's budget, skill and experience of artist, and how work will be used when establishing payment.
Tips: Especially looks for "creativity, craftsmanship and quality of presentation" when reviewing a portfolio. Changes in the field include "big influence by computers, both in concept work and execution. Computer knowledge is helpful."

THE HOYT GROUP, INC., 5 Harrison Ave., Waldwick NJ 07463. President: Earl Hoyt. Specializes in corporate identity and packaging. Clients: *Fortune* 500 firms.
Needs: Works with 10-15 freelance artists/year. Seeks experienced professionals. Works on assignment only. Uses artists for design, mechanicals, airbrushing, model making, lettering and logos.
First Contact & Terms: Send brochure to be kept on file. Send reproductions only as samples—no original art. Reports only if interested. Write for appointment to show portfolio. Considers client's budget, and skill and experience of artist when establishing payment.

***HUSTON DESIGN CONSULTANTS**, 120 Lake St., Burlington VT 05402-1034. (802)864-5928. Principal: B. Huston. Specializes in displays, interior design, packaging, publications and signage. Clients: manufacturers, communication departments, museums and corporations.
Needs: Works with 24-50 freelance artists/year. Works on assignment only. Uses artists for design, illustrations, books, P-O-P displays, mechanicals, model making, charts/graphs and AV materials.
First Contact & Terms: Send query letter with resume. Samples not filed are returned only if requested. Reports only if interested. Call to show a portfolio, which should include thumbnails, roughs and photographs. Pays for design by the hour, $9-15. Pays for illustration by the hour, $25-75. Considers complexity of project, client's budget, skill and experience of artist, and turnaround time when establishing payment.

IDENTITY CENTER, 955G N. Plum Grove Rd., Schaumburg IL 60195. (312)843-2378. President: Wayne Kosterman. Specializes in brand identity, corporate identity, publications, signage and brochures. Clients: hospitals and corporations.

Needs: Works with up to 12 freelance artists/year. Artist must have at least 3 years' experience. Uses artists for illustration, mechanicals, retouching, airbrushing, model making, keyline and paste-up.

First Contact & Terms: Send query letter with photocopies to be kept on file. Samples not filed are returned only if requested. Reports within 2 weeks. Pays for illustration by the hour, $12 minimum; by the project, $100 minimum. Considers complexity of project, client's budget, skill and experience of artist, how work will be used and turnaround time when establishing payment.

IMAGES, 1835 Hampden Ct., Louisville KY 40205. (502)459-0804. Creative Director: Julius Freedman. Specializes in annual reports, corporate identity, poster design and publications. Clients: corporate.

Needs: Works with approximately 100 freelance artists/year. Prefers experienced artists only. Uses artists for advertising illustration and layout, brochure and catalog design and illustration, brochure layout, mechanicals, retouching, poster design, book design and illustration, charts/graphs, lettering and logo design.

First Contact & Terms: Send brochure/flyer or resume and business card as samples to be kept on file. Samples not filed returned by SASE. Works on assignment only; reports whether to expect possible future assignments. Pays by the project for design and illustration.

INNOVATIVE DESIGN & GRAPHICS, Suite 252, 708 Church St., Evanston IL 60201. (312)475-7772. Contact: Tim Sonder and Maret Thorpe. Specializes in publications. Clients: magazine publishers, corporate communication departments, associations.

Needs: Works with 3-15 freelance artists/year. Local artists only. Uses artists for illustration and airbrushing.

First Contact & Terms: Send query letter with brochure showing art style or resume, tear sheets, photostats, slides and photographs. Reports only if interested. Write to schedule an appointment to show a portfolio, which should include original/final art, final reproduction/product, tear sheets and photostats. Pays for illustation by the project, $100-700 average. Considers complexity of project, client's budget and turnaround time when establishing payment.

Tips: "Interested in meeting new illustrators, but have a tight schedule. Looking for people who can grasp complex ideas and turn them into high-quality illustrations. Ability to draw people well is a must."

***INTERSPACE INC.**, A660, 2502 Rocky Point Dr., Tampa FL 33607. Specializes in interior architecture, interior design, furniture design and signage.

Needs: Works with 6 freelance artists/year. Uses artists for design, illustrations, brochures, books, magazines, newspapers, P-O-P displays, mechanicals, retouching, airbrushing, posters, model making, charts/graphs, AV materials, lettering, logos and advertisements.

First Contact & Terms: Send query letter with brochure showing art style or resume, tear sheets, photostats, photographs and photocopies. Samples not filed are not returned. Reports only if interested. To show a portfolio, mail appropriate materials, which should include thumbnails, roughs, original/final art, final reproduction/product, color, tear sheets, photostats, and b&w photographs. Pays for design by the hour, $20-70; by the project, based on scope; by the day, $200-500. Pays for illustrations by the hour, $20-75; by the project, based on scope; by the day, $200-500. Considers complexity of project, client's budget, skill and experience of artist, how work will be used, turnaround time and rights purchased.

Tips: "Concentrate on interior architecture and design renderings. Include complete samples of work in portfolio."

JMH CORPORATION, Suite 300, 247 S. Meridian, Indianapolis IN 46225. (317)639-2535. President: Michael Hayes. Specializes in corporate identity, packaging and publications. Clients: publishing, consumer products, corporate and institutional.

Needs: Works with 10 freelance artists/year. Prefers experienced, talented and responsible artists only. Works on assignment only. Uses artists for advertising, brochure, catalog design, illustration and design, P-O-P displays, mechanicals, retouching, charts/graphs and lettering.

First Contact & Terms: Send query letter with brochure/flyer, resume and slides. Samples returned by SASE, "but we prefer to keep them." Reporting time "depends entirely on our needs." Write for appointment. Pay is by the project for design and illustration. Pays $100-1,000/project average; also negotiates. Considers complexity of project, client's budget, skill and experience of artist, how work will be used, turnaround time and rights purchased when establishing payment.

Tips: "Prepare an outstanding mailing piece and 'leave-behind' that allows work to remain on file."

JOHNSON DESIGN GROUP, INC., 3426 N. Washington Blvd., Arlington VA 22201. (703)525-0808. Art Director: Leonard A. Johnson. Specializes in publications. Clients: corporations, associations and public relations firms.

Needs: Works with 12 freelance artists/year. Works on assignment only. Uses artists for brochure and book illustration, mechanicals, retouching and lettering. Especially needs line illustration and a realistic handling of human figure in real life situations.
First Contact & Terms: Send query letter with brochure/flyer and samples (photocopies OK) to be kept on file. Samples are not returned. Negotiates payment by the project.

JONES MEDINGER KINDSCHI INC., Fields Ln., RFD 2, North Salem NY 10560. Contact: Wynn Medinger. Specializes in annual reports, corporate identity and publications. Clients: corporations.
Needs: Works with 15 freelance artists/year. Works on assignment only. Uses artists for illustration.
First Contact & Terms: "*No* phone calls!" Send query letter with tear sheets, slides, photostats or photocopies to be kept on file. Samples not kept on file are returned by SASE only. Reports only if interested. Pays for illustration by the project $250-5,000 average. Considers client's budget, skill and experience of artist and how work will be used when establishing payment.
Tips: "We mainly use editorial-style illustration for corporate house organs."

JONSON PEDERSEN HINRICHS & SHAKERY, 141 Lexington Ave., New York NY 10016. Clients: corporations and publishers.
Needs: Prefers local artists. Uses artists and photographers for annual reports, publications, catalogs, etc. Pays $15-20, mechanicals and paste-up. Negotiates pay for color separations, illustrations, lettering, retouching and technical art.
First Contact & Terms: Query. SASE.

FREDERICK JUNGCLAUS, Designer/Illustrator, 145 E. 14th St., Indianapolis IN 46202. (317)636-4891. Owner: Fred Jungclaus. Specializes in annual reports, corporate identity, displays, architectural renderings and 3-D photo props. Clients: ad agencies and architects.
Needs: Works with 3-5 freelance artists/year. Works on assignment only. Uses artists for retouching and airbrushing. Seeks artists capable of illustrating Indy-type race cars or antique cars.
First Contact & Terms: Send samples to be kept on file. Prefers slides or tear sheets as samples. Samples not filed are returned only if requested. Reports by SASE only if interested. Call for appointment to show portfolio. Pays by the project. Considers skill and experience of artist and turnaround time when establishing payment.

DAVID KAGEYAMA, DESIGNER, 2119 Smith Tower, Seattle WA 98104. Contact: David Kageyama. Specializes in annual reports, brand and corporate identity, displays, packaging, publications and signage. Clients: advertising agencies, public service agencies, corporations, banking and insurance, attorneys and other professionals.
Needs: Works with 12 freelance artists/year. Works on assignment only. Uses artists for advertising, brochure, poster, direct mail package, book and catalog illustration; mechanicals, retouching, AV presentations and lettering. Especially needs good, quick line/wash, humorous illustrator.
First Contact & Terms: Send brochure/flyer or resume, business card and samples to be kept on file for possible future assignments. Prefers photos (prints), actual illustrations and printed pieces as samples. Call for appointment. Pays $100-300 average/project for illustration. Considers client's budget, skill and experience of artist and turnaround time when establishing payment.
Tips: "We are much more apt to respond to the artist with a specific style or who specializes in a particular topic rather than the generalist. Keep in touch with your latest work. I like to see rough sketches as well as finished work. My firm buys all photography and virtually all illustration used for our clients."

AL KAHN GROUP, 221 W. 82nd St., New York NY 10024. (212)580-3517. Contact: Al Kahn. Specializes in annual reports, corporate identity, packaging and publications. Clients: industrial, high tech, entertainment, fashion and beauty.
Needs: Works with 36 freelance artists/year. Works on assignment only. Uses artists for advertising design and layout, brochure and catalog design, illustration and layout; poster design and illustration, model making, charts/graphs, lettering and logo design. Prefers 3-dimensional construction style.
First Contact & Terms: Send brochure/flyer or resume, slides, b&w photos and color washes. Samples returned by SASE. Reports in 1 week. To show a portfolio, mail roughs, original/final art, final reproduction/product, tear shees and photographs or call to schedule an appointment. Pays for design by the hour, $15 minimum; by the project, $250 minimum. Pays for illustration by the hour, $20 minimum; by the project, $250 minimum.
Tips: "We specialize in 'emotional response' advertising and image building."

KEITHLEY & ASSOCIATES, INC., 32 W. 22nd St., New York NY 10010. (212)807-8388. Studio Manager/Art Director: Nancy P. Danahy. Specializes in publications. Primary clients: publishing (book and promotion departments); secondary clients: small advertising agencies.

Close-up

Martin Pedersen
Designer
New York, New York

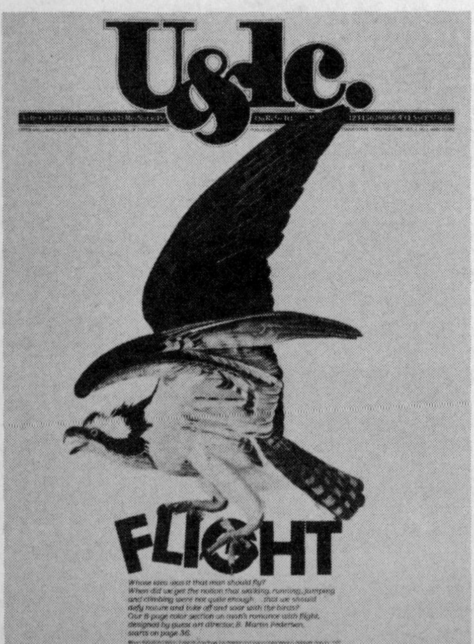

Artist: Lee Hammond

"The day you become completely satisfied with your work, you're not growing." That's the best advice Martin Pedersen, head of the New York office of Jonson Pedersen Hinrichs & Shakery design firm, can give to illustrators and designers.

Over the last two and a half decades, the Norwegian-born artist must have followed this advice, because he is considered one of the top designers in this country—and the partnership he helped found is among the most prestigious.

His work has earned Pedersen over 300 national awards in the area of graphic design and has helped give Jonson Pedersen Hinrichs & Shakery (which is also based in Connecticut and San Francisco) a reputation for completely participating in assignments and appropriately balancing aesthetics with business for their corporation and publishing clients.

"You should constantly throw out the worst piece in your portfolio," the art director continues. "What I look for in an illustrator's portfolio is consistency of style and execution. When commissioning an illustrator for the first time, the bottom line of what I can expect is the weakest piece in the portfolio."

Pedersen has frequently acted as guest art director and designer for individual sections or the entirety of the journal U&lc. This cover design relates to the featured article on flight.

Pedersen applies similar criteria when judging a designer's portfolio, adding, "When you hire a designer, you're really buying taste."

Most art directors, like Pedersen, are so busy that they can only spend a minute or so with each portfolio they get—all the more reason to include samples that will grab their attention immediately. And, according to him, resumes and personal interviews are largely unnecessary and unadvisable. "I don't mean this as a disservice to artists, but I have to maintain a drop-off policy for portfolios," he says. "It isn't necessary for illustrators or designers to see me personally when they deliver their portfolio. That's suspect. Their work is not going to be sold on the basis of their personality. If the work is good, it doesn't require elaborate conversation."

Though this advice Pedersen offers on portfolio submissions holds true for both illustrators and designers, he stresses that the paths to success and the payment terms are somewhat different for these two types of artists.

Illustrators primarily earn their living as freelancers, so it is crucial that their financial interests be protected. Thus, when one of his clients wants to commission an illustrator, Pedersen is careful about handling the payment terms in a way that is fair to the artist. "I don't feel that selling illustrations is like selling real estate," he says. "With real estate, the agent sets a price he knows is on the high side, so it's open for negotiation. But with illustrators, the prices they state are usually fair, and, in most cases, I like to have the client pay them at least what they ask for."

For designers, price isn't as big an issue. "Designers have to work their way up more, and learn certain procedures of the trade," Pedersen says, "so they should try to get apprenticeships or jobs with design studios. Money should not be the priority under these circumstances. What is important is that you aspire to work at a good place."

One thing common to designers and illustrators is that they both face a tough, competitive job market today—Pedersen alone receives about 15 to 20 portfolios a week from freelancers and job hunters.

"There's no easy way to achieve success," the art director stresses. "You have to love what you do and you've got to work hard at it."

—Betsy Schoellkopf

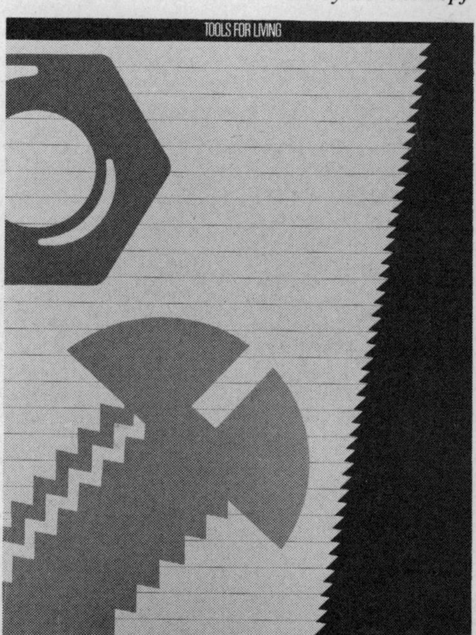

Pedersen's ability to capture the essence of a design, as in this bold 'Tools for Living' folder, has garnered over 300 major awards.

Needs: Works with 3-6 freelance artists/year. "Except for artists doing retouching and some design work, all work must be done in our studio. We prefer experienced artists (2 years minimum)." Uses artists for design, brochures, catalogs, books (design and dummy), mechanicals, retouching and charts/graphs.
First Contact & Terms: Call for appointment to show portfolio. Do not send samples. Reports only if interested. Pays for design by the hour $10-15 average. Pays for mechanicals by the hour, $6-15 average. Considers client's budget, and skill and experience of artist when establishing payment.
Tips: "We will be most likely to use you if you can handle the assignment completely—concept, presentation comps, type specs, mechanicals—or efficiently pick up a project in mid-course." A mistake artists make in presenting their portfolio is "not pointing out the obstacles they had to overcome during the course of a job."

LARRY KERBS STUDIOS INC., 419 Park Ave. S., New York NY 10016. (212)686-9420. Contact: Larry Kerbs or Jim Lincoln. Specializes in sales promotion design, some ad work and placement, annual reports, corporate identity, publications and technical illustration. Clients: industrial, chemical, insurance and public relations.
Needs: Works with 3 illustrators and 1 designer/month. New York, New Jersey and Connecticut artists only. Uses artists for direct mail, layout, illustration, slide sets, technical art, paste-up and retouching for annual reports, trade magazines, product brochures and direct mail. Especially needs freelance comps through mechanicals; type specification.
First Contact & Terms: Mail samples or call for interview. Prefers b&w line drawings, roughs, previously published work as samples. Provide brochures, business card and resume to be kept on file for future assignments. No originals returned to artist at job's completion. Pays $14-18/hour, paste-up; $18-20/hour, comprehensive layout; $18-22/hour average, design; negotiates payment by the project for illustration.
Tips: "Improve hand lettering for comps; strengthen typographic knowledge and application."

***KNT PLUSMARK INC.**, Suite A, 1200 Main St., Irvine CA 92715. (714)979-3051. Vice President Creative: Lois Hinds. Specializes in brand identity, corporate identity and packaging. Clients: Fortune 500 companies.
Needs: Works with 5-8 freelance artists/year. Uses artists for design, illustrations, mechanicals, retouching, airbrushing, model making, lettering, logos and marker comps.
First Contact & Terms: Send query letter with resume. Samples not filed are returned by SASE. Reports only if interested. Call to schedule an appointment to show a profolio, which should include roughs, original/final art, final reproduction/product, color, photographs and b&w. Pays for design by the hour, $12-18; by the project. Pays for illustration by the project. Considers client's budget, skill and experience of artist and turnaround time when establishing payment.

ARVID KNUDSEN AND ASSOCIATES, 592 A Main St., Hackensack NJ 07601. (201)488-7857. Contact: Arvid Knudsen. Specializes in publications. Clients: publishing companies.
Needs: Works with 12 freelance artists/year. Artists with "creativity, technical skills, experience and dependability" only. Uses artists for catalog design, illustration and layout; book and magazine design and illustration, mechanicals.
First Contact & Terms: Send tear sheets of full color work, photocopies of b&w work, to be kept on file. Samples not kept on file are returned by SASE only if requested. Reports only if interested. Works on assignment only. Pay for all work "is negotiated and related to client's budget," also complexity of project.
Tips: "First, find out precisely what kind of work we are interested in. Then, if possible, send in tear sheets or photocopies of work that comes close to that need."

KOVACH ASSOCIATES INC., Suite 800, 150 E. Huron, Chicago IL 60611. (312)266-0286. President: Ronald Kovach. Specializes in annual reports, corporate identity, packaging, publications and signage. Clients: real estate, industrial manufacturers, public relations and retail manufacturers.
Needs: Uses artists for advertising, brochure, poster and direct mail package illustration. Prefers a classic look for annual reports and packaging; "probably includes illustration for logotype or company mark when appropriate."
First Contact & Terms: Send query letter with brochure/flyer or resume. Prefers finished art or finished products as samples. Samples returned by SASE. Reports within 2 weeks. Provide resume, business card and brochure/flyer to be kept on file for possible future assignments. Call or write for appointment. Pays $100-3,000 average/project for design or illustration; also negotiates.
Tips: "Most good work relationships center on the personal relationship between parties. Although direct mail solicitation is effective, if you see a company you like, visit with them personally as often as possible."

F. PATRICK LA SALLE DESIGN/GRAPHICS, 225 Sheridan St., Rockford IL 61103. (815)963-2089. Contact: F. Patrick La Salle. Specializes in corporate identity, displays, direct mail, packaging, publications and signage. Clients: small corporations, ad agencies, book publishers and hospitals.
Needs: Works with 10-15 freelance artists/year. Experienced artists only. Uses artists for design, illustration, brochures, catalogs, books, magazines, newspapers, P-O-P displays, mechanicals, photography (studio and on-location), retouching, airbrushing, posters, direct mail packages, model making and AV materials.
First Contact & Terms: Send query letter with brochure and samples to be kept on file. Call for appointment to show portfolio. "Photocopies as samples okay if technique is clear." Samples not kept on file are not returned. Reports back only if interested. Pays for design by the hour, $10-25 average. Pays for illustration by the hour, $20-35 average. Considers complexity of project, client's budget and turnaround time when establishing payment. "Artist will be paid after client has paid invoice."
Tips: "Most freelancers work here at the studio with provided supplies. Payment schedules set up with client *before* work is begun. Frequently, there is a 45-60 day wait for payment after billing has been completed. Recently, our clients have depended a great deal on our co-ordination and consultation with small to elaborate audiovisual presentations. Some have included live actors with slide support for demonstrations. Many artists, in the form of freelance support and production companies, have been involved."

***LEE GRAPHICS DESIGN**, 395 19th St. NE, Salem OR 97301. (503)364-0907. Owner/Art Director: Lee Ericksen. Specializes in annual reports, brand identity, corporate identity, displays, landscape design, interior design, direct mail, packaging, publications, signage and technical illustrations. "We are a full service graphics studio." Clients: individuals, ad agencies and PR firms.
Needs: Works with approximately 3-5 freelance artists/year. Artist must have talent, creativity and basic design ability. Uses design, illustrations, brochures, catalogs, books, magazines, newspapers, P-O-P displays, mechanicals, airbrushing, posters, direct mail packages, charts/graphs, AV materials, lettering, logos, advertisements and anything that appears in print form.
First Contact & Terms: Send query letter with resume. Reports only if interested. Call to schedule an appointment to show a portfolio, which should include thumbnails, roughs, original/final art, final reproduction/product, color, tear sheets, photostats, photographs and b&w. Pays for design by the hour, $10-25; by the project, $10-25. Pays for illustrations by the hour, $10-25; by the project, $10-25. Considers complexity of project, client's budget, skill and experience of artist, how work will be used, turnaround time and rights purchased when establishing payment.
Tips: "Always show respect to your artwork with presentation; follow directions. Be versatile in all areas of graphics."

LEGAL ARTS, 711 Twelfth Ave., San Diego CA 92101. (619)231-1551. Contact: James Gripp. Specializes in displays; technical illustration; and forensic exhibits including: medical illustration, scale diagrams and models; and charts and graphs. Clients: law firms.
Needs: Works with 3-5 freelance artists/year. Prefers "degreed artists (AA or BA); local to San Diego County." Works on assignment only. Uses artists for illustration, airbrushing, model making, charts/graphs and AV materials. Especially needs medical illustrator and model maker.
First Contact & Terms: Send query letter with resume and samples to be kept on file. Write for appointment to show portfolio. "Samples may be shown by appointment in lieu of portfolio. Artist must send at least 5 photocopy samples with query letter." Reports back within 5 days. Pays for design and illustration by the hour, $7.50 minimum. Considers skill and experience of artist, and turnaround time when establishing payment. "Always 'work for hire' due to legal application of original art."
Tips: Especially looks for "diversity of media, specific applications towards my needs and superior craftsmanship" in samples for portfolio. "If you are a 'generalist', good! We do work that will be used as evidence in court—it must be accurate *every* time. In the legal field, the background of the artist (i.e. degrees), is of great importance to the courts. One must qualify as being educationally capable rather than just physically capable of preparing exhibits for trial use. Hence, the freelancer must have some documented background that a non-artist (judge or juror), will deem as being necessary before the artist can truthfully, accurately and honestly portray whatever is in the exhibit."

THE LEPREVOST CORPORATION, Suite #6, 29350 Pacific Coast Hwy., Malibu CA 90265. (213)457-3742. President: John LePrevost. Specializes in corporate identity, record covers, television and film design. Clients: corporations—CBS television, Metromedia Producers Corporation, P.M. Magazine/Westinghouse Broadcasting.
Needs: Works with 10 freelance artists/year. Prefers "talented and professional" artists only. Works on assignment only. Uses artists for animation and film design and illustration; lettering and logo design. Animation and design becoming more sophisticated.
First Contact & Terms: Call for appointment. Samples not returned. Provide information to be kept on file for possible future assignments; reports back. Payment by the project for both design and illustra-

tion. Considers complexity of project, client's budget, skill and experience of artist, how work will be used, turnaround time and rights purchased when establishing payment.

***WES LERDON ASSOCIATES, INDUSTRIAL DESIGN**, 3070 Riverside Dr., Columbus OH 43221. (614)486-8188. Owner: W.E. Lerdon. Specializes in corporate identity and technical illustrations. Clients: manufacturers.
Needs: Works with 4 freelance artists/year. Prefers Ohio area designers with skill. Uses artists for design, illustrations, brochures, mechanicals, model making and logos.
First Contact & Terms: Send query letter with resume. Samples not filed are returned only if requested. Reports only if interested. Call or write to schedule an appointment to show a portfolio, which should include thumbnails, roughs, original/final art and photographs. Pays for design by the hour, $10-25. Pays for illustrations by the hour, $12-30. Considers complexity of project, client's budget, skill and experience of artist, and turnaround time when establishing payment.

LESLEY-HILLE, INC., 32 E. 21st St., New York NY 10010. (212)677-7570. President: Valrie Lesley. Specializes in annual reports, corporate identity, publications, advertising and sales promotion. Clients: financial, fashion, nonprofit organizations, hotels, restaurants, investment firms, oil and real estate firms.
Needs: Works with "many" freelance artists/year. "Experienced and competent" artists only. Uses artists for illustration, mechanicals, airbrushing, model making, charts/graphs, AV materials and lettering.
First Contact & Terms: Send query letter with resume, business card and samples to be kept on file. Accepts "whatever best shows work capability" as samples. Samples not filed are returned by SASE. Reports only if interested. Call or write for appointment to show portfolio. Pay varies according to project. Considers complexity of project, client's budget, skill and experience of artist, and turnaround time when establishing payment.
Tips: Artists must "be *able to do* what they say they can and agree to do . . . professionally and on time!"

LIGATURE INC., 165 N. Canal St., Chicago IL 60606. (312)648-1233. Design Director: Josef Godlewski. Specializes in annual reports, corporate identity, displays, publications, signage and technical illustration. Clients: educational publishers, general book and magazine publishers, financial institutions and corporations.
Needs: Works with 100 freelance artists/year. Works on assignment only. Uses artists for advertising, brochure and book illustration; mechanicals and lettering.
First Contact & Terms: "All publishing work is rented as work-for-hire and upon acceptance becomes the property of the publisher." Send query letter with resume, samples and/or tear sheets to be kept on file except original samples. Any form of samples are acceptable. Samples not kept on file are returned. Reports only if interested. Write for appointment to show portfolio. Pay based on project. Considers complexity of project, client's budget, skill and experience of artist, how work will be used, turnaround time and rights purchased.

LIKA ASSOCIATES INC., 160 E. 38th St., New York NY 10016. (212)490-3660. President: Art Lika. Specializes in annual reports, brand identity, corporate identity, displays, direct mail, packaging, publications, signage and technical illustration. Clients: corporations, banks, public relation firms, ad agencies and publishers.
Needs: Works with 1-6 freelance artists/year. Works on assignment only. Uses artists for design, illustration, brochures, catalogs, books, magazines, newspapers, P-O-P displays, mechanicals, retouching, airbrushing, posters, direct mail packages, model making, charts/graphs, AV materials, lettering, logos and advertisements. Especially needs designers and mechanical artist.
First Contact & Terms: Send query letter with resume and business card to be kept on file. Prefers roughs, comps, finished art and final printed materials as samples. Samples not kept on file returned by SASE. Reports within 1 week. Call for appointment to show portfolio. Pays for design by the hour, $20-100 average. Considers complexity of project, client's budget and how work will be used when establishing payment.

JAN LORENC DESIGN, INC., A460, 3475 Lenox Rd., Atlanta GA 30326. (404)266-2711. President: Mr. Jan Lorenc. Specializes in corporate identity, displays, packaging, publications, architectural signage design and industrial design. Clients: developers, product manufacturers, architects and institutions.
Needs: Works with 10 freelance artists/year. Local artists only—senior designers. Uses artists for design, illustration, brochures, catalogs, books, P-O-P displays, mechanicals, retouching, airbrushing, posters, direct mail packages, model making, charts/graphs, AV materials, lettering and logos. Especially needs architectural signage designers.

First Contact & Terms: Send brochure, resume and samples to be kept on file. Prefers slides as samples. Samples not kept on file are returned. Call or write for appointment to show portfolio, which should include thumbnails, roughs, orignal/final art, final reproduction/product, color, photostats and photographs. Pays for design by the hour $10-25 average; by the project, $100-3,000 average. Considers complexity of project, client's budget, and skill and experience of artist when establishing payment.

JACK LUCEY/ART & DESIGN, 84 Crestwood Dr., San Rafael CA 94901. (415)453-3172. Contact: Jack Lucey. Art agency. Specializes in annual reports, brand identity, corporate identity, publications, signage, technical illustration and illustrations/cover designs. Clients: businesses, agencies and freelancers.
Needs: Works with 1 illustrator/month. Uses mostly local artists. Uses artists for illustration and lettering for newspaper work. Especially needs agricultural painting and corporation illustrations.
First Contact & Terms: Query. Prefers photostats and published work as samples. Provide brochures, business card and resume to be kept on file for future assignments. No originals returned to artist at job's completion. Payment is negotiated by the project.
Tips: "We would like to see an upgrade of portfolios."

MCGRAPHICS DESIGN, Suite 206, 1010A W. Magnolia Blvd., Burbank CA 91506. (213)841-1266. Owner: Kathleen McGuinness. Specializes in brand identity, corporate identity, direct mail, packaging and publications. Clients: corporations (manufacturers and distributors), some public relation firms and printers.
Needs: Works with 10 freelance artists/year. "Local artists only, personable and presentable in the corporate environment." Works on assignment only. Uses artists for illustration, catalogs, mechanicals, retouching, airbrushing and newsletters. Especially needs b&w line illustration.
First Contact & Terms: Send brochure, business card and samples to be kept on file. Call or write for appointment to show portfolio. Prefers brochures with some information about artist and samples of work. Samples not kept on file are not returned. Reports back "only if the artist calls and follows up." Pays for design by the hour, $20-30 average. Pays for illustration line products by the project, $100-250 average. Considers complexity of project, client's budget, and skill and experience of artist when establishing payment.
Tips: "Send samples first then make an appointment. Show up on time and *follow up* if we say we are interested."

MCGUIRE WILLIS & ASSOCIATES, 249 E. Cook Rd., Columbus OH 43214. (614)262-8124. Contact: Sue Willis. Specializes in annual reports, audiovisual and publications. Clients: schools, training departments of companies, sales and banking.
Needs: Works with 20 freelance artists/year. Works on assignment only. Uses artists for advertising, brochure, catalog, poster, direct mail package and book design and illustration, and mechanicals.
First Contact & Terms: Send query letter with photostats, slides brochure/flyer and samples to be kept on file. Samples returned by SASE if not kept on file. Reports in 2 weeks. Reports back on whether to expect possible future assignments. Negotiates payment.

ROB MacINTOSH COMMUNICATIONS, INC., 93 Massachusetts Ave., Boston MA 02115. President: Rob MacIntosh. Specializes in annual reports, advertising design and collateral. Clients: manufacturers, graphic arts industry, nonprofit/public service agencies.
Needs: Works with 12 freelance artists/year. Portfolio and work experience required. Uses artists for advertising and brochure design, illustration and layout; mechanicals, retouching and charts/graphs. Occasionally uses humorous and cartoon-style illustrations.
First Contact & Terms: Send samples to be kept on file. Irregular sizes or abundant material will not be filed. "Never send original work unless it's a printed sample. A simple, compact presentation is best. Often photostats are adequate." Reports only if interested and "generally only when we require more information and/or services." Pays for design by the day, $100 minimum. Write for appointment to show portfolio. Pays for illustration by the project, $100 minimum. Considers complexity of project, client's budget, skill and experience of artist and turnaround time when establishing payment.

MCS, 600 Valley Rd., Wayne NJ 07470. (201)628-9630. Director: Pamela K. Johnson. Specializes in brand identity, corporate identity, displays and packaging. Clients: consumer product companies.
Needs: Works with 10 freelance artists/year. Prefers local artists. Works on assignment only. Uses artists for illustration, retouching, airbrushing and AV materials.
First Contact & Terms: Call or write for appointment to show portfolio. Prefers slides and printed material as samples. Samples not kept on file returned by SASE. Reports only if interested. Pays for design and illustration by the hour. Considers complexity of project, client's budget and turnaround time when establishing payment.

Tips: "The cool-fine artist approach is a turn-off. Professionalism, clean work, originality and a cooperative attitude is a plus. If excessive verbal explanation of work is necessary, then obviously the visual doesn't communicate on its own."

***MCS MARK COLOR STUDIOS**, Box 116, Glen Mills PA 19342. (215)459-5163. Art Director: Lisa Toscani. Specializes in brand indentity, corporate identity, direct mail, packaging and publications. Clients: consumer products.
Needs: Works with 3 freelance artists/year. Works with local artists only, on assignment only. Prefers a realistic style and particularly needs airbrushing/graphic design work. Uses artists for design, illustrations, retouching, airbrushing and mechanical art.
First Contact & Terms: Send query letter with brochure showing art style or tear sheets, photostats, photocopies, slides and photographs. Samples not filed are returned only if requested. Reports only if interested. Call to schedule an appointment to show a portfolio, which should include thumbnails, original/final art, final reproduction/product, color and tear sheets. Pays for design by the hour, $6-9. Considers client's budget and turnaround time when establishing payment.
Tips: "Be as *professional* as possible and not cute."

DONYA MELANSON ASSOCIATES, 437 Main St., Boston MA 02129. Contact: Donya Melanson. Art agency. Clients: industries, associations, publishers, financial and government.
Needs: Most work is handled by staff, but may occasionally use illustrators and designers. Local artists only. Uses artists for stationery design, direct mail, brochures/flyers, annual reports, charts/graphs and book illustrations.
First Contact & Terms: Query with brochure, resume, photostats and photocopies. Reports in 1-2 months. Provide materials (no originals) to be kept on file for future assignments. Originals returned to artist after use only when specified in advance. To show a portfolio, call or write to schedule an appointment or mail thumbnails, roughs, original/final art, final reproduction/product, color, tear sheets, photostats, photographs and b&w. Pays $10-25/hour, cartoons, design, illustrations, lettering, retouching, technical art and logo design. Pays $10-20/hour, mechanicals. Considers complexity of project, client's budget, skill and experience of artist and how work will be used when establishing payment.
Tips: "Be sure your work reflects concept development."

MG DESIGN ASSOCIATES INC., 824 W. Superior, Chicago IL 60622. (312)243-3661. Contact: Michael Grivas or design director. Specializes in trade show exhibits, museum exhibits, expositions and commercial interiors. Clients: industrial manufacturers, consumer-oriented product manufacturers, pharmaceutical firms, state and federal government, automotive parts manufacturers, etc.
Needs: Works with 4-6 freelance artists/year. Artists must be local exhibit designers with minimum of five years' experience. Works on assignment only. Uses artists for design, illustration, detail drawings and model making.
First Contact & Terms: Send resume slides and photocopies to be evaluated. Samples not kept on file are returned only if requested. Write for appointment to show portfolio. Considers complexity of project, client's budget, and skill and experience of artist when establishing payment.

E.M. MITCHELL, INC., 820 2nd Ave., New York NY 10017. (212)986-5595. Vice President: Steven E. Mitchell. Specializes in brand identity, corporate identity, displays, direct mail and packaging. Clients: major corporations.
Needs: Works with 20-25 freelance artists/year. "Most work is done in our studio." Uses artists for design, illustration, mechanicals, retouching, airbrushing, model making, lettering and logos.
First Contact & Terms: Send query letter with brochure, resume, business card, photostats, photographs and slides to be kept on file. Reports only if interested. Call or write for appointment to show portfolio, which should include roughs, original/final art, final reproduction/product, color, photostats and photographs. Pays for design by the hour, $20 minimum; by the project, $150 minimum. Pays for illustration by the project, $250 minimum. Considers complexity of project, client's budget, skill and experience of artist, how work will be used, turnaround time and rights purchased when establishing payment.
Tips: "Call first."

MIZEREK ADVERTISING, 48 E. 43rd St., New York NY 10017. (212)986-5702. President: Leonard Mizerek. Specializes in catalogs, fashion and technical illustration. Clients: corporations—various service-oriented clientele.
Needs: Works with 25-30 freelance artists/year. Experienced artists only. Works on assignment only. Uses artists for design, illustration, brochures, retouching, airbrushing and logos.
First Contact & Terms: Send query letter with tear sheets and photostats. Reports only if interested. Call to schedule an appointment to show a portfolio, which should include original/final art and tear

sheets. Pays by the project, $200-1,000. Considers client's budget and turnaround time when establishing payment.
Tips: "Contact by mail; don't press for interview. Let the work speak for itself. Show commercial product work not only magazine editorial."

MOODY GRAPHICS, 639 Howard St., San Francisco CA 94105. (415)495-5186. President: Carol Moody. Specializes in annual reports, corporate identity, direct mail, publications and technical illustration. Clients: executives, printers and printing brokers.
Needs: Works with 3-5 freelance artists/year. "Artists work in my studio. They should have mechanical experience and good mechanical abilities; stat camera experience helpful." Works on assignment only. Uses artists for design, illustration, brochures, catalogs, mechanicals, retouching, airbrushing, direct mail packages, charts/graphs, lettering, logos and advertisements.
First Contact & Terms: Call or write for appointment to show portfolio. Samples not kept on file returned by SASE. Reports only if interested. Pays for design, mechanical assembly by the hour, $12-18 average. Pays for illustration, technical drawing by the hour, $12-18 average. Considers skill and experience of artist when establishing payment.
Tips: "Show paste-ups as well as printed samples."

MARTIN MOSKOF & ASSOCIATES, INC., 154 W. 57th St., New York NY 10019. (212)333-2015. President: Martin Moskof. Specializes in annual reports, corporate identity, exhibits and shows, publications and signage. Clients: corporations and institutions, colleges (e.g., IBM, Carnegie Hall).
Needs: Works with 30-40 freelance artists/year. Local artists only, 2-3 years' experience. Works on assignment only. Uses artists for brochure and catalog design, illustration and layout; book design and illustration; mechanicals, retouching, direct mail packages, charts/graphs, AV presentations and logos.
First Contact & Terms: Send query letter with tear sheets, photocopies, slides and photographs to be kept on file. Reports only if interested. Call or write for appointment to show portfolio, which sould include roughs, final reproduction/product, color and tear sheets. Pays for design by the hour, $20-30 average; by the project, $300-5,000 average; by the day, $125-200 average. Pays for illustration by the project, $250 minimum. Considers complexity of project, client's budget and skill and experience of artist when establishing payment.

MOSSMAN DESIGN ASSOCIATES, (formerly Mossman Associates), 2514 N. Charles St., Baltimore MD 21218. (301)243-1963. Account Supervisor: Hilary J. Mossman. Specializes in corporate identity, direct mail, publications, health care institution brochures, book jacket and book design. Clients: publishers, manufacturers, hospitals, agencies, nonprofit institutions, etc.
Needs: Works with 3-5 freelance artists/year. Interested in "local artists with strong portfolio, a few years' experience, neat work and understanding of mechanicals." Uses artists for design, mechanicals, charts/graphs and photography.
First Contact & Terms: Send query letter with resume, business card and samples to be kept on file. Prefers copies, tear sheets and mock-ups as samples. Reports back within 5 days. Call or write for appointment to show portfolio. Pays for design and illustration by the hour, $5-20 average. Considers complexity of project, and skill and experience of artist when establishing payment.
Tips: Especially looks for creative samples or portfolio, clean and organized. A mistake artists make is "not knowing their own limitations, not being honest about their skills."

MURAMATSU INCORPORATED, (formerly Halsted & Muramatsu), 1762 N. Neville St., Orange CA 92665. (714)921-1630. Contact: Art Director. Specializes in displays and trade show exhibits. Clients: various manufacturers in consumer electronics field.
Needs: Works with 10-15 freelance artists/year. Local artists preferred. Works on assignment. Uses artists for exhibit design, technical illustration, P-O-P displays, mechanicals and posters.
First Contact & Terms: Send query letter with brochure, resume and business card to be kept on file. Samples not kept on file are returned by SASE only if requested. Reports only if interested. To show a portfolio, mail appropriate materials or call or write to schedule an appointment. Pays by the hour, $10-35. Considers complexity of project, client's budget, skill and experience of artist, how work will be used, turnaround time and rights purchased when establishing payment.
Tips: "Contemporary design philosophy."

SID NAVRATIL ART STUDIO, 1305 Clark Bldg., Pittsburgh PA 15222. Contact: Sid Navratil. Specializes in annual reports, corporate identity, direct mail, publication, signage, technical illustration and 3-dimensional designs. Clients: ad agencies and corporations.
Needs: Works with 5 freelance artists/year. Experienced artists only with a minimum of 5 years' experience; "I prefer artist to work on my premises at least during revision work, if that is possible." Works on assignment only. Uses artists for design, illustration, brochures, mechanicals, retouching, airbrushing,

charts/graphs, lettering, logos and advertisements.
First Contact & Terms: Send resume, photocopies and business card to be kept on file. Material not filed is returned only if requested. Reports within 10 days. Write for appointment to show portfolio. Pays for design and illustration by the hour, $20-30 average. Considers complexity of project, client's budget, and skill and experience of artist when establishing payment.
Tips: "In illustration, we prefer the daring, innovative approach. The subject is usually industrial in nature, done for corporations such as PPG, USS, Alcoa, Rockwell. Do not send expensive photos and brochures. A brief resume with few photocopies of work is sufficient."

LOUIS NELSON ASSOCIATES INC., 80 University Pl., New York NY 10003. (212)620-9191. Contact: Judy Moskowitz. Specializes in brand identity, corporate identity, displays, interior design, packaging, publications, signage, product design, exhibitions and marketing. Clients: corporations, associations and governments.
Needs: Works with 8 + freelance artists/year. Works on assignment only. Uses artists for design, illustration, mechanicals, model making and charts/graphs.
First Contact & Terms: Considers "quality, point-of-view for project and flexibility." Send query letter with brochure showing art style or tear sheets, slides and photographs. Samples are returned only if requested. Reports within 2 weeks. Write to schedule an appointment to show a portfolio, which should include roughs, final reproduction/product, color and photographs. Pays for design by the hour, $8-35 average; by the project, $60-5,000 average. Pays for illustration by the project, $100-500 average. Considers complexity of project, client's budget, skill and experience of artist and rights purchased when establishing payment.
Tips: "I want to see how the person responded to the specific design problem and to see documentation of the process—the stages of development. The artist must be versatile and able to communicate a wide range of ideas. Mostly, I want to see the artist's integrity reflected in his/her work."

NIIMI DESIGN ASSOCIATES INC., 451 N. Racine, Chicago IL 60622. (312)666-8383. Contact: B. Hoolihan. Clients: hardware consumer products.
Needs: Assigns 20-100 jobs/year. Uses mostly local artists. Uses artists for design, illustrations, layout, lettering, paste-up, retouching and technical art for catalogs, charts/graphs, exhibits, packaging, P-O-P displays and print media advertising.
First Contact & Terms: Query with samples or arrange interview. SASE. Pay determined by job.

NOTOVITZ & PERRAULT DESIGN, INC., 47 E. 19 St., New York NY 10003. (212)677-9700. President: Joseph Notovitz. Specializes in corporate design (annual reports, literature, publications), corporate identity and signage. Clients: finance and industry.
Needs: Works with 10 freelance artists/year. Uses artists for brochure, poster, direct mail and booklet illustration, mechanicals, charts/graphs and logo design.
First Contact & Terms: Send resume, slides, printed pieces and tear sheets to be kept on file. Samples not filed are returned by SASE. Reports in 1 week. Call for appointment to show portfolio, which should include roughs, original/final art and final reproduction/product. Pays for design by the hour, $15-50; by the project, $200-1,500. Pays for illustration by the project, $100-2,000; also negotiates.
Tips: "Send pieces which reflect our firms's style and needs. They should do a bit of research in the firm they are contacting. If we never produce book covers, book cover art does not interest us."

OPTASONICS PRODUCTIONS, 186 8th St., Creskill NJ 07626. (201)871-0068. President: Jim Brown. Specializes in multi-image, audio for AV, displays, exhibits, print media and graphics. Clients: industry, theatre.
Needs: Works with varied number of freelance artists/year. Prefers local artists. Works on assignment

> **❝** *I see more use of innovative type design on covers. There are more sophisticated illustrations in curriculum materials. These changes have led to a need for more experienced freelance designers and illustrators.* **❞**
>
> *Amy S. Rood, Winston Press*

only. Uses artists for advertising, brochure and catalog design and illustration; and for graphics for multi-image slide show.
First Contact & Terms: Send query letter with brochure/flyer, business card or resume which may be kept on file. Negotiates payment.

PERSECHINI & COMPANY, 357 S. Robertson Blvd., Beverly Hills CA 90211. (213)657-6175. Contact: Phyllis Persechini. Specializes in annual reports, corporate identity, displays, packaging, publications and signage. Clients: ad agencies, public relations firms, and internal communications departments.
Needs: Works on assignment basis only. Uses artists for design, illustration, mechanicals, retouching, airbrushing and lettering. Occasionally uses humorous and cartoon-style illustrations.
First Contact & Terms: Send query letter with brochure, business card and photostats and photocopies to be kept on file. Samples not kept on file are returned by SASE. Reports back only if interested. Pays for design by the hour $10-20 average. Pays for illustration by the project $100-2,500 average. Considers complexity of project, client's budget, skill and experience of artist, how work will be used, turnaround time and rights purchased when establishing payment.
Tips: "Our clients seem to want a very sophisticated look for their ads, brochures, etc. Occasionally we have a call for humor."

PHARES ASSOCIATES INC., Consultant Designers-Industrial Design, 37624 Hills Tech Dr., Farmington Hills MI 48018. (313)553-2232. Administrative Assistant: Penelope Phares. Specializes in interior design and product design. Clients: manufacturing and architectural firms and advertising agencies.
Needs: "At least 2 years' experience, speed and accuracy a must." Works on assignment only. Uses artists for design, illustration and model making. Special needs include architectural rendering, product design and drafting.
First Contact & Terms: Send query letter with brochure, resume, business card, slides, tear sheets or photographs to be kept on file. Samples not filed are returned by SASE. Reports within 2 weeks. Call or write for appointment to show portfolio. Pays for design by the hour, $8-20 average. Pays for illustration by the hour, $8-15 average. "Speed and quality are the determining factors regarding pay." Considers complexity of project, and skill and experience of artist when establishing payment.
Tips: "Our firm likes to use the work of artists who can take direction and meet short deadlines with quality work."

PILCHER & ASSOCIATES, 1045 San Juan, Tustin CA 92680. Art Director: Joel Pilcher. Specializes in corporate identity, advertising design, brochures, data sheets and catalogs. Clients: book publishers, educational institutions, hospitals and industrial firms.
Needs: Works with about 10 freelance artists/year. Works on assignment only. Uses artists for illustration, brochures, catalogs, retouching, airbrushing, lettering and advertisements.
First Contact & Terms: Send query letter with brochure, resume, slides, photocopies and tear sheets to be kept on file. Samples not filed are returned by SASE only if requested. Reports back only if interested. Call for appointment to show portfolio, which should include original/final art, color and tear sheets. Pays for design and illustration by the project, $50-1,500 average. Considers client's budget when establishing payment.
Tips: "I look for freelance work that keeps pace with our changing field—high technology. Clients are very aware of changes in the field. Plan to come in and show your portfolio and talk for about 30 minutes (not 60 or 90)." When reviewing work, looks for "quality, the details. Is it creative or just a spin off?" Artists shouldn't show too much; stick to only the best. Projects they liked 10 years ago are often included; they're not important to me. I can tell with about ten items if the artist is the one I want or not."

PROFESSIONAL GRAPHICS, 80 A Belvedere St., San Rafael CA 94901. (415)459-5300. Contact: Zai Zatoon. Design studio providing camera ready illustration and graphic design. Clients: corporate and private businesses of all sizes.
Needs: Number of freelance artists used/year varies. Works on assignment only. Uses artists for advertising, brochure and catalog design, illustration and layout, signage and copywriting.
First Contact & Terms: Send query letter with resume and printed sample pieces only (no originals) to be kept on file. Call or write for appointment to show portfolio. Samples not kept on file are returned by SASE only if requested. Reports only if interested. Pays by the hour, $8-10; "volunteers welcome for nonprofit, tax-exempt projects." Considers complexity of project, skill and experience of artist, client's budget and turnaround time when establishing payment.

PULSE COMMUNICATIONS, 2445 N. Sayre Ave., Chicago IL 60635. (312)622-7066. Creative Director: Frank G. Konrath. Specializes in annual reports, corporate identity, displays, landscape design,

interior design, packaging, publications, signage and technical illustration. Clients include corporations.
Needs: Works with 5-15 freelance artists/year. "Local artists preferred. I will always consider talent over experience." Works on assignment only. Uses artists for projects involving many different specialities.
First Contact & Terms: Send query letter with resume and business card to be kept on file. "Please don't call. Send your business card and give me an idea of what you're best at; I'll call you to arrange an interview when something comes up in your area. Save your samples until I ask to see them." Reports only if interested. Considers complexity of project, client's budget, turnaround time and rights purchased when establishing payment.
Tips: "Know what area you want to work in. We hire freelance artists for their talent in specific areas of discipline and for what they can produce consistently. I've noticed that many artists seem overly occupied with primary colors; I like design that's not locked in or trendy."

***THE PUSHPIN GROUP**, 67 Irving Place, New York NY 10003. (212)674-8080. Senior Vice President: Phyllis Rich Flood. Specializes in annual reports, brand identity, corporate identity, packaging, publications and signage. Clients: individuals, ad agencies, corporations, PR firms, etc.
Needs: Works with 5-6 freelance artists/year. Generally prefers designers to illustrators. Uses artists for design, illustrations, brochures, books, magazines, mechanicals, retouching, airbrushing, charts/graphs and lettering.
First Contact & Terms: Send query letter with resume, tear sheets, photostats and photocopies. Samples not filed are returned only if requested. Reports only if interested. Drop-off policy for portfolios. Portfolio should include roughs, original/final art, final reproduction/product, color, tear sheets, photostats, photographs and b&w. Pays for design by the hour, $15-20. Considers complexity of project, client's budget, skill and experience of artist, and turnaround time when establishing payment.

QUALLY & COMPANY INC., #2502, 30 E. Huron, Chicago IL 60611. (312)944-0237. Creative Director: Robert Qually. Specializes in advertising, graphic design and new product development. Clients: major corporations.
Needs: Works with 20-25 freelance artists/year. "Artists must be good and have the right attitude." Works on assignment only. Uses artists for design, illustration, mechanicals, retouching and lettering.
First Contact & Terms: Send query letter with brochure, resume, business card and samples to be kept on file. Samples not kept on file are returned by SASE. Reports back within several days. Call or write for appointment to show portfolio. Considers complexity of project, client's budget, skill and experience of artist, how work will be used, turnaround time and rights purchased when establishing payment.
Tips: Looks for talent, point of view, style, craftsmanship, depth and innovation in portfolio or samples. Sees "too many look-a-likes. Very little innovation. Few people who understand how to create an image, who know how to conceptualize, who can think." Artists often "don't know how to sell or what's involved in selling."

THE QUARASAN GROUP, INC., Suite 7, 1845 Oak St., Northfield IL 60093. (312)446-4777. Director of Creative Services: Randi S. Brill. Production Manager: Joy Christensen. Specializes in books. Clients: book publishers.
Needs: Works with 100-300 freelance artists/year. Artists with publishing experience only. Uses artists for illustration, books, mechanicals, charts/graphs, lettering and production.
First Contact & Terms: Send query letter with brochure or resume and samples to production manager to be kept on file. Prefers "anything that we can retain for our files; photostats, photocopies, tear sheets or dupe slides that do not have to be returned" as samples. Reports only if interested. Pays for production by the hour, $8-15 average; for illustration by the project, $75-3,500 average. Considers complexity of project, client's budget, how work will be used and turnaround time when establishing payment. "For illustration, size and complexity are the key factors."
Tips: "More publishers are finding that solid publishing service groups, with strength in art procurement, are an asset. They want us to work with the artists. This is good for artists, too. By working with us their work and talents can be displayed to all of our clients. It works well!"

COCO RAYNES GRAPHICS, INC., 35 Newbury St., Boston MA 02116. President: Coco Raynes. Specializes in brand identity, corporate identity, displays, direct mail, packaging, publications and signage. Clients: corporations, institutions (private and public) and architects.
First Contact & Terms: Send query letter with resume, tear sheets, and photocopies to be kept on file. Reports only if interested. Write to schedule an appointment to show a portfolio, which should include original/final art, photographs and b&w. Pays for design by the hour, $5-50. Pays for illustration by the project, $50-5,000. Considers client's budget, and skill and experience of artist when establishing payment.
Tips: "Be on time, present yourself well. Show only your best pieces, smile, laugh."

RENAISSANCE COMMUNICATIONS, INC., 7835 Eastern Ave., Silver Spring MD 20910. (301)587-1505. Art Director: Joseph Giacalone. Specializes in corporate identity, publications, technical illustration, general illustrations and audio visual presentations. Clients: government design and graphic departments, high tech firms.
Needs: Works with 30-40 freelance artists/year. Uses artists for design, illustration, mechanicals, retouching, airbrushing, charts/graphs, AV materials and lettering.
First Contact & Terms: Send query letter with resume to be kept on file. Reports back only if interested. Pays for design and illustration by the hour, $10-20 average; for art production by the hour, $6-15 average. Considers complexity of project, skill and experience of artist and turnaround time when establishing payment.

***RENQUIST/ASSOCIATES, INC.**, 2300 Washington Ave., Racine WI 53405. (414)634-2351. Vice President/Design: Dick Huennekens. Specializes in annual reports, brand identity, corporate identity, displays, landscape design, interior design, direct mail, fashion, packaging, publications, signage and technical illustrations. Clients: consumer and industrial.
Needs: Works with 10-12 freelance artists/year. Uses artists for illustrations, retouching, airbrushing, AV materials and lettering.
First Contact & Terms: Send query letter with brochure showing art style or resume, slides and photographs. Samples not filed are returned only if requested. Reports within 2 weeks. Call or write to schedule an appointment to show a portfolio, which should include thumbnails, roughs, original/final art, final reproduction/product, color and tear sheets. Pays for design by the hour, $15-50. Pays for illustration by the hour, $15-50. Considers complexity of project, client's budget and turnaround time when establishing payment.

***WILLIAM REYNOLDS DEPICTION & DESIGN INC.**, 314 W. Reno Ave., Bismarck ND 58501. (701)258-1864. President: William Reynolds. Specializes in corporate identity, displays, landscape design, interior design, signage and technical illustrations. Clients: sign companies, outdoor advertisers, architects and miscellaneous businesses.
Needs: Works with 2 freelance artists/year. Uses artists for mechanicals and lettering.

RICHARDS DESIGN GROUP, INC., (formerly Richards Graphic Design), 4722 Old Kingston Pk., Knoxville TN 37919. (615)588-9707. Contact: Stephanie Dixon. Specializes in corporate identity. Clients: ad agencies, magazine publisher, industrial and consumer business.
Needs: Works on assignment only. Uses artists for illustration, mechanicals, retouching and lettering.
First Contact & Terms: Send query letter with tear sheets to be kept on file. Call for appointment to show portfolio. Samples not kept on file are returned only if requested. Reports only if interested. Pays for design by the project, $50-150 average. Considers complexity of project, how work will be used, turnaround time and rights purchased when establishing payment.

***ROY RITOLA, INC.**, 714 Sansome, San Francisco CA 94111. (415)788-7010. President: Roy Ritola. Specializes in brand identity, corporate identity, displays, direct mail, packaging and signage. Clients: manufacturers.
Needs: Works with 6-10 freelance artists/year. Uses artists for design, illustrations, airbrushing, model making, lettering and logos.
First Contact & Terms: Send query letter with brochure showing art style or resume, tear sheets, slides and photographs. Samples not filed are returned only if requested. Reports only if interested. To show a portfolio, mail final reproduction/product. Pays for design by the hour, $15-40. Considers complexity of project, client's budget, skill and experience of artist, turnaround time and rights purchased when establishing payment.

***ROSENBAUM ENTERPRISES**, 41 Glen Avon Dr., Riverside CT 06878. (203)637-1088. Chief Designer: Jeanette Rosenbaum. Specializes in interior design and posters. Clients: corporate headquarters and our own projects.
Needs: Works with 3-4 freelance artists/year. Uses artists for illustrations, books, magazines, newspapers, retouching, airbrushing, posters, model making and lettering.
First Contact & Terms: Send query letter with brochure showing art style or photographs. Samples not filed are returned by SASE. Reports only if interested. To show a portfolio, mail original/final art and final reproduction/product. Pays for illustration by the hour, $25-75; by the day, $200-500. Considers complexity of project, client's budget, skill and experience of artist, how work will be used, turnaround time and rights purchased when establishing payment.
Tips: "We like to see various styles of work and often can either use right away on project but other times it takes longer to use an artist. We welcome different types of illustrations."

THE ANDREW ROSS STUDIO INC., 148 W. 28th St., New York NY 10001. (212)807-6699. Contact: Andrew Ross. Graphic design studio. Clients: magazines, AV, sales presentations, sales promotions and direct mail.
Needs: Works with 1 or 2 illustrators/month. Local artists only. Uses artists for direct mail, slides, brochures/flyers, trade magazines, illustration, paste-up, lettering and retouching.
First Contact & Terms: Send brochures and tear sheets to be kept on file. Originals returned to artist upon request. Call for interview. Pays for illustration by the project, $100-1,000 average. Pays for mechanicals and paste-up approximately $10-15/hour. Doesn't buy design.

PHILLIP ROSS ASSOCIATES LTD., (formerly Beda Ross Design Ltd.), 310 W. Chicago Ave., Chicago IL 60610. Creative Director: Phillip Ross. Specializes in brand identity, corporate identity, displays, posters, direct mail, fashion, packaging, publications and signage. Clients: ad agencies, public relation firms, corporations and poster publishers.
Needs: Works with 10 freelance artists/year. Prefers artists with three years' experience. Uses artists for design, illustration, brochures, catalogs, P-O-P displays, mechanicals, retouching, airbrushing, posters, direct mail packages, lettering, logos and advertisements. Especially needs experienced artists for graphic design and art production.
First Contact & Terms: Send query letter with resume, photostats and slides to be kept on file. Reports within 30 days. Call for appointment to show portfolio. Pays for design by the hour, $10-20 average. Considers complexity of project and client's budget when establishing payment.
Tips: "Especially looks for "visual impact, simplicity, sensitivity to typography and color, and clean line when reviewing work."

JOHN RYAN & COMPANY, 12400 Whitewater Dr., Minnetonka MN 55343. (612)936-9900. Senior Designer: Stevan L. Olson. Specializes in brand identity, corporate identity, displays, interior design, fashion, packaging and signage. Clients: major national retail chains, book publishers and retailers, food, clothing and hi-tech manufacturers and retailers.
Needs: Works with 30-50 freelance artists/year. "Local and regional artists are preferred, but I will work with talented people anywhere. Professionalism is more important than experience; quality must be of the highest. Artists much be fast and priced within normal market rates." Uses artists for illustration, brochures, books, P-O-P displays, mechanicals, retouching, airbrushing, posters, direct mail packages, AV materials, lettering, logos and advertisements. Especially looking for "fresh new talent in black-and-white, graphic, airbrush and classic painterly styles, plus people working in new media such as 3.0 and paper sculpture."
First Contact & Terms: Send query letter with brochure, resume, business card and samples to be kept on file. Accepts color stats, slides, photocopies, photostats or printed samples, "preferably in 8½x11" format so that they are filable." Samples not filed are returned by SASE only if requested. Reports within 1 month. Call for appointment to show portfolio. Pays for design by the hour, $30-75 average; by the project, $50-300 average. Pays for illustration by the project, $200-3,000 average. Considers complexity of project, client's budget, skill and experience of artist, turnaround time and rights purchased when establishing payment.
Tips: "Artist's work should be fresh in approach, superlative in execution, turned around in reasonable deadline, priced along normal rate guidelines. Creative problem solving and dazzling execution are premiums here."

SANTORO DESIGN CONSULTANTS LTD., 503 W. 27th St., New York NY 10001. (212)714-9207. President: Joseph L. Santoro. Specializes in annual reports, corporate identity, direct mail, packaging, publications and signage. Clients: major corporations, public relation firms, book publishers, not-for-profit institutions, real estate developers and architects.
Needs: Works with 2 freelance designers/year. "Designers must be local, willing to perform services that support a small business, open-minded and have strong drawing ability."
First Contact & Terms: Send query letter with brochure showing art style to be kept on file. "Save your samples. I'd prefer to meet artists as I review work." Samples not kept on file are not returned. Call for appointment to show portfolio. Pays for design by the hour, $12-20. Considers client's budget, and skill and experience of artist when establishing payment.
Tips: "Don't assume the needs of a client! *Find out!*"

JACK SCHECTERSON ASSOCIATES INC., 6 E. 39th St., New York NY 10016. (212)889-3950. Contact: Jack Schecterson. Art/ad agency. Specializes in packaging, product design, annual reports, brand identity, corporate identity, displays, exhibits and shows, publications and signage. Clients: manufacturers of consumer/industrial products.
Needs: Uses local artists. Works on assignment only. Uses artists for annual reports, catalogs, direct mail brochures, exhibits, flyers, packaging, industrial design, slide sets, album covers, corporate de-

sign, graphics, trademark, logotype design, sales promotion, audiovisuals, P-O-P displays and print media advertising. Especially needs package and product designers.
First Contact & Terms: Send query letter with brochure showing art style or resume and tear sheets, or write for appointment. Samples returned by SASE. Reports "as soon as possible." Pays by the project for design and illustration; negotiates payment. Reproduction rights purchased.

***SCHROEDER BURCHETT DESIGN GROUP**, 40 Park Ave., New York NY 10016. Design Consultant: Carla Schroeder. Specializes in packaging. Clients: manufacturers.
Needs: Works on assignment only. Uses artists for design, mechanicals, lettering and logos.
First Contact & Terms: Send resume and photostat to be kept on file. Samples not kept on file are returned. Reports within 5 days. Write for appointment to show portfolio, thumbnails, final reproduction/product and photographs. Pays for design by the project, $10-25 average. Considers skill and experience of artist when establishing payment.
Tips: "Creativity depends on each individual; it cannot be paid on hours fees. In graphics, the trend is toward bold colors.

SEAY GROUP INTERNATIONAL, 4651-A Roswell Rd., Atlanta GA 30342. (404)257-0263. Director Design/Development: Don Kaminski. Specializes in corporate identity, displays, packaging, technical illustration, product design and graphics. Clients: manufacturers and publishers.
Needs: Works with 5-6 freelance artists/year. Prefers local artists for fast turnaround. Works on assignment only. Uses artists for design, illustration, brochures, books, P-O-P displays, mechanicals, direct mail packages, model making, charts/graphs and logos.
First Contact & Terms: Send query letter with resume. Samples not kept on file are returned by SASE only if requested. Reports back only if interested. Call to schedule an appointment to show a portfolio, which should include final reproduction/product. Pays for design by the hour, $5-100 average. Considers complexity of project, client's budget, skill and experience of artist, and turnaround time when establishing payment.
Tips: "Send a few quality examples of current works."

SHERIN & MATEJKA, INC., 400 Park Ave. S, New York NY 10016. (212)686-8410. President: Jack Sherin. Specializes in corporate communications, publications and sales promotion. Clients: banks, consumer magazines and insurance companies.
Needs: Works with 25 freelance artists/year. Prefers artists located nearby with solid professional experience. Works on assignment only. Uses artists for advertising and brochure design and illustration, mechanicals, retouching, model making, charts/graphs and lettering.
First Contact & Terms: Send query letter with brochure showing art style to be kept on file. Samples returned by SASE. Reports in 1 week. Call to schedule an appointment to show a portfolio, which should include original/final art and tear sheets. Pays $15-40/hour for design; negotiates illustration payment method. Considers complexity of project, client's budget, skill and experience of artist, and how work will be used when establishing payment.
Tips: "We buy many humorous illustrations for use in corporate publications."

SMALLKAPS ASSOCIATES, INC., 40 E. 34th St., New York NY 10016. (212)683-0339. Creative Directors: Marla Kaplan and Guy Smalley. Specializes in brand identity, corporate identity, brochures and posters. Clients: publishers, major corporations and large ad agencies.
Needs: Works with 5 freelance artists/year. "Artists must do accurate, clean work and have great mechanical skills." Works on assignment only. Uses artists for mechanicals, retouching, charts/graphs and AV materials.
First Contact & Terms: Send query letter with resume, business card and samples to be kept on file. Samples not kept on file are returned by SASE only. Reports back only if interested. Call for appointment to show portfolio. Pays for illustration by the project, $50-300 average; mechanicals, $8-15. Considers complexity of project, client's budget, skill and experience of artist, how work will be used and turnaround time when establishing payment.
Tips: "Artist must do fast, *clean* mechanicals and have good work habits."

SMITH & DRESS, 202 E. Main St., Huntington NY 11743. (516)427-9333. Contact: A. Dress. Specializes in annual reports, corporate identity, displays, direct mail, packaging, publications and signage. Clients: corporations.
Needs: Works with 3-4 freelance artists/year. Local artists only. Works on assignment only. Uses artists for illustration, retouching, airbrushing and lettering.
First Contact & Terms: Send query letter with brochure showing art style or tear sheets to be kept on file (except for works larger than 8½x11). Pays for illustration by the project. Considers client's budget and turnaround time when establishing payment.

SMYTHE GRAPHICS, 1125 Camino Del Mar, Del Mar CA 92014. (619)755-0842. Specializes in annual reports, corporate identity, brochures and publications. Clients: industrial, research and development, medical products and hospitals, consulting firms, high technology firms.
Needs: Works with 10-12 freelance artists/year. Artists must be "conveniently located since they pick up and deliver to/from us. They must do neat, clean work." Works on assignment only. Uses artists for advertising layout, brochure and catalog illustration and layout; mechanicals, retouching, posters, direct mail packages and charts/graphs.
First Contact & Terms: Send query letter with resume, photocopies and tear sheets to be kept on file. Samples returned by SASE only if requested. Reports only if interested. Call or write for appointment to show portfolio, which should include thumbnails, roughs, original/final art, final reproduction/product, color and b&w. Pays for design by the hour, $20-40 average. Pays for illustration by the hour, $15-40 average. Considers complexity of project, and skill and experience of artist when establishing payment. Estimated completion time required from artist. Reproduction rights are purchased with payment for work done.

***PATRICK SOOHOO INC.**, Suite A, 8800 Venice Blvd., Los Angeles CA 90034. (213)836-8800. Senior Design Director: Phillip Komai. Specializes in annual reports, brand and corporate identity and marketing support material. Clients: ad agencies, manufacturers, retailers and the entertainment industry.
Needs: Works with freelance artists as needed. Prefers local artists. "We prefer to have freelance artists work in our studio; the exception would be illustrators." Uses artists for advertising illustration, brochure and catalog illustration, mechanicals, retouching and lettering. Especially needs a good production artist, who can do fast, clean, accurate mechanicals with a sense of design.
First Contact & Terms: Call for appointment. Prefers printed samples, actual art pieces and transparencies as samples. Samples returned by SASE. Provide business card and tear sheets to be kept on file for possible future assignments. All fees are negotiable. Considers client's budget, and skill and experience of artist when establishing payment.
Tips: "Work should be neat and clean and professionally presented." In Los Angeles, "the trend is towards *fun* design—more color and innovative typography."

SPLANE DESIGN ASSOCIATES, 10850 White Oaks Ave., Granada Hills CA 91344. (818)366-2069. Contact: Robson Lindsay Splane. Specializes in product design, corporate identity, displays, packaging, exhibitry and furniture design.
Needs: Local artists only. Works on assignment only. Uses artists for illustration, mechanicals, and model making.
First Contact & Terms: Send query letter with brochure showing art style to be kept on file. Reports only if interested. To show a portfolio, mail appropriate materials, which should include thumbnails, roughs, original/final art and photographs. Pays for design and illustration by the hour, $7. Considers complexity of project, client's budget, skill and experience of artist, and turnaround time when establishing payment.

STEPAN DESIGN, 317 S. Prairie Ave., Mt. Prospect IL 60056. (312)364-4121. Designer: J. Stepan. Specializes in annual reports, brand identity, corporate identity, direct mail, packaging, publications and signage. Clients: corporations, ad agencies, arts organizations and hospitals.
Needs: Works with 4 freelance artists/year. Works on assignment only. Uses artists for illustration, P-O-P displays, mechanicals, retouching, model making, lettering and gift items. Currently seeks production-oriented designers on a freelance basis.
First Contact & Terms: "Must see folio or examples of art for reproduction as well as finished product." Send query letter with brochure, resume and samples to be kept on file. Call for appointment to show portfolio. Samples not filed are returned by SASE. Reports back within 2 months. Pays for design by the hour, $10-25, average; for illustration by the project, $50-500, average. Considers complexity of project, client's budget, skill and experience of artist, how work will be used, turnaround time and rights purchased when establishing payment.

LINDA STILLMAN INC.,, 114 E. 91st St., New York NY 10128. (212)410-3225. Art Director: Linda Stillman. Specializes in promotion, brochures and publications. Clients: cultural and art organizations, publishers, insurance companies and financial companies.
Needs: Works with numerous freelance artists. Local artists only. Uses artists for design, illustration, lettering, mechanicals, photography and retouching. "We mostly need mechanical artists."
First Contact & Terms: Send query letter, resume, tear sheets or photocopies to be kept on file. Considers complexity of project, client's budget, skill and experience of artist, how work will be used, turnaround time and rights purchased when establishing payment. Payment varies.

GORDON STROMBERG DESIGN, 5423 N. Artesian, Chicago IL 60625. (312)275-9449. President: Gordon Stromberg. Specializes in corporate identity, publications, interior design, direct mail and signage. Clients: advertising agencies, book publishing, small businesses, manufacturers, public relations firms, nonprofit organizations, Christian groups/charities and magazine publishers.
Needs: Works with variable number of artists/year. Uses artists for illustration, brochures, promotion, calligraphy, retouching and charts/graphs.
First Contact & Terms: Looks for "quality, price and appropriateness in artists' work." Works on assignment only. Send query letter with brochure, resume and samples—"anything that will give me insight into your ability"—to be kept on file; write for appointment to show portfolio. "A phone call will only delay the process until you send brochure or samples or photocopies of samples." Prefers slides; accepts photocopies. Samples are returned by SASE only if requested. Considers complexity of project, client's budget, skill and experience of artist, how work will be used, and turnaround time when establishing payment.

SYNTHEGRAPHICS CORPORATION, 940 Pleasant Ave., Highland Park IL 60035. (312)432-7774. President: Richard Young. Specializes in publications. Clients: PR agencies, ad agencies and book publishers.
Needs: Works with 4-5 freelance artists/year. "Prefer local artists, particularly ones good at juvenile, multi-ethnic illustrations." Works on assignment only. Uses artists for advertising and brochure design, illustration and layout; book design and illustration, mechanicals and charts/graphs.
First Contact & Terms: Send resume and photocopies to be kept on file. Reports only if interested. Call for appointment to show portfolio, which should include thumbnails, roughs, original/final art, color, tear sheets and photostats. Pays for design by the hour, $15-25 average. Pays for illustration by the hour, $10-15 average. Considers complexity of project, client's budget, and skill and experience of artist when establishing payment.

***TEAM 4 & CO., INC.**, 2239 Front St., Cuyahoga Falls OH 44221. (216)928-9048. Vice President: Larry Walker. Specializes in annual reports, corporate identity, displays, interior design, direct mail, packaging, publications and architecture. Clients: small diversified industry.
Needs: Works with various freelance artists/year. Specializes in illustrations and mechanicals.
First Contact & Terms: Send query letter with resume and slides. Samples not filed are returned only if requested. Reports within 2 weeks. Call to schedule an appointment to show a portfolio, which should include roughs and final reproduction/product. Considers complexity of project, client's budget, skill and experience of artist, and turnaround time when establishing payment.

DOUGLAS R. TERCOVICH ASSOC. INC., 575 Madison Ave., New York NY 10022. (212)838-4800. President: Douglas Tercovich. Specializes in packaging, brand identity, displays, sales promotion and fashion. Clients: cosmetic companies, industry and corporations.
Needs: Works with 15 freelance artists/year. Works on assignment only. Uses artists for design, illustration, brochures, P-O-P displays, mechanicals, retouching, airbrushing, posters, lettering and logos.
First Contact & Terms: Send resume and samples to be kept on file. Prefers photostats or tear sheets as samples. Reports back only if interested. Write for appointment to show portfolio. Pays by the project: design $75 minimum; illustration $150-1,100 average. Considers complexity of project and client's budget when establishing payment.
Tips: "Mechanicals should be of packaging quality."

TESA DESIGN INC., 7015 Carroll Rd., San Diego CA 92121. (619)453-2490. President: Thomas E. Stephenson. Specializes in brand identity, corporate identity, packaging, signage and technical illustration. Clients: original equipment manufacturers.
Needs: Works with 4 freelance artists/year. Works on assignment only. Uses artists for design, illustration, brochures, catalogs, P-O-P displays, mechanicals, airbrushing, model making and logos.
First Contact & Terms: Send brochure and resume to be kept on file. Samples not kept on file are returned by SASE. Reports only if interested. Call for appointment to show portfolio. Pays for design and illustration by the project. Considers complexity of project, skill and experience of artist, and how work will be used when establishing payment.
Tips: "Portfolio should include industrial or mechanical subject matter."

TOKYO DESIGN CENTER, Suite 928, 548 S. Spring St., Los Angeles CA 90013. (213)680-1294. Creative Art Director: Mac Watanabe. Specializes in corporate identity, advertising and packaging. Clients: fashion, cosmetic, architectural and industrial firms.
Needs: Works with 4 freelance artists/year. Uses artists for design, illustration, brochures, catalogs, books, P-O-P displays, mechanicals, airbrushing, charts/graphs and advertisements.
First Contact & Terms: Send samples to be kept on file. Samples not kept on file not returned. Reports

only if interested. Pays for design and illustration by the project. Considers client's budget when establishing payment.

TOKYO DESIGN CENTER, Suite 252, 703 Market St., San Francisco CA 94103. Contact: Curtis Tsukano. Specializes in annual reports, brand identity, corporate identity, packaging and publications. Clients: consumer products, travel agencies and retailers.
Needs: Uses artists for design and illustration.
First Contact & Terms: Send business card, slides, tear sheets and printed material to be kept on file. Samples not kept on file are returned by SASE only if requested. Reports only if interested. Pays for design by the project, $50-1,000 average. Pays for illustration by the project, $100-1,500 average. Considers client's budget, skill and experience of artist, turnaround time and rights purchased when establishing payment.

***THE T-SHIRT GALLERY LTD.**, 154 E. 64 St., New York NY 10021. (212)838-1212. Vice President: Flora Azaria. Specializes in t-shirts.
Needs: Works with 10 freelance artists/year. Uses artists for design and illustrations.
First Contact & Terms: Send query letter with resume and samples. Samples not filed are returned only if requested. Reports within weeks. To show a portfolio, mail appropriate materials. Pays for design by the project, $50-500. Pays for illustrations by the project, $50-500. Considers how work will be used when establishing payment.

UNIT 1, INC., 1556 Williams St., Denver CO 80218. (303)320-1116. President: Chuck Danford. Specializes in annual reports, brand identity, corporate identity, direct mail, packaging, publications and signage.
Needs: Uses artists for design, brochures, catalogs, P-O-P displays, mechanicals, posters, direct mail packages, charts/graphs, logos and advertisements.
First Contact & Terms: Send resume and samples to be kept on file. Samples not kept on file are returned. Reports only if interested. Call or write for appointment to show portfolio. Pays for design by the hour. Considers skill and experience of artist when establishing payment.

UNIVERSAL EXHIBITS, 9517 E. Rush St., South El Monte CA 91733. (213)686-0562. Design and Sales Administrator: Frank Meyer. Specializes in displays and interior design. Clients: ad agencies and companies.
Needs: Works with 5 freelance artists/year. Prefers local artists, up to 40 miles, with excellent sketching abilities. Works on assignment only. Uses artists for design and model making.
First Contact & Terms: Send resume and samples to be kept on file. Prefers slides as samples; reviews original art. Samples not kept on file are returned only if requested. Reports back within 5 days. Call for appointment to show portfolio. Pays for design by the hour, $10-25 average. Considers clients's budget and turnaround time when establishing payment.

WALTER VAN ENCK DESIGN LTD., 3830 N. Marshfield, Chicago IL 60613. (312)935-9438. President: Walter Van Enck. Specializes in annual reports, brand identity, corporate identity, displays, direct mail, packaging, publications and signage. Clients: book publishers, financial associations, health care institutions, investment advisory corporations and medium-sized corporations.
Needs: Works with 2-3 freelance artists/year. Prefers local artists. Works on assignment only. Uses artists for design, illustration, mechanicals, retouching, model making and lettering.
First Contact & Terms: Send query letter with business card and "slides or photostats that do justice to line art" to be kept on file. Samples not kept on file are returned only if requested. Reports within 1 week. Call or write for appointment to show portfolio. Pays for design by the hour, $8-15 average. Pays for illustration by the project, $500-2,500 average. Considers client's budget, and skill and experience of artist when establishing payment.

VIE DESIGN STUDIOS, INC., 830 Xenia Ave., Yellow Springs OH 45387. (513)767-7293. President: Read Viemeister. Specializes in corporate identity, packaging, publications and signage.
Needs: Works with 2 freelance illustrators/photographers per year. Artists must be local, or have a "very special style." Works on assignment only. Uses keyliners for mechanicals and charts/graphs.
First Contact & Terms: Send query letter with resume to be kept on file. Prefers to review photostats and prints. Samples not kept on file are returned by SASE. Reports only if interested. Write for appointment to show portfolio. Pays for illustration by the hour, $20-30 average; or by the project. Considers turnaround time when establishing payment.
Tips: "Smaller budgets require that design solutions be designed around existing resources, thus freelancer must be a known quantity."

***ALAN WELNER DESIGNS**, 3110 N. 16th St., Phoenix AZ 85006. President: Alan Welner. Specializes in signage. Clients: architects and developers.
Needs: Works with 4 freelance artists/year. Uses artists for design, illustrations, brochures, mechanicals, logos and signage design.
First Contact & Terms: Send query letter with brochure showing art style or resume, photocopies and slides. Samples not filed are returned only if requested. Reports only if interested. Write to schedule an appointment to show a portfolio, which should include thumbnails, roughs, original/final art, final reproduction/product, tear sheets and photographs. Pays for design by the hour, $10 minimum. Pays for illustration by the project, $100 minimum. Considers client's budget, and skill and experience of artist when establishing payment.

***WEST & WOHER ASSOCIATES INC.**, A3, 115 King St., Alexandria VA 22314. Art Directors: Luanne G. Woher and Stephanie D. West. Specializes in annual reports, corporate identity, direct mail and publications. Clients: associations, corporations, health care, retail, PR firms and educational.
Needs: Works with 2 freelance artists/year. "Artist must be local and willing to work in our offices and must have technical knowledge of preparing art for printing." Uses artists for illustrations and mechanicals.
First Contact & Terms: Send query letter with resume and samples to be kept on file. Reports only if intersted. Write to schedule an appointment to show a portfolio, which should include original/final art and final reproduction/product. Pays for design by the hour, $8-15. Pays for illustration, by the project. Considers complexity of project, client's budget, and skill and experience of artist when establishing payment.
Tips: "Since we do not hire a lot of freelance work it is important to send up-to-date materials. We always go through our files before we hire someone."

WHITEFLEET DESIGN INC., 440 E. 56th St., New York NY 10022. (212)319-4444. Contact: Design Production. Specializes in annual reports, brand and corporate identity, displays, exhibits and shows, packaging, publications, signage and slide shows. Clients: large corporation in computers, software computer, retail stores, hospitals, banks, architects and industry.
Needs: Works with 8 freelance artists/year. Uses artists for brochure and catalog layout, mechanicals, retouching, model making, charts/graphs, AV presentations, lettering and logo design. Especially needs good artists for mechanicals for brochures and other print. Prefers Swiss graphic style.
First Contact & Terms: Send brochure/flyer and resume; submit portfolio for review. Prefers actual printed samples or color slides. Samples returned by SASE. Reports within 1 week. Provide brochure/flyer, resume and tear sheets to be kept on file for possible future assignments. Pays $10-15 average/hour for mechanicals; pays/project for illustration.
Tips: Artists should "not start so high if unknown; give a break on the first 2 days to work in."

WISNER ASSOCIATES, Advertising, Marketing & Design, 1991 Garden Ave., Eugene OR 97403. (503)683-3235. Creative Director: Linda Wisner. Specializes in brand identity, corporate identity, direct mail, packaging and publications. Clients: small businesses, manufacturers, restaurants, service businesses and book publishers.
Needs: Works with 7-10 freelance artists/year. Prefers experienced artists and "fast clean work." Works on assignment only. Uses artists for illustration, books, mechanicals, airbrushing and lettering.
First Contact & Terms: Send query letter with resume, photostats, photocopies, slides and photographs to be kept on file. Prefers "examples of completed pieces, which show the abilities of the artist to his/her fullest." Samples not kept on file are returned by SASE only if requested. Reports only if interested. To show a portfolio, mail appropriate materials or call to schedule an appointment; portfolio should include thumbnails, roughs, original/final art and final reproduction/product. Pays for illustration by the hour, $10-20 average. Pays for paste-up/production by the hour, $8.50-10. Considers complexity of project, client's budget, skill and experience of artist, how work will be used and turnaround time when establishing payment.
Tips: "Bring a complete portfolio with up-to-date pieces."

BENEDICT NORBERT WONG MARKETING DESIGN, 55 Osgood Pl., San Francisco CA 94133. (415)781-7590. President/Creative Director: Ben Wong. Specializes in annual reports, corporate identity, direct mail and marketing design for financial services. Clients: financial services companies (banks, savings and loans, insurance companies, stock brokerage houses) and direct mail marketing firms (ad agencies, mail houses).
Needs: Works with 15 freelance artists/year. Uses artists for design, illustration, brochures, catalogs, P-O-P displays, mechanicals, retouching, posters, direct mail packages, charts/graphs, lettering, logos and advertisements. Especially needs "experienced mechanical artists in area of direct mail production."

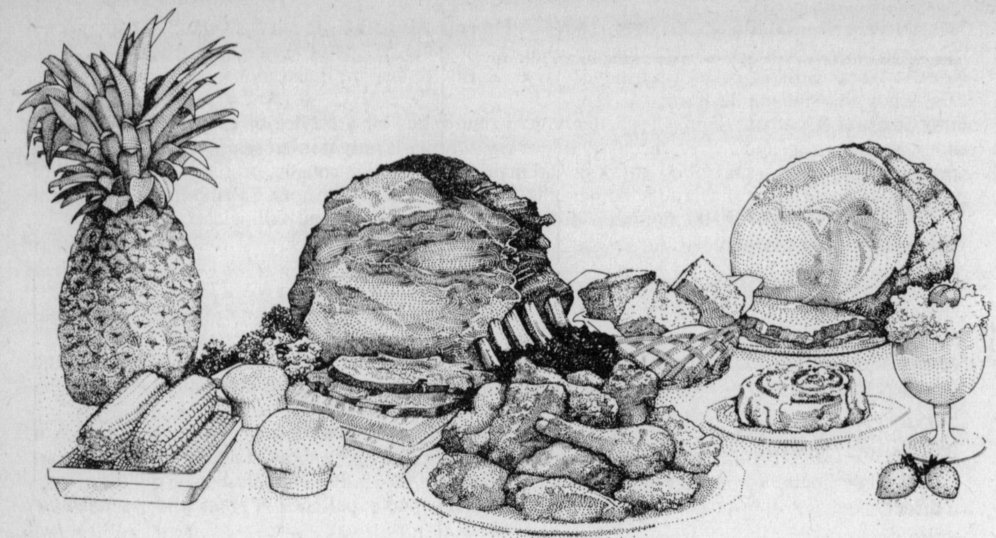

Linda Wisner, creative director of Wisner Associates in Eugene, Oregon, assigned freelance artist Kathy Kifer, also of Eugene, to illustrate the buffet-style dining of International King's Table, a local restaurant. Kifer says, "I have received other assignments of product illustration in stipple style, because the completed piece is now in my portfolio." Kifer received $250 for the pen & ink drawing.

First Contact & Terms: Send query letter with resume, business card and samples to be kept on file. Prefers tear sheets as samples. Reports back only if interested. Call for appointment to show portfolio. "Payment depends on experience and portfolio." Considers complexity of project, client's budget, skill and experience of artist, how work will be used, turnaround time and rights purchased when establishing payment.
Tips: "Please show imaginative problem solving skills which can be applied to clients in the financial services industry."

***WORDGRAPHICS, INC.**, Suite 208, 1372 Peachtree St. NE, Atlanta GA 30309. Art Director: Dixie Wilson. Specializes in typesetting, mechanical art, corporate identity, publications, slides, maps, ads and all graphics. Clients: printers, ad agencies, sales organizations, PR firms, publishers and manufacturers.
Needs: Works with varied number of freelance artists/year. Works on assignment only. Uses artists for mechanical preparation, layout, design and illustration and typesetting.
First Contact & Terms: Send query letter with resume to be kept on file. Call for appointment to show portfolio, which should include thumbnails, roughs, original/final art and final reproduction/product. Pays for design by the hour, $15-30; pays for illustration, $10-15.

X-GROUP, INC., 636 Avenue of the Americas, New York NY 10011. (212)255-5900. Art Director: Ernie Bellico. Specializes in marketing communications, brand identity, corporate identity, displays, audiovisual slide presentations and video and film animation. Clients: advertising agencies, public relation firms and corporations.
Needs: Works with 20 freelance artists/year. Uses artists for illustration, mechanicals, retouching, airbrushing, model making, charts/graphs, AV materials and animation.
First Contact & Terms: Send query letter with brochure, resume, business card and samples to be kept on file. Prefers slides and tear sheets as samples. Reports back only if interested. Pays for design by the hour, $5-15 average. Pays for illustration by the project, $75-3,000 average. Considers complexity of project, client's budget, skill and experience of artist, how work will be used, turnaround time and rights purchased when establishing payment.
Tips: "Be professional, direct and to the point. No fluff."

Associations & Institutions

The ideals of our culture are embodied in the charters of associations and institutions. The purposes of these groups vary—from soliciting funds for education to the preservation of animal welfare—but they all seek to promote and enrich humanitarian values.

To promote their concerns, associations rely on artwork to deliver their messages. Because of tight budgets, they are unable to support a fulltime art staff and thus turn to freelancers. Their needs range from occasional spot art to complex audiovisual presentations. Service-oriented associations rely heavily on various print media, including magazines, newsletters, posters, invitations, brochures and catalogs.

Art directors (or public relations directors) seek bold and simple visuals that communicate a direct message in symbolic terms. Many times one piece of artwork is used to thematically unite several printed pieces. Portfolio samples should reproduce well in print, exhibit low-cost design solutions and be flexible enough for application to several uses.

Some projects, such as layout and campaign designs, call for local artists to faciliate quick turnaround times. Other projects, however, such as magazine illustration or spot art for membership literature, often can be discussed, assigned and submitted via the mail.

Some associations ask artists to contribute their work; the exposure gained through widely-disseminated literature and posters often leads to referrals and paying jobs. Also, the work provides pieces for your portfolio, which is especially important if you are just beginning to build one.

For additional information, consult the *Encyclopedia of Associations*, *Barron's Profiles of American Colleges*, *Comparative Guide to American Colleges*, and *Directory of World Museums*.

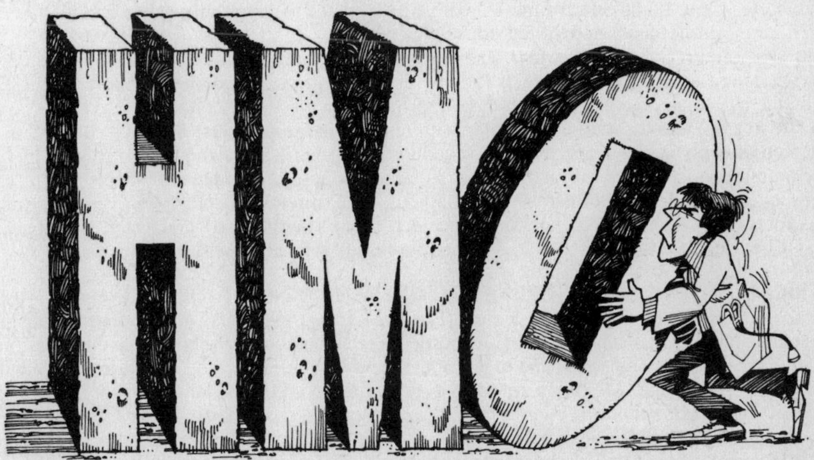

Michael J. Burke of the American Academy of Pediatrics in Elk Grove Village, Illinois, asked freelance artist Chuck Bracke of Chicago to "illustrate a commentary on how pediatricians should cooperate with the development of Health Maintenance Organizations." The artwork, created in pen & ink, appeared in the Academy's monthly membership newspaper to convey the message, as Burke says, that "for many had been a burdensome problem."

ADRENAL METABOLIC RESEARCH SOCIETY OF THE HYPOGLYCEMIA FOUNDATION, INC., 153 Pawling Ave., Troy NY 12180. (518)272-7154. President: Marilyn Hamilton Light. Nonprofit association providing information and research on functional hypoglycemia and related endocrine disorders for lay and professional persons.
Needs: Works with 1 freelance artist/year. Prefers design representative of content of material—medical designs, etc. Works on assignment basis only.
First Contact & Terms: Send query letter with brochure, samples and resume. "Photostats are acceptable as samples." Samples returned by SASE if not kept on file. Reports in 2 weeks. Provide brochure and samples to be kept on file for possible future assignments. Write for appointment. Payment is negotiable; varies according to client's budget.

AESTHETICIANS INTERNATIONAL ASSOCIATION, INC., Suite D, 3606 Prescott, Dallas TX 75219. (214)526-0752. Chairman of the Board: Ron Renee. Promotes education and public awareness of skin care, make-up and body therapy. Produces seminars and holds an annual congress; produces a magazine, *Dermascope*, published bimonthly.
Needs: Works with 6 freelance artists/year. Works on assignment only. Uses artists for advertising design, illustration and layout, brochure and magazine/newspaper design, exhibits, displays and posters.
First Contact & Terms: Send query letter with brochure showing art style, tear sheets, photostats, photocopies, slides or photographs to be kept on file. Samples not kept on file are returned by SASE. Reports only if interested. Call or write to schedule an appointment to show portfolio, which should include tear sheets, photostats and photographs. Pays by the hour, $3.75-6 average. Considers available budget when establishing payment.

AFFILIATE ARTISTS INC., 37 W. 65 St., New York NY 10023. Director, Communications: Katharine Walling. A national not-for-profit organization, producing residencies for performing artists of all disciplines. "Through residencies, Affiliate Artists supports the professional development of exceptionally talented performers and builds audiences for live performance. Residencies are sponsored by corporations and corporate foundations, and presented locally by arts institutions and community organizations. Roster represents every discipline."
Needs: Works with 3 freelance artists/year. Works on assignment only. Uses artists for advertising and brochure design, illustration and layout.
First Contact & Terms: Send query letter with resume and photostats. Samples returned only if requested. Reports only if interested. Pays by the project. Considers available budget when establishing payment.

***AMERICAN ACADEMY OF PEDIATRICS**, 141 Northwest Point Blvd., Elk Grove Village IL 60007. Publications Editor: Michael Burke. "A professional organization serving more than 28,000 pediatricians in North, Central and South America who are dedicated to the health, safety and well-being of infants, children, adolescents and young adults."
Needs: Works with 6 freelance artists/year. "Local artists only, please." Works on assignment only. Quick turnaround necessary. Uses artists for newspaper illustration, and annual report design. Especially needs themes related to child health care improvement.
First Contact & Terms: Send query letter with resume and tear sheets. Samples not filed are not returned. Reports only if interested. Write to schedule an appointment to show a portfolio, which should include thumbnails, roughs, original/final art, final reproduction/product, tear sheets, photostats, photographs and b&w. Pays for illustration by the hour, $100 minimum. "Payment varies considerably; will pay for talent." Considers complexity of project, client's budget, skill and experience of artist, how work will be used, turnaround time and rights purchased when establishing payment.

***AMERICAN ANTHROPOLOGICAL ASSOCIATION**, 1703 New Hampshire Ave NW, Washington DC 20009. (202)232-8800. Managing Editor: Thomas Krizay. "World's largest nonprofit organization of individuals interested in anthropology. Its purposes are to encourage scholarly and professional communication among anthropologists and to promote the public understanding of anthropology and its use to solve human problems. Members are from every subfield and every employment setting—anyone with a professional or scholarly interest in anthropology."
Needs: Works with several freelance artists/year. "We have little use for graphic artists, and have in the past used a couple of local artists whose work we are satisfied with." Uses artists for brochure design, illustration and layout; magazine/newspaper design, illustration and layout.
First Contact & Terms: Send query letter with resume and samples. Reports only if interested. Considers skill and experience of artist and turnaround time when establishing payment.

AMERICAN BONSAI SOCIETY, INC., Box 358, Keene NH 03431. (603)352-9034. Executive Secretary: Anne D. Moyle. Nonprofit educational corporation and organization of individuals interested in

the art of miniature trees; a journal and newsletter published quarterly.
Needs: Works with 2-3 freelance artists/year.
First Contact & Terms: Send query letter to be kept on file.

*AMERICAN CETACEAN SOCIETY, Box 2639, San Pedro CA 90731. (215)548-6279. Executive Director: Patricia Warhol. ACS is a marine mammal conservation/education organization serving marine scientists, educators and interested lay persons.
Needs: Works with 8-10 freelance artists/year. "Work must show whales, dolphins, or other marine mammals with anatomical accuracy." Uses artists for advertising, brochure and magazine/newspaper design and illustration.
First Contact & Terms: Send query letter with samples. Samples not filed are returned only if requested. Reports back within 1 month. To show portfolio, mail appropriate materials or call to schedule an appointment. "ACS is a nonprofit, volunteer organization. Publication in our journal pays no money, but is an excellent way to have one's work seen by interested people."
Tips: "We work with numerous artists and are always pleased to find new talent. We respond to letters or phone calls."

*AMERICAN GEM SOCIETY, 5901 West Third St., Los Angeles CA 90036. Contact: Editor. "AGS is a nonprofit professional organization of jewelers and educators which seeks to build consumer confidence in the retail jeweler through promotion of ethical business standards and continuing advancement of the gemological professional (nationwide) serving retail jewelers, jewelry suppliers and jewelry consumers."
Needs: Works with 5 freelance artists/year. Artist must have "ability to portray beauty and romance of jewlery." Uses artists for brochure design, illustration and layout; AV presentations and exhibits. Prefers "an effective blend of simplicity, quality, and the tastefulness exemplified by fine jewelry stores."
First Contact & Terms: Send query letter with brochure showing art style or resume and tear sheets. Samples not filed are returned by SASE. Reports only if interested. Write to schedule an appointment to show a portfolio, which should include roughs and final reproduction/product. "Bids are taken on projects." Considers client's budget, bids and satisfaction with previous work when establishing payment.
Tips: "Visit AGS stores (listed in the Yellow pages) to see the kind of clientele we serve."

AMERICAN PAINT HORSE ASSOCIATION, Box 18519, Forth Worth TX 76118. (818)439-3400. Magazine Editor: Bill Shepard. Art Director: Vicki Day. Breed registry for Paint horses. Publishes magazine for people who raise, breed and show Paint horses. Circ. 10,500. Receives 4-5 cartoons and 2-3 illustrations/week from freelance artists. Original artwork returned after publication. Sample copy $1; artist's guidelines free for SASE.
Cartoons: Buys 3-5 cartoons/issue, all from freelancers. Interested in horses; single panel with gagline. Send finished cartoons. Material returned by SASE only if requested. Reports in 1 month. Buys first rights. Pays $10, b&w line drawings; on acceptance.
Illustrations: Uses 2-3 illustrations/issue; buys few/issue from freelancers. Receives few submissions/week from freelancers. Especially needs youth drawings with Paint horses. Send business card and samples to be kept on file. Prefers original art or photostats as samples. Samples returned by SASE if not kept on file. Reports within 1 month. Buys first rights. Pays $7.50, b&w, inside; $50 color.
Tips: "Be sure horses included in artwork are Paint horses! We've lowered the prices we pay for freelance work as we now employ 3 fulltime artists."

*AMERICAN SCIENCE FICTION ASSOCIATION, Suite 95, 421 E. Carson, Las Vegas NV 89101. Vice President: M. Silvers. Promotion and publishing of *all* facets of science fiction and fantasy literature for science fiction fans mostly.
Needs: Works with 20-40 freelance artists/year. Uses artists for brochure and magazine design, illustration and layout; AV presentation, exhibits, displays, signage and posters. Prefers futuristic themes.
First Contact & Terms: Send query letter with resume and samples. Samples not filed are not returned. Reports back within 3 weeks. To show a portfolio, mail original/final art. Pays for design by the hour, $18.50 minimum; by the project, $500 minimum; by the day, $88 minimum. Pays for illustration by the project, $250 minimum. Considers complexity of project and rights purchased when establishing payment.
Tips: "Past experience seems to indicate that the more material submitted the better the chance of our using the artist's services."

AMERICAN SOCIETY FOR THE PREVENTION OF CRUELTY TO ANIMALS, 441 E. 92nd St., New York NY 10128. (212)876-7700. Contact: Head of Publications. A nonprofit humane society which cares for 200,000 animals annually. Its members are animal lovers and those concerned about humane issues.

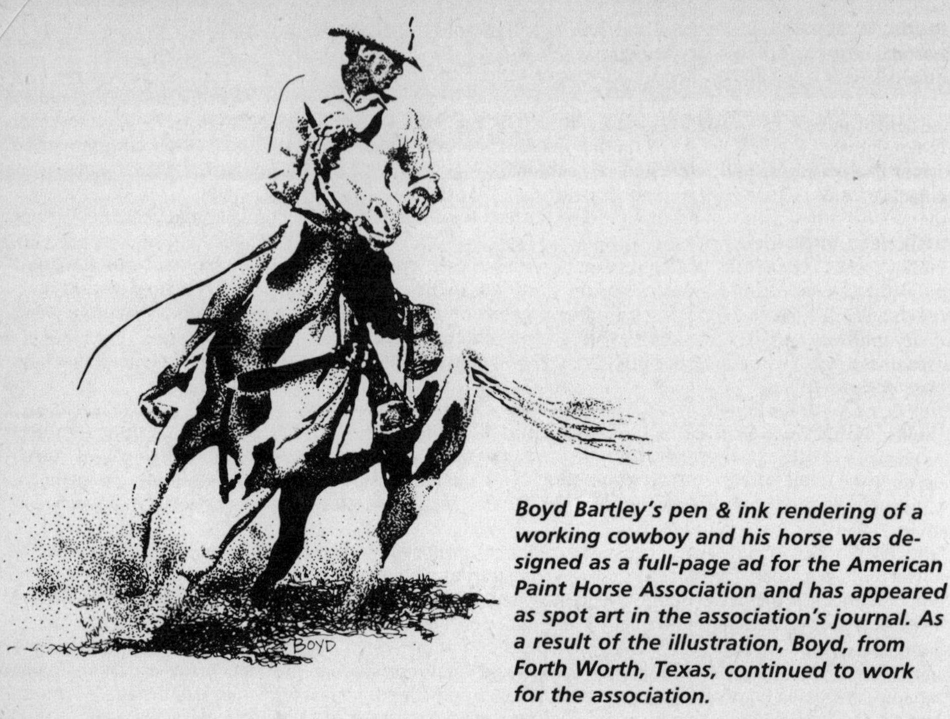

Boyd Bartley's pen & ink rendering of a working cowboy and his horse was designed as a full-page ad for the American Paint Horse Association and has appeared as spot art in the association's journal. As a result of the illustration, Boyd, from Forth Worth, Texas, continued to work for the association.

Needs: Often uses illustrations for posters, booklets and newsletters. "We prefer realistic depictions of animals rather than cartoons."
First Contact & Terms: Write with samples. Samples returned by SASE. Provide resume, brochure/flyer and tear sheet samples to be kept on file for future assignments. Reports within 3 weeks. Pays $25/small illustration for a pamphlet. Pay for product design and illustration depends on job required and funds available.

AMUSEMENT AND MUSIC OPERATORS ASSOCIATION, Suite 600, 111 E. Wacker Dr., Chicago IL 60601. (312)644-6610. Executive Vice President: William W. Carpenter. Represents the coin-operated games, music and vending industry (primarily jukeboxes, electronic darts and videogames) with 3,000 member companies, operators, distributors, suppliers and manufacturers.
Needs: Works with 4 freelance artists/year. Local artists only. Works on assignment basis only. Uses artists for magazine/newspaper design, illustration and layout; exhibits, signage and posters. Prefers themes revolving around the coin-op entertainment industry.
First Contact & Terms: Send query letter with brochure, resume, business card, samples and tear sheets to be kept on file; do not call. Accepts photostats, original work, slides or photographs as samples. Reports only if interested. Negotiates pay by the project. Considers complexity of project, available budget, turnaround time and rights purchased when establishing payment.

BIKECENTENNIAL, INC., Box 8308, Missoula MT 59807. (406)721-1776. Art Director: Greg Siple. Service organization for touring bicyclists; 18,000 members.
Needs: Works on assignment only. Uses artists for illustration. Considers various styles.
First Contact & Terms: Send query letter with brochure showing art style or resume, tear sheets, photostats, photocopies, slides and photographs to be kept on file. Samples not filed are returned. Reports within 4 weeks. To show a portfolio, mail thumbnails, roughs, final reproduction/product, tear sheets, photostats, photographs and b&w. Pays by the project, $25-75. Considers complexity of project, available budget, skill and experience of artist and how work will be used when establishing payment.
Tips: "We assign specific illustrations and usually provide reference material."

BROWARD COMMUNITY COLLEGE, 225 E. Las Olas Blvd., Ft. Lauderdale FL 33301. (305)761-7490. Director of Cultural Affairs: Dr. Ellen Chandler. Assigns 2 jobs/year.

Needs: Works with 1 illustrator and 1 designer/year. Mostly local artists. Works on assignment only. Seasonal illustration needs during concert season: October-March. Uses artists for exhibits/displays. Especially needs season brochure and/or poster.
First Contact & Terms: Send query letter with photographs or call for interview. Looks for "imaginative design and clean, clear work." Reports in 1 month. Samples returned by SASE. Pay varies. Considers complexity of project and available budget when establishing payment.
Tips: "Our own college art students and printing department have become more actively involved in our projects."

BUCKNELL UNIVERSITY, Lewisburg PA 17837. (717)523-3200. Director of Public Relations and Publications: Sharon Poff. 3,400-student university; public relations department serves students, alumni (31,000), donors and students' parents.
Needs: Works with 3-4 freelance artists/year. Prefers freelancers with strong experience in college/university graphics and located within a 3-hour drive from campus. Uses artists for brochure, catalog and magazine/newspaper design, illustration and layout; graphic design and posters. Especially needs brochure design.
First Contact & Terms: Send query letter with samples, brochure/flyer and resume. Accepts any type samples. Looks for innovation, appropriateness of design concept to target audience and "sensitivity to our particular 'look'—rather classic and dignified, but not boring" when reviewing artist's work. Samples returned by SASE. Reports in 1 month. Call or write for appointment to show portfolio. Payment is by the project, $50-3,000 average or by the hour, $10-20 average; method is negotiable. Considers complexity of project, available budget and turnaround time when establishing payment.
Tips: "Artists should "be able to help me produce graphically strong and cost-effective pieces."

CALIFORNIA BAPTIST COLLEGE, 8432 Magnolia Ave., Riverside CA 92504. (714)689-5771. Vice President for Public Affairs: Dr. Jay P. Chance.
Needs: Assigns 3-5 jobs/year. Local artists only. Uses artists for annual reports, catalog covers/layouts, direct mail/publicity brochures, displays, newspaper ad layouts, lettering, recruitment literature and company publications.
First Contact & Terms: Send query letter with samples to Division of Public Information on campus. SASE. Reports in 3 weeks. Call to schedule an appointment to a show a portfolio, which should include final reproduction/product. Pays by hour.
Tips: "Call for appointment with Ken Miller."

***CANCER CARE INC.**, 1180 Avenue of the Americas, New York NY 10036. (212)221-3300. Creative Services Director: F. Critchlow. Health agency for cancer patients and their family, "helping emotionally and financially."
Needs: Works with two freelance artists/year. Prefer local artists only. Uses artists for the design, illustration and layout of advertising and brochure and for posters. Prefers modern, contemporary styles.
First Contact & Terms: Send query letter with brochure. Samples not filed are returned if requested. Reports back only if interested. Pays for design and illustration by the project. Considers skill and experience of artists when establishing payment.

CHAPMAN COLLEGE, 333 N. Glassell, Orange CA 92666. Director of Publications: Annie P. Long. A 4-year private liberal arts college producing publications for use by donors and approximately 1,800 students enrolled on the home campus and the surrounding community.
Needs: Works with 2 full-time and 2 part-time artists and occasionally freelancers. Prefers artists who "live in the surrounding area to be available for meetings." Works on assignment only. Uses artists for catalog design, illustration and layout; exhibits, displays, signage and calligraphy. Especially needs freelance illustrations, photographs and production artists/designers.
First Contact & Terms: Send query letter, resume and business card with photos or photocopies to be kept on file; write for appointment. Looks for "quality, creative, clean and cost-conscious design" when reviewing artist's work. Samples not filed are returned by SASE. Payment varies according to job. Considers complexity of project, available budget, and skill and experience of artist when establishing payment.
Tips: CASE, The Council for the Advancement of Secondary Education, and UCDA, The University & College Designers Association, and local community organizations such as public relations societies or business associations are helpful organizations to join for education art contacts. "The ability to communicate clearly is important. Administrators at institutions are involved in so many meetings and other tasks that the opportunity to catch them anytime with questions is not always there. Artists need to be versatile and able to illustrate, design and have a working knowledge of production and printing processes." Artists should avoid "underselling themselves by asking for less than they deserve, or overselling by asking for much more than their experience shows."

CHILD AND FAMILY SERVICES OF NEW HAMPSHIRE, 99 Hanover St., Box 448, Manchester NH 03105. (603)668-1920. Contact: Public Relations Director. "Our purposes are to reduce social problems, promote and conserve wholesome family life, serve children's needs and guard children's rights."
Needs: Works with 1 illustrator and designer/year; February-May only. Uses artists for annual reports, direct mail brochures, exhibits/displays, posters, publicity brochures and trademarks/logotypes. Especially needs illustrations of children and/or families. Prefers realistic portrayals of family life.
First Contact & Terms: Query with business card and tear sheets to be kept on file or arrange interview. Looks for human interest appeal when reviewing artist's work. Reports in 2 weeks. Works on assignment only. Samples returned by SASE. Considers complexity of project and available budget when establishing payment.
Tips: "In black-and-white work, we look for a balance—nothing too stark or horrific—but a snapshot of real people, children, families."

COACHING ASSOCATION OF CANADA, 333 River Rd., Ottawa, Ontario K1L 8H9 Canada. (613)748-5264. Editor: Vic Mackenzie. National nonprofit organization dedicated to coaching development and the profession of coaching.
Needs: Works with 18 freelance artists/year. Works on assignment only. Uses artists for advertising, brochure, catalog and magazine illustration. Prefers coaching (sport) themes in realistic styles.
First Contact & Terms: Send brochure and samples to be kept on file. Prefers slides or photographs as samples. Samples not kept on file are returned. Reports within 3 weeks. Pays by the project, $50-500 average. Considers complexity of project, available budget, skill and experience of artist, how work will be used and rights purchased when establishing payment.
Tips: "Artists must have a good understanding of sport."

COLLEGE OF THE SOUTHWEST, 6610 Lovington Highway, Hobbs NM 88240. (505)392-6561. Contact: Public Information Officer. Privately supported, independently governed 4-year college offering professional studies on a foundation of arts and sciences, emphasizing Christian principles and the private enterprise system.
Needs: Works with varying number of freelance artists/year. Prefers to work with artists in the Southwest. Works on assignment only. Uses artists for advertising, brochure and graphic design; advertising and brochure illustration; and posters. Especially needs artwork "relating to Southwestern heritage."
First Contact & Terms: Send query letter; submit portfolio for review. Prefers 5-10 photostats or slides as samples. Samples returned by SASE. Reports within 2 weeks. Provide resume and samples to be kept on file for possible future assignments. Negotiates payment.

THE CONTEMPORARY ARTS CENTER, 115 E. 5th St., Cincinnati OH 45202. (513)721-0390. Publications Coordinator: Carolyn Krause. The Center is a small organization (8-10 full time positions) with changing exhibitions of contemporary art surveying individuals, movements, regional artists, etc., in all media. "We have a growing membership which is geared toward contemporary art and design."
Needs: Works with 2-5 freelance artists/year. Works on assignment only. Uses artists for advertising, brochure and catalog design, illustration and layout; magazine/newspaper design and layout; signage and posters. Prefers contemporary styles.
First Contact & Terms: Send query letter with brochure and resume to be kept on file. Reports only if interested. Pays by the project; "other payment arrangements can be devised as needed." Considers complexity of project, available budget, skill and experience of artist, and turnaround time when establishing payment.

CORE PUBLICATIONS, 236 W. 116th St., New York NY 10026. (212)316-1577. Communications Coordinator: George Holmes. Nonprofit association providing civil rights publications.
Needs: Works with 20-30 freelance artists/year. Works on assignment only. Uses artists for advertising and magazine/newspaper design, illustration and layout.
First Contact & Terms: Send query letter with samples and resume. Especially looks for artistic skill, imagination, reproduction ability and originality when reviewing work. Samples not filed returned by SASE. Reports within 6 weeks. Negotiates payment by the project.

***CYSTIC FIBROSIS FOUNDATION**, Suite 510, 6000 Executive Blvd., Rockville MD 20852. (301)881-9130. Field Material/Information Coordinator: Ms. Robbye Wilson. National, nonprofit organization. National office oversees activities of 60 chapters throughout the country.
Needs: Works with 3 freelance artists/year. "Because we're a nonprofit organization, cost is a crucial factor-we must contract with artist that gives lowest bid, but we still strive for quality." Uses artists for brochure design and illustrations; magazine/newspaper design, illustration and layout; AV presentations, exhibits, displays and posters. Especially needs artwork for promotional, fund raising pieces and for corporate solicitations. Prefers simple, yet professional styles.

First Contact & Terms: Send query letter with brochure showing art style or resume and samples. Samples not filed are returned only if requested. Reports only if interested. Call to schedule an appointment to show a portfolio, which should include roughs, original/final art and color. Pays for design and illustration by the hour, $50 maximum. Considers complexity of project, client's budget and turnaround time when establishing payment.
Tips: "We see more nonprofit organizations competing for less dollars, which means fund raising pieces will become slicker, more professional and business-oriented."

DISCOVERY: THE ARTS WITH YOUTH IN THERAPY, 3977 2nd Ave., Detroit MI 48201. (313)832-4357. Director: Fr. Russ Kohler. "We fund self-employed artists to work for 15 weekly house calls to youth with cancer and long-term illnesses."
Needs: Works with "artists as we need them upon referral of patients by physicians and medical social workers. We prefer artists who are somewhat isolated in their medium and willing to enter the isolation of the child overly identified with his disease. Prefer a minimum of psychological and medical jargon; emphasis on the language of art and visual expression and experience."
First Contact & Terms: Write with resume to be kept on file for future assignments.

DREXEL UNIVERSITY, Dept. of Public Relations, 32nd and Chestnut Sts., Philadelphia PA 19104. (215)895-2613. Director: Philip Terranova. Assigns 20 jobs and buys 10 illustrations/year.
Needs: Works with 3 illustrators and 6 designers/year. Seasonal needs: September-June. Uses designers for books, pamphlets and posters; illustrators for covers, jacket covers, spot art, etc. Also uses artists for advertising, annual reports, charts, direct mail brochures, exhibits/displays, handbooks, publicity, recruitment literature, magazines, newsletters and trademarks/logos.
First Contact & Terms: Send query letter with resume, b&w tearsheets (no slides) or arrange interview. Looks for originality and sound production skills. SASE. Reports in 1 week. Pays for design by the project, $50-750; for illustration by the project, $50-400. Considers available budget and skill and experience of artist when establishing payment.

EDUCATIONAL FILM LIBRARY ASSOCIATION, INC., Suite 301, 45 John St., New York NY 10038. (212)227-5599. Executive Director: Marilyn Levin. "The leading professional association concentrating on 16mm films, video and other nonprint media for education and community use." Members include: public libraries, universities/colleges, museums, community groups, film programmers, filmmakers, film teachers, etc.
Needs: Works with 1 artist/year for all illustrations; 1 for ad design. "Artists must work within strict guidelines."
First Contact & Terms: Query by mail or write with samples. Works on assignment only. Samples returned by SASE. Reports back on future assignment possibilities. Provide resume, business card, brochure/flyer, tear sheet samples or "anything that gives a good idea of work experience" to be kept on file for future assignments. Pay is negotiable.
Tips: "Send samples that apply to film/video technology, film librarians, independent video and filmmakers."

EPILEPSY FOUNDATION OF AMERICA, Suite 406, 4351 Garden City Dr., Landover MD 20785. (301)459-3700. Director of Administrative Services: Hugh S. Gage. Nonprofit association providing direct and indirect programs of advocacy, public health education and information, research, government liaison and fundraising to persons with epilepsy, their families and professionals concerned with the disorder.
Needs: Works with 3-4 freelance artists/year. Prefers local artists "because of tight deadlines. Sometimes this is not a problem. However it depends on the job." Works on assignment only. Uses artists for advertising layout, brochure design, illustration and layout; graphic design, exhibits, displays, signage, AV presentations, annual reports, illustrations and layouts for fundraising materials. Themes must be suitable to a publicly funded, charitable organization. Especially needs slide presentations, exhibit panels and brochure covers.
First Contact & Terms: Provide business card to be kept on file. Looks for "diversity, taste, 'non-cute' approaches." Samples returned by SASE. Reports back on whether to expect possible future assignments. Call for appointment. Payment is by the project. Considers complexity of project and available budget when establishing payment.
Tips: "We're looking for the most value for our money. Don't bring banged up, poorly printed samples."

***ESSEX COMMUNITY COLLEGE**, 7201 Rossville Blvd., Baltimore County MD 21237. (301)682-6202. Contact: Managing Director. Performing arts center; presents musicals, cabaret plays, open-air Shakespearean and other classical plays, Renaissance Festival, and seminars. "Cockpit is in residence

at Essex Community College. We try to use the services of the school graphics department as much as possible but sometimes must use freelance artists because the staff at the school is too overloaded or they are unable to give us what we want."
Needs: Works with 2 illustrators and 2 designers/year. "Our brochure is our most important tool for publicity as it creates an image for our theatre. Work on the brochure begins in early fall for the following summer season." Uses artists for advertising, billboards, designer-in-residence, direct mail brochures, flyers, graphics, posters, sets and technical art.
First Contact & Terms: Local artists only. Query with samples or arrange interview. SASE. Reports within 2 weeks. Works on assignment only. Samples returned by SASE; and reports back on future assignment possibilities. Provide resume, business card, brochure, flyer and tear sheets to be kept on file for future assignments. Negotiates payment.
Tips: "Cockpit in Court Summer Theatre is a rarity. We are self-supporting through subscription sales, nearly every production area and seldom require the services of a freelance artist as college faculty and staff members can usually produce what we want." To those artists interested in working in the performing arts field, "keep artwork simple! Graphics and typeface must be reproducible, will most likely be reduced for flyers, newspapers ads, etc. The simpler the typeface the better."

***FEDERAL BAR ASSOCIATION**, Suite 408, 1815 H. St. NW, Washington DC 2006. (202)638-0252. Director of Publications: Jamie Loomis. "Our 15,000 member association was created 65 years ago to further the goals of the federal legal profession." Serves lawyers, magistrates, judges, district attorneys and members of the JAG.
Needs: Works with 4 freelance artists/year. Uses artists for magazine design and illustration.
First Contact & Terms: Send query letter with resume and samples. Samples not filed are returned by SASE. Reports only if interested. Call or write to schedule an appointment to show a portfolio, which should include roughs, original/final art and final reproduction/product. Pays for illustration by the project, $400 maximum. Considers client's budget when establishing payment.

THE FINE ARTS CENTER, CHEEKWOOD, Forrest Park Dr., Nashville TN 37205. (615)352-8632. Director: Kevin Grogan. Art musuem; full-time staff of 7; collects, preserves, exhibits and interprets art with special emphasis on American painting. The Tennessee Botanical Gardens and Fine Arts Center, Inc., has a membership in excess of 8,000 drawn primarily from Nashville (Davidson County) and neighboring counties in the middle-Tennessee, southern Kentucky region.
Needs: Works with 1-3 freelance artists/year. Prefers local artists. Uses artists for advertising, brochure and catalog design and layout; signage and posters.
First Contact & Terms: Send query letter with resume, business card, slides and photographs to be kept on file; "slides, if any, will be returned." Reports within 4 weeks. Write to schedule an appointment to show portfolio and for artists' guidelines. Pays by the hour, $5-20 average. Considers complexity of project, available budget, skill and experience of artist, how work will be used and turnaround time when establishing payment.

FLORIDA MEMORIAL COLLEGE, 15800 NW 42nd Ave., Miami FL 33054. (305)625-4141. Public Affairs Director: Nadine Drew. Baptist-related, 4-year, accredited liberal arts college located on a 50-acre site with enrollment of 1,800 multi-racial students.
Needs: Works with 2-3 freelance artists/year. Works on assignment only. Uses artists for advertising, brochure and catalog design, illustration and layout.
First Contact & Terms: Send brochure/flyer with printed material, tear sheets and actual work. Samples returned upon request only with SASE. Reports immediately.

***FOUNDATION OF HUMAN UNDERSTANDING**, Box 811, 111 NE Evelyn St., Grants Pass OR 97526. (503)479-0549. Managing Editor: David Masters. "Nonprofit, Judeo-Christian church, whose daily radio program reaches millions of listeners nationwide. Purpose is to teach people how to control their emotions through observation/meditation exercise taught by Founder/President Roy Masters. We reach out and help people of all faiths."
Needs: Works with 100 freelance artists/year. Uses artists for advertising and brochure design and illustration; magazine design, illustration and layout. Prefers thought-provoking, iconolastic, controversial b&w, pen & ink, photos, cartoons, modern, classic, etc; variety of artwork designed to shock or stimulate ideas surrounding article content.
First Contact & Terms: Send query letter with tear sheets, photostats, photocopies, slides, photographs and original artwork. Samples not filed are not returned. Reports within 2 weeks. To show a portfolio, mail thumbnails, roughs, original/final art, final reproduction/product, color, tear sheets, photostats, photographs and b&w.
Tips: "The more controversial the subject matter, the better."

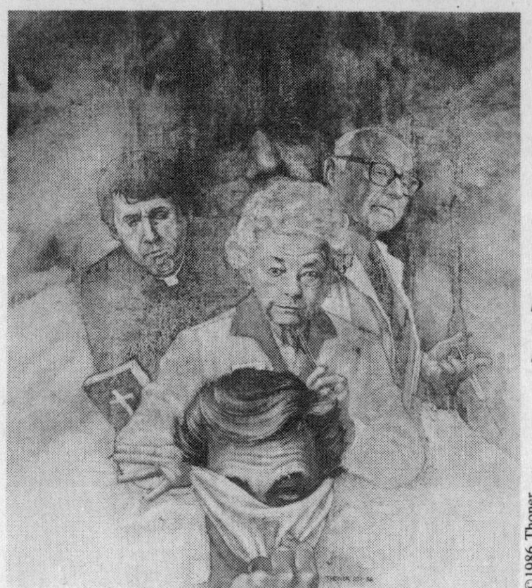

Dan Thoner created this painting to convey "the destructive effect that so-called experts have on people when trying to help them solve their problems." The painting illustrates the cover of the Foundation of Human Understanding's magazine, Iconoclast. The illustration, painted in oils on linen, was based on the theme of the magazine's feature article. Thoner, of San Diego, California, says that the publication of his artwork "helped to establish my validity as an illustrator among reps."

FRANKLIN PIERCE COLLEGE, Public Relations Office, Rindge NH 03461. Director/Public Relations: Richard W. Kipperman.
Needs: Regional artists only. Uses artists for cover illustrations for brochure and catalog covers, occasionally for brochure design and logo/institutional identity designs.
First Contact & Terms: Query with previously published work. Looks for "quality, artistic ability" when reviewing samples. Works on assignment only. Samples returned by SASE; and reports back on future possibilities. Provide resume and business card to be kept on file for future assignments. Pays per completed assignment (includes concept/roughs/comps/mechanicals).

GEORGIA INSTITUTE OF TECHNOLOGY, Office of Publications, Alumni/Faculty House, Atlanta GA 30332. (404)894-2450. Director: Thomas Vitale. University with 11,000 students; publications serving alumni, graduate and undergraduate students and faculty.
Needs: Works with 5 freelance artists/year. Works on assignment only. Uses artists for brochure design and illustration, magazine/newspaper illustration and posters. Themes and styles vary with each project.
First Contact & Terms: Send query letter with brochure and samples to be kept on file. Samples not filed are returned only if requested. Reports only if interested. Call or write for appointment to show portfolio. Pays by the hour, $25-100 average. Considers complexity of project, available budget, skill and experience of artist, how work will be used, turnaround time and rights purchased when establishing payment.
Tips: "We are a state school—budgets are tight, but the work is very high-quality."

GIRL SCOUTS OF THE USA, 830 3rd Ave., New York NY 10022. Director, Graphics & Design: Michael Chanwick.
Needs: New York City area artists only. Uses artists for design, direct mail brochures, annual reports, promotions, publications, exhibits, catalogs and posters. "Very interested in illustration and photography showing young people in various activities."
First Contact & Terms: Submit published samples.

HAMPDEN-SYDNEY COLLEGE, Hampden-Sydney VA 23943. (804)223-4382. Director of Publications: Dr. Richard McClintock. Nonprofit all-male liberal arts college of 750 students in a historic zone campus.
Needs: Works with 5-6 freelance artists/year. Works on assignment only. Uses artists for advertising, brochure, catalog and graphic design; brochure and magazine/newspaper illustration; brochure, catalog and magazine/newspaper layout; AV presentations and posters. Especially needs illustrations and mechanical preparations.
First Contact & Terms: Send query letter with resume and actual work. Write for appointment to show

portfolio. Samples returned by SASE. Reports in 1 week. Negotiates payment.
Tips: "Changes in art and design include more formality, careful design and quality of 'look.' "

***HARDWOOD PLYWOOD MANUFACTURERS ASSN.**, Box 2789, Reston VA 22090. (703)435-2900. President: Clark E. McDonald. National trade association of hardwood plywood and veneer manufacturers and prefinishers of hardwood plywood and suppliers to the industry. Prefinishers, printer, vinyl overlayers, paper overlayers, embossers, etc. of imported and domestic hardwood plywood wall paneling.
Needs: Works with 1 freelance artist/year. Uses artists for brochure and catalog illustration.
First Contact & Terms: Send query letter with resume and samples. Samples not filed are returned only if requested. Reports only if interested. To show a portfolio, mail appropriate materials. Considers association's budget when establishing payment.

***INSTITUTE OF INTERNAL AUDITORS**, 249 Maitland Ave., Altamonte Spgs. FL 32701. (305)830-7600, ext. 263. Art Director: W.P. Dolle. Professional association for accountants and auditors with 30,000 members in 128 countries around the world.
Needs: Works with 8-10 freelance artists/year. Artist must have 3-5 years' experience. Works on assignment only. Regional artists used but it is not necessary to be local. Uses artists for advertising, brochure and catalog design and illustration; magazine design and illustration, and photography. Prefers business/international theme.
First Contact & Terms: Send query letter with resume, tear sheets, photostats and photocopies. Samples not filed are returned by SASE. Reports within days. Call or write to schedule an appointment to show a portfolio, which should include roughs, original/final art, final reproduction/product, color, photographs and b&w. Pays for design and illustration by the project, $200-600. Considers complexity of project, client's budget, and skill and experience of artist when establishing payment.
Tips: "When deadline is established, work should be delivered by that date, no excuses."

***INSTITUTE OF INTERNATIONAL EDUCATION**, Communications Division, 809 United Nations Plaza, New York NY 10017. Senior Production Editor: Ellen L. Goodman. Specializes in information flyers, paperback catalogs and statistical analysis; also annual report. Publishes 11 titles/year.
Needs: Works with many freelance artist/year. Works on assignment only.
First Contact & Terms: Send query letter with brochure, resume and samples to be kept on file. Samples returned by SASE. Reports within 2 weeks. Call to schedule an appointment to show a portfolio. Originals sometimes returned to artist after job's completion. Pays by the project. Rights purchased vary.

INTERNATIONAL ASSOCIATION OF INDEPENDENT PRODUCERS, Box 2801, Washington DC 20013. (202)775-1113. Executive Director/Editor: Dr. Edward VonRothkirch. Associate Director: Ted Edwards.
Needs: Works with 15-25 illustrators and 3-4 designers/year. Works on assignment only. Uses graphic designers for art which pertains to motion pictures, TV, records, tapes, advertising and book/record cover illustrations. Specific needs include layouts, logos and column heads.
First Contact & Terms: Send resume, brochure and tear sheet to be kept on file; also send tear sheets, photocopies or transparencies as samples. Samples returned by SASE; reports back on future assignment possibilities. Pays by job. Usually buys all rights.

***INTERNATIONAL PLATFORM ASSN.**, 2564 Berkshire Rd., Cleveland Hts. OH 44106. (216)932-0505. Newsletter Editor: Dose Hill, 2126 Saddleback, Mosreau OK 73072. "Approximately 200 artists within the organization, among some 40 exhibits at annual art shows." Serves all types of patrons from all parts of the country and some foreign.
Needs: Works with 50 freelance artists/year. "Most freelance artists are painters that we work with but many prizes have been awarded to photographers in the past." Uses artists for art shows.
First Contact & Terms: "Each artist must be a member of I.P.A. (International Platform Assoc). Artists get a mention in the *Talent* magazine when they win our award."

***INTERNATIONAL RACQUET SPORTS ASSOCIATION**, 132 Brookline Ave., Boston MA 02215. (617)236-1500. Editor: Pamela Worner. Trade association for commercially operated, investor-owned racquet and fitness clubs.
Needs: Works with 6 freelance artists/year. Prefers local artists. Uses artists for advertising, brochure and magazine/newspaper design, illustration and layout; posters. Prefers fitness club operations, business scenes and club sports as themes.
First Contact & Terms: Send query letter with brochure showing art style. Samples not filed are returned by SASE. Reports only if interested. Call or write to schedule an appointment to show a portfolio.

Pays for design by the project, $200 minimum. Pays for illustation by the project, $100 minimum. Considers complexity of project, client's budget, skill and experience of artist, and turnaround time when establishing payment.

Tips: "We have only begun budgeting for design and illustration work fairly recently, so our rates are low. We are looking to build a stable of contacts—if you start with us, you can probably take on work from a variety of sources within our organization: monthly magazine, marketing department, meeting planning, etc. Opportunity to grow with us (we've jumped from 8 staff and $500,000 budget 2 years ago to 20 employees and $2 million budget)."

***INTERNATIONAL RADIO AND TELEVISION SOCIETY, INC.**, Suite 531, 420 Lexington Ave., New York NY 10170. (212)867-6650. Director of Sales: Linda Miller. Membership organization for executives in radio, television, cable, advertising, public relations and allied fields serving executives, on-air talent, students and professors.

Needs: Works with 2-3 freelance artists/year. Uses artists for brochure design.

First Contact & Terms: Send resume and tear sheets. Samples not filed are returned by SASE. Reports only if interested. Call or write to schedule an appointment to show a portfolio, which shoud include final reproduction/product. Pays for design by the project. Considers complexity of project, client's budget, and skill and experience of artist when establishing payment.

Tips: "Call or write for an appointment, be on time, bring samples, and follow up additional requests if necessary."

***INTER-TRIBAL INDIAN CEREMONIAL ASSOCIATION**, Box 1, Church Rock NM 87311. (505)863-3896. WATS Line: 1-800-233-4528. Executive Director: L.D. Linford. Teaches Indian culture to Indians and nonIndians.

Needs: Assigns 1 art job/year. Uses artists for direct mail brochures and posters. Indian artists only. Especially needs posters and advertising art. Prefers Indian motifs by Indian artists.

First Contact & Terms: Send query letter with brochure showing art style. SASE. Reports within 1 month. Write to schedule an appointment to show a portfolio, which should include original/final art and photographs. Pays $500 maximum/job, design.

IPI ADVERTISING GROUP, (formerly Invitational Promotions, Inc.), 6930 Owensmouth Ave., Canoga Park CA 91303. (818)999-6515. Vice President, Creative: John A. Buchanan. National agency serving over 2,500 financial institutions, and 2,500 auto dealers in over 120 cities. Works in areas of auto, loan promotion, furniture, travel promotion; also deals in incentives and sales promotion, credit card systems and insurance.

Needs: Works on assignment only. Uses artists for advertising, brochure, magazine/newspaper and catalog design, illustration and layout; exhibits, displays, signage, posters and retouching. Especially needs "life-style types, four-color illustrations and layouts for financial promotions, i.e. IRA, ATM, loans, savings and checking printed pieces."

First Contact & Terms: Send query letter with brochure showing art style or resume and tear sheets, photostats and photocopies to be kept on file. "No originals." Samples not kept on file are returned. Reports within 1 week. Call or write to schedule an appointment to show portfolio, which should include thumbnails, roughs, final reproduction/product, color, tear sheets, photostats, photographs, b&w and slides of work if available. Pays by the hour, $3.85 minimum; by the project, rate varies, generally normal L.A. freelance rates. "Projects are generally quoted as a result of the scale; artists must work in a do-not-exceed price structure." Considers complexity of project, available budget, skill and experience of artist and turnaround time when establishing payment.

Tips: Artists should "make sure their books are concise and self-explanatory, and show as wide a range of work as possible. We look for versatility in style. Since we work with over 2,500 banks, savings & loans and credit unions, each piece must be unique. We will work with artists on a national basis because we use printing facilities in over 120 cities. We have rapidly expanded into fullscale advertising and marketing in the financial marketplace. There has been radid deregulation, thus more advertising."

***KOFFLER GALLERY**, (Jewish Community Centre of Toronto), 4588 Bathurst St., North York, Ontario M2R 1W6 Canada. (416)636-1880. Contact: Director or Public Relations. "The Koffler Gallery is a public gallery, a non-profit organization whose mandate is to show the fine arts, decorative arts and design and judaica. It is an educational institution aimed on making the visual arts available to the public."

Needs: Needs freelance artists when a catalogue needs to be designed, for a major public relations campaign etc. "This is never known in advance." Works on assignment only. Uses artists for brochure and catalog design, illustration and layout, poster design and illustration and set design.

First Contact & Terms: Send query letter with resume, samples, tear sheets, photostats, photocopies, slides and photographs to be kept on file. Write for appointment to show a portfolio, which should include "everything an artist feels that would benefit us for our choice." Samples returned only if request-

ed. Reports within 2 months. Pays for design and illustration according to "artist's quote for each job." Considers available budget when establishing payment.
Tips: "People are becoming more capable in design, not necessarily with a design background. Contemporary design is moving very fast and with an interesting outlook."

***LABAN GUILD**, 1 Parkwood Court, Bulwell Nottinghamshire NE6 9SP UK. Administrator: E. Johnson. A guild of members who work in professional, recreative dance, education, therapy, industry and seek to advance the principles of movement provided by the late Rudolph Laban.
Needs: Works with 500 freelance dance/movement artists/year. "The Laban Guild produces two magazines and 4 newsletters, various advertising brochures and exhibitions. These are 'inhouse'; only printing is contracted out."

LANE COLLEGE, 545 Lane Ave., Jackson TN 38301. (901)424-4600, ext. 241. Public Relations Director: Ms. Martha Robinson. Predominantly black church-affiliated institution.
Needs: Assigns 5-10 jobs/year. Local artists only. Uses artists for advertising, exhibits/displays, publicity brochures, recruitment literature and trademarks/logos.
First Contact & Terms: Send query letter with brochure showing art style or resume, business card and samples to be kept on file. SASE. Reports within 2 weeks. To show a portfolio, mail appropriate materials. Payment by job: $10-75, design; $30-80, illustration; $40-100, layout; $40-80, production.

LOYOLA UNIVERSITY OF CHICAGO, 820 N. Michigan Ave., Chicago IL 60611. (312)670-2974. Assistant Vice President/University Public Relations: James Reilly. One of the largest private universities in Illinois providing higher education to 15,000 students on 3 Chicago area campuses and one in Rome, Italy.
Needs: Works with 6-7 freelance artists/year. Works on assignment basis only. Uses artists for brochure and catalog design and layout; graphic design, exhibits, displays, signage, AV presentations and posters.
First Contact & Terms: Send query letter. Prefers original work as samples. Samples returned. Reports in 6 weeks. Write for appointment to show portfolio. Payment varies according to job.
Tips: "Keep up with the latest trends."

***LYCOMING COLLEGE**, College Place, Williamsport PA 17701. (717)321-4037. Contact: Director of Public Relations. Nonprofit, small liberal arts and sciences college of 1,250 students.
Needs: Works with 1-2 freelance artists/year. Prefers artists with "some feel for or experience with educational institutions." Uses artists for advertising and brochure design, illustration and layout; graphic design and posters. Especially needs illustrations for college magazine.
First Contact & Terms: Prefers work that shows originality—"a feel for the unusual but effective message and an awareness of what the typical, common person can relate to and appreciate." Send query letter with 2-3 photocopies and resume. Samples not returned. Call or write to schedule an appointment to show a portfolio, which should include roughs and original/final art. Negotiates payment.
Tips: "There is a trend toward more use of high-quality, tasteful advertising. Artists should keep work simple. We're always interested in good freelance art."

MACALESTER COLLEGE, Office of Public Relations & Publications, 1600 Grand Ave., St. Paul MN 55105. (612)696-6203. Director: Nancy A. Peterson. Designer: Marnie Baehr. Four-year liberal arts college "with reputation as one of nation's finest." Produces materials for student recruitment, academic use, alumni relations, fundraising, etc.
Needs: Works with a few freelance artists/year. Works on assignment only. Uses artists for advertising, brochure and catalog design, illustration and layout; graphic design, magazine/newspaper design and illustration; and posters. Prefers variety of themes and styles. Especially needs b&w illustrations and photographs.
First Contact & Terms: Send query letter with resume, tear sheets, photocopies, photographs and printed samples. Reports back on whether to expect possible future assignments. Call or write for appointment to show portfolio. Samples not kept on file are returned. Payment varies according to job and client's budget.
Tips: "We're conservative in our approach to design, but we like something fresh and clean."

***McALLEN CHAMBER OR COMMERCE**, Box 790, McAllen TX 78501. (512)682-2871. Public Relations Manager: Rick Arriola. Promotes conventions, tourism, community programs, industry and legislation for McAllen.
Needs: Assign 8-15 jobs and buys 12 illustrations/year. Uses artists for advertising, magazines, newsletters, publicity brochures, exhibits/displays and trademarks/logos. Especially needs economic/business oriented artwork; international trade and commerce themes; and Hispanic-related art and information.

First Contact & Terms: Send query letter with samples. SASE. Reports in 1 week. Pays $10-20/illustration. Considers turnaround time when establishing payment.
Tips: "We have expanded our monthly newsletter to a monthly economic report."

MARCH OF DIMES BIRTH DEFECTS FOUNDATION, 1275 Mamroneck Ave., White Plains NY 10605. (914)428-7100. Print Production Supervisor: Susan Lynn. Nonprofit organization dedicated to the prevention of birth defects.
Needs: Works with 12 freelance artists/year. Works on assignment only.Uses artists for advertising, brochure, catalog and magazine/newspaper design, illustration and layout; AV presentations, exhibits, displays and posters.
First Contact & Terms: Send query letter with business card and samples to be kept on file. Prefers "current jobs completed by the artist pertaining to brochures, ads, newsletters, etc." as samples. Samples not kept on file are not returned. Call for appointment to show portfolio.

***METASCIENCE FOUNDATION**, Box 32, Kingston RI 02881. Associate Editor/Art Director: Robert Adsit. "We publish a scholarly academic periodical covering all areas of consciousness research. Topics covered include telepathy, precognition, psychokinesis, astrology, graphology, ufology, metaphysics, neurophysiology and the quantum physics of consciousness."
Needs: Works with 4 freelance aritsts/year. Uses artists for advertising design, illustration and layout; exhibits, displays and features artists within periodicals. Prefers Egyptian, occult, futuristic themes; creative, abstract, representational styles.
First Contact & Terms: Send query letter with photostats, slides and photographs possibly to be kept on file. Samples not kept on file are returned by SASE if requested. Reports within 2 months. Pays $15; "our journal goes out to over 30 countries and over 50 libraries. Payment is more in exposure and opportunity than in direct pecuniary rewards."
Tips: Current trends include "surreal, metyphysical, extradimensional and futuristic themes."

METHODIST COLLEGE, Raleigh Rd., Fayetteville NC 28301. (919)488-7110. Director of Publications: Al Robinson. Nonprofit, small liberal arts college of 1,000 students.
Needs: Works with 2 freelance artists/year. Works on assignment basis only. Uses artists for advertising, brochure and catalog design, illustration and layout; regularly buys cartoons for college newspaper and humorous illustrations; occasionally buys cartoon-style illustrations. Especially needs cover design for admissions material; pen & inks of campus buildings, and graphics to accompany news and feature stories. Looks for clarity, style and reproduction quality when reviewing samples.
First Contact & Terms: Send query letter with samples, brochure/flyer and resume. Prefers photostats as samples. Samples returned by SASE. Reports in 2 weeks. Provide resume and business card to be kept on file for possible future assignments. Call for appointment to show portfolio. Negotiates payment. Considers complexity of project, available budget and how work will be used when establishing payment.
Tips: "Bring fresh perspective. You will be paid as much for your perception as your performance."

MID-AMERICA BIBLE COLLEGE, 3500 S.W. 119th, Oklahoma City OK 73170-9797. (405)691-3881. Director of College Relations: Bill Cissna. A single purpose institution that prepares leadership for Christian service; serves approximately 350 students (55% male, 45% female and 32% married).
Needs: Works with 2-3 freelance artists/year. Artists must be sympathetic with the Christian philosophy of life and have a well-balanced portfolio. Works on assignment basis only. Uses artists for advertising, brochure, catalog and magazine/newspaper design; advertising, brochure, catalog and magazine/newspaper illustration; brochure and catalog layout; signage and posters. Prefers religious themes; "lots of people." Especially needs posters for distribution to local churches nationwide; brochures and response card for each degree program.
First Contact & Terms: Send query letter with samples, brochure/flyer and resume; submit portfolio for review. Prefers "whatever is most convenient and economical for the artist" as samples. "Appeal to Christian high school student; work in sympathy with a conservative college." Samples returned. Reports in 5 weeks. Provide business card, brochure, flyer and samples to be kept on file for possible future assignments. Negotiates payment. Considers available budget and how work will be used when establishing payment.
Tips: "We like one artistic concept to do a multiple number of things." There has been "addition of new degree programs" here.

MODERN LANGUAGE ASSOCIATION, 10 Astor Place, New York NY 10003. Production Manager: Judith Altreuter. Not-for-profit professional organization; membership consists of 25,000 professors of English and foreign languages in universities.
Needs: Works with 2-5 freelance artists/year. Works on assignment only. Uses artists for brochure de-

sign. Prefers 2-color graphics; classic; "interesting, but not trendy."
First Contact & Terms: Send query letter with brochure, resume and business card to be kept on file. Reports only if interested. Write for appointment to show portfolio. Pays by the project, $150-500 average. Considers complexity of project, available budget, skill and experience of artist, how work will be used and turnaround time when establishing payment.
Tips: Artists should be "reliable and patient."

***NAMSB SHOW**, 535 Fifth Ave., New York NY 10017. Advertising Manager: Massimo Iacoboni. Men's wear trade shows serving men's wear retailers.
Needs: Works with 2-3 freelance artists/year. Artist must have a good fashion sense. Uses artists for advertising design and illustration; brochure design and illustration; catalog design and illustration; magazine/newspaper illustration, exhibits, displays and posters. "Prefers fashion illustration/photography. All styles can be considered."
First Contact & Terms: Send query letter with brochure showing art style or tear sheets, photostats, photocopies, slides and photographs. Samples not filed are returned only if requested. Reports only if interested. Write to schedule an appointment to show a portfolio, which should include original/final art, final reproduction/product, color, tear sheets, photographs and b&w. Pays for illustration by the project, $100-350. Considers complexity of project, client's budget, skill and experience of artist, and rights purchased when establishing payment.
Tips: Artist should have a "strong fashion sense/modern to avant-garde feeling."

NATIONAL AESTHETICIAN AND NAIL ARTISTS ASSOCIATION, 16 N. Wabash, Chicago IL 60602. (312)782-1329. Executive Director: Phyllis Monier. Association for manicure, pedicure, skin care cosmetics.
Needs: Works with 3 freelance artists/year. Works on assignment only. Uses artists for advertising design and illustration, displays, signage and posters. Prefers line drawings.
First Contact & Terms: Send brochure showing art style or photostats or original work to be kept on file. Samples not filed returned by SASE. Reports only if interested. Write for appointment to show portfolio. Considers available budget when establishing payment.

***THE NATIONAL ASSOCIATION FOR CREATIVE CHILDREN & ADULTS**, 8080 Springvalley Dr., Cincinnati, OH 45236. Editor: Ann Isaacs.
Needs: Works with 1 artist/year for advertising design. Also uses artists for books and brochures.
First Contact & Terms: Send query letter with samples. Samples returned by SASE. Reports back on future assignment possibilities. Provide business card, brochure and/or tear sheet samples to be kept on file for future assignments. Reports in 3 months. Payment is in copies of publications.

NATIONAL ASSOCIATION OF EVANGELICALS, Box 28, Wheaton IL 60189. (312)665-0500. Director of Information: Donald R. Brown. Voluntary fellowship of evangelical denominations, churches, schools, organizations and individuals; seeks to be a means of cooperative effort between its various members; provides evangelical identification for 43,000 churches and 4 million Christians.
Needs: Works with 1-5 freelance artists/year. Uses artists for advertising illustrations and layout, and brochure design. Themes are specified per project.
First Contact & Terms: Send query letter with photostats, photocopies and photographs. Samples are returned by SASE. Reports within 2 months. Call or write to schedule an appointment to show a portfolio. Pay varies according to assignment. Considers complexity of project, available budget, skill and experience of artist, how work will be used, turnaround time and rights purchased when establishing payment.
Tips: Artists should have "an understanding of the National Association of Evangelicals: its history, current projects and ministries; and its objectives and purpose." Currently using more line art.

THE NATIONAL ASSOCIATION OF LIFE UNDERWRITERS, 1922 F St. NW, Washington DC 20006. (202)331-6070. Editor: Edward Keenan. Publishes *Life Association News*, the monthly official association magazine with a circulation of 140,000. Subscriptions are limited to members and affiliated organizations, schools and libraries. Also publishes numerous brochures and catalogs. Serves life underwriters (life insurance agents), financial brokers and consultants, and businesspersons associated with insurance in general.
Needs: Works with 5-10 freelance artists/year. DC metropolitan area artists only. Works on assignment only. Uses artists for brochure, catalog and magazine illustration. Prefers pen & ink, washes, drybrush and airbrush. Especially needs editorial calendar. Looks for "clarity, expression, realism and freshness" in themes and styles.
First Contact & Terms: Send query letter with resume, original work, photostats or tear sheets to be kept on file. Material not filed returned by SASE only if requested. Reports only if interested. Write for

Close-up

Gordon Bieberle
Director of Publications
National Safety Council
Chicago, Illinois

In theme-oriented associations, such as the National Safety Council in Chicago, prolific output of print materials and publications requires reliable freelance sources for graphic art of all kinds.

According to Gordon Bieberle, director of publications for this nongovernmental, nonprofit safety education society, discovering and working with new talent is a priority.

"Going after new artists is a relatively new activity since I have been here," Bieberle says, pointing out that the Council has worked most often with Chicago-based artists simply because "it was more expedient."

However, in pursuit of his objective to infuse print materials with a fresh, contemporary look, Bieberle will consider any artist, local or not, who can meet the Council's current needs.

"If an artist has the ability and style we are seeking, then five or ten years' experience isn't a factor," he says, adding that he has no preconceived notions that time in the field equals talent. "We are not looking for absolute 'top' people . . . We can't afford 'top.' " Most associations look for high quality—in summarizing concepts, being able to translate them visually in the simplest, most direct ways and turning in finished art correct and on time.

Among the Council's numerous print materials are educational and promotional brochures, posters, magazines, hardcover books, an annual calendar and every other year, an atlas.

Just within the magazine area, the Council publishes eight different safety-related titles. Each magazine has its own visual identity . . . for now, he says.

Each year many associations select a theme which they promote on many levels. For instance, the Safety Council's theme for 1986 was Team Safety, aimed at increasing awareness of personal and joint responsibility for safety of co-workers in industrial environments.

"Visuals have to be bold and simple. Grab the readers, make them think or they'll turn the page. The Council is promoting an attitude: the regard for safety. In my mind, a strong visual communicates a strong message. Anything else misses the goal," he says.

Bieberle points out that he is personally pushing for art and photographs that have striking symbolism.

"Symbols enable you to pose questions, not necessarily to answer them, that you cannot conveniently or politely put into words," he explains, adding that piquing the reader's curiosity and making him think is always the objective.

As for artists contacting associations, Bieberle prefers a more informal approach.

"The inquiry doesn't have to be very formal—I'm not very formal myself," he reassures. "Dispensable tear sheets of printed work with a cover letter are the best method. If someone sends an SASE, a return is possible. But I can't even guarantee that.

"We would be comfortable working out a contract with artists whose work we like a lot after they have done three or four projects for us," he says. The main criteria for artwork used by associations would be continuity in style and quality, variety of techniques in the artist's repertoire, and reliability.

—Sam A. Marshall

appointment to show portfolio. Pays by the project, $50-75 average for spot art. Considers complexity of project and turnaround time when establishing payment.

***NATIONAL ASSOCIATION OF PHYSICAL THERAPISTS, INC.**, Box 367, West Covina CA 91793. (818)919-7836. Executive Director: Shela Denton. International association for physical therapists.
First Contact & Terms: Send query letter with brochure showing art style or resume and samples. Samples not filed are returned only if requested. Reports back within 3 weeks. To show a portfolio, mail appropriate materials.

NATIONAL BUFFALO ASSOCIATION, Box 565, Ft. Pierre SD 57532. (605)223-2829. Executive Director-Editor: Judi Hebbring. Breed organization representing commercial producers of buffalo (bison); also caters to collectors, historians, etc. Publishes bimonthly magazine of interest to buffalo enthusiasts, collectors and producers; circulation 1,400. Membership: 1,000.
Needs: Works with 4-5 freelance artists/year. "We feature artists in the magazine (must paint, sketch, sculpt, etc., buffalo); also feature artwork on cover."
First Contact & Terms: Send query letter with brochure and photographs. Material is kept on file until used, then it is returned to artist. Samples not kept on file are returned. Reports within 2-3 weeks. No pay; "we trade magazine exposure for use of photos and story about the artist in _Buffalo!_ magazine.
Tips: Especially looks for "a good representation of the American buffalo, as well as a well-rounded subject portfolio. Awards and credentials are also looked at but not as primary criteria—talent and salability of the work is number one." Current trends include "a back-to-basics movement where artists are doing native animals rather than the exotics that were the vogue a few years ago."

***NATIONAL CAVES ASSOCIATION**, Rt. 9, Box 106, McMinnville TN 37110. (615)668-3925. Secretary/Treasurer: Barbara Munson. "The NCA is an organization of show caves owners and operators, established to set and maintain standards of operation and to promote the visitation of show caves."
Needs: "As an organization, the NCA offers little opportunity for freelance artists."

NATIONAL COMMITTEE FOR CITIZENS IN EDUCATION, 410 Wilde Lake Village Green, Columbia MD 21044. (301)997-9300. Editor: Chrissie Bamber. Purpose is to improve the education of children by mobilizing and assisting citizens, including parents, to strengthen public schools; an advocate for citizens helping them gain and use information and skills to influence the quality of public education.
Needs: Works with 3-4 freelance artists/year. Local artists preferred except for newspaper illustration. Works on assignment only. Uses artists for advertising, brochure and catalog design and layout; brochure illustration, magazine/newspaper design and illustration, and AV presentations.
First Contact & Terms: Send query letter with samples and tear sheets to be kept on file. Write for artists' guidelines. Prefers photostats as samples. Samples not kept on file returned by SASE. Reports within 2 weeks. Pays by the project, $25-50 average for single illustration for newspaper; rates for "design of bookcover, brochure, AV aids, etc, are higher." Considers complexity of project, available budget, skill and experience of artist, how work will be used, turnaround time and rights purchased when establishing payment.
Tips: Artists should exhibit an "understanding of current education issues" in their work.

NATIONAL GALLERY OF ART, DEPARTMENT OF EXTENSION PROGRAMS, National Gallery Plaza, Washington DC 20565. Curator: Ruth R. Perlin. Clients: schools, museums and libraries.
Needs: Works with 2-3 designers/year. Uses artists for design of text brochures, programs, catalogs and posters. Local artists only. Works on assignment only.
First Contact & Terms: Send query letter with resume, brochures, pamphlets and posters. Samples returned by SASE.

***NATIONAL INSTITUTE FOR AUTOMOTIVE SERVICE EXCELLENCE**, 1920 Association Dr., Reston VA 22091. (703)648-3838. Contact: Berry McNulty.
Needs: Uses artists for magazine graphics, audiovisual materials, recruitment literature and public information brochures.
First Contact & Term: Call or write. Looks at "quality and price" when reviewing artist's work. Buys all rights.

***NATIONAL SAFETY COUNCIL**, 444 N. Michigan, Chicago IL 60611. Director of Publications: Gordon Bieberle. Director of Art: Frank Waszak. Non-governmental, not-for-profit public service organization aimed at saving lives in industry and private sectors through education serving primarily manufacturing industry.
Needs: Works with 24 freelance artists/year. Local artists preferred. "Contemporary style important. Superior technique and conceptual abilities essential." Uses artists for the design, illustration and layout

of advertising, brochures, magazines and posters.

First Contact & Terms: Send query letter with brochure showing art style or tear sheets and slides. Samples not filed are returned by SASE. Reports back only if interested. To show portfolio, mail appropriate materials or "if in area," call or write to schedule an appointment; portfolio should include thumbnails, roughs, final reproduction/product and color. Payment "determined solely on project size negotiated at time of assignment." Considers complexity of project and how work will be used when establishing payment.

Tips: "Interested artists should query with samples of work (tearsheets) by mail."

NATIONAL SKEET SHOOTING ASSOCIATION, Box 68007, San Antonio TX 78268. (512)688-3371. Editor, *Skeet Shooting Review* Magazine: Phil Murray. Emphasizes shotgun target shooting, particularly "skeet" shooting; approximately 15,000 members.

Needs: Works with 3-6 freelance artists/year. Uses artists for brochure and magazine illustration. Prefers shooting sports themes; primarily b&w illustrations (pen & ink, charcoal, etc.).

First Contact & Terms: Send query letter. Reports within 1 week. Write for appointment to show portfolio. Pays by the project, $50-200 average. Considers available budget, and skill and experience of artist when establishing payment.

Tips: "This is an excellent opportunity for inexperienced artists to get published in a national publication."

***THE NEW ALCHEMY INSTITUTE**, 237 Hatchville Rd., E. Falmouth MA 02540. (517)563-2655. Publications: Kate Eldred. A nonprofit research and educational institution working on ecologically sound methods of producing food, energy, and shelter for about 2,000 members and another 5,000 visitors who come by each year to the farm site on Cape Cod.

Needs: Works with 0-3 freelance artists/year. Uses artists for brochure design and magazine/newspaper design and illustration; postcard designs. Prefers themes emphasizing alternative technology such as gardening, solar design, compost, and green houses; prefers b&w line drawings, also schematics.

First Contact & Terms: Send query letter with brochure showing art style or photocopies. Samples not filed are returned by SASE. Reports only if interested. To show a portfolio, mail appropriate materials. Pays for design by the hour, $10 minimum; by the project, $25 minimum. Pays for illustrations by the hour, $10 minimum; by the project, $25 minimum. "We use donated skill whenever possible."

Tips: "We have to use mostly students and people who believe in us rather than pros."

***NEW JERSEY ASSOCIATION OF OSTEOPATHIC PHYSICIANS & SURGEONS**, 1212 Stuyvesant Ave., Trenton NJ 08618. Executive Director: Elenore A Farley. Nonprofit association serving a membership of approximately 1,000 osteopathic physicians and medical students.

Needs: Works with 1 freelance artist/year. Works on assignment only. Uses artists for brochure and magazine/newspaper design, illustration and layout; graphic design, and signage. Prefers themes which are in keeping with the medical profession.

First Contact & Terms: Send query letter with photostats of original work and actual work. Looks for "quality and originality" when reviewing artist's work. Samples returned by SASE. Reports in 1 month. Write for appointment. Negotiates payment according to client's budget.

NORML, National Organization for the Reform of Marijuana Laws, Suite 640, 2035 S St. NW, Washington DC 20009. (202)483-5500. National Director: Kevin Zeese. Nonprofit consumer educational organization working for reform of marijuana laws.

Needs: Works on assignment only. Uses artists for advertising, brochure, catalog and magazine/newspaper design, graphic design, public service announcements, original artwork for auction, AV presentations and posters. Especially needs magazine ads. "Work should relate to issue of marijuana law reform."

First Contact & Terms: Send query letter with tear sheets to be kept on file. Reports within 1 week. Payment varies according to job and available budget.

Tips: "Opportunity for major national coverage at initial public interest group rate of pay."

***NORTH AMERICAN NATIVE FISHES ASSOCIATION**, 123 W. Mt. Airy Ave., Philadelphia PA 19119. (215)247-0384. President: Bruce Gebhardt. "A 400-member group dedicated to study of fishes (mostly non-game) native to North America. It serves ichthyologists, biologists, government officials, aquarists and naturalists."

Needs: Uses artists for magazine/newspaper illustration. Especially needs accurate, realistic sketches of North American fish, non-game. "We need realistic b&w sketches of fishes (non-game, mostly, native to North America)." Prefers accuracy, realism.

First Contact & Terms: Send query letter with resume and photocopies; include SASE. Samples not filed are returned by SASE. Reports back within 1 week. To show a portfolio, mail appropriate materials or call to schedule an appointment; portfolio should include photostats. "Better to call first." "We can't commission artwork; however, if someone had drawn a particular fish, for another assignment and could legally and ethically use it again, it would be a way to pick up a couple of bucks." Considers client's budget and how work will be used when establishing payment.

Tips: "We may be expanding our operations and art needs in the next few years. We're no major market, but artists who draw fish for other clients might try us as a second user."

OCCIDENTAL COLLEGE, 1600 Campus Rd., Los Angeles CA 90041. (213)259-2677. Contact: Director of Public Information and Publications. Educational institution with approximately 1,600 students providing a liberal arts education and serving current students, alumni, faculty, administration, trustees, staff and the community.

Needs: Publishes a quarterly magazine, currently ranked as one of the "Top Five College Magazines" in the country. Magazine often showcases a single illustrator, who provides artwork for cover and four feature articles related by a common theme. Excellent exposure for aspiring illustrators in need of impressive portfolio piece. Occasionally uses illustrators for other publications, such as catalogs and fundraising brochures. "We mostly use students or alumni. Perhaps use freelancers 3 or 4 times a year." Works on assignment only.

First Contact & Terms: Send query letter with business card and original work or photocopies. Looks for "originality, nice clean layout and realistic renderings, as opposed to fantasy pieces" when reviewing artist's work. Samples not returned. Reports in 2 weeks. Submit portfolio for review. Magazine showcase illustrators are paid $400 for the series of cover and feature illustrations. For other publications, artists must be willing to furnish high-quality illustrations or photographs at very modest cost. Payment varies according to job and client's budget.

Tips: "Tight financial picture demands development of one comprehensive illustration/publication that has components which can be reproduced on their own throughout the publication."

PGA OF AMERICA, 100 Avenue of the Champions, Palm Beach Gardens FL 33418. (305)626-3600. Editor/Advertising Sales Director: William A. Burbaum. Circulates to 14,500 golf club professionals and amateur golfers nationwide.

Needs: Works with 2 artists/year for magazine illustrations. Artists "should know something about golf and golf tournaments." Interested in title page art and golf tip illustrations for magazine that circulates to 14,500 professionals and 25,000 amateur golfers nationwide. Works on assignment most of the time.

First Contact & Terms: Write with tear sheets to be kept on file. Samples returned by SASE. Reports in 2 weeks. Reports back on future assignment possibilities. Negotiates pay by prior agreement.

Tips: "Read our magazine, and read and check the artwork in golf's two major national publications: *Golf Magazine* and *Golf Digest*."

***PLAN AND PRINT**, Box 879, 9931 Franklin Ave., Franklin Park IL 60131. (312)671-5356. Editor: James C. Vebeck. Serves architects, engineers, design/drafters/computer-aided design users, reprographic firm owners and managers.

Needs: Works with 7-10 artists/year. Works on assignment only. Uses magazine article illustrations. Especially needs cover art.

First Contact & Terms: Send query letter with brochure showing art style or samples. Samples not filed are returned. Reports back within 10 days. Call or write to schedule an appointment to show a portfolio, which should include final reproduction/product, color, tear sheets and b&w. Pays for illustration by the project, $300-500. Considers compelxity of project, client's budget and rights purchased when establishing payment. Buys all rights.

***QUINNIPIAC COLLEGE**, Mt. Carmel Ave., Hamden CT 06518. Contact: College Editor.
Needs: Works with freelance designers and artists as needed. Works on assignment only.
First Contact & Terms: Arrange interview. Send resume, brochure, and flyer to be kept on file.

RIPON COLLEGE, Box 248, Ripon WI 54971. (414)748-8115. Director of College Relations: Andrew G. Miller. Four-year, coeducational, liberal arts college serving 950 students, alumni and prospective students.
Needs: Works with 3-4 freelance artists/year. Works on assignment basis only. Uses artists for advertising, brochure and magazine/newspaper illustration; graphic design and AV presentations; photography. Especially needs graphic design and photography. Buys 1-2 cartoon-style illustrations/year.
First Contact & Terms: Send query letter with resume and samples. Samples returned by SASE. Reports back on whether to expect possible future assignments. Call for appointment to show portfolio. Negotiates payment.

ROWAN COUNTY HISTORICAL SOCIETY, INC., 104 Main St., Morehead KY 40351. (606)784-9145. Public Relations Director: Lloyd Dean. "A society that studies the history of Rowan County and Morehead and collects pictures, prints, histories, diaries and items of historical interest."
Needs: "We might need artists to draw pictures of historical places in Rowan County and Morehead."
First Contact & Terms: Send a query letter with resume, business card, brochure and flyer to be kept on file. SASE. Reports in 5 weeks.
Tips: There is a trend toward "more concern for the historical past."

ST. VINCENT COLLEGE, Latrobe PA 15650. (412)539-9761. Director/Publications and Publicity: Don Orlando.
Needs: Assigns 25 jobs/year. Uses artists for advertising, annual reports, direct mail brochures, exhibits, flyers, graphics, posters and programs.
First Contact & Terms: Send query letter with samples. SASE. Reports in 1 month. Pays $10 minimum/hour, design, illustration and layout.

SAN FRANCISCO AFRICAN AMERICAN HISTORICAL AND CULTURAL SOCIETY, Building C-165, Fort Mason Center, San Francisco CA 94123. (415)441-0640. Executive Director: Jule C. Anderson. Membership organization established to promote an accurate account of the contributions to world development by people of African descent. Gallery, museum and library are open to the public. Publications and lectures/class workshops are available. Serves "people of all ages and ethnic backgrounds who are interested in acquiring knowledge on culture and contributions of people of African descent."
Needs: Works with 20 freelance artists/year. Works on assignment only. Uses artists for brochure design and layout; AV presentations, exhibits, displays, posters, invitations and designs. Prefers African or African-American themes.
First Contact & Terms: Send query letter with brochure to be kept on file. Samples returned only if requested. Reports within 30 days. Write to schedule an appointment to show a portfolio, which should include final reproduction/product, color, photostats and b&w. Considers complexity of project, available budget, skill and experience of artist and references, how work will be used, turnaround time and rights purchased when establishing payment.
Tips: "Write a letter and send photos of work. Request return of photos if so desired."

SLOCUMB GALLERY, East Tennessee State University, Department of Art, Box 23740A, Johnson City TN 37614-0002. (615)929-4247. Gallery Director: M. Wayne Dyer. Nonprofit university gallery.
Needs: Works with 0-2 freelance artists/year. Works on assignment only. Uses artists for advertising design, illustration and layout; brochure and catalog design; exhibits, signage and posters.
First Contact & Terms: Send query letter with slides to be kept on file. Samples not filed are returned only if requested. Reports within 1 month. Negotiates payment. Considers complexity of project and available budget when establishing payment.

SOCIETY FOR INTERNATIONAL DEVELOPMENT, Suite 1100, 1401 New York Ave. NW, Washington DC 20005. Send *all* correspondence to: Kim Winnard, Visual Media Specialist, 107 N. Jackson St., Arlington VA 22201. Organization focusing on international development issues.
Needs: Works with 3 freelance artists/year. Works on assignment only. Uses artists for design and illustration of brochures, reports and magazines.
First Contact & Terms: Send query letter with tear sheets or photocopies to be kept on file. Samples not filed are returned by SASE. Reports within 1 month. Returns original artwork after job's completion. Pays by the project, $150-450 average for design; $50 average/drawing for illustration. Considers project's budget when establishing payment. Rights purchased vary according to project.

***SPACE WORLD MAGAZINE**, Suite 203 W, 600 Maryland Ave. SW, Washington DC 20024. (202)484-1111. Editor: Tony Reichhardt. Membership organization popularizing and advancing space exploration for the general public interested in all aspects of space program.
Needs: Works with 15-20 freelance artists/year. Uses artists for magazine illustraton. "We are looking for original artwork on space themes, either conceptual or representing specific designs, events, etc."
First Contact & Terms: Send query letter with photographs, "color prints are best." Samples not filed are returned by SASE. Reports within 1 month. To show portfolio, mail appropriate materials, which should include color and photographs. Pays for illustration by the project, $25-50. "We do not generally commission original art. These fees are for one-time reproduction of existing artwork. Considers rights purchased when establishing payment.
Tips: "We know there are a lot of talented "space artists" out there. Give us a chance to showcase your work."

SPIRIT OF THE FUTURE CREATIVE INSTITUTE, Box 40296, San Francisco CA 94110. (415)821-7800. Creative Director: Gary Marchi. Provides information on future science and technology/space innovations, free enterprise system (new business ventures development, vital growth industries), mental development (applied logic, creativity, learning improvement systems), conservation, survival and self-reliance planning, and natural health. Operates Central Library Archive, Information Clearinghouse, Creative Innovation Center and Media Network Systems to serve innovators, pioneers, inventors, futurists, investigative researchers, research and development groups, selected media, educators, and all creative, self-reliant, future consumers—applied thinkers.

Needs: San Francisco Bay area artists only. Works on assignment only. Uses freelance artists for brochure design, illustration and layout; AV presentations, displays, posters and television computer graphics. Themes of institute image design (letters structure and logos), celestial/space, nature, futuristic designs.

First Contact & Terms: Send query letter with brochure, resume, business card or color photographs or photostats to be kept on file. Samples not kept on file are returned by *SASE*. Reports within 3 weeks. To show a portfolio, mail tear sheets, photostats and photographs. Payment is "mutual exchange trading (barter)—advisory service on marketing and promoting their work, skills, for albums, cassette covers, book covers, acquiring an agent." Considers complexity of project, skill and experience of artist, how work will be used, rights purchased, available budget and "a strong interest in our institute, goals, purpose, future plans. Artists should clearly state their purpose, objectives and interests in writing."

SUNDAY SCHOOL BOARD OF THE SOUTHERN BAPTIST CONVENTION, 127 9th Ave. N., Nashville TN 37234. (615)251-2365. Supervisor, Curriculum Design Section: Mrs. Doris Mae Adams. Religious publisher of periodicals, books, Bibles, records, kits, visual aids, posters, etc. for churches.

Needs: Works with 45-50 freelance artists/year. Artists must be "people with experience that meet our quality requirements." Works on assignment only. Uses artists for illustration. Especially needs four-color Biblical illustrations in a realistic style.

First Contact & Terms: Send query letter with brochure showing art style. Call or write for appointment to show portfolio, which should include original/final art, final reproduction/product and color. Originals are preferred, tear sheets are acceptable; do not send slides. Samples are returned. Reports within 2 weeks. Pays by the illustration, $80-150 average. "For the price range quoted here, we buy all rights and retain the work." Considers complexity of project, skill and experience of the artist and how the work will be used when establishing payment.

***SWEDISH HOSPITAL MEDICAL CENTER**, 747 Summit Ave., Seattle WA 98104. (206)386-2738. Assistant Director for Communications: Julie Hanger.

Needs: Works with 2 illustrators and 6 designers/year. Works on assignment only. Uses artists for brochures, reports and posters.

First Contact & Terms: Query with photocopies. SASE. Contacts artists as needs arise. To show a portfolio, mail final reproduction/product, photographs and b&w. Negotiates pay.

***TECHNICAL ASSISTANCE PROJECT (TAP)**, 20th Floor, 570 7th Ave., New York NY 10018. (212)302-6709. Director: Donna Brady. Nonprofit organization serving the performing arts community as well as film, TV, advertising and fashion through referrals of qualified production personnel (designers, stage managers and technicians). TAP also maintains information files with wide ranging details on hard-to-find equipment.

Needs: Works with 50 freelance artists/year. Uses freelance artists for AV presentation, displays, signage, posters and theatrical application.

First Contact & Terms: Send query letter with brochure showing art style or resume. Samples not filed are returned by SASE. Call to schedule an appointment to show a portfolio, which should include original/final art, final reproduction/product and color. Payment varies. Considers complexity of project, client's budget, skill and experience of artist, how work will be used, turnaround time and rights purchased when establishing payment.

THE TEXTILE MUSEUM, 2320 S St. NW, Washington DC 20008. (202)667-0441. Public Relations Manager: Joan Wessel. Private, nonprofit museum dedicated to the collection, study, preservation, education and exhibition of historic and handmade textiles and carpets.

Needs: Works with 1-2 freelance artists/year. Local artists only. Works on assignment only. Uses artists for brochure illustration and layout, catalog design and layout, exhibits, displays and posters.

First Contact & Terms: Send query letter with samples to be kept on file. Prefers original work as samples. Reports only if interested. Negotiates pay according to project.

Tips: "Send samples of newsletters, invitations, catalogs or posters as these are items most often used by the institution; keep in mind the low budget of client."

UNITED HOSPITAL, 333 N. Smith Ave., St. Paul MN 55102. (612)292-5531. Assistant Public Relations Director: Sandra Hansen.

Needs: Works with 5 illustrators and designers/year. Local artists only. Works on assignment only. Uses artists for brochure and newsletter design, programs and general publications artwork. Especially needs logo design, publication and brochure design and keyline.
First Contact & Terms: Query with resume. SASE. Looks for "fast service, reasonable price, and creative and well thought-out approaches to project goals" when reviewing artist's work. Reports in 2 weeks. Samples returned by SASE. Provide resume and business card to be kept on file for possible future assignments. Pays by hour. Considers complexity of project, available budget and turnaround time when establishing payment.
Tips: Especially likes "clean, uncluttered, simple, striking design."

***U.S. SPACE EDUCATION ASSOC., NEWS OPERATIONS DIV.**, 746 Turnpike Rd., Elizabethtown PA 17022-1161. Editor, Space Age Times: Stephen M. Cobaugh. International grassroots association dedicated to the promotion of the peaceful uses of outer space. Serves both laymen and professionals concerned with all aspects of space education and news.
Needs: Works with 3 freelance artists/year. "Artist should be able to demonstrate knowledge of current space issues—both domestic and foreign." Uses artists for magazine/newspaper design and illustration; exhibits; displays and particularly editorial cartoons. Prefers space-related topics; particularly space shuttle, space station, commercialization, spinoffs, etc.
First Contact & Terms: Send query letter with brochure showing art style or resume, tear sheets, photostats and photocopies. Samples not filed are returned by SASE. Reports only if interested. To show a portfolio, mail roughs and original/final art. Pays for design and illustration by the project, $25 minimum. Considers complexity of project, client's budget, turnaround time and rights purchased when establishing payment.

UNIVERSITY OF LOWELL, ART DEPARTMENT, 1 University Dr., Lowell MA 01854. (617)452-5000. Chairperson Art Department: Dr. Liana Cheney. Teaching institution, granting a BA degree and BFA in commercial art and drawing/painting degrees.
Needs: Works with 2 freelance artists/year. Local artists only. Works on assignment only. Uses artists for advertising, brochure and catalog design, illustration and layout. Prefers college-related themes, single style.
First Contact & Terms: Send resume to be kept on file for 1 year; mail slides. Slides are returned. Reports within 1 month. Pays by the hour, $9 minimum. Considers available budget when establishing payment.
Tips: "Be patient."

UNIVERSITY OF NEW HAVEN, West Haven CT 06516. (203)932-7000. Public Relations Director: Sally Devaney.
Needs: Works with illustrators for catalogs, magazines, newsletters, direct mail brochures, schedules, booklets, exhibits/displays, handbooks, publicity brochures and recruitment literature. Looks for "simplicity of reproduction. Prefers b&w line art for illustrations. Contemporary style that would appeal to students (18-34)." Works on assignment only.
First Contact & Terms: Query with samples (brochures and other publications, especially those for educational or service organizations; cover designs; illustrations). SASE. No samples returned. Provide resume if available, business card, fee structure, and samples of work to be kept on file for future assignments. Considers complexity of project, available budget, skill and experience of artist and turnaround time when establishing payment.
Tips: "Our budget is modest. Most pieces are one or two colors. We'd like to see work that would appeal to younger and older students. We're interested in variety of styles. Also interested in area talent."

UNIVERSITY OF SAN FRANCISCO, 2130 Fulton St., San Francisco CA 94117. Contact: Managing Editor. Largest private university in San Francisco with eight colleges and professional schools providing the principles of humanistic Jesuit education to 6,500 students, alumni, parents and the general public.
Needs: Works with 20 freelance artists/year. Local artists only. Works on assignment only. Uses artists for advertising, brochure and catalog design and layout; graphic design, displays and posters. Prefers designs that can be coordinated under a university integrated design concept, using Times Roman type, certain standard formats, university logo, etc.
First Contact & Terms: Send query letter with resume and samples. Looks for "professionalism, that is, ability to work within established budgets and editorial guidelines; ability to meet deadlines; accuracy and creativity in solving design problems." Samples returned by SASE. Reports in 2 weeks. Reports back on whether to expect possible future assignments. Write to schedule an appointment to show a portfolio, which should include final reproduction/product. Payment varies according to job.

VERIFICATION GALLERY, MAYNARD LISTENER LIBRARY, 171 Washington, Taunton MA 02780. (617)823-3783. Executive Director: Merrill A. Maynard. Nonprofit free service organization for the blind and physically handicapped, served through The Maynard Listener Library.
Needs: Prefers artist with "motivation." Uses artists for graphic design, exhibits and displays. Especially needs calendar material. Prefers mobility information theme.
First Contact & Terms: Send query letter with samples. Prefers photostats or slides as samples. Samples returned by SASE. Reports within 2 months. Provide samples to be kept on file for possible future assignments. Negotiates payment.
Tips: "We are creating a demand for our product; therefore artists should realize its potential."

WASHINGTON UNIVERSITY IN ST. LOUIS, Campus Box 1070, St. Louis MO 63110. Art Director: Lewis Glaser. Educational institution publication office serving alumni development (alumni magazines) and various schools' recruiting and promotional needs.
Needs: Works with 20 freelance artists/year. Works on assignment only. Uses artists for advertising, brochure, catalog, and magazine/newspaper illustration. Especially needs layout and pasteup mostly, some design *with* art direction and illustration. Looks for diversity, versatility.
First Contact & Terms: Send query letter with brochure, resume, photostats, slides, photographs and tear sheets to be kept on file. Samples not filed are returned by SASE only if requested. Reports only if interested. Call for appointment to show portfolio, which should include original/final art, final reproduction/product, color, tear sheets and b&w. Pays by the project, $50 minimum. Considers complexity of project, available budget, skill and experience of artist, how work will be used, turnaround time and rights purchased when establishing payment.
Tips: "Present a neat and clean portfolio, showing as much diversity as possible. Better to have only five strong pieces than twenty-five weak ones."

***WOLF TRAP FARM FOR THE PERFORMING ARTS**, The Wolf Trap Foundation, 1624 Trap Rd., Vienna VA 22180. Director of Public Affairs and Communications: Beverly Jackson. Provides programming and publicity for Wolf Trap Farm Park. The Foundation serves as the administrative arm of the Park with the National Park Service maintaining the Park grounds. Wolf Trap is the only national park for the performing arts. "As a national park, Wolf Trap serves the nation as well as international visitors."
Needs: Works with 5 freelance artists/year. Uses artists for the design, illustration and layout of advertising, brochures, and magazines plus AV presentations, exhibits and displays.
First Contact & Terms: Send a query letter with resume and tear sheets, which will be kept on file. Samples not filed are returned only if requested. Reports back within 3-4 weeks. Call or write for an appointment to show a portfolio. Pays by the project. Considers available budget, skill and experience of the artist, and turnaround time when establishing payment.
Tips: "We are a nonprofit organization and do not have a large budget for outside services."

WORCESTER POLYTECHNIC INSTITUTE, 100 Institute Rd., Worcester MA 01609. (617)793-5609. Director of Publications: Kenneth McDonnell. Third oldest college of engineering and science in US with 3,500 students in undergraduate and graduate programs.
Needs: Works with 2-6 freelance artists/year. Prefers local artists. Works on assignment only. Uses artists for advertising illustration; brochure design, illustration and layout; catalog illustration and layout; AV presentations, exhibits, displays, signage and posters.
First Contact & Terms: Send query letter with resume, photostats, slides, photographs and tearsheets. Write for appointment to show portfolio. Samples are returned by SASE. Reports within 2 weeks. Negotiates payment. Considers complexity of project, available budget, skill and experience of artist, turnaround time and rights purchased when establishing payment.

YOUTH LAW NEWS/NATIONAL CENTER FOR YOUTH LAW, 5th Floor, 1663 Mission St., San Francisco CA 94103. (415)543-3307. Editor, *Youth Law News*: Marsha Henry.
Needs: Works with 8 freelance artists and photographers/year. Artists "must have lower price rate for nonprofit organization." Works on assignment only. Uses artists and photographers for brochure design and magazine/newspaper illustrations and layout. Prefers themes involving children's issues.
First Contact & Terms: Send query letter with resume and samples to be kept on file. Write for artists' guidelines. Open to any type of sample; "artist's preference." Reports back as soon as possible. Pays by the project. Considers complexity of project, available budget, skill and experience of artist, how work will be used and turnaround time when establishing payment.

Approximately 47,000 books went to press last year as the book industry continued to increase production and sales. Diet and health, business and travel books as well as sagas, romances and classics headed the bestselling categories for the past year. Popular collaterals such as video story tapes, calendars and posters provided additional freelance opportunities for artists within the industry.

The book publishing industry classifies publishers according to subject matter or field of activity, and each classification requires different art treatments. A realistic approach is needed for romance and historical novels, whose covers usually focus on one or two of the story's main characters. A look at nonfiction titles reveals a tendency toward pure, simplistic design, often with an emphasis on typography. Specialized publishers who produce books geared to one topic like cooking or gardening often want traditional, very detailed art/design representing their main focus. Figurative work has been popular in children's books lately. Educational titles require simple graphic design and two-color printing.

Although books are released in only two seasons, Spring/Summer and Fall/Winter, book design and production continue throughout the year. Book publishers primarily use the talents of freelance artists in book design, jacket/cover design and illustration and text illustration. Through typography and page layout, the book designer creates an easy-to-read book. Dust covers are in reality small posters which advertise the book's content; jacket designers/illustrators must have a dramatic flair. Requirements for text illustration vary from realistic pen-and-ink drawings to full-color fantasy landscapes. As publishing houses compete for sales, they look for increasingly innovative treatments and vivid color.

Don't discount a firm because it publishes only a few books a year. Small presses are making an impact on the publishing industry as many of these publishers have commercial aspirations and are growing in that direction. With an emphasis on quality, many small press books are award winners, often because of the special attention given to the illustrations.

Visit bookstores and examine the type of artwork each publisher favors. Write and request a catalog of the firm's products—there's hardly a book publisher that won't send you one. Also read the advice of Chris Van Allsburg, winner of two Caldecott Awards for his children's books, in the Close-up in this section.

For additional information on this market, refer to *Writer's Market 1987*, *Literary Market Place*, *Books in Print*, and *International Directory of Little Magazines and Small Presses*. The trade magazine *Publisher's Weekly* provides weekly updates on book publishing.

***ACS PUBLICATIONS, INC.**, Box 16430, San Diego CA 92116-0430. (619)297-9203. Editoral Director: Maritha Pottenger. Specializes in trade paperbacks and originals especially in astrology, metaphysics and holistic health. Pubilshes 10 titles/year.
First Contact & Terms: Works with 3 freelance artists/year. Prefers local artists ony. Works on assignment only. Send query letter with tear sheets, photostats, photocopies and photographs. Samples not filed are returned by SASE. Reports only if interested. Original work returned after job's completion. Considers complexity of project, skill and experience of artist, project's budget (biggest factor) and turnaround time when establishing payment. Buys first rights or reprint rights.
Jackets/Covers: Assigns 10 book covers/year to freelancers. Pays by the project, $200-400.
Tips: "Most of our covers involve people. Artist must be excellent with faces."

A.D. BOOK CO., 6th Floor, 10 E. 39th St., New York NY 10157-0002. (212)889-6500. Art Director: Doris Gordon. Publishes hardcover and paperback originals on advertising design and photography. Publishes 12-15 titles/year; 4-5 of which require designers, 1-2 use illustrators.

First Contact & Terms: Send query letter which can be kept on file and arrange to show portfolio (4-10 tear sheets). Samples returned by SASE. Buys first rights. Originals returned to artist at job's completion. Free catalog. Advertising design must be contemporary. Pays $100 minimum/book design.
Jackets/Covers: Pays $100 minimum.

ACROPOLIS BOOKS LTD., 2400 17th St. NW, Washington DC 20009. Production Manager: Lloyd Greene. Publishes how-to, self help, educational, political and Americana.
Needs: Uses artists for jacket design and illustration and advertising layouts.
First Contact & Terms: Local artists only. Send query letter with information on your background and specialties.

ADDISON-WESLEY, Jacob Way, Reading MA 01867. (617)944-3700. Art Dircetor: Marshall Henrichs. Publishes adult trade books. Publishes 100 titles/year; 50% require freelance designers. Handles higher educational books.
First Contact & Terms: Send proofs. Buys all rights. Works on assignment only. Reports back on future assignment possibilities. Provide resume, business card and tear sheet to be kept on file for future assignments. Check for most recent titles in bookstores.
Jackets/Covers: Needs trade cover designers. Pays $500-800.

AIR-PLUS ENTERPRISES, Box 190, Garrisonville VA 22463. (609)881-0724. Specializes in hardcover and paperback originals on women's interest (particularly case histories of abortion complications—physical or other) and human sexuality. Publishes 2 titles/year.
First Contact & Terms: Works with 2 freelance artists/year. "We give anybody a chance." Send query letter with original sketches or photographs to be kept on file "unless unsuitable." Samples not kept on file are returned by SASE. Reports within 2 months. No originals returned to artist at job's completion. Considers project's budget when establishing payment. Buys all rights.
Jackets/Covers: Assigns 2 freelance illustration jobs/year. Pays by the project, $35-100 average.
Text Illustration: Assigns 2 freelance jobs/year. Pays by the project, $25-250 average.
Tips: Uses medical illustrations. "We see an increased need for technical work and have found that our best people in this field don't do cartoons well at all, so we now seek cartoonists."

ALLYN AND BACON INC., College Division, 7 Wells Ave., Newton MA 02159. (617)964-5530. Cover Administrator: Linda Knowles Dickinson. Publishes hardcover and paperback textbooks. Publishes 75-85 titles/year; 75% require freelance cover designers.
First Contact & Terms: Needs artists/designers experienced in preparing art and mechanicals for print production. Designers must be strong in book cover design and contemporary type treatment.
Jackets/Covers: Assigns 50-65 freelance design jobs/year; assigns 2-3 freelance illustration jobs/year. Pays by the project, $475-575.
Tips: "Keep stylistically and technically up to date. Learn *not* to over-design: read instructions, and ask questions. Introductory letter must state experience and include at least photocopies of samples of your work. We prefer designers/artists based in the Boston area. Calligraphers—please send samples."

***ALYSON PUBLICATIONS, INC.**, 40 Plympton St., Boston MA 02118. Publisher: Sasha Alyson. Book publisher emphasizing gay and lesbian concerns. Publishes 15 titles/year. Circ. 800. Sample copy catalog free for SASE with 45¢ postage.
First Contact & Terms: Buys 10 illustrations/book. Works on assignment only. Send query letter with brochure showing art style or tear sheets, photostats, photocopies and photographs. Samples returned by SASE. Reports only if interested. Pays $200-500, b&w, $300-500, color, cover; on acceptance.

ANTIOCH PUBLISHING COMPANY, Box 28, Yellow Springs OH 45387. Art Director: Jean Rudegeair. Publishes calendars, bookmarks, bookplates, greeting cards and children's books. Also has separate religious/inspirational line.
First Contact & Terms: Buys 100 or more illustrations/year. Works on assignment only. Send SASE, attention Creative Guidelines, for copy of Antioch Artist's Guidelines before sending samples of any kind. Send query letter with brochure showing art style or tear sheets and slides. Write to schedule an appointment to show a portfolio, which should include roughs, original/final art, final reproduction/product and tear sheets. "We generally do not view portfolios—we review slides, etc. by mail." Buys vari-

"When I received this assignment," says Michael Fleishman of Yellow Springs, Ohio, "I set out to create drawings for young eyes—large, playful forms, bright colors, fuzzy warm tones." Antioch Publishing Company of Yellow Springs paid Michael $2,000 for the cover and 13 illustrations for Favorite Bible Stories, Vol. 1. This was Michael's first book assignment.

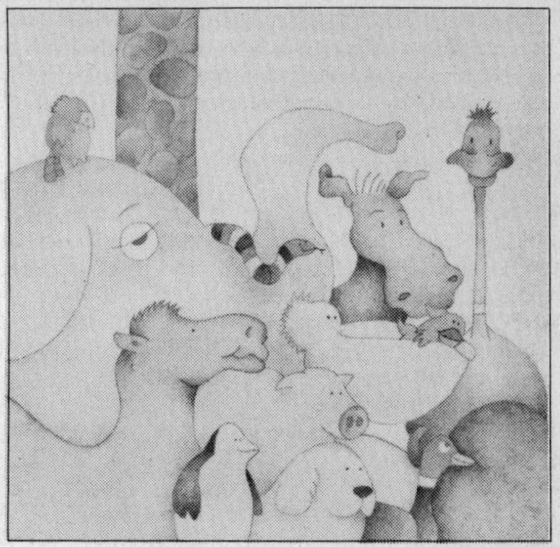

ous rights. Pays $100-200/illustration, depending on use and inhouse preparation time.

Text Illustration: Uses artists for illustrations. "Most of our needs are of the full-color, magical-unicorn-rainbow-charming-whimsical-humorous variety. I want art from people who know how to use color for good reproduction. I want to work with professionals who know the importance of deadlines, flexibility and marketability. Because of this I prefer working with experienced, previously published artists, although I've also worked with relative newcomers who have a high degree of professionalism." Buys occasional science fiction/fantasy artwork.

Tips: "Color is playing a more important part with 'trendy' colors more apparent. More new, fresh ideas appearing more quickly than before. Everything seems to change faster. Looser styles."

APPLEZABA PRESS, Box 4134, Long Beach CA 90804. (213)591-0015. Publisher: D.H. Lloyd. Specializes in paperbacks on poetry and fiction. Publishes 2-4 titles/year.

First Contact & Terms: Works on assignment only. Send query letter with brochure, tear sheets and photographs to be kept on file. Samples not filed are returned by SASE. Reports only if interested. Originals returned to artist at job's completion. Considers project's budget and rights purchased when establishing payment. Rights purchased vary according to project.

Jackets/Covers: Assigns 1 freelance design job/year. Pays by the project, $30-100 average.

ARCO PUBLISHING INC., One Gulf and Western Plaza, New York NY 10023. Editorial Director: William Mlawer. Art Director: Hal Siegel. Publishes hardcover and paperback reference originals and reprints.

First Contact & Terms: Will keep on file submitted art samples. Will return samples if return postage is provided. Relevant resumes will be kept on file.

***ARCsoft PUBLISHERS**, Box 132, Woodsboro MD 21798. (301)845-8856. President: A.R. Curtis. Specializes in original paperbacks, especially in space science, computers, miscellaneous high-tech subjects. Publishes 12 titles/year.

First Contact & Terms: Works with 5 freelance artists/year. Works on assignment only. Send query letter with brochure, resume and non-returnable samples. Samples not filed are not returned. Reports back within 3 months only if interested. Original work not returned after job's completion. Considers complexity of project, skill and experience of artist, project's budget and turnaround time when establishing payment. Buys all rights.

Book Design: Assigns 5 freelance illustration jobs/year. Pays by the project.

Jackets/Covers: Assigns 1 freelance design and 5 freelance illustration jobs/year. Pays by the project.

Text Illustration: Assigns 5 freelance jobs/year. Pays by the project.

Tips: "Artists should not send in material they want back. All materials received become the property of ARCsoft Publishers."

ARCUS PUBLISHING COMPANY, Box 228, Sonoma CA 95476. (707)996-9529. Owner: Betty Gordon. Estab. 1983. Specializes in hardcover and paperback originals. "We are not confining our publish-

ing efforts to any one category of subject matter. We expect to do some children's books, non-fiction books on various subjects, humor and, when meeting our standards, some fiction."
First Contact & Terms: Works on assignment only. Send query letter with brochure and resume to be kept on file. Prefers photographs, tear sheets or photocopies as samples. Samples returned by SASE only if requested. Reports only if interested. Originals returned to artist at job's completion. Call or write for appointment to show portfolio. Consider complexity of the project, skill and experience of artist and project's budget when establishing payment. Buys variable rights according to project.

ART DIRECTION BOOK CO., 6th Floor, 10 E. 39th St., New York NY 10157-0002. (212)889-6500. Art Director: Doris Gordon. Specializes in hardcover and paperback books on advertising art and design. Publishes 15 titles/year; 50% require freelance designers.
First Contact & Terms: Works with 5 freelance artists/year. Professional artists only. Call for appointment. Drop off portfolio. Samples returned by SASE. Originals returned to artist at job's completion. Buys one-time rights.
Book Design: Assigns 10 jobs/year. Uses artists for layout and mechanicals. Pays by the job, $100 minimum.
Jackets/Covers: Assigns 10 design jobs/year. Pays by the job, $100 minimum.

ARTIST'S MARKET, Writer's Digest Books, 9933 Alliance Rd., Cincinnati OH 45242. (513)984-0717. Contact: Editor. Annual hardcover directory of freelance markets for graphic artists. Send b&w samples—photographs, photostats or good quality photocopies—of artwork. "Since *Artist's Market* is published only once a year, submissions are kept on file for the next upcoming edition until selections are made. Material is then returned by SASE." Buys one-time rights.
Needs: Buys 50-60 illustrations/year. "I need examples of art that has sold to one of the listings in *Artist's Market*. Thumb through the book to see the type of art I'm seeking. The art must have been freelanced; it cannot have been done as staff work. Include the name of the listing that purchased the work, what the art was used for, and the payment you received." Pays $25 to holder of reproduction rights and free copy of *Artist's Market* when published.

ARTS END BOOKS, Box 162, Newton MA 02168. (617)965-2478. Editor and Publisher: Marshall Brooks. Specializes in hardcover and paperback originals and reprints of contemporary literature. Publishes 2 titles/year.
First Contact & Terms: Works with 2-3 freelance artists/year. Send query letter with photostats and tear sheets to be kept on file. Samples not filed are returned by SASE. Reports within a few days. Return of original work depends on arrangement with artist. Considers complexity of the project, skill and experience of artist, project's budget, turnaround time and rights purchased when establishing payment. Rights purchased vary according to project.
Book Design: Pays by the project.
Jackets/Covers: Assigns 2 freelance jobs/year. Pays by the project.
Text Illustration: Prefers pen and ink work. Pays by the project.

ASHLEY BOOKS INC., Box 768, Port Washington NY 11050. (516)883-2221. President: Billie Young. Publishes hardcover originals; controversial, medical and timely, fiction and nonfiction. Publishes 50 titles/year; 40% require freelance designers or freelance illustrators. Also uses artists for promotional aids.
First Contact & Terms: Metropolitan New York area residents only; experienced artists with book publisher or record album jacket experience. Arrange interview to show portfolio. Buys first rights. Negotiates pay. Free catalog.
Book Design: Assigns 35 jobs/year. Uses artists for layout and paste-up.
Jackets/Covers: Assign 35 jobs/year. "Covers are less busy; those that have a stark quality seem to be dominating."
Tips: "As a result of an upsurge in consumer interest in cooking, more cookbooks will be produced generating more illustrations and more artwork."

AUGSBURG PUBLISHING HOUSE, Box 1209, 426 S. 5th St., Minneapolis MN 55440. (612)330-3300. Manager, Editorial/Design Services: James Lipscomb. Publishes paperback Protestant/Lutheran books (45 titles/year); religious education materials; audiovisual resources; periodicals. Also uses artists for catalog cover design, advertising circulars; advertising layout, design and illustration. Negotiates pay, b&w and color.
First Contact & Terms: "We don't have a rule to only work locally, but the majority of the artists are close enough to meet here on assignments." Works on assignment only. Call, write, or send slides or photocopies. Reports in 5-8 weeks. Samples not filed are returned by SASE. Reports back on future assignment possibilities. Provide brochure, flyer, tear sheet, good photocopies and 35mm transparencies;

if artist willing to have samples retained, they are kept on file. Buys all rights on a work-for-hire basis except for cartoons. May require artist to supply overlays on color work.
Book Design: Assigns 45 jobs/year. Uses artists primarily for cover design; occasionally inside illustration, sample chapter openers. Pays $500-900 for cover design.
Text Illustrations: Negotiates pay, 1-, 2-, and 4-color.
Tips: Buys 20 cartoons/year. Uses material on family, church situation and social commentary. Pays $15-20 minimum for one-time use.

AVON BOOKS, Art Department, 1790 Broadway, New York NY 10019. (212)399-4500. Publisher: Walter Meade. Art Director: Matthew Tepper. Publishes paperback originals and reprints—mass market, trade and juvenile. Publishes 300 titles/year; 80% require freelance illustrators.
First Contact and Terms: Works with 100 freelance artists/year. Works on assignment only. Send query letter with resume and samples to be filed. Call or write for an appointment to show a portfolio. Accepts any type sample. Samples returned only by request. Reports within 1 month. Works on assignment only. Original work returned to the artist after job's completion. Considers complexity of the project, skill and experience of the artist and project's budget when establishing payment.
Book Design: Assigns 20 jobs/year. Uses artists for all aspects. Payment varies.
Jackets/Covers: Assigns 150 freelance design and 150 freelance illustration jobs/year.
Text Illustrations: Assigns 20 freelance jobs/year.
Tips: "Look at our books to see if work is appropriate for us before submitting."

AZTEX CORP., Box 50046, 1126 N. 6th Ave., Tucson AZ 85703. (602)882-4656. President: W. R. Haessner. Publishes hardcover and paperback originals on sports, mainstream and how-to. Publishes 9-12 titles/year.
First Contact & Terms: Works on assignment only. Send query letter with resume and/or brochure showing art style and samples. Especially looks for realism and detail when reviewing samples. Reports in 6 weeks. Samples returned by SASE. Buys reprint or all rights. No originals returned to artist at job's completion. Free catalog.
Jackets/Covers: Assigns 4 jobs/year. "We need technical drawings and cutaways." Pays $50-150, opaque watercolors and oils.

***BAKER BOOK HOUSE**, 6030 E. Fulton Rd., Ada MI 49301. (616)676-9185. Art Director: Dwight Baker. Specializes in hardcovers, paperbacks, originals and reprints of religious trade and textbooks. Publishes 75 titles/year.
First Contact & Terms: Works with 10 freelance artist/year. Works on assignment only. Send query letter with brochure showing art style or resume, tear sheets, photostats, photocopies, slides and photographs. Samples not filed are returned by SASE only if requested. Reports only if interested. Original art work not returned after the job's completion. Considers complexity of project, skill and experience of artist, and project's budget when establishing payment. Buys all rights.
Jackets/Covers: Assigns 5 freelance design and 12 freelance illustration jobs/year. Pays by the project, $250-350.
Text Illustration: Assigns 2 freelance jobs/year. Prefers pen & ink cartoons and line drawings. Pays $10/spot drawing.
Tips: "We are always looking for jacket designers who work primarily with type for our academic book covers."

WILLIAM L. BAUHAN, PUBLISHER, Dublin NH 03444. Art Director: W.L. Bauhan. Publishes hardbound and paperback books on New England. Publishes 6-8 titles/year.
Needs: Uses artists for jackets, covers, text illustrations. Uses line drawings and block prints, all b&w.
First Contact & Terms: Works on assignment only. Send query letter. SASE. Reports in 4 weeks. Send resume and samples or just samples of work to be kept on file for future assignments; do not send originals. Check for most recent titles in bookstores. Purchases outright.

BENGAL PRESS, INC., 1885 Spaulding SE, Grand Rapids MI 49506. (616)949-8895. President: John Ilich. Specializes in paperback and hardcover originals and reprints of nonfiction (business, history, law, how-to) and fiction (science fiction, religious, inspirational). Publishes 1-4 titles/year; 100% require freelance designers; 25% require freelance illustrators.
First Contact & Terms: Send query letter with samples to be kept on file. Accepts any samples the artist deems relevant to show quality and type of work. Reports only if interested. Works on assignment only. No originals returned to artist at job's completion. Considers complexity of project, skill and experience of artist and project's budget when establishing payment. Buys all rights.
Book Design: Assigns 1-3 freelance jobs/year. Pays by the project with fee negotiated at the time artist is hired.

Jackets/Covers: Assigns 1-3 freelance design and 1-4 freelance illustration jobs/year. Pays by the project with fee negotiated at the time artist is hired.
Text Illustration: Assigns 1-3 freelance jobs/year. Pays by the project with fee negotiated at the time artist is hired.

***THE BENJAMIN/CUMMINGS PUBLISHING CO.**, 2725 Sand Hill Rd., Menlo Park CA 94025. Contact: Production Manager. Specializes in college textbooks in biology, chemistry, computer science and mathematics. Publishes 40 titles/year; 90% require freelance design and illustration.
Illustration: Works with 15-20 freelance artists/year. Mostly line drawings, one and two-color mechanicals. "Our biologic texts require trained bio/med illustrators. Proximity to Bay Area is a plus, but not essential." Works on assignment only. Original artwork not returned to artist at job's completion. Send query letter with resume and samples. Samples returned only if requested. Pays by piece, $20-80 average and job maximum.
Book Design: Assigns 30 jobs/year. "From manuscript, designer prepares specs and layouts for review. After approval, final specs and layouts are required. On our books which are dummied, very often the designer is contracted as dummier at a separate per page fee." Pays by the job, $500-1,000.
Cover: Assigns 40 jobs/year. Pays by the job, $300-900.

***BENNETT & MCKNIGHT PUBLISHING**, 809 W. Detweiller, Peoria IL 61615. (309)691-4454. Director of Art/Design/Production: Donna M. Faull. Specializes in original hardcovers and paperbacks, especially in vocational education (industrial art/high tech/home economics/career education textbooks, filmstrips, software). Publishes over 100 titles/year.
First Contact & Terms: Works with over 30 freelance artists/year. Works on assignment only. Send query letter with brochure, resume, and "any type of samples." Samples not filed are returned if requested. Reports back in weeks. Original work not returned after job's completion; work-for-hire basis with rights to publisher. Considers complexity of the project, skill and experience of the artist, project's budget, turnaround time and rights purchased when establishing payment. Buys all rights.
Book Design: Assigns over 30 freelance design and over 30 freelance illustration jobs/year. Pays by the hour, $10-40; pays by the project, $300-3,000 and upward (very technical art, lots of volume).
Jackets/Covers: Assigns over 50 freelance design/jobs/year. Pays by the project, $200 for 1-color—4,000 for complete cover/interiors for textbooks.
Text Illustration: Assigns over 50 freelance jobs/year. Pays by the hour, $10-40; amount varies widely.
Tips: "Try not to call or never drop in without an appointment."

BLACKTHORNE PUBLISHING INC., 786 Blackthorne Ave., El Cajon CA 92020. (619)463-9603. Art Director: Steven J. Schanes. Estab. 1983. Specializes in paperback originals and reprints, comic books, signed prints, and trade books. Publishes 48 titles/year.
First Contact & Terms: Works with 50 freelance artists/year. "We look for professional standards in artists we work with." Send query letter with brochure, resume, and samples to be kept on file; originals will be returned. Prefers slides and photostats as samples. Samples not filed are returned. Reports within 3 weeks. Originals returned to artist after job's completion. Considers complexity of the project, skill and experience of artist, project's budget and turnaround time when establishing payment. Rights purchased vary according to project.
Book Design: Assigns 50 jobs/year. Pays by the project, depending on the job, from $50 for a spot illustration to $15,000 for a complete comic book series.
Jackets/Covers: Assigns 15 freelance design and 30 freelance illustration jobs/year. Pays by the hour, $5-40 average; by the project, $50-10,000 average.
Text Illustration: Assigns 15 jobs/year. Prefers pen & ink. Pays by the hour, $5-40 average; by the project, $50-10,000 average.

BLACKWELL SCIENTIFIC PUBLICATIONS, INC., 52 Beacon St., Boston MA 02108. (617)720-0761. Production Manager: Elizabeth O'Neill McGuire. Specializes in hardcovers of medical and nursing books. Publishes 5 titles/year.
First Contact & Terms: Artists must have experience in medical illustration. Send query letter with brochure, resume, photocopies and photostats to be kept on file. Samples not kept on file are returned by SASE. Reports only if interested. Works on assignment only. No originals returned to artist at job's completion. Considers project budget and turnaround time when establishing payment. Buys all rights.
Jackets/Covers: Assigns 3 freelance design jobs/year.
Tips: Artists should "investigate the potential purchaser to see if their work is even appropriate."

BLUEJAY BOOKS INC., Suite 306, 1123 Broadway, New York NY 10010. (212)206-1538. Publisher: James Frenkel. Specializes in hardcover and paperback originals and reprints of science fiction and fantasy. Publishes 35 titles/year.

First Contact & Terms: Works with 20 freelance artists/year. Works on assignment only. Send query letter with samples to be kept on file; call for appointment to show portfolio. Prefers Cibachromes as samples. Samples not filed are returned by SASE. Reports only if interested. Original work returned after job's completion. Considers project's budget when establishing payment. Rights purchased vary according to project.
Jackets/Covers: Assigns 35 freelance illustration jobs/year. Pays by the project, $500 minimum.
Text Illustration: Assigns 5 freelance jobs/year. Prefers b&w illustrations. Pays by the project, $50 minimum.

BOWLING GREEN UNIVERSITY POPULAR PRESS, Bowling Green University, Bowling Green OH 43403. (419)372-2981. Managing Editor: Pat Browne. Publishes hardcover and paperback originals on popular culture, folklore, women studies, science fiction criticism, detective fiction criticism, music and drama. Publishes 15-20 titles and 8 journals/year.
First Contact & Terms: Send previously published work. SASE. Reports in 2 weeks. Buys all rights. Free catalog.
Jackets/Covers: Assigns 20 jobs/year. Pays $50 minimum, color washes, opaque watercolors, gray opaques, b&w line drawings and washes.

BRADY COMMUNICATIONS COMPANY, INC., a Prentice-Hall Company, 14999 Annapolis Rd., Bowie MD 20715. (201)592-2000. Executive Art Director: Jo DiDomenico, AMI. Publishes medical, allied health, emergency care, nursing and home computer textbooks.
First Contact & Terms: Artists must be experienced cover designers (high-tech computer covers for home computer books) or experienced textbook illustrators. Works on assignment only. Send resume and samples to be kept on file. Prefers tear sheets of illustrations or printed flat sheets of covers, both computer and medical, as samples. Samples not filed are returned by SASE. Reports back only if interested. Pays by the project; cover designs, rough comprehensive full color to size; text illustrations, rough and final inking. Considers the complexity of the project, skill and experience of artist, turnaround time and rights purchased when establishing payment.
Needs: Works with 50 freelance artists/year. Uses artists for textbook illustration and cover design.
Tips: "Work must be of a high quality, neat, clean. We prefer previously published examples only; no school work."

GEORGE BRAZILLER INC., 1 Park Ave., New York NY 10016. (212)889-0909. Contact: Herman Figatner. Publishes hardcover and paperback originals on history of art and architecture; philosophy and religion. Publishes 20 titles/year. Also uses artists for advertising, paste-up, catalog layout and design, posters. Query with resume; local artists only. Works on assignment only. Provide resume and samples to be kept on file. Buys one-time rights.
Book Design: Assigns 25 jobs/year. Designer is responsible for type spec, composition arrangements, through finished mechanicals. Pays by the project, $2,000 maximum.
Jackets/Covers: Uses freelance designers and illustrators. Prefers line drawings, color wash, prints (wood blocks) as cover illustrations. Pays for design and illustration by the project, $150-300 average.
Tips: "Show work directly geared to a particular publisher."

BRIARCLIFF PRESS, 11 Wimbledon Court, Jericho NY 11753. (516)681-1505. Editorial/Art Director: Trudy Settel. Publishes hardcover and paperback cookbook, decorating, baby care, gardening, sewing, crafts and driving originals and reprints. Publishes 18 titles/year; 100% require freelance designers and illustrators. Uses artists for color separations, lettering and mechanicals; assigns 25 jobs/year, pays $5-10/hour. Also assigns 5 advertising jobs/year for catalogs and direct mail brochures; pays $5-10/hour.
First Contact & Terms: Send query letter; no samples until requested. Artists should have worked on a professional basis with other firms of this type. SASE. Reports in 3 weeks. Buys all rights. No advance. Pays promised fee for unused assigned work.
Book Design: Assigns 25/year. Pays $6 minimum/hour, layout and type spec.
Jackets/Covers: Buys 24/year. Pays $100-300, b&w; $250-500, color.
Text Illustrations: Uses artists for text illustrations and cartoons. Buys 250/year. Pays $10-30, b&w; $25-50, color.

***BRIDGE PUBLISHING, INC.**, 2500 Hamilton Blvd., South Plainfield NJ 07080. (201)754-0745. Art Director: Mary Irwin. Publisher of Christian books. Emphasizes novels and book-length essays with a Christian world view; books dealing with the practical aspects of the Christian life for a broad spectrum of Christian denominations and theological viewpoints; mainly adults. Publishes 25 titles/year. Catalog available, $1.
First Contact & Terms: Buys 10-15 illustrations/year. Prefers Christian themes, figurative work. Send query letter with brochure, resume, photostats, photocopies, slides, photographs and samples of

book covers. Samples not filed are returned by SASE. Reports back only if interested. To show a portfolio, call or write to schedule an appointment or mail thumbnails, roughs, original/final art, final reproduction/product and color. Buys first rights or reprint rights; "we are paying the artist for rights to reproduce their work on book covers as well as any promotional materials." Payment is negotiable; on acceptance.

BROADMAN PRESS, 127 9th Ave. N., Nashville TN 37234. (615)251-2630. Art Director: Jack Jewell. Religious publishing house.
First Contact & Terms: Artist must be experienced, professional illustrator or book cover designer. Works on assignment only. Send query letter with brochure and samples to be kept on file. Call or write for appointment to show portfolio. Send slides, tear sheets, photostats or photocopies; "samples *cannot* be returned." Reports only if interested. Pays by the project, $50-600 average. Considers complexity of the project, client's budget and rights purchased when establishing payment. Buys all rights.
Needs: Works with 50 freelance artists/year. Uses artists for illustration and occasionally graphic design. "We publish for all ages in traditional and contemporary styles, thus our needs are quite varied."
Tips: "The quality of design in the Christian book publishing market has greatly improved in the last five years. We actively search for 'realist' illustrators who can work in a style that looks contemporary."

WILLIAM C. BROWN PUBLISHERS, 2460 Kerper Blvd., Dubuque IA 52001. (319)588-1451. Vice President and Director, Production and Design: David A. Corona. Design Director: Marilyn A. Phelps. Publishes hardbound and paperback college textbooks. Publishes 200 titles/year; 3% require freelance designers, 50% require freelance illustrators. Also uses artists for advertising. Pays $35-350, b&w and color promotional artwork.
First Contact & Terms: Works on assignment only. Send query letter with resume, brochure, tear sheets or 8½x11" photocopies or finished 11x14" or smaller (transparencies if larger) art samples or call for interview. Reports in 4 weeks. Samples returned by SASE if requested. Reports back on future assignment possibilities. Buys all rights. Pays half contract for unused assigned work.
Book Design: Assigns 10-15 freelance design jobs/year; assigns 75-100 freelance illustration jobs/year. Uses artists for all phases of process. Pays by the project, $500 minimum; varies widely according to complexity. Pays by the hour, mechanicals.
Jackets/Covers: Assigns 15-25 freelance design jobs and 20-30 freelance illustration jobs/year. Pays $100-350 average and negotiates pay for special projects.
Text Illustrations: Assigns 75-100 freelance jobs/year. Uses b&w and color work. Prefers mostly continuous tone, some line drawings; ink preferred for b&w. Pays $25-300. Artwork includes medical illustration.
Tips: "In the field, there is more use of color. There is need for sophisticated color skills—the artist must be knowlegeable about the way color reproduces in the printing process. The designer and illustrator must be prepared to contribute to content as well as style. Tighter production schedules demand an awareness of overall schedules. *Must* be dependable."

***ARISTIDE D. CARATZAS, PUBLISHER**, Box 210, 481 Main St., New Rochelle NY 10802. (914)632-8487. Managing Editor: John Emerich. Publishes books about archaeology, art histroy, natural history and classics for specialists in the above fields in universities, museums, libraries and interested amateurs. Accepts previously published material. Send query letter with brochure showing art style. Samples not filed are returned by SASE. Reports only if interested. To show a portfolio, mail appropriate materials or call or write to schedule an appointment. Buys all rights or negotiates rights purchased.

CAREER PUBLISHING, INC., Box 5486, Orange CA 92613-5486. (714)771-5155. Secretary/Treasurer: Sherry Robson. Specializes in paperback original textbooks on trucking, medical office management, medical insurance billing, motorcycle dictionary, real estate dictionary, micro computer courses and guidance for jobs. Uses artists for advertising, direct mail and posters.
First Contact & Terms: Works with 3 freelance artists/year. Works on assignment only. Send query letter with brochure/flyer or resume, photostats and line drawings or actual work to be kept on file. Submit portfolio for review. Guidelines given for each project. Samples returned by SASE. Reports in 2 months. No originals returned to artist at job's completion. Buys all rights.
Book Design: Assigns 12 jobs/year. Negotiates payment by the job.
Jackets/Covers: Assigns 12 design and 150 illustration jobs/year. Prefers line drawings, paintings and cartoons for illustrations. Negotiates payment by the job.
Text Illustration: Assigns approximately 10 jobs/year. Negotiates payment by the job.
Tips: Uses some medical illustrations.

CARNIVAL ENTERPRISES, Box 19087, Minneapolis MN 55419. (612)870-0169. Director of Operations: Gregory N. Lee. "Carnival is a book producer, not a publisher. The titles we create are for clients who market them in many outlets and editions. Produces juvenile fiction and nonfiction. Produces 25-45 titles/year.

First Contact & Terms: Works with 25-45 freelance artists/year. "Experience in children's literature is *crucial*, including past published children's books and experience in picturebook design." Works on assignment only. Send query letter with brochure, resume, photocopies, slides, printed excerpts—anything except original work to be kept on file. "Carnival uses a file system and only contacts artists on an assignment basis. No specific submissions will be accepted; no queries are followed upon by Carnival due to the volume of our mail. We literally match up artists with appropriate styles. All samples are welcome, but bulk should be kept to a minimum for easy filing." Samples not filed are returned *only* by request with an SASE. Does not report back to the artist. Considers complexity of the project, skill and experience of artist, project's budget, (vital) turnaround time, rights purchased and going rates when establishing payment. Rights purchased vary from client to client.

Text Illustration: Assigns 25-45 titles/year. Considers watercolor, markers, colored pencil and gouache—any "flexible" medium for laser separation. Pays by the project, $2,000-6,000 for color. B&w line art pays less.

CATHOLIC BOOK PUBLISHING CO., 257 W. 17th St., New York NY 10011. (212)243-4515. Manager: Robert W. Cavalero. Specializes in hardcover and paperback originals. Publishes 10 titles/year; 50% require freelance illustrators.

First Contact & Terms: Works with 6 freelance artists/year. Works on assignment only. Send samples and tear sheets to be kept on file; call or write for appointment to show portfolio. Reports within 1 week. No originals returned to artist at job's completion. Considers skill and experience of artist when establishing payment. Buys all rights.

Text Illustration: Assigns 10 freelance jobs/year.

THE CHILD'S WORLD, INC., Box 989, Elgin IL 60120. Editor: Diane Dow Suire. Specializes in hardcover originals on early childhood education. Publishes 40 titles/year; 50% require freelance designers; 100% require freelance illustrators.

First Contact & Terms: Works with 20 freelance artists/year. Prefers artists who have experience illustrating for children. Works on assignment only. Send samples and tear sheets to be kept on file except for original work. "Correspond please. Don't call." Reports only if interested. No originals returned to artist at job's completion. Considers complexity of project, skill and experience of artist, and project's budget when establishing payment. Buys all rights.

Book Design: Assigns 4-6 (by series) freelance jobs/year. Pays by the project for design and illustration.

Jackets/Covers: Assigns 4-6 (by series) freelance design jobs/year. Pays by the project for design and illustration.

Text Illustration: "We do about 40 books in series format. We publish in full-color and use very little black-and-white art." Pays by the project.

Tips: Looks for "art geared for the very young child—there's a big demand for more quality books for preschool children."

CHILTON BOOK CO., 201 King of Prussia Rd., Radnor PA 19089. (215)964-4711. Art Director: Edna H. Jones. Publishes hardbound and paperback arts and crafts, business, computer, technical, trade and automotive books. Publishes 80 titles/year; 50% require freelance designers, fewer than 5% require freelance illustrators.

First Contact & Terms: Query. "I prefer to deal in person rather than through the mail." Reports within 3 weeks. Buys world rights. No originals returned at job's completion. Works on assignment only. Samples returned by SASE. Provide resume, business card, flyer and tear sheet to be kept on file for future assignments. Check for most recent titles in bookstores. Artist sometimes supplies overlays for color work. Full payment for unused assigned work. Pays on acceptance.

Book Design: Assigns 40 jobs/year. Uses artists for layout, type spec and scaling art, castoffs. Pays by the project, $300-800 upon completion and acceptance. Price is discussed at beginning of the job with the designer.

Jackets/Covers: Assigns 80 freelance design and 30 freelance illustration jobs/year. Pays $400-1,000.

Text Illustrations: Assigns 1-2 freelance jobs. Pays by the project.

CHRISTIAN BOARD OF PUBLICATION, Box 179, St. Louis MO 63166. Director of Product Development, Design and Promotion: Guin Tuckett. Publishes several paperbacks annually. Also publishes magazines, curriculum, catalogs and advertising pieces. Uses artists for design and illustration of curriculum, books, direct mail brochures and display pieces.

First Contact & Terms: Send query letter with resume, brochure or copies of work to be kept on file. SASE. Reports in 6-8 weeks. Buys all rights. No originals returned to artist at job's completion. Works

on assignment only. Samples returned by SASE.
Jackets/Covers: Assigns a few jobs/year. Pays $100 minimum, 2-color and 4-color.
Text Illustrations: Assigns many jobs/year. Pays $40 minimum, 2-color; $55 minimum, 4-color. "In a teen-age monthly magazine we use about 8-10 cartoons/issue."

CHRONICLE BOOKS, Suite 806, One Hallidie Plaza, San Francisco CA 94102. (415)777-7240. Production and Art Director: David Barich. Publishes hardcover and paperback originals on California and the West Coast, how-to, architecture, contemporary fine art books and cookbooks, California history, urban living, guidebooks, art and photography; some paperback reprints. Publishes 35-45 titles/year; 75% require freelance designers, 10% require freelance illustrators.
First Contact & Terms: Personal contact required. Query with resume or arrange interview to show portfolio. SASE. Reports within 2 weeks. Buys various rights. Free catalog.
Book Design: Assigns 25 jobs/year. Uses artists for layout, type spec and design. Pays by the project, $225-550 average. Payment upon completion of project.
Jackets/Covers: Assigns 40 jobs/year. Pays by the project, $225-550 average for design; by the project, $125-400 average for illustrations, b&w line drawings, washes and gray opaques; $400-650, color washes and opaque watercolors.
Text Illustrations: Pays by the project, $200 minimum.

***DIXIE CLARK PRODUCTION**, 47 Orient Ave., Melrose MA 02176. Produces hardcover and paperback text and trade book originals. Publishes 30-40 titles/year.
First Contact & Terms: Send query letter with resume, art and representative prices. SASE. Reports in 2 weeks.
Book Design: Assigns 6 freelance design and 8 freelance illustration jobs/year. Pays by the project, $200-350.
Jackets/Covers: Assigns 2 freelance design jobs/year. Pays by the project, $100-250 average.
Text Illustrations: Prefers pen & ink with overlays for color if necessary. Pays by the project, $7-40 technical art; $7-10/hour, or by the page, mechanicals and paste-up.
Tips: "I'm more apt to deal with Northeastern US suppliers because of scheduling."

CLIFFS NOTES INC., Box 80728, Lincoln NE 68501. Contact: Michele Spence. Publishes educational and trade (Centennial Press) books. Uses artists for educational posters.
First Contact & Terms: Works on assignment only. Samples returned by SASE. Reports back on future assignment possibilities. Send brochure, flyer and/or resume. No originals returned to artist at job's completion. Buys all rights. Artist supplies overlays for color art.
Jackets/Covers: Uses artists for covers and jackets.
Text Illustrations: Uses technical illustrators for mathematics, science, miscellaneous.

COASTAR PUBLISHING, Subsidiary of Newtek Industries, Box 46116, Los Angeles CA 90046. (213)874-6669. Publisher: Jules Brenner. Estab. 1984. Publishes 1 original paperback—the *Brenner Restaurant Index*—each year. Also publishes a software program for home and office computers.
First Contact & Terms: "We are not yet working with artists, but would consider doing so." Send query letter with resume and samples to be kept on file. Accepts any type sample. Samples not filed are returned by SASE. Reports within 3 weeks. Original work returned to artist "if artist insists." Rights purchased vary according to project.
Jackets/Covers: Will probably assign 1 freelance illustration job/year. Pays 3 copies of book.
Text Illustration: Will consider using text illustration.

COLOR-A-STORY, Box 99, Burley WA 98322. Art Director: J. Scott. Specializes in paperback originals, juvenile fiction and nonfiction. Publishes 12 titles/year.
First Contact & Terms: Works with 7 freelance artists/year. Artist "must be capable of producing illustrations compatible with the Color-A-Story series." Works on assignment only. Send resume and samples to be kept on file, except for "those which do not interest us." Prefers photocopies as samples, although slides and/or photographs are acceptable. Samples not filed are returned by SASE. Reports only if interested. Original work may be returned to the artist. Considers complexity of the project, skill and experience of artist, project's budget, turnaround time and rights purchased when establishing payment. Rights purchased vary according to project.
Jackets/Covers: Assigns 12 freelance illustration jobs/year.
Text Illustration: Assigns 12 jobs/year. Prefers pen & ink illustrations. "Artist is assigned text and cover." Pays royalty up to 15%.
Tips: "We are happy to assign work to new artists provided they produce quality work, on time, and follow outlines provided with assignments."

***COMPACT PUBLICATIONS, INC.**, 2500 Hollywood Blvd., Hollywood FL 33020. (305)925-5242. President: Donald L. Lessne. Specializes in hardcovers, paperbacks and magazines—mostly trade books. Publishes 20 titles/year.
First Contact & Terms: Works with 5 freelance artists/year. Prefers local artists only. Works on assignment only. Send brochure showing art style or photocopies. Samples not filed are returned only if requested. Reports within 30 days. No originals returned to artist at job's completion "unless specifically requested that they need it back." Considers rights purchased when establishing payment. Rights purchased vary according to project.
Book Design: Assigns 20 freelance design and 20 freelance illustration jobs/year. Pays by the project, $400-1,000.
Jackets/Covers: Assigns 20 freelance design and a variable amount of freelance illustration jobs/year. Pays by the project, $400-1,000.
Tips: "We are looking for fresh approaches to creative art in the trade area. We are looking for contemporary artists; we are looking for self-starters that are able to complete total job ready for typesetting."

COMPCARE PUBLICATIONS, 2415 Annapolis Ln., Minneapolis MN 55441. (800)328-3330. Publisher: Margaret Marsh. Specializes in personal growth books including alcohol/chemical dependency, stress management, parenting and weight control. Publishes 6-8 titles/year. Uses artists for text illustrations and cover art.
First Contact & Terms: Works with 4 freelance artists/year. "We only consider artists who have illustrated for trade books." Works on assignment only. Send query letter with tear sheets. Negotiates payment arrangement with artist.
Book Design: Assigns 1-2 freelance design and 1-2 freelance illustration jobs/year.
Jackets/Covers: Assigns 6-8 freelance design and 2 freelance illustration jobs/year.
Text Illustration: Assigns 1-2 freelance jobs/year. Prefers line art—pencil illustration.

COMPUTER SCIENCE PRESS INC., 1803 Research Blvd., Rockville MD 20850. (301)251-9050. Publishes hardcover and paperback computer science, engineering, computers and math textbooks. Publishes 18 titles/year; 100% require freelance illustrators. Also uses artists for technical drawings using templates and form letters or Leroy lettering.
First Contact & Terms: Works on assignment only. Call or send query letter with template work, an illustration or line drawing as well as an upper and lower case alphabet and some words in Leroy or Berol lettering. Photocopy of work is OK. Samples not returned. Buys all rights. No originals returned to artist at job's completion. Check for most recent titles in bookstores. Artist supplies overlays for cover artwork. Send artwork to the attention of Ilene Hammer.
Book Design: Assigns 12 freelance design and 12 illustration jobs/year. Pays by the hour, $8 minimum.
Jackets/Covers: Assigns 12 freelance design jobs/year. Pays by the project, $100 minimum.
Text Illustration: Buys text illustrations (artist "reproduces our rough art"), jacket designs and cover designs. Assigns 12 freelance text illustration jobs/year; prefers pen & ink drawings. Pays by the hour, $8 minimum.
Tips: "We would like to develop a file of freelance technical draftsmen familiar with Leroy or Berol lettering. Local artists preferred. We provide rough art to copy."

CONCH MAGAZINE LTD., PUBLISHERS, 102 Normal Ave., Buffalo NY 14213. (716)885-3686. Creative Director: Don Robertson. Specializes in hardcover and paperback originals, scholarly and educational. Publishes 10-20 titles/year 99% require freelance designers and illustrators.
First Contact & Terms: Send query letter with brochure, business card, samples and tear sheets to be kept on file. Samples should be whatever is convenient and available. Reports only if interested. Works on assignment only. Considers complexity of project, skill and experience of artist and turnaround time when establishing payment.
Book Design: Assigns 10 freelance jobs/year. Pays by the project, $25-50 average.
Jackets/Covers: Assigns 10 freelance design and 10 freelance illustration jobs/year. Pays by the project, $25-50 average. Artwork includes medical illustration.

DAVID C. COOK PUBLISHING COMPANY, Book Division, 850 N. Grove Ave., Elgin IL 60120. (312)741-2400. Managing Editor: Catherine L. Davis. Publishes religious books spanning ages infant-junior high. Publishes 50 titles/year; 60% require freelance illustrators.
First Contact & Terms: Prefers artists with publishing experience. Send photocopies of work or 35mm slides with return package and postage. Samples returned by SASE. Provide "anything that can be kept or photocopied" to be kept on file for future assignments. Check for most recent titles in bookstores. Artist sometimes supplies overlays on inside illustrations.
Book Design: Assigns 20-35/year. Buys realistic illustrations. Uses artists for layout and full-color art.

Close-up

Chris Van Allsburg
Children's book illustrator
Providence, Rhode Island

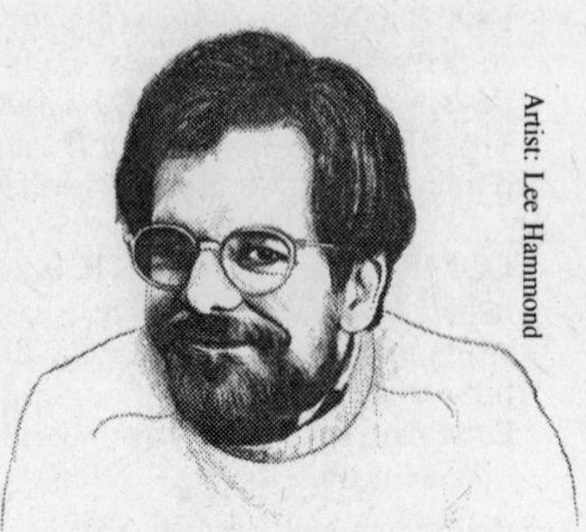

Chris Van Allsburg knows what's special about childhood. "I have a vivid memory of my childhood. It doesn't seem all that long ago." His children's books, which he both writes and illustrates, capture a child's sense of wonder, that sense of being suspended between reality and illusion. A librarian tells the true story of a mother who watched from another room as her son opened one of Van Allsburg's books, carefully placed it on the floor and literally tried to step into the picture.

Van Allsburg has won two Caldecott Medals, the highest honor for illustrated children's books. He applies fine-art techniques and his training as a sculptor to illustration; by controlling perspective and juggling black-and-white contrast, he creates velvet spaces of illusion.

In his picture books, Van Allsburg keeps in mind that illustrations should illuminate text. "I think about stories with telling power. I see a story unfold, I see the images." Striking images usually trigger a narrative idea for him. He writes the story, then draws the illustrations sequentially to establish a rhythm. His books usually consist of 14 pictures; he does twenty or more thumbnail sketches for each illustration, then refines them by using live models. His finished drawings are rendered in whatever medium suits the subject; either charcoal and pencil, Conte dust or pastels. He associates color with landscapes, black-and-white images with interiors.

The process from thumbnails to finished sketches is not complete without Van Allsburg's final test, a question he feels illustrators must ask themselves: "Is it making a sincere and honest statement from the artist?" He feels there are too many artists who copy ideas from popular illustrators. "They're not feeding off their own emotional impact."

Van Allsburg encourages his students at the Rhode Island School of Design to draw every

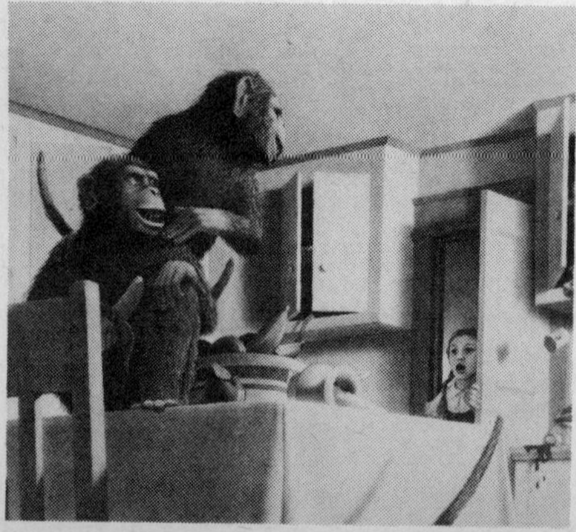

Van Allsburg won his first Caldecott Award with Jumanji. Drawn with carbon pencil, the illustrations for the book bring to life the dilemma of two children who change a game to reality.

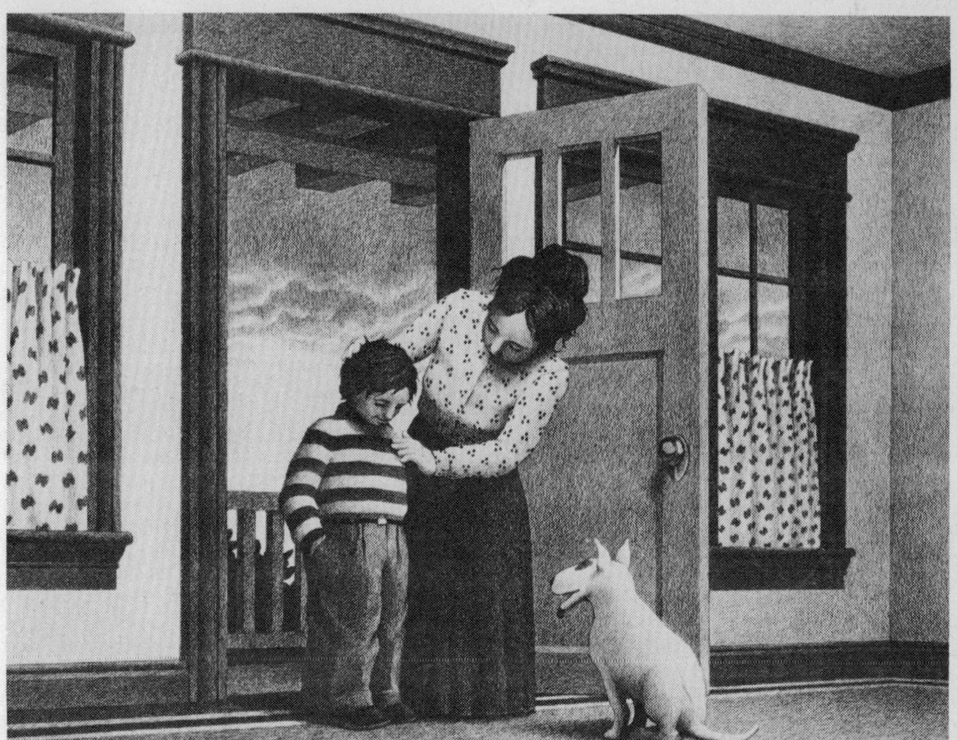

Working with carbon pencil on Strathmore paper, Van Allsburg produced for his first book,
The Garden of Abdul Gahazi, intricately detailed drawings. Here, the main character is con-
soled by his mother as he returns from Gahazi's magical garden.

day to strengthen their own sense of style. The teacher follows his own prescription by drawing seven or eight hours a day. When illustrating a book, he tries to finish a drawing a day, but
he usually takes four or five months to complete a project.

Before exploring children's book illustration, Van Allsburg was a sculptor. "I drew for
kicks." His wife submitted some of his drawings to book publishers, which led to meetings
with several editors, then a contract with Houghton-Mifflin. "I have a good relationship with
my editor. Now I call and say I have an idea for a book, and then I show up some months later
with the finished product."

He tells his illustration students that they must carefully assemble a portfolio reflecting
good draftsmanship. Art directors at book publishers usually look for portraiture skills and
the ability to capture a mood. Your portfolio should contain examples of black-and-white art,
suitable for both line and halftone reproduction. Some color work should have a limited color
range, suggesting your potential for executing pre-separated art.

His final advice to illustrators is to follow your own star. "Keep working with the goal of
self-discovery through making a picture that's important to yourself. Good art is truly
personal."

Illustrated books usually have an advance and royalty.
Jackets/Covers: Assigns 20-35/year. Buys realistic illustrations; prefers b&w and full-color. Uses artists for layout and full-color art. Pays by the job.

CORNERSTONE PRESS image magazine, Box 28048, St. Louis MO 63119. (314)296-9662. Art-Graphics Editor: Bob Bangert. Specializes in paperbacks of poetry, fiction, fantasy and science fiction.
First Contact & Terms: Works with 5-10 freelance artists/year. Send query letter with samples; write for artists' guidelines. Samples not kept on file are returned by SASE. Reports within 8 weeks. Occasionally works on assignment. Originals returned to artist at job's completion. Considers complexity of project, project's budget and turnaround time when establishing payment. Negotiates rights purchased.
Book Design: Assigns 1-4 freelance jobs/year. Pays by the project $5-100 average.
Jackets/Covers: Assigns 3-5 freelance design and 10-60 freelance illustration jobs/year. Pays by the project, $5-100 average.
Text Illustration: Prefers pen and ink, collage and prints. Pays by the project, $5-100 average.

CPI, 223 E. 48th St., New York NY 10017. (212)753-3800. Contact: Sherry Olan. Publishes hardcover originals, workbooks and textbooks for ages 4-14. Publishes 40 titles/year; 100% require freelance illustrators. Also uses artists for instructional materials, workbooks, textbook and scientific illustration.
First Contact & Terms: Local artists only. Works on assignment only. Send query letter with flyer, tear sheets and photocopies. Reports in 2 weeks. Samples returned by SASE. Reports back on future assignment possibilities. No originals returned to artist at job's completion. Buys all rights. Free artist's guidelines.
Text Illustrations: Assigns 75 freelance jobs/year. "Submit color samples of action subjects. In general, realistic and representational art is required." Pays $100-900, opaque watercolors or any strong color medium. Also buys b&w line drawings.

CRAFTSMAN BOOK COMPANY, 6058 Corte del Cedro, Carlsbad CA 92008. (714)438-7828. Art Director: Bill Grote. Specializes in paperback technical construction books. Publishes 12 titles/year; 50% require freelance illustrators.
First Contact & Terms: Works with 6 freelance artists/year. Send query letter with brochure/flyer or resume, photocopies or tear sheets to be kept on file. Reports back on whether to expect future assignments. Originals returned to artist at job's completion. Buys all rights.
Book Design: Assigns 6 freelance design and 6 freelance illustration jobs/year. Pays by the project, $6-12 average.
Jackets/Covers: Assigns 6 freelance design and 6 illustration jobs/year. Prefers color comps for illustrations. Pays by the job, $50-350 average.
Tips: "List prices up front. We are using more 4-color. We need artists with full-color background and experience."

THE CROSSING PRESS, Box 640, Trumansburg NY 14886. (607)387-6217. Publishers: John and Elaine Gill. Publishes hardcover and paperback cookbooks, how-to, feminist/gay literature, and greeting cards and calendars. Publishes 15 titles/year. Free catalog.
First Contact & Terms: Send query letter. SASE. Reports within 4 weeks.
Jackets/Covers: Assigns 6 jobs/year. Pay varies up to $200, b&w line drawings and washes.
Text Illustrations: Assigns 3-4 jobs/year. Pays $20 and up/illustration or $300-1,000/book for b&w line drawings and washes.

***CROSSWAY BOOKS/GOOD NEWS PUBLISHERS**, 9825 West Roosevelt Rd., Westchester IL 60153. Trade book publisher emphasizing contemporary issues, fine fiction, science fantasy and conservative viewpoints for well-educated evangelical Christians, families and professionals.
First Contact & Terms: Send query letter with 8½x11" samples of style to be kept on file. Samples returned by SASE. Buys first rights. Works on assignment only. Reports within 2-3 months. Negotiates rights purchased, usually first rights.
Jackets/Covers: Assigns 6 out of 15 new covers/list a year to freelance illustrators. Pays $300-1,000 for photograh or illustrated color cover. Pays $250-600 for b&w multiple text illustrations or photographs. Pays $15-50 for b&w illustrations or photographs in text.

***CROWN PUBLISHERS, INC.**, 225 Park Ave. S., New York NY 10003. Design Director: Ken Sansone. Specializes in hardcovers, paperbacks and originals, especially general trade—fiction, nonfiction and illustrated nonfiction. Publishes 250 titles/year.
First Contact & Terms: Works with 50 artists/year. Prefers local artists. Works on assignment only. Contact only through artist's agent, who should send query letter with brochure showing art style. Samples not filed are returned by SASE. Reports only if interested. Original work returned at job's comple-

tion. Considers complexity of project, skill and experience of artist, project's budget, turnaround time and rights purchased when establishing payment. Negotiates rights purchased; rights purchased vary according to project.
Book Design: Assigns 20-30 freelance design and very few freelance illustration jobs/year. Pays by the project.
Jackets/Covers: Assigns 150 freelance design and 150 freelance illustration jobs/year. Pays by the project.
Text Illustration: Assigns very few jobs/year.

CURRICULUM ASSOCIATES, INC., 5 Esquire Rd., North Billerica MA 01862. (617)667-8000. Vice President of Production/Manufacturing: Kerry Donovan. Educational publisher of el/hi materials (textbooks).
First Contact & Terms: Works on assignment only. Send query letter with resume and samples to be kept on file; call for appointment to show portfolio. Samples not filed returned by SASE.
Needs: Uses artists for advertising, brochure and catalog illustration and layout.

CUSTOM COMIC SERVICES, Box 50028, Austin TX 78763. Art Director: Scott Deschaine. Estab. 1985. Specializes in educational comic books for promotion and advertising for use by business, education, and government. "Our main product is full-color comic books, 16-32 pages long." Publishes 12 titles/year.
First Contact & Terms: Works with 24 freelance artists/year. "We are looking for artists who can produce finished artwork for educational comic books from layouts provided by the publisher. They should be able to produce consistently high quality illustrations for mutually agreeable deadlines, with no exceptions." Works on assignment only. Send query letter with business card and nonreturnable samples to be kept on file. *Samples should be of finished comic book pages*; prefers photostats. Reports within 6 weeks. Considers complexity of project and skill and experience of artist when establishing payment. Buys all rights.
Text Illustration: Assigns 18 freelance jobs/year. "Finished artwork will be black-and-white, clean, and uncluttered. Artists can have styles ranging from the highly cartoony to the highly realistic."

*** DATA COMMAND**, Box 548, 329 E. Court, Kankakee IL 60901. (815)933-7735. Editor: Patsy Gunnels. Specializes in educational software, teacher's guides, supplements to school curriculum in the language arts, math, science and social studies. Publishes 6 titles/year.
First Contact & Terms: Works with 4 freelance artists/year. Prefers artists with experience in marketing and cover design. Works on assignment only. Send resume and tear sheets, photocopies, slides and photographs. Samples not filed are returned by SASE. Reports back within 3 weeks. Original work not returned after job's completion. Considers complexity of project, skill and experience of artist and project's budget when establishing payment. Buys all rights.
Book Design: Pays by the project.
Jackets/Covers: Assigns 3-4 freelance design and 1-2 freelance illustration jobs/year. Pays by the project, $100 minimum.
Text Illustration: Assigns 1-2 freelance jobs/year. Pays by the project.
Tips: "All our products are aimed at educators and students from kindergarten to twelfth grade."

***DAWN SIGN PRESS**, #501, 2490 Channing Way, Berkley CA 94704. Art Director: Joe Dannis. Specializes in paperback on education, juvenile fiction and parenting, sign language and deaf culture. Publishes 4 titles/year.
First Contact & Terms: Works with 2 freelance artists/year. All artists must go through interview process. Works on assignment only. Send query letter with resume, tear sheets, photostats, photocopies, slides and photographs. Samples not filed returned only if requested. Reports within 90 days. Considers project's budget when establishing payment. Rights purchased vary according to project.
Book Design: Assigns 2 freelance designer jobs/year and 2 freelance illustration jobs/year. Pays by the project, $250-550 average.
Jackets/Covers: Assigns 2 freelance design jobs/year and 2 freelance illustration jobs/year. Pays by the project, $250-550 average.
Text Illustration: Assigns 2 freelance jobs/year. Pays by the project, $20-45 average.
Tips: Artist should "specify their talents: i.e. graphic, cartoonist, illustrator, etc."

DAWNWOOD PRESS, Suite 2650, 2 Park Ave., New York NY 10016. (212)532-7160. President: Ms. Kathryn Drayton. Specializes in hardcover originals of fiction with contemporary themes of social significance. Publishes 1-2 titles/year.
First Contact & Terms: Works with 1 freelance artist/year. Highly experienced, local artists only. Works on assignment only. Send query letter with brochure to be kept on file. Write for appointment to

show portfolio, which should include photographs. Contact through artist's agent preferred. Reports within 10 days. No original work returned after job's completion. Considers complexity of project and project's budget when establishing payment. Buys all rights.
Jackets/Covers: Assigns 1 freelance job/year. Pays by the project, $400-700 average.

DECALOGUE BOOK INC., Box 2212, Mount Vernon NY 10550. (914)664-7944. Art Director: Rosemary Campion. Publishes paperback educational materials. Publishes 10 titles/year. Also uses artists for posters, direct mail brochure illustration, catalog and letterhead design. Negotiates pay.
First Contact & Terms: Send resume and samples; local and experienced artists only. SASE. Reports within 1 month. Works on assignment only. Reports back on whether to expect future assignments. Provide business card, flyer and tear sheet to be kept on file for possible future assignments. Originals not returned after completing assignment. "Samples supplied to artists we wish to consider." Buys all rights unless negotiated.
Book Design: Assigns 5-10 jobs/year. Uses artists for layout and type spec. Negotiates pay.
Jackets/Covers: Assigns 2 jobs/year. Buys color washes, opaque watercolors, gray opaques, b&w line drawings and washes. Negotiates pay.
Text Illustrations: Assigns 5 jobs/year. Buys opaque watercolors, color washes, gray opaques, b&w line drawings and washes. Negotiates pay.
Tips: Buys small number of cartoons for use as cover art in educational material. Negotiates pay.

***DELMAR PUBLISHERS INC.**, Box 15-015, 2 Computer Dr. W., Albany NY 12212. Art Director: Ron L. Blackman. Specializes in original hardcovers and paperbacks, especially textbooks—science, computers, health and mathematics, professions and trades. Publishes 50 titles/year.
First Contact & Terms: Works with 35 freelance artists/year. Prefers artists with "professional technical art and photo preparation skills; dummy and page make-up skills; book publishing experience." Works on assignment only. Send query letter with brochure, resume, tear sheets, photostats, photocopies, slides and photographs. Samples not filed are returned by SASE. Reports back only if interested. Original work not returned after job's completion. Considers complexity of project, project's budget and turnaround time when establishing payment. Buys all rights.
Book Design: Assigns 15 freelance design and 4-5 freelance illustration jobs/year. Pays by the project, $300-600.
Jackets/Covers: Assigns 15 freelance design and 15 freelance illustration jobs/year. Pays by the project, $200-400.
Text Illustration: Assigns 35 freelance jobs/year. Prefers ink and mylar or vellum; simplified style (axonometrics, schematics, diagrams and anatomical art). Pays by the project, $1,000-20,000.
Tips: "Quote prices for samples shown."

DILLON PRESS, 242 Portland Ave. S, Minneapolis MN 55415. (612)333-2691. Publisher: Uva Dillon. Specializes in hardcovers of juvenile fiction (Gemstone Books) and nonfiction for school library and trade markets. Publishes 40 titles/year.
First Contact & Terms: Works with 5 freelance artists/year. Works on assignment only. Send query letter with resume and samples to be kept on file. Call or write for appointment to show portfolio. Prefers slides and tear sheets as samples. Samples not filed are returned by SASE. Reports within 6 weeks. Originals not returned to artist. Considers complexity of the project, skill and experience of artist and project's budget when establishing payment. Rights purchased vary according to project.
Book Design: Assigns 10 jobs/year. Pays by the hour or by the project, negotiated so as competitive with other publishers in area.
Jackets/Covers: Assigns 10 freelance design and 10 freelance illustration jobs/year. Pays by the hour or by the project, negotiated so as competitive with other publishers in area.
Text Illustration: Assigns 10 jobs/year. Seeks a variety of media and styles. Pays by the hour or by the project, negotiated so as competitive with other publishers in area.

THE DONNING COMPANY/PUBLISHERS, 5659 Virgnia Beach Blvd., Norfolk VA 23502. Publishes hardcover and paperback originals on pictorial histories, science fiction, fantasy and horror, illustrated cookbooks, general and regional. Publishes 30-35 titles/year. Free catalog.
First Contact & Terms: Works on assignment only. Send query letter to be kept on file for future assignments. Samples returned by SASE. Reports in 4 weeks. Buys first rights. Originals returned to artist at job's completion. Artist supplies overlays for cover artwork.

***DORCHESTER PUBLISHING CO., INC. (publishers of Leisure Books)**, Suite 900, 6 E. 39th St., New York NY 10016. (212)725-8811. Production Manager: Lesley Poliner. Specializes in paperbacks, originals and reprints, especially mass market category fiction—historical romance, contemporary women's fiction, western, adventure, horror, mystery, romantic suspense, war. Publishes 144 titles/year.

First Contact & Terms: Works with 24 freelance artists/year. "Should have experience doing paperback covers, be familiar with current design trends." Works on assignment only. Send brochure showing art style or resume, photostats, slides and photographs. Samples not filed are returned by SASE. Reports within 2 weeks. Call for appointment to show portfolio. Original work returned after job's completion. Considers complexity of project and project's budget when establishing payment. Usually buys first rights but rights purchased vary according to project.
Jackets/Covers: Pays by the project, $500 minimum.
Tips: "Talented new artists are welcome. Be familiar with the kind of artwork we use on our covers. If it's not your style, don't waste your time and ours."

DOUBLEDAY AND CO. INC., 245 Park Ave., New York NY 10167. (212)984-7561. Head Art Director: Alex Gotfryd. Publishes general adult, juvenile, western, science fiction, mystery, religious and special interest titles. Call Doug Bergstresser and Diana Klemin for interview.
Needs: Uses artists for jackets, inside illustrations.

DRAMA BOOK PUBLISHERS, 821 Broadway, New York NY 10003. (212)228-3400. Editor-in-Chief: Ralph Pine. Contact: Judith Holmes. Publishes hardcover and paperback originals and reprints on performing arts. Publishes 20 titles/year; 80% require freelance designers, 20% require freelance illustrators. Also uses artists for direct mail brochures and advertising layouts. Free catalog.
First Contact & Terms: Works on assignment only. "Nonreturnable copies, no matter how primitive, preferred to returnable copies, no matter how slick." Send samples of work—particularly samples showing type treatments with or without illustration for use on jackets or covers, whether or not the designs were actually used; samples are kept on file and reviewed when future assignments come in. Check for most recent titles in bookstores. Artist supplies overlays for cover artwork. Reports back to artist on future assignment possibilities. Buys various rights.
Book Design: Assigns 20 freelance jobs/year. Pays by the project.
Jackets/Covers: Assigns 20 freelance design jobs/year. Pays by the project.
Text Illustrations: Pays by the project.

THE ECONOMY COMPANY, 1200 N.W. 63rd St., Oklahoma City OK 73116. (405)840-1444. Art Director: William Mathison. Specializes in hardcover and paperback original and reprint textbooks in the language arts (K-8th grade). Publishes 2,000 titles; 75% require freelance illustrators. Also uses artists for occasional posters and other teaching aids.
First Contact & Terms: Works with 100 artists/year. Works only with published artists experienced in book illustration. Send brochure/flyer and samples or actual work; submit portfolio for review. Prefers color illustrations, either originals or tear sheets, as samples. Samples returned by SASE. Reports in 2 weeks. Works on assignment only. No originals returned to artist at job's completion. Buys all rights.

***WM. B. EERDMANS PUBLISHING COMPANY**, 255 Jefferson Ave SE, Grand Rapids MI 49503. (616)459-4591. Art Director: Randy Albosta. Specializes in hardcovers, paperbacks, originals and reprints. Publishes 70 titles/year.
First Contact & Terms: Works on assignment only. Send query letter with slides and photographs. Samples not filed are returned. Reports within 5 days. To show a portfolio, an artist should mail appropriate materials or call or write to schedule an appointment; portfolio should include original/final art. Buys one-time rights.
Book Design: Assigns 40-50 freelance design jobs/year, 4 or 5 illustration jobs/year. Payment depends on the project.
Jackets/Covers: Uses 40-50 freelance designs/year, 4 or 5 illustrations/year. Payment depends on the project.
Text/Illustration: Payment depends on the project.
Tips: "Anything can happen in this field. The quality of freelance art has dropped."

EMC PUBLISHING, 300 York Ave., St. Paul MN 55101. (612)771-1555. Editor: Eileen Slater. Specializes in educational books and workbooks for schools and libraries. Uses artists for book design and illustration.
First Contact & Terms: Works with 1-2 freelance artists/year. Prefers local artists with book experience. Works on assignment only. Send query letter with resume, business card and samples. Call for appointment to show a portfolio. Reports in 3 weeks. Buys all rights. Negotiates payment by the project.

***ENSLOW PUBLISHERS**, Box 777, Bloy St. & Ramsey Ave., Hillside NJ 07205. Contact: Patricia Culleton. Specializes in hardcovers, juvenile young adult nonfiction; popular science. Publishes 30 titles/year.
First Contact & Terms: Works with 10 freelance artists/year. Works on assignment only. Send query

letter with brochure or photocopies. Samples not filed are not returned. Does not report back. Considers skill and experience of artist when establishing payment. Rights purchased vary according to project.
Book Design: Assigns 5 freelance design jobs/year. Pays by the project. $20-500 average.
Text Illustration: Assigns 10 freelance jobs/year. Pays by the project, $20-1,000 average.
Tips: "We're interested in b&w india ink work. We keep a file of samples by various artists to remind us of the capabilities of each."

ENTELEK, Ward-Whidden House/The Hill, Box 1303, Portsmouth NH 03801. Editorial Director: Albert E. Hickey. Publishes paperback education originals; specializing in computer books and software. Clients: business, schools, colleges and individuals.
First Contact & Terms: Query with samples. Prefers previously published work as samples. SASE. Reports in 1 week. Free catalog. Works on assignment only. Provide brochure, flyer and tear sheets to be kept on file for possible future assignments. Pays $300, catalogs and direct mail brochures.
Needs: Works with 1 artist for ad illustrations; 1, advertising design; and 1, illustration, for use on 6 products/year. Especially needs cover designs/brochure designs.

ESPress, Inc., Box 55482, Washington DC 20011. (202)723-4578. President: Rev. Henry J. Nagorka. Specializes in nonfiction in the area of parapsychology, frontiers of science and holistic inner development. Publishes 4-8 titles/year; 5% require freelance designers, 10% require freelance illustrators.
First Contact & Terms: Works with 1-2 freelance artists/year. Works on assignment only. Send query letter with resume, slides, photographs and tear sheets to be kept on file. Especially looks for clarity of concept, effective technique in realizing it and maturity/experience/authority when reviewing samples. Reports within 2 weeks. No originals returned to artist at job's completion. Considers project's budget when establishing payment. Buys first rights or reprint rights.
Jackets/Covers: Assigns 3-4 freelance design and 1-2 freelance illustration jobs/year. Pays by the project, $50-100 average.
Text Illustration: Assigns 1-2 freelance jobs/year. "Guidelines set for each book."

***EXPOSITION PRESS OF FLORIDA, INC.**, Suite C., 1701 Blount Rd., Pompano Beach FL 33069. (305)979-3200. Vice-President: Adam Uhlan. Specializes in original and reprint hardcovers and paperbacks, particularly romance fiction, juvenile fiction, science textbooks; all subject except pornography and anti-ethnic material." Publishes 300 titles/year.
First Contact & Terms: Works with 5-10 freelance artists/year. Prefers, "but not restricted to," local artists. Works on assignment only. Send query letter with brochure, resume, and samples. Samples not filed are returned by SASE if requested. Reports back only if interested. Original work is returned but "depends on the specific needs of the assignment." Considers complexity of the project, skill and experience of the artist and the project's budget when establishing payment. Rights purchased vary according to project, but will buy all rights.
Book Design: Assigns 3 freelance design and 3 freelance illustration jobs/year. Pays by the hour.
Jackets/Cover: Assigns 5 freelance design and 5 freelance illustration jobs/year.

THE FAMILY WORKSHOP INC., Box 52189, Tulsa OK 74152. (918)366-6532. Art Director: Wanda Young. Book publisher of 14-15 titles/year plus 2 how-to columns weekly on woodworking, fabric work, crafts, etc.
First Contact & Terms: Works on assignment only. Send query letter with brochure, resume, business card and samples to be kept on file; call or write for appointment to show portfolio. Samples not filed are returned by SASE only if requested. Reports only if interested. Pays on acceptance and publication. Considers skill and experience of artist, salability of artwork, client's preferences and rights purchased when establishing payment. Buys all rights.
Text Illustration: Assigns 5 freelance jobs/year for b&w and color cartoons (single, double and multi-panel), illustations and spot drawings. Payment open.

FARRAR, STRAUS & GIROUX INC., 19 Union Square W., New York NY 10003. Contact: Dorris Janowitz. Publishes general fiction, nonfiction, biography and juveniles. Publishes 90 titles/year; 75% require freelance designers, 20% require freelance illustrators. Send samples.
Needs: Uses artists for jacket designs and inside illustrations. Pays $550, pre-separated 3-color jacket, and $600-750 full-color illustration, with type.
Book Design: Assigns 65 jobs/year. Requires castoff from mss, layouts, type spec sheets and follow through on proofs.
Tips: "Learn how to do the jacket typography as well as illustrate."

FOREIGN SERVICES RESEARCH INSTITUTE/WHEAT FORDERS, Box 6317, Washington DC 20015-0317. (202)362-1588. Director: John E. Whiteford Boyle. Specializes in paperback originals of

modern thought; nonfiction and philosophical poetry.
First Contact & Terms: Works with 2 freelance artists/year. Artist should understand the principles of book jacket design. Works on assignment only. Send query letter to be kept on file. Reports within 15 days. No originals returned. Considers project's budget when establishing payment. Buys first rights or reprint rights.
Book Design: Assigns 1-2 freelance jobs/year. Pays by hour, $25-35 average.
Jackets/Covers: Assigns 1-2 freelance design jobs/year. Pays by the project, $250 minimum.
Tips: "Submit samples of book jackets designed for and accepted by other clients. SASE, please."

***THE FREE PRESS, A DIVISION OF MACMILLAN, INC.**, 866 Third Ave., New York NY 10022. Manufacturing Director: W.P. Weiss. Specializes in hardcover and paperback originals, concentrating on professional and tradebooks in the social sciences. Publishes 70 titles/year.
First Contact & Terms: Works with around 10 artists/year. Prefers artists with book publishing experience. Works on assignment only. Send query letter with brochure showing art style or resume and nonreturnable samples. Samples not filed are returned by SASE. Reports only if interested. Original work returned after job's completion. Considers complexity of project, skill and experience of artist, project's budget, turnaround time and rights purchased when establishing payment. Buys all rights.
Book Design: Assigns around 70 freelance design and around 35 freelance illustration jobs/year. Pays by the project.
Jackets/Covers: Assigns around 70 freelance design and illustration jobs/year. Pays by the project, $250-750.
Text Illustration: Assigns around 35 freelance jobs/year. "It is largely drafting work, not illustration." Pays by the project.

C.J. FROMPOVICH PUBLICATIONS, RD 1, Chestnut Rd., Coopersburg PA 18036. (215)346-8461. Publisher: Catherine Frompovich. Specializes in self-help and technical books on nutrition, especially natural nutrition. Publishes 3 titles/year. Uses artists for jacket/cover design and illustration, text illustrations, games, cards, pamphlets.
First Contact & Terms: Works with 3 freelance artists/year. Send query letter with finished work and tear sheets; no sketches. Samples returned by SASE. Pays by the project.
Tips: "Do not solicit via telephone. Send a written resume and photocopies of some recently completed work."

FUNKY PUNKY AND CHIC, Box 601, Cooper Sta., New York NY 10276. (212)533-1772. Creative Director: R. Eugene Watlington. Specializes in paperback originals on poetry, celebrity photos and topics dealing with new wave, high fashion. Publishes 4 titles/year; 50% require freelance designers; 75% require freelance illustrators.
First Contact & Terms: Works with 20 freelance artists/year. Send query letter with business card, photographs and slides. Samples not kept on file are returned by SASE. Reports only if interested. Write for appointment to show portfolio. No originals returned to artist at job's completion. Considers complexity of project and project's budget when establishing payment. Buys all rights.
Book Design: Assigns 1 freelance job/year. Pays by the project, $100-300 average.
Jackets/Covers: Assigns 3 freelance illustration jobs/year. Pays by the project, $50-75 average.
Text Illustration: Assigns 2 freelance jobs/year. Pays by the project, $50-75 average.

GALISON BOOKS, 25 W. 43rd St., New York NY 10036. (212)354-8840. President: Gerald Galison. Specializes in hardcover and paperback originals on soft science and the arts. Publishes 5-10 titles/year.
First Contact & Terms: Local artists only. Send query letter with resume to be kept on file; call or write for appointment to show portfolio. Reports only if interested. Works on assignment only. Originals returned at job's completion. Considers complexity of project, skill and experience of artist, project's budget, turnaround time and rights purchased when establishing payment. Negotiates rights purchased.
Book Design: Assigns 10 freelance jobs/year. Pays by the project, $500 average minimum.
Jackets/Covers: Assigns 10 freelance design jobs/year. Pays by the project, $500 average minimum.

GENERAL HALL INC., 23-45 Corporal Kennedy St., Bayside NY 11360. Editor, for editorial and advertising work: Ravi Mehra. Publishes hardcover and paperback originals; college texts and supplementary materials. Publishes 4-6 titles/year; 100% require freelance designers, 10% require freelance illustrators.
First Contact & Terms: Local artists only. Query. SASE. Reports in 1-2 weeks. No originals returned to artist at job's completion. Works on assignment only. Provide brochure/flyer to be kept on file for future assignment. Artist provides overlays for color artwork. Buys all rights. Free catalog and artist's guidelines.
Book Design: Assigns 4-6 jobs/year. Uses artists for layout. Pays on job basis.

Jackets/Covers: Assigns 3-5 jobs/year. Pays by the project, $50-100 for design; $25-50 for illustration, b&w line drawings, washes, gray opaques and color washes.
Text Illustrations: Assigns 1-2 jobs/year. Pays by the project, $10-25, b&w line drawings, washes and gray opaques.

***GLENCOE PUBLISHING COMPANY**, 17337 Ventura Blvd., Encino CA 91316. Design Director: Gary Hespenheide. Specializes in hardcovers and paperbacks, especially textbooks in all subjects. Publishes 120-150 titles/year.
First Contact & Terms: Works with 50-60 freelance artists/year. Looking for "quality work." Works on assignment only. Send resume and tear sheets. Samples not filed are returned by SASE. Reports back only if interested. Original work not returned after job's completion. Considers project's budget when establishing payment. Negotiates rights purchased but generally buys all rights.
Book Design: Assigns 20 freelance design and 50 freelance illustration jobs/year. Pays by the project, $300-1,500.
Jackets/Covers: Assigns 20 freelance design and 30 freelance illustration jobs/year. Pays by project, $200-600.
Text Illustration: Assigns 50 freelance jobs/year. Pays by the project, $50-200.

***GORSUCH SCARISBRICK, PUBLISHERS**, 8233 Via Paseo del Norte, E-400, Scottsdale AZ 85258. Production Manager: Gay L. Orr. Specializes in college textbooks for all disciplines.
First Contact & Terms: Works with 5 freelance artists/year. Works on assignment only. Send query letter with resume, photocopies or "any suitable sample." Samples not filed are not returned. Reports only if interested. Original work not returned after job's completion. Considers complexity of project, skill and experience of artist, project's budget and turnaround time when establishing payment. Buys all rights.
Book Design: Assigns 1-5 freelance design jobs/year. Pays by the project, $200-500.
Jackets/Covers: Assigns 15-18 freelance design and 15-18 freelance illustration jobs/year. Pays by the project, $150-600.
Text Illustration: Assigns 5 freelance jobs/year. Pays by the project, $100-600.
Tips: "We do not have a lot of work, but would like to establish some long-term working arrangments with a few good artists."

***GOSPEL LIGHT PUBLICATIONS**, 2300 Knoll Dr., Ventura CA 93003. (805)644-9721. Book Designer: Ted Killan. Specializes in Bible study and Christian message.
First Contact & Terms: Works on assignment only. Send brochure showing art style and tear sheets, photostats, photocopies, slides and photographs. Samples not filed are returned. Reports within 1 month. To show a portfolio, mail appropriate materials, which should include original/final art, final reproduction/product, tear sheets, photostats, photographs and b&w. Negotiates rights purchased. Pays $300-700 for b&w; $700-1,000 for color, cover. Payment varies.

GRAPHIC IMAGE PUBLICATIONS, Box 6417, Alexandria VA 22306. Assistant Art Director: Ann Ross. Specializes in hardcover, paperback originals, mass market romance, calendars. Publishes 5-10 titles/year.
First Contact & Terms: Works with 5-10 freelance artists/year, on assignment only. Send query letter with brochure or resume, business card and samples to be kept on file; write for appointment to show portfolio. Prefers 2-5 slides, photostats or photographs as samples. Samples not filed are returned by SASE. Reports within 3 months. Original work returned to artist unless all rights purchased. Considers complexity of the project, project's budget and rights purchased when establishing payment. Rights purchased vary according to project.
Book Design: Assigns 5-10 jobs/year. Pays by the hour, $10-50; by the project, up to $5,000.
Jackets/Covers: Assigns 2-5 freelance design and 2-5 freelance illustration jobs/year. Pays by the hour, $10-50; by the project, up to $1,000.
Text Illustration: Assigns 20-30 jobs/year. Pays by the hour, $10-50; by the project, negotiable.
Tips: Seeks "innovative designs. Artist should accept constructive criticism."

GREAT COMMISSION PUBLICATIONS, 7401 Old York Rd., Philadelphia PA 19126. (215)635-6515. Art Director: John Tolsma. Publishes paperback original educational and promotional materials for two Presbyterian denominations and one seminary.
First Contact & Terms: Works with 6 freelance artists/year. Seeks experienced illustrators, usually local artists, but some may be from out-of-state. Works on assignment only. Send query letter with brochure, resume, business card and tear sheets to be kept on file. Material not filed is returned only if requested. Reports only if interested. No originals returned at job's completion. Considers complexity of project, skill and experience of artist, and the project's budget when establishing payment. Buys all rights.

Text Illustration: Assigns 100-150 jobs per year. Prefers stylized and humorous illustration, primarily figure work with some Biblical art; 1-, 2- and 4-color art. Pays by the project, $300 maximum. Assigns from 1-13 projects at one time.

***GREEN HILL PUBLISHERS, INC./Jameson Books**, 722 Columbus St., Ottawa IL 61350. (815)434-7905. Assistant to Publisher: Mrs. Sahadi. Specializes in hardcover and paperback originals and reprints. Specializes in politics/economics, Chicago themes and early American history, authentic pre-1840 fiction and nonfiction books. Publishes 10-20 titles/year.
First Contact & Terms: Works on assignment only. Send query letter with brochure showing art style or resume, slides and photographs. Samples not filed are returned by SASE if requested by artist and accompanied by SASE. Reports within 2 weeks. To show a portfolio, mail appropriate materials. Negotiates rights purchased. Pays $600-800 for color cover.
Book Design: Assigns 5-10 freelance design and 5-10 freelance illustration jobs/year. Pays by the project, $500 minimum.
Jackets/Covers: Assigns 5-10 freelance designs and 5-10 freelance illustration jobs/year. Pays by the project, $500 minimum.

THE GREEN TIGER PRESS, 1061 India St., San Diego CA 92101. Art Director: Sandra Darling. Specializes in original paperback gift and children's books with "imaginative plus unusual themes and illustrations." Publishes 8-10 titles/year.
First Contact & Terms: Works with 3-4 freelance artists/year. Works on assignment only. Send query letter with samples to be kept on file "only if it's work we're interested in." Write for artists' guidelines. Prefers slides and photographs as samples. Never send originals. Samples not filed are returned by SASE. Reports back to the artist within 8 weeks. Originals returned at job's completion. Considers project's budget and rights purchased when establishing payment. Rights purchased vary according to project.
Text Illustration: Assigns 3-6 freelance jobs/year. Payment is usually on a royalty basis.
Tips: "We are looking for artists who have a subtle style and imagination that reflect our aesthetic views."

GUERNICA EDITIONS, Box 633, Station N.D.G., Montreal, Quebec, H4A 3R1 Canada. President: Antonio D'Alfonso. Specializes in hardcover and paperback originals of poetry, juvenile and essays. Publishes 8 titles/year.
First Contact & Terms: Works with 5 local freelance artists/year. Works on assignment only. Send query letter with brochure and photographs to be kept on file. Samples not filed are returned by SASE. Reports only if interested. Write for appointment to show portfolio. Originals returned to artist at job's completion depending on royalty agreement. Buys all rights.
Book Design: Assigns 3 freelance jobs/year. Pays by the project, $200-500 average.
Jackets/Covers: Assigns 3 freelance design and 3 freelance illustration jobs/year. Pays by the project, $200-500 average.
Text Illustration: Assigns 1-2 freelance jobs/year. Pays by the project, royalties, $200 maximum.

***HARPER & ROW PUBLISHERS, INC.**, 10 East 53rd St., New York NY 10022. (212)207-7036. Art Director: Harriet Barton. Specializes in fiction and nonfiction hardcover, paperback and picture books for young adults and children. Publishes 165 hardcover and 69 paperback titles/year.
First Contact & Terms: Works with 40 freelance artists/year. Works on assignment only. Send query letter with resume and photocopies (no originals). Samples not filed returned only if requested. Reports only if interested. Originals returned to artist at job's completion. Buys all rights.
Jackets/Covers: Assigns 40 freelance illustration jobs/year. Pays by the project.
Tips: "If possible, visit publishers in person to show a portfolio or go to your library or bookstores to see which books are publishing your type of art. Your work has to hold up to competitor's work—and it has to hold up on its own. Remember, your art is for children."

HAYDEN BOOK CO. INC., 10 Mulholland Dr., Hasbrouck Heights NJ 07604. Art Director: Jim Bernard. Publishes computer technology and theory, electronics books. Publishes 75 titles/year.
First Contact & Terms: NJ/NY area artists only. Prefers "mostly printed samples—a few original composite sketches." Buys all rights. Originals returned to artist at job's completion. Works on assignment only. Samples returned by SASE. Reports back on future assignment possibilities. Send business card to be kept on file for future assignments. Check for most recent titles in bookstores and "compare to competitive material."
Needs: Buys cover designs, illustrations, text design, and special effects photography. Pays $650 minimum, cover design, plus mechanicals and art costs.
Tips: "Prefer trade book experience. *Don't* like to see 'school projects.' "

D.C. HEATH AND CO., Division of Raytheon, 125 Spring St., Lexington MA 02173. (617)862-6650. Contact: School Division Design Dept. Publishes elementary and secondary textbooks. (Separate College Division at same address also buys illustrations and cover designs.)
First Contact & Terms: Submit samples. Prefers copies or tear sheets which can be kept on file. May show portfolio in person by appointment. Provide flyer, tear sheet or brochure to be kept on file for future assignments. (Photocopies OK.) Buys textbook rights. Originals usually returned.
Needs: Uses artists for inside illustrations and cover design. "Must be relevant to textbook subject and grade level." Occasionally uses freelance book designers. "Recent major el/hi series have used thousands of 4-color cartoon-type illustrations, as well as realistic scientific paintings, and a variety of 'story' pictures for reading books; also black line work for workbooks and duplicating masters." Payment is usually by project, and varies greatly, "but is competitive with other textbook publishers."

T. EMMETT HENDERSON, PUBLISHER, 130 W. Main St., Middletown NY 10940. (914)343-1038. Contact: T. Emmett Henderson. Publishes hardcover and paperback local history, American Indian, archaeology, and genealogy originals and reprints. Publishes 2-3 titles/year; 100% require freelance designers, 100% require freelance illustrators. Also assigns 5 advertising jobs/year; pays $10 minimum.
First Contact & Terms: Send query letter. No work returned. Reports in 4 weeks. Buys book rights. Originals returned to artist at job's completion. Works on assignment only. Send resume to be kept on file for future assignments. Check for most recent titles in bookstores. Artist supplies overlays for cover artwork. No advance. No pay for unused assigned work.
Book Design: Assigns 2-4 jobs/year. Uses artists for cover art work, some text illustration. Prefers representational style.
Jackets/Covers: Buys 2-4/year. Uses representational art. Pays $20 minimum, b&w line drawings and color-separated work.
Text Illustrations: Pays $10 minimum, b&w. Buys 5-15 cartoons/year. Uses cartoons as chapter headings. Pays $5-12 minimum, b&w.

HOLIDAY HOUSE, 18 E. 53rd St., New York NY 10022. (212)688-0085. Editor: Margery Cuyler. Publishes hardcover originals for juveniles; fiction, nature, nonfiction and picture books. Publishes 35 titles/year.
First Contact & Terms: Arrange interview to show portfolio to art director, David Rogers. Must have samples of color separations. SASE. Buys all rights. Originals returned at job's completion. Works on assignment only. Provide flyer and brochure to be kept on file for future assignments. Check for most recent titles in bookstores. Artist supplies overlays for cover artwork and inside illustrations. Negotiates pay. Free catalog.
Jackets/Covers: Assigns 5-10 jobs/year. Uses mostly "young adult-oriented themes (humor and problems)." Buys full-color and color-separated work.
Text Illustrations: Assigns 5-10 jobs/year. Uses illustrations for nonfiction and picture books. Buys color-separated work and b&w line drawings. Offers advance.

HOLLOWAY HOUSE PUBLISHING COMPANY, 8060 Melrose Ave., Los Angeles CA 90046. (213)653-8060. President: Ralph Weinstock. Specializes in paperbacks directed to the black reader, i.e., romance books, biographies, fiction, nonfiction, gambling-game books. Publishes 30-50 titles/year.
Needs: Assigns 25-50 book design and jacket/cover illustration jobs/year.
First Contact & Terms: Works with 6-10 freelance artists/year. Professional artists only. Works on assignment only. Send query letter with resume, slides, photostats, photographs or tear sheets to be kept on file. Samples not filed are returned by SASE only if requested. Reports only if interested. Call for appointment to show portfolio. Considers project's budget when establishing payment. Rights purchased vary according to project.

HOMESTEAD PUBLISHING, Box 193, Moose WY 83012. Art Director: Carl Schreier. Specializes in hardcover and paperback originals of nonfiction, natural history, Western art and general Western regional literature. Publishes 3 + titles/year.
First Contact & Terms: Works with 16 freelance artists/year. Works on assignment only. Send query letter with samples to be kept on file or write for appointment to show portfolio. Prefers to receive as samples "examples of past work, if available (such as published books or illustrations used in magazines, etc.). For color work, slides are suitable; for b&w technical pen, photostats. And one piece of original artwork which can be returned." Samples not filed are returned by SASE only if requested. Reports within 10 days. No original work returned after job's completion. Considers complexity of project, skill and experience of artist, project's budget and turnaround time when establishing payment. Rights purchased vary according to project.
Book Design: Assigns 6 freelance jobs/year. Pays by the project, $50-3,500 average.

Jackets/Covers: Assigns 2 freelance design and 4 freelance illustration jobs/year. Pays by the project, $50-3,500 average.
Text Illustration: Assigns 26 freelance jobs/year. Prefers technical pen illustrations, maps (using airbrush, overlays, etc.), watercolor illustrations for children's books, calligraphy and lettering for titles and headings. Pays by the hour, $5-20 average; by the project, $50-3,500 average.
Tips: "We are using more graphic, contemporary designs."

HUMANICS LIMITED, Suite 201, 1389 W. Peachtree St., Atlanta GA 30309. (404)874-2176. Editor: David A. Strawn. Specializes in original paperback textbooks on early childhood education and development. Publishes 10 titles/year. Also uses artists for advertising, direct mail pieces, catalogs and posters.
First Contact & Terms: Works with 5 freelance artists/year. Prefers local artists. Send query letter with resume and business card to be kept on file. Call or write for appointment to show portfolio. Prefers line drawings, finished work, published ads and brochures as samples. Samples returned by SASE. Reports within 2 weeks. Works on assignment only. No originals returned after job's completion. Buys all rights.
Book Design: Assigns 10 freelance jobs/year. Pays by the job; "we solicit bids on jobs and give the job to the lowest bidder; $75 minimum."
Jackets/Covers: Assigns 10 design and 10 illustration jobs/year. Prefers b&w line drawings and mechanical designs suitable for PMS colors. Pays for illustration by the project, $150-200 average.
Text Illustrations: Assigns 10 jobs/year. Prefers line illustrations. Pays by the job; "we negotiate a per illustration rate; $75 minimum."

CARL HUNGNESS PUBLISHING, Box 24308, Speedway IN 46224. (317)638-1466. Editorial Director: Carl Hungness. Publishes hardcover automotive originals. Publishes 2-4 titles/year. Send query letter with samples. SASE. Reports in 2 weeks. Offers $100 advance. Buys book, one-time or all rights. No pay for unused assigned work. Free catalog.

HURTIG PUBLISHERS LTD., 10560 105th St., Edmonton, Alberta T5H 2W7 Canada. (403)426-2359. Editor-in-Chief: Elizabeth Munroe. Specializes in hardcover and paperback originals of nonfiction, primarily on Canadian-oriented topics. Publishes 10-20 titles/year.
First Contact & Terms: Artists must have "considerable experience and be based in Canada." Send query letter to be kept on file; "almost all work is specially commissioned from current sources." Reports within 3 months. Considers complexity of project, skill and experience of artist, project's budget, turnaround time and rights purchased when establishing payment. Rights purchased vary according to project.

***IGNATIUS PRESS, Catholic Publisher**, Box 18990, San Francisco CA 94118. Production Editor: Carolyn Lemon. Catholic theology and devotioal books for lay people, priests and religious readers.
First Contact & Terms: Works on assignment only. Will send art guidelines "if we are interested in the artist's work." Accepts previously published material. Send brochure showing art style or resume and photocopies. Samples not filed are not returned. Reports only if interested. To show a portfolio, mail appropriate materials; "we will contact you if interested." Pays on acceptance.
Jackets/Covers: Buys cover art from freelance artists. Prefers Christian symbols/calligraphy and religious illustrations of Jesus, saints, etc. (used on cover or in text).

INSTITUTE FOR THE STUDY OF HUMAN ISSUES (ISHI PUBLICATIONS), 210 S. 13th St., Philadelphia PA 19107. (215)732-9730. Marketing Director: Edward A. Jutkowitz. Publishes hardcover and paperback political science, anthropology, folklore, drug studies, and history—originals and paperback reprints. Uses artists for dust jackets, covers, maps, flowcharts, graphs, catalogs and advertising flyers. Publishes 16-20 titles/year.
First Contact & Terms: Prefers local artists. Especially likes artists with "directly related experience in needed areas and whose estimated charges are appropriate to the job in question. Most jobs involve jacket design and mechanicals; text art limited. Mostly black and white; some 2-color, little 4-color work." Send query letter with resume and samples. Reports in 2 weeks. Buys all rights. No originals returned to artist at job's completion. Works on assignment only. Samples returned by SASE. Artist supplies overlays for cover artwork and advertising art. Pays promised fee for unused assigned work. Free catalog.
Book Design: Assigns 4 freelance design and illustration jobs/year. Pays by the project, $100-350 average.
Jackets/Covers: Assigns approximately 12 freelance design and 9 illustration jobs/year. Prefers line drawings or mezzotint and screened photos for cover illustrations. Pays by the project, $75-275 average; $250-350 for jacket mechanicals.

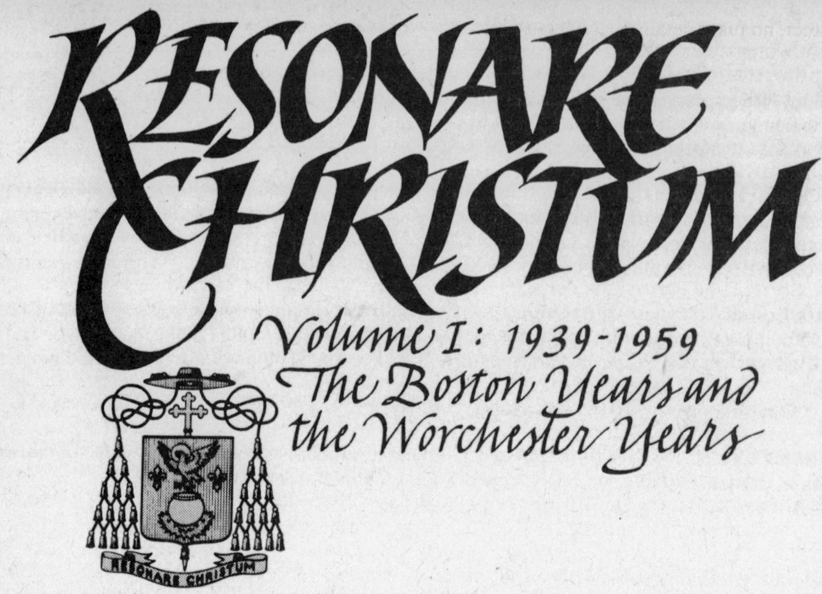

Darlene Lawless of Ignatius Press in San Francisco, California, asked calligrapher Victoria Hoke Lane of Alameda, California to capture the dignity of Cardinal John Wright's thoughts in a book jacket design. "Resonare Christum," which means "resounding in Christ," was printed in silver, which reminded Lawless of a bell.

Text Illustrations: Assigns approximately 4 freelance jobs/year. Prefers line art. Pays by the project, $100-300 average. Includes "maps, charts, graphs, other simple line art and labeling."
Tips: "In the nonfiction area the new emphasis is on simplicity of design; the use of decorative typefaces and strong color combinations is very much in evidence."

***JALMAR PRESS**, Bldg. 2, 45 Hitching Post Dr., Rolling Hill Estates CA 90274-4297. (213)547-1240. President: Bradley L. Winch.
First Contact & Terms: Works with 5-10 freelance artists/year. Works on assignment only. Send query letter with brochure showing art style. Samples not filed are returned by SASE. Reports only if interested. Considers complexity of project, client's budget and turnaround time when establishing payment. Buys all rights.

JANUS BOOK PUBLISHERS, 2501 Industrial Pkwy. W., Hayward CA 94545. (415)785-9625 or (415)887-7070. Production Manager: Carol Gee. Publishes hardcovers and remedial reading materials and soft-cover workbooks for high school and basic adult education. Publishes 25 titles/year.
First Contact & Terms: Works on assignment only. Send samples or arrange interview to show portfolio; prefers local artists. SASE. Reports within 3 weeks. Buys various rights. Provide resume and "photocopies of samples" to be kept on file for future assignments. Artist supplies overlays for 2-color cover artwork; sometimes for advertising art. Free catalog. Also uses artists for catalog design. Pays $25/hour.
Book Design: Assigns 10 jobs/year. Layout done inhouse. Offers advance "upon completion of acceptable roughs."
Jackets/Covers: Uses "2-color and 4-color, very direct and very simple designs" Pays for design and illustration by the project, $1,500-2,000 average.
Text Illustrations: Assigns 12-15 jobs/year. Especially seeks realistic drawings. Pays $40-50 for ¼ or ½-page spot drawings; also pays by the project, $50 (single drawing)-2,400 (entire book). Buys b&w line drawings and washes. Offers advance "upon completion of acceptable roughs." Also uses a realistic type of cartoon. "Our 'cartoons' are used to illustrate meaning of words and phrases, either line or halftone wash work. Artist is given specifications, and asked to supply rough, revised, rough and finished art." Pays $35-50, b&w.
Tips: "Clear, concise, figure work with emphasis on minority groups (black, Chicano, Asian). Simple

and direct, no fussy detail. Beginners should show their work to anyone who will take the time to look at it. Keep trying.''

JUDSON PRESS, American Baptist Churches USA, Board of Educational Ministries, Publishing Division, Valley Forge PA 19481. Assistant Advertising/Graphics Manager: David E. Monyer. Specializes in paperbacks on religious themes (inspirational, Christian education, church administration, missions). Publishes 10-12 titles/year; 90% require freelance cover designers.
First Contact & Terms: Works with 4 or more freelance artists/year. Artists with book cover experience only. Send query letter, brochure/flyer, resume and samples to be kept on file. Prefers examples of book cover designs as samples. Samples not kept on file are returned by SASE. ''We don't report on acceptance or rejection, but keep samples on file.'' Works on assignment only. No originals returned to artist at job's completion.
Jackets/Covers: Assigns 8-10 design and 1-2 illustration jobs/year. Prefers 2-color, usual bold graphics, title dominant, for cover designs. Pays by the job, $300-500 average; ''We pay for type and stats.''
Text Illustration: Assigns 1-2 freelance jobs/year. Prefers line drawings. Pays by the project, $100 minimum.
Tips: ''Stay with bold graphics, up-to-date typography.''

KAR-BEN COPIES, INC., 6800 Tildenwood Ln., Rockville MD 20852. Editor: Madeline Wikler. Specializes in hardcovers and paperbacks on juvenile Judaica. Publishes 8 titles/year.
First Contact & Terms: Works with 3 freelance artists/year. Send query letter with photostats or tear sheets to be kept on file or returned. Samples not filed are returned by SASE. Reports within 2 weeks only by SASE. Originals returned after job's completion. Considers skill and experience of artist and turnaround time when establishing payment. Buys all rights.
Text Illustration: Assigns 3 freelance jobs/year. Pays by the project, $500-1,500 average, or royalty.

***KENT STATE UNIVERSITY PRESS**, 101 Franklin Hall, Kent State University, Kent OH 44242. (212)672-7913. Design/Production Manager: Donna Palchesko. Specializes in original and reprint hardcovers and paperbacks, especially in history, literature and archaeology. Publishes 15-17 titles/year.
First Contact & Terms: Works with 1 freelance artist/year. Prefers local artists with at least three years' experience in design. Prefers book experience. Works on assignment only. Send query letter. Samples not filed are returned only if requested. Reports back only if interested. Original work not returned after job's completion. Considers complexity of project, skill and experience of artist, project's budget, turnaround time and rights purchased when establishing payment. Buys all rights.
Book Design: Assigns 2 freelance design jobs/year. Pays by the project, $400-500.
Jackets/Covers: Assigns 2 freelance design jobs/year. Pays by the project, $400-500.

***THE KRANTZ COMPANY PUBLISHERS**, 2210 N. Burling, Chesye IL 60616. (312)472-6900. President: Les Krantz. Book publisher specializing in art, photography and general publishing. Publishes 5-7 titles/year. Circ. 10,000. Accepts previously published material. Original artwork returned after publication. Material not filed is returned by SASE.
First Contact & Terms: Works on assignment only. Send query letter. Buys one-time rights. Negotiates payment.
Book Design: Assigns 10 freelance design and 3-5 illustration jobs/year. Pays by the hour, $15-30 average.
Jackets/Covers: Assigns 5 freelance design and 3 illustration jobs/year for covers only. Pays by the hour, $15-30 average.

LACE PUBLICATIONS, INC., Box 10037, Denver CO 80210-0037. Managing Editor: Artemis Oak-Grove. Specializes in paperbacks of lesbian fiction. Publishes 5 titles/year.
First Contact & Terms: Works with 10-15 freelance artists/year. Lesbians or sexually sensitive women only. Works on assignment only. Send query letter with resume, b&w photographs or photocopies to be kept on file except for ''the ones I don't like.'' Samples not filed are returned by SASE. Reports within 1 month. Original work returned after the job's completion; cover art returned only if requested. Considers complexity of project, skill and experience of artist, and project's budget when establishing payment. Rights purchased vary according to project; all rights purchased on cover art.
Jackets/Covers: Assigns 5 freelance design and varying number of freelance illustration jobs/year. Pays by the project, $75 minimum.

LAKE VIEW PRESS, Box 578279, Chicago IL 60657. Director: Paul Elitzik. Specializes in hardcover and paperback nonfiction originals on film and political science. Publishes 4-6 titles/year; 100% require freelance designers.

First Contact & Terms: Works with 3 freelance artists/year. Prefers artists with Chicago residence and experience in book design or printing. Works on assignment only. Send query letter with resume to be kept on file. Reports only if interested. Originals returned to artist at job's completion. Considers project's budget when establishing payment. Buys all rights.
Book Design: Assigns 4-6 freelance jobs/year. Pays by the project, $100-300 average.
Jackets/Covers: Assigns 4 freelance design jobs/year. Pays by the project, $200-300 average.

***LIBRARIES UNLIMITED**, Box 263, Littleton CO 80160-0263. (303)770-1220. Marketing Director: Shirley Lambert. Specializes in hardcover and paperback original reference books concerning library science and school media for librarians, educators and researchers. Publishes 45 titles/year.
First Contact & Terms: Works with 4-5 freelance artists/year. Works on assignment only. Send query letter with resume and photocopies. Samples not filed are returned only if requested. Reports within 2 weeks. No originals returned to artist at job's completion. Considers complexity of project, skill and experience of artist, and project's budget when establishing payment. Buys all rights.
Book Design: Assigns 2-4 freelance illustration jobs/year. Pays by the project, $100 minimum.
Jackets/Covers: Assigns 45 freelance design jobs/year. Pays by the project, $250 minimum.
Tips: "There is more use of design for covers of reference materials. No longer plain green, blue, maroon, etc. Greater need for graphic design."

***LIFE CYCLE BOOKS**, Box 792, Lewiston NY 14092-0792. (416)690-5860. Manager: Paul Broughton. Specializes in reprint paperbacks, pamphlets and brochures. Publishes 4-8 titles/year.
First Contact & Terms: Works with 2-3 freelance artists/year. Works on assignment only. Send query letter with resume, tear sheets, photostats, photocopies, slides and photographs. Samples not filed are returned by SASE. Reports back only if interested. Original work not returned after job's completion. Considers complexity of project, skill and experience of artist and project's budget when establishing payment. Negotiates rights purchased.
Jackets/Covers: Assigns 2-3 freelance illustration jobs/year. Pays by the project, $200-500.

LITTLE, BROWN AND COMPANY ADULT TRADE DIVISION, 34 Beacon St., Boston MA 02106. (617)227-0730. Publishes mainstream hardcover originals. Publishes 125 titles/year.
First Contact & Terms: Send samples or arrange interview to show portfolio. Reports within 2-3 weeks. Buys first and reprint rights. "We have no artist's guidelines but will gladly answer questions."
Jackets/Covers: Assigns 100 jobs/year. Buys graphic design, color washes, opaque watercolors, gray opaques, oils, b&w line drawings and washes. Negotiates pay.

***THE LITURGICAL PRESS**, Collegeville MN 56321. (612)363-2218. Art Director: Don Bruno. Specializes in hardcovers and paperbacks. Publishes about 35-50 books/year concerning liturgy (worship) and scripture.
First Contact & Terms: Send query letter with resume and photostats. Samples not filed are returned. Reports within 1 month. To show a portfolio, an artist should mail appropriate materials such as original/final art. Buys one-time rights.
Book Design: Assigns 5-10 freelance design and 2-5 freelance illustration jobs/year. Pays by the project, $500-1,000.
Jackets/Covers: Assigns 5-10 freelance design and 2-5 freelance illustration jobs/year. Pays by the project, $300-500.
Text Illustration: Assigns 2 freelance jobs/year. Prefers line art. Pays by the project, $300 minimum.

LLEWELLYN PUBLICATIONS, Box 64383, St. Paul MN 55164. Art Director: Terry Buske. Specializes in paperback originals. Publishes metaphysical, astrology and New Age books. Works with at least 6 freelance artists/year. Uses artists for book cover designs and inside art, color and b&w.
First Contact & Terms: Works on assigment only. Send query letter with samples to be kept on file. No preference regarding types of samples, but "must be professionally submitted. No roughs, fragments or photocopies of other than excellent quality. Do not send actual artwork." Samples not kept on file are returned by SASE only if requested. Reports within 2 weeks after receipt of submission if SASE is supplied. Negotiates payment. Considers project's budget, skill and experience of artist, and rights purchased when establishing payment. Negotiates rights purchased.
Book Design: Assigns 5 freelance illustration jobs/year. Pays by the project, $20-40.
Jackets/Covers: Assigns 15 freelance illustration jobs/year. Pays by the project, $100-600.
Text Illustration: Assigns 5 freelance jobs/year. Prefers pen & ink. Pays per illustration, $20-40.
Tips: "People expect more of a high-tech, photo realistic or refined look for the product. We are interested in artists who express our themes in more general terms reaching a broad audience. We are interested in realistic (photo-realism) art." Especially looks for "technique and professionalism" in artist's work. Uses many airbrush paintings.

LODESTAR BOOKS, division of E.P. Dutton, 2 Park Ave., New York NY 10016. (212)725-1818. Associate Editor: Rosemary Brosnan. Publishes young adult fiction (12-16 years) and nonfiction hardcovers, and fiction and nonfiction for ages 9-11 and 10-14 years. "No picture books." Publishes 16-20 titles/year.
First Contact & Terms: Send query letter with samples or arrange interview. Especially looks for "knowledge of book requirements, previous jackets, good color, strong design and ability to draw people" when reviewing samples. Prefers to buy all rights.
Jackets/Covers: Assigns approximately 10-12 jackets/year. Pays $600 minimum, color.
Tips: In young adult fiction, there is a trend toward "covers that are more realistic with the focus on one or two characters. In nonfiction, strong, simple graphic design, often utilizing a photograph. Two color jackets are popular for nonfiction; occasionally full-color is used."

McGRAW-HILL RYERSON LIMITED, 330 Progress Ave., Scarborough, Ontario M1P 2Z5 Canada. (416)293-1911. Art Supervisor: Dan Kewley. Publishes educational books for school and college levels, and professional and reference books. Publishes 126 titles/year. Works with 10 freelance artists/year. Uses artists for book production, paste-up, line illustrations (technical and interpretive); medical, biology and science text illustration; one and 2-color mechanical preparation.
First Contact & Terms: Local artists only with experience in publishing. Works on assignment only. Send resume, business card and photostats or photocopies to be kept on file. Especially looks for "flexibility of style, application to company needs, and quality of work and of presentation" when reviewing samples. Reports only if interested. Call for appointment to show portfolio. Considers complexity and quantity of project, how work will be used, and turnaround time when establishing payment.
Jackets/Covers: Assigns 8 freelance jobs/year. Pays by the project, $450-1,300, "depending on the medium and technique, i.e., computer graphics."
Test Illustration: Assigns 35-50 freelance jobs/year. Prefers "art to be prepared camera-ready mechanicals, one- to two-color black-line with overlays." Pays by the hour, $10-15; by the project, $500 minimum. Considers "complexity of project, quantity and time."
Tips: "Freelance artists must follow design established by designer using the best materials available to supply the best artwork possible."

***MACMILLAN PUBLISHING CO.**, Professional Books Division, 866 3rd Ave., New York NY 10022. Manufacturing Director: W.P. Weiss. Publishes hardcover and paperback originals as professional books in the social sciences and the technical sciences. Publishes 80-100 titles/year; 20-30% require freelance designers, 25-45% require freelance illustrators.
First Contact & Terms: Works with 10-20 freelance designers and/or artists/year. Prefers artists in proximity of Macmillan offices for easier contact. Works on assignment only. Send query letter with resume and samples of actual work; no slides. Call or write for appointment. Samples not returned. Originals returned to artist at job's completion. Buys all rights; copyright Macmillan Publishing Co., Inc.
Book Design: Assigns 80-100 jobs/year. Uses designers primarily for type spec; some dummy and mechanical work. Pays by the job, $75-450 range.
Jackets/Covers: Assigns 80-100 freelance designs. Pays by the job, $175-650 range.
Text Illustrations: Assigns 24-45 jobs/year. Mostly line drafting. Pays by the job according to content.
Tips: "Prefer people with book publishing experience."

***MASTERY EDUCATION**, 85 Main St., Watertown MA 02172. Managing Editor: Elena Wright. Specializes in paperback originals of teacher-directed instruction books. Publishes 100 titles/year.
First Contact & Terms: Works with 10 artists/year. Artists should have experience in educational textbooks. Works on assignment only. Send resume, tear sheets and photocopies. Samples not filed are returned by SASE. Reports only if interested. No originals returned to artist at job's completion. Considers complexity of project and project's budget when establishing payment. Buys all rights.
Book Design: Assigns 2 freelance design jobs/year. Pays by the project.
Text Illustration: Assigns hundreds of jobs/year. Pays by the project.
Tips: "Look at what is good in children's trade book art and show how you can transplant that excitement into elementary textbooks."

***MEDIA PROJECTS INCORPORATED**, 201 E. 16th St., New York NY 10003. (212)777-4510. Assistant Editorial Director: Ellen Coffey. Specializes in hardcover and paperback originals on juveniles, lifestyles and cookery. Publishes 15 titles/year.
First Contact & Terms: Works with 3-6 freelance artists/year. Works on assignment only. Send query letter with brochure showing art style or resume and tear sheets, photostats, photocopies, slides and photographs. Samples not filed are returned by SASE. Reports within 2 weeks. Original work returned at job's completion. Considers project's budget when establishing payment. Negotiates rights purchased.

Book Design: Assigns 10 freelance design and 10 freelance illustration jobs/year. Pays by the project, negotiable amount.
Jackets/Covers: Assigns 10 freelance design and 10 freelance illustration jobs/year. Pays by the project, negotiable amount.
Text Illustration: Assigns 10 freelance jobs/year. Prefers line drawings. Pays by the project, negotiable amount.

***MERCURY HOUSE**, Suite 700, 300 Montgomery St., San Francisco CA 94901. (415)488-4005. Executive Editor: Alev Lytle. Publishes quality fiction and nonfiction. Uses artists for designing and producing art for book covers.
First Contact & Terms: Send query letter with brochure showing art style and/or resume and samples. Samples not filed are returned by SASE. Reports within 60 days. To show a portfolio, mail thumbnails, roughs, original/final art, final reproduction/product, color, tear sheets, photostats, photographs and b&w. Prefers color. Considers complexity of project, skill and experience of artist, turnaround time, rights purchased, budget and number of books to be printed bearing the artist's work on cover when establishing payment. Rights purchased vary according to project.

METAMORPHOUS PRESS, Suite 67, Box 1712, 4 SW Touchstone, Lake Oswego OR 97034. (503)635-6709. Publisher: Victor Roberge. Specializes in hardcover and paperback originals, general trade books, mostly nonfiction. "We are a general book publisher for a general audience in North America." Publishes at least 12 titles/year.
First Contact & Terms: Works with a varying number of freelance artists/year. "We're interested in what an artist can do for us—not experience with others." Works on assignment only. Send query letter with brochure, business card, photostats, photographs, and tear sheets to be kept on file. Samples not filed are returned by SASE. Reports within a few days usually. Originals returned to artist at job's completion if requested. Considers complexity of project and project's budget when establishing payment. Rights purchased vary according to project.
Book Design: Rarely assigns freelance jobs. "We negotiate payment on an individual basis according to project."
Jackets/Covers: Will possibly assign 5-10 jobs in both freelance design and freelance illustration this year. Payment would vary as to project and budget.
Text Illustration: Assigns 5-10 freelance jobs/year. Payment varies as to project and budget.

MILADY PUBLISHING CORP., 3839 White Plains Rd., Bronx, New York NY 10467. (800)223-8055. Editor: Mary Healy. Publishes textbooks and audiovisual aids for vocational schools.
First Contact & Terms: Works on assignment only. Send query letter with samples to be kept on file; write for appointment to show portfolio. Prefers photostats as samples. Samples not filed are returned by SASE. Reports only if interested. Pays by the hour, $5 minimum; by the project depending on nature of project and length of time needed for completion. Considers complexity of the project, client's budget and skill and experience of artist when establishing payment. Buys all rights. Catalog costs $1.
Needs: Works with 3 freelance artists/year during overloads. Especially important is ability to produce accurate and neat mechanicals and clean line illustrations. Uses technical and "fashion features and hairstyles" illustrations.
Tips: "Build up skills in illustrating hands and hair."

MINNE HA! HA!, Box 14009, Minneapolis MN 55414. Editor/Publisher: Lance Anger. Specializes in paperback originals on political humor, cartoons and cartooning. Publishes 1-3 titles/year.
First Contact & Terms: Works with 3-10 freelance artists/year. "Fine artists encouraged to showcase here." Send query letter with brochure, resume, business card, samples and tear sheets to be kept on file. Send only photocopies as samples which do not have to be returned. Samples not kept on file are NOT returned. Reports only if interested. Write for appointment to show portfolio. Originals returned to artist at job's completion. Considers project's budget and cooperative profit-sharing when establishing payment. Buys one-time rights.
Book Design: Assigns 1-3 freelance jobs/year. Pay is negotiable.
Jackets/Covers: Assigns 1-3 freelance design jobs/year.
Text Illustration: Assigns 1-3 freelance jobs/year.
Tips: "We are using more art integrated with words/text."

BARRY LEONARD STEFFAN MIRENBURG, DESIGN, 413 City Island Ave., New York NY 10464. Design Director: Barry L.S. Mirenburg. Specializes in hardcover and paperback nonfiction originals. Publishes 10 titles/year; 20% require freelance designers; 80% require freelance illustrators. Also uses artists for posters, annual reports, graphic design, trademarks, etc.
First Contact & Terms: Works with 12 freelance artists/year. Works on assignment only. Send bro-

chure/flyer or resume and samples; samples not returned. Sometimes reports back whether to expect possible future assignments. Negotiates rights purchased.
Book Design: Assigns 12 jobs/year. Uses artists for layout, type spec and mechanicals. Pays "going rates."
Jackets/Covers: Assigns 20% to freelance designers and 80% of needs to freelance illustrators. Prefers b&w line drawings, paintings, color washes, gray opaques; no cartoon style. Payment varies.
Text Illustrations: Number of jobs assigned/year varies. Prefers b&w line drawings, paintings, color washes, gray opaques; no cartoon style. Payment varies.

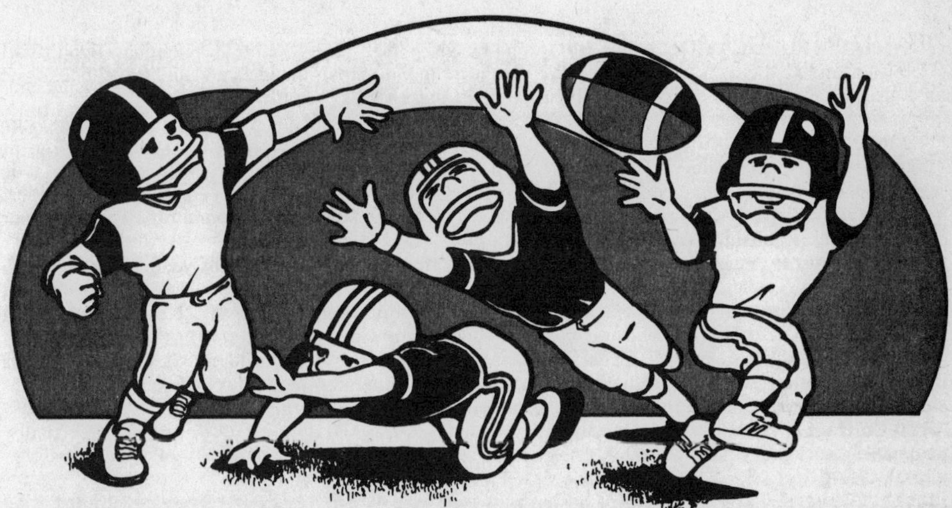

Learning should be a fun experience, and that's what freelance artist Gary Rittenour of Munroe Falls, Ohio, was asked to convey in his illustrations for Modern Curriculum Press of Cleveland, Ohio. The publishing company's art director, John K. Crum, says, "Gary is able to capture action and humor in his style."

MODERN CURRICULUM PRESS, 13900 Prospect Rd., Cleveland OH 44136. (216)238-2222. Art Director: John K. Crum. Specializes in supplemental text books, readers and workbooks. Publishes 100 titles/year. Also uses local artists for advertising and mechanicals.
First Contact & Terms: All freelance. Works on assignment only. Send resume and drawings of various aged children and animals to be kept on file. Samples not kept on file are returned by SASE. Reports within 2-3 weeks. Buys all rights.
Book Design: Assigns 2-3 freelance jobs/year. Uses artists for layout, mechanicals, type specs. Pays by the project, $20 minimum.
Jackets/Covers: Pays by the project.
Text Illustrations: Prefers real life themes "nothing too cartoony; must be accurate." Pays by the project; $25-700.

***MODERN PUBLISHING**, 155 East 55th St., New York NY 10022. (212)826-0850. Art Director: Jill Steinberg. Specializes in hardcovers and paperbacks and coloring books. Publishes approximately 20 titles/year.
First Contact & Terms: Works with 15 freelance artists/year. Works on assignment only. Send query letter with resume and samples. Samples not filed are returned only if requested. Reports only if interested. Original work not returned at job's completion. Considers turnaround time and rights purchased when establishing payment. Buys all rights.
Jackets/Covers: Pays by the project, $100-200 average per cover, "usually 4 books per series."
Text Illustration: Pays by the project, $15-20 average per page (line art), "48-382 pages per book, always 4 books in series."

MONUMENT PRESS, 513 S. Rosemont St., Dallas TX 75208. (214)948-7001. General Editor: Dr. Arthur Ide. Estab. 1984. Specializes in books on women—historical and scholarly. Publishes 5 titles/year.

First Contact & Terms: Works with 3 freelance artists/year. Send query letter with photos and tear sheets. Samples not filed are returned by SASE. Reports within 3 weeks. Write for appointment to show portfolio. Considers complexity of project, skill and experience of artist, project's budget, turnaround time and rights purchased when establishing payment. Negotiates rights purchased.
Book Design: Assigns 5 jobs/year. Pays by the project, $5,000 maximum.
Jackets/Covers: Assigns 5 freelance design and 5 freelance illustration jobs/year. Pays by the project, $5,000 maximum.
Text Illustration: Assigns 5 titles/year. Pays by the project, $500 maximum. Contact Samantha Gonzoles for graphics.

JOHN MUIR PUBLICATIONS, Box 613, Santa Fe NM 87501. (505)982-4078. President: Ken Luboff. Publishes trade paperback nonfiction. "We specialize in auto repair manuals and and travel books and are always actively looking for new illustrations in these fields." Publishes 10 titles/year.
First Contact & Terms: Works with 5-6 freelance artists/year. Send query letter with resume and samples to be kept on file. Write for appointment to show portfolio. Accepts any type of sample "as long as it's professionally presented." Samples not filed are returned by SASE. Reports within months; "it depends on how harried our schedule is at the time." Originals returned at job's completion. Considers complexity of project, skill and experience of artist, project's budget, turnaround time and rights purchased when establishing payment. Buys all rights.
Jackets/Covers: Assigns 6-8 freelance design and freelance illustration jobs/year. Negotiates payment.
Text Illustration: Assigns 6-8 freelance jobs/year. Usually prefers pen & ink. Negotiates payment.

NELSON-HALL INC., 111 N. Canal St., Chicago IL 60606. Vice President: Stephen A. Ferrara. Publishes 85 titles/year; 100% require freelance designers, 50% require freelance illustrators. Also uses artists for technical illustration, advertising layout and catalog illustration.
First Contact & Terms: Submit resume and photocopies. Buys all rights. Pays on acceptance. Catalog available.
Book Design: Assigns 100 jobs/year.
Jackets/Covers: Pays $300, jacket design plus type.

NEW SOCIETY PUBLISHERS, 4722 Baltimore Ave., Philadelphia PA 19143. (215)726-6543. Production Director: T.L. Hill. Specializes in hardcover and paperback originals and reprints on nonviolent social change. Publishes 15 titles/year.
First Contact & Terms: Works with 4 freelance artists/year. Works on assignment only. Send query letter with samples to be kept on file. Call for appointment to show portfolio. Prefers photostats and photographs as samples. Samples not filed are returned only by SASE. Reports only if interested. Original work may or may not be returned to the artist. Considers complexity of the project, project's budget and rights purchased when establishing payment. Negotiates rights purchased.
Book Design: Usually "done in-house with occasional exceptions." Pays by the hour, $5-100.
Jackets/Covers: Assigns 8-10 freelance design jobs/year. Pays by the project, $50 for 3 sketches. "If one is accepted then $150 for completed mechanicals. Additional must be negotiated—normally on 2-color jobs only.
Text Illustration: Assigns 1-2 jobs/year. Prefers pen & ink line drawings. Pays by the hour, $5-10 or negotiated by the project.

NICHOLS PUBLISHING COMPANY, Box 96, New York NY 10024. (212)580-8079. President: Linda Kahn. Specializes in hardcover professional and reference books in architecture, business, education, technology, energy and international relations. Publishes 30 titles/year.
First Contact & Terms: Works with 4 freelance artists/year. Works on promotion assignment only. Artists must be in New York area. Send query letter with brochure and resume. Samples not kept on file are returned only if requested. Reports only if interested. Call or write for appointment to show portfolio, which should include promotion brochures. Considers complexity of project, skill and experience of artist and project's budget when establishing payment. Rights purchased vary.

NORTHWOODS PRESS, Box 88, Thomaston ME 04861. Editor: Robert Olmsted. Part of the Conservatory of American Letters. Specializes in hardcover and paperback originals of poetry; fiction in novelette form. Publishes approximately 20 titles/year.
First Contact & Terms: Works with 1-2 freelance artists/year. Send query letter to be kept on file. Reports within 10 days. Originals returned to artist at job's completion. Considers complexity of project, skill and experience of artist, project's budget, turnaround time and rights purchased when establishing payment. Buys one-time rights and occasionally all rights.
Jackets/Covers: Assigns 4-5 freelance design jobs and 4-5 freelance illustration jobs/year. "The author provides the art work and payment."

NOYES PRESS, Noyes Building, Park Ridge NJ 07656. Contact: Robert Noyes. Publishes academic and technical books on chemistry, chemical engineering, food, environment, art, electronics, archaeology and classical studies.
Needs: Uses artists for jacket design. Pays $250 minimum, 2-color camera-ready art.

***OCTAMERON PRESS**, 2873 Duke St., Alexandria VA 22314. President: Anna Leider. Specializes in paperbacks—college money and college admissions guides and travel guides. Publishes 10-15 titles/year.
First Contact & Terms: Works with 1 or 2 artists/year. Prefers local artists only. Works on assignment only. Send query letter with brochure showing art style or resume and photocopies. Samples not filed are returned. Reports within 1 week. Original work returned at job's completion. Considers complexity of project and project's budget when establishing payment. Rights purchased vary according to project.
Jackets/Covers: Works with variable number of freelance designer/year. Pays by the project $75-250.
Text Illustration: Works with variable number of freelance artist/year. Prefers line drawings from photographs. Pays by the project, $35-75.

ODDO PUBLISHING, INC., Box 68, Fayetteville GA 30214. (404)461-7627. Vice President: Charles W. Oddo. Specializes in hardcovers on juvenile fiction. Publishes 6-10 titles/year; 100% require freelance illustration.
First Contact & Terms: Works with 3 freelance artists/year. Send query letter with brochure, resume, business card, samples or tear sheets to be kept on file; write for appointment to show portfolio. Accepts "whatever is best for artist to present" as samples. Samples not kept on file are returned by SASE only if requested. Reports only if interested. Works on assignment only. No originals returned to artist at job's completion. Pay is negotiated. Buys all rights.
Book Design: Assigns 3 freelance jobs/year. Pay is negotiated.
Text Illustration: Assigns 3 freelance jobs/year. Artwork purchased includes science fiction/fantasy.

ONCE UPON A PLANET, INC., 65-42 Fresh Meadow Lane, Fresh Meadows NY 11365. Art Director: Alis Jordan. Publishes trade paperback originals, greeting cards, pads and novelty books (humor). Uses artists for book design, cover and text illustration, mechanicals, displays, brochures and flyers.
First Contact & Terms: Prefers local artists. Send query letter with brochure showing art style or resume, tear sheets, photocopies and/or slides. Works on assignment only. If originals are sent, SASE must be enclosed for return. Reports in 3-5 weeks. Prefers to buy all rights, but will negotiate. Payment is negotiated.
Book Design: Assigns 8-12 jobs/year. Uses artists for layout, type specifications.
Jackets/Covers: Assigns 6 jobs/year. Uses 2-color art, occasionally 4-color art.
Text Illustration: Assigns 8-12 jobs/year. Uses b&w line drawings and washes.

101 PRODUCTIONS, 834 Mission St., San Francisco CA 94103. Art Director: Lynne O'Neil. Specializes in paperback cookbooks, travel guides and restaurant guides. Publishes 10-12 titles/year; 40% require freelance illustrators.
First Contact & Terms: Works with 4 freelance artists/year. Send query letter with resume and samples to be kept on file. Prefers good-quality photocopies of b&w line drawings, etc., related to food and architecture; do not send original art. Samples returned with SASE only.
Jackets/Covers: Inhouse cover design done in cooperation with illustrator. Illustrator does both cover and text art on one book. Payment usually on royalty basis.
Tips: "Know your market—I look for food and architecture subjects and don't want to see portfolios that lack these."

OTTENHEIMER PUBLISHERS, INC., 300 Reisterstown Rd., Baltimore MD 21208. (301)484-2100. Art Director: Diane Parameros. Specializes in mass market-oriented hardcover and paperback originals and reprints—encyclopedias, dictionaries, self-help books, cookbooks, children's coloring and activity books, story books and novelty books. Publishes 200 titles/year.
First Contact & Terms: Works with 15-20 freelance artists/year. Local artists only, preferably professional graphic designers and illustrators. Works on assignment only. Send query letter with resume, slides, photostats, photographs, photocopies or tear sheets to be kept on file except for work style which is unsuitable for us. Samples not filed are returned by SASE. Reports only if interested. Call or write for appointment to show portfolio. Original work not returned at job's completion. Considers complexity of project, project's budget and turnaround time when establishing payment. Buys all rights.
Book Design: Assigns 20-40 freelance design jobs/year and 25 illustration jobs/year. Pays by the project, $75-300 average.
Jackets/Covers: Assigns 25 + freelance design and 25 + freelance illustration jobs/year. Pays by the project, $50-400 average, depending upon project, time spent and any changes.

Text Illustration: Assigns 30+ jobs/year. Prefers water-based color media and b&w line work. Prefers graphic approaches as well as very illustrative. "We cater more to juvenile market." Pays by the project, $50-2,000 average.

OUTDOOR EMPIRE PUBLISHING INC., Box C-19000, 511 Eastlake Ave. E., Seattle WA 98109. (206)624-3845. Vice President/General Manager: Alec Purcell. Publishes paperback outdoor and how-to books on all aspects of outdoor recreation. Publishes 40 titles/year: 10% require freelance designers, 50% require freelance illustrators. Also uses artists for advertising layout and illustration. Minimum payment: $10-15, b&w; $25-50, color.
First Contact & Terms: Arrange interview or mail art. Especially looks for style, accuracy in rendering figures and technical illustrations when reviewing samples. Reports within 3 weeks. Buys all rights. No originals returned at job's completion. Works on assignment only. Samples returned by SASE; and reports back on future assignment possiblities. Send resume, flyer, business card, tear sheet, brochure and photocopies of samples that show style to be kept on file. Artist sometimes supplies overlays for color artwork. Gives minimum payment for unused assigned work. Pays on publication.
Book Design: Uses artists for layout and type spec. Pays by the hour, $10-35 average; by the project, $10-1,500; "depends upon project."
Jacket/Covers: Pays for design by the hour, $10-35 average; by the project $50-1,000 average. Pays for illustration by the hour, $10-35 average; by the project, $10-500 average.
Text Illustrations: Pays by the hour, $10-35 average; by the project, $10-100 average. Occasionally uses cartoons; buys 6 cartoons/year. Pays $10, b&w.
Tips: "Assignments sometimes depend upon timing—right style for the right project. Availability is important, especially with 'rush' projects. The competition is getting tougher. More people are trying to break into the field."

OXFORD UNIVERSITY PRESS, ELT Department, 200 Madison Ave., New York NY 10016. (212)679-7300. Art Director: Shireen Nathoo. Specializes in hardcover and paperback originals; educational materials for English as a second language. Publishes 15-20 titles/year: 25% require freelance designers; 100% require freelance illustrators.
First Contact & Terms: Works with 25 freelance artists/year. Prefers artists with experience in juvenile or educational publishing. Send query letter with resume, samples and tear sheets to be kept on file. Call to show portfolio. Prefers photostats, photocopies or printed samples. Samples not kept on file are returned by SASE. Reports only if interested. Works on assignment basis only. Considers complexity of project, skill and experience of artist and project's budget when establishing payment. Buys all rights.
Book Design: Assigns 5 freelance artists/year. Pays by the project.
Book Advertising and Promotion: Assigns 15-20 freelance projects/year. Pays by the project.
Text Illustration: Assigns 15-20 freelance projects/year. Pays by the project.
Tips: Looks for "a developed sense of style, a good understanding of the problem and its visual solution, creativity within a set of tight specs and good renderings of children and ethnic features" when reviewing samples.

***PADRE PRODUCTIONS**, Box 1275, San Luis Obispo CA 93406. Editor/Publisher: Lachlan P. MacDonald. Publishes county and area, especially California, guidebooks. Publishes 6-10 titles/year; 5% require freelance designers; 40% require freelance illustrators.
First Contact & Terms: Query. Answers queries in 10 days; book decisions, 2 months. Samples returned by SASE. Provide resume, flyer, tear sheet, brochure and book jacket samples to be kept on file for future assignments. Artist provides overlays for color art. "We typeset all text, but want the artist to be responsible for complete preparation of art." Artists who produce quality, clarity and neat work only. "Actively seeking quality ink drawings in categories of: Western Americana, mystical, science fiction and contemporary humor." Need illustrations for short stories and novellas. Works on assignment only. Usually buys all book rights. Originals returned to artist at job's completion. Pays $10-1,000.
Book Design: Assigns 1-2 jobs/year. Uses artists to prepare mechanicals from roughs. Pays by agreed arrangement.
Tips: "Too few artists are familiar with book production, effects of reduction on their art, printing of process color, etc. Always query first. We are still in the market for complete basics and want to see the manuscripts along with simple line drawings."

PALADIN PRESS, Box 1307, Boulder CO 80306. (303)443-7250. Art Director: Fran Porter. Publishes hardcover and paperback originals and reprints; military-related (weaponry, self-defense, martial arts and survival) and titles of general interest. Publishes 40 titles/year. Free catalog for SASE.
First Contact & Terms: Local artists only for book design. Works on assignment only. Send query letter with good quality photocopies of sample work to be kept on file. Reports in 1 month. Samples returned by SASE; reports back on future assignment possiblities. Artist supplies overlays for all color artwork. Buys all rights.

Text Illustration: Assigns 8/year. Uses "99% pen & ink, b&w. Often technical." Buys b&w line drawings, washes and color washes. Negotiates pay.
Tips: "We prefer working with artists who have a strong background in mechanical and production skills (have they ever worked with a printer?). There is continued expansion into the martial arts market, financial survival, outdoor skills, etc. Also an increased demand for high caliber execution of how-to photo layouts."

PANJANDRUM BOOKS, Suite 1, 11321 Iowa Ave., Los Angeles CA 90025. (213)477-8771. Editor and Publisher: Dennis Koran. Publishes hardcover and paperback original nonfiction (cookbooks, philosophy, health, music, drama, herbs and vegetarianism), fiction (fantasy, European works), and poetry. Publishes 4-5 titles/year; 50% require freelance designers, 20% require freelance illustrators.
First Contact & Terms: Works with 2 freelance artists/year. Prefers local artists, but not mandatory. Works on assignment only. Send query letter with brochure, slides, photostats, tear sheets, photographs or original art as samples to be kept on file; call or write for an appointment to show portfolio. Reports within 1 month. Sometimes returns original work after job's completion. Considers complexity of the project, skill and experience of the artist and project's budget when establishing payment. Buys all rights "for the book involved."
Book Design: Assigns 4-5 jobs/year. Pays by the project, $150-750 average.
Jackets/Covers: Assigns 2 freelance design jobs/year. Pays by the project, $150-500 average.
Text Illustration: Assigns 1-2 jobs/year. Prefers line drawings. Pay varies by the project.

***PAULIST PRESS**, 997 MacArthur Blvd., Mahwah NJ 07430. Specializes in hardcovers, paperbacks and originals—academic theology, philosophy, self-help, inspirational. Publishes 90-100 titles/year.
First Contact & Terms: Works with 20-30 freelance artists/year. "We look for local people. New York City and North New Jersey." Works on assignment only. Send resume, tear sheets, photostats and photocopies. Samples not filed are returned only if requested. Reports only if interested. Original work returned at job's completion "if requested." Considers complexity of project and project's budget when establishing payment. Rights purchased vary according to project.
Book Design: Assigns 5-10 freelance design and 10-12 freelance illustration jobs/year. "With illustrators we often like to work out a royalty arrangement. For design, payment depends on the complexity."
Jackets/Covers: Assigns 9-10 freelance design and 5-10 freelance illustration jobs/year. Pays by the project, $100-250.
Text Illustration: Assigns "very few" jobs/year.
Tips: "We use little or no four-color art inside books. We look for artists with style that can be reproduced as b&w line art."

***PEANUT BUTTER PUBLISHING**, Suite 401, 911 Western Ave., Seattle WA 98104. (206)628-6200. Specializes in paperback regional cookbooks and also specialty cookbooks for people who like to dine in restaurants and try the recipes at home. Publishes 30 titles/year.
First Contact & Terms: Works on assignment only. Send brochure showing art style or tear sheets, photostats and photocopies. Samples not filed are returned only if requested. Reports only if interested. To show a portfolio, mail appropriate materials. Negotiates rights purchased. Payment depends on project.

PELICAN PUBLISHING CO., Box 189, 1101 Monroe St., Gretna LA 70053. (504)368-1175. Production Manager: Sam Buddin. Publishes hardcover and paperback originals and reprints. Publishes 70 titles/year.
First Contact & Terms: Works on assignment only. Send query letter and 3-4 samples. SASE. No samples returned. Reports back on future assignment possibilities. No originals returned at job's completion. Buys complete rights.
Book Design: Assigns variable number of freelance artists. Payment varies.
Jackets/Covers: Assigns variable number of freelance artists. Payment varies.
Text Illustration: Assigns variable number of freelance artists. Payment varies.

PENUMBRA PRESS, 920 S. 38th St., Omaha NE 68105. (319)455-2182. Contact: Bonnie O'Connell. Specializes in limited editions of hand printed books—generally contemporary poetry with graphics or original prints as illustration. Subjects include contemporary poetry, very short fiction, graphics and original prints. Publishes 1-3 titles/year.
First Contact & Terms: Works with 1 artist every 2 years. Works on assignment only. Send query letter with good photocopies of line work, color slides which can be returned; material not suitable for letterpress book production will not be kept on file. Samples not kept on file are returned by SASE or adequate return postage. Reports within 4 weeks. Originals returned to artist at job's completion. Considers complexity of project and skill and experience of artist when establishing payment.

Book Design: Assigns 1-2 freelance illustration jobs/year. Pays by the project.
Text Illustration: Assigns 1-2 freelance jobs/year. Prefers pen & ink, high contrast work, original relief prints, collage and mixed media work. Pays price requested by artist and/or royalty copies.
Tips: "I provide hand printed, hand bound books in limited editions. I see more exciting styles of illustration in mixed media techniques entering fine press books."

PERGAMON PRESS INC., Fairview Park, Elmsford NY 10523. (914)592-7700. Art Department Manager: Angela Langsten. Publishes scientific, technical, scholarly, educational, professional and business books. Publishes 120 titles/year: 5% require freelance designers, 5% require freelance illustrators. Also uses artists for jacket designs, cover designs, text illustrations, advertising design, advertising illustrations and direct mail brochures; 1- and 2-color.
First Contact & Terms: Prefers local artists. Works on assignment only. Call for interview. No originals returned at job's completion. Check for most recent titles in bookstores.
Book Design: "15% of work load goes to outside." Uses artists for design and mechanicals, when necessary. Prefers "scholarly" style. Pays net 90 days.
Tips: There has been a formation of an internal art department. Rarely needs freelance work now.

***PICTURE BOOK STUDIO**, 60 North Main St., Natick MA 01760. Editor: Robert Saunders. Produces children's picture books.
Needs: Publishes 25 books per year with 10-12 illustrations in each.
First Contact & Terms: Send query letter with slides. Samples not filed returned by SASE. Reports within 1 month. "We always must see slides first. Do not call." Originals returned to artist at job's completion. Buys worldwide book rights.
Tips: Artist should "write us for a catalog to see if their work fits. Never call."

***PLAYERS PRESS**, Box 1132, Studio City CA 91604. Associate Editor: Marjorie Clapper. Specializes in childrens books, covers to books, jackets, etc.
First Contact & Terms: Buys up to 300 illustrations/year from freelancers. Works on assignment only. Send query letter with brochure showing art style or resume and samples. Samples not filed are returned by SASE. Reports only if interested. To show a portfolio, mail appropriate materials, which should include thumbnails, original/final art, final reproduction/product, tear sheets, photographs and as much information as possible. Buys all rights. Payment varies.

***PLAYMORE INC. PUBLISHERS**, 1107 Broadway, New York NY 10010. (212)924-7447. President: Robert Horwich. Publishes hardcover and paperback juvenile, adult and mass market originals and reprints. Publishes 50 titles/year; 100% require freelance illustrators.
First Contact & Terms: Send query letter with samples. SASE. Reports in 2 weeks. Negotiates pay for design and illustration.

PLYMOUTH MUSIC CO., INC., 170 NE 33rd St., Ft. Lauderdale FL 33334. (305)563-1844. General Manager: Bernard Fisher. Specializes in paperbacks dealing with all types of music. Publishes 60-75 titles/year; 100% require freelance designers, 100% require freelance illustrators.
First Contact & Terms: Works with 10 freelance artists/year. Artists "must be within our area." Works on assignment only. Send brochure, resume and samples to be kept on file; call for appointment to show portfolio. Samples not kept on file are returned. Reports within 1 week. No originals returned to artist at job's completion. Considers complexity of project when establishing payment. Buys all rights.
Jackets/Covers: Assigns 5 freelance design and 5 freelance illustration jobs/year. Pays by the project.

POCKET BOOKS, Art Department, Simon & Schuster Bldg., 1230 Avenue of the Americas, New York NY 10020. (212)246-2121, ext. 166. Art Director: Bruce Hall. Publishes paperback romance, science fiction, Westerns, young adult, fiction, nonfiction and classics. Publishes 250 titles/year; 80% require freelance illustrators.
First Contact & Terms: Works with 30 freelance artists/year. "We prefer artists who live close enough that they are able to deliver and discuss their work in person. We judge them on their portfolio work. We prefer color illustration." Send brochure/flyer and samples; submit portfolio for review, no appointment necessary. Prefers color slides, transparencies and prints as samples. Samples not kept on file are returned by SASE. Reports in weeks. Works on assignment only. Provide brochure/flyer, samples, tear sheets to be kept on file for possible future assignments. Originals returned to artist at job's completion. Buys all rights.
Jackets/Covers: Assigns 220 freelance illustration jobs/year. Prefers paintings and color washes. Pays by the job, $800-4,000 average.

PORTER SARGENT PUBLISHERS, INC., 11 Beacon St., Boston MA 02108. (617)523-1670. Coordinating Editor: Peter Casey. Specializes in hardcover and paperback originals and reprints of college texts

in the social sciences, particularly political science, sociology and history. Publishes 4-5 titles/year; 20% require freelance designers, 20% require freelance illustrators.
First Contact & Terms: Works with 2-4 freelance artists/year. Local artists only. Works on assignment only. Send query letter with resume, business card and tear sheets to be kept on file; write for appointment to show portfolio. "We are basically looking for samples of dust jacket cover designs." Samples not kept on file returned by SASE. Reports only if interested. No originals returned at job's completion. Considers complexity of project, and skill and experience of artist when establishing payment. Buys all rights.
Jackets/Covers: Assigns 1-2 freelance design jobs/year. Pays by the project, $200 minimum; negotiates.

CLARKSON N. POTTER INC., 1 Park Ave., New York NY 10016. (212)532-9200. Art Director: Gael Towey. Publishes hardbound and paperback books on Americana, fiction, fashion, interior decoration, satire, art, cooking, photographs, life style. Publishes 35 titles/year; 90% require freelance designers, 10% require freelance illustrators.
First Contact & Terms: Prefers minimum of three years' experience, New York location. Send query letter with photocopies or call for an appointment. SASE. Reports within 2 weeks "if we like samples." Buys all rights.
Book Design: Assigns 30 jobs/year. Uses artists for all aspects of the book as a package. Pays $300-800 for jacket design, $450 for simple text design, more for lifestyle photography books, $50 full page illustration and $15-20 for spot illustration.

PRENTICE-HALL, INC., Children's Book Division, Englewood Cliffs NJ 07632. (201)592-2618. Editor-in-Chief and Art Director: Barbara Francis. Specializes in hardcover juvenile trade books. "We specialize in high quality full-color picture books for children aged 4-8." Publishes 30 hardcovers and 15 paperback reprints/year.
First Contact & Terms: Works with 30 freelance artists/year. Send samples to be kept on file. "Follow up with a call or write for an appointment to show portfolio." Prefers tear sheets or photocopies of b&w art. Samples not filed are not returned. Reports only if interested. Original work returned after the job's completion. Considers complexity of the project, skill and experience of artist and project's budget when establishing payment. Buys all book rights.
Text Illustration: Assigns 30 jobs/year. Pays an advance against royalty.

***PRUETT PUBLISHING COMPANY**, 2928 Pearl St., Boulder CO 80301. Project Editor: Jim Pruett. Specializes in hardcovers, paperbacks and originals on western history, outdoor themes, Americana and railroads. Publishes 20 titles/year.
First Contact & Terms: Works with 4-5 freelance artists/year. Prefers local artists. Works on assignment only. Send query letter with brochure showing art style. Samples not filed are returned only if requested. Reports within 10 days. Original work returned at job's completion. Considers complexity of project, skill and experience of artist, project's budget and turnaround time when establishing payment. Rights purchased vary according to project.
Book Design: Assigns 20 freelance design and 0-1 freelance illustration jobs/year. Pays by the hour, 15-25.
Jackets/Covers: Assigns 20 freelance design and 5-10 freelance illustratin jobs/year. Pays by the project $250-450.
Text Illustration: Assigns 0-1 freelance jobs/year. Pays by the project, $75-400.

***PUBLISHERS ASSOCIATES**, Box 160361, Las Colinas TX 75016. (817)478-8564. Chief Operating Officer: Nicholas Lashment. Established 1985. Specializes in paperback originals on feminist/liberal subject. Publishes 10 titles/year.
First Contact & Terms: Works with 3 freelance artists/year. Send query letter with brochure showing art style or photocopies. Samples not filed are returned by SASE only if requested. Reports within 45 days. "Never send original work until requested." Considers skill and experience of artist, project's budget and rights purchased when establishing payment. Buys all rights.
Book Design: Works with 10 freelance designers and 10 freelance illustrators/year. Pays by the project, $50 on up.
Jackets/Covers: Works with 10 freelance desingers and 10 freelance illustrators/year. Pays by the project $50 on up. "We are beginning a medieval series of 200 volumes. We need quality/realistic work for medieval books—primarily on women, some men illustrations."
Text Illustration: Works with 10 freelance artists/year. Prefers line drawings, ink only. Pays by the project $100 on up. "We are in desperate need of artists who can draw men with/without clothing (no porno) in historic settings for our newest press (a division) to be started. Will pay well. Our staff artists currently are capable only in area of women. Need freelance here, too."

Tips: "Never send original work. We do not use cartoons, unless commissioned first. Cartoons are political (liberal) in nature. All other work must be realistic in style. Our primary emphasis is women—we will not accept "Gibson Girl" or "clip art" style work. Historic/period brings top dollars."

***PULSE-FINGER PRESS**, Box 488, Yellow Springs OH 45387. Contact: Orion Roche or Raphaello Farnese. Publishes hardbound and paperback fiction, poetry and drama. Publishes 5-10 titles/year. Also uses artists for advertising design and illustrations. Pays $25 minimum for direct mail promos.
First Contact & Terms: Send query letter. "We can't use unsolicited material." SASE. "Inquiries without SASE will not be acknowledged." Prefers local artists. Works on assignment only. Reports in 6 weeks. Samples returned by SASE; reports back on future assignment possibilities. Send resume to be kept on file for future assignments. Artist supplies overlays for all color artwork. Originals returned to artist at job's completion. Buys first serial and reprint rights.
Jackets/Covers: "Must be suitable to the book involved; artist must familiarize himself with text. We tend to modernist/abstract designs. Try to keep it simple, emphasizing the thematic material of the book." Pays $25-100, b&w jackets, on acceptance.

G.P. PUTNAM'S SONS, (Philomel Books), 51 Madison Ave., New York NY 10010. (212)689-9200. Art Director, Children's Books: Nanette Stevenson. Publishes hardcover and paperback juvenile books. Publishes 100 titles/year.
First Contact & Terms: "We take drop-offs on Tuesday mornings. Please call Alice Groton in advance with the date you want to drop off your portfolio." Originals returned to artist at job's completion. Works on assignment only. Samples returned by SASE. Provide flyer, tear sheet, brochure and photocopy or stat to be kept on file for possible future assignments. Artist often supplies overlays for cover artwork and inside illustrations. Free catalog.
Jackets/Covers: "Full-color paintings, tight style."
Text Illustrations: "A wide cross section of styles for story and picture books."

QUINTESSENCE PUBLICATIONS, 356 Bunker Hill Mine Rd., Amador City CA 95601. (209)267-5470. Proprietor: Marlan Beilke, aka Linomarl. Specializes in letter-press hardcover and paperback originals and reprints on literature, literary criticism, poetry and art history. Publishes 2 titles/year. "Largest linotype museum in the West; hot metal typography specialists."
First Contact & Terms: Works with 1 freelance artist/year. Send query letter with business card and line drawings. Samples not kept on file are returned by SASE. Reports in 1 month. Originals returned to artist at job's completion. Considers project's budget when establishing payment. Negotiates rights purchased.
Book Design: Assigns 1 freelance job/year. Pays by the project.
Jackets/Covers: Assigns 1 freelance illustration job/year. Pays by the project.
Text Illustration: Assigns 1 freelance job/year. Prefers line drawings for letter-press reproduction. Pays by the project.
Tips: Artists should "seek a long-time, cooperative association with flexibility on a number of projects. Line drawings reproduce best in letter-press work." Especially looks for "clean line and crisp detail in samples or a portfolio. Do try to avoid the trendy. We prefer the old look—art nouveau and classic."

RAINTREE PUBLISHERS GROUP, 310 W. Wisconsin Ave., Milwaukee WI 53203. (414)273-0873. Art Director: Suzanne Beck. Specializes in educational material for children. Publishes 40 titles/year; 90% require freelance illustrators.
First Contact & Terms: Works with 12 freelance artists/year. Send samples or submit portfolio for review. Do not call in person. Prefers slides, tear sheets or photocopies as samples. Provide samples to be kept on file for possible future assignments. Samples not kept on file are returned by SASE. Reports in 2-3 weeks. Works on assignment only. Originals sometimes returned to artist at job's completion. Buys all rights.
Jackets/Covers: Assigns 12 illustration jobs/year. Pays by the job, $3,500-5,500 average.
Text Illustrations: Assigns 12 jobs/year. Pays by the job, $2,000-3,500 average.

***RESOURCE PUBLICATIONS INC.**, Suite 290, 160 E. Virginia, San Jose CA 95112. Editorial Director: Kenneth Guensert. Art Director: George F. Collopy. Publishes paperback religious originals. Publishes 12 titles/year. Also uses artists for advertising and production. Assigns 4 advertising jobs/year. Pays $4-25/hour; catalogs, direct mail brochures, letterhead and magazines. Assigns 12-16 production jobs/year. Pays $5-10/hour, paste-up.
First Contact & Terms: Send query letter with samples. SASE. Reports in 6-8 weeks. No advance. Buys all rights. Free catalog.
Book Design: Assigns 1-4/year. Pays $5-25/hour, layout and type spec.
Jackets/Covers: Buys 1-4/year. Pays $45-125, b&w; $50-250, color.

ROSSEL BOOKS, 44 Dunbow Dr., Chappaqua NY 10514. (914)238-8954. President: Seymour Rossel. Specializes in hardcover and paperback originals, reprints and textbooks on Judaism and Jewish culture, adult and juvenile—juvenile fiction historical, mystery, romance and science fiction. Publishes 6-8 titles/year.
First Contact & Terms: Works with 10 freelance artists/year. Artists must have experience in graphic design (covers and illustrations) and book design (text and type design). Works on assignment only. Send query letter with resume and samples (no originals) to be kept on file. Call for appointment to show portfolio. Prefers tear sheets and photocopies (no originals) as samples. Samples not filed are returned by SASE. Reports only if interested. Original work not returned to artist. Considers skill and experience of artist, project's budget and turnaround time when establishing payment. Buys all rights.
Book Design: Assigns 4 jobs/year. Pays by the project, $250-1,000 maximum.
Jackets/Covers: Assigns 6-8 freelance design and 1 freelance illustration job/year. Pays by the project, $250 minimum.
Text Illustration: Assigns 1 job/year. Prefers pen & ink and line illustrations. Pays by the project, $250 minimum.

***ROUNDTABLE PUBLISHING, INC.**, 933 Pico Blvd., Santa Monica CA 90405. (213)450-9777. Publisher: Michel Fattah. Specializes in hardcovers, general fiction and non-fiction, biographics, Hollywood stories, children's books. Publishes 6 titles/year.
First Contact & Terms: Works with 6 freelance artists/year. Works on assignment only. Send query letter with brochure. Samples not filed are returned by SASE if requested. Reports back only if interested. Original work not returned after job's completion. Considers skill and experience of artist and project's budget when establishing payment. Rights purchased vary according to the project.
Book Design: Assigns 2 freelance design and 4 freelance illustration jobs/year. Pays by the project, $50 minimum.
Jackets/Covers: Assigns 6 freelance design and 4-6 freelance illustration jobs/year. Pays by the project, $200 minimum.
Text Illustration: Assigns 1-2 freelance jobs/year. Pays by the project, "no established minimum at this date."
Tips: "We are open to artists just starting out since we are a small publisher and have limited budgets."

ROWAN TREE PRESS, 124 Chestnut St., Boston MA 02108. (617)523-7627. Specializes in paperback originals and reprints on poetry, mystery, juvenile and memoir. Publishes 6 titles/year; 100% require freelance designers, 50% require freelance illustrators.
First Contact & Terms: Area artists only. Send query letter with brochure, resume and samples to be kept on file; call or write for appointment to show portfolio. Prefers photographs as samples. Samples not kept on file are returned by SASE. Reports within 2 months. Works on assignment only. Originals returned to artist at job's completion. Considers complexity of project, skill and experience of artist and project's budget when establishing payment. Negotiates rights purchased. Material not copyrighted.
Jackets/Covers: Assigns 6 freelance design and 2 freelance illustration jobs/year. Pays by the project, $200-300 average.
Text Illustration: Pays by the project, $100 maximum.

ROYAL HOUSE PUBLISHING CO., INC., Book Division of Recipes-of-the-Month Club, 9465 Wilshire Blvd., Box 5027, Beverly Hills CA 90210. (213)277-7220 or 550-7170. Director: Mrs. Harold Klein. Publishes paperbacks on entertaining, humor, sports and cooking. Publishes 3 titles/year. Also uses artists for brochures, ads, letterheads and business forms.
First Contact & Terms: Query with samples; local artists only. SASE. Reports in 4-6 weeks. Purchases outright. No originals returned to artist at job's completion. Works on assignment only. Provide brochure to be kept on file for future assignments. Check for most recent titles in bookstores. Negotiates pay.
Book Design: Assigns 8-12 jobs/year. Uses artists for layout and type spec.
Jackets/Covers: Assigns 8-12 jobs/year. Uses "4-color art; old-fashioned heirloom quality." Buys color washes, opaque watercolors and b&w line drawings.
Text Illustrations: Assigns 8-12 jobs/year. Buys b&w line drawings.

WILLIAM H. SADLIER INC., 11 Park Place, New York NY 10007. (212)227-2120. Art Director: Grace Kao. Publishes hardcover and paperback Catholic adult education, religious, mathematics, social studies and language arts books. Publishes 60 titles/year. Also uses artists for direct mail pieces and catalogs. Pays $12-15/hour or $175-350/job.
First Contact & Terms: Query with samples. SASE. Reports within 2 weeks. Buys all rights.
Book Design: Assigns 40 jobs/year. Uses artists for layout, type spec and mechanicals. Pays $10-15/hour.

Text Illustrations: Assigns 30 jobs/year. Pays $75-200, color washes and opaque watercolors; $60-200, gray opaques, b&w line drawings and washes.

SANTILLANA PUBLISHING CO. INC., 257 Union St., Northvale NJ 07647. (201)767-6961. President: Sam Laredo. Specializes in hardcover and paperback juvenile, textbooks and workbooks. Publishes 20 titles/year.
First Contact & Terms: Works with 5 freelance artists/year. Works on assignment only. Send query letter with brochure, tear sheets or "anything we don't have to return" to be kept on file. Call or write for appointment to show portfolio. Samples not filed are returned by SASE. Reports only if interested. No originals returned to artist at job's completion. Considers skill and experience of artist, project's budget and rights purchased when establishing payment. Buys all rights or negotiates rights purchased.
Text Illustration: All jobs assigned to freelancers. Pays by the project, $200-5,000 average.

***SCHIFFER PUBLISHING, LTD.**, 1469 Morstien Rd., West Chester PA 19380. (215)696-1001. President: P. Schiffer. Specializes in books for collectors and artists.
First Contact & Terms: Works on assignment only. Send query letter with resume and tear sheets, photostats, photocopies, slides and photographs. Samples not filed are returned by SASE. Reports only if interested. Negotiates rights purchased.

SCHOCKEN BOOKS INC., 62 Cooper square, New York NY 10003. (212)475-4900. Production/Art Director: Millicent Fairhurst. Trade and academic, paperback and hardcover publisher. Publishes 50 titles/year; 40% require freelance designers.
First Contact & Terms: Works with 30-40 freelance artists/year. Send query letter with samples to be kept on file; call or write for appointment to show portfolio. Prefers best reproductions possible as samples. Samples not kept on file are returned by SASE. Reports within 10 days. Works on assignment only. Originals returned to artist at job's completion. Considers complexity of project and project's budget when establishing payment. Buys one-time rights.
Book Design: Assigns 15-20 freelance jobs/year. Pays by the hour, $15 minimum; by the project, $350-500 average.
Jackets/Covers: Assigns 15-20 freelance design jobs/year. Pays by the project, $450 minimum.

SCHOLIUM INTERNATIONAL INC., 265 Great Neck Rd., Great Neck NY 11021. (516)466-5181. President: A. L. Candido. Publishes scientific and technical books.
First Contact & Terms: Send photocopies or transparencies. Uses artists for jacket design, direct mail brochures and advertising layouts/art.

***SCOTT, FORESMAN AND CO.**, 1900 E. Lake Ave., Glenview IL 60025. Design Manager: John Mayahara. Specializes in hardcover and paperback originals and reprints on elementary and high school text books for major subject areas. Publishes over 100 titles/year.
First Contact & Terms: Works with over 200 artists/year. Works on assignment only. Send query letter with slides or "any material that can be filed; *no* original art." Samples not filed are returned by SASE. Reports within 1 month. No originals returned to artist at job's completion. Considers complexity of project, skill and experience of artist and project's budget when establishing payment. Buys all rights.

CHARLES SCRIBNER'S SONS, 115 Fifth Ave., New York NY 10003. (212)614-1300. Art Director for adult books: Ruth Kolbert. Art Director for children's books: Vikki Sheatsley. "Send in nonreturnable samples of work (machine copies OK) before calling for appointment."
Needs: Uses illustrators for jacket designs and inside illustrations. Pays $650 for "mainly full-color jacket illustration for young adult novels." Adult book division uses illustrators and graphic designers for trade and paperback jackets and covers. Uses some freelance book designers for interior design.
Tips: "We have a very large list, and prices vary, types of illustration and design vary as well."

SEVEN SEAS PRESS, 2 D Ave., Newport RI 02840. (401)849-9610. Editor: Jim Gilbert. Specializes in hardcover and paperback originals of nautical subject matter. Publishes 12 titles/year; 25% require freelance illustrators.
First Contact & Terms: Works with 7-10 freelance artists/year. "Marine illustrating experience necessary. Our requirements generally are for technical illustrations." Send resume, samples and/or tear sheets to be kept on file; write for appointment to show portfolio. Prefers photostats as samples. Samples not kept on file are returned only if requested. Reports only if interested. Originals returned to artist at job's completion. Considers complexity of project, skill and experience of artist, project's budget, turnaround time and rights purchased when establishing payment. Negotiates rights purchased.
Book Design: "All book design done inhouse."
Jackets/Covers: Assigns 12 freelance design and 12+ freelance illustration jobs/year. Pays by the project, $500-1,200 average.

Text Illustration: Assigns 12+ freelance jobs/year. Prefers line drawings, mechanical. Pays $35 minimum/illustration.
Tips: "A superb technical illustration, to me, is one that presents the complex clearly and at the same time does not threaten those who may be inclined to be put off by technical subject matter. Besides ability, the next most important criterion for an artist is setting and meeting deadlines."

SHARON PUBLICATIONS, EDREI COMMUNICATIONS, 1086 Teaneck Rd., Teaneck NJ 07666. (201)569-5055. Art Director in Chief: Paul Castori. Publishes Star books, Sharon Romances for teens, Bambi Classic series for 10-12 year olds, board books for toddlers, coloring books, and more. Also publishes music entertainment and teen oriented magazines (see D.S. Magazines listing in Magazines section).
First Contact & Terms: Send query letter with brochure, resume, business card and samples to be kept on file; call for appointment to show portfolio. Accepts photostats, photographs, photocopies, slides or tear sheets as samples. Samples not filed returned only by SASE. Reports only if interested. Payment varies according to project; "we have a wide range." Considers the complexity of project, how work will be used and turnaround time. Pays on publication.
Needs: Works with 5 freelance artists/year. Uses artists for brochure layout, product illustrations, paste-up and mechanicals.

HAROLD SHAW PUBLISHERS, Box 567, 388 Gundersen Dr., Wheaton IL 60189. (312)665-6700. General Manager and Vice President: Steve Board. Production Manager: Joyce Schram. Publishes original cloth and paperback Christian literature for adults, Bible study guides for adults and teens and literary criticism series. Publishes 20-25 titles/year; 10% require freelance designers; 10% require freelance illustrators.
First Contact & Terms: Local artists only; must be experienced. Query with samples. Reports in 3-4 weeks. Usually buys one-time rights. Works on assignment only. Samples returned by SASE. Provide resume, brochure and one or two samples to be kept on file for future assignments. Check for most recent titles in bookstores. Negotiates pay.
Book Design: Assigns 2-3 jobs/year. Uses artists for layout, type spec and covers. Pays by the project.
Jackets/Covers: Assigns 2-3 jobs/year. Buys photographs and b&w line drawings. Pays for design and illustration by the project.
Text Illustrations: Assigns 2 jobs/year. Buys b&w line drawings. Pays by the project.
Tips: "Be acquainted with our full line of books; show samples already published."

SIERRA CLUB BOOKS, 730 Polk St., San Francisco CA 94109. Publisher: Jon Beckmann. Editorial Director: Daniel Moses. Design Director: Eileen Max. Publishes books on natural history, science, ecology, conservation issues and related themes, calendars and guides.
First Contact & Terms: Send query letter with resume, tear sheets and/or business card to be kept on file.
Needs: Uses artists for book design and illustration (maps, juvenile art) and jacket design. Pays by the project, $450-700 for book design. Pays by the project, $450-1,000 for jacket/cover design; $175-500 for jacket/cover illustration; $1,000-2,000 average for text illustration. Buys US or world rights.

***SILVER BURDETT CO.**, 250 James St., Morristown NJ 07690. (201)285-8104. Designer: Carolyn Meeker. Specializes in elementary and high school text books.

***SINAUER ASSOCIATES, INC.**, North Main St., Sunderland MA 01375. (413)665-3722. Production Manager/Art Director: Joseph J. Vesely. Specializes in hardcover and paperback originals on biology, neurology, immunology and sociology. Publishes 8 titles/year.
First Contact & Terms: Works with 3 freelance artists/year. Works on assignment only. "Certainly we only buy art that we've assigned to artists for the text of our books but we may (seldom) buy rights to use something striking for a book cover." Send query letter with brochure showing art style or resume, tear sheets, photostats or photocopies, slides and photographs. Samples not filed are returned only if requested. Reports only if interested. No originals returned to artist at job's completion "unless requested and agreed to." Considers complexity of project, project's budget, turnaround time and quality of the artwork when establishing payment. Rights purchased vary according to project.
Book Design: Assigns 2 freelance design and 4 freelance illustration jobs/year. Pays by the project, $250-500.
Jackets/Covers: Assigns 2 freelance design jobs/year. Pays by the project, $150-300.
Text Illustration: Assigns 4 freelance jobs/year. Prefers "graphs and charts with sharp, clean, thin lines, usually on film (mylar or acetate), generally stippling for other jobs." Pays by the hour, $12-25.
Tips: "Forget about 'fine art' renderings. Our major requirement is for efficient creation of charts and graphs in simple line renderings, with well-defined lines, clean corners, and accuracy."

SINGER COMMUNICATIONS, INC., 3164 Tyler Ave., Anaheim CA 92801. (714)527-5650. Contact: Natalie Carlton. Licenses paperback originals and reprints; mass market, Western, romance, doctor/nurse, mystery, science fiction, nonfiction and biographies. Licenses 200 titles/year through affiliates, 95% require freelance designers for book covers. Also buys 3,000 cartoons/year to be internationally syndicated to newspaper and magazine publishers—also used for topical books. Pays 50% of fee received.
First Contact & Terms: Send query letter with photocopies and tear sheets to be kept on file. Do not send original work. Material not filed is returned by SASE. Reports in 2 weeks. Buys first and reprint rights. Originals returned to artist at job's completion. Artist's guidelines $1.
Book Design: Assigns "many" jobs/year. Uses artists for reprints for world market. Prefers clean, clear uncluttered style.
Jackets/Covers: Popular styles include Western, romance, mystery, science fiction/fantasy, war and gothic. "We are only interested in color transparencies for paperbacks." Duplicates only. Offers advance.
Tips: "Study the market. Study first the best seller list, the current magazines, the current paperbacks and then come up with something better if possible or something new. We now utilize old sales for reprint." Looking for "new ideas, imagination, uniqueness. Every artist is in daily competition with the best artists in the field. A search for excellence helps. We get hundreds of medical cartoons, hundreds of sex cartoons. We are overloaded with cartoons showing inept office girls but seldom get cartoons on credit cards, senior management, aerobics, fitness, romance. We have plenty on divorce, but few on nice romance and love. We would like more positive and less negative humor. Can always use good travel cartoons around the world."

***SOUTH END PRESS**, 116 Botolph St., Boston MA 02115. (617)266-0629. Contact: Editorial Department. Specializes in hardcover and paperback books on contemporary problems, alternatives to oppression, movements for change. Publishes 15 titles/year. Uses artists for jacket/cover illustration.
First Contact & Terms: Works with varying number of freelance artists/year. "Artist must read the book and understand theme of leftist issues." Send samples of jacket covers of similar books. Prefers photostats as samples. Negotiates payment arrangement with artist.

STANDARD PUBLISHING, 8121 Hamilton Ave., Cincinnati OH 45231. Advertising Manager: John Weidner. Art Director: Frank Sutton. Publishes religious, self-help and children's books.
First Contact & Terms: Artists with at least 4 years' experience. Send query letter with business card to be kept on file. SASE. Reports in 2 weeks. Buys all rights. Free catalog.
Needs: Art director uses artists for illustrations only. Advertising manager uses artists for advertising, books, catalogs, convention exhibits, decorative spots, direct mail brochures, letterheads, magazines, packages and posters.

***STAR PUBLISHING**, Box 68, Belmont CA 94002. Managing Editor: Stuart Hoffman. Specializes in original paperbacks and textbooks. Publishes 16 titles/year.
First Contact & Terms: Works with 10 artists/year. Send query letter with resume, tear sheets and photocopies. Samples not filed are returned only if requested. Reports back only if interested. Original work returned after job's completion "if arrangements are made." Rights purchased vary according to project but does buy one-time rights.
Book Design: Assigns 3 freelance design and 4 freelance illustration jobs/year. Pays by the project.
Jackets/Covers: Assigns 3 freelance design and 3 freelance illustration jobs/year. Pays by the project.
Text Illustration: Assigns 3 freelance jobs/year.

STEIN AND DAY, Scarborough House, Briarcliff Manor NY 10510. Art Director: Janice Rossi. Publishes hardcover, paperback, original and reprint mass market fiction and nonfiction. Publishes 100 titles/year; 10% require freelance designers, 20% require freelance cover illustrators.
First Contact & Terms: Prefers local artists with experience with other publishers, but young unpublished artists are welcome to submit. Send query letter with brochure showing art style or resume and nonreturnable samples. Especially looks for clean, smooth art, good color design and layout; also a variety of technical skills. SASE. Works on assignment only. Reports back on future assignment possibilities. Portfolios accepted at Westchester office for review. Artist provides overlays for color covers. Buys all rights. Negotiates pay for unused assigned work. Pays on publication. Free catalog.
Jackets/Covers: Assigns 15 freelance design and 25 illustration jobs/year. Pays by the project, $500-1,200 average; mass market cover illustration, $700-1,500 average.
Text Illustrations: Assigns 3-5 jobs/year. Pays by the project, $150-500 average. "We use very little text illustration but on occasion we require maps or b&w line drawings."
Tips: "Art today seems to reflect the style of today. Bold colors, bizarre subject matter, futuristic at times. In publishing, books are selling by covers. The most enticing and interesting jackets are selling the books. I see more of a mass market treatment being given to hardcover jackets."

STEMMER HOUSE PUBLISHERS, INC., 2627 Caves Rd., Owings Mills MD 21117. (301)363-3690. President: Barbara Holdridge. Specializes in hardcover and paperback fiction, nonfiction, art books, juvenile and design resource originals. Publishes 20 titles/year; 50% require freelance designers, 75% require freelance illustrators.
First Contact & Terms: Works with 10 freelance artists/year. Works on assignment only. Send brochure/flyer, tear sheets, photocopies or color slides to be kept on file; submission must include SASE; do not send original work. Material not filed is returned by SASE. Call or write for appointment to show portfolio. Reports in 6 weeks. Works on assignment only. Originals returned to artist at job's completion on request. Negotiates rights purchased.
Book Design: Assigns 1 freelance design and 5 illustration jobs/year. Uses artists for design. Pays by the project, negotiable amount.
Jackets/Covers: Assigns 12 freelance design jobs/year. Prefers paintings. Pays by the project, $300 minimum.
Text Illustration: Assigns 12 jobs/year. Prefers full-color artwork for text illustrations. Pays by the project on a royalty basis.
Tips: "We are seeing more black-and-white illustrations. It is more difficult to find good book designs in our area."

STONE WALL PRESS INC., 1241 30th St. NW, Washington DC 20007. Publisher: Henry Wheelwright. Publishes paperback and hardcover environmental, backpacking, fishing, beginning and advanced outdoor originals, also medical. Publishes 2-4 titles/year; 10% require freelance illustrators.
First Contact & Terms: Prefers artists who are accessible. Works on assignment only. Send query letter with resume and brochure to be kept on file. Samples returned by SASE. Reports in 2 weeks. Buys one-time rights. Originals returned to artist at job's completion.
Book Design: Assigns 1 job/year. Uses artists for composition, layout, jacket design. Prefers generally realistic style—photo, color or b&w. Artist supplies overlays for cover artwork. Pays cash upon accepted art.
Text Illustrations: Buys b&w line drawings.

*****SWORDSMAN PRESS**, Suite 10, 15445 Ventura Blvd., Sherman Oaks CA 91413. (213)342-1422. President: Bob Monaco. Specializes in paperbacks on music. Publishes 2 titles/year.
First Contact & Terms: Works with 3 freelance artists/year. Local artists only. Send query letter with resume and photostats to be kept on file. Samples not kept on file are returned by SASE. Reports only if interested. Call or write for appointment to show portfolio. Originals returned to artist at job's completion. Considers complexity of project and project's budget when establishing payment. Buys all rights.

TEN SPEED PRESS, Box 7123, Berkeley CA 94707. (415)845-8414. Editorial Director: Phil Wood. Publishes hardcover and paperback cookbook, history, sports, gardening, career and life planning originals and reprints. Publishes 50 titles/year. Assigns 15 advertising jobs/year. Pays $1,500 maximum/job, catalogs; $1,000 maximum/job, direct mail brochures.
First Contact & Terms: Submit query. Reports within 4 weeks. Works on assignment only. Samples returned by SASE. Provide resume, flyer and/or sample art which may be kept on file for future assignments. Buys all rights, but may reassign rights to artist after publication. Pays flat fee. Offers advance. Pays promised fee for unused assigned work. Free catalog.
Book Design: Assigns 20 jobs/year. Pays by the hour, $20 minimum; by the project, $200 minimum.
Jackets/Covers: Assigns 50 freelance design and 20 freelance illustration jobs/year. Pays by the hour, $20 minimum; by the project, $200 minimum.
Text Illustrations: Assigns 20 jobs/year. Pay varies.

*****TEXAS MONTHLY PRESS**, Box 1569, Austin TX 78767. (512)476-7085. Design & Production Director: Cathy S. Casey. Specializes in hardcover and paperback originals and reprints on general trade books. Publishes 25-28 titles/year.
First Contact & Terms: Works with 15 freelance artists/year. Works on assignment only. Send resume, tear sheets and photostats. Samples not filed are returned only if requested. Reports within 3 weeks. Originals returned at job's completion. Considers complexity of project and project's budget when establishing payment. Buys first rights.
Book Design: Assign 25-28 freelance design and 3 freelance illustration jobs/year. Pays by the project, $350-1,000.
Jackets/Covers: Assigns 25-28 freelance design and 3 freelance illustration jobs/year. Pays by the project, $350-1,200.
Text Illustration: Assigns 2 freelance jobs/year. Pays by the project, $200-500.

*****THORNDIKE PRESS**, Box 159, Thorndike ME 04986. (207)948-2962. Senior Editor: Tim Loeb. Specializes in hardcover and paperback originals and reprints—large print books for the visually impaired. Publishes 136 titles/year.

First Contact & Terms: Works with 15-18 freelance artists/year. Prefers local artists. "Demand experience in preparation of mechanicals for four-color process." Works on assignment only. Send query letter with tear sheets and slides. Samples not filed returned by SASE. Reports only if interested. Considers project's budget when establishing payment. Rights purchased vary according to project.
Book Design: Assigns 12 freelance design jobs and 6 freelance illustration jobs/year. Payment is negotiable.
Jackets/Covers: Works with 16 freelance designers/year. Pays by the project, negotiable amount.
Text Illustration: Works with 6 freelance artists/year. Prefers pen & ink. Payment is negotiable.
Tips: "We are looking for artists/designers who have experience in four-color process on the trade book publishing level; textbook or magazine experience is *not* sufficient in most cases."

THUNDER'S MOUTH PRESS, Box 780, New York NY 10025. (212)595-2025. President: Neil Ortenberg. Specializes in hardcovers and paperbacks of poetry, plays and translations; fiction—ethnic, science fiction, historical and humorous. Publishes 6 titles/year; 100% require freelance designers, 25% require freelance illustrators.
First Contact & Terms: Works with 10 freelance artists/year. Works on assignment only. Send query letter with brochure and resume to be kept on file. Samples not kept on file are returned by SASE. Reports within 2 months. Originals returned to artist at job's completion. Write for appointment to show portfolio. Considers complexity of project, skill and experience of artist, and project's budget when establishing payment. Buys one-time rights.
Book Design: Assigns 6 freelance jobs/year. Pays by the hour.

TOR BOOKS, 49 W. 24th St., New York NY 10018. Editor-in-Chief: Beth Meacham. Specializes in hardcover and paperback originals and reprints: espionage, thrillers, horror, mysteries and science fiction. Publishes 180 titles/year; heavy on science fiction.
First Contact & Terms: All covers are freelance. Works on assignment only. Send query letter with color photographs, slides or tearsheets to be kept on file "unless unsuitable"; call for appointment to show portfolio. Samples not filed are returned by SASE. Reports only if interested. Original work returned after job's completion. Considers skill and experience of artist, and project's budget when establishing payment. "We buy the right to use art on all editions of book it is commissioned for and in promotion of book."
Jackets/Covers: Assigns 180 freelance illustration jobs/year. Pays by the project, $500 minimum.

TRADO-MEDIC BOOKS, division of Conch Magazine Ltd., Publishers, 102 Normal Ave., Buffalo NY 14213. (716)885-3686. Managing Editor: Lynda S. Anozie. Publishes hardcover and paperback originals on health, medicine and culture in the Third World, Africa in particular. Publishes 10 titles/year. Also uses artists for catalog, letterhead and envelope design and brochure illustrations. Themes include Africa, traditional medicine of all kinds, botany, etc. Pays $25-50/job, b&w or color. Free catalog if available.
First Contact & Terms: Send query letter with brochure showing art style or resume and "as wide a variety of samples as the artist has; tear sheets preferred to originals." Artist should be professional, with a feel for African local color. Works on assignment only. Reports within 2 weeks. Buys all rights. No originals returned at job's completion. Samples returned by SASE. Reports back on future assignment possibilities. Artist supplies overlays for all color artwork.
Book Design: Assigns 4/year. Themes include Africa, traditional medicine of all kinds, botany, etc. Pays $25-50/job, layout.
Jackets/Covers: Assigns 4/year. Pays $25-50, b&w line drawings, gray opaques and 2-color designs.
Text Illustrations: Buys over 1,000/year. Also uses cartoons. Number cartoons bought/year varies. Themes include Africa, traditional medicine of all kinds, botany, etc. Pays $25-50, b&w line drawings, gray opaques and 2-color designs.

TROLL ASSOCIATES, Book Division, 320 Rt. 17, Mahwah NJ 07430. Vice President: Marian Schecter. Specializes in hardcover and paperbacks for juveniles 5 to 15 years. Publishes 100 + titles/year; 30% require freelance designers and illustrators.
First Contact & Terms: Works with 30 freelance artists/year. Send query letter with brochure/flyer or resume and samples. Prefers photostats or photocopies as samples. Samples "usually" returned by SASE. Reports in 3 weeks. Works on assignment only. Originals "usually not" returned to artist at job's completion. Negotiates all rights.

TROUBADOR PRESS INC., Suite 205, 1 Sutter St., San Francisco CA 94104. (415)397-3716. Editorial Director: Malcolm K. Whyte. Publishes mostly children's paperback project and activity books (coloring, cut-out, maze, puzzle, and paperdoll books), also science fiction/fantasy. Publishes 4-6 titles/year.

First Contact & Terms: Send query letter with resume, tear sheets and copies of b&w art outline of work. SASE must accompany submissions. Reports in 4 weeks. Originals returned to artist at job's completion, upon request. Check most recent titles in toy, art supply and bookstores for current style. All rights may be purchased or royalty contract arranged. Pays 4-6% royalty. Offers advance. Pays promised fee for unused assigned work. Catalog and artist's guidelines for SASE with 39¢ postage.
Needs: Uses artists for design and illustrations for coloring, game, cut-out books and some art books. Pays $25-100/illustration.
Tips: "Study our existing books in print for style, quality and interest range before sending material. See that it *fits* the publisher."

***TURRET PUBLISHING**, 5346 N. Enid, Azusa CA 91702. President: Mitch Persons. Specializes in paperbacks of juvenile fiction. Publishes 3 titles/year; 100% require freelance designers and freelance illustrators.
First Contact & Terms: Works with varied number of freelance artists/year. Send query letter with samples to be kept on file; write for appointment to show portfolio. Samples not kept on file are returned by SASE. Reports within 2 months. Works on assignment only. Originals returned to artist at job's completion. Considers project's budget when establishing payment. Negotiates rights purchased.
Book Design: Assigns 1 freelance job/year. Pays by the project.
Jackets/Covers: Assigns 1 freelance design and 1 freelance illustration job/year. Pays by the project.
Text Illustration: Assigns 1 freelance job/year. Pays by the project.

TYNDALE HOUSE PUBLISHERS, 336 Gundersen Dr., Wheaton IL 60189. (312)668-8300. Art Director: Tim Botts. Publishes hardcover and paperback originals and reprints on Christian beliefs, family, Bible study, missions, wholesome fiction, contemporary issues for adult and juveniles; also Bible products. Publishes 100 titles/year; 25% require freelance illustrators; "design is handled inhouse." Uses artists for *The Christian Reader* magazine, and *Have a Good Day* leaflet. Also buys 25 cartoons/year. Payment: $50 and up, b&w; $75 and up, color.
First Contact & Terms: Works with 20-30 freelance illustrators/year. Artists must be able to meet deadlines. Send brochure/flyer and samples, preferably 8½x11", to be kept on file. "We only want to see an illustrator's best work, so quality is more important than quantity." Samples not returned. Reports only if interested. Publisher retains original art unless otherwise negotiated.
Book Design: "Nearly all of this work is done inhouse." Uses artists for total design only by special agreement with some authors.
Jackets/Covers: Assigns 25 freelance illustration jobs/year. Various media used; style is according to subject matter of book. Pays by the job, $100 and up, b&w; $400 and up, full-color cover illustration.
Text Illustrations: Assigns 25-30 jobs/year. Medium and style vary according to subject matter and budget available for reproduction. Pays by the job, $50 and up, b&w; $100 and up, color.
Tips: Especially looks for "an artist's ability to tell a story visually. I would rather see three or four samples than one to give me a better sense of the artist's consistency. Successful illustrators seem to be those who come to a manuscript with an open mind and then faithfully communicate what they find."

UNDERWOOD-MILLER, 651 Chestnut St., Columbia PA 17512. (717)684-7335. Publisher: Chuck Miller. Specializes in hardcover originals and reprints on science fiction, fantasy, romance and popular literature. Publishes 12-20 titles/year.
First Contact & Terms: Works with 5 freelance artists/year. Works on assignment only. Send query letter with photostats, photos and tearsheets (not original art) to be kept on file. Samples not filed are returned by SASE. Reports only if interested. Original work returned to artist. Considers complexity of project, project's budget and rights when establishing payment. Usually buys one-time rights, but can vary according to project.
Book Design: Assigns 2 jobs/year. Pays by the project, $250 minimum.
Jackets/Covers: Assigns 15 freelance illustration jobs/year. Pays by the project, $250 minimum.
Text Illustration: Assigns 4 jobs/year. Prefers b&w line drawings. Pays by the project, $250 minimum.

***THE UNICORN PUBLISHING HOUSE, INC.**, 1148 Parsippany Blvd., Parsippany NJ 07054. (201)334-0353. Associate Editor: Heidi K.L. Corso. Specializes in original and reprint hardcovers, especially juvenile, issue-oriented, music books. Publishes 14 titles/year.
First Contact & Terms: Works with 8 freelance artists/year. Send query letter with brochure, resume, tear sheets and photocopies. Samples not filed are returned by SASE. Reports back within 3 months. Original work returned after job's completion. Considers complexity of project, experience of artist, and project's budget when establishing payment. Negotiates rights purchased.
Book Design: Assigns 5 freelance design and 8 freelance illustration jobs/year. Pays by the project "payment depends on job."

Text Illustration: Assigns 8 jobs/year. "No preference in medium—art must be detailed and realistic." Pays by the project, "depends on the number of pieces being illustrated."
Tips: "Send duplicates. No work returned without a SASE."

UNION OF AMERICAN HEBREW CONGREGATIONS, 838 5th Ave., New York NY 10021. (212)249-0100. Director of Publications: Stuart L. Benick. Produces books, filmstrips and magazines for Jewish school children and adult education. Free catalog.
First Contact & Terms: Send samples or write for interview. SASE. Reports within 3 weeks. Pays $50-200, illustrations.
Needs: Buys book covers and illustrations.

UNIVELT INC., Box 28130, San Diego CA 92128. (619)746-4005. Manager: H. Jacobs. Publishes hardcover and paperback originals on astronautics and related fields; occasionally publishes science fiction/fantasy. Publishes 10 titles/year; all have illustrations.
First Contact & Terms: Prefers local artists. Works on assignment only. Send query letter with resume, business card and/or flyer to be kept on file. Samples not filed are returned by SASE. Reports in 4 weeks on unsolicited submissions. Buys one-time rights. Originals returned to artist at job's completion. Artist supplies overlays for cover artwork. Free catalog.
Book Design: Assigns 10 jobs/year. Uses artists for covers, title sheets, dividers, occasionally a few illustrations. Pays $50-100/book design; also per assignment.
Tips: "Designs have to be space-related."

UNIVERSITY OF IOWA PRESS, University of Iowa, Iowa City IA 52242. Director: Paul Zimmer. Publishes scholarly works and short fiction series. Publishes 20 titles/year; 15 require freelance scholarly book designers, 2 require freelance illustrator or photographer.
First Contact & Terms: "We use freelance book designers." Query with "two or three samples; originals not required." Works on assignment only. Samples returned by SASE. Check for most recent titles in bookstores. Free catalog.
Book Design: Assigns 15 freelance jobs/year, 250 to draw specifications and prepare layouts. Pays $300 minimum, book design; $250, jacket.

UNIVERSITY OF NEBRASKA PRESS, 901 N. 17th St., Lincoln NE 68588-0520. (402)472-3581. Production Manager: Debra K. Turner. Publishes hardcover and paperback books on Western and literary history. Buys 5 designs/year.
First Contact & Terms: Send query letter with brochure showing art style and 4-5 tear sheets. Buys various rights. Originals returned to artist at job's completion. Works on assignment only. No samples returned. Check for most recent titles in bookstores. Negotiates pay for unused assigned work. Pays on acceptance.
Book Design: Pays by the project, $200-500 average.
Jackets/Covers: Pays for design by the project, $100-200 average; pays for illustration by the project, $100-250 average.
Text Illustration: Pays by the project, $30-60; "varies widely."
Tips: "Be familiar with the best of university press publishing by examining catalogs of the American Association of University Press Book Show, an annual event."

THE UNIVERSITY OF WISCONSIN PRESS, 114 N. Murray St., Madison WI 53715. (608)262-4978. Production Manager: Gardner R. Wills. Publishes scholarly hardcover and paperback books. Publishes 40-50 titles/year; 85% require freelance designers.
First Contact & Terms: Works on assignment only. Query first. Reports in 2 weeks. Buys all rights. No originals returned to artist at job's completion. Samples returned by SASE. Reports back on future assignment possibilities. Provide letter of inquiry and samples as agreed upon to be kept on file. Check for most recent titles in bookstores. Designer supplies overlays for cover artwork. No advance.
Book Design: Assigns 20-25/year. Pays upon completion of design. Pays by the project, $200-300 average.
Jackets/Covers: Assigns 30-40 freelance design and 2 freelance illustration jobs/year. Pays for design by the project, $175-250, average; b&w line drawings, washes, halftones and color-separated work "only if part of the jacket/cover design package. We do not purchase individual items of art."

VITACHART, INC., 3446 Fort Independent St., Bronx NY 10463. (212)796-7413. President: Carolyn West. Specializes in nutrition and health charts. Publishes 1 title/year. Uses artists for layout and design plus spot drawings of herbs, foods.
First Contact & Terms: Works with 1 freelance artist/year. Greater New York City area artists only. Send photostats and tear sheets. Negotiates payment arrangement with artist. Especially needs mechanical artists.

J. WESTON WALCH, PUBLISHER, Box 658, Portland ME 04104-0658. (207)772-2846. Managing Editor: Richard Kimball. Specializes in supplemental secondary school materials including books, poster sets, filmstrips and computer software. Publishes 120 titles/year.
First Contact & Terms: Works with 20 freelance artists/year. Works on assignment only. Send query letter with resume and samples to be kept on file unless the artist requests return. Write for artists' guidelines. Prefers photostats as samples. Samples not filed are returned only by request. Reports within 6 weeks. Original work not returned to the artist after job's completion. Considers project's budget when establishing payment. Rights purchased vary according to project.
Jackets/Covers: Assigns 20 freelance design and 20 freelance illustration jobs/year. Pays by the project, $100 minimum.
Text Illustration: Assigns 10 freelance jobs/year. Prefers b&w pen & ink. Pays by the project, $100 minimum.

WALKER & COMPANY, 720 Fifth Ave., New York NY 10019. (212)265-3632. Cable address: REKLAWSAM. Art Director: Laurie McBarnette. Publishes hardcover originals and reprints on mysteries, regency romance, children's science, adult trade, etc. Publishes 200 titles/year; 60% require freelance designers, 80% require freelance illustrators. Also uses artists for catalog design and layout (educational).
First Contact & Terms: Works with 20-30 freelance artists/year. Illustrators must be within 2 hours of New York; designers must have textbook experience. Works on assignment only. Send business card and samples to be filed. Prefers any sample except slides. Samples are returned by SASE. Reports only if interested. Buys all rights. Originals returned to artist at job's completion (except in special instances).
Book Design: Assigns 7 jobs/year. Uses freelance artists for complete follow-through on job, layout, type spec. Prefers classic style—modern conservative. Pays by the hour, $7.50-15 average, or by the project $200-600 average 60 days upon completion.
Jackets/Covers: Assigns 40 freelance illustration jobs/year. Pays by the project, $100 minimum.
Text Illustration: Assigns 3 freelance jobs/year. Prefers b&w line drawings or pencil. Pays by the project $500 minimum.

***WARNER BOOKS INC.**, 666 Fifth Ave., New York NY 10103. (212)484-3151. Art Director: Jackie Meyer. Publishes 400 titles/year; 20% require freelance designers, 80% require freelance illustrators.
First Contact & Terms: Works on assignment only. Query or call. Buys first rights. Originals returned to artist at job's completion (artist must pick up). Provide tear sheets to be kept on file for future assignments. Check for most recent titles in bookstores.
Jackets/Covers: Uses realistic jacket illustrations. Payment subject to negotiation.
Tips: Industry trends include "more graphics and stylized art. Looks for "photorealistic style with imaginative and original design and use of eyecatching color variations." Artists shouldn't "talk too much. Good design and art should speak for themselves."

WESTBURG ASSOC., PUBLISHERS, 1745 Madison St., Fennimore WI 53809. (608)822-6237. Editor/Publisher: John Westburg. Specializes in paperback originals of essays, criticism, short fiction, poetry, in the fields of literature and humanities. Publishes 1-3 titles/year.
First Contact & Terms: Works with 3-5 freelance artists/year. Send query letter with brochure and business card to be kept on file. Do not send samples until requested; do not send original work. Samples not filed are returned by SASE. No originals returned at job's completion. Considers project's budget when establishing payment. Buys all rights or negotiates rights purchased.
Jackets/Covers: Assigns 1-3 freelance design and illustration jobs/year. Pays by the project, $25-50 average.
Text Illustration: Assigns 1 + freelance illustration jobs/year. Prefers b&w line drawings. Pays by the project, $25-50 average.

WHITCOULLS PUBLISHERS, Private Bag, Christchurch, New Zealand, 794580. Art Director: Tonni Wojtas. Specializes in hardcover and paperback originals. Publishes 30-35 titles/year.
First Contact & Terms: Works with approximately 8 freelance artists/year. Works on an assignment basis only. Send query letter with business card and samples to be kept on file. Call or write for appointment to show portfolio. Prefers photostats, photographs and tear sheets as samples. Samples not filed are returned only if requested by artist. Reports back to the artist only if interested. Original work returned to the artist after the job's completion. Considers project's budget when establishing payment. Purchases all rights.
Jackets/Covers: Assigns approximately 4 freelance illustration jobs/year. Pays by the project.
Text Illustration: Assigns 2-3 freelance jobs/year. Pays by the project.

WHITE EAGLE PUBLISHER, Dept. A-0111, Box 1332, Lowell MA 01853. President: Jack Loisel. Specializes in paperbacks on religion and poetry. Publishes 5 titles/year; 100% require freelance designers, 100% require freelance illustrators.

First Contact & Terms: Works with 7 freelance artists/year. Artists should have experience. Send query letter with brochure or photographs and photostats to be kept on file. Reports only if interested. Works on assignment only. No originals returned to artist at job's completion. Considers complexity of project and project's budget when establishing payment. Buys one-time or all rights. Material not copyrighted.
Book Design: Assigns 5 freelance jobs/year. Pays by the project, $500 minimum.
Jackets/Covers: Assigns 5 freelance design and 10 freelance illustration jobs/year. Pays by the project, $400 minimum.
Text Illustration: Assigns 2 freelance jobs/year. Pays by the project, $300 minimum.

ALBERT WHITMAN & COMPANY, 5747 W. Howard St., Niles IL 60648. Editor: Kathleen Tucker. Specializes in hardcover original juvenile fiction and nonfiction—many picture books for young children. Publishes 21 titles/year; 100% require freelance illustrators.
First Contact & Terms: Works with 18 freelance artists/year. Prefers working with artists who have experience illustrating juvenile trade books. Works on assignment only. Send brochure/flyer or resume and "a few slides and photocopies of original art and tear sheets that we can keep in our files. Do *not* send original art through the mail." Samples not returned. Reports to an artist if "we have a project that seems right for him. We like to see evidence that an artist can show the same children in a variety of moods and poses." Original work returned to artist at job's completion "if artist holds the copyright." Rights purchased vary.
Cover/Text Illustration: Cover assignment is usually part of illustration assignment. Assigns 18 jobs/year. Prefers realistic art. Pays by flat fee or royalties.
Tips: Especially looks for "an artist's ability to draw people, especially children."

***WILLIAMS & WILKINS**, (formerly Nuresco, Inc.), Suite 105, 984 Monument, Pacific Palisades CA 90272. (213)454-6597. Production Editor: Nora Galvin. Specializes in books for nurses. "We have 23 books in production now."
First Contact & Terms: Buys 2-20 illustrations/book from freelancers. Works on assignment only. Prefers technical (medical) themes, except for covers. Send query letter with brochure showing art style or resume and photocopies. Samples not filed are returned by SASE. Reports back. Call or write to schedule an appointment to show a portfolio. Buys all rights. Pays on acceptance.

WILSHIRE BOOK CO., 12015 Sherman Rd., North Hollywood CA 91605. (213)875-1711 or (818)983-1105. President: Melvin Powers. Publishes paperback reprints on psychology, self-help, inspirational and other types of nonfiction. Publishes 25 titles/year.
First Contact & Terms: Local artists only. Call. Buys first, reprint or one-time rights. Negotiates pay. Free catalog.
Jackets/Covers: Assigns 25 jobs/year. Buys b&w line drawings.

WINSTON PRESS, 600 First Ave. North, Minneapolis MN 55403. (612)338-3000. Contact: Art Department with book jacket design and with photographs or illustrations. Specializes in paper originals. Pubilshes approximately 100 titles/year.
First Contact & Terms: Works on assignment only. Send slides or samples of work and SASE.
Book Design: Assigns 3 freelance design and 12 freelance illustation jobs/year. Pays by the hour, $12-50.
Jackets/Covers: Assigns 60 freelance design and 30 freelance illustration jobs/year. Pays $600-900.
Text Illustration: Assigns 6 freelance jobs/year. Prefers line art. Pays by the project, $200-1,500.
Tips: "There is more use of innovative type design on covers. More sophisticated illustrations in curriculum materials. These changes have led to a need for more experienced freelance designers and illustrators."

WISCONSIN TALES & TRAILS, INC., Box 5650, Madison WI 53705. (608)231-2444. Publisher: Howard Mead. Publishes adult trade books. Specializes in hardcover and paperback originals and reprints. "Only those that relate in some way to Wisconsin." 3 categories: Wisconsiana, guides, nature/environment. Publishes 1-2 titles/year.
First Contact & Terms: Works on assignment only. Send query letter and samples to be kept on file for future assignments. Samples returned by SASE "if requested." Reports back on future assignment possibilities. Buys one-time rights. Return of original artwork "depends on individual contract or agreement negotiated."
Book Design: Pays by the project, $300-1,000.
Jackets/Covers: Pays by the project, $200 minimum.
Text Illustration: Assigns 1-2 freelance jobs/year. Pays by the project, $300-1,000.
Tips: Also publishes bimonthly magazine, *Wisconsin Trails*. "We have been using freelance artwork regularly in our magazine, b&w and color."

WOMEN'S AGLOW FELLOWSHIP, Publications Division, Box I, Lynnwood WA 98036. (206)775-7282. Art Director: Kathy Boice. Specializes in Bible studies and Christian literature, and a bimonthly magazine offering Christian women's material. Publishes 20 titles/year; 25% require freelance illustrators and calligraphers.
First Contact & Terms: Works with 20 freelance artists/year. Send samples; call or write for appointment to show portfolio. Prefers slides, photostats, line drawings and reproduced art as samples. Samples returned by SASE. Reports in 6 weeks. Provide resume, business card, brochure/flyer, samples and tear sheets to be kept on file for possible future assignments. Originals returned to artist at job's completion. Buys one-time rights.
Jackets/Covers: Prefers b&w line drawings. Pays for design and illustration by the job, $80-250 average.
Magazine Illustrations: Pays $80-175, b&w line drawings; $200-325, color, inside; $500, color, cover.
Text Illustrations: Prefers b&w line drawings. Pays by the job, $35-200 average.
Tips: "Be aware of organization's emphasis. Be motivated to work for a women's organization."

WOODALL PUBLISHING COMPANY, 500 Hyacinth Pl., Highland Park IL 60035. (312)433-4550. Directory Manager: Debby Spriggs. Specializes in paperback annuals on camping. Publishes 2 titles/year.
First Contact & Terms: Works with 4 freelance artists/year. Works on assignment only. Call for appointment to show portfolio. Reports within 4 weeks. No original work returned at job's completion. Considers complexity of project, skill and experience of artist, and project's budget when establishing payment. Rights purchased vary according to project.
Book Design: Assigns 3-4 jobs/year. Pays by the project.
Jackets/Covers: Assigns 2 freelance design and illustration jobs/year. Pays by the project.
Text Illustration: Pays by the project.

WOODSONG GRAPHICS INC., PO Box 238, New Hope PA 18938. (215)794-8321. President: Ellen Bordner. Specializes in paperback originals covering a wide variety of subjects, "but no textbooks or technical material so far." Publishes 6-10 titles/year.
First Contact & Terms: Works with 1-5 freelance artists/year depending on projects and schedules. Works on assignment only. Send query letter with brochure and samples to be kept on file. Any format is acceptable for samples, except originals. Samples not filed are returned by SASE. Reports only if interested. Originals returned to artist at job's completion. Considers complexity of the assignment, skill and experience of artist, project's budget and turnaround time when establishing payment. Rights purchased vary according to project.
Book Design: Assigns 2-3 freelance jobs/year. Pays by the project, $400 minimum.
Jackets/Covers: Assigns 3-6 freelance illustration jobs/year. Pays by the project, $100 minimum.
Text Illustration: Assigns 2-3 freelance jobs/year. Medium and style vary according to job. Pays by the project, $250 minimum.

THE WORDSHOP, Division of Slawson Communications, 3719 6th Ave., San Diego CA 92103. (619)291-9126. Art Director: Ed Roxburgh. Specializes in paperback computer books and childrens color books. Subjects include computers, childrens teaching books and literary. Publishes 25 titles/year.
First Contact & Terms: Works with 20-25 freelance artists/year. Works on assignment only. Send query letter with resume and samples to be kept on file. Samples not filed are returned by SASE. Reports only if interested. Call for appointment to show portfolio. Considers complexity of project and project's budget when establishing payment. Rights purchased vary according to project.
Jackets/Covers: Assigns 10 freelance design and 20 freelance illustration jobs/year. Pays by the project, $300-600 average.
Text Illustration: Assigns 20 jobs/year. Pays by the illustration, $25-80 average depending on complexity, color, etc.

WRITER'S DIGEST BOOKS/NORTH LIGHT, F&W Publishing, 9933 Alliance Rd., Cincinnati OH 45242. Art Director: Carol Buchanan. Publishes 25-30 books annually for writers, artists, photographers, plus selected trade titles. Send query letter with samples or request appointment to show portfolio. "Prefer that artist has had work published in area of assignment." SASE. Reports in 3 weeks. Assigns 25-50/year. Payment by job: $50-350, catalogs; $50 minimum, direct mail brochures; $25 minimum, magazines.
Jackets/Covers: Buys 8-10/year. Pays $350-500 for concept through mechanical art.
Text Illustration: Uses artists for text illustration and cartoons. Pays $5 minimum.
Tips: Also uses artists for ad illustration and design.

YE GALLEON PRESS, Box 25, Fairfield WA 99012. (509)283-2422. Editorial Director: Glen Adams. Publishes rare western history, Indian material, antiquarian shipwreck and old whaling accounts, and town and area histories; hardcover and paperback originals and reprints. Publishes 30 titles/year; 20% require freelance illustrators.
First Contact & Terms: Query with samples. SASE. No advance. Pays promised fee for unused assigned work. Buys book rights. Free catalog.
Text Illustrations: Buys b&w line drawings, some pen & ink drawings of a historical nature; prefers drawings of groups with facial expressions and some drawings of sailing and whaling vessels. Pays $5-35.
Tips: " 'Wild' artwork is hardly suited to book illustration for my purposes. Many correspondents wish to sell oil paintings which at this time we do not buy. It costs too much to print them for short edition work."

***ZONDERVAN CORPORATION**, 1415 Lake Dr. S.E., Grand Rapids MI 49506. Advertising Director: Art Jacobs. Specializes in hardcovers, paperbacks and reprints—religious and romance books. Publishes 250 titles/year.
First Contact & Terms: Works with 12-15 freelance artists/year. Artists "must be of professional caliber." Works on assignment only. Send query letter with brochure showing art style or tear sheets. Samples not filed are returned by SASE. Reports only if interested. Original work returned at the job's completion "if artist requests." Considers project's budget when establishing payment. Buys all rights.
Book Design: Assigns 150-175 freelance design and 50 freelance illustration jobs/year. Pays by the project, $250-750.
Jackets/Covers: Assigns 150 freelance design and 50 freelance illustration jobs/year. Pays by the project, 250-750.
Tips: Artists "must have previous book jacket and illustration experience—samples a must of artists best work. Creative artists only . . ."

> **❝There is not much good in sending a SASE that is not large enough to return your artwork. Also, U.S. writers should remember that their neighbors to the North can't use U.S. stamped envelopes. Use UPU (Universal Postal Union) coupons.❞**
>
> *David Golden, Angler & Hunter Magazine*

"The business of America is business," said Calvin Coolidge. And artists are often surprised at how much business awaits them in this section. There is a wide assortment of business occupations and art/design needs that range from the ordinary to the unexpected. Frozen seafood processors, motivational program producers, dental supply distributors, manufacturers of collectible plates, ski resorts, amusement parks, insurance companies—these are but a few of the businesses providing freelance opportunities that might otherwise be overlooked by artists.

Besides requiring artists for layout duties, manufacturers need industrial and package designers. Industrial designers shape products, determining the characteristic look and quality one "feels' about a product. This designer must have skills that combine artistic talent with manufacturing know-how; his portfolio should show samples that reflect a consistency of design, a sense of pure graphics and knowledge of manufacturing processes. Some industrial designers move into toy designing, in which they work with miniature projects. A package designer must combine the three-dimensional skills of an industrial designer with the two-dimensional design sense of a graphic designer. He creates graphic symbols and works with the color and design of labels; his portfolio should demonstrate that he is a visual problem-solver.

The business world also has needs for fine art. We've included in-depth information on the collectibles market in this section, featuring a Close-up with Janet Jensen of The Bradford Exchange. Learn what collectibles manufacturers look for in artwork and how to approach this market.

There are constants in the ever-changing world of fashion illustration, as Margaret Volker-Ferrier points out in the Close-up that appears in the Fashion subsection. With international experience, this fashion illustrator describes the demands of this fast-paced world and stresses that freelancers can work anywhere in this field.

If you're interested in a particular product area, check the Yellow Pages and ask at your local library for suggestions of trade periodicals dealing with that specific interest. Additional manufacturers can be obtained from the *Thomas Register of Manufacturers*, which lists companies alphabetically and according to product.

To increase your knowledge of the exhibit, display and sign field, refer to the trade magazine *Visual Merchandising & Store Design* and consult your Yellow Pages for local firms.

Refer to the *Standard Rate and Data Services*'s annual directories of consumer and trade publications for magazines which use fashion illustration. Keep up with fashion trends by referring to *Women's Wear Daily* or its "sister" magazine *W.*, and *Homesewing Trade News* to keep current with the housesewing industry.

Collectible manufacturers are found in *The Bradford Book of Collector's Plates* and in *Plate World*.

***ABBEY PRESS**, Hill Dr., St. Meinrad IN 47577. Creative Director: Jo Anne Calucchia. Manufacturer/distributor/mail order catalog providing Christian products, greeting cards, wall decor and sculpture. Clients: Christian bookstores and retail catalog.
Needs: Works with 50 freelance artists/year. Buys 200-300 freelance designs/illustrations/year. Artist must have knowledge of art preparation for reproduction; prefers 3 years' experience in greeting cards. Works on assignment only. Uses artists for 3-dimensional product design, illustration on product and model making. "Quick turnaround time is required."
First Contact & Terms: Send query letter with resume, tear sheets, slides and photographs. Samples not filed are returned by SASE. Reports back within 1 month.
Tips: "Our products are of a religious and/or inspirational nature. We need full-color illustrations from experienced artists who know how to prepare art for reproduction. Familiarize yourself with current looks and trends in the Christian market."

***ABRACADABRA MAGIC SHOP**, Box 450, Scotch Plains NJ 07076. (201)668-1313. President: Robert Bokor. Manufacturer/mail order specializing in fun products for boys, marketed via mail order. Clients: boys, as well as hobby and magic shops.
Needs: Works with 2-3 freelance artists/year. Local artists only. Works on assignment only. Uses artists for advertising and catalog design, illustration and layout; packaging design and layout.
First Contact & Terms: Send query letter with resume and photocopies. Samples not filed are returned by SASE. Reports back within 1 month. To show a portfolio, mail appropriate materials. Pays for design by the project, $50-1,000. Considers client's budget when establishing payment.
Tips: "Freelancers with past experience designing products/ads for boys and/or hobby products is a plus."

ADELE'S II, INC., 17300 Ventura Blvd., Encino CA 91316. (818)990-5544. Contact: Shirley Margulis. Franchisor and retailer of personalized gifts including acrylic and oak desk accessories, novelty clocks, personalized gift items from any medium. Sells to "high-quality-conscious" customers.
Needs: Works with 100-150 freelance artists/year. Uses artists for product design, model making and lettering. "We always will consider any type of item that can be personalized in some way, shape or form."
First Contact & Terms: Send query letter with brochure or photocopies and photos to be kept on file. Samples not filed are returned by SASE. Reports only if interested. Write for appointment to show portfolio, which should include thumbnails and photographs. Negotiates payment. Considers rights purchased when establishing payment.
Tips: "Consider first that we only purchase items we can sell personalized. A beautiful picture can't be personalized."

AERO PRODUCTS RESEARCH INC., 11201 Hindry Ave., Los Angeles CA 90045. Director of Public Relations: J. Parr. Aviation training materials producer. Produces line of plastic greeting cards, religious and inspirational cards, credit and business cards.
Needs: Works with about 2 illustrators/month. Prefers local artists. Uses artists for brochures, album covers, books, catalogs, filmstrips, advertisements, graphs and illustrations.
First Contact & Terms: Send query letter with resume, brochure/flyer, resume and tear sheets to be kept on file. No originals returned to artist at job's completion. Negotiates pay according to experience and project.

AHPA ENTERPRISES, Box 506, Sheffield AL 35660. Marketing Manager: Allen Turner. Media products producer/marketer. Provides illustrations, fiction, layouts, video productions, computer-printed material, etc. Specializes in adult male, special-interest material. Clients: limited-press publishers, authors, private investors, etc.
Needs: Seeking illustrators for illustration of realistic original fiction or concepts. Wants only those artists "who are in a position to work with us on an intermittent but long-term basis." Works on assignment only.
First Contact & Terms: Send query letter with resume and photocopies or tear sheets, photostats, photographs and new sketches to be kept on file. Samples not filed are returned by SASE only if requested. Reports back only if interested (within 3-7 days). Pays for illustration by the project, $30-1,000 average. Considers complexity of the project and number and type of illustrations ordered when establishing payment. Buys all rights.
Tips: "Samples should indicate capability in realistic (if 'glamorized') face-and-figure illustration. Continuity-art experience is preferred. This is an excellent place for capable amateurs to 'turn pro' on a part-time, open-end basis."

AK INTERNATIONAL, 40 N. Water St., Lititz PA 17543. (717)626-0505. President: O. Ali Akincilar. Produces brass photo frames and ornaments. Clients: the gift industry.
Needs: Buys approximately 10 designs/year from freelance artists. Prefers line drawings for illustrations. Artists must have a knowledge of photo etching. Works on assignment only.
First Contact & Terms: Send query letter with brochure, resume and photographs to be kept on file. Samples not filed are returned only if requested. Reports only if interested. Call for appointment to show portfolio. Original art not returned after reproduction. Pays by the project, $50-500 average. Buys all rights.

ALBEE SIGN CO., 561 E. 3rd St., Mt. Vernon NY 10553. (914)668-0201. President: William Lieberman. Produces interior and exterior signs and graphics. Clients are commercial accounts, banks and real estate companies.
Needs: Works with 6 artists for sign design, 6 for display fixture design, 6 for P-O-P design and 6 for custom sign illustration. Local artists only. Works on assignment only.

First Contact & Terms: Query with samples (pictures of completed work). Previous experience with other firms preferred. SASE. Reports within 2-3 weeks. No samples returned. Reports back as assignment occurs. Provide resume, business card and pictures of work to be kept on file for future assignments. Pays by job.

ALL-STATE LEGAL SUPPLY CO., One Commerce Dr., Cranford NJ 07016. (201)272-0800. Advertising Manager: Paul Ellman. Manufacturer and distributor of supplies, stationery, engraving, printing. Clients: lawyers.
Needs: Works with 6 freelance artists/year. Experienced, local artists and designers only. Works on assignment only. Uses artists for advertising, brochure and catalog design, illustration and layout; display fixture design, and illustration on product. Especially needs cover illustrations and catalog work.
First Contact & Terms: Send query letter with photostats to be kept on file. Reports only if interested. Call for appointment to show portfolio. Pays by the project, $350-1,500 average. Considers complexity of project, skill and experience of artist and turnaround time when establishing payment.

***ALVIMAR MANUFACTURING CO., INC.**, 51-02 21st St., Long Island City NY 11101. (212)937-0404. President: Alan P. Friedlander. Display firm and manufacturer of plastic inflatable swim toys, such as beach balls, rings, pools, mats. Also premium items, such as product replicas. Ex: Little Green Sprout and Wrigley Spearmint Chewing Gum. Clients: service advertising agencies, food and cosmetic manufacturers, "any category as we make product replicas."
Needs: Uses artists for product and P-O-P design and model making.
First Contact & Terms: Call for appointment. Prefers to see originals or photostats of work. Samples returned by SASE. Reports in 4 months. Provide resume and tear sheets to be kept on file for possible future assignments. Payment method is negotiable and varies according to client's budget.

***AMERICAN ADVERTISING DISTRIBUTORS**, 170 Changebridge Rd., Montville NJ 07045. (201)227-4607. President: Joesph O'Dowd. Distributor of direct mail advertising for retail and professional business.
Needs: Works with 3 freelance artists/year. Local artists only. Uses artists for advertising design and layout.
First Contact & Terms: Send query letter with brochure showing art style. Reports only if interested. Write to schedule an appointment to show a portfolio, which should include roughs and original/final art. Pays for design by the hour $5-20. Considers complexity of project and turnaround time when establishing payment.

AMERICAN ARTISTS, Division of Graphics Buying Service, 225 W. Hubbard St., Chicago IL 60610. (312)828-0555. Advertising Coordinator: Lorraine Light. Manufacturer of limited edition plates and figurines. Specializes in horse, children, and cat themes, but considers others. Clients: wholesalers and retailers.
Needs: Works with 3 freelance artists/year. Does not work on assignment only. Uses artists for plate and figurine design and illustration; brochure design, illustration and layout. Open to most art styles.
First Contact & Terms: Send query letter with resume and samples to be kept on file unless return is requested or artwork is unsuitable. Prefers transparencies or slides but will accept photos—color only. Samples not filed are returned only if requested or if unsuitable. Reports within 1 month. Call or write for appointment to show portfolio. Payment varies and is negotiated. Rights purchased vary. Considers complexity of project, skill and experience of artist, how work will be used and rights purchased when establihsing payment.

AMERICAN BOOKDEALERS EXCHANGE, Box 2525, La Mesa CA 92041. Editor: Al Galasso. Publisher of *Book Dealers World* targeted to self-publishers, writers and mail order book dealers. Clients: self-publishers, writers, business opportunity seekers.
Needs: Works with 3 freelance artists/year. Prefers artists with at least a year's experience. Works on assignment only. Uses artists for advertising, brochure and catalog design and illustration.
First Contact & Terms: Send query letter with photostats to be kept on file. Samples not kept on file are returned only if requested. Reports only if interested. Pays by the project, $25-200 average. Considers complexity of project, skill and experience of artist, turnaround time and rights purchased when establishing payment.

***AMERICAN EAGLE COMPANY**, 1130 E. Big Beaver, Troy MI 48083. (800)521-1455. Creative Director: Dodi Sikevitz. Provides teaching aid products and marketing products/programs for hospitals and nurses and foreign language teachers.
Needs: Works with 6 freelance artists/year. Local artists only. Works on assignment only. Uses artists for advertising, brochure and catalog design, illustration and layout; product design, illustration on product, posters and model making.

First Contact & Terms: Send query letter with resume and photocopies. Samples not filed are not returned. Reports only if interested. To show a portfolio, mail appropriate materials or call or write to schedule an appointment. Pays for design and illustration by the hour, $10-15. Considers complexity of project, skill and experience of artist, and how work will be used when establishing payment.
Tips: Artist should "show their best samples—our interview time is limited. Have a resume if possible."

***AMERICAN PERMANENT WARE, INC. (APW)**, 729 Third Ave. Dallas TX 75226. (214)421-7366. Director of Advertising and Marketing: Mary M. Cardone. Manufacturer of stainless steel food service equipment for dealers, distributors and national accounts.
Needs: Works with 4 freelance artists/year. Prefers local artists. Works on assignment only. Uses artists for the design, illustration and layout of advertising brochures and catalogs plus P-O-P displays and trade publication ad layouts.
First Contact & Terms: Send query letter with brochure showing art style or photocopies. Samples not filed are returned only if requested. Reports back only if interested. Write to schedule an appointment to show a portfolio, which should include final reproduction/product and color. Considers complexity of project and client's budget when establishing payment. Buys all rights.
Tips: "See more sophistication in the field."

***"JIMMY ANGEL" MODELING AGENCY, INC.**, Box 2544, Baton Rouge LA 70821. (504)924-6865. Director: Jimmy Angel. Modeling agency providing art, photos, layouts for album covers, videos, covers, fashion magazines, etc.
Needs: Works with 15 freelance artists/year. Works on assignment only. Uses freelance artists for the design, illustration and layout of advertising, brochure, and catalogs plus product design, P-O-P displays, posters, model making and signage.
First Contact & Terms: Send query letter with brochure showing art style or resume, photocopies and photographs. Samples not filed are returned. Reports back within 2 weeks. To show a portfolio, mail appropriate materials or write to schedule an appointment; portfolio should include original/final art, final reproduction/product, color and photographs. Pays for design and illustration by the project, $100-1,000. Considers complexity of project, client's budget, skill and experience of artist and when establishing payment how work will be used.
Tips: "Be able to provide us with artwork on any subject and be a professional."

ARMSTRONG'S, 150 E. 3rd St., Pomona CA 91766. (714)623-6464. President: David W. Armstrong. Wholesale and retail manufacturer/gallery of collector plates, figurines and lithographs. Clients: wholesale and retail customers of all age groups.
Needs: Works on assignment only. Uses professional artists for plate design; limited edition art prints; advertising posters; advertising, brochure and catalog design, illustration and layout.
Contact & Terms: Send query letter with brochure, resume, business card and photographs, transparencies and tear sheets to be kept on file. Samples not filed are returned. Reports within 2 weeks. Payment is determined on a case-by-case basis. Considers skill and experience of the artist and rights purchased when establishing payment.
Tips: "Make your initial contact by letter and do not make excessive telephone calls to our offices."

***ARTISTS OF THE WORLD**, 2915 N. 67th Place, Scottsdale AZ 85251. National Sales Manager: Thomas R. Jackson. Producer of plates, figurines and miniature plates and figurines. Clients: wholesalers and retailers.
Needs: Works with a variable number of freelance artists/year. Works on assignment only. Uses artists for the design and illustration of plates and figurines.
First Contact & Terms: Send query letter with brochure showing art style. Samples not filed are returned only if requested. Reports back within 2 weeks. To show a portfolio, mail appropriate materials, which should include original/final art, final reproduction/product and color. Pays for design by the project. Considers how work will be used when establishing payment.

***ART-PHYL CREATIONS**, 16250 NW 48th Ave., Hialeah FL 33014. Contact: Barry Spatz. Manufacturer and display firm.
Needs: Works with 3-5 freelance artists/year. Works on assignment basis only. Uses artists for advertising, brochure and catalog design, illustration and layout; display fixture for P-O-P design.
First Contact & Terms: Send query letter and write for appointment. Samples not returned. Reports in 2 weeks. Provide business card to be kept on file for possible future assignments. Negotiates payment.

***THE ASHTON-DRAKE GALLERIES**, 9333 Milwaukee Ave., Niles IL 60648. (312)966-2770, ext. 300. Product Development: Ed Bailey-Mershon. Marketer of limited edition collectibles, such as dolls,

figurines, ornaments, and other uniquely executed artwork sold in thematic series. Clients: Collectible consumers represent all age groups.
Needs: Works with 200 freelance doll artists, costume designers, illustrators, artists, sculptors a year. Works on assignment only. Uses artists for concept illustrations, collectible designs, prototype specifications and construction. Prior experience in giftware design, greeting card and book illustration a plus. Subject matter is children and mothers, animals nostalgia scenes.
First Contact & Terms: Send query letter with resume, copies of samples to be kept on file, except for copyrighted slides which are duplicated and returned. Prefers slides, photographs, tear sheets, or photostats (in that order) as samples. Samples not filed are returned. Reports within 45 days. Illustrations are done "on spec" to $200 maximum. Contract for length of series on royalty basis. Considers complexity of the project, project's budget, skill and experience of the artist, and rights purchased.

AUTOMATIC MAIL SERVICES, INC., 30-02 48th Ave., Long Island City NY 11101. (212)361-3091. Contact: Michael Waskover. Manufacturer and service firm. Provides printing and direct mail advertising. Clients: publishers, banks, stores, clubs.
Needs: Works with 5-10 freelance artists/year. Uses artists for advertising, brochure and catalog design, illustration and layout.
First Contact & Terms: Send business card and photostats to be kept on file. Call for appointment to show portfolio. Samples not kept on file are returned only if requested. Works on assignment only. Pays by the project, $10-1,000 average. Considers skill and experience of artist and turnaround time when establishing payment.

***AVALON FORGE**, 409 Gun Rd., Baltimore MD 21227. (301)242-8431. Owner: John White. Mail order seller providing 18th century replicas for historical education programs. Clients: parks, historical societies, historical re-enactors and restored homes.
Needs: Works with 1 freelance artist/year. Uses artists for illustration on product.
First Contact & Terms: Send query letter with photocopies. Samples not filed are returned by SASE. Reports only if interested. Write to schedule an appointment to show a portfolio, which should include photostats. Considers client's budget when establishing payment.
Tips: "Artist should be totally familiar with historic artifacts."

AVALON INDUSTRIES, 95 Lorimer St., Brooklyn NY 11206. R&D Director: Anne Pitrone. Manufacturer of toys.
Needs: Works with 4-5 freelance artists/year. Seeks artists with "toy experience." Works on assignment only. Uses artists for advertising, brochure and catalog design.
First Contact & Terms: Send query letter with brochure showing art style and photographs, slides or tear sheets to be kept on file. Samples not filed are returned. Reports only if interested. Call or write for appointment to show portfolio. Pays by the project. Considers complexity of the project and skill and experience of the artist when establishing payment.

BAKER STREET PRODUCTIONS LTD., Box 3610, Mankato MN 56001. (507)625-2482. Contact: Karyne Jacobsen. Service-related firm providing juvenile books to publishers.
Needs: Works with 2 freelance artists/year. Artists must be able to meet exact deadlines. Works on assignment only. Uses artists for advertising illustration, illustration on product and book illustration.
First Contact & Terms: Send query letter with resume and tear sheet. Reports back within 3 months. Write to schedule an appointment to show a portfolio, which should include roughs, final reproduction/product, color and photographs. Fee is determined by the size of the project involved. Pays for design and illustration by the project. Considers complexity of the project and how work will be used when establishing payment. Buys all rights.

BANKERS LIFE & CASUALTY COMPANY, 1000 Sunset Ridge Rd., Northbrook IL 60062. (312)498-1500. Manager-Communications/Graphics: Charles S. Pusateri. Insurance firm.
Needs: Works with 5-10 freelance artists/year. Works on assignment only. Uses artists for advertising and brochure displays, illustration and layout; posters and signage.
First Contact & Terms: Send query letter with resume and printed pieces to be kept on file. Samples returned only if requested. Reports within 2 weeks only if interested. Write to schedule an appointment to show a portfolio, which should include thumbnails, roughs and final reproduction/product. Pays for design by the hour, $25-50 average. Considers complexity of project, skill and experience of artist, and turnaround time when establishing payment. Rights purchased vary according to project.
Tips: "Follow rules but don't give up. Timing is essential."

***BENJAMIN DIVISION, THOMAS INDUSTRIES**, Box 180, Rte. 70 S. Rd., Sparta TN 38583. (615)738-2241. Advertising Manager: Cindy Jarvis. Manufacturer of commercial/industrial fluores-

Close-up

Janet Jensen
Artist Liaison
The Bradford Exchange
Niles, Illinois

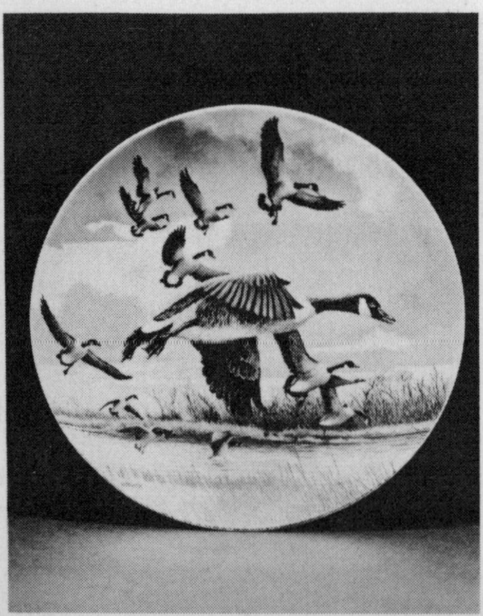

Chicago may be known as the Second City, but in terms of collector's plates, it is Number One in the world.

The reason for its international supremacy is tucked away in the quiet suburb of Niles where The Bradford Exchange is headquartered. Its international office is the world's largest trading center for limited edition collector's plates, handling more than 13,000 transactions each day. In 1984, over $100 million worth of plates was traded on the Exchange.

There are eight million plate collectors in the world, the majority of them in the U.S. The Bradford Exchange accommodates them through its computerized trading floor, its museum (which houses the world's largest permanent exhibit of limited edition plates) and the marketing of collector's plates.

Bradford extends a welcoming attitude to emerging artists. "I see the work of hundreds of artists," said Janet Jensen, Bradford's artist liaison. "We look for illustrators who have not only good technique but also creative ideas." There are only so many metaphors to draw upon for inspiration, but there is an infinite amount of variations—in style, media and technique.

For manufacturers and distributors of collector's plates, the hunt for good artists is never ending. Jensen is not content merely to receive interesting artwork through the mail via slides

The Bradford Exchange was granted worldwide distribution rights for the plate series "Wings Upon the World." The series, painted by wildlife painter and naturalist Donald Pentz, is sponsored by the Canadian Wildlife Federation.

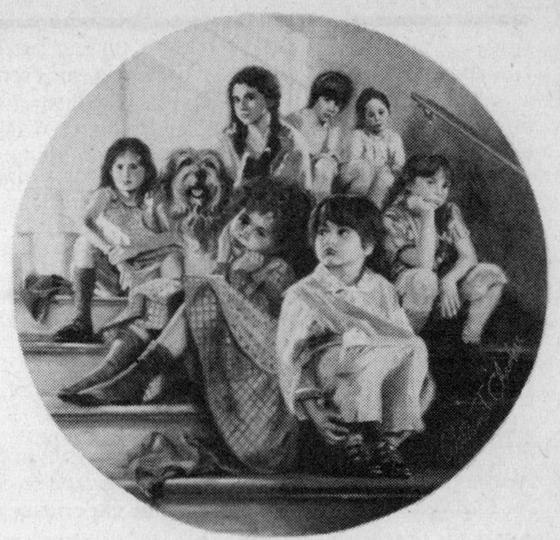

and brochures. She conducts a nationwide search by visiting galleries, fairs and exhibitions. An artist herself, who has run a gallery, this personable woman knows what to spot. "Pictures with people that somehow tell a story sell the best. I look at how the artist deals with figurative features; whether the artist is good at portraiture. I particularly look for realistic treatment of the frontal view of faces. Of course, the women must be pretty and the men very handsome. The image is always positive or pleasant."

The subject matter is not restricted to people. Jensen also works with landscape artists and sculptors. Whatever the media or milieu, the artist must convey a sense of proportion, perspective and composition.

Through her talent searches, Jensen finds a variety of prospects. Together with Bradford's program managers, she examines the sketches of two to three artists for a certain project.

Jensen, like many representatives of collector plate manufacturers, is mainly interested in finding good technique and creative style rather than specific subject matter. Portfolios, which include original artwork, are shown during an interview.

Bradford pays $150 for two or three sketches to determine how an artist deals with specific subject matter. The selected artist will sign a contract to complete a series of plates; payment is generally an advance against royalties, and a royalty payment per plate sold. The artist is paid the advance as soon as final art is approved. Royalties are paid quarterly for each plate sold.

A plate series is marketed through direct response, space ads and sometimes TV commercials. Selected artists are requested to appear at conventions and dealer openings, all expenses paid.

Collector's plates are the world's most traded art form. Not only are the plates collected and displayed in homes, but they also can be bought, sold and resold many times over the years. Therefore, a plate artist can enjoy endless exposure and continued royalties. For an emerging illustrator, figurative painter or landscape specialist, collector's plates are an ideal introduction to an international audience.

cent/incandescent lighting, produce HID lighting for lighting distributors, architects, engineering firms, government agencies, schools, industrial firms and national chains.
Needs: Works with 1-2 freelance artists/year. Prefers artists with three years' experience. Works on assignment basis only. Uses artists for the illustration layout of advertising, brochures and catalogs.
First Contact & Terms: Send query letter with brochure showing art style. Reports back only if interested. Call or write to schedule an appointment to show a portfolio, which should include original/final art, final reproduction/product, color and photographs. Pays for design and illustration by the project. Considers how work will be used and turnaround time when establishing payment.

BERMAN LEATHERCRAFT INC., 25 Melcher St., Boston MA 02120. (617)426-0870. President: Robert S. Berman. Manufacturer/importer/mail order firm providing leathercraft kits and leather supplies, diaries and notepads. Clients: shops, hobbyists, schools and hospitals. "We mail to 5,000-25,000 people every six weeks."
Needs: Works with 2-4 freelance artists/year. Local artists only "for the convenience of both parties." Uses artists for brochure design, illustration and layout; "we produce two- to four-page fliers." Especially needs line drawings with dimension.
First Contact & Terms: Send query letter with printed brochures; "follow up with a phone call three to five days later." Samples not filed are returned by SASE only if requested. Pays by the project. Considers complexity of project, and skill and experience of artist when establishing payment. Buys all rights.

BEROL, Berol Corp., Eagle Rd., Danbury CT 06810. (203)744-0000. Art Product Group Manager: Lance Hopkins. Manufactures writing instruments and drawing materials (Prismacolor Art Pencils and Art Markers, Art Stix artist crayons).
Needs: Uses artists for illustrations and layout for catalogs, ads, brochures, displays, packages. Artists must use Prismacolor and/or Verithin products only.
First Contact & Terms: Query with photographs and slides to be kept on file. Samples returned only by request. Reports within 2 weeks. Call or write to schedule an appointment to show a portfolio; portfolios not necessary. Pays by the project, $300 maximum. Rights purchased vary according to project.
Tips: "Hand-colored photographs (with Prismacolor Art Pencils) becoming very popular."

BEST WESTERN INTERNATIONAL INC., Best Western Way, Box 10203, Phoenix AZ 85064. (602)957-5763. Art Director: Barbara Lanterman. Motel inn/hotel resort chain. Clients: motels, hotels, resorts.
Needs: Assigns 200 jobs/year. Especially needs photography, illustration, production art, design.
First Contact & Terms: Query with samples. Prefers samples of printed or published pieces, illustrations.

***BING & GRONDAHL**, 111 North Lawn Ave., Elmsford NY 10523. Creative Director: Cami Messina. Wholesale manufacturer of collectibles, figurines, plates and dinnerware. Clients: wholesalers, retailers, corporations.
Needs: Uses artists for limited and unlimited edition plate and figurine design, model making, mechanicals, advertising posters and design, illustration and layout of advertising and brochures. "We prefer a Scandinavian look."
First Contact & Terms: Send a query letter with a brochure, resume and a sample, either a tear sheet, a slide or photograph. Samples not filed are returned by SASE. Reports back only if interested. Write to schedule an appointment to show a portfolio or mail roughs, original/final art, color, tear sheets, photographs and b&w. Payment depends "on the project and what is involved." Considers complexity of project, client's budget, skill and experience of artist, how work will be used; turnaround time and rights purchased.

BLONDER-TONGUE LABORATORIES INC., 1 Jake Brown Rd., Old Bridge NJ 08857. (201)679-4000. Vice President: James Fitzpatrick. Manufactures TV signal distribution equipment for schools, hotels, hospitals and communities.
Needs: Uses artists for catalog cover designs, spec sheet layouts, P-O-P display designs and direct mail brochures.
First Contact & Terms: Send query letter with resume. Reports within 2 weeks. Write to schedule an appointment to show a portfolio, which should include original/final art, final reproduction/product and b&w. Buys all rights.
Tips: Artists should have "industiral and electronic experience."

THE BRADFORD EXCHANGE, 9333 Milwaukee, Niles-Chicago IL 60648. (312)966-2770, ext. 302. Artist Liaison: Janet Jensen. Marketers of collectible plates. Clients: plate collectors in all age groups and income groups.

Needs: Works with 200 freelance artists/year. Works on assignment only. Uses artists for plate design; interested in all media, 2-D, 3-D. Subject matter is predominately mothers, children; new areas: animals and movie themes. Especially needs professional artists of portraiture, landscape, sculptors, still life, wildlife, fantasy, nautical and religious. "Quality painting reproduced on plate."
First Contact & Terms: Send query letter with brochure, 18-20 slides, resume and samples to be kept on file. Prefers slides, photographs, photocopies, tear sheets or photostats (in that order) as samples. Samples not filed are returned. Reports within 45 days. Call or write for appointment to show portfolio; portfolio should include roughs, original/final art, final reproduction/product, tearsheets, photographs and slides or transparencies. Pays "on spec"; $200 maximum. Contract negotiated for series. Considers complexity of the project, project's budget, skill and experience of the artist and rights purchased when establishing payment.
Tips: Artists "need good reference material illustrating ability to render the human figure and faces realistically. Include a resume or biography."

CANTERBURY DESIGNS, INC., Box 4060, Martinez GA 30907. (800)241-2732 or (404)860-1674. President: Angie A. Newton. Publisher and distributor of charted design books; counted cross stitch mainly. Clients: needlework specialty shops, wholesale distributors (craft and needlework), department stores and chain stores.
Needs: Works with 12-20 freelance artists/year. Uses artists for product design.
First Contact & Terms: Send query letter with samples to be kept on file. Prefers stitched needlework, paintings, photographs or charts as samples. Samples not filed are returned. Reports within 1 month. Call for appointment to show portfolio. Payment varies. "Some designs purchased outright, some are paid on a royalty basis." Considers complexity of project, salability, customer appeal and rights purchased when establishing payment.
Tips: "When sending your work for our review, be sure to photocopy it first. This protects you. Also, you have a copy from which to reconstruct your design should it be lost in mail. Also, send your work by certified mail. You have proof it was actually received by someone."

KEN CAPLAN PRODUCT DESIGN, 4651 Fitch Ave., Lincolnwood IL 60646. (312)674-2643. Art Director: Ken Caplan. Product development of hobbycrafts, activity toys, Christmas ornaments, leather crafts, clock kits and toys. "We create, invent, design the product, its color and 'look' for child and adult shelf appeal." Clients: manufacturers.
Needs: Works on assignment only. Uses artists for advertising and catalog illustration and layout, brochure illustration, product design, illustration on product and model making. "We use whimisical illustrations that are conducive to game boards, cards and all children's products."
First Contact & Terms: Send query letter with resume photocopies, photographs, tear sheets or proofs to be kept on file. Samples not returned. Reports within 10 days. To show a portfolio, mail appropriate material, which should include thumbnails, roughs and original/final art. Pays by the project. Considers complexity of project, how work will be used and rights purchased when establishing payment. Buys all rights.
Tips: "There is a large "do-it-yourself" adult market and also juvenile market. There is a trend more towards the *fine-detail* illustration. Show-n-tell days are over. Let your work do *all* the talking for you."

CENIT LETTERS, INC., 7438 Varna Ave., North Hollywood CA 91605. (818)983-1234 or (213)875-0880. President: Don Kurtz. Sign firm producing custom cutout letters. Clients: building managers and their tenants (high rise), designers and architects. Assigns 25 jobs/year.
Needs: Local artists only. Works on assignment only. Works with artists for sign design, exhibit design, P-O-P design, and custom sign artwork. Also uses artists for layout and gold leaf work.
First Contact & Terms: Send query letter with resume. SASE. Reports in 1 week. Samples returned by SASE. Call to schedule an appointment to show a portfolio, which should include original/final art and photographs. Pays $100 minimum gold leaf. Pays for design and illustration by the hour, $10-12. Buys one time rights.
Tips: Especially looks for "proficiency in hand lettering and accurate full-scale layouts. Find an end-user for their artwork (e.g. a buyer for 3-dimensional graphics) and we could produce the end product."

***CETEC GAUSS**, 9130 Glenoaks Blvd., Sun Valley CA 91352. Director of Marketing and Sales: Peter Horsman. Manufacturer.
Needs: "We have not worked with freelance artists in some years. This is a new project for us." Minimal experience required of freelance artists; inexpensive, no major projects are assigned, mostly lay up, mechanicals, etc. Works on assignment only. Uses artists for brochures, mechanicals, charts/graphs and advertisements. "Artists should have mechanical lay up skills."
First Contact & Terms: Send resume, tear sheets and photocopies. Samples not filed are returned only if requested. Reports back within 10 days. To show a portfolio, write to schedule an appointment. Pays

for mechanicals by the hour, $10-15. Considers complexity of project, client's budget, skill and experience of artist, how work will be used and turnaround time when establishing payment. Buys all rights.

***C.I.T.S. RECORDS DISTRIBUTORS**, Box 2544, Baton Rouge LA 70821. (504)924-6856. Director: E. Harrison. Manufacturer and distributor of phonograph records, cassettes, video tapes and albums. "We are a distributor (nationwide and all foreign countries)."
Needs: Works with 12 or more freelance artists/year. Works on an assignment basis only. Uses artists for advertising and catalog design, illustration and layout plus product design, illustration on product, P-O-P displays, display fixture design and posters.
First Contact & Terms: Send brochure showing art style or resume and tear sheets, photocopies and photographs and catalog. Samples not filed are returned by SASE. Reports back within 2 weeks. To show a portfolio, mail appropriate materials or call or write to schedule an appointment; portfolio should include roughs, original/final art, final reproduction/product, color, tear sheets, photographs and catalog. Pays for design and illustration by the project $100-1,000. Also offers royalties from sales. Considers complexity of project, skill and experience of artist, how work will be used, rights purchased and sales when establishing payment.

CLYMER'S OF BUCKS COUNTY, 141 Canal St., Nashua NH 03061. (603)882-2180. President: Joan B. Litle. Mail order catalog of gifts and collectibles, primarily American made. Clients: consumers.
Needs: Works with 12 freelance artists/year. Prefers local artists with experience in direct mail catalogs. Works on assignment only. Uses artists for advertising, brochure and catalog design, illustration and layout.
First Contact & Terms: Send query letter with brochure, references, photostats and tear sheets to be kept on file. Samples not kept on file are returned by SASE. Reports only if interested. Pay varies according to project. Considers skill and experience of artist and turnaround time when establishing payment.

CMA MICRO COMPUTER, 55722 Santa Fe Trail, Yucca Valley CA 92284. (619)365-9718. Director/Advertising: Phyllis Wattenbarger. Manufacturer/distributor of computer software. Clients: computer software manufacturers and distributors.
Needs: Works with 10 freelance artists/year. Uses artists for advertising and brochure design and illustration.
First Contact & Terms: Send query letter with photostats, photographs, photocopies or tear sheets to be kept on file. Samples not filed returned only if requested. Reports only if interested. To show a portfolio, mail appropriate materials, which should include tear sheets and photostats. Pays for design by the hour, $8 minimum. Considers complexity of project, skill and experience of the artist, how work will be used and turnaround time ("very important") when establishing payment. Buys all rights.
Tips: "Just mail material appropriate to the computer industry. If we wish to respond, we will call or write."

***COLLINS-LACROSSE SIGN CORP.**, 222 Pine St., LaCrosse WI 54601. (608)784-8200. President/Manager: Charles C. Collins. Outdoor advertising sign firm. Clients: food manufacturers, beer and soft drink bottlers, oil companies; "any commercial enterprise."
Needs: Works with artists for sign design and custom sign illustration. Works on assignment only. Also uses artists for billboards, displays, neon signs and sign redesign.
First Contact & Terms: Send brochure showing art style, resume, tear sheets or photographs. Write to schedule an appointment to show a portfolio, which should include thumbnails, roughs, original/final art and photographs. Reports in 3 days. Samples returned by SASE. Pays $25-75, full color sketches; $6, rough pencil-$30, accurate pencil; by the hour, $8-12 average. Considers complexity of project, skill and experience of artist, and turnaround time when establishing payment. Rights purchased vary according to project.
Tips: "There is a trend toward animation. Freelance artists need to be able to provide fast service. Determine a need, supply roughs to start and get an okay for precise work."

COLORSCAN SERVICES, INC., 241 Stuyvesant Ave., Lyndhurst NJ 07071. (201)438-6729. President: J. Principato. Graphic services firm providing separations and printing services. Clients: ad agencies, printers, manufacturers and publishers.
Needs: Works with 3 freelance artists/year. Works on assignment only. Uses artists for advertising, brochure and catalog design, illustration and layout; product design; illustration on product; P-O-P displays; display fixture design; posters; model making; and signage.
First Contact & Terms: Send resume and tear sheets to be kept on file. Samples not filed are returned by SASE. Reports only if interested. Write for appointment to show portfolio. Pays by the project. Considers complexity of the project and rights purchased when establishing payment.

COMMUNICATION SKILL BUILDERS, INC., Box 42050, Tucson AZ 85733. (602)323-7500. Production Manager: Sharon Walters. Publisher of education materials for special education (K-12), gifted education and microcomputer education. Clients: teachers, special education professionals, hospitals, clinics, etc.
Needs: Works with 10 freelance artists/year. Prefers local artists, but "can work with out-of-town artists as well. Must have experience." Works on assignment only. Uses artists for advertising, brochure and catalog design, illustration and layout; product and display fixture design; illustration on product; and posters.
First Contact & Terms: Send query letter with brochure and slides, photos and printed work to be kept on file. Write for appointment to show portfolio. Reports within 2 weeks. Considers complexity of project, turnaround time and rights purchased when establishing payment.
Tips: "Artists should have experience doing materials for educational publishers."

COMMUNICATIONS ELECTRONICS, Dept. AM, Box 1045, Ann Arbor MI 48106-1045. (313)973-8888. Editor: Ken Ascher. Manufacturer, distributor and ad agency (10 company divisions). Clients: electronics, computers.
Needs: Works with 150 freelance artists/year. Uses artists for advertising, brochure and catalog design, illustration and layout; product design, illustration on product, P-O-P displays, posters and renderings.
First Contact & Terms: Send query letter with brochure, resume, business card, samples and tear sheets to be kept on file. Samples not kept on file returned by SASE. Reports within 1 month. Call or write for appointment to show portfolio. Pays by the project, $25-350 average. Considers complexity of project, skill and experience of artist, how work will be used, turnaround time and rights purchased when establishing payment.

CONIMAR CORPORATION, Box 1509, Ocala FL 32678. (904)732-7235. Manufactures placemats, coasters, table hot pads, calendars, recipe cards, note cards, postcards.
Needs: Buys 10-15 designs/year. Designs range from floral to abstract and children's designs. Especially needs illustrations. Artist quotes price to be considered by Conimar. "Our designs are based a lot on designs of dinnerware, glassware and stationery items." Works on assignment only.
First Contact & Terms: Send query letter, resume and tear sheets, photocopies, slides and photographs. Reports in 1 week. Samples returned by SASE. To show portfolio, mail appropriate materials, which should include color, tear sheets, photostats and photographs. Pays for design by the hour, $15-25; pays for illustration by the project, $50-350. Buys all rights.

CONSOLIDATED MOUNTING & FINISHING, 50-10 Kneeland St., Elmhurst NY 11373. Chief Designer: C. Sutnar. Display firm.
Needs: Assigns 60-100 jobs/year. Uses artists for exhibit design, display fixture design, model-making, P-O-P design, print advertising and scale models. Works on assignment.
First Contact & Terms: Send a query letter with photostats. SASE. Reports in 3 weeks. To show a portfolio, a freelance artist should mail appropriate materials, which should include photographs and photostats. Pays $16/hour. Considers complexity of project, and skill and experience of artist when establishing payment. Negotiates rights purchased; rights vary according to project.

CONSOLIDATED STAMP MFG. CO., 7220 W. Wilson Ave., Harwood Heights IL 60656. (312)867-5800. Advertising/Marketing Manager: Paula Phillips. Manufacturer and distributor of customized stationery embossers and notarial seals, marking devices of all types, security badges, advertising medallions, transportation tokens, premiums for banks, store chains, etc. Clients: office and stationery supply stores, department stores, direct mail chains, security outfits, transportation systems, consumer direct mail.
Needs: Works with 2-3 freelance artists/year. Local, experienced artists only; "must not work for our competition." Works on assignment only. Uses artists for advertising design, illustration and layout; brochure, catalog and display fixture design; and P-O-P displays. There is a trend in the field toward "a simplification of overall design with the use of more open spaces."
First Contact & Terms: Send query letter with resume, business card and samples to be kept on file. Prefers "whatever artist has available, original art, printed brochures, etc." as samples. Samples not filed are returned by SASE. Reports only if interested. Call or write for appointment to show portfolio. Pays by the project. "We prefer the artist to quote on the entire job." Considers complexity of project, and skill and experience of artist when establishing payment.
Tips: "At least be familiar with our product line. An artist who comes in and inquires as to what we do is given little consideration. Many artists make a fatal mistake of bringing dirty, worn-out samples, or poor examples of their work. Most come ill-prepared to explain their capabilities. An artist is a salesman. In a large firm like ours we can't gamble with the unknown factors." When reviewing samples, especially looks for "originality, certainly, but of more importance is an artist's ability to understand our specific art problems or our promotional communication problems. His flexibility is also important."

***CORMAN & ASSOCIATES, INC.**, 881 Floyd Dr., Lexington KY 40505. (606)233-05444. Vice President: Stanley T. Baugh. Manufacturer. "We design and build displays and store fixtures for all forms of visual merchandising." Clients: all types of clothing stores; any business that needs specialized promotional decor, architectural facades, fixturing, exhibits, etc.
Needs: Has not worked with freelancers previously but is interested. "Artist must be familiar with in-store display, visual merchandising, fashion trends and fixturing."
First Contact & Terms: Send query letter to be kept on file. Prefers sketch work as samples. Reports within 1 week. Call or write for appointment. "Since I have not worked with freelance people before, payment will have to be negotiated."
Tips: "Above all else, artists should have a feeling of what is necessary to design props that can be manufactured by our company and used in all aspects of merchandising."

COVERDELL INSURANCE GROUP, 2015 Peachtree Rd. NE, Atlanta GA 30309. (404)355-8880. Director of Production: Ruth Lasky. Insurance marketing. Provides direct mail marketing of insurance plans. Clients: banks, savings and loans, finance companies, rural electric cooperatives.
Needs: Works with 6 freelance artists/year. Prefers local artists with direct mail materials experience. Works on assignment only. Uses artists for advertising and brochure design, illustration and layout.
First Contact & Terms: Call or write for appointment to show portfolio. Pays by the project, $50-2,000 average. Considers complexity of project, skill and experience of artist and how work will be used when establishing payment.
Tips: Artists "should have some design samples of direct mail materials or projects."

CREATE YOUR OWN, INC., R.R. A2, Box 201A, Hickory Corner Rd., Milford NJ 08848. (201)479-4015. President: Catherine C. Knowles. Vice President: George S. Wetteland. Manufactures needlework and craft kits, including needlepoint, crewel, fabric, dolls, crochet, stamped cross stitch and counted cross stitch, plastic canvas, candlewicking and lace net darning. Clients: catalog houses, department store chains, needlework chains, retail stores, etc.
Needs: Works with 2-3 freelance artists/year. Prefers local artists with some experience in needleworking design, if possible. Works on assignment only. Uses artists for product design in needlework area only and model making.
First Contact & Terms: Send query letter with brochure, resume, business card and samples to be kept on file, except for original art work. Prefers photographs or tear sheets as samples. Samples returned only if requested. Pays by the project. Considers skill and experience of the artist, how work will be used, turnaround time and rights purchased when establishing payment.

CREATIVE AWARDS BY LANE, 1575 Elmhurst Rd., Elk Grove IL 60007. (312)593-7700. Contact: Don Thompson. Distributor of recognition incentive awards consisting of trophies, plaques, jewelry, crystal, ad specialties and personalized premiums. Clients: companies, clubs, associations, athletic organizations.
Needs: Works with 3-4 freelance artists/year. Local artists only. Uses artists for advertising, brochure and catalog design, illustration and layout; and signage.
First Contact & Terms: Send query letter to be kept on file. Write for appointment to show portfolio, which should include photostats, photographs or photocopies. Reports within 10 days. Pays by the project. Considers complexity of project when establishing payment.

***CUSTOM HOUSE**, Box 38, Owls Head ME 04854. (207)594-5984. Owners: George Thompson and Alice Thompson. Fine art bronzes and custom wood carving providing wildlife, bird and animal casting for fountains, light fixtures and sculptures, also inwood (cherry and pine) and ornamental designs. Clients: architects, interior decorators, galleries, contractors and private commissions.
Needs: Works with 5-6 freelance artists/year. Uses artists for product design, model making, wood carvings, pattern makers.
First Contact & Terms: Send query letter with brochure showing art style or resume, photographs or model. Reports back within 30 days only if interested. Call or write to schedule an appointment to show a portfolio, which should include photographs and b&w.

CUSTOM HOUSE OF NEEDLE ARTS, INC., 200 Stow Rd., Marlborough MA 01752. (617)485-6699. Owner/President: Carolyn Purcell. Manufacturer of traditional crewel embroidery kits. Clients: needlework shops and catalogs.
Needs: Uses artists for product design. "We hope that artist is a crewel stitcher and can produce sample model."
First Contact & Terms: Send query letter with samples and any pertinent information to be kept on file. Prefers colored drawings or photos (if good closeup) as samples. Samples not filed are returned by SASE only if requested. Reports within 1 month. Pays royalty on kits sold.

Tips: "We emphasize *traditional* designs; use *some* current 'cutesy' type designs, but only if exceptional, for pictures, pillows, bellpulls, chair seats and clock faces."

CUSTOM STUDIOS, 1337 W. Devon Ave., Chicago IL 60660. (312)761-1150. President: Gary Wing. Custom T-shirt manufacturer. "We specialize in designing and screen printing of custom T-shirts for schools, business promotions, fundraising and for our own line of stock."
Needs: Works with 4 illustrators and 4 designers/month. Assigns 50 jobs/year. Especially needs b&w illustrations (some original and some from customer's sketch). Uses artists for direct mail and brochures/flyers, but mostly for custom and stock T-shirt designs.
First Contact & Terms: Send query letter with resume, photostats, photocopies or tear sheets; "do not send originals as we will not return them." Reports in 3-4 weeks. To show a portfolio, mail appropriate materials or call or write to schedule an appointment; portfolio should include tear sheets, photostats and b&w to be kept on file. Pays by the hour, $5-25 average. Considers turnaround time and rights purchased when establishing payment. On designs submitted to be used as stock T-shirt designs, pays 5-10% royalty. Rights purchased vary according to project.
Tips: "Send good copies of your best work. Do not get discouraged if your first designs sent are not accepted."

***DEKA PLASTICS, INC.**, 914 Westfield Ave., Elizabeth NJ 07208. (201)351-0900. Director of Marketing: David M. Hummer. Manufacturer and distributor of toys and children's products for trade-toy retailers and distributors.
Needs: Works with 6 freelance artists/year. Works on assignment only. Uses artists for the design, illustration and layout of advertising brochures and catalogs plus product design, illustration on product, P-O-P displays, display fixture design, model making and signage.
First Contact & Terms: Send query letter with brochure showing art style or resume, tear sheets, photocopies, slides and photographs. Samples not filed are returned by SASE. Reports back only if interested. Write to schedule an appointment to show a portfolio, which should include roughs, original/final art, final reproduction/product, photostats and photographs. Considers complexity of project, skill and experience of artist, turnaround time and rights purchased when establishing payment.

DISPLAYCO, 2055 McCarter Hwy., Newark NJ 07104. (201)485-0023. Creative Art Director: Chris Boyd. Designers and producers of P-O-P displays in all materials. Clients: "any consumer products manufacturers."
Needs: Works with 12 freelance artists/year. Prefers artists experienced in P-O-P or display/exhibit. Works on assignment only. Uses artists for advertising layout, brochure illustration and layout, display fixture and P-O-P design, and model making. Especially needs P-O-P designers with excellent sketching and rendering skills.
First Contact & Terms: Send samples, brochure/flyer and resume. Submit portfolio for review or call for appointment. Prefers renderings, models, produced work, photos of models, work, etc., as samples. Samples not returned. Reports back on whether to expect possible future assignments. Provide resume, business card, brochure, flyer or tear sheets to be kept on file for possible future assignments. Payment is determined by the project; method is negotiable and varies according to job.
Tips: There is a "need for greater creativity and new solutions. Freelancers should have knowledge of P-O-P materials (plastics, wire, metal, wood) and how their designs can be produced."

DUKE'S CUSTOM SIGN CO., 601 2nd St. NE, Canton OH 44702. (216)456-2729. Clients: banks, merchants, architects, hospitals, schools and construction firms.
Needs: Assigns 5-10 jobs/year. Works with 1-2 artists/year for sign design. Prefers local artists. Works on assignment only. Especially needs sign shapes for outdoor and free-standing displays.
First Contact & Terms: Send query letter with resume to be kept on file. SASE. Reports within 2 weeks. Call to schedule an appointment to show a portfolio, which should include thumbnails. Pays for design by the hour, $4.50-10. Considers complexity of project, skill and experience of artist, and how work will be used when establishing payment.
Tips: "Please bring samples of what you think are quality sign displays. Know current graphic designing."

EARTHWARE COMPUTER SERVICES, Box 30039, Eugene OR 97403. (503)344-3383. President: Donna J. Goles. Manufacturer of software for home and school. The educational products are geared for jr. high through college ages.
Needs: Works with 2 freelance artists/year. Prefers local or regional artists. Works on assignment only. Uses artists for advertising design, illustration and layout; and product design.
First Contact & Terms: Send query letter with brochure, resume, business card, photostats, photographs, photocopies, slides or tear sheets to be kept on file. Samples not filed are returned. Reports with-

in 1 month. Pays by the project. Considers complexity of project when establishing payment.
Tips: "Do not over supply us with samples."

***EBERSOLE ARTS & CRAFT SUPPLY**, 11417 W. Highway 54, Wichita KS 67208. (316)722-4771. Buyer/Manager: Carolyn Hendryx. Art supply store providing full line of art supplies: brushes, canvas, paints (many kinds), easels, frames, wood products—some needlework, calligraphy supplies, books and some classes. Clients: other art stores and general public—mostly women from 20 to 60 age group.
Needs: Works with 4-6 freelance artists/year. Uses artists to teach classes.
First Contact & Terms: Send query letter with brochure showing art style. Samples not filed are returned by SASE. Reports only if interested. Call or write to schedule an appointment to show a portfolio. Payment varies. Considers skill and experience of artist when establishing payment. Rights purchased vary according to project.

EMBOSOGRAPH DISPLAY MFG. CO., 1430 W. Wrightwood, Chicago IL 60614. (312)472-6660. Vice President/Personnel: Lee Frizane. Specializes in "complete creative art services and manufacturing in litho, silk screen, plastic molding of all kinds, spray, hot stamping, embossing, die cutting, metal work and assembly." Clients: brewery, beverage, food, automotive, hardware, cosmetics, service stations, appliances and clocks, plus consumer wall decor.
Needs: Assigns 50-100 jobs/year. Works with 15 artists for sign design, display fixture design, costume design, model-making, P-O-P design, print advertising and custom sign illustration. Especially needs P-O-P design. Works on assignment only.
First Contact & Terms: Query with resume or call. Prefers roughs and previously published work as samples. Reports in 2 weeks. Samples returned by SASE. Provide resume and brochure to be kept on file for possible future assignments. Pays $25-45/hour.
Tips: "We have added consumer items, mostly wall decor." There is a trend toward "counter and wall cases and stands" in this business field.

***EMERSON RADIO CORPORATION**, One Emerson Lane, North Bergen NJ 07047. Advertising Manager: Sharon Fenster. Distributor.
Needs: Works with 3-5 freelance artists/year. Prefers New York, New Jersey-area artists. Works on assignment only. Uses artists for the design, illustration and layout of advertising, brochures and catalogs.
First Contact & Terms: Send query letter with brochure showing art style. Samples not filed are returned only if requested. Reports back only if interested. Write to schedule an appointment to show a porfolio, which should include final reproduction/product and color.

***ENVIRONMENTAL TECTONICS CORP.**, County Line Industrial Park, Southhampton PA 18966. (215)355-9100. Art Director: Larry Keffer. Manufacturer of environmental systems, hospital and industrial sterilizers, hyperbaric systems, aeromedical physiological training systems for clients in medicine, industry and government.
Needs: Works with a various amount of freelance artists/year. Works on assignment only. Uses artists for the design and illustration of advertising, brochures, and catalogs, plus technical illustration.
First Contact & Terms: Send query letter with brochure, resume, tear sheets, photostats and photocopies. Samples not filed are returned if requested. Reports back within 2 weeks. Call or write to schedule an appointment to show a portfolio or mail roughs, original/final art, final reproduction/product, color, tear sheets and photostats. Pays for design by the hour, $15 minimum; pays for illustration by the project, $50 minimum. Considers complexity of project, client's budget, skill and experience of artist, how work will be used, turnaround time and rights purchased when establishing payment.
Tips: Looking for "strong, clean, well-educated design and illustration shouting superior quality and originality capable of competing in high-tech international market."

EXHIBIT BUILDERS INC., 150 Wildwood Rd., Deland FL 32720. (904)734-3196. Contact: J.C. Burkhalter. Produces custom exhibits, displays, scale models, dioramas, sales centers and character costumes. Clients: primarily manufacturers, ad agencies and tourist attractions.
Needs: Works on assignment only. Uses artists for exhibit/display design and scale models.
First Contact & Terms: Provide resume, business card and brochure to be kept on file. Samples returned by SASE. Reports back on future possibilities. Considers complexity of project, skill and experience of artist, how work will be used, turnaround time and rights purchased when establishing payment.
Tips: "Wants to see examples of previous design work for other clients; not interested in seeing school-developed portfolios."

***EUREKA**, Box 977, Scranton PA 18501. Marketing Manager: John A. Yourishen. Manufactures decorations and school and stationery supplies. Uses artists for party decorations, package design, greeting cards and lettering. Send samples. Reports in 30 days. Pays on acceptance.

GEORGE E. FERN CO., 1100 Gest St., Cincinnati OH 45203. (513)621-6111. General Manager: George J. Budig. Exposition service contractor/display firm.
Needs: Very limited art needs; "almost zero." Works on assignment only. Sometimes uses artists for backdrop displays, trade show exhibit/design, convention entrances and special room decorations.
First Contact & Terms: Query by phone. Reports in 1 week. Samples returned by SASE. Pays by the hour, $20-35 average; by the project, $100-500 average. Considers complexity of project, skill and experience of artist, how work will be used and turnaround time when establishing payment.
Tips: "We need some names, addresses and phone numbers so we can call."

***FRANKLIN ELECTRIC**, 400 Spring St., Bluffton IN 46714. Manager of Corporate Communications: Mel Haag. Manufacturer of submersible and fractional H.P. motors for original equipment manufacturers and distributors.
Needs: Works with 8 freelance artists/year. "Freelance artists must be proven." Works on assignment only. Uses artists for the design, illustration and layouts of advertising and brochures, the design and layout of catalogs and for posters.
First Contact & Terms: Send query letter with brochure showing art style or resume, tear sheets, slides and photographs. Samples not filed are returned only if requested. Reports only if interested. Call to schedule an appointment to show a portfolio, which should include roughs, original/final art, final reproduction/product, color and tear sheets. Pays for design and illustration by the hour, the amount being negotiable.

FRELINE, INC., Box 889, Hagerstown MD 21740. Contact: Art Director. Manufacturer and developer of library promotional aids—posters, mobiles, bookmarks, reading motivators and other products to promote reading, library services and resources. Clients: school and public libraries, classroom teachers.
Needs: Works with 6 freelance artists/year. Works on assignment only. Uses artists for advertising design, illustration and layout; catalog design, illustration and layout; product design, illustration on product and posters.
First Contact & Terms: Experienced designers or illustrators only. Send query letter with brochure, resume photographs, slides or tear sheets to be kept on file. Samples not filed are returned. Reports within 15 days. Pays by the project, $250-800 average. Considers complexity of the project, skill and experience of the artist, turnaround time and rights purchased when establishing payment.
Tips: "We love good idea and concept artists."

***FROG TOOL CO. LTD.**, 700 W. Jackson Blvd., Chicago IL 60606. (312)648-1270. President: R. Watkins. Distributor selling woodworking tools over the counter and by mail order. Clients: hobbyists and woodworking shops.
Needs: Works with 1 freelance artist/year. Artist must understand tools and mail order business. Use artists on full-time basis only.
First Contact: Reports only if interested. Call to schedule an appointment to show a portfolio, which should include thumbnails, roughs, original/final art, final reproduction/product, color, tear sheets, photostats, photographs and b&w. Considers skill and experience of artist when establishing payment.
Tips: "We hire full-time people to make up catalog. They must also be able to write."

G.A.I. AND ASSOCIATES, INC., Box 30309, Indianapolis IN 46230. (317)257-7100. President: William S. Gardiner. Licensing agents. "We represent artists to the collectibles industry, i.e., manufacturers of high-quality prints, collector's plates, figurines, bells, etc. There is no up-front fee for our services. We receive a commission for any payment the artist receives as a result of our efforts." Clients: manufacturers of high-quality prints and lithographs, porcelain products.
Needs: Works with 30-40 freelance artists/year. Works on assignment only. "We are not interested in landscapes, still lifes, or modern art. We are looking for 'people-oriented' art that will appeal to the average person."
First Contact & Terms: Send query letter with resume and color photographs; do *not* send original work. Samples not kept on file are returned by SASE. Reports in 1 month. Payment: "If we are successful in putting together a program for the artist with a manufacturer, the artist is usually paid a royalty on the sale of the product using his art. This varies from 4%-10%." Considers complexity of project, skill and experience of artist, how work will be used and rights purchased when establishing payment; "payment is negotiated individually for each project."
Tips: "We are looking for art with broad emotional appeal."

GADSDEN COUNTY CHAMBER OF COMMERCE, Box 389, Quincy FL 32351. (904)627-9231. Executive Director: Ben Ellinor.
Needs: Assigns 2 jobs/year. Uses artists for direct mail/publicity brochures, newspaper ad layouts, trade magazine ads and publications.

First Contact & Terms: Arrange interview or mail art. SASE. Reports in 1 month. Negotiates payment.

***GALLERY CLASSICS**, 13735 Iroquis Pl., Chino CA 91710. (714)627-8533. President: Robert A. Perkins. Manufacturer of wholesale and retail ceramic collector items (plates, bowls, etc.). Clients: wholesalers, retailers and consumers (direct mail) age 30-65 female.
Needs: Works with 3 freelance artists/year. Works on assignment only. Uses artists for plate and figurine design and illustration. Prefers "realistic wildlife (water fowl, baby animals endangered species, etc.) generally in their natural habitat and children (cute, soft, gentle) real, not animated."
First Contact & Terms: Send query letter with brochure showing art styles or slides. Samples not filed returned only if requested. Reports within 10 days. To show a portfolio, mail appropriate materials or call or write to schedule an appointment. Portfolio should include original/final art and photographs. Pays for design by the project, $1,500/subject, plus royalties. Considers complexity of project, skill and experience of artist, how work will be used and rights purchased when establishing payment.
Tips: "We deal with series of 2-4 subjects. Artists must think of continuity of subjects."

GARDEN STATE MARKETING SERVICES, INC., Box 343, Oakland NJ 07436. (201)337-3888. President: Jack Doherty. Service-related firm providing public relations and advertising services, mailing services and fulfillment. Clients: associations, publishers, manufacturers.
Needs: Works with 6 freelance artists/year. Works on assignment only. Uses artists for advertising and brochure design, illustration and layout; display fixture design, P-O-P displays and posters.
First Contact & Terms: Send query letter with resume, business card and copies to be kept on file. Samples not kept on file are returned. Reports only if interested. To show a portfolio, mail appropriate materials, which should include thumbnails, original/final art, final reproduction/product, color, tear sheets, photographs and b&w. Pays for design by the hour, $8-15. Considers complexity of project, skill and experience of artist and how work will be used when establishing payment.
Tips: "We have noticed a movement toward one color with use of bendays."

GARON PRODUCTS INC., 1924 Highway 35, Wall NJ 07719. (201)449-1776. Marketing Manager: Christy Karl. Industrial direct marketers of maintenance products, i.e., concrete repair, roof repair. Clients: maintenance departments of corporations, government facilities, small businesses.
Needs: Works with 3 freelance artists/year. Uses artists for brochure and catalog design, illustration and layout. Seeks "local artists and ones who will work within the organization so that corrections and additions can be done on the spot."
First Contact & Terms: Send query letter with brochure, resume, business card, photographs or photostats to be kept on file. Reports only if interested. Pays by the page or by the project. Considers complexity of project, and skill and experience of artist when establishing payment.
Tips: "Professionalism is a must! Work should be camera-ready for commercial printing upon completion. I need experienced catalog artists with creative ideas."

GARTH PRODUCTS, INC., 32-4 Littell Rd., East Hanover NJ 07936. (201)887-8487. President: Garth Patterson. Manufacturer of silkscreened ceramic and glass souvenirs. Clients: banks, museums, amusement parks, restored villages, tourist attractions, resorts, hotels and retail stores.
Needs: Works with 5 artists per year. Uses artists for illustrations on products. Especially needs line drawings of buildings, statues, flowers and songbirds.
First Contact & Terms: Send query letter, photostats, brochure/flyer or actual work. Samples returned by SASE. Reports within 3-4 weeks. Provide business card, brochure and samples to be kept on file for possible future assignments. Payment is by the project; $25-100 average and varies according to complexity of job and skill and experience of artist.
Tips: "Understand the type of line work needed for silkscreening. We now also use pencil work. Better artwork is more appreciated."

GEORGIA-PACIFIC CORP., 133 Peachtree St., Atlanta GA 30303. (404)521-4758. Director of Marketing Communications, Building Products: Allen Thielman. Manufactures building products, pulp, paper and resin.
Needs: Works with 5-10 artists/year for ad illustrations; 15-20, advertising design; 3, product design; and 4-5, illustrations for use on products. Also uses artists for direct mail brochures, annual reports, billboards, interior design, posters, catalogs, spec sheets and print collateral. Prefers local artists.
First Contact & Terms: Query with resume and printed samples. Provide resume, business card, brochure and flyer to be kept on file for future assignments. Pays $35-50/hour, design; $25-30/hour, finish. Fees on large projects are estimated by artist—"generally runs at $35-50/hour."

GOLDBERGS' MARINE, 202 Market St., Philadelphia PA 19106. (215)829-2200. Vice President Marketing: Richard Goldberg. Produces 9 mail order catalogs of pleasure boating equipment and watersport gear for the active family.

Needs: Works with 6 freelance artists/year. Artists must be "flexible with knowledge of 4-color printing, have a willingness to work with paste-up and printing staff, and exhibit the ability to follow up and take charge." Uses artists for brochure and catalog design, illustration and layout; and signage.
First Contact & Terms: Send query letter with brochure, business card, printed material and tear sheets to be kept on file. Original work (mechanicals) may be required at portfolio showing." Reports only if interested. Call for appointment to show portfolio. Pays by the project. Considers complexity of project, how work will be used and turnaround time when establishing payment.
Tips: "Boating experience is helpful and a willingness to do research is sometimes necessary. Long-term relationships usually exist with our company."

***THE GREAT MIDWESTERN ICE CREAM COMPANY**, Box 1717, 209 N. 16 St., Fairfield IA 52556. (515)472-7595. President: Fred Gratzon. Manufacturer and franchiser. "We manufacture an excellent ice cream which we feel is the new standard in the industry. We sell it through supermarkets and our beautiful franchise stores." Clients are grocery shoppers and ice cream lovers.
Needs: Works with 15+ freelance artists/year. Uses freelance artists for the design, illustration and layout of advertising, brochures and catalogs plus product design, illustration of the product, P-O-P displays, display fixture design, posters, model making, signage, and fashion clothing design for franchise employees and customers (t-shirts, etc.).
First Contact & Terms: Send query letter with resume and samples. Samples not filed are returned with SASE. Reports back only if interested. Call to schedule an appointment to show a portfolio. Pays for design by the project, $3,000; pays for illustration by the project, $1,000. Considers complexity of project, client's budget, skill and experience of artists, how work will be used and rights purchased when establishing payment.
Tips: "We are a highly creative company that prefers art on the cutting edge. We are looking for all types of art—from painting to cartoons—that uses ice cream as the theme."

GUILFORD PUBLICATIONS INC., 200 Park Ave. S., New York NY 10003. (212)674-1900. Marketing Manager: Marian Robinson. Produces professional, educational and industrial audiovisuals and books.
Needs: Assigns 20 jobs/year. Local artists only. Uses artists for catalog design, book jackets and ads.
First Contact & Terms: Query. SASE. Reports within 4 weeks. Pays by job.

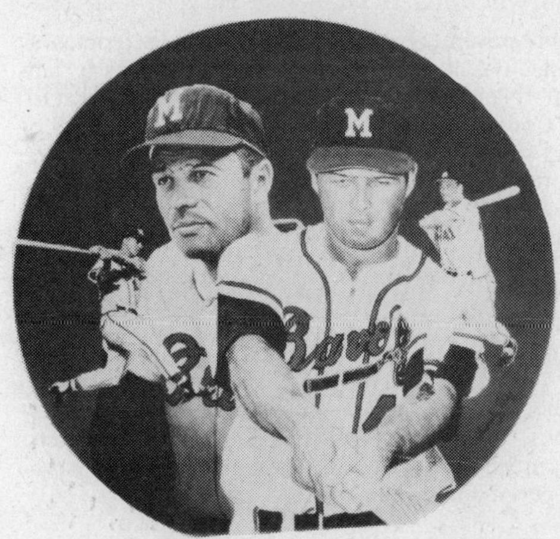

Freelance artist Christopher Paluso used an airbrush to capture the hitting power of slugger Eddie Matthews in this limited edition collectors plate issued by Hackett American of Fort Lauderdale, Florida. Paluso received $2,000 for the single-issue release.

HACKETT AMERICAN, (formerly DMP Hackett American), 6700 Griffin Rd., Ft. Lauderdale FL 33314. (305)791-1264. President: James. R. Hackett. Manufacturer and art publisher of wholesale collector plates, lithographs, figurines and miniatures. Clients: wholesalers, dealers and consumers.
Needs: Works with 20-30 freelance artists/year. Uses freelance artists for plate design and illustration; figurine design; and limited edition fine art prints. Seeks illustrative, realistic style artwork.
First Contact & Terms: Works on assignment basis only. Send query letter with slides and photographs to be kept on file. Samples not kept on file are returned only if requested. Reports within 30 days. Write for appointment to show portfolio. Pays by the project, $500-2,000 or on a royalty basis. Considers skill and experience of artist when establishing payment. Negotiates rights purchased.

THE HAMILTON COLLECTION, Suite 1000, 9550 Regency Square Blvd., Jacksonville FL 32211. Vice President, Product Development: Melanie Hart; Art Director (for commercial art/advertising): Debra Levine. Direct mail/marketing firm for collectibles and limited edition art, plates, sculpture. Clients: general public and specialized lists of collectible buyers.
Needs: Works with 5 freelance artists in creative department and 15 in product development/year. Only local artists with three years' experience for mechanical work. For illustration and product design, "no restrictions on locality, but must have *quality* work and flexibility regarding changes which are sometimes necessary. Also, a 'name' and notoriety help." Uses artists for advertising mechanicals, brochure illustration and mechanicals, product design and illustration on product.
First Contact & Terms: Send query letter with samples to be kept on file, except for fine art which is to be returned (must include a SASE or appropriate container with sufficient postage). Samples not kept on file are returned only if requested by artist. Reports within 2-4 weeks. Call or write for appointment to show portfolio. Pays by the hour for mechanicals, $20 average. Considers complexity of project, skill and experience of artist, how work will be used and rights purchased when establishing payment.
Tips: "Be prepared to offer sketches on speculation."

HARTMAN CARDS, 839 N. Woodstock St., Philadelphia PA 19130. (215)236-4944. Contact: Louis Hartman. Distributor of greeting cards, calendars, stationery, gifts and t-shirts.
Needs: Buys finished products from artists; prefers a "contemporary, trendy" look. "Artists sell me the product once it's produced."
First Contact & Terms: Call for appointment to show portfolio. Prefers to review photographs. "Don't send material. Call only if you have produced a product and developed it into a business yourself."
Tips: "Artists should have initiative, flexibility, and the ability to develop a product line. We are looking for artists who will start their own business."

HERFF JONES, Box 6500, Providence RI 02940-6500. (401)331-1240. Art Director: Fred Spinney. Manufacturer of class ring jewelry; motivation/recognition/emblematic awards—service pins, medals, medallions and trophies. Clients: high school and college level students; a variety of companies/firms establishing recognition programs.
Needs: Works with 6 freelance artists/year. "Previous experience in this field helpful but not necessary. Must be strong in illustration work." Works on assignment only. Uses artists for illustration of product.
First Contact & Terms: Send query letter with brochure, resume, business card and samples (copies of original work) to be kept on file; originals will be returned if sent. Prefers slides and photographs as samples. Samples not kept on file returned by SASE. Reports only if interested. Write for appointment to show portfolio. Pays by the project, $25-100 average. Considers complexity of project, skill and experience of artist, and turnaround time when establishing payment.
Tips: Artists approaching this firm "should be of a professional level. The artist should have a good versatile background in illustrating as well as having some mechanical drawing abilities, such as hand lettering."

***HOUSTON INSTRUMENT**, 8500 Cameron, Austin TX 78753. Manager, Graphics Production: James Haining. Manufacturer of computer peripherals.
Needs: Works with 4 freelance artist/year. Uses artists for advertising design and illustration and brochure illustration.
First Contact & Terms: Send query letter with resume, slides and photographs. Samples not filed are returned only if requested. Reports back within 3 weeks. To show a portfolio, mail appropriate materials, which should include color, photostats and photographs. Pays for design and illustration by the project, negotiable amount. Considers use of computer peripherals when establishing payment.

***HOWARD-COOPER CORP.**, 8501 NE Killingsworth St., Portland OR 97220. (503)256-5600. Advertising Manager: Kent Cooper. Distributor providing sales and service construction, logging and mining equipment. Directed towards 21 years and up. Dresser construction and mining equipment, FMC link-belt, Timberjack, Prentice, OK and Wagner labels.
Needs: Works with 1 freelance artists/year. Local artists with industrial experience only. Uses artists for advertising and brochure design, illustration and layout; paste-up, mechanicals and direct mail. Prefers industrial theme.
First Contact & Terms: Send query letter with resume and samples. Samples not filed are returned only if requested. Reports only if interested. Call to schedule an appointment to show a portfolio, which should include tear sheets. Pays for design and illustration by the project, $200-1,000. Considers client's budget when establishing payment.
Tips: Artist should "be creative and know our industry."

HOWARD JOHNSON CO., Braintree Hill Office Park, 35 Rockdale Rd., Braintree MA 02184. Graphics/Design Director: Robert C. Downing. Services/Products: Food and lodging and specialty restaurant concepts.
Needs: Works with illustrators, graphic design shops, product designers and 2-3 freelancers/year. Prefers local artists. Must have professional experience in lodging industry. Uses artists for product illustrations, sales promotion literature, catalog covers/illustrations, exhibit designs and displays.
First Contact & Terms: Send query letter with brochure showing art style or resume, slides and photographs. Samples will be returned if requested. "Illustrators should submit samples which will be returned. Would especially like to see architectual and interior design style illustrations, color and/or black and white." Call or write to schedule an appointment to show a portfolio, which should include thumbnails, roughs, original/final art, final reproduction/product, color, photographs and b&w. Pays for design by the hour, $35-100; by the project, $250-2,000. Pays for illustration by the hour, $35-100; by the project, $250-2,500. Rights purchased vary according to project.
Tips: "Know field that the customer is in—don't show children's illustrations to a business of commercial customers—see style they've used lately—show same *and* next step beyond for "new look." Consider also what their competition is doing."

HUTCHESON DISPLAYS, INC., 517 S. 14th St., Omaha NE 68102. (402)341-0707. President: Wm. S. Hutcheson. Manufacturer of screen printed display materials. Clients: advertisers.
Needs: Works with 6 freelance artists/year. Uses artists for advertising layout. Especially needs graphic design.
First Contact & Terms: Send query letter with brochure showing art style. Samples returned. Portfolio should include photographs. Pays by the project. Pays for design and illustration by the project. Considers complexity of project when establishing payment. Buys one-time rights.

IGPC, 48 W. 48th St., New York NY 10036. (212)869-5588. Postage Stamp Art Director: Dick King. Agent to foreign governments; "we produce postage stamps and related items on behalf of thirty different foreign governments."
Needs: Works with 25-35 freelance artists/year. Artists must be within metropolitan (NY) or tri-state area. "No actual experience required except to have good tight art skills (four-color) and excellent design skills." Works on assignment only. Uses artists primarily for postage stamp design; sometimes uses them for advertising, brochure and catalog design, illustration and layout.
First Contact & Terms: Call for appointment to show portfolio. Reports immediately. Pays by the project, $500-15,000 average. Considers government allowance per project when establishing payment.
Tips: "Artists considering working with IGPC must have excellent 4-color abilities (in general or specific topics, i.e., flora, fauna, transport, famous people, etc.); sufficient design skills to arrange for and position type; the ability to create artwork that will reduce to postage stamp size and still hold up to clarity and perfection. 90% of the work we require is realistic art and 10% is graphic. In most cases, we supply the basic layout and reference material; however, we appreciate an artist who knows where to find references and can present new and interesting concepts. Initial contact may be made by mail only if you live in the NY tri-state area and can come in to receive and discuss commissions. If you live outside the tri-state area, please don't bother making contact as your material will not be reviewed or returned to you."

INCOLAY STUDIOS INCORPORATED, 445 N. Fox St., Box 592, San Fernando CA 91340. (818)365-2521. Curator: Brenda Lynch-Silvestri. Manufacturer of wholesale Incolay stone bas-relief giftware. Clients: high-end jewelry and gift stores.
Needs: Works with 6 freelance artists/year. Works on assignment only. Uses freelance artists to sculpt bas-relief designs.
First Contact & Terms: Send query letter with photographs or slides to be kept on file. Reports back to the artist within 2 weeks. Call or write to schedule an appointment to show a portfolio, which should include photographs and b&w. Payment is by the project on a royalty basis (% of wholesale). Considers complexity of the project and project budget when establishing payment. Buys all rights.

***INSTAR**, 11 East 26 St., New York NY 10010. Contact: Bruce Andolfo. Manufacturer of open stock and custom ceramic and glass decals; collectable quality decals for ceramics and glass; finished products in ceramic and glass. Clients: wholesalers, corporations and manufacturers.
Needs: Works with 15-20 freelance artist/year. Uses artists for plate and figurine design. Send query letter with brochure showing art style or slides and photographs. Samples not filed returned only if requested. Reports only if interested. Write to schedule an appointment to show a portfolio, which should

include original/final art, final reproduction/product, color and photographs. Pays for design by the project, $60-600. Considers complexity of project, skill and experience of artist, turnaround time and rights purchased when establishing payment.

INTERNATIONAL RESEARCH & EVALUATION, 21098 Ire Control Ctr., Eagan MN 55121. (612)888-9635. Art Director: Ronald Owon. Private, nonpartisan, interdisciplinary research firm that collects, stores and disseminates information on line, on demand to industry, labor and government on contract/subscription basis.
Needs: Works with 30-40 freelance artists/year. Works on assignment only. Uses artists for advertising, brochure and catalog design, illustration and layout; product design and P-O-P displays.
First Contact & Terms: Artists should request "Capabilities Analysis" form from firm. Reports only if interested. Pays by the hour, $50-250 average. Considers how work will be used when establishing payment.

***JARVIS DESIGN & DISPLAY, LTD.**, 350 Kirkwood Ave., Ottawa, Ontario, Canada K1Z 8P1. (613)722-4162. Production Manager: Chris Dixon. Manufacturer of 3-D letters (high density foam, plexiglass, vinyl); "custom work our specialty." Clients: large department stores, grocery stores, any retail outlet, shopping centers, anyone requiring display in trade shows.
Needs: Works with 2 freelance artists/year. Uses artists for brochure, catalog and product design; P-O-P displays, and signage.

JOULÉ INC., 54 Oakwood Ave., Orange NJ 07051. (201)672-2000. Marketing Manager: Carl Tuosto. Engineering firm.
Needs: Works on assignment only. Uses artists for advertising gimmicks, graphic sales promotion, audiovisual presentations and exhibit equipment. Needs artists for general design, layout and comps.
First Contact & Terms: Send query letter, brochure and resume to be kept on file for possible future assignments. Reports back. Call or write to schedule an appointment to show a portfolio, which should include thumbnails, roughs, final reproduction/product, photographs and b&w. Pays $500-1,000 average for camera-ready art.

***DAVID KAHN INC. "WEAVER"**, Rt. 61, Deer Lake PA 17961-0280. (717)366-1011. President: Alvin A. Kahn. Manufacturer writing instruments.
Needs: Uses artists for advertising, brochure and catalog design; and package design.
First Contact & Terms: Send query letter with brochure showing art style. To show a portfolio, mail appropriate materials.

***KELCO**, Division of Merck & Co., Inc., 8355 Aero Dr., San Diego CA 92123. (619)292-4900. Advertising and Communcations: Yolanda Nuñez. Specialty chemical firm. Clients: food companies, industrial users and oil field companies.
Needs: Works with 1-2 freelance artists per year. Works on assignment only. Uses artists for advertising and brochure design and illustration; employee annual report, and AV presentations.
First Contact & Terms: Send query letter. Reports in 3 weeks. Negotiates payment.

KERN COLLECTIBLES, 1987 Industrial Blvd., Box 366, Stillwater MN 55082. (612)733-9442. Contact: Manager. Art publisher of wholesale and retail collector plates and figurines featuring children, birds, wildlife, and fantasy art. Clients: retail stores and consumers.
Needs: Works with 6 freelance artists/year. Uses artists for plate and figurine design and illustration. Prefers realistic styles.
First Contact & Terms: Send query letter with brochure and samples; brochure only is filed. Prefers slides and photographs as samples. Samples are returned. Reports back within 30 days. Negotiates payment. Considers skill and experience of the artist and rights purchased when establishing payment.

***KIMBALL SYSTEMS**, 151 Cortlandt St., Belleville NJ 07109. Art Director: John Corimer. Manufacturer providing artwork pertaining to the airline sortation industry. Clients: airlines, steam ships, hotels and trains.
Needs: Works with 20 freelance artist/year. Local artists only with 5 years' experience minimum. Works on assignment only. Uses artists for brochure design and illustration; catalog layout; and P-O-P displays.
First Contact & Terms: Send query letter with resume and slides. Samples not filed are not returned. Reports only if interested. Write to schedule an appointment to show a portfolio, which should include thumbnails, roughs, original/final art, final reproduction/product, photostats and photographs. Pays for design by the project, $10-250. Pays for illustration by the project, $25-500. Considers complexity of project, skill and experience of artist, turnaround time and rights purchased when establishing payment.

KLITZNER IND., INC., 44 Warren St., Providence RI 02901. (401)751-7500, ext. 242. Design Director: Louis Marini. Manufacturer; "four separate divisions that serve uniquely different markets: ad specialty, fraternal, direct mail and retail."

Needs: Works with "several" freelance artists/year. Artists must be "qualified to provide the desired quality of work within our time frame." Works on assignment only. Uses artists for product design, illustration on product and model making.

First Contact & Terms: Send query letter with resume to be kept on file. Reviews photostats, photographs, photocopies, slides or tear sheets; "they must clearly illustrate the quality, detail, etc. of artist's work." Materials not filed are returned by SASE. Reports back only if interested. Write for appointment to show portfolio. Pays by the project; "a mutually agreed upon figure *before* the project is undertaken."

Tips: "Turn-around time on most projects has been virtually cut in half. More competitive market warrants quick, dependable service. This change has created a bigger need for outside assistance during heavy backlog periods."

***KRISCH HOTELS, INC.**, Box 14100, Roanoke VA 24022. (703)342-4531. Director of Communications: Julie Becker. Estab. 1985. Service-related firm providing all advertising, in-room and P-O-P pieces for camping (inhouse department). Clients: hotel/motels and restaurants/lounges.

Needs: Works with 10-20 freelance artists/year. Prefers local artists. Works on assignment only. Uses artists for advertising and brochure illustration; illustration on product, P-O-P displays, posters and signage.

First Contact & Terms: Send query letter with resume and photocopies. Samples not filed are not returned. Reports only if interested. Call or write to schedule an appointment to show a portfolio, which should include roughs, original/final art, tear sheets and photostats. Pays for design and illustration by the hour, $25 minimum; by the project, $75 minimum; by the day, $200 minimum. Considers complexity of project, client's budget, how work will be used, turnaround time and rights purchased when establishing payment.

Tips: "Increased competition in all markets leads to more sophisticated work atitudes on the part of our industry. Artists should know their own abilities and limitations and be able to interact with us to achieve best results."

KRON-TV, NBC, 1001 Van Ness Ave., San Francisco CA 94119. (415)441-4444. Design Director: Judy Rosenfeld. TV/film producer. Produces videotapes and still photos.

Needs: Works with 1-2 artists/year for ad illustrations, 1-2 for advertising design and 1-5 for product design. Local artists only. Uses artists for design and production of all types of print advertising, direct mail brochures, promotion and sales pieces. Especially needs computer graphic art.

First Contact & Terms: Query. Provide resume and business card to be kept on file for future assignments.

Tips: "We're looking for experienced designers with heavy production knowledge that would enable them to handle a job from design concept through printing."

***KUTSUWA (AMERICA) INC.**, 2295 Jefferson St., Torrance CA 90501. (213)618-1513. Executive President: Tad Katayama. Manufacturer of stationery, gift and novelty products. Clients: retailers (gift shop, candy shop, boutique, stationery shop).

Needs: Works with 4 freelance artists/year. Works on assignment only. Uses artists for mechanicals, advertising, brochure and catalog design, graphic designs on products. Prefers trendy, high-fashion and high-tech as looks.

First Contact & Terms: Send query letter with resume and photographs. Samples not filed are returned. Reports only if interested. Call or write to schedule an appointment to show a portfolio, which should include final reproduction/product, color and photographs. Pays for design by the hour, $20 minimum. Pays for design by the hour, $20 minimum. Pays for illustrations by the hour, $20 minimum. Considers how work will be used when establishing payment.

KVCR—TV/FM RADIO, 701 S. Mount Vernon Ave., San Bernardino CA 92410. (714)888-6511 or 825-3103. Program Director: Lew Warren. Specializes in public and educational radio/TV.

Needs: Works with 1 ad illustrator and 2 product illustrators/year. Assigns 1-10 jobs/year. Works on assignment only. Works on assignment only. Uses artists for graphic/set design, set design painters and camera-ready cards.

First Contact & Terms: Query and mail photos or slides. Reports in 2 weeks. Samples returned by SASE. Pays $20-30, camera-ready cards.

***LARAMI CORPORATION**, 340 North 12 St., Philadelphia PA 19107. (215)923-4900. Vice President: Myung Song. Produces toys.

Needs: Uses local artists only. Works on assignment only. Uses artists for mechanicals.
First Contact & Terms: Send query letter with brochure showing art style and/or resume and samples. Samples not filed are not returned. Reports only if interested. To show a portfolio, mail thumbnails, roughs, original/final art, final reproduction/product, color, tear sheets, photostats, photographs and b&w.

***LASER ART DIVISION-LASER LABORATORY**, Laser Art Gallery-The Light Fantastic, Laser Research Laboratory, Cincinnati OH 45208. (513)321-4804. Director: Leon Goldman, MD. Develops all phases of laser art. Members are those interested in training, in laser art and art for laser companies. Special exhibits of many forms of laser art.
Needs: Works with 4 freelance artists/year. Artists must have training or interest in laser technology. Uses artists for advertising, exhibits, brochure and catalog design, illustration and layout, exhibits, displays, signage and posters. Prefers any phase of laser art design, sculpture, photography, interferommentry: holography, lapidary.
First Contact & Terms: Schedule at times available for training in laser art. Send query letter with photocopies and slides to be kept on file. Samples are returned. Reports within 2 weeks. Write to schedule an appointment to show a portfolio, which should include original/final art, color, photostats and photographs. Considers complexity of project and available budget when establishing payment.
Tips: "Accepts exhibits for laser art in laser art gallery, the Light Fantastic."

LEISURE AND RECREATION CONCEPTS INC., 2151 Fort Worth Ave., Dallas TX 75211. (214)942-4474. President: Michael Jenkins. Designs and builds amusement and theme parks.
Needs: Assigns 200 jobs/year. Uses artists for exhibits/displays and sketches of park building sections and bird's eye views of facilities.
First Contact & Terms: Query with samples or previously used work, or arrange interview. SASE. Reports in 1 week. Pay determined by job.

LEISURE LEARNING PRODUCTS INC., 16 Division St. W., Box 4869, Greenwich CT 06830. (203)531-8700. Advertising/Sales Promotion Manager: Richard Bendett. Manufactures children's games, activities, books and educational products.
Needs: Uses artists for illustration and design for sales literature, inhouse publications, recruitment literature, catalogs, exhibits and displays. Also needs cartoon-type color illustrations similar to the style of Walt Disney illustrations, Peanuts and Nancy strips. Must appeal to the 3-8 year old range.
First Contact & Terms: Query with photocopies or art. Pays $10-25 minimum, product illustration.

LILLIAN VERNON CORP., 510 S. Fulton Ave., Mount Vernon NY 10550. (914)699-4131. Vice President: David Hochberg. Direct mail giftware firm that produces greeting cards, giftwrap, calendars, stationery and paper tableware products. Also produces toiletries, housewares, textiles, dinnerware and toys. Two divisions: one serves general consumers, the other serves retail stores.
Needs: Buys 250 designs and 100 illustrations/year from freelance artists. Only artists within 250 miles "for ease in communication." Works on assignment only. Also uses artists for P-O-P displays. Considers all types of media for illustrations. "We are heavily oriented toward Christmas merchandise"; submit seasonal artwork in January or February.
First Contact & Terms: Send query letter with brochure, resume photostats, photographs or tear sheets to be kept on file. "Please don't call!" Samples not filed are returned only if requested. Reports within 2 weeks. Original art not returned after reproduction. Pays flat fee. Buys first rights.
Tips: "We are *always* on the lookout for good talent!"

LOON MOUNTAIN RECREATION CORP., Kancamagus Hwy., Lincoln NH 03251. (603)745-8111. Marketing Director: Rick Owen. Ski resort with inn, restaurants and lounges.
Needs: Works with 2 advertising designers/year. Assigns 6 jobs and buys 2 illustrations/year. Uses artists for design and illustration of brochures, signs, displays, mailings and other promotional materials. Especially needs renderings of future projects.
First Contact & Terms: Arrange interview. SASE. Reports within 2 weeks. Negotiates pay; pays by the hour, $10 average. Considers skill and experience of artist, and turnaround time when establishing payment.

***LOVELADY ENTERPRISES**, 2045 W. 236th Pl., Torrance CA 90501. President: Janet Lovelady. Works on assignment only. Send query letter with brochure showing art style or resume, tear sheets, photostats and photocopies.

***McCULLEY MARKETING**, 17910 Los Alamos, Saratoga CA 95070. President: Jean McCulley. Estab. 1985. Service related firm providing advertising, data sheets, catalogs, and public relations for electronics manufacturers.

Needs: Works with 3 freelance artists/year. Prefers local artists only. Works on assignment only. Uses artists for the design, illustrations and layout of advertising, brochures and catalogs.
First Contact & Terms: Send resume and photocopies. Samples not filed are returned only if requested. Reports only if interested. Call or write to schedule an appointment to show a portfolio, which should include roughs and photocopies. Pays for design by the hour, $10-30. Pays for illustration by the hour $10-30. Considers complexity of project, client's budget, and skill and experience of artist when establishing payment.

***MARKETECHS INC.**, 630 Loucks Mill Rd., York PA 17403. Contact: Mary Popovich. Exhibits firm.
Needs: Uses artists for advertising, exhibits, display design and scale models. Especially needs freelance exhibit and display designers.
First Contact & Terms: Write to schedule an appointment to show a portfolio, which should include roughs, tear sheets, photographs and b&w. Pays up to $300 for 15' exhibit. Buys all rights.

MARURI USA CORP., 15145 Califa St., Van Nuys CA 91411. Director/Sales and Marketing: Edward J. Purcell. Manufacturer of wholesale limited edition porcelain figurines and ceramic giftware. Clients: retailers.
Needs: Works with 3-5 freelance artists/year. Works on assignment only. Uses artists for figurine design and illustration; advertising, brochure and catalog design and illustration.
First Contact & Terms: Send query letter with brochure, resume, photographs and tear sheets to be kept on file. Samples not filed are returned only if requested. Reports only if interested. Write for appointment to show portfolio. Pays for design by project, $500 minimum; for illustration by the project, $100 minimum. Considers complexity of the project and how work will be used when establishing payment.

***METROPOLITAN WATER DISTRICT OF SOUTHERN CALIFORNIA (MWD)**, Box 54153, 1111 Sunset Blvd., Los Angeles CA 90054. (213)250-6496. Graphic Arts Designer: Mario Chavez. Supplies water for southern California. "MWD imports water from the Colorado River and Northern California through the state water project, it imports about half of all the water used by some 13 million consumers in urban Southern California from Ventura to Riverside to San Diego counties. MWD wholesales water to 27 member public agencies which, along with about 130 subagencies, deliver it to homes and businesses in MWD's 5,200-square-mile service area."
Needs: Works with 4-6 freelance artists/year. "Color artwork for publication is separated on scanner, it should be flexible; final agreement (contract) is purchase order, based upon verbal agreement of artist accepting assignment. All artwork is vested in Metropolitan Water District unless agreed upon." Works on assignment only. Uses artists for brochure/publications design, illustration and layout.
First Contact & Terms: Send query letter with brochure showing art style. Samples not filed are returned by SASE. Reports only if interested. Call to schedule an appointment to show a portfolio, which should include roughs, original/final art, color, tear sheets and b&w. Pays for design by the project, $100 minimum. Pays for illustration by the project, $50 minimum. Considers complexity of project, client's budget, skill and experience of artist, how work will be used, turnaround time and rights purchased when establishing payment.
Tips: "Phone calls should be kept short and to a minimum. Public affairs of MWD is interested in skillful execution of conceptual artwork to illustrate articles for its publication program. Number of projects is limited."

MILWAUKEE SIGNS CO., 1964 Wisconsin Ave., Grafton WI 53024. (414)377-8920. Director of Marketing: Bob Aiken.
Needs: Local artists only. Works on assignment only. Works with 3 artists for sign design and P-O-P design. Also uses artists for custom sign faces, brochure and ad design.
First Contact & Terms: Arrange interview to show portfolio. Samples returned by SASE. Reports back on future possibilities. Send resume, business card and brochure to be kept on file. Considers complexity of project, skill and experience of artist, and how work will be used when establishing payment.

MURPHY INTERNATIONAL SALES ORGANIZATION, 11444 Zelzah Ave., Granada Hills CA 91344. (818)363-1410. President: F.S. Murphy. Distributor and service-related firm providing retrofit, covering materials, new products and patents. Clients: building and home owners.
Needs: Works with 2 freelance artists/year. Uses artists for advertising, brochure and catalog design, and illustration on product.
First Contact & Terms: Send samples to be kept on file. Write for art guidelines. Prefers photocopies as samples. Samples not filed are not returned. Reports back only if interested. Pays by the project. Considers how work will be used when establishing payment.
Tips: "Design should be realistic. Art is becoming more simple and less dramatic."

MURRAY HILL PRESS, 43 N. Village Ave., Rockville Centre NY 11570. (516)764-6262. President: Ralph Ceisler. Printer. Clients: paint manufacturers, window treatment magazines and general commercial.
Needs: Assigns 12 jobs/year; uses mostly local artists. Uses artists for catalogs, direct mail brochures, flyers and P-O-P displays. Especially needs P-O-P displays in retail stores, paint and hardware stores in particular. "Need good catalog-brochure art. Must be creative. We compete with originals by supplying full package. Artist preferably should be from Long Island for better access."
First Contact & Terms: Send query letter with tearsheets. SASE. Reports in 2 weeks. Call or write to schedule an appointment to show a portfolio, which should include thumbnails, roughs, original/final art and final reproduction/product. Pays for design and illustration by the project, $100 minimum. Pay depends strictly on job and is negotiable. Considers complexity of project, skill and experience of artist, and how work will be used when establishing payment. Rights purchased vary according to project.
Tips: "Have samples showing rough thru completion."

NEIBAUER PRESS, INC., 20 Industrial Dr., Warminister PA 18974. (215)322-6200. Contact: Nathan Neibauer. Publishers and printers of religious publications.
Needs: Works with 12 freelance artists/year. Works on assignment only. Uses artists for advertising, brochure and catalog design, illustration and layout; illustration on product, and posters.
First Contact & Terms: Send query letter with photocopies. Reports only if interested. Write for appointment to show portfolio. Pays by the hour, $10 minimum; or by the project. Considers skill and experience of artist when establishing payment.

NORTON OUTDOOR ADVERTISING, 5280 Kennedy Ave., Cincinnati OH 45213. (513)631-4864. Contact: Tom Norton. Outdoor advertising firm.
Needs: Assigns 30-60 jobs/year. Local artists only. Uses artists for billboards.
First Contact & Terms: Call for interview. Pays $25 minimum, roughs; $75-100, finished sketch.

NOT-POLYOPTICS, 13721 Lynn St., Woodbridge VA 22191. (703)491-5543. General Partner: Michael Capobianco. Manufacturer/distributor of software and hardware for the Texas Instruments 99/4(A) home computer. Clients: individuals, distributors, software stores.
Needs: Works with 3-4 freelance artists/year. Works on assignment only. Uses artists for advertising design, illustration and layout; catalog design and illustration; illustration on product and art co-ordination for total effect.
First Contact & Terms: Send query letter with brochure showing art style. Samples not filed are returned by SASE. Reports within 1 month. To show a portfolio, mail final reproduction/product and color. Pays by the project, $100-500 average; terms of payment are negotiable. Considers complexity of project, skill of artist, turnaround time and rights purchased when establishing payment. Buys all rights.
Tips: "We are particularly interested in high-quality color and b&w renditions of game situations. Airbrush skill is important."

O'DONNELL-USEN FISHERIES, 255 Northern Ave., Boston MA 02210. (617)542-2700. Executive Vice President: Arnold S. Wolf. Processes frozen seafoods.
Needs: Assigns 20-30 jobs and buys 15 illustrations/year. Uses artists for packaging, point of sale material and letterheads, etc. Especially needs new packaging design.
First Contact & Terms: Query with samples (rough sketches, mock up design). SASE. Reports in 3 weeks. Provide resume to be kept on file for possible future assignments. Pays compensation based on agreement by the project. Considers complexity of project and rights purchased when establishing payment.
Tips: "Present boxes are being redesigned and made more modern." Artists should "have past experience in design of packaging."

***PENNSYLVANIA FIREBACKS, INC.**, 1011 East Washington Ln., Philadelphia PA 19138. Art Director/President: J. Del Conner. Manufacturer of sculpted cast iron products and custom made hand-painted wood products. Clients: mail order catalogs, gift shops and department stores.
Needs: Works with 6-7 freelance artists/year. Works on assignment only. Uses artists for advertising and catalog design and illustration; brochure design, illustration and layout; product design, illustration on product and model making.
First Contact & Terms: Send query letter with resume, photocopies, slides and photographs. Samples not filed are returned only if requested. Reports back. To show a portfolio, mail photographs or write to schedule an appointment. Pays for illustration by the project, $50-500. Considers how work will be used when establishing payment.

PERFECT PEN & STATIONERY CO. LTD., A42, 1241 Denison St., Markham, Ontario L3R 4B4 Canada. (416)474-1866. President: S. Szlrtes. Distributor of advertising specialties, office specialties and

gifts. Clients: "all businesses across Canada."
Needs: Works with 6 freelance artists/year. Artists must have a minimum of 5 years' experience and references. Works on assignment only. Uses artists for advertising, brochure and catalog design and layout; photography and film work.
First Contact & Terms: Send query letter with brochure to be kept on file. Prefers tear sheets as samples. Samples not filed are not returned. Reports back only if interested. Write for appointment to show portfolio. Pays by the project. Considers complexity of the project when establishing payment.
Tips: "Apply only if you're experienced in direct mail advertising or a closely related area."

PHILADELPHIA T-SHIRT MUSEUM, 235 N 12th St., Philadelphia PA 19107. (215)625-9230. President: Marc Polish. Manufacturer and distributor of imprinted t-shirts and sweatshirts for retail shops and national mail order firms.
Needs: Uses artists for imprinted sportwear.
First Contact & Terms: Send query letter with brochure showing art style or photocopies. Samples not filed are returned. Reports within 1 week. To show a portfolio, mail roughs and photostats. Pays in percent of sales or outright purchase.

PICKARD, INC., 782 Corona Ave., Antioch IL 60002. Contact: Product Development Manager. Manufacturer of wholesale fine china dinnerware and collector plates. Clients: retailers.
Needs: Works with 3-4 freelance artists/year. Works on assignment only. Uses artists for patterns for dinnerware and fine art for collector plates. Prefers realistic and classical styles. Seeks "fine art as opposed to illustration for our limited edition plates."
First Contact & Terms: Send query letter with brochure, resume and slides or printed brochure. Samples not filed are returned only if requested. Reports within 1 month. Negotiates payment; generally a flat fee and/or royalties. Considers complexity of project, project's budget, skill and experience of the artist, how work will be used, turnaround time and rights purchased when establishing payment.

PICTURESQUE PRODUCTS, Box 41630, Tucson AZ 85717. President: B.B. Nelson. Mail order firm of general gift items. Clients: consumers.
Needs: Works with 2 freelance artists/year. Uses artists for advertising, brochure and catalog design, illustration and layout; and P-O-P displays.
First Contact & Terms: Send query letter to be kept on file. Reports only if interested. Pays by the project, $100-500 average. Considers skill and experience of artist, how work will be used and rights purchased when establishing payment.
Tips: "Originality in the presentation sells me."

PITTSBURGH DISPLAY, 200 Federal St., Pittsburgh PA 15212. (412)322-5800. President: Art Pearlman. Distributes decorative material, fabrics, papers, plastics, and photographic arts. Clients: malls, shopping centers, banks, utilities and retail merchants.
Needs: Works with 8-12 freelance artists/year. Uses artists for brochure and catalog design, illustration and layout; P-O-P displays; display fixture design; posters; and signage.
First Contact & Terms: Send query letter with brochure and samples to be kept on file. Prefers photographs, photocopies and tear sheets as samples. Samples not filed are returned by SASE. Does not report back. Call for appointment to show portfolio. Pays by the project, $60-200 average. Considers complexity of the project when establishing payment. Amount allowed within bid to customer.

PLANET-TRANS, INC., 5 Blake Ave., Brooklyn NY 11212. (718)773-3332. President: Marino Bonilla. Manufacturer of iron-on heat transfers in all types of design—adults, children, souvenir, babies—with worldwide distribution.
Needs: Works with 10 freelance artists/year. Works on assignment only. Uses artists for advertising illustration.
First Contact & Terms: Send query letter with original work, slides or photos to be kept on file. Samples not filed are returned by SASE. Reports only if interested. Call or write for appointment to show portfolio. Pays by the project, $125-200 average. Considers skill and experience of artist when establishing payment.
Tips: Prefers airbrush artwork on boards.

***POURETTE MFG. INC.**, 6910 Roosevelt Way NE, Seattle WA 98115. (206)525-4488. President: Don Olsen. Manufacturer and distributor specializing in candle making supplies and soap making supplies. Clients: anyone interested in selling candle making supplies or making candles.

***PRECISION GRAPHICS**, 119 W. Washington St., Champaign IL 61820. (217)359-6655. Contact: Jeff Mellander. Specializes in technical illustration for book publishers.

Needs: Works with 1-5 freelance artists/year. Uses artists for one-color, two-color and four-color work including airbrush illustration.
First Contact & Terms: Seeks artists experienced in drawing with technical pens and with highly developed skills in the area of technical illustration. Send query letter with brochure showing art style or resume, tear sheets, photostats, photocopies and slides to be kept on file. Samples not filed are returned by SASE only if requested. Reports only if interested. Write for appointment to show portfolio, which should include original/final art. Pays according to accepted job bid of artist. Considers complexity of project, skill and experience of artist, and turnaround time when establishing payment.
Tips: Looks for "quality-not quantity-and consistency" when reviewing work. "Beginning artists just out of school tend to show too much; try to hit on too many areas. Show what you *like* to do and what you do best."

PRESTIGELINE INC., 5 Inez Dr., Brentwood NY 11717. (516)273-3636. Director of Marketing: Ken Golden. Manufacturer of lighting products.
Needs: Buys various illustrations from freelance artists/year. Uses artists for advertising and catalog design, illustrations and layout; and illustration on product. Prefers b&w line drawings. Produces seasonal material for Christmas, Mother's Day, Father's Day, Thanksgiving, Easter, back-to-school and graduations; submit work 3-4 months before season.
First Contact & Terms: Send resume, business card and photostats. Call for appointment. Samples returned by SASE. Reports within 2 weeks. Buys all rights. Payment method is negotiable.
Tips: "There is an increased demand for b&w line art for newspaper advertisements."

PUCCI MANIKINS, 578 Broadway, New York NY 10012. (212)219-0142. Manufacturer of manikins—art work on faces, clay for sculptures. Clients: department stores.
Needs: Uses artists for model making.

PULPDENT CORPORATION OF AMERICA, 75 Boylston St., Brookline MA 02147. (617)232-2380. Director of Product Information: Jane Hart Berk. Manufacturer/distributor of dental supplies including instruments, pharmaceuticals, X-ray supplies, sterilizers, needles, articulating paper, etc. Clients: dental supply dealers and dentists.
Needs: Works with 3-5 freelance artists/year. Prefers local artists. Works on assignment only. Uses artists for advertising, brochure and catalog design, illustration and layout; photography and technical illustration.
First Contact & Terms: Send query letter with business card, photostats and tear sheets. Samples returned by SASE if not kept on file. Reports within 6 weeks. Call or write for appointment to show portfolio. Pays by the project, $40 minimum. Considers complexity of project, and skill and experience of artist when establishing payment; "how much our product is worth determines to some extent the amount we are willing to invest in designing, etc."
Tips: "We prefer simple, not-too-trendy designs aimed at the dental professional."

***RBW GRAPHICS**, 1749 20th St. E, Owen Sound, Ontario, N4K 5R2 Canada. Art Director: Thomas Hakala. Large volume, full-service printer with five print divisions: magazines, books, catalogs, directories and Data Graphics.
Needs: Works on assignment only. Prefers artists living in general area, but for some projects will consider anyone with the ability to create style needed.
First Contact & Terms: Send query letter with resume and photostats for b&w artwork; photographs or painted samples for color to be kept on file. Samples not kept on file are not returned. Reports only if interested. Pays $5 minimum/illustration, if in a series, for simple b&w (i.e., coloring books, cartoons) and $25 minimum for cover illustration, "depending on complexity and style." Considers complexity of project, skill and experience of artist, how work will be used and rights purchased when establishing payment.
Tips: "We don't use outside art on a regular basis—only for volume work and special projects. Don't expect immediate results. Our need is only occasional and generally we deal with the first name available as the need arises. We are involved in electronic page make up, pagination and word processor to type conversions, all which involve some amount of knowledge by the artist. Our film and press departments are now involved in computer conversion on a large scale."

***REALTORS NATIONAL MARKETING INST.**, Suite 500, 430 N. Michigan, Chicago IL 60611-4092. (312)670-3780. Production Assistant: Lisa Sulgit. Trade organization for real estate brokers.
Needs: Works with 4-8 freelance artists/year. Prefers local artists. Works on assignment only. Uses artists for advertising and brochure illustration.
First Contact & Terms: Send query letter with resume, tear sheets and photocopies. Samples not filed are not returned. Reports only if interested. Call or write to schedule an appointment to show a portfolio,

which should include original/final art, final reproduction/product and b&w. Pays for illustration by the hour, $10-50; by the project, $25-250. Considers complexity of project, how work will be used and turnaround time when establishing payment.

RECO INTERNATIONAL CORPORATION, Collector's Division, Box 951, 138-150 Haven Ave., Port Washington NY 11050. (516)767-2400. Manufacturer/distributor of limited editions collectors plates, lithographs and figurines. Clients: stores.
Needs: Works with 4 freelance artists/year. Uses artists for plate and figurine design, and limited edition fine art prints. Prefers romantic and realistic styles.
First Contact & Terms: Send query letter and brochure to be filed. Write for appointment to show a portfolio. Reports within 3 weeks. Negotiates payment.

RECO INTERNATIONAL CORPORATION, Kitchen Gourmet Accessories Division, 138-150 Haven Ave., Port Washington NY 11050. (516)767-2400. President: Heio W. Reich. Publisher and manufacturer.
Needs: Designers to design houseware and kitchen utensils on an exclusive basis for production according to designs. Works on assignment only.
First Contact & Terms: Send query letter brochure showing art style or resume; submit portfolio for review. Prefers to see "anything that will show artist's ability." Reports "when needed." Negotiates payments.

BOB ROBINSON MARKETING INC., 366 N. Broadway, Jericho NY 11753. (516)334-8600. President: Bob Robinson.
Needs: Assigns 100 jobs/year. Uses artists for display/P-O-P design and scale models.
First Contact & Terms: Arrange interview to show portfolio. SASE. Reports in 2 weeks. Pays $50-300/sketch or $100-1,000/job for design of permanent displays.

RSVP MARKETING, Suite 5, 450 Plain St., Marshfield MA 02050. (617)837-2804. President: Edward C. Hicks. Direct marketing consultant services—catalogs, direct mail and telemarketing. Clients: primarily industry and distributors.
Needs: Works with 7-8 freelance artists/year. Desires "primarily local artists; must have direct marketing skills." Uses artists for advertising, copy brochure and catalog design, illustration and layout.
First Contact & Terms: Send query letter with resume and finished, printed work to be kept on file. Reports only if interested. Pays by the job, $250-500 minimum. Considers skill and experience of artist when establishing payment.

***S.E. RYKOFF & CO.**, 761 Terminal St., Los Angeles CA 90021. (213)622-4131. Advertising Manager: Brad Sattler. Distributor of wholesale food and equipment to restaurants and institutions nationwide, serving restaurants, hospitals, schools and food establishments.
Needs: Works with 2 or 3 freelance artists/year. Prefers local artists. Works on assignment only. Uses artists for catalog design and layout, and also signage.
First Contact & Terms: Send query letter with resume. Reports only if interested. Write to schedule an appointment to show a portfolio, which should include final reproduction/product. Pays for design by the hour. Considers complexity of project when establishing payment.

SANTA FE PARK SPEEDWAY, 9100 S. Wolf Rd., Hinsdale IL 60521. (312)839-1050. Public Relations: Mary Lou Tiedt. Stock car racetrack. Clients: "We are a public family entertainment establishment and service a wide variety of manufacturers, patrons and small businesses locally. A large portion of advertisers, which need the work of our artists, are auto shops, motorcycle shops and restaurants."
Needs: Works with 2 artists/year for advertising design. Uses artists for advertising, direct mail brochures, posters, publicity brochures, yearly programs, bumper stickers and road signs. "We are looking for new original layouts and designs for racing." Especially needs speedway logo to be used on t-shirts, mailings and the program cover.
First Contact & Terms: Mail art. Will review basic pencil sketches or photos; previously published work is preferred. SASE. Reports in 2-4 weeks. Provide business card to be kept on file for possible future assignments. Call or write to schedule an appointment to show a portfolio, which should include original art, final reproduction, color or photographs. Negotiates pay. Considers how work will be used, turnaround time and rights purchased when establishing payment. Rights purchased vary according to project.
Tips: "Artist must keep up to date on the car models on the market for designs as we run a 'late model stock car' division; also on trends in t-shirt design and what will work well for printing (silk screen). Keep in touch and be persistent, as we get very busy. Send samples with envelope to return work in-…this allows a quick return and response to work. The best time to contact us for work is in November or late January. The spring season is much too late. By March, we are already set for the summer season."

***SEVEN CONTINENTS ENTERPRISES, INC.**, 350 Wallace Ave., Toronto, Ontario M6P 3P2 Canada. (416)535-5101. 1-800-387-0301 in USA. Creative Director: Sinclair Russell. Manufacturer providing display products, silk yardage, accessories to home furnishings. Materials used: silk, teakwood, cotton, bamboo, brass. Clients: department stores—window display, store interiors, fashion coordinators, furnishings; hotels-upholstery, urns.
Needs: Works with 5 freelance artists/year. Artists must possess "unusual creativity using much color and wild sizes." Uses artists for advertising, brochure and catalog design, illustration and layout; product and display fixture design, illustration on product, P-O-P displays, model making and signage.
First Contact & Terms: Send query letter with brochure, resume and samples to be kept on file or write for appointment to show portfolio. Samples returned only by request. Prefers color photographs and drawings as samples. Reports only if interested. Pays by the project, $200 minimum; or by the hour, $8-30. Considers complexity of project, skill and experience of artist, how work will be used, turnaround time and rights purchased when establishing payment.
Tips: "If you are not creative and terribly energetic, forget it."

SLADE CREATIVE MARKETING, Box 484, Santa Barbara CA 93102. (805)687-5331. President: S. Richard Slade. Service-related firm providing graphics, brochures, technical drawings, collateral material and general advertising. Clients: technical and consumer.
Needs: Works with 10-12 freelance artists/year. Artists must be able to communicate directly with company. Works on assignment only. Uses artists for advertising, brochure and catalog design, illustration and layout; illustration on product, P-O-P displays, signage, photography and technical writing.
First Contact & Terms: Send query letter with resume, photostats, photographs, photocopies, slides or tear sheets to be kept on file. Samples not filed are returned by SASE only if requested. Reports only if interested. Write for appointment to show portfolio. Pays by project, $100-750 average. Considers complexity of project, how work will be used and rights purchased when establishing payment.
Tips: "Be flexible and open to any job within your range."

***SNAP-ON TOOLS CORP.**, 1801-80th St., Kenosha WI 53140-2801. (414)656-5348. Advertisng Supervisor: Lee L. Hagopian. Manufacturer of tools and provides retouching of hand tool photos for dealers and marketing needs.
Needs: Works with 5 freelance artists per year on a daily basis, 5 outside freelancers. Prefers artists with three years' experience. Uses artists for the design, illustration and layout of advertising brochures and catalogs plus product design, illustration on product, P-O-P displays, display fixture design, posters, model making and signage.
First Contact & Terms: Contact only through artist's agent. Samples not filed are not returned. Reports back only if interested. Call or write to schedule an appointment to show a porfolio, which should include thumbnails, roughs, original/final art, final reproduction/product, color, tear sheets, photostats, photographs and b&w. Pays for design by the hour, $15-55. Pays for illustration by the hour $15-55. Considers complexity of project, client's budget, skill and experience of artist, how work will be used, turnaround time and rights purchased when establishing payment.

SOFTSYNC, INC., 162 Madison Ave., New York NY 10016. (212)685-2080. Director of Creative Services: Linda Schupack. Manufacturer of software for a variety of home computers. Subject matter includes education, personal productivity. Clients: computer and mass market retail stores.
Needs: Works with 5 freelance artists/year. Works on assignment only. Uses artists for advertising and brochure design, illustration and layout; illustration on product, P-O-P displays and posters.
First Contact & Terms: Send query letter with brochure and photographs, slides or tear sheets to be kept on file. Samples not filed are returned only if requested. Reports within days. Call or write for appointment to show portfolio. Pays by the hour, $10-15 average, or by the project, $350-1,000 average. Considers complexity of project, skill and experience of artist and how work will be used when establishing payment.
Tips: "For mechanicals artists, we need people who are quick and accurate. For illustrators, bring us samples that are colorful, zippy and innovative."

SPENCER GIFTS, INC., 1050 Black Horse Pike, Pleasantville NJ 08232. (609)645-5526. Art Director: James Stevenson. Retail gift chain located in approximately 440 malls in 43 states; gifts range from wall decorations to 14k gold jewelry.
Needs: Assigns 150-200 jobs/year. Prefers artists with professional experience in their field of advertising art. Uses artists for package design illustration, hard line art, fashion illustration, newspaper ads and toy, poster, package and product design, T-shirt design and other soft goods.
First Contact & Terms: Query with samples, previously published work or arrange interview to show portfolio. With samples, enclose phone number where you can be reached during business hours. Reports within 2 weeks. Negotiates pay.

STAMP COLLECTORS SOCIETY OF AMERICA, Box 3, W. Redding CT 06896. Executive Vice President and Creative Director: Malcolm Decker. Philatelic marketing firm. Develops mail order/direct response buyers of stamps using publications and mailing lists.
Needs: Works with 6 freelance artists/year. Prefers local (Westchester, New Haven, Fairfield County and New York City) artists; "experience requirement is determined by the job complexity." Works on assignment only. Uses artists for advertising and brochure design, illustration and layout; product design, album and editorial design, and "full-dress" direct mail packages.
First Contact & Terms: Send query letter and resume; "if interested, we'll call you. Show your portfolio and leave behind or send in samples or photocopies as requested." Pays by the hour, by the project, or offers a retainer. Considers complexity of project, and skill and experience of the artist when establishing payment.
Tips: "Send a comprehensive, detailed resume listing all the clients served, noting those for whom the most work was done."

***STOODY COMPANY**, 16425 Gale, Industry CA 91745. (818)968-0717. Advertising Manager: Thomas Chavez. Manufacturer providing welding consumables for end users and distributors.
Needs: Works on assignment only. Uses artists for advertising and catalog design, illustration and layout; P-O-P displays and signage.
First Contact & Terms: Send query letter with resume and photocopies. Samples not filed are returned only if requested. Reports back within 10 days. Call to schedule an appointment to show a portfolio, which should include thumbnails, roughs, final reproduction/product, color and tear sheets. Pays for design by the hour, $50-75. Pays for illustration by the hour, $20-50. Considers complexity of project, client's budget, skill and experience of artist, and turnaround time when establishing payment.
Tips: "Show me industrial applications. Not impressed by layouts with sexy ladies!"

***SURCO PRODUCTS, INC.**, Box 777, Braddock PA 15104. General Manager: Arnold Howard. Manufacturer of air fresheners, cleaners and related products.
Needs: Works with 3 freelance artists/year. Uses artists for advertising, brochure and catalog design, illustration and layout; product design, illustration on product, P-O-P displays, display fixture design, posters, model making and signage.
First Contact & Terms: Send query letter with brochure showing art style or resume, tear sheets, photostats and photocopies. Samples not filed are not returned. Reports only if interested. Write to schedule an appointment to show a portfolio, which should include original/final art, final reproduction/product, tear sheets, photographs and b&w. Negotiates payment. Considers complexity of project, client's budget, skill and experience of artist, how work will be used and turnaround time when establishing payment.

***SWEET STOP INC.**, 11 Tompkins Ave., S.I. NY 10304. (718)447-8400. President: G. Feldman. Produces candy novelties for card and gift shops.
Needs: Buys 4 designs and 4 illustrations from freelance artists/year. Prefers local artists only. Also uses artists for P-O-P displays and mechanicals. Prefers watercolors.
First Contact & Terms: Send resume, tear sheets and photographs. Samples not filed are returned. Reports within 10 days. Call to schedule an appointment to show a portfolio, which should include thumbnails and photographs. Original artwork returned. Pays flat fee. Negotiates rights purchased.

SYSTEMS PLUS, INC., 500 Clyde Ave., Mountain View CA 94043. Media Relations: Norman Stephens. Software publisher of vertical and horizontal business software for microcomputers.
Needs: Works with less than 5 freelance artists/year. Prefers local artists with extensive experience in the computer field and marketing. Works on assignment only. Uses artists for advertising design and illustration; brochure design, illustration and layout; product design, illustration on product and P-O-P displays.
First Contact & Terms: Send query letter with brochure and business card to be kept on file; "samples should be sent only on request." Samples not filed returned *if* accompanied by SASE. Reports only if interested, "usually." Pays by the project. Considers complexity of project, skill and experience of the artist, and turnaround time when establishing payment.

TEACH YOURSELF BY COMPUTER SOFTWARE, INC., 2128 W. Jefferson Rd., Pittsford NY 14534. (716)427-7065. President: Lois B. Bennett. Publisher of educational software for microcomputers. Clients: schools, individuals, stores.
Needs: Local artists only. Works on assignment only. Uses artists for advertising, brochure and catalog design, illustration and layout; and illustration on product.
First Contact & Terms: Send query letter with brochure, resume, photostats, photographs, photocopies, slides or tear sheets to be kept on file. Samples not filed are returned by SASE. Reports within 6

weeks. Write for appointment to show portfolio, which whould include roughs, photostats and photographs. Pays for design and illustration by the hour. Considers complexity of project, skill and experience of artist, how work will be used, turnaround time and rights purchased when establishing payment. Buys all rights.

THOMAS NELSON PUBLISHERS, Box 141000, Nelson Place, Elm Hill Pike, Nashville TN 37214. (615)889-9000. Vice President Advertising and Marketing: Robert J. Schwalb. Manufacturer and distributor of religious materials, Bibles, Christian books; also secular markets from subsidiary companies. Clients: retailers, book stores.
Needs: Works with 60 freelance artists/year. Works on assignment only. Uses artists for advertising, brochure and catalog design, illustration and layout; product and display fixture design, illustration on product, P-O-P displays, posters, model making and signage.
First Contact & Terms: Send query letter with brochure showing art style or tear sheets, photostats, photocopies, slides and photographs. Samples not kept on file are returned. Reports only if interested. Call or write to schedule an appointment to show a portfolio, which should include original/final art, final reproduction/product and photographs. No set pay range; "project budget sets price." Payment terms of 10 days or 30-day turnaround. Firm reserves publishing rights. Buys all rights.
Tips: Industry trends are toward "a clean-cut motif with simple design." When reviewing work, evaluates "presentation of work, cleaness and creative concept." Artists should "research the type of work or creative needs of the business they interview with."

***THUMB FUN AMUSEMENT PARK**, Box 128, Hwy. 42, Fish Creek WI 54212. (414)868-3418. Contact: Doug Butchart. Send samples.
Needs: Uses artists for direct mail brochures, posters, newspaper ads, costume design, signs, bumper stickers, designs for t-shirt printing and tie-in products.
First Contact & Terms: Send query letter with brochure showing art style or resume and photocopies. To show a portfolio, mail appropriate materials or write to schedule an appointment; portfolio should include roughs, photostats and photographs. Rights purchased varies according to project. Pays by the project. Considers complexity of project, skill and experience of artist, how work will be used, turnaround time and rights purchased when establishing payment.

TRI-COMMUNITY AREA CHAMBER OF COMMERCE, 111 Main St., Southbridge MA 01550. (617)764-3283. Contact: Richardson K. Prouty Jr. The tri-community area consists of Southbridge, a primarily industrial community; Sturbridge, a restored historical village and tourist mecca; and Charlton, an agricultural community.
Needs: Works with 3 ad illustrators and 2 advertising designers/year. Prefers local artists. Works on assignment only. Uses artists for ad illustrations.
First Contact & Terms: Send brochure to be kept on file. Reports back on future assignment possibilities. Call for interview to show portfolio. Pays $500, brochure design.

***TRW OPTOELECTRONICS DIVISION**, 1207 Tappan Circle, Carrollton TX 75006. (214)323-2200. Marketing Manager: J. Scott Bechtel. Manufacturer providing optoelectronic components for electronic equipment. Clients: manufacturers of electronic equipment, e.g. computers.
Needs: Works with 10 freelance artists/year. Artist must have experience in technology-related areas such as electronics or mechanical illustration. Uses artists for illustration on product.
First Contact & Terms: Send query letter with resume. Samples not filed are not returned. Reports only if interested. Write to schedule an appointment to show a portfolio, which should include original/final art, photostats and photographs. Pays for design and illustration by the hour, $25-45. Considers skill and experience of artist, and how work will be used when establishing payment.
Tips: "All successful candidates must be significantly more competitive than existing vendors. Names are kept on file and called in to bid on project."

TURNROTH SIGN CO., 1207 E. Rock Falls Rd., Rock Falls IL 61071. (815)625-1155. Contact: R. Neil Turnroth. Clients: banks, business, retail and industry.
Needs: Works with artists for billboards ($25-50), neon signage ($20-75), sign redesign ($20-100). Works primarily with out-of-town artists. Assigns 15-20 jobs/year.
First Contact & Terms: Send query letter with samples. SASE. Reports within 1 week. Payment by job.
Tips: Artists should have some nice photos of sketch work.

UMSI INCORPORATED, Box 450, Scotch Plains NJ 07076. (201)668-1313. President: Robert Bokor. Mail order firm. Offers magic tricks and novelties marketed to children, primarily boys, ages 8-15.
Needs: Works with 2 freelance artists/year. Local artists only "who have samples of similar product

links (hobbies or children's products)." Works on assignment only. Uses artists for advertising and catalog design, illustration and layout.
First Contact & Terms: Send query letter with brochure, resume and samples to be kept on file "unless the samples exhibit that the artist does not have closely related experience." Prefers samples that need not be returned. Samples not kept on file are returned by SASE. Reports only if interested. Call for appointment to show portfolio. Pays by the project, $500 minimum for catalog design and typesetting, less for smaller projects (ads, etc.). Considers complexity of project and skill and experience of artist when establishing payment.

***UNIVERSAL CLAMP CORP.**, 6905 Cedros Ave., Van Nuys CA 91405. (818)780-1015. President: Harry Van Gelder. Manufacturer of clamps for home and industry plus a jig (UC-805) for mitered frame assembly. Clients: Cabinet and home shops.
Needs: Works with 1 freelance artist/year. Uses artists for advertising design, illustration and layout; brochure design.
First Contact & Terms: Send query letter with brochure showing art style. Samples not filed are returned only if requested. Reports only if interested. To show a portfolio, mail appropriate materials. Pays for design by the hour, $35 minimum. Considers complexity of project when establishing payment.

THE VANESSA-ANN COLLECTION, Box 9113, Ogden UT 84409. (801)621-2777. President: Jo P. Buehler. Publishes needlework books, charts and designs. Clients: needlework and craft shops.
Needs: Works with 5 freelance artists/year. Considers pen & ink line drawings, oil and acrylic paintings, pastels, watercolors and mixed media—all to be converted into needlework charts/designs. Especially likes children, holiday and kitchen themes.
First Contact & Terms: Send query letter with samples to be kept on file. Samples not filed are returned by SASE with sufficient postage. Reports within 1 month. Buys all rights. Negotiates payment; offers advance.

***VARCO, INC.**, 121 N, Ninth St., Dekalb IL 60115. Advertising Manager: Melinda Newtson. Direct mail catalog providing computer supplies and business forms to businesses with computers.
Needs: Works with 1-2 freelance artists/year. Works on assignment only. Uses artists for brochure design and layout, catalog layout and cover designs.
First Contact & Terms: Send query letter with resume, tear sheets and photocopies. Samples not filed are returned only if requested. Reports only if interested. To show a portfolio, mail roughs, final reproduction/product and tear sheets. Pays for design by the project, $100 minimum. Considers complexity of project, skill and experience of artist, and turnaround time when establishing payment.

***VISION IMPACT ASSOCIATES**, Suite 223, 6860 Gulfport Blvd. S., St Petersburg FL 33707. (813)367-3911. Creatvie Co-ordinator: Sarah Markham. Stock library for art, paintings, drawings and photography marketing pictures of all mediums to publishers and product manufacturers world-wide including greeting cards, calendars, and printed products in general, advertising agencies, poster companies etc.
Needs: Works with 100 or more freelance artists/year. We will supply guidelines." Uses artists for advertising design and illustration, brochure and catalog illustration, illustration on product, posters and greeting card subjects.
First Contact & Terms: Send query letter with tear sheets, photocopies, slides and photographs. Samples not filed returned by SASE. Reports back within 14 days. Call or write to schedule an appointment to show a portfolio, which should include final reproduction/product, color, tear sheets and photographs. Pays 50% commission on any sales made, payment in the month following payment by client. "Payment is a reproduction fee based on use of subject."
Tips: "Study subjects-pictures used on greeting cards, paperback books, calendars and reproduced art in general. Allow space for title and greetings, etc. (majority of subjects are vertical)."

VISUAL AID/VISAID MARKETING, Box 4502, Inglewood CA 90309. (213)473-0286. Manager: Lee Clapp. Distributes sales promotion (aids), marketing consultant (service)—involved in all phases. Clients: manufacturers, distributors, publishers and graphics firms (printing and promotion) in 23 zip code areas.
Needs: Works with 3-5 freelance artists/year. Uses artists for advertising, brochure and catalog design, illustration and layout; product design, illustration on product, P-O-P displays, display fixture design and posters. Buys some cartoons and humorous and cartoon-style illustrations. Additional media: fiber optics, display/signage, design/fabrication.
First Contact & Terms: Works on assignment only. Send query letter with brochure, resume, business card, photostats, duplicate photographs, photocopies and tear sheets to be kept on file. Originals returned by SASE. Reports within 2 weeks. Write for appointment to show portfolio. Negotiates payment

by the project. Considers complexity of project, skill and experience of artist and turnaround time when establishing payment.
Tips: "Do not say 'I can do anything.' We want to know best media you work in (pen/ink, line, illustration, layout, etc.)."

***WM. K. WALTHERS, INC.**, 5601 W. Florist Ave., Milwaukee WI 53218. (414)527-0770. Art Director: John Sanheim. Manufacturer/distributor of hobby products—primarily model railroading. Clients: hobby shops.
Needs: Works with 2 freelance artists/year. Local artists only. Works on assignment only. Uses artists for brochure and catalog design, illustration and layout; product design and signage.
First Contact & Terms: Send query letter with brochure showing art style or resume and samples. Samples not filed are returned only if requested. Reports only if interested. Call or write to schedule an appointment to show a portfolio, which should include thumbnails, roughs, original/final art, final reproduction/product, color and b&w. Pays for design by the hour, $8 minimum. Pays for illustration by the hour, $6 minimum. Considers complexity of project, client's budget, skill and experience of artist, and turnaround time when establishing payment.

***WELLS CONCRETE PRODUCTS, PRESTRESSED BUILDINGS DIV.**, Box 308, Hwy. 109 E., Wells MN 56097. Advertising Manager: Bruce Borkenhagen. Manufacturer of commercial/industrial/office buildings, building components and bridges. Clients: business owners, developers, architects and government.
Needs: Works with 6 freelance artists/year. Works on assignment only. Uses artists for advertising, brochure and catalog design, illustration and layout; illustration on product and signage.
First Contact & Terms: Send query letter. Samples not filed are returned by SASE. Reports only if interested. Call or write to schedule an appointment to show a portfolio, which should include roughs. Pays for design and illustration by the hour, $10 minimum; by the project, $30 minimum. Considers complexity of project when establishing payment.
Tips: "Outside work would be primarily doing line perspective drawings by photographs supplied by us (work on buildings by quote)."

WEST SUPPLY, INC., 319 N. Appleton St., Appleton WI 54911. (414)734-2313. Vice President: Mark H. West. Manufactures wall hangings with pen-and-ink artwork reproduced on wood, and several lines of belt buckles. Clients: retail stores, distributors and wholesalers.
Needs: Works with 7 freelance artists/year. Uses artists for illustration on product; black on white pen & ink art to be reproduced on belt buckles and wall hangings.
First Contact & Terms: "We prefer to purchase reproduction rights." Send query letter with brochure and samples to be kept on file, except for originals which will be returned if not used; write for art guidelines. Accepts photocopies as samples. Samples not filed are returned if requested. Reports within 2 weeks. Pays per piece by mutual agreement. Considers complexity of project, how work will be used and rights purchased when establishing payment.
Tips: "We are price conscious, but easy to work with, and we are happy to review your work."

THE WILD SIDE INC., 7300 SW 42nd St., Miami FL 33155. (305)264-7320. Contact: Chris Fowler. Imprinted sportswear company.
Needs: Assigns 50+ jobs/year. Needs artists for t-shirt design. Prefers beach and resort designs, "or anything vaction/travel-related."
First Contact & Terms: Query with resume and samples. "Don't call on the telephone. We must see samples of your work." Prefers samples of color work; slides or original art samples returned. Reports within 1 week. No original art returned at job's completion. Pays $100 for each design used.

***WINDSOR ART PRODUCTS, INC.**, 9101 Perkins St., Pico Rivera CA 90660. (213)723-6301. Design Director: Pauline Raschella. Manufacturer of decorative framed artwork and miorrors for retail stores.
Needs: Works with 5 freelance artists/year. Prefers local artists. Works on assignment only. Uses artists for product design.
First Contact & Terms: Send query letter with brochure showing art style and photographs. Samples not filed are returned only if requested. Reports only if interested. Call or write to schedule an appointment to show a portfolio, which should include roughs, original/final art, final production/product and photographs. Pays by the project, amount negotiated with artist. Considers complexity of project when establishing payment.

WOODMERE CHINA INC., Box 5305, New Castle PA 16105. (412)658-1630. President: L.E. Tway. Manufacturer and importer of all types of collectible plate and porcelain figurines, dinnerware and gift-

ware. Clients: wholesalers, retailers and corporations.
Needs: Works with 2-4 freelance artists/year. Works on assignment only. Uses artists for plate and figurine design; mechanicals; advertising, brochure and catalog design, illustration and layout.
First Contact & Terms: Send query letter with resume and samples to be filed unless returned requested. Accepts any type sample. Reports within 2 weeks. Pays by the project, $50-1,000 or on a royalty basis. Considers complexity of the project, skill and experience of the artist and reputation of artist in market when establishing payment.
Tips: Be professional. Seeks "only art styles that fit our markets and that are good, tight quality work."

YORK DISPLAY FINISHING CO., INC., 240 Kent Ave., Brooklyn NY 11211. (718)782-0710. President: Stanley Singer. Manufacturer and display firm providing P-O-P advertising displays in vacuum formed plastics, cardboard, corrugated and paper. Clients: display agencies, printers, artists, etc.
Needs: Works with 2 freelance artists/year. New York City metro area artists only, thoroughly experienced in P-O-P design. Uses artists for P-O-P design and model making.
First Contact & Terms: Send query letter with resume or business card to be kept on file. Reports in 3 weeks. Samples returned by SASE. Pays by the project, $100-1,500 average.

Fashion

ACROPOLIS BOOKS LTD., 2400 17th St. NW, Washington DC 20009. Art Director: Robert Hickey. Specializes in hardcover and paperback originals on adult nonfiction, self help and general interest. Publishes 25 titles/year.
Needs: Assigns 1-2 jobs/year. "Local artist preferred for convenience." Prefers b&w line art—fashion and food only. Pays by the project.
First Contact & Terms: Send business card and photocopies with SASE to be kept on file except for those that are too bulky. Samples not filed are returned by SASE. Does not report back to the artist. Original work is not returned to artist. Considers project's budget when establishing payment. Purchases all rights.

ACT YOUNG IMPORTS INC., 49 W. 37th St., New York NY 10018. (212)354-8894. Executive Vice President: Joe Hafif. Manufacturers and importers of printed totes, diaper bags, knapsacks, school bags, ladies handbags, clutches made of canvas, vinyl, oxford, nylon, etc.
Needs: Buys 300-600 designs/year. Especially needs experienced designers. Local artists only.
First Contact & Terms: Query with samples. Designs on paper only, no sample manufacturing necessary.

***ADVERTIR, LTD.**, 80 West 40 St., New York NY 10018. (212)840-2710. President: Eve Denbaum.
Needs: Works with many freelance artists/year. Local artists only. Works on assignment only. Uses artists for illustrations, brochures, catalogs, magazines, newspapers, mechanicals, retouching, airbrushing and advertisements.
First Contact & Terms: Send query letter with brochure showing art style or samples. Samples not filed are returned only if requested. Reports only if interested. Call to schedule an appointment to show a portfolio, which should include final reproduction/product, color, tear sheets and b&w. Pays by the project. Considers complexity of project, client's budget, skill and experience of artist, and how work will be used when establishing payment.
Tips: "Respond only if professional."

LILLIAN ALBUS SHOPS INC., 139 Kings Hwy. E., Haddonfield NJ 08033. (609)429-1875. General Manager: Mr. S. Ross. Women's retail specialty chain. Sells better ready-to-wear, sportswear and gifts.
Needs: Works with 1 freelance illustrator or designer/year. Especially needs fashion illustrations. Local artists only.
First Contact & Terms: Arrange interview to show portfolio. Reports within 1 week. Works on assignment only. Samples returned by SASE; and reports back on future assignment possibilities. $30 minimum per design; $30 minimum per illustration.

***APPAREL WORLD**, 386 Park Ave. S., New York NY 10016. (212)683-7520. Fashion Editor: Alison Fendel. Official publications of the National Knitwear and Sportwear Association emphasizing apparel manufacturing, management and marketing. It covers the latest trends in fabrics, color and technology. Monthly. Circ. 11,000.

Needs: Local artists with a knowledge of fashion to do interpretive work in the editorial area. "Artists must be able to do interpretive work, to use their imagination. If I tell them I want a long dress or a tunic sweater over a short skirt, they have to know what I need. If you can only work with figure models, you can't work with me." Prefers an "interesting" contemporary look but no avant garde.
First Contact & Terms: Send a query letter with photocopies. Samples are filed for future reference. "Artists must show the ability to meet tight deadlines." Call to schedule an appointment to show a portfolio.

ARKANSAS GAZETTE, Box 1821, Little Rock AR 72203. (501)371-3723. Fashion Editor: Mardi Epes. Weekly newspaper woman's section featuring fashion and beauty. Circ. 130,000. Accepts previously published material. Returns original artwork to the artist after publication. Sample copy and art guidelines available.
Needs: Buys a varying number of fashion illustrations per issue. Seek styles "with a 'feel' rather than catalogue details." Color and b&w possibilities. Works on an assignment basis only.
First Contact & Terms: Send query letter with samples to be kept on file. Accepts any type sample. Samples not kept on file are returned if accompanied by an SASE. Reports back to the artist. Purchases first rights. Pays on publication.

***AVALON LTD.**, 2657 Jolly Rd., Okemos MI. (517)332-4902. Vice President: Susan Zussman. Estab. 1984. Importer/distributor/retailer of rattan and bamboo home fashions and furniture. Directed toward ages 20-45.
Needs: Works with 2-4 freelance artists/year. Uses artists for brochure and catalog design, illustration and layout; P-O-P displays, posters and direct mail.
First Contact & Terms: Send query letter with resume and samples. Samples not filed are returned only if requested. To show a portfolio, mail roughs, original/final art, color and tear sheets. Pays for design and illustration by the project, $10-100. Considers complexity of project and budget when establishing payment.

BAIMS, 408 Main, Pine Bluff AR 71601. (501)534-0121. Contact: David A. Shapiro. Retailer. Carries Haggar, Van Heusen and other labels.
Needs: Works with 2-3 illustrators/designers/year. Assigns 25-100 jobs/year. Uses artists for ad illustrations.
First Contact & Terms: Send a query letter with resume, business card and samples to be kept on file. Reports in 2 weeks. Call or write to arrange an appointment to show a portfolio. Pays $5-20/job.

***BEACON SHOE COMPANY, INC.**, Lions Estates Dr., Jonesburg MO 63351. (314)488-5444. Advertising Manager: Jennifer Turnbaugh. Manufacturer of women's casual footwear for department stores, independent merchants and mail order firms.
Needs: Works with 2 freelance artists/year. Works on assignment only. Uses artists for illustration on product, the design and layout of advertising and catalogs and also advertising illustrations. Especially needs line art and wash drawings.
First Contact & Terms: Send query letter with tear sheets, photostats and photocopies. Samples not filed are returned only if requested. Reports within 10 days. Call to schedule an appointment to show a portfolio, which should include roughs, original/final art, tear sheets, b&w photostats and photographs. Pays for illustration by the shoe, $10-65. Considers complexity of project, client's budget, skill and experience of artist, how work will be used and turnaround time. Buys all rights or reprint rights.
Tips: "The shoe industry—at least domestically—is becoming harder and harder each year. Because of that the advertising has had to become much more aggressive. Trade advertising has become much more sophisticated. Obviously our company must follow those changes with our work. Be flexible!"

BENO'S, 1515 Santee St., Los Angeles CA 90015. (213)748-2222. Director of Advertising and Sales Promotion: Gregg Seaman. Department and family apparel chain in California and Oregon.
Needs: Works with 4-5 freelance artists/year. Local artists only. Uses artists for illustrations of men's, women's and children's fashions, some hard lines and domestics (pillows, blankets, sheets) for newspapers ads and direct mail coupon books.
First Contact & Terms: Arrange interview to show portfolio. Prefers b&w line drawings, airbrush, charcoal, and previously published work as samples. SASE. Reports in 1-2 weeks. Pays by the project, $10-75 average; negotiates payment based on experience and skill of artist, and turnaround time.

BODY FASHIONS/INTIMATE APPAREL, 545 5th Ave., New York NY 10017. (212)503-2910. Editor/Associate Publisher: Jill Gerson. Information for merchandise managers, buyers, manufacturers and suppliers about men's and women's hosiery and underwear and women's intimate apparel and leisurewear. Monthly. Circ. 13,500.

Illustrations: Interested in fashion illustrations of intimate apparel. Do not mail artwork. Arrange interview to show portfolio. Works on assignment only. Keeps file consisting of editor's comments on portfolio review and samples of work. Reports in 4 weeks. Pays on publication.

***THE BRITCHES OF GEORGETOWN**, Extension 229 Adver. Agency, 2213 Mt. Vernon Ave., Alexandria VA 22301. (703)548-0200. Art Director: Janet K. Daniel. Upscale retailer and manufacturer of men's and women's clothing, providing exclusive designs at the best possible prices. High level of customer service. Casual, business and formal wear. Clothing "reflects a level of taste that makes building a Britches wardrobe a continual investment in quality, fashion and enjoyment that will last for years to come." Produces casual and rugged outerwear and also elegant and sophisticated business and evening wear.
Needs: Works with 6-8 freelance artists/year. Works on assignment only. Uses artists for advertising, brochure and product illustration, model making and signage.
First Contact & Terms: Send query letter with brochure showing art style or resume, tear sheets, photostats, photocopies, slides and photographs. Samples not filed are returned only if requested. Reports only if interested. Call or write to schedule an appointment to show a portfolio, which should include original/final art, final reproduction/product, color, tear sheets, photostats, photographs, b&w, slides and prints. Pays for design by the project, $50 minimum. Pays for illustration by the project, $50-1,000. Considers complexity of project, client's budget, skill and experience of artist, how work will be used, turnaround time and rights purchased when establishing payment.

CATALINA/Division of Kayser Roth, 6040 Bandini Blvd., Los Angeles CA 90040. (213)726-1262, ext. 281. Art Director: Rhonda Thomason. Manufacturer of women's, men's, juniors, and girls' swimwear and sportswear; Catalina.
Needs: Works with 10 freelance artists/year. Uses artists for fashion illustration, paste-up and mechanicals. Seeks "contemporary but not 'high' fashion look" in art styles. Prefers b&w work, in markers or wash with charcoal pencil line. Watercolors and markers are generally used in color work.
First Contact & Terms: Local artists only. Send samples photostats and photographs to be kept on file. Reports to the artist only if interested. Call for appointment to show portfolio. Pays by the hour, $18-25 for production; by the project, $125-250 for illustration/per figure. "For catalogs that are totally illustrated, we would like to make arrangements according to budget." Considers complexity of project, available budget and how work will be used when establishing payment.

EARNSHAW'S REVIEW, 393 7th Ave., New York NY 10001. (212)563-2742. Publisher: Thomas Hudson. Managing Editor: Christina Gruber. Art Director: Bette Gallucci. For designers, manufacturers, buyers and retailers in the children's fashion industry. Monthly. Circ. 10,000.
Needs: Buys 180 illustrations/year on fashion (infants to pre-teenagers). Works with 12-15 illustrators/year. Especially needs color fashion sketches.
First Contact & Terms: Send tear sheets with an SASE or call. Reports in 1 week. Call to schedule an appointment to show a portfolio, which should include original/final art, color, tear sheets, photographs and b&w. Pays for design by the project, $20-250; for illustration by the project, $15-250.
Tips: "There is more fashion orientation and color in the field. We are interested in new people. Know children's body shapes, size, and age differences."

***SHIRLEY GADOL CO. INC.**, 5801 NE 14th Ave., Ft. Lauderdale FL 33334. 771-5414. Vice President/Secretary Treasurer: A. Gadol. Manufacturer of women's sportswear, embroidered motifs and commercial embroidery for junior and missey sizes styles. Labels: Shirley Gadol, Gadol, Chez Gadol.
Needs: Works with 4 freelance artists/year. Uses artists for advertising illustration, brochure design, product and fashion design, fashion illustration, textile design and direct mail.
First Contact & Terms: Contact only through artist's agent; agent should send tear sheets. Samples not filed are returned only if requested. Reports only if interested. Call to schedule an appointment to show a portfolio, which should include final reproduction/product. Pays by the hour, $15-35; occasionally by the project, $100-300. Considers skill and experience of artist when establishing payment.
Tips: "Do your homework—be prepared."

GARLAND CORPORATION, 6th Floor, 1411 Broadway, New York NY 10018. Technical Coordinator: Tamara Lenkeit. Manufacturer of sweaters, updated classics. Labels are Garland and Yves Jennet.
Needs: Works with 1 freelance artist/year. Seeks local artists only with previous experience. Uses artists for brochure illustration.
First Contact & Terms: Send query letter with business card and photographs to be kept on file. Reports to the artist only if interested. Write for appointment to show portfolio. Pays by the project, $10-150 for illustration. Considers complexity of project when establishing payment.

Close-up

Margaret Volker-Ferrier
Fashion Illustrator
Cincinnati, Ohio

The latest fashions always premiere in New York, Paris or Milan—not in Cincinnati, Ohio, where Margaret Volker-Ferrier has set up shop as one of America's top fashion illustrators.

"It doesn't matter if I'm in Cincinnati in a rather conservative environment. I live in the world. I have access to Paris, New York, California, anywhere I want. In fact, this is a central location." Because of today's technology and communication, artists can maintain an international network of contacts yet live wherever they want.

Having already proved herself on the international scene, Volker-Ferrier has returned to her alma mater, the University of Cincinnati, to teach fashion illustration and design and to freelance. She has maintained her European connections and her network of college friends. "Your fellow graduates are very valuable as they move into 'Positions.' They will remember you when a job comes up. A friend from school just called me from Chloe with a need to illustrate something 'very different.' And she remembered I did very different things in our classes."

Throughout her classroom experiences at U.C., she acquired the essentials of fashion illustration—speed and flexibility ("being able to handle as many situations as possible"), knowledge of fabrics ("memorizing how fabrics move, how they fold"), anatomy ("it frees you to make anything you want") and design ("I know how garments are put together, I know what they're supposed to look like"). From experience she learned the intangibles of her craft. "You have to have an emotional response to what the clothing is trying to say. You're drawing that response, even more than you're drawing clothing."

Depending upon the type of artwork you do, there is a variety of opportunities in the fashion world. Retail illustration requires a realistic style, because its purpose is to sell garments for department stores, boutiques and catalogs. "The audience is mass-market people who want to see every button." Margaret's specialty, editorial art, requires a loose style; the audience consists of fashion-educated buyers. "You're doing trends, showing the way a garment should look." Print advertisements which stress a certain look or style use this approach. Almost a lost art, croquis (design) sketches depict "something that doesn't exist" to seamstresses in design houses.

Margaret has found that trade publications such as *Women's Wear Daily, Promostyl* and *Here & There* are excellent sources for freelance submissions. The White Pages of major metropolitan areas and *Women's Wear Daily* provide the phone numbers of design houses or showrooms. Most entry-level jobs are found in retail stores as layout artists; names and numbers of the stores can be found in the *Directory of Department Stores.*

When contacting art directors of department stores or houses, Margaret advises making appointments in advance for portfolio presentations. Don't make impromptu visits because "you take the chance of being considered terribly rude and will never be called. Most people want to look at portfolios and are very kind about it." With your first appointment, introduce yourself and your work; if the art director likes your work, you will be kept in mind for future assignments.

"Never put anything in your portfolio that you don't want to do," Margaret advises. While students need to show a variety of work to get a job, "any job," a professional should represent himself with work that he is comfortable with. Find out what the prospective client wants by examining advertisements and catalogs.

Gaining recognition as a fashion illustrator requires originality. "Only Antonio does Antonio well," Margaret points out. "You don't become national by copying. As a student, it's good to imitate what's been done as a learning experience, but it's best not to become dependent on other people's work." In fact, Margaret herself has pioneered the new trend of using cut paper instead of the usual mediums of pencil, pastel or wash.

Asked to describe her own style, she says, "Somebody was critiquing my work and said, 'Your heads look like little birds,' " Those little birds have flown a long way in the fashion world.

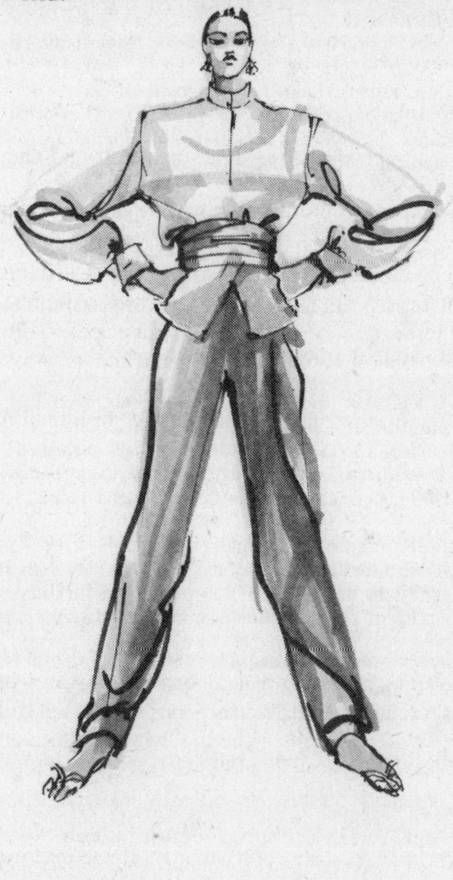

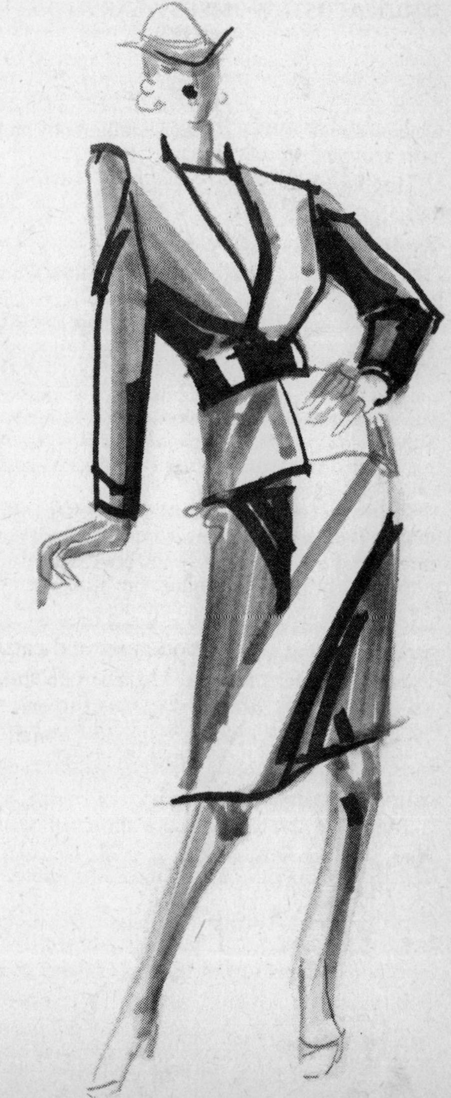

Two portfolio pieces by Volker-Ferrier demonstrate her ability to use markers, which facilitates the quick turnaround time needed by trade magazines and department stores.

GELMART INDUSTRIES, INC., 180 Madison Ave., New York NY 10016. (212)889-7225. Vice President and Head of Design: Ed Adler. Manufacturer of high fashion socks, gloves, headwear, scarves, and other knitted accessories. "We are prime manufacturers for many major brands and designer names."
Needs: Uses artists for fashion accessory design.
First Contact & Terms: Call for appointment to show portfolio.
Tips: "Keep the products in mind and show us how your ideas can adapt."

HOSIERY AND UNDERWEAR, 545 Third Ave., New York NY 10017. (212)503-2910. Managing Editor: Lynn Rhodes. Magazine emphasizing hosiery; directed to hosiery buyers (from department and specialty stores mass merchandisers, etc.) and hosiery manufacturers nationwide. Monthly. Circ. 10,000. Returns original artwork after publication if requested. Sample copy free for SASE; art guidelines available.
Illustrations: Considers illustrations of hosiery; "we look for a clean style that pays attention to detail, but has a fresh, '80s look." Works on assignment only. Send query letter with brochure, resume and samples to be kept on file; or write for appointment to show portfolio. Accepts photostats, tear sheets or photocopies as samples; no slides and photographs. Samples not filed are returned only if requested. Reports back. Buys all rights. Pays $8/b&w figure; $75-100 for color spread. Pays on acceptance.

***IZOD LACOSTE WOMENSWEAR**, 11 Penn Plaza, 6th Floor, New York NY 10001. Advertising PR: Beckey Roy. Manufacturer of knit sportwear (shirts, bottoms, outerwear) with classic, updated traditional styling, alligator emblem, for ages 25-50 and up. Labels: Izod, Izod Lacoste (alligator).
Needs: Works with 5-6 freelance artists/year. Prefers artists experienced with sportswear. Uses artists for the design and illustration of advertising and brochures, the layout of brochures, fashion illustration, window design, P-O-P displays, calligraphy and mechanicals. Prefers "sophisticated, traditional, realistic, feminine styles.
First Contact & Terms: Send query letter with brochure showing art style or resume and tear sheets, slides and photographs. Samples not filed are returned by SASE. Reports only if interested. To show a portfolio, mail appropriate materials; portfolio should include final reproduction/product, color, tear sheets and photographs. Pays for illustration by the project, $200 minimum. Considers complexity of project, skill and experience of artist, how work will be used and turnaround time when establishing payment.
Tips: "We need very good turnaround; consultation during development of project."

KOALA ARTS INC., 3450 Channel Way, San Diego CA 92110. (619)223-2555. President: Ken Klempan. Specializes in fashion, promotional sportswear (imprinted). Clients: corporations (directly), agencies and wholesale distributors.
Needs: Works with 6-10 freelance artists/year. "Local southern California artists only with experience in imprinted sportswear design." Works on assignment only. Uses artists for design, mechanicals, lettering and logos.
First Contact & Terms: Send query letter with brochure, resume and samples, if available, to be kept on file. "Screen printed samples preferred; if not available slides are acceptable." Reports back only if interested. Pays for design by the hour, $10-50 average; by the project, $25 minimum. Pays for illustration by the project, $25 minimum. Considers complexity of project, client's budget, and rights purchased when establishing payment.

LEE CO., Division of Lee Byron Corp., Suite 2819, Empire State Building, New York NY 10118. (212)244-4440. Contact: Dan L. Lieberfarb. Produces belts and personal leather goods. Mail samples or call for interview; prefers New York City artists.
Needs: Uses artists for fashion design of men's ladies' and boys' belts, sales promotion/ad layouts, package design and direct mail brochures.

***MAYFAIR INDUSTRIES INC.**, 1407 Broadway, New York NY 10018. President: Robert Postal. Manufacturer of T shirts, sweat shirts and sportswear. Prefers screen printed tops and bottoms (fun tops). Directed towards ages 2 to 21. B. J. Frog, Jane Colby and Rrribbit Rrribbit labels.
Needs: Works with 10 freelance artists/year. Uses artists for pattern design. Prefers cartoon style, young in look.
First Contact & Terms: Send query letter with brochure showing art style. Samples not filed are returned only if requested. Reports only if interested. To show a portfolio, mail appropriate materials. Pays for illustrations by the project, $100-500. Considers complexity of project when establishing payment.

***NAMSB SHOW**, 535 Fifth Ave., New York NY 10017. Advertising Manager: Massimo Iacoboni. Menswear trade shows serving menswear retailers.

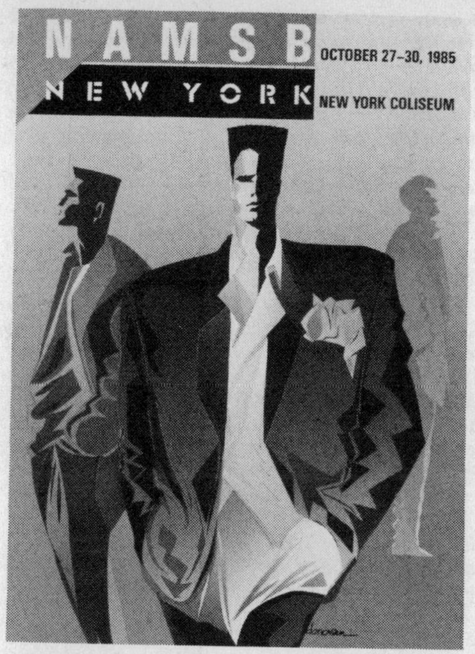

Freelance illustrator donovan of Philadelphia, Pennsylvania used paper collage to create a stylish illustration for an advertisement announcing the NAMSB menswear trade show, which features the latest fashions from around the world. donovan's illustration captures "a spring fashion mood mixed with sophistication and elegance," according to NAMSB's advertising manager Massimo Iacoboni of New York City.

Needs: Works with 2-3 freelance artists/year. Artist must have a good fashion sense. Uses artists for advertising design and illustration; brochure design and illustration; catalog design and illustration; magazine/newspaper illustration, exhibits, displays and posters. "Prefers fashion illustration/photography. All styles can be considered."

First Contact & Terms: Send query letter with brochure showing art style or tear sheets, photostats, photocopies, slide and photographs. Samples not filed are returned only if requested. Reports only if interested. Write to schedule an appointment to show a portfolio, which should include original/final art, final reproduction/product, color, tear sheets, photographs and b&w. Pays for illustration by the project, $100-350. Considers complexity of project, client's budget, skill and experience of artist, and rights purchased when establishing payment.

Tips: Artist should have a "strong fashion sense/modern to avant-garde feeling."

NAZARETH/CENTURY MILLS, 350 5th Ave., New York NY 10118. (212)613-0500. Designers: Lisa Goerke (girls'/ladies' sportswear); Eileen Kornbluh (boys'/mens' sportswear); Martha Deutsch (sleepwear). Manufactures children's sleepwear, men's, boys', girls' and ladies' sportswear and underwear; cotton and polyester/cotton; Nazareth Mills, Savage and Lady Nazareth labels.

Needs: Buys 50-100 illustrations/year. Works with 6 local freelance artists/year.

First Contact & Terms: Query with samples. Reports within 4 weeks. Works on assignment only. Samples returned by SASE; and reports back on future assignment possibilities. Provide flyer to be kept on file for future assignments. Pays $100-200/job, artwork for screen printing.

***NETWORK IND./CLASS KID LTD.**, 350 Fifth Ave., New York NY 10118. Design Director: Debbie Kuhfahl. Importer of men's and boys wearing apparel.

Needs: Works with 4-6 seasonal freelance artists/year. Uses artists for fashion, textile, and graphic screen print design.

First Contact & Terms: Send query letter with resume and photocopies. Samples not filed are not returned. Reports back ony if interested. To show a portfolio, mail appropriate materials; portfolio should include roughs (concepts), original/final art and color. Pays for design and illustration by the project, $10-75. Considers complexity of project and skill and experience of artist when establishing payment.

NEUVILLE INDUSTRIES INC., (formerly Neuville Mobil-Sox Inc.), 200 Madison Ave., New York NY 10016. (212)532-2510. Contact: Dom Esposito. Specializes in anklets and knee-hi socks for all ages.

Needs: Works with 3-4 freelance artists/year. Uses artists for sales promotion/ad layouts, package design and direct mail brochures.

First Contact & Terms: Query with brochure and tear sheets to be kept in file for possible future assignments. SASE. Reports within 2 weeks. Pays by the project for design and illustration.

***LOUIS NICHOLE, INC.**, Office and showroom location 105 E 29th St., New York NY 10016. (212)685-0395. Design studio location 54 New Haven Rd., Prospect CT 06712. (203)758-3160. President: Louis Nichole. Design company for home furnishings and decorative arts products providing very detailed romantic European 18th and 19th century designing of wallcovering, fabrics, dinnerware, glassware, statonery, greeting cards, dolls, furniture lace, bridal and children apparel.
Needs: Works with 20 freelance artists/year. Uses artists for product design, illustration on product, posters, signage and illustration.
First Contact & Terms: Artists must have only quality, European style and detail craftsmanship. Send query letter with brochure, resume, samples and tear sheets to be kept on file or call for appointment to show a portfolio. Samples returned by SASE only if requested by artist. Reports within 1 week. Pays by the hour, $10-50 average. Considers complexity of project, skill and experience of artist, and turn-around time when establishing payment.

***PACIFIC TRAIL**, 1310 Mercer St., Seattle WA 98109. Director of Advertising: Mary Chernis. Importer/distributor of clothing; men's, women and children's outerwear and sportswear. Directed towards all ages—infants on up. Pacific Trail label.
Needs: Works with 10 freelance artists/year. Uses artists for advertising design, illustration and layout; catalog design and illustration; fashion illustration, paste-up, mechanicals, posters and direct mail.
First Contact & Terms: Send query letter. Samples not filed are returned by SASE. Reports only if interested. To show a portfolio, mail appropriate materials. Considers complexity of project, client's budget, skill and experience of artist, and how work will be used when establishing payment.

PENDLETON WOOLEN MILLS, 218 SW Jefferson, Portland OR 97201. Menswear Communications Manager: Carolyn A. Zelle; Womenswear Communications Manager: Pat McKevitt. Manufacturer of men's and women's sportswear, blankets and piece goods; all 100% pure virgin wool. Pendleton Woolen Mills.
Needs: Works with 1 or 2 freelance artist/year directly "through our agency more." Seeks local artist for line art. Uses artists for advertising illustration.
First Contact & Terms: Send query letter with samples to be kept on file. Call for appointment to show portfolio. Reports to the artist within 3 weeks. Considers complexity of project, available budget and how work will be used when establishing payment. Pays for illustration by the project, $40 minimum.

PERSONAL LEATHER DESIGN, INC., Box 9155, Wethersfield CT 06109. (203)721-0270. President: Larry Bell. Manufactures leather bags, clothing, etc.
Needs: Works on assignment only. Works with fashion illustrators in New York and the Northeast for advertising and promotional material. Buys 10-15 sketches/year. Especially needs illustrations for newspaper ads and direct mail. Needs unique fashion style. Prefers illustrators with a new approach.
First Contact & Terms: Query. SASE. Reports in 2 weeks. Provide resume and b&w line drawings of work to be kept on file for future assignment possibilities. Pays by the project.

PINEHURST TEXTILES INC., Box 1628, Asheboro NC 27204. (919)625-2153. Contact: Lloyd E. Milks Jr. Manufactures ladies' lingerie, sleepwear and leisurewear; nylon tricot, woven polyester/cotton, brushed tricot and fleece; Pinehurst Lingerie label.
Needs: Works with 2 illustrators/year. Seasonal needs: spring and summer due September 1; fall and winter due March 1.

PLYMOUTH MILLS, INC., 330 Tompkins Ave., Staten Island NY 10304. (718)447-6707. President: Alan Elewson. Manufacturer of imprinted sportswear—t-shirts, sweatshirts, fashionwear, caps, aprons and bags. Clients: mass merchandisers/retailers.
Needs: Works with 6 freelance artists/year. Uses freelance artists for advertising and catalog design, illustration and layout; product design.
First Contact & Terms: Send brochure and resume. Reports back only if interested. Negotiates payment; pays by the project. Considers complexity of the project and how work will be used when establishing payment.

***PROPHECY CORP.**, 1302 Champion Circle, Carrollton TX 75006. (214)245-7807. Director of Advertising: Jayme Stoutt. Manufacturer of missy and petite fashions: jackets, blouses, skirts, sweaters, pants and dresses in the upper moderate price range. Prefers a variety of themes from casual, career, to dressy. Directed toward 25-60 years. Prophecy label.
Needs: Works with 6 freelance artists/year. Artists must constantly produce professional work quickly. Uses artists for brochure and fashion illustration, textile and pattern design, calligraphy, paste-up, mechanicals and direct mail.
First Contact & Terms: Send query letter with any type of sample that does not need to be returned.

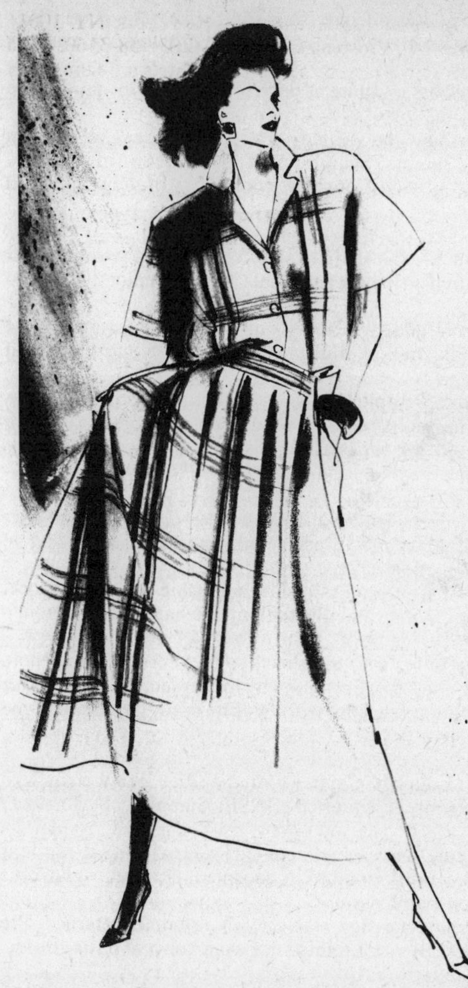

Jayme Stoutt of Prophecy Corporation, Carrollton, Texas, chose the artwork of Jacques Alschek to illustrate a spring press release and additional advertisements. Jacques used pastels, markers and charcoal to convey a "casual but crisp look" of Prophecy's line of office attire.

Samples not filed are not returned. Reports only if interested. Call to schedule an appointment to show a portfolio. Pays for design by the project, $60-100. Pays for illustration by the project, $60-300. Considers complexity of project, skill and experience of artist, and turnaround time when establishing payment.

Tips: "Quick turnaround is an absolute must; for example . . . five fashion figures would be expected to be completed and returned in two days."

QUEEN CASUALS, INC., 1411 Broadway, New York NY 10018. (212)398-9977. Advertising Director: Tillie Smith. Manufacturer of misses and women's coordinated sportswear, misses sizes 8-20, womens sizes 38-46 in polyester knits; Queen Casuals, Lady Queen and Smith, Smith & Jones misses sizes, Smith & Jones for Her, Smith & Jones Petites labels.

Needs: Works with a varied number of freelance artists/year. Works on assigment only. Prefers artists in New York, New Jersey, Pennsylvania and Connecticut areas primarily. Uses artists for fashion illustration and mechanicals.

First Contact & Terms: Send query letter with resume, tear sheets and photocopies. To show a portfolio, mail appropriate materials or call or write to schedule an appointment; portfolio should include original/final art, b&w or color, and tear sheets. Samples returned by SASE. Does not report on acceptance or rejection; "artist should call." Pays for design by the project, $2-300; pays for illustration by the project.

Tips: "Check the kind of work done by the client."

R-TEX DECORATIVES CO., INC., 59 Sea Cliff Ave., Glen Cove NY 11542. (516)671-7600. President: Lillian Sturm. Manufacturer of high-fashion decorative yard goods, posters, panels and banners. Clients: department stores.
Needs: Works with 3-4 freelance artists/year. Works on assignment only. Uses artists for product design and posters.
First Contact & Terms: Send query letter with brochure and samples to be kept on file. Call or write for appointment to show portfolio. Accepts any type sample. Samples not filed are returned only if requested. Reports back only if interested. Pays by the project. Considers complexity of the project and artist's bid when establishing payment.

SHIREY COMPANY, 1917 Stanford St., Greenville TX 75401. (214)455-5235. Vice President, Merchandising: Michelle Jenkins. Manufacturer of children's sleepwear, infants through juniors, boys and girls, in a variety of fabrics; Shirey label.
Needs: Works with 5-8 freelance artists/year. Prefers Dallas area artists only. Works on assignment only. Uses artists for advertising, brochure and catalog illustration, illustration on products and direct mail promotions.
First Contact & Terms: Send resume and actual work. Samples returned. Write for appointment. Pays for design and illustration by the hour, $5 minimum; by the project, $400-1,000 average. Provide resume, business card and brochure/flyer to be kept on file for possible future assignments.
Tips: "I need to see sketches of 'cute' kids."

PRESTON STUART ART SERVICES, 12 E. 97 St., New York NY 10029. (212)722-6637. Director: Preston Stuart. Specializes in fashion. Clients: fashion manufacturers, retail stores, magazines and ad agencies.
Needs: Works with 10 freelance artists/year. Desires "a professional relationship and good work." Works on assignment only. Uses artists for advertising design and illustration, mechanicals and retouching.
First Contact & Terms: Send query letter with samples and tear sheets to be kept on file. "Photocopied samples are best." Reports only if interested. Pays for illustration by the project, $150-800 average. Considers client's budget, skill and experience of artist, how work will be used, turnaround time and rights purchased when establishing payment.

***STITCH 'N SEW**, Box 497, Contocook NH 03229. Editor-in-Chief: Mildred T. Rice. For women who like to sew. Original artwork returned after publication if requested. SASE. Sample copy for 9x12 SASE with 66¢ postage.
Cartoons: Uses 1 cartoon/issue. Interested in needle work; single panel. Prefers finished cartoons. SASE. Reports ASAP if not accepted. "May hold several months" if accepted. Buys all rights on a work-for-hire basis. Pays $15-20; line drawings; on publication.
Illustration: Interested in b&w line drawings. Works on assignment only. No samples returned. Provide resume to be kept on file for future assignments. Buys all rights on a work-for-hire basis. Inside: pays $5 minimum, b&w line drawings; on publicaton.

TRIBORO QUILT MFG. CORP., 172 S. Broadway, White Plains NY 10605. (914)428-7551. Sales Manager: Alvin Kaplan. Produces infants' wear and bedding under the Triboro label; for chain and department stores.
Needs: Works with 3 designers, 3 textile designers and 3 illustrator/designers/year. Works on assignment only. Uses artists for advertising/catalog layouts, direct mail brochures, fabric and fashion design, hang tags, inserts, iron-ons and package design for infant items.
First Contact & Terms: Call for interview or provide resume, business card and brochure to be kept on file. Reports in 1 week. Samples returned by SASE; and reports back on future assignment possibilities.

UNIFORMS MANUFACTURING INC., Box 5336, W. Bloomfield MI 48033. (313)332-2700. President: L.P. Tucker. Manufacturer of all types of wearing apparel—smocks, lab coats, shirts, trousers, coveralls, dresses, aprons, gloves in cotton, polyester and knits; Uniform label.
Needs: Works with 3 freelance artists/year. Works on assignment only. Uses artists for advertising, brochure and catalog design; advertising illustration and direct mail promotions.
First Contact & Terms: Send brochure/flyer and slides as samples. Samples returned by SASE. Reports as soon as possible. Reports back whether to expect possible future assignments. Negotiates payment.

U.S. SHOE CORPORATION, One Eastwood Dr., Cincinnati OH 45227. (513)527-7000. Promotion Services Director: Philip Gleeson. Manufacturer of shoes featuring current fashion trends; Red Cross, Socialites, Cobbies, Joyce, Selby, Pappagallo and Capezio.

Needs: Works with 3 freelance artists/year. "Experience is normally necessary." Uses artists for advertising, brochure and catalog design, illustration and layout; fashion design and illustration; paste-up and mechanicals.
First Contact & Terms: Send query letter with samples to be kept on file. Call or write for appointment to show portfolio. Accepts any type sample. Samples not kept on file are returned only if requested by artist. Reports to the artist only if interested. Pays by the hour, $25-30 for design; $30-35 for illustration. Considers complexity of project, available budget and turnaround time when establishing payment.

***VOGUE/BUTTERICK PATTERNS**, 161 Sixth Ave., New York NY 10013. (212)620-2733. Assistant Art Director: Steve Isoz. Manufacturer of clothing patterns with the Vogue, Butterick labels.
Needs: Works with 4-6 freelance artists/year. "Artists must be proficient in fashion illustration." Uses artists for catalog illustration and fashion illustration. "The nature of this illustration is specialized; every button, every piece of top-stitching has to be accurately represented."
First Contact & Terms: Send query letter with resume and tearsheets, slides photographs. Samples not filed are returned by SASE. Reports back within one month. Call or write to schedule an appointment to show a portfolio, which should include original/final art, final reproduction/product, color and tear sheets. Pays by the project. Considers complexity of the project and turnaround time when establishing payment.

WHITE STAG MFG. CO., 5100 SE Harney Dr., Portland OR 97206. Vice President Advertising: Robert Zwald. Manufacturer of women's sportswear, men's and women's warmups and ski-wear; White Stag, Mountain Goat.
Needs: Works with 8-10 freelance artists/year. Uses artists for advertising and design illustration; catalog illustration; fashion illustration; and direct mail.
First Contact & Terms: "Most pieces require quick-turnaround and/or daily coordination." Send query letter with resume and samples to be kept on file. Call for appointment to show portfolio after mail contact. Prefers transparencies, photographs or printed work as samples. Samples not kept on file are returned only if requested by artist. Reports to the artist only if interested. Pays by the hour, $25-60 for design and illustration. Considers complexity of project, available budget, skill and experience of artist, how work will be used, turnaround time and rights purchased when establishing payment.

WILROY INC., 530 7th Ave., New York NY 10018. (212)221-2200. Women's apparel manufacturer specializing in sportswear and dresses sizes 6 through 20 of fine fabrics; Setiage and Wilroy sport labels.
Needs: Works with 6 freelance artists/year. Artists should be in New York City limits. Uses artists for advertising illustrations. Prefers soft, sophisticated, elegant illustrations, color only.
First Contact & Terms: Send query letter with brochure/flyer or resume; all artists should present a portfolio at appointment. Samples returned. Works on assignment only. Provide information to be kept on file for possible future assignment. Negotiates payment.

***WIN-TEX INC.**, 2760 Satsuma, Dallas TX 75229. Design Director: Kathryn Inman. Manufacturer/importer of kitchen textiles. Needs designs with *broad* market appeal.
Needs: Works with 5 freelance artists/year. Uses artists for advertising, brochure and catalog design, illustration and layout; product, accessory, textile, pattern, and package design, P-O-P displays, paste-up, mechanicals, direct mail, package inserts and photography.
First Contact & Terms: Send query letter with brochure showing art style or resume, tear sheets and photostats. Pays for design by the hour, $15 minimum. Prefers quotes by artist/agent for specific job. Considers complexity of project, client's budget, skill and experience of artist, how work will be used and marketability of design.
Tips: Artist should have "knowledge of our market by researching the market on their own—knowing who is doing what."

Greeting Cards and Paper Products

Greeting card publishers have a common goal—to offer cards that express every conceivable sentiment. Publishers create cards for every occasion and nonoccasion, in fact, every social and personal situation possible. Modern cards celebrate days of the week, bemoan a lost pet or announce ownership of a new car.

This billion-dollar industry seems to possess an insatiable appetite for ideas and artwork. With small entrepeneurs expanding the market with personal-expression cards, the doors have been opened for every artistic style, medium and technique. Traditional cards favor fine art treatments while cartoons spice the everyday or nonoccasion cards, which feature an unusual look at contemporary lifestyles. Study what "looks" are out in the marketplace and which ones certain retailers choose to promote. Also examine what occasions get the most shelf space.

Publishers look for work that elicits an immediate emotional response. The artwork must first catch the consumer's eye, with the text hooking the appropriate sentiment. Shoppers buy cards because they are too busy to write a letter or note but nevertheless want to express themselves personally. In the case of greeting cards, the medium has become the message.

Most publishers prefer contact by mail. Your mailing package should include a cover letter, resume or brochure, 10-12 samples and an SASE that is large enough to return your work. Send slides, photostats and tearsheets to show how your work appears in printed form. For a line of cards revolving around a central theme or character, submit 8x10" dummies, or actual-size cards with artwork and verse. Keep in mind standard sizes and the company "image"; write to the card publisher and request catalogs and art guidelines before submitting your work.

Payment is usually a flat fee for each illustration or a royalty. Remember that many publishers also merchandise popular card characters through what is called social-expression items such as mugs, collector's plates, miniatures and giftware. Your contract should state payment terms concerning these peripherals if applicable.

As new products are developed and trends change, artists need to update their ideas and styles. To keep current with the greeting card industry, consult *Greetings Magazine*. *Thomas Register of Manufacturers* lists paper product manufacturers and can be found in your local library. Ron Lister's *Designing Greeting Cards and Paper Products* and Susan Evart's *The Art & Craft of Greeting Cards* give overviews of the industry. *A Guide to Greeting Card Writing* by Larry Sandman points out the opportunities in the field.

***ABEL CARDS**, 28 W. Sixth St., Media PA 19063. (215)891-9119. President: Madaline Tomlinson. Produces greeting cards.
Needs: Buys 25-30 designs and illustrations from freelance artists/year. Prefers final art to be 5x3¾" of slightly larger. Submit seasonal material one year before holiday.
First Contact & Terms: Send query letter with brochure, photographs and actual work. Samples not filed are returned by SASE. Reports back within 1 month. To show a portfolio, mail roughs and final reproduction/product. Original work not returned after publication. Payment averages $50/accepted design. Buys all rights.
Tips: "We prefer old-fashioned, non-flashy cards."

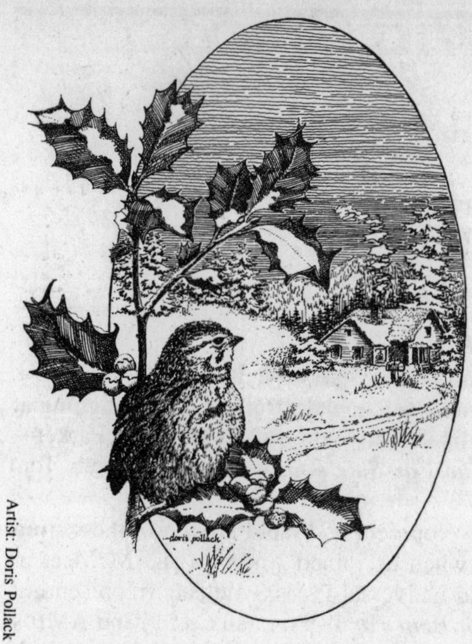

Artist: Doris Pollack

Maggie La Noue of Albion Cards in Albion, Michigan, chose this artwork by Doris Pollack of Concrete, Washington, for a Christmas card design or as a general winter scene. "We arranged to pay 5% royalties on all card sales," says LaNoue. Pollack's pen & ink rendering was chosen because it "conveyed the warmth and comfort of home."

ALBION CARDS, Box 102, Albion MI 49224. Owners: Maggie and Mike LaNoue. Produces greeting cards, prints, note cards, postcards, catalogues and brochures. Uses b&w, line art, realistic, detailed, old fashioned, clear; must hold line quality when reduced—to "jump out"—high contrast. Directs products to women, older people, tourists, nostalgia buffs and sports enthusiasts.

Needs: Buys approximately 200 designs from freelance artists/year. Uses artists for calligraphy and mechanicals. Considers pen & ink and watercolors. Size of originals 9x12" or proportionate; important elements of design and artist's signature should be one inch from all edges of the drawing. Produces material for Christmas and summer (skiing, golfing, bicycling, boating); other subjects: animals (cats & ducks especially), landscapes, wild flowers and herbs. Catalog $2; art guidelines free for SASE. Theme must be "upbeat" and positive, but not cutesy.

First Contact & Terms: Send query letter with brochure, showing art style and photocopies. Samples not filed are not returned. Reports back within 2 months. Originals returned to show a portfolio, mail color photographs, b&w and photocopies. Pays for illustration by the project, 5% minimum. Payment depends entirely on sales; artists can boost sales and earn sales commission as well. Buys copyright outright to be used for cards only; artist retains rights for other items; negotiates rights for prints. Buys only scenes that have not been published as cards to date.

Tips: "We are interested in producing series of cards relating to scenic tourist areas, seascapes, street scenes and landmarks. We can help promote other artists' works in their own locale. The card market is expanding; nostalgia is gaining in popularity. Our needs for freelance work have increased dramatically. There is a greater appreciation of quality work—we can no longer produce all the new card scenes that our customers would like to purchase—so we are using more freelace work. We are interested in serious artists. Please do not send quick sketchy work or designs that display bad taste. Work must reproduce well and give the viewer a good feeling."

AMBERLEY GREETING CARD CO., Box 36159, Cincinnati OH 45236. Art Director: Ned Stern. Publishes studio, humorous, and everyday greeting cards.

Needs: Assigns 200 jobs/year. Local artists only. Uses freelance artists for product illustration. Especially needs humorous cards.

First Contact & Terms: Call first. Buys all rights. No original work returned at job's completion. Call or write to schedule an appointment to show a portfolio, which should include original/final art and final reproduction/product. Pays for design and illustration by the project, $10-60; on acceptance.

Tips: Visit greeting card shops to get a better idea of the types of cards published by Amberley. When reviewing an artist's work, "the first thing I look for is the professionalism of the presentation, i.e. samples neatly displayed (no loose drawings, scraps of paper, etc.); creativity—what has the artist done differently and effectively; use of color, and lettering." An artist's biggest mistake is having a sloppy portfolio; "I'd rather see 5 good examples of work than 25 poorly done."

Close-up

George Parker
President, Andrews/McMeel & Parker

"America's No. 1 Publisher of Humor is in Fairway, Kansas."
The slogan is enough to make even the most serious artist snicker. But noboby's laughing at the success of the three-year-old Oz card and gift line from Andrews, McMeel and Parker—which represents heavyweight humorists like *The Far Side's* Gary Larsen, *Ziggy's* Tom Wilson, and *Herman's* Jim Unger.

George Parker provided the impetus for the development and rapid growth of the stationery, greeting card, and gift line at the company when he joined Andrews and McMeel in 1983. The strengths of the company's 10-year-old Universal Press Syndicate (representing such innovative cartoon strips as *Doonesbury, For Better or Worse,* and *Cathy*) and AMP's book publishing division, coupled with Parker's 12 years of creative work at Hallmark, proved to be a winning combination.

Parker moved the company into specialized, alternative humor lines that have spelled success for the company—and brought new definitions to everyday humor. This success, according to Parker, can be attributed to Oz's recognition of the changing social climate that has a great effect on the social expression business as well.

"There are all kinds of cross-currents in the land today; you see a segmentation of interests everywhere. Like cable television, for instance, where the Dr. Ruths and Jim Bakers of the world can co-exist within the same society. And I think what has revolutionized the greeting card business is that it has segmented itself as well—to meet these needs."

As a young line unbound by the image constraints that confront some of the major, highly entrenched and established companies, Oz was able to seek out unique styles of humor. "Some of the larger [social expression] companies, by nature of their size and power are actually weak because they are so rigid, so locked into the apple-pie, motherhood image.

"We look for humor that is as different and diverse as Gary Larsen's *Far Side* is from Tom Wilson's *Ziggy.*" You can't get much more diverse than Larsen's wry images of dinosaurs smoking cigarettes and the sweet, lovably insecure bumble of Ziggy. "I'm looking for anybody who has a funny idea that's fresh and new.

"We *aren't* just looking for artists—we can find plenty of good artists in this town. Artwork is almost impossible without putting ideas down on paper. So we're constantly looking for people . . . to discover how well they write, how well they illustrate—to see if they have any greeting card ideas that we can go with. Think—is it a *fresh* idea?"

Serious artists who want to submit their work should send a letter with general information first—*not* actual art. "We first assess if your greeting card idea is something we might want to look into. If we're interested in your idea, we'll ask you to sign a waiver that will let us review your work—not sign it away to us, but to protect your idea. The greeting card business is beset by people who have already written what you're just about to publish—and all serious creative people *and* companies have to protect themselves. It gives us a chance to review new ideas—the last thing we want to do is turn away people with good ideas.

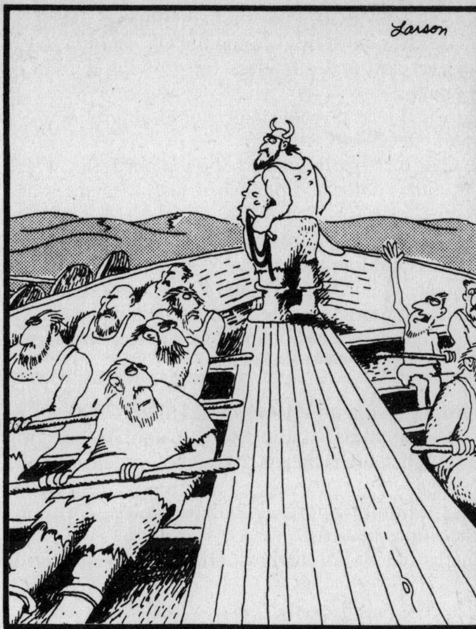

The off-beat humor of Gary Larsen has been featured by Andrews McMeel & Parker in greeting cards, social expression items and calendars. There are over three million of The Far Side books in print, and the cartoon panel is syndicated in over 300 newspapers.

"There's no doubt that we're very few people here at Oz, and we *need* freelancers. We can't act like the larger companies who create entirely from within. Something really important is going on in humor, and I want to give people some real encouragement to come to us with it."

What new ventures will Oz be developing this next year? "We're taking some chances and going national with good cartoonists who aren't known outside the local level." After all, that's the way the company hit big with Gary Larsen just four years ago.

—Lisa Hulse

Sniglets, "any word that doesn't appear in the dictionary but should," appear on magnetic memo pads, notepads and mugs, as well as greeting cards and books published by AMP.

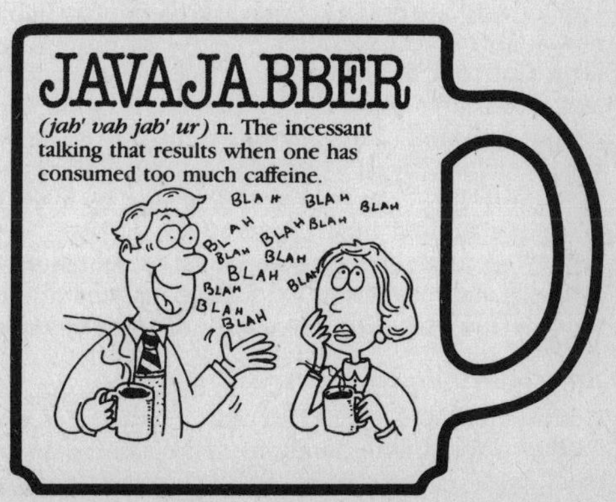

AMCAL INC., 1050 Shary Ct., Concord CA 94518. (415)689-9930. Publishes and imports calendars and greeting cards. Markets to all major gift, book and department stores throughout US, Europe and Japan. Rapidly expanding company looking for distinctive card and gift ideas for growing market demand. "All subjects considered that fit our quality image."
Needs: Prefers work submitted in 5x7" vertical card format with possible suggestions of printing methods and paper stock. Send query letter, slides and published work.
First Contact & Terms: Responds within 2 weeks. Call for appointment to show a portfolio, which should include original/final art, final reproduction/product, color and published work. Payment and terms negotiable. No portfolios, please.
Tips: "Artwork must be suitable for an expandable line of greeting cards for a multitude of occasions and holidays. The minimum number of cards in a greeting card line is around 24. We find that any less than that number doesn't make a significant enough impact with buyers to make a line successful. New card ideas using embossing, hot stamping and die-cuts are of particular interest to us. Know the market. Go to gift shows and visit lots of stationery stores. Read all the trade magazines. Talk to store owners to find out what's selling and what isn't."

AMERICAN GREETINGS CORP., 10500 American Rd., Cleveland OH 44102. (216)252-7300. Director Creative Personnel: Kathy McConaughy. Publishes humorous, studio and conventional greeting cards, calendars, giftwrap, posters, stationery and paper tableware products. Manufactures candles and ceramic figurines.
First Contact & Terms: Query with resume. Forms for submitting portfolio will be mailed. Portfolios received without necessary paperwork will be returned unreviewed.
Tips: "We are staffed to generate our own ideas internally, but we will review portfolios for full-time or freelance employment."

***ANDREWS, MCMEEL & PARKER**, 4400 Johnson Dr., Fairway KS 66205. (913)362-1523. Contact: Joyce Schulte. "We're the nation's No. 1 publisher of humor," AMP consists of the Universal Press Syndicate, Universal Licensing and a book publishing concern. Universal Press Syndicate distributes popular cartoons such as "Doonesbury," "Ziggy," and "The Far Side." The syndicate's wholly owned subsidiary. Universal Licensing, markets hundreds of tie-ins, such as coffee mugs and knicknacks.
Needs: Buys 50 ideas/year from freelance artists. AMP is seeking artists mainly for its Oz line of greeting cards and stationery.
First Contact & Terms: Query first with an idea, not actual art. "We can first assess if your greeting card idea is something we might want to look into. If we're interested in your idea, we'll ask you to sign a waiver that will let us review your work—not to sign it away to us, but to protect your ideas." Payment is negotiable, whether it is for art or for an idea; the amount also depends upon the rights purchased. Will agree on a share of the royalty, or even a direct buyout if the artist prefers.

ANTIOCH PUBLISHING COMPANY, Box 28, Yellow Springs OH 45387. Art Director: Jean Rudegeair. Publishes calendars, bookmarks, bookplates, greeting cards and children's books. Also has separate religious/inspirational line.
Needs: Buys 100 or more illustrations per year. Works on assignment only. Uses artists for illustrations. "Most of our needs are of the full color, magical-unicorn-rainbow-charming-whimsical-humorous variety. I want art from people who know how to use color for good reproduction. I want to work with professionals who know the importance of deadlines, flexibility and marketability. Because of this I prefer working with experienced, previously published artists, although I've also worked with relative newcomers who have a high degree of professionalism."
First Contact & Terms: Send query letter with brochure showing art style or tear sheets and slides. Send SASE, attention Creative Guidelines, for copy of Antioch artist's guidelines before sending samples of any kind. Buys various rights. Write to schedule an appointment to show a portfolio, which should include roughs, original/final art, final reproduction/product and tear sheets; we generally do not view portfolios—we review slides, etc., by mail. Pays $100-200/illustration, depending on use and in-house preparation time.
Tips: "We appreciate a professional presentation of work by an artist who is creative, familiar with our products and responsive to ideas of marketability and will work with us to achieve desired results on time." This year, "trendy color are more apparent—looser styles."

ARGUS COMMUNICATIONS, INC., Division of DLM, One DLM Park, Allen TX 75002. Creative Administration: Janice O'Bryant. Produces greeting cards, postcards, calendars, posters, etc.
Needs: Works with hundreds of freelance artists/year. Must be professional artist. Works on assignment only. Uses artists for roughs, layouts and final art. Particularly interested in new humorous approaches to greeting card illustrations.

First Contact & Terms: Send query letter with resume and samples to be kept on file. Samples not filed are returned by SASE. Reports only if interested. To show a portfolio, mail thumbnails, roughs, tear sheets, photostats and photographs. Payment depends on project. Considers complexity of the project, turnaround time and rights purchased when establishing payment. Negotiates rights purchased.
Tips: "Be familiar with our product line before contacting us. Remember that greeting cards are a consumer product and must meet a consumer need to be successful."

***ART 101 LTD.**, 1401 Chattahoochee, Atlanta GA 30318. (404)351-9146. President: Jules Stine. Produces greeting cards, games, calendars, posters, stationery, paper tableware products, t-shirts and totes for retail, premium and ad-specialty.
Needs: Buys 12-15 designs and 3-5 illustrations from freelancers/year. Uses artists for P-O-P displays and mechanicals. Prefers 10¼x3¼ or 16/20 (20/16). Seasonal material should be submitted 6 months in advance.
First Contact & Terms: Send query letter with resume and photographs. Samples not filed are returned by SASE. Reports back within 1 month. Call or write to schedule an appointment to show a portfolio. No originals returned to artist at job's completion. Negotiates payment. Buys all rights.
Tips: "Do not be afraid to be 'off the wall'."

***BARNSTABLE ORIGINALS**, 50 Harden Ave., Camden ME 04843. (207)236-8162. Art Director: Marsha Smith. Produces greeting cards, posters, gift books, paper sculpture cards and memo pads. Directed towards tourists travelling in New England, and sailors or outdoors people—"nature and wildlife lovers."
Needss: Buys 50 designs and illustrations from freelance artists/year. Prefers 5x7 cards, vertical or horizontal. Produces material for Christmas; submit 1 year before holiday.
First Contact & Terms: Send query letter with brochure showing art style or resume, tear sheets, photostats, photocopies, slides or photographs. Samples not filed are returned by SASE. Reports back within 1 month. To show a portfolio, mail tear sheets, photostats, color photographs or slides of originals. No originals returned to artist at job's completion. Pays $50 minimum per design/illustration. Pays on acceptance. Buys all rights.
Tips: "We're looking for quality art work—any creative and fresh ideas also cute and whimiscal."

BARTON-COTTON INC., 1405 Parker Rd., Baltimore MD 21227. (301)247-4800. Contact: Creative/ Art Department. Produces religious greeting cards, commercial Christmas cards, and spring note cards. Free guidelines and sample cards; specify area of interest: religious, Christmas, spring, etc.
Needs: Buys 150-200 illustrations each year. Submit seasonal work "any time of the year."
First Contact & Terms: Send query letter with resume, tear sheets, photocopies, photostats, slides and photographs. Previously published work and simultaneous submissions accepted. Reports in 4 weeks. To show a portfolio, mail original/final art, final reproduction/product, color and tear sheets. Submit full-color work only (watercolors, gouache, pastels, oils and acrylics); pays $150-500/illustration; on acceptance.
Tips: "Fresh approaches are needed for traditional Christmas card designs. Good draftsmanship is a must, particularly with figures and faces. Spend some time studying market trends in the greeting card industry to determine current market trends." There is an increased need for creative ways to paint traditional Christmas scenes with up-to-date styles and techniques.

BEACH PRODUCTS, 1 Paper Pl., Kalamazoo MI 49001. (616)349-2626. Art Director: Jude Beattie. Publishes paper tableware products; general and seasonal, birthday, special occasion, invitations, announcements, stationery, wrappings and thank you notes for children and adults.
Needs: Buys 100 designs/year from freelance artists. Uses artists for product design and illustration. Sometimes buys humorous and cartoon-style illustrations. Prefers flat 4-color designs; 5¼ wide x 5½" high for luncheon napkins. Produces seasonal material for Christmas, Mother's Day, Thanksgiving, Easter, Valentine's Day, St. Patrick's Day, Halloween and New Year's Day. Submit seasonal material before June 1; everyday (not holidays) material before March.
First Contact & Terms: Send query letter with SASE (9x12" envelope) so catalog can be sent with response. Samples returned. Reports in 6-8 weeks. Call or write to schedule an appointment to show a portfolio, which should include original/final art and final reproduction/product. Previously published work OK. Originals not returned to artist at job's completion; "all artwork purchased becomes the property of Beach Products. Items not purchased are returned." Buys all rights. Pays average flat fee of $100/design; on acceptance. Considers product use when establishing payment.
Tips: "When asking for specifications and catalog, the SASE should be large enough to accommodate the catalog, for example, a 9x12" envelope. Artwork should have a clean, professional appearance and be the specified size for submissions, as well as a maximum of four flat colors."

BLOOMIN' IMAGES, 70 W. Cedar St., Box H, Poughkeepsie NY 12602. (914)471-3110. Administrative Services Manager: Vera Lawrence. Estab. 1983. Produces a unique variety of greeting cards and stationery sold primarily on the east coast.
Needs: Buys 20 designs and illustrations from freelance artists/year. Works on assignment only. Uses artists for calligraphy and paste-up. Prefers pen & ink.
First Contact & Terms: Send query letter with samples to be kept on file. Prefers tear sheets as samples. Samples not filed are returned. Reports within 2 months. Returns original artwork after reproduction. Negotiates payment and rights purchased.

BRETT-FORER GREETINGS, INC., 105 73rd St., New York NY 10021. Art Director: Barbara T. Schaffer. Publishes cute and whimsical greeting cards; Christmas and everyday.
Needs: Uses artists for design of 6x9'' and 4½x6'' Christmas cards, and 4¾x6½'' everyday cards. Considers all media. Produces seasonal cards for Valentine's Day and Mother's Day.
First Contact & Terms: Send samples. Reports in 4 weeks. No originals returned to artist at job's completion. Buys all rights. Pays average flat fee of $125/design. Considers complexity of project when establishing payment.

BRILLIANT ENTERPRISES, 117 W. Valerio St., Santa Barbara CA 93101. Art Director: Ashleigh Brilliant. Publishes postcards.
Needs: Uses up to 300 designs/year. Artists may submit designs for word-and-picture postcards, illustrated with line drawings.
First Contact & Terms: Submit 5½x3½'' horizontal b&w line drawings. SASE. Reports in 2 weeks. Buys all rights. "Since our approach is very offbeat, it is essential that freelancers first study our line. Ashleigh Brilliant's books include *I May Not Be Totally Perfect, But Parts of Me Are Excellent* and *Appreciate Me Now and Avoid the Rush*. We supply a catalog and sample set of cards for $2." Pays $40 minimum, depending on "the going rate" for camera-ready word-and-picture design.
Tips: "Since our product is highly unusual, freelancers should familiarize themselves with it by sending for our catalog ($2 plus SASE). Otherwise, they will just be wasting our time and theirs."

BURGOYNE, INC., (formerly Sidney J. Burgoyne & Sons Inc.), 2030 E. Byberry Rd., Philadelphia PA 19116. (215)677-8000. Art Director: Jon Harding. Publishes greeting cards and calendars; Christmas, winter and religious themes.
Needs: Buys 75-100 designs/year. Prefers artists experienced in greeting card design. Uses freelance artists for products design and illustration, and calligraphy. Will review any media; prefers art proportional to 5¼x7⅛''. Produces seasonal material for Christmas; will review new work at any time.
First Contact & Terms: Send query letter with original art or published work or actual work. Samples returned by SASE. Simultaneous submissions OK. Reports in 2 weeks. No originals returned to artist at job's completion. To show a portfolio, mail appropriate materials or call to schedule an appointment; portfolio should include original/final art and final reproduction/product. Pays for design by the project, $100-300. Buys all rights; on acceptance.
Tips: "Familiarize yourself with greeting card field. Spend time in card stores."

CAPE SHORE PAPER PRODUCTS, INC., 42A N. Elm St., Box 537, Yarmouth ME 04096. Art Director: Anne W. Macleod. Produces notes, giftwrap and stationery predominantly nautical in theme. Directs products to gift and stationery stores/shops.
Needs: Buys 25-50 designs and illustrations/year from freelance artists. Prefers watercolor, acrylics, cut paper and gouache. Specific sizes for final art listed in guideline letter. Produces material for Christmas cards; June deadline for finished artwork.
First Contact & Terms: Send query letter with brochure to be kept on file. Reports within several weeks. Pays by the project, $25-200. Prefers to buy all rights. Originals returned to artist if not purchased.
Tips: "We do not use black-and-white artwork, photographs, greeting card prose. Please pay close attention to specification requirements—otherwise, problems can occur."

CAROLYN BEAN PUBLISHING, LTD., 120 2nd St., San Francisco CA 94105. (415)957-9574. Art Director: Tom Drew. Publishes greeting cards and stationery; diverse themes.
Needs: Buys 500-800 designs/illustrations per year from freelance artists. Uses artists for product design. Produces greatly expanded occasions and holiday images; submit material 12-18 months in advance.
First Contact & Terms: Send query letter with slides or photocopies. Samples returned by SASE. Reports in 4 weeks. Originals returned to artist at job's completion. Do not call or write to schedule an interview. Provide samples, business card and tear sheets to be kept on file for possible future assignments. Negotiates rights purchased; prefers royalty arrangement. "To date, we have offered small ad-

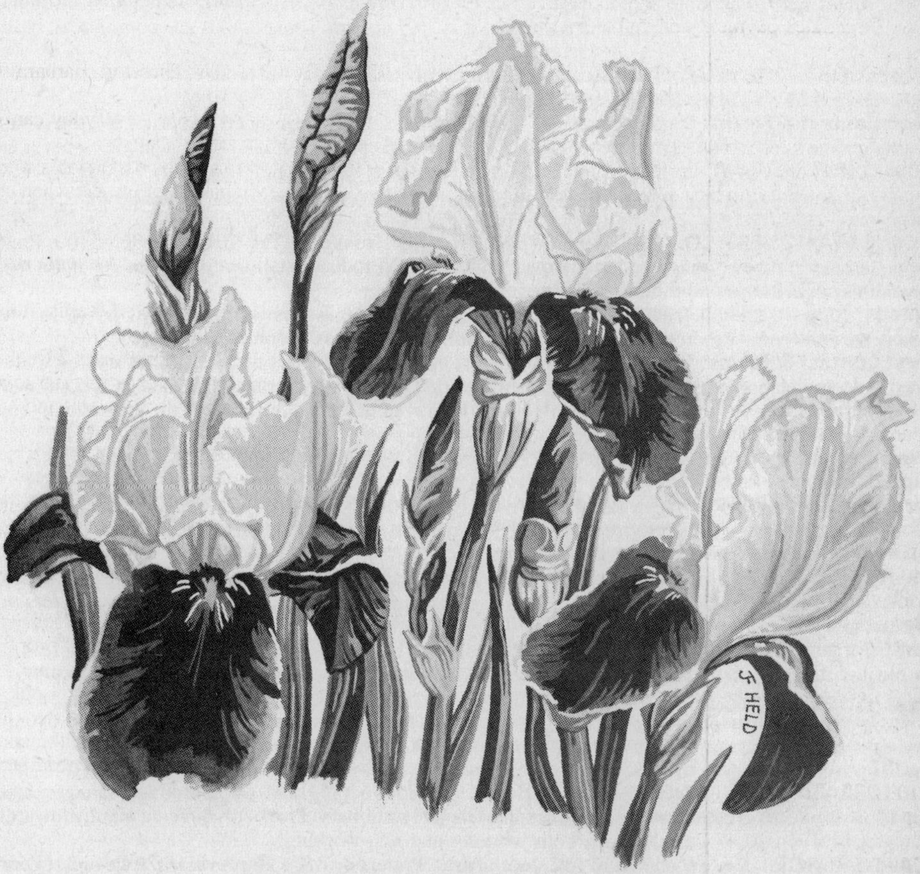

Freelance artist Jackie Held of Hayward, California, submitted this floral watercolor to Cape Shore Paper Products, Yarmouth, Maine, after reading the company's listing in Artist's Market. Cape Shore paid Jackie $100 for the design, which was used for notecards, The message Jackie wanted to convey is "a happy mood and a general message of 'I like spring and iris and I think you will too when you get this card.' "

vances against royalties that range from 5% of wholesale." Payment is made according to time schedule established in contract.
Tips: "Think about *cards*. I see good work all the time, but rarely things that have been created with greeting cards in mind."

CAROUSEL DESIGNS, INC., 369 NE 59th St., Miami FL 33137. (305)751-1100. Marketing Director: Cynthia Huffling. Wallpaper and decorative fabrics firm. Products are "eclectic with emphasis on the more contemporary for residential and commercial customers furnishing homes and commercial buildings."
Needs: Buys 12-20 designs from freelance artists/year. Uses artists for product design and mechanicals. Prefers 27" wide by 25½" vertical repeat.
First Contact & Terms: Send query letter with brochure, samples, tear sheets and original work (color washes) to be kept on file. Samples not filed are returned. Reports within 14 days. Call or write for appointment to show portfolio. No originals returned to artist at job's completion. Pays $300-500 per design; will consider royalty agreement for full program. Buys all rights.

***CASE STATIONERY CO. INC.**, 179 Saw Mill River Rd., Yonkers NY 10701. (914)965-5100. President: Jerome Sudwow. Vice President: Joyce Blackwood. Produces stationery and tins for mass merchandisers in stationery and housewares departments.
Needs: Buys 50 designs from freelance artists/year. Works on assignment only. Uses artists for mechanicals and ideas. Produces materials for Christmas; submit six months in advance.
First Contact & Terms: Send query letter with resume and tear sheets, photostats, photocopies, slides and photographs. Samples not filed are returned. Reports back. Call or write to schedule an appointment to show a portfolio. Original artwork is not returned. Pays a flat fee, by the hour, by the project or by royalties. Buys first rights or one-time rights.
Tips: "Get to know us. We're people who are creative who know how to sell a product."

H. GEORGE CASPARI, INC., 225 Fifth Ave., New York NY 10010. (212)685-9726. President: Douglas H. Stevens. Publishes greeting cards, Christmas cards, invitations, giftwrap and paper napkins. The line maintains a very traditional theme.
Needs: Buys 80-100 illustrations/year from freelance artists. Prefers watercolors, color pencil, and other color media. Produces seasonal material for Christmas, Mother's Day, Father's Day, Easter and Valentine's Day.
First Contact & Terms: Arrange an appointment with Lisa Fingeret to review portfolio. Prefers unpublished original illustrations as samples. Reports within 4 weeks. Negotiates payment on acceptance; pays for design by the project, $200 minimum.
Tips: "Caspari and many other small companies rely on freelance artists to give the line a fresh, overall style rather than relying on one artist. We feel this is a strong point of our company."

***CELEBRATION GREETINGS**, Box 9500, Boulder CO 80301. (303)530-1442. Product Manager: Jane Knutson. Produces greeting cards, calendars, posters and stationery. Product is directed mainly towards females between 20-45 years of age, both working and non-working.
Needs: Buys 100 designs/year from freelance artists. Prefers artists with previous publication experience and/or knowledge of reproduction and of the greeting card industry. Works on assignment only. Also uses freelance artists for calligraphy and greeting card illustration. Considers watercolors, acrylics, airbrush and torn paper. Prefers sizes proportionate to 5x7" with space for 1" bleeds. Seasonal material includes Christmas cards; submit material for the holiday any time of the year.
First Contact & Terms: Send query letter with brochure, resume, tear sheets, slides, photographs and originals. Samples not filed are returned. Reports back within 3 weeks. Call or write to schedule an appointment to show a portfolio, which should include original/final art; final reproduction/product, color, tear sheets and photographs. Original work sometimes returned after publication. Pays a flat fee, $150-200/illustration. Payment is also negotiable. Artists will receive 25 free samples of each illustration. Buys all rights.
Tips: "Most of our accounts are Christian bookstores. Our product tends to have a warm and friendly feel, as opposed to a highly graphic feel. Art may suggest a religious theme, but not usually unless it is specifically for Christmas. We are looking for contemporary art, not dated or traditional themes."

***THE COLORTYPE COMPANY**, 1640 Market St., Coronua CA 91720. (714)734-7410. Vice President/Marketing: Mike Gribble. Produces greeting cards, stationery, mugs and bulletin boards.
Needs: Buys 150 designs from freelance artists/year. Experienced artists only. Uses artists for P-O-P displays, paste-up and mechanicals. Prefers pen & ink, watercolors and acrylics.
First Contact & Terms: Send query letter with brochure showing art style or samples. Samples not filed are returned by SASE. Reports back within 2 weeks. To show a portfolio, mail appropriate materi-

als. No originals returned to artist at job's completion. Pays average flat fee of $120/design and illustration.
Tips: Artist should "be knowledgeable about the card business."

***CPS INDUSTRIES, INC.**, Columbia Highways, Franklin IN 37064. (615)794-8000. Art Director: Michelle Rosenberg. Produces giftwrap.
Needs: Buys 70-75 designs from freelance artists/year. "We solicit speculatives at the concept stage." Prefers pattern repeat, an even division of 18. Produces 50% of material for Christmas, the rest for occasions such as weddings, showers, baby, etc.; submit 1½ years in advance.
First Contact & Terms: Send query letter with resume and photocopies. Samples not filed are returned by SASE. Reports only if interested; will always send guidelines. Call for an appointment to show a portfolio, which should include original/final art, roughs, tear sheets and photostats. Original artwork is returned sometimes. Pays by the project, $100-300 average. Buys rights for giftwrap.
Tips: "Initial work begins with pencil concepts with an indication of color feel. We prefer to work with designs that allow changes at the printing stage. Not interested in complicated, elaborate designs. Ask for a copy of artist's guidelines and send *non-returnable* samples of work."

CRABWALK, INC., 648 Broadway, New York NY 10012. (212)260-1901. Art Director: Alan Gabay. Produces greeting cards, calendars and novelty items with contemporary theme for all ages.
Needs: Purchases only complete lines. Also uses artists for P-O-P displays, paste-up and mechanicals. Considers all media. Finished greeting card 5½x7½". Produces material for Christmas and Valentine's Day; submit 6-9 months before holiday.
First Contact & Terms: Send query letter with samples to be kept on file; write for art guidelines. Prefers tear sheets and photocopies as samples. Samples not filed are returned by SASE. Reports within 2 months. Call or write for appointment to show portfolio. Originals sometimes returned to artist at job's completion. Pays by the project. Negotiates rights purchased.
Tips: "We are only interested in card lines with 30-36 pieces in the line. All other ideas looked at."

CREATIVE PAPER PRODUCTS, INC., 1523 Prudential, Dallas TX 75235. (214)634-1283. President: David Hardenbergh. Novelty pens, pencils etc. for children; 6-14 year olds costume jewelry, "Hello Kitty"—type merchandise. Everyday themes for women.
Needs: Buys "simplistic flat art that is very colorful" from freelance artists. Uses artists for product design and illustration. Produces seasonal material; submit art 6 months before holiday.
First Contact & Terms: Send samples. Prefers photostats and slides as samples. Samples returned on request. Reports within 3 weeks. Provide samples to be kept on file for possible future assignments. Material not copyrighted. Negotiates payment on acceptance.

CREATIVE PAPERS BY C.R. GIBSON, The C.R. Gibson Co., Knight St., Norwalk CT 06856. (203)847-4543. Vice President Creative Papers: Steven P. Mack. Publishes stationery, note paper, invitations and silk-screened giftwrap. Interested in material for lines of products. "Two to three designs are sufficient to get across a concept. We don't use too many regional designs. Stationery themes are up-to-date, fashion oriented. Designs should be somewhat sophisticated without being limiting. Classic designs and current material from the giftware business do well."
Needs: Buys 100-200 designs/year. Especially needs new 4-color art for note line and invitations; "we need designs that relate to current fashion trends as well as a wide variety of illustrations suitable for boxed note cards. We constantly update our invitation line and can use a diverse selection of ideas." Uses humorous illustrations especially for invitation line. Speculation art has no size limitations. Finished size of notes is 4x5½" and 3¾x5"; folded invitations, 3¾x5"; card style invitations 4¾x6"; and giftwrap repeat, 8x8" minimum.
First Contact & Terms: Send query letter with brochure showing art style or resume, photocopies and slides. Prefers 4-6 samples (slides or chromes of work or originals), published or unpublished. Previously published, photocopied and simultaneous submissions OK, if they have not been published as cards and the artist has previous publishers' permissions. SASE. Reports in 6 weeks. Call or write to schedule an appointment to show a portfolio, which should include thumbnails, roughs, original/final art and tear sheets. Pays $35 for rough sketch. Pays for design by the hour, $20 minimum; by the project, $35 minimum. Pays for illustration by the project, $175 minimum. Negotiates payment. Considers complexity of project, skill and experience of artist, reproduction expense and rights purchased. Usually buys all rights; sometimes buys limited rights.
Tips: "Almost all of the artists we work with or have worked with are professional in that they have a background of other professional assignments and exhibits as well as a good art education. We have been fortunate to make a few 'discoveries,' but even these people have been at it for a number of years and have a very distinctive style with complete understanding of printing specifications and mechanicals. More artists are asking for royalties and are trying to develop licensed characters. Most of the work is not

worthy of a royalty and people don't understand what it takes to make a 'character' sell. Keep your presentation neat and don't send very large pieces of art. Keep the submission as varied as possible and neat. Good quality slides also will show the artwork in a better light."

***THE CROCKETT COLLECTION**, Rt. 7, Box 1428, Manchester Center VT 05255. (802)362-2913. President: James Alden. Publishes mostly traditional, some contemporary, humorous and whimsical Christmas and everyday greeting cards, postcards, note cards. Christmas themes geared to sophisticated, upper-income individuals. Free artist's guidelines.
Needs: Buys up to 100 designs/year from freelance artists. Produces products by silkscreen method exclusively.
First Contact & Terms: Send query letter. Request guidelines which are mailed out once a year in January, one year in advance of printing. Submit unpublished, original designs only. Art should be in finished form. Art not purchased returned by SASE. Buys all rights. Pays $70-125 per design.
Tips: "Designs must be suitable for silkscreen process. Airbrush and watercolor techniques are not amenable to this process. Bold, well-defined designs only. Our look is mostly traditional and realistic, so that is a must. Artists should find out what a company specializes in and submit only appropriate work."

***CURRENT INC.**, 1005 E. Woodmen Rd., Colorado Springs CO 80901. Art Director: Pierre De Bernay. Produces greeting cards, giftwrap, calendars and stationery for working women and housewives—all ages.
Needs: Buys 25 designs and illustrations from freelancers/year. Experienced, professional artists only. Uses artists for calligraphy, paste-up and mechanicals. Prefers full color illustrations—no pen & ink. Produces material for all seasons and holidays; submit 2 months before.
First Contact & Terms: Send query letter with brochure showing art style or slides. Samples not filed are returned by SASE. Reports back within 2 weeks. Mail appropriate materials or call or write to schedule an appointment to show a portfolio, which should include original/final art, final reproduction/product and color. Originals sometimes returned to artist at job's completion. Pays average flat fee of $250/design and illustration.
Tips: "Send only small sampling of best art showing variety of styles and quality illustration."

***DECORAL INC.**, 232 Route 109, Farmingdale NY 11735. In NY (516)752-0076; outside NY (800)645-9868. President: Walt Harris. Produces decorative, instant stained glass plus sports and wildlife decals.
Needs: Buys 50 designs from freelance artists/year; buys 50 illustrations from freelance artists/year. Uses artists for P-O-P displays. Prefers watercolors.
First Contact & Terms: Send query letter with brochure showing art style or resume and samples. Samples not filed are returned. Reports back within 30 days. To show a portfolio, mail appropriate materials or call or write to schedule an appointment; portfolio should include original/final art, final reproduction/product and photostats. Original artwork is not returned. Pays average flat fee. Buys all rights.

DESIGNERS STUDIO, 157 Centre St., Brockton MA 02403. (617)583-6775. President: Edward Y. Walker. Produces Christmas cards only.
Needs: Buys 50 designs/year from freelance artists. Considers watercolors for illustrations, and other Christmas card art. Submit seasonal material 15 months in advance.
First Contact & Terms: Send query letter with samples; prefers to receive original artwork. Samples are returned by SASE. Reports back only if interested. Call to schedule an appointment to show a portfolio. Does not return original art after reproduction. Pays by the project $50-75. Buys all rights.
Tips: "Send sample prints only—just a few, to give flavor of work."

DICKENS COMPANY, 59-47 Fresh Meadow Lane, Flushing NY 11365. (718)357-5700, (800)445-4632. Vice President: James Chou. Art Director: David Podwal. Produces greeting cards including musical greetings.
Buys: Buys 100 designs from freelance artists/year; also buys illustrations. Prefers watercolors mainly. Final art size 5¾x8". Produces material for Valentine's Day, Mother's Day, Father's Day and Christmas; submit 9 months in advance.
First Contact & Terms: Prefers local artists with experience in greeting card design. Send resume and samples to be kept on file; call or write for appointment to show portfolio. Prefers photographs or slides as samples. Samples not filed are returned only if requested. Reports within 1 month. Originals returned to artist at job's completion. Pays average flat fee of $100-500/design; $20-100/illustration; or royalties. Negotiates rights purchased.
Tips: "We need experienced artists for greeting card artwork badly."

THE DRAWING BOARD GREETING CARDS, INC., 8200 Carpenter Freeway, Dallas TX 75247. (214)638-4800 ext. 226. Design Director: Richard Hunt. Produces greeting cards, calendars, giftwrap, paper tableware products and stationery.
Needs: Number bought/year varies. Uses color washes, opaque watercolors and oil or acrylics.
First Contact & Terms: Submit seasonal work 6-12 months in advance. Interested in 10-20 of any kind of samples of style. SASE. Reports in 1 week. Buys all rights. Pays $125 minimum for color; on acceptance.
Tips: "Have prior greeting card experience and an unusual style or technique."

***EARTH CARE PAPER CO.**, 325 Beech Lane, Harbor Springs MI 49740. (616)526-7003. Art Director: John Magee. Produces greeting cards, giftwrap, notecards and stationery. "All of our products are printed on recycled paper."
Needs: Buys 25-40 illustrations from freelance artists/year. Considers all media. Produces Christmas cards; seasonal material should be submitted 10 months before the holiday.
First Contact & Terms: Send query letter with samples. Samples not filed are returned by SASE. Reports back within 1 month. To show a portfolio, mail appropriate materials. Original artwork is sometimes returned after publication. Pays a flat fee, $50-100/illustration; royalties vary. "We pay a flat fee plus possible royalties. Negotiates rights purchased.
Tips: "We primarily use a nature theme but will consider anything."

THE EVERGREEN PRESS, INC., 3380 Vincent Rd., Pleasant Hill CA 94523. (415)933-9700. Art Director: Malcolm K. Nielsen. Publishes greeting cards, giftwrap, and stationery; high quality art reproductions, Christmas cards and Christmas postcards.
Needs: Buys 200 designs/year from freelance artists. Uses artists for product design (any design that can be used to produce greeting cards, giftwrap, stationery and other products sold through book, stationery, card and gift stores). Uses only full-color artwork in any media in unusual designs, sophisticated art and humor or series with a common theme. No super-sentimental Christmas themes, single greeting card designs with no relation to each other, or single color pen or pencil sketches. Roughs may be in any size to get an idea of work; final art must meet size specifications. Produces seasonal material for Christmas, Easter and Valentine's Day; "we examine artwork at any time of the year to be published for the next following holiday."
First Contact & Terms: Send query letter with brochure showing art style or slides and actual work; write for art guidelines. Samples returned by SASE. Reports within 2 weeks. To show a portfolio, mail roughs and original/final art. Originals returned at job's completion. Negotiates rights purchased. "We usually make a cash down payment against royalties; royalty to be negotiated. Royalties depend upon the type of product that is submitted and the state of readiness for publication." Considers product use and reproduction expense when establishing payment. Pays on publication.

EXCLUSIVE HANDPRINTS INC., 96 NW 72nd St., Miami FL 33150. (305)751-0281. Vice President: Stanley Bercovitch. Wallpaper firm.
Needs: Buys 12 designs from freelance artists/year. Artists who are "well experienced in wallpaper and fabric designs" only. Uses artists for wallpaper and fabric patterns. If design is repeated, accepts 18" repeat pattern; will also consider nonrepeated designs.
First Contact & Terms: Call or write for appointment to show portfolio. No originals returned at job's completion. Pays flat fee/design. Buys all rights.

***FRAN MAR**, 587 Main St., New Rochelle NY 10801. (914)632-2232. President: Stan Cohen. Produces greeting cards and paper products.
Needs: Buys 150 designs and illustrations from freelance artists/year. Uses artists for full color art or mechanicals. Produces material for all seasons.
First Contact & Terms: Send query letter with brochure showing art style or resume and samples. Samples not filed are returned by SASE. Reports back within 2 weeks. Call or write to schedule an appointment to show a portfolio, which should include original/final art and photostats. No originals returned to artist at job's completion. Pays by the project, $150-300 average. Buys all rights.

***FRAVESSI-LAMONT INC.**, 11 Edison Place, Springfield NJ 07081. Art Director: Helen M. Monahan. Publishes greeting cards; general, cute and some humorous.
Needs: Buys "thousands" of designs and "few" illustrations/year from freelance artists. Uses artists for greeting card design and illustration. Especially needs seasonal and everyday designs; prefers color washes or oil paintings for illustrations. Pays $50 minimum.
First Contact & Terms: Send query letter and samples of work. Prefers roughs as samples. Produces seasonal material for Christmas, Mother's Day, Father's Day, Thanksgiving, Easter, Valentine's Day and St. Patrick's Day; submit art 10 months before holiday. SASE. Reports in 2-3 weeks. No originals

returned to artist at job's completion. Provide samples to be kept on file for possible future assignments. To show a portfolio, mail roughs and color. Buys all rights. Negotiates payment; pays $60-100 average/design; pays on acceptance. Considers product use and reproduction expense when establishing payment. Free artist's guidelines.
Tips: "Just send a few samples of type of work to see if it fits in with our line."

FREEDOM GREETINGS, Box 715, Bristol PA 19007. (215)945-3300. Vice President: Jay Levitt. Produces greeting cards featuring flowers and scenery.
Needs: Buys 100 designs from freelance artists/year. Works on assignment only. Considers watercolors, acrylics, etc. Call for size specifications. Produces material for all seasons and holidays; submit 14 months in advance.
First Contact & Terms: Send query letter with resume and samples. Samples are returned by SASE. Reports within 10 days. To show a portfolio, mail roughs and original/final art. Originals returned to artist at job's completion. Pays for design by the project, $150-200. Buys all rights.

THE C.R. GIBSON CO., 32 Knight St., Norwalk CT 06856. (203)847-4543. Director of Creative Services: Gary E. Carpenter. Publishes stationery, baby and wedding books, paper tableware and other gift products. SASE. Reports in 6 weeks. No finished art, paid for, is returned. Buys all rights.
Needs: Buys 200 designs/year. Uses artists for illustration and calligraphy. Assigns specific art needs for individual projects. Does not usually buy unsolicited finished art.
First Contact & Terms: Send query letter with samples to the attention of Creative Services Coordinator: Marilyn Schoenleber.

THE C.R. GIBSON CO., Creative Papers and Greeting Cards, 32 Knight St., Norwalk CT 06856. (203)847-4543. Product Manager: John C.W. Carroll. Produces greeting cards.
Needs: Buys 100-200 designs and illustrations from freelance artists/year. Considers most media except collage. Scale work to a minimum of 5x7". Prefers vertical image. Submit seasonal material 9-12 months before the holiday.
First Contact & Terms: Send query letter with brochure showing art style and or resume and tear sheets, photostats, photocopies, slides, photographs and other private materials. Prefers any sample. Do not send originals. Samples not filed are returned by SASE. Reports in 6-8 weeks. Call or write for appointment to show portfolio, which should include final reproduction/product, color, tear sheets, photostats, photographs and transparencies. Write for art guidelines. Original artwork returned at job's completion. Pays by the project, $150 minimum. Negotiates rights purchased.
Tips: "If your images are appropriate for card use ("sendability"), then accompanying text should follow relatively easily; artists *can* write . . . it's a complete concept. In the field there is some tendency toward fashion. Also some concentration on the manufacturing side; "merging companies. Marginal operations aren't able to compete—big gets bigger."

GRAND RAPIDS CALENDAR CO., 906 S. Division Ave., Grand Rapids MI 49507. (616)243-1732. Art Director: Rob Van Sledright. Publishes calendars; pharmacy, medical and family themes.
Needs: Buys approximately 15 designs/year. Uses artists for advertising art and line drawings.
First Contact & Terms: Send query letter and SASE for information sheet. Reports in 2 weeks. Previously published, photocopied and simultaneous submissions OK. Pays $10 minimum.

GRAND SLAM GREETINGS, INC., 35 York St., Brooklyn NY 11201. President: Kent Wood. Produces t-shirts, sweatshirts and children's wear.
Needs: Buys 30 designs/year from freelance artists. Local artists only. Also uses artists for paste-up and mechanicals. Considers pen & ink for illustrations.
First Contact & Terms: Send query letter with resume and photographs to be kept on file; "I'll make contact when interview time is available." Samples not filed are returned by SASE. Reports back only if interested. Pays by the hour, $10-15 average; by the project, $100-350 average. Negotiates rights purchased.
Tips: "Stop expecting me to pay a good hourly rate when you don't know your craft. Learn painting, learn about separations. Don't expect me to pay for your education."

GRANDMA JENNY GREETING CARDS, 16120 Cohasset, Van Nuys CA 91406. President: Benson Goldenberg. Produces greeting cards with cartoon themes.
Needs: Buys illustrations from freelance artists/year. Uses artists for calligraphy. Prefers pen & ink, watercolors, color pencils and acrylics. Prefers larger than 5x7" for final art. Produces material for Christmas, Hanukkah, Valentine's Day, Mother's and Father's Day—"all in addition to everyday cards"; submit 9 months in advance.
First Contact & Terms: Send query letter with resume, photostats and tear sheets to be kept on file.

Samples not filed are not returned. Reports within 2 weeks. No originals returned to artist at job's completion. Pays average flat fee of $100-250/illustration. Buys all rights.

THE GRAPHIC ARTISAN, LTD., 3 Cross St., Box 388, Suffren NY 10901. (914)368-1700. Art Director: Peter A. Aron. Publishes stationery, greeting cards, invitations, calendars, posters, diplomas and certificates; general, romantic and Biblical. Mail samples or arrange interview; submit Christmas and Jewish New Year's designs 9 months in advance. SASE. Reports within 1 month. Previously published and simultaneous submissions OK. Buys all rights.
Needs: Buys 50-100 designs/year. Pays $10-100, illustrations. Present needs are predominantly in realistic/cartoon pen & ink sketches of people "in action"—playing games, sports, partying, etc. Also needs animal sketches—single, cartoon type. "Please do not submit original art; photo or photocopy will do."

GREAT LAKES CONCEPTS DESIGNED, Box 2107, Traverse City MI 49685. (616)941-1372. General Manager: Ardana J. Titus. Estab. 1983. Produces greeting cards. Seeks "simple romantic and humorous designs with one or two subjects—no detailed designs. We need colorful and imaginative designs for all-occasion notecard line." No landscapes. Sample card $3.
Needs: Buys 12 designs from freelance artists/year. Considers primarily watercolor—bright, distinct colors and designs—no washes. Final art size 8x11"; allow ¼" on all sides for trim. Prefers vertical designs but will consider horizontal.
First Contact & Terms: Prefers Michigan artists; will consider work from Great Lakes area. Send query letter with samples to be kept on file. Write for art guidelines with SASE. Prefers photographs or originals as samples. Samples not filed are returned by SASE. Reports back within 3 months. Original art returned after reproduction. Pays flat fee of $50 for design. Purchases first rights and/or reprint rights.
Tips: "When submitting material, send bright designs using imaginative approaches. An example is a white lily on a bright yellow background. We will consider a series. We're looking for designs of one or two children as subjects. Designs must be of easily recognizable subjects. Customers want designs of distinct subject work, landscapes don't seem to do well on stationery cards."

THE GREAT NORTHWESTERN GREETING SEED COMPANY, Box 776, Oregon City OR 97045. (503)631-3425. Art Director: Betty Barrett. Produces greeting cards. Uses pastel watercolor, black overlay; whimsical, botanical and natural themes.
Needs: Prefers to work on assignment with local artists. Uses artists for calligraphy, P-O-P displays, paste-up and mechanicals. Prefers pen & ink and watercolor. Produces material for Christmas, Mother's Day, Father's Day and Valentine's Day.
First Contact & Terms: Send query letter with samples to be kept on file. Accepts slides, photostats, photographs, photocopies and tear sheets as samples. Samples not filed are returned. Reports within several weeks. No originals returned to artist at job's completion. Buys all rights.

GREEN TIGER PRESS, 1061 India St., San Diego CA 92101. (619)238-1001. Art Director: Sandra Darling. Publishes greeting cards, giftwrap, calendars, posters, stationery and books; fantasy, nostalgia, The World of the Child themes.
Needs: Buys 50 designs and 100 illustrations/year from freelance artists. Uses artists for product, book and calendar illustration. Prefers b&w drawings and full-color painting. Produces seasonal material for Christmas, Easter and Valentine's Day; submit art 1 year before holiday.
First Contact & Terms: Send samples or actual work. Provide samples to be kept on file for possible future assignments. Samples not kept on file are returned by SASE. Reports in 2 months. Submit portfolio for review. "For first contact any examples of work will serve." Originals returned to artist at job's completion. Negotiates rights purchased. Negotiates payment.
Tips: Artists should have a "good variety of samples; include human figures if available."

***GREETING SEEDS**, Box 776, Oregon City OR 97045. (503)631-3425. Contact: Betty Barrett. Produces greeting cards.
Needs: Buys 24 illustrations from freelance artists/year. Prefers local artists only. Works on assignment only. Uses artists for calligraphy, P-O-P displays, paste-up and mechanicals. Prefers watercolors. Prefers final size of art to be equal to 150% of product. Produces material for Christmas, Mothers Day and Fathers Day; submit 6 months in advance.
First Contact & Terms: Send query letter with resume and samples. Samples not filed are returned by SASE. Reports back ony if interested. Call or write to schedule an appointment to show a portfolio, which should include thumbnails, roughs, original/final art, final reproduction/product and color. Original artwork is not returned. Pays by the project. Buys all rights.
Tips: "Artist should be familiar with our products, botanical subjects, watercolor, whimsical designs and black line."

GREETWELL, D-23, M.I.D.C., Satpur, Nasik 422 007 India. Chief Executive: H.L. Sanghavi. Produces greeting cards, calendars and posters. Specializes in wildlife, flowers, landscapes; general purpose only.
Needs: Buys 100 designs from freelance artists/year. Will review any media; final art is acceptable any size. Accepts seasonal material "any time during the year, but preferably before April."
First Contact & Terms: Send resume and samples to be kept on file. Prefers printed proofs as samples; color photographs or photostats are acceptable. Samples not filed are returned only if requested. Reports within 4 weeks. Original art returned after reproduction. Pays flat fee of $60/design. Buys reprint rights.
Tips: "Submit printed proof of past work so that we can send guidelines and a sample of our requirements."

H.W.H. CREATIVE PRODUCTIONS, INC., 87-53 167th St., Jamaica NY 11432. (212)297-2208. President: Willis Hogans, Jr. Publishes greeting cards, stationery; humorous, designer, primitive art themes, high-tech and New Wave designs.
Needs: Buys 5 designs and 10 illustrations/year from freelance artists. Uses artists for product illustrations, calligraphy plus advertising and catalog illustration and layout. Prefers b&w line drawings and watercolor for product illustrations; 8½x11" and 3 11/16x5¼". Produces seasonal material for Christmas, Thanksgiving, Valentine's Day and Halloween; submit art 6 months before holiday. Also mod humorist illustrations.
First Contact & Terms: Send query letter with continuous tone photos, color slides and brochure/flyer. Samples not kept on file are returned by SASE. Reports in 2 weeks. Originals returned to artist at job's completion. Write to schedule an appointment to show a portfolio, which should include roughs, original art, final reproduction, color and photographs. Negotiates rights purchased but materials not copyrighted sometimes. Pays for design by the project, $50 minimum; pays for illustration by the project, $80 minimum.
Tips: "Know your design abilities and your specialties. Use them."

***IDEA SOURCE**, 77 Park Ave., New York NY 10016. (212)532-5831. President: Ted Tamarkin. Produces greeting cards, stationery, plastic glassware, ceramics, giftware and lighting.
Needs: Buys 100 designs from freelance artists/year; buys 120 illustrations from freelance artists/year. Prefers local artists only. Works on assignment only. Uses artists for P-O-P displays. Submit material 10 months to a year in advance.
First Contact & Terms: Send query letter with brochure showing art style, photostats and photographs. Samples not filed are returned by SASE. Reports within 1 month. Call or write to schedule an appointment to show a portfolio, which should include thumbnails, roughs, original/final art and final reproduction/product. Original artwork is returned sometimes. Pays average flat fee; pays by the hour, $30-60 average; by the project, $50-200 average. Buys all rights.

INTERCONTINENTAL GREETINGS LTD., 176 Madison Ave., New York NY 10016. (212)683-5830. Creative Marketing Director: Robin Lipner. Sells reproduction rights on a per country per product basis. Licenses and syndicates to 4,500-5,000 publishers and manufacturers in 50 different countries. Industries include greeting cards, calendars, prints, posters, stationery, books, textiles, heat transfers, giftware, china, plastics, toys and allied industries, scholastic items and giftwrap.
Needs: Assigns 400-500 jobs and 1,500 designs and illustrations/year. "The trend is to more graphic— clean, modern work." Uses some humorous and cartoon-style illustrations. Prefers full-color original artwork, C-prints or transparencies.
First Contact & Terms: Send query letter and/or resume, tear sheets, slides and photographs. SASE. To show a portfolio, mail appropriate materials or call or write to schedule an appointment; portfolio should include original/final art, color, tear sheets, photographs and originals. Pays for design and illustration by the project $30-500 + . Pays by the project, design and illustration. "Royalties and/or commission; minimum advances." Pays royalties upon sale of reproduction rights on all selected designs. Contractual agreements made with artists and licensing representatives, will negotiate reasonable terms. Considers skill and experience of artist, product use, turnaround time and rights purchased when establishing payment. Provides promotion, color separation and portfolio samples, worldwide trade show display.
Tips: "More and more of our clients need work submitted in series form, so we have to ask artists for work in a series or possibly reject the odd single designs submitted. Make as neat and concise a presentation as possible with commerical application in mind."

JOLI GREETING CARD CO., 2520 W. Irving Park Rd., Chicago IL 60618. (312)588-3770. President: Joel Weil. Produces greeting cards and stationery.
Needs: Number of designs and illustrations bought/year varies. Artists must not have worked for Joli's immediate competition. Uses artists for P-O-P displays. Considers airbrush for product illustration. Pre-

fers finished art of 4x9'' for studio cards and 5x7'' for 5x7'' line. Publishes seasonal material for Christmas, St. Valentine's Day, Mother's Day, Father's Day.
First Contact & Terms: Send query letter with samples to be kept on file. Accepts "whatever is available" as samples. Samples not filed are returned by SASE. Reports within 1 month. Sometimes returns original art after reproduction. Pays flat fee; "open, depending on project." Buys all rights.
Tips: "We are looking for a 'today-look' primarily in the medium of airbrushing."

***KOGLE CARDS, INC.**, Box 3744, Englewood CO 80155. President: Patty Koller. Produces greeting cards.
Needs: Buys 50 designs from freelance artists/year; buys 50 illustrations from freelance artists/year. Works on assignment only. Considers all media for illustrations. Prefers 5x7'' for final art. Produces material for Christmas and all major holidays plus birthdays; material accepted all year round.
First Contact & Terms: Send resume and slides. Samples not filed are returned by SASE. Reports back within 2 weeks. To show a portfolio, mail appropriate materials which should include original/final art, color, photostats, photographs and b&w. Original artwork is not returned. Pays on royalty basis. Buys all rights.

LAFF MASTERS STUDIOS INC., 557 Oak St., Copiague NY 11726. (516)789-8361. Also: Robin Lane Art Studios (counter card division), same address and phone number. Creative Art Director: Sylvia Hacker. Publishes greeting cards: humorous, sophisticated, conventional and youth-oriented. "Robin Lane is concerned with all categories of everyday counter cards, from birth congratulations to formal sympathy cards. Its art standards are extremely high and its freelance work and inhouse requirements are handled by top professionals." In most cases, prefer artists who are nearby and can work with inhouse staff.
Needs: Buys 150-250 illustrations/year. Especially needs humorous and conventional art on assignment only. Artists must be well-versed in knowledge of latest greeting card printing and finishing techniques. Also requires artists who are skilled in juvenile style artwork for future juvenile lines.
First Contact & Terms: Submit published samples only. "Never send unsolicited unpublished material. All samples submitted must have SASE. We cannot return unsolicited samples which do not have SASE and correct postage." Reports within 1 week. No originals returned at job's completion. Pays $75 and up; on acceptance. Buys all rights.
Tips: "We assign work. We never buy unsolicited art. We require artists who are familiar with all phases of greeting card finishing and printing requirements. We see a trend toward more sophisticated and stylized art."

***LEANIN' TREE PUBLISHING CO.**, Box 9500, Boulder CO 80301. (303)530-1441. Product Manager: Jane Knutson. Publishes greeting cards, calendars, posters and stationery. Product is directed mainly towards females between 20-45 years of age, both working and non-working.
Needs: Buys 100 designs/year from freelance artists. Prefers artists with previous publication experience and/or knowledge of reproduction and of the greeting card industry. Works on assignment only. Also uses freelance artists for calligraphy and greeting card illustration. Considers watercolors, acrylics, airbrush and torn paper. Prefers sizes proportionate to 5x7'' with space for 1'' bleeds. Seasonal material includes Christmas cards; submit material for the holiday any time of the year.
First Contact & Terms: Send query letter with brochure, resume, tear sheets, slides, photographs and originals. Samples not filed are returned. Reports back within 3 weeks. Call or write to schedule an appointment to show a portfolio, which should include original/final art; final reproduction/product, color, tear sheets and photographs. Original work sometimes returned after publication. Pays a flat fee, $150-200/illustration; payment is also negotiable. Artists will receive 25 free samples of each illustration. Buys all rights.
Tips: "The majority of our product has a warm, friendly feel, as opposed to a slick, graphic feel. Be sure to take a look at our product."

PAUL LEVY-DESIGNER, 2993 Lakewood Lane, Hollywood FL 33021. (305)981-9550. President: Paul Levy. Produces wallpaper and fabrics.
Needs: Buys 12-24 designs from freelance artists/year. Uses artists for original designs for wallcovering and fabric. Prefers gouache - watercolor designers colors for illustrations; side repeats divisible into 27'' and down repeats 18'' to 27''.
First Contact & Terms: Send resume and original sketches. Call or write to schedule an appointment to show a portfolio, which should include original/final art, final reproduction/product and color. Pays for design by the hour, $8-10; "price depends on experience of artist."
Tips: "Designs in fabrics and wall covering will continue in a contemporary fashion with a modest blending of 'transitional' which is a combination of traditional and contemporary. It is most critical to be as original as possible. Designs of "me too" nature will not be acceptable in marketplace. Have eyes ev-

erywhere as design is universal. Search out the unusual and try to apply it to the medium and field you are designing for. Keep up with color trends as color is as important if not more so than design."

MAINE LINE COMPANY, Box 418, Rockport ME 04856. (207)236-8536 or 1-800-624-6363. Contact: Liz Stanley or Chris Van Dusen. Publishes greeting cards for contempory women from college age up, with primary concentration on women in their 30s. Most of the cards are humorous and deal with women's contemporary concerns. Also publishes humorous products.
Needs: Buys 300-400 illustrations a year from freelance artists; most work is commissioned. "We're looking for illustrators with a wacky sense of humor, whose style is contemporary, funky and colorful. You need not write your own copy to illustrate cards for us, but we're also looking for illustrators who write as well." Most often commissions a group or series of cards, rather than a single card. Also reviews artists or designers concepts for greeting card and postcard series.
First Contact & Terms: Send query letter with photocopies, photostats, tearsheets, slides and photographs. SASE needed for return of samples. Sample card $1 each; creative guidelines for SASE with 60¢ postage. Turnaround time 4-6 weeks. To show a portfolio, mail appropriate materials, which should include final reproduction/product, color, tear sheets, photographs, b&w and slides. Pays advance against royalties for commissioned work.
Tips: "We will be developing a new postcard line in the future, possibly using photographs. We are using more and more full-color art and have more need for illustrators and designers. Please send organized work, labeled, with SASE."

***ALFRED MAINZER INC.**, 27-08 40th Ave., Long Island City NY 11101. (212)392-4200. Art Director: Arwed H. Baenisch. Publishes calendars, greeting cards and postcards; religious, traditional and ethnic European. Submit seasonal work 12 months in advance. Previously published work OK. SASE. Reports in 2 weeks. Originals returned to artist at job's completion. Purchases outright.
Needs: Buys 500-1,000 illustrations/year. Pays $25-250, color; on acceptance.
Tips: Does not accept unsolicited artwork sent by *registered* mail.

MARCEL SCHURMAN CO. INC., 954 60th St., Oakland CA 94608. (415)428-0200. Art Director: Philip Schurman. Produces greeting cards, giftwrap and stationery. Specializes in "very fine art work with many different looks: classical, humorous, children's illustration."
Needs: Buys 50-75 designs/year from freelance artists. Considers watercolors and acrylics for product illustrations. Prefers final art sizes of 5x7", 4x6"; "all can be made 100%-150% larger and reduced." Produces seasonal material for Valentine's Day, Easter, Mother's Day, Father's Day, graduation, Halloween, Christmas, Hanukkah and Thanksgiving. Submit art by March for Valentine's Day and Easter, end of June for Mother's and Father's Day, graduation; November for Christmas, Halloween, Thanksgiving and Hanukkah. Interested in all-occasion cards also.
First Contact & Terms: Send query letter with samples to be kept on file. Prefers slides or photographs as samples. Samples not filed returned by SASE. Reports within 2 weeks. Returns original art after reproduction. Call or write for appointment to show portfolio. Buys all rights.
Tips: "Please send work; we are very open to see new designs."

MARK I INC., 1733 W. Irvine Park Rd., Chicago IL 60613. (312)281-1111. Art Director: Kevin Lahvic. Produces calendars and posters directed to adults 18-35 years old.
Needs: Buys 200 designs from freelance artists/year. Works on assignment only. Uses artists for calligraphy. Considers all media. Produces material for Valentine's Day and Christmas; submit 1 year before holiday.
First Contact & Terms: Send query letter to be kept on file. Write for art guidelines. Samples not filed are returned by SASE. Reports within 2 weeks. Originals returned to artist at job's completion. Write for appointment to show portfolio. Pays by the hour, by the project, or royalties. Buys all rights.

MASTERPIECE STUDIOS, 5400 W. 35th St., Chicago IL 60650. (312)656-4000. Vice President/Creative Director: George Major. Publishes Christmas cards, stationery and notes. Free artist's guidelines. Buys all rights.
Needs: Interested in original material for lines of cards and stationery. "We are interested in reviewing any Christmas art on spec, regardless of experience." Submit seasonal work "any time."
First Contact & Terms: Send query letter with brochure showing art style or resume and samples. Prefers samples of unpublished Christmas cards and stationery. SASE. Reports in 3-4 weeks. Write to schedule an appointment to show a portfolio, which should include original/final art and final reproduction/product. No originals returned to artist at job's completion. Pays for design by the project, $50-75; pays for illustration by the project, $150-350. Considers complexity of project and skill and experience of artist when establishing payment.
Tips: "Originate highly stylized, updated designs with plenty of emphasis on originality, color and design."

***MICHEL'S DESIGNS, INC.,—DIVISION OF THE VIOLA GROUP, INC.**, 8 Engineers Lane, Farmingdale, Long Island NY 11735. (516)249-7722. Creative Coordinator: Arthur D. Viola. Produces period and high fashion (contemporary) hand-silk screen wallcoverings for interior designers/interior decorators; home-furnishings; showrooms; and major wallcovering distribution companies.
Needs: Buys 18-36 designs from freelance artists/year. Priority to local artists having contacts and a presence in the home furnishings and or Interior Decorator/Interior Designer markets. Ability to create artwork; produce color separations on acetate, thus creating camera-ready artwork. Uses artists for paste-up and mechanicals. Prefers watercolor or color pencils initially, and subsequently reproduction on acetates to produce the wallcovering design samples at our factory. Prefers 28'' to 32'' pattern repeat, initially on notepaper, and subsequently reproduced on acetate in color separations by creating freelance artists. Coloring of designs must be current and applicable to the season the line is launched—which is usually fall or spring.
First Contact & Terms: Contact only through artist's agent, who should send query letter with resume, tear sheets, photostats, photocopies and photographs. Samples not filed are returned by SASE. Reports back within 4 weeks. To show a portfolio, mail appropriate materials or call or write to schedule an appointment. Portfolio should include thumbnails, original/final art, final reproduction/product, color, photostats and photographs. No originals returned to artist at job's completion. Payment is reimbursement of reasonable expenses, a royalty arrangement which includes publicly trading common stock in our parent company; and if the line (you help create) goes, a permanent creative consulting position in the division created to house your line and others. Buys all rights.
Tips: "We are looking for a freelancer with sufficient business acumen and commitment to act as manager of a division of a small public company. This division of our parent company will be created around the line her artwork helps to create. A block of stock in the company may be available at the "insider" price to the right candidate should her creative ability produce a profitable line. She will gain through capital gains on the stock and through profit-sharing percentage on the line created."

***MILANO SERIES**, Box 216, 385 Warburton, Hastings on Hudson NY 10706. (914)478-5540. President: Bruce Parisi. Produces giftwrap, posters, paper tableware products, luggage, totes, canvas products, beach and outdoor products and furniture. Directed towards contemporary life style and good design stores.
Needs: Buys 150 designs and 25 illustrations from freelance artists/year. Uses artists for P-O-P displays and mechanicals. Produces material for summer and Christmas; submit 1 year before holiday.
First Contact & Terms: Send query letter with resume, tear sheets, photostats, photocopies, slides and photographs. Samples not filed are returned. Reports only if interested. To show a portfolio, mail appropriate materials or write to schedule an appointment. Portfolio should include thumbnails, roughs, original/final art, final reproduction/product, color, tear sheets, photostats, photographs and b&w. Originals sometimes returned to artist at job's completion. Pays by the hour, $15-22 or royalties of 2-5%. Buys all rights.
Tips: "Our products are all very clean, straightforward products with very clean straightforward graphics. We work on very precise and sometimes tight deadlines."

MILLEN CARDS INC., 45 Ranick Dr. E., Amityville NY 11701. (516)842-2276. Art Director: Mrs. Lois Millner. Produces traditional greeting cards. Submit seasonal work 10 months in advance. SASE. Simultaneous submissions OK. Free artist's guidelines.
Needs: Assigns over 50/year. All artwork is freelanced.
First Contact & Terms: Query with samples of previously published work. Reports within 4 weeks. Samples returned by SASE. Provide business card and samples to be kept on file. Pays average flat fee of $85/design; average flat fee of $85/illustration. Considers complexity of project, skill and experience of artist, reproduction expense, turnaround time and rights purchased when establishing payment.

MORNING STAR, INC., 6800 College Blvd., Overland Park KS 66215. (913)764-3400. Creative Director: Dianne Deckert. Produces greeting cards, giftwrap, calendars, posters, stationery, announcements, invitations, buttons, stickers, boxed Christmas cards and seasonal counter cards. "We publish Christian greeting cards and stationery products featuring the highest quality and fresh, contemporary colors and designs." Directs products primarily to the evangelical Christian and religious markets.
Needs: Buys designs and illustrations from freelance artists. Also uses artists for calligraphy. Prefers primarily watercolors (interested in full-color work), but have used some acrylic and some pen & ink. Wrapping paper repeats: 18''; average greeting card: 4⅞x7'' vertical ("leave bleed room, please"). Produces material for Easter, Mother's Day, Father's Day, Graduation, Confirmation, Grandparent's Day, Thanksgiving, Christmas and Valentine's Day; submit 9 months in advance.
First Contact & Terms: Send query letter with printed samples to be kept on file or original art. Original art and samples not filed are returned only if requested. Reports as soon as possible. No originals returned to artist at job's completion. Call for appointment to show portfolio. Pays flat fee. Buys all rights.

Tips: "Work on flexible board, as white as possible. Do not draw outline around suggested cropping. Leave plenty of bleed room all the way around art. Send by registered mail."

MUSICAL IMAGE DESIGNS, 1212 Ardee Ave., Nashville TN 37216. (615)226-1509. Creative Director: Stacy Slocum. Estab. 1985. Produces greeting cards, giftwrap, stationery and banners. "We cater to the music business. We want musical themes—piano, staff, banjo, any musical instrument."
Needs: Uses artists for designs, illustration, calligraphy and P-O-P displays. Considers pen & ink. Produces material for all holidays. "Music should be integrated into the holiday theme." Submit seasonal material 3 months in advance.
First Contact & Terms: Send resume and samples to be kept on file. Write or call for art guidelines. Prefers photocopies or tear sheets as samples. Samples not filed are returned only by request with SASE. Reports within 1 month. No originals returned at job's completion. Pays by the project. "If they are great ideas and followed through with care this will be a factor. Complexity does not necessarily make it more valuable to us." Buys all rights or first rights.
Tips: "I am most interested in what you can do now. Send me samples of musical designs. What you've done in the past is of no real interest to me. I would like all work in black ink on 8½x5½" white paper."

OATMEAL STUDIOS, Box 138, Rochester VT 05767. (802)767-3325. Art Director: Helene Lehrer. Publishes greeting cards; creative ideas for everyday cards and holidays.
Needs: Buys 100-150 designs/illustrations per year from freelance artists. Uses artists for greeting card design and illustration. Considers all media; prefers 5x7", 6x8½", vertical composition. Produces seasonal material for Christmas, Mother's Day, Father's Day, Easter, Valentine's Day and Hanukkah. Submit art in October for Christmas and Hanukkah, in March for other holidays.
First Contact & Terms: Send query letter with slides, roughs, printed pieces, brochure/flyer to be kept on file; write for artists' guidelines. "If brochure/flyer is not available, we ask to keep one slide or printed piece." Samples returned by SASE. Reports in 2-4 weeks. Negotiates payment arrangement with artist.
Tips: "We're looking for exciting and creative illustrations and graphic design for greeting cards. Also, light humor with appeal to college age and up."

***PACIFIC PAPER GREETINGS, INC.**, (formerly Snap Dragon Floral Design), Box 2249, Sidney British Columbia V8L 3S8 Canada. (604)656-0504. President: Louise Rytter. Produces greeting cards and stationery.
Needs: "Prefers experience and artists that will develop a theme to their artwork thus creating a series for greeting cards." Uses artists for paste-up. Prefers illustrations for cake reproductions only. Prefers greeting cards of stand-up size, 5x7". Produces material for Christmas and Valentines Day; submit 1 year before holiday.
First Contact & Terms: Send query letter with brochure showing art style or resume tear sheets, photostats, photocopies, slides and photographs. Samples not filed returned by SASE. Reports within 6 weeks. To show a portfolio, mail appropriate materials. no originals returned to artist at job's completion. Negotiates payment. Negotiates rights purchased.
Tips: "Remember we are looking for a theme artist to create a card line."

PAPEL, INC., Box 9879, North Hollywood CA 91609. (818)765-1100. Art Coordinator: Helen Scheffler. Produces souvenir and seasonal ceramic giftware items: mugs, photo frames, greeting tiles.
Needs: Buys 500 illustrations from freelance artists/year. Artists with minimum 3 years' experience in greeting cards only; "our product is ceramic but ceramic experience not necessary." Uses artists for product and P-O-P design, illustrations on product, calligraphy, paste-up and mechanicals. Produces material for Christmas, Valentine's Day, Easter, St. Patrick's Day, Mother's and Father's Day; submit one year before holiday.
First Contact & Terms: Send query letter with brochure, resume, photostats, photocopies, slides, photographs and tear sheets to be kept on file. Samples not kept on file are returned by SASE if requested. Reports within 2 weeks. No originals returned to artist at job's completion. To show a portfolio, mail appropriate materials, which should include final reproduction/product, color, tear sheets, photostats, photographs and b&w. Pays by the project, $50-350 average. Buys all rights.
Tips: "As art styles change, it may affect which artists we pick, but it certainly does not affect the amount of freelance artwork we require. We still depend a tremendous amount on freelance talent. Send samples of as many different styles as you are capable of doing well. Versatility is a key to having lots of work."

***PAPER ART COMPANY INC.**, 3500 N. Arlington Ave., Indianapolis IN 46218. (800)428-5017. Creative Director: Jo Anne Madry. Produces stationery, paper tableware products, invitations and party decor.

Needs: Buys 10% of line from freelance artists/year. Prefers flat watercolor, designer's gouache for designs. Prefers 5x5" design area for luncheon napkin design; 4x4" for cocktail napkins; 9¼" for plate design. Produces general everyday patterns for birthday, weddings, baby and bridal showers; St. Patrick's Day, Easter, Valentine's Day, Fall, Halloween, Thanksgiving, Christmas and New Year; submit 8-10 weeks in advance.

First Contact & Terms: Send query letter with brochure showing art style, photocopies and printed samples. Samples not filed are returned. Reports back within 2 weeks. Call to schedule an appointment to show a portfolio, which should include original/final art, final reproduction/product, color and designs. Original artwork is not returned if purchased. Pays by the project, $150 minimum.

Tips: "Color coordinating and the mixing and matching of patterns are prevalent. There are more sophisticated designs. In paper products, the biggest change is in non-drinking type cocktail napkins. For us, we require professional, finished art that would apply to our product."

PECK INC., 3963 Vernal Pike, Box 1148, Bloomington IN 47402. Art Director: Trisha Vollmer. Manufactures Christmas tags; Christmas, Halloween, Valentine and Easter cutouts; and educational bulletin board aids.

Needs: Uses artists for product design and illustrations. Specific needs include juvenile characters, animals, traditional Christmas, Halloween and/or all occasion design.

First Contact & Terms: Send a query letter with color samples or slides. SASE. Reports in approximately 2 months. Pays by the project; negotiates payment according to complexity of project and product use.

Tips: Especially looks for "full-color work and emphasis on clarity of color and design."

PICKHARDT & SIEBERT (USA) INC., 16201 Trade Zone Ave., Upper Marlboro MD 20772. (301)249-7900. Produces wallcovering and companion fabrics.

Needs: Uses artists for product design, illustration on product, calligraphy, paste-up and mechanicals. "Wallcovering manufacturing being done in Germany; some wallcovering textile designs are purchased in the US. We do find the need for *local* freelance artists."

First Contact & Terms: Send query letter with resume; tear sheets and photostats to be kept on file. Reports only if interested. To show a portfolio, mail original/final art or call or write to schedule an appointment. Negotiates pay.

Tips: "Need complete package as soon as possible—prefer approach with total concept."

***PLYMOUTH INC.**, 361 Benigno Blvd., Bellmawr NJ 08031. Art Director: Nancy Yarnall. Produces greeting cards, posters, stationery and paper products, such as 3x5 wire-bound memo books, wire-bound theme books, porfolios, scribble pads, book covers, pencil tablets, etc., all with decorative covers for school, middle grades and high school. "We use contemporary illustrations. Some of our work is licensed. We are expanding into the gift trade with various paper products aimed toward an older age group 19 and up."

Needs: Buys 300 designs and 300 illustrations from freelance artists/year. Works on assignment only. Uses artists for calligraphy, P-O-P displays, paste-up and mechanicals. Prefers full color.

First Contact & Terms: Send query letter with brochure showing art style or resume, tear sheets, photostats, photocopies, slides and photographs. Samples returned by SASE. Reports only if interested. Mail appropriate materials or write to schedule an appointment to show a portfolio, which should include final reproduction/product, color and tear sheets. Pays according to project and based upon experience. Buys all rights or negotiates rights purchased.

Tips: "Plymouth is looking for professional illustrators and designers. The work must be top notch. It is the art that sells our products. We use many different styles of illustration and design and are open to new ideas."

***POTPOURRI PRESS**, 6210 Swiggett Rd., Greensboro NC 27410; mailing address: Box 19566, Greensboro NC 27419. (919)852-8961. Director of New Product Development: Barbara Kelley. Produces giftwrap, paper tableware products, tins, plastics, stoneware and fabric items for giftshops, the gourmet shop trade, and department stores.

Needs: Buys 10-20 designs from freelance artists/year; buys 10-20 illustrations from freelance artists/

> ❝ *Portfolios should be comprehensive but not too large. Organization of portfolios is as important as the samples.* ❞
>
> *Mort Gower, Art Administrator*
> *J. Walter Thompson USA*

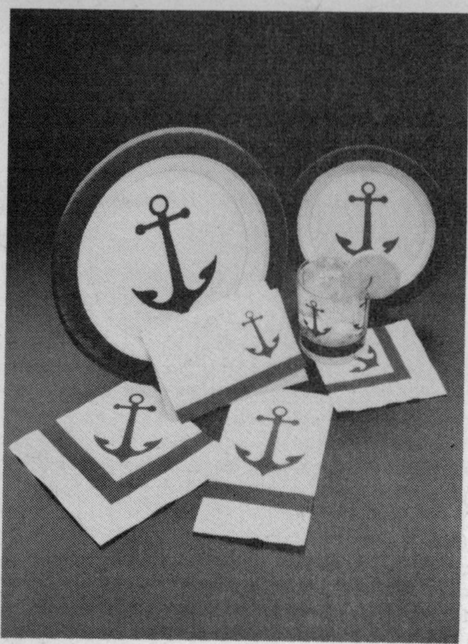

Freelance artist Tom Cathay of New York City received an assignment from Barbara Kelley of Potpourri Press in Greensboro, North Carolina, to convey "fun, summer, relaxation at the poolside." He used a nautical theme for the "Dockside" line of tins, paper and plastic items. Kelley purchased first rights to the design.

year. Works on assignment only. Uses artists for calligraphy, mechanicals and art of all kinds for product reproduction. Prefers watercolor, acrylics and mechanical work. Produces material for Valentine's Day, Mother's and Father's Day and Christmas; submit 1½ years before holiday.

First Contact & Terms: Send query letter with resume and tear sheets, photostats, photocopies, slides and photographs. Samples not filed are returned by SASE. Reports back as soon as possible. Call or write to schedule an appointment to show a portfolio which should include anything to show ability. "Artist must have good portfolio showing styles the artist is comfortable in." Original artwork not returned. Pays average flat fee. Buys all rights.

Tips: "Give us maximum information to help us make our decision. Provide references that can tell us if you meet deadlines, are easy, medium or tough to work with, etc."

PREFERRED STOCK, INC., 1020 Turnpike St., Canton MA 02021. (617)244-7558. President: Ann C. Cohen. Produces greeting cards, stationery, bags, pads, pencils and invitations using graphics and illustrations.

Needs: Buys 200 designs and 150 illustrations from freelance artists/year. Also uses artists for calligraphy and mechanicals. Works on assignment only. Considers watercolors, acrylics, etc. Prefers 5x7" size for final art. Produces material for Christmas, Valentine's Day, Mother's Day, Father's Day, Graduation, Chanukkah and Jewish New Year; submit 1 year in advance.

First Contact & Terms: Send query letter with brochure, resume, business card and samples to be kept on file. Prefers slides, colored photostats and printed pieces as samples. Samples not filed are returned by SASE. Reports only if interested. Originals sometimes returned to artist at job's completion. To show a portfolio, mail non-returnable roughs. Pays by the project, $100-200. Buys all rights.

Tips: Especially wants "humorous cards, *colorful* illustrations and professionalism."

***PRELUDE DESIGNS**, 1 Hayes St., Elmsford NY 10523. Art Director: Franco Maida. Produces paper tableware products and wallpaper/fabric.

Needs: Buys 10 designs and 1-5 illustrations from freelance artists/year. Local artists only. Works on assignment only. Uses artists for paste-up and color paint-ups. Prefers tempera, oil, watercolor and acrylic. Prefers 36x27" (or frations thereof).

First Contact & Terms: Send query letter with resume. Samples not filed are returned. Reports within 7 days. To show a portfolio, which should include original/final art, final reproduction/product, color and photographs. Originals sometimes returned to artist at job's completion. Pays average flat fee of $200-500. Negotiates rights purchased.

THE PRINTERY HOUSE OF CONCEPTION ABBEY, Conception MO 64433. Art Director: Rev. Norbert Schappler. A publisher of religious greeting cards; religious Christmas and all occasion themes for people interested in religious yet contemporary expressions of faith. "Our card designs are meant to touch the heart and feature strong graphics, calligraphy and other appropriate styles."
Needs: Works with 25 freelance artists/year. Uses artists for product illustrations. Prefers silk-screen, oil, watercolor, line drawings; classical and contemporary calligraphy. Produces seasonal material for Christmas and Easter.
First Contact & Terms: Send query letter with brochure showing art style or resume, tear sheets, photostats, photocopies, slides and photographs. Samples returned by SASE. Reports within 3 weeks. To show a portfolio, mail appropriate materials only after query has been answered. Portfolio should include final reproduction/product, color, tear sheets and photographs. "In general, we continue to work with artists year after year once we have begun to accept work from them." Pays by the project; $100-250. Usually purchases exclusive reproduction rights; for a specified format; occasionally buys complete reproduction rights.
Tips: "We are seeing a revival of interest in classically-clean designs, along with an interest in new colors, better graphics, mixed-media work, appropriate Biblical quotations, etc. Computerized graphics are beginning to have an impact in our field; multi-colored calligraphy is a new development. Remember our specific purpose of publishing greeting cards with a definite Christian/religious dimension but not piously religious. Wedded with religious dimension, it must be good quality artwork. We sell mostly via catalogs so artwork has to reduce well for catalog."

PRODUCT CENTRE-S.W. INC./THE TEXAS POSTCARD CO., Box 708, Plano TX 75074. (214)423-0411. Art Director: Susan Hudson. Produces greeting cards, calendars, posters, melamine trays, coasters and postcards. Themes range from nostalgia to art deco to pop/rock for contemporary buyers.
Needs: Buys 150 designs from freelance artists/year. Uses artists for P-O-P display, paste-up and mechanicals. Considers any media, "we do use a lot of acrylic/airbrush designs." Final art must not be larger than 8x10. "Certain products require specific measurements; we will provide these when assigned. Produces Christmas material; submit 1 year in advance.
First Contact & Terms: Send resume, business card slides, photostats, photographs, photocopies and tear sheets to be kept on file. Samples not filed are returned only by request with SASE including return insurance. Reports within 1 month. No originals returned to artist at job's completion. Call or write for appointment to show portfolio. Pays average flat fee of $100/design maximum. Buys all rights.
Tips: "Artist should be able to submit camera-ready work and understand printer's requirements. The majority of our designs are assigned."

***P.S. GREETINGS**, (formerly Fantus Paper Products), 4459 W. Division St., Chicago IL 60651. Art Director: Rudy Schwarz. Publishes greeting and note cards; everyday and Christmas.
Needs: Uses freelance work. Uses artists for greeting and note cards.
First Contact & Terms: Mail in letter of introduction with samples of artwork for consideration. Will respond with artist's guidelines letter and samples and possibly arrange for interview to show portfolio. Prefers 5½x7½" or 4½x6½" for greeting cards; 3½x5½" for note cards. Submit seasonal work 1 year in advance. SASE. Reports in 4 weeks. Simultaneous submissions and previously published work OK. Call or write to schedule an appointment to show a portfolio, which should include original/final art and photograph. Buys first or reprint rights. Pays for design by the project, $150 maximum; on acceptance.
Tips: "Of course, we look for originality and ingenuity, but also concentration on detail and marketability."

RAINBOW ARTS, 488 Main St., Fitchburg MA 01420. (617)345-4476. Art Director: Ian Michaels. Produces greeting cards, specializing in everyday, all occasion and Valentine's Day cards.
Needs: Buys 100-125 designs/illustrations from freelance artists/year. Uses artists for product design and illustration on product. Considers wide variety of media for illustrations; "we've used just about every medium—watercolor, acrylics, colored line work, markers, airbrush, gouache, silkscreen, batik, etc. We *do not* use still lifes, nature studies or abstract art. Prefers artwork "larger than our 5⅛x6½" format, but in direct proportion; otherwise you have a card with disproportionate borders or have to crop part of the artwork." Produces seasonal material for Valentine's Day, Mother's Day, Father's Day, Easter and Christmas, but "each work should be able to relate to other occasions, such as, blanks (cards with no verse), birthday, anniversary, etc." Submit seasonal material 6-12 months before holiday. "We also design and manufacture stickers."
First Contact & Terms: Send query letter with brochure showing art style or tear sheets, photocopies, slides and photographs; possibly to be kept on file. "We can't be responsible for original art unless otherwise stated." Samples not kept on file are returned by SASE *provided* by the artist. Usually reports within 1 month, but does vary during the year. Originals returned to artist at job's completion. To show a portfolio, mail appropriate materials, which should include final reproduction/product, color, tear

sheets and slides; "we prefer to view slides." Pays royalties of 8% and advances ranging from $100-200. Buys reprint rights for greeting cards and we do licensing. Pays for design by the project 5%-8%..
Tips: "With new freelance artists we look more for new looks. The market surge is in cartoon-style illustration, in both the cute category and the risque market. Send us your samples with a *self addressed stamped envelope*. Request it and we'll send you *The Artist's Guide to the Freelance Market* by Ian Michaels with our response. Include a self-addressed stamped post card with your work. Write on it: "Date received," so you can keep track of your work without the worry. An artist should first have this work okayed as being relevent to what a card company is currently producing before taking the time to tailor this work to that company's size and schedule. There are a lot of fine artists that are finding it harder and harder to get published in cards. Art is becoming secondary to the message. We have had to cease producing some art from artists that we have worked with in the past."

RAINBOWORLD INC., 319 A St., Boston MA 02210. (617)350-0260. Contact: Sallie Horton, production department. Publishes greeting cards, giftwrap, calendars and stationery; general themes.
Needs: Buys 20 designs and 50 illustrations/year from freelance artists. Works on assignment only. Uses artists for advertising illustration. Considers any color media sized 10x14" or larger. Produces seasonal material for Christmas and Valentine's Day; submit art 6-12 months before holiday.
First Contact & Terms: Send resume and brochure/flyer *which do not need to be returned*. No originals or slides. "If work is suitable, we will arrange to review portfolio and other work." Reports as soon as possible. Originals returned to artist at job's completion. Buys first rights and reprint rights. Negotiates payment, $250 and up/project; on publication. Considers complexity of project, skill and experience of artist, product use and rights purchased when establishing payment.
Tips: "For initial contact, artists should submit copies of their work which we can *keep* on file—even photocopies. This allows us to keep a 'review' file to use as projects develop and allows us to quickly discover which artists are suitable for our market with a minimum of inconvenience to both parties. Do not send resumes without samples and do not bother to write asking for further information on firm. Send samples. This is a visual medium, not verbal."

RECYCLED PAPER PRODUCTS INC., 3636 N. Broadway, Chicago IL 60613. Art Director: Audrey Christie. Publishes greeting cards, calendars, posters and stationery; unique subjects. Artist's guidelines available.
Needs: Buys 500 designs and 1,000-2,000 illustrations/year from freelance artists. Uses artists for product design and illustrations, calligraphy and P-O-P design. Considers b&w line and color—"no real restrictions." Prefers 5x7" for cards, 10-14" maximum. "Our primary concern is card design." Produces seasonal material for Christmas, Hanukkah, Mother's Day, Father's Day, Thanksgiving, Easter, Valentine's Day, St. Patrick's Day and Halloween. Submit seasonal material 12-18 months in advance for Christmas or send at holidays for following year.
First Contact & Terms: Send query letter with slides, roughs and printed pieces or actual work. Samples returned by SASE. Reports in 2 months. Original work usually not returned at job's completion, but "negotiable." Provide samples and tear sheets to be kept on file for possible future assignments. Buys all rights. Pays average flat fee of $150/design or illustration; also negotiates payment "if we have major interest"; on acceptance.
Tips: "Sophisticated, light humor is our keynote. We're trend setters, not followers."

RED FARM STUDIO, 334 Pleasant St., Box 347, Pawtucket RI 02862. (401)728-9300. Creative Director: Mary M. Hood. Produces greeting cards, giftwrap, coloring books, paper dolls, story coloring books, napkins, Christmas cards, gift enclosures, notes, postcards and paintables. Specializing in nautical and country themes and fine watercolors. Art guidelines available upon request if SASE is provided.
Needs: Buys approximately 200 designs and illustrations/year from freelance artists. Considers watercolor artwork. Prefers final art of $6\frac{3}{4}$x$8\frac{7}{16}$" ($\frac{3}{16}$" bleed) for Christmas cards; $4\frac{3}{4}$x$6\frac{3}{4}$" ($\frac{1}{8}$" bleed) for everyday cards; and $6\frac{3}{16}$x$8\frac{13}{16}$" ($\frac{3}{16}$" bleed) for notes. Submit Christmas artwork 1 year in advance.
First Contact & Terms: Send query letter with slides, photographs, photocopies or tear sheets to be kept on file. Call for appointment to show portfolio, which should include brochure showing art style and tear sheets, photocopies and slides. Samples not filed are returned by SASE. Reports within 1-2 weeks. Original artwork not returned after reproduction. "Our pay scale starts at $150/design. Pays for illustration by the project, $150 minimum. Buys all rights.
Tips: "We are interested in realistic, fine art watercolors. We do not reproduce photography. Our line consists of realistic, fine art watercolors."

C.A. REED, INC., 99 Chestnut St., Box 3128, Williamsport PA 17701-0128. Art Director: Bob Crain. Publishes paper tableware products; birthday, everyday, seasonal and holiday.
Needs: Buys 150-200 designs/year. Uses artists for product design and illustration. Interested in material for paper tableware, i.e. plates, napkins, cups, etc. No greeting cards.

First Contact & Terms: Query with samples. SASE. Reports in 6 weeks. Photocopied and simultaneous submissions OK. "Buys all rights within our field of publication." Pays $100-150, product design.
Tips: Artist should visit stationery shops and/or request artist's guidelines.

REED STARLINE CARD CO., Box 26247, Los Angeles CA 90026. Purchases slightly risque, humorous, everyday and seasonal greeting card copy and art.
First Contact & Terms: Send query letter with photocopies. To show a portfolio, mail appropriate materials, which should include roughs, final reproduction/product and photostats. Pays for illustration by the project, $100-125.
Tips: "Cartoons only, want neuter characters."

REGENCY & CENTURY GREETINGS, 1500 W. Monroe St., Chicago IL 60607. (312)666-8686. Art Director: David Cuthbertson. Publishes Christmas cards; traditional and some religious Christmas.
Needs: Buys 200 illustrations and designs/year.
First Contact & Terms: Send query letter with samples. Submit seasonal art 8 months in advance. Reports in 4-6 weeks. Previously published work OK. Buys *exclusively Christmas* card reproduction rights. Originals returned to artist at job's completion. Pays $90 minimum, b&w; $125, color; $90-150, design. Pays on acceptance.
Tips: Artist should visit stationery shops for ideas, and request artist's guidelines to become familiar with the products. "Traditional still sells best in more expensive lines."

RENAISSANCE GREETING CARDS, Box 127, Springvale ME 04083. Creative Director: Robin Kleinrock. Publishes greeting cards; "current approaches" to all occasion cards, seasonal cards, Christmas cards and nostalgic Christmas themes.
Needs: Buys 600 illustrations/year from freelance artists. Full-color illustrations only. Prefers art proportional to 8½x11". Produces everyday occasions—birthday, Get Well, friendship and seasonal material for Christmas, Valentine's Day, Mother's Day, Father's Day, Easter, graduation, St. Patrick's Day, Halloween, Thanksgiving, Passover, Jewish New Year and Hanukkah; submit art 18 months in advance for Christmas material; approximately 1 year for other holidays.
First Contact & Terms: Send query letter with printed pieces, tear sheets and/or slides; write for artists' guidelines. Samples returned by SASE. Reports in 3 months. To show a portfolio, mail appropriate materials, which should include original/final art, color tear sheets and slides or transparencies. Originals returned to artist at job's completion. Negotiates payment amount.
Tips: "Start by sending a small (10-12) sampling of 'best' work, preferably printed samples or slides of your best work (with SASE for return). This allows a preview for possible fit, saving time and expense."

***REPRODUCTA CO. INC.**, 11 E. 26th St., New York NY 10010. Art Director: Thomas B. Schulhof. Publishes stationery, postcards and greeting cards; religious and general.
Needs: Buys 750 designs/year. Works with all occasions—religious plus floral, wildlife and "cutes."
First Contact & Terms: Mail art. SASE. Seasonal: Christmas, Mother's Day, Easter and Father's Day themes. No originals returned to artist at job's completion. Request artist's guidelines. Buys all rights. Pays $50-200; payment negotiated.

***RIVERSIDE PAPER COMPANY**, Box 179, Appleton WI 54912-0179. (414)733-6651. Marketing Manager: Scott Priby. Produces fine printing papers.
Needs: Buys 10 designs for freelance artists/year; buys 4-5 illustrations from freelance artists/year. Works on assignment only. Prefers brochures, top sheets, etc.

ROCKSHOTS, INC., 8th Floor, 632 Broadway, New York NY 10012-2416. (212)420-1400. Art Director: Tolin Greene. Publishes greeting cards, calendars, posters and stationery; humorous, erotic and satirical themes for "anyone who loves well-designed, outrageous, humorous, sexy cards."
Needs: Buys 150 designs and 150 illustrations/year from freelance artists. Uses artists for card, calendar and catalog illustration layout and catalog design. No airbrush, prefer cartoon—bright, full-color artwork. Produces seasonal material for birthday, Christmas, Mother's Day, Father's Day, Easter, Valentine's Day and Halloween; submit art 10 months before holiday.
First Contact & Terms: Send resume and actual work. Prefers slides and examples of artist's style of original work as samples. Samples returned by SASE. Reports within 2 weeks. Originals returned to artist at job's completion. Provide tear sheets to be kept on file for possible future assignments. Call for appointment, submit portfolio for review. Buys all rights. Negotiates payment; on acceptance.

***RONNIES GREETING CARDS LIMITED**, 245 Acton Lane, Park Royal, London NW10 England. 44-01-965-6135. Managing Director: Mr. P. Patel. Produces greeting cards, giftware and gift tags; humorous and graphic designs, plus "cuties."

Needs: Buys 100-200 designs/year from freelance artists. Works on assignment only. Produces seasonal material for St. Valentine's Day, Mother's Day, Easter, and Christmas; submit 1 year in advance.
First Contact & Terms: Send query letter with brochure and samples to be kept on file. Prefers slides or photographs as samples. Samples not filed are returned by SASE (nonresidents include IRC) or only if requested. Reports within 4 weeks. Sometimes returns original artwork after reproduction. Payment varies. Buys all rights.
Tips: "We are a very fast-growing company."

ROUSANA CARDS, 28 Sager Pl., Hillside NJ 07205. Art Director: Dorothy Chmielewski. Produces seasonal (all) and everyday greeting cards.
Needs: Established greeting card designers only.
First Contact & Terms: "Submit printed samples of your style, no original art. Write to schedule an appointment to show a portfolio, which should include final reproduction/product and color. Pays for illustration by the project, $150 minimum; varies with complexity of project.
Tips: We see a leaning towards smart, shophisticated designing."

THE ROYAL STATIONERY, INC., Minneapolis Industrial Park, 13000 County Rd. 6 at Hwy. 55, Minneapolis MN 55441. (612)559-3671. National Sales: Larry Gallaf. Produces stationery, postcards, note cards, mugs, key chains and soaps; floral, scenic, animal, children and novelty. Interested in material for lines of products.
Needs: Buys 50 designs/year. Uses artists for product design, and b&w and color illustrations.
First Contact & Terms: Submit 4-5 illustrations. Prefers unpublished samples. SASE. Reports within 4 weeks. No originals returned at job's completion. Buys all rights. Pays by the project, $25 minimum, camera-ready designs. Considers complexity of project, skill and experience of artist, and reproduction expense when establishing payment.

SACKBUT PRESS, 2513 E. Webster Place, Milwaukee WI 53211. Contact: Angela Peckenpaugh. Publishes poem postcards and notecards.
Needs: "A few line drawings for very specific themes."
First Contact and Terms: Send query letter with photostats. Samples returned. Reports in 1 month. Send photostats. Buys one-time rights. Pays for illustration by the project, $10; on publication.
Tips: "I went from publishing a literary magazine to publishing poem postcards and notecards. I have little time or money to market my product. I sell at fairs. Produce sporadic direct mail ads and classifieds. Usually my prices only appeal to beginners or hobbyists."

ST. CLAIR PAKWELL, 120 25th Ave., Bellwood IL 60104. (312)547-7500 ext. 262. Design Art Director: Elaine Brochocki. Publishes gift boxes, giftwrap and graphic packaging.
Needs: Buys 50-150 designs/year. Uses artists for giftwrap designs. Especially needs Christmas giftwrap designs. Prefers giftwrap pattern repeat in an even division or 24" from top to bottom.
First Contact & Terms: Query. SASE. Reports in 3 weeks. Buys all rights. Negotiates payment.

ST. CLAIR-PAKWELL PAPER PRODUCTS, Box 800, Wilsonville OR 97070. (503)638-9833. Art Director: Anna Mack. Publishes gift boxes, giftwrap and various packaging.
Needs: Buys 100 designs/year. Uses artists for product design and illustration. "For use in department stores as courtesy wrap or used for pre-wrapped box coverings."
First Contact & Terms: Send query letter with resume and tear sheets, photostats, photocopies, slides, photographs and "anything available." Prefers 15" repeat and even divisions thereof for giftwrap. SASE. Reports in 2 weeks. Call or write to schedule an appointment to show a portfolio, which should include original/final art and final reproduction/product. No originals returned to artist at job's completion. Pays for design by the hour, $4.50 minimum; pays for illustration by the project, $50-500. Buys all rights.
Tips: "We're seeing more and more use of freelance artists. Work should be geared toward the resale market—not the fine arts."

***SAY IT WITH A SONG, INC.**, 243 Church St. NW, Vienna VA 22180. (703)255-9500. Vice President: Eugene Stouse. Estab. 1985. Produces greeting cards and posters for a record-buying audience.
Needs: Buys 200 designs from freelance artists/year; buys 150 illustrations from freelance artists/year. Considers all media. Prefers a manageable size for final art. Produces material related to songs and lyrics.
First Contact & Terms: Send query letter with brochure showing art style. Samples not filed are returned. Reports back within 10 days. To show a portfolio, mail appropriate materials or call or write to schedule an appointment. Original artwork returned. Payment is negotiated. Buys first rights or reprint rights.

***W.N. SHARPE LTD.—CLASSIC CARDS**, Bingley Rd., Bradford, West Yorkshine BD9 6SD England. 44-02-744-1365. Publishing Director: Roger Hutchings. Produces greeting cards and giftwrap.
Needs: Buys 800 designs from freelance artists/year. Considers watercolors and acrylics for illustrations. Prefers final art size of 9⅛x6⅜". Produces seasonal material for St. Valentine's Day, Christmas; submit artwork 6 months in advance.
First Contact & Terms: Artists must have a minimum 3 years' experience in greeting cards. Works on assignment only. Send query letter with resume and samples; write for art guidelines. Prefers printed cards or finished art as samples. Samples not filed are returned. Reports within 2 weeks. Original art not returned after reproduction. Pays flat fee of $200/design. Buys all rights.
Tips: "Send samples similar to those published by the three main USA publishers. We are a part of the Hallmark group and require designs in a similar vein suitable for the 'popular' market."

STONEWAY LTD., Box 548, Southeastern PA 19399. (215)272-4400. Art Director: Rose Flynn. Publishes coloring books and brochures, children cartoon themes for 2-8 year-olds.
Needs: Buys 10 designs and 125 illustrations/year from freelance artists. Needs artists experienced in children's illustration line. Uses artists for product design and illustrations plus advertising and catalog design, illustration and layout. Prefers b&w line drawings and color washes; 17x22" for coloring books, 11x17", 8½x11", 17x22" for brochures. Also produces seasonal material.
First Contact & Terms: Send query letter with samples and resume to be kept on file; write for appointment. Prefers roughs as samples. Samples not kept on file are returned by SASE. Reports in 3 weeks. No originals returned to artist at job's completion. Buys all rights. Payment varies per type of job or project. Pays on acceptance *only*.

***STUART HALL CO., INC.**, Box 1381, Kansas City MO 64141. Art Director: Judy Riedel. Produces stationery, school supplies and office supplies.
Needs: Buys 40 designs and illustrations from freelance artists/year. Artist must be experienced—no beginners. Works on assignment only. Uses artists for design, illustration, calligraphy, paste-up and mechanicals. Considers pencil sketches, rough color, layouts, tight comps or finished art; watercolor, gouache, or acrylic paints are preferred for finished art. Avoid fluorescent colors. "All art should be prepared on heavy white paper and lightly attached to illustration board. Allow at least one inch all around the design for notations and crop marks. Avoid bleeding the design. In designing sheet stock, keep the design small enough to allow for letter writing space. If designing for an envelope, first consult us to avoid technical problems."
First Contact & Terms: Send query letter with resume, tear sheets, photostats, slides and photographs. Samples not filed returned by SASE. Reports only if interested. To show a portfolio, mail roughs, original/final art, final reproduction/product, color, tear sheets, photostats and photographs. No originals returned to artist at job completion. Pays average flat fee of $150/design and illustration. "Stuart Hall may choose to negotiate on price but generally accepts the artist's price." Buys all rights.

SUNRISE PUBLICATIONS INC., Box 2699, Bloomington IN 47402. (812)336-9900. Manager of Creative Services: Lorraine Merriman Farrell. Publishes greeting cards. Art guidelines available.
Needs: Generally works on assignment but picks up existing pieces from unsolicited submissions. Purchases 300-350 designs and illustrations/year. Considers any medium. Full-color illustrations scaled to 5x7" vertical, but these can vary. "We are interested in full range of styles for everyday and seasonal use, from highly illustrated to simple and/or humorous." Produces seasonal material for Christmas, Valentine's Day, St. Patrick's Day, Easter, Mother's Day, Father's Day, graduation, Halloween and Thanksgiving.
First Contact & Terms: Send query letter with brochure, business card and slides as samples, but any type is acceptable. "Indicate whether or not samples may be kept on file." Reports in 4-6 weeks. Samples returned only by SASE. Originals returned to artist at job's completion. Call or write for appointment to show portfolio. Offers an advance against royalty program.
Tips: "First, study our cards in your local card shops or send for our catalogs to get an idea of our look. To best fulfill the consumers' needs, we have begun to purchase rights to a much broader scope of contemporary subject matter and application with current emphasis on humor."

THOUGHT FACTORY, Box 55515 Sherman Oaks CA 91413. Contact: Creative Director. Produces greeting cards, calendars, posters, stationery, notepads, books and mugs. "Promotional line—try to place designs (a look) across all product lines—trendy." Directs products to middle America.
Needs: Buys variable number of designs and illustrations from freelance artists/year. Uses artists for design illustration, calligraphy and production. Considers full-color art and photography. Produces material for Valentine's Day and Christmas.
First Contact & Terms: Prefers artists with background in the gift/stationery market. Send query letter with resume, business card, slides and tear sheets to be kept on file. Samples not filed are returned by

SASE if requested. Originals sometimes returned to artist at job's completion. Negotiates payment and rights purchased.

Tips: "No students. Artists should have at least 1 year experience in the gift/stationery market."

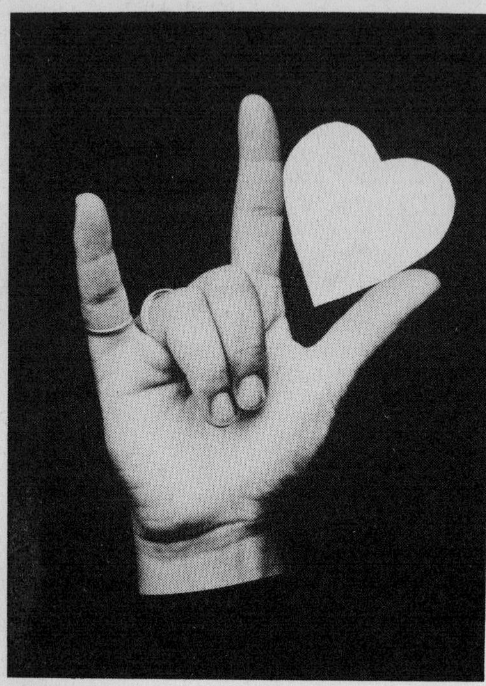

Liza Cowan is both artist and publisher of this design created for the Deaf. Liza, who is publisher of White Mare, Inc., has created a greeting card line designed for the Deaf. She focused on the 'I love you' sign in this collage because it is recognized internationally as a message of Deaf pride. The design also appears on buttons and key tags.

***WHITE MARE, INC.**, 57B Glasco Tpk., Woodstock NY 12498. President: Liza Cowan. Produces greeting cards, buttons, posters and postcards. All products are in American Sign Language and are of particular interest to deaf and hearing impaired people, families and friends of the Deaf, teachers and students of American Sign Language.

Needs: Buys 5 dozen designs from freelance artists/year. Prefers Deaf and hearing-impaired artists only. Designs must include American Sign Language and/or visual refrence to a part of Deaf culture. Also must include message in English. Works on assignment only. Considers all media. Prefers 5x7" vertical for final art. Produces Christmas, Valentine's, New Year and birthday cards.

First Contact & Terms: Send query letter with resume and tear sheets, photocopies and photographs. Samples are not returned. Reports back within weeks. To show a portfolio, mail appropriate materials; "do not send original artwork." Pays average flat fee of $100/design.

Tips: "A knowledge of Deaf culture is essential. We are looking for stylish, polished, saleable work. It would be best to send samples of work done and if we like it, we will discuss what type of cards we are looking for."

WILD CARD, Box 3960, Berkeley CA 94703-0960. Art Director: Leal Charonnat. Publishes greeting cards, and stationery; current, avant-garde themes for 20-40 year olds—"young, upwardly mobile urbanites." Send $2 for sample cards and additional information. Many designs die-cut.

Needs: Imaginative die-cut designs that fit the basic greeting card market themes (birthday, Christmas, Valentine's, friendship, etc.); must be very graphic as opposed to illustrated. Specializes in die-cut, 3-D cards."

First Contact & Terms: Send samples, SASE, and brochure/flyer or resume to be kept on file. All materials 8½x11 only. Prefers brochure of work with nonreturnable pen & ink photostats or photocopies as samples; do not send original work. "If your project is accepted, we will contact you. But we cannot always promise to contact everyone who submits." Pays for design by the project or royalties, $75-250 average; average flat fee of $75-250/illustration. Also pays royalties for card line ideas. Considers complexity of project, product use and reproduction expense when establishing payment. "We will have all publishing rights for any work published. Artist may retain ownership of copyright." Pays on publication.

Tips: "Present only commercially potential examples of your work. *Do not* present work that is not of a professional nature or what one would expect to see published. Know what is already in the market and have a feeling for the subjects the market is interested in. Go out and look at *many* card stores before submitting. Ask the owner or buyer to 'review' your work prior to submitting.''

CAROL WILSON FINE ARTS, INC., Box 17394, Portland OR 97217. (503)283-2338 or 281-0780. Contact: Gary Spector. Produces greeting cards, postcards, posters and stationery that range from contemporary to nostalgic. "At the present time we are actively looking for unusual humor to expand our contemporary humor line. We want cards that will make peole laugh out loud! Another category we also wish to expand is fine arts.''
Needs: Uses artists for product design and illustration. Considers all media. Produces seasonal material for Christmas, Valentine's Day, and Mother's Day; submit art preferably 1 year in advance.
First Contact & Terms: Send query letter with resume, business card, tear sheets, photostats, photocopies, slides and photographs to be kept on file. No original artwork on initial inquiry. Write for an appointment to show portfolio or for artists' guidelines. "All approaches are considered but, if possible, we prefer to see ideas that are applicable to specific occasions, such as birthday, anniversary, wedding, new baby, etc. We look for artists with creativity and ability.'' Samples not filed are returned by SASE. Reports within 2 months. Negotiates return of original art after reproduction. Payment ranges from flat fee to royalties. Buys all rights.
Tips: "We have noticed an increased emphasis on humorous cards for specific occasions, specifically, feminist and 'off-the-wall' humor. We are also seeing an increased interest in fine arts cards.''

> ❝*Records are out, compact discs in. Videos will service us in all areas of education, trade, sales and entertainment. Design changes will relate to high-tech in the music and entertainment areas.*❞
>
> *Ron Warwell, Audiofidelity Enterprises, Inc.*

If you could count the number of magazines published today, you would begin to see the possibilities they offer as a market for artwork. *The Standard Periodical Directory* lists 65,000 entries from the United States and Canada. There is a magazine to cover every conceivable subject, from lifestyles to quarry products. Most people are familiar with the publications found on the newsstands, but there are thousands of trade journals read exclusively by the business world they serve.

Understanding a magazine's category is important. There are three basic categories. First of all, the consumer magazine is geared towards the general public. Though we are most familiar with these magazines, such as *Sports Illustrated*, *Time* and *Good Housekeeping*, the second and largest category consists of trade or business publications. These are directed towards a certain profession, trade or industrial group. The third category is inhouse publications (or company publications) produced by companies for their employees.

After deciding the type of magazine most suited to your interests, focus the subject matter of your artwork in that area. Read at least four to six issues of each publication you plan to submit work to, reviewing its topics, themes and styles of artwork. Keep in mind that the wider a magazine's audience, the keener the art competition. As a newcomer, start with the less-circulated and more focused publications to increase your chance for sales.

There are two types of artwork that magazines purchase most often—illustrations and cartoons. Illustrations are used for covers, editorial content and also for spot art. Spot illustrations are usually a column wide and are needed on demand, meaning they are more likely to be bought from your samples. Illustrations range from pen-and-ink renderings to paintings. Send nonreturnable photostats or photocopies for black-and-white work and photos or slides to represent color.

Illustrators often specialize in a certain area, such as science fiction or medicine. Art directors look for artists with a certain style or treatment when they assign work, and specialists have a better chance of developing unique approaches to an often esoteric subject.

More and more magazines use freelance cartoons, not just as fillers but as unique parts of the editorial content. Art directors prefer to receive original work and will often buy cartoons unsolicited. Send twelve to sixteen finished or rough cartoons, each cartoon labeled on the back with the artist's name, address and phone number plus a cartoon reference number. When an art director selects one or more cartoons, he notifies the artist and refers to the cartoon by the number or caption.

Check the mastheads of the magazines you are focusing on to note any changes in the staff, particularly the art director. Consult the following directories for further names and addresses, but no marketing information: the *Standard Periodical Directory*, the *Internal Publications Directory*, the *Gebbie Press All-in-One Directory*, *Ayer Directory of Publications* and *Ulrich's International Periodical Directory*.

***ACA JOURNAL OF CHIROPRACTIC**, 8229 Maryland Ave., St. Louis MO 63105. Editor: Kathleen Z. Brown. Emphasizes chiropractic for doctors of chiropractic in US who are members of the American Chiropractic Association. Monthly. Circ. 19,200. Accepts previously published material and simultaneous submissions. Original artwork returned after publication. Sample copy and art guidelines available.

Illustrations: Uses 3 illustrations/issue. Prefers chiropractic or general themes. Send query letter to be kept on file or write for appointment to show portfolio. Prefers photographs as samples. Samples returned if not kept on file. Reports within 30 days.

ACCENT, Box 10010, Ogden UT 84409. (801)394-9446. Editor: Robyn Walker. Articles on travel. Circ. 90,000.
First Contact & Terms: Sample copy $1. Buys color transparencies to accompany articles. Send query letter with resume, tear sheets and photocopies. Samples returned by SASE. Reports in 6 weeks. Pays $35 color, inside; $50 color, cover; on acceptance.

ACCENT ON LIVING, Box 700, Bloomington IL 61702. Editor: Betty Garee. Emphasis on success and ideas for better living for the physically handicapped. Quarterly. Original artwork returned after publication, if requested. Sample copy $2.
Cartoons: Buys approximately 12 cartoons/issue from freelancers. Receives 5 submissions/week from freelancers. Interested in people with disabilities in different situations. Send finished cartoons. SASE. Reports in 2 weeks. Buys first-time rights (unless specified). Pays $20 b&w; on acceptance.
Illustrations: Uses 3-5 illustrations/issue. Interested in illustrations that "depict articles/topics we run." Works on assignment only. Provide samples of style to be kept on file for future assignments. Samples not kept on file are returned by SASE. Reports in 2 weeks. To show a portfolio, mail color and b&w. Buys all rights on a work-for-hire basis. Pays $250, color, cover; on acceptance.
Tips: "Send a sample and be sure to include various styles of artwork that you can do."

***ACCESS 86**, 11754 Jollyville, Austin TX 78759. (517)250-1255. Production Director: Fred Graber. Magazine emphasizing Wang computers. Monthly. Circ. 27,000. Accepts previously pubished material. Original artwork returned after publication. Art guidelines available.
Illustrations: Buys 3 illustrations/issue from freelancers. Works on assignment only. Prefers computer graphics and pen & ink. Send query letter with resume, tear sheets and photocopies. Samples not filed are not returned. Reports only if interested. To show a portfolio, mail appropriate materials. Buys first rights. Pays $350, b&w, and $400, color, cover; and $100, b&w and $100, color, inside; on publication.

ACROSS THE BOARD, 845 Third Ave., New York NY 10022. (212)759-0900. Art Director: Josef Kozlakowski. Emphasizes business-related topics for Chief Executive Officers in the business field and industry. Monthly. Returns original artwork after publication. Sample copy free for SASE.
Illustrations: Buys 4-6 illustrations/issue from freelancers. Works on assignment only. Send brochure and samples to be kept on file. Prefers tear sheets or photocopies as samples. Samples not filed are returned by SASE. Reports back only if interested. Call for appointment to show portfolio. Buys first rights. Pays $400 for color cover; $200 for b&w inside; on publication.

ACTION, 901 College Ave., Winona Lake IN 46590. (219)267-7656. Contact: Vera Bethel. For ages 9-11. Circ. 25,000. Weekly. SASE. Reports in 1 month. Pays on acceptance.
Cartoons: Buys 1/issue on school, pets and family. Pays $10, b&w. Send finished artwork.
Illustrations: Uses color illustrations on assignment. Send samples or slides. Pays $75 for full-color drawings (no overlays).

ADIRONDAC, 172 Ridge St., Glens Falls NY 12801. Editor: Neal Burdick. Emphasizes the Adirondack Mountains and conservation for members of Adirondack Mountain Club, conservationists and outdoor-oriented people in general. Published 10 times/year. Circ. 9,000. Accepts previously published material and simultaneous submissions. Original artwork returned after publication. Sample copy $1.75; art guidelines free for SASE.
Cartoons: Interested in environmental concerns, conservation, outdoor activities as themes. Prefers single panel with gagline; b&w line drawings. Send query letter to be kept on file. Reports within 4 weeks. Negotiates rights purchased. No payment.
Illustrations: Prefers maps, specific illustrations for articles. Send query letter to be kept on file. Reports within 4 weeks. No payment.

***AEROBICS & FITNESS**, Suite 802, 15250 Ventura Blvd., Sherman Oaks CA 91403. (818)905-0040. Editor: Peg Angsten. Magazine emphasizing fitness, health and exercise for sophisticated, college-educated, very active lifestyles. Bimonthly. Circ. 50,000. Accepts previously pubilshed material. Original artwork returned after publication. Sample copy $1.
Cartoons: Buys 1 cartoon/issue from freelancers. Material not kept on file is returned if requested. Buys one-time rights. Pays $35, b&w; $45, color.

The asterisk before a listing indicates that the listing is new in this edition. New markets are often the most receptive to freelance contributions.

Illustrations: Buys 1-2 illustrations/issue from freelancers. Works on assignment only. Prefers very sophisticated line drawings. Send query letter with brochure showing art styles and tear sheets. Reports back within 2 months. To show a portfolio, mail thumbnails and roughs. Buys one-time rights. Pays $50, b&w; $80, color, cover; on publication.

AFTA-THE ALTERNATIVE MAGAZINE, Second Floor, 153 George St., New Brunswick NJ 08901. (201)828-5467. Editor: Bill-Dale Marcinko. Emphasizes rock music, films, TV and books for young (18-35) male readers who are regular consumers of books, records, films and magazines; and socially and politically aware. 60% are gay; 50% are college educated or attending college. Quarterly. Circ. 25,000. Receives 10 cartoons and 30 illustrations/week from freelance artists. Previously published material and simultaneous submissions OK. Original work returned after publication. Sample copy $3.50. Especially needs political satire; rock and film illustrations, surreal, erotic work.
Cartoons: Uses 50 cartoons/issue; buys all from freelancers. Interested in satires on social attitudes, current political events, films, TV, books, rock music world, sexuality; single and multiple-panel with gagline, b&w line drawings. No color work accepted. Send query letter with samples of style. Samples returned. Buys one-time rights. Pays in contributor copies; on publication.
Illustrations: Uses 75 illustrations/issue; buys all from freelancers. Interested in illustrations from films, rock music stars, books and TV programs. No color work accepted. Send query letter with samples of style to be kept on file. Samples not kept on file are returned. Reports in 1 week. Buys one-time rights. Pays in contributor copies; on publication.
Tips: "Read a sample copy of *AFTA* before submitting work."

AIM, Box 20554, Chicago IL 60620. (312)874-6184. Editor-in-Chief: Ruth Apilado. Managing Editor: Dr. Myron Apilado. Art Director: Bill Jackson. Readers are those "wanting to eliminate bigotry and desiring a world without inequalities in education, housing, etc." Quarterly. Circ. 16,000. Sample copy $3; artist's guidelines for SASE. Reports in 3 weeks. Previously published, photocopied and simultaneous submissions OK. Receives 12 cartoons and 4 illustrations/week from freelance artists.
Cartoons: Uses 1-2 cartoons/issue; all from freelancers. Interested in education, environment, family life, humor through youth, politics and retirement; single panel with gagline. Especially needs "cartoons about the stupidity of bigotry." Mail finished art. SASE. Reports in 3 weeks. Buys all rights on a work-for-hire basis. Pays $5-15, b&w line drawings; on publication.
Illustrations: Uses 4-5 illustrations/issue; half from freelancers. Interested in current events, education, environment, humor through youth, politics and retirement. Provide brochure to be kept on file for future assignments. No samples returned. Reports in 4 weeks. Prefers b&w for cover and inside art. Buys all rights on a work-for-hire basis. Pays $25 for b&w illustrations, cover; on publication.
Tips: "Because of the possibility of nuclear war, people are seeking out ways for survival. They are feeling more alienated from society and are more conscious of the importance of getting together. Their submissions reflect their concern. For the most part, artists submit material omitting black characters. We would be able to use more illustrations and cartoons with people from all ethnic and racial backgrounds in them. We also use material of general interest."

ALFRED HITCHCOCK MYSTERY MAGAZINE, Davis Publications, 380 Lexington Ave., New York NY 10017. (212)557-9100. Art Director: Jerry Hawkins. Art Editor: Ron Kuliner. Emphasizes mystery fiction.
Needs: Line drawings, minimum payment: $100.
First Contact & Terms: Call for interview. Reports in 1 week. Pays on acceptance. Buys first rights.

ALIVE!, Christian Board of Publication, Box 179, St. Louis MO 63166. Editor: Mike Dixon. For junior high students. Monthly. Sample copy $1.
Cartoons: Buys 6-7 cartoons/issue on life and teenage problems. Prefers to see finished cartoons. SASE. Reports in 2 weeks. Buys one-time rights. Pays $10.
Illustrations: Buys 3 illustrations/issue from freelance artists. Illustrations should appeal to junior high. Interested in inks, line drawings and washes. Send query letter with brochure, resume, tear sheets and photocopies. Prefers to see finished art and samples of style; samples returned by SASE. Provide business card, brochure and/or tear sheets to be kept on file. Reports in 2 weeks. To show a portfolio, send tear sheets and photostats. Buys first North American serial rights. Pays $30-50; on acceptance.

ALTERNATIVE HOUSING BUILDER MAGAZINE, 16 1st Ave., Corry PA 16407. Managing Editor: Harry Calhoun. Emphasizes alternative housing: log homes, domes, earth shelters, post & beam construction and any other type of non-conventional housing for kit package manufacturers and builder-dealers of these homes. Published 9 times/year. Circ. 11,000. Original artwork returned after publication if requested. Sample copy and art guidelines free for SASE.
Cartoons: Buys 1-2 cartoons/issue from freelancers. Considers anything pertaining to log homes, geo-

desics, earth shelters, post & beam construction or the problems faced by the men and women who are building these homes. Prefers single panel with or without gagline; b&w line drawings or b&w washes. Send query letter with finished cartoons, slides and photographs to be kept on file. Material not filed is returned only if requested. Reports within 2 weeks. Buys all rights. Pays $10-15, b&w; on publication.
Illustrations: Buys 1-2 illustrations/issue. Send query letter with slides, photographs and illustrations. To show a portfolio, mail appropriate materials.
Tips: "We're sprucing up the appearance of our magazine and, as such, may be more receptive to freelancers' work."

AMATEUR GOLF REGISTER, 2843 Pembroke Rd., Hollywood FL 33020. (305)921-0881. Managing Editor; Bernard Block. Estab. 1985. Emphasizes golf for golfers. Monthly. Circ. 7,000. Original artwork returned after publication. Sample copy and art guidelines free for SASE.
Cartoons: Buys 1 cartoon/issue from freelancers. Prefers single panel with gagline; b&w line drawings. Send finished cartoons to be kept on file for 3 months. If not used, returned by SASE. Buys first rights. Pays $5, b&w; on publication.
Illustrations: Buys 3-5 illustrations/issue from freelancers. Prefers golf-oriented theme. Send query letter with tear sheets, slides or photographs. Samples not filed are returned by SASE. Reports within 1 month. Buys first rights.

AMELIA, 329 "E" St., Bakersfield CA 93304. (805)323-4064. Editor: Frederick A. Raborg, Jr. Estab. 1983. Magazine; also publishes 2 supplements—*Cicada* (haiku) and *SPSM&H* (sonnets) and illustrated postcards. Emphasizes fiction and poetry for the general review. "Our readers are drawn from a cross-section of reading tastes and educational levels, though the majority tend to be college-educated." Quarterly. Circ. 1,000. Accepts some previously published material from illustrators. Original artwork returned after publication if requested with SASE. Sample copy $4.75; art guidelines for SASE.
Cartoons: Buys 3-5 cartoons/issue from freelancers for *Amelia*. Prefers sophisticated or witty themes (see Wayne Hogan's work in January 1986 issue). Prefers single panel with or without gagline (will consider multi-panel on related themes); b&w line drawings, b&w washes. Send query letter with finished cartoons to be kept on file. Material not filed is returned by SASE. Reports within 1 week. Buys first rights or one-time rights; prefers first rights. Pays $5-25, b&w; on acceptance.
Illustrations: Buys 80-100 illustrations and spots annually from freelancers for *Amelia;* 24-30 spots for *Cicada*; 15-20 spots for *SPSM&H*; and 50-60 spots for postcards. Considers all themes; "no taboos except no explicit sex; nude studies in taste are welcomed, however." Send query letter with resume, photostats and/or photocopies to be kept on file; unaccepted material returned immediately by SASE. "See work by H. E. Knickerbocker, Wayne Hogan, Walt Phillips, Gregory Powell, Steve Del Monte, Cliff Johnson, Ford Button, L. John Creslinski, Richard Dahlstrom in our January 1986 issue." Reports in 1 week. Buys first rights or one-time rights; prefers first rights; Pays $25, b&w, $100, color, cover; $5-25, b&w, inside; on acceptance, "except spot drawings which are paid for on assignment to an issue."
Tips: "We try to use as many advances in print technology as our limited funds allow. Computer art seems to be the most rapidly advancing of the new forms, though I cannot say I'm yet overly enthused about it. I still prefer the human element and its aesthetic distance. Send us your best work and keep trying. H.E. Knickerbocker received his first assignment to fully illustrate our first chapbook because of his persistent reliability and adaptability. He offered us diversity of product, artistic insight and deadline assurance. Offer clean, professional work. If the work is good and we can use it, we'll make an offer."

AMERICAN AGRICULTURIST, Box 370, Ithaca NY 14851. (607)273-3507. Production Manager: Andrew Dellava. Emphasizes agriculture in the Northeast, specifically New York, New Jersey and New England. Monthly. Circ. 72,000. Original artwork not returned after publication. Art guidelines free for SASE.
Cartoons: Buys 3 cartoons/issue from freelancers. Prefers agriculture theme. Single panel, 2⅛" wide by 2¾-3¼" high or similar proportions, with gagline; b&w line drawings. Send query letter with finished cartoons. Material returned. Reports within 3 weeks. Buys first rights or one-time rights. Pays $10, b&w; on acceptance.

THE AMERICAN ATHEIST, Box 2117, Austin TX 78768. (512)458-1244. Editor: R. Murray-O'Hair. For atheists, agnostics, materialists and realists. Monthly. Circ. 30,000. Simultaneous submissions OK. Free sample copy.
Cartoons: Buys 10 cartoons/issue. Cartoons, $15 each. Especially needs 4-seasons art for covers and greeting cards. Send query letter with resume and samples.
Illustrations: Buys 1 illustration/issue on acceptance. "All illustrations must have bite from the atheist point of view and hit hard." To show a portfolio, mail original/final art, final reproduction/product, photographs and b&w. Pays on acceptance. Line drawings, $25. Four-color art and photos, $100.
Tips: "*The American Atheist* looks for clean lines, directness and originality. We are not interested in

side-stepping cartoons and esoteric illustrations. Our writing is hard-punching and we want artwork to match." Examine a sample copy before submitting work.

AMERICAN BABY INC., 575 Lexington Ave., New York NY 10022. (212)752-0775. Art Director: Blair Davis. Four publications emphasizing babies, children and parents. Monthly, quarterly and annually. Circ. 1,000,000. Returns original artwork after publication. Sample copy free for SASE, art guidelines available.
Illustrations: Buys 3-5 illustrations/issue from freelancers. Works on assignment only. Send business card and samples to be kept on file. Samples not filed are not returned. Reports back only if interested. Buys one-time rights. Pays on publication.

AMERICAN BANKERS ASSOCIATION-BANKING JOURNAL, 345 Hudson St., New York NY 10014. (212)620-7256. Art Director: Rob Klein. Emphasizes banking for middle and upper level banking executives and managers. Monthly. Circ. 42,000. Accepts previously published material. Returns original artwork after publication.
Illustrations: Buys 2 illustrations/issue from freelancers. Themes relate to stories, primarily, financial; styles vary, realistic, cartoon, surreal. Works on assignment only. Send query letter with brochure and samples to be kept on file. Prefers tear sheets, slides or photographs as samples. Samples not filed are returned by SASE. Negotiates rights purchased. Pays $350-500 for color cover and $75-100 for b&w or color inside; on acceptance.

THE AMERICAN BAPTIST MAGAZINE, Box 851, Valley Forge PA 19482-0851. (215)768-2441. Managing editor: Ronald Arena. Manager of Print Media Services: Richard Schramm. National publication of American Baptist Churches in the USA. Contains feature articles, news and commentary of interest to the American Baptist (1.5 million) constituency. Circ. 100,000. Bimonthly. Guidelines available.
Illustrations: All artwork on assignment for specific themes/subjects. (May make occasional use of freelance line art and cartoons.) Compensation negotiable. Portfolio samples and resume welcomed; enclose SASE for material to be returned.
Tips: "Artists should be willing to work promptly and creatively within stated guidelines for both specific and thematic art work."

AMERICAN BIRDS, National Audubon Society, 950 3rd Ave., New York NY 10022. (212)546-9191. Editorial Assistant: F. Baumgarten. Emphasizes ornithology — migration, distribution, breeding and behavior of North and South American birds, including Hawaii and the West Indies. Journal for the scientific community, serious birders. Publishes 5 issues/year. Circ. 10,000, paid. Sample copy $3.50; art guidelines for SASE.
Illustrations: Uses a few illustrations/issue from freelancers. Prefers North and South American birds drawn with strict adherence to anatomical detail. Occasionally uses stylized drawings. Send query letter with samples to be kept on file. Write for appointment to show portfolio. Prefers sharp photostats or original pen & ink drawings; occasionally publishes color. Samples returned by SASE if not kept on file.

AMERICAN BOOKSELLER, Booksellers Publishing Inc., Suite 1410, 122 E. 42nd St., New York NY 10168. (212)867-9060. Editor-in-Chief: Ginger Curwen. Art Director: Amy Bogert. For booksellers interested in trends, merchandising, recommendations, laws and industry news. Monthly. Circ. 8,700. Original artwork returned after publication. Sample copy $3.
Cartoons: Uses 4 cartoons/year; buys all from freelancers. Receives 5-10 submissions/week from freelancers. Interested in bookselling, authors and publishing; single panel with gagline. Send finished cartoons. SASE. Reports in 2 weeks. Buys first North American serial rights.
Illustrations: Uses 4 illustrations/issue; buys 4/issue from freelancers. Receives 10 submissions/week from freelancers. Looks for strong concepts and an original style. Interested in books, inventory or material for specific assignments. Works on assignment only. Provide business card, flyer and tear sheet to be kept on file for future assignments. Prefers finished art, samples of style or portfolio. SASE. Reports in 2 days. Buys first North American serial rights. Pays $45 minimum for b&w line drawings, washes and gray opaques; on acceptance.
Tips: "I have a greater and greater need for strong conceptual work. Yet the mailing pieces I get don't give me enough sense of the artist's ability to solve a visual problem with a visual idea. Please be more specific in this—don't just send nice drawings!"

AMERICAN DEMOGRAPHICS, Box 68, Ithaca NY 14851. (607)273-6343. Managing Editor: Caroline Arthur. Emphasizes demographics and population trends. Readers are business decision makers, advertising agencies, market researchers, newspapers, banks and professional demographers and business analysts. Monthly. Circ. 10,000. Original artwork returned after publication. Sample copy $6.

Cartoons: Uses 1-3 cartoons/issue, all from freelancers. Receives 5-10 submissions/week from freelancers. Interested in population trends including moving, aging, families, birth rate, the census, surveys, changing neighborhoods, women working, data (use, computers, etc.), market research, business forecasting and demographers. Format: single panel b&w line drawings and b&w washes with gagline. Prefers to see finished cartoons. SASE. Reports in 2 weeks. Buys one-time rights. Pays $50-100 on publication.
Illustrations: Uses 2 illustrations/issue. Interested in demographic themes. Needs "styles that reproduce best in b&w. Spare statements with a light approach to the subject." Prefers to see portfolio; contact Caroline Arthur. SASE. Provide photocopies of work to be kept on file for future needs. Reports in 1 month. Buys one-time rights. Inside: pays $50, under ½ page; $75, ½ page; $100, full page. Cover: pay is negotiable ($100-300).

THE AMERICAN LEGION MAGAZINE, Box 1055, Indianapolis IN 46206. Cartoon Editor: Margaret Bradbury. Emphasizes the historical development of the world at present, and milestones of history; general interest magazine for veterans and their families. Monthly. Original artwork not returned after publication.
Cartoons: Uses 2-3 cartoons/issue, all from freelancers. Receives 100 submissions/week from freelancers. Especially needs general humor, in good taste. "Generally interested in cartoons with a broad, mass appeal. Prefer action in the drawing, rather than the illustrated joke-type gag. Those which have a beguiling character or ludicrous situation that attract the reader and lead him to read the caption rate the highest attention. No-caption gags purchased only occasionally. Because of the tight space problem, we're not in the market for the spread-type or multipanel cartoon, but use both vertical and horizontal format single panel cartoons. Themes should be home life, business, sports and everyday Americana. Cartoons which pertain only to one branch of the service may be too restricted for this magazine. The service-type gag should be recognized and appreciated by any ex-serviceman or woman. Cartoons in bad taste, off-color or which may offend the reader not accepted. Liquor, sex, religion and racial differences are taboo. Ink roughs not necessary, but are desirable. Finish should be line, Ben-Day." Send query letter with brochure showing art style with promotional material that will not be returned. Usually reports within 30 days. Call to schedule an appointment to show a portfolio, which should include final reproduction/product. Buys first rights; "pays on receipt of Ben-Day acceptance." Pays $95-125; on publication.
Tips: "Artists should submit their work as we are always seeking a new slant or more timely humor. Black-and-white representational art is primarily what we seek. Note: Cartoons are a separate department from the art department."

AMERICAN MOTORCYCLIST, American Motorcyclist Association, Box 6114, Westerville OH 43081-6114. (614)891-2425. Executive Editor: Greg Harrison. Associate Editors: Bill Wood and John Van Barriger. Monthly. Circ. 130,000. For "enthusiastic motorcyclists, investing considerable time and money in the sport." Sample copy $1.50.
Cartoons: Uses 2-3 cartoons/issue; all from freelancers. Receives 5-7 submissions/week from freelancers. Interested in motorcycling; "single panel gags." Prefers to receive finished cartoons. SASE. Reports in 2 weeks. Buys all rights on a work-for-hire basis. Pays $15 minimum, b&w washes; on publication.
Illustrations: Uses 1-2 illustrations/issue, almost all from freelancers. Receives 1-3 submissions/week from freelancers. Interested in motorcycling themes. Works on assignment only. Provide resume and tear sheets to be kept on file. Prefers to see samples of style and resume. Samples returned by SASE. Reports in 3 weeks. Buys first North American serial rights. Pays $75 minimum, color, cover: $30-100, b&w and color, inside; on publication.

AMERICAN SALON, Suite 1102, 261 Madison Ave., New York NY 10016. Art Director: Richard Schemm. Editor: Jody Byrne. Concerns the art of cosmetology and related fashion; for beauty salons. Monthly. Circ. 158,000. Simultaneous submissions OK "if trade exclusive." Receives 1-2 cartoons and 2-3 illustrations/month.
Illustrations: Buys themes on hairstyling. Especially needs drawings of men and women with current or avante garde hairstyles. Uses b&w line drawings and photos. Query with resume and samples or arrange interview to show a portfolio. SASE. Reports in 3-4 weeks. Negotiates pay. Buys all rights.
Tips: Work "must have a professional look."

***THE AMERICAN SHOTGUNNER MAGAZINE**, Box 3351, Reno NV 89505. Story Editor: Simon Grimes. Emphasizes high-grade and competition shotguns; hunting and the outdoors; trap and skeet competitions; industry news; reloading for upscale hunters, collectors and outdoorsmen; competition shooters. Monthly. Circ. 120,000. Original artwork returned after publication.
Illustrations: Uses approximately 4 b&w line drawings and 7 wildlife paintings or bronze sculptures.

Prefers skeet or trap shooters; hunters (with dogs) as themes. Send query letter with resume, business card and samples to be kept on file. To show a portfolio, mail final reproduction/product, color, photostats, photographs, b&w ad Kodachrome slides or high-grade wildlife art and wildlife bronze sculptures. Samples not kept on file are returned by SASE. Reports within 2 months. Buys first rights. Pays $10-20, b&w; $30-50, color, inside; $75 color, cover, on publication.
Tips: "Our art editor is constantly looking for new names in the field so we can profile them as the up-and-coming wildlife artist."

***THE AMERICAN SPECTATOR**, Box 10448, Arlington VA 22210. Managing Editor: Wladyslaw Pleszcynski. Concerns poltics and literature. Monthly. Circ. 43,000. Original artwork returned after publication. Sample copy $1.25.
Illustrations: Uses 2-3 illustrations/issue, all from freelancers. Interested in "caricatures of political figures (for portraits with a point of view)." Works on assignment only. Samples returned by SASE. Reports back on future assignment possibilities. Provide resume, brochure and tear sheets to be kept on file for future assignments. Prefers to see portfolio and samples of style. Reports in 2 weeks. Buys first North American serial rights. Pays $150 minimum, b&w line drawings, cover. Pays $35 minimum, b&w line drawings, inside; on publication.

AMERICAN TRUCKER MAGAZINE, Box 6366, San Bernardino CA 92412. Editor: Steve Sturgess. Emphasizes trucks and trucking topics of interest to the single truck owner operator and the small truck fleet businessman. Monthly. Circ. 46,800. Accepts previously published material only in exceptional circumstances. Does not return original artwork after publication. Sample copy free for SASE.
Illustrations: Buys 1 illustration/issue from freelancers. Prefers realistic styles. Works on assignment only. Send query letter. Write for appointment to show portfolio. Buys first rights. Pays $100/page for b&w; on publication.

***THE AMHERST REVIEW**, Box 486, Station 2, Amherst MA 01002. Art Editor: Carolyn McNiven. Editor-in-Chief: Ruth Abbe. Magazine emphasizing literary and fine arts for the college community. Annual. Circ. 1,000-2,000. Original artwork returned after publication. Sample copy $6. Art guidelines available.
Illustrations: "The Amherst Review publishes 15 original prints and drawings and 4 color paintings per issue. Payment is in copies. We also publish up to 15 b&w and color photographs. Submissions are reviewed from Sept. to March only. Deadline for submissions is February 1."

***AMIGA WORLD**, 80 Pine St., Peterborough NH 03458. Art Director: Glenn Suokko. Estab. 1984. Magazine emphasizing computing for business and families who own and operate a Commodore computer or Commodore Amiga. Monthly. Circ. 225,000. Accepts previously published material. Sample copy and art guidelines available.
Illustrations: Buys 5 illustrations/issue from freelancers. Works on assignment only. Prefers exciting, creative themes or styles. Send query letter with brochure showing art style or resume and brochure, business card and samples. Samples not filed are returned by SASE. Reports back only if interested. Negotiates rights purchased. Pays $300-600, b&w; $500-1,000, color, cover; $300-600, b&w; $500-1,200, color, inside; on acceptance.

ANGLER & HUNTER MAGAZINE, 169 Charlotte St., Box 1541, Peterborough, Ontario K9J 7H7 Canada. (705)748-3891. Art Director: David Golden. Emphasizes angling, hunting and conservation of natural resources. Monthly except November/December and January/February are published as single issues. Circ. 51,000. Accepts some previously published material. Original artwork returned after publication. Sample copy and art guidelines free for SASE.
Cartoons: Buys up to 3 or 4 cartoons/issue. Prefers angling, hunting or conservation themes; single panel with or without gagline; b&w line drawings. Send query letter with samples of style or finished cartoons to be kept on file. Material not filed is returned if requested. Reports within 3 weeks. Buys one-time rights. Pays $30, b&w; on publication.
Illustrations: Buys 1-2 illustrations/issue. Prefers angling, hunting and conservation themes; humorous and cartoon-style illustrations are presently a potential market. Works on assignment only. Send query letter with brochure, resume, business card and 3 samples to be kept on file. Prefers tear sheets, slides or photographs as samples. Samples not filed are returned if requested. Reports back within 3 weeks. To show a portfolio, mail appropriate materials or write to schedule an appointment; portfolio should include thumbnails, roughs, original/final art, final reproduction/product, color and b&w. Buys one-time rights. Pays on publication.
Tips: "Industry trends appear to be toward utilizing materials that enhance and clarify editorial stands. Our present search for illustrators and cartoonists reflects our desire to present our readership with a more attractive, more interesting, more comprehensively understandable package. Send/show widest

variety of samples to reflect their speciality, preference, etc. If you are submitting work that measures 8½x11, don't send #10 SASE. Also, U.S. writers should remember to use UPU (Universal Postal Union) coupons.''

***ANOTHER CHICAGO MAGAZINE**, Box 11223, Chicago IL 60611. Fiction Editor: Sharon Solwitz. Magazine emphasizing poetry and fiction for people interested in contemporary literature and art. Published twice a year. Circ. 1,000. Accepts previously published material. Original artwork returned after publication. Sample copy $3.50.
Illustrations: Buys 8 illustrations/issue from an individual artist. Send query letter with resume, photocopies and photographs. Samples not filed are returned by SASE. Reports within 2 months. Buys one-time rights. Pays $25-50; on acceptance.

***ANTIC, The Atari Resource**, 524 Second St., San Francisco CA 94107. Art Director: Marni Tapscott. Magazine emphasizing computers for Atari enthusiasts. Monthly. Circ. 100,000. Original artwork returned after publication.
Illustrations: Buys 3-5 illustrations/issue from freelancers. Works on assignment only. Prefers sophisticated, highly realistic styles using airbrush, colored pencil, pastels, or acrylics. Send brochure showing art style or resume and tear sheets, photostats, photocopies, slides and photographs; "color work should be in color though." Samples not filed are returned. Reports back only if interested. To show a portfolio, mail appropriate materials, which should include original/final art, final reproduction/product, color and tear sheets. Buys one-time rights. Pays $800-1,000, color, cover; $50-150, b&w; $75-700, color, inside; 30 days from acceptance date.

THE ANTIQUARIAN, Box 798, Huntington NY 11743. (516)271-8990. Editors: Marguerite Cantine and Elizabeth Kilpatrick. Concerns antiques, arts, shows and news of the market; for dealers and collectors. Monthly. Circ. 15,000.
Illustrations: Receives 2 illustrations/week from freelance artists. "We are one magazine that hates the use of photography but it's more available to us than good illustrations. We ran a complete history of the teddy bear and would have used all drawings if we could have found an illustrator. Instead we had to use photos. We've also recently started using many illustrations of colonial and Victorian buildings." Buys b&w line drawings. Especially needs illustration for ad designs. Query with resume, samples and SASE. "No phone calls, please!" Include 8½x11" SASE with $1.25 if sample copy is requested. Reports in 4-8 weeks. Buys all rights. Pay "depends on the size of the article. We commission the entire article or issue if possible to one artist. I like for the artist to quote his/her rates." Pays $10 maximum, b&w; on acceptance.
Tips: "Our covers are us. They are children's illustrations from fine, usually German, books circa 1850-1875. If an artist can get the feel of what we're trying to convey with our covers, the rest is easy. We specialize in totally designed magazines. I think we're a leader in the antiques trade field and people will follow the trend. We are heavily illustrated—we use few photos. Send 5-10 illustrations *after* reviewing the publications. Suggest a price range. If the illustration is good, needed, usable, the price is never a problem. So suggest one. Only the artist knows the time involved. We buy *all rights only*. Please quote prices accordingly."

ANTIQUES DEALER, 1115 Clifton Ave., Clifton NJ 07013. (201)779-1600. Editor: Nancy Adams. For antiques dealers. Monthly. Circ. 7,500. Query first. Receives 4 cartoons/year from freelance artists.
Cartoons: Buys 4/year on antiques theme. Query or mail art. SASE. Reports in 4 weeks. Buys all rights. Pays $25, b&w line drawings, washes and half tones. "We're looking for sophisticated, sublime humor; avoid derogatory tone."

AOPA PILOT, 421 Aviation Way, Frederick MD 21701. (301)695-2353. Emphasizes general aviation (no military or airline) for aircraft owners and pilots. Monthly. Circ. 270,000. Original artwork returned after publication. Sample copy $2.
Illustrations: Buys 1-3 illustrations/issue. Uses illustrations specifically for manuscripts. Works on assignment only. Send query letter with tear sheets, photostats, photocopies, slides and photographs. Samples returned by SASE. Reports only if interested. Call to schedule an appointment to show a portfolio, which should include original/final art and tear sheets. Buys first rights. Pays on acceptance.
Tips: "Avoid duplicating photographs, as such an illustration is an unnecessary extra step. If I can use photography, I will."

APPALACHIAN TRAILWAY NEWS, Box 807, Harpers Ferry WV 25425. (304)535-6331. Editor: Judith Jenner. Emphasizes the Appalachian Trail for members of the Appalachian Trail Conference. 5 issues/year. Circ. 22,000. Sometimes accepts previously published material. Returns original artwork after publication. Sample copy $1 for serious inquiries; art guidelines free for SASE with 22¢ postage.

Cartoons: Buys 0-1 cartoons/issue from freelancers. Prefers themes on hikers and trailworkers on Applachian Trail. Open to all formats. Send query letter with roughs and finished cartoons. Only materials pertinent to Appalachian Trail are considered. Material not filed is returned by SASE. Reports within 1 month. Negotiates rights purchased. Pays $25-50 for b&w; on acceptance.
Illustrations: Buys 2-5 illustrations/issue from freelancers. Themes/styles are assigned to particular story ideas. Send query letter with samples to be kept on file. Write for appointment to show portfolio. Prefers photostats, photocopies or tear sheets as samples. Samples not filed are returned by SASE. Reports within 1 month. Negotiates rights purchased. Pays $75-150, b&w and $150 up, color (watercolor only) for covers; $25-100, b&w and color for inside; pays on acceptance.

***ARARAT**, 585 Saddle River Rd., Saddle Brook NJ 07662. Contact: Leo Hamalian. For those interested in Armenian life and culture, for Americans of Armenian descent, and Armenian immigrants. Quarterly. Circ. 2,000.
Illustrations: SASE. Pays on publication.

***ARIZONA LIVING MAGAZINE**, Suite C, 5046 N. 7th St., Phoenix AZ. (602)264-4295. Art Director: Margie Diguiseppe. Magazine emphasizing Arizona lifestyle and strong issues for 28-45 age group; salary of $30,000 or more a year; yuppie type. Monthly. Circ. 18,000. Accepts previously published material. Original artwork returned after publication. Sample copy free for SASE with 50¢ postage. Art guidelines free for SASE with 25¢ postage.
Cartoons: Buys 0-1 cartoon/issue from freelancers. Prefers funny yet strong themes. Prefers single or multiple panel with gagline; b&w washes. Send samples of style to be kept on file. Call for appointment to show a portfolio. Samples not filed returned only if requested. Reports only if interested. Buys one-time rights. Payment is credit in magazine only.
Illustrations: Buys 3 illustrations/issue from freelancers. Works on assignment only. Prefers themes dealing with people and subjects pertaining to story. Send query letter with resume, tear sheets and photostats. Samples not filed returned only if requested. Reports only if interested. Call or write to schedule an appointment to show a portfolio, which should include original/final art, tear sheets and photostats. Buys one-time rights. "Payment is only credit to artists unless a very intricate or cover illustrations." Pays on illustration.

ART DIRECTION, 10 E. 39th St., 6th Floor, New York NY 10157-0002. (212)889-6500. Editor: Loren Bliss. Emphasizes advertising for art directors. Monthly. Circ. 12,000. Original work returned after publication. Sample copy $2.50. Receives 7 illustrations/week from freelance artists.
Illustrations: Uses 2-3 illustrations/issue; all from freelancers. Interested in themes that relate to advertising. Send query letter. Provide information to be kept on file for possible future assignments. Samples not returned. Reports in 1 month. No payment for cover or editorial art.

ART MATERIAL TRADE NEWS, 6255 Barfield Rd., Atlanta GA 30328. (404)256-9800. Editor: Jeff Abugel. Emphasizes art material business, merchandising and selling trends, products, store and manufacturer profiles for dealers, manufacturers, wholesalers of artist supplies. Monthly. Circ. 11,500. Accepts previously published material. Original artwork returned after publication. Sample copy $2.
Cartoons: Themes and styles open. Send query letter with samples of style to be kept on file "if desired by artist." Write for appointment to show portfolio. Material not kept on file returned by SASE. Reports "as soon as possible." Negotiates rights purchased. Payment negotiable. Pays on publication.
Illustrations: Works on assignment only. Send brochure, resume, samples and tear sheets to be kept on file. Write for an appointment to show portfolio. Prefers "anything but originals" as samples. Samples returned by SASE if not kept on file. Reports "as soon as possible." Negotiates rights purchased. Pays on publication.

THE ARTIST'S MAGAZINE, 9933 Alliance Rd., Cincinnati OH 45242. (513)984-0717. Editor: Mike Ward. Estab. 1984. Emphasizes the techniques of working artists for the serious beginning and amateur artist. Published 12 times/year. Circ. 185,000. Occasionally accepts previously published material. Returns original artwork after publication. Sample copy $2 with SASE and $1.25 postage.
Cartoons: Buys 4-5 cartoons/issue from freelancers. Prefers single-panel finished cartoons with or without gagline; b&w line drawings, b&w washes. Cartoons should be artist-oriented, appealing to the working artist (versus the gallery-goer), and should not denigrate art or artists. Avoid cliche situations. Vertical-format cartoons are always welcome. Send query letter with preferably 4 or more finished cartoons; write for appointment to show portfolio. Material not filed is returned by SASE. Reports within 1 month. Pays $50 for b&w; on acceptance.
Illustrations: Contact Carol Buchanan, art director. Buys 3-4 illustrations/issue from freelancers. Themes depend on editorial copy being illustrated; "mostly humorous, but most important, well-composed art that appeals to artists." Works on assignment only. Send query letter with brochure, resume

and samples to be kept on file. Write for appointment to show portfolio. Prefers photostats or tear sheets as samples. Samples not filed are returned by SASE. Reports within 1 month. Buys first rights. Pays on acceptance.

***ARTSLINE**, 2518 Western Ave., Seattle WA 98121. (206)441-0786. Editor: Alice Copp Smith. Magazine emphasizing performing and visual arts. Monthly. Circ. 79,000. Original artwork returned after publication. Sample copy free for SASE and 1 first class stamp; art guidelines free for SASE with 1 first class stamp.
Cartoons: Buys 6 cartoons/year from freelancers. Prefers single panel with or without gagline; b&w line drawings. Send query letter with finished cartoons to be kept on file except for finished cartoons "which will be returned if accompanied by SASE." Samples not filed are returned by SASE. Reports within 6 weeks. Buys first rights. Pays $25-50, b&w.
Illustrations: Buys 1 illustration/issue from freelancers. Works on assignment only. Prefers spot art, "Seattle scenes; arts-related themes; *New Yorker*-style spot art." Send query letter with brochure showing art style or tear sheets and photostats. Samples not filed are returned by SASE. Reports back within 6 weeks. To show a portfolio, mail appropriate materials or call to schedule an appointment. Buys first rights. Pays $25-50, b&w, inside; on acceptance.

ASSOCIATION AND SOCIETY MANAGER, Brentwood Publishing Corp., 825 S. Barrington Ave., Los Angeles CA 90049. Publishers: Martin H. Waldman and Hal Spector. Art Director: Tom Medsger. Devoted to the interests of managers of professional membership societies.
First Contact & Terms: Send brochure/flyer to be kept on file for possible future assignment. Reports only when assignment available. Buys all rights. Pays $60 and up, spot art; $400, full-color cover; on acceptance.

ATLANTIC CITY MAGAZINE, 1637 Atlantic Ave., Atlantic City NJ 08401. (609)348-6886. Art Director: Jeff Roth. Emphasizes the growth, people and entertainment of Atlantic City for residents and visitors. Monthly. Circ. 50,000.
Illustrations: Buys 2-4 illustrations/issue. Mainly b&w, some 4-color. Works on assignment only. Send query letter with brochure showing art style and tear sheets, slides and photographs to be kept on file. Send samples of style. Call or write to schedule an appointment to show a portfolio, which should include original/final art, final reproduction/product, color, tear sheets, photographs and b&w. Buys first rights. Pays $50-250, b&w, $150-400, color; on publication.
Tips: "We are looking for intelligent, reliable artists who can work within the confines of our budget and time frame. Deliver good art and receive good tear sheets."

ATLANTIC SALMON JOURNAL, 1435 St. Alexandre, Montreal, Quebec H3A 2G4 Canada. (514)842-8059. Managing Editor: Joanne Eidinger. Emphasizes conservation and angling of Atlantic salmon; travel, biology and cuisine for educated, well-travelled, affluent and informed anglers and conservationists, biologists and professionals. Quarterly. Circ. 20,000. Does not accept previously published material. Returns original artwork after publication. Sample copy free for SASE. Art guidelines available.
Cartoons: Uses 2-4/issue. Prefers environmental or political themes, specific to salmon resource management, travel and tourism—light and whimsical. Prefers single panel with or without gagline; b&w line drawings. Send query letter with samples of style to be kept on file. Material not filed is returned. Reports within 8 weeks. Buys first rights and one-time rights. Pays $50-100, b&w; on publication.
Illustrations: Uses 4-6/issue. Prefers themes on angling, environmental scenes and biological drawings. Send query letter with samples to be kept on file. Prefers photostats, tear sheets, slides or photographs as samples. Samples not filed are returned. Reports within 8 weeks. Buys first rights and one-time rights. Pays $50-150, b&w, and $100-250, color, inside; on publication.

***AURA LITERARY/ARTS REVIEW**, Box 76, University Center, UAB, Birmingham AL 35210. (205)934-3216. Editor: Andrea Mathews. Magazine emphasizing literature and art for largely academic, literary minded and artistic people. Biannually. Circ. 500. Accepts previously published material. Original artwork returned after publication. Sample copy $2.50. Art guidelines free for SASE with 22¢ postage.
Illustrations: "We use art that is thematic in its own right; it is not illustration."

AUTO TRIM NEWS, 1623 Grand Ave., Baldwin NY 11510. Contact: Nat Danas. Does not return original artwork after publication. Pays on publication. Especially needs P-O-P posters "for the small businessman."
Cartoons: Buys 2/issue from freelancers. Prefers to see roughs; reports in 2 weeks.
Illustrations: Buys 1/issue from freelancers. Works on assignment only. Send query letter with roughs

and samples of style; samples returned. Reports in 2 weeks. Buys all rights on a work-for-hire basis. Pays $10, spot drawings; $25-50, cover design; on publication.
Tips: Artists should "visit a shop" dealing in this field.

***AUTOMATIC MACHINING MAGAZINE**, 100 Seneca Ave., Rochester NY 14621. (716)338-1522. Editor: Donald Wood. For metalworking technical management. Readers are management and engineering personnel. Monthly. Circ. 16,000. Purchased artwork not returned.
Cartoons: Uses 3-4 cartoons/issue, all from freelancers. Receives 1 submission/week from freelancers. Interested in engineering and metalworking. Prefers single panel b&w line drawings with gag lines. Prefers finished cartoons. SASE. Reports in 1 week. Buys one-time rights. Pays $5-10; on acceptance.
Tips: There is a trend toward "use of computers and numerical control" in our field. Artists should "get a copy of our magazine" before making submissions.

AUTOMOBILE QUARTERLY, 221 Nassau St., Princeton NJ 08542. (609)924-7555. Contact: L. Scott Bailey. Concerns autos and auto history. Circ. 30,000. Quarterly. Original artwork returned after publication, by arrangement.
Illustrations: Uses 8-10 illustrations/issue, all from freelancers. Interested in antique, classic cars and cutaway technical illustrations. Works on assignment only. Send query letter with photostats, photocopies, slides and photographs. Provide "sample of rendering" to be kept on file for future assignments. SASE. Reports in 2 weeks. Buys various rights. Negotiates pay (part of payment may be posters of work); pays on publication.

AUTOMOTIVE AGE, THE DEALER BUSINESS MAGAZINE, 6931 Van Nuys Blvd., Van Nuys CA 91405. (818)997-0644. Art Director: Chris Gallison. Emphasizes car dealership for car and truck dealers. Monthly. Circ. 34,000. Accepts previously published material. Sample copy available.
Illustrations: Buys 2-3 illustrations/issue from freelancers. Prefers realism. Works on assignment only. Send query letter with samples to be kept on file. Call for appointment to show portfolio. Prefers tear sheets or slides as samples. Samples are returned only if requested. Reports only if interested. Pays $350, b&w and $350-600, color, cover; $150, b&w and $300, color, inside; on publication.

AXIOS, The Orthodox Journal, 800 S. Euclid Ave., Fullerton CA 92632. (714)526-2131. Editor: David Gorham. Emphasizes "challenges in ethics and theology, some questions that return to haunt one generation after another, old problems need to be restated with new urgency. *Axios* tries to present the 'unthinkable.' " Works from an Orthodox Catholic viewpoint. Monthly. Circ. 5,308. Accepts previously published material and simultaneous submissions. Original artwork returned after publication. Sample copy $2.
Illustrations: Buys 5-10 illustrations/issue from freelancers. Prefers bold line drawings, seeks icons, b&w; "no color *ever*; use block prints—do not have to be religious, but must be *bold*!" Send query letter with brochure, resume, business card or samples to be kept on file. Samples not filed are returned by SASE. Reports within 5 weeks. To show a portfolio, mail final reproduction/product and b&w. Buys one-time rights. Pays $100, b&w cover and $50-75, b&w inside; on acceptance.
Tips: "Realize that the Orthodox are *not* Roman Catholics, nor Protestants. We do not write from those outlooks. Though we do accept some stories about those religions, be sure *you* know what an Orthodox Catholic is. Know the traditional art form—we prefer line work, block prints, lino-cuts."

BAJA TIMES, Box 755, San Ysidro CA 92073. (706)612-1244. Editorial Consultant: John W. Utley. Emphasizes Baja California, Mexico for tourists, other prospective visitors and retirees living there. Monthly. Circ. 50,000. Accepts previously published material. Original artwork returned after publication. Sample copy for 9x12 or larger SASE with 85¢ postage.
Cartoons: All must be Baja California-oriented. Prefers single panel with gagline; b&w line drawings. Send query letter with sample of style to be kept on file. Material not filed returned by SASE. Reports within 1 month. Buys one-time rights. Payment not established. Pays on publication.
Illustrations: Theme: Baja California. Send query letter with samples, tear sheets or photocopies to be kept on file. Samples not filed are returned by SASE. Reports within 1 month. Buys one-time rights. Payment not established. Pays on publication.
Tips: "We have not used art, mostly because it has not been offered to us. If properly oriented to our theme (Baja California), we would consider on an occasional basis."

BAKERSFIELD LIFESTYLE MAGAZINE, 123 Truxtun Ave., Bakersfield CA 93301. (805)325-7124. Editor: Steve Walsh. City magazine aimed at local lifestyles of college-educated males/females, ages 25-65. Monthly. Circ. 10,000. Accepts previously published material. Original artwork returned after publication. Sample copy $3; art guidelines free for SASE.

Cartoons: Buys 4 cartoons/issue from freelancers. No political humor. Prefers single panel with gagline; b&w line drawings or b&w washes. Send finished cartoons to be kept on file. Material not filed is returned by SASE. Reports only if interested. Buys one-time rights or reprints rights. Pays $5, b&w; on publication.

Illustrations: Buys 6 illustrations/issue from freelancers. Send photostats, tear sheets or photocopies to be kept on file. Write for appointment to show portfolio. Samples not filed are returned by SASE. Reports only if interested. Buys one-time rights or reprint rights. Pays $100, b&w and $150, color, cover; $50, b&w and $75, color, inside; on publication.

***BALTIMORE JEWISH TIMES**, 2104 North Charles St., Baltimore MD 21218. (301)752-3504. Art Director: Kim Muller-Thym. Assistant Art Director: Carol Steuer. Tabloid emphasizing special interest to the Jewish community for largely local readership. Weekly. Circ. 20,000. Returns original artwork after publication, if requested. Sample copy available.

Illustrations: Buys 2-3 illustrations/issue from freelancers. Works on assignment only. Prefers high-contrast b&w illustrations. Send query letter with brochure showing art style or tear sheets and photocopies. Samples not filed are returned by SASE. Reports back only if interested. To show a portfolio, mail appropriate materials or write to schedule an appointment; portfolio should include original/final art, final reproduction/product, color, tear sheets and photostats. Buys first rights. Pays $100-150, b&w, cover and $200-300, color, cover; $30-100, b&w, inside; on publication.

BANJO NEWSLETTER, INC., Box 364, Greensboro MD 21639. (301)482-6278. Editor/Publisher: Hub Nitchie. Emphasizes banjo 5-string music for musicians and instrument collectors. Monthly. Circ. 7,000. Accepts previously published material. Original artwork returned after publication. Sample copy $1; deductible on subscription..

Cartoons: Buys 1 cartoon/issue from freelancers. Prefers single panel; b&w line drawings. Send query letter with sample of style to be kept on file. Material not filed is returned by SASE. Reports within 2 weeks. To show a portfolio, mail thumbnails. Buys one-time rights. Pays $20-25, b&w; on publication.

Illustrations: Buys 1-2 illustrations/issue from freelancers. Send query letter to be kept on file. Samples returned by SASE. Reports within 2 weeks. Buys one-time rights. Pays approximately $30, b&w, cover; $20-30, b&w, inside; on publication.

***BANKERS MONTHLY**, Tower Suite, 870 Seventh Ave., New York NY 10019. (212)399-1084. Contact: Elaine Kursch. Magazine emphasizing banking for top management of banks. Monthly circ. 16,000. Accepts previously published material. Returns original artwork after publication "unless we bought." Sample copy available.

Cartoons: Prefers gagline; b&w line drawings. Send query letter with samples of style to be kept on file. Write or call for appointment to show portfolio. Samples not filed are returned only if requested. Reports within 1 month. Buys all rights or one-time rights. Pays $25-100, b&w; $500, color.

Illustrations: Buys 1-3 illustrations/issue from freelancers. Works on assignment only. Prefers banking and finance-related themes. Send query letter with brochure showing art style. Samples not filed are returned only if requested. Reports back within 1 month. To show a portfolio, mail appropriate materials. Buys one-time rights or all rights.

BAY AND DELTA YACHTSMAN, Recreation Publications, 2019 Clement Ave., Alameda CA 94501. (415)865-7500. Editor: Dave Preston. Art Director: David Hebenstreit. Concerns boating and boat owners in northern California. Monthly. Circ. 20,000. Previously published and simultaneous submissions OK (if not published in northern California). Original artwork returned after publication if requested. Sample copy $1.50.

Cartoons: Buys 4-5/year on boating. Prefers to see roughs. SASE. Reports in 2 weeks. Buys all rights on a work-for-hire basis. Pays $5 minimum, b&w line drawings; on publication.

Illustrations: Uses 2-3 charts and technical drawings/issue on boating. Prefers to see roughs. SASE. Send query letter with resume to be kept on file. Reports in 2 weeks. Buys all rights on a work-for-hire basis. Pays $5 minimum, b&w line drawings; on publication.

BEND OF THE RIVER MAGAZINE, Box 239, 143 W. Third St., Perrysburg OH 43551. Editors-in-Chief: Chris Raizk Alexander and R. Lee Raizk. For local history enthusiasts. Monthly. Circ. 3,000. Previously published and photocopied submissions OK. Original artwork returned after publication. Sample copy $1.

Cartoons: Buys 12 cartoons/issue from freelancers. Interested in early Americana; single panel with gagline. SASE. Buys first North American serial rights or all rights on a work-for-hire basis. Pays $1-3, b&w line drawings.

Illustrations: Buys 20 illustrations/year. Interested in "historic buildings for ads." Works on assignment only. Prefers to see roughs. SASE. No samples returned. Reports in 6 weeks. Buys first North

American serial rights or all rights on a work-for-hire basis. Pays $10-15, b&w line drawings, inside. Especially needs antiques, nostalgic items, landscapes and riverscapes.

***THE BERKELEY MONTHLY**, 910 Parker St., Berkeley CA 94710. Art Director: Laura Cirolia. Tabloid emphasizing art/ad mix and exciting graphics for Bay area residents. Monthly. Circ. 80,000. Accepts previously published material. Original artwork returned after publication. Sample copy free for SASE.
Cartoons: Buys 1-2 cartoons/issue from freelancers. Prefers single, double or multiple panel; b&w line drawings. Send samples of style to be kept on file. Material not filed is returned by SASE. Reports only if interested. Buys one-time rights. Pays $50-75.
Illustrations: Buys 5 illustrations/issue from freelancers. Works on assignment only. Send query letter. Samples not filed are returned by SASE. Reports only if interested. To show a portfolio, mail final reproduction/product, tear sheets and photographs. Buys one-time rights. Pays $200, color, cover; $50-100, b&w, and $100, color, inside; on publication.

BETTER HOMES & GARDENS, Meredith Corp., 1716 Locust, Des Moines IA 50336. Contact: Cartoon Editor. For "middle-and-up income, homeowning and community-concerned families." Monthly. Circ. 8,000,000. Original artwork not returned after publication. Free artist's guidelines.
Cartoons: Uses 2 cartoons/issue; buys all from freelancers. Receives 50-75 submissions/week from freelancers. Interested in current events, education, environment, family life, humor through youth, politics, religion, retirement, hobbies, sports and businessmen; single panel with gag line. Prefers finished cartoons. SASE. Reports in 2 weeks. Buys all rights. Pays $300 minimum, b&w line drawings; on acceptance.

BEVERAGE WORLD MAGAZINE, 150 Great Neck Rd., Great Neck NY 11021. (516)829-9210. Art Director: Andrew Patapis. Managing Editor: Jeannie Lukasick. Emphasizes beverages (beers, wines, spirits, bottled waters, soft drinks, juices) for soft drink bottlers, breweries, bottled water/juice plants, wineries and distilleries. Monthly. Circ. 30,000. Accepts simultaneous submissions. Original artwork returned after publication if requested. Sample copy $2.50.
Illustrations: Uses 5 illustrations/issue; buys 3-4 illustrations/issue from freelancers. Works on assignment only. Send query letter with photostats, slides or tear sheets to be kept on file. Write for appointment to show portfolio. Reports only if interested. Negotiates rights purchased. Pays $350 color, cover; $30, b&w, inside; on acceptance. Uses color illustration for cover. Usually black-and-white for sport illustrations inside.

BICYCLE GUIDE, 711 Boylston St., Boston MA 02116. (617)236-1885. Editor: Ted Costantino. Art Director: Cindy Davis. Estab. 1984. Magazine emphasizes bicycles for bicycle enthusiasts. Published 9 times/year; Sept./Oct., Nov./Dec. and Jan./Feb. are combination issues. Circ. 150,000. Original artwork returned after publication. Sample copy for SASE with $1.37 postage.
Cartoons: Generally doesn't use cartoons, but will consider submissions. Prefers upscale cycling oriented themes. Send query letter with samples of style to be kept on file; write for appointment to show portfolio. Material not filed is returned by SASE. Reports only if interested. Negotiates rights purchased. Payment is negotiable; pays on publication.
Illustrations: Buys 1-10 illustrations/issue from freelancers. Prefers technical themes. Works on assignment only. Send query letter with brochure, resume, business card, photostats, tear sheets, photocopies, slides, photographs, etc. to be kept on file. Samples not filed are returned by SASE. Reports within 1 month. To show a portfolio, mail appropriate materials or write to schedule an appointment; portfolio should include final reproduction/product, tear sheets, slides or anything we don't have to return. Negotiates rights purchased. Pays negotiable rate on publication.
Tips: "Remember that even the most casual pieces we use must be technically accurate."

BICYCLE USA, Suite 209, 6707 Whitestone Rd., Baltimore MD 21207. (301)944-3399. Editor: Karen Missavage. Readers are members of BICYCLE USA; publication is also sold in bicycle stores. Monthly. Circ. 16,000. Previously published material OK "if not in overlapping market." Original artwork returned after publication. SASE.
Cartoons: Uses 1-2 cartoons/issue; buys all from freelancers. Interested in recreational or utilitarian use of bicycles, road design, legislation and technical topics; single panel with gagline. Send query letter with brochure showing art style or photocopies, slides and photographs. Reports in 3 weeks. To show portfolio, mail appropriate materials, which should include appropriate material and an SASE. Buys one-time rights. Pays in copies of magazine; on publication.
Illustrations: Buys 1-2 illustrations/issue.
Tips: "Bicycling is growing! Next new trend-after tennis and jogging. Bicycle geometry is critical. Illustrations of real bicycles are preferable to ones with funny frames and parts missing."

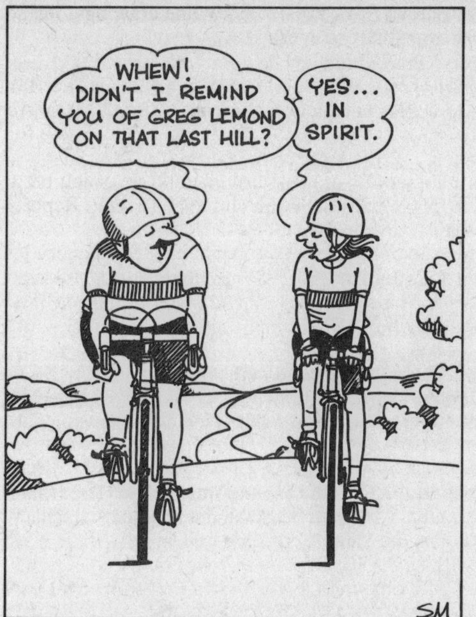

Sal Murdocca of New York City, created this panel in pen & ink "to create a small laugh," in Bicycle U.S.A. *"I have been a very successful illustrator for many years," says Murdocca. "I did this for fun." A persistent editor asked him to draw a cartoon, and Sal was paid in "warm thanks and complimentary copies."* Bicycle U.S.A. *claimed one-time rights to the artwork.*

***BIFROST**, Box 1180, Milford DE 19963. Editor/Acting Art Director: Ann Wilson. Re-established 1985. Emphasizes science fiction/fantasy for intelligent, creative people of both sexes and all ages. Quarterly. Circ. 1,000w. Sometimes accepts previously published material. Original artwork returned after publication. Sample copy $5.50; art guidelines free for SASE with 22¢ postage.
Cartoons: Would like to buy 3-5 cartoons/issue from freelancers. Prefers science fiction/fantasy themes. Prefers single panel with gagline; b&w line drawings. Send finished cartoons to be kept on file for 1 year, then returned if not used (and accompanied by SASE.) Samples returned by SASE. Reports within 2-3 weeks. Buys first rights. Payment is 1 copy.
Illustrations: Buys 15-20 illustrations from freelancers. Prefers science fiction/fantasy-type style. Send query letter with tear sheets, photostats and photocopies. Samples not filed are returned by SASE. Reports within 2-3 weeks. To show a portfolio, mail photostats or photocopies of finished work. Buys first rights. Pays in copies on publication.
Tips: "Prefers art that is as 'realistic' as possible with sf/fantasy subjects; avoid heavy blacks, especially large heavy blacks."

***THE BIG REEL**, Rt. 3, Box 239A, Madison NC 27025. (919)427-5850. Publisher: Donald R. Key. Tabloid. Emphasizes motion picture films, videotapes, movie photos and material for movie buffs and serious movie material collectors. Monthly. Circ. 5,000. Accepts previously published material. Original artwork returned after publication if requested. Sample copy available upon request.
Cartoons: Uses up to 3 cartoons/issue. Format open. Send query letter with finished cartoons to be kept on file. Material not kept on file returned by SASE only if requested. To show a portfolio, mail appropriate materials, which should include original/final art and photographs. No pay.
Illustrations: Accepts 4 or more/issue.
Tips: "Submit movie, TV and entertainment materials . . . only!"

BIKEREPORT, Box 8308, Missoula MT 59807. (406)721-1776. Editor: Daniel D'Ambrosio. Magazine. Emphasizes long-distance bicycle touring for bicycle enthusiasts. Circ. 18,000. Accepts previously published material. Original artwork returned after publication. Sample copy and art guidelines free for SASE.
Illustrations: Uses 3-6 illustrations/issue. Themes/styles are open. Works on assignment only. Send query letter with samples to be kept on file. Samples not kept on file are returned. Reports within 1 month. To show a portfolio, mail tear sheets and photostats. Buys first rights. Pays $75, b&w, cover; $20-50, b&w, inside; on publication.

***BIRD TALK**, Box 6050, Mission Viejo CA 92690. (714)240-6001. Managing Editor: Karyn New. Magazine emphasizing information about caring for pet birds, plus entertainment for birds for owners of

pet birds. Monthly. Circ. 70,000. Accepts previously published material. Original artwork returned after publication. Sample copy $3. Art guidelines free for SASE with 22¢ postage.
Cartoons: Buys 2-8 cartoons/issue from freelancers. Prefers themes dealing with pet birds (some wild). No "Polly want a cracker" takeoffs! Prefers single-panel, with gagline; b&w line drawings. Send query letter with finished cartoons to be kept on file. Samples not filed are returned by SASE. Reports within 30 days. Buys one-time rights. Pays $25, b&w.
Illustrations: Buys 1 illustration/issue from freelancers. Prefers pet birds (fairly lifelike) as themes. Send query letter with brochure showing art style or photocopies only, no originals. Samples not filed are returned by SASE. Reports within 30 days. No portfolios. Only a few drawings need to be sent in the mail. Buys one-time rights. Pays $20-150, b&w, inside; after publication.

BIRD WATCHER'S DIGEST, Box 110, Marietta OH 45750. (614)373-5285. Editor: Mary B. Bowers. Emphasizes birds and bird watchers for "bird watchers and birders (backyard and field; veteran and novice)." Bimonthly. Circ. 40,000. Previously published material OK. Original work returned after publication. Sample copy $2.
Cartoons: Uses 1-3 cartoons/issue; buys all from freelancers. Interested in themes pertaining to birds and/or bird watchers. Single panel with or without gagline, b&w line drawings. Send roughs. Samples returned by SASE. Reports in 1 month. Buys one-time rights and reprint rights. Pays $10, b&w; on publication.

BLACK AMERICAN LITERATURE FORUM, Parsons Hall 237, Indiana State University, Terre Haute IN 47809. (812)237-3169. Editor-in-Chief: Joe Weixlmann. Concerns black American writers and their work. Quarterly. Circ. 1,050. Simultaneous submissions OK. Sample copy $4; free artist's guidelines.
Illustrations: Buys 3/issue on black life. Mail art with an SASE. Reports in 2 weeks. Buys all rights, but may reassign rights to artist after publication. Pays $15 maximum, b&w line drawings for cover and inside; on acceptance.
Tips: "We get, and need, relatively little work."

***BLACK BEAR PUBLICATIONS**, 1916 Lincoln St., Croydon PA 19020-8026. (215)788-3543. Editors: Jeanne or Ron. Estab. 1984. Magazine emphasizing social, political, ecological, environmental subjects for a mostly well-educated audience, any age group. Semiannual. Circ. 400. Accepts previously published material. Original artwork returned after publication with SASE. Sample copy $2 (for back issues); art guidelines free for SASE with 22¢ postage.
Illustrations: Buys 6 illustrations/issue from freelancers. Prefers collage, woodcuts, pen & ink. Send query letter with SASE, resume and photocopies. Samples not filed returned by SASE. Reports within 10 days. To show a portfolio, mail photocopies. Buys one-time rights or reprint rights. Pays in copies; on publication.

THE BLACK COLLEGIAN MAGAZINE, 1240 S. Broad St., New Orleans LA 70125. (504)821-5694. Art Director: Mike Hancock. For black college students and recent graduates with a concentration on career-oriented subjects and job opportunities. Bimonthly. Circ. 171,000. Previously published material and simultaneous submissions accepted. Sample copy available; art guidelines free for SASE.
Illustrations: Uses 6 illustrations/issue; buys 4/issue from freelancers. Send query letter with samples to be kept on file; original work is returned. Prefers photostats or tear sheets as samples. Samples not kept on file are returned by SASE only if requested. Reports within 30 days. Call or write for appointment to show portfolio. Buys one-time rights or reprint rights. Pays $150, b&w and $275, color, for covers; $20 and up for b&w and color, inside. Pays on publication.

THE B'NAI B'RITH INTERNATIONAL JEWISH MONTHLY, B'nai B'rith, 1640 Rhode Island Ave. NW, Washington DC 20036. (202)857-6645. Editor: Marc Silver. Emphasizes a variety of articles of interest to the Jewish family. Published 10 times/year. Circ. 200,000. Original artwork returned after publication. Sample copy $1. Also uses artists for "design, lettering, calligraphy on assignment. We call or write the artist, pay on publication."
Illustrations: Buys 2 illustrations/issue from freelancers. Theme and style vary, depending on tone of story illustrated. Works on assignment only. Write or call for appointment to show portfolio, which should include tear sheets, slides or photographs. Reports within 3 weeks. Samples returned by SASE. Buys first rights. Pays $150, b&w and $250, color, cover; $100, b&w and color, inside; rates vary regarding size of illustration; on publication.

BOATING, 1 Park Ave., New York NY 10016. (212)503-3500. Art Director: Victor Mazurkiewicz. Emphasizes boating for boat owners. Monthly. Circ. 180,000. Accepts simultaneous submissions. Original artwork returned after publication.
Illustrations: Occasionally uses illustrations; buys all from freelancers. Works on assignment only.

Send samples and tear sheets to be kept on file. Write or call for appointment to show portfolio. Prefers photostats or photographs as samples. Samples returned only by SASE if not kept on file. Buys first rights. Pays $1,000, color, cover. Pays $100-500, b&w, inside; $1,000, color, 2-page spread, inside. Pays after publication.

***BOSTON MAGAZINE**, 300 Massachusetts Ave., Boston MA 02115. Associate Art Director: Suzanne Heine Peterman. Emphasizes regional/city subjects/issues of the Boston area for young professionals. Monthly. Circ. 110,000. Original artwork returned after publication.
Illustrations: Uses 8 illustrations/issue. Works on assignment only. Send query letter with brochure showing art style or resume and tearsheets to be kept on file. Call for appointment to show portfolio, which should include final reproduction/product, color and tear sheets. Samples not filed are returned by SASE. Reports only if interested. Buys first rights. Pays on publication.

***BOTH SIDES NOW**, Rt. 6, Box 28, Tyler TX 75704. (214)592-4263. Contact: Editor. Magazine emphasizing the new age for people seeking holistic alternatives in spiritual, lifestyle and politics. Irregular publication. Circ. 2,000 printed. Accepts previously published material. Original artwork returned by SASE. Sample copy 75¢.
Cartoons: Buys various number of cartoons/issue from freelancers. Prefers fantasy, political satire, religion and exposes of hypocrisy as themes. Prefers single or multiple panel; b&w line drawings. Send query letter with samples of style such as good photocopies. Samples not filed are returned by SASE. Reports within 3 months. Pays in copies only.
Illustrations: Buys variable amount of illustrations/issue from freelancers. Prefers fantasy, surrealism, spirituality and realism as themes. Send query letter with resume and photocopies. Samples not filed are returned by SASE. Reports back within 3 months. Pays in copies; on publication.

BOW & ARROW MAGAZINE, Box HH, Capistrano Beach CA 92624. (714)493-2101. Managing Editor: Roger Combs. Emphasizes bowhunting and bowhunters. Bimonthly. Original artwork not returned after publication. Art guidelines available.
Cartoons: Uses 2-3 cartoons/issue; buys all from freelancers. Prefers single panel, with gag line; b&w line drawings. Send finished cartoons. Material not kept on file returned by SASE. Reports within 2 months. Buys all rights. Pays $7.50-$10, b&w. Pays on acceptance.
Illustrations: Uses 1-2 illustrations/issue; buys all from freelancers. Prefers live animals/game as themes. Send samples. Prefers photographs or original work as samples. Especially looks for perspective, unique or accurate use of color and shading, and an ability to clearly express a thought, emotion or event. Samples returned by SASE. Reports in 2 months. Buys all rights or negotiates rights purchased. Pays $100-150, color, cover; payment for inside b&w varies. Pays on acceptance.

BOWHUNTER, Editorial Offices, 3150 Mallard Cove Lane, Fort Wayne IN 46804. (219)432-5772. Editor-in-Chief: M.R. James. For "readers of all ages, background and experience. All share two common passions—hunting with the bow and arrow and a love of the great outdoors." Bimonthly. Circ. 185,000.
Cartoons: Uses few cartoons; but considers all submissions. Interested in "bowhunting and wildlife. No unsafe hunting conditions; single panel." Prefers to see roughs. SASE. Reports in 4 weeks. Buys all rights on a work-for-hire basis; will reassign rights. Pays $15-25, line drawings; on acceptance.
Illustrations: Buys b&w and color illustrations/issue, all from freelancers. Interested in "wildlife-bowhunting scenes." Send query letter with slides and photographs. SASE. Reports in 4 weeks. To show a portfolio, mail roughs. Buys first rights. Pays $200 color, cover; $20 + and $50 + color, inside; on acceptance.
Tips: "We are presently overstocked with cartoons but need good wildlife art." Artist must convey "a feeling and understanding for the game represented. Call it atmosphere or mood, or whatever, it's something that is either there or not. The art we select for publication has this extra something the viewer immediately senses. We are using more color on inside pages. This opens up additional possibilities for freelance artists with good wildlife art. Study the magazine before contacting us. Know what we use before making suggestions or submitting ideas. Know the subject down to the finest details."

BOWLERS JOURNAL, John Hancock Center, 875 N. Michigan Ave., Chicago IL 60611. (312)266-7171. Managing Editor: Jim Dressel. Monthly. Circ. 22,000. Emphasizes bowling. Also uses artist for design; specific assignments to suit editorial themes. Query with previously published work.
Illustrations: Needs art to illustrate specific articles. Send query letter with brochure showing art style. SASE. Reports in 2 months. Buys one-time rights. Call to schedule an appointment to show a portfolio, which should include a representative variety of their work." Pays $200 b&w; $325 color cover; $100 b&w; $150 color, inside; on acceptance.
Tips: "We've stepped up our use of illustration for our more conceptual articles. We've been bearing

down to customize the artwork to the article rather than depend so heavily on our file of stock art. Art or illustration projects were assigned to a tight coterie of those who have worked with us in the past, but with turnover and increased demands, we would like to see samples or portfolios of those who would like to work in the bowling arena. Humorous and cartoon-style illustrations are assigned on a need basis.''

BREAD, 6401 The Paseo, Kansas City MO 64131. (816)333-7000. Editor-in-Chief: Gary Sivewright. Christian leisure reading magazine for ages 12-17 with denominational interests. Monthly. Circ. 25,000. Previously published and simultaneous submissions OK. Free sample copy and artist's guidelines *with* SASE.
Cartoons: Buys 10 cartoons/year; buys all from freelancers. Receives 10 submissions/week from freelancers. Interested in humor through youth—teen, school, religious, dating. Prefers single panel with gagline. Prefers to see finished cartoons. Reports in 4-6 weeks. Buys first rights. Pays $6-15, b&w line drawings; on acceptance.
Illustrations: Uses 15 illustrations/year. Works on assignment only. Prefers to see samples. Pays $150-200, color, cover; $35-80, b&w, inside; on acceptance.

***BREAKFAST WITHOUT MEAT**, Room 188, 1827 Haight St., San Francisco CA 94117. Art Director: G. Obo. Magazine emphasizing music and satire. We have world-wide distribution, mainly to fans of humor and punk music. Quarterly. Circ. 600. Sample copy $1.25. Art guidelines free for SASE with 22¢ postage.
Cartoons: Buys 2 cartoons/issue from freelancers. Prefers single or multiple panel with gagline; b&w line drawings. Send query letter with finished cartoons. Samples not filed are returned by SASE. Reports back within 4 weeks. Negotiates rights purchased. Pays $10, b&w.

BRIGADE LEADER, Box 150, Wheaton IL 60189. (312)665-0630. For Christian laymen and adult male leaders of boys enrolled in the Brigade man-boy program. Circ. 14,000. Published 4 times/year. Original artwork returned after publication. Sample copy for $1.50 and large SASE; artist's guidelines free for SASE.
Cartoons: Contact: Cartoon Editor. Uses 1 cartoon/issue, all from freelancers. Receives 3 submissions/week from freelancers. Interested in sports, nature and youth; single panel with gagline. "Keep it clean." SASE. Buys first rights only. Pays $20, b&w line drawings; on publication.
Illustrations: Art Director: Lawrence Libby. Uses 2 illustrations/issue. Interested in man and boy subjects, sports, camping—out of doors, family. Works on assignment only. Samples returned by SASE. Reports back on future assignment possibilities. Provide resume and flyer to be kept on file for future assignments. Prefers to see portfolio and samples of style. Reports in 2 weeks. Pays $50-85, for inside use of b&w line drawings and washes; on publication.

BROTHERHOOD OF MAINTENANCE OF WAY EMPLOYES JOURNAL, 12050 Woodward Ave., Detroit MI 48203. Associate Editor/Director of Public Relations: R.J. Williamson. For members of international railroad workers' union who build, repair and maintain tracks, buildings and bridges. Monthly. Circ. 120,000. Previously published, photocopied and simultaneous submissions OK. Original artwork returned after publication. Free sample copy available.
Cartoons: Buys 2 cartoons/year from freelancers. Receives less than 1 submission/week from freelancers. Interested in railroad/trackwork themes; single panel with gagline, b&w line drawings. Send query letter with photocopies. Samples returned by SASE. Reports in 1 week. Buys one-time rights. Pays $10, b&w; on acceptance.

BRUCE JENNER'S BETTER HEALTH & LIVING MAGAZINE, 800 2nd Ave., New York NY 10017. (212)986-9026. Editorial Director: Julie Davis. Art Director: May Sugano-Koto. Estab. 1985. Emphasizes health, nutrition, exercise, eating, sleeping and living for men and women, business people, ages 25-50. Bimonthly. Circ. 200,000. Does not accept previously published material. Returns original artwork after publication. Sample copy free for SASE.
Illustrations: Uses a varying number/issue. Works on assignment only. Send samples to be kept on file. Prefers tear sheets as samples. Samples not filed are returned by SASE. Does not report back. Negotiates payment and rights purchased. Pays on publication.

BUILDER MAGAZINE, Suite 475, 655 15th St. NW, Washington DC 20005. (202)737-0717. Associate Art Director: Debra A. Burkhead. Emphasizes the housing industry for the National Association of Home Builders members and subscriptions. Monthly. Circ. 185,000. Original artwork not returned after publication unless requested. Sample copy and art guidelines available.
Illustrations: Uses 4-7 illustrations/issue. Prefers b&w line drawings. Works on assignment only. Send query letter with samples to be kept on file. Prefers tear sheets, photostats or photocopies as sam-

ples. Looks for "originality, a distinct style and creativity" when reviewing samples. Reports only if interested. Buys one-time rights. Call for appointment to show portfolio. Pays $75-150, b&w; payment negotiable for color, inside. Pays on acceptance.

"I wanted to express the feelings of frustration and helplessness most of us feel when up against the impersonal complexities and dangers in the nuclear arms race," says Ken Shooshan-Stoller of Avon, Connecticut. Ken created this pen & ink illustration for The Bulletin of Atomic Scientists, *which he discovered in the Artist's Market. Ken received $25 for one-time rights plus "an outlet for my serious side in illustration rather than my humor in cartoons."*

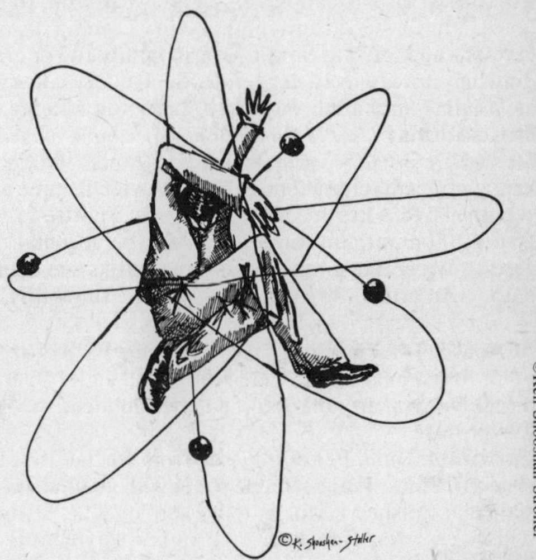

BULLETIN OF THE ATOMIC SCIENTISTS, 5801 S. Kenwood, Chicago IL 60637. (312)363-5225. Art Director: Lisa Grayson. Emphasizes arms control; science and public affairs for audience of 40% scientists, 40% politicians and policy makers, and 20% interested, educated citizens. Monthly. Circ. 25,000. Original artwork returned after publication. Sample copy $2.50; free artist's guidelines for SASE.

Cartoons: Buys about 5-10 cartoons/issue including humorous illustrations from freelancers. Considers arms control and international relation themes. "We are looking for new ideas. Please, no mushroom clouds or death's heads." Prefers single panel without gagline; b&w line drawings. Send finished cartoons. Cartoon portfolios are not reviewed. Material returned by SASE. Reports within 1 month. Buys first rights. Pays $25, b&w; on acceptance.

Illustrations: Buys 5-8 illustrations/issue from freelancers. Considers serious b&w themes; check 1986 issues for samples. "Do not even consider sending work until you have viewed a few issues. The name of the magazine misleads artists who don't bother to check; they wind up wasting time and postage." Works on assignment only. Send query letter with brochure and samples to be kept on file, except for completely unsuitable work which is returned promptly by SASE. Artist may write or call for appointment to show portfolio but prefers mailed samples. Prefers tear sheets or photostats as samples. Samples not filed are returned by SASE. Reports within 1 month. Buys first world-wide rights. Pays $300, b&w, cover; $100/¼ page, $150/½ page, $250/full page, b&w, inside; on acceptance.

BUSINESS TODAY, Aaron Burr Hall, Princeton NJ 08540. (609)921-1111. Contact: Production Manager. For college undergraduates interested in business, politics and careers in those fields. Published 3 times/academic year. Circ. 205,000. Receives 10 cartoons and 2 illustrations/week from freelance artists. Especially needs illustrations and political cartoons. Query with samples to be kept on file; do not send originals, photocopies only. Will contact artists as needed. Previous work as magazine illustrator preferred. Reports in 2 months. Previously published, photocopied, and simultaneous submissions OK. Buys one-time, reprint or simultaneous rights. Pays on publication. Original artwork returned after publication. Sample copy $2.

Cartoons: Buys 4-5/issue on current events, education, environment, politics, business, college life and careers. "Keep the student readership in mind; *no typical scenes with executives and secretaries.*"

Illustrations: Buys 4-5/issue on current events, education, environment, politics, college life and careers. "We like the style of *The New Yorker* and op-ed cartoons in *The New York Times*." Prefers to have samples of style and topic areas covered. Provide business card and letter of inquiry to be kept on file for future assignments. Cover: Pays $50 minimum, color; $10-20, b&w. Inside: Pays $20 minimum, color; $10 minimum, b&w; on publication.

Tips: There is a trend toward "more quality, less quantity of artwork; we like to have artwork that says something. We need both concrete and abstract photos, as long as they are of quality and in sharp focus."

***BUTTER FAT MAGAZINE**, Box 9100, Vancouver B.C., V6B 4G4 Canada. (604)420-6611. Editor: Carol A. Paulson. Emphasizes dairy farming, dairy product processing, marketing and distribution for dairy cooperative members and employees in British Columbia. Monthly. Circ. 3,500. Free sample copy and art guidelines for SASE.
Cartoons: Uses 2 cartoons/issue; buys all from freelancers. Receives 10 submissions/week from freelancers. Interested in agriculture, dairy farming, farming families and Canadian marketing systems. No cartoons unrelated to farming, farm family life or critical of food prices. Prefers single panel b&w line drawings or washes with gagline. Send query letter with finished cartoons. Reports in 2 weeks. Negotiates rights purchased. Pays $10, b&w; on acceptance.
Illustrations: Uses 1 llustration/issue; buys all from freelancers. Interested in making assignments for specific issues—variable technical, food. Works on assignment only. Send brochure. Samples not kept on file are returned by SASE. Provide resume and samples to be kept on file for possible future assignments. Reports in 2 weeks. To show a portfolio, mail original/final art. Negotiates rights purchased. Pays $100 minimum for b&w inside; on acceptance.
Tips: "We prefer to meet artists as well as see their work. Most assignments are short notice: 10-14 days." An artist's work should reflect "suitability of tone and style" to the publication.

***CALLI'S TALES**, Box 1224, Palmetto FL 33561. Editor: Annice E. Hunt. Magazine emphasizing wildlife and pets for animal lovers of all ages. Quarterly. Circ. 100. Accepts previously published material. Original artwork returned after publication. Sample copy $2. Art guidelines free for SASE with 22¢ postage.
Cartoons: Buys 1 cartoon/issue from freelancers. Prefers animals, wildlife and environment in good taste as themes. Prefers single panel with gagline; b&w line drawings. Send query letter with samples of style and finished cartoons to be kept on file. Samples not filed are returned by SASE. Reports back within 2 weeks. Buys one-time rights. Payment is one free copy of issue.
Illustrations: Buys 2-3 illustrations/issue from freelancers. Prefers wildlife, pets and nature scenes as themes. Send query letter with resume and tear sheets. Samples not filed are returned by SASE. Reports within 2 weeks. Payment is one free copy of issue.

CAMPUS LIFE, 465 Gundersen Dr., Carol Stream IL 60188. Senior Editors: Gregg Lewis and Jim Long. For high school and college students. "Though our readership is largely Christian, *Campus Life* reflects the interests of all kids—music, activities, photography and sports." Monthly. Circ. 175,000. Original artwork returned after publication. "No phone calls, please. Show us what you can do."
Cartoons: Uses 3-5 single-panel cartoons/issue plus cartoon features (assigned). Receives 5 submissions/week from freelancers. Buys 50/year on high school and college education, environment, family life, humor through youth, and politics; apply to 13-23 age groups; prefers single panel, especially vertical format. Prefers to receive finished cartoons. Reports in 4 weeks. Pays $50 minimum, b&w; on acceptance.
Illustrations: Art Director: Jeff Carnehl. Uses 2 illustrations/issue; buys all from freelancers. Receives 5 submissions/week from freelancers. Works on assignment only. Send query letter, brochure, resume and samples; sample transparencies returned by SASE, brochures and tear sheets not returned. Reporting time varies; is at least 2 weeks. Buys first North American serial rights; also considers second rights. Pays $250-400, color; $225-300, b&w; on acceptance.
Tips: "The best way to see what we can use is to ask for several sample copies ($2 each)."

CANADIAN FICTION MAGAZINE, Box 946, Station F, Toronto, Ontario M4Y 2N9 Canada. Editor: Geoffrey Hancock. Anthology devoted exclusively to contemporary Canadian fiction. Quarterly. Canadian artists or residents only. Sample copy $5.50.
Illustrations: Uses 16 pages of art/issue; also cover art. SASE (nonresidents include IRC). Reports in 4-6 weeks. Pays $10/page; $25, cover. Uses b&w line drawings, photographs.
Tips: "Portraits of contemporary Canadian writers in all genres are valuable for archival purposes."

CANOE, Canoe America Association, Box 597, Camden ME 04843. Managing Editor: George Thomas. Art Director: Faith Hague. "Readers are lifestyle canoeists and kayakers; they're interested in touring, camping, sailing, racing and whitewater river running." Bimonthly. Circ. 55,000. Previously published work OK (if published in unrelated or noncompeting magazine). Original artwork usually not returned after publication unless previously arranged. Free sample copy and artist's guidelines with 9x12 SASE.
Illustrations: Uses 6 illustrations/issue; buys 1-2/issue from freelancers. Interested in canoeing, kayaking and camping "as fits the subject." Prefers to see finished art. Provide resume, tear sheet and samples to be kept on file for future assignments. SASE. Reports in 3-5 weeks. Buys various rights. Inside: Pays $50 minimum, b&w line drawings and gray opaques; on acceptance.
Tips: "Above all, look at recent back issues for the type of material we're currently using. As for car-

toon material, it should fit in with our specialized approach to the sport of paddling . . . aimed at *paddlers*, not just a general audience."

***CAPE COD LIFE**, Box 222, Osterville MA 02655. (617)428-5706. Art Director: Betsy Morin. Magazine emphasizing Cape Cod people, places, arts and concerns for a wide range of ages, from 40-70. Bimonthly. Circ. 32,000. Original artwork returned to artists after publication. Sample copy $3; art guidelines available.
Illustrations: Buys 8-10 illustrations/issue from freelancers. Prefers Cape Cod scenes, a realistic style. "When subject is an identifiable area or building, we are more likely to use the illustration." Send query letter with tear sheets and photocopies. Samples not filed are returned by SASE. Reports only if interested. Call or write to schedule an appointment to show a portfolio, which should include original/final art, final/reproduction/product and tear sheets. Buys one-time rights. Pays $15-30, b&w; $20-40, color, inside; on publication.

CAR CRAFT, Petersen Publishing Co., 8490 Sunset Blvd., Los Angeles CA 90069. (213)657-5100. Editor-in-Chief: Jeff Smith. Managing Editor: Tracey Hurst. Art Director: Todd Westover. "We feature articles on automotive modifications and drag racing. Monthly. Circ. 425,000. Original artwork not returned unless prior arrangement is made. Free sample copy and artist's guidelines.
Illustrations: Uses 1 or more illustrations/issue; buys 1/issue from freelancers. Interested in "automotive editorial illustration and design with a more illustrative and less technical look." Works on assignment only. Query with business card, brochure, flyer and tear sheet to be kept on file for future assignments. SASE. Reports in 2 weeks. Buys all rights on a work-for-hire basis.

CASE CURRENTS, Suite 400, 11 Dupont Circle, Washington DC 20036. (202)328-5944. Art Director: Ellen Cohen. Emphasizes education for professionals at colleges, universities, and independent schools who work in fund raising, alumni relations and educational communications. Monthly. Circ. 14,500. Accepts previously published material. Original artwork returned after publication. Sample copy free for SASE.
Illustrations: Uses 2-3 illustrations/issue; buys all from freelancers. Uses wide variety of themes and styles, "but must be very high quality." Send query letter with brochure, business card and samples to be kept on file. Prefers photocopies only of printed work; "please no slides, photos, stats or originals. Samples not kept on file are returned by SASE. Reports only if interested. Buys first or reprint rights or negotiates. Pays $250, color, cover; $150, b&w, inside; on acceptance.
Tips: Especially seeks "concise conceptualization" in artwork. Current trends include a "simplistic, contemporary look; illustrations which are a bit looser and more 'fun.' "

CAT FANCY, Fancy Publications Inc., Box 6050, Mission Viejo CA 92690. (714)240-6001. Editor: Linda W. Lewis. For cat owners, breeders and fanciers. Readers are men and women of all ages interested in all phases of cat ownership. Monthly. Circ. 130,000. Simultaneous submissions and previously published work OK. Sample copy $3; free artist's guidelines.
Cartoons: Buys 12/year; single, double and multiple panel with gagline. "Central character should be a cat." Send query letter with photostats or photocopies as samples. SASE. Reports in 6 weeks. Pays $20-50, b&w line drawings; on publication. Buys first rights.
Illustrations: Buys 12/year of domestic and wild cats. Send query letter with resume and samples. SASE. Reports in 6 weeks. Inside: Pays $50-125, b&w line drawings; on publication. Buys first rights.
Tips: "We need good cartoons."

CATHOLIC FORESTER, 425 W. Shuman Blvd., Naperville IL 60566. (312)983-4920. Editor: Barbara Cunningham. Magazine. "We are a fraternal insurance company but use general interest art and photos. Audience is middle-class, many small town as well as big city readers, patriotic, somewhat conservative. We are distributed nationally." Bimonthly. Circ. 150,000. Accepts previously published material. Original artwork returned after publication. Sample copy for SASE with 56¢ postage.
Cartoons: Considers "anything *funny* but it must be clean." Prefers single panel with gagline; b&w line drawings. Send query letter with roughs. Material returned by SASE. Reports within 3 months; "we try to do it sooner." Buys one-time rights or reprint rights. Pays $25, b&w; on acceptance.
Illustrations: Send query letter with photostats, tear sheets, photocopies, slides, photographs, etc. to be kept on file. Samples not filed are returned by SASE. Reports within 3 months. Write for appointment to show portfolio. Buys one-time rights or reprint rights. Payment depends on work and negotiation with artist. "We have large and small needs, so it's impossible to say." Pays on acceptance.

***CATHOLIC SINGLES MAGAZINE**, Box 1920, Evanston IL 60204. (312)731-8769. Founder: Fred C. Wilson. Magazine for single, widowed, separated and divorced Catholic persons. Circ. 3,000. Accepts previously published material. Original artwork returned after publication by SASE. Sample copy

$1. Art guidelines free for SASE with 20¢ postage.
Cartoons: Buys approximately 6/issue from freelancers. Prefers anything that deals with being single (no porn) as themes. Send query letter with finished cartoons to be kept on file. Write or call to schedule an appointment to show a portfolio. Material not filed returned by SASE only if requested. Reports only if interested. Buys one-time rights. Pays $10, b&w.
Illustrations: Works on assignment only. Prefers anything dealing with singledom as themes. Send query letter with samples. Samples not filed returned by SASE. Reports only if interested. To show a portfolio, mail original/final art. Buys one-time rights. Pays $25, b&w cover; $10, b&w inside; on publication.

THE CATTLEMAN, 1301 W. Seventh St., Fort Worth TX 76102. (817)332-7155. For Southwestern cattle producers and cattlemen. Monthly. Circ. 22,000. Sample copy $2.
Cartoons: Contact Kipp Shackelford. Uses 3 cartoons/issue. Receives 10 submissions/week from freelancers. Interested in beef cattle raising and the Old West. Prefers single panel with gagline. Prefers to see finished cartoons. SASE. Reports in 1 month. Buys first North American serial rights. Pays $10 minimum, b&w line drawings; on acceptance.
Illustrations: Contact Dale Segraves, editor. Buys limited number of illustrations. Interested in beef cattle, raising cattle and horses, western art. Send query letter with resume and samples to be kept on file. Samples not kept on file are returned by SASE. Reports in 2 weeks. Buys first North American serial rights or buys all rights on a work-for-hire basis. Pays $100 minimum, color washes, cover. Pays $15-25, color washes and opaque watercolors; $15-20, b&w line drawings, washes and gray opaques, inside; on acceptance.

CAVALIER, Dugent Publishing Corp., 2355 Salzedo St., Coral Gables FL 33134. Contact: Nye Willden. "For young men and college students interested in good fiction, articles and sex." Monthly. Circ. 250,000. Sample copy $2.50; guidelines free. Receives 50-75 cartoons and 3-4 illustrations/week from freelance artists. Original work only; no simultaneous submissions.
Cartoons: Buys 5/issue on erotica; single panel with gagline. Send query letter with samples. SASE. Reports in 2 weeks. Buys first rights. Pays $50-100, b&w line drawings and washes; 30 days before publication.
Illustrations: Buys 3/issue on erotica and assigned themes, including some humorous and cartoon-style illustrations. Works on assignment only. Send query letter with samples. SASE. Reports in 2 weeks. Buys first rights. Pays $150 minimum, b&w line drawings and washes; $200/page, $300/spread, color washes and full-color work, inside; 30 days before publication.
Tips: "Send 35mm slide samples of your work that art director can *keep* in his file, or tear sheets of published work. We have to have samples to refer to when making assignments. Large portfolios are difficult to handle and return. Also send samples *related* to our publication, i.e., erotica or nude studies. We are an excellent market for unpublished but very talented artists and cartoonists. Many of the top people in both fields — Mort Drucker, Peter Max, Ed Arno, Sid Harris—started with us, and many of them still work for us. Study *our* magazine for samples of acceptable material. *Do not submit* original artwork for our evaluation; slides, photos or stats only."

***CENEX MARKETING INSIGHT**, Box 64089, St. Paul MN 55164. Manager, Marketing Publications: Susan Winsor. Emphasizes business management and agri-marketing for managers and employees of 1,500 agribusinesses/dealers. Quarterly. Circ. 261,000. Accepts previously published material.
Cartoons: Send query letter with samples of style. Reports only if interested. Pays on acceptance.
Illustrations: Uses 2-3 illustrations/issue. Seeks themes to illustrate business or marketing management. Send samples—"anything that applies to above themes and target audience." Pays on acceptance.

***CENTRAL FLORIDA MAGAZINE**, Box 8434, 341 N. Maitland Ave., Maitland FL 32751. (305)628-8850. Art Director; Charles Utz. Magazine emphasizing lifestyle of Central Floridians for an upwardly mobile, educated, high spending, good male-female ratio and affluent audience. Monthly. Circ. 25,000. Accepts previously published material. Original artwork returned after publication. Sample copy and art guidelines available.
Cartoons: Write or call for appointment to show a portfolio. Material not kept on file is returned. Reports within 10 days. Buys one-time rights. Pays $100-250, color (negotiable).
Illustrations: Buys 1-2 illustrations/issue from freelancers. Works on assignment only. Send query letter with resume, tear sheets, photostats, photocopies, slides and photographs. Samples not filed are returned. Reports back within 10 days. Call or write to schedule an appointment to show a portfolio. Buys one-time rights. Pays $500, b&w, and $500, color, cover; $100, b&w, and $250, color, inside; on publication.

***CENTRAL PARK/A JOURNAL OF THE ARTS & SOCIAL THEORY**, Box 1446, New York NY 10023. (212)382-9151. Co-editor; Stephen-Paul Martin. Magazine emphasizing experimental or politically progressive statements of art and social theory for intellectuals and artists of all kinds. Twice/year. Circ. 1,000. Accepts previously published material. Original artwork returned after publication. Sample copy $5. Art guidelines free for SASE with 22¢ postage.
Illustrations: Also accepts photographs and collages. Buys 20 illustrations/issue from freelancers. Prefers social realism, surrealism and expressionism as themes. Send resume and photographs. Samples not filed returned by SASE. Reports within 6 weeks. Buys first rights. "Until further notice, payment is one copy of the issue in which the work appears."
Tips: "Artists should keep in mind that our medium is the 8x10" page and that their artwork will be considered in relation to experimental and political literary texts."

CHAIN STORE AGE, 425 Park Ave., New York NY 10022. (212)371-9400. Emphasizes retail stores. Readers are buyers, retail executives, merchandise managers, vice presidents of hard lines and store personnel. Monthly. Circ. 30,000.
Cartoons: Occasional use of line art *by assignment only*. Send samples of style to art director. SASE. Keeps file on artists. Pays $50-125 on publication for b&w cartoons. Buys all rights on a work-for-hire-basis.
Illustrations: Uses 1-2 illustrations/issue, all from freelancers. We "keep samples on file; must be in NY area. Must see portfolio." Uses inside b&w line drawings and washes, cover color washes and pre-separated art. Send roughs, tear sheets and samples of style, and/or arrange personal appointment to show portfolio to art director. SASE. Reports in 1 week. Pays $50-125 on publication for inside b&w, $300 maximum for color cover, $150-250 for inside color. Buys all rights.

CHANGING TIMES, 1729 H St. NW, Washington DC 20006. Cartoon Editor: Joseph Yacinski. For general, adult audience interested in personal finance, family money management and career advancement. Monthly.
Cartoons: Buys 1 cartoon/issue from freelancers. Receives 800 submissions/month from freelancers. Interested in financial topics, home budgeting, insurance, stocks, taxes, etc. or of seasonal nature. Uses 1 cartoon/month on letters to editor page. Send query letter with tear sheets. Prefers to see finished drawings. SASE. Reports in 1 month. Pays $250, b&w; on acceptance.

CHARIOT, Ben Hur Life Association, Box 312, Crawfordsville IN 47933. Editor: Loren Harrington. Emphasizes fraternal activities and general interest for members of the Association, a fraternal life insurance benefit society. Quarterly. Circ. 11,000. Accepts previously published material. Original artwork returned after publication if requested. Sample copy free for 9x12 SASE with 88¢ postage; art guidelines for #10 SASE with 22¢ postage.
Cartoons: Rarely buys cartoons from freelancers. Considers humor and some satire. Prefers single panel with gagline; b&w line drawings or washes. Send finished cartoons to be kept on file. Material not filed is returned by SASE. Reports within 1 month. Negotiates rights purchased. Pays $1-20, b&w; on acceptance.
Illustrations: Rarely buys illustrations from freelancers but may work on assignment basis. Prefers line and wash, b&w only. Send query letter with resume and samples to be kept on file. Write for appointment to show portfolio. Accepts any type of sample that portrays quality of work. Reports in 1 month. Negotiates rights purchased and payment. Pays on acceptance, sometimes on publication.

CHARLOTTE MAGAZINE, Box 221269, Charlotte NC 28222. (704)375-8034. Editor: Chuck Duritsch. Emphasizes local people and local places. Monthly. Circ. 20,000. Original artwork returned after publication, if requested. Free sample copy and art guidelines.
Illustrations: Usually 3-4/issue; buys all from freelancers. Prefers b&w line drawings and b&w graphic art. Works on assignment only after acceptance of thumbnail or rough. Arrange appointment to show portfolio to editor. Buys first rights. Pays $35-75, b&w; 30 days after publication.

CHESS LIFE, 186 Route 9W, New Windsor NY 12550. (914)562-8350. Art Director: Bruce R. Helm. Official publication of the United States Chess Federation. Contains news of major chess events with special emphasis on American players, plus columns of instruction, general features, historical articles, personality profiles, cartoons, quizzes, humor and short stories. Monthly. Circ. 56,000. Accepts previously published material and simultaneous submissions. Sample copy for SASE with $1.07 postage; art guidelines for SASE with 22¢ postage.
Cartoons: Buys 1-2 cartoons/issue from freelancers. All cartoons must have a chess motif. Prefers single panel, with gagline; b&w line drawings. Send query letter with brochure showing art style. "We may keep a few cartoons on hand, but most are either bought or returned." Material not kept on file returned by SASE. Reports within 2-4 weeks. Negotiates rights purchased. Pays $10-25, b&w; on publication.

Illustrations: Buys 1-2 illustrations/issue from freelancers. All must have a chess motif; uses some humorous and occasionally cartoon-style illustrations. "We use mainly b&w." Works on assignment, but will also consider unsolicited work. Send query letter with photostats or original work for b&w; slides for color, or tear sheets to be kept on file. Reports within 4 weeks. Call to schedule an appointment to show a portfolio, which should include roughs, original/final art, final reproduction/product and tear sheets. Negotiates rights purchased. Pays by the project, $25-150 average. Pays on publication.
Tips: "I look for work that is clean, well-executed, well thought out and which will reproduce well in print."

CHIC, Larry Flynt Publications, Suite 3800, 2029 Century Park E., Los Angeles CA 90067. (213)556-9200. Cartoon/Humor Editor: Dwaine Tinsley. For affluent men, 25-30 years of age, college-educated and interested in current affairs, luxuries, investigative reporting, entertainment, sports, sex and fashion. Monthly. Returns original art.
Cartoons: Publishes 20/month; 10 full-page color, 4 color spots and 6 b&w spots. Receives 300-500 cartoons from freelancers. Especially needs "outrageous material. Mainly sexual, but politics, sports OK. Topical humor and seasonal/holiday cartoons good." Mail samples. Prefers 8½x11" size; avoid crayons, chalks or fluorescent colors. Also avoid, if possible, large, heavy illustration board. Samples returned by SASE only. Place name, address and phone number on back of each cartoon. Reports in 3 weeks. Buys first rights with first right to reprint. Pays $150, full page color; $75 spot color; $50 spot b&w. Pays on acceptance.
Tips: Especially needs more cartoons, cartoon breakaways or one-subject series. "Send outrageous humor—work that other magazines would shy away from. Pertinent, political, sexual, whatever. We are constantly looking for new artists to complement our regular contributors and contract artists. An artist's best efforts stand the best chance for acceptance!"

CHICAGO, 3 Illinois Center., Chicago IL 60601. (312)565-5100. Editor-in-Chief: Don Gold. Art Director: Bob Post. For active, well-educated, high-income residents of Chicago's metropolitan area concerned with quality of life and seeking insight or guidance into diverse aspects of urban/suburban life. Monthly. Circ. 220,000. Original artwork returned after publication.
Cartoons: Uses 8 cartoons/issue, all from freelancers. Receives 90 submissions/week from freelancers. Interested in "social commentary, urban life, arts and dining." Single panel. Line preferred; halftones and washes OK. Prefers to receive finished cartoons. SASE. Reports in 6 weeks. Buys first North American serial rights. Minimum payment: $100, b&w.
Illustrations: Uses 7-8 illustrations/year, all from freelancers. Interested in "subjective approach often, but depends on subject matter." Works on assignment only. Query with brochure, flyer and tear sheets, photostats, photocopies, slides and photographs to be kept on file. Accepts finished art, roughs, transparencies or tear sheets as samples. Samples not filed are returned by SASE. Reports in 4 weeks. Call to schedule an appointment to show a portfolio, which should include original/final art, tear sheets and photostats. Buys first North American serial rights. Negotiates pay for covers, color-separated and reflective art. Inside: Pays $450 minimum, color; $250 minimum, b&w ($75 for spot illustrations); on publication.

***CHIEF FIRE EXECUTIVE**, 33 Irving Place, New York NY 10003. (212)475-5400. Editor: W. Porter. Estab. 1986. Magazine emphasizing management issues relative to community fire protection for fire chiefs, corporate safety officers, fire marshals, architects and engineers. Bimonthly. Circ. 35,000. Accepts previously published material. Sample copy and art guidelines free for SASE.
Cartoons: Uses various cartoons/issue. Send query letter with finished cartoons. Call to schedule an appointment to show a portfolio. Material not filed is returned by SASE. Reports only if interested. Buys one-time rights.
Illustrations: Buys various illustrations/issue from freelancers. Works on assignment only. Send query letter with resume and tear sheets. Samples not filed are not returned. Reports only if interested. Call to schedule an appointment to show a portfolio, which should include tear sheets. Buys one-time rights. Pays on publication.

CHILD LIFE, 1100 Waterway Blvd., Box 567, Indianapolis IN 46206. (317)636-8881. Art Director: Edward F. Cortese. For children 7-9. Monthly except bimonthly February/March, April/May, June/July and August/September. Receives 3-4 submissions/week from freelance artists. Sample copy 75¢.
Illustrations: Buys 25 (average)/year on assigned themes. Especially needs health-related (exercise, safety, nutrition, etc.) themes, and stylized and realistic styles of children 7-9 years old. Send query letter with brochure showing art style or resume and tear sheets, photostats, photocopies, slides, photographs and SASE. Especially looks for an artist's ability to draw well consistently. SASE. Reports in 4 weeks. To show a portfolio, mail appropriate materials or call or write to schedule an appointment; portfolio should include original/final art, b&w and 2-color pre-separated art. Buys all rights. Pays $225/il-

lustration, color, cover. Pays for illustrations inside by the job, $60-125 (4-color), $50-100 (2-color), $25-65 (b&w); thirty days after completion of work. "All work is considered work-for-hire."
Tips: Trends in the field include "updates on realistic illustrations of people and stylized illustrations. There is a greater number of highly creative people giving rise to a diversity of styles and techniques. Changes in our operation include that we have thirty two 4-color pages available inside, and sixteen b&w only inside." Artists should "obtain copies of current issues to insure proper submission of art styles needed."

CHILDREN'S DIGEST, Box 567, Indianapolis IN 46206. (317)636-8881. Art Director: Lisa A. Nelson. Special emphasis on health, nutrition, safety and exercise for boys and girls 8-10 years of age. Monthly except bimonthly February/March, April/May, June/July and August/September. Accepts previously published material and simultaneous submissions. Sample copy 75¢; art guidelines free for SASE.
Illustrations: Uses 25-35 illustrations/issue. Works on assignment only. Send query letter with brochure, resume, samples and tear sheets to be kept on file. Write for appointment to show portfolio. Prefers photostats, slides and good photocopies as samples. Samples returned by SASE if not kept on file. Reports within 1 week. Buys all rights. Pays $225, color, cover; $25-65, b&w; $50-100, 2-color; $60-125, 4-color, inside. Pays on acceptance. "All artwork is considered work-for-hire."
Tips: Likes to see situation and story-telling illustrations with more than 1 figure. When reviewing samples, especially looks for artists' ability to bring a story to life with their illustrations. "Contemporary artists, by and large, are more experimental in the use of their mediums, and are achieving a greater range of creativity. We are aware of this, and welcome the artist who can illustrate a story that will motivate a casual viewer to read."

CHILDREN'S PLAYMATE, Box 567, Indianapolis IN 46206. (317)636-8881. Editorial Director: Beth Wood Thomas. Art Director: Linda Simmons. For ages 5-7; special emphasis on health, nutrition, exercise and safety. Published 8 times/year. Sample copy sent if artist's work might be used.
Illustrations: Uses 25-35 illustrations/issue; buys 10-20 from freelancers. Interested in "stylized, humorous, realistic themes; also nature and health." Especially needs b&w and 2-color artwork for line or halftone reproduction; text and full-color cover art. Works on assignment only. Prefers to see portfolio and samples of style. SASE. Provide brochure, flyer, tear sheet, stats or good photocopies of sample art to be kept on file. Buys all rights on a work-for-hire basis. Pays $225, color, cover; $25-65, inside; 2-color, $50-100; full-color, $125-160. Will also consider b&w art, camera-ready for puzzles, such as dot-to-dot, hidden pictures, crosswords, etc. Payment will vary. "All artwork is considered work for hire."
Tips: "Look at our publication prior to coming in; it is for *children*. Also, gain some experience in preparation of two-color and four-color overlay separations."

CHINA PAINTER, 2641 N.W. 10th St., Oklahoma City OK 73107. (405)521-1234 or (405)943-3841. Founder/Trustee: Pauline Salyer. Emphasizes porcelain china painting for those interested in the fine art. Bimonthly. Circ. 9,000. Original artwork returned after publication. Sample copy $2.75 plus 95¢ postage.
Illustrations: Send query letter. Prefers art designs in color or photographs of hand painted porcelain china art as samples. Samples returned by SASE only if requested.

THE CHRISTIAN CENTURY, 407 S. Dearborn St., Chicago IL 60605. (312)427-5380. Advertising/Production Manager: Kathleen Wind. Emphasizes religion and comments on social, political and religious subjects; includes news of current religious scene, book reviews, humor. Weekly. Circ. 38,000. Original artwork not returned after publication. Sample copy free for SASE.
Cartoons: Occasionally uses cartoons. Prefers social, political, religious (non-sexist) issues. Prefers single panel with gagline; b&w line drawings. Send query letter with finished cartoons to be kept on file unless "we can't possibly use them." Material not filed is returned only if requested. Reports only if interested. Buys all rights. Pays $15-20, b&w; on publication.
Illustrations: Uses 4 illustrations/issue; buys 1-2 from freelancers. Prefers religious and general scenes, people at various activities, books. Send query letter with resumes and photocopies to be kept on file. Samples not filed are returned by SASE. Reports only if interested. Buys all rights. Pays $50, cover and $20, inside b&w; on publication.
Tips: "Because of our newsprint, bold, uncluttered styles work the best. Too much detail gets lost."

CHRISTIAN HERALD, 40 Overlook Dr., Chappaqua NY 10514. (914)769-9000. Editor: Dean Merrill. Grassroots magazine for Christian adults (30 and up); specializes in people stories, real-life examples. Monthly. Circ. 205,000. Original artwork returned after publication. Receives 3 illustrations/week from freelance artists. Sample copy $2.
Cartoons: Rarely uses cartoons.
Illustrations: Uses 2-3 illustrations/issue; buys all from freelancers. Prefers pen & ink, airbrush, wash-

es, oils, acrylics; "pencil drawings are unacceptable." Works on assignment only. Send query letter with resume and tear sheets, photostats and slides. Samples not kept on file are returned by SASE. Reports in 4 weeks or less. Negotiates rights purchased. Pays $75-200 inside, b&w line drawings or b&w washes; $100-350 inside, color washes; upon publication.
Tips: "Present your best work only, and make contacting you as easy as possible."

CHRISTIAN HOME & SCHOOL, 3350 E. Paris Ave. SE, Grand Rapids MI 49508. (616)957-1070. Assistant Editor: Judy Zylstra. Emhasizes current, crucial issues affecting the Christian home for parents who support Christian education. Published 8 times/year. Circ. 13,000. Original artwork returned after publication. Sample copy free for SASE with 75¢ postage; art guidelines free for SASE with 22¢ postage.
Illustrations: Buys approximately 2 illustrations/issue from freelancers. Prefers family or school life themes. Works on assignment only. Send query letter with resume, tear sheets, photocopies or photographs. Samples returned by SASE. Reports only if interested. Buys first rights. Pays on publication.

THE CHRISTIAN MINISTRY, 407 S. Dearborn St., Chicago IL 60605. (312)427-5380. For the professional clergy (primarily liberal Protestant). Bimonthly. Circ. 12,000.
Cartoons: Buys 3 cartoons/issue on local church subjects. Send query letter with brochure showing art style or resume, tear sheets, photostats, photocopies and photographs. SASE. Reports in 2 weeks. Pays $20 minimum, b&w; on publication.
Illustrations: Uses 4 spot drawings/issue on local church issues; preaching, counseling, teaching, etc. Illustrations and cartoons should reflect the diversity of professional clergy—male, female, black, white, young, old, etc. To show a portfolio, mail thumbnails, original/final art, final reproduction/product, photostats, photographs and b&w. Pays $50, b&w, cover; $20, b&w; inside; on publication.
Tips: "We tend to use more abstract than concrete artwork. We insist on a balance between portrayals of male and female clergy."

THE CHRONICLE OF THE HORSE, Box 46, Middleburg VA 22117. Editor: John Strassburger. Emphasizes horses and English horse sports for dedicated competitors who ride, show and enjoy horses. Weekly. Circ. 21,000. Accepts previously published material. Sample copy available.
Cartoons: Buys 1-2 cartoons/issue from freelancers. Considers anything about English riding and horses. Prefers single panel with or without gagline; b&w line drawings or b&w washes. Send query letter with finished cartoons to be kept on file. Material not filed is returned. Reports within 2 weeks. Buys first rights. Pays $20, b&w; on publication.
Illustrations: "We use a work of art on our cover every week. The work must feature horses, but the medium is unimportant. We do not pay for this art, but we always publish a short blurb on the artist and his or her equestrian involvement, if any." Send query letter with samples to be kept on file. If accepted, insists on high-quality, b&w 8x10 photographs of the original artwork. Samples are returned. Reports within 2 weeks.

THE CHURCHMAN, 1074 23rd Ave. N., St. Petersburg FL 33704. (813)894-0097. Editor: Edna Ruth Johnson. Published 9 times/year. Circ. 10,000. Original artwork returned after publication. Sample copy available.
Cartoons: Uses 2-3 cartoons/issue. Interested in religious, political and social themes. Prefers to see finished cartoons. SASE. Reports in 1 week. Pays on acceptance.
Illustrations: Uses 2-3 illustrations/issue. Interested in themes with "social implications." Prefers to see finished art. Provide tear sheet to be kept on file for future assignments. SASE. Reports in 1 week. Pays $5, b&w spot drawings; on acceptance.
Tips: "Read current events news so you can apply it humorously."

CINCINNATI MAGAZINE, Suite 300, 35 E. 7th St., Cincinnati OH 45202. (513)421-4300. Editor: Laura Pulfer. Art Director: Thomas Hawley. Emphasizes Cincinnati living. For college-educated, ages 25+ with an excess of $35,000 incomes. Monthly. Circ. 30,000. Previously published and simultaneous submissions OK. Original artwork returned after publication. Buys all rights. Pays on acceptance.
Cartoons: Uses 2 cartoons/issue, all from freelancers. Receives 3 submissions/week from freelancers. Interested in current events, education and politics; single panel. Send finished cartoons. SASE. Reports in 3 weeks. Buys all rights on a work-for-hire basis. Pays $15-25, b&w washes; on acceptance.
Illustrations: Uses 3 illustrations/issue, all from freelancers. Receives 3 illustrations/week from freelance artists. Buys cover art and article illustrations on assigned themes. Works on assignment only. Prefers to see portfolio or samples of style. Samples returned by SASE. Reports in 3 weeks. Buys all rights on a work-for-hire basis.

CINEFANTASTIQUE, Box 270, Oak Park IL 60303. Editor-in-chief: Frederick S. Clarke. Emphasizes science fiction, horror and fantasy films for "devotees of 'films of the imagination.'" Bimonthly. Circ.

20,000. Original artwork not returned after publication. Sample copy $6.
Cartoons: Buys 0-1 cartoon/issue; buys all from freelancers. Interested in a variety of themes suited to magazine's subject matter; formats vary. Send query letter with resume and samples of style. Samples not returned. Reports in 3-4 weeks. Buys all rights. Pays $75/page or proportionally for fraction thereof; b&w; on publication.
Illustrations: Uses 1-2 illustrations/issue; buys all from freelancers. Interested in "dynamic, powerful styles, though not limited to a particular look." Works on assignment only. Send query letter with resume, brochure and samples of style to be kept on file. Samples not returned. Reports in 3-4 weeks. Buys all rights. Pays $75 maximum, inside b&w line drawings; $75 maximum, inside b&w washes; $150 maximum, cover color washes; $75 maximum, inside color washes; on publication.

***CIRCLE TRACK MAGAZINE**, 8490 Sunset Blvd., Los Angeles CA 90069. (213)854-2350. Art Director: Mike Austin. Magazine emphasizing oval-track racing for enthusiasts, ages 18-40. Monthly. Circ. 100,000. Original artwork returned after publication. Sample copy and art guidelines available.
Cartoons: Buys 3-4 cartoons/issue from freelancers. Prefers technical, automative themes. Prefers single panel, b&w line drawings. Send samples of style to be kept on file. Call for appointment to show portfolio. Material not filed is returned. Reports only if interested. Negotiates rights purchased. Pays $100, b&w; $200, color.
Illustrations: Buys 0-1 illustrations/issue from freelancers. Works on assignment only. Prefers automotive themes. Send resume. Samples not filed are returned. Reports only if interested. Call to schedule an appointment to show a portfolio, which should include original/final art. Negotiates rights purchased. Pays $200, b&w; $400, color, inside; on publication.

CIVIL WAR TIMES ILLUSTRATED, Box 8200, 2245 Kohn Rd., Harrisburg PA 17105. (717)657-9555. Art Director: Jeanne Collins. For the general public interested in well-researched historical articles. Monthly except July and August. Circ. 120,000.
Illustrations: Works on assignment only. Prefers American history (1861-1865) themes. Send query letter with photostats of historical illustration work to be kept on file. Provide rates and deadline requirements with work samples. SASE. Reports in 4 weeks. Pays $10-500, b&w or color; on acceptance or publication.
Tips: "Please send photostatic samples of historical illustration work, to be kept on file. We accept no unsolicited submissions. All freelance work is on assignment. All freelancers should provide their rates and deadline requirements with work samples. We use no cartoons."

CLAVIER, 200 Northfield Rd., Northfield IL 60093. Editor: Barbra Barlow Kreader. For teachers and students of keyboard instruments. Published 10 times/year. Buys all rights. Pays on publication for articles. Sample copy available with magazine-sized SASE.
Cartoons: Buys 10-20/year on music, mostly keyboard music. Receives 1 set of cartoons/week from freelance artists. Pays $15 on acceptance.

CLEANING MANAGEMENT, Harris Communications, 17911-C Sky Park Blvd., Irvine CA 92714. (714)261-7192. Editor-in-Chief/Art Director: R.D. Harris, Jr. Managing Editor: Teri Fivecoat-Wilhelm. For managers of in-plant cleaning maintenance crews. Monthly. Circ. 33,000. Query with samples. SASE. Receives 2-3 cartoons and 1-2 illustrations/week from freelance artists. Especially needs cover illustrations. Reports in 3 weeks. Simultaneous submissions OK. Buys first rights. Pays on publication. Free sample copy.
Cartoons: Buys 2-3/issue; single and multiple panel with gaglines. Pays $10-15, b&w line drawings.
Illustrations: Just beginning to use illustrations on the custodial field. "We used to have an illustrator do our covers 6 months out of the year's 12 issues. We could use an illustrator's services for cover work periodically." Send tear sheets, photostats, photocopies, slides and photographs. To show a portfolio, mail appropriate materials or call or write to schedule an appointment; portfolio should include thumbnails, roughs, original/final art, final reproduction/product, color, tear sheets, photostats, photographs and b&w. Pays $300-500, b&w, cover; on publication.
Tips: "Interested in offering cover assignments (four-color). We could use hi-tech material—we are a trade publication for the cleaning industry, which is reliant on equipment and chemicals for their operations. Hi-tech style is more appropriate than casual."

CLEARWATER NAVIGATOR, 112 Market St., Poughkeepsie NY 12603. (914)454-7673. Graphics Coordinator: Nora Porter. Emphasizes sailing and environmental matters for middle-upper income Easterners with a strong concern for environmental issues. Bimonthly. Circ. 8,000. Accepts previously published material. Original artwork returned after publication. Sample copy free with SASE.
Cartoons: Buys 1 cartoon/issue from freelancers. Prefers editorial lampooning—environmental themes. Prefers single panel with gaglines; b&w line drawings. Send query letter with samples of style

to be kept on file. Material not filed is returned only if requested. Reports within 1 month. Buys first rights. Pays negotiable rate, b&w; on publication.

CLEVELAND MAGAZINE, 1621 Euclid Ave., Cleveland OH 44115. (216)771-2833. City magazine emphasizing local news and information. Monthly. Circ. 50,000.
Illustrations: Buys 5-6 editorial illustrations/issue on assigned themes. Sometimes uses humorous illustrations. Send query letter with brochure showing art style or samples. Call or write to schedule an appointment to show a portfolio, which should include original/final art, final reproduction/product, color, tear sheets and photographs. Payment varies.
Tips: "Artists used on the basis of talent. We use many talented college graduates just starting out in the field. We do not publish gag cartoons but do print editorial illustrations with a humorous twist. Full page editorial illustrations usually deal with local politics, personalities and stages of general interest. Generally, we are seeing more intelligent solutions to illustration problems and better techniques."

CLUBHOUSE, Box 15, Berrien Springs MI 49103. (616)471-9009. Editor: Elaine Meseraull. Magazine emphasizing stories, puzzles and illustrations for children ages 9-15. Published 10 times/year. Circ. 17,000. Accepts previously published material. Returns original artwork after publication if requested. Sample copy for SASE with postage or 3 oz.
Cartoons: Buys 2/issue. Prefers animals, kids and family situation themes; single panel with gagline, vertical format; b&w line drawings. Accepts previously published material. Pays $10-12 on acceptance.
Illustrations: Buys 19-20/issue on assignment only. Assignments made on basis of samples on file. Send query letter with resume and samples to be kept on file. Samples returned by SASE within 1 month. Portfolio should include final reproduction/product, tear sheets, photostats and b&w. Usually buys one-time rights. Pays according to published size: $30 b&w, cover; $25 full page, $18 half page, $15 third page, $12 quarter page, $7.50 spots, b&w inside; on acceptance.

COACHING REVIEW, 333 River Rd., Ottawa, Ontario K1L 8H9 Canada. (613)746-0036. Editor: Steve Newman. Emphasizes volunteer as well as paid sports coaching. Bimonthly. Circ. 15,000. Receives 2-3 cartoons and 2-3 illustrations/week from freelance artists. Especially needs good practical applied information that is original; creative illustration; sport specific and life-like illustration. Original artwork returned after publication. Free sample copy.
Cartoons: Buys 4 cartoons/issue from freelancers. Interested in coaching-related situations. Prefers single panel b&w line drawings with or without gaglines. Send query letter with brochure showing art style or slides. Reports in 2 weeks. Pays $25-50, b&w; on publication. Buys one-time rights.
Illustrations: Buys 2-8 illustrations/issue from freelancers. Illustrations should be in the style of "creative realism . . . depicting athletes in action." Prefers color washes for cover and inside; b&w line drawings for inside. Reports in 2 weeks. Call to schedule an appointment to show a portfolio, which should include color, tear sheets, photostats and b&w. Pays $400, b&w, and $600, color, cover; $250-450, b&w; on acceptance.
Tips: There is a trend toward "realistic illustration showing coaching techniques. Read the magazine before sending in work."

COBBLESTONE MAGAZINE, 20 Grove St., Peterborough NH 03458. (603)924-7209. Editor: Carolyn Yoder. Emphasizes American history; features stories, supplemental nonfiction, fiction, biographies, plays, activities, poetry for children between 8 and 14. Monthly. Circ. 45,000. Accepts previously published material and simultaneous submissions. Sample copy $2.95. Material must relate to theme of issue; subjects/topics published in guidelines which are free with SASE.
Illustrations: Uses variable number of illustrations/issue; buys 1-2/issue from freelancers. Prefers historical theme as it pertains to a specific feature. Works on assignment only. Send query letter with brochure, resume, business card, samples or tear sheets to be kept on file. Call or write for appointment to show portfolio. Prefers photocopies as samples. Samples not kept on file are returned by SASE. Buys all rights. Payment varies. Artists should request illustration guidelines. Pays on publication.
Tips: "Study issues of the magazine for style used. Send samples and update samples once or twice a year to help keep your name and work fresh in our minds."

COINS MAGAZINE, 700 E. State St., Iola WI 54990. (715)445-2214. Editor: Arlyn G. Sieber. Emphasizes coin collecting as a hobby or business for collectors of all forms of coins, paper money, medals, etc. Monthly. Circ. 70,000. Previously published material and simultaneous submissions OK. Original artwork not returned after publication. Free sample copy for SASE.
Illustrations: Buys 1-2/issue from freelancers. Works on assignment only. Provide brochure and samples to be kept on file. Reports in 2 weeks. Buys first rights and reprint rights. Pays $10-50, inside b&w line drawings; $10-50, inside b&w washes; $75-200, cover color washes; $25-100, inside color washes; on acceptance.

COLLISION, Box M, Franklin MA 02038. (617)528-6211. Audience is autobody repair, dealers and towing companies. For management in small businesses. Published 9 times/year. Circ. 21,000. Accepts previously published material. Sample copy $2 (postage); guidelines free.
Cartoons: Buys 1 cartoon/issue. Prefers themes that are "positive or corrective attitudes." Considers single panel with gagline; b&w line drawings. Send roughs or finished cartoons. Material is returned by SASE. Reports within 2 weeks. Buys first rights and reprint rights. Pays $12.50/cartoon for b&w line art; on acceptance.
Illustrations: Buys 1 illustration/issue from freelancers. Themes and styles depend on editorial content (2 year advance). Send query letter with tear sheets and photocopies. Samples are returned. Reports within 2 weeks. Write to schedule an appointment to show a portfolio, which should include roughs, original/final art, color, tear sheets, photographs and b&w. Buys first rights and reprint rights. Pays $25 and up for b&w inside; on acceptance.
Tips: "Send photocopies of any work so we can see what they have to offer in style, capability and technique."

***THE COLORADO ALUMNUS**, Koenig Alumni Center, University of Colorado, Boulder CO 80309. (303)492-8484. Editor: Ronald A. James. For university administrators, alumni, librarians and legislators. Published 6 times/year. Circ. 90,000. Previously published work and simultaneous submissions OK. Original artwork not returned after publication. Free sample copy.
Cartoons: Uses 1 cartoon/issue from freelancers. Receives 2-3 submissions/week from freelancers. Interested in sports, humor through youth, environment, campus and problems in higher education. Prefers to see finished cartoons. SASE. Reports in 2 weeks. "Work becomes the property of the University of Colorado." Pays $25 minimum, line drawings and halftones; on acceptance.
Illustrations: Uses 2-3 illustrations/issue from freelancers. Receives 1-2 submissions/week from freelancers. Interested in sports, campus and higher education. Send query letter with samples. SASE. Reports in 2 weeks. "Work becomes the property of the University of Colorado." Call or write to schedule an appointment to show a portfolio, which should include roughs, original/final art and final reproduction/product. Pays $25 minimum, b&w line drawings cover and inside; on acceptance.

COLUMBIA, Drawer 1670, New Haven CT 06507. (203)772-2130, ext. 263-64. Editor: Elmer Von Feldt. Art Director: John Cummings. Fraternal magazine of the Knights of Columbus; indepth interviews on family life, social problems, education, current events and apostolic activities as seen from the Catholic viewpoint. Monthly. Circ. 1,374,257. Original artwork not returned after publication. Buys all rights. Sample copy available.
Cartoons: Buys 3 cartoons/issue from freelancers. Interested in pungent, captionless humor. Send roughs or finished cartoons to be kept on file. SASE. Reports in 2 weeks. Buys all rights. Pays $50; on acceptance.
Illustrations: Buys 1 cover illustration/issue; buys all from freelancers. Send query letter with tear sheets or slides to be kept on file for future assignments. SASE. Reports in 4 weeks. To show a portfolio, mail color, tear sheets and photographs. Buys all rights. Pays $1,000, full-color cover design; on acceptance.

***COLUMBIA JOURNALISM REVIEW**, 700 Journalism Bldg., Columbia University, New York NY 10027. Contact: Managing Editor or Art Director. Emphasizes analysis of the performance of various communications media. For professional journalists, government leaders and students. Bimonthly. Circ. 40,000. Query with resume and samples. Previously published work OK. Original artwork returned after publication.
Illustrations: Uses 1-6 illustrations/issue, all from freelancers. Interested in political and satirical themes and caricatures. Works on assignment only. Samples returned "only if necessary"; prefers "photocopies or other disposable material." Reports back on future assignment possibilities. Provide calling card, brochure, flyer, tear sheet or photocopies to be kept on file for future assignments. Prefers to see portfolio or samples of style. Reporting time varies. Buys one-time reproduction rights. Pays $500-800; 4-color. Inside: Pays $100-200, spot drawings; on publication.

COLUMBUS MONTHLY, Columbus Monthly Publishing Corp., 171 E. Livingston Ave., Columbus OH 43215. (614)464-4567. Editor: Max S. Brown. Associate Publisher: Sanford Meisel. Regional/city publication. Emphasizes subjects of general interest primarily to Columbus and central Ohio. Circ. 40,000. Sample copy $1.75.
Illustrations: Uses 4-6 illustrations/month; buys most from freelancers. Interested in contemporary editorial illustration. Works on assignment only. Samples returned with SASE. Provide resume, business card, letter of inquiry and brochure to be kept on file for future assignments. Prefers to see portfolio (finished art). Buys publication rights. Pays $200-350, color washes and full-color art, cover; $60 minimum, b&w line drawings and washes, inside.

***COMMON LIVES/LESBIAN LIVES**, Box 1553, Iowa City IA 52264. Contact: Editorial Collective. Magazine emphasizing lesbian lives for lesbians of all ages, races, nationalities, and sizes. Quarterly. Circ. 2,000. Original artwork returned after publication if SASE provided. Sample copy $4.
Cartoons: Prefers lesbian themes. Send finished cartoons to be kept on file. Material not kept on file is returned only if SASE provided. Reports within 4 months.
Illustrations: Prefers lesbian themes. Samples not filed are returned only if SASE provided. Reports back within 3 months.

COMMONWEAL, 232 Madison Ave., New York NY 10016. (212)683-2042. Editor: Peter Steinfels. National journal published by Catholic laypeople emphasizing political, social, cultural and religious issues. Biweekly. Circ. 18,000. Accepts previously published material. Original artwork not returned after publication.
Cartoons: Buys 1-3 cartoons/issue from freelancers. Prefers single panel without gagline; b&w line drawings. Send finished cartoons to be kept on file. Material not filed is not returned. Reports only if interested. Buys one-time rights. Pays $10-15, b&w; on publication.
Illustrations: Buys 0-1 illustration/issue from freelancers. Prefers political/social/religious themes; simple drawings. Send query letter with brochure showing art style or samples and tear sheets. Samples not filed are not returned. Reports only if interested. Write to schedule an appointment to show a portfolio, which should include original/final art. Buys one-time rights. Pays $25, cover, b&w; $10-15, inside, b&w; on publication.

COMMUNICATION WORLD, c/o IABC, Suite 940, 870 Market St., San Francisco CA 94102. (415)433-3400. Managing Editor: Gloria Gordon. Emphasizes communication, public relations (international) for members of International Association of Business Communicators: corporate and nonprofit businesses, hospitals, government communicators, universities, etc. who produce internal and external publications, press releases, annual reports and customer magazines. Monthly except June/July combined issue. Circ. 17,000. Accepts previously published material. Original artwork returned after publication. Sample copy available.
Cartoons: Buys 1-5 cartoons/issue from freelancers. Considers international communication and publication themes. Prefers single panel with or without gagline; b&w line drawings or washes. Send query letter with samples of style or finished cartoons to be kept on file. Material not filed is returned only if requested. Reports only if interested. Write or call for appointment to show portfolio. Buys first rights, one-time rights or reprint rights; negotiates rights purchased. Pays $25-50, b&w; on publication.
Illustrations: Buys 3-10 illustrations/issue from freelancers. Theme and style are compatible to individual article. Send query letter with samples to be kept on file; write or call for appointment to show portfolio. Accepts photostats, tear sheets, photocopies, slides or photographs as samples. Samples not filed are returned only if requested. Reports only if interested. Buys first rights, one-time rights or reprint rights; negotiates rights purchased. Pays $175, b&w and $250, color, cover; $150, b&w and $200, color, inside; on publication.
Tips: Artwork "must be professionally displayed. Show understanding of subject, disciplined in use of media, general knowledge of working with editorial design problems."

COMPUTER DECISIONS, 10 Mulholland Dr., Hasbrouck Heights NJ 07604. Art Director: Bonnie Meyer. For computer-involved management in industry, finance, academia, etc.; well-educated, sophisticated and highly paid. Monthly. Circ. 175,000.
Illustrations: Buys 2-3/issue. Assigned to illustrate columns and some feature stories. Works on assignment only. Prefers to see portfolio or samples of style. Send query letter with brochure or samples to be kept on file. Reports in 1 week. Call or write to schedule an appointment to show a portfolio, which should include original/final art, final reproduction/product, color and tear sheets. Buys all rights. Pays $150, b&w and $350, color, inside; on acceptance.
Tips: "Chartists with good ideas needed. No cartoons—realistic, slick drawings/renderings only. Ability to draw people well."

***COMPUTER LIVING/NEW YORK**, 5793 Tyndall Ave., Riverdale NY 10741. Publisher: Andrew Wolf. Newspaper emphasizing personal computers for personal computer users in New York metro area. Monthly. Circ. 30,000. Accepts previously published material. Original artwork returned after publication. Sample copy and art guidelines available.
Cartoons: Buys 3-4 cartoons/issue from freelancers. Prefers single panel with gagline; b&w line drawings. Send query letter with samples of style and finished cartoons to be kept on file. Material not filed is returned. Reports only if interested. Buys one-time rights.
Illustrations: Buys 3-4 illustrations/issue from freelancers. Works on assignment only. Send query letter with brochure showing art style or resume and photocopies. Samples not filed are returned only if interested. Write to schedule an appointment to show a portfolio, which should include tear sheets and photostats. Buys one-time rights. Negotiates payment; pays on publication.

COMPUTER MERCHANDISING, Eastman Publishing, Suite 660, 3550 Wilshire Blvd., Los Angeles CA 90010. (213)383-5800. Art Director: Michael Walters. Emphasizes computers; "we publish trade magazines directed to reach retailers of high-technology products." Semimonthly. Circ. 25,000. Accepts previously published material. Does not return original artwork after publication.
Illustrations: Buys 10-15 illustrations/issue from freelancers. Prefers pen & ink, airbrush, watercolor. Works on assignment only. Send brochure and samples to be kept on file. Call for appointment to show portfolio. Prefers tear sheets, photostats or photocopies as samples. Samples not filed are not returned. Reports back only if interested. Buys all rights. Pays $75 for b&w and $125 for color, inside; on publication.

CONNECTICUT MAGAZINE, 636 Kings Hwy., Fairfield CT 06430. (203)576-1207. Art Director: Lori Bruzinski Wendin. Emphasizes issues and entertainment in Connecticut for "upscale, 40-50's, Connecticut residents." Monthly. Circ. 66,000. Accepts previously published material. Original artwork returned after publication.
Illustrations: Uses 1-3 illustrations/issue; buys all from freelancers. Works on assignment only. Send query letter with brochure, business card, samples or tear sheets to be kept on file. Call for appointment to show portfolio. Samples not filed are not returned. Pays $200-600, color, cover; $75-400, b&w, $200-600, color, inside; on publication.

CONSERVATIVE DIGEST, Suite 800, National Press Building, Washington DC 20045. (202)662-8919. Editor: Scott Stanley. Concerns activities and political issues for "new right" conservatives. Circ. 40,000. Monthly. Simultaneous submissions and previously published work OK. Original artwork returned after publication. Buys one-time and reprint rights. Sample copy $2.25.
Cartoons: Uses 6 cartoons/issue. Receives 80 submissions/week from freelancers and syndicates. Interested in current events and politics (conservative view). Send finished cartoons or veloxes. SASE. Reports in 3 weeks. Buys reprint rights. Pays $15-100, b&w line drawings; on publication.

***CONSERVATORY OF AMERICAN LETTERS**, Box 123, South Thomaston ME 04858. (207)354-6550. Editor: Bob Olmsted. Estab. 1986. Newsletter emphasizing literature for literate, cultured adults. Quarterly. Accepts previously published material with proper written evidence of right to re-use. Original artwork returned after publication. Sample copy free for SASE with 22¢ postage.
Illustrations: Expects to need approximately 6 covers in '86. Send brochure showing art style or samples. Samples not filed are returned by SASE. Reports back within 15 days. To show a portfolio, mail appropriate materials, which should include photographs. Buys first rights, one-time rights or reprint rights. Pays $100, color, cover; on acceptance.

CONSTRUCTION EQUIPMENT OPERATION AND MAINTENANCE, Construction Publications, Inc., Box 1689, Cedar Rapids IA 52406. (319)366-1597. Editor-in-Chief: C.K. Parks. Concerns heavy construction and industrial equipment for contractors, machine operators, mechanics and local government officials involved with construction. Bimonthly. Circ. 67,000. Simultaneous submissions OK. Original artwork not returned after publication. Free sample copy.
Cartoons: Uses 8-10 cartoons/issue, all from freelancers. Interested in themes "related to heavy construction industry" or "cartoons that make contractors and their employees 'look good' and feel good about themselves"; multiple panel. Send finished cartoons. SASE. Reports within 2 weeks. Buys all rights but may reassign rights to artist after publication. Pays $10-15, b&w.
Illustrations: Uses 20+ illustrations/issue; "very few" are from freelancers. Pays $80-125; on acceptance.

THE CONSTRUCTION SPECIFIER, 601 Madison St., Alexandria VA 22314. (703)684-0300. Editor: Kimberly C. Smith. Emphasizes commercial (*not* residential) design and building for architects, engineers and other A/E professionals. Monthly. Circ. 18,000. Returns original artwork after publication if requested. Sample copy free for SASE with $2.07 postage.
Illustrations: Buys 1-2 illustrations/issue from freelancers. Works on assignment only. Send query letter with photostats, tear sheets, photocopies, slides or photographs. Samples not filed are returned by SASE. Reports back only if interested. Buys one-time rights. Pays on publication.

***CONSUMERS DIGEST**, 5705 N. Lincoln Ave., Chicago IL 60659. (312)275-3590. Senior Art Director: Lori Weber. Magazine emphasizing consumer products for post 30 consumers. Monthly. Circ. 1,200,000. Accepts previously published material. Original artwork returned after publication. Sample copy available.
Illustrations: Buys 5-10 illustrations/issue from freelancers. Works on assignment only. "No restraints except we buy more realistic art than cartoon art." Send query letter with brochure showing art style or tear sheets, photostats and slides. Samples not filed are returned by SASE. Does not report back.

To show a portfolio, mail original/final art, final reproduction/product, color, tear sheets, photostats and photographs. Buys reprint rights. Pays $1,000, color, cover; $100-700, b&w; and $200-900, color, inside; on acceptance.

CONTACTS, Box 407, North Chatham NY 12132. Editor: Joseph Strack. For dental laboratory owners and managers and dental technician staffs. Bimonthly.
Cartoons: Buys 3-4/issue on the dental laboratory industry. Mail art. Reports in 1 week. Buys first serial rights. Pays $25; on acceptance.

***CONTEMPORARY CHRISTIAN MAGAZINE**, Box 6300, Laguna Hills CA 92653. Art Director: Lynn Rassol. Reviews and comments on personalities, music, arts, entertainment and issues relevant to Christian adults. Emphasis on music. Monthly. Circ. 40,000. Accepts previously published material and simultaneous submissions if so specified and with which publications. Originals returned to artist after publication only if requested and accompanied by required postage. Sample copy $1.95 and music.
Cartoons: Interested in using cartoons as editorial fillers. Should be music oriented. Prefers single panel with hand-lettered gagline; *New Yorker* style. Mail prints or reproducible photocopies of finished cartoons to be kept on file; do not call. Material not kept on file is not returned. Reports only if cartoon is used. Buys one-time rights or negotiates. Pays $15-25, b&w; 30 days after publication. Return address, phone and credit information must be on the back of each cartoon.
Illustrations: Buys 1 illustration/issue from freelancers. Works on assignment only. Send query letter with brochure showing art style or photocopies to be kept on file. Samples not kept on file are returned by SASE. Reports only if interested. Call to schedule an appointment to show a portfolio, which should include original/final art, final reproduction/product and b&w. Buys one-time rights or negotiates. Pays $50-150, b&w, inside; 30 days after publication.
Tips: "Include a self-addressed stamped postcard as a response card. That way it will be sent back (usually right away). Type inquiries, it looks more professional."

***CONTRACT**, Gralla Publications, 1515 Broadway, New York NY 10036. Editor: Len Corlin. Executive Editor: Roberta Walton. Provides "ideas for interior installations, product information, and news on developments in the commercial interior design industry." Monthly. Circ. 35,000.
Illustrations: Buys 2-4/year on interior design; all on assignment only. Mail art or samples, or arrange interview to show portfolio. SASE. Reports in 3 weeks. Buys one-time rights. Pays $300, full-color renderings, cover; pays $150-250, b&w line drawings and washes, inside; on publication.
Tips: "Illustrators should not be shy. Call editor(s) to show portfolio."

DAVID C. COOK PUBLISHING CO., 850 N. Grove Ave., Elgin IL 60120. (312)741-2400. Director of Design Services: Gregory Eaton Clark. Publishers of magazines, teaching booklets, visual aids and film strips. For Christians, "all age groups."
Illustrations: Buys about 30 illustrations/week from freelancers, b&w line drawings and full-color art. Send tear sheets, slides or photocopies of previously published work; include self-promo pieces. No samples returned unless requested and accompanied by SASE. Reports in 2-4 weeks to personal queries only. Works on assignment only. Pays on acceptance $50 minimum for inside b&w; $275-300, for color cover and $100 minimum for inside color. Considers complexity of project, skill and experience of artist and turnaround time when establishing payment. Buys all rights. Originals can be returned in most cases.
Tips: "We do not buy illustrations or cartoons on speculation. We welcome those just beginning their careers, but it helps if the samples are presented in a neat and professional manner. Our deadlines are generous but must be met. We send out checks as soon as final art is approved, usually within 2 weeks of our receiving the art. We want art radically different from normal Sunday School art. Fresh, dynamic, the highest of quality is our goal; art that appeals to preschoolers to senior citizens; realistic to humorous, all media."

COOKBOOKS FOR CAUSES, Drawer 5007, Bend OR 97708. (503)382-6878. Contact: Kenneth Asher. Produces cookbooks for fundraisers. Buys 10-15 covers/year. Write for guidelines; submit color photographs of art. Reports in 6 weeks. Negotiates payment. Buys all rights.

CORPORATE FITNESS & RECREATION, 825 S. Barrington Ave., Los Angeles CA 90049. Publisher: Martin Waldman. Art Director: Tom Medsger. Emphasizes health/fitness corporate programs and professional news.
First Contact & Terms: Submit brochure/flyer to be kept on file for possible future assignment. Reports only when assignment available. Buys all rights. Pays $60-up, spot art; $400, full-color cover; on acceptance.

***CORPORATE MONTHLY**, 105 Chestnut St., Philadelphia PA 19106. (215)629-1611. Publisher: Bruce Anthony. Magazine emphasizing regional business in Philadelphia area for senior level executives. Monthly. Circ. 25,000. Accepts previously published material. Original artwork returned after publication. Sample copy free for 9x12 SASE with 78¢ postage.
Cartoons: Buys 5 cartoons/issue from freelancers. Prefers single panel. Send query letter with samples of style to be kept on file. Call to schedule an appointment to show a portfolio. Material not kept on file is returned only if requested. Reports only if interested. Negotiates payment.
Illustrations: Buys 0-3 illustrations/issue from freelancers. Works on assignment only. Send query letter with samples. Samples not filed are returned by SASE. Reports only if interested. Call to schedule an appointment to show a portfolio. Negotiates payment; on publication.

CORVETTE FEVER MAGAZINE, Box 44620, Fort Washington MD 20744. (301)839-2221. Editor: Patricia Stivers. For "Corvette owners and enthusiasts, average ages: 25-55." Bimonthly. Circ. 35,000. Original artwork not returned after publication. Sample copy $2; general art guidelines for SASE.
Cartoons: Uses 2 cartoons/issue; buys 2-4 from freelancers. Themes "must deal with Corvettes"; single panel with gagline, b&w line drawings. Send roughs. Samples returned by SASE. Reports in 6 weeks. Buys first rights and reprint rights. Pays $15-35, b&w; on publication.
Illustrations: Uses 4-6 illustrations/issue; buys 3-6 from freelancers. Themes "must deal with Corvettes." Provide resume, brochure and tear sheets to be kept on file for possible future assignments. Send roughs with samples of style. Samples returned by SASE. Reports in 6 weeks. Buys first rights and reprint rights. Pays $10-75, inside, b&w line drawings; on publication.

COSMOPOLITAN, 224 W. 57th St., New York NY 10019. Cartoon Editor: Stephen Whitty. For career women, ages 18-34.
Cartoons: Works largely with extensive present list of cartoonists. Receives 200 cartoons/week from freelance artists. Especially looks for "light, sophisticated, female-oriented cartoons."
Tips: "Less and less freelance work is purchased—the competition is tougher. Choose your topics and submissions carefully. We buy only sophisticated cartoons that stress a *positive* view of women—females as the subject of the cartoon but not the butt of the joke. Please read the magazine—there are only about 20 cartoonists who really understand our needs. I can't stress this enough." When reviewing an artist's work, "appropriateness to the magazine comes first. Sense of humor comes next, then quality of art. We like pretty people to be featured in our magazine—even in the cartoons. Be aware of *all* the outlets available to you—papers, ad agencies—then study the market *you're* trying to break into. Every magazine has its own slant. Read half a dozen issues and then ask yourself—can I describe, in two or three sentences, a typical reader's concerns, interests, age and economic background?"

THE COVENANT COMPANION, 5101 N. Francisco Ave., Chicago IL 60625. (312)784-3000. Editor: James R. Hawkinson. Emphasizes Christian life and faith. Monthly. Circ. 27,500. Original artwork returned after publication if requested. Sample copy $1.50.
Illustrations: Uses b&w drawings or photos about Easter, Advent, Lent, and Christmas. Works on assignment only. Write or submit art 10 weeks in advance of season. SASE. Reports "within a reasonable time." Buys first North American serial rights. Pays in month after publication.

CREATIVE CHILD & ADULT QUARTERLY, The National Association for Creative Children and Adults, Teachers College 910, Ball State University, Muncie IN 47306. Editor: Dr. Wallace D. Draper. Emphasizes creativity in *all* its applications for parents, teachers, students, administrators in the professions. Quarterly. Original artwork returned after publication if SASE is enclosed. Sample copy, special price $8; regular price $10.
Cartoons: Uses 1 cartoon/issue. Prefers single panel; b&w line drawings. Send samples of style or finished cartoons to be kept on file. Material not kept on file is returned by SASE. Reports within weeks. Pays in copies of publication.
Illustrations: Uses various number of illustrations/issue, including some humorous and cartoon-style illustrations. Send query letter and original work. Samples returned by SASE. Reports within weeks. Pays in copies of publication.

***CREATIVE IDEAS FOR LIVING**, 820 Shades Creek Pkwy., Birmingham AL 35202. (205)877-6000. Art Director: Lane Gregory. Magazine emphasizing lifestyle for women 28-40. Monthly. Circ. 750,000. Original artwork returned after publication. Sample copy free for SASE.
Cartoons: Buys 1 cartoon/issue. Prefers b&w line drawings; b&w or color washes. Send samples of style to be kept on file. Write or call for an appointment to show a portfolio. Material not filed is returned only if requested. Reports only if interested. Negotiates rights purchased. Negotiates payment.
Illustrations: Buys 3-4 illustrations/issue from freelancers. Send query letter with brochure showing art style or resume and samples. Samples returned only if requested. Reports only if interested. To show

a portfolio, mail final reproduction/product, color and tear sheets. Negotiates rights purchased. Negotiates payment. Pays on acceptance.

CREDITHRIFTALK, Box 59, 601 NW Second St., Evansville IN 47701. (812)464-6638. Editor: Gregory E. Thomas. Emphasizes consumer finance for employees of Credithrift Financial. Monthly. Circ. 4,200+. Free sample copy and art guidelines for SASE (60¢ in stamps).
Cartoons: "We use illustrative cartoons done on an assignment basis only." Send samples of style. Samples not returned. Reports in 2 weeks. Negotiates rights purchased. Pays $25 minimum/cartoon; on acceptance.
Illustrations: Works on assignment only. Send business card, samples or tear sheets, or photocopies of samples or tear sheets to be kept on file for possible future assignments. Likes "variety in samples." Samples not returned. Reports in 2 weeks. Negotiates rights purchased. Pays $50 minimum/b&w illustration.
Tips: "We are using more two-color and more process color. I am looking for sources for airbrush and other types of color illustration."

CROSSCURRENTS, 2200 Glastonbury Rd., Westlake Village CA 91361. Graphic Arts Editor: Michael Hughes. "This is a literary quarterly that uses graphic art as accompaniment to our fiction and poetry. We are aimed at an educated audience interested in reviewing a selection of fiction, poetry and graphic arts." Circ. 3,000. Original artwork returned after publication. Sample copy $5; art guidelines available for SASE.
Illustrations: Uses 5-7 illustrations/issue; buys 75% from freelancers. Considers "any work of high quality and in good taste that will reproduce b&w, 5x7", with clarity, including but not limited to line drawings, charcoal sketches, etchings, lithographs, engravings; vertical format. No pornography." Send brochure, resume, tearsheets, photostats, slides and photographs. No simultaneous submissions or previously published material. SASE. Reports in 3 weeks. To show a portfolio, mail appropriate material. Buys first rights. Pays $10 minimum cover or inside b&w line drawings and b&w washes; $15 minimum cover, color washes; on acceptance.
Tips: "Study a sample copy of our publication and read our guidelines to understand what it is that we use, and what styles we publish." When reviewing an artist's work, "we look for technical excellence, strength of style, something of worth. A professional, neat submission is a must, of course."

***CRUISING WORLD**, 524 Thames St., Newport RI 02840. (401)847-1588. Assistant Art Director: Rachel Cocroft. Magazine emphasizing cruising sailboats for an audience with a $98,000 average income, most own their own boat, approx. 40-50 years old. Circ. 118,000. Returns original artwork after publication. Sample copy and art guidelines available "if we're interested in their work."
Illustrations: Buys 10 or more illustrations/issue from freelancers. Works on assignment only. Prefers b&w or four-color marine, boat-oriented editorial illustrations as well as b&w technical line illustrations. Send query letter with brochure showing art style or tear sheets, photostats, photocopies, slides and photographs. Samples not filed are returned by SASE. To show a portfolio, mail final product, color, tear sheets, photostats, photographs, b&w. Buys first rights. Pays $100-300, b&w; $150-650, color, inside; on publication.
Tips: "There is a wider appeal of boat ownership and cruising. For the magazine, freelance artists must be familiar with boats, what they look and feel like when sailing. An artist must have ability to render human anatomy accurately in scale with marine equipment and also to interpret editorial matter."

CRUSADER, Box 7259, Grand Rapids MI 49510. (616)241-5616. Editor: G. Richard Broene. For boys ages 9-14. Published 7 times/year by the Calvinist Cadet Corps. Previously published work OK. Sample copy and art guidelines for SASE.
Cartoons: Buys 1/issue. Submit resume. Reports in 6 weeks. Minimum payment: $10, single panel; $20, double panel; $25, full page. "We especially look for originality and quality. If artists care about their work, they send it in clean, neat, appropriate packaging."
Illustrations: Buys 1 story illustration/issue.
Tips: "Too many artists copy existing styles. We are looking for fresh approaches."

CRUSADER, Baptist Brotherhood Commission, 1548 Poplar, Memphis TN 38104. (901)272-2461. Art Director: Herschel Wells. Christian-oriented mission magazine for boys grades 1-6. Monthly. Circ. 100,000. Photocopied and simultaneous submissions OK. Original artwork returned after publication, if requested.
Illustrations: Uses 10 illustrations/issue; buys 2/issue from freelancers. Interested in boys' youth and boys' activities. Works on assignment only. Sample copy provided "if we consider using the artist after we've seen samples." Send roughs or samples of style, which may be returned or duplicated to be kept on file. Samples not filed are returned by SASE. Reports in 3 weeks. To show a portfolio, mail original/

final art, tear sheets and photostats. Buys first North American serial rights. Pays $100, b&w, and up to $250, color, cover; up to $120, b&w, inside; on acceptance.
Tips: "Please send several samples if you have more than one style. We must see figure work as most of our art requires this."

CRYPTOLOGIA, Rose-Hulman Institute of Technology, Terre Haute IN 47803. (812)877-1511. Managing Editor: Brian J. Winkel. Emphasizes all aspects of cryptology: data (computer) encryption, history, military, science, ancient languages, secret communications for scholars and hobbyists. Quarterly. Circ. 1,000. Accepts previously published material and simultaneous submissions. Original artwork returned after publication.
Cartoons: Uses 2-3 cartoons/issue. Prefers plays on language, communication (secret), ancient language decipherment, computer encryption. Prefers single, double or multi panel, with or without gagline; b&w line drawings or b&w washes. Send query letter with samples of style, roughs, or finished cartoons to be kept on file. Material not kept on file is returned by SASE. Reports within 2 weeks. Negotiates rights purchased. Pays on acceptance.

***CURRENTS**, Box 6847, 314 N. 20th St., Colorado Springs CO 80904. Editor: Eric Leeper. Magazine emphasizing whitewater river running for kayakers, rafters and canoeists; from beginner to expert; middle-class, college-educated. Bimonthly. Circ. 10,000. Accepts previously published material. Original artwork returned after publication. Sample copy 75¢. Art guidelines free for SASE with 22¢ postage.
Cartoons: Buys 0-1 cartoon/issue from freelancers. Themes *must* deal with whitewater rivers or river running. Prefers single panel with gagline; b&w line drawings. Send query letter with roughs of proposed cartoon(s) to be kept on file. Samples not kept on file are returned by SASE. Reports within 6 weeks. Buys one-time rights. Pays $10-35, b&w.
Illustrations: Buys 0-2 illustrations/issue from freelancers. Works on assignment only. Themes must deal with rivers or river running. Send query letter with proposed illustrations. Samples not filed returned by SASE. Reports within 6 weeks. To show a portfolio, mail appropriate materials, which should include "whatever they feel is necessary." Buys one-time rights. Pays $10-35, b&w; inside. Pays on publication.
Tips: "Make sure you have seen a sample copy of *Currents* and our guidelines. Be sure you know about rivers and whitewater river sports."

CURRICULUM REVIEW, 517 S. Jefferson St., Chicago IL 60607. (312)939-3010. Editor-in-Chief: Irene M. Goldman. Emphasizes material of interest to teachers, superintendents, curriculum coordinators, librarians (schools of education and school libraries). Bimonthly. Circ. 10,000. Original artwork returned after publication. Sample copy free for SASE ($1.75 postage).
Cartoons: Uses variable number of cartoons/issue. Prefers single, double or multiple panel with gagline; b&w line drawings. Send query letter with samples of style to be kept on file. Material not kept on file is returned by SASE. Reports only if interested. Write for appointment to show portfolio. Negotiates payment. Pays on publication.
Illustrations: Send query letter with photostats and tear sheets to be kept on file. Samples not kept on file are returned by SASE. Reports within 1 month only if interested. Buys reprint rights. Negotiates payment. Pays on publication.

CWC/PETERBOROUGH, 80 Pine St., Peterborough NH 03458. (617)924-9471. Creative Director: Christine Destrempes. "We publish 3 microcomputing monthlies and one bi-monthly: *AmigaWorld*, *80 Micro*, *RUN*, and *inCider*." Circ. 140,000-550,000. Accepts previously published material. Returns original artwork after publication. Sample copy free for SASE; art guidelines available.
Cartoons: Minimal number of cartoons purchased from freelancers. Prefers single panel without gaglines; b&w line drawings, b&w washes or color washes. Send query letter with samples of style or finished cartoons to be kept on file. Material not filed is returned only if requested. Reports within 5 weeks. Rights purchased and payment varies; pays within 30 days.
Illustrations: Buys 8-20 illustrations/issue from freelancers. Works on assignment only. Send query letter with resume, and tear sheets to be kept on file. Samples not filed are returned only if requested. Reports within 5 weeks. To show a portfolio, mail final reproduction/product, color and b&w or call or write to schedule an appointment. Rights purchased and payments vary; pays on acceptance.
Tips: "The quality of presentation is very important."

CYCLE WORLD, 1499 Monrovia Ave., Newport Beach CA 92663. (714)720-5300. For active motorcyclists who are "young, affluent, educated, very perceptive." Monthly. Circ. 375,000. "Unless otherwise noted in query letter, we will keep spot drawings in our files for use as future fillers." Previously published work OK. Free sample copy and artist's guidelines.
Cartoons: Uses 6 cartoons/year, all from freelancers. Receives 1 submission/week from freelancers.

Interested in motorcycling; single or double panel with gagline. Send resume or finished art or arrange interview. Buys all rights. Pays $50-250, b&w line drawings, washes and gray opaques; $50-400, color.
Illustrations: Art Director: Elaine Anderson. Uses 7-8 illustrations/issue, all from freelancers. Receives 25-30 submissions/week from freelancers. Interested in motorcycling and assigned themes. Works on assignment only. Prefers to see resume and samples. Samples returned, if originals; kept if photocopies. Reports back on future assignment possibilities to artists who phone. Does not report back to artists who contact through mail. Call or write to schedule an appointment to show a portfolio, which should include original/final art, final reproduction/product, color, tear sheets and b&w. Provide brochure, tear sheet, letter of inquiry and business card to be kept on file for future assignments. Buys all rights. Pays $300-500, cover. Pays $25-150, b&w; $100-400, color; $75, spot drawings, inside; on publication.
Tips: "We use a lot of spot drawings as fillers. black-and-white motorcyle illustrations used mostly. Call or write. Do not send original art or unsolicited art."

D.S. MAGAZINES, Sharon Publications, Edrei Communications, 1086 Teaneck Rd., Teaneck NJ 07666. (201)569-5055. Art Director in Chief: Paul Castori. Publisher of *Tiger Beat*, *Tiger Beat Star*, *Right On!*, *Focus*, *Class*, *Lovebook*, *Rock!*, *HitMag*, *ZapMag*, *TufMag*, *MaxMag*, *Daytimers*, and more. Also publishes books (see listing under Sharon Publications in Book Publishers section).
Needs: Works with 5 freelance artists/year. Uses artists for magazine layout, illustrations, paste-up and mechanicals.
First Contact & Terms: Send query letter with brochure, resume, business card and samples to be kept on file. Accepts photostats, photographs, photocopies, slides or tear sheets as samples. Samples not filed are returned only if accompanied by SASE. Reports back only if interested. Call for appointment to show portfolio. Payment varies according to project; "we have a wide range." Considers the complexity of the project, how the work will be used and the turnaround time. Pays on publication.

THE DALE CORP., 2684 Industrial Row, Troy MI 48084. (313)288-9540. Contact: Art Director. Publishes law enforcement, corrections and fire fighting publications. Circ. 240,000. Send query letter with previously published work. SASE. Reports in 4 weeks. Buys all rights, but may reassign rights to artist after publication. Pays on acceptance. Free sample copies and art guidelines.
Illustrations: Buys 12/year. Cover: Pays $100-200, b&w line drawings; $75-200, color-separated work.

DANCE MAGAZINE, 33 W. 60th St., New York NY 10023. Editor-in-Chief: William Como. Emphasizes performance, education, personalities, books, records, films and lifestyle, all pertaining to the dancer or the dance aficionado. Monthly. Works on assignment only. Original artwork not returned after publication. Sample copy $3.50.
Illustrations: Buys 3-4 illustrations/issue from freelancers. Prefers dance-related themes (ballet, modern, ethnic, etc.). Send query letter with resume. SASE. Reports in 2 weeks. Buys all rights on a work-for-hire basis. Pays on publication.

DASH, Box 150, Wheaton IL 60189. (312)665-0630. Art Director: Lawrence Libby. Senior Graphic Designer: Roy Green. For Christian boys ages 8-11 in the church's Brigade program. Published 6 times/year. Circ. 24,000. Simultaneous submissions and previously published work OK. Original artwork returned after publication. Sample copy for $1.50 and SASE. Free artist's guidelines with SASE.
Cartoons: Send to attention of Cartoon Editor. Buys 1-3 cartoons/issue from freelancers. Receives 10 submissions/week from freelancers. Interested in family life, humor through youth, nature, school, sports; single panel with gagline. "Keep it clean." Prefers finished cartoons. SASE. Reports in 2-4 weeks. Buys first time rights. Pays $20 minimum, b&w line drawings; on publication.
Illustrations: Contact: Art Director. Buys 2 illustrations/issue from freelancers. B&w only; clean/professional look. Works on assignment only. Samples returned by SASE. Reports back on future assignment possibilities. Send resume, business card or photocopy of samples to be kept on file. SASE. Reports in 2 weeks. Buys first time rights. Pays $100-150 for inside use of b&w line drawings and washes; on publication.

DATAMATION MAGAZINE, 12th Floor, 875 Third Ave., New York NY 10022. (212)605-9711. Art Director: Kenneth Surabian. Emphasizes computers for data processing professionals. Bimonthly. Circ. 165,000. Original artwork returned after publication.
Cartoons: Uses 8 cartoons/issue. Prefers computers, business themes in *New Yorker* magazine style. Send query letter with finished cartoons. Call for appointment to show portfolio. Material not kept on file is returned by SASE. Reports within 2 weeks. Buys first or one-time rights. Pays $50-75, b&w; on acceptance.
Illustrations: Uses 6 illustrations/issue; buys all from freelancers. Works on assignment only. Send

photostats or promotional cards and tear sheets to be kept on file. Does not report back. Call for appointment to show portfolio. Buys first or one-time rights. Pays $500-700, b&w, and 500-1,000, color, cover; $400, b&w, $500, color, inside; on acceptance.

***DEATH RATTLE**, No. 2 Swamp Rd., Princeton WI 54968. (414)295-6922. Story Editor: Dave Schreiner. Serious comic book emphasizing science fiction and horror for serious readers and collectors of quality fantasy, science fiction and horror comics. Bimonthly. Circ. 20-25,000. Does not accept previously published material unless obscure publications. Original artwork returned after publication. Sample copy $2.50 postpaid; art guidelines free for SASE with 22¢ postage.
Cartoons: "We *never* buy "gag" on single panel cartoons. This is a comic book featuring fully developed graphic stories." Prefers b&w line drawings. Send query letter with samples of style, roughs or photocopies of finished cartoons to be kept on file. Samples not filed are returned only by SASE. Does not send original art on query. Reports within 2 weeks. Negotiates rights purchased. Pays $75-150, b&w; $100-400, color.
Illustrations: For cover only; "balance is fully-developed graphic stories.." Generally works on assignment only. Preferred style is simplified realism. Send query letter with brochure showing art styles or tear sheets, photostats and photocopies. Samples returned by SASE. Reports within 2 weeks. "Portfolio presentations unrealistic for geographic reasons." Negotiates rights purchased. Pays $200-400, b&w, cover. Pays one-half on acceptance, one-half on publication.

DECOR, 408 Olive, St. Louis MO 63102. (314)421-5445. Assistant Editor: Sharon Shinn. "Trade publication for retailers of art, picture framing and related wall decor. Subscribers include gallery owners/directors, custom and do-it-yourself picture framers, managers of related departments in department stores, art material store owners and owners of gift/accessory shops." Monthly. Circ. 20,000. Simultaneous submissions and previously published work OK. Original artwork not returned after publication. Sample copy $4.
Cartoons: Uses 6-10 cartoons/year; buys all from freelancers. Receives 5-10 submissions/week from freelancers. Interested in themes of galleries, frame shops, artists and small business problems; single panel with gagline. Especially needs cartoons for January business planning and forecast issue. Using more art-merchandising cartoons than in past. "We need cartoons as a way to 'lighten' our technical and retailing material. Cartoons showing gallery owners' problems with shows, artists and the buying public, inept framing employees, selling custom frames to the buying public and running a small business are most important to us." Send finished cartoons. SASE. Reports in 2 weeks. Buys various rights. Pays $20, b&w line drawings and washes; on acceptance.
Illustrations: Assigns illustration work to local artists.
Tips: "Most of our cartoons fill one-quarter-page spaces. Hence, cartoons that are vertical in design suit our purposes better than those which are horizontal. Send good, clean drawings with return envelopes; no more than 6 cartoons at a time."

DEER & DEER HUNTING, Box 1117, Appleton WI 54912. (414)734-0009. Art Director/Publisher: Jack Brauer. Emphasizes whitetail deer, deer hunting, outdoor themes for bow, camera, gun hunters. Bimonthly. Circ. 125,000. Accepts previously published material and simultaneous submissions. Original artwork returned after publication. Sample copy $2.95; art guidelines free for SASE.
Illustrations: Uses 2-3 illustrations/year; buys some from freelancers. Prefers b&w scenery or hunting-related illustrations; artwork of whitetail deer. Send resume, business card, photocopies or photostats to be kept on file. Samples not filed are returned by SASE. Reports only if interested. Buys one-time rights. Pays $20-50, b&w, and $50-75, color, cover; $20-35, b&w, and $35-50, color, inside; on publication.
Tips: "We prefer vertical work in b&w and especially look for the correct anatomy of deer when reviewing work. Follow instructions—SASE, don't call us."

DELAWARE TODAY, 120A Senatorial St., Wilmington DE 19807 (302)995-7146. Art Director: Ingrid Lynch. Emphasizes the most well-known people, places and events in the area. Monthly. Circ. 17,000. Free sample copy.
Illustrations: Uses 2-3 illustrations/issue; buys all from freelancers. Interested in blackline, ink washes, spots on current events and environment. Works on assignment only. Query with resume and samples. Samples returned by SASE. Provide business card, brochure, flyer and tear sheet to be kept on file for future assignments. Cover: Pays $250, color. Inside: Pays $75, b&w and color; on publication. Arrange interview to show portfolio. SASE. Reports in 1 week. Buys first North American serial rights.
Tips: "I have noticed a lot of illustrators are using flat color and shapes, I would like to find illustrators that do this; also illustrators that draw loosely (not cartoony)."

DENTAL HYGIENE, Suite 3400, 444 N. Michigan, Chicago IL 60611. Contact: Division Director. Emphasizes "professional concerns and issues involving dental hygienists and scientific topics concerning

dental hygiene" for "a primarily female audience of dental hygientists." Monthly. Circ. 30,000. Original artwork returned after publication. Sample copy available.
Illustrations: Uses 1 illustration/issue; buys 1/issue from freelancers. Prefers a variety of styles. "The theme depends on the individual issue. Past issues have dealt with government, hospital dental care, job opportunities abroad, and dental health education in public schools." Works on assignment only. Send query letter with brochure, resume, samples and tear sheets to be kept on file. Prefers slides or photographs of color work "although photostats would be OK." Reports within 1 month. Write for appointment to show portfolio. Buys one-time rights. Payment depends on the artwork. Pays on publication.

DERBY, Box 5418, Norman OK 73070. (405)364-9444. Editor: G.D. Hollingsworth. Estab. 1983. Emphasizes thoroughbred horse racing and breeding for owners, breeders and trainers of thoroughbred race horses. Monthly. Circ. 5,000. Accepts previously published material. Original artwork returned after publication. Sample copy $3; art guidelines available.
Illustrations: Buys cover illustration each issue from freelancer. Send query letter with samples to be kept on file. Prefers photos of artwork as samples. Samples not filed are returned. Reports within 2 weeks only if interested. Negotiates rights purchased. Pays $450, color, cover; on publication.

DETROIT MAGAZINE, 321 W. Lafayette, Detroit MI 48231. (313)222-6446. Art Director: Sheila Young Tomkowiak. Sunday magazine of major metropolitan daily newspaper emphasizing general subjects. Weekly. Circ. 800,000. Original artwork returned after publication. Sample copy available.
Illustrations: Buys 1-2 illustrations/issue from freelancers. Uses a variety of themes and styles, "but we emphasize fine art over cartoons." Works on assignment only. Send query letter with samples to be kept on file unless not considered for assignment. Send "whatever samples best show artwork and can fit into 8½x11" file folder." Samples not filed are not returned. Reports only if interested. Buys first rights. Pays $250-300, color, cover; up to $200, color and up to $175, b&w, inside; on publication.

DETROIT MONTHLY MAGAZINE, 1400 Woodbridge, Detroit MI 48207. (313)446-6000. Emphasizes "features on local political, economic, style, cultural, lifestyles, culinary subjects, etc., relating to Detroit and region" for "middle and upper-middle class, urban and suburban, mostly college-educated professionals." Monthly. Circ. approximately 45,000. "Very rarely" accepts previously published material. Sample copy free for SASE.
Illustrations: Uses 10 illustrations/issue; buys 10/issue from freelancers. Works on assignment only. Send query letter with samples and tear sheets to be kept on file. Call for appointment to show portfolio. Prefers anything *but* original work as samples. Samples not kept on file are returned by SASE. Reports only if interested. Pays $75-300, b&w, and $100-350, color, inside; on publication.

***DHARMART DESIGNS**, 2425 Hillside Ave., Berkeley CA 94704. (415)548-5407. Contact: Rima Tamar. Catalog of stationery items, emphasizing fine art. Accepts previously published material. Returns original artwork after publication. Sample copy available.
Illustrations: Works on assignment only. Send query letter with brochure showing art style or photographs. Samples not filed are returned by SASE. Reports back only if interested. To show a portfolio, mail appropriate materials. Negotiate rights purchased. Pays on publication.

DIABETES SELF-MANAGEMENT, 42-15 Crescent St., Long Island City, NY 11101. (718)937-4283. Production Director: Ms. Maryanne Schott. Estab. 1983. Magazine. Emphasizes diabetes self-care for diabetics. Bi-monthly. Circ. 250,000. Original artwork not returned after publication. Sample copy $3.
Cartoons: Buys 6-8 cartoons/issue from freelancers. Themes or styles dependent on editorial content. Prefers single panel or multiple panel; b&w washes, color washes. Send query letter with samples of style to be kept on file. Material not filed is returned by SASE. Reports only if interested. Buys all rights. Pays on publication.
Illustrations: Buys 20-30 illustrations/issue from freelancers. Themes or styles vary from issue to issue based on editorial. Send query letter with tear sheets, phototstats, slides and photos to be kept on file. Samples not filed are returned by SASE. Reports only if interested. Buys all rights. Pays on publication.

THE DISCIPLE, Christian Board of Publication, Box 179, St. Louis MO 63166. Editor: James L. Merrell. For ministers and laypersons. Monthly. Circ. 57,500. Photocopied and simultaneous submissions OK. Original artwork returned after publication, if requested. Sample copy $1.25; free artist's guidelines.
Cartoons: Buys 1 cartoon/issue from freelancers. Receives 10 submissions/week from freelancers. Interested in family life and religion; single panel. Church material only. "Originality in content and subject matter stressed. No clergy collars—ties or robes preferred." Especially needs "good religious cartoons along the lines of those which appear in *TV Guide*." Prefers to see finished cartoons. SASE. Re-

ports in 4 weeks. Buys first North American serial rights. Pays $15 minimum, b&w line drawings and washes; on acceptance.
Illustrations: Uses 2 illustrations/issue; buys 1/issue from freelancers. Receives 10 submissions/week from freelancers. Interested in "seasonal and current religious events/issues." Also uses 4 cartoon-style illustrations/year. Send query letter with tear sheets, photocopies and photographs. SASE. Reports in 2 weeks. To show a portfolio, mail tear sheets, photostats and photographs. Buys first North American serial rights. Payment depends on quality. Pays on acceptance.
Tips: "We would be very happy to look at samples of artists' work (covers), in case we want to commission. Read the magazine before submitting material. Send seasonal art, especially Easter and Christmas, at least six months in advance."

***DISCIPLESHIP JOURNAL**, Box 6000, Colorado Springs CO 80934. (303)598-1212, ext. 298. Art Director: Naomi Trujillo. Magazine/journal emphasizing Christian living and discipleship. Bi-monthly. Works with 15 freelance artists/year.
Illustrations: Buys 4-5 illustrations/issue from freelance artists. Pays by the project, $150-1,000. Buys one-time rights. Send resume, tear sheets, photostats, photocopies, slides, photographs. Samples not filed are returned if requested by SASE. Reports back only if interested.

DISTRIBUTOR, Box 745, Wheeling IL 60090. (312)537-6460. Editorial Director: Steve Read. Emphasizes HVAC/R wholesaling for executives at management level in the wholesale field. Bimonthly. Circ. 10,000. Returns original artwork after publication. Sample copy $4; art guidelines available.
Illustrations: Works on assignment only. Send query letter with brochure, photostats, tear sheets, photocopies, slides or photographs to be kept on file; *no original work*. Reports within 2 weeks. To show a portfolio, mail tear sheets, photostats, photographs and b&w. Buys first rights. Negotiates payment; pays on publication.

DIVER MAGAZINE, 8051 River Rd., Richmond, British Columbia V6X 1X8 Canada. (604)273-4333. Editor: N. McDaniel. Emphasizes scuba diving, ocean science and technology (commercial and military diving) for a well-educated, outdoor-oriented readership. Published 9 times yearly. Circ. 25,000. Sample copy $3; art guidelines free for SASE. Nonresidents must include International Reply Coupons.
Cartoons: Buys 1 cartoon/issue from freelancers. Interested in diving-related cartoons only. Prefers single panel b&w line drawings with gagline. Send samples of style. SASE. Reports in 2 weeks. Buys first North American serial rights. Pays $15 for b&w; on publication.
Illustrations: Uses 25 illustrations/issue; buys 20 from freelancers. Interested in diving related illustrations of good quality only. Prefers b&w line drawings for inside. Send samples of style. SASE. Reports in 2 weeks. Buys first North American serial rights. Pays $7 minimum for inside b&w; $75 minimum for color cover and $15 minimum for inside, color. Payment four weeks after publication.

DOG FANCY, Box 6050, Mission Viejo CA 92690. (714)240-6001. Editor: Linda Lewis. For dog owners and breeders of all ages, interested in all phases of dog ownership. Monthly. Circ. 95,000. Simultaneous submissions and previously published work OK. Sample copy $3.; free artist's guidelines with SASE.
Cartoons: Buys 12 cartoons/year; single, double or multiple panel. "Central character should be a dog." Mail finished art. SASE. Prefers photostats or photocopies as samples. Reports in 6 weeks. Buys first rights. Pays $20-50, b&w line drawings; on publication.
Illustrations: Buys 12 illustrations/year on dogs. Query with resume and samples. SASE. Reports in 6 weeks. Buys first rights. Pays $50-100, b&w line drawings, inside; on publication.
Tips: Artists should have "originality and intimacy with their subject."

***DOLLS—THE COLLECTOR'S MAGAZINE**, 170 5th Ave., New York NY 10010. Art Director: Lisa Dayton. Magazine emphasizing antique and collectible dolls for doll collectors. Bimonthly. Circ. 52,500. Original artwork returned after publication. Sample copy $2. Art guidelines free for SASE and 22¢ postage.
Illustrations: Buys 1-2 illustrations/issue from freelancers. Works on assignment only. Prefers realistic presentations. Send query letter with resume, tear sheets and photocopies. Samples not filed returned by SASE. Reports only if interested. Write to schedule an appointment to show a portfolio, which should include roughs, original/final art, final reproduction/production, color, tear sheets, photographs and b&w. Negotiates rights purchased. Payment varies. Pays on publication.

***DOLLSTARS**, Room 1300, 10 Columbus Circle, New York NY 10019. (212)541-7300. Design Director: Altemus. Estab. 1985. Magazine for children 6-13. Quarterly. Circ. 200,000. Accepts previously published material. Returns original artwork after publication. Send samples of style to be kept on file. Call for appointment to show portfolio. Material not filed is returned by SASE. Buys first rights.

Illustrations: Buys 10 illustrations/issue. Works on assignment only. Prefers stylized, graphic, light styles. Send tear sheets. Samples not filed are returned by SASE. Does not report back. To show a portfolio, mail appropriate materials or call to schedule an appointment; portfolio should include tear sheets and photostats. Buys first rights. Pays $300, b&w; $300, color, cover; $75, b&w; $100, color, inside; on publication.

THE DOLPHIN LOG, The Cousteau Society, 8440 Santa Monica Blvd., Los Angeles CA 90069. (213)656-4422. Editor: Pamela Stacey. Educational magazine covering "all areas of science, history and the arts related to our global water system, including marine biology, ecology, the environment, and natural history" for children ages 7-15. Quarterly. Circ. 58,000. Original artwork returned after publication. Sample copy for $2 and SASE with 56¢ postage; art guidelines for SASE with 22¢ postage.
Cartoons: Considers themes or styles related to magazine's subject matter. B&w line drawings or b&w or color washes. Send query letter with samples of style to be kept on file; write or call for appointment to show portfolio. Material not filed is returned by SASE. Reports within 1 month. Buys one-time rights and translation rights. Pays $25-50, b&w and color; on publication.
Illustrations: Buys 4-6 illustrations/issue from freelancers. Uses simple, biologically and technically accurate line drawings and scientific illustrations. Subjects should be carefully researched. Send query letter with tear sheets and photocopies to be kept on file unless otherwise notified. "No original artwork, please." Samples not filed are returned by SASE. Reports within 1 month. To show a portfolio, mail final reproduction/product, tear sheets and b&w. Buys one-time rights and worldwide translation rights. Pays $100, color, cover; $25-50, b&w and color, inside; on publication.
Tips: "Biological/technical accuracy a must. Stay within concept of magazine. If any fun is to be had, it should be by making people, not animals, look silly."

DOWN EAST, Box 679, Camden ME 04843. (207)594-9544. Art Director: F. Stephen Ward. Concerns Maine's people, places, events and heritage. Monthly. Circ. 75,000. Previously published work OK. Buys first North American serial rights. Sample copy $2.
Illustrations: Buys 50/year on current events, environment, family life and politics. Query with resume and samples or arrange interview to show portfolio. SASE. Reports in 4-6 weeks. Cover: Pays $75, color paintings in any medium; "must have a graphic, poster-like feel and be unmistakably Maine." Inside: Pays $25-200, b&w or color; on publication.
Tips: "Neatness in presentation is as important as the portfolio itself."

DRAGON MAGAZINE, Dragon Publishing, Box 110, Lake Geneva WI 53147. Editor: Kim Mohan. For readers interested in game-playing, particularly fantasy and science fiction role-playing games. Circ. 110,000. Query with samples. SASE. Usually buys first rights only. Pays within 30-45 days after accetpance. Sample copy $3.50 (cover price).
Cartoons: Buys 20-30/year on science fiction and fantasy role-playing. Pays $25, b&w minimum; color cartoons not used.
Illustrations: Buys at least 100/year on fantasy and science fiction subjects. Pays $500 minimum, color, cover; $150/page, b&w; and $250/page, color, inside.

EARTHWISE: A JOURNAL OF POETRY, Box 680-536, Miami FL 33168. (305)688-8558, 823-5973. Publisher: Barbara Holley. Art Editor: Kathryn L. Vilips. Emphasizes poetry, art and literature for an eclectic group of literate writers, artists and poets, mainly academic, collegiate and aimed at excellence in the field. Quarterly. Circ. 3,000 + . Sometimes accepts previously published material; simultaneous submissions OK. Original artwork returned after publication. Sample copy $4; art guidelines for SASE.
Illustrations: Uses 4-8 illustrations/issue; buys some from freelancers. Send query letter with velox copies or originals (please insure). "We especially prefer samples, photocopies or stats which we can purchase and/or keep on file for future publication; our themes occasionally change depending on submissions." Samples returned by SASE "but would like something to keep on file." Reports in 3 months. Write to schedule an appointment to show a portfolio, which should include thumbnails, roughs, original/final art, final reproduction/product, color, tear sheets, photostats, photographs and especially b&w. Buys first rights. Pays $10-50/b&w line drawings, cover; $10-25/b&w line drawings, inside. "Very negotiable depending on size, availability, etc." Pays on publication.
Tips: "We lean toward the environmental, nature, creatures, humankind. Send 4-6 black-and-white samples, either veloxes or insured originals with proper return envelope and appropriate postage for their prompt return. We use black-and-white in both the annual calendar and the newsletter also."

EASYRIDERS, Box 52, Malibu CA 90265. Contact: Art Director. For adult bikers. Monthly. "Need art and cartoons, scenes with choppers in them, sexy women—in other words, 'bikes, booze and broads,'

or scenes depicting the good times derived from owning a Harley-Davidson (if a cycle is illustrated)." Sample copy $3.
Cartoons: Buys 30/month. SASE. Reports in 2 weeks. Buys all rights. Pays $35, small b&w gags; $150, full-page b&w; on acceptance.
Illustrations: Buys 3 illustrations/issue. "Subject matter is more important than the medium. We use more b&w than color." Send query letter with tear sheets, photostats and photocopies. SASE. Reports in 2 weeks. Call or write to schedule an appointment to show a portfolio. Pays $150, b&w, and $350, color, inside; on acceptance. Buys all rights.
Tips: "Check out our magazine."

***80 MICRO**, 80 Pine St., Peterborough NH 03458. (603)924-9471. Art Director: Anne Fleming. Magazine for users of Tandy TRS-80 computers. Monthly. Circ. 90,000. Original artwork returned after publication. Sample copy and art guidelines available.
Cartoons: Buys 4 cartoons/issue from freelancers. Prefers single panel without gagline; b&w line drawings or b&w washes. Send query letter with samples of style to be kept on file. Write or call for appointment to show a portfolio. Material not kept on file is returned only if requested. Reports only if interested. Buys first or one-time rights. Payment varies with size.
Illustrations: Buys 2-3 illustrations/issue from freelancers. Works on assignment only. Prefers creative, original and new themes and styles. Send query letter with brochure showing art style or tear sheets, photostats and photocopies. Samples not filed are returned only if requested. Reports only if interested. Call or write to schedule an appointment to show a portfolio, which should include original/final art, final reproduction/product and tear sheets. Buys first or one-time rights. Pays $700-850/page, color, inside; on acceptance.

ELECTRIC COMPANY MAGAZINE, 1 Lincoln Plaza, New York NY 10023. (212)595-3456, ext. 512. Art Director: Bob Feldgus. For ages 6-11.
Illustrations: Buys 60/year. Query with photocopied samples. SASE. Reports in 2 weeks. Buys one-time rights. Pays $150 minimum/page, b&w; $250/page, $450/spread, color; on acceptance.

ELECTRICAL APPARATUS, Barks Publications, Inc., 400 N. Michigan, Chicago IL 60611. Contact: Elsie Dickson. Emphasizes industrial electrical maintenance and repair.
Cartoons: Receives 2-3 cartoons/week from freelance artists. "Always looking for applicable cartoons, as we use a strip (assigned), plus 4-6 individual column-size cartoons in every issue." Query with resume.
Tips: Artists should "know the magazine!"

ELECTRICAL WORLD, McGraw-Hill Inc., 1221 Avenue of the Americas, New York NY 10020. (212)512-2440. Art Director: Kiyo Komoda. Emphasizes operation, maintenance and use of electric utility facilities. For electric utility management and engineers. Monthly. Original artwork returned after publication, on request. Pays $50-150 b&w, $80-200 color; on acceptance.
Cartoons: Buys 1 cartoon/issue from freelancers, works on assignment only. Interested in industry-related situation cartoon, usually related to editorial articles. Buys one-time and reprint rights. Pays on acceptance.
Illustrations: Uses 20 illustrations/issue, buys ⅓ from freelancers. Interested in energy systems; 90% are mechanical line drawings, maps, flow designs, graphs and charts. Works on assignment only. Samples returned by SASE. Provide resume or business card to be kept on file for future assignments. Prefers to see portfolio or finished art. Reports in 1 week. Buys one-time and reprint rights. Cover: Pays $10-200, b&w line drawings, inside; $20-300 color, inside; on acceptance.
Tips: "We prefer artists with clean and crisp line work. They should know about color separation and overlays. Young artists welcomed."

***ELECTRONIC COMMUNICATION, INC.**, Suite 220, 1311 Executive Center Dr., Tallahasee FL 32303. (904)878-4178. Art Director: Faye Howell. Three publications emphasizing educational technology for kindergarten to high school principals, teachers, and administrators and also college and upper educational teachers and administrators. Monthly, bimonthly and quarterly. Circ. 275,000; 70,000; 34,000. Original material not returned after publication. Sample copy free for SASE with 56¢ postage.
Illustrations: Buys 0-3 illustrations/issue from freelancers. Works on assignment only. Send query letter with brochure showing art style. Samples not filed are returned only if requested. Reports only if interested. To show a portfolio, mail appropriate materials, which should include final reproduction/product, color and tear sheets. Negotiates rights purchased. Payment "varies widely;" on publication.

***THE ELKS MAGAZINE**, 425 W. Diversey Pkwy., Chicago IL 60614. Editor: Judith Keogh. Emphasizes general interest with family appeal. For members of the Elks. Monthly. Circ. 1,600,000. Original

artwork not returned after publication. Pays on acceptance. Free sample copy with 9x12 SASE.
Cartoons: Uses 1 cartoon/issue, buys from freelancers. Receives 50 submissions/week from free-lancers. Buys 8-10/year; single panel. "Must have family appeal." Interested in general interest car-toons. Prefers to see finished cartoons. Reports in 2 weeks. Buys first and North American serial rights. Pays $50, line drawings; on acceptance.
Tips: "Many cartoonists are specializing in 'put-down' or 'insult' humor. Our publication has no use for this type of material; thus many technically excellent artists find themselves the recipients of our rejec-tion slips." Needs "clean, well-rendered art; appropriate or adaptable subject matter; fresh, succinct captions."

ELLERY QUEEN'S MYSTERY MAGAZINE, Davis Publications, 380 Lexington Ave., New York NY 10017. (212)557-9100. Editor: Eleanor Sullivan. Emphasizes mystery stories and reviews of mystery books. Reports within 1 month. Pays $25 minimum, line drawings. All other artwork is done inhouse. Pays on acceptance.

EMERGENCY MEDICINE MAGAZINE, 475 Park Ave. S, New York NY 10016. (212)686-0555. Art Director: Lois Erlacher. Emphasizes emergency medicine for primary care physicians, emergency room personnel, medical students. Bimonthly. Circ. 139,000. Returns original artwork after publication.
Illustrations: Buys 3-4 illustrations/issue from freelancers. Works on assignment only. Send tear sheets, transparencies, original art or photostats to be kept on file. Samples not filed are not returned. To show a portfolio, mail appropriate materials. Reports only if interetsed. Buys first rights. Pays $700 for color, cover; $250-500, b&w and $500-600, color, inside; on acceptance.
Tips: "Portfolios may be dropped off any day of the week. Art Director prefers to keep overnight—call first."

EMPLOYEE SERVICES MANAGEMENT MAGAZINE, NESRA, 2400 S. Downing Ave., Westchester IL 60153. (312)562-8130. Editor: Joan Price. Emphasizes the field of employee services and recreation, which is one aspect of human resources, for human resource professionals, and employee services and recreation managers and leaders within corporations, industries or units of government. Published 10 times/year. Circ. 5,000. Accepts previously published material. Returns original artwork after publica-tion. Sample copy free for SASE with 56¢ postage; art guidelines free for SASE with 22¢ postage.
Illustrations: Buys 0-1 illustration/issue from freelancers. Works on assignment only. Send query let-ter with resume and tear sheets or photographs to be kept on file. Samples not filed are returned only if requested. Reports within 1 month. Buys one-time rights. Pays $100-200 for b&w and $300-400 for col-or covers; on acceptance.
Tips: "We have noticed a change to a simpler, more dramatic style in art and design, one that is not so 'busy.' We have used freelancers who embrace this style."

***ENDLESS VACATION PUBLICATIONS, INC.**, Box 80260, Indianaplis IN 46280-0260. Art Direc-tor: Lisa Krassick. Magazine emphasizing travel for timeshare owners. Bimonthly. Circ. 500,000. Ac-cepts previously published material. Original artwork returned after publication.
Illustrations: Buys 1 illustration/issue from freelancer. Works on assignment only. Send query letter with brochure showing art style. Samples not filed are not returned. Reports only if interested. Call to schedule an appointment to show a portfolio, which should include final reproduction/product, tear sheets and photographs. Buys one-time rights. Pays on publication.

THE ENSIGN, Official Publication of the United States Power Squadrons, Box 31664, Raleigh NC 27622. (919)821-0892. Editor: Carol Romano. Emphasizes boating safety and education for members of the United States Power Squadrons, a nonprofit organization of boating men and women across the country. Monthly. Circ. approximately 50,000. Returns original artwork after publication. Sample copy and art guidelines free for SASE.
Cartoons: Prefers single panel, with gagline; b&w line drawings. Send query letter with finished car-toons; "material is reviewed and used or returned by SASE." Reports within 2 weeks. Acquires all rights.
Illustrations: Prefers boating themes. Send query letter with photocopies; "material is reviewed and used or returned by SASE." Reports within 2 weeks. Acquires all rights.
Tips: "We are happy to accept cartoons and drawings for use in the magazine and provide artists with copies of the magazine at no charge, a letter of appreciation and a certificate of appreciation for their contributions. We provide an opportunity for beginning freelancers to get nationwide exposure, but we have no freelance budget to pay artists at this time."

ENVIRONMENT, 4000 Albemarle St., Washington DC 20016. (202)362-6589 or 6445. Production Graphics Editor: Ann Rickerich. Emphasizes energy, conservation, pollution, ecology and scientific, technological, and environmental policy issues. Readers are "high school students and college under-grads to scientists and business and government executives." Circ. 12,500. Published 10 times/year. Original artwork returned after publication if requested. Sample copy $4; cartoonist's guidelines available.

Cartoons: Uses 0-1 cartoon/issue; buys all from freelancers. Receives 2 submissions/week from freelancers. Interested in single panel b&w line drawings or b&w washes with or without gagline. Send finished cartoons. SASE. Reports in 2 weeks. Buys first North American serial rights. Pays $35, b&w cartoons; on acceptance.

Illustrations: Buys 5/year from freelance artists. Send query letter, brochure, tear sheets and photocopies. To show a portfolio, mail original/final art, final reproduction/product and b&w. Pays $200 b&w, cover; $50-200 b&w, inside; on publication.

Tips: "Regarding cartoons, we prefer the witty to the slapstick. For illustrations, "we are looking for an ability to communicate complex ideas."

***ESPIONAGE MAGAZINE**, Box 1184, Teaneck NJ 07405. Art Director: Laura Avello. Estab. 1984. Magazine emphasizing spying and espionage for upscale male. Bimonthly. Sample copy $3. Art guidelines free for SASE with 20¢ postage.

Cartoons: Buys various cartoons/issue from freelancers. Prefers single panel; b&w line drawings. Send query letter with finished cartoons to be kept on file. Write to schedule an appointment to show a portfolio. Material not kept on file is returned by SASE. Reports only if interested. Buys first rights. Pays $15, b&w.

Illustrations: Buys 10-12 illustratios/issue from freelancers. Send query letter with brochure showing art style or samples. Samples not filed are returned by SASE. Reports only if interested. Write to schedule an appointment to show a portfolio, which should include original/final art, final reproduction/product, color, photostats and b&w. Buys first rights. Pays $100, color, cover; $30, inside; on publication.

ESQUIRE, 2 Park Ave., New York NY 10016. (212)561-8100. Art Director: Wendall Harrington (Ms.). Emphasizes politics, business, the arts, sports and the family for American men.

Illustrations: Buys 1-10 illustrations/issue, depending on special sections. Send brochure showing art style or resume and tear sheets. To show a portfolio, mail original/final art, final reproduction/product, color, tear sheets, photographs and b&w. Pays on acceptance.

ETERNITY MAGAZINE, 1716 Spruce St., Philadelphia PA 19103. (215)546-3696. Design Coordinator: Robin Burnham. Emphasizes cultural analysis from a Christian viewpoint for business people, 30-60 years of age. Monthly. Circ. 45,000. Accepts previously published material. Original artwork returned after publication. Sample copy $2; art guidelines available.

Illustrations: Buys 3-4 illustrations/issue from freelancers. Considers variety of media, serious style—not cartooning. Themes range from war to education to androgeny. Works on assignment only. Send query letter with resume, tear sheets, photostats, photocopies, slides and photographs. "Please do not send original work." Samples returned by SASE. Reports only if interested. Call or write to schedule an appointment to show a portfolio, which should include original art, final reproduction/product, color, tear sheets and b&w. Buys one-time rights. Pays $100-200, b&w, and $150-250, color, cover; $50-150, b&w, inside; on acceptance.

Tips: "I like unusual techniques, texture and tone. I am not interested in seeing storybook, cartoony illustrations. The work should be neat, sloppy art degrades the art, artists and project. Please call for an appointment."

EUROPE, MAGAZINE OF THE EUROPEAN COMMUNITY, Seventh Floor, 2100 M St. NW, Washington DC 20037. (202)862-9500. Editor: Webster Martin. Emphasizes European affairs, US-European relations—particularly economics, trade and politics. Readers are businessmen, professionals, academics, government officials and consumers. Bimonthly. Circ. 65,000. Free sample copy.

Cartoons: Occasionally uses cartoons, mostly from a cartoon service. "The magazine publishes articles on US-European relations in economics, trade, business, industry, politics, energy, inflation, etc." Considers single panel b&w line drawings or b&w washes with or without gagline. Send resume plus finished cartoons and/or samples. SASE. Reports in 3-4 weeks. Buys one-time rights. Pays $25; on publication.

Illustrations: Uses 3-5 illustrations/issue. "At present we work exclusively through our designer and set up charts and graphs to fit our needs. We would be open to commissioning artwork should the need and opportunity arise. We look for economic graphs, tables, charts and story-related statistical artwork"; b&w line drawings and washes for inside. Send resume and photocopies of style. SASE. Reports in 3-4 weeks. To show a portfolio, mail original/final art. Buys all rights on a work-for-hire basis. Payment varies; on publication.

EVANGEL, 901 College Ave., Winona Lake IN 46590. (219)267-7656. Contact: Vera Bethel. Readers are 65% female, 35% male; ages 25-31; married; city-dwelling; mostly non-professional high school graduates. Circ. 35,000. Weekly.
Cartoons: Buys 1/issue on family subjects. Pays $10, b&w; on publication. Mail finished art.
Illustrations: Buys 1/issue on assigned themes. Pays $40, 2-color; on acceptance. Query with samples or slides. SASE. Reports in 1 month.

THE EVENER, Box 7, Cedar Falls IA 50613. (319)277-3599. Managing Editor: Susan Salterberg. Magazine. Emphasizes draft horses (*some* mules and oxen). "*The Evener*'s subscribers are primarily farmers, craftsmen, showmen and women. They are interested in horses, nostalgia—and, oftentimes—self-sufficiency. Some subscribers work horses, mules or oxen on their farm or ranch and look for features and quality artwork and photographs about people in the industry." Quarterly. Circ. 10,400. Accepts previously published material. Original artwork returned after publication. Sample copy for SASE with $1.07 postage, cover; art guidelines for SASE with 39¢ postage.
Cartoons: Buys 1 cartoon/issue from freelancers.
Illustrations: Buys 2 illustrations/issue from freelancers. Usually works on assignment. Send query letter with brochure or photostats, photographs and slides as samples. Samples not filed are returned by SASE. Reports within 3 months by SASE only. Negotiates rights purchased; prefers first-time rights. Pays $40-100, b&w, cover; $10-60, b&w, inside; on acceptance.

EVENT, Douglas College, Box 2503, New Westminster, British Columbia V3L 5B2 Canada. (604)520-5400. Editor: Ken Hughes. For "those interested in literature and writing." Published semiannually. Circ. 1,000. Original artwork returned after publication. Sample copy $4.
Illustrations: Receives 3 illustrations/week from freelance artists. Buys 16-20 illustrations/issue from freelancers. Interested in experimental drawings and prints, and thematic or stylistic series of 12-20 works. SASE (nonresidents include IRC). Reporting time varies; at least 2 weeks. To show a portfolio, mail original/final art, b&w and color. Buys first North American serial rights. Pays $40 maximum, b&w line drawings, photographs and lithographs for cover and inside; work must reproduce well in one color. Pays on publication. Payment includes free copy.
Tips: "No photocopies—otherwise we welcome almost anything—no cartoons—no nudies."

***THE EXCEPTIONAL PARENT**, 605 Commonwealth Ave., Boston MA 02215. (617)536-8961. Managing Editor: Ellen Herman. "A national consumer publication for parents and professionals who are concerned with the education of children and young audlts with disabilities. We publish on a wide range of topics: health care, education, technology, recreation, employment, etc." 8 issues/year. Circ. 35,000. Accepts previously published material. Original artwork returned after publication. Sample copy and editorial guidelines $2 with SASE.

***EXCLUSIVELY YOURS MAGAZINE**, Suite 4032, 161 W. Wisconsin Ave., Milwaukee WI 53092. Creative Director; Miriam Hansen. Magazine emphasizing general interest of Wisconsin for selected upper-income households. Monthly. Circ. 40,000. Accepts previously published material. Original artwork returned after publication if one-time rights. Sample copy $2.10.
Illustrations: Buys 1 illustration/issue from freelancers. Prefers non-violent and non-sexually explicit themes. Primarily uses photos. Send query letter with brochure showing art style. Samples not filed are returned by SASE. Reports only if interested. To show a portfolio, mail appropriate materials. Local artists write to schedule an appointment. Negotiates rights purchased. Payment varies. Pays on publication.

***EXECUTIVE DIGEST FOR TOURIST ATTRACTIONS AND PARKS**, 401 N. Broad St., Philadelphia PA 19108. (215)925-9744. Contact: President. Concerns amusement and theme parks, museums, zoos, landmarks, caves and attractions. Bimonthly newsletter. Circ. 20,000. Uses artists for cover. Freelance paste up person needed with each issue.
Cartoons: SASE. Reports in 3-4 weeks. Buys all rights. Pays $50 minimum, gray opaques; on publication.
Illustrations: Buys 1 illustration/issue; "must be tied to reader business." Send query letter with resume and samples. SASE. Reports in 3-4 weeks. Buys all rights. Pays $50 minimum, b&w, cover; on publication.

EXPECTING MAGAZINE, 685 Third Ave., New York NY 10017. Art Director: Ruth M. Kelly. Emphasizes pregnancy, birth and care of the newborn for pregnant women and new mothers. Quarterly. Circ. 1.2 million distributed through obstetrician and gynecologist offices nationwide. Original artwork returned after publication.
Illustrations: Buys approximately 6/issue. Color only. Works on assignment. "We have a drop-off

policy for looking at portfolios; include a card to be kept on file." Buys one-time rights. Pays within 30 days after publication.

***THE EYE MAGAZINE**, 11th & Washington Sts., Wilmington DE 19801. (302)571-6977. Art Director: Paul A. Miles. Tabloid for high school students; all writing, cartoons, photographs, etc. are produced by high-school age cartoonists and artists. Monthly October through May. Circ. 25,000. Accepts previously published material. Original artwork returned after publication. Sample copy free for SASE with 37¢ postage.
Cartoons: Uses 1 cartoon/issue. Prefers single panel with gagline; b&w line drawings. Prefers themes showing resourcefulness of young people. "We prefer ones that do not show teens in a derogatory manner." Send query letter with samples of style to be kept on file. Material not kept on file is returned by SASE. Reports within 30 days. Buys one-time rights.
Illustations: Buys 1 illustration/issue from freelancers. Works on assignment only. Primary theme is teenagers; artist must be a teenager. Send query letter with resume and photocopies. Samples not filed are returned by SASE. Reports within 30 days. "We do not see portfolios." Buys one-time rights. Pays $25, b&w, cover; $10, b&w, inside. "Our publication is a non-profit publication to give students a voice to their peers and adults. We are a training ground and as such do not pay very much for editorial or artwork. We will gladly give copies of publication and letters of recommendations to high school students interested in getting something published."
Tips: "Don't expect very much from us. We are small and like to help artists; not monetarily, but through public work."

FACT MAGAZINE, 305 E. 46th, New York NY 10017. Art Director: Christopher Goldsmith. Emphasizes consumer money management and investment. Monthly. Returns original artwork after publication.
Cartoons: Buys 8-10 cartoons/issue. Pays $75, b&w; $200, color.
Illustrations: Buys 10-12 illustrations/issue from freelancers. Always works on assignment. Contact only through artist's agent, who should send photostats, tear sheets, photocopies, slides or photographs to be kept on file. Samples not filed are returned only if requested. Reports only if interested. Write for appointment to show portfolio, which should include final reproduction/product, color, tear sheets, photostats, photographs and b&w. Buys first rights or reprint rights. Pays $500-800 for cover; $300-600 inside.

FAMILY PLANNING PERSPECTIVES, 111 5th Ave., New York NY 10003. (212)254-5656. Production Manager: Dore Hollander. Magazine. Emphasizes family planning/population for health care providers, educators and policy-makers. Bimonthly. Circ. 15,000. Original artwork returned after publication. Sample copy available.
Cartoons: Buys 0-1 cartoon/issue from freelancers. Prefers political/social aspects of family planning issues as themes. Prefers single panel without gagline; b&w line drawings. Send query letter with samples of style. Material returned by SASE. Reports only if interested. Negotiates rights purchased. Pays on publication.
Illustrations: Buys 0-1 illustration/issue from freelancers. Prefers political/social aspects of family planning issues as themes. Works on assignment only. Send query letter with samples. Samples returned by SASE. Reports only if interested. Negotiates rights purchased. Pays on publication.

***FANFARE**, Box 720, Tenafly NJ 07670. (201)567-3908. Editor: Joel Flegler. Magazine emphasizing classical record reviews for classical record collectors. Bimonthly. Circ. 20,000. Accepts previously published material. Original artwork returned after publication. Sample copy $5.
Illustrations: Buys 1 illustration/issue from freelancers. Prefers anything to do with music as themes. Send query letter with resume and samples. Samples not filed are returned by SASE. Reports only if interested. Call to dicuss artwork; no appointments. Buys one-time rights. Pays $100, color, cover; on acceptance.

FANTASY REVIEW, College of Humanities, Florida Atlantic University, Boca Raton FL 33431. (305)393-3839. Editor: Robert A. Collins. Emphasizes fantasy and science fiction for "collectors, book dealers, libraries, academics and fans in general." Monthly. Circ. 3,000. Original artwork returned after publication. Sample copy $2.50. Receives very few cartoons ("could use more") and 10 illustrations/week from freelance artists.
Cartoons: Horror, fantasy and science fiction subjects (no space hardware). "Publishing is caught in the Reaganomics squeeze; rates will stay the same or go down."
Illustrations: Uses 5-6 illustrations/issue; buys all from freelancers. Interested in themes pertaining to fantasy, science fiction, and horror. "Artists should *not* send originals on speculation—send PMT's, stats, or quality photocopies. Don't send copies larger than 9x12 inches. If we need originals (as for

cover illustration), we ask for them. All art is eventually returned, but we assume no responsibility for it." Samples returned "with SASE only." Reports in 4 weeks. Buys one-time publication rights only; all other rights retained by artist. Pays $50-100 cover (b&w with one-color overlays), $10-25 inside (various sizes), all media; pays 3 weeks after acceptance.
Tips: *"Fantasy Review* is now published through the Division of Continuing Education at Florida Atlantic University, a state institution. Payments to artists are slower (red-tape) and nudity is restricted: female, upper body only; no genitalia."

***FANTASY TALES**, 130 Park View, Wembley, Middx., HA9 6JU England. Editor: Steve Jones. Magazine emphasizing fantasy/horror fiction for science fiction/fantasy/horror fans. Approximately bi-annually. Circ. 1,500. Accepts previously published material. Original artwork returned after publication. Sample copy $4 (including postage & packing). Art guidelines free for SASE with $1 postage.
Illustrations: Buys 7-12 illustrations/issue from freelancers. Works on assignment only. Uses artists for manuscript illustration. Send query letter with tear sheets, photostats and photocopies. Samples not filed are returned by SASE only if requested. Reports within 14 days. Buys one-time rights. Negotiates payment; pays on publication.

***FARM COMPUTER NEWS**, Locust at 17th, Des Moines IA 50336. (515)284-2702. Art Director: Curt Goettsch. Magazine emphasizing computer use in agriculture for successful Class I farmers interested in computer technology and how it can be a business tool. Bimonthly. Circ. 16,000.
Cartoons: Buys 1 cartoon/issue from freelancers. Prefers computer technology themes. Send query letter with roughs to be kept on file. Material not kept on file is returned by SASE. Reports only if interested. Buys all rights.
Illustrations: Buys 2 illustrations/issue from freelancers. Works on assignment only. Prefers computer technology themes. Send query letter with brochure showing art style or resume, tear sheets, slides and photographs. Samples not filed are returned by SASE. Reports only if interested. Buys all rights. Pays $300, b&w, and $500, color, cover; $150, b&w, and $300, color, inside; on acceptance.

FARMFUTURES, Agridata Resources, Inc., 330 E. Kilbourn Ave., Milwaukee WI 53202. (414)278-7676. Art Director: Geri Strigenz. Farm business marketing and managing magazine. Monthly.
Illustrations: Buys 20 illustrations/issue from freelancers. Send query letter with brochure showing art style or tear sheets, photocopies and slides. Samples not kept on file are returned by SASE. Works on assignment only. To show a portfolio, mail final reproduction/product, color, tear sheets and b&w. "No phone calls." Buys exclusive rights. Originals returned by special arrangement only. Pays $500-800 color, cover; $150-300 b&w and $200-400 color, inside; on publication.

FARMSTEAD MAGAZINE, Box 111, Freedom ME 04941. (207)382-6200. Publisher: George Frangoulis. Focuses on home gardening and country living. Published 6 times a year. Circ. 125,000. Free sample copy and artist's guidelines with 8½x11 SASE.
Illustrations: Buys 2 illustrations/issue. Receives 5 submissions/week from freelancers. Interested in farming, gardening, plants, livestock, wildlife, etc. (pen & ink, wood block, etching). Works on assignment only. Call to schedule an appointment to show a portfolio, which should include roughs, original/final art or final reproduction/product. SASE. Reports in 8 weeks. Buys all rights on a work-for-hire basis. Pays $125 color, cover; $25-100 b&w; $50-100 color, inside; on publication.
Tips: "Send attractive resume that is short and simple, and several samples (photocopies preferred) of work, slides for color work. Creative brochures are eye-catching. Artist should include a telephone number—we often call on short notice. No samples returned without SASE."

FARM SUPPLIER, Watt Publishing Co., Mount Morris IL 61054. Managing Editor: Marcella Sadler. For retail farm suppliers and dealers throughout the US. Monthly.
Illustrations: "We use color slides that match editorial material. They should relate to the farm supply retail business, including custom application of chemicals and fertilizers." Send query letter with slides. To show a portfolio, mail photographs and slides. Pays $150 color, cover; on acceptance.

THE FIDDLEHEAD, Old Arts Bldg, University of New Brunswick, Frederiction, New Brunswick E3B 5A3 Canada. (506)454-3591. Editor: Michael Taylor. Emphasizes poetry, short stories, essays and book reviews for a general audience. Quarterly. Circ. 1,050. Original artwork returned after publication. Sample copy $4.25 plus postage.
Illustrations: Buys 3-5 illustrations/issue from freelancers. Send query letter with tear sheets, photostats and photocopies to be filed "if considered suitable." Samples returned by SASE (Canadian stamps or IRC). Reports within 6-8 weeks. Buys first rights. Pays $50, b&w and $75, color, cover; $20, b&w, inside; on publication.
Tips: "There is a trend away from cartoons to line drawings and much more brush work; abstract work

is becoming more desirable. When sending samples, doodles aren't acceptable; there needs to be some purpose.''

***FIELD & STREAM MAGAZINE**, 1515 Broadway, New York NY 10036. (212)719-6552. Art Director: Victor J. Closi. Magazine emphasizing wildlife hunting and fishing. Monthly. Circ. 2 million. Original artwork returned after publication. Sample copy and art guidelines free for SASE.
Illustrations: Buys 9-12 illustrations/issue from freelancers. Works on assignment only. Prefers "good drawing and painting ability, realistic style, some conceptual and humorous styles are also used depending on magazine article." Send query letter with brochure showing art style or tear sheets and slides. Samples not filed are returned only if requested. Reports only if interested. Call or write to schedule an appointment to show a portfolio, which should include roughs, original/final art, final reproduction/product and tear sheets. Buys first rights. Payment varies: $75-300 on simple spots; $500-1,000 single page; $1,000 and up on spreads, and $1,500 and up on covers; on acceptance.

FIGHTING WOMAN NEWS, Box 1459, Grand Central Station, New York NY 10163. Art Director: Muskat Buckby. Emphasizes women's martial arts for adult women actively practicing some form of martial art; 90% college graduates. Quarterly. Circ. 5,000. Accepts previously published material, "but we must be told about the previous publication." Sample copy $3.50; art guidelines for SASE with 39¢ postage.
Cartoons: Buys 0-1 cartoon/issue from freelancers. Cartoon format open; no color. Send query letter with samples of style to be kept on file. Material not filed is returned by SASE. Reports as soon as possible. Buys one-time rights. Pays in copies.
Illustrations: Buys 3-4 illustrations/issue from freelancers. "No woman black-belt beating up men or 'sexy' themes—done to death!" Send query letter with tear sheets and photostats to be kept on file. Samples not filed are returned by SASE. Reports as soon as possible. Write to schedule an appointment to show a portfolio. Buys one-time rights. Pays $10, b&w, cover; in copies, b&w, inside; on publication.
Tips: "We *strongly* suggest artists examine a sample copy before submitting! When requesting a sample copy, tell us you are an artist or cartoonist so we can send an appropriate sample."

FIRST HAND LTD., 310 Cedar Ln., Teaneck NJ 07666. (201)836-9177. Art Director: Jeff Madden. Emphasizes homoerotica for a male audience. Monthly. Circ. 60,000. Original artwork can be returned after publication. Sample copy $3; art guidelines available for SASE.
Cartoons: Buys 5 cartoons/issue from freelancers. Prefers single panel with gagline; b&w line drawings. Send finished cartoons to be kept on file. Material not filed is returned by SASE. Reports within 2 weeks. Buys first rights. Pays $15 for b&w; on acceptance.
Illustrations: Buys 20 illustrations/issue from freelancers. Prefers "nude men in a realistic style; very basic, very simple." Send query letter with photostats or tear sheets to be kept on file. Samples not filed are returned. Reports within 2 weeks. Call or write for appointment to show portfolio. Buys all magazine rights. Pays $25-50 for inside b&w; on acceptance.
Tips: When reviewing a portfolio, looks for "porportion and skill—proof that the artist has seen a human body naked. Don't send artwork that is too large. The closer the art is to the size of the magazine, the better."

FISHING WORLD, 51 Atlantic Ave., New York NY 11001. (516)352-9700. Editor: Keith Gardner. Emphasizes angling. Readers are adult male US sport fishermen. Bimonthly. Circ. 335,000. Original artwork returned after publication. Sample copy $1.
Illustrations: Buys 1 illustration/issue from freelancers. Interested in realistic illustrations. Uses inside color washes. Works on assignment only. No samples returned. Send brochure, flyer and tear sheets to be kept on file for future assignments. SASE. Reports in 3 weeks. Buys first North American serial rights. Pays $300 for cover color; on acceptance.

FLING, Relim Publishing Co., 550 Miller Ave., Mill Valley CA 94941. (415)383-5464. Editor: Arv Miller. Bimonthly. Emphasizes sex, seduction, sports, underworld pieces, success stories, travel, adventure and how-to's for men, 18-34. Sample copy for $4.
Cartoons: Prefers sexual themes. "The female characters must be pretty, sexy and curvy, with extremely big breasts. Sytles should be sophisticated and well-drawn." Pays $30, b&w, $50-100, color; on acceptance.

FLORIST, Florists Transworld Delivery Association, Box 2227, Southfield MI 48037. (313)355-9300. Editor-in-Chief: William Golden. Production Manager: Kim Segula. Managing Editor: Susan Nicholas. Emphasizes information pertaining to the operation of the floral industry. For florists and floriculturists. Monthly. Circ. 24,000. Reports in 1 month. Accepts previously published material. Does not return original artwork after publication.

Cartoons: Buys 3 cartoons/issue. Interested in retail florists and floriculture themes; single panel with gagline. Mail samples or roughs. SASE. Buys one-time rights. Pays $20, b&w line drawings; on acceptance.
Illustrations: Works on assignment only. Send query letter with photostats, tear sheets, photocopies, slides or photographs. Samples not filed are returned by SASE. Reports within 3 months. To show a portfolio, mail final reproduction/product, tear sheets, photostats and photographs. Buys first rights.

FLOWER AND GARDEN, 4251 Pennsylvania, Kansas City MO 64111. (816)531-5730. Editor: Rachel Snyder. Emphasizes "gardening for avid home gardeners." Bimonthly. Circ. 500,000. Sample copy $2.
Cartoons: Uses 1 cartoon/issue. Receives about 10 submissions/week. Needs cartoons related to "indoor or outdoor home gardening." Format: single panel b&w line drawings or washes with gagline. Prefers to see finished cartoons. SASE. Reports in 4 weeks. Buys one-time rights. Pays $20, b&w cartoon; on acceptance.

FLY FISHERMAN, Editorial Offices, Box 8200, 2245 Kohn Rd., Harrisburg PA 17105. (802)867-5951. Art Director: Jeanne Collins. Emphasizes fly fishing. Readers are 99% male; 79% are college graduates; 79% are married. Published 6 times a year. Circ. 143,988. Original artwork returned after publication. Sample copy $3; art guidelines for SASE.
Illustrations: Uses spots, maps and diagrams. Receives about 20 submissions/week from freelancers. Interested in "saltwater and freshwater fly-fishing or stream-scene in all areas of the country. Scenics including insects, fish—preferably not dead or braces of—and related subjects." Prefers b&w line drawings, b&w washes and color washes for inside magazine. Freelancers are selected from "samples and spot-filler-work kept on file." Send query letter or a sample of work preferably in the fly-fishing or stream area to be kept on file for future assignments. Prefers to see samples of style or arrange personal appointment to show portfolio. SASE. Reports in 4-6 weeks. Buys one-time North American magazine rights. Pays $25-200 for b&w "depending on size and use inside the magazine"; color payment negotiated; on publication.

THE FLYFISHER, 1387 Cambridge Dr., Idaho Falls ID 83401. (208)523-7300. Editor: Dennis G. Bitton. For members of the Federation of Fly Fishers. Concerns fly fishing and conservation. Quarterly. Circ. 10,000. Buys first North American serial rights. Sample copy $3 from Federation of Fly Fishers main office, Box 1088, West Yellowstone, MT 59758.
Cartoons: Buys 3-4 cartoons/issue. Pays $25 b&w; $25-150 color.
Illustrations: Interested in fly-fishing themes. Send query letter with tear sheets, photostats and photocopies. Samples returned by SASE. Reports in 2 weeks. To show a portfolio, mail appropriate materials. Buys first North American serial rights. Pays $150-200 b&w and; $150-200 color, cover; $25-150 b&w and; $35-150 color, inside; on publication.
Tips: "We always encourage freelancers to submit material. The possibility for a sale is good with good material. We especially look for an artist's ability to illustrate an article by reading the copy. See a current issue of the magazine. In general there is better line art. There are more artists, yes I use more."

FOOD & WINE, 1120 Avenue of the Americas, New York NY 10036. (212)382-5702. Art Director: Elizabeth Woodson. Emphasizes food and wine for "an upscale audience who cook, entertain and dine out stylishly." Monthly. Circ. 600,000.
Illustrations: Buys all from freelancers. Interested in sophisticated style. Works on assignment and pick up. Send brochure and samples of style to be kept on file; drop portfolio off on third Tuesday of the month only. Reports when assignment is available. Buys one-time rights or all rights. Pays $100 minimum, inside, b&w line drawings; on acceptance.

FOOD ENGINEERING MAGAZINE, Chilton Way, Radnor PA 19089. (215)964-4459. Art Director: Scott Stephens.Emphasizes food processing and packaging materials and methods for food processing executives. Monthly. Circ. 50,000. Accepts previously published material. Does not return original artwork after publication. Sample copy available.
Cartoons: Buys 12-15 cartoons/issue from freelance artists. Send query letter with samples. Pays $75, b&w; $150 color; on publication.
Illustrations: Buys 30-40 illustrations/issue. Works on assignment only. Send query letter with tear sheets, slides and photographs to be kept on file. Samples not filed are returned by SASE. Reports only if interested. To show a portfolio, mail final reproduction/product, color and photographs. Buys all rights. Pays $100 b&w; $200 color, inside; on publication.
Tips: "There are more high-tech style illustrations and design trends. We need better quality work to meet today's standards. Be technically accurate and precise."

FOOD PROCESSING, Putman Publishing Co., 301 E. Erie, Chicago IL 60611. Editor/Publisher: Roy Hlavacek. Emphasizes equipment, new developments, laboratory instruments and government regulations of the food processing industry. For executives and managers in food processing industries. Monthly. Circ. 68,000. Photocopied submissions OK. Original artwork not returned after publication. Free sample copy and artist's guidelines.
Cartoons: Buys 1-2 cartoons/issue from freelancers. Receives 10-15 submissions/week from freelancers. Interested in "situations in and around the food plant (e.g., mixing, handling, transporting, weighing, analyzing, government inspection, etc.)"; single panel with gagline. Prefers to see finished cartoons. SASE. Reports in 1 week. Buys all rights. Pays $20 minimum, b&w line drawings.
Tips: "Avoid most 'in-the-home' and all retailing cartoon situations. Stick to in-the-food-plant situations—meat packing, vegetable and fruit canning, candymaking, beverage processing, bakery, dairy—including any phase of processing, inspecting, handling, quality control, packaging, storage, shipping, etc."

FORMAT: ART AND THE WORLD, Seven Oaks Press, 405 S. 7th St., St. Charles IL 60174. (312)584-0187. Editor: Ms. C.L. Morrison. Emphasizes art, society, artist's lives and social role, criticism and political critiques. Quarterly.
Illustrations: Assigns 3 freelance jobs for covers and 5 for text illustrations/year. "Material accepted must be philosophically or idea-oriented, not slick. May be abstract or accompanied by writing; symbolic, personal sketchbook-type work. Also embarking on a new project in which layouts for a whole issue are given to a single artist who will then do artwork throughout the issue for direct, one-time publication." Send small b&w sketches (photocopies acceptable) with SASE. Do not send slides and do not query. Reports within 8 weeks. Original work returned to artist after job's completion. Considers the project's budget when establishing payment. Pays by the project, $5-15.

FORUM MAGAZINE, 1965 Broadway, New York NY 10023-5965. (212)496-6100. Art Director: John Arocho. Emphasizes medicine/human relations/sexuality. Monthly. Circ. 350,000. Returns original artwork after publication. Art guidelines available.
Illustrations: Buys 3-6 illustrations/issue from freelancers. Works on assignment only. Prefers graphic b&w, variable subject matter. Send query letter with tear sheets, photostats and photocopies to be kept on file. Call for appointment to show portfolio, which should include original/final art, final reproduction/product, color and b&w. Samples not filed are returned only if requested. Reports only if interested. Negotiates rights purchased. Pays $800 for b&w and $1,200 for color, inside; on acceptance.
Tips: "There is a large number of young illustrators in the field right now who have added a vitality to the business. The changes with these young illustrators give me a chance to be more selective. Use a variety of styles and put your best work forward."

4-H LEADER-THE NATIONAL MAGAZINE FOR 4-H, 7100 Connecticut Ave., Chevy Chase MD 20815. (301)656-9000. Editor: Suzanne Carney Harting. Emphasizes techniques for working with children, and interests of children, for adult and teenaged 4-H volunteers. Receives few cartoons and 2-3 illustrations/week from freelance artists.
Illustrations: Especially needs themes on families, teen interest and adults interacting with youngsters. Send query letter with brochure showing art style or photostats, tear sheets or photocopies to be kept on file. No originals. May be any type b&w technique, watercolor, charcoal sketch, scratchboard, pen & ink or woodcuts. "Art should suggest rather than show literal detail." SASE. Reports in 1 month. Buys one-time rights. Pays $10-50; on acceptance.

***4 WHEEL & OFF-ROAD MAGAZINE**, 8490 Sunset Blvd., Los Angeles CA 90069. Art Director: Karen Hawley. Magazine emphasizing 4-wheel drive vehicles for males aged 16-35. Monthly. Circ. 350-400,000.
Cartoons: Buys 1-3 cartoons/issue from freelancers. Prefers single or multiple panel; b&w line drawings. Send samples of style to be kept on file. Call to schedule an appointment to show a portfolio. Material not kept on file is returned only if requested. Reports only if interested. Buys all rights.
Illustrations: Buys 0-3 illustrations/issue from freelancers. Works on assignment only. Send query letter with resume, tear sheets, photostats and photocopies. Samples not filed are returned only if requested. Reports only if interested. Call or write to schedule an appointment to show a portfolio, which should include original/final art and final reproduction/product. Buys all rights. Pays on publication.

***FREEWAY**, Box 632, Glen Ellyn IL 60138. (312)668-6000. Designer: Mardelle Ayers. Sunday School paper emphasizing Christian living for teenagers for high school and college age teens from a conservative, evangelical Christian upbringing. Published 4 quarters a year, 13 issues per quarter. Circ. 60,000. Accepts previously published material. Returns originals after publication. Sample copy free for SASE with 22¢ postage.

Cartoons: Buys 4-5 cartoons/quarter. Prefers any style or theme that appeals to teens. Prefers single, double or multiple panel with gagline; b&w line drawings or b&w washes. Send query letter with finished cartoons. Material not kept on file is returned by SASE. Reports within 4 weeks. Buys first rights. Pays $15, b&w.

Illustrations: Buys 1-3 illustrations/issue from freelancers. Works on assignment only. Prefers any theme or style appealing to teens. Send query letter with resume, photostats and photocopies. Samples not filed are returned by SASE if requested. Reports only if interested. To show a portfolio, mail photostats and b&w photos. Payment is variable on acceptance.

***FRETS MAGAZINE, THE MAGAZINE FOR ACOUSTIC STRING MUSICIANS**, 20085 Stevens Creek, Cupertino CA 95014. (408)446-1105. Art Director: Lachlan Throndson. Magazine emphasizing acoustic string instrument playing, building and teaching for acoustic string instrument builders, players, teachers and salesmen. Monthly. Circ. 70,000. Accepts previously published material. Original artwork returned after publication. Sample and/or art guidelines free for SASE with 22¢ postage.

Cartoons: Rarely buys cartoons from freelancers. Send query letter with samples of style to be kept on file. Material not kept on file is returned only if requested. Does not report back. Buys one-time or reprint rights. Pays $35-50, b&w."

THE FRIEND, 50 E. North Temple, Salt Lake City UT 84150. (801)531-2210. Contact: Art Director. Children's publication of the Church of Jesus Christ of Latter-day Saints. Emphasizes the cultures and children of different countries. Original artwork returned after publication, usually after about 1 year.

Illustrations: Uses 30-35 illustrations/issue; buys about 12/issue from freelancers. Interested in themes mostly specific to individual art assignments from our concepts (child-related, dealing with ages 1-12); excellent, competitive quality. Covers often emphasize seasons and holidays; wide spectrum of styles and ideas. Works with freelancers on assignment basis only except for activity related things. Samples returned if artist requests. Provide printed samples to be kept on file for future assignments. Prefers roughs of ideas before finish art. SASE. Report depends on specific art assignment. Need to retain art for about a year. Pays $200-600, b&w, 2-color and full-color; on acceptance.

***FRIENDS OF WINE/LES AMIS DU VIN'S MAGAZINE OF WINE AND FOOD**, 2302 Perkins Pl., Silver Spring MD 20910. Administrative Assistant to Managing Editor: Lila Mensh. Magazine emphasizing wine and food for "highest profile, pre-selective audience of wine and spirits buyers. Over 80 percent are professionals with graduate school education." Circ. 87,000. Accepts previously published material. Original artwork returned after publication. Sample copy available.

Illustrations: Buys 3 illustrations/issue from freelancers. Works on assignment only. Prefers wine and food themes. Send slides and photographs. Samples not filed are returned only if requested. Reports only if interested. To show a portfolio, mail appropriate materials; portfolio should include color and b&w. Buys reprint rights. Pays $200, b&w; $350, color; cover; $100, b&w; $150, color, inside; on publication.

FRONT PAGE DETECTIVE, RGH Publications, 20th Floor, 460 W. 34th St., New York NY 10001. Editor: Rose Mandelsberg. For mature adults—law enforcement officials, professional investigators, criminology buffs and interested laymen. Monthly.

Cartoons: Must have crime theme. Submit finished art. SASE. Reports in 10 days. Buys all rights. Pays $25; on acceptance.

Tips: "Make sure the cartoons submitted do not degrade or ridicule law enforcement officials. Omit references to supermarkets/convenience stores."

FUR-FISH-GAME, A.R. Harding Publishing Co., 2878 E. Main St., Columbus OH 43209. (614)231-9585. Editor/Art Director: Ken Dunwoody. Monthly magazine with circulation of 180,000 for practical outdoorsmen, emphasizing hunting, fishing, trapping and camping. Previously published work OK in some cases. Sample copy $1; free artists' guidelines.

Covers: Uses 12/year, mostly from freelancers. Receives about 1 submission/week. Interested in game animals, gamebirds, gamefish and furbearers. Prefers to see color photograph or transparency of art. SASE. Reports in 4 weeks. Painting must be able to crop into square format for cover. Pays $75 for one-time rights for full-color covers; on acceptance.

Illustrations: Uses 12-40 b&w/year, mostly from freelancers responding to assigned work. Interested freelancers should send query letter with specific submissions or samples of work. Photostats or other reproductions preferred as submissions. SASE if needed. Pays $15-25 for most, on acceptance.

Tips: "We are seeking quality color paintings for our covers. We work at least 10 weeks in advance with covers and attempt to keep them seasonal. Subjects such as small game, common game fish and furbearers have the best chance of acceptance. Prefer artist's signature on right side of painting. Credit will be given in table of contents. We are looking for very realistic work that contains a certain freshness and vitality, especially for our covers. The work must not only be visually appealing, but also painstakingly accurate in its detail of wild animals or birds. Familiarize yourself with the magazine before making queries or sending samples."

FUTURIFIC MAGAZINE, Suite 1210, 280 Madison Ave., New York NY 10016. Publisher: B. Szent-Miklosy. Emphasizes future-related subjects for highly educated, upper income government, corporate leaders of the community. Monthly. Circ. 10,000. Previously published material and simultaneous submissions OK. Original artwork returned after publication. Free sample copy for SASE with $1 postage and handling.
Cartoons: Buys 5/issue from freelancers. Prefers positive, upbeat, futuristic themes; no "doom and gloom." Prefers single, double or multiple panel with or without gagline, b&w line drawings. Send finished cartoons. Samples returned by SASE. Reports within 4 weeks. Will negotiate rights and payment. Pays on publication.
Illustrations: Buys 5 illustrations/issue from freelancers. Prefers positive, upbeat, futuristic themes; no "doom and gloom." Send finished art. Samples returned by SASE. Reports within 4 weeks. Call or write to schedule an appointment to show a portfolio. Will negotiate rights and payment. Pays on publication.
Tips: "Only optimists need apply. Looking for good, clean art. Interested in future development of current affairs, but not sci-fi."

THE FUTURIST, 4916 St. Elmo Ave., Bethesda MD 20814. (301)656-8274. Art Director: Cynthia Fowler. Assistant Editor: Tim Willard. Emphasizes all aspects of the future for a well-educated, general audience. Bimonthly. Circ. 30,000. Accepts simultaneous submissions. Return of original artwork following publication depends on individual agreement. Sample copy available.
Illustrations: Buys 3-4 illustrations/issue from freelancers. Uses a variety of themes and styles "usually line-drawings, often whimsical. We like an artist who can read an article and deal with the concepts and ideas." Works on assignment only. Send query letter with brochure, samples or tear sheets to be kept on file. Call or write for appointment to show portfolio. "Photostats are fine as samples; whatever is easy for the artist." Reports only if interested. Rights purchased negotiable. Pays $300-500, color, cover; $100-125, b&w, inside; on acceptance.

GALLERY MAGAZINE, 800 2nd Ave., New York NY 10017. (212)986-9600. Creative Director: Michael Monte. Emphasizes sophisticated men's entertainment for the middle-class, collegiate male. Monthly. Circ. 700,000. No art guidelines, editorial content dictates illustration style.
Cartoons: Buys 5 cartoons/issue from freelancers. Interested in sexy humor; single, double, or multiple panel with or without gagline, color and b&w washes, b&w line drawings. Send finished cartoons. Reports in 1 month. Buys first rights. Pays on publication. Enclose SASE. Contact: J. Linden.
Illustrations: Buys 4 full-page illustrations and 4 spots/issue from freelancers. Works on assignment only. Interested in the "highest creative and technical styles." Especially needs slick, high quality, 4-color work. Send flyer, samples and tear sheets to be kept on file for possible future assignments. Send samples of style or submit portfolio. Samples returned by SASE. Reports in several weeks. Negotiates rights purchased. Pays $800 maximum for inside color washes; on publication.

GAMES, 515 Madison Ave., New York NY 10022. (212)421-5984. Contact: Art Director. Emphasizes games, puzzles, mazes, brain teasers, etc. for teachers, students, computer analysts and mathematicians interested in paper-and-pencil games. Monthly. Circ. 750,000.
Cartoons: Buys 1 cartoon/issue from freelancers. Pays $100 b&w and $200 color.
Illustrations: Buys 5-15 illustrations/issue from freelancers. Illustrations should be lighthearted but not childish. Prefers b&w line drawings and color renderings for inside and cover. Send query letter with brochure showing art style or tear sheets. To show a portfolio, mail tear sheets or call to schedule an appointment. Buys one-time rights. Pays $1,500 b&w, cover; $400 b&w and $500 color, inside; on acceptance.
Tips: "We encourage artists to create games or puzzles that they can execute in their own style after editorial approval. Illustrations are often required to be based on specific puzzles but can also be conceptual in nature."

GARDEN, New York Botanical Garden, Bronx NY 10458. Associate Editor: Anne Schwartz. Emphasizes all aspects of the plant world—botany, horticulture, the environment, etc. for "members of botanical gardens and arboreta—a diverse readership, largely college graduates and professionals, with a common interest in plants." Bimonthly. Circ. 30,000. Accepts previously published material. Original artwork returned after publication. Sample copy $2.50.
Illustrations: Buys 0-1 illustration/issue from freelancers. Works on assignment only. Local artists preferred. Send query letter with photostats, photographs, tear sheets, slides or photocopies. Especially

Close-up

George Stavrinos
Illustrator
New York City

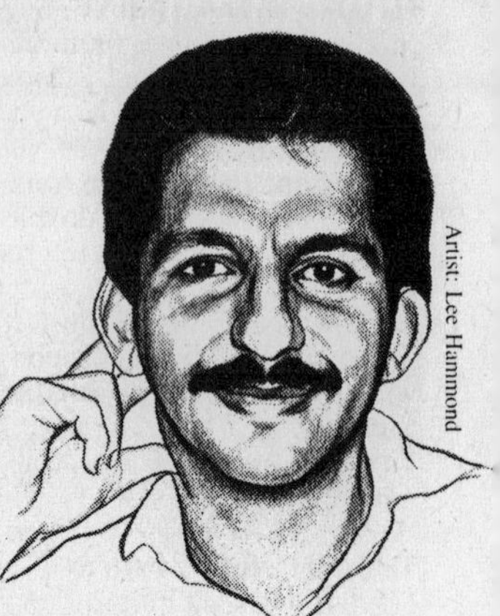

Though he regularly illustrates the pages of top fashion magazines, George Stavrinos does not consider himself a fashion illustrator. "I don't do fashion illustration. I do art that contains fashion information." He relies on his trained eye as an illustrator to catch the nuances of his subjects—whether they are fashion models in *Vogue* or *Gentleman's Quarterly* or celebrities such as John Cougar Mellencamp for *Playboy*. "I'm a stickler for conveying the feeling of an object. The better I got in drawing, the better these things were conveyed."

Stavrinos is the master of the graphite pencil, one of the most fundamental tools of a draftsman. He emphasizes the importance of students learning solid draftsmanship and graphic skills. "A lot of people put down graphic art, but I feel my graphics background helped me a lot with layout." A drawing class he took as a student at the Rhode Island School of Design helped him "draw the part we see and understand the part we don't see."

Most artistic types complain about deadlines, but Stavrinos thrives under the discipline of art studio and print time frames. "The more I draw under deadline supervision, the more I learn." He came to New York with a heavy portfolio and set up appointments at places he thought best suited his style. Push Pin Studios hired him as a fulltime freelancer. Then he took his work to the *New York Times*, where he illustrated the book review, travel and magazine sections. "I was at the right place at the right time. I came to New York with black-and-white work when color was used a lot. My layout was very strong, and the people at the *Times* got very excited about it, because it gave them a new thing to work with."

To approach the magazine and newspaper market, Stavrinos suggests that freelance artists should "hit everybody that could use the work that you like to do and the ones that look like they hire a lot of people." He added that the *New York Times* proved to be very helpful because it has such a large circulation. "That's the nice thing about magazines and newspapers—you get immediate results and you're so visible. I would get a week's worth of calls from one piece in the *Times*. People were able to follow my work, people who would not normally be looking at fashion art."

Over the years he has developed a reputation as an expert draftsman who not only meets deadlines but is also a thoroughly professional businessman. He answers calls promptly, keeps appointments and maintains a forthright manner—etiquette which all artists must observe to be successful.

He conducts business during the day, making appointments and sketching, then draws his finished products at night without so many distractions. He begins a project with a small sketch, referring to a photographic file for background information. "I go through a lot of sketches before the final product. I try out a lot of ideas." He then hones his sketches into a polished perfection with his graphite pencils, occasionally using tempera for backgrounds or watercolors for washes. While he is drawing, Stavrinos listens to Puccini, Cole Porter and movies—"I listen to movies after I've watched them."

It has been said that success is a journey, not a destination, and Stavrinos' aspirations prove this to be true. Besides illustrating for magazines and recently for the New York City Opera, he has been experimenting with computer art. He feels it is challenging because "I can't do the same things I'm doing in drawing. So it's forcing me to try something new." He would also like to draw visualizations for films, having worked on one already. "People say my black-and-white work reminds them of movie stills."

What is his ultimate advice to freelance artists? "Draw every day. The only times I see improvement in my work is when I am constantly working."

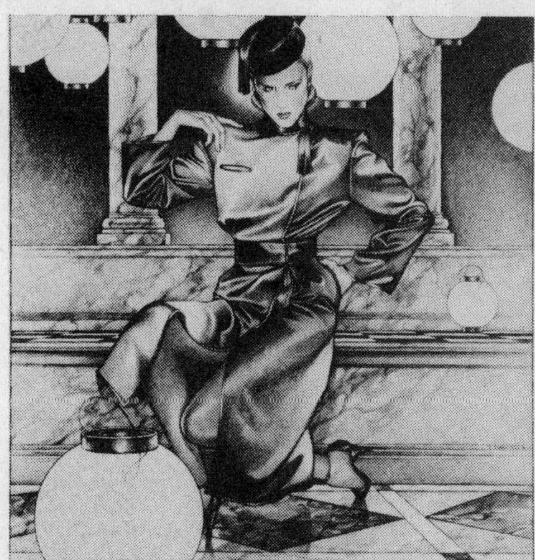

Bergdorf Goodman commissioned Stavrinos to illustrate an advertisement for the store in the New York Times. *Rendered with tempera and graphite pencils on Strathmore paper, the figure shows the classic lines and attention to detail that mark Stavrinos' work.*

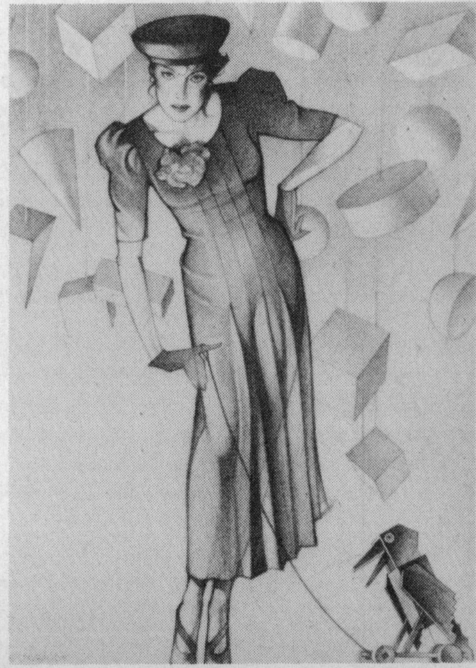

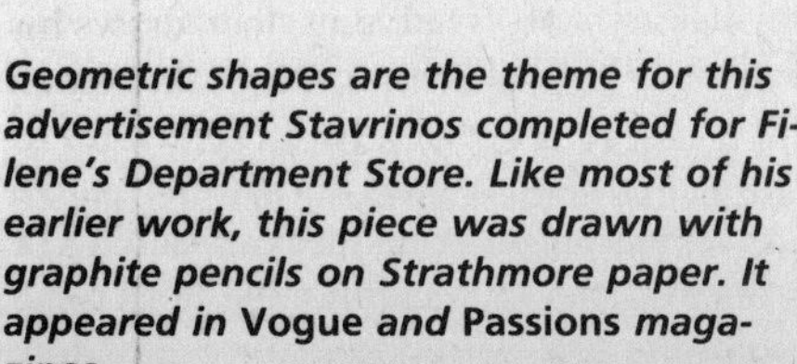

Geometric shapes are the theme for this advertisement Stavrinos completed for Filene's Department Store. Like most of his earlier work, this piece was drawn with graphite pencils on Strathmore paper. It appeared in Vogue *and* Passions *magazines.*

looks for "quality, botanical accuracy and style." Samples not kept on file are returned by SASE. Reports only if interested. To show a portfolio, mail appropriate materials. Buys one-time rights. Pays $25 minimum, b&w, inside; on publication.

GENERAL LEARNING CORPORATION, (formerly Curriculum Innovations), 3500 Western Ave., Highland Park IL 60035. (312)432-2700, (800)323-5471. Photo & Graphics Editor: Barbara A. Bennett. Associate Photo Editor: Kelly Mountain. Produces 10 magazines—*Current Health 1*, *Current Health 2*, *Career World*, *Writing!* and *Current Consumer & Lifestudies* published monthly during the school year and *New Driver* published quarterly. Readership is 7-12th grade students. Remaining four titles are *Your Health & Fitness* and *Your Health & Safety*, both bimonthly, *Energy Sense* and *Money Plan* both quarterly. The readership is a general audience. Accepts previously published material. Original artwork returned after publication. Sample copy free for 8x10 SASE.
Illustrations: Student publications use a varying number of b&w illustrations/issue. General magazines use 5-10 b&w and color illustrations/issue and work on an assignment basis only. Send query letter with photocopies or slides. Samples are returned only by request with SASE. Reports within 2-4 weeks. Buys one-time rights for student magazines, negotiates payment, pays on publication. Negotiates rights purchased and payment for general magazines; on acceptance.

GENT, Dugent Publishing Co., 2355 Salzedo St., Coral Gables FL 33134. Publisher: Douglas Allen. Editor: John Fox. Managing Editor: Nye Willden. For men "who like big women."
Cartoons: Buys humor and sexual themes; "major emphasis of magazine is on large D-cup-breasted women." Mail cartoons. Buys first rights. Pays $50, b&w spot drawing; $75/page.
Illustrations: Buys 3-4 illustrations/issue on assigned themes. Submit illustration samples for files. Buys b&w only. Buys first rights. Pays $100-150.
Tips: "Send samples designed especially for our publication. Study our magazine. Be able to draw erotic anatomy. Write for artist's guides and cartoon guides *first*, before submitting samples, since they contain some helpful suggestions."

GENTLEMANS QUARTERLY, 350 Madison Ave., New York NY 10017. (212)880-6691. Art Director: Mary Shanahan. Emphasizes "men's fashions and lifestyles for middle-to upper-income professional males ranging in age from 20 to 40." Monthly. Circ. 650,000. No cartoons.
Illustrations: Uses less than 10 illustrations/issue, all supplied by freelancers. Selection based on review of portfolios ("we have a strict first time drop-off policy") and by reviewing files maintained on freelancers. Send copied samples of b&w and color drawings to art assistant; do not send original work. SASE. Reports in 1 week. Pays 30 days after work is completed. Buys all rights on a work-for-hire basis.

GLAMOUR, 350 Madison Ave., New York NY 10017. (212)880-8800. Art Director: George Hartman. Emphasizes fashion, beauty, travel, lifestyle for women ages 18-35. Query with resume and arrange to show portfolio.
Needs: "All work done here is freelance." Pays $225/page.

GLASS DIGEST, 310 Madison Ave., New York NY 10017. Editor: Charles B. Cumpston. For management in the distribution, merchandising, and installation phases of the flat glass, architectural metal, and allied products industry (including stained, art glass and mirrors). Original artwork not returned after publication. Free sample copy.
Cartoons: Uses 0-3 cartoons/issue; buys about 2/issue from freelancers. Receives 5 submissions/week from freelancers. Interested in storefront and curtain wall construction and automotive glass industry. Prefers to see finished cartoons. SASE. Reports in 1 week. Pays $7.50; on acceptance.
Illustrations: Works on assignment only. Prefers to see roughs. Samples returned by SASE. Reports in 1 week. Buys first North American serial rights. Pays on acceptance.
Tips: "Stick to the subject matter."

***GLASS NEWS**, (formerly National Glass Budgets) Box 7138, Pittsbrugh PA 15213. (412)362-5136. Manager: Liz Scott. Emphasizes glass manufacturing and industry news for glass manufacturers, dealers, and others involved in making, buying, and selling glass items and products. Semimonthly. Circ. 1,600. Free sample copy with 1st class stamp.
Cartoons: Uses 1 cartoon/issue. Receives an average of 1 submisson/week from freelancers. Cartoons should pertain to glass manufacturing (flat glass, fiberglass, bottles and containers; no mirrors). Prefers single and multiple panel b&w line drawings with gagline. Prefers roughs or finished cartoons. SASE. Reports in 1 month. Buys all rights. Pays $25; on acceptance.
Tips: "Learn about making glass of all kinds."

***GLIMPSES OF GUAM AND MICRONESIA**, Box 8066, Tamuning, Guam 96911. 477-3483. Editor: Dr. Pedro C. Sanchez. "A regional publication for Micronesia lovers, travel buffs, and readers interested in America's last frontier. Our audience covers all age levels and is best described as well educated and fascinated by our part of the world." Quarterly. Circ. 10,000. Original artwork returned after publication. Sample copy $3.
Cartoons: "Use very little, but willing to look at Pacific-related themes."
Illustrations: "We are interested in story illustration, both color and b&w." Works on assignment only. Send brochure showing art style or resume and tear sheets and photocopies. SASE. Buys all rights on a work-for-hire basis, or first North American rights if work was not solicited by us. Payment varies; $30 for full-page b&w; $15-100 for cover illustration.

***GOLDEN YEARS MAGAZINE**, 233 E. New Haven Ave., Melbourne FL 32901. Art Director: Debbie Billington. Magazine for the mature market (50 and over). Monthly. Circ. 700,000. Accepts previously published material. Original artwork returned after publication. Sample copy $1. Art guidelines available.

GOLF JOURNAL, Golf House, Far Hills NJ 07931. (201)234-2300. Managing Editor: George Eberl. Readers are "literate, professional, knowledgeable on the subject of golf." Published 8 times/year. Circ. 140,000. Original artwork not returned after publication. Free sample copy.
Cartoons: Buys 2-3 cartoons/issue from freelancers. Receives 50 submissions/week from freelancers. "The subject is golf. Golf must be central to the cartoon. Drawings should be professional, and captions sharp, bright and literate, on a par with our generally sophisticated readership." Formats: single or multi-panel, b&w line drawings with gagline. Prefers to see finished cartoons. SASE. Reports in 1 month. Buys one-time rights. Pays $25, b&w cartoons; on acceptance.
Illustrations: Buys several illustrations/issue from freelancers. "We maintain a file of samples from illustrators. Our needs for illustrations—and we do need talent with an artistic light touch—are based almost solely on assignments, illustrations to accompany specific stories. We would assign a job to an illustrator who is able to capture the feel and mood of a story. Most frequently, it is light-touch golf stories that beg illustrations. A sense of humor is a useful quality in the illustrator; but this sense shouldn't lapse into absurdity." Uses color washes. Send samples of style to be kept on file for future assignments. SASE. Reports in 1 month. Buys all rights on a work-for-hire basis. Payment varies, "usually $300/page.
Tips: "We often need illustrations supporting a story. Knowledge of the game and a light touch, however, are imperative and, too often, sadly lacking. I can't call it a trend, but at times it seems that self expression supersedes the ability and willingness to underscore a point artistically."

***GOLF MAGAZINE**, Times Mirror Magazines, 380 Madison Ave., New York NY 10017. Art Director: Ron Ramsey. Emphasizes golf. Monthly. Circ. 850,000. Original artwork returned after publication. Art guidelines free for SASE.
Illustrations: Uses 3-6 illustrations/issue; buys 2-3/issue from freelancers. Works on assignment only. Send 35mm photographs or tear sheets to be kept on file. Samples not kept on file are returned by SASE. Reports only if interested. Buys first or all rights. Write for appointment to show portfolio; drop off policy. Pays $700, b&w and $1,000, color, cover; $300, b&w and $700, color, inside; on acceptance.

GOLF SHOP OPERATIONS, 5520 Park Ave., Trumbull CT 06611. (203)373-7000. Editor: Nick Romano. Art Director: Karen Polaski. For golf professionals at public and private courses, resorts and driving ranges. Published 6 times/year. Circ. 13,000. Original artwork returned after publication. Free sample copy.
Illustrations: Buys 4-6 illustrations/issue. Works on assignment only. Soft goods oriented. Illustrations often used for conceptual pieces. Send query letter with brochure showing art style or tear sheets, slides and photographs. Samples returned by SASE. Reports back on future assignment possibilities. Reports in 2 weeks. Call to schedule an appointment to show a portfolio, which should include thumbnails, roughs, original/final art, final reproduction/product, color, tear sheets and b&w. Buys one-time reproduction rights on a work-for-hire basis. Pays $50-750; on acceptance.

GOOD HOUSEKEEPING, Hearst Corp., 959 8th Ave., New York NY 10019. (212)262-5700. Editor-in-Chief: John Mack Carter. Contact: Art Director. For homemakers. Emphasizes food, fashion, beauty, home decorating, current events, personal relationships and celebrities. Monthly. Circ. 5,000,000.
Cartoons: Buys 150/year on family life, animals and humor through youth; single panel. Arrange an interview to show portfolio. Buys all reproduction rights. Pays $250 maximum, b&w line drawings and washes; on acceptance.
Illustrations: Buys 15 illustrations/issue on romantic themes. "Drop off" policy for portfolios. Reports in 3 weeks. Buys all reproduction rights. Inside: pay for b&w line drawing and washes depends on complexity of job, $1,000-2,000, color washes and full-color renderings; on acceptance.

GOOD NEWS BROADCASTER, Box 82808, Lincoln NE 68501. Managing Editor: Norman Olson. Interdenominational magazine for adults ages 16 and up. Monthly. Circ. 150,000. Previously published work OK. Original artwork returned after publication. Sample copy $1.50.
Illustrations: Interested in themes that are "serious, related to the subjects of the articles about the Christian life." Works on assignment only. Send query letter with brochure showing art style. Samples returned by SASE. "Helps to know if person is a Christian, too, but not necessary." Reporting time varies. Buys first North American serial rights. Pays $80 color, cover; $20 b&w and $50 color, inside; on publication.
Tips: Trends in the field today include "more realism, more primary colors and more oil painting than pencil/pen." When reviewing work, "we ask how well does it fit the story and does it have a truly professional look? Artists should think of the publication's needs and pay attention to small, but important, details in artwork that will complement the details in the writing."

GOOD READING MAGAZINE, Box 40, Litchfield IL 62056. (217)324-3425. "Nonfiction magazine which emphasizes travel, business, human interest and novel occupations." Monthly. Circ. 12,000. Original artwork returned after publication, only if requested.
Cartoons: Buys 1 cartoon/issue from freelancers. Receives 15 submissions/week from freelancers. Interested in "business, points of interest, people with unusual hobbies and occupations, and wholesome humor." Send query letter with resume and samples. Prefers to see finished cartoons. SASE. Reports in 6-8 weeks. To show a portfolio, mail original/final art. Buys first North American serial rights. Pays $15 b&w; on acceptance.

GRADUATING ENGINEER, 1221 Ave. of the Americas, New York NY 10020. (212)512-3796. Art Director: Vincent Lomonte. Directed to the young engineer in his last year of school, who is about to enter job market. Quarterly with 3 special issues; computer, women, minority. Circ. 85,000. Returns original artwork after publication. Art guidelines available.
Cartoons: Buys 1-2 cartoons/issue from freelancers. Call for appointment to show portfolio. Pays $135-150, b&w; $300-350, color; on acceptance.
Illustrations: Buys 10-15 illustrations/issue from freelancers. Works on assignment only. Send brochure and business card to be kept on file. Will review photostats, tear sheets, photocopies, slides or photographs. Reports back only if interested. Call art director for appointment to show portfolio. Negotiates rights purchased. Pays $200-300 for b&w and $500 for color, cover; $125-225 for b&w inside; on acceptance.

GRAND RAPIDS MAGAZINE, Gemini Publications, Suite 1040, Trust Building, 40 Pearl St. NW, Grand Rapids MI 49503. (616)459-4545. Editor: Ronald E. Koehler. Managing Editor: William Holm. Graphics Editor: Stephen Allie. For greater Grand Rapids residents. Monthly. Circ. 13,500. Original artwork returned after publication. Local artists only.
Cartoons: Buys 2-3 cartoons/issue from freelancers. Prefers Michigan, Western Michigan, Lake Michigan, city, issue or consumer/household themes. Send query letter with samples. Samples not filed are returned by SASE. Reports within 1 month. Buys all rights. Pays $25-35 b&w.
Illustrations: Buys 2-3 illustrations/issue from freelancers. Prefers Michigan, Western Michigan, Lake Michigan, city, issue or consumer/household themes. Send query letter with samples. Samples not filed are returned by SASE. Reports within 1 month. To show a portfolio, mail original/final art and final reproduction/product or call to schedule an appointment. Buys all rights. Pays $100 color, cover; $20-30 b&w and $30-50 color, inside; on publication.
Tips: "Approach only if you have good ideas."

GRAPHIC ARTS MONTHLY, 875 3rd Ave., New York NY 10022. (212)605-9548. Editor: Roger Ynostroza. Managing Editor: Peter Johnston. For management and production personnel in commercial and specialty printing plants and allied crafts. Monthly. Circ. 90,000. Sample copy $5.
Cartoons: Buys 15 cartoons/year on printing, layout, paste-up, typesetting and proofreading; single panel. Mail art. SASE. Reports in 3 weeks. Buys first rights. Pays on acceptance.

GRAY'S SPORTING JOURNAL, 205 Willow St., So. Hamilton MA 01982. (617)468-4486. Editor-in-Chief: Ed Gray. Art Director: DeCourcy Taylor. Concerns the outdoors, hunting and fishing. Published 4 times/year. Circ. 35,000. Sample copy $6.50; free artist's guidelines. SASE.
Illustrations: Buys 10 illustrations/year, 2-6/issue, on hunting and fishing. Send query letter with tear sheets or slides. SASE. Reports in 4 weeks. To show a portfolio, mail tear sheets and photographs. Buys one-time rights. Pays $350, color art; $100-200, b&w line drawings, inside.

GREAT LAKE SPORTSMAN GROUP, Box 2266, Oshkosh WI 54903. Contact: Art Director. Publishes five regional outdoor publications: *Michigan Sportsman, Minnesota Sportsman, Pennsylva-*

nia Outdoors, *New York Afield*, and *Wisconsin Sportsman*. Bimonthlies. Circ. 200,000. Mail art or query with samples or previously published work. SASE. Material is purchased for use in any or all publications at discretion of editor. Reports in 3 weeks. Photocopied submissions OK. Buys one-time rights. Pays on acceptance. Free sample copy. Especially needs good cover material and multi-media illustrators who can work with one-month deadlines.
Cartoons: Buys 50 cartoons/year on the environment, wildlife, hunting and fishing; single, double and multiple panel with or without gaglines. Pays $80-100, b&w and color.
Illustrations: Buys 15-20 illustrations/year on the environment, wildlife and outdoors. "No Disney-type animals. Must be geographically and anatomically correct. No palm trees, snow-capped mountains." Cover: Pays $250 minimum, color. Inside: Pays $50 minimum, b&w; $100 minimum, color.
Tips: "Study the magazines and send SASE with all work."

***GREAT LAKES TRAVEL & LIVING**, 108 W. Perry St., Port Clinton OH 43452. (419)734-5774. Associate Editor: Carol B. Brown. Estab. 1986. Magazine emphasizing travel and tourism in the Great Lakes region for people who enjoy living and vacationing in the Great Lakes region. Monthly. Circ. 30,000. Accepts previously published material. Original artwork returned after publication. Sample copy free for SASE with 37¢ postage. Art guidelines free for SASE with 22¢ postage.
Cartoons: Prefers b&w line drawings. Send query letter with samples of style to be kept on file except for items artist requests back. Write or call for appointment to show a portfolio. Material not kept on file is returned by SASE. Reports within 4 weeks. Buys one-time rights. Negotiates payment.
Illustrations: Buys 1-3 illustrations/issue from freelancers. Works on assignment only. Prefers b&w line drawings, usually rendered from photos of locations featured in the editorial material. Send query letter with brochure showing art style. Samples not filed are returned by SASE. Reports within 4 weeks. Call or write to schedule an appointment to show a portfolio. Buys one-time rights or negotiates rights purchased. Negotiates payment. Pays on publication.

***GREATER HARTFORD BUSINESS**, City Place, HQ 31, Hartford CT 06103. (203)275-6555. Editor: Gerald Brittle. Estab. 1986. Magazine emphasizing business and finance in Connecticut for top CEO's, business owners and professionals in the Greater Hartford region. Monthly. Circ. 20,000. Original artwork returned after publication. Sample copy $1.
Cartoons: Buys 2-3 cartoons/issue from freelance artists. Prefers single-panel with gagline, b&w line drawings. Send roughs, which will be kept on file. Material not filed is returned by SASE. Reports back. Buys first rights. Pays $50, b&w.

GREATER PORTLAND MAGAZINE, 142 Free St., Portland ME 04101. (207)772-2811. Editor: Daniel W. Weeks. The city magazine for Portland, Maine. Includes fiction, interviews, theater and restaurant reviews, and features. "Our contemporary graphics and illustrations are aimed at the upscale consumer market—heavy art emphasis." Quarterly. Circ. 10,000. Accepts previously published material if new to this area. Returns original artwork after publication. Sample copy for $1.75.
Cartoons: "I am open to *New Yorkerish* cartoons, but like our stories, they need a local focus." Also looking for a series with local appeal. Send query letter with samples of style to be kept on file. Write or call for appointment to show portfolio. Materials not kept on file are returned by SASE. Reports within 2 weeks if SASE enclosed. Purchases first rights. Negotiates payment; pays on acceptance.
Illustrations: Buys 2/issue. Prefers "airbrush for our fiction section, but like a baby *Esquire*, we like any interpretive stuff. Try for the unusual." Works on assignment only "so far." Uses humorous and cartoon-style illustrations whenever they fit in with a story already planned. Send query letter with brochure, tear sheets, slides or photographs to be kept on file. Write or call for appointment to show portfolio. Samples not kept on file are returned by SASE. Reports within 2 weeks. Pays $150 for color, cover; $150 for color, inside; on acceptance.
Tips: "We particularly enjoy dealing with artists committed to developing a working relationship with us, and who are sensitive to the subject and point of view of individual articles."

GREEN FEATHER MAGAZINE, Box 2633, Lakewood OH 44107. Editor: Gary S. Skeens. Emphasizes fiction and poetry for general audience. Annually. Circ. 150-200. Accepts previously published material. Original artwork returned after publication. Sample copy $1.50; art guidelines free for SASE.
Cartoons: Buys 1 cartoon/issue from freelancers. Prefers single panel with gagline; b&w line drawings. Send query letter with samples of style to be kept on file. Material not filed is returned by SASE. Reports in 1 month. Buys first rights or reprint rights. Negotiates payment, $5 maximum; on publication.
Illustrations: Buys 1 illustration/issue from freelancers. Send query letter with resume, tear sheets or photocopies to be kept on file. Samples not filed are returned by SASE. Reports within 1 month. To show a portfolio, mail tear sheets and b&w. Buys first rights or reprint rights. Negotiates payment. Pays on publication.

THE GRENADIER MAGAZINE, 3833 Lake Shore, Oakland CA 94610. (415)763-0928. Senior Editor: S.A. Jefferis-Tibbets. Emphasizes military simulation and its historical context for military professionals, war gamers and game theorists. Bimonthly. Circ. 5,600. Original artwork not returned after publication. Sample copy for 9x12 SASE with $1.25 postage; art guidelines for SASE with 22¢ postage.
Cartoons: Buys 0-1 cartoon/issue from freelancers. Military simulation theme. Prefers single panel with gagline; b&w line drawings or b&w washes. Send query letter with samples of style or finished cartoons to be kept on file. Material not filed is returned by SASE. Reports within 1 month. To show a portfolio, mail appropriate materials. Buys all rights. Pays $10-5, b&w; open rate, color; on acceptance.
Illustrations: Buys 0-12 illustration/issue from freelancers. Works on assignment only. Send query letter with brochure and samples to be kept on file. Photocopies OK as samples if they show the artist's style and capability. Samples not filed are returned by SASE. Reports within 1 week. To show a portfolio, mail appropriate materials. Buys all rights. Pays $250 + , color, cover; $10-25, b&w, inside; on acceptance.

GROUP, Thom Schultz Publications, Inc., Box 481, Loveland CO 80539. (303)669-3836. Editor: Gary Richardson. Art Director: Jean Bruns. For adult leaders of high-school-age Christian youth groups. Published 8 times/year. Circ. 60,000. Previously published, photocopied and simultaneous submissions OK. Original artwork returned after publication, if requested. Sample copy $1.
Cartoons: Buys 3 cartoons/issue from freelancers. Interested in humor through youth and religion. Send finished artwork. Reports in 2 weeks. Buys first, reprint or all rights, but may reassign rights to artist after publication. Pays on acceptance.
Illustrations: Buys 8 illustrations/issue; buys all from freelancers. Send query letter with finished art, roughs or tear sheets to be kept on file for future assignments. Reports in 2 weeks. Call to schedule an appointment to show a portfolio, which should include original/final art, tear sheets and photograph. Cover: Pays $100 minimum, color. Inside: Pays $25-300, b&w line drawings and washes, color. Buys first publication rights and occasionally additional rights.

***GULFSHORE LIFE MAGAZINE**, 3620 N. Tamiami Trail, Naples FL 33940. (813)262-6425. Art Director: Alyce Mathias. Magazine emphasizing lifestyle of southwest Florida for an affluent, sophisticated audience. Monthly. Circ. 18,000. Accepts previously published material. Original artwork returned after publication. Sample copy $3.
Illustrations: Send query letter with brochure, resume, tear sheets, photostats and photocopies. Samples not filed are returned by SASE. Reports back only if interested. Write to schedule appointment to show a portfolio, which should include thumbnails, original/final art, final/reproduction/product and tear sheets. Negotiates rights purchased. Payment negotiated; pays on acceptance.

***GYMNASTICS TODAY**, 2006 Pine St., Philadelphia PA 19103. (215)235-4917. Publisher: Ron Alexander. Tabloid emphasizing gymnastics and fitness for teen gymnastic athletes, coaches, officials and fans. Bimonthly. Circ. 130,000. Accepts previously published material. Returns original artwork after publication. Sample copy free for SASE with 60¢ postage; art guidelines free for SASE with 22¢ postage.
Cartoons: Buys 1 cartoon/issue from freelancers. Prefers single panel; b&w line drawings or b&w washes. Send samples of style or roughs to be kept on file. Call for appointment to show portfolio. Material not kept on file is returned by SASE if requested. Buys one-time rights. Payment is negotiable.
Illustrations: Buys 3-5 illustrations/issue from freelancers. Prefers b&w line drawings and washes. Send query letter with resume, tear sheets, photostats, photocopies, slides and photographs. Samples not filed are returned by SASE. Reports only if interested. Call or write to schedule an appointment to show a portfolio, which should include thumbnails, roughs, tear sheets, photostats and b&w. Buys one-time rights. Pays $200-500, b&w; $300-600, color, cover; $150-300, b&w; $200-400, color, inside; on publication.

HADASSAH MAGAZINE, 50 W. 58th St., New York NY 10019. (212)355-7900. Editor-in-Chief: Alan M. Tigay. Advertising Director: Nancy Margolis. Art Director: Meyer Fecher. For American Jewish families; deals with social, economic, political and cultural developments in Israel and Jewish communities in the U.S. and elsewhere. Monthly. Circ. 370,000. Sample copy $1.50. SASE. Reports in 6 weeks. Buys first rights. Pays on acceptance.

HAM RADIO, Greenville NH 03048. (603)878-1441. Editor-in-Chief: Rich Rosen. Assistant Editor: Dorothy Rosa. Art Director: Susan Shorrock. Address inquiries to Dorothy Rosa. For licensed amateur radio operators and electronics experimenters. Monthly. Circ. 50,000.
Illustrations: Buys drafting (on assignment), cover art, illustration. Prefers to see photocopied samples; do not send original art unless requested to do so. Reports in 30 days. Minimum payment: cover art, $100; illustration, $20; on publication.

Tips: "On our covers we favor strong graphic interpretations of concepts in electronics. The use of bright, bold colors sets us apart from other publications in our field."

***HANDS-ON ELECTRONICS**, 500 B Bi-County Blvd., Farmingdale NY 11735. (516)293-3000. Editor: Julian Martin. Magazine emphasizing hobby electronics for consumer and hobby-oriented electronics buffs. Bimonthly—will be monthly in November 1986. Circ. 120,000. Original artwork not returned after publication. Sample copy free.

Cartoons: Buys 3-5 cartoons/issue from freelancers. Prefers single panel with or without gagline; b&w line drawings and b&w washes. Send finished cartoons; "we purchase and keep! Unused ones returned." Works on assignment only. Send query letter with brochure showing art style. Samples are returned. Reports within 1 week. Buys all rights. Pays $25 b&w.

Illustrations: Does not buy illustrations currently, "but would like to start." Works on assignment only. Send query letter with brochure showing art style. Samples not filed are returned. Reports within 1 week. Write to schedule an appointment to show a portfolio, which should include thumbnails, roughs, original/final art, final reproduction/product, color, tear sheets, photographs and b&w. Buys all rights. Pays $400, color, cover; payment depends on usage for inside; on acceptance.

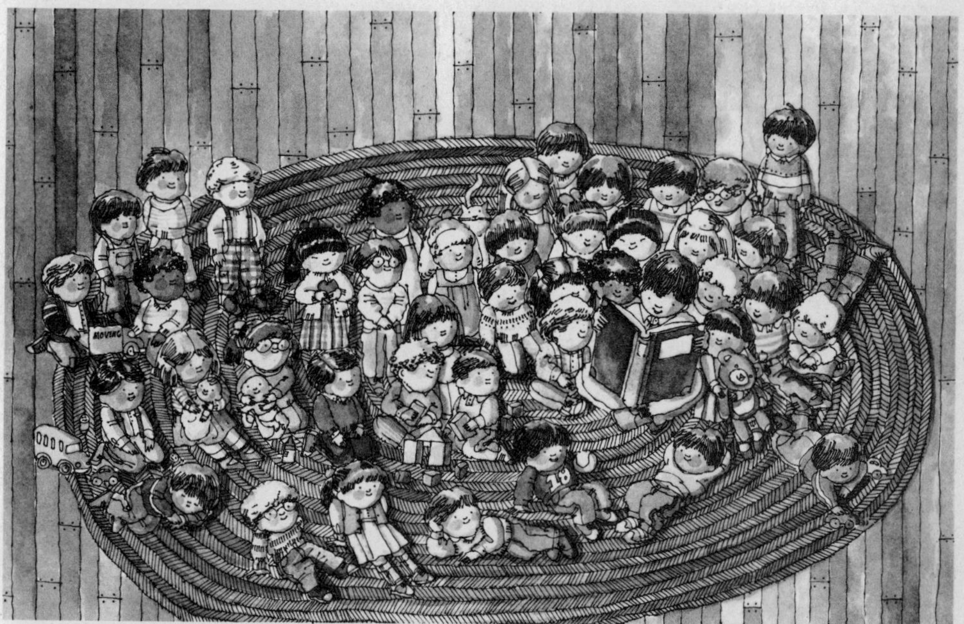

Elise Niven Black of Provo, Utah, used pen and watercolor to capture the pleasure young children derive from stories. This assignment from Happy Times Magazine *gave Black "experience, income and fun." Black sold one-time rights to the magazine.*

HAPPY TIMES MAGAZINE, 5600 N. University Ave., Provo UT 84604. (801)225-9000. Managing Editor and Art Director: Colleen Hinckley. Associate Art Director: Mark Robison. Emphasizes moral values in a non-religious way for children ages 3-7. Publishes 10 times/year. Circ. 85,000. Accepts previously published material. Returns original artwork after publication. Sample copy $1.10.

Illustrations: Buys 10-15/issue. "Artists must be able to draw children well—whether it be a realistic or cartoon style with good use of color. Oil paintings are unacceptable due to color separation problems. We also encourage puzzle and activity artists to submit hidden pictures, dot-to-dots, mazes, and folding activities that help reinforce our monthly themes. Theme lists are available on request with SASE." Works on assignment only. Send query letter with brochure, tear sheets, slides, photostats and photocopies to be kept on file. "Originals are acceptable only if artist brings a portfolio in person." Samples not filed are returned by SASE. Reports only if interested. Usually buys first North American serial rights. To show a portfolio, mail appropriate materials or call to schedule an appointment; portfolio should include roughs, final reproduction/product, color slides, I prefer transparencies." Pays $250, color, inside double spread. Pays 30-60 days after acceptance. "I am interested in slide of three dimen-

sional work as well although we don't purchase large amounts of this type of work. Please have them mail samples I can keep and not to query by mail."
Tips: "Write for our guidelines first. We are primarily a puzzle magazine. Send us only upbeat and positive work."

HARROWSMITH, Camden House Publishing Ltd., Ontario K0K 1J0 Canada. (613)378-6661. Editor-in-Chief: James Lawrence. Associate Art Director: Pamela McDonald. Concerns alternative lifestyles, energy sources and architecture, the environment, country living and gardening. Publishes 6 issues/year. Circ. 164,000. Sample copy $5. Receives 4 cartoons and 6 illustrations/week from freelance artists.
Cartoons: Uses 2-3 cartoons/issue, all from freelancers. Single panel with gagline. Prefers roughs, samples for files and business card; nonresidents include SAE and IRC. Reports in 6 weeks. Pays $25-100 on acceptance.
Illustrations: Uses 12 illustrations/issue, all from freelancers. Interested in "high quality color, drawings and some fine art on country living theme. Many have won awards." Works on assignment only. Likes to have samples on file. Reports back on future assignment possibilities; nonresidents include SAE and IRC. Reports in 6 weeks. Buys first North American serial rights. Cover: Pays $500-1,200, color. Inside: Pays $250-1,000 color; $150-500, b&w; on acceptance.

***HARROWSMITH MAGAZINE**, The Creamery, Charlotte VT 05445. (802)425-3961. Managing Editor: Tom Rawls. Estab. 1986. Magazine emphasizing country living in the northern U.S. for sophisticated, well-educated, between 25-45 years of age interested in country living. Bimonthly. Circ. 150,000. Original artwork returned after publication. Sample copy $4. Art guidelines free for SASE with 39¢ postage.
Cartoons: Buys 1 cartoon/issue from freelancers. Prefers b&w line drawings. Send query letter with samples of style to be kept on file. Write to schedule an appointment to show a portfolio. Samples not filed returned by SASE. Reports within 4 weeks. Buys first or reprint rights. Negotiates payment.

***THE HERB QUARTERLY**, Box 275, Newfane VT 05345. (802)365-4392. Associate Editor: Jeanne Turner. Magazine emphasizing horticulture for middle to upper class, affluent men and women with an ardent enthusiasm for herbs and all their uses—gardening, culinary, crafts, etc. Most are probably home-owners. Quarterly. Circ. 20,000. Accepts previously published material. Original artwork returned after publication if requested. Sample copy $5. Art guidelines available.
Illustrations: Prefers pen & ink illustrations, heavily contrasted. Illustrations of herbs, garden designs, etc. Artist should be able to create illustrations drawn from themes of manuscripts sent to them. Send query letter with brochure showing art style or resume, tear sheets, photocopies, slides and photographs. Samples not filed are returned by SASE only if requested. Reports within weeks. To show a portfolio, mail original/final art, final reproduction/product, photographs or b&w. Buys reprint rights. Pays on publication.

***HIBISCUS MAGAZINE**, Box 22248, Sacramento CA 95822. Editor: Margaret Wensrich. Estab. 1985. Magazine for "people who like to read poetry and short stories." Published three times a year. Circ. 1,000. Original artwork returned after publication if requested. Sample copy $3; art guidelines free for SASE with 39¢ postage.
Illustration: Buys 3-4 illustrations/issue from freelancers. Works on assignment only. Send query letter with resume and samples. Samples not filed are returned by SASE. Reports back only if interested. To show a portfolio, mail original/final art or photocopy of finished work. "We use pen & ink drawings only. No color, slides, etc." Buys first rights. Pays $10 and up for cover and inside; on acceptance.

***HIGHLIGHTS FOR CHILDREN**, 803 Church St., Honesdale PA 18431. Art Director: John R. Crane. Cartoon Editor: John Lansingh Bennett. For ages 2-12. Monthly, bimonthly in July/August. Circ. 1,600,000.
Cartoons: Buys 2-4 cartoons/issue from freelancers. Receives 20 submissions/week from freelancers. Interested in upbeat, positive cartoons involving children, family life or animals; single panel. Send roughs or finished cartoons. SASE. Reports in 4-6 weeks. Buys all rights. Pays $20-25, line drawings; on acceptance. "One flaw in many submissions is that the concept or vocabulary is too adult, or that the experience necessary for its appreciation is beyond our readers. Frequently, a wordless self-explanatory cartoon is best."
Illustrations: Uses 30 illustrations/issue; buys 25 from freelancers. Works with freelancers on assignment only. "We are always looking for good hidden pictures. We require a picture that is interesting in itself and has the objects well hidden. Usually an artist submits pencil sketches. In no case do we pay for any preliminaries to the final art." Also needs "original ideas and illustrations for covers and 'What's Wrong' illustrations for back cover. Send samples of style and flyer to be kept on file. SASE. Reports in

4-6 weeks. Buys all rights on a work-for-hire basis. Pays on acceptance.
Tips: No cartoons or artwork that uses sex-role sterotypes, "sick" humor or mocks authority. "We use very limited amounts of 'cartooning' type art."

HIS MAGAZINE, Box 1450, Downers Grove IL 60515. (312)964-5700. Art Director: Kathy Burrows. Emphasizes editing for students on the college campus for Christian college students. Monthly during school year (9 issues—October through June). Accepts simultaneous submissions. Original artwork returned after publication. Sample copy and art guidelines available.
Cartoons: Buys cartoons from freelancers. Send query letter with samples of style. Write for appointment to show portfolio. Material not kept on file is returned. Reports within 1 month. Buys one-time rights. Pays $50-100, b&w; on acceptance.
Illustrations: Buys illustrations from freelancers. Usually works on assignment. Send query letter with samples. Write for appointment to show portfolio. Prefers photostats as samples. Samples not kept on file are returned. Reports within 4 weeks. Buys one-time rights. Pays $250, b&w and color, cover; $150, b&w, inside; on acceptance.

HOME GYM & FITNESS MAGAZINE, 16200 Ventura Blvd., Encino CA 91436. Art Director; J.R. Martinez. Emphasizes home gym equipment and general fitness. Also has articles directed toward sports, endurance and sports medicine. Monthly. Circ. 80,000. Original art becomes property of publisher. Sample copy and artist guidelines available for SASE.
Illustrations: Buys 1-2 illustrations/issue from freelancers. Full-page, any medium on health, fitness, sport and equipment. Works on assignment only. Send query letter with resume, tear sheets, photostats, photocopies, slides, photographs or veloxes to be kept on file. Write or call for appointment to show portfolio, which should include original/final art and final reproduction/product. Buys all rights. Pays $100-300, b&w; per assignment for 4-color; on publication.
Tips: "Considers circulation before establishing editorial rate. Small companies cannot pay *Playboy* magazine fees."

HOME LIFE, 127 9th Ave. N, Nashville TN 37234. Editor: Reuben Herring. Emphasizes Christian family life. For married adults and parents of all ages, but especially newlyweds and middle-aged marrieds. Monthly. Send 75¢ for sample copy and art guidelines.
Cartoons: Buys 2-4 cartoons/issue on family life situations; particularly interested in cartoons on marriage and parenting. Receives 50 cartoons/week from freelance artists. No sex. Send query letter. To show a portfolio, mail appropriate materials. Reports in 45 days. Buys all rights. Pays $38 minimum, line drawings and halftones; on acceptance.
Illustrations: Buys 15-20 illustrations. Send query letter. To show a portfolio, mail appropriate materials.
Tips: "Submit cartoons to editor; other artwork and illustrations to artist-designer, David Wilson."

THE HORROR SHOW, 14848 Misty Springs Ln., Oak Run CA 96069-9801. (916)472-3540. Editor: David B. Silva. Magazine emphasizing short horror fiction for "anyone who enjoys a good chill up their spine." Quarterly. Circ. 2,200. Original artwork not returned after publication. Sample copy $4.95; art guidelines free for SASE with 22¢ postage.
Cartoons: Buys 1-2 cartoons/issue. Pays $3 b&w; on acceptance.
Illustrations: Buys 13-20 b&w illustrations/issue from freelancers. Works on assignment only. Send query letter with tear sheets and photocopies to be kept on file, except for slides, which will be returned. Samples not filed are returned by SASE. Reports within 2 weeks. Buys first rights or reprint rights. To show a portfolio, mail tear sheets, photographs and b&w. Pays $10, color, cover; $5, b&w, inside; on acceptance.

HORSE ILLUSTRATED, Box 6050, Mission Viejo CA 92690. (714)240-6001. Editor: Jill-Marie Jones. For people of all ages who own, show and breed horses, who are interested in all phases of horse ownership. Monthly. Circ. 50,000. Sample copy $3.; free art guidelines.
Cartoons: Buys several cartoons/issue. Prefers single, double or multiple panel. "Central character should be a horse." Send finished art. SASE. Reports within 6 weeks. Buys first rights. Pays $10-35, b&w line drawings; on publication.
Illustrations: Buys several illustrations/year on horses. Send query letter with resume and samples. SASE. Reports within 6 weeks. Buys first rights. Pays $20-50, b&w line drawings, inside; on publication.
Tips: When reviewing an illustrator's work, "we look for realism and accurate portrayal of the horse. We don't use 'fantasy' or 'surrealistic' art. For cartoons, we look for drawing ability and humor. We will, however, accept good humor with adequate illustration over good illustration with poor humor. Generally, we use free-standing illustrations as art rather than going to the illustrator and commissioning

a work, but this is impossible if the artist sends us poor reproductions. Naturally, this also lessens his chance of our seeking out his services.''

***HORTICULTURE, THE MAGAZINE OF AMERICAN GARDENING**, 755 Boylston St., Boston MA 02116. (617)247-4100. Illustration Editor: Sarah Boortyn Schwartz. Magazine geared to homeowners. Monthly. Circ. 140,000. Very occasionally accepts previously published material. Original artwork returned after publication. Sample copy and art guidelines available.
Illustrations: Buys 15 illustrations/issue from freelancers. Works on assignment only. Prefers gardening as a theme, 'how-to' illustrations and color floral pieces. Send query letter with tear sheets, photostats, photocopies, slides and photographs. Samples not filed are returned. Reports within 2 months. To show a portfolio, mail appropriate materials or call or write to schedule an appointment. Buys one-time rights. Payment depends on complexity of style and the amount of material; on publication.
Tips: "Show as many different styles as possible. Bring in (or send in) lots of work—don't really care to see only gardening or horticulture material. I look for ability to render hand manipulations and figures. We are doing far more how-to, step-by-step sorts of illustration to gear ourselves to the new gardeners.''

HOSPITAL PRACTICE, 10 Astor Place, New York NY 10003. (212)477-2727. Design Director: Robert S. Herald. Emphasizes clinical medicine and science for practicing physicians throughout the US. 18 issues/year. Circ. 200,000. Original artwork returned after publication if requested.
Illustrations: Uses 40-50 illustrations/issue; buys 15-20 illustrations/issue from freelancers. Uses only medical and scientific (conceptual) illustrations. Works on assignment only. Send query letter with brochure showing art style, resume, photostats, photographs and tear sheets to be kept on file. Does not report unless called. Call for appointment to show portfolio, which should include original/final art, color, tear sheets, photostats and b&w. Returns material if SASE included. Negotiates rights purchased. Pays $800, color, cover; $150 and up, b&w, inside; on publication.
Tips: "If possible, review the publication before submitting work, to understand specific editorial style.''

HOUSE & GARDEN, 350 Madison Ave., New York NY 10017. (212)880-8800. Art Director: Karen Gant. Readers are upper income home owners or renters. Monthly. Circ. 500,000.
Illustrations: Uses minimum number of illustrations/issue; all of which are commissioned by the magazine. Selection based on "previous work, samples on file, and from seeing work in other publications. Illustrations are almost always assigned to fit specific articles.'' Themes "vary with our current format and with article we want illustrated.'' Format: b&w line drawings or washes. Portfolios viewed on a drop-off basis or send samples of style to Lloyd Ziff, Editorial Design Director. SASE. Reports "from immediately to 4 weeks.'' Payment on acceptance "varies depending on artist, size and type of illustration.'' Buys all rights.

HUMPTY DUMPTY'S MAGAZINE, Box 567, Indianapolis IN 46206. (317)636-8881. Editor: Christine French Clark. Art Director: Lawrence Simmons. Special emphasis on health, nutrition, safety and exercise for girls and boys, ages 4-6. Monthly except bimonthly February/March, April/May, June/July and August/September. Sample copy 75¢; art guidelines free for SASE.
Illustrations: Uses 25-35 illustrations/issue. Works on assignment only. Send query letter with brochure, resume, photostats, slides, good photocopies and tear sheets to be kept on file. Samples returned by SASE if not kept on file. Reports within 3-4 weeks. Buys all rights. To show a portfolio, mail original/final art, final reproduction/product, color, b&w and 2-color. Pays $225, cover; and $25-65, b&w; $50-100, 2-color; $60-125, 4-color, inside; on publication.
Tips: Illustrations should be figurative and should be composed of story telling situations. "Be familiar with the magazines before submitting artwork or samples that are completely inappropriate.''

HUSTLER, Larry Flynt Publications, Suite 3800, 2029 Century Park E., Los Angeles CA 90067. (213)556-9200. Cartoon/Humor Editor: Dwaine Tinsley. For middle income men, 18-35 years of age, interested in current affairs, luxuries, investigative reporting, entertainment, sports, sex and fashion. Monthly. Original artwork returned after publication.
Cartoons: Publishes 23 cartoons/month; 10 full-page color, 4-color spots, 8 b&w and 1 "Most Tasteless.'' Receives 300-500 cartoons/week from freelance artists. Especially needs "outrageous material, mainly sexual, but politics, sports acceptable. Topical humor and seasonal/holiday cartoons good.'' Mail samples. Prefers 8½x11'' size; avoid crayons, chalks or fluorescent colors. Prefers original art submissions to roughs. Avoid, if possible, large, heavy illustration board. Samples returned by SASE only. Place name, address and phone number on back of each cartoon. Reports in 3 weeks to 1 month. Adheres to Cartoonists Guild guidelines. Pays $300, full-page color; $125 ¼-page color; $100 ¼-page b&w; $100, ¼-page "Most Tasteless.'' Pays on acceptance.
Tips: Especially needs more cartoons, cartoon breakaways or one-subject theme series. "Send outra-

geous humor—work that other magazines would shy away from. Pertinent, political, sexual, whatever. We are constantly looking for new artists to compliment our regular contributors and contract artists. Let your imagination and daring guide you. We will publish almost anything as long as it is funny."

HUSTLER HUMOR MAGAZINE, Larry Flynt Publications, Suite 3800, 2029 Century Park E., Los Angeles CA 90067. (213)556-9200. Cartoon/Humor Editor: Dwaine Tinsley. Bimonthly. Circ. 150,000.
Cartoons: Uses 150-180 cartoons/issue; buys 30% from freelancers. Prefers "outrageous sexual, social, political" themes. Prefers single or multiple panel, with or without gag line; b&w line drawings, b&w washes. Send finished cartoons to be kept on file. Material not kept on file returned by SASE. Reports within 1 month. Buys first rights. Pays $7.50 b&w spot, $75 b&w strips/page. Original artwork returned after publication. Payment on acceptance.
Illustrations: Uses 2 covers, full-color sight gags. Prefers soft sexual themes; realistic cartoon styles. Send samples and tear sheets to be kept on file. Reports within 2 weeks. Pays $500, front; $200, back. Pays on acceptance.
Tips: This is a "humor magazine consisting of jokes and cartoons exclusively. The material is primarily sexual in nature—but the scope is wide-ranging. We need work *badly* to build our inventory."

***IDEALS MAGAZINE**, Box 141000; Nelson Place at Elm Hill Pike, Nashville TN 37214. (615)889-9000. Editor: Ramona Richards. Magazine emphasizing poetry and light prose for women, 50 and up. Published 8 times/year. Circ. 175,000. Accepts previously published material. Original artwork returned depending on rights purchased. Sample copy $1; art guidelines free for SASE with 22¢ postage.
Illustrations: Buys 1 illustration/issue from freelancers. Prefers seasonal themes rendered in a realistic style. Send query letter with brochure showing art style or tear sheets and slides. Samples not filed are returned by SASE. Reports within 2 months. To show a portfolio, mail appropriate materials; portfolio should include final reproduction/product and tear sheets. Negotiate rights purchased. Pays on publication.

INCENTIVE TRAVEL MANAGER, Brentwood Publishing Corp., 825 S. Barrington Ave., Los Angeles CA 90049. Publishers: Martin H. Waldman and Hal Spector. Art Director: Tom Medsger.
Illustrations: Submit brochure/flyer to be kept on file for possible future assignment. Reports only when assignment available. Buys all rights. Pays $60 and up, spot art; $400 and up, full-color cover. Pays on acceptance.

***INCIDER-THE APPLE II MAGAZINE**, CW Communications-80 Pine St., Peterborough NH 03458. (603)924-9471. Art Director: Donna Wohlfarth. Magazine emphasizing Apple II computing. Monthly. Circ. 150,000. Original artwork returned after publication. Sample copy free for SASE. Art guidelines available.
Illustrations: Buys 5-7 illustrations/issue from freelancers. Works on assignment only. Send query letter with resume and samples. Samples not filed are returned only if requested. Reports only if interested. Call or write to schedule an appointment to show a portfolio, which should incude original/final art or tear sheets. Buys first rights. Negotiates payment; on acceptance.

INDIANAPOLIS 500 YEARBOOK, Box 24308, Speedway IN 46224. (317)638-1466. Publisher: Carl Hungness. Emphasizes auto racing for auto racing fans. Annually. Circ. 50,000. Previously published material OK. Original artwork returned after publication. Sample copy $12.95.
Illustrations: Works on assignment only. Send query letter plus information to be kept on file for possible future assignments. Samples returned by SASE. Reports in 2 weeks. Buys one-time rights. Pays on publication.

INDIANAPOLIS MAGAZINE, 32 E. Washington St., Indianapolis IN 46204. (317)639-6600. Editor: Nancy Comiskey. Emphasizes any Indianapolis-related problems/features or regionally related topics. Readers have "high income and are highly educated." Monthly. Circ. 20,000. Sample copy $1.75.
Cartoons: "We are just beginning to accept and publish cartoons and *New Yorker* type illustrations. Will buy all from freelance artists." Needs art related to the "consumer, tourist-business-related or city-related." Receives 5 cartoons/week from freelance artists. Format: single panel b&w line drawings or b&w washes, with or without gagline. Send roughs or photocopied finished cartoons. SASE. Rejects in 2 weeks. "Possibles kept until used which can be a long time. Number published varies." Pays $15 on publication per b&w cartoon. Buys one-time rights.
Illustrations: Uses 2-5 illustrations/issue, 50% of which are supplied by freelancers. Works on spec or assignment basis. Needs illustrations that are "broad, general interest or Indianapolis-related." Format: b&w line drawings or b&w washes. Send photocopied finished art or roughs. SASE. Reports in 2 weeks, "but depends on production schedule and influx of material." Pays $35 on publication per inside

b&w or color illustration. Buys one-time rights.
Tips: The trend is toward "more sophisticated, mature cartoons. Please, no Farmer Bill cartoons—we're a *city*. Orient cartoons and illustrations to a *professional audience*. Always need food-related, dining cartoons."

INDUSTRIAL ENGINEERING, 25 Technology Park, Norcross GA 30092. (404)449-0460. Editor/Publisher: E.F. Cudworth. Emphasizes engineering. Monthly. Circ. 47,000.
Illustrations: Uses 0-7 illustrations/issue; buys 0-7/issue from freelancers. Prefers airbrush, full color, some b&w line styles. Works on assignment only. Send query letter with brochure and samples to be kept on file. No preference for samples. Samples not kept on file are returned by SASE. Does not report back. Buys all rights. Call for appointment to show portfolio. Pays $400-1,200, color, cover ("we run no b&w on cover"); $50-500, b&w, and $400-1,000, color, inside; on publication.

INDUSTRIAL LAUNDERER, Suite 613, 1730 M St. NW, Washington DC 20036. (202)296-6744. Editor: David A. Ritchey. For decision makers in the industrial laundry business. Monthly. Circ. 3,000. Sample copy $1.
Cartoons: Submit resume. Reports as soon as possible. Buys first industry rights. Pays on publication. Negotiates pay for b&w line drawings and washes.

INDUSTRIAL MACHINERY NEWS, division of Hearst Business Media Corp., Box 5002, 29516 Southfield Rd., Southfield MI 48086. (313)557-0100. Contact: L.D. Slace. For those in the metalworking industry responsible for manufacturing, purchasing, engineering, metalworking, machinery, equipment and supplies.
Cartoons: Receives 10 cartoons/week from freelance artists. Interested in themes of metalworking or personal relationships. Buys one-time rights. Pays $5 for line ink work; on publication.
Tips: "We have been purchased by the Hearst Corp. If interested in submitting artwork other than cartoons, call or write first. Do not send original art. A photocopy in many cases will do. Think industrial (metalworking) plants, factories, firms and the people who work and manage them."

INDUSTRY WEEK, 1111 Chester Ave., Cleveland OH 44114. (216)696-7000. Editor: Stanley J. Modic. Examines top- and middle-management problems in industry. Biweekly. Circ. 350,000. Original artwork returned after publication if requested. Buys first and reprint rights. Sample copy $2.
Cartoons: News Editor: John Carson. Uses freelance cartoons rarely. Receives 10 submissions/week from freelancers. Interested in management themes; single panel. SASE. Reports in 2 weeks. Buys various rights. Pays $35 minimum, b&w line drawings or washes; pays on acceptance.
Illustrations: Art Director: Nick Dankovich. Buys 2-4 illustrations/issue. Works on assignment only. Buys various rights. Cover and inside: buys b&w and color work, all media; pays on acceptance.
Tips: "Read and examine our magazine."

INSIDE, 226 S. 16th St., Philadelphia PA 19102. (215)893-5760. Art Director: Lenore Chorney. Quarterly. Circ. 70,000. Original artwork returned after publication.
Illustrations: Buys 3 or more illustrations/issue from freelancers. Prefers color and b&w drawings. Works on assignment only. Send samples and tear sheets to be kept on file; call for appointment to show portfolio. Samples not kept on file are not returned. Reports only if interested. Buys first rights. Pays from $100, b&w, and from $300 full-color, inside; on acceptance. Prefers seeing sketches.

INSIDE DETECTIVE, RGH Publications, 20th Floor, 460 W. 34th St., New York NY 10001. (212)947-6500. Editor: Rose Mandelsberg. For mature adults—law enforcement officials, professional investigators, criminology buffs and interested laymen. Monthly.
Cartoons: Receives approximately 20 cartoons/week from freelance artists. Must have crime theme. Submit finished art. SASE. Reports in 10 days. Buys all rights. Pays $25; on acceptance.
Tips: "Make sure that the humor in the cartoons is *not* at the expense of police officers or law enforcement officials. Omit references to supermarket/convenience stores."

INSTANT AND SMALL COMMERCIAL PRINTER, Box 368, Northbrook IL 60062. Editor: Daniel Witte. Emphasizes the instant/quick and small commercial printing business and successful, profitable, technical and promotional methods for owners and/or managers of print shops, as well as interested employees. Bimonthly. Circ. 25,000. Accepts previously published work and simultaneous submissions "if material is so indicated." Sample copy $3.
Cartoons: Buys 1 cartoon/issue from freelancers. Prefers single panel with gagline; b&w line drawings. Send query letter with samples of style, roughs or finished cartoons to be kept on file. Material not kept on file is returned by SASE only if requested. Reports within 1 month. Buys all rights. Pays $25, b&w; on publication.

Illustrations: Buys 2 illustrations/issue from freelancers. Works on assignment only. Send query letter with brochure, resume, business card, samples and tear sheets to be kept on file. Samples not kept on file are returned by SASE only if requested. Reports within 1 month. Buys all rights. Pays $50-150, b&w, and $150-250, color, covers; $50-100, b&w, and $50-200, color, inside; on publication.

THE INSTRUMENTALIST, 200 Northfield Rd., Northfield IL 60093. (312)328-6000. Contact: Anne Driscoll. Emphasizes music education for "school band and orchestra directors and teachers of the instruments in those ensembles." Monthly. Circ. 22,500. Original artwork may be returned after publication. Sample copy $2.
Cartoons: Buys 3 cartoons/issue; buys all from freelancers. Interested in themes stating "music is wonderful." No themes stating "music is a problem"; single panel with gagline, "if needed"; b&w line drawings. Send finished cartoons. Samples not returned. Reports in 1-2 months. Buys all rights. Pay $8-15, b&w; on acceptance.

INSURANCE SALES, Rough Notes Publishing Co. Inc., Box 564, Indianapolis IN 46206. (317)634-1541. Editor: Roy Ragan. For life and health insurance salespeople; "emphasis on sales and marketing methods, and on the uses of life and health insurance to solve personal and business financial situations." Monthly. Circ. 25,000. Sample copy $1. Receives 15-20 cartoons/week from freelance artists.
Cartoons: Buys 50-60 cartoons/year from freelancers. Interested in life insurance salesmanship, tax payer and IRS situations, inflation, recession, vagaries of bankers and stock market; single panel. "No cartoons which show salesman holding prospect on ground, twisting arm, knocking doors down, etc." Send finished cartoons with SASE. Reports in 1 week. Buys all rights. Pays $15, b&w line drawings; on acceptance.

***INTERNATIONAL BUSINESS MONTHLY**, Box 87339, Houston TX 77287. (713)641-0201. Publisher: T. George Pratt. Tabloid emphasizing business and industry for upper management, executives, government, business and industry. Monthly. Circ. 130,000. Original artwork returned after publication. Sample copy $5 and SASE.
Cartoons: Currently buys no cartoons from freelancers. Samples not filed are returned by SASE. Reports within 30 days. Buys all rights. Pays $50, b&w; $100, color.
Illustrations: Buys 10% of illustrations/issue from freelancers. Works on assignment only. Send brochure showing art style and photographs. Samples not filed are returned by SASE. Reports within 1 month. To show a portfolio, mail appropriate materials, which should include original/final art, final reproduction/product, color and b&w. Buys all rights. Payment based upon quality of work. Pays on publication.

***INTERNATIONAL MEDICAL CENTER JOURNAL**, 1515 NW 167th St., Miami FL 33169. (305)623-1091. Art Director: David Rison. Magazine emphasizing health, fitness, preventative medicine and fulfilled living for senior citizens and middle age professionals. Quarterly. Circ. 200,000. Accepts previously published material. Original artwork returned after publication. Sample copy free for SASE with 40¢ postage.
Illustrations: Prefers modern, contemporary and trend aware themes or styles. Send query letter with brochure showing art style or tear sheets, photostats, photocopies, "or any sample that is non-returnable." Samples not filed are returned only if requested. Reports only if interested. Call to show portfolio, which should include final reproduction/product, original/final art, photographs and tear sheets. Buys one-time rights. Payment varies. Pays on publication.

INTERRACIAL BOOKS FOR CHILDREN BULLETIN, 1841 Broadway, New York NY 10023. Managing Editor: Ruth Charnes. Emphasizes "bias-free children's literature and learning materials" for teachers, librarians, parents, authors, and others concerned with children's materials. Published 8 times/year. Circ. 5,000. Accepts previously published material. Original artwork returned after publication. Sample copy $3.50; art guidelines free for SASE.
Cartoons: Rarely uses cartoons. Prefers b&w line drawings. Send query letter with samples of style; samples will be kept on file if relevant. Material not kept on file is returned by SASE. Reports within 2 months.
Illustrations: Uses up to 15 illustrations/issue. Send query letter with photostats and photographs; material will be kept on file if relevant. Samples returned by SASE if not kept on file. Reports within 4 weeks. Buys one-time rights. Pays $50, b&w, cover; $25, b&w, inside; on publication.

***INVESTMENT DECISIONS**, 11 Elm Pl., Rye NY 10580. (914)921-0230. Publications Director: George G. Lindsey. Magazine emphasizing professional investing for upscale, investment and financial/managers. Monthly. Circ. 40,000. Accepts previously published material. Original artwork returned after publication. Sample copy available.

Cartoons: Buys 1 cartoon/issue from freelancers. Prefers single panel without gagline; b&w line drawings. Send query letter with samples of style to be kept on file. Call for appointment to show portfolio. Samples are returned only if requested. Reports only if interested. Negotiates rights purchased.
Illustrations: Buys 3 illustrations/issue from freelancers. Works on assignment only. Send query letter with resume and samples. Samples not filed are returned only if requested. Reports only if interested. Call or write to schedule an appointment to show a portfolio, which should include thumbnails, roughs, original/final art and tear sheets. Negotiates rights purchased. Pays on publication.

***IOWA MUNICIPALITIES**, League of Iowa Municipalities, Suite 100, 900 Des Moines St., Des Moines IA 50309. Editor-in-Chief: Robert W. Harpster. Managing Editor/Art Director: Sandy Pollard. Magazine for city officials. Monthly. Circ. 10,400. Previously published, photocopied and simultaneous submissions OK. Sample copy $1.
Cartoons: Buys none except from local artists; "would consider some really good political cartoons relating to the federal government and cities."
Illustrations: Buys 12 illustrations/issue from freelancers. Send query letter with tear sheets and photostats. To show a portfolio, mail photostats and b&w. Pays $75 b&w, cover; on publication.

JACK AND JILL, Box 567, 1100 Waterway Blvd., Indianapolis IN 46206. (317)636-8881. Art Director: Edward F. Cortese. Emphasizes entertaining articles written with the purpose of developing the reading skills of the reader. For ages 6-8. Monthly except bimonthly February/March, April/May, June/July and August/September. Buys all rights. Original artwork not returned after publication (except in case where artist wishes to exhibit the art. Art must be available to us on request.) Sample copy 75¢.
Illustrations: Buys 25 illustrations/issue; buys 10-15/issue from freelancers. Receives 3-4 submissions/week from freelancers. Interested in "stylized, realistic, humorous, mystery, adventure, science fiction, historical and also nature and health." Works on assignment only. Send query letter with brochure showing art style or resume, tear sheets, photostats, photocopies, slides and photographs to be kept on file; include SASE. Reports in 4 weeks. To show a portfolio, mail appropriate materials or call or write to schedule an appointment; portfolio should include original/final art, color, tear sheets, b&w and 2-color pre-separated art. Buys all rights on a work-for-hire basis. Pays $225, color, cover; $60-125, 4-color; $50-100, 2-color, $25-65, b&w, inside; thirty days after completion of work.
Tips: "There are more updates on realistic illustrations of people and stylized illustrations." Artists should "obtain copies of our current issues to insure proper submission of art styles needed. Likes to see situation and story telling illustrations with more than 1 figure.

JAPANOPHILE, Box 223, Okemos MI 48864. (517)349-1795. Editor: Earl R. Snodgrass. Emphasizes cars, bonsai, haiku, sports, etc. for educated audience interested in Japanese culture. Quarterly. Circ. 800. Accepts previously published material. Original artwork not returned after publication. Sample copy $3; art guidelines free for SASE.
Cartoons: Buys 1 cartoon/issue from freelancer. Prefers single panel with gagline; b&w line drawings. Send finished cartoons. Material returned only if requested. Reports only if interested. Buys all rights. Pays $5; on publication.
Illustrations: Buys 1-5 illustrations/issue from freelancers. Prefers sumie or line drawings. Send photostats or tear sheets to be kept on file if interested. Samples returned only if requested. Reports only if interested. Buys all rights. Pays $15, cover and $5, inside, b&w; on publication.

JEMS JOURNAL OF EMERGENCY MEDICAL SERVICES, Box 1026, Solana Beach CA 92075. (619)481-1128. Senior Editor: Rick Minerd. Emphasizes emergency medical services for emergency room physicians, nurses, paramedics, emergency medical technicians and administrators. Monthly. Circ. 30,000. Accepts previously published material. Original artwork returned after publication. Sample copy for SASE with $1.07 postage; art guidelines for SASE with 22¢ postage.
Illustrations: Buys 3-5 illustrations/issue from freelancers. Works on assignment only. Send query letter with photostats, tear sheets, photocopies, slides or photos to be kept on file. Samples not filed are returned by SASE. Reports within 2 weeks. Buys one-time rights. Pays $150-200, color, cover; $35-50, b&w, and $50-75, color, inside; on publication.

***JOURNAL OF ACCOUNTANCY**, 1211 Avenue of the Americas, New York NY 10036. (212)575-5268. Art Coordinator: Jeryl Costello. Magazine emphasizing accounting for certified public accountants. Monthly. Circ. 300,000. Original artwork returned after publication.
Illustrations: Buys 2 illustrations/issue from freelancers. Works on assignment only. Send query letter with brochure showing art style. Samples not filed are not returned. Reports only if interested. Call to schedule an appointment to show a portfolio, which should include original/final art, color, tear sheets and b&w. Buys first rights. Pays $900, color, cover; $150-500, color (depending on size), inside; on publication.

***JOURNAL OF READING**, Int'l Reading Assn., Box 8139, Newark DE 19714-8139. (302)731-1600. Graphic Design Co-ordinator: Larry Husfelt. Magazine emphasizing teaching for teachers, reading specialists and professors. Published monthly Oct.-May (8 issues/year). Circ. 19,000. Sample copy free for SASE with 60¢ postage. Art guidelines available.
Cartoons: Buys 1 cartoon/issue from freelancers. Prefers double panel with or without gagline; b&w line drawings. Send finished cartoons. "We buy what we want immediately and return the rest." Reports within 14 days. Buys one-time rights. Pays $20, b&w.
Illustrations: Buys 1 illustration/issue from freelancers. Works on assignment only. Prefers themes about schools and reading. Send query letter with brochure showing art style or resume and photocopies. Samples not filed are returned only if requested. Reports within 20 days. Call to schedule an appointment to show a portfolio, which should include original/final art. Buys first rights. Pays $250-350, color, cover; on acceptance.

JOURNAL OF THE WEST, 1531 Yuma, Manhattan KS 66502. (913)532-6733. Editor: Robin Higham. Emphasizes the West for readers in public libraries and classrooms. Quarterly. Circ. 4,500 (readership). Original artwork returned after publication. Sample copy and art guidelines available.
Illustrations: Uses cover illustrations only; artist supplies 4-color separation. Send query letter with brochure or samples and/or tear sheets to be kept on file. Prefers either photographs, prints or preferably duplicate slides as samples. Samples not filed are returned only if requested. Reports within 4 days. Negotiates rights purchased. Payment: "We make a trade."
Tips: There is a trend toward "pastels with sometimes interesting and eye-catching results in Western scenes." Looks for work that is "original and not copied from a photograph; and is evidence of artistic talent and ability. We also are concentrating on the twentieth century. Artists send material that is unsuitable to our publication, often because they have never bothered to look at it or to send for a sample copy."

***JUDICATURE**, Suite 1600, 25 E. Washington, Chicago IL 60602. Contact: David Richert. Journal of the American Judicature Society. Published 6 times/year. Circ. 30,000. Accepts previously published material. Original artwork returned after publication. Sample copy free for SASE with $1.07 postage.
Cartoons: Buys 1-2 cartoons/issue. Interested in "sophisticated humor revealing a familiarity with legal issues, the courts and the administration of justice." Send query letter with samples of style. SASE. Reports in 2 weeks. Buys one-time rights. Pays $35 for unsolicited cartoons.
Illustrations: Buys 2-3 illustrations/issue. Works on assignment only. Interested in styles from "realism to light cartoons." Prefers subjects related to court organization, operations and personnel. Send query letter with brochure showing art style. SASE. Reports within 2 weeks. Write to schedule an appointment to show a portfolio, which should include roughs and original/final art. Buys one-time rights. Negotiates payment. Pays $250, b&w, cover; $175, b&w, inside.

KEYNOTER, Kiwanis International, 3636 Woodview Trace, Indianapolis IN 46268. Executive Editor: Jack Brockley. Art Director: Jim Patterson. Official publication of Key Club International, nonprofit high school service organization. Published 7 times/year. Copyrighted. Circ. 115,000. Previously published, photocopied and simultaneous submissions OK. Original artwork returned after publication. Free sample copy.
Illustrations: Buys 3 illustrations/issue from freelancers. Works on assignment only. "We only want to work with illustrators in the Indianapolis area because it is otherwise too inconvenient because of our production schedule. SASE. Reports in 2 weeks. "They should call our Production and Art Department for interview." Buys first rights. Pays on publication.

KIWANIS, 3636 Woodview Trace, Indianapolis IN 46268. (317)875-8755. Executive Editor: Chuck Jonak. Art Director: James Patterson. Magazine emphasizing civic and social betterment, business, education, religion and domestic affairs for business and professional men. Uses cartoons, illustrations, and photos from freelancers. Original artwork returned after publication. Published 10 times/year.
Cartoons: Buys 1-2 cartoons/issue, all from freelancers. Interested in "daily life at home or work. Nothing off-color, no silly wife stuff, no blue-collar situations." Prefers finished cartoons. Send query letter with brochure showing art style or tear sheets, slides and photographs. SASE. Reports in 3-4 weeks. Pays $50, b&w; on acceptance.
Illustrations: Buys 6-8 illustrations/issue from freelancers. Interested in themes that correspond to themes of articles. Works on assignment only. Keeps material on file after in-person contact with artist. Prefers portfolio, "anything and everything." SASE. Reports in 2 weeks. To show a portfolio, mail appropriate materials (out of town/state) or call or write to schedule an appointment; portfolio should include roughs, original/final art, final reproduction/product, color, tear sheets, photostats, photographs and b&w. Buys first North American serial rights or negotiates. Pays $1,000, full-color, cover; $400-700, full-color, inside; $50-75, spot drawings; on acceptance.
Tips: "We deal direct—no reps. Have plenty of samples, particulary those that can be left with us."

LACMA PHYSICIAN, Box 3465, Los Angeles CA 90054. (213)483-1581. Managing Editor: Howard Bender. "Membership publication for physicians who are members of the Los Angeles County Medical Association; covers association news and medical issues." Published 20 times/year, twice monthly except January, July, August and December. Circ. 11,000. Does not accept previously published material. Original artwork returned after publication "if requested." Sample copy for SASE with $1.50 postage.
Illustrations: "Occasionally use illustrations for covers." These are "generally medical, but can relate to a specific feature story topic." Works on assignment only. Send query letter with business card and samples to be filed. Samples not kept on file are returned by SASE. Reports only if interested. Call or write for appointment. Negotiates pay; pays on acceptance. Buys all rights."

LANDSCAPE ONTARIO/LANDSCAPE TRADES, 1293 Matheson Blvd., Mississauga, Ontario Canada. (416)629-1184. Jim Bradley. Readers are landscapers, nursery garden centers, grounds maintenance firms, wholesale growers, suppliers of goods to the landscaping industry, parks and recreation officials, horticulturists and others. Monthly. Circ. 2,700. Free sample copy.
Cartoons: Uses 1 cartoon/issue which should relate to the industry and have appeal to readers mentioned above. Prefers single or multiple panel b&w line drawings or washes with or without gag line but will also consider color cartoons. Send finished cartoons or samples of style. Buys one-time rights. Pays $20/b&w on publication.
Illustrations: Uses 1 illustration/issue; buys 0-1 from freelancers. "I'd be happy to keep samples on file and request illustrations when a particular need or idea comes up." Prefers b&w line drawings or washes for inside. Send finished art or samples of style. Pays $20 for inside b&w; on publication.

LE BUREAU, Suite 1000, 1001 de Maisonneuve West, Montreal, Quebec H3A 3E1 Canada . (514)845-5141. Editor-in-Chief: Paul Saint-Pierre. For corporate and financial executives, office managers, electronic data processing experts and systems analysts. Bimonthly. Circ. 10,500. Free sample copy if artist sends samples.
Illustrations: Buys 12 illustrations/year on calculators, small computers, in-plant printing and word processing. All covers are freelance illustrations. Especially needs "outstanding drawings illustrating an office situation. We appreciate humor in good taste." Query with samples. SAE (nonresidents include IRC). Reports in 2 weeks. Buys all rights, but may reassign rights to artist after publication. Pays $125-200, color; on acceptance.

***LEATHER CRAFTSMAN**, (formerly Make It With Leather), Box 1386, Fort Worth TX 76101. (817)560-2396. Editor: Stanley Cole. For persons interested in leather crafts. 60% of articles are how-to-do-it, 20% are profiles of people producing leatherwork. Bimonthly. Circ. 25,000. Previously published, photocopied and occasionally, simultaneous submissions OK. Free sample copy.
Illustrations: Buys leathercraft themes. "We are how-to-do-it oriented. Make the art relevant to the audience, and do some research on tools and terminology of the craft. The more accurate, the more usable." Send query letter with samples. SASE. Reports in 6-8 weeks. To show a portfolio, mail appropriate materials. Buys all rights. Pays $10-100, b&w line drawings, washes and reflective art; on publication.
Tips: "Most often we require a whole package, including an article and photographs or illustrations. Basically we are looking for journalists who can write a how-to-do-it or profile article who can also illustrate their piece, or for an artist who has teamed up with a writer to illustrate his/her submission. We do have an illustrator on staff who can draw good, clear photographs."

THE LEATHERNECK MAGAZINE, Magazine of the Marines, Box 1775, Quantico VA 22134. (703)640-6161. Art Director: John De Grasse. Emphasizes activities of Marines—air, land, sea ships, tanks, aircraft, physical fitness, etc. for Marines, dependents, retired, friends of the Corps, plus former Marines. Monthly. Circ. 95,000. Occasionally accepts previously published material. Only original cover artwork returned after publication. Sample copy available.
Cartoons: Uses 8 cartoons/issue; buys all from freelancers. Prefers Marine-related subjects and "correctly pictured uniforms particularly." Prefers single panel with gagline; b&w line drawings. Send query letter with samples of style. Material not kept on file is returned by SASE. Reports within 30 days. Buys first rights. Pays $25, b&w; on acceptance.
Illustrations: Uses 4 illustrations/issue. Send query letter with samples. Prefers illustrations for covers only. Pays $100-150, b&w, cover; on acceptance.

LEGAL ECONOMICS, The Magazine of Law Office Management, Box 11418, Columbia SC 29211. (803)754-3563 or 359-9940. Managing Editor/Art Director: Delmar L. Roberts. For the practicing lawyer. 8 issues (monthly, Jan., Feb., Sept., Oct.; bimonthly Mar./Apr., May/June, Jul./Aug., Nov./Dec.). Circ. 27,000. Previously published work rarely used. Pays on publication.
Needs: Primarily interested in cartoons "depicting situations inherent in the operation and manage-

ment of a law office, e.g., operating word processing equipment and computers, interviewing, office meetings, lawyer/office staff situations, and client/lawyer situations. We have rarely used cartoons, primarily because the calibre of the work we have received has not been suitable for our sophisticated audience. We almost never use material relating to trial law." Send query letter with resume. Reports in 90 days. Usually buys all rights. Pays $30-60 for all rights; on publication.

Illustrations: Uses inside illustrations and, infrequently, cover designs. Send query letter with resume. Reports in 90 days. Usually buys all rights. Pays $75-125; more for covers and for 4-color; on publication.

Tips: "There's an increasing need for artwork to illustrate high-tech articles."

LEGION, 359 Kent St., Ottawa, Ontario K2P 0R6 Canada. (613)235-8741. Editor-in-Chief: Jane Dewar. Art Director: Dick Logan. For Royal Canadian Legion members. Monthly. Circ. 558,071. Original artwork returned after publication. Free sample copy.

Illustrations: Buys 6-8 illustrations/issue from freelancers. Interested in "various techniques." Works on assignment only. Provide 35mm slides to be kept on file for possible future assignments. Prefers to see portfolio. Reports immediately. Buys various rights. Cover: Pays $450-1,500, color. Inside: Pays $100-1,200, b&w; $100-1,500, color; on acceptance.

LEISURE WHEELS, Box 7302, Station E, Calgary, Alberta T3C 3M2 Canada. (403)263-2707. Publisher: Murray Gimbel. Emphasizes recreational vehicles, travel and outdoors for upper income, ages 30-65. Monthly. Circ. 100,000. Sample copy 50¢; free art guidelines.

Cartoons: Uses 4 cartoons/issue; buys all from freelancers. Receives 1 submission/month from freelancers. Especially needs cartoons. Subject matter should concern traveling and camping as it relates to trailering, motorhoming, fishing or hiking. Prefers b&w line drawings with gag line. Send samples of style. SASE (nonCanadians include International Reply Coupons). Reports in 2 weeks. Cartoons can appear in other publications. Pays $25 for b&w.

Illustrations: Uses 4 illustrations/issue; buys all from freelancers. Receives 1 submission/week from freelancers. Usually works on assignment. Illustration needs identical to cartoons. Prefers b&w line drawings for inside. Send samples of style. SASE (nonCanadians include International Reply Coupons). Reports in 3 weeks. "Prefer illustrations not appear in a similar magazine." Pays $50-100 for inside b&w on publication.

Tips: "We now feature a broader range of editorial content. Basically, any subject that applies to recreational activity outdoors."

***LET'S LIVE**, 444 N. Larchmont, Los Angeles CA 90004. (213)469-3901. Managing Editor: Keith Stepro. Emphasizes nutrition, health and recreation. Monthly. Circ. 140,000. Sample copy $1.50; free art guidelines.

Illustrations: Uses 8-12 illustrations/issue; buys 2/issue from freelancers. Receives 2 illustrations from freelancers/week. Works on assignment only. "We like to check newspapers and magazines to find samples of the style we like to use or, we check the *Creative Black Book* for artists." Needs illustrations of inanimate objects: (e.g., salt shaker, vitamin bottles), sports action, charts, graphs, montages, spot illustrations, medical scenes (facilities, equipment), people, faces. "No mod or avant-garde styles, please." Especially needs good illustrations of various organs. Query first. Prefers samples, tear sheets and/or roughs. Originals should be sent certified mail. SASE. "Our medically-oriented graphics must be simple, non-technical, but accurate depictions of parts and their functional relationships in the body." Format: color and b&w washes. Reports in 2 weeks. Buys first North American serial rights. Pays $150-200 for color cover; $75-150 for inside color; $50-125 for inside b&w; on publication.

Tips: "There is more interest in preventive medicine and the use of natural foods and supplements, more interest among readers in seeing graphics explaining how their systems work, and more interest in exercise or therapeutic regimens. Also greater emphasis on top-flight rendering ability in illustrators doing expository and/or instructional graphics; we don't want "artistes" of the avant-garde school—we want artists who can illustrate with diagrammatic skills that can replace a lot of extraneous verbiage."

PETER LI, INC./PFLAUM PRESS, 2451 E. River Rd., Dayton OH 45439. (513)294-5785. Art Director: Jim Conley. Publishes three monthly magazines—*The Catechist*, *Classroom Computer Learning* and *Today's Catholic Teacher*.

Illustrations: Works with 20 freelance artists/year. "Local artists are, of course, more preferable but it's not an absolute." Uses artists for 4-color cover illustrations and b&w and 2-color spot illustrations. "We are only interested in *professional* illustrators, especially those with fresh, innovative styles. Experience a plus but not necessary." Works on assignment only. Send query letter with photostats, photographs, slides or tear sheets. Samples returned by SASE. Reports only if interested. Pays by the project, $100-600 average. Considers complexity of the project when establishing payment. Buys all rights.

LIGHT & LIFE, 901 College Ave., Winona Lake IN 46590. (219)267-7656. Contact: Art Director. "Emphasizes evangelical Christianity with Wesleyan slant for a cross-section readership." Readers are mostly of Free Methodist denomination. Monthly. Circ. 48,000. Original artwork returned after publication, if requested and postage included. Sample copy $1.50.
Cartoons: Rarely used. Interested in religious themes. Format: single panel b&w line drawings with or without gagline. Prefers finished cartoons. SASE. Reports in 4 weeks. Buys all rights. Pays $5-20; on acceptance.
Illustrations: Buys 2-4 illustrations/issue from freelancers. Interested in art that illustrates themes of articles. Works on assignment only. Send query letter with brochure showing art style or resume and tear sheets. Reports in 4 weeks. To show a portfolio, mail original/final art, final reproduction/product, color and tear sheets. Buys all rights on a work-for-hire basis. Pays $25 and up, inside b&w and 2-color; on publication.
Tips: "Art and design are becoming much more important in the Christian field. So there is a great need for experienced and quality illustrators in the area of Christian publications. Artists need to be able to illustrate concepts and create moods with their illustrations. Seeks someone "who wants to be a contributor partly because its fun.""

***LIGHTING DESIGN & APPLICATION MAGAZINE**, 345 E. 47th St., New York NY 10017. (212)644-7922. Emphasizes lighting design and engineering. Readers are "lighting designers, engineers, architects, researchers, and scientists." Monthly. Circ. 13,000.
Illustrations: Buys 10 illustrations/issue from freelancers. "Most are graphs, charts and line drawings. We have a regular contributor for most work. Special assignments occasionally require additional artists." Prefers b&w line drawings. Freelancers should send samples of style to the editor. SASE. Reports in 1 month. Pays on acceptance. Buys first North American serial rights.

LOG HOME GUIDE FOR BUILDERS & BUYERS, Exit 447, I-40, Hartford TN 37753. (615)487-2256. Editor: Doris Muir. Emphasizes buying and building log homes; energy-efficiency. Audience: ages 25-60, college educated, middle- upper-middle income; prefer country life. Quarterly. Circ. 125,000. Sometimes accepts previously published material. Original artwork returned after publication. Sample copy $3.50; art guidelines for SASE.
Cartoons: Buys 1-4 cartoons/issue from freelancers. Themes include renderings of log homes; warmth of log home living; amusing aspects of building with logs; and country living. Prefers single panel without gagline; b&w line drawings, b&w and color washes. Send query letter with samples of style or roughs to be kept on file. Material not filed is returned if accompanied by SASE. Reports within 6 weeks. Negotiates rights purchased. Pays $10-25, b&w; $25-50, color; on publication.
Illustrations: Buys 1-4 illustrations/issue from freelancers. Themes include log home renderings; log homes in rural scenes; and beavers and badgers in natural settings. Send query letter with brochure, resume, business card and samples to be kept on file. Prefers tear sheets, slides and photographs as samples. Samples not filed are returned by SASE. Reports within 6 weeks. Negotiates rights purchased. Pays $250, color, cover; $15-35, b&w and $25-50, color, inside; on publication.

LONE STAR HUMOR DIGEST, Lone Star Publications of Humor, Suite 103, Box 29000, San Antonio TX 78229. Editor/Publisher: Lauren Barnett Scharf. "Book-by-subscription" (magazine-type format). Emphasizes "comedy connoisseurs," and "others who like to laugh." Published about 3 times/year. Circ. 1,200. Sometimes accepts previously published material. Original artwork returned after publication. Inquire for update on sample copy; art guidelines for SASE with 22¢ postage.
Cartoons: Buys 20-25 cartoons/issue from freelancers. Prefers single, double or multiple panel with or without gagline; b&w line drawings. Send roughs or finished cartoons. Material returned by SASE. Reports within 3 months. Negotiates rights purchased. Pays on publication ("but we try to pay before"). Inquire for update on pay scale.

THE LOOKOUT, 8121 Hamilton Ave., Cincinnati OH 45231. (513)931-4050. Editor-in-Chief: Mark A. Taylor. For conservative Christian adults and young adults. Weekly. Circ. 140,000. Original artwork not returned after publication, unless requested. Sample copy and artists' guidelines available for 50¢.
Cartoons: Uses 1 cartoon/issue; buys 20/year from freelancers. Interested in church, Sunday school and Christian family themes. Send roughs or finished cartoons. Samples returned by SASE. Reports in 2 weeks. Buys one-time rights.
Illustrations: Buys 3-4 illustrations/issue. Interested in "adults, families, interpersonal relationships; also, graphic treatment of titles." Works on assignment only. Send query letter with brochure, flyer or tear sheets to be kept on file for future assignments to Frank Sutton, art director, at above address. Reporting time varies. Buys all rights but will reassign. Inside: Pays $100 for b&w, $125 for full-color illustrations, firm; on acceptance. Cover: "Sometimes more for cover work."

LOS ANGELES, 1888 Century Park E, Los Angeles CA 90067. (213)552-1021. Design Director: William Delorme. Emphasizes lifestyles, cultural attractions, pleasures, problems and personalities of Los Angeles and the surrounding area. Monthly. Circ. 160,000. SASE. Reports in 2-3 weeks. Especially needs very localized contributors—custom projects needing person-to-person concepting and implementation. Previously published work OK. Pays on publication. Sample copy $3.
Cartoons: Contact Geoff Miller, editor-in-chief. Buys 5-7/issue on current events, environment, family life, politics, social life and business; single, double or multiple panel with gagline. Mail roughs. Pays $25-50, b&w line drawings.
Illustrations: Buys 10/issue on assigned themes. Send brochure showing art style or tear sheets, photostats, photocopies and slides. To show a portfolio, mail original/final art, final reproduction/product, color, tear sheets, photostats, photographs, etc. Pays $300-500, color, cover; $150-500, b&w and $200-750, color, inside; on publication.
Tips: "Show work similar to that used in the magazine—a sophisticated style. Study a particular publication's content, style and format. Then proceed accordingly in submitting sample work." There is a trend toward "imaginative imagery and technical brilliance with computer-enhanced art being a factor. Know the stylistic essence of a magazine at a gut level as well as at a perceptive level. Identify with Los Angeles or Southern California."

LOST TREASURE, 15115 S. 76th East Ave., Bixby OK 74008. (918)366-4441. Managing Editor: James D. Watts, Jr. Emphasizes treasure hunting for treasure hunters, coinshooters, metal detector owners. Monthly. Circ. 50,000. Sample copy for 9x12 SASE.
Cartoons: Buys 1-2 cartoons/issue; all from freelancers. Receives 10 cartoons from freelancers/month. Cartoons should pertain to treasure hunting, people using metal detectors, prospecting, etc. Prefers single panel b&w line drawings or b&w washes with gagline. Send query letter with finished cartoons. SASE. Reports in 6-8 weeks. Pays 15 on publication. Buys first North American serial rights.
Tips: "Cartoon should be very treasure-hunting oriented and funny. Prefer irony to slap stick."

***LOTTERY PLAYER'S MAGAZINE**, Box 5013, Cherry Hill NJ 08034. Editor/Publisher: S.W. Valenza, Jr. Emphasizes lottery, gaming. Monthly. Circ. 200,000. Accepts previously published material and simultaneous submissions. Sample copy $1.
Cartoons: Occasionally uses cartoons. Prefers single panel, with gagline; b&w line drawings. Send samples of style to be kept on file. "If in the area, an appointment *may* be possible." Material not kept on file is returned by SASE. Reports in 4 weeks. Buys one-time rights. Pays $15-40, b&w; on publication.
Illustrations: Uses illustrations occasionally; occasionally buys from freelance artists. Themes or styles depend on content of issue; "we are 2-color." Send query letter with business card and photostats or photocopies to be kept on file; no slides. Samples returned by SASE if not kept on file. Reports within 4 weeks. Buys one-time rights. To show a portfolio, mail appropriate materials. Pays $20-100, b&w, inside; on publication.

LOUISIANA LIFE MAGAZINE, 4200 S. I-10 Service Rd., Metairie LA 70001. (504)456-2220. Art Director: Tessa Tilden-Smith. Emphasizes the lifestyle of Louisiana (food, entertainment, work, etc.) for the upper-income Louisianian, "proud of the state and its diversity." Bimonthly. Circ. 50,000. Accepts previously published material. Original artwork returned after publication. Art guidelines available.
Illustrations: Buys 1-2 illustrations/issue from freelancers. Prefers watercolor illustrations. Works on assignment only. Send query letter with resume, photocopies and tear sheets to be kept on file. Samples not kept on file are returned by SASE. Reports within 2 weeks. Call or write to schedule an appointment to show a portfolio, which should include original/final art (if possible), final reproduction/product and tear sheets. Buys first rights. Pays $150/page, color, inside; on publication.
Tips: "Be very selective when assembling a portfolio. Show only your best. Don't overwhelm us with volume."

***THE LUTHERAN**, 2900 Queen Lane, Philadelphia PA 19129. (215)438-6580. Editor-in-Chief: Edgar R. Trexler. Associate Editor: Walter A. Kortrey. General interest magazine of the Lutheran Church in America. Biweekly; monthly in July, August and December. Circ. 546,000. Previously published work OK. Original artwork returned after publication. Free sample copy.
Cartoons: Buys 1 cartoon/issue from freelancers. Receives 30 submissions/week from freelancers. Interested in humorous or thought-provoking cartoons on religion or about issues of concern to Christians; single panel. Prefers roughs or finished cartoons. SASE. Reports usually within a week. Buys first rights. Pays $10-50, b&w line drawings and washes; on publication.
Illustrations: Buys 2 illustrations/issue from freelancers. Interested in church-related family scenes, Christmas, Advent, Baptism, Communion, Confirmation, church entering, leaving, interior, exterior, choirs, funerals, Easter and Lent. Works on assignment only. Prefers to see portfolio or samples of style. Reports in 2 weeks. Buys all rights on a work-for-hire basis. Samples returned by SASE. Send resume or

tear sheets to be kept on file for future assignments. Buys 30-40/year on assigned themes. Pays $150, b&w; on publication.

THE LUTHERAN STANDARD, Box 1209, 426 S. 5th St., Minneapolis MN 55440. (612)330-3300. Editor: Lowell G. Almen. Managing Editor: Donn S. McLellan. Emphasizes news in the world of religion, dealing primarily with the Lutheran church. For members of the American Lutheran Church. Published 20 times/year. Circ. 579,000. Free sample copy.
Cartoons: Buys 1-2 cartoons/issue; buys all from freelancers. Receives 10 submissions/week from freelancers. Interested in current events, education, family life, humor through youth and religious themes. Send finished cartoons. SASE. Reports in 3-4 weeks. Buys first or simultaneous rights. Pays $10-25, b&w line drawings and washes; on acceptance.
Illustrations: Buys 4 illustrations/issue from freelancers. Works on assignment only. Send query letter with photocopies and SASE. Reports in 3-4 weeks. Buys all rights on a work-for-hire basis. Inside: Pays $50-150, b&w and 2-color line drawings and washes.

***LYNN, THE NORTH SHORE MAGAZINE**, 45 Forest Ave., Swampscott MA 01907. CEO: Paula R. Hastings. Estab. 1984. Magazine emphasizing the general consumer, some emphasis on local geographical area (North Shore of Boston) for upscale homeowners, age 30 and up. Bimonthly. Circ. 75,000. Accepts previously published material. Original artwork returned after publication if requested. Sample copy free for SASE with $1 postage.
Cartoons: Prefers lifestyle themes, human issues, sports or the ocean and wildlife. Prefers single panel with gagline; b&w line drawings and b&w washes. Send query letter with samples of style and finished cartoons. Samples not filed are returned by SASE. Reports only if interested. Buys one-time rights. Pays $50, b&w.
Illustrations: Buys 5 illustrations/issue from freelancers. Works on assignment only. Prefers "a generally realistic style, lifestyle material and mixed media. Send query letter with brochure showing art style or resume, tear sheets and photocopies. Samples not filed are returned by SASE. Reports only if interested. Buys one-time rights. Pays $300, b&w and $300, color, cover; $200, b&w and $200, color (full page), inside. Smaller pieces negotiable. Pays on publication.

***MACUSER MAGAZINE**, 25 W. 39th St., New York NY 10018. (212)302-2626. Art Director: Lisa Orsini. Estab. 1985. Magazine emphasizing MacIntosh computers for MacIntosh computer owners who use programs for business or personal means. Monthly. Circ. 100,000. Accepts previously published material. Returns original artwork after publication. Sample copy and art guidelines available.
Illustrations: Buys 12 illustrations/issue from freelancers. Works on assignment only. Send query letter with tear sheets, photostats and photocopies. Samples not filed are returned only if requested. Reports only if interested. Call to schedule an appointment to show a portfolio, which should include original/final art and tear sheets. Negotiates rights purchased. Pays $500, b&w, and $500, color, cover; $300, b&w and $350, color, inside; on publication.

MADE TO MEASURE, 300 W. Adams St., Chicago IL 60606. (312)263-6355. Publisher: William Halper. Emphasizes uniforms, career clothes, men's tailoring and clothing. Magazine distributed to retailers, manufacturers and uniform group purchasers. Semiannually. Circ. 24,000. Art guidelines available.
Cartoons: Buys 15 cartoons/issue from freelancers. Prefers themes relating to subject matter of magazine; also general interest. Prefers single panel with or without gagline; b&w line drawings. Send query letter with samples of style or finished cartoons. Any cartoons not purchased are returned to artist. Reports back. Buys first rights. Pays $20-25 b&w, on acceptance.

MAGIC CHANGES, 8 Huntington Cr. West, #14, Naperville IL 60540. (312)355-3275. Editor: John Sennett. Emphasizes fantasy and poetry for college students, housewives, teachers, artists and musicians: "People with both interesting and artistic slant." Annually. Circ. 500. Accepts previously published material. Original artwork returned after publication. Sample copy $4; art guidelines free for SASE.
Cartoons: Buys 2 cartoons/issue from freelancers. Considers space, art, animals and street activity themes. Single, double, or multiple panel with or without gagline; b&w line drawings. Send query letter with finished cartoons. Material returned by SASE. Reports within 2 weeks. Acquires first rights. Pays in copies.
Illustrations: Buys 10 illustrations/issue from freelancers. Considers city, wilderness, bird, space and fantasy themes. Send query leter with samples. Samples returned by SASE. Reports within 2 weeks. To show a portfolio, mail original/final art, final reproduction/product or b&w. Acquires first rights. Pays in copies.
Tips: "Send imaginative b&w drawings."

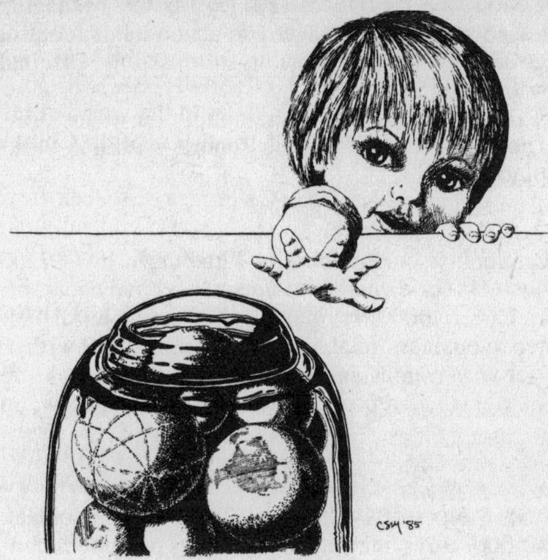

Cheryl Mandus of Dunwoody, Georgia, queried Magic Changes *magazine about an article to write and illustrate. Editor John Sennet assigned Mandus a cover design, requesting a "space theme" to convey a sense of depth. Publication of the pen & ink rendering resulted in more work references and further exposure for the artist. Sennet bought reprint rights for the work.*

MAGICAL BLEND, Box 11303, San Francisco CA 94101. Emphasizes the psychic, occult and spiritual. Quarterly. Circ. 12,000. Original artwork returned after publication. Sample copy $4; art guidelines for SASE.
Cartoons: Buys 3 cartoons/issue from freelancers. Send query letter with photostats.
Illustrations: Buys 60 illustrations/issue from freelancers. Receives 5 submissions/week from freelancers. Interested in fantasy and sorcery. "We keep samples on file and work by assignment according to the artists and our time table and workability. We accept b&w line drawings, also pencil and pre-separated color work. We tend towards fantasy and new age styles. We look for pieces with occult, psychic and spiritual subjects with positive, inspiring, uplifting feeling. No dark, bizarre, or negative material will be considered." Especially needs Oriental themes and strong cultural themes, i.e., African, Latin American, Zen brush work, Indian, etc. Send query letter with photostats to be kept on file. Prefers to see portfolio or samples of style. SASE. Reports in 3 months. Buys first North American serial rights. Rights revert to artist. Pays in copies. Also needs "comics and/or comix about occult, sorcery, magic, psychic subjects with positive, uplifting endings."
Tips: "We now are printing color and will consider pre-separated color work. We are getting wider recognition, and thus, more professional. Send good reproductions—not photocopies, not originals. Read the magazines."

MAINE LIFE, Suite 8, Pierre St., Lewiston ME 04240. (207)782-5952. Publisher: Garry Owen Bowles. Editor: Nancy Marcotte. Emphasizes the State of Maine for the general public. Monthly. Circ. 30,000. Previously published material OK. Original artwork returned after publication. Free sample copy for 8½x11 SASE.
Illustrations: Uses 2-3 illustrations/issue. Send query letter with resume and samples. Samples returned by SASE. Reports in 6 weeks. Buys first rights. To show a portfolio, mail final reproduction/product, photostats and photographs. Pays $25-35 minimum, inside b&w line drawings; on publication.
Tips: Looking for "illustrations of people in action, wildlife indigenous to Maine, good quality, strong line, well presented package with all components identified and labeled. Two of our regular features *Umcolcus Charlie* and *Main Street* will almost always use line art. Artists should be able to transform popularly photographed places in Maine and Maine animals into line art."

***THE MAINE SPORTSMAN**, Box 365, Augusta ME 04330. Editor: Harry Vanderweide. Emphasizes Maine outdoors for hunters and fishermen. Monthly tabloid. Circ. 23,000. Original work returned after publication.
Cartoons: Uses some. Buys 1-3 cartoons/month from freelancers. Prefers to buy 10-12 at a time. Samples returned by SASE. Reports in one week. B&w only. Pays $15 on acceptance.
Illustrations: Buys 1-3 illustrations/month from freelancers. Especially wildlife scenes. Most issues feature drawing on cover. Send query letter with brochure showing art style and samples. Samples returned by SASE. Reports in one week. Buys first rights, pays when illustration is published. B&w only. Pays $50 for cover drawing, $10-20 for illustrations used inside.
Tips: "We prefer cartoons that are actually humorous, especially if they don't require a caption line."

MANAGEMENT ACCOUNTING, 10 Paragon Dr., Montvale NJ 07645. (201)573-6269. Managing Editor: Robert F. Randall. Emphasizes management accounting for management accountants, controllers, chief accountants, treasurers. Monthly. Circ. 95,000. Accepts simultaneous submissions. Original artwork not returned after publication. Sample copy free for SASE.
Cartoons: Buys 1 cartoon/issue from freelancers. Prefers single panel with gagline; b&w line drawings. Send finished cartoons. Material not kept on file is returned by SASE. Reports within 2 weeks. Buys one-time rights. Pays $15-25, b&w; on acceptance.
Illustrations: Buys 1 illustration/issue.

***MANAGING**, Graduate School of Business, University of Pittsburgh, Pittsburgh PA 15260. (412)648-1644. Editor: Karen B. Hoy. Emphasizes business for "middle- to upper-level managers, primarily in the Pittsburgh area." Published 2 times/year. Circ. 7,000. Previously published material OK.
Cartoons: Number of cartoons/issue varies. Interested in business-related themes; single panel with or without gagline, b&w line drawings. Send query letter with roughs and samples of style. Samples returned on request. Reports in 2 months. Buys one-time rights and reprint rights. Pays $10-30, b&w; on acceptance.
Tips: "We don't publish much freelance artwork."

MARRIAGE AND FAMILY LIVING, Abbey Press, St. Meinrad IN 47577. (812)357-8011. Contact: Art Director. For Christian families. Monthly. Circ. 40,000. Buys one-time rights. Pays on publication.
Cartoons: "We try to use one cartoon per month."
Illustrations: Buys 200 illustrations/year.

***MATURE YEARS**, United Methodist Publishing House, 201 8th Ave. S., Nashville TN 37202. (615)749-6000. Art Director: Dave Dawson. For retired persons and those facing retirement; persons seeking help on how to handle problems and privileges of retirement. Quarterly. Circ. 103,000. Free catalog and artist's guidelines.
Cartoons: Buys 4 cartoons/year. Interested in current events relate to aging, religion and retirement. Send query letter with samples. SASE. Reports in 4 weeks. Buys all rights. Pays $25 minimum, b&w; on publication.
Illustrations: Buys 1 and 2-color inside illustrations according to manuscript needs. Using more illustrations depicting intergenerational activities. Works on assignment only. Pays $60-80 depending on complexity.

MEDIA & METHODS, 1511 Walnut St., Philadelphia PA 19102. (215)563-3501. Emphasizes the methods and technologies of teaching for all school teachers and administrators. Bimonthly. Circ. 40,000+. Accepts previously published material. Returns original artwork after publication. Sample copy for SASE.
Cartoons: Buys 0-1 cartoons/issue from freelancers. Prefers education themes. Prefers single panel with gagline; b&w line drawings, b&w washes. Send query letter with samples of style to be kept on file. Material not filed is returned by SASE. Reports back only if interested. Buys first rights or reprint rights; pays on publication.
Illustrations: Buys 1-2 illustrations/issue from freelancers. Send query letter with brochure, business card and samples to be kept on file. Prefers slides, photostats or photographs as samples. Material not filed is returned by SASE. Reports back only if interested. Buys first rights or reprint rights. Pays $175 for b&w and $250 for color, cover; $150 for b&w and $175 for color, inside; on publication.
Tips: "We are willing to work through the mail and look for unique styles."

***MEDICAL ECONOMICS FOR SURGEONS**, 680 Kinderkamack Rd., Oradell NJ 07649. (201)267-3030. Art Administrator: Ms. Grady Olley. Magazine for physicians, surgeons and financial specialists. Monthly. Circ. 45,000. Accepts previously published material. Original artwork returned after publication. Sample copy free for SASE.
Cartoons: Buys 5-7 cartoons/issue from freelancers. Prefers medically-related themes. Prefers single panel with gagline; b&w line drawings and b&w washes. Send query letter with finished cartoons. Samples not filed are returned by SASE. Reports within 2 months. Buys all rights. Pays $50, b&w.
Illustrations: Buys 10-23 illustrations/issue from freelancers. Works on assignment only. Send query letter with resume, tear sheets, and slides. Samples not filed are returned by SASE. Reports back only if interested. Call to schedule an appointment to show a portfolio, which should include original/final art (if possible) and tear sheets. Buys one-time rights. Pays $300-1,000, color, cover; $50-300, b&w, $200-500, color, inside; on acceptance.

***MEDICAL ECONOMICS MAGAZINE**, 680 Kinderkamack Rd., Oradell NJ 07649. (201)262-3030. Art Administrator: Ms. Grady Olley. Magazine for those interested in the financial and legal aspects of

running a medical practice. Bimonthly. Circ. 182,000. Accepts previously published material. Original artwork returned after publication. Sample copy free for SASE.
Cartoons: Buys 10 cartoons/issue from freelancers. Prefers medically-related themes. Prefers single panel, with gagline; b&w line drawings and b&w washes. Send query letter with finished cartoons. Material not filed is returned by SASE. Reports within 8 weeks. Buys all rights. Pays $50, b&w.
Illustrations: Buys 12-15 illustrations/issue from freelancers. Works on assignment only. Send query letter with resume and samples. Samples not filed are returned by SASE. Reports only if interested. Call to schedule an appointment to show a portfolio, which should include original/final art (if possible) and tear sheets. Buys one-time rights. Pays $300-1,000, color, cover; $75-300, b&w and $250-600, color, inside; on acceptance.

MEDICAL TIMES, 80 Shore Rd., Port Washington NY 11050. Executive Editor: Susan Carr Jenkins. Emphasizes clinical medical articles. Monthly. Circ. 105,000. Sample copy $5.
Cartoons: Buys 5-6 cartoons/year from freelancers. Prefers medical themes, "but nothing insulting to our audience." Accepts single panel with gagline; b&w line drawings. Send query letter with finished cartoons; "we'll either accept and pay or return them within one month." Negotiates rights purchased. Pays $25, b&w; on acceptance.
Illustrations: Buys 2 or 3 illustrations/issue, 24-36/year from freelancers. Works on assignment only. Send query letter with resume and medical samples such as tear sheets, photostats, photocopies, slides and photographs. Samples not filed are returned. Reports within 1 month. Write to schedule an appointment to show a portfolio, which should include original art (1 or 2 pieces only) and printed material "so we can see how the artist's work reproduces. Most of the portfolio should consist of printed pieces." Negotiates rights purchased. Payment varies; pays on acceptance.
Tips: "With the ever-increasing number of medical journals competing for the same ad budgets, competition and cost controls are becoming fierce. This may mean a cutback in the amount of artwork purchased by some of the marginally successful journals. I've noticed a trend away from the 'sci-fi' look that was so popular a couple of years ago. As for *Medical Times*, don't send me any samples that aren't medical in nature. You may be a wonderful portrait artist, but that doesn't help me at all in deciding if you could draw a lung."

***MEDICAL WORLD NEWS**, Suite 112, 7676 Woodway, Houston TX 77063. Art Director: Melanie McMullen. The newsmagazine of medicine for all doctors: family practitioners, general practitioners and internal medicine. Semi-monthly. Circ. 123,000. Original artwork returned after publication.
Cartoons: Buys 2 cartoons/issue from freelancers. Prefers single panel without gagline. Send samples of style to be kept on file. Material not kept on file is returned by SASE. Reports within 2 weeks. Buys one-time rights. Pays $50-100, b&w.
Illustrations: Buys 1 illustration/issue from freelancers. Works on assignment only. Send query letter with brochure showing art style or tear sheets and photocopies. Samples not filed are returned by SASE. Reports only if interested. Write to schedule an appointment to show a portfolio, which should include tear sheets. Buys one-time rights. Pays $500-800, color, cover; $50-100, b&w, inside; on publication.

***MEDICENTER MANAGEMENT**, (fomerly Vascular Diagnosis & Therapy), Brentwood Publishing Corp., 825 S. Barrington Ave., Los Angeles CA 90049. Publisher: Martin Waldman. Art Director: Tom Medsger. Emphasizes technological, medical and professional news. Send brochure/flyer to be kept on file for possible future assignment. Reports only when assignment available. Buys all rights. Pays $60 and up, spot art; $400, full-color cover; on acceptance.

MEMCO NEWS, Box 1079, Appleton WI 54912. Editor: Richard F. Metko. Emphasizes "welding applications as performed with Miller Electric equipment. Readership ranges from workers in small shops to metallurgical engineers." Quarterly. Circ. 44,000. Previously published material and simultaneous submissions OK. Original artwork not returned after publication.

MENDOCINO REVIEW, Box 888, Mendocino CA 95460. (707)964-3831. Editor: Camille Ranker. Literary journal emphasizing short stories, poetry, photographs and artwork. Annual. Circ. 5,000. Returns original work after publication. Sample copy available when "requested on letterhead or with sample submissions." Art guidelines available.
Cartoons: Have published none to date, but "would love to!" Send query letter with samples of style to be kept on file. Material not filed is returned by SASE. Reports within 1 month. Acquires one-time rights. Prefers single, double or multiple panel with gagline; b&w line drawings or washes. Pays in contributor's copies; on publication.
Illustrations: " We would like to have 'lots' in the magazine, but because we're unable to pay, we've had few. We retain submissions on file and attempt to match the illustrations to stories and poetry as needed." Send query letter and samples; "good quality copies are fine. If accepted we contact for a re-

production or the original as needed." Samples not filed are returned by SASE. Reports within 1 month. Acquires first rights or one-time rights. Pays in contributor's copies; on publication.

THE MERCEDES-BENZ STAR, 1235 Pierce St., Lakewood CO 80214. (303)235-0116. Editor: Frank Barrett. Magazine emphasizing new and old Mercedes-Benz automobiles for members of the Mercedes-Benz Club of America and other automotive enthusiasts. Bimonthly. Circ. 20,000. Does not usually accept previously published material. Returns original artwork after publication. Sample copy for SASE with $1.75 postage.
Illustrations: Buys 0-1/issue. Prefers Mercedes-Benz related themes. Send query letter with resume, slides or photographs to be kept on file except for material requested to be returned. Write for appointment to show portfolio. Samples not filed are returned by SASE. Reports within 3 weeks. Buys first rights. Negotiates payment; pays on publication.

MERCURY MAGAZINE, Astronomical Society of the Pacific, 1290 24th Ave., San Francisco CA 94122. (415)661-8660. Editor: Andrew Fraknoi. Emphasizes astronomy for students, teachers, lay people. Bimonthly. Circ. 6,000. Accepts previously published material. Original artwork returned after publication, "but we need to keep photo." Sample copy $2.
Cartoons: Uses 3 cartoons/year. Prefers astronomy theme. Send query letter with a copy of finished cartoons to be kept on file. Material not kept on file is returned by SASE. Buys first rights.
Illustrations: Uses various number of illustrations/issue. Prefers astronomy theme only. Send query letter with samples and tear sheets to be kept on file. Samples not kept on file are returned by SASE. Buys first rights.

MESSENGER OF ST. ANTHONY, Basilica del Santo, Via Orto Botanico, 35123 Padua, Italy. Executive Editor: Fr. Livio Poloniato. "Ours is basically a religious, family-oriented magazine." Monthly. Circ. 20,000. Accepts previously published material. Original artwork returned after publication. Sample copy available.
Illustrations: Prefers couples, families, children. Samples returned only if requested. Reports only if interested. Buys one-time rights. Pays $10, b&w and $15, color, inside; on publication.

***METALSMITH MAGAZINE**, 6707 N. Santa Monica Blvd., Milwaukee WI 53217. (414)351-2232. Editor: Sarah Bodine. Magazine emphasizing development and appreciation of metal arts for jewelers, designers, metal sculptors, teachers and students. Quarterly. Circ. 6,000. Sample copy free for SASE.
Illustrations: Buys various illustrations/issue from freelancers. Works on assignment only. Prefers technical and mechanical illustrations. Send query letter with resume, tear sheets and photographs. Samples not filed are returned by SASE. Reports only if interested. To show a portfolio, mail final reproduction/product, tear sheets and photographs. Negotiates rights purchased. Pays on publication.

MICHIGAN OUT OF DOORS, Box 30235, Lansing MI 48909. Contact: Kenneth S. Lowe. Emphasizes outdoor recreation, especially hunting and fishing; conservation; and environmental affairs. Sample copy $1.
Illustrations: "Following the various hunting and fishing seasons we have a need for illustration material; we consider submissions 6-8 months in advance." Reports as soon as possible. Pays $15 for pen & ink illustrations in a vertical treatment; on acceptance.
Tips: "Our magazine has shifted from newsprint to enamel stock. We have our own art department and thus do not require a great deal of special material."

***MILITARY LIFESTYLE MAGAZINE**, (formerly Ladycom), 1732 Wisconsin Ave. NW, Washington DC 20007. Art Director: Judi Connelly. Emphasizes active-duty military lifestyles for military wives and families. 10 times/year. Circ. 500,000. Original artwork returned after publication.
Illustrations: Buys 2-6 illustrations/issue from freelancers. Theme/style depends on editorial content. Works on assignment only. Send brochure and business card to be kept on file. Accepts photostats, tear sheets, photocopies, slides, photographs, etc. as samples. Samples returned only if requested. Reports only if interested. Buys first rights. Payment depends on size published, cover and inside; pays on publication.

MILITARY MARKET MAGAZINE, Springfield VA 22159-0210. (703)750-8676. Editor: Nancy M. Tucker. Emphasizes "the military's PX and commissary businesses for persons who manage and buy for the military's commissary and post exchange systems; also manufacturers and sales companies who supply them." Monthly. Circ. 11,000. Simultaneous submissions OK. Original artwork not returned after publication.
Cartoons: Buys 3-4 cartoons/issue from freelancers. Interested in themes relating to "retailing/buying of groceries and general merchandise from the point of view of the store managers and workers"; single

panel with or without gagline, b&w line drawings. Send finished cartoons. Samples returned by SASE. Reports in 6 months. Buys all rights. Pays $25, b&w; on acceptance.
Tips: "We use freelance cartoonists only—*no* other freelance artwork."

MPLS. ST. PAUL MAGAZINE, Suite 1030, 12 S. 6th St., Minneapolis MN 55402. (612)339-7571. Contact: Tara Christopherson. City/regional magazine. For "professional people of middle-upper income levels, college educated, interested in the arts, dining and the good life of Minnesota." Monthly. Circ. 48,000. Original artwork returned after publication.
Illustrations: Uses 12 illustrations/issue. Works on assignment only. Arrange interview to show portfolio. Provide business card, flyer or tear sheet to be kept on file for future assignments. Reports in 2 weeks. Buys first North American serial rights, and all rights on a work-for-hire basis. Pays $75-200, b&w; $600 maximum/full-page, color; on acceptance.

MISSOURI LIFE, 710 N. Tucker, St Louis MO 63101. (314)342-1281. Editor: Debra Gluck. Magazine about Missouri. Readers are people interested in where to go, what to do in the state, and the beauty and fascination of Missouri places and faces. Bimonthly. Circ. 30,000. Original artwork returned after publication. Sample copy $3; art guidelines for SASE.
Cartoons: Used to illustrate some departments and features.
Illustrations: Uses original artwork depicting Missouri places or people. Receives 2 illustrations/week from freelance artists. Especially needs variety of b&w and color line art and other types of art for illustration of specific stories, on assignment; interested in a variety of styles. Format: b&w, color cover washes, inside and cover color washes and original art that will reproduce for offset printing/web. Samples returned by SASE. Provide letter of inquiry, tear sheet, proposal and sample of work to be kept on file for future assignments. Reports in 4 weeks. Buys first North American serial rights. Pays $25-50 for b&w, on publication.
Tips: "Send samples of work that show the styles and media you are experienced and good at. We prefer artists in the mid-Missouri, Kansas City and St. Louis areas."

MISSOURI RURALIST, Suite 600, 2103 Burlington, Columbia MO 65202. (314)474-9557. Contact: Editor. For Missouri farm families. Biweekly (except monthly June, July, December). Circ. 80,000. Previously published material OK. Original artwork not returned after publication.
Cartoons: Buys 2 cartoons/issue from freelancers. Interested in farm and rural themes; single panel with gagline. Send finished cartoons. Samples returned by SASE. Reports in 4 weeks. Negotiates rights purchased. Negotiates pay; pays on publication.
Tips: There is a "definite need for good agricultural cartoonists who understand the agriculture business. They must be able to write as well as draw. Puns on farming and agriculture are taboo. Good agricultural cartoonists are scarce. Most are artists, but not good gag writers."

MODEL RETAILER, Clifton House, Clifton VA 22024. (703)830-1000. Editor: Geoffey A. Wheeler. For hobby store owners. Monthly. Circ. 6,100. Previously published and simultaneous submissions ("must be notified") OK. Original artwork returned after publication. Also interested in art for covers, article illustrations, and headline/blurb blocks.
Cartoons: Buys 3 cartoons/issue, all from freelancers. Receives 10 submissions/month from freelancers. Interested in themes pertaining to hobbies, hobby stores or small businesses; double panel. "Query first, with brief summary of types of work done (ads, covers, headline art, cartoons, etc.); after positive response from us send samples of work (photocopies, etc.) and some references." SASE. Reports in 2 weeks. Buys "first time rights in our field." Pays $25 minimum, line drawings; on publication.
Tips: We are "trying to improve the look of the magazine to gain attention for articles and help emphasize key points through imaginative use of graphics. We want good artwork that could be used to dress up

> **There is a good use of hand-lettered title type and more graphic style of illustrations such as vignettes and collage setups. Simplicity in design gives a clean look, with brighter and untraditional color combinations being used.**
>
> **Candice V. Lichty, Stein and Day**

feature articles, especially artwork for the headline/blurb block. Basically, artwork that would look good as line or with color overlays.''

MODERN DRUMMER, 870 Pompton Ave., Cedar Grove NJ 07009. (201)239-4140. Editor-in-Chief: Ronald Spagnardi. Art Director: David Creamer. For drummers, all ages and levels of playing ability with varied interests within the field of drumming. Monthly. Circ. 50,000. Previously published work OK. Original artwork returned after publication. Sample copy $2.75.
Cartoons: Buys 5-10 cartoons/year. Uses 1 cartoon/issue. Interested in drumming; single and double panel. ''We want strictly drummer-oriented gags.'' Prefers finished cartoons or roughs. SASE. Reports in 3 weeks. Buys first North American serial rights. Pays $5-25; on publication.

***MODERN LITURGY**, #290, 160 E. Virginia St., San Jose CA 95112. Editor: Kenneth Guentert. Art Editor: Mary Hicks. For religious artists, musicians and planners of workship services for Catholic and Protestant liturgical traditions. Published 9 times/year. Circ. 15,000. Sample copy $4.
Illustrations: Buys 4 illustrations/year from freelancers on assigned themes. Send query with samples. SASE. Reports in 4-6 weeks. Buys all rights but may reassign rights to artist after publication. Pays $25-50, color-separated art.

MODERN MACHINE SHOP, 6600 Clough Pike, Cincinnati OH 45230. (513)231-8020. Editor: Ken M. Gettelman. Emphasizes the metalworking industry for production and engineering management in the metalworking industry. Monthly. Circ. 106,000. Free sample copy.
Cartoons: Uses 1 cartoon/issue; buys 1 from freelancers. Receives 5 cartoons/week from freelance artists. Interested in themes relating to the manufacturing environment; single panel with gag line. A topical cartoon can still be appropriate. Send finished cartoons. Samples returned. Reports in 2 weeks. Buys all rights. Pays $25-35, b&w; on acceptance.
Illustrations: Uses 25 illustrations/issue; industrial material only. Prefers illustrations with articles; especially needs those relating to the new trends of computer-assisted design and manufacturing. Provide samples and tear sheets to be kept on file for possible future assignments. Call for appointment. Samples returned. Buys all rights. Pays $300-500 for illustrations with articles; on acceptance.
Tips: ''We see growth of manufacturing capabilities around the world and growth of computer-assisted manufacturing.''

MODERN MATURITY, 3200 East Carson, Lakewood CA 90712. (213)496-2277. Picture Editor: Ms. M.J. Wadolny. Emphasizes health, lifestyles, travel, sports, finance and contemporary activities for members of American Association of Retired Persons. Bimonthly. Previously published work OK. Original artwork returned after publication. Sample copy available.
Cartoons: Uses 4 cartoons/issue; buys 2/issue from freelancers. Receives 50 submissions/week from freelancers. Interested in general interest themes. Send finished cartoons, color and b&w. SASE. Reports in 2 months. Buys all rights on a work-for-hire basis. Pays $150, 8x10 finished cartoons.

***MODERN TIRE DEALER**, 110 N. Miller Rd., Akron OH 44313. (216)867-4401. Editor: David L. Burkhart. Circ. 33,000. For owners-operators of independent retail/wholesale tire shops. Buys all rights. Pays on publication.
Cartoons: Buys themes relating to automotive and tire services. Send actual cartoons with gagline. SASE. ''When a cartoonist sends cartoons that are already complete and asks us to consider them, chances are good we will use them. If we don't, after a few months we return them.'' Pays $50, pen & ink, approximately 8x10'' to be shot down to about 3x5'' on publication.
Illustrations: Buys automotive services and tire-related themes, using line drawings of men performing services on tires, brakes, shocks and mufflers. Send query letter with samples of artistic style. SASE. Assignments given based on samples. Reports in 1 week. Pays $100-200, color, cover; pays $20-50, drawings inside; on publication.

***MOMENT MAGAZINE**, 462 Boylston St., Boston MA 02116. Assistant Editor: Josh Gamson. Magazine for American Jews, largely affluent and well-educated. Monthly. Circ. 27,000. Original artwork returned after publication. Sample copy $4.
Illustrations: Buys approximately 4 illustrations/year from freelancers. Works on assignment only. Usually prefers illustrated fiction. Send query letter with brochure showing art style or resume and samples. Samples not filed are returned by SASE. Reports back within weeks. Call or write to schedule an appointment to show a portfolio. Negotiates first rights purchased. Payment varies. Pays on publication.

***MONEY MAKER**, 5705 N. Lincoln Ave., Chicago IL 60659. Art Director: Craig Smith. Magazine emphasizing financial investments. Bimonthly. Circ. 300,000. Accepts previously published material.

Original artwork returned after publication.
Illustration: Buys 15 illustrations/issue. Works on assignment only. Prefers financial themes in any art style. Send query letter with brochure showing art style, tear sheets, photostats, photocopies and slides. Samples not filed, returned by SASE. Reports only if interested. To show a portfolio, mail appropriate materials or write to schedule an appointment; portfolio should include original/final art and tear sheets. Buys reprint rights or negotiates rights purchased. Pays $750, b&w; $900, color, inside; on acceptance.

THE MORGAN HORSE, Box 1, Westmoreland NY 13490. (315)735-7522. Production Manager: Carol Misiaszek. Emphasizes all aspects of the Morgan horse breed including educating Morgan owners, trainers and enthusiasts on breeding and training programs; the true type of the Morgan breed, techniques on promoting the breed, how-to articles, as well as preserving the history of the breed. Monthly. Circ. 9,000. Accepts previously published material and simultaneous submissions. Original artwork returned after publication. Sample copy $3; art guidelines free for SASE.
Cartoons: Buys 3-6 cartoons/issue from freelancers. "Since most of our issues have specific themes, cartoons relating to those themes are most welcome, i.e., our June issue is devoted to youth involved in the breed." Prefers single panel, with gagline; b&w line drawings. Send query letter with finished cartoons to be kept on file "only if purchased and until publication." Samples not filed are returned by SASE. Reports within 6-8 weeks. Buys one-time rights. Pays $10, b&w; negotiates, color; pays on acceptance.
Illustrations: Uses 2-5 illustrations/issue. "Line drawings are most useful for magazine work. We also purchase art for promotional projects dealing with the Morgan horse—horses should look like *Morgans*." Send query letter with samples and tear sheets. Accepts "anything that clearly shows the artist's style and craftsmanship" as samples. Samples are returned by SASE. Reports within 6-8 weeks. Call or write for appointment to show portfolio. Buys all rights or negotiates rights purchased. Pays $50 minimum, color cover; $10 minimum, b&w inside; on acceptance.

***THE MOTHER EARTH NEWS**, Box 70, Hendersonville NC 28791. Art Director: Mark J. Wilson. Magazine emphasizing self-reliant living, do-it-yourself products, natural foods, organic gardening, etc. for suburban, rural, small town, upper-middle income, family folks. Bimonthly. Circ. 800,000. Accepts previously published material. Original artwork returned after publication. Sample copy free for SASE with $2.40 postage.
Cartoons: Buys 1 cartoon/issue from freelancers. Prefers single panel with or without gagline; b&w line drawings and b&w washes. Send query letter with samples of style and finished cartoons to be kept on file except for finished cartoons. Write or call for appointment to show portfolio. Material not kept on file is returned by SASE. Reports only if interested. Negotiates rights purchased. Pays $200, b&w.
Illustrations: Buys 1-2 illustrations/issue from freelancers. Works on assignment only. Send query letter with brochure showing art style or tear sheets, photostats and photocopies. Samples not filed are returned by SASE. Reports only if interested. To show a portfolio, mail appropriate materials or write to schedule an appointment; portfolio should include roughs, original/final art, color, tear sheets and photographs. Negotiates rights purchased. Pays $200-400, b&w, and $300-500, color, inside; on acceptance.

MOTOR MAGAZINE, 555 W. 57th St., New York NY 10019. Art Director: Harold A. Perry. Emphasizes automotive technology, repair and maintenance for auto mechanics and technicians. Monthly. Circ. 135,000. Accepts previously published material. Original artwork returned after publication if requested. Never send unsolicited original art.
Illustrations: Buys 5-15 illustrations/issue from freelancers. Works on assignment only. Prefers realistic/technical line renderings of automotive parts and systems. Send query letter with resume and photocopies to be kept on file. Will call for appointment to see further samples. Samples not filed are not returned. Reports only if interested. Buys one-time rights. Write to schedule an appointment to show a portfolio, which should include final reproduction/product, color and tear sheets. Payment negotiable for cover, basically $300-1,500; pays $50-500, b&w, inside; on acceptance.
Tips: "*Motor* is an educational, technical magazine and is basically immune to illustration trends because our drawings *must* be realistic and technical. As design trends change we try to incorporate these into our magazine (within reason). Though *Motor* is a trade publication, we approach it, design-wise, as if it were a consumer magazine. We make use of white space when possible and use creative abstract and impact photographs and illustration for our opening pages and covers. But we must always retain a 'technical look' to reflect our editorial subject matter. There are more and more *Folio* and *Forbes* clones. A few of the elite say what is good and the rest fall into line. Publication graphics is becoming like TV programming, more calculating and imitative and less creative."

MOTOR TREND, 8490 Sunset Blvd., Los Angeles CA 90069. (213)854-2222. Art Director: William Claxton. Emphasizes automobiles, world-wide automotive field. Monthly. Circ. 900,000. Sometimes

returns original artwork after publication; depends on agreement with artist. Sample copy available.
Cartoons: Buys 1-2 cartoons/issue from freelancers. Prefers any automotive theme, sophisticated style. Considers single or double panel with gagline; b&w line drawings, b&w washes. Send roughs to be kept on file. Material not filed is returned only if requested. Reports only if interested. Negotiates rights purchased. Payment varies; pays on acceptance.
Illustrations: Buys 3-4 illustrations/issue from freelancers. Themes are automotive (both technical and general illustrations); personality portraits. Send query letter with samples to be kept on file. Accepts "only high-quality samples and examples" to review. Samples not filed are returned only if requested. Reports only if interested. Call for appointment to show portfolio. Negotiates rights purchased. Payment varies; pays on acceptance.

***MOVING OUT**, Box 21249, Detroit MI 48221. Contact: Editors. Annual magazine emphasizing feminist literature and arts for college women, people interested in the women's movement." Circ. 500. Original artwork not returned after publication. Sample copy $3.50. Art guidelines free for SASE.
Cartoons: Uses few cartoons/issue. Prefers themes concerned with women's aesthetic. Send query letter with samples of style. Samples not filed are returned by SASE. Reports within 6 months if SASE enclosed. Buys first rights and reprint rights. Pays on publication.
Illustrations: Buys 5-10 illustrations/issue from freelancers; also front and sometimes back covers. Prefers themes dealing with women's aesthetic in a high-contrast b&w; no pornography. Send query letter with resume and photographs which will not be kept on file. Samples returned by SASE. Reports within 6 months if SASE enclosed. To show a portfolio, mail original/final art, final reproduction/product, photostats, photographs and b&w. Buys first or reprint rights. Pays on publication with a contributor copy.
Tips: "We are interested in work that develops the women's/feminist aesthetic."

MUSCLE MAG INTERNATIONAL, Unit 2, 52 Bramsteel Rd., Brampton, Ontario L6W 3M5 Canada. (416)457-3030. Editor-in-Chief: Robert Kennedy. For 16- to 50-year-old men and women interested in physical fitness and overall body improvement. Published 12 times/year. Circ. 210,000. Previously published work OK. Original artwork not returned after publication. Sample copy $3.
Cartoons: Buys 6 cartoons/issue from freelancers. Receives 30 submissions/week from freelancers. Interested in weight training and body building; single panel; "well-drawn work—professional." Send finished cartoons. SASE (nonresidents include IRC). Send $3 for return postage. Reports in 3 weeks. Buys all rights on a work-for-hire basis. Pays $15-25, color; $10-20, b&w; on acceptance. More for superior work.
Illustrations: Uses 2 illustrations/issue; buys 1/issue from freelancers. Receives 20 submissions/week from freelancers. Interested in "professionally drawn exercise art of body builders training with apparatus." Send query letter with tear sheets, photocopies, slides, photographs, and preferably finished art. SASE (nonresidents include IRC). Send $4 for return postage. Reports in 2 weeks. Call to schedule an appointment to show a portfolio, which should include original/final art. Buys all rights on a work-for-hire basis. Pays $300, color, cover; $100, color and $80, b&w, inside; on acceptance. "Pay can be triple for really professional or outstanding artwork."
Tips: "We only want to see top line work—we want only the best. Study our publication, then submit material to us."

MUSCULAR DEVELOPMENT, Box 1707, York PA 17404. (717)767-6481. Advertising Manager: Philip Redman. Emphasizes body building, powerlifting and strength sports. Bimonthly. Circ. 100,000. Accepts previously published material. Original artwork returned after publication. Sample copy for SASE with $1 postage; art guidelines available.
Illustrations: Buys variable number of illustrations/issue from freelancers. Prefers styles other than line art. Works on assignment only. Send query letter with resume and photocopies or any other good representation to be kept on file; originals and printed material in person. Samples returned by SASE. Reports only if interested. Buys one-time rights. Call for appointment to show portfolio. Pays on publication as determined by artist and negotiations.

MUSIC EDUCATORS JOURNAL, 1902 Association Dr., Reston VA 22091. (703)860-4000. Editor: Rebecca Grier Taylor. Production Manager: Pamela Halonen. Art Director: Charlene Gridley. For music educators in elementary and secondary schools and universities. Monthly (September-May). Circ. 56,000.
Illustrations: Uses illustrations from freelancers. Interested in collages, drawings, paintings, designs on music education subjects. "Artwork should be geared toward people, faces, etc., in music—not very many abstracts are used. Depictions of instruments must be true to form, correct playing positions." Works on assignment. Send brochure, flyer or tear sheets to be kept on file for future assignments. Reports in "up to 6 months." Buys one-time rights on a work-for-hire basis. Cover: Pays $100-250, full-

color art. Inside: Pays $25-100 per item: b&w line drawings, washes, gray opaques and color-separated work; on acceptance.
Tips: "Contact the art director (preferrably during April-June). We favor artists from the greater Washington, D.C., area who can come in and show us a portfolio. This market provides opportunities for new artists, but their work must be top-notch. Sometimes we don't have an appropriate subject at the time that an artist sends a sample or brochure. Eventually, though, we find a use for most types of art. Artwork must be clean and appropriate for offset reproduction. Instruments must be accurately drawn and postures and fingerings must be correct. Artwork should show teaching, not just performing. Call for appointment."

***MY WEEKLY "THE MAGAZINE FOR WOMEN EVERYWHERE"**, 80 Kingsway East, Dundee 0D4 8SL Scotland. Editor: Stewart D. Brown. Magazine emphasizing women's interests for family-oriented women of all ages. Weekly. Circ. 696,275. Accepts previously published material. Original artwork returned after publication. Art guidelines free for SASE with postage.
Illustrations: Buys 2 illustrations/issue from freelancers. Prefers romantic, family . . . "up-dated Rockwell" themes. Send query letter with brochure showing art style or resume, tear sheets and photographs. Samples not filed are returned only if requested. Reports within 2 months. Buys British rights. Pays on acceptance.

THE NATIONAL FUTURE FARMER, Box 15130, Alexandria VA 22309. (703)360-3600. Editor-in-Chief: Wilson W. Carnes. For members of the Future Farmers of America who are students of vocational agriculture in high school, ages 14-21. Emphasizes careers in agriculture/agribusiness and topics of general interest to youth. Bimonthly. Circ. 460,000. Reports in 3 weeks. Buys all rights. Pays on acceptance. Sample copy available.
Cartoons: Buys 15-20 cartoons/year on Future Farmers of America or assigned themes. Receives 30 cartoons/week from freelance artists. Pays $15, cartoons; more for assignments.
Illustrations: "We buy a few illustrations for specific stories; almost always on assignment." Send query letter with tear sheets or photocopies. Write to schedule an appointment to show a portfolio, which should include final reproduction/product, tear sheets and photostats. Negotiates payment.
Tips: "We suggest you send samples of work so we can keep your name on file as the need arises. We prefer b&w line art. Please include rates. We are a bimonthly publication and buy very little art-study back issues and offer suggestions for improvement through the use of art."

NATIONAL GEOGRAPHIC, 17th and M Sts. NW, Washington DC 20036. (202)857-7000. Contact: Art Director. Monthly. Circ. 10,500,000. Original artwork returned after publication, in some cases.
Illustrations: Number of illustrations bought/issue varies. Interested in "full-color, representational renderings of historical and scientific subjects. Nothing that can be photographed is illustrated by artwork. No decorative, design material. We want scientific geological cutaways, maps, historical paintings." Works on assignment only. Prefers to see portfolio and samples of style. Samples are returned by SASE. "The artist should be familiar with the type of painting we use." Provide brochure, flyer or tear sheet to be kept on file for future assignments. Reports in 2 weeks. Minimum payment: Inside: $1,000, color; $200, b&w; on acceptance.

NATIONAL MOTORIST, Suite 300, One Market Plaza, San Francisco CA 94105. (415)777-4000. Graphic Artist: Lana Peters. Editor: Jane Offers. Emphasizes travel on the West Coast for all members of the National Automobile Club in California. Bimonthly. Circ. 205,000. Original artwork returned after publication. Sample copy 50¢.
Cartoons: Uses 1 cartoon/issue; buys 1/issue from freelancer. Prefers auto- or travel-related themes. Prefers b&w line drawings with gaglines. Send query letter with roughs to be kept on file. Material not kept on file is returned. Reports within days. Buys first rights. Pays "on request", b&w and color; on acceptance.
Illustrations: Uses very few illustrations/issue. Prefers auto- or travel-related themes. Send query letter with samples to be kept on file. Prefers original work as samples. Samples not kept on file are returned. Buys first rights. Pays "all on request"; on acceptance.

THE NATIONAL NOTARY, 23012 Ventura Blvd., Box 4625, Woodland Hills CA 91365-4625. (818)347-2035. Contact: Production Editor. Emphasizes "notaries public and notarization—goal is to impart knowledge, understanding, and unity among notaries nationwide and internationally." Readers are notaries of varying primary occupations (legal, government, real estate and financial), as well as state and federal officials and foreign notaries." Bimonthly. Circ. 45,000. Original artwork not returned after publication. Sample copy $5.
Cartoons: May use. Cartoons "must have a notarial angle"; single or multiple panel with gagline, b&w line drawings. Send samples of style. Samples not returned. Reports in 4-6 weeks. Call to schedule

an appointment to show a portfolio. Buys all rights. Negotiates pay; on publication.
Illustrations: Uses about 5 illustrations/issue; buys all from local freelancers. Works on assignment only. Themes vary, depending on subjects of articles. Send business card, samples and tear sheets to be kept on file. Samples not returned. Reports in 4-6 weeks. Call for appointment. Buys all rights. Negotiates pay; on publication.
Tips: "We are very interested in experimenting with various styles of art in illustrating the magazine. We generally work with Southern California artists, as we prefer face-to-face dealings."

NATIONAL REVIEW, 150 E. 35th St., New York NY 10016. Contact: Anna Lieber. Emphasizes world events from a conservative viewpoint. Bimonthly. Original artwork returned after publication.
Cartoons: Buys 15 cartoons/issue from freelancers. Interested in "political, social commentary." Prefers to receive finished cartoons. SASE. Reports in 2 weeks. Buys first North American serial rights. Pays $25 b&w; on publication.
Illustrations: Uses 15 illustrations/issue. Especially needs b&w ink illustration, portraits of political figures and conceptual editorial art (b&w line plus halftone work). "I look for a strong graphic style; well-developed ideas and well-executed drawings." Works on assignment only. Send query letter with brochure showing art style or tear sheets and photocopies. No samples returned. Reports back on future assignment possibilities. Call to schedule an appointment to show a portfolio, which should include original/final art, final reproduction/product, tear sheets and b&w. SASE. Also buys small decorative and humorous spot illustrations in advance by mail submission. Buys first North American serial rights. Pays $15, small spots, $35, larger spot, $40; assigned illustration; $40 b&w, inside; $250 color, cover; on publication.
Tips: "Tear sheets and mailers are helpful in remembering an artist's work. Artists ought to make sure their work is professional in quality of idea and execution. Printed samples alongside originals help. Changes in art and design in our field include fine art influence and use of more half-tone illustration."

NATIONAL RURAL LETTER CARRIER, Suite 100, 1448 Duke St., Alexandria VA 22314. (703)684-5545. Managing Editor: RuthAnn Saenger. Emphasizes news and analysis of federal law and current events. For rural letter carriers and family-oriented, middle-Americans; many are part-time teachers and businessmen. Weekly. Circ. 68,000. Mail art. SASE. Reports in 4 weeks. Original artwork returned after publication. Previously published, photocopied and simultaneous submissions OK. Buys first rights. Sample copy 24¢. Receives 1 cartoon and 2 illustrations/month from freelance artists.
Illustrations: Buys 12 covers/year on rural scenes, views of rural mailboxes and rural people. Buys 1 illustration/issue from freelancers. Interested in pen & ink or pencil on rural, seasonal and postal matter. Especially needs rural mailboxes and sketches of scenes on rural delivery. Works on assignment only. Send query letter with brochure showing art style or resume, tear sheets, photocopies, slides and photographs. Samples returned by SASE. Reports in 1 week, if accepted; 1 month if not accepted. Write to schedule an appointment to show a portfolio, which should include original/final art, final reproduction/product, color, tear sheets, photostats, photographs and b&w. Buys all rights on a work-for-hire basis. Pays $50-75; on publication.
Tips: "Please send in samples when you inquire about submitting material." Have a definite need for "realistic painting and sketches."

NATIONAL SAFETY AND HEALTH NEWS, (formerly *National Safety News*), National Safety Council, 444 N. Michigan Ave., Chicago IL 60611. (312)527-4800. Editor: Roy Fisher. For those responsible for developing and administering occupational safety and health programs. Monthly. Circ. 56,000. Original artwork returned after publication. Free sample copy and artist's guidelines. Also uses artists for 4-color cover design, publication redesign and layout mock-ups. Contact: Gordon Bieberle, Director of Publications Department.
Cartoons: Contact: Susan-Marie Kelly. Uses 4-6 cartoons/issue, all from freelancers. Interested in occupational safety and health; single, double or multipanel with gagline. Prefers to see roughs. SASE. Reports in 4 weeks. Buys first North American serial rights or all rights on a work-for-hire basis. Pays $10 minimum, b&w line drawings.

***NATIONAL SOCIETY OF PUBLIC ACCOUNTANTS**, 1010 North Fairfax St., Alexandria VA 22314. Contact: Managing Editor. Send samples.
Illustrations: Buys assigned themes on accounting, business, finances, taxes and economics. Pays $20 minimum, line drawings. "Only send items relating to tax issues or small business."

NATIONAL WILDLIFE, INTERNATIONAL WILDLIFE, 8925 Leesburg Pike, Vienna VA 22180. Art Director: Dan Smith. Emphasize wildlife. For those concerned with the future of wildlife and the environment. Bimonthlies. Circ. 800,000.
Illustrations: Assigns art on 1-2 stories/issue. Works on assignment only. Prefers to see samples of

style. SASE. Provide flyer, slides or tear sheets to be kept on file. Reports in 3 weeks. Usually buys first, reprint and promotion rights. Pays competitive rates; on acceptance.

NATURAL HISTORY, American Museum of Natural History, Central Park W. and 79th St., New York NY 10024. (212)873-1300. Editor-in-Chief: Alan Ternes. Art Director: Tom Page. Emphasizes social and natural sciences. For well-educated professionals interested in the natural sciences. Monthly. Circ. 500,000. Previously published work OK.
Illustrations: Buys 10-15 illustrations/year; 20-30 maps or diagrams/year. Interested in current events and environment. Works on assignment only. Query with samples. Samples returned by SASE. Provide "any pertinent information" to be kept on file for future assignments. Reports in 1 week. Buys one-time rights. Inside: Pays $100, b&w line drawings and washes; on publication.
Tips: "Be familiar with the publication and the trend toward human ecology."

NAVAL INSTITUTE PROCEEDINGS, U.S. Naval Institute, Annapolis MD 21402. (301)268-6110. Editor-in-Chief: Fred H. Rainbow. Emphasizes the Navy, Marine Corps, Coast Guard and related maritime and military topics. Monthly. Circ. 100,000. Returns original artwork after publication. Free sample copy and art guidelines.
Illustrations: Buys about 5 illustrations/issue from freelancers. Themes vary but are mainly military/political. Works on assignment only. Send query letter with sketches to be kept on file. Samples not filed are returned only if requested. Reports within a few weeks. Write or call for appointment to show portfolio. Negotiates rights purchased and payment. Pays on acceptance.

NEGATIVE CAPABILITY, 6116 Timberly Rd. N, Mobile AL 36609. Editor: Sue Walker. Journal. Emphasizes fiction, poetry, art, music and essays. Audience is interested in art/literature. Quarterly. Circ. 800. Original artwork returned after publication. Sample copy $3.50.
Cartoons: Buys 3 cartoons/issue from freelancers. Theme or style open. Prefers single or double panel with gagline; b&w line drawings, b&w washes. Send finished cartoons to be kept on file. Material not filed is returned by SASE. Reports within 6 weeks. To show a portfolio, mail original/final art, final reproduction/product, photographs and b&w. Acquires one-time rights. Pays in 2 contributor's copies.
Illustrations: Buys 8-10 illustrations/issue from freelancers. Themes or styles open. Send query letter with brochure showing art style and samples to be kept on file. Samples not filed are returned by SASE. Reports within 6 weeks. To show a portfolio, mail original/final art, final reproduction/product, photographs and b&w. Acquires one-time rights. Pays in 2 contributor's copies.

NEW AGE JOURNAL, 342 Western Ave., Brighton MA 02135. (617)787-2005. Art Director: Greg Paul. Emphasizes alternative lifestyles, holistic health, ecology, personal growth, human potential, planetary survival for highly educated young professionals with an interest in their health, personal potential and quality of life. Monthly. Circ. 150,000. Accepts previously published material and simultaneous submissions. Original artwork returned after publication. Sample copy $2.50.
Illustrations: Uses 8 illustrations/issue. Illustrations accompany specific manuscripts. Send query letter with samples or tear sheets to be kept on file. Call for appointment to show portfolio. Prefers photostats, photocopies or slides as samples. Samples returned by SASE if not kept on file. Buys one-time rights.

***NEW ENGLAND BUILDER, THE JOURNAL OF LIGHT CONSTRUCTION**, Box 278, Montpelier VT 05602. Editor: Michael Reitz. Tabloid emphasizing residential, light commercial construction and renovation/restoration for builders, contractors, architects and engineers. Monthly. Circ. 12,000. Accepts previously published material. Original artwork returned after publication. Sample copy $2.
Cartoons: Buys 1-2 cartoons/issue from freelancers. Prefers single panel without gagline; b&w line drawings. Send query letter with samples of style or finished cartoons to be kept on file. Material not filed is returned. Reports within 1 month. Negotiates rights purchased and payment.
Illustrations: Buys 4-5 illustrations/issue from freelancers. Works on assignment only. Send query letter with photocopies. Samples not filed are returned. Reports within 1 month. To show a portfolio, mail appropriate materials. Negotiates rights purchased and payment. Pays on publication.

NEW ENGLAND SAMPLER, Box 306, Belfast ME 04915-0306. (207)525-3575. Editor/Publisher: Virginia M. Rimm. Emphasizes New England (rural). Audience is over-30, high school or college level educated, interested in rural New England, traditional family values; large percentage of professionals. "We're an upbeat family-style publication." Published 9 times/year. Circ. 2,000. Accepts previously published material. Original artwork returned after publication. Sample copy $1; art guidelines free for SASE.
Illustrations: Buys 2-3 illustrations/issue from freelancers. Send query letter with resume and samples to be kept on file. Prefers tear sheets or photocopies as samples. Samples returned by SASE. Reports within 6-8 weeks. Acquires one-time rights. Pays in copies only.

NEW MEXICO MAGAZINE, Bataan Memorial Bldg., Santa Fe NM 87503. (505)827-6180. Art Director: Mary Sweitzer. Emphasizes the state of New Mexico for residents, and visiting vacationers and businesspersons. Monthly. Circ. 100,000. Accepts previously published material and simultaneous submissions. Original artwork returned after publication. No printed artists' guidelines, but may call for information. Also interested in calligraphers.
Cartoons: Uses 12-20 cartoons/year, 1-2/issue. Prefers single panel; b&w line drawings, b&w washes. Send resume, tear sheets, photostats, photocopies and slides. Call to schedule an appointment to show a portfolio, which should include original/final art, final reproduction/product, color, tear sheets, photographs and b&w. Material not kept on file is returned only if requested. Reports only if interested. Buys one-time rights. Pays $25-50, b&w; $50-100, color; two weeks after acceptance, on publication for stock material.
Illustrations: Uses 2 illustrations/issue. Works on assignment only. Send query letter with samples to be kept on file. Samples not kept on file are returned only if requested. Reports only if interested. Buys one-time rights. Pays $40 for small illustrations to $300 for 4-color work, usually all inside; on acceptance.
Tips: Contact verbally or with written material first. Send appropriate materials and samples.

NEW OREGON REVIEW, 537 NE Lincoln St., Hillsboro OR 97123. Editor: Steven Dimeo, Ph.D. For college students, professors and those interested in the humanities. Published semiannually. Circ. 300. Sample copy $3 (mention *Artist's Market*). Receives 1 illustration/month from freelance artists. Would like to receive more freelance submissions.
Illustrations: Buys 2-5 illustrations/year. Primarily purchases photos. "We like drawings that deal uncommonly with the common, surrealistic landscapes of the mind featuring nudes, portraits or nature." Send query letter with samples and 3-5 sentence biographical statement. SASE. Reports in 2-3 months. Buys all rights. Pays $10, b&w line drawings and washes; $25, commissioned work; on publication. We offer $100 prize for best illustration published.
Tips: "A neat presentation of an artist's samplings by means of a flyer or portfolio is almost mandatory."

NEW ORLEANS, ARC Publishing Co., 6666 Morrison Rd., New Orleans LA 70126. (504)246-2700. Art Director: David Maher. Editor: Sandy Shilstone. Emphasizes entertainment, travel, sports, news, business and politics in New Orleans. For readers with high income and education. Monthly. Circ. 44,000. Previously published and photocopied submissions OK. Sample copy $2.50.
Illustrations: Query with samples. SASE. Buys assigned illustrations and cartoons on current events, education and politics. Especially needs assigned feature illustrations "specifically relating to and illustrating a concept in one of our main feature stories." Pays $40-100, spot drawings; $75-200, feature illustrations; on publication.
Tips: "Do not send unassigned, unsolicited work on speculation. It creates a burden for me to sift through work and return it. However, do send nonreturnable photocopies or stats of work so I can keep them on file when work becomes available."

***NEW ORLEANS BUSINESS**, Box 354, Gretna LA 70054. (504)362-4310. Editor: Lan Sluder. Newspaper emphasizing regional business for high-income executives. Weekly. Circ. 20,000. Accepts previously published material. Sample copy $1.
Cartoons: Buys 10 cartoons/year from freelancers. Send query letter with samples of style to be kept on file. Material not kept on file is returned by SASE. Reports only if interested. Buys one-time rights. Pays $10-40, b&w.
Illustrations: Buys 1 illustration/issue from freelancers. Works on assignment only. Send query letter with resume and samples. Samples not filed are returned by SASE. Reports only if interested. To show a portfolio, mail appropriate materials. Buys one-time rights. Pays $75, b&w, and $150, color, cover; $50, b&w, and $75, color, inside; on acceptance.

NEW ORLEANS REVIEW, Box 195, Loyola University, New Orleans LA 70118. (504)865-2294. Editor: John Mosier. Journal of literature and culture. Published 4 times/year. Sample copy $7.
Illustrations: Uses 5-10 illustrations/issue. Cover: uses color, all mediums. SASE. Reports in 2 months. Inside: uses b&w line drawings, photos/slides of all mediums.

NEW REALITIES, Suite 408, 680 Beach St., San Francisco CA 94109. Editor/Publisher: James Bolen. Managing Editor: Shirley Christine. Concerns "holistic health and personal growth." Bimonthly. Pays on publication.
Cartoons: Buys 2 cartoons/issue on assigned themes. Send roughs. Pays $35 minimum, b&w.
Illustrations: Buys 4 illustrations/issue on assigned themes. Arrange interview to show portfolio. Minimum payment: Cover, $150-300, 4-color. Inside: $75-150, b&w and color.

***the new renaissance**, 9 Heath Rd., Arlington MA 02174. Contact: Louise T. Reynolds. Magazine emphasizing literature arts and opinion for "the general, literate public which has an aesthetic sensibility and which has an interest in provocative ideas or opinion pieces." Bi-annual (Spring & Fall). Circ. 1,600. Returns original artwork after publication if SASE is enclosed. Sample copy $4.75.
Illustrations: Buys 5-8 illustrations/issue from freelancers. Works on assignment only. Send resume, samples and SASE. Samples not filed are returned by SASE. Reports within 1 month. To show a portfolio, mail appropriate materials; portfolio should include roughs, photographs and b&w. Buys one-time rights. Pays $25, b&w, cover; on publication.

THE NEW REPUBLIC, 1220 19th St. NW, Washington DC 20036. (202)331-7494. Copy Editor: Jamie Baylis. Emphasizes politics and culture for a "well-educated, well-off audience with a median age of 40." Weekly. Circ. 100,000. Accepts previously published material and simultaneous submissions. Original artwork returned after publication.
Cartoons: Buys 1 cartoon month from freelancers. Send query letter with samples of style, finished cartoons and color work, if possible, to be kept on file. Material not kept on file returned only if requested and only if accompanied by SASE. Write or call for appointment to show portfolio. Reports only if samples are accompanied by cover letter or written inquiry. Negotiates rights purchased. Pays $50 b&w; on publication.
Illustrations: Uses 1 illustration/issue. Prefers political, literary themes. Works on assignment only. Send query letter with brochure, resume, business card, samples and tear sheets to be kept on file. Call or write for appointment to show portfolio. Negotiates rights purchased and payment. Pays on publication.

NEW WOMAN MAGAZINE, 215 Lexington Ave., New York NY 10016. (212)685-4790. Magazine emphasizing emotional self-help for women ages 25-34, 66% married. Most have attended college but not graduated. Medium personal income is $14,000. Published monthly. Circ. 1 million. Accepts previously published material. Returns original artwork to the artist.
Cartoons: Uses approximately 20 freelance cartoons/issue. Prefers single panel, with or without gagline; b&w line drawings. "We have changed quite a bit. We are still pro-women, but not as hard-hitting or as sexist in putting men down. We use cartoons in our sections on food (no gagline), word power, book reviews and letters to the editor. Look at recent issues of the magazine." Contact Rosemarie Lennon, cartoon editor, for more information. Send finished cartoon and SASE. Reports back to the cartoonist. Purchases all serial rights. Pays $225 on acceptance.
Illustrations: Uses 3-4 freelance illustrations/issue. Works on assignment only. Send query letter with tear sheets and photocopies to be kept on file. Samples not kept on file are not returned. Reports only if interested. Payment varies. Pays on acceptance.

NEW YORK MAGAZINE, 755 Second Ave., New York NY 10017. (212)880-0700. Design Director: Robert Best. Art Director: Patricia Bradbury. Emphasizes New York City life; also covers all boroughs for New Yorkers, upper middle income; business people interested in what's happening in the city. Weekly. Original artwork returned after publication.
Illustrations: Works on assignment only. Send query letter with tear sheets to be kept on file. Prefers photostats as samples. Samples returned if requested. Call or write for appointment to show portfolio (drop-offs). Buys first rights. Pays $1,000, b&w and color, cover; $600 for 4-color, $400 b&w full page, inside; $225 for 4-color, $150 b&w spot, inside. Pays on publication.

***NEW YORK/PHILADELPHIA ACTION**, Suite 144, 1601 Easton Rd., Willow Grove PA 19090. Managing Editor: George Finster. Tabloid emphasizing sex and adult entertainment for adult males. Monthly. Circ. 10,000. Sample copy free for SASE with $1.50 postage. Cartoon guidelines free for SASE with 22¢ postage.
Cartoons: Buys 12 cartoons/issue from freelancers. Prefers sex as themes. Prefers single panel with gagline; b&w line drawings. Send query letter with brochure showing art style or resume, tear sheets, photostats, photocopies and finished cartoons. Material not kept on file is returned by SASE. Reports within 12-14 weeks. To show a portfolio, mail original/final art and b&w. Buys first rights or reprint rights. Pays $9.50, b&w; on publication or 30 days after acceptance, whichever comes first.
Tips: "No interest in non-sexual cartoons."

THE NEW YORKER, 25 W. 43rd St., New York NY 10036. Contact: Art Editor. Emphasizes news analysis and lifestyle features.
Needs: Buys cartoons, spots and cover designs. Receives 3,000 cartoons/week. Mail art or deliver sketches on Wednesdays. SASE. "Spots are now purchased every 4 months." Strict standards regarding style, technique, plausibility of drawing. Especially looks for originality. Pays $500 minimum, cartoons; top rates for spots and cover designs.
Tips: "Familiarize yourself with your markets."

THE NEWS CIRCLE, Box 3684, Glendale CA 91201. (818)240-1918. Contact: Laila Haiek. For Arab-Americans. Monthly magazine. Circ. 5,000.
Cartoons: Buys 5-8 cartoons/issue. Needs b&w. Send roughs. Reports in 3 weeks. Negotiates pay; pays on publication.
Illustrations: Buys b&w Arabic and arabesque designs. Send query letter with samples. Reports in 3 weeks. Negotiates pay; pays on publication.

NEXUS, 1110 N. Fillmore, Amarillo TX 79107. (806)376-6229. Editor: Vance Buck. Emphasizes games for game players. Quarterly. Circ. 10,000. Usually does not accept previously published material. Returns original artwork after publication with SASE. Sample copy for $5; art guidelines for SASE.
Illustrations: Buys 10-30/issue. Prefers themes related to games produced by Task Force Games Company—Star Fleet Battles, StarFire, History of WWII and Battlewagon, etc. Send query letter with photostats, photocopies, slides and photographs. Reports within 3 weeks. To show a portfolio, mail color, tear sheets, photostats, photographs and b&w. Buys one-time rights. Pays $200-300, color, cover; $3/column inch, b&w, inside; on publication.
Tips: "Artists should be familiar enough with our games to be able to do artwork which is consistent with game concepts."

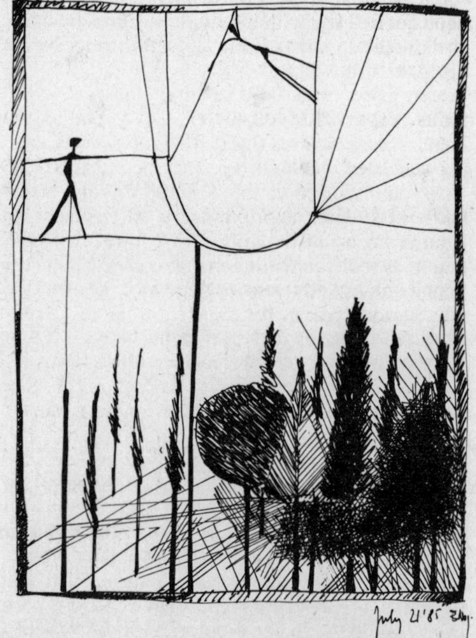

This pen & ink piece is one of many that Ewa Nogiec-Smith has published in Nit & Wit, _a literary magazine based in Chicago. The piece conveys a trascendent, suspended state of "dreaming and walking in the sky," according to Nogiec-Smith, who is from Geneva, Illinois. She discovered_ Nit & Wit _through the_ Artist's Market. _The literary magazine purchased one-time rights to the artwork._

***NIT&WIT**, Box 627, Geneva IL 60134. (312)232-9496. Publisher: Harrison McCormick. Magazine emphasizing the cultural arts for an affluent, art-oriented audience, 50% male, 50% married, median age 35. Bimonthly. Circ. 10,000 plus original artwork returned after publication. Samples copy, $2.50; art guidelines available.
Cartoons: Prefers themes revolving around the cultural arts. Prefers b&w line drawings. Send query letter with samples of style, which will be kept on file. Write for an appointment to show a portfolio. Samples not filed are returned by SASE. Reports back within 2 weeks. Buys first rights. Payment is copies.
Illustrations: Buys 6-10/issues from freelance artists. Prefers cultural arts themes. Send query letter with brochure, resume, tear shets, photostats and photocopies. Samples not filed are returned by SASE. Reports back within 2 weeks. To show a portfolio, mail roughs and photostats. Buys first rights. Pays in copies.

NJEA REVIEW, 180 W. State St., Box 1211, Trenton NJ 08607. Editor-in-Chief: Martha O. DeBlieu. Nonprofit, for New Jersey public school employees. Monthly. Circ. 120,000. Previously published work OK. Original artwork not returned after publication. Free sample copy.
Cartoons: Buys 3-4/year from freelancers. Receives 20 submissions/week from freelancers. Interested

in b&w cartoons with an "education theme—do not make fun of school employees or children"; single panel. Prefers to see finished cartoons. Buys all rights on a work-for-hire basis. Pays on acceptance. Limited budget.

Illustrations: Buys 1-2 illustrations/issue from freelancers. Receives 1-2 submissions/week from freelancers. Especially needs education-related spot art. Send query letter with brochure showing art style or resume, tear sheets, photostats, photocopies and photographs. Reports as soon as possible. To show a portfolio, mail appropriate materials, which should include original/final art, tear sheets, photographs and b&w. Buys all rights on a work-for-hire basis. Pays $25 b&w, cover; $10 b&w, inside; on acceptance.

Tips: "Like bigger and bolder art rather than intricate work. Too much artwork we see is too finely detailed or on the other extreme, too simplistic, amateur looking. Look at our magazine and don't send us material not related to our type of magazine."

NORTH AMERICAN HUNTER, Box 35557, Minneapolis MN 55435. (612)941-7654. Editorial Assistant: Carolyn Ehler. Publishes hunting material only for avid hunters of both small and big game in North America. Bimonthly. Circ. 100,000. Accepts previously published material. Original artwork returned after publication unless all rights are purchased. Sample copy $1; art guidelines available.

Cartoons: Buys 3-6 cartoons/issue from freelancers. Considers humorous hunting situations. Prefers single panel with gagline; b&w line drawings or washes. Send query letter with tear sheets, photostats, photocopies, slides, photographs or finished cartoons. Returns unpurchased material immediately. Reports within 5 days. Buys all rights. Pays $15, b&w; on acceptance.

Illustrations: Buys 1-5 illustrations/issue from freelancers; usually includes 1 humorous illustration. Prefers game animal and hunter themes. Samples not filed are returned. Reports within 5 days. Buys all rights. Pays $250, color, cover; $75-100, b&w or color, inside; on acceptance.

Tips: "Send only art that deals with hunting, hunters, wildlife or hunting situations. North American big and small game only."

NORTH AMERICAN MENTOR, Drawer 69, Fennimore WI 53809. (608)822-6237. Editor-in-Chief: John Westburg. Managing Editor: Mildred Westburg. Send art submissions to Martial R. Westburg, art editor, North American Mentor, Box 558, Old Chelsea Station, New York NY 10011. For professional people, half of whom are age 60 or over. Quarterly. Circ. 400. Previously published, photocopied and simultaneous submissions OK. Original artwork not returned after publication. Sample copy $2.

Illustrations: Buys 1 (cover) illustration/issue. Receives less than 10 submissions/year from freelancers. Interested in b&w line drawings only. Send resume, brochure, flyer and tear sheets to be kept on file. Samples are not returned. Reports in "6 months or more." Buys all rights. Pays $25 minimum, b&w line drawings; on publication.

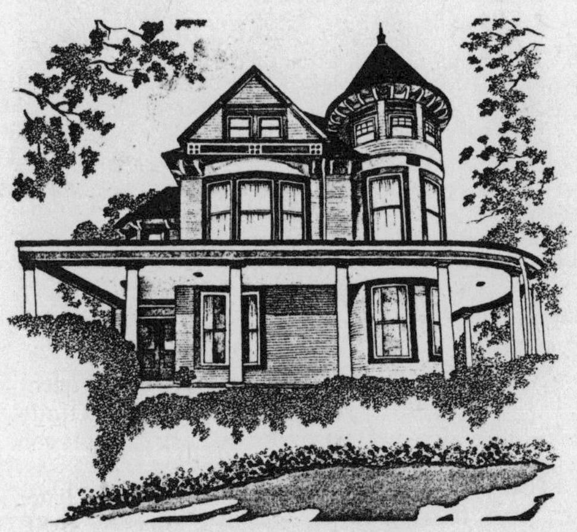

Freelance artist Kathleen O'Malley of Chicago, Illinois, received the assignment from North Shore Magazine *to illustrate the Victorian charm of a property advertised in the magazine. Kathleen received $535 for the illustration completed in water colors with pen & ink. As a result of the piece being published, "I received recognition in the northern suburbs as an architectural watercolorist."*

NORTH SHORE MAGAZINE, 874 Green Bay Rd., Winnetka IL 60093. (312)441-7892. Contact: Art Director. City/regional magazine; upscale readership. Monthly. Circ. 37,000 subscribers. Occasionally accepts previously published material. Returns original artwork after publication. Sample copy free for SASE with $1 postage.

Cartoons: Buys 1-5 cartoons/issue from freelancers. Prefers single panel with gagline; b&w line draw-

ings. Send query letter with samples of style or finished cartoons to be kept on file. Material not filed is returned by SASE. Reports within 1 week. Buys first rights. Payment varies; pays on publication.
Illustrations: Buys 1-3 illustrations/issue from freelancers. Works on assignment only. Send query letter with resume, tear sheets and slides. Samples not filed are returned by SASE. Reports within 1 week. Call to schedule an appointment to show a portfolio, which should include original/final art, final reproduction/product, color and b&w. Buys first rights. Pays on acceptance.

NORTHEAST OUTDOORS, Box 2180, Waterbury CT 06722-2180. (203)755-0158. Editorial Director: John Florian. For camping families in the Northeastern states. Monthly. Circ. 14,000. Original artwork returned after publication, if requested. Previously published material and simultaneous submissions OK if noted in cover letter. Editorial guidelines for SASE with 1 first class stamp; sample copy for 9x12 SASE with 6 first class stamps.
Cartoons: Buys 1 cartoon/issue on camping and recreational vehicle situations. Send query letter with samples. Reports in 2 weeks. Pays $10, b&w; on acceptance.
Illustrations: Buys 2-3 illustrations/year with manuscripts. To show a portfolio, mail appropriate materials. Pays $40 b&w, cover; $10-30 b&w, inside; on publication.
Tips: "Make it neat. Felt-tip pen sketches won't make it in this market any more. Query or send samples for illustration ideas. We occasionally buy or assign to accompany stories. Artists who have accompanying manuscripts have an extra edge, as we rarely buy illustrations alone."

THE NORTHERN LIGHT, Box 519, Lexington MA 02173. (617)862-4410. Editor: Richard H. Curtis. Emphasizes the fraternal order for Scottish Rite Masons and their families. Published 5 times/year. Circ. 475,000. Original artwork returned after publication.
Cartoons: Number of cartoons used/issue "depends on space and availability." Prefers fraternal themes. Prefers single, double or multipanel with or without gagline; b&w line drawings or b&w washes. Send query letter with samples of style to be kept on file. Write or call for appointment to show portfolio. Material not kept on file is returned only if requested. Reports only if interested. Negotiates rights purchased. Pays on acceptance.
Illustrations: Number of illustrations used/issue "depends on space and availability." Prefers varied styles and themes. Send query letter with samples to be kept on file. Call or write for appointment to show portfolio. Samples not kept on file are returned only if requested. Reports only if interested. Negotiates rights purchased. Pays on acceptance.

THE NORTHERN LOGGER & TIMBER PROCESSOR, Northeastern Loggers Association Inc., Box 69, Old Forge NY 13420. (315)369-3078. Editor: Eric A. Johnson. Emphasizes methods, machinery and manufacturing as related to forestry. "For loggers, timberland managers and processors of primary forest products." Monthly. Circ. 13,000. Previously published material OK. Free sample copy; guidelines sent upon request.
Cartoons: Uses 1 cartoon/issue, all from freelancers. Receives 1 submission/week from freelancers. Interested in "any cartoons involving forest industry situations." Send finished cartoons with SASE. Reports in 1 week. Pays $10 minimum, b&w line drawings; on acceptance.
Tips: "Keep it simple and pertinent to the subjects we cover. Also, keep in mind that on-the-job safety is an issue that we like to promote."

NORTHWEST REVIEW, 369 PLC, University of Oregon, Eugene OR 97403. (503)686-3957. Editor: John Witte. Art Editor: Deb Casey. Emphasizes literature. "We publish material of general interest to those who follow American/world poetry and fiction." Original artwork returned after publication. Published 3 times/year. Sample copy $3.
Illustrations: Uses b&w line drawings, graphics and cover designs. Receives 20-30 portfolios/year from freelance artists. Arrange interview or mail slides. SASE. Reports as soon as possible. Acquires one-time rights. Pays in contributor's copies. Especially needs high-quality graphic artwork. "We run a regular art feature of the work of one artist, printed in b&w, 133-line screen on quality coated paper. A statement by the artist often accompanies the feature."

***NOSTALGIA WORLD FOR COLLECTORS AND FANS**, Box 231, North Haven CT 06473. Editor: Bonnie Roth. Collector's magazine for records, comics, toys, movie memorabilia, baseball cards, sheet music, etc. Bimonthly. Circ. 4,000. Accepts previously published material and simultaneous submissions. Original artwork returned after publication. Sample copy $2; art guidelines free for SASE.
Cartoons: Uses 24-page comic strips presently bought through syndication. Prefers b&w line drawings. Send query letter with roughs to be kept on file. Material not kept on file is returned by SASE. Reports within 2-4 weeks. Buys all rights. Pays $7-15, b&w; on acceptance.
Illustrations: Uses 2-5 illustrations/issue; number bought from freelancers varies. Prefers topics relating to collectors. Send query letter with photocopies to be kept on file. Reports within 2-4 weeks. Buys

all rights. Pays $35, b&w, cover; $15, b&w, inside; on publication.
Tips: "We are looking for outrageous concepts in the form of comic strip art as we are planning to publish more comic books in the future. We presently purchase comic strip art through syndication. Be bold, be daring, but have an original style."

NOTRE DAME, University of Notre Dame, 415 Main Bldg., Box M, Notre Dame IN 46556. Art Director: Don Nelson. For university alumni. Quarterly. Circ. 98,000. Uses 6 illustrations/issue, all from freelancers. Professional artists only. "Please don't request sample copies." Accepts previously published material. Original artwork returned after publication.
Illustrations: Seeks " 'graphic' solutions to communication problems." Buys 6 illustrations/issue from freelancers. Send query letter with brochure showing art style or tear sheets, photostats and photocopies. Works on assignment only. Samples returned by SASE. Buys one-time rights. Pays $800-1,200, color, cover; pays $175-375, b&w inside; on acceptance.

NUCLEAR TIMES MAGAZINE, Room 512, 298 5th Ave., New York NY 10001. (212)563-5940. Managing Editor: Renata Rizzo. Provides straight news coverage of the anti-nuclear weapons movement. Bimonthly. Circ. 70,000. Accepts previously published material. Returns original artwork after publication. Sample copy $1; art guidelines available.
Cartoons: Buys up to 10 cartoons/issue from freelancers. Accepts single, double or multiple panel with or without gagline; b&w line drawings, b&w washes. Send query letter with photocopies of samples of style, roughs and finished cartoons to be kept on file. Material not kept on file returned by SASE only if requested. Reports within 2 weeks. Write or call for appointment to show portfolio. Buys one-time rights. Pays $25 for b&w; on publication.
Illustrations: Buys 10 + illustrations/issue from freelancers. Only anti-nuclear issues as themes. Primarily works on assignment. Send query letter with brochure, resume, business card and samples to be kept on file. Write or call for appointment to show portfolio. Prefers to review photocopies and tear sheets in mail submissions; originals when shown portfolio at office. Samples not filed are returned only if requested. Reports within 2 weeks. Buys one-time rights. Pays $25-40 for b&w cover; $25 for b&w inside; on publication.

NUGGET, Dugent Publishing Co., 2355 Salzedo St., Coral Gables FL 33134. Editor: John Fox. Illustration Assignments: Nye Willden. For men and women with fetish interests.
Cartoons: Buys 10 cartoons/issue, all from freelancers. Receives 100 submissions/week from freelancers. Interested in "funny fetish themes." B&w only for spots, b&w and color for page. Prefers to see finished cartoons. SASE. Reports in 2 weeks. Buys first North American serial rights. Pays $35, spot drawings; $50, page.
Illustrations: Buys 4 illustrations/issue from freelancers. Interested in "erotica, cartoon style, etc." Works on assignment only. Prefers to see samples of style. No samples returned. Reports back on future assignment possibilities. Send brochure or flyer to be kept on file for future assignments. Buys first North American serial rights. Pays $100-125, b&w.
Tips: Especially interested in "the artist's anatomy skills, professionalism in rendering (whether he's published or not) and drawings which relate to our needs." Current trends include "a return to the 'classical' realistic form of illustration which is fine with us because we prefer realistic and well-rendered illustrations."

OCEANS, 2001 W. Main St., Stanford CT 06902. Editor: Michael W. Robbins. "For those interested in the beauty, science, adventure and conservation of the oceans and the life forms which live therein." Bimonthly. Circ. 65,000. Original artwork returned after publication. Sample copy $2; free contributor guidelines.
Cartoons: Interested in sea-oriented themes. Prefers roughs. SASE. Buys first North American serial rights.
Illustrations: Interested in the environment, ocean dwellers and subjects pertaining to oceans. Samples returned by SASE. Reports in 1 week. Buys first North American serial rights.

OFF DUTY, Suite C-2, 3303 Harbor Blvd., Costa Mesa CA 92626. Art Director: John Wong. Three editions: Europe, Pacific and America. Emphasizes general interest topics, e.g. leisure, sports, travel, food, photography, music, finance for military Americans stationed around the world. Combined circ: 708,000. Accepts previously published material and simultaneous submissions if not submitted to other military magazines. Assignment artwork returned after publication. Sample copy $1.
Cartoons: Uses occasional cartoons in two categories. First must relate to military personnel, families and military life. Off-duty situations preferred. Send to Bruce Thorstad, U.S. Editor. Second category relates to hobbies of audio, video, computers or photography. "A military angle in this category is ideal, but not necessary." Send to Mike Michels. Technical Editor. "Keep in mind that all readers are active

duty military, not retirees or vets." Pays $40 minimum b&w; more by negotiation.

Illustrations: *Off Duty's* America edition uses several illustrations per issue, by assignment only. Accepts photocopies or tearsheets of previous work that can be kept on file, but does not want originals or anything that must be returned. Pays $50-150 on acceptance for assignments.

***OHIO FAMILY MAGAZINE**, Box 183, Yellow Springs OH 45322. (513)767-3421. Contact: Teri Schoch. Estab. 1985. Magazine emphasizing families of central & southwest Ohio for women of childbearing age with families. Bimonthly. Circ. 30,000. Accepts previously published material. Original artwork returned after publication. Sample copy free for SASE with $1.10 postage. Art guidelines available.

Cartoons: Buys 2-6 cartoons/issue from freelancers. Prefers families of all types; different races, nationalities, single parent families, elderly and children as themes. Prefers b&w line drawings. Send samples of style to be kept on file. Call to schedule an appointment to show a portfolio. Samples not filed are returned by SASE. Reports within 2 weeks. Negotiates rights purchased and payment.

Illustrations: Prefers families of all types and situations as themes. Send query letter with resume and samples. Samples not filed returned by SASE. Reports within 2 weeks. Call to schedule an appointment to show a portfolio, which should include final reproduction/product, color and tear sheets. Negotiates rights purchased and payment. Pays on acceptance.

OHIO MAGAZINE, 40 S. Third St., Columbus OH 43215. (614)461-5083. Managing Editor: Ellen Stein. Emphasizes feature material of Ohio for an educated, urban and urbane readership. Monthly. Circ. 100,000. Previously published work OK. Original artwork returned after publication. Sample copy $2.

Illustrations: Buys 1-3/issue from freelancers. Interested in Ohio scenes and themes. Works on stock and assignment. Send query letter with brochure showing art style or tear sheets, slides and photographs. SASE. Reports in 2 weeks. Pays $75-150, b&w; $100-250, color, inside; on publication. Buys one-time publication rights.

Tips: Magazine is now realizing an "increased use of stock photography and artwork (illustration, paintings, prints). Artwork should exhibit a fine arts 'bent,' but not 'slick.' Uncontrived elegance, rich, noncommercial images which elevate 'real life' in Ohio."

OLD WEST, Box 2107, Stillwater OK 74076. (405)743-0130. Editor: John Joerschke. Emphasizes American western history from 1830 to 1910 for a primarily rural and suburban audience, middle-age and older, interested in Old West history, horses, cowboys, art, clothing and all things western. Quarterly. Circ. 90,000. Accepts previously published material and considers some simultaneous submissions. Original artwork returned after publication. Sample copy and art guidelines free for SASE.

Illustrations: Uses 5-10 illustrations/issue, including 2 or 3 humorous illustrations; buys all from freelancers. "Inside illustrations are usually, but need not always be pen & ink line drawings; covers are western paintings." Send query letter with samples to be kept on file; "we return anything on request." Call or write for appointment to show portfolio. "For inside illustrations, we want samples of artist's line drawings. For covers, we need to see full-color transparencies." Reports within 1 month. Buys one-time rights. Pays $100-150 for color transparency for cover; $15-40, b&w, inside; on acceptance.

Tips: "*Old West* has begun moving away from the action-oriented, animated appearance on its cover in recent years. We think the mainstream of interest in Western Americana has moved in the direction of fine art, and we're looking for more material along those lines. A recent cover that we were very pleased with is Summer 1985."

***1001 HOME IDEAS**, 3 Park Ave., New York NY 10011. (212)340-9258. Art Director: Robert Thornton. Magazine emphasizing home furnishings for an audience with a median age at 36, female, interested in decorating." Monthly. Circ. 1,150,000. Original artwork returned after publication. Art guidelines available.

Illustrations: Buys 7-9 illustrations/issue from freelancers. Work on assignment only. Prefers "graphic, contemporary styles." Contact "any way." Samples not filed are returned. Reports back. Call to schedule an appointment to show a portfolio. Buys first rights. Payment varies; on publication.

ONE WORLD, Box 1351, State College PA 16804. (814)238-0793. Vice President: Dana Stuchell. Emphasizes animal rights for "the general public involved in the protection of animals and promotion of animal rights and the philosphical public interested in animal rights as a philosophical/ethical issue." Periodic. Circ. 5,000. Accepts previously published material. Original artwork returned after publication. Sample copy $1.

Cartoons: Prefers animal rights or environmental issue themes. Send query letter with tear sheets, photostats, photocopies and finished cartoons to be kept on file. Material not filed is returned by SASE. Reports only if interested. Buys reprint rights. Pays negotiable rate, b&w and color; on publication.

Illustrations: Prefers animal rights and environmental issue as themes. Send query letter with tear sheets, photostats, photocopies and photographs to be kept on file. Samples returned by SASE. Reports only if interested. Buys reprint rights. Pays negotiable rate, b&w and color, cover and inside; on publication.
Tips: "Artwork should have an immediate relevance to animal rights."

ONLINE-TODAY MAGAZINE, 5000 Arlington Centre Blvd., Columbus OH 43220. (614)457-8600. Art Director: Thom Misiak. Edited for people and businesses on the leading edge of the personal computing and videotext industries. "*Online-Today* helps people maximize the potential of their personal computing equipment by examining how personal computers can be used to increase productivity, manage financial resources, communicate, inform and educate." Monthly. Circ. 265,000.
Illustrations: Works with 10 freelance artists/year. Works on assignment only. Uses artists for magazine illustration; also for advertising and brochure design, illustration and layout. Send query letter with brochure showing art style and samples to be kept on file. "I look for a professional, clean and organized presentation demonstrating good draughtsmanship and skill in the application of the selected media." Material not filed is returned by SASE. Reports only if interested. Call for appointment to show portfolio, which should include roughs, original/final art and tear sheets. Pays $500-1,000 color, cover; $75-150 b&w and $100-500 color, inside; on publication. Considers complexity of project, available budget, skill and experience of artist, and turnaround time when establishing payment.
Tips: "The biggest mistake an artist makes is not offering his creative input to the solution of a graphic problem. The artist is not only selling his illustrative talent but also his creative thinking. This should be part of any presentation the artist makes. I see a trend towards freer styles. These techniques at times appear to disguise poor draughtsmanship. I hope to see a return to anatomically correct figures."

***ONTARIO OUT OF DOORS**, 7th Floor, 777 Bay St., Toronto, Ontario M5W 1A7 Canada. (416)368-3011. Editor-in-Chief: Burton Myers. Emphasizes hunting, fishing, camping and conservation. Published 10 times/year. Circ. 55,000. Previously published work OK. Original artwork not returned after publication. Free sample copy and artist's guidelines.
Cartoons: Buys 2 cartoons/issue, all from freelancers. Receives 10-20 cartoons/month from freelance artists. Interested in fishing, hunting and camping themes; single panel. Send roughs. SASE (nonresidents include IRC). Reports within 6 weeks. Buys one time rights. Pays $50, b&w line drawings; 4 weeks after acceptance.
Illustrations: Uses 1-2 color illustrations plus 2-4 b&w line drawings/issue, all from freelancers. Interested in wildlife and fish themes. Especially needs cover artwork. Prefers to see roughs. SAE (nonresidents include IRC). Provide business card to be kept on file for future use. Reports in 6 weeks. Pays $250-500, color, cover; 4 weeks after acceptance.
Tips: "Strive for realism. Take the time to research the publication. Ask for a sample copy first before sending submissions." Especially looks for "the ability to depict nature or an activity in a clear-cut, informative fashion that supports the article."

OPPORTUNITY MAGAZINE, 6 N. Michigan Ave., Chicago IL 60602. Editor: Jack Weissman. Features articles dealing with direct (door-to-door) selling and on ways to start small businesses. For independent salesmen, agents, jobbers, distributors, sales managers, franchise seekers, route salesmen, wagon jobbers and people seeking an opportunity to make money full- or part-time. Monthly. Original artwork not returned after publication. Sample copy free for SASE with 50¢ postage.
Cartoons: Buys 2-3 cartoons/issue from freelancers. Interested in themes dealing with humorous sales situations affecting door-to-door salespeople. Considers single panel with gagline; b&w line drawings. Prefers roughs or finished cartoons. SASE. Buys all rights. Pays $5 on publication.
Tips: "Get sample copy beforehand and have an idea of what is appropriate."

OPTICAL INDEX, 633 3rd Ave., New York NY 10017. (212)741-4736. Art Director: Rebecca Brackett. Emphasizes eyewear fashion and dispensing for opticians and optometrists. Monthly. Circ. 27,000. Does not return original artwork after publication unless requested. Sample copy for SASE; art guidelines available.
Illustrations: Buys 1-2 illustrations/issue from freelancers. Themes and styles are dependent upon assignment; "usually color, highly stylized." Works on assignment only. Send query letter with brochure showing art style or photostats, tear sheets, photocopies, slides or photographs to be kept on file. Call for appointment to show portfolio. Samples not filed are not returned. Reports only if interested. Negotiates rights purchased. Pay varies; pays on acceptance.

THE OPTIMIST MAGAZINE, 4494 Lindell Blvd., St. Louis MO 63108. Editor: Dennis R. Osterwisch. Emphasizes activities relating to Optimist clubs in US and Canada (civic-service clubs). "Magazine is mailed to all members of Optimist clubs. Average age is 42, most are management level with some

college education." Circ. 160,000. Accepts previously published material. Sample copy free for SASE.
Cartoons: Buys 3 cartoons/issue from freelancers. Prefers themes of general interest; family-oriented, sports, kids, civic clubs. Prefers single panel, with gagline. No washes. Send query letter with samples. Submissions returned by SASE. Reports within 1 week. Buys one-time rights. Pays $30/b&w; on acceptance.

ORANGE COAST MAGAZINE, Suite 8, 245-D Fischer Ave, Costa Mesa CA 92626. (714)545-1900. Creative Director: Suzanne Reid. General interest city magazine. Monthly. Circ. 30,000. Returns original artwork after publication. Sample copy and art guidelines available.
Illustrations: Buys 3 illustration/issue from freelancers. Considers airbrush. Works on assignment only. Send brochure showing art style or tear sheets, slides or transparencies to be kept on file. Samples not filed are returned only if requested. Reports only if interested. To show a portfolio, mail original/final art, final reproduction/product, color, tear sheets and photographs. Buys one-time rights. Payment is negotiable; on publication.
Tips: There is a need for "fluid free-style illustration and for more photojournalistic expression within an artists mode—i.e. the art meets needs to express a story exactly, yet in a creative manner. Please send samples soon."

ORGANIC GARDENING, 33 E. Minor St., Emmaus PA 18049. (215)967-5171. Contact: Art Director. Emphasizes organic gardening and self-sufficiency. Monthly. Circ. 1,300,000.
Cartoons: Buys 1-2 cartoons/issue from freelancers. Interested in gardening, health, wood stove and alternative energy subjects; single panel, b&w line drawings and b&w washes. Send brochure showing art style and samples of style. SASE. Buys all rights. Pays $100-125.
Illustrations: Uses 20 + illustrations/issue. Interested in gardening, insects, flowers and vegetables and energy themes. Especially needs line work with very good figure drawings, (people in their gardens). Works on assignment only. Prefers b&w line drawings and washes, some color work for inside. Send brochure showing art style and business card with samples of style. SASE. Reports in 1 month. Call to schedule an appointment to show a portfolio, which should include original/final art, final reproduction/product and tear sheets. Prefers to buy all rights. Pays $65 + , spot illustrations; $125 + , color, inside; on acceptance.
Tips: "I like to see good figure drawing—if you can handle people realistically, you can handle most anything."

THE ORIGINAL NEW ENGLAND GUIDE, Historical Times, Inc., Box 8200, 2245 Kohn Rd., Harrisburg PA 17105. Editor: Kathie Kull. Consulting Editor: Mimi E.B. Steadman. Art Director: Jeanne Collins. Emphasizes New England travel of all kinds. Readers are "those planning on going on vacation trips, weekend jaunts, mini-holidays, day trips. For North American and overseas visitors to New England." Annually. Circ. 160,000. Sample copy $5.
Illustrations: "*The Guide* is almost always able to make its few assignments for artwork locally. However, we are certainly happy to know about freelancers and their special abilities, and welcome letters and/or samples (clips are fine)." Pays $50-150 on publication for inside b&w, depending on use. Send correspondence to Art Director.

THE OTHER SIDE, 300 W. Apsley St., Philadelphia PA 19144. (215)849-2178. Editor: Mark Olson. Art Director: Cathleen Boint. "We are read by Christians with a radical commitment to social justice and a deep allegiance to Biblical faith. We try to help readers put their faith into action." Published 10 times/year. Circ. 15,000. Receives 3 cartoons and 1 illustration/week from freelance artists. Sample copy $3.
Cartoons: Buys 2 cartoons/year on current events, environment, economics, politics and religion; single and multiple panel. Pays $25, b&w line drawings; on publication. "Looking for cartoons with a radical political perspective."
Illustrations: Especially needs b&w line drawings illustrating specific articles. Send query letter with tear sheets, photocopies, slide, photographs and SASE. Reports in 6 weeks. Photocopied and simultaneous submissions OK. To show a portfolio, mail appropriate materials or call to schedule an appointment; protfolio should include roughs, original/final art, final reproduction/product and photographs. Pays "within 4 weeks of publication." Pays $125-200, 4-color. Pays $40-175, b&w line drawings inside, on publication.
Tips: "We're looking for illustrators who share our perspective on social, economic and political issues, and who are willing to work for us on assignment."

OTTAWA MAGAZINE, 192 Bank St., Ottawa, Ontario K2P 1W8 Canada. (613)234-7751. Art Director: Peter de Gannes. Emphasizes lifestyles for sophisticated, middle and upper income, above average education professionals; most readers are women. Monthly. Circ. 42,500. Accepts previously published material. Sample copy available; include $1.06 Canadian funds to cover postage (nonresidents include 2 IRCs).

Illustrations: Buys 6-8 illustrations/issue from freelancers. Receives 3-4 submissions/week from freelancers. "Illustrations are geared to editorial copy and run from cartoon sketches to *Esquire*, *New York* and *Psychology Today* styles. Subjects range from fast-food franchising to how civil servants cope with stress. Art usually produced by local artists because of time and communication problems." Open to most styles including b&w line drawings, b&w and color washes, collages, photocopy art, oil and acrylic paintings, airbrush work and paper sculpture for inside. Also uses photographic treatments. Send query letter with resume and photocopies. "Do not send original artwork." No samples returned. Reports in 1 month. To show a portfolio, mail appropriate materials, which should include tear sheets and photostats. Buys first-time rights, or by arrangement with artist. Pays $35-150 for inside b&w; and $75-250 for inside color; on publication.

Tips: Prefers "work that shows wit, confidence in style and a unique approach to the medium used. Especially in need of artists who can look at a subject from a fresh, unusual perspective. There is a trend toward more exciting illustration, use of unusual techniques like photocopy collages or collages combining photography, pen & ink and watercolor. Freedom given to the artist to develop his treatment. Open to unusual techniques. Have as diversified a portfolio as possible. Remember that our average reader is an upper middle class woman, married, with children, aged 40-50."

OUI MAGAZINE, 6th Floor, 300 W. 43rd St., New York NY 10036. (212)397-5889. Executive Editor: Barry Janoff. Men's entertainment magazine: music, movies, erotically-oriented lifestyle for the '80s and '90s, for ages 18-35, "mostly but not all male, high school and/or college educated, upwardly mobile, trendsetters." Monthly. Circ. 500,000. Original artwork returned after publication. Sample copy $5 (check or money order); art guidelines for SASE.

Cartoons: Buys 2-5 cartoons/issue from freelancers. Considers erotically oriented or off-beat themes. Prefers single panel with gagline; b&w line drawings. Send finished cartoons; call for appointment to show portfolio. Material returned by SASE. Reports within 6 weeks. Negotiates rights purchased. Pays $30, b&w; $75, color; on publication.

Illustrations: Buys 0-2 illustrations/issue from freelancers. Theme or style depends on article or fiction. "Artist works with art director and editor to focus on topic being illustrated, 90% of input comes from artist." Works on assignment only. Send query letter with brochure and samples if possible (or copies) to be kept on file; call for appointment to show portfolio. Prefers tear sheets, slides or photostats as samples. Samples not filed are returned by SASE. Reports only if interested. Negotiates rights purchased. Pays $400+, color, inside; on publication.

OUR FAMILY, Oblate Fathers of St. Mary's Province, Box 249, Battleford, Saskatchewan S0M 0E0 Canada. (306)937-2663. Art Editor: Albert Lalonde O.M.I. Inspirational, educational magazine. Monthly. Circ. 14,265. Previously published, photocopied and simultaneous submissions OK. Original artwork not specifically commissioned by *Our Family* returned after publication. Artwork commissioned for *Our Family* is retained by magazine. Sample copy $2.85 to cover cost of magazine and postage.

Cartoons: Buys 5 cartoons/issue on family situations, especially parent-children relationships; single panel with gagline. Send query letter with resume, tear sheets, photostats and photocopies. To show a portfolio, mail tear sheets, photostats and photocopies. SAE and personal check, postal money order or International Reply Coupon because U.S. postage cannot be used in Canada. Reports in 2-4 weeks. Pays $15-20, b&w line drawings and washes; on acceptance.

Illustrations: Buys 1-2 illustrations/issue from freelancers. Receives several submissions/month from freelancers. Subject "depends on the article we want illustrated. We usually commission this work to a specific artist." Works on assignment only. Send samples of work for review. Samples returned by SAE and personal check, postal money order or International Reply Coupon because U.S. postage cannot be used in Canada. Send brochure and tear sheet to be kept on file for future assignments. Reports in 2-4 weeks. To show a portfolio, mail tear sheets, photostats and photocopies. "We will let the artist know what work he can do for us." Buys all rights to commissioned work. Inside: Pays $100 and up for commissioned art.

Tips: "Request sample copy of the magazine for study of our style. Enclose $2.85 to cover cost. Then submit portfolio of appropriate material."

OUTDOOR AMERICA MAGAZINE, Suite 1100, 1701 N. Ft. Meyer Dr., Arlington VA 22209. Editor: Carol Dana. Emphasizes conservation and outdoor recreation (fishing, hunting, etc.) for sportsmen and conservationists. Quarterly. Circ. 45,000. Accepts previously published material. Original artwork returned after publication. Sample copy $1.50.

Cartoons: Buys 0-1 cartoon/issue from freelancers. Considers conservation and outdoor recreation themes. Prefers single panel with gagline; b&w line drawings. Send query letter with samples of style to be kept on file. Material not filed is returned by SASE. Buys one-time rights or reprint rights. Pays $25 and up, b&w; on publication.

Illustrations: Buys 2-3 illustrations/issue from freelancers. Send query letter with samples to be kept on file. Prefers tear sheets or photocopies as samples. Samples not filed are returned. Reports within 2 months. Buys one-time rights or reprint rights. Pays on publication.

OUTDOOR LIFE, 380 Madison Ave., New York NY 10017. (212)687-3000. Art Director: Jim Eckes. Emphasizes hunting, fishing, boating and camping for "male and female, young and old who enjoy the outdoors and what it has to offer." Monthly. Circ. 1.5 million. Original artwork returned after publication "unless we buy all rights." Sample copy available "if work is going to be published."
Cartoons: Very seldom uses cartoons. Send finished cartoons to be kept on file, except for "those we won't ever use." Material not kept on file is returned by SASE. Reports only if interested. Buys first rights. Pays on publication.
Illustrations: Uses 2-3 illustrations/issue. Prefers "realistic themes, realistic humor." Works on assignment only. Send query letter with samples and tear sheets to be kept on file except "those which do not meet our standards." Prefers slides, tear sheets and originals as samples. Samples not kept on file are returned. Reports only if interested. Call for appointment to show portfolio. Negotiates rights purchased. Pays $800, color spread, $1,000, cover; on publication. Payment "depends on size and whether it is a national or regional piece."
Tips: "First of all, we're looking for 'wildlife, realists'—those who know how to illustrate a species realistically and with action."

***OUTDOOR SPORTS & RECREATION**, 2306 S. Broadway, Alexandria MN 56308. (612)762-1142. Editor-in-Chief: John Hall. Magazine emphasizing hunting, fishing and outdoor recreation for fishermen and hunters in the upper Midwest (emphasis in Minnesota and Wisconsin). Bimonthly. Circ. 30,000. Original artwork returned after publication. Sample copy free for SASE with 39¢ postage.
Cartoons: Buys 1 cartoon/issue from freelancers. Prefers fishing/hunting humor themes. Prefers single panel with gagline; b&w line drawings. Send query letter with samples of style or roughs to be kept on file. Material not kept on file is returned by SASE. Reports back within 2 weeks. Buys one-time rights. Pays $15, b&w.

OUTREACH PUBLICATIONS, INC., Box 1010, Siloam Springs AR 72761. (501)524-9301. Art Director: Darrell Hill. Emphasizes Christian/religious themes. Original artwork not returned after publication. Sample copy and art guidelines available.
Illustrations: Uses 250-350 illustrations/year; buys 150-250 illustrations/year from freelancers. Send query letter with photostats, photographs, slides and original work to be kept on file. Samples returned only if requested. Reports only if interested. Material not copyrighted. Call or write for appointment to show portfolio. Negotiates payment. Pays within 30 days of receipt.
Tips: Especially looks for "creative concepts and unique style" in artwork.

OUTSIDE, 1165 N. Clark St., Chicago IL 60610. (312)951-0990. Managing Editor: John Rasmus. Design Director: John Askwith. Concerns enjoyment and participation in the great outdoors. Published 12 times/year. Circ. 240,000 + .
Illustrations: Uses 60 illustrations/year; buys 60/year from freelancers. Works on assignment only. Receives 3-4 submissions/week from freelancers. Ask for artists' guidelines. Especially needs spot (less than ½ page) 4-color art; "contemporary, communicative, powerful illustration. We are also interested in seeing any contemporary stills for assignment purposes." Send "good slides" or previously published work as samples. SASE. Reports in 2 weeks. Send samples or tear sheet to be kept on file for future assignments. Buys one-time rights. Pays $100-750, b&w line drawings, washes and full-color renderings, inside; on publication.
Tips: "Observe the 'front runners' for style and trends. We presently don't use cartoons."

OVERSEAS!, Kolpingstr 1, 6906 Leimen, West Germany. Editorial Director: Charles L. Kaufman. Managing Editor: Greg Ballinger. "*Overseas!* is the leading lifestyle magazine for the U.S. military male stationed throughout Europe. Primary focus is on European travel, with regular features on music, sports, video, audio and photo products, and men's fashion. The average reader is male, age 24." Sample copy for SAE and 4 IRCs; art guidelines for SAE and 1 IRC.
Cartoons: Buys 3-5 cartoons/issue. "Always looking for humorous cartoons on travel and being a tourist in Europe. Best bet is to send in a selection of 5-10 for placement of all on one-two pages. Looking for more *National Lampoon* or *Playboy*-style cartoons/humor than a *Saturday Evening Post*-type cartoon. Anything new, different or crazy is given high priority. On cartoons or cartoon features don't query, send nonreturnable photocopies. Pay is negotiable, $25-75/cartoon to start."
Illustrations: Uses 3-5 illustrations/month. Send query letter with nonreturnable photocopies. "We will assign when needed." To show a portfolio, mail appropriate materials or call or write to schedule an appointment. Pays $75-200, negotiable.
Tips: "Not enough cartoonists send samples of work for consideration."

OZARK MAGAZINE, East-West Network, Inc., Suite 800, 5900 Wilshire Blvd., Los Angeles CA 90036. (213)937-5810. Editor: Laura Dean Bennett. Art Director: Carla Schrad. Emphasizes culture, sports, business and personalities in the Midwest. For the executive. Monthly. Sample copy $2. Accepts previously published material. Originals returned to artist after publication.
Illustrations: Works on assignment only. Send query letter with resume, tear sheets, slides and photographs to be filed. Samples returned only by request with SASE. Reports only if interested. Buys first rights. Call or write to schedule an appointment to show a portfolio. Pays $800 color, cover; $300 b&w and $500 color, inside; on acceptance.
Tips Sees "less cartoon and/or nostalgic-type artwork, more avante and/or modern work need. Be professional."

PACIFIC COAST JOURNAL, Box 254822, Sacramento CA 95865. Editor-in-Chief: Jill Scopinich. For horse breeders, trainers and owners interested in performance, racing and showing of quarter horses. Monthly. Circ. 7,800. Previously published and simultaneous submissions OK "if we are notified."
Cartoons: Buys 24 cartoons/year on horses; single panel. Send query letter with samples. SASE. Reports in 4 weeks. Buys first, reprint, all or simultaneous rights. Pays $7.50-20, washes; on acceptance.

PAINT HORSE JOURNAL, Box 18519, Fort Worth TX 76118. (817)439-3400. Editor: Bill Shepard. Art Director: Vicki Day. Official publication of breed registry for Paint horses. For people who raise, breed and show Paint horses. Monthly. Circ. 11,200. Receives 4-5 cartoons and 2-3 illustrations/week from freelance artists. Original artwork returned after publication if requested. Sample copy $2; artist's guidelines free for SASE.
Cartoons: Buys 1 or 2 cartoons/issue, all from freelancers. Interested in *Paint* horses; single panel with gagline. Material returned by SASE only if requested. Reports in 1 month. Buys first rights. Pays $10, b&w line drawings; on acceptance.
Illustrations: Uses 1-3 illustrations/issue; buys few/issue from freelancers. Receives few submissions/week from freelancers. Especially needs youth drawings with Paint horses. Send business card and samples to be kept on file. Prefers original art or photostats as samples. Samples returned by SASE if not kept on file. Reports within 1 month. Send query letter with brochure showing art style or photocopies and finished art. Buys first rights. Pays $5-25, b&w, inside; $50 color, cover; on publication.
Tips: "We use a lot of different styles of art, but no matter what style you use-you *must* include Paint horses with acceptable (to the APHA) conformation. As horses are becoming more streamlined-as in race-bred Paints, the older style of horse seem so out dated. I get a lot of art from older artists who still draw the Paint as stocky and squatty—which they are not."

PANDORA, %Empire Books, Box 625, Murray KY 42071-0625. Editor: Jean Lorrah. Emphasizes science fiction and fantasy. Semiannually. Circ. 700. Accepts previously published material. Original artwork returned after publication but prefers photostat. Sample copy $3.50.
Cartoons: Buys 1-2 cartoons/year from freelancers. Considers science fiction themes. Prefers single panel; b&w line drawings. Send query letter with roughs to be kept on file. Material not filed is returned by SASE. Reports within 6 weeks. Buys first North American serial rights. Pays $5, b&w; on acceptance.
Illustrations: Buys 5-7 illustrations/issue from freelancers. Style should suit story. Works on assignment only. Send query letter with tear sheets or photocopies to be kept on file. Samples not filed are returned by SASE. Reports in 6 weeks. Buys first North American serial rights. Pays $10, b&w, cover and inside; on acceptance. "We pay $15 for a photostat, to avoid the hassles of handling originals."

PARADE MAGAZINE, 750 Third Ave., New York NY 10017. (212)573-7187. Director of Design: Ira Yoffe. Photo Editor: Brent Petersen. Emphasizes general interest subjects. Weekly. Circ. 31 million (readership is 60 million). Original artwork returned after publication. Sample copy and art guidelines available.
Illustrations: Uses varied number of illustrations/issue. Prefers various themes. Works on assignment only. Send query letter with brochure, resume, business card and tear sheets to be kept on file. Call or write for appointment to show portfolio. Reports only if interested. Buys first rights, and occasionally all rights.
Tips: "Provide a good balance of work."

***PARAPLEGIA NEWS**, Suite 111, 5201 N. 19th Ave., Phoenix AZ 85015. Art Director: Carol Beiriger. Magazine emphasizing wheelchair living for wheelchair users, rehabilitation specialists. Monthly. Circ. 24,000. Accepts previously published material. Original artwork not returned after publication. Sample copy free for SASE with 96¢ postage; art guidelies free for SASE with 22¢ postage.
Cartoons: Buys 1 cartoon/issue from freelancers. Prefers line art with wheelchair theme. Prefers single panel with gagline; b&w line drawings. Send query letter with samples of style or finished cartoons to be

kept on file. Write for appointment to show portfolio. Material not kept on file is returned by SASE. Reports only if interested. Buys all rights. Pays $10, b&w.
Illustrations: Buys 1 illustration/issue from freelancers. Prefers wheelchair living or medical and financial topics as themes. Send query letter with brochure showing art style or tear sheets, photostats, photocopies and photographs. Samples not filed are returned by SASE. Reports only if interested. To show a portfolio, include final reproduction/product, color, tear sheets, photostats, photographs and b&w. Negotiates rights purchased. Pays on acceptance.

PARTNERSHIP, 465 Gundersen Dr., Carol Stream IL 60188. (312)260-6200. Art Director: Joan Nickerson. Estab. 1984. Emphasizes ministry wives. Bimonthly. Circ. 45,000. Accepts previously published material. Original artwork returned after publication only if requested. Sample copy free for SASE.
Cartoons: Buys 6-10 cartoons/issue from freelancers. Prefers inside humor having to do with the parish ministry. Prefers single panel with gagline; b&w line drawings. Send finished cartoons; call for appointment to show portfolio. All cartoons are returned. SASE. Reports within 2 weeks. Buys first rights. Pays $100, b&w; on acceptance.
Illustrations: Buys 5-6 illustrations/issue from freelancers. Works on assignment only. Send query letter; write for appointment to show portfolio. Accepts photostats, tear sheets, photocopies, slides, photographs, etc. as samples. Samples not filed are returned. Reports within 1 week. Negotiates rights purchased. Pays on acceptance.

PARTS PUPS, 2999 Circle 75 Parkway, Atlanta GA 30339. Editor: Don Kite. For automotive repairmen. Circ. 270,000. Monthly plus annual publication. Original artwork not returned after publication. Previously published material and simultaneous submissions OK. Free sample copy and artist's guidelines.
Cartoons: Buys 144/year on "girlie" themes, auto repairmen, general interest; single panel with gagline, b&w line drawings and washes. Receives 400 cartoons/week from freelance artists. Send finished artwork with SASE. Reports in 6 weeks. Pays $30, b&w line drawings and washes; on acceptance.
Tips: "Look over our publication before submitting material."

PASTORAL LIFE, The Magazine for Today's Ministry, Rt. 224, Canfield OH 44406. (216)533-5503. Editor: Rev. Jeffrey Mickler. Emphasizes religion and anything involving pastoral ministers and ministry for Roman Catholic priests (70%); the remainder are sisters, brothers, laity and ministers of other denominations. Monthly. Circ. 7,000. Original artwork returned after publication. Sample copy available.
Illustrations: Prefers religious, pastoral themes. Works on assignment only. Send query letter with photographs. Call or write for appointment to show portfolio, which should include b&w or photographs. Samples not kept on file are returned by SASE only if requested. Reports within 3 weeks. Buys first rights. Payment varies; on publication.

PEDIATRIC ANNALS, 6900 Grove Rd., Thorofare NJ 08086. (609)848-1000. Managing Editor: Donna Carpenter. Emphasizes pediatrics for practicing pediatricians. Monthly. Circ. 33,000. Original artwork returned after publication. Sample copy and art guidelines available.
Illustrations: Buys 4-5 illustrations/issue from freelancers. Send query letter with tearsheets, slides and photographs to be kept on file except for those specifically requested back. Reports within 2 months. Buys one-time rights or reprint rights. Pays $150, b&w and $200-300, color, cover; $25-30, b&w and $50-100, color, inside; on publication.

PENNSYLVANIA ANGLER, Box 1673, Harrisburg PA 17105-1673. (717)657-4520. Editor: Art Michaels. Emphasizes fishing in Pennsylvania, published by the Pennsylvania Fish Commission. Monthly. Circ. 68,000. Sample copy and art guidelines free for 9x12" SASE with 73¢ postage.
Illustrations: Uses 12 illustrations/issue; buys 4/issue from freelancers. Send query letter with samples and tear sheets to be kept on file. Accepts slides or photocopies as samples. Samples not kept on file are returned by SASE. Reports back. Write for appointment to show portfolio. Buys all rights, but rights can be reassigned after publication on written request. Pays $50-300, color, cover; $5-25, b&w, and $25-100, color, inside; on acceptance.

PENNSYLVANIA MAGAZINE, Box 576, Camp Hill PA 17011. (717)761-6620. Editor-in-Chief: Albert Holliday, for college-educated readers, ages 36-60+, interested in self-improvement, history, and civic and state affairs. Quarterly. Circ. 24,000. Query with samples. SASE. Reports in 3 weeks. Previously published, photocopied and simultaneous submissions OK. Buys first serial rights. Pays on publication or on acceptance for assigned articles/art. Sample copy $2.50.

Illustrations: Buys 12 illustrations/year on history-related themes. Minimum payment for cover, $100, inside color, $25-50; inside b&w, $5-50.

PENNWELL PUBLISHING CO., 1421 S. Sheridan, Tulsa OK 74112. (918)835-3161. Art Director: Mike Reeder. Emphasizes dental economics for practicing dentists; 24-65 years of age. Monthly. Circ. 100,000. Original artwork not returned after publication. Sample copy free for SASE; art guidelines available.
Cartoons: Uses about 1 cartoon/2 issues. Prefers dental related themes. Prefers single panel, with or without gagline; b&w line drawings. Send query letter with samples of style to be kept on file. Material not filed is returned by SASE. Reports only if interested. Negotiates rights purchased and payment. Pays on acceptance.
Illustrations: Currently uses no illustrations/issue. Works on assignment only. Send query letter with brochure to be kept on file. Prefers photostats and photographs as samples. Samples not filed are returned by SASE. Negotiates rights purchased. Pays on acceptance.
Tips: "When reviewing samples especially looks for diversification. For the most part, I like to see a variety of samples to show me that this artist has a firm grasp on the skills needed for this profession!"

PERSONAL COMPUTING MAGAZINE, 10 Mulholland Dr., Hasbrouck Heights NJ 07604. (201)393-6000. Associate Art Director: Peter Herbert. Emphasizes personal computers for managerial/professional; upper income audience. Monthly. Circ. 525,000. Original artwork returned after publication. Art guidelines free for SASE.
Illustrations: Buys several illustrations/issue from freelancers. Works on assignment only. Send query letter with tear sheets or slides to be kept on file. Samples not filed are returned only if requested. Buys first rights. Pays on acceptance.

Brad Veley of Marquette, Michigan, received $50 for first rights to this single-panel cartoon which appeared in Personnel Journal. *The magazine has a regular single-panel cartoon accompanying the editor's column each issue. "I just love drawing pictures that make me chuckle," says Veley. "That's my only criteria for a good cartoon."*

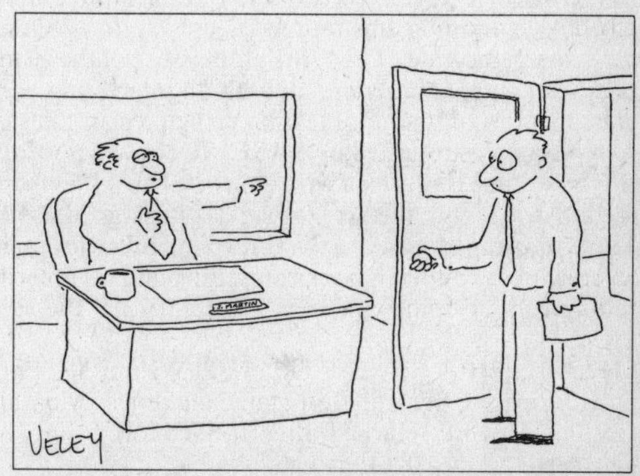

"Well, the buck used to stop here, but lately, thank gosh, it's been cruising right on by, down to Gunderson in Personnel!"

PERSONNEL JOURNAL, Suite B2, 245 Fischer, Costa Mesa CA 92626. (714)751-1883. Art Director: Susan Overstreet. Emphasizes the hiring, firing, training, recruiting of employees. Directed to directors or managers of corporate personnel departments in organizations with 500 or more employees. Monthly. Circ. 20,000. Original artwork returned after publication. Sample copy and art guidelines free for SASE.
Cartoons: Buys 1 cartoon/issue; buys 1/issue from freelancer. Prefers theme of the world of work, jobs, careers. "Please, no sexist or racist cartoons." Prefers single panel with gagline; b&w line drawings or b&w washes. Send query letter with samples of style to be kept on file. Reports within 3 weeks. Buys one-time rights. Pays $50, b&w; on acceptance.
Illustrations: Buys 3 illustrations/issue; buys all from freelancers. Prefers professional themes such as the workplace, office equipment, professionals (line drawings). Works on assignment; will also accept previously published material. Send query letter with resume, business card and photostats to be kept on file. Call or write for appointment to show portfolio. Samples not kept on file are returned only if requested. Reports only if interested. Negotiates rights purchased. Pays $150-200, b&w, inside; on acceptance.

PET BUSINESS, 5400 N.W. 84th Ave., Miami FL 33166. Editor-in-Chief: Robert Behme. For those in the pet trade: manufacturers, importers, exporters, wholesalers, retailers and livestock breeders.

Monthly news magazine. Circ. 14,500. Sample copy $1. Also uses artists for layout and book art.
Cartoons: Buys 2 cartoons/issue on pet-related themes; single panel. Query. SASE. Reports in 3 weeks. Pays $15-25, b&w line drawings and halftones; on acceptance.
Illustrations: Buys 20 illustrations/year on assigned themes. Query. SASE. Reports in 3 weeks. Pays $25-40, b&w; on acceptance.

PETERSENS HUNTING MAGAZINE, Petersen Publishing Co., 8490 Sunset Blvd., Los Angeles CA 90069. (213)854-2222. Editor: Craig Boddington. Art Director: C. A. Yeseta. Emphasizes sport hunting for hunting enthusiasts. Monthly. Circ. 275,000. Sometimes returns originals after publication. Sample copy $1.75. Occasionally uses production paste-up artists on an hourly wage.
Cartoons: Uses 1-2 cartoons/year from freelancers on hunting scenes and wildlife. Prefers to see finished cartoons. Reports in 1 week. Pays on publication.
Illustrations: Buys 8-10 illustrations/year on "very realistic wildlife themes and action hunting scenes"; some "how-to" drawings. Works on assignment only. Prefers to see finished art, roughs, portfolio, samples of style or previously published work. Arrange interview to show portfolio. Samples returned by SASE. Provide resume, business card, letter of inquiry; also brochure or flyer containing examples of work to be kept on file for future assignments. Reports in 4 weeks. Buys various rights. Inside: Pays $75-150, b&w line drawings; on publication.

PHI DELTA KAPPAN, Box 789, Bloomington IN 47402. Editor-in-Chief: Robert W. Cole, Jr. Design Director: Kristin Herzog. Emphasizes issues, policy, research findings and opinions in the field of education. For members of the educational organization Phi Delta Kappa and subscribers. Published 10 times/year. Circ. 135,000. Considers unpublished artists on a speculative basis. SASE. Reports in 2 weeks. Previously published work OK; "specify where item appeared. We return cartoons after publication." Sample copy $2.50—"the journal is available in most public and college libraries."
Illustrations: Uses 2-5 b&w illustrations/issue, all from freelancers, on education subjects. Occasionally buys humorous illustrations (about 4/year). "Quality of drawing and good concepts most important aspect-i.e., the kind of line, the graphic use of the space. Next is ability to depict appropriate image from editorial content and come up with an interesting concept. Most illustrations depict teachers or principals, theories of learning, testing principles, studies of excellence, international comparisons of education." Samples returned by SASE. To show a portfolio, mail a few slides and photocopies with SASE. Buys one-time rights on a work-for-hire basis. Payment varies all over the place depending on the skill of the artist, whether the art was stock or assigned, whether it's been published before," on acceptance.
Tips: "You need to take a lot of responsibility for marketing your work. I'd suggest going to the library and reading a couple of books on selling and salemanship. It doesn't matter if the books are talking about selling cars or homes or soap—the skills are the same."

PHILADELPHIA MAGAZINE, 1500 Walnut St., Philadelphia PA 19102. Contact: Art Director. For a professional, upper-middle-income audience. Monthly. Circ. 142,000. Simultaneous submissions OK. Original artwork returned after publication.
Cartoons: Buys 0-1 cartoons/issue.
Illustrations: Uses 10-16 illustrations/issue; buys all from freelancers. Interested in a variety of themes and styles. Works on assignment only. Send query letter with resume and tear sheets, photostats, photocopies, slides and photographs to be kept on file. Samples not returned. Buys one-time rights. To show a portfolio, mail appropriate materials, which should include original/final art, final reproduction/product, color, tear sheets and b&w. Pays for illustrations $75-375 b&w; $100-500 color, inside; on acceptance.
Tips: "Variety is the key word. Accurate and intelligent interpretation of the editorial message is essential. Look at several issues of the magazine in the library. Understand the level of work expected."

PHOENIX HOME/GARDEN, 3136 N. 3rd Ave., Phoenix AZ 85013. (602)234-0840. Editor: Manya Winsted. Managing Editor: Nora Burba. Emphasizes homes, entertainment and gardens for Phoenix area residents interested in better living. Monthly. Circ. 33,000. Original artwork not returned after publication. Sample copy $2.50.
Illustrations: Uses 6-12 illustrations/year; buys 1-5 from freelancers. Interested in botanical illustrations and spot art relevant to topics. Also uses illustrations for promotional material in conjunction with the magazine. Works on assignment only. Send samples of style. Reports in 6 weeks. Provide tear sheets to be kept on file for possible future assignments. Buys all rights on assignments. Pays $30-50 average inside, b&w line drawings. Pays on publication.

PHOTO MARKETING MAGAZINE, 3000 Picture Pl., Jackson MI 49201. (517)788-8100. Executive Editor/Associate Publisher: Bruce Aldrich. Managing Editor: Nancy Brent. Emphasizes the photographic industry. Readers are camera store dealers, photofinishers, photo processors, manufacturers

and distributors of photographic equipment. Monthly. Circ. 16,000. Free sample copy; art guidelines for SASE.
Cartoons: Needs vary each issue. Freelancers are selected for particular subject matter or story topic. Format: b&w line drawings without gagline. Send samples of style and resume. SASE. Reports in 1 week. Pays on publication. Buys first North American serial rights.
Illustrations: Seldom run illustration; buys 1-2 illustrations/issue. "Selection is made from freelancers on file, per assignment basis only." Uses inside b&w line drawings and color washes. Send brochure showing art style. SASE. Reports in 1 week. To show a portfolio, mail appropriate materials, which should include original/final art, b&w. Pays on publication; on acceptance. Buys first North American serial rights.
Tips: "Magazines have more need for bold graphics and charts with less cartooning." Concerning approaching this market, "Consider the professional appearance of book and artist. Always return calls and keep appointment."

PHYSICIAN'S MANAGEMENT, 7500 Old Oak Blvd., Cleveland OH 44130. (216)243-8100, ext. 808. Editor: Robert A. Feigenbaum. Art Director: David Komitau. Published 12 times/year. Circ. 110,000. Emphasizes business, practice management and legal aspects of medical practice for primary care physicians.
Cartoons: Receives 50-70/week from freelancers. Buys 10 cartoons/issue. Themes typically apply to medical and financial situations "although we do publish general humor cartoons." Prefers single and double panel; b&w line drawings with gagline. Uses "only clean-cut line drawings." Send query letter with brochure showing art style or resume and tear sheets, photostats, photocopies, slides and photographs. SASE. Reports in 2 weeks. Call or write to schedule an appointment to show a portfolio, which should include final reproduction/product and photographs. Buys one-time rights. Pays $80 for b&w; on acceptance. No previously published material and/or simultaneous submissions.
Illustrations: Buys 5 illustrations/issue. Accepts b&w and color illustrations. All work done on assignment. Send a query letter to editor or art director first or send examples of work. Fees negotiable. Buys first rights. No previously published and/or simultaneous submissions.
Tips: "First, become familiar with our publication, second, query the art director. Cartoons should be geared toward the physician—not the patient. No cartoons about drug companies or medicine men. No sexist cartoons. Illustrations should be appropriate for a serious business publication. We do not use cartoonish or comic book styles to illustrate our articles. We work with artists nationwide."

PIG IRON, Box 237, Youngstown OH 44501. (216)783-1269. Editor-in-Chief: Jim Villani and Rose Sayre. Emphasizes literature/art for writers, artists and intelligent lay audience with emphasis in popular culture. Annually. Circ. 1,000. Previously published and photocopied work OK. Original artwork returned after publication. Sample copy $2.50.
Cartoons: Uses 1-15 cartoons/issue, all from freelancers. Receives 1-3 submissions/week from freelancers. Interested in "the arts, political, science fiction, fantasy, alternative lifestyles, psychology, humor"; single and multiple panel. Especially needs fine art cartoons. Prefers finished cartoons. SASE. Reports in 1 month. Buys first North American serial rights. Pays $2 minimum, b&w halftones and washes; on acceptance.
Illustrations: Uses 15-30 illustrations/issue, all from freelancers. Receives 1-3 submissions/week from freelancers. Interested in "any media: pen and ink washes, lithographs, silk screen, charcoal, collage, line drawings; any subject matter." B&w only. Prefers finished art or velox. Reports in 2 months. Buys first North American serial rights. Minimum payment: Cover: $4, b&w. Inside: $2; on publication.
Tips: "*Pig Iron* is a publishing opportunity for the fine artist; we publish art in its own right, not as filler or story accompaniment. The artist who is executing black-and-white work for exhibit and gallery presentations can find a publishing outlet with *Pig Iron* that will considerably increase that artist's visibility and reputation." Current themes include "humor," and the "Wild West." Looking for Third World artists for Third World anthology.

***THE PILOTS LOG**, New England Mutual Life Insurance Co., 501 Boylston St., Boston MA 02117. (617)266-3700, ext. 2020. Editor: Patrick Crowley. Emphasizes insurance sales; "*The Pilot's Log* is New England Life's feature magazine for its 5,000-member sales force." Bimonthly. Circ. 5,000. Simultaneous submissions OK. Original art work returned after publication. Free sample copy for SASE.
Illustration: No unsolicited submissions. Works on assignment only. Uses 2 inside b&w illustrations/issue; also occasional full-color illustration; buys all from freelancers. "We buy b&w and color illustrations as well as sculptures, models, etc. to accompany stories on a variety of themes-buyers, sellers, business, professional, etc." Reports back whether to expect possible future assignments. Samples not returned. Reports in 4 weeks. Negotiates rights purchased. Pays $300-600, cover b&w line drawings; $350-650, cover b&w color washes; $100-300, inside b&w line drawings; $150-350, inside b&w or color lunches; on acceptance.

PITTSBURGH MAGAZINE, 4802 5th Ave., Pittsburgh PA 15213. (412)622-1360. Art Director: Michael Maskarinec. Emphasizes culture, feature stories and material with heavy Pittsburgh city emphasis; public broadcasting television and radio schedule. Monthly. Circ. 58,000. Sample copy $2.
Illustrations: Uses 5-10 illustrations/issue; all from freelancers; inside b&w and 4-color illustrations. Works on assignment only. Prefers to see roughs. SASE. Buys one-time rights on a work-for-hire basis. Pays on publication.

PLANE & PILOT MAGAZINE, 16200 Ventura Blvd., Encino CA 91436. Art Director: J.R. Martinez. Emphasizes business and personal aviation for private and small business pilots. Monthly. Circ. 70-100,000. Does not return original artwork after publication. Sample copy available; art guidelines free for SASE.
Illustrations: Prefers business and aircraft oriented work, b&w line, wash or airbrush. Works on assignment only. Send query letter with photostats, tear sheets and slides to be kept on file. Reports back. Buys all rights. Write for appointment to show portfolio. Pays $100-300 for b&w and per assignment for color, inside; on acceptance.
Tips: "Fewer artists have portfolios oriented toward b&w work. It makes it more difficult to evaluate who would be best for a b&w assignment."

PLANNING, American Planning Association, 1313 E. 60th St., Chicago IL 60637. (312)955-9100. Editor-in-Chief: Sylvia Lewis. Art Director: Richard Sessions. For urban and regional planners interested in land use, housing, transportation and the environment. Monthly. Circ. 25,000. Previously published work OK. Original artwork returned after publication, upon request. Free sample copy and artist's guidelines.
Cartoons: Buys 2 cartoons/year on the environment, city/regional planning, energy, garbage, transportation, housing, power plants, agriculture and land use. Prefers single, double and multiple panel with gaglines ("provide outside of cartoon body if possible"). SASE. Reports in 2 weeks. Buys all rights. Pays $25 minimum, b&w line drawings; on publication.
Illustrations: Buys 20 illustrations/year on the environment, city/regional planning, energy, garbage, transportation, housing, power plants, agriculture and land use. Prefers to see roughs and samples of style. SASE. Reports in 2 weeks. Buys all rights. Pays $200 maximum, b&w drawings, cover. Pays $25 minimum, b&w line drawings inside; on publication.

PLAYBILL, Suite 320, 71 Vanderbilt Ave., New York NY 10169. (212)557-5757. Editor-in-Chief: Joan Alleman. Concerns theater in New York City. Monthly. Circ. 1,040,000.
Cartoons: Buys b&w line drawings on New York City theater. SASE. Reports in 4 weeks. Buys all rights. Pays on acceptance.
Illustrations: Assigns work on New York City theater. SASE. Reports in 4 weeks. Buys all rights. Pays on acceptance.

PLAYBOY, 919 Michigan Ave., Chicago IL 60611. Executive Art Director: Tom Staebler. Emphasizes celebrities, beautiful women, dining, humor and fiction. For the sophisticated, urban male. All work generally done on assignment. Reports in 3-4 weeks.
Cartoons: Submit roughs with one finished drawing to Michelle Urry, cartoon editor. Buys 40/month on satirical, sophisticated, and other situations. Prefers cartoons that deal with sex and are slanted toward young, urban male market. Also looking for one-line "strips" for Funnies section. "Style and technique very important." Pays $350, b&w; $600, full-page color.
Illustrations: Submit samples to Kerig Pope, managing art director. Pays $1,200/page or $2,000/spread; $200-250, spot drawings.

PLAYGIRL, Suite 3000, 3420 Ocean Park Blvd., Santa Monica CA 90405. (213)450-0900. Assistant Art Director: Mark D'Antoni. Emphasizes entertainment, fiction, reviews, beauty, fashion, cooking and travel for women ages 18-40. Monthly. Circ. 850,000.
Cartoons: Uses 6-18 cartoons/issue; all by freelancers. Receives 200+ cartoons from freelancers/month. Cartoons should be "slanted towards women's problems, intellectual humor, and topical issues." Format: Single panel b&w washes with gagline. Especially needs 6-inch square, b&w cartoons

dealing with women's issues, experiences. Prefers finished cartoons or excellent photocopies. SASE. Reports in 60 days. Pays on publication; $75 for b&w. Buys first North American serial rights. Call Cartoon Editor Jeanie Barnett for appointment to show a portfolio.
Illustrations: Works on assignment only. Uses 4-12 illustrations/issue; all by freelancers. Artists are selected from "walk-ins" doing editorial artwork to illustrate fiction. Format: b&w line drawings and color washes for inside. Especially needs vertical color and b&w. Arrange personal appointment to show portfolio and/or send samples of style and tear sheets. SASE. Reports only if interested. Pays on publication. Buys all rights.
Tips: "There is a trend toward humor with a subliminal sexuality slant. Women are being depicted in a more liberal light, particularly regarding male nudity and in other sexual contexts. We want as strong and contemporary a visual style as possible."

***POCKETS**, Box 189, 1908 Grand Ave., Nashville TN 37202. (615)327-2700, ext. 455. Associate Editor: Janet Bugg. Devotional magazine for children 6 to 12. Monthly magazine except Jan/Feb. Circ. 68,000. Accepts previously published material. Original artwork returned after publication. Sample copy free for SASE with 73¢ postage.
Illustrations: Uses variety of styles; 4-color, 2-color, flapped art appropriate for children. Realistic fable and cartoon styles. We will accept tear sheets, photostats and slides. Samples not filed are returned by SASE. Reports only if interested. Buys one-time or reprint rights. Pays $50-500 depending on size. Pays on acceptance.

PODIATRY MANAGEMENT MAGAZINE, 401 N. Broad St., Philadelphia PA 19108. (215)925-9744. President: Scott Borowsky. Emphasizes practice management for podiatrists, faculty and students. Published 8 times/year. Circ. 11,000. Original artwork returned after publication. Also uses paste-up artists; pays $7/hour.
Illustrations: Buys 2-3 b&w illustrations/issue from freelancers. Themes tie in with stories. Works on assignment only. Send query letter with resume to be kept on file; write for appointment to show portfolio. Prefers photostats and tear sheets as samples. Samples returned by SASE. Reports only if interested and if SASE is included. Buys all rights. Pays $100-175, b&w and $250, color, cover; $100, b&w, inside; on publication.

POPULAR SCIENCE, Times Mirror Magazines, Inc., 380 Madison Ave., New York NY 10017. Art Director: David Houser. For the well-educated adult male, interested in science, technology, new products. Receives 3 illustrations/week from freelance artists. Original artwork returned after publication.
Illustrations: Uses 30-40 illustrations/issue; buys 30/issue from freelancers. Works on assignment only. Interested in technical 4-color art and 2-color line art dealing with automotive or architectural subjects. Especially needs science and technological pieces as assigned per layout. Samples returned by SASE. Reports back on future assignment possibilities. Provide tear sheet to be kept on file for future assignments. "After seeing portfolios, I photocopy or photostat those samples I feel are indicative of the art we might use." Reports whenever appropriate job is available. Buys first publishing rights.
Tips: "More and more scientific magazines have entered the field. This has provided a larger base of technical artists for us. Be sure your samples relate to our subject matter, i.e., no rose etchings, and be sure to include a tear sheet for our files."

POPULAR WOODWORKING, 1300 Galaxy Way, Concord CA 94520. Editor: David Camp. Emphasizes woodworking for the small shop woodcraftsperson or advanced hobbyist. Bimonthly. Circ. 25,000. Prefers simultaneous submissions "only if clearly indicated." Original artwork returned after publication if requested. Sample copy $2.95; art guidelines free for SASE.
Cartoons: Uses 2 cartoons/issue; buys all from freelancers. Accepts themes of woodworking frustrations, problems, mistakes, etc. Accepts single, double or multiple panel with or without gagline; b&w line drawings. Send query letter with roughs or finished cartoons to be kept file; will not be kept more than a year. Material not kept on file is returned by SASE. Reports within 6 weeks. Buys all rights or negotiates. Payment varies ($5-10/cartoon); on publication.
Illustrations: Buys illustrations or diagrams that accompany articles. Send query letter to be kept on file. Reports within 6 weeks. Buys all rights or negotiates. Payment varies; on publication.
Tips: "You'll never know until you try. We always appreciate your time and effort, and we review each submission carefully. We do our very best to assist you in any way we can with your article, and know, through your experience, you have a lot to share with other woodworkers. So—put down your planes, pick up your typing paper, and tell us all about it."

POWER, McGraw-Hill, Inc., 1221 Avenue of the Americas, New York NY 10020. (212)512-2440. Art Director: Kiyo Komoda. Emphasizes the systems and equipment for the use and conservation of energy.

For power generation and plant energy systems. Monthly plus 2 annuals. Original artwork returned after publication, on request only.
Illustrations: Uses 30 illustrations/issue on energy systems. Buys 30%/issue from freelancers; most are graphs, charts and mechanical line drawings. Especially needs "graphs, charts, diagrams with more imagination or creative dramatization of what they represent." Works on assignment only. Send query letter with brochure showing art style or tear sheets and photostats. Samples returned by SASE. Reports in 1 week. Call to schedule an appointment to show a portfolio, which should include original/final art, final reproduction/product and tear sheets. Buys one-time and reprint rights. Cover: Pays $150-500, color. Inside: Pays $30-300, color; $10-200, b&w line drawings; on acceptance.
Tips: "We prefer artists with clean and crisp line works. They should know about color separation and the use of Zipatone. Young artists welcomed. Follow the specs—especially those arts with deadlines. I'll never recall any artist if he or she fails to meet specs or deadlines."

***POWER TRANSMISSON DESIGN**, 1111 Chester Ave., Cleveland OH 44114. (216)696-0300. Contact: Managing Editor. Readers are designers, users and maintainers of industrial power transmission equipment. Monthly. Circ. 50,500.
Cartoons: Uses 1 cartoon/issue; buys 50% from freelancers. Themes "should relate to design, manufacture, use, maintenance or government regulation of such power transmission components as bearings, controls, drives or motors." Also uses editorial cartoons; "please query." Prefers single panel b&w line drawings with gagline. Send finished cartoons. SASE. Reports in 2 weeks. Buys one-time rights. Pays $25 for b&w on publication.

PRAYING, Box 410335, Kansas City MO 64141. (816)531-0538. Editor: Arthur N. Winter. Estab. 1983. Emphasizes spirituality for everyday living for lay catholics and members of mainline Protestant churches; primarily Catholic, non-fundamentalist. "Starting point: The daily world of living, family, job, politics, is the stuff of religious experience and Christian living." Bimonthly. Circ. 15,000. Accepts previously published material. Original artwork not returned after publication. Sample copy and art guidelines available.
Cartoons: Buys 1-2 cartoons/issue from freelancers. Especially interested in cartoons that spoof fads and jargon in contemporary spirituality, prayer and religion. Prefers single panel with gagline; b&w line drawings. Send query letter with samples of style to be kept on file. Material not filed is returned by SASE. Reports within 2 weeks. Buys one-time rights. Pays $25, b&w; on acceptance.
Illustrations: Buys 2-3 illustrations/issue from freelancers. Prefers contemporary interpretations of traditional Christian symbols to be used as incidental art; also drawings to illustrate articles. Send query letter with samples to be kept on file. Prefers photostats, tear sheets and photocopies as samples. Samples returned if not interested or return requested by SASE. Reports within 2 weeks. Buys one-time rights. Pays $25, b&w; on acceptance.

THE PRESBYTERIAN RECORD, 50 Wynford Dr., Don Mills, Ontario M3C 1J7 Canada. (416)441-1111. Production Editor: Mary Visser. Published 11 times/year. Deals with family-oriented religious themes. Circ. 75,771. Original artwork returned after publication. Simultaneous submissions and previously published work OK. Free sample copy and artists' guidelines.
Cartoons: Buys 1-2 cartoons/issue; buys from freelancers. Interested in some theme or connection to religion. Send roughs. SASE. Reports in 2 weeks. Pays on publication.
Illustrations: Buys 1 illustration/year on religion. "We use freelance material, and we are interested in excellent color artwork for cover." Any line style acceptable— should reproduce well on newsprint. Works on assignment only. Send query letter with brochure showing art style or tear sheets, photocopies and photographs. Samples returned by SASE. Reports in 2 weeks. To show a portfolio, mail appropriate materials; portfolio should include original/final art, color, tear sheets and b&w. Buys all rights on a work-for-hire basis. Pays $50, color washes and opaque watercolors, cover; pays $10-20, b&w line drawings, inside; on publication.
Tips: "We don't want any 'cute' samples (in cartoons). Prefer some theological insight in cartoons; some comment on religious trends and practices."

PRESBYTERIAN SURVEY, 341 Ponce de Leon Ave. NE, Atlanta GA 30365. (404)873-1549. Art Director: Linda Colgrove. Emphasizes Presbyterian-related features and news, issues facing the church, Christian life. Monthly. Circ. 200,000. Sample copy available.
Cartoons: Runs 1/issue on topics which speak to the issues of the day. Prefers finished cartoons. Reports in 6 weeks. Pays 20, b&w.
Illustrations: Buys 2/issue. Works on assignment only. Send query letter with brochure showing art style or tear sheets and photocopies. Samples not returned. Reports only if interested. To show a portfolio, mail final reproduction/product, tear sheets and photostats. Negotiates rights purchased. Pays $250 b&w, cover; $250 b&w, inside; on acceptance.

PREVENTION, 33 E. Minor St., Emmaus PA 18049. (215)967-5171. Executive Art Director: Wendy Ronga. Emphasizes health, nutrition, fitness, cooking. Monthly. Circ. 3 million. Returns original artwork after publication. Sample copy available.
Cartoons: Buys 2-3 cartoons/issue from freelancers. Prefers themes of health, pets, fitness. Considers single panel with gagline; b&w line drawings, b&w washes. Samples of style are filed; unused roughs or finished cartoons are returned by SASE within 2 weeks. Reports back only if interested. Buys one-time rights.
Illustrations: Buys about 20 illustrations/issue from freelancers. Themes are assigned on editorial basis. Works on assignment only. Send samples to be kept on file. Prefers tear sheets or slides as samples. Samples not filed are returned by SASE. Reports back only if interested. Buys one-time rights.

PREVIEWS MAGAZINE, Suite 245, 919 Santa Monica Blvd., Santa Monica CA 90401. (213)458-3376. Editor: Jan Loomis. Emphasizes community events for upper middle-class, well-educated, sophisticated audience. Monthly. Circ. 37,000. Original artwork returned after publication. Sample copy and art guidelines free for SASE.
Cartoons: Buys 1-2 cartoons/issue from freelancers. Prefers single panel with gagline; b&w line drawings or washes. Send query letter with samples of style or roughs to be kept on file. Material not filed is returned by SASE. Reports within 1 month. Negotiates rights purchased. Write for appointment to show portflio. Pays $17.50, b&w; on publication.
Illustrations: Specific topics illustrated. Works on assignment only. Send query letter with brochure, resume, business card and photocopies to be kept on file. Samples not filed are returned by SASE. Reports within 1 month. Negotiates rights purchased. Write or call for appointment to show portfolio. Pays $100, b&w and $200, color, cover; $50, b&w and $100, color, inside/page; on publication.

PRIMAVERA, University of Chicago, 1212 E. 59th St., Chicago IL 60637. (312)684-2742. Contact: Editorial Board. Emphasizes art and literature by women for readers interested in contemporary literature and art. Annual. Circ. 800. Original artwork returned after publication. Sample copy $4; art guidelines available for SASE.
Illustrations: Buys 15-20 illustrations/issue from freelancers. Receives 5 illustrations/week from freelance artists. "We are open to a wide variety of styles and themes. Work must be in b&w with strong contrasts and should not exceed 7" high x 5" wide." Especially needs work with women figures. Send finished art. Reports in 1-2 months. "If the artist lives in Chicago, she may call us for an appointment." Acquires first rights. "We pay in 2 free copies of the issue in which the artwork appears"; on publication.
Tips: "It's a good idea to take a look at a recent issue. Artists often do not investigate the publication and send work which may be totally inappropriate. We publish a wide variety of women artists. We have increased the number of graphics per issue. Send us a variety of prints. It is important that the graphics work well with the literature and the other graphics we've accepted. Our decisions are strongly influenced by personal taste and the work we know has already been accepted. Will consider appropriate cartoons and humorous illustrations."

***PRINTING IMPRESSIONS**, 401 N. Broad St., Philadelphia PA 19108. (215)238-5366. Design Director: Albert Gaspari. Magazine for printing and graphic arts industry. Monthly. Circ. 95,000. Accepts previously published material. Original artwork returned after publication. Sample copy and art guidelines available.
Ilustrations: Buys 1 illustration/issue from freelancers. Send query letter with brochure showing art style or photocopies and photographs. Samples not filed are returned only if requested. Reports only if interested. Write to schedule an appointment to show a portfolio, which should include original/final art, final reproduction/product and tear sheets. Negotiates rights purchased. Pays on acceptance.

PRIVATE PILOT/AERO/KITPLANES, Box 6050, Mission Viejo CA 92690. (714)240-6001. Contact: Editor. For owners/pilots of private aircraft, student pilots and others aspiring to attain additional ratings and experience. Circ. 80,000. Monthly. Receives 5 cartoons and 3 illustrations/week from freelance artists.
Cartoons: Buys 2-4 cartoons/issue on flying. Send finished artwork. SASE. Reports in 3 months. Pays $35, b&w; on publication.
Illustrations: Send query letter with samples. SASE. Reports in 3 months. Pays $50-100, b&w; $75-150, color. "We also use spot illustrations as column fillers; buys 1-2 spot illustrations/issue. Pays $25/spot."
Tips: "Know the field you wish to represent; we get tired of 'crash' gags submitted to flying publications."

PRIVATE PRACTICE, Suite 470, 3535 NW 58th St., Oklahoma City OK 73112. (405)943-2318. Art Director & Design Director: Rocky C. Hails. Editorial features "maintenance of freedom in all fields of

medical practice and the effects of socioeconomic factors on the physician." Monthly. Circ. 180,000. Free sample copy and artists' guidelines.
Cartoons: Buys cartoons regularly, approximately 3/issue. Send query letter with resume and samples or arrange interview to show portfolio. SASE. Reports in 2-3 weeks. Negotiates pay; pays on acceptance.
Illustrations: Buys 1-4 illustrations/issue on politics, medicine, finance and physicians' leisure activities. Also uses artists for 4-color cover illustration. Uses some humorous illustrations and occasionally cartoon-style illustrations. Especially looks for "craftsmanship, combined with an ability to communicate complex concepts." Send a brochure showing art style or tear sheets, photostats, slides and photographs. Reports in 2-3 weeks. Call to schedule an appointment to show a portfolio, which should include original/final art, final reproduction/product, color, tear sheets, photostats, photographs and b&w. Buys first and reprint rights. Cover: Pays $200-400, unlimited to media, all forms, cover; pays $60-110, color washes and opaque watercolors; $40-100, b&w line drawings and washes inside; on acceptance.
Tips: "Provide reproductions of several illustrations (that demonstrate the uniqueness of your style) to leave with the art director. Include a postcard requesting my response to the applicability of their work to Private Practice. This is efficient for both the art director and artist. It is encouraging to see the wide variety of 'accepted' styles and the design revisions going on in major journals. There is a rapid movement toward interactive production techniques freeing the designer for greater experimentation and creativity."

PROBE, Baptist Brotherhood Commission, 1548 Poplar, Memphis TN 38104. (901)272-2461. Art Director: Herschel Wells. Christian-oriented mission magazine for boys grades 7-12. Monthly. Original artwork returned after publication, if requested. Circ. 50,000. Previously published, photocopied and simultaneous submissions OK.
Illustrations: Uses 3 illustrations/issue; buys 1/issue from freelancers. Interested in family life with emphasis on boys and their interests. "Our freelance needs are usually directed toward a specific story; we frequently use humorous illustrations and sometimes use cartoon-style illustrations; we very seldom use art submitted on spec." Send brochure showing art style or resume and roughs to be kept on file. Reports in 3 weeks. Samples returned by SASE. Buys first North American serial rights. Cover: Pays $200-250, full-color; $100-180, b&w line drawings, washes and gray opaques. Inside: Pays $45-120, b&w line drawings, washes and gray opaques. Pays on acceptance.

PROCEEDINGS, U.S. Naval Institute, Annapolis MD 21402. (301)268-6110. Editor-in-Chief: Fred H. Rainbow. Emphasizes Navy, Marine Corps, Coast Guard, and related maritime and military topics for sea service professionals. Monthly. Circ. 100,000. Original artwork returned after publication. Sample copy and art guidelines available.
Cartoons: Buys a few cartoons/issue on various themes from freelancers. No rigid format guidelines. Prefers b&w line drawings. Send query letter with samples of style to be kept on file, except for rejections. Material not filed is returned only if requested. Reports within a few weeks. Negotiates rights purchased. Pays $25-50, b&w and color; on acceptance.
Illustrations: Buys approximately 5 illustrations/issue on varied themes from freelancers. Works on assignment only. Send query letter with tear sheets or photocopies. Samples returned only if requested. Reports within a few weeks. Negotiates rights purchased. Pays $200, color, cover; $25-50, b&w and color, inside; on acceptance.

PROFESSIONAL AGENT, 400 N. Washington St., Alexandria VA 22314. (703)836-9340. Editor and Publisher: Janice J. Artandi. For independent insurance agents and other affiliated members of the American Agency System. Monthly. Circ. 40,000. Original artwork returned after publication. Free sample copy.
Illustrations: Buys 3/issue from freelancers. Local artists preferred. Provide samples to be kept on file for future assignments. Buys first-time North America rights.
Tips: Conceptual approach often required. Trends are toward "more realism and fewer cartoons." Looks for "whether an artist's work is reproducible. Editorial experience is helpful."

PROFESSIONAL ELECTRONICS, 2708 W. Berry St., Ft. Worth TX 76109. (817)921-9062. Editor-in-Chief: Wallace S. Harrison. For professionals in electronics, especially owners, technicians and managers of consumer electronics sales and service firms. Bimonthly. Circ. 10,000. Samples of previously published cartoons furnished on request.
Cartoons: Buys themes on electronics sales/service, association management, conventions and directors' meetings. Prefers single panel with gagline. Submit art with SASE. Reports in 2 weeks. Buys first rights. Pays $10, b&w line drawings; on acceptance.
Illustrations: Buys assigned themes. Submit art and SASE. Reports in 2 weeks. Buys first rights. Pays $30-60, b&w line drawings, cover. Pays $10-15, b&w line drawings, inside; on acceptance.

***PROFILES MAGAZINE**, 533 Stevens Ave., Solana Beach CA 92075. (619)481-4352. Art Director: Lorraine Leung. Magazine emphasizing computers. Monthly. Circ. 95,000. Original artwork returned after publication. Sample copy and art guidelines available.
Cartoons: Buys 4 cartoons/issue. Prefers multiple panel, with or without gagline; b&w line drawings. Send finished cartoons to be kept on file. Write for appointment to show portfolio. Samples not filed are not returned. Does not report back. Buys first rights or one-time rights.
Illustrations: Buys 4 illustrations/issue from freelancers. Works on assignment only. Send tear sheets, photostats, photocopies, slides and photographs. Samples not filed are not returned. Reports only if interested. To show a portfolio, mail original/final art, final reproduction/product, color, tear sheets, photostats, photographs and b&w. Buys one-time rights. Payment varies.

***PROFIT**, Box 1132, Studio City CA 91604. (818)789-4980. Associate Editor: Marjorie Clapper. Magazine emphasizing business news for the business community. Circ. 10,000/month. Original artwork not returned after publication. Sample copy $1.
Cartoons: Prefers single-panel; b&w line drawings or b&w washes. Send query letter with samples of style to be kept on file if acceptable. Write for appointment to show portfolio. Samples not filed are returned by SASE. Reports only if interested. Buys all rights. Payment varies.
Illustrations: Buys 0-12 illustrations/issue from freelancers. Works on assignment only. Send query letter with brochure showing art style or resume and samples. Samples returned by SASE. Reports only if interested. To show a portfolio, mail thumbnails, original/final art, final reproduction/product, tear sheets, b&w photographs and as much information as possible. Buys all rights. Payment varies. Pays on publication.

THE PROGRESSIVE, 409 E. Main St., Madison WI 53703. (608)257-4626. Art Director: Patrick JB Flynn. Monthly. Circ. 50,000. Free sample copy and artists' guidelines.
Illustrations: Buys 15 b&w illustrations/issue from freelancers. Works on assignment only. Send query letter with tear sheets and photocopies. Samples returned by SASE. Reports in 2 months. Portfolio should include final reproduction/product and tear sheets. Cover pays $250, b&w. Inside pays $75-150, b&w line or tone drawings/paintings, inside; on publication, cover. Buys first rights.
Tips: Do not send original art. Send appropriate return postage. "The most obvious trend in editorial work is toward more artistic freedom in idea and individual style. I think the successful art direction of a magazine allows for personal interpretation of an assignment."

***PSYCHIC GUIDE MAGAZINE**, Box 701, Providence RI 02901. (401)351-4320. Publisher: Paul Zuromski. Magazine emphasizing new age, natural living and metaphysical topics for people looking for tools to improve body, mind and spirit. Quarterly. Circ. 125,000. Original artwork returned after publication. Sample copy free for SASE with 90¢ postage.
Cartoons: Prefers new age, natural living and metaphysical themes. Prefers single panel with gagline; b&w line drawings. Send query letter with samples of style and roughs to be kept on file. Write to show a portfolio. Material not kept on file is returned by SASE. Reports within 3 months. Buys one-time reprint rights. Negotiates payment.
Illustrations: Buys 5-10 illustrations/issue from freelancers. Works on assignment only. Prefers line art with new age, natural living and metaphysical themes. Send query letter with resume, tear sheets, photostats, photocopies, slides and photographs. Samples not filed are returned by SASE. Reports within 3 months. To show a portfolio, mail original/final art and tear sheets. Buys one-time reprint rights. Negotiates payment. Pays on publication.

PUBLIC CITIZEN, #605, 2000 P St., Washington DC 20036. (202)293-9142. Editor: Elliott Negin. Emphasizes consumer issues for the membership of Public Citizen, a group founded by Ralph Nader in 1971. Bimonthly. Circ. 50,000. Accepts previously published material. Returns original artwork after publication. Sample copy available.
Cartoons: Buys 1/issue from freelancer. Prefers single panel with gagline; b&w line drawings. Send query letter with samples of style to be kept on file. Call for appointment to show portfolio. Material not filed is returned by SASE. Reports only if interested. Buys first rights or one-time rights. Pays on publication.
Illustrations: Buys up to 10/issue. Send query letter with samples to be kept on file. Write or call for appointment to show portfolio, which should include tear sheets or photocopies. Samples not filed are returned by SASE. Reports only if interested. Buys first rights or one-time rights. Pays $275, b&w, cover; and $40-150, b&w, inside; on publication.

QUARRY MAGAZINE, Box 1061, Kingston, Ontario K7L 4Y5 Canada. (613)376-3584. Editor: Bob Hilderley. Emphasizes poetry, fiction, short plays, book reviews—Canadian literature. Audience: Canadian writers; libraries (public, high school, college, university); persons interested in current new

writing. Quarterly. Circ. 1,000. Original artwork returned after publication. Sample copy $3.
Illustrations: Buys 3-5 illustrations/issues from freelancers. No set preference on themes or styles; "we need high quality line drawings." Send query letter with originals or good photostats to be kept on file. Contact only by mail. Reports within 12 weeks. Buys first rights. Pays $25, b&w, cover; $25, b&w, inside. Pays on publication.

QUICK PRINTING, 3255 South US 1, Ft. Pierce FL 33482. (305)465-9450. Publisher: Robert Schweiger. Emphasizes quick printing for owners/managers of quick print, copying and small commercial printshops. Monthly. Circ. 28,500. Returns original artwork after publication. Sample copy free for SASE with 80¢ postage; call for art guidelines.
Cartoons: Buys 1 cartoon/issue from freelancers. Prefers themes related to quick printing/copying, the plight of managers and computers. Prefers double panel with gagline; b&w line drawings. Send query letter with roughs to be kept on file. Material not filed is returned by SASE only if requested. Reports within 1 month. Negotiates rights purchased. Pays $10 for b&w; on acceptance.
Illustrations: Buys 3 illustrations/issue from freelancers. Works on assignment only. Send query letter to be kept on file. "No samples necessary." Reports within 1 week. Negotiates rights purchased. Pays $100 for b&w and $150 for color, cover; $25 for b&w and $40 for color, inside; on acceptance.

***QUILT WORLD**, Box 337, Seabrook NH 03874. Editor: Sandra L. Hatch. Concerns patchwork and quilting. Bimonthly. SASE. Previously published work OK. Original artwork not returned after publication. Sample copy with 9x12" SASE with 66¢ postage.
Cartoons: Buys 2 cartoons/issue from freelancers. Receives 25 submissions/week from freelancers. Uses themes "poking gentle fun at quilters." Send finished cartoons. Reports in 3 weeks if not accepted. "I hold cartoons I can use until there is space." Buys all rights. Pays on acceptance.

R-A-D-A-R, 8121 Hamilton Ave., Cincinnati OH 45231. Editor: Margaret Williams. For children 3rd-6th grade in Christian Sunday schools. Original artwork not returned after publication.
Cartoons: Buys 1 cartoon/month on animals, school and sports. Prefers to see finished cartoons. Reports in 6 weeks. Pays $10-15; on acceptance.
Illustrations: Uses 5 or more illustrations/issue. "Art that accompanies nature or handicraft articles may be purchased, but almost everything is assigned." Send tear sheets to be kept on file. Samples returned by SASE. Reports in 6 weeks. Buys all rights on a work-for-hire basis. Pays $60, line drawing, cover; pays $35-40, inside.

RADIO-ELECTRONICS, 500-B Bi-County Blvd., Farmingdale NY 11735. (516)293-3000. Editorial Director: Arthur Kleiman. Monthly. For electronics professionals and hobbyists. Circ. 211,000. Previously published work OK. Free sample copy.
Cartoons: Buys 3 cartoons/issue on electronics, service, hi-fi, computers and TV games; single panel. Mail art. SASE. Reports in 1 week. Buys first or all rights. Pays $35 minimum, b&w washes; on acceptance.

***RAG MAG**, Box 12, Goodhue MN 55027. Contact: Beverly Voldseth. Emphasizes poetry, graphics, fiction and reviews for small press, writers, poets and editors. Semiannually: fall and spring. Circ. 300. Accepts previously published material. Original artwork returned after publication. Sample copy $3; art guidelines free for SASE.
Cartoons: Buys 2 cartoons/issue from freelancers. Any theme or style. Prefers single panel or multiple panel with gagline; b&w line drawings. Send samples of styles or finished cartoons. Material returned in 2 months by SASE if unwanted. Reports within 2 months. Write for appointment to show a portfolio. Acquires first rights. Pays in copies only.
Illustrations: Buys 6 illustrations/issue from freelancers. Any style or theme. Send samples. Prefers tear sheets, photocopies, photostats as samples. Samples returned by SASE. Reports within 1 month. Write for appointment to show portfolio, which should include thumbnails, final reproduction/product, photostats, photographs, b&w PMTs. Acquires first rights. Pays in copies for b&w cover and inside.
Tips: "Realize I publish only 2 issues per year. I can use only 10-12 art pieces per year. I don't hold a lot in my files because I think artists should be sending their art work around. And even if I like someone's art work very much, I like to use new people."

RAILROAD MODEL CRAFTSMAN, Box 700, Newton NJ 07860. (201)383-3355. Editor: William Schaumburg. Emphasizes scale model railroads for all levels of enthusiasts. Covers full range of model railroading, including narrow-gauge, traction, period and modern-day equipment. Monthly. Buys all rights.
Illustrations: Uses scale line drawings of railroad equipment and structures requiring extensive knowledge of real/scale model railroading; 5x7 minimum. Write for payment rates.
Tips: "Freelancers should be active in the field of model railroading."

RAVE COMMUNICATIONS, 850 7th Ave., New York NY 10019. (212)977-7745. Creative Director: Cliff Sloan. Publishes program books: *Rock Bill*, *Soundcheck*, *Radio City Music Hall*, *Miller Time Concerts* and others. Emphasizes music, youth-oriented topics, fashion, film and trends for an audience 18-35 years old, clubgoers, trendsetters with musical interests. Monthly. Circ. 500,000. Returns original artwork after publication. Sample copy free for SASE with 35¢ postage.
Cartoons: Rarely buys cartoons. Prefers youth or musically oriented themes. Accepts single, double or multiple panel with gagline; b&w line drawings, b&w washes, color washes. Send query letter with samples of style to be kept on file. Write for appointment to show portfolio. Material not filed is returned by SASE. Reports only if interested. Buys first rights. Negotiates payment; pays on publication.
Illustrations: Buys 2 illustrations/issue from freelancers. Themes and styles are geared specifically to articles. Also buys "musical" cover art. Works on assignment only. Send query letter with brochure showing art style or photostats, tear sheets, photocopies, slides or photographs to be kept on file. Do not send unsolicited original work. Samples not filed are returned by SASE. Reports only if interested. Call to schedule an appointment to show a portfolio, which should include final reproduction/product, color, tear sheets, photostats, b&w and "anything they think is good." Buys first rights. Negotiates payment; pays on publication.

***READER**, 8471 Melrose Ave., Los Angeles CA 90069. Art Director: Miriam King. Newspaper emphasizing general interest/entertainment with emphasis on local stories for young professional adults. Weekly. Circ. 82,000. Accepts previously published material. Original artwork returned after publication if requested. Sample copy $1. Art guidelines free for SASE with 22¢ postage.
Illustrations: Buys 3 illustrations/issue from freelancers. Works on assignment only. Prefers illustrations that show "thinking." Send query letter with brochure showing art style. Samples not filed are returned by SASE. Reports only if interested. Call to schedule an appointment to show a portfolio, which should inlcude original/final art, final reproduction/product and b&w. Buys one-time rights. Pays $75, b&w, $125, 2-color and $200, 4-color, cover; $30, b&w and $50, color, inside; on publication.

***READERS NUTSHELL**, 1776 Lake Worth Rd., Lake Worth FL 33460. Concerns insurance and safety. Bimonthly.
Cartoons: Buys 3-4/issue on family, office and general themes. Send finished art. SASE. Reports in 2 weeks. Pays $10, b&w; on publication.

***REASON MAGAZINE**, Box 40105, Santa Barbara CA 93103. (805)963-5993. Contact: Art Director. Emphasizes current affairs, public policy from libertarian point of view for the "intelligent, literate person concerned with public issues." Monthly. Circ. 28,000. Original artwork returned after publication.
Cartoons: Uses 1 cartoon/issue ("could use more if funny"); buys all from freelancers. "Jokes should be *funny*, well-drawn, with an irreverent view toward government." Prefers single-panel, with gagline; b&w line drawings, b&w washes. Send query letter with samples of style to be kept on file. Material not kept on file returned by SASE. Reports only if interested. Buys first rights. Call for appointment to show a portfolio. Payment depends on size, $25 and up.
Illustrations: Uses 8 illustrations/issue; buys all from freelancers. Works on assignment only. Send query letter with brochure showing art style, tear sheets, photocopies, slides or photographs to be kept on file. Write for appointment to show a portfolio, which should include original/final art, final reproduction/product, color, tear sheets, photographs and b&w. Samples returned by SASE if not kept on file. Reports in 3 weeks. Buys first rights. Pays color, cover, depending on size; $100 b&w; $175 color, inside; on publication.

***RELIGION TEACHER'S JOURNAL**, Box 180, Mystic CT 06355. (203)536-2611. Design Artist: William Baker. Magazine emphasizing how to teach religion for primarily volunteer catechists (religion teachers) who need practical suggestions for teaching religion. Published 7 times year. Circ. 40,000. Accepts previously published material. Original artwork returned after publication. Sample copy and art guidelines free for SASE.
Cartoons: Buys 1-2/issue from freelancers. Prefers humorous situations with children in religion class as themes. Send query letter with samples of style and finished cartoons to be kept on file only as per arrangement with artist. Write for appointment to show portfolio. Samples not filed are returned by SASE. Reports within 2 weeks. Buys first rights or one-time rights. Pays $25, b&w.
Illustrations: Not presently in need of illustrations.

Market conditions are constantly changing! If this is 1988 or later, buy the newest edition of Artist's Market *at your favorite bookstore or order directly from* Writer's Digest Books.

RESIDENT AND STAFF PHYSICIAN, 80 Shore Rd., Port Washington NY 11050. (516)883-6350. Executive Editor: Anne Mattarella. Emphasizes hospital medical practice from clinical, educational, economic and human standpoints. For hospital physicians, interns and residents. Monthly. Circ. 100,000.
Cartoons: Buys 3-4 cartoons/year. "We occasionally publish sophisticated cartoons in good taste dealing with medical themes." Interested in "inside" medical themes. Contact only through artist's agent; agent should send query letter with brochure showing art style or resume, tear sheets, photostats, photocopies, slides and photographs. Call or write to schedule an appointment to show a portfolio, which should include final reproduction/product, color, tear sheets and b&w. Reports in 2 weeks. Buys all rights. Pays $25; varies for color; also buys spots; pays $10-50; on acceptance.
Illustrations: "We commission qualified freelance medical illustrators to do covers and inside material. Artists should send sample work." Pays $600, color, cover; payment varies for inside work; on acceptance.
Tips: "We like to look at previous work to give us an idea of the artist's style. Since our publication is clinical, we require highly qualified technical artists who are very familiar with medical illustration. Sometimes we have use for nontechnical work. We like to look at everything. We need material from the *doctor's* point of view, *not* the patient's."

RESPIRATORY THERAPY, 1640 5th St., Santa Monica CA 90401. Publisher: Martin Waldman. Art Director: Tom Medsger. Emphasizes technological, medical and professional news.
First Contact & Terms: Send brochure/flyer to be kept on file for possible future assignment. Reports only when assignment is available. Buys all rights. Pays $60 and up, spot art; $400, full-color cover; on acceptance.

RESTAURANT BUSINESS MAGAZINE, 633 Third Ave., New York NY 10017. (212)986-4800. Art Director: Michael Delia. Emphasizes restaurants/hotels for restaurateurs. Monthly. Circ. 110,000. Original artwork returned after publication. Art guidelines available.
Illustrations: Uses 8-10 illustrations/issue. Works on assignment only. Call Tracey J. Grant for appointment to show a portfolio. Prefers to see b&w portfolio with a few samples of color work. Negotiates rights purchased and payment. Pays $500-1,000 b&w and $500-1,000 color, cover; $100-250 b&w inside; within 60 days.

RESTAURANT HOSPITALITY, 1100 Superior Ave., Cleveland OH 44114. (216)696-7000. Associate Editor: David Farkas. Emphasizes commercial foodservice industry for owners, managers, chefs, etc. Circ. 121,000. Accepts previously published material "if exclusive to foodservice trade press." Original artwork returned after publication. Sample copy $4.
Illustrations: "We want to build a file of freelance illustrators to whom we can assign projects." Works on assignment only. Send query letter with brochure, resume, business card, samples and tear sheets to be kept on file. Prefers photographs as samples, 5x7" or larger, but will accept photostats. Reports back to the artist. Pays $250-400, cover; $100-300, inside; on acceptance.

THE RETIRED OFFICER, 201 N. Washington St., Alexandria VA 22314. (703)549-2311. Art Director: M.L. Woychik. For retired officers of the seven uniformed services; concerns recent military, history, humor, holiday anecdotes, travel, human interest, second career opportunities and current affairs. Monthly. Circ. 350,000.
Illustrations: Buys illustrations on assigned themes. (Generally uses Washington DC area artists.) Send query letter with resume and samples.

REVIEW, East-West Network Inc., 34 E. 51st St., New York NY 10022. (212)888-5900. Art Director: Kevin Fisher. "In-flight Eastern Airlines publication; features fiction and nonfiction articles on art, sports, travel, the media, business, self-improvement and health." Monthly. Simultaneous submissions and previously published work OK. Sample copy $2.
Illustrations: Buys 1-4 illustrations/issue on current events, sports, travel, the media and self-improvement. Call or query with portfolio. Buys first rights. Inside: Pays $450, color; $50-350, b&w; on publication.

THE REVIEW OF THE NEWS, 345 Concord Ave., Belmont MA 02178. (617)489-0605. Editor: Scott Stanley. "News magazine with a conservative and free market orientation for people interested in conservative oriented news in capsulated form." Weekly. Circ. 60,000. Free sample copy (mention *Artist's Market*).
Cartoons: Uses 3 + cartoons/issue, most by freelancers. Receives 1,000 submissions/week from freelancers. Interested in general humor for a conservative family audience. Format: single panel b&w line drawings with gagline. Sizes must be 2x2½ or 4½x2¼. Prefers finished cartoons. SASE. Reports in 8 weeks. Will send tear sheets. Buys all rights. Pays $25; on acceptance.

RISK MANAGEMENT, 205 E. 42nd St., New York NY 10017. (212)286-9292. Production Manager: Edith Reimers. Emphasizes the insurance trade for insurance buyers of *Fortune 500* companies. Monthly. Circ. 10,500. Sample copy available.
Illustrations: Uses 3-4 illustrations/issue; buys 2-4 every issue from freelancers. Prefers color illustration or line with color styles; no humorous themes. Works on assignment only. Send brochure showing art style or tear sheets, photostats, photocopies, slides and photographs. Call for appointment to show portfolio, which should include final reproduction/product, color and tear sheets. Prefers printed pieces as samples; original work will not be kept on file after 1 year. Samples not kept on file are returned only if requested. Buys one-time rights. Pays $100 color, cover (2nd use); $175-225 b&w and $250-300 color, inside; on acceptance.
Tips: When reviewing an artist's work, looks for "neatness, strong concepts, realism with subtle twists and sharply defined illustrations."

RN MAGAZINE, 680 Kinderkamack Rd., Oradell NJ 07649. (201)262-3030. Readers are registered nurses. Monthly. Circ. 330,000. Sample copy $2.
Cartoons: "We are not currently buying cartoons but plan to in the future.
Illustrations: Buys 10 illustrations/issue from freelancers. Works on assignment only. Provide promo material to be kept on file for future assignments. Samples returned by SASE. Prefers b&w line drawings and washes for inside and color washes, oils, acrylics, etc. for cover. Editorial and medical art is bought. Buys first world serial rights, reprints and promotional rights. Pays $50-300 for inside b&w, $300-1,000 for color cover and $200-500 for inside color; on publication.
Tips: "The art director sees very little need for outside freelance design help but is willing to accept new ideas and their execution by freelancers if the need arises. Freelance artists should contact the art administrator to schedule an appointment."

ROAD KING MAGAZINE, Box 250, Park Forest IL 60466. (312)481-9240. Editor: George Friend. Emphasizes services for truckers, news of the field, CB radio and fiction; leisure oriented. Readers are over-the-road truckers. Quarterly. Circ. 224,000.
Cartoons: Uses 4 cartoons/issue; buys all from freelancers. Receives 1-2 submissions/week from freelancers. Interested in over-the-road trucking experiences. Prefers single panel b&w line drawings with gagline. Send finished cartoons. SASE. Reports in 2-4 months. Buys first North American serial rights. Pays $25 for b&w; on acceptance.
Tips: "Stick to our subject matter. No matter how funny the cartoons are, we probably won't buy them unless they are about trucks and trucking."

***ROCKBILL MAGAZINE**, 850 7th Ave., New York NY 10019. (212)977-7745. Creative Director: Cliff Soan. Magazine emphasizing music, movies and youth oriented topics for young entertainment-oriented trendsetters, nightclub goers. Monthly. Circ. 500,000. Original artwork returned after publication. Sample copy free for SASE.
Illustrations: Buys 1 illustration/issue from freelancers. Works on assignment only. Send query letter with tear sheets, photostats and slides. Samples not filed are returned by SASE. Reports only if interested. Call to schedule an appointment to show a portfolio, which should include original/final art, final reproduction/product and tear sheets. Buys first rights. Negotiates payment. Pays on publication.

RODALES NEW SHELTER, 33 E. Minor St., Emmaus PA 18049. (215)967-5171. Art Director: John Pepper. Emphasizes "do-it-yourself energy conservation, home design, repair and management for 30-40-year-old, college-educated males; homeowners, handymen." Published 9 times/year. Circ. 700,000. Receives 1-2 cartoons and 5 illustrations/week from freelance artists. Previously published material OK. Original artwork returned after publication "if requested." Free sample copy for SASE "and samples of artist's work"; art guidelines available for SASE.
Cartoons: Presently uses 1-2/issue—"we're very interested in more. We're open to all styles. We always have an eye open for energy-related cartoons." Prefers single or double panel. Send finished cartoons (or published cartoons as sample of style). Samples returned by SASE. Reports in 2-4 weeks. Buys all rights. Pays up to $40, b&w; on publication.
Illustrations: Buys 15-20 illustrations/issue from freelancers. Works on assignment only, "although we have used cold submissions in the past." Send business card, brochure, flyer, samples, and tear sheets—"anything to help us decide to use an artist"—to be kept on file for possible future assignments; call or write for appointment to show portfolio. Samples not kept on file are returned by SASE. Reports in 2-4 weeks. Buys all rights. Pays $15-200, inside b&w line drawings; $15-200, inside b&w washes; $50-300, inside color washes; "just prior to publication."
Tips: "Become familiar with the needs and style of publication. Have a unique, innovative style that works with the nature of the magazine."

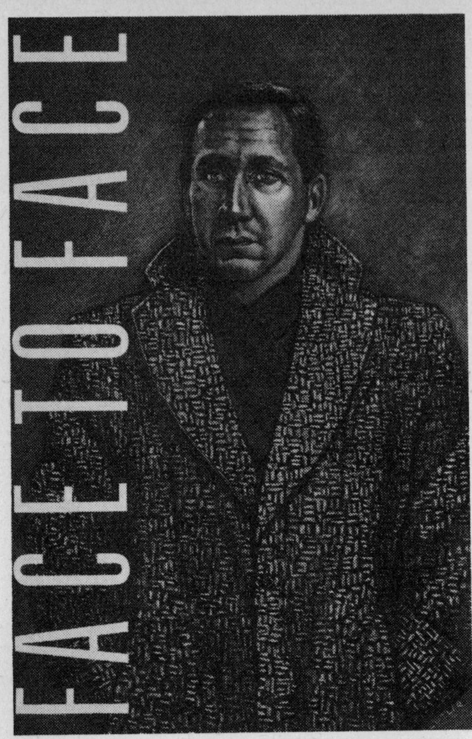

Cliff Sloan, editor of Rockbill Magazine, asked freelance artist David Cutler "to capture the aging Townshend, grown out of his bad boy image, and convey a sense of mileage in his eyes and also an air of responsibility." Cutler, of Spring Valley, New York, received $400 for one-time rights to the artwork, which was completed in oils and colored pencils.

ROOM OF ONE'S OWN, Box 46160, Station G, Vancouver, British Columbia V6R 4G5 Canada. Contact: Editor. Emphasizes feminist literature for general and academic women, and libraries. Quarterly. Circ. 1,200. Original artwork returned after publication. Sample copy $2.75; art guidelines free for SAE (nonresidents include IRC).
Illustrations: Buys 3-5 illustrations/issue from freelancers. Prefers good b&w line drawings. Send samples to be kept on file. Accepts photostats, photographs, slides or original work as samples. Samples not kept on file are returned by SAE (nonresidents include IRC). Reports within 1 month. Buys first rights. Pays $50, b&w, cover; $25, b&w, inside; on publication.

ROSICRUCIAN DIGEST, Rosicrucian Order, AMORC, San Jose CA 95191. (408)287-9171, ext. 320. Editor/Art Director: Mr. Robin M. Thompson. Fraternal magazine featuring articles on science, philosophy, psychology, metaphysics, mysticism, and the arts for men and women of all ages—"inquiring minds seeking answers to the important questions of life." Monthly. Circ. 70,000. Does not accept previously published material. Returns original artwork to the artist. Sample copy available.
Illustrations: Buys a maximum of 10/year. Send query letter with samples. Prefers photostats, tear sheets and photocopies as samples. Samples returned with SASE. Reports back within 30-60 days. Negotiable payment. Pays on acceptance.

THE ROTARIAN, 1600 Ridge Ave., Evanston IL 60201. Editor: Willmon L. White. Associate Editor: Jo Nugent. Art Director: P. Limbos. Emphasizes general interest and business and management articles. Service organization for business and professional men, their families, and other subscribers. Monthly. Sample copy and editorial fact sheet available. Also uses artists for cover illustration. Most illustrative work, apart from knockout designs that might be considered as covers, is assigned.
Cartoons: Buys 4-5 cartoons/issue. Interested in general themes with emphasis on business. Avoid topics of sex, national origin, politics. Send query letter with brochure showing art style. Reports in 1-2 weeks. Buys all rights. Pays $50 on acceptance.
Illustrations: Buys assigned themes. Most editorial illustrations are commissioned. Buys average 3 or more illustrations/issue; 6 humorous illustrations/year. Send query letter with brochure showing art style. Reports within 10 working days. Buys all rights. Call to schedule an appointment to show a portfolio, which should include original/final art, final reproduction/product, color and photographs. Pays on acceptance.

Tips: "Artists should set up appointments with art director to show their portfolios. Preference given to area talent." Conservative style and subject matter.

***RUBICON**, 853, rue Sherbrooke ouest, Montréal Québec H3A 2T6 Canada. (514)286-0652. Art Director: Su Schnee. Magazine emphasizing contemporary writing and visual art for artists and writers. Bi-annual. Circ. 750. Sample copy $4; art guidelines free for SASE with International Reply Coupon.
Illustrations: Buys 50 illustrations/issue from freelancers. Prefers contemporary themes and styles. Send resume, tear sheets, photostats, photocopies, slides and photographs, ("*not* originals"). Samples not filed are returned by SASE. Reports within 3 months. To show a portfolio, mail appropriate materials, which should include thumbnails, roughs, tear sheets, photostats, photographs and b&w. Buys first rights. Payment is "minimal;" on publication.

RUN CW, Communications/Peterborough, 80 Pine St., Peterborough NH 03458. Art Director: Glenn Suokko. Estab. 1984. Emphasizes computing for business and families who own and operate a Commadore computer. Monthly. Circ. 225,000. Accepts previously published material. Original artwork returned after publication. Sample copy and art guidelines available.
Illustrations: Buys 5 illustrations/issue from freelancers. Prefers exciting, creative themes or styles. Works on assignment only. Send query letter with brochure, resume, business card, tear sheets, photographs, or promotional material. Samples not filed are returned by SASE. Reports only if interested. Negotiates rights purchased. Pays $300-600, b&w; $500-1,000, color, cover; $300-600, b&w; $500-1,200, color, inside; on acceptance.

***RUNNER'S WORLD**, 135 N. 6th St., Emmaus PA 18049. (215)967-5171. Art Director: Kay Douglas. Emphasizes serious, recreational running. Monthly. Circ. 350,000. Returns original artwork after publication. Sample copy available.
Cartoons: Buys 2/issue from freelancers. Prefers themes on running. Considers single panel with gagline; b&w line drawings, b&w washes. Samples of style are filed; unused roughs or finished cartoons are returned by SASE within 1 month. Buys one-time rights. Pays $100, b&w on acceptance.
Illustrations: Buys average of 4/issue from freelancers. Themes assigned are humorous, related to running and medical basis. Works on assignment only. Send samples to be kept on file. Prefers tear sheets or slides and samples. Samples not filed are returned by SASE. Reports back only if interested. Buys one-time rights.

RUNNING TIMES, Suite 20, 14416 Jefferson Davis Hwy., Woodbridge VA 22191. (703)643-1740. Emphasizes distance running. Readers include road runners, cross country and adventure runners; people interested in fitness. Monthly. Sample copy $1.95.
Illustrations: Uses 3-5 illustrations/issue, all from freelancers. Prefers b&w line drawings for inside, and color illustrations for inside and cover. Especially needs color illustrations for feature articles and small b&w drawings. Prefers to see finished art, portfolio or tear sheet to be kept on file. SASE. Reports in 4 weeks. Buys all rights on a work-for-hire basis. Pays $35-200 for inside and $250 minimum for cover; on publication. Buys first North American serial rights.
Tips: "We need more art and would like to see more samples or portfolios!"

***RURAL KENTUCKIAN**, Box 32170, Louisville KY 40232. Editor: Gary Luhr. Magazine emphasizing Kentucky-related and general feature material for Kentuckians living outside metropolitan areas. Monthly. Circ. 293,000. Accepts previously published material. Original artwork returned after publication if requested. Sample copy available. All artwork is solicited by the magazine to illustrate upcoming articles.
Illustrations: Buys 2-3 illustrations/issue from freelancers. Works on assignment only. Prefers b&w line art. Send query letter with resume and samples. Samples not filed are returned only if requested. Reports within 2 weeks. Buys one-time rights. Pays $50, b&w, cover, $30-50, b&w, inside; on acceptance.

***RV'N ON**, 10417 Chandler Blvd., N. Hollywood CA 91601. Editor/Publisher: Kim Quimet. Emphasizes camping and recreational vehicles for full- and part-time RVers. Monthly. Circ. 5,500. Original work returned after publication by SASE. Sample copy $1 with SASE.
Cartoons: Uses cartoons occasionally as filler; buys all from freelancers. Receives 4 cartoons/week from freelance artists. Interested in camping, children, RVs, etc. themes; single panel with or without gagline, b&w line drawings. Send query letter with samples of style. Samples returned by SASE. Reports in 6 weeks. Buys reprint rights. Pays $5, b&w; 60 days after publication.
Illustrations: Currently uses none but "would be interested." Especially needs illustrations for holidays as well as small "logo" type items for various columns. Would like illustrations for Christmas cover and other holidays. Interested in camping, outdoors and RV themes. Provide resume, brochure, flyer

and samples to be kept on file for possible future assignments. Send query letter with roughs or samples of style. Samples returned by SASE. Reports in 6 weeks. Buys first and reprint rights. Pays in copies only.

Tips: "RVers are reading more on how to save energy, but still use their RVs.

SACRAMENTO MAGAZINE, Box 2424, Sacramento CA 95811. (916)446-7548. Art Director: Chuck Donald. Emphasizes Sacramento city living for audience 25-54 years old, executives/professionals, married, middle-upper income. Monthly. Circ. 30,000. Accepts previously published material and simultaneous submissions. Sample copy free for SASE.
Cartoons: Buys 6 cartoons/issue. Pays $25 b&w.
Illustrations: Uses 5 illustrations/issue. Send query letter with brochure showing art style or tear sheets, photostats, slides and photographs to be kept on file. Accepts any type of samples which fairly represent artist's work. Reports only if interested. Negotiates rights purchased. Call or write to schedule an appointment to show a portfolio, which should include original/final art and final reproduction/product. Pays $300 color, cover; $125 b&w and $200 color, inside; on acceptance.

SAILING, 125 E. Main St., Port Washington WI 53074. (414)284-3494. Editor: William F. Schanen III. Emphasizes all aspects of sailing (sailboats only). Monthly. Circ. 30,000. Original artwork returned after publication upon special request. Previously published work OK. Sample copy $2.50.
Illustrations: Uses very few illustrations/year. Interested in action sailing only. Works on assignment. Send resume, finished art, or samples of style. Samples returned by SASE, if requested. Provide letter of inquiry to be kept on file for future assignments. Reports in 2-3 weeks. Buys one-time rights.

THE ST. LOUIS JOURNALISM REVIEW, 8606 Olive Blvd., St. Louis MO 63132. (314)991-1699. Contact: Charles L. Klotzer. Features critiques of St. Louis media—print, broadcasting, TV, cable, advertising, public relations and the communication industry. Monthly. Circ. 12,000.
Cartoons: "We have never bought a cartoon, but will consider." Subject should pertain to the news media; preferably local. Query. SASE. Reports in 4-7 weeks. Pays on publication.
Illustrations: Query with samples. SASE. Reports in 4-6 weeks. Pays $15-25 each (negotiable) for b&w and color illustrations pertaining to the news media (preferably local); on publication.

SALES AND MARKETING MANAGEMENT, 633 3rd Ave., New York NY 10017. (212)986-4800. Art Director: Tom Loria. For sales managers. Biweekly. Circ. 50,000. Simultaneous submissions OK. Pays on acceptance.
Cartoons: Buys 36 cartoons/year. Interested in sales management and selling; single panel. Prefers art. SASE. Reports in 1 week. Buys all rights but may reassign rights to artist after publication. Pays $30-45, b&w; on acceptance.
Illustrations: Buys 2 illustrations/issue. SASE. Reports in 1 week. Buys all rights but may reassign rights to artist after publication. Pays $30-50, b&w spot line drawings; on acceptance.

SALT LICK PRESS, 1804 E. 38½ St., Austin TX 78722. Editor/Publisher: James Haining. Published irregularly. Circ. 1,500. Previously published material and simultaneous submissions OK. Original artwork returned after publication. Sample copy $3.
Illustrations: Uses 12 illustrations/issue; buys 2 from freelancers. Receives 2 illustrations/week from freelance artists. Interested in a variety of themes. Send brochure showing art style or tear sheets, photostats, photocopies, slides and photographs. Samples returned by SASE. Reports in 6 weeks. To show a portfolio, mail roughs photostats, photographs and b&w. Negotiates payment; on publication. Buys first rights.

SALT WATER SPORTSMAN, 186 Lincoln St., Boston MA 02111. (617)426-4074. Editor-in-Chief/Art Director: Barry Gibson. Emphasizes resorts, areas, techniques, equipment and conservation. For saltwater fishermen, fishing equipment retailers and resort owners. Monthly. Circ. 116,000. Original artwork returned after publication. Free sample copy and artists' guidelines.
Illustrations: Buys 3 illustrations/issue from freelancers. Receives 3 submissions/week from freelancers. Works on assignment only. Interested in themes covering all phases of salt water sport fishing—mood, how-to, etc. Send query letter with brochure to be kept on file. SASE. Reports in 4 weeks. Reports back on future assignment possibilities. Write to schedule an appointment to show a portfolio, which should include final reproduction/product. Buys first North American serial rights. Pays $400 b&w, cover, payment varies for inside; on acceptance.
Tips: "Let us see samples of work relevant to our topics/areas. New artists should strive for accuracy in portraying fish, equipment, etc."

SAN FRANCISCO FOCUS MAGAZINE, 680 8th St., San Francisco CA 94103. (415)553-2800. Art Director: Laura Lamar. The city magazine for the San Francisco Bay area including PBS program guide.

Audience is 45-year-old average, male/female, professional-managerial, post-graduate, homeowner; average income $70-160,000. Monthly. Circ. 190,000. Sometimes accepts previously published material. Original artwork returned after publication.

Illustrations: Uses 3-6 illustrations/issue; buys 2-6 illustrations/issue from freelancers. Uses a variety of styles according to editorial content; top-level professional artists *only*. Assignments made on basis of individual style and proficiency. Send resume, business card and samples to be kept on file. No original work—only reproductions (prints, slides, tear sheets, photocopies, stats) as samples. Samples returned by SASE only if requested; prefers to keep on file. No "guidelines" sent. Reports only if interested. Please; no calls—only letters. Send samples to "Attn: Artists File". Buys one-time rights. Pays $100-500 color, cover; $50-150, b&w and $150-400, color, inside; on publication (30 days after receipt of invoice).

Tips: "Send samples for us to keep on file; please don't call or just send letter or resume—we need to see the *work*."

SAN FRANCISCO MAGAZINE, 450 Sansome St., San Francisco CA 94111. (415)956-6262. Contact: Design Director. Emphasizes general interest topics of local or national scope for San Francisco, Northern California Bay area and residents. Monthly. Circ. 55,000.

Illustrations: Uses 8-10 spot illustrations, 3-4 illustrations for major pieces; buys all from freelancers. Theme and style depend on the article. Works on assignment only. Send brochure, samples and tear sheets to be kept on file; call for appointment, submit portfolio. Samples not filed are returned only by SASE. Buys one-time rights.

SAN JOSE STUDIES, San Jose State University, San Jose CA 95192. (408)277-2841. Editor: Fauneil J. Rinn. Emphasizes the arts, humanities, business, science, social science; scholarly. Published 3 times/year. Circ. 500. Original artwork returned after publication. Sample copy $5.

Cartoons: Number of cartoons/issue varies. Interested in "anything that would appeal to the active intellect." Prefers single panel b&w line drawings. Send slides. SASE. Reports in 2 weeks. Buys first North American serial rights. Pays in 2 copies of publication, plus entry in $100 annual contest.

Illustrations: Number of illustrations/issue varies. Prefers b&w line drawings. Send slides. SASE. Reports in 2 weeks. To show a portfolio, mail photostats, photographs and b&w. Buys first North American serial rights. Pays in 2 copies of publication, plus entry in $100 annual contest.

Tips: "We would be interested in cartoons, and humorous and cartoon-style illustrations especially if accompanied by some description of the artist's techniques, purpose, conception and development of the artwork."

***SANTA BARBARA MAGAZINE**, 123 W. Padre St., Santa Barbara CA 93105. Art Director: Trish Reynales. Magazine emphasizing Santa Barbara culture and community. Bimonthly. Circ. 11,000. Original artwork returned after publication if requested. Sample copy $2.95.

Illustrations: Buys about 3 illustrations/issue from freelance artists. Works on assignment only. Send query letter with brochure, resume, tear sheets and photocopies. Reports back within 6 weeks. To show a portfolio, mail original/final art, final reproduction/product/color, tear sheets and b&w, will contact if interested. Buys first rights. Payment varies; on acceptance.

***SATELITE ORBIT, SATELITE DEALER**, Box 53, Boise ID 83707. (208)322-2800. Executive Art Director: Brian Larkowski. Magazine emphasizing satellite television industry for home satelite dish owners and dealers. Monthly. Circ. Satellite Orbit—300,000; Satellite Dealer—20,000. Accepts previously published material. Original artwork returned after publication. Sample copy available.

Cartoons: Buys 1-3 cartoons/issue from freelancers. Prefers single panel, with gagline; b&w washes. Send query letter with samples of style to be kept on file. Material not kept on file is returned by SASE. Reports within 1 month. Negotiates rights purchased. Pays $150, b&w; $200-250, color.

Illustrations: Buys 5-15 illustrations/issue from freelancers. Works on assignment only. Send query letter with tear sheets, photocopies, slides and photographs. Samples not filed are returned only if requested. Reports within 1 month. To show a portfolio, mail color, tear sheet, photographs and b&w. Negotiates rights purchased. Pays $500-1,500, b&w and $500-1,500, color, cover; $100-1,000, b&w and $100-1,000, color, inside; on publication.

THE SATURDAY EVENING POST, The Saturday Evening Post Society, 1100 Waterway Blvd., Indianapolis IN 46202. (317)636-8881. General interest, family-oriented magazine. Published 9 times/year. Circ. 600,000. Sample copy $1.

Cartoons: Cartoon Editor: Timothy Ehrgott. Buys 10 cartoons/issue. Prefers single panel with gaglines. Receives 100 batches of cartoons/week from freelance cartoonists. "We look for cartoons with neat line or tone art. The content should be in good taste, suitable for a general-interest, family magazine. It must not be offensive while remaining entertaining. We prefer that artists first send SASE

Close-up

Chris Wilhoite
Art Director
Saturday Evening Post

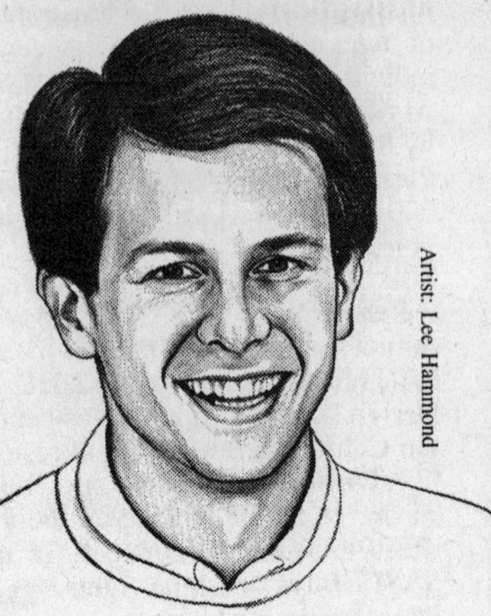

Chris Wilhoite, art director of *The Saturday Evening Post*, says he'd rather do most of his shopping at a department store than browse in and out of dozens of specialty shops. He feels the same way about commissioning freelance artists for his magazine.

"If you are really good, you can have a specialty," says Wilhoite, "but today, it is best not to get tied down to having only one style that you can present all the time. If you have control over different mediums and techniques, and are willing to explore different subject matter, you'll get more work."

You also should study the particular style and content of each magazine before submitting samples of your work. "*The Saturday Evening Post* is a very traditional, nostalgic, Americana magazine," he says of the Indianapolis-based publication. "There's quite a difference between its style and that of *Rolling Stone* or *Smithsonian*."

In its 200-plus years of existence, *The Post* has printed millions of cartoons and illustrations—some by the likes of Norman Rockwell, Mark English and countless other art world heavyweights. "Many of our articles and illustrations deal with history, medicine and religion, and we use a lot of portraits and humorous pieces," Wilhoite continues. "We appeal to, say, the 44-year-old farmer in Des Moines, Iowa or the suburban housewife in Indiana."

This traditional atmosphere colors the technical aspects of *The Saturday Evening Post* as well. "Since I've become art director, we've made a few minor stylistic changes like putting captions closer to pictures, but the overall design of the magazine stays the same," he says. "Therefore, we would not use airbrush or New Wave-type designs."

Besides making sure *The Saturday Evening Post* keeps its characteristic look every month, Wilhoite spends two or three days per issue reviewing resumés and portfolios from freelancers all over the United States who hope to get an illustration or two in the magazine. He estimates that 150 inquiries come across his desk each month.

"We have about three artists in house," the art director explains, "so the majority of our work is done by freelancers. I'm amazed at the high quality of illustration now. People are really trying hard—so the market is very competitive."

When searching for people who have an edge over everyone else, Wilhoite looks at experience as well as style. "I'm afraid to use new artists if they're not accustomed to deadlines," he explains. "I also want people who can do, on the first try, an illustration pretty close to what I want.

"Generally, I initiate the idea for each illustration," Wilhoite continues. "I'll send the artist the manuscript he is to illustrate, and then I like him to call me when he receives it, so we can discuss it and I can answer any questions he might have. After I set the deadline and payment terms, the illustrator sends me a rough sketch for approval and then goes on with the finished art."

The first part of this procedure is especially important to remember, because the art director says that many freelancers send their original artwork to him out of the blue, thinking he'll publish it in *The Saturday Evening Post* if it fits the magazine's style and is executed well. There is only a slim chance that the piece will match one of the topics in an upcoming issue. Wilhoite prefers not to receive originals.

"It seems like twice a week I get a painting from somebody," he says. "Even if it's good, I always have to send it back, because it won't fit in my accordion file folders. I like to receive expendable material that I can keep for future reference, and believe me, I *do* keep files on artists who have potential."

Slides, photocopies and tearsheets are the types of materials that Wilhoite and other art directors like to receive. "Personally, I like to see something really slick with a nice design on a good, coated stock of paper," he adds. "And above all, I like to see each sample illustration intact with the actual ad or printed page where it appeared, so I can see if it accomplished what it was supposed to do."

—Betsy Schoellkopf

Wilhoite appreciates the "fresh, loose, creative style" of humorous illustrator Don Twain of Montclair, New Jersey. "His illustrative interpetations of the manuscripts I send him are always of the highest calibre."

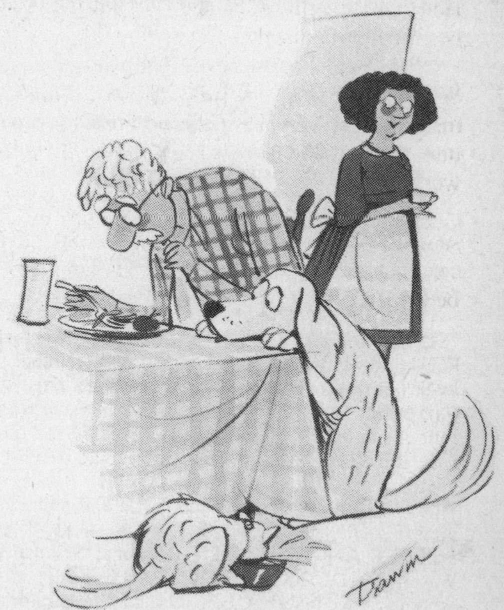

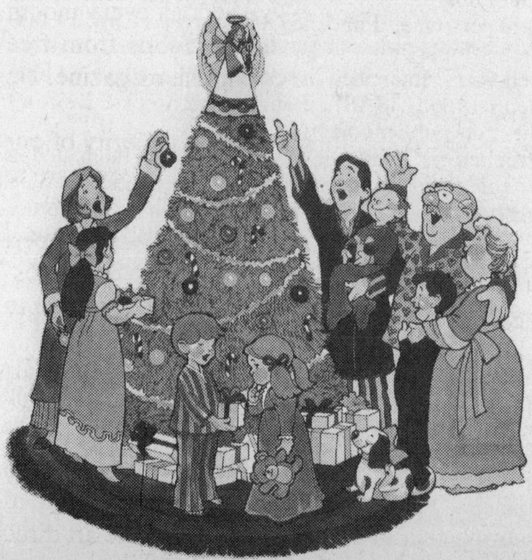

Frank Cotham, from Bartlett, Tennessee, is "a great humorous cartoonist," says Wilhoite. "He also does illustrations but is more of a cartoonist." Cotham's Christmas scene reflects the family orientation of the Saturday Evening Post.

for guidelines and then review recent issues. Political or violent cartoons are not used." SASE. Reports in 3 weeks. Buys all rights. Pays $125, b&w line drawings and washes, no pre-screened art; on publication.
Illustrations: Art Director: Chris Wilhoite. Uses average of 3 illustrations/issue; buys 90% from freelancers. Send query letter with brochure showing art style or resume and samples. To show a portfolio, mail original/final art. Buys all rights, "generally. All ideas, sketchwork and illustrative art are handled through commissions only and thereby controlled by art direction. Do not send original material (drawings, paintings, etc.) or 'facsimiles of' that you wish returned." Cannot assume any responsibility for loss or damage. "If you wish to show your artistic capabilities, please send unreturnable, expendable/sampler material (slides, tear sheets, xeroxes, etc.)."

SAVINGS INSTITUTIONS, 111 E. Wacker Dr., Chicago IL 60601. (312)644-3100. Art Director: George Glatter. Emphasizes the savings and loan business for people in savings and loan or related businesses. Monthly. Circ. 35,000. Accepts previously published material. Original artwork returned after publication. Sample copy available.
Cartoons: Buys 0-1 cartoon/issue from freelancers.
Illustrations: Buys 0-2 illustrations/issue from freelancers; some are humorous or cartoon-style illustrations. Works on assignment only. Send query letter with samples to be kept on file. Call for appointment to show portfolio. Samples not kept on file are returned only if requested. Reports only if interested. Buys first rights, one-time rights, reprint rights or negotiates rights purchased. Negotiates payment. Pays on acceptance.

SCHOLASTIC INC., 730 Broadway, New York NY 10003. (212)505-3000. Editorial Design Director: Dale E. Moyer. Emphasizes educational classroom supplements dealing with almost all curriculum areas: reading, writing, science, math, social studies, art, computers, home economics for K-12; professional teaching magazine. Weekly, monthly and bimonthly. Circulation varies per publication. Original artwork returned after publication. Sample copy available.
Illustrations: Themes depend on editorial content. Works on assignment only. Call for appointment to show portfolio. Prefers tear sheets in portfolio. Reports only if interested. Buys one-time rights or negotiates rights purchased. Pays $250-300, b&w, and $400, color, cover; $100 minimum, b&w, and $250, color, inside; on acceptance.

***SCHOOL SHOP**, Box 8623, Ann Arbor MI 48107. Publisher and Executive Editor: Alan H. Jones. For industrial and technical education personnel. Published 10 times/year. Circ. 45,000. Original artwork not returned after publication. Free artist's guidelines.
Cartoons: Buys 1 + cartoons/issue; buys all from freelancers. Interested in vocational/industrial education; single, double or multiple panel. Send query letter, resume and finished cartoons. SASE. Reports in 6 weeks. To show a portfolio, mail roughs, tear sheets and b&w. Buys all rights. Pays $20, b&w line drawings; on publication.
Tips: "Must be related to industrial and technical education."

SCIENCE AND CHILDREN, National Science Teachers Association, 1742 Connecticut Ave. NW, Washington DC 20009. (202)328-5800. Editor-in-Chief: Phyllis Marcuccio. For elementary and middle school science teachers, educators, administrators and personnel. Published 8 times/year. Circ. 17,000. Original artwork not returned after publication. Free sample copy.
Cartoons: Buys 1 cartoon/issue; buys all from freelancers. Interested in science-technology and environment; multi-panel with gaglines. Prefers finished cartoons. SASE. Reports in 2 weeks. Buys all rights. Pays $15-25, b&w line drawings and washes; on publication.
Illustrations: Buys 10-15 illustrations/issue from freelancers. Works on assignment only. Interested in education and environment; light, stylized, realistic science illustrations (no stock illustrations). Samples returned by SASE. Send resume, brochure, flyer or photocopy of work to be kept on file for future assignments. Prefers to see portfolio with samples of style. Reports in 2 weeks. Buys all rights on a work-for-hire basis. Pays $50-150, b&w line drawings, washes and color, cover. Pays $10-100, b&w line drawings and washes, inside; on publication.
Tips: "Looking for new talent. Realistic drawings of children important—scientific renderings secondary."

SCIENCE NEWS, 1719 N St. NW, Washington DC 20036. (202)785-2255. Art Director: Wendy McCarren. Emphasizes all sciences for teachers, students and scientists. Weekly. Circ. 175,000. Accepts previously published material. Original artwork returned after publication. Sample copy free for SASE with 39¢ postage.
Illustrations: Buys 10 illustrations/year from freelancers. Prefers realistic style, scientific themes; uses some cartoon-style illustrations. Works on assignment only. Send query letter with photostats or pho-

tocopies to be kept on file. Samples returned by SASE. Reports only if interested. Buys one-time rights. Write to schedule an appointment to show a portfolio, which should include original/final art. Pays variable rates; on acceptance.
Tips: Uses some cartoons and cartoon-style illustrations.

***SCOTT STAMP MONTHLY MAGAZINE**, Box 828, Sidney OH 45365. Art Director: Edward Heys. Magazine emphasizing stamp collecting for beginning through advanced collectors. Monthly. Circ. 22,000. Accepts previously published material. Original artwork returned after publication. Sample copy available for SASE ($1.24 postage).
Cartoons: Buys 1-2 cartoons/issue. Prefers single, double or multiple panel with gagline; b&w line drawings; b&w washes. Send query letter with brochure showing art style, resume, tear sheets, photostats, photocopies and slides. Material not kept on file is returned by SASE. Reports only if interested. Buys reprint rights. Pays $10-25, b&w.
Illustrations: Works on assignment only. Reports only if interested. To show a portfolio, mail roughs, photostats and tear sheets. Samples not filed are returned by SASE. Buys one-time and reprint rights. Pays $300, color, cover; $25-100, b&w, and $50-200, color, inside; on acceptance.

SCREEN PRINTING MAGAZINE, 407 Gilbert Ave., Cincinnati OH 45202. (513)421-2050. Art Director: Ann Campbell. Emphasizes screen printing for screen printers, distributors and manufacturers of screen printing equipment and screen printed products. Monthly. Circ. 12,000. Accepts previously published material and simultaneous submissions in noncompeting magazines. Sometimes returns original artwork after publication. Sample copy available.
Illustrations: Uses 3 illustrations/issue; buys all from freelancers. Send query letter with samples and tear sheets. Prefers photostats as samples. Samples returned by SASE if requested. Reports only if interested. Call for appointment to show portfolio. Negotiates rights purchased. Payment is open. Pays on acceptance.
Tips: "Ask for sample copy of the magazine."

SEA, Box 1337, Newport Beach CA 92663, (714)646-3963. Contact: Art Director. Emphasizes recreational boating for owners or users of recreational boats, both power and sail, primarily for cruising and general recreation; some interest in boating competition; regionally oriented to 13 Western states. Monthly. Circ. 50,000. Whether original artwork returned after publication depends upon terms of purchase. Free sample copy for SASE.
Illustrations: Uses 6-8 illustrations/issue; buys 90% from freelancers. "I often look for a humorous illustration to lighten a technical article." Works on assignment only. Send query letter with business card and tear sheets to be kept on file. Samples returned. Reports in 6 weeks. Negotiates rights purchased and payment. Pays on publication (negotiable).
Tips: "We will accept students for portfolio review with an eye to obtaining quality art at a reasonable price. We will help start career for illustrators and hope that they will remain loyal to the publication which helped launch their career."

SECURITY MANAGEMENT, c/o ASIS, Suite 1200, 1655 N. Fort Myer Dr., Arlington VA 22209. (703)522-5800. Managing Editor: Pamela James Blumgart. For security managers who protect assets, personnel and information of organizations. Monthly. Circ. 25,000. Previously published and simultaneous submissions acceptable if not submitted to competitors. "Want exclusive in security market. Please state where else work has been submitted." Original artwork not returned after publication. Sample copy sent without charge.
Cartoons: Rarely use cartoons. Receives 10-20 submissions/week from freelancers. Interested in "management and protection—avoid emphasizing 'dumb-guard' aspect—our readers are fighting that image and don't appreciate it." Prefers to see roughs. SASE. Reports within 1 month. Negotiates rights purchased. Pays $10-15, b&w; on acceptance.
Illustrations: Buys 1-3 illustrations/issue; buys all from freelancers. Works on assignment only. Send query letter with brochure, business card and photostats to be kept on file. Reports in 1 month. Negotiates rights purchased. Pays $400-500, color, cover; $50-225, b&w and $100-400, color, inside; on publication.
Tips: There is an "increasing use of color in our operation. Artists should get a couple of copies and try to get to know the orientation of the content. We aren't interested in the 'clip art' look or sunset scenes or beautiful women. Send samples of illustrations from other professional/business publications."

SEEK, 8121 Hamilton, Cincinnati OH 45231. (513)931-4050, ext. 365. Emphasizes religion/faith. Readers are young adult to middle-aged adults who attend church and Bible classes. Quarterly in weekly issues. Circ. 45,000. Free sample copy and guidelines; SASE appreciated.
Cartoons: Editor: Eileen H. Wilmoth. Uses 1-2 cartoons/quarter. Buys "church or Bible themes—

contemporary situations of applied Christianity." Prefers single panel b&w line drawings with gagline. Send finished cartoons, photocopies and photographs. SASE. Reports in 1-3 weeks. Buys first North American serial rights. Pays $10-15 on acceptance.
Illustrations: Art Director: Frank Sutton. Buys 13-15 illustrations/issue. Uses cover & inside b&w line drawings and washes. Works on assignment only; needs vary with articles used. Arrange appointment to show portfolio. Reports in 1 week. Pays $60, cover or full page art; $40, inside pieces; on acceptance. Buys first North American serial rights.
Tips: "We use only 2-color work. The art needs to be attractive as well as realistic. I look for detail, shading and realism."

SELLING DIRECT, 6255 Barfield Rd., Atlanta GA 30328. (404)256-9800. Editor: Robert C. Rawls. Emphasizes selling as a profession and ways for sales persons to improve their techniques and their overall businesses. "For independent businessmen and women who sell door-to-door, by the party-plan method, through direct mail or phone solicitation; products or services are bought directly from manufacturers and sold by our readers." Monthly. Circ. 500,000. Free sample copy and artists' guidelines.
Cartoons: Uses 1-2 cartoons/issue, all from freelancers. Interested in current events, direct selling, salespeople not employed by retailers and self-employed entrepreneurs without employees; single panel. "Cartoons should illustrate the typical door-to-door or office-to-office salesperson, those who sell party-plan, or phone solicitors." SASE. Reports in 6-8 weeks. Buys all rights. Pays $15 minimum, b&w line drawings; on publication.
Tips: "Freelance cartoonists should submit their work along with complete mailing information and a Social Security number. I am interested in cartoons that present a positive aspect of direct selling, and not those whose main purpose is to downgrade salespeople or the industry."

THE SENSIBLE SOUND, 403 Darwin Dr., Snyder NY 14226. Editor: John A. Horan. Emphasizes audio equipment for hobbyists. Quarterly. Circ. 4,900. Accepts previously published material and simultaneous submissions. Original artwork returned after publication. Sample copy $2.
Cartoons: Uses 4 cartoons/year. Prefers single panel, with or without gagline; b&w line drawings. Send samples of style and roughs to be kept on file. Material not kept on file is returned by SASE. Reports within 30 days. Negotiates rights purchased; pay rate varies; on publication.

SERVICE BUSINESS, 1916 Pike Pl. #345, Seattle WA 98101. (206)622-4241. Publisher: Bill Griffin. Managing Editor: Martha M. Ireland. Technical, management and human relations emphasis for self-employed cleaning and maintenance service contractors. Quarterly. Circ. 4,500. Prefers first publication material, simultaneous submissions OK. Original artwork returned after publication if requested by SASE. Sample copy $1.
Cartoons: Buys 1-2 cartoons/issue from freelancers. Must be relevant to magazine's readership. Prefers b&w line drawings.
Illustrations: Buys approximately 12 illustrations/issue, including some humorous and cartoon-style illustrations, from freelancers. Send query letter with samples. Samples returned by SASE. Buys first publication rights. Reports only if interested. Payment modest, on publication.
Tips: "Art and design trends include more interest in using graphics."

***73 MAGAZINE**, Peterborough NH 03458. Publisher: Wayne Green. For amateur radio operators and experimenters. Sample copy $2. 50. Especially needs work for covers.
Illustrations: Uses 15 illustrations/issue. Receives 3 illustrations/week from freelance artists. Works on assignment only. Does not return samples. Does not report back on possible future assignments. Send query letter with resume to be kept on file for future assignments. Buys all rights on a work-for-hire basis. Submit rough line drawings for assignment as oil, watercolor or pastel covers. Pays $5-20, spot art; $75/page, finished art; on acceptance.

THE SHINGLE, One Reading Center, Philadelphia PA 19107. (215)238-6300. Managing Editor: Nancy L. Hebble. Law-related articles, opinion pieces, news features, book reviews, poetry and fiction for the Philadelphia Bar Association membership (9,400 members). Quarterly. Circ. 10,000. Sample copy free for SASE.
Illustrations: Buys 2 illustrations/issue. Works on assignment only. Prefers fine line drawings; themes vary with editorial content. Send query letter with brochure, resume, business card and photostats to be kept on file. Samples not kept on file are not returned. Reports only if interested. To show a portfolio, mail appropriate materials, which should include original/final art and final reproduction/product. Buys first or one-time rights. Pay rate varies; pays on acceptance.

SHUTTLE SPINDLE & DYEPOT, 65 LaSalle Rd., West Hartford CT 06117. (203)233-5124. Art Director: Tracy McHugh. Emphasizes weaving and fiber arts for hobbyists and professionals. Quarterly.

Circ. 18,500. Accepts simultaneous submissions. Original artwork returned after publication. Sample copy $4.75; art guidelines free for SASE.
Illustrations: Uses 20-30 illustrations/issue; buys "very few" from freelancers. Prefers b&w line drawings. Works on assignment only. Send query letter with resume, tear sheets, photocopies and slides to be kept on file. Reports within 6 weeks. To show a portfolio, mail color and b&w or write to schedule an appointment. Buys first American serial rights. Honorarium only; no payment; on publication. Credit line given.

SIERRA—THE SIERRA CLUB BULLETIN, 730 Polk St., San Francisco CA 94109. (415)776-2211. Art Director: Bill Prochnow. Emphasizes conservation and environmental politics for young adults on up who are well educated, activists, outdoor oriented and politically well informed with a dedication to conservation. Bimonthly. Circ. 310,000. SASE. Reports in 4 weeks.
Illustrations: Buys 1-2 illustrations/issue from freelancers. Interested in all styles—images of politically aware environmental concerns and also humorous illustrations. Works on assignment only. Send resume, business card, tear sheets and copies of illustrations to be kept on file for future assignments. SASE if material is to be returned. Buys one-time rights. Pay varies; on publication.

***SIGN OF THE TIMES—A CHRONICLE OF DECADENCE IN THE ATOMIC AGE**, Box 70672, Seattle WA 98107-0672. Contact: M. Souder. Magazine emphasizing fiction, photography and graphics for sleazy up-scale college-educated readers. Published twice yearly. Circ. 750. Accepts previously published material. Original artwork returned after publication if requested. Sample copy $3.50.
Cartoons: Buys 1-2 cartoons/issue from freelancers. Prefers single or multiple panel with or without gagline; b&w line drawings. Send query letter to be kept on file. Material not kept on file is returned by SASE. Reports within 6 weeks. Buys reprint rights. Negotiates payment.
Illustrations: Buys 1-2 illustrations/issue from freelancers. Prefers amusing themes. Send query letter with photocopies. Samples not filed are returned by SASE. Reports within 6 weeks. To show a portfolio, mail original/final art. Buys reprint rights. Negotiates payment; on publication.

THE SINGLE PARENT, Suite 1008, 7910 Woodmont Ave., Bethesda MD 20814. (301)654-8850. Editor: Donna Duvall. Assistant Editor: Liz Bostick. Emphasizes family life in all aspects—raising children, psychology, divorce, remarriage, etc.—for all single parents and their children. Bimonthly. Circ. 210,000. Accepts simultaneous submissions and occasionally accepts previously published material. Original artwork returned after publication. Sample copy available.
Cartoons: Uses 1-2 cartoons/issue; buys all from freelancers. Prefers divorce, children, family life topics with single parenthood as the theme. Prefers cartoons with gag line; b&w line drawings, b&w washes. Send finished cartoons to be kept on file. Material not kept on file returned by SASE. Reports within 6 weeks. Write or call for appointment to show portfolio. Negotiates rights purchased. Pays $15, b&w; on publication.
Illustrations: Uses 5-6 illustrations/issue; buys all from freelancers. Works on assignment only for specific stories. Assignments based on artist's style. Send query letter with brochure, resume, samples to be kept on file. Write or call for appointment to show portfolio. Prefers photostats, photographs, tear sheets as samples. Samples returned by SASE if not kept on file. Reports within 6 weeks. Negotiates rights purchased. Pays $75, b&w, cover; $50-75, b&w, inside. Pays on publication.

SKI, 380 Madison Ave., New York NY 10017. Editor: Richard Needham. Emphasizes instruction, resorts, equipment and personality profiles. For new and expert skiers. Published 8 times/year. Previously published work OK "if we're notified."
Cartoons: Especially needs cartoons of skiers with gagline. "Artist/cartoonist must remember he is reaching experienced skiers who enjoy 'subtle' humor." Mail art. SASE. Reports immediately. Buys first serial rights. Pays $50, b&w skiing themes; on publication.
Illustrations: Mail art. SASE. Reports immediately. Buys one-time rights. Pays $100-300, full-color art; on acceptance.

SKIING, 1 Park Ave., New York NY 10016. (212)503-3900. Art Director: Barbara Rietschel. Emphasizes skiing, ski areas, ski equipment, instruction for young adults and professionals; good incomes. Published 7 times a year, September-March. Circ. 445,000. Original artwork returned after publication. Sample copy free for SASE.
Cartoons: Uses 1 cartoon/issue. Prefers single panel with or without gagline; b&w line drawings or washes. Send query letter with samples of style to be kept on file. Material returned by SASE if not kept on file. Reports only if interested. Write or call for appointment. Buys first or one-time rights. Pays $35-50; on acceptance.
Illustrations: Uses 2 illustrations/issue on average. Works on assignment basis. Send query letter with samples to be kept on file. Call for appointment to show portfolio. Prefers photostats or photocopies as

samples. Samples returned by SASE if not kept on file. Reports only if interested. Buys first or one-time rights. Pays $75-250, b&w, inside; on acceptance.
Tips: "Know the magazine. I find it very annoying when artists come in, never having looked at a copy of *Skiing*."

SKY AND TELESCOPE, 49 Bay State Rd., Cambridge MA 02238. Editor: L.J. Robinson. Art Director: Penny Margolskee. Concerns astronomy, building telescopes and space exploration for enthusiasts and professionals. Monthly. Circ. 75,000. Buys all rights. Pays on publication.
Cartoons: Buys 4/year on astronomy, telescopes and space exploration; single panel preferred. Pays $25, b&w line drawings, washes and gray opaques. Send query letter with samples.
Illustrations: Buys assigned themes. Send query letter with previously published work. Pays $50-150.

***SLIMMER MAGAZINE**, Suite 3000, 3420 Ocean Park Blvd., Santa Monica CA 90405. (213)450-0900. Art Director: Mark D'Antoni. Magazine emphasizing woman's fitness and lifestyle for women 25-45 years old, active. Bimonthly. Circ. 200,000. Original artwork returned after publication. Art guidelines available.
Illustrations: Buys 2-5 illustrations/issue from freelancers. Works on assignment only. Prefers various fitness, food, excercise themes. Send tear sheets and color photocopies. Samples not filed are returned only if requested. Reports only if interested. Call to schedule an appointment to show a portfolio, which should include original/final art, color, tear sheets and photographs. Negotiates rights purchased. Pays on publication.

THE SMALL POND MAGAZINE OF LITERATURE, Box 664, Stratford CT 06497. Emphasizes poetry and short prose. Readers are people who enjoy literature—primarily college educated. Published 3 times/year. Circ. 300. Sample copy $2.50; art guidelines for SASE.
Illustrations: Editor: Napoleon St. Cyr. Uses 1-5 illustrations/issue. Receives 50-75 illustrations/year. Uses "line drawings (inside and on cover) which generally relate to natural settings, but have used abstract work completely unrelated." Especially needs line drawings; "fewer wildlife drawings and more unrelated-to-wildlife material." Send query letter with finished art or production quality photocopies, 2x3" minimum 8x11" maximum. SASE. Reports in 2 weeks. Pays 2 copies of issue in which work appears on publication. Buys copyright in convention countries.
Tips: "Need cover art work, but inquire first or send for sample copy." Especially looks for "smooth clean lines, original movements, an overall impact. Don't send a heavy portfolio, but rather 4-6 black-and-white representative samples with SASE. Better still, send for copy of magazine ($2.50)."

SOAP OPERA DIGEST, 254 W. 31st St., New York NY 10001. Art Director: Andrea Wagner. Emphasizes soap opera and prime-time drama synopses and news. Biweekly. Circ. 825,000. Accepts previously published material. Returns original artwork after publication upon request. Sample copy available, with SASE.
Cartoons: Publishes 3/issue. Seeks humor on soaps, drama or TV. Accepts single or double panel with or without gagline; b&w line drawings, b&w washes. Send query letter with samples of style to be kept on file. Material not filed is returned by SASE. Pays $35, b&w; on publication.
Illustrations: Buys 1 illustration/issue from freelancers. Works on assignment only. Prefers humor, caricatures or realistic portraits from a photo. Send query letter with brochure showing art style or resume, tear sheets and photocopies to be kept on file. Call to schedule an appointment to show a portfolio, which should include original/final art and tear sheets. Negotiates rights purchased. Pays $150-250 for b&w and $250-500 for color, inside; on publication. All original artwork is returned after publication.
Tips: Familiarize yourself with the magazine before submitting your samples. They should be relevant to our topics and styles.

***SOARING**, Soaring Society of America, Box 66071, Los Angeles CA 90066. Editor: Robert Said. "We are a low-budget magazine and depend on society members for art, but I'd like to have the names of some artists to whom I could send a manuscript and description of what we need and figure on getting the work back in time for the next month's issue." Monthly. Circ. 19,500. Receives 1 cartoon and 1 illustration/week from freelance artists. Original artwork returned after publication, if requested. Sample copy $1.10.
Cartoons: Uses less than 1 cartoon/issue. Prefers to see finished cartoons. Reports in 1 month. Buys one-time rights. Pays on publication.
Illustrations: Uses less than 1 illustration/issue. Interested in cutaway 3-dimension technical illustrations and illustrations for realism in flight stories. Send brochure showing art style and tear sheets to be kept on file for future assignments; "offer samples. We will return promptly. Good copies OK to judge style." SASE. Reports in 1 week. Buys one-time rights. Cover: Pays $50. Inside: Negotiates payment for line drawings, pen and ink, and washes.

NEW! For the Graphic Arts Professional

Graphic Tools & Techniques

by John Laing & Rhiannon Saunders-Davies

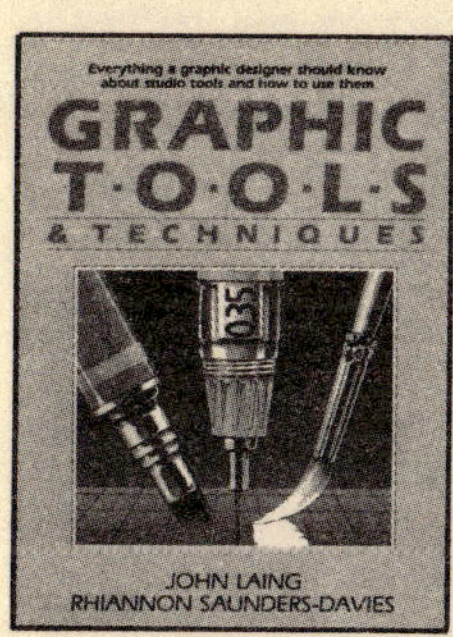

This comprehesive guide to tools and techniques will help you locate the materials and equipment best suited to your graphic design/art project *and* illustrates such basic techniques as how to draw a box with rounded corners, correct mistakes made with ink, and mask for airbrushing. Includes tool manufacturers' names and addresses for ordering purposes. 160 pages/100 color illus./$24.95

Studio Secrets for the Graphic Artist

by Jacqui Graham, Roger Hicks & Peter Brookesmith

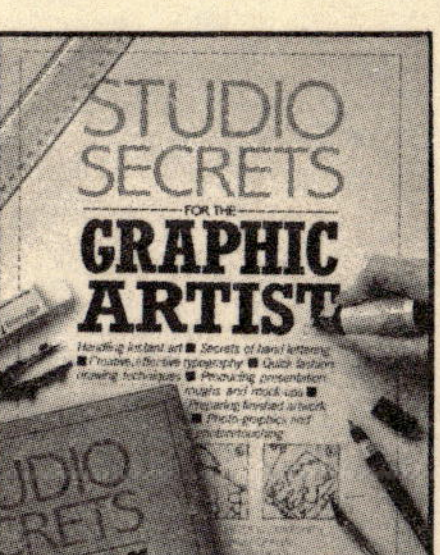

Here's a goldmine of inside art and design tricks and techniques to help you produce sharper, faster, better art immediately—such "secrets" as how to make a "slide sandwich" by superimposing one slide over another; intensify color by using markers on the back of the paper; and sand the edges of a cut print with fine glass paper to hide the join lines. 192 pages/100 color, 100 b&w illus./$27.50

(See back for more graphics books)

To order, drop this postpaid card in the mail.

YES! Please send me:

______ (7326) Complete Airbrush & Photoretouching Manual, $21.95

______ (7407) Design Rendering Techniques, $24.95

______ (7625) Graphic Tools & Techniques, $24.95

______ (8486) Studio Secrets for the Graphic Artist, $27.50

Please include $2.00 postage and handling for one book, 50¢ for each additional book. (Ohio residents add 5½% sales tax.)

☐ Payment enclosed (Slip this card and your payment into an envelope.)

☐ Please charge my: ☐ Visa   ☐ MasterCard

Account #_______________________ Exp. Date_______________________

Signature_______________________

Name_______________________

Address_______________________

City_______________________ State__________ Zip__________

Send to: **Writer's Digest Books/North Light**   2161
9933 Alliance Road
Cincinnati, Ohio 45242

Tips: "Readership is nuts-and-bolts oriented. We are leery of nonrepresentational art, though not adamant. We receive many flight stories which call for illustration. Occasional articles offer opportunity for quick sketch or cartoon-type treatment. Technical cutaway drawing for display of aircraft very desirable."

SOCIAL POLICY, 33 W. 42nd St., New York NY 10036. (212)840-7619. Managing Editor: Audrey Gartner. Emphasizes the human services—education, health, mental health, self-help, consumer education, neighborhood movement, employment. For social action leaders, academics, social welfare practitioners. Quarterly. Circ. 5,000. Accepts simultaneous submissions. Original artwork returned after publication. Sample copy $2.50.
Cartoons: Accepts b&w only, "with social consciousness." Sometimes uses humorous illustrations; often uses cartoon-style illustrations. Call for appointment to show portfolio. Reports only if interested. Buys one-time rights. Pays on publication.
Illustrations: Buys 4-6 illustrations/issue from freelancers. Accepts b&w only, "with social consciousness." Send query letter and tear sheets to be kept on file. Call for appointment to show portfolio, which should include original/final art, final reproduction/product, tear sheets and b&w. Reports only if interested. Buys one-time rights. Pays $100, cover; $25, b&w, inside. Pays on publication.
Tips: When reviewing an artist's work, looks for "sensitivity to the subject matter being illustrated."

SOLDIERS MAGAZINE, Cameron Station, Alexandria VA 22304-5050. (202)274-6671. Editor-in-Chief: Lt. Col. Charles G. Cavanaugh, Jr. Lighter Side Compiler: Mr. Steve Hara. Provides "timely and factual information on topics of interest to members of the Active Army, Army National Guard, Army Reserve and Department of Army civilian employees." Monthly. Circ. 207,000. Previously published material and simultaneous submissions OK. Samples available upon request.
Cartoons: Purchases approximately 60 cartoons/year. Should be single panel with gagline. Prefers military and general audience humor. Submit work; reports within 3 weeks. Buys all rights. Pays $25/cartoon on acceptance.
Tips: "We are actively seeking new ideas, fresh humor and looking for new talent—people who haven't been published before. We recommend a review of back issues before making submission. Issues available upon request. Remember that we are an inhouse publication—anti-Army humor, sexist or racist material is totally unacceptable."

SOLIDARITY MAGAZINE, Published by United Auto Workers, 8000 E. Jefferson, Detroit MI 48214. (313)926-5291. Editor: David Elsila. "1.5 million member trade union representing US and Canadian workers in auto, aerospace, agricultural-implement and other industries."
Illustrations: Works with 10-12 artists/year for illustrations. Uses artists for posters and magazine illustrations. Interested in graphic designs of publications, topical art for magazine covers with liberal-labor political slant. Especially needs illustrations for articles on unemployment, economy. Prefers Detroit area artists, but not essential. Looks for "ability to grasp publication's editorial slant" when reviewing artist's work. Send query letter with resume, flyer and/or tear sheet. Samples to be kept on file. Pays $75/small b&w spot illustration: up to $400 for color covers; $400+/designing small pamphlet.

SOUTH CAROLINA WILDLIFE, Box 167, Columbia SC 29202. (803)758-0001. Editor: John Davis. Art Director: Linda Laffitte. Deals with wildlife, outdoor recreation, natural history and environmental concerns. Bimonthly. Circ. 65,000. Previously published work OK. Sample copy and guidelines available.
Illustrations: Uses 10-20 illustrations/issue. Interested in wildlife art; all media; b&w line drawings, washes, full-color illustrations. "Particular need for natural history illustrations of good quality. They must be technically accurate." Subject matter must be appropriate for South Carolina. Prefers to see finished art, portfolio, samples of style, slides, or transparencies. Send resume, brochure, or flyer to be kept on file. SASE. Reports in 2-8 weeks. Acquires one-time rights. Does not buy art; accepts donations.
Tips: "We are interested in unique illustrations—something that would be impossible to photograph. Make sure proper research has been done and that the art is technically accurate."

SOUTH FLORIDA LIVING MAGAZINE, Bldg. 3, Suite 102, 700 W. Hillsboro Blvd., Deerfield Beach FL 33441. (305)428-5602. Managing Editor: Dee Krams. Emphasizes real estate (new developments) and is directed to newcomers to South Florida; homebuyers. Bimonthly. Circ. 80,000. Accepts previously published material. Does not return original artwork after publication. Sample copy available.
Cartoons: Send query letter with samples of style to be kept on file. Material not filed is returned by SASE. Reports within 1 month. Write for appointment to show portfolio. Buys first rights. Negotiates payment; pays on acceptance.
Illustrations: Buys "a few" illustrations/issue from freelancers. Works on assignment only. Send que-

ry letter with samples to be kept on file. Write for appointment to show portfolio. Prefers tear sheets or photographs as samples. Samples not filed are returned by SASE. Reports within 1 month. Buys first rights. Negotiates payment; pays on acceptance.

SOUTHERN ANGLER'S & HUNTER'S GUIDE, Box 2188, Hot Springs AR 71913. (501)623-8437. Editor: Don J. Fuelsch. Covers hunting and fishing in southern states. Circ. 125,000. Annual. SASE. Reports in 4 weeks. Pays on acceptance.
Cartoons: Buys 25/issue on fishing and hunting. Mail roughs or finished art.
Illustrations: Buys 300/issue on fish and game. Prefers pen-and-inks or scratchboards. Query with samples.

SOUTHERN GRAPHICS, Box 2028, 410 W. Verona St., Kissimmee FL 32742. (305)846-2800. Editor: George Meyer. Emphasizes news events and developments in the graphic arts industry. For commercial printing plant management in 14 southern states. Monthly. Circ. 10,000. Previously published work OK. Sample copy $1.25.
Cartoons: Buys 6 cartoons/year on printing industry; single panel with gagline. Mail finished art. SASE. Reports in 4 weeks. Negotiates payment.
Illustrations: Send query letter with previously published work. Uses 4-color cover design. SASE. Reports in 4 weeks.

***SOUTHERN MOTOR CARGO**, Box 4169, Memphis TN 38104. Contact: Thomas R. Stone. For trucking management and maintenance personnel of private, contract and for-hire carriers in 16 southern states (Alabama, Arkansas, Delaware, Florida, Georgia, Kentucky, Louisana, Maryland, Mississippi, North Carolina, Oklahoma, South Carolina, Tennessee, Texas, Virginia and West Virginia) and the District of Columbia. Special issues include "ATA Conventions," October; "Transportation Graduate Directory," February. Monthly. Circ. 55,000.
Cartoons: Buys 1-2 cartoons/issue on truck management situations. "Stay away from stereotyped 'truckin' on' theme." Mail roughs. Pays $20, b&w; on publication. SASE. Reports in 6 weeks.

SOYBEAN DIGEST, Box 41309, 777 Craig Rd., St. Louis MO 63141. (314)432-1600. Editor: Gregg Hillyer. Concerns agricultural and ag-business, specifically soybean production and marketing. Audience: high-acreage soybean growers. Monthly except semi-monthly in February and March, bi-monthly in June/July and August/September. Circ. 200,000. Previously published work OK. Original artwork returned after publication. Sample copy $3.
Cartoons and Illustrations: Buys maximum 6 cartoons/year and 3 illustrations/year on agriculture, soybean production and marketing. Send query letter or original art. SASE. Reports in 2-3 weeks. Buys all rights, but may reassign rights to artist after publication.

SPACE AND TIME, 4B, 138 W. 70th St., New York NY 10023-4432. Editor: Gordon Linzner. Emphasizes fantasy and science fiction stories. "Readers are sf/fantasy fans looking for an alternative to the newsstand magazines." Biannually. Circ. 450. Original artwork returned after publication. Sample copy $4.
Cartoons: Buys 1-2 cartoons/issue from freelancers. Considers sf/fantasy themes—any style. Prefers single panel with or without gagline; b&w line drawings. Send finished cartoons to be kept on file if accepted for publication; write for appointment to show portfolio. Material not filed is returned by SASE. Reports within 3 months. Buys first rights. Pays $2, b&w; on acceptance.
Illustrations: Buys 20-25 illustrations from freelancers. Assigns themes or styles illustrating specific stories. "We use all styles, but could use more representational material." Works on assignment only. Send query letter with brochure showing art style. Samples not filed are returned by SASE. Reports within 3 months. To show a portfolio, mail original/final art, photostats and b&w. Buys first rights. Pays $2, b&w, inside; on acceptance.

***SPACE WORLD MAGAZINE**, Suite 203 W. 600 Maryland Ave. SW, Washington DC 20024. (202)484-1111. Title Editor: Tony Reichardt. Feature magazine popularizing and advancing space exploration for the general public interested in all aspects of space program.
Needs: Works with 15-20 freelance artist/year. Uses artists for magazine illustration. "We are looking for original artwork on space themes, either conceptual or representing specific designs, events, etc."
First Contact & Terms: Send query letter with photographs, "color prints are best." Samples not filed are returned by SASE. Reports back within 1 month. To show a portfolio, mail appropriate materials, which should include color and photographs. Pays for illustration by the project, $25-50. "We do not generally commission original art. These fees are for one-time reproduction of existing artwork. Considers rights purchased when establishing payment.
Tips: "We know there are a lot of talented "space artists" out there. Give us a chance to showcase your work."

SPECTRUM STORIES, Box 58367, Louisville KY 40258. Editor: Walter Gammons. Emphasizes short stories, poems of science fiction, fantasy, experimental and horror and suspense; interviews, essays for a mostly well-educated professional adult audience. Quarterly. Circ. 2,500-3,000. Accepts previously published art only. Original artwork returned after publication. Sample copy $5.45; art guidelines for SASE with 44¢ postage.
Cartoons: Buys 4 cartoons/issue from freelancers. Science fiction, science, high tech, writing, publishing (small press angle), fantasy and horror (no gore) themes. Prefers single panel with gagline; b&w line drawings. Send query letter with samples of style or finished cartoons to be kept on file. Material not filed is returned by SASE only if requested. Reports within 2 months. Buys first rights. Pays $5-15, b&w; on publication.
Illustrations: Buys 12 illustrations/issue from freelancers. Prefers science fiction, fantasy, horror and experimental themes. Send query letter with resume, photostats, slides or photographs to be kept on file. Samples not filed are returned by SASE only if requested. Reports within 2 months. Buys first rights. Pays $50-75, b&w and $75-100, color, cover; $10-25, b&w and $50, color, inside; on publication.

SPIRIT MAGAZINE, (formerly *Solo Magazine*), Box 1231, Sisters OR 97759. (503)549-0442. Art Director: Denis Mortenson. "Our purpose is to encourage, entertain, assist and challenge readers to be all God wants them to be." Audience is primarily Christians with careers—baby boomers. Articles relate to maintaining a Christian lifstyle in a secular workplace. Circ. 50,000. Accepts previously published material. Original artwork returned after publication. Sample copy $2 and magazine-size SASE.
Cartoons: Buys 8-10 cartoons/issue from freelancers. Prefers cartoons that relate to career relationship and lifestyle; single panel, with or without gagline; b&w line drawings or b&w washes. Send query letter with samples of style or finished cartoons to be kept on file. Material not filed is returned by SASE. Reports within 1 month. Buys first rights. Pays $15-50, b&w; on publication.
Illustrations: Buys 1-2 illustrations/issue from freelancers. "Usually illustrations are tailored to particular articles, so theme and style varies." Send query letter with brochure showing art style or tear sheets, photostats, photocopies slides and photographs to be kept on file. To show a portfolio, mail appropriate materials, which should include final reproduction/product, color and tear sheets. Samples returned by SASE. Reports within 1 month. Buys first rights. Pays $50-200, 2-color, and $25-150, b&w, inside; on publication.
Tips: "Be experienced, able to meet deadlines—willing to work for less money than the norm."

***SPITBALL, the Literary Baseball Magazine**, 1721 Scott Blvd., Covington KY 41011. (606)261-3024. Editor: Mike Shannon. Magazine emphasizing baseball exclusively, for well-educated, literate baseball fans. Quarterly. Accepts previously published material. Returns original artwork after publication if the work is donated; does not return if purchases work. Sample copy $1; art guidelines free for SASE with 22¢ postage.
Cartoons: "We have never used cartoons, but are open to using them in the future." Prefers single-panel without gagline, b&w line drawings. Query with samples of style, roughs and finished cartoons. Samples not filed are returned by SASE. Reports back within 1 week. Negotiates rights purchased.
Illustrations: We need three types of art: cover work, illustration (for a story, essay or poem), and filler. All must be b&w ink. Sometimes we assign the cover piece on a particular subject; sometimes we just use a drawing we like. Interested artists should write to set out needs for future covers and specific illustration." Buys 3 or 4 illustration/issue. Send query letter with original b&w illustrations. Samples not filed are returned by SASE. Reports back within 1 week. To show a portfolio, mail appropriate materials. Negotiates rights purchased. Pays $10 minimum; on acceptance.

***SPORTING CLASSICS**, Box 1017, Camden SC 29290. (803)425-1003. Design Director: Duncan Grant. Magazine emphasizing outdoor sports such as hunting and fishing for "sophisticated, educated high-income, well-traveled sportsmen" who love art, decoys, collect guns, knives, etc. Circ. 85,000. Accepts previously published material. Original artwork returned after publication. Sample copy free for SASE with 80¢ postage.
Illustrations: Uses 10-15 illustrations/issue. Works on assignment only. Prefers sporting, wildlife, outdoor, hunting and fishing themes. Send query letter with brochure showing art style or samples, tear sheets, photostats, photocopies, slides and photographs. Reports only if interested. Write to schedule an appointment to show a portfolio, which should include color, tear sheets and photographs. Buys one-time rights. Pays $500, b&w and $1,200, color, cover; $50-250, b&w and $250-1,000, color, inside on publication.

SPORTS AFIELD MAGAZINE, 250 W. 55th St., New York NY 10019. (212)262-8839. Art Director: Gary Gretter. Magazine emphasizing outdoor activities—fishing, hunting and camping. Monthly. Circ. 600,000. Does not accept previously published material. Returns original artwork after publication.
Illustrations: Buys 2-3/issue. Works on assignment only. Send query letter with samples to be kept on

file except for material not of interest. Prefers slides as samples. Samples not filed are returned by SASE. Call for appointment to show portfolio. Buys first rights or negotiates rights purchased. Pays $1,000 spread, color.

***SPORTS PARADE**, Box 10010, Ogden UT 84409. Editor: Robyn C. Walker. Monthly magazine covering sports and general interest items. Readers are generally business and family-oriented. Sample copy $1.
Cartoons: Send query letter with photocopies. Samples returned by SASE. Reports in 1-2 weeks. Pays on acceptance.

STARWIND, Box 98, Ripley OH 45167. Contact: Editor. Emphasizes science fiction, fantasy and nonfiction of scientific and technological interest. Quarterly. Circ. 2,500. Sample copy $2.50; art guidelines for SASE.
Cartoons: Buys 5-8 cartoons/issue from freelancers. Interested in science fiction and fantasy subjects. Format: single and multiple panel b&w line drawings. Prefers finished cartoons. SASE. Reports in 6-8 weeks. Buys first North American serial rights. Pays on publication.
Illustrations: Uses 10-15 illustrations/issue. Sometimes uses humorous and cartoon-style illustrations depending on the type of work being published. Works on assignment only. Samples returned by SASE. Reports back on future assignment possibilities. Send resume or brochure and samples of style to be kept on file for future assignments. Illustrates stories rather extensively (normally an 8x11" and an interior illustration). Format: b&w line drawings (pen & ink and similar media). SASE. Reports in 6-8 weeks. Buys first North American rights. Pays for cover; on publication.
Tips: "We select artists on quality of workmanship and a dependable turnaround time. We also appreciate reasonable rates, as we have a limited budget. We encourage new artists to contact us. Artists are using dry transfer lettering, screens, etc. more to their advantage. This enables them to produce more professional, polished work. They also produce more camera-ready art. We prefer artwork to be camera-ready so we appreciate this trend."

STEREO REVIEW, 1515 Broadway, New York NY 10036. (212)719-6007. Art Director: Sue Llewellyn. Emphasizes stereo equipment, classical and popular music for music enthusiasts. Monthly. Circ. 600,000.
Illustrations: Uses about 6 illustrations/issue; 3 supplied by freelancers. Illustrators "must be local and fast. Our lead time is very short. We are always looking for new talent." Especially interested in artwork and charts to accompany articles on technical subjects. Format: b&w line drawings and color washes for inside. Send samples of style and photocopies. SASE. Reports in 1 week or when assignment is needed. Payment on acceptance is negotiated. Buys one-time rights plus promotional use.
Tips: "Call for appointment around 20th of month to show portfolio."

***STERLING MAGAZINE**, 355 Lexington Ave., New York NY 10017. Art Director: Larry Matthews. Magazine emphasizing sports, music and black romance for people interested in sports, ages 13-30; music, ages 13-17; black romance, ages 16-20. Monthly. Circ. 160,000. Original artwork returned after publication. Sample copy and art guidelines available.
Cartoons: Write for appointment to show a portfolio. Material not kept on file is returned by SASE. Buys all rights.
Illustrations: Send query letter with brochure showing art style or samples. Samples not filed are returned by SASE. Reports only if interested. Call or write to schedule an appointment to show a portfolio, which should include roughs, original/final art, final reproduction/product and color. Buys first or one-time rights. Pays $250, color, cover; on acceptance.

***STICKERS & STUFF**, Rm 1300, 10 Columbus Circle, New York NY 10019. (212)541-7300. Design Director: Altemus. Magazine for children 6-13. Quarterly. Circ. 200,000. Accepts previously published material. Returns original artwork after publication.
Illustrations: Buys 5-10 illustrations/issue. Works on assignment only. Prefers stylized, graphic, light styles. Send tear sheets. Samples not filed are returned by SASE. Does not report back. To show a portfolio, mail appropriate materials or call to schedule an appointment; portfolio should include tear sheets and photostats. Buys first rights. Pays $300, b&w and $300, color, cover; $75, b&w and $100, color, inside; on publication.

STONE COUNTRY, Box 132, Menemsha MA 02552. Editor-in-Chief: Judith Neeld. Art Editor: Pat McCormick. Submit to 69 Central Ave., Madison NJ 07940. For serious poets and poetry supporters. Published 2 times/year. Circ. 1,000. Previously published artwork OK. Sample copy $3.50; $2.50 for tear sheets and sample covers (postage included).

Illustrations: Uses 1 cover/year and 6-7 illustrations/issue. Receives 1 illustration/week from freelance artists. Must be camera-ready. Cover design should fit 8½x5½, "no lettering" inside drawings no larger than 3x4. Interested in b&w drawings only, no washes or pencil shading; to achieve shading, use fine b&w lines. Any style or theme; size is important. "We are interested in abstract as well as representational work. Art students welcome." Send query letter with brochure showing art style or resume, tear sheets, photostats and photocopies, "submit completed work directly." Reports in 6-8 weeks. "We don't view portfolios." Buys first North American serial rights. Cover: Pays $15, b&w; on publication. Inside: Pays 1 contributor's copy, b&w.
Tips: "Send original graphics directly to Art Editor with SASE. Or, to save both of us if the work isn't what we look for, order samples through General Editor."

STONE IN AMERICA, 6902 N. High St., Worthington OH 43085. (614)885-2713. Managing Editor: Robert Moon. Journal of the American Monument Association; deals with design, marketing and sales of memorial stones. Circ. 2,600. Monthly. Reports in 4 weeks. Buys first rights. Pays on acceptance. Free sample copy.

***STRAIGHT**, Standard Publishing, 8121 Hamilton Ave., Cincinnati OH 45231. Art Director: Frank Sutton. Magazine emphasizing religious/inspirational topics for Christian teenagers, ages 13-19, who receive the magazine at church. Produced quarterly. Circ. 75,000. Does not return original artwork after publication. Sample copy free for SASE with 39¢ postage.
Cartoons: Not accepting any at this time.
Illustratons: Buys 1-3 illustrations/issue from freelancers. Works on assignment only. Prefers contemporary style with an appeal to teenagers. Send query letter with brochure showing art style. Samples not filed are returned by SASE. Reports only if interested. Write to schedule an appointment to show a portfolio, which should include roughs, original/final art, final reproduction/product and examples of Bible characters, Bible story illustrations; teenagers; people of all ages; children. Buys all rights. Pays $50, b&w, cover; $35, b&w, inside; on acceptance.

THE STUDENT, 127 9th Ave. N., Nashville TN 37234. (615)251-4580. Photo Librarian: Dot Garner. Magazine emphasizing all facets of college life. Monthly. Circ. 22,000. Accepts previously published material. Returns original artwork after publication. Art guidelines available.
Cartoons: Buys 3/issue. Prefers anything to do with college life. Prefers single panel with gagline; b&w line drawings. Send samples of style. Call for appointment to show portfolio. Material not filed returned by SASE. Reports within 1 month. Buys one-time rights. Pays $15-20, b&w; on acceptance.
Illustrations: Buys 4/issue. Prefers mostly realistic styles with some caricatures. Works on assignment only. Send samples to be kept on file. Call for appointment to show portfolio. Prefers photocopies as samples. Samples not filed are returned. Reports within 1 month. Buys all rights. Pays $125, b&w, cover; and $60-120, b&w, inside; on acceptance.

***THE SUN**, 412 W. Rosemary, Chapel Hill NC 27514. (919)942-5282. Editor: Sy Safransky. Magazine of ideas. Monthly. Circ. 2,000. Accepts previously published material. Original artwork returned after publication. Sample copy $3. Art guidelines free for SASE with 22¢ postage.
Cartoons: Buys various cartoons/issue from freelancers. Send finished cartoons. Material not kept on file is returned by SASE. Reports within 1 month. Buys first rights. Pays $5, b&w; plus copies and subscription.
Illustrations: Buys various illustrations/issue from freelancers. Works on assignment only. Send query letter with samples. Samples not filed are returned by SASE. Reports within 1 month. To show a portfolio, mail appropriate materials. Buys first rights. Pays $5; plus copies and subscription. Pays on publication.

***THE SUNDAY OREGONIAN'S NORTHWEST MAGAZINE**, 1320 SW Broadway, Portland OR 97201. 221-8235. Graphic Coordinator: Kevin Murphy. Estab. 1984. Magazine emphasizing stories with Northwest orientation for aged 25-45 and upwardly mobile people. Weekly. Circ. 430,000. Original artwork returned after publication. Sample copy free for SASE.
Illustrations: Buys 1 illustration/issue from freelancers. Works on assignment only. Send query letter with brochure showing art style or resume and slides. Samples not filed are returned only if requested. Reports only if interested. Call or write to schedule an appointment to show a portfolio, which should include original/final art, color, photographs and slides. Buys first or one-time rights. Negotiates payment. Pays on publication.

SUPERMARKET BUSINESS, Suite 707, 25 W. 43rd St., New York NY 10036. (212)354-5169. Editor: Ken Partch. Concerns merchandising methods, industry trends and issues, and surveys of the supermarket industry. Monthly. Circ. 80,000.

Cartoons: "Cartoons are almost never used unless they express a specific idea." Query with samples. SASE. Reports in 1 month. Pays $35 minimum, gray opaques, b&w line drawings and washes; on acceptance.
Illustrations: Buys 12-15/year, usually after working with artist to illustrate a specific story. Query with resume and samples or arrange interview to show portfolio. SASE. Reports in 1 month. Inside: Pays $50 minimum, gray opaques, b&w line drawings and washes; on acceptance.

SURFER MAGAZINE, Box 1028, Dana Point CA 92629. Art Director: Jeff Girard. Emphasizes surfing: the sport, the lifestyle. Monthly. Circ. 100,000. Accepts previously published material. Original artwork returned after publication. Free art guidelines.
Cartoons: Buys 1 cartoon/issue from freelancers. Considers surfing and surf lifestyle themes. Reviews all formats. Send query letter with samples of style to be kept on file; write for appointment to show portfolio. Material not filed is not returned. Reports only if interested. Buys one-time rights. Pays $100/page, b&w; $350/page, color; on publication.
Illustrations: Buys 3 illustrations/issue from freelancers. Prefers surfing and surf lifestyle themes; hand lettering or editorial illustrations. Works primarily on assignment. Send query letter with brochure, resume, business card and samples to be kept on file. Prefers tear sheets or 35mm slides as samples for color, photocopies for b&w. "We do not guarantee return of unsolicited material." Samples not filed are not returned. Reports only if intersted. Buys one-time rights. Pays $100/page, b&w, and $350/page, color, inside; on publication.
Tips: "We are doing more feature-type articles, so we may be buying a few more illustrations/year."

***SURFING MAGAZINE**, 2720 Camino Capistrano, San Clemente CA 92672. Managing Art Director: Dave Vecker. Magazine emphasizing surfing. Monthly. Circ. 115,000. Original artwork returned after publication.
Illustrations: Buys 1 illustration/issue from freelancers. Works on assignment only. Send query letter with brochure showing art style or resume, tear sheets, slides and photographs. Samples not filed are returned by SASE. Reports within 3 weeks. Call or write to schedule an appointment to show a portfolio, which should include roughs, original/final art, final reproduction/product, color and photographs. Buys reprint rights. Pays on publication.

TECHNOLOGY REVIEW, Massachusetts Institute of Technology, Cambridge MA 02139. (617)253-8255. Design Director: Nancy L. Cahners. Design Manager: Kathleen Sayre. Emphasizes technology and its implications. Published 8 times/year. Circ. 80,000. Accepts previously published material and simultaneous submissions. Original artwork returned after publication. Sample copy $3; art guidelines available.
Illustrations: Uses 10 + illustrations/issue; buys all from freelancers. Works on assignment only. Send query letter with brochure, resume, business card, samples and tear sheets to be kept on file. Prefers tear sheets or facsimile as samples. Samples not kept on file are returned by SASE. Reports only if interested. Call or write for appointment to show portfolio. Buys one-time rights. Pays on publication.

'TEEN, Petersen Publishing Co., 8490 Sunset Blvd., Los Angeles CA 90069. (213)854-2222. Art Director: Laurel Watson. Deals with self-development for girls 12-19. Circ. 1,000,000.
Illustrations: Buys 2-3 illustrations/issue for fiction, fashion and beauty sections. Contact only through artist's agent or send query letter with brochure showing art style or tear sheets, slides and photographs. Works on assignment only. Will see artists and photographers with finished and professional portfolios. Call to schedule an appointment to show a portfolio, which should include original/final art, final reproduction/product, color, tear sheets, photographs and b&w. Buys all rights. Pays $25-150, b&w and $150-250, color, inside; on acceptance. Other assignments are negotiable.
Tips: "Youth today are more involved and the keyword is *active*. Prefer youthful upbeat look. We're appealing to an audience that is bright, young and active."

TENNIS, 5520 Park Ave., Trumbull CT 06611. (203)373-7000. Contact: Art Director. For young, affluent tennis players. Monthly. Circ. 500,000.
Cartoons: Buys 3 cartoons/issue from freelancers. Receives 6 submissions/week from freelancers on tennis. Prefers finished cartoons, single panel. Reports in 2 weeks. Pays $75, b&w.
Illustrations: Buys 5 illustrations/issue from freelancers. Works on assignment only. Send query letter with tear sheets. To show a portfolio, mail appropriate materials or call to schedule an appointment; portfolio should include original/final art, final reproduction/product, color, tear sheets and photographs. Pays $400, color; on acceptance.
Tips: "There is a return to clean design, strong images, and purer color. I use illustrations whose work reflects these elements. They should first look through an issue of the magazine to make sure their style is appropriate for us."

TEXAS FOOD & SERVICE NEWS,Box 1429, Austin TX 78767. (512)444-6543. Editor: Kim Goodwin. "As the official trade publication of the Texas Restaurant Association, we are interested in materials which deal with the problems faced by restaurant owners and operators primarily in Texas; some members are managers of clubs, bars and hotels." Published 10 times/year. Circ. 6,000. Simultaneous submissions OK. Original artwork returned after publication. Free sample copy and art guidelines for SASE.

Cartoons: Interested in "cartoons that deal with the problems of restaurant owners or employees. We are not interested in cliched fly-in-soup jokes about food or other digs at restaurants. Humor should be from the point of operators and employees. Understanding of food service is helpful." Prefers single, double or multiple panel with or without gagline, b&w line drawings, b&w washes. Send finished cartoons. Samples returned. Reports in 3 weeks. Negotiates rights purchased. Pays $20, b&w; on acceptance.

Illustrations: "We are not set in style, as long as art is high quality black-and-white or color. However, we would like to see a variety of art styles, including airbrush, watercolor, pastel and pen & ink. We are looking for versatile artists who can illustrate articles about the food service industry in Texas, particularly as it pertains to management. Topics: financing, employee relations, computers, food, decor, etc." Works on assignment only. Send query letter with resume, samples and tear sheets to be kept on file. Samples not kept on file are returned. Reports in 3 weeks. Call for appointment to show a portfolio. Negotiates rights purchased. Pays $25-50, inside b&w line drawings; $25-50, inside b&w washes; $40-60, cover color washes; $30-50, inside color washes; on acceptance.

THE TEXAS OBSERVER, 600 W. 7th, Austin TX 78701. (512)477-0746. Contact: Art Director. Emphasizes Texas political, social and literary topics. Biweekly. Circ. 12,000. Accepts previously published material. Returns original artwork after publication. Sample copy free for SASE with 39¢ postage; art guidelines free for SASE with 22¢ postage.

Cartoons: Buys 2 cartoons/issue from freelancers. Prefers current political and social issues as themes. Considers single or double panel with or without gagline, b&w line drawings, b&w washes. Send samples of style to be kept on file. Material not filed is returned by SASE. Reports within 1 month. Write or call for appointment to show portfolio. Buys one-time rights. Pays $10-50 for b&w; on publication.

Illustrations: Buys 2 illustrations/issue from freelancers. "We only print black and white, so pen & ink is best, washes are fine." Send photostats, tear sheets, photocopies, slides or photographs to be kept on file. Samples not filed are returned by SASE. Reports within 1 month. Write or call for appointment to show portfolio. Buys one-time rights. Pays $35 for b&w cover; $20, inside; on publication.

THRUST—Science Fiction & Fantasy Review, 8217 Langport Terrace, Gaithersburg MD 20877. Publisher/Editor: D. Douglas Fratz. Emphasizes science fiction and fantasy literature for highly knowledgeable science fiction professionals and well-read fans. Biannually. Circ. 1,500. Accepts previously published material. Returns original artwork after publication. Sample copy $2.50. Art guidelines free for SASE with 22¢ postage.

Cartoons: Buys 1-2/issue from freelance artists. Themes must be related to science fiction or fantasy. Prefers single panel; b&w line drawings. Send query letter with samples of style to be kept on file unless SASE included. Reports within 4 weeks. Buys one-time rights. Pays $2-4, b&w; on publication.

Illustrations: Buys 9-10/issue from freelance artists. Science fiction or fantasy themes only. Send query letter with tear sheets, photostats or photocopies to be kept on file unless SASE included. Accepts any style. Samples not filed are returned by SASE. Reports within 4 weeks. To show a portfolio, mail appropriate materials, which should include original/final art, final reproduction/product, tear sheets and b&w. Buys one-time rights. Pays $25, b&w, cover; and $10/page, b&w, inside; on publication.

TIC, Box 407, North Chatham NY 12132. Editor: Joseph Strack. For dentists.

Cartoons: "Remember, it's for dentists, not patients—so no pain or 'open wide' cliche gags, please." Reports in 10 days. Buys exclusive dental publication rights; will release reprint rights. Pays $25 for washes, pen & inks and line drawings; on acceptance.

TODAY'S CHRISTIAN PARENT, 8121 Hamilton Ave., Cincinnati OH 45231. Editor: Mildred Mast. Emphasizes the pleasures and problems of parenting from a Christian perspective. Quarterly. Circ. 30,000. No simultaneous submissions. Sample copy available for SASE, 7x9 or larger.

Cartoons: Uses 1 cartoon/issue (6 in summer); from freelancers. Interested in family and seasonal themes. Prefers to see finished cartoons. SASE. Buys all rights on a work-for-hire basis. Pays $10-15, b&w; on acceptance.

Illustrations: Uses 3-4 illustrations/issue, mostly on assignment, some from freelancers. Interested in "various aspects of family life." Especially needs family activities, including older children and adults. Send query letter with tear sheets, photostats, photocopies and photographs. Enclose SASE for return of pieces. To show a portfolio, mail appropriate materials. Buys all rights on a work-for-hire basis. Negotiates pay; pays on acceptance.

TODAY'S POLICEMAN, Box 875108, Los Angeles CA 90087. Contact: Editor. For persons employed in and interested in police services. Semiannualy. Circ. 10,000.
Cartoons: Buys 6 cartoons/issue dealing with law enforcement and politics. Send finished art. SASE. Pays $2.50 for b&w.

TOURIST ATTRACTIONS AND PARKS, Suite 226, 401 N. Broad St., Philadelphia PA 19108. (215)925-9744. President: Scott Borowsky. Deals with arenas, attractions, fairgrounds, stadiums, concerts, theme and amusement parks. Published 6 times/year. Circ. 20,000. Also uses freelance artists for cover, layout and paste-up (each issue).
Illustrations: Buys 6/issue. Send query letter with resume and samples. SASE. Buys all rights. Cover: Pays $50 minimum, gray opaques; on publication. Inside: Buys gray opaques.

TOW-AGE, Box M, Franklin MA 02038. Contact: J. Kruza. For readers who run their own tow service business. Circ. 15,000. Published every 6 weeks.
Cartoons: Pays $12.50 average/cartoon.
Illustrations: Pays $15-60, b&w illustrations preferably in line technique on assigned subjects or themes. Write for lists. Send copies of style. SASE.

TRADITION, 106 Navajo, Council Bluffs IA 51501. Editor-in-Chief/Art Director: Robert Everhart. "For players and listeners of traditional and country music. We are a small, nonprofit publication and will use whatever is sent to us. A first time gratis use is the best way to establish communication." Monthly. Circ. 2,000. Simultaneous submissions and previously published work OK. Buys one-time rights. Free sample copy.
Cartoons: Buys 1/issue on country music; single panel with gagline. Receives 10-15 cartoons/week from freelance artists. Mail roughs. Pays $5-15, b&w line drawings; on publication.
Illustrations: Buys 1/issue on country music. Query with resume and samples. SASE. Cover: Pays $5-15, b&w line drawings. Inside: Pays $5-15, b&w line drawings; on publication. Reports in 4 weeks.
Tips: "We'd like to see an emphasis on traditional country music."

TRAINING: THE MAGAZINE OF HUMAN RESOURCES DEVELOPMENT, 50 S. Ninth St., Minneapolis MN 55402. Editor: Jack Gordon. Art Director: Jodi Scharff. Covers "job-related training and education in business and industry, both theory and practice." Audience: "training directors, pesonnel managers, sales and data processing managers, general managers, etc." Monthly. Circ. 51,000. Especially needs cartoons and adult education on the job. Original artwork returned after publication "on request." Sample copy $3 plus 9x11 SASE.
Cartoons: Buys 3-8 cartoons/issue from freelancers. Prefers b&w drawings that reproduce well. Samples not filed are returned by SASE only if requested. Reports in 4 weeks. Buys reprint rights. Pays $25, b&w, on acceptance.
Illustrations: Buys 2-6 illustrations/issue from freelancers. Send query letter with photocopies or photostats to be kept on file. Call (612)333-0471 or write art director for appointment to show portfolio. Samples not filed are returned only if requested and only by SASE. Reports within 4 weeks. Buys reprint rights. Pays $300 and up for color, cover; $75-200 for b&w, inside; on acceptance.

TRANSAMERICA, Transamerica Corp., 600 Montgomery St., San Francisco CA 94111. (415)983-4295. Editor: Beth Quartarolo. For employees. Quarterly. Circ. 42,000. SASE. Previously published work OK. Pays on acceptance.
Illustrations: Buys 3-4/year on assigned themes. Cover: Uses color illustrations. Query with previously published work or arrange interview to show portfolio. Negotiates pay.
Tips: "When trying to sell your work, give some general rates. I need some idea of what the artist is going to charge."

TRAVEL & LEISURE, 1120 6th Ave., New York NY 10036. (212)382-5600. Design/Art Director: Adrian Taylor. Associate Art Directors: Ken Kleppert and Joan Ferrell. Emphasizes travel, resorts, dining and entertainment. Monthly. Circ. 1,000,000. Original artwork returned after publication. Art guidelines for SASE.
Cartoons: Rarely uses cartoons. Interested in travel or leisure related themes. Format: b&w line drawings and b&w and color washes without gaglines. Prefers to see roughs. SASE. Reports in 1 week. Buys World serial rights. Pays $200-800, b&w; on publication.
Illustrations: Uses 1-15 illustrations/issue, all from freelancers. Interested in travel and leisure related themes. "Illustrators are selected by excellence and relevance to the subject." Works on assignment only. Provide business card to be kept on file for future assignment; samples returned by SASE. Reports in 1 week. Buys World serial rights. Pays a minimum of $150 inside b&w and $800-1,500 maximum, inside color; on publication.

TRIQUARTERLY, Northwestern University, 1735 Benson Ave., Evanston IL 60201. (312)491-3490. Editor: Reginald Gibbons. Design Director: Gini Kondziolka. Emphasizes "serious contemporary fiction primarily—subject matter varies. Readers are well-read, well-educated and interested in new trends and directions in art, writing, photography, illustration—the arts in general." Published 3 times/year. Circ. 5,000. Original artwork usually returned after publication—"negotiated with the artist." Sample copy $3.
Illustrations: Very occasionally uses illustrations from freelancers. "Themes and styles vary according to editorial focus of issue." Works on assignment only. Reports in 6-8 weeks. Buys one-time rights. "Fee negotiated on a per issue basis with artist." Pays on "acceptance of artwork and approval of bill, then it's submitted for payment to Northwestern University."

TROPIC MAGAZINE, The Miami Herald, 1 Herald Plaza, Miami FL 33101. (305)376-3432. Art Director: Philip Brooker. Emphasizes general (local) interests for Sunday newspaper magazine readers. Weekly. Circ. 555,000. Original artwork returned after publication. Sample copy free with SASE; art guidelines available.
Illustrations: Buys 0-2 illustrations/issue from freelancers. Works on assignment only. Send query letter with slides to be kept on file. Reports within 2 weeks. Call for appointment to show portfolio. Pays $300, b&w and $400-500, color, cover; $75-250, b&w and $300, color, inside; on acceptance.

TRUE WEST/Frontier Times, Box 2107, Stillwater OK 74076. Editor: John Joerschke. Emphasizes American western history from 1830 to 1910 for a primarily rural and suburban audience, middle-age and older, interested in Old West history, horses, cowboys, art, clothing, and all things western. Monthly. Circ. 90,000. Accepts previously published material and considers some simultaneous submissions. Original artwork returned after publication. Sample copy and art guidelines free for SASE.
Illustrations: Buys 5-10 illustrations/issue from freelancers. "Inside illustrations are usually, but not always, pen & ink line drawings; covers are western paintings." Send query letter with samples to be kept on file; "we return anything on request. For inside illustrations, we want samples of artist's line drawings. For covers, we need to see full-color transparencies." Reports within 30 days. Call or write for appointment to show portfolio. Buys one-time rights. Pays $100-150, for color transparency for cover; $15-40, b&w, inside; on acceptance.

TURF AND SPORT DIGEST, 511-513 Oakland Ave., Baltimore MD 21212. Publisher: Allen L. Mitzel Jr. Emphasizes thoroughbred racing coverage, personalities, events and handicapping methods for fans of thoroughbred horseracing.
Cartoons: Interested in horse racing themes. Pays $10; on publication.

TURTLE MAGAZINE FOR PRESCHOOL KIDS, 1100 Waterway Blvd., Box 567, Indianapolis IN 46206. (317)636-8881. Art Director: Lawrence Simmons. Emphasizes health, nutrition, exercise and safety for children 2-5 years. Monthly except bimonthly February/March, April/May, June/July and August/September. Accepts previously published material and simultaneous submissions. Original artwork not returned after publication. Sample copy 75¢; art guidelines free for SASE.
Illustrations: Buys 15-30 illustrations/issue from freelancers. Interested in "stylized, humorous, realistic and cartooned themes; also nature and health." Especially needs b&w and 2-color artwork for line or halftone reproduction; full-color text and cover art. Works on assignment only. Send query letter with resume, stats or good photocopies, slides and tear sheets to be kept on file. Samples not kept on file returned by SASE. Reports only if interested. Buys all rights. To show a portfolio, mail final reproduction/product, color, tear sheets, b&w and 2-color. Pays $225, 4-color, cover; $25-100, b&w and 2-color and $60-125, 4-color, inside; on publication.
Tips: "Be sure to send in appropriate material for the magazine (example: do not send New Yorker illustrations for a children's magazine for ages 2-5)."

TV GUIDE, Radnor PA 19088. Cartoon Editor: M.E. Bilisnansky. Emphasizes news, personalities and programs of television for a general audience. Weekly. Query. Reports in 2 weeks. Buys all rights. Pays on acceptance.
Cartoons: Buys about 35 cartoons/year on TV themes. Pays $200, single cartoon. Also uses cartoons for editorial features. Line drawings and halftones. Buys only single panel cartoons. No cartoon strips.

***TWIN CITIES**, 7831 East Bush Lake Rd., Minneapolis MN 55435. (612)835-6855. Art Director: Marcia Wright. Magazine emphasizing lifestyle and general local interest for upscale, wealthy, well-educated, men and women. Monthly. Circ. 37,000. Original artwork returned after publication. Sample copy $3.
Illustrations: Buys 2-6 illustrations/issue from freelancers. Works on assignment only. Prefers original styles that illuminate the editorial theme. Send query letter with resume, tear sheets and photocopies.

Samples not filed are returned by SASE. Reports only if interested. Call to schedule an appointment to show a portfolio, which should include roughs, original/final art, final reproduction/product, color, tear sheets, photostats, photographs and b&w. Buys one-time rights. Pays on publication.

***II COMPUTING, For Apple II Users**, 524 Second St., San Francisco CA 94107. Art Director: Marni Tapscott. Magazine emphasizing computers for Apple II enthusiasts. Bimonthly. Circ. 50,000. Original artwork returned after publication.
Illustrations: Buys 3-5 illustrations/issue from freelancers. Works on assignment only. Prefers sophisticated, highly realistic styles using airbrush, colored pencil, pastels or acrylics. Send brochure showing art style or resume, tear sheets, photostats, photocopies, slides and photographs; "color work should be in color, though." Samples not filed are returned. Reports only if interested. To show a portfolio, mail original/final art, final reproduction/product, color and tear sheets. Buys one-time rights. Pays $800-1,000, color, cover; $50-150, b&w; $75-700, color, inside; 30 days after acceptance date.

UNITED EVANGELICAL ACTION, Box 28, Wheaton IL 60189. (312)665-0500. Editor: Donald R. Brown. Magazine emphasizing religious news for leaders, pastors, laypeople in the evangelical church. Bimonthly. Circ. 10,500. Accepts previously published material. Original artwork returned after publication. Sample copy for SASE with 45¢ postage.
Cartoons: Buys 1-3 cartoons/year from freelancers. Religion-in-the-news themes. Prefers single panel with gagline; b&w line drawings. Send query letter with samples of style to be kept on file; write for appointment to show portfolio. Material not filed is returned by SASE. Reports within 1 month. Buys first rights. Pays $35-50, b&w; on publication.
Illustrations: Buys 1-2 illustrations/year from freelancers. Theme: religion confronting current issues. Send query letter with brochure and tear sheets to be kept on file; write for appointment to show portfolio. Samples not filed are returned by SASE. Reports within 1 month. Buys first rights. Payment is negotiable; on publication.

THE UNITED METHODIST PUBLISHING HOUSE, Graded Press Division, 201 Box 801, Eighth Ave. S, Nashville TN 37202. Art Procurement Supervisor: David Dawson. Publishes 60 + magazines, and church and home leaflets for ages 1½ years and up. Uses 30-40 illustrations/publication. Assigns 500-1,000 jobs/year.
First Contact & Terms: Works with 25-50 freelance artists/year. Seeks "artists with editorial and publishing experience. Also seeks artists of ethnic background—Korean, Hispanic and black." Works on assignment only. Send brochure showing art style or slides, photostats, photographs and tear sheets to be kept on file. Samples not filed are returned only if requested. Reports only if interested. Considers complexity of project, skill and experience of artist, project's budget and rights purchased when establishing payment. Buys all rights.
Magazine Covers: Pays by the project, $150-200 for full-color.
Magazine Text Illustration: Pays by the project, $5-40 for simple illustrations, $60-125 for full color.
Tips: "The ability to render the human figure is a must. Artists must be able to handle varied and numerous illustrations."

UNMUZZLED OX, 105 Hudson St., New York NY 10013. (212)226-7170. Editor: Michael Andre. Emphasizes poetry, stories, some visual arts (graphics, drawings, photos) for poets, writers, artists, musicians and interested others. Circ. 18,000. Whether original artwork is returned after publication "depends on work—artist should send SASE." Sample copy $4.95 plus $1 postage.
Cartoons: Number used/issue varies. Send query letter with copies. Reports within 10 weeks. No payment for cartoons.
Illustrations: Uses "several" illustrations/issue. Themes vary according to issue. Send query letter and "anything you care to send" to be kept on file for possible future assignments. Reports within 10 weeks.
Tips: Magazine readers and contributors are "highly sophisticated and educated"; artwork should be geared to this market.

THE UNSPEAKABLE VISIONS OF THE INDIVIDUAL, Box 439, California PA 15419. Editors-in-Chief: Arthur and Kit Knight. For people with a better-than-average education interested in "beat" literature. Annually. Circ. 2,000. Sample copy $3.50.
Illustrations: Uses 3-6 illustrations/issue. Number illustrations/issue bought from freelancers varies. Receives 1 submission/month from freelancers. Interested in "beat" related themes, such as writers Jack Kerouac, William S. Burroughs, Allen Ginsberg, Gary Snyder and Carolyn Cassady. Prefers to see finished art. SASE. "Work without SASE will be destroyed." Reports in 2 weeks-2 months. Buys first North American serial rights. Pays 2 contributor's copies, minimum; $10 maximum; on publication.
Tips: "See a sample copy."

USA TODAY, 1860 Broadway, New York NY 10023. (212)265-6680. Contact: Bob Rothenberg. For intellectual college graduates. Monthly. Circ. 200,000. Free sample copy.
Illustrations: Buys 70-80 illustrations/year on assigned themes. Uses only New York artists in the metropolitan area. Send query letter with samples. SASE. Reports in 1 week. Buys all rights. Cover: pays $150, color. Inside: Pays $15-50, b&w line drawings; on publication.

USA WEEKEND FAMILY WEEKLY, (formerly Family Weekly), c/o Gnotte Co, 1000 Wilson Blvd., Arlington VA 22209. (703)276-3400. Director of Photography: Jackie Greene. Emphasizes general topics. Weekly. Circ. 13 million. Returns original artwork after publication.
Illustrations: Buys illustrations from freelancers. Considers b&w line drawings and color. Works on assignment only. Send tear sheets to be kept on file; call for appointment to show portfolio. Samples not filed are returned by SASE. Buys first rights. Payment negotiable.

VEGETARIAN TIMES, Box 570, Oak Park IL 60303. (312)848-8120. Editor/Publisher: Paul Obis. Consumer food magazine with emphasis on fitness and health for readers 30-50, 75% women. Monthly. Circ. 80,000. Accepts previously published material. Original artwork returned after publication. Sample copy $2.
Illustrations: Buys 4 illustrations/issue from freelancers. Send query letter with brochure showing art style and tear sheets. To show a portfolio, mail appropriate materials or call to schedule an appointment; portfolio should include roughs, original/final art, color, tear sheets, photographs and b&w. Pays $100-300, inside; on publication.

VENTURE, Box 150, Wheaton IL 60189. (312)665-0630. Art Director: Lawrence Libby. Senior Graphic Designer: Roy Green. For boys 12-18. "We seek to promote consciousness, acceptance of and personal commitment to Jesus Christ." Published 6 times/year. Circ. 13,000. Simultaneous submissions and previously published work OK. Original artwork returned after publication. Sample copy $1.50 with large SASE; artists' guidelines with SASE.
Cartoons: Send to attention of Cartoon Editor. Uses 1-3 cartoons/issue; buys all from freelancers. Receives 2 submissions/week from freelancers, on nature, sports, school, camping, hiking; single panel with gagline. "Keep it clean." Prefers finished cartoons. SASE. Reports in 2-4 weeks. Buys first-time rights. Pays $20 minimum, b&w line drawings; on acceptance.
Illustrations: Contact Art Director. Uses 3 illustrations/issue; buys 2/issue from freelancers, on education, family life and camping; b&w only. Works on assignment only. Send business card, tear sheets and photocopies of samples to be kept on file for future assignments. Samples returned by SASE. Reports back on future assignment possibilities. SASE. Reports in 2 weeks. Buys first time rights. Pays $100-150 for inside use of b&w line drawings and washes; on publication.

VERDICT MAGAZINE, 124 Truxtun Ave., Bakersfield CA 93301. (805)325-7124. Editor: Steve Walsh. Emphasizes law for insurance defense lawyers. Circ. 5,000. Accepts previously published material. Original artwork returned after publication. Sample copy for SASE with $3 postage; art guidelines for SASE with 22¢ postage.
Cartoons: Buys 4 cartoons/issue from freelancers. Legal themes. Prefers single panel with gagline; b&w line drawings or b&w washes. Send finished cartoons to be kept on file. Material not filed is returned by SASE. Reports only if interested. Buys one-time rights or reprint rights. Write for appointment to show portfolio. Pays $5, b&w; on publication.
Illustrations: Buys 4 illustrations/issue from freelancers. Themes: law, legal. Send photostats, tear sheets or photocopies to be kept on file. Samples not filed are returned by SASE. Reports only if interested. Write for appointment to show portfolio. Buys one-time rights or reprint rights. Pays $10, color, cover; $5, b&w, inside; on publication.

***VERMONT BUSINESS NEWSMAGAZINE**, Box 6120, Brattleboro VT 05301. (802)257-4100. Production Manager: Valarie Rozokat. Newspaper emphasizing Vermont businesses for firms located or doing business in Vermont. Monthly. Circ. 14,000. Accepts previously published material. Original artwork returned after publication. Sample copy free with SASE; art guidelines available.
Cartoons: Prefers b&w line drawings. Send query letter with samples of style to be kept on file. Material not filed is returned only if requested. Does not report back. Call for an appointment to show portfolio. Negotiates rights purchased. Payment is "subject to various material."
Illustrations: Buys various amounts of illustrations. Works on assignment only. Send query letter. Samples not filed are returned only if requested. Reports only if interested. Call or write to schedule an appointment to show a portfolio, which should include final reproduction/product. Negotiates rights purchased. Pays on acceptance.

VICTIMOLOGY: AN INTERNATIONAL JOURNAL, Box 39045, Washington DC 20016. (703)528-8872. Editor-in-chief: Emilio Viano. For professionals, lawyers, criminologists, medical personnel and

others helping child/spouse abuse programs, hotlines, rape crisis centers and other victim programs. "By 'victim,' we mean not only those victimized by crime but earthquakes, the environment, accidents, pollution and the state." Quarterly. Circ. 2,500. Send query letter with samples. SASE. Reports in 4 weeks. Buys all rights. Pays on publication. Sample copy $5. Write to be put on mailing list to receive periodical announcements.
Illustrations: Buys several illustrations/year on victimization. "We like to see illustrations on what is done in behalf of the victim." Pays $150, color, cover; $50, b&w. Pays $30, b&w, inside. Pays $50 for brochure work.

VIDEOGRAPHY, 50 W. 23rd St., New York NY 10010. (212)645-1000. Art Director: Jean Fujisaki. Audience is video professionals. Monthly. Circ. 25,000 + . Original artwork returned after publication.
Cartoons: Number of cartoons used/issue varies. Themes vary. Prefers b&w line drawings. Send query letter with samples of style to be kept on file.
Illustrations: Number of illustrations used/issue varies. Send query letter with brochure showing art style or tear sheets, slides and photographs to be kept on file. Write to schedule an appointment to show a portfolio, which should include original/final art, final reproduction/product, color, tear sheets, photostats, photographs and b&w. Pays on publication.
Tips: "There's a greater and greater sophistication in computer-generated graphics. We try to keep abreast on the latest techniques."

VIDEO MOVIES™ MAGAZINE, 3841 W. Oakton, Skokie IL 60076. (312)676-3470. Art Director: Jeff Hapner. Estab. 1983. Emphasizes movies available on video tape or disc for home viewing. Monthly. Circ. 200,000. Does not return original artwork after publication. Sample copy $1.95.
Illustrations: Works on assignment only. Send samples to be kept on file. "Photocopies are fine as samples, whatever the artist usually sends." Samples not filed are returned only if requested. Reports back only if interested. Write for appointment to show portfolio. Buys all rights. Payment varies according to project; pays on acceptance.

VIDEO REVIEW, 902 Broadway, New York NY 10010. (212)477-2200. Art Director: Orit. Emphasizes home video for owners and prospective owners of home video equipment. Monthly. Circ. 475,000. Original artwork returned after publication.
Cartoons: Uses 1-2 cartoons/issue; buys all from freelancers. Accepts "anything humorous" concerning home video use; single panel. Send photocopies of finished cartoons. Samples not returned. Reports in 1 month if requested. Buys first reproduction rights. Pays $35-100, b&w. Pays 4-6 weeks after publication.
Illustrations: Uses 3-5 illustations/issue; buys all from freelancers. Prefers airbrush, line drawings, sculpture and color for cover. Works on assignment only. Provide resume and samples to be kept on file for possible future assignments. Send samples of style. Samples not returned. Reports when an assignment is available. Call or write for appointment. Negotiates rights purchased. Pays $250-950; 6-8 weeks after publication.

***VIRGINIA BAR NEWS**, Suite 1000, Ross Building, 801 East Main St., Richmond VA 23219. (804)786-2061. Coordinator of Public Information and Publications: Cathe Kervan. Magazine emphasizing legal profession for members of the bar throughout the state. Bimonthly. Circ. 20,000. Sample copy free for SASE.
Illustrations: Buys various illustrations/issue from freelancers. Works on assignment only. Send query letter with resume, tear sheets, photostats, photocopies and photographs. Samples not filed are returned only if requested. Reports within 1 month. Portfolio should include original/final art, photographs and b&w. Pays $150-200, b&w, cover; $25-75, b&w, inside; on publication.

***VIRTUE MAGAZINE**, Box 850, Sisters OR 97759. (503)549-8261. Art Director: Ann Staatz. Magazine aimed at Christian homemakers. The majority are ages 25-45, married, and have children living at home. Publishes 10 issues/year. Circ. 125,000. Accepts previously published material. Original artwork returned after publication. Sample copy $2 plus postage or SASE. Art guidelines free for SASE with 22¢ postage.
Cartoons: Buys 1-4 cartoons/issue from freelancers. Cartoons should involve family, children, homemaking, marriage or incidents in a woman's everyday life. They should be aimed at women. Prefers single panel with or without gagline; b&w line drawings or b&w washes. Send samples of style and finished cartoons. Samples not filed are returned by SASE. Reports within 5-10 days. Buys first rights. Pays $25, b&w.
Illustrations: Buys 4-6 illustrations/issue from freelancers. Works on assignment only. Send query letter with brochure showing art style or resume, tear sheets, photostats, photocopies, slides or photographs. Prefers samples that be filed. Samples not filed are returned by SASE. To show a portfolio, mail

appropriate materials or call to schedule an appointment; portfolio should include original/final art and tear sheets. Buys first rights. Pays $50-75, b&w, and $100-150, color, inside; on publication.

VISIONS, THE INTERNATIONAL MAGAZINE OF ILLUSTRATED POETRY, Black Buzzard Press, 4705 S. 8th Rd., Arlington VA 22204. Editors: Bradley R. Strahan, Ursula Gill and Shirley Sullivan. Emphasizes literature and the illustrative arts for "well educated, very literate audience, very much into art and poetry." Published 3 times/year. Circ. 650. Sometimes accepts previously published material under special circumstances. Original artwork returned after publication only if requested. Sample copy $2.50 (latest issue $3); art guidelines free for SASE.
Illustrations: Buys approximately 16/issue, 50 illustrations/year from freelancers. Works on assignment only. Representational to surrealistic and some cubism style. Send query letter with SASE and samples to be kept on file. Samples should clearly show artist's style and capability; no slides or originals. Samles not filed are returned by SASE. Reports within 2 months. Buys first rights. "For information on releases on artwork, please contact the editors at the above address." Payment varies.
Tips: "We don't follow trends. We publish imaginative, skillful artworks no matter what the style. We strongly recommend reviewing a recent issue before submitting work."

VOGUE, 350 Madison Ave., New York NY 10017. Art Director: Roger Schoening. Emphasizes fashion, health, beauty, culture and decorating for women. Write and send resume; will then review portfolio; works primarily with New York area artists. Leave photocopies for referral.

VOLKSWAGEN'S WORLD, Volkswagen of America, Troy MI 48099. (313)362-6770. Editor: Ed Rabinowitz. For Volkswagen owners. Quarterly. Circ. 250,000. Receives 2-3 cartoons and 2-3 illustrations/week from freelance artists. Previously published and photocopied submissions OK. Free sample copy.
Cartoons: Seldom purchases cartoons unless the subject matter is particularly unique. Send query letter with samples. SASE. Reports in 6 weeks. Buys all rights. Pays $15 minimum, halftones and washes; on acceptance.
Illustrations: Buys 12/year on assigned themes. Send query letter with samples. SASE. Reports in 6 weeks. Buys all rights. Cover: Pays $250 minimum, color. Inside: Pays $15 minimum, b&w and color; on acceptance.
Tips: "We're happy to send sample issues to prospective contributors. It's the best way of seeing what our needs are."

WASHINGTON FOOD DEALER MAGAZINE,8288 Lake City Way NE, Seattle WA 98115. Managing Editor/Advertising Director: T.J. Robison. Emphasizes the food industry, particularly retail grocers (independents). Monthly. Circ. 3,800. Accepts previously published material. Does not return original artwork after publication. Sample copy $1; art guidelines available.
Cartoons: Interested in cartoons on food industry trends with an editorial message. Prefers single panel with b&w line drawings. Send query letter with samples of style to be kept on file. Write for appointment to show portfolio. Material not filed is returned only if requested. Reports only if interested. Negotiates rights purchased. Negotiates pay; pays on publication.
Illustrations: Buys 1-2 illustrations/issue from freelance. Prefers food industry themes. Works on assignment only. Send query letter with resume and tear sheets to be kept on file. Write for appointment to show portfolio. Samples not filed are returned by SASE. Reports only if interested. Negotiates rights purchased and payment. Pays on publication.

THE WASHINGTON MONTHLY, 1711 Connecticut Ave. NW, Washington DC 20009. (202)462-0128. Art Director: Kitry Krause. For journalists, government officials and general public interested in public affairs. "We examine government's failures and suggest solutions." Monthly. Circ. 39,000. Previously published and photocopied submissions OK.
Illustrations: Buys 20-40 illustrations/year on politics and government. Local artists preferred. Send query letter with samples or arrange interview to show portfolio. SASE. Reports in 4 weeks. Buys one-time rights. Pays $50-125, b&w line drawings and washes, inside; pay is negotiable for color-separated work; $100 minimum, b&w, cover; on publication.
Tips: "We need fast turn-around; artist should read articles before attempting work."

THE WASHINGTONIAN MAGAZINE, Suite 200, 1828 L St. NW, Washington DC 20036. (202)296-3600. Emphasizes politics, cultural events, personalities, entertainment and dining. About Washington, for Washingtonians. Monthly. Circ. 144,000. Simultaneous submissions and previously published work OK. Original artwork returned after publication if requested. No artists' guidelines available.
Cartoons: Cartoon Editor: Howard Means. Buys 5 cartoons/issue from freelancers, on "sophisticated topics, urban life"; single and double panel with gagline. Uses b&w line drawings, gray opaques, b&w

washes, and opaque watercolors. Prefers finished cartoons. Reports in 4-6 weeks. Buys one-time rights. Pays $50, b&w; on publication.

Illustrations: Design Director: Linda Otto. Uses 5 illustrations/issue; buys 3/issue from freelancers, on a variety of subjects. Works on assignment only. Uses b&w line drawings, gray opaques, b&w washes, color washes and opaque watercolor. Send resume, business card and tear sheets to be kept on file. Returns samples if requested. Does not report back on future assignment possibilities. Prefers to see portfolio and samples of style. SASE. Reports in 1 week. Buys one-time rights. Pay is negotiable; on publication. Also uses freelance pasteup artists.

***WATERFRONT MAGAZINE**, Box 1337, Newport Beach CA 92663. Art Director: Jeffrey Fleming. Magazine emphasizing boating for Southern Californians who own a boat or like to go boating. Monthly. Circ. 38,000. Accepts previously published material. Original artwork returned after publication. Sample copy free for SASE with $1.75 postage.

Cartoons: Buys 2 cartoons/year from freelancers. Prefers single panel without gagline; b&w line drawings. Send query letter with samples of style to be kept on file. Samples not filed are returned by SASE. Reports only if interested. Write to schedule an appointment to show a portfolio. Negotiates rights purchased. Pays $75, b&w.

Illustrations: Buys 2 illustrations/issue from freelancers. Prefers boat-related themes (power or sail). Send query letter with resume, tear sheets, photostats, photocopies, slides and photographs. Samples not filed are returned by SASE. Reports only if interested. To show a portfolio, mail appropriate materials. Negotiates rights purchased.

WATER SKI MAGAZINE, Box 2456, Winter Park Fl 32790. (305)628-4802. Publisher: Terry Snow. Send query letters to: Terry Temple, editor. Emphasizes water skiing for an audience generally 18-34 years old, 80% male, active, educated, affluent. Published 8 times/year. Circ. 56,000. Accepts previously published material and simultaneous submissions. Original artwork returned after publication. Query for guidelines.

Cartoons: Uses 1-4 cartoons/issue, buys all from freelancers. 90% assigned. Prefers single panel with gagline, color or b&w washes or b&w line drawings. Prefers to receive query letter with samples or roughs first, but will review finished work. Samples returned. Reports within 3 weeks. Negotiates rights purchased. Negotiates payment, usually $15-30, b&w; up to $300, color, depending on topic. Pays 30 days after publication.

Illustrations: Uses 10 illustrations/issue; buys 5 illustrations/issue from freelancers. Prefers strong lines in a realistic style. Works on assignment "most of the time." Send query letter with resume, samples and tear sheets to be kept on file. Samples returned by SASE if not kept on file. Reports within 3 weeks. May also submit portfolio. Negotiates payment and rights purchased. Pays on publication.

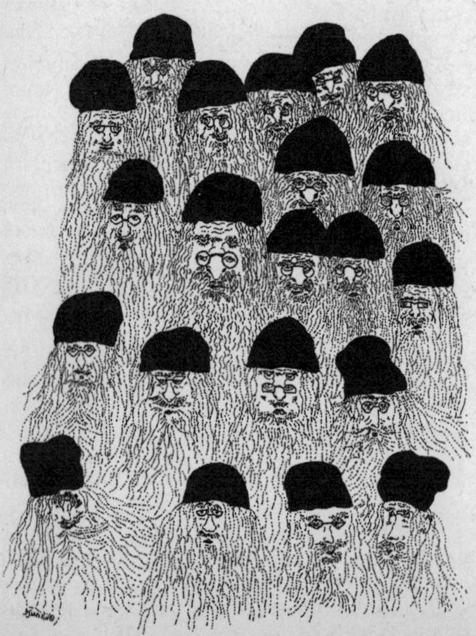

Freelance illustrator David Sheshkin of Bethel, Connecticut, "gets personal satisfaction when I see any of my drawings published," as he did with the spot drawing he published in Waves, *a Canadian literary journal. Bernice Lever, editor of the magazine, bought one-time rights to the piece, which is entitled "Holy Reunion I". Sheshkin discovered the magazine in the* Artist's Market.

WAVES, (Fine Canadian Writing), 79 Denham Dr., Richmond Hill, Ontario L4C 6H9 Canada. (416)889-6703. Editor: Bernice Lever. Emphasizes literature for readers of contemporary poetry and fiction. Published trianually. Circ. 1,100. Returns original artwork after publication. Sample copy for SASE (nonresidents include IRC). Art guidelines available.
Illustrations: Uses 3-15/issue. Themes and styles are open. "Art does not relate to the literature printed. It can contrast or harmonize." Send query letter with samples to be kept on file for 6 months. Prefers photostats or tear sheets as samples—high contrast line drawings. Samples not filed are returned by SASE (nonresidents include IRC). Reports within 1 month. Write for appointment to show portfolio. Buys one-time North American rights. Pays $6.50, b&w, inside; and $25, b&w, cover; on publication.

WEEDS TREES & TURF, 7500 Old Oak Blvd., Cleveland OH 44130. Editor: Jerry Roche. Emphasizes landscape management, i.e., golf courses, estates, parks, schools, and private landscape contractors for golf course superintendents, landscape contractors, park supervisors, athletic field directors, estate managers, staff groundskeepers. Monthly. Circ. 46,000. Accepts previously published material. Sample copy free for SASE.
Illustrations: Buys 2 illustrations/issue from freelancers. Prefers line art and color art. Works on assignment only. Send query letter with photostats, photographs, slides or original work to be kept on file. Write to schedule an appointment to show a portfolio, which should include thumbnails, roughs, original/final art, final reproduction/product, color, tear sheets, photostats, photographs and b&w. Samples not kept on file are returned. Reports within 30 days. Negotiates rights purchased. Pays $300-500, color, cover; $50, b&w, $200, color, inside; on publication.

WEIGHT WATCHERS MAGAZINE, 360 Lexington Ave., New York NY 10017. (212)370-0644. Art Director: Alan Richardson. Emphasizes food, health, fashion, beauty for the weight and beauty conscious, 25-45 years old. Monthly. Circ. 875,000. Original artwork returned after publication.
Illustrations: Uses 6 illustrations/issue. Works on assignment only. Send query letter with brochure to be kept on file. Reports only if interested. Portfolios seen by drop-off only. Buys one-time rights. Pays on acceptance.

THE WEIRDBOOK SAMPLER, Box 149, Amherst Branch, Buffalo NY 14226. Editor-in-Chief: W. Paul Ganley. An irregular companion publication to *Weirdbook* for those interested in fantasy, adventure and horror. Irregular publications. Circ. 200. Buys first or all rights. Sample copy $3.75.
Illustrations: Buys 10-20 illustrations/year. Interested in weird, macabre, supernatural and fantastic themes. "Illustrate scenes from famous weird writers like Bradbury, Lovecraft, Poe, etc." Mail art. Photocopies OK. Must be suited to photocopy. SASE. Reports within 3 months. Cover: Pays $10, b&w; Inside: Pays $5/page; on publication. *Currently overstocked.*
Tips: "Plan to reduce art to 85% of actual size; column width of 4" or double column width of 8¼" 'intermediate sizes can be used.' Art that does not require half-toning preferred, particularly on interiors. Leave at least ¼" around interiors for cropping (⅜" on full page sizes). No pencil drawings or slides. Copies OK if suitable for reproduction. All due care will be used in handling, but send a reminder letter when you want them back (about 6 weeks after publication). B&w artwork only, no color."

WEST, 750 Ridder Park Dr., San Jose CA 95190. (408)920-5602. Editor: Jeffrey Klein. Art Director: Bambi Nicklen. General interest magazine for subscribers of the *San Jose Mercury News*. Circ. 307,000. Weekly. Free sample copy.
Illustrations: Buys 2-3/issue on all themes except erotica. Query with resume and samples or previously published work, or arrange interview to show portfolio. Cover: Pays up to $500, opaque watercolors, oils, acrylics or mixed media. Inside: Pays $125-400, b&w line drawings, washes and gray opaques; $150-400, color washes, opaque watercolors, oils, acrylics or mixed media. Pays on acceptance.

***WEST COAST REVIEW**, English Dept., Simon Fraser University, Burnaby, British Columbia V5A 1S6 Canada. (604)291-4287. Editor: F. Candelaria. Magazine emphasizing arts and literature for university libraries, writers and artists. Quarterly. Circ. 700. Original artwork returned after publication. Sample copy $4. Art guidelines free for SASE with 37¢ Canadian postage.
Illustrations: Buys 4 illustrations/issue from freelancers. Send query letter with photographs. Samples not filed are returned by SASE. Reports within 2 months. To show a portfolio, mail appropriate materials. Buys first rights. Pays $50-100, b&w, cover; $50-100, b&w, inside; on acceptance.

***WEST MICHIGAN MAGAZINE**, 7 Ionia S.W., Grand Rapids MI 49503. Art Director: Becky McWilliams. Magazine emphasizing people, places and issues related to West Michigan for upscale-higher than average incomes and education. Monthly. Circ. 22,000. Accepts previously published material. Original artwork returned after publication. Sample copy $2 with 98¢ postage.

Cartoons: Buys at least 2 cartoons/issue from freelancers. Prefers double panel with or without gagline; b&w line drawings. Send query letter with samples of style to be kept on file except for unacceptable quality artwork. Material not kept on file is returned by SASE. Reports only if interested. Buys one-time or reprint rights.

Illustrations: Buys 1-3 illustrations/issue from freelancers. Works on assignment only. Send query letter with brochure showing art style. Samples not kept on file are returned by SASE. Reports only if interested. Call to schedule an appointment to show a portfolio, which should include original/final art, final reproduction/product, color and b&w. Buys one-time rights. Pays on publication.

WESTERN HUMANITIES REVIEW, University of Utah, Salt Lake City UT 84112. (801)581-7438. Literary magazine. Readers are "highly educated and interested in all aspects of the humanities. Most of our subscribers are libraries." Quarterly. Circ. 1,100. Original artwork returned after publication. Sample copy $4. "We also need covers, for which we pay $150 each. Artists should look at past issues to see the sort of things we use."

Cartoons: Buys 4 cartoons/issue; buys all from freelancers. Receives 4 submissions/week from freelancers. Format: b&w line drawings with a touch of wit preferred. Single panel *without gagline*. "Art-

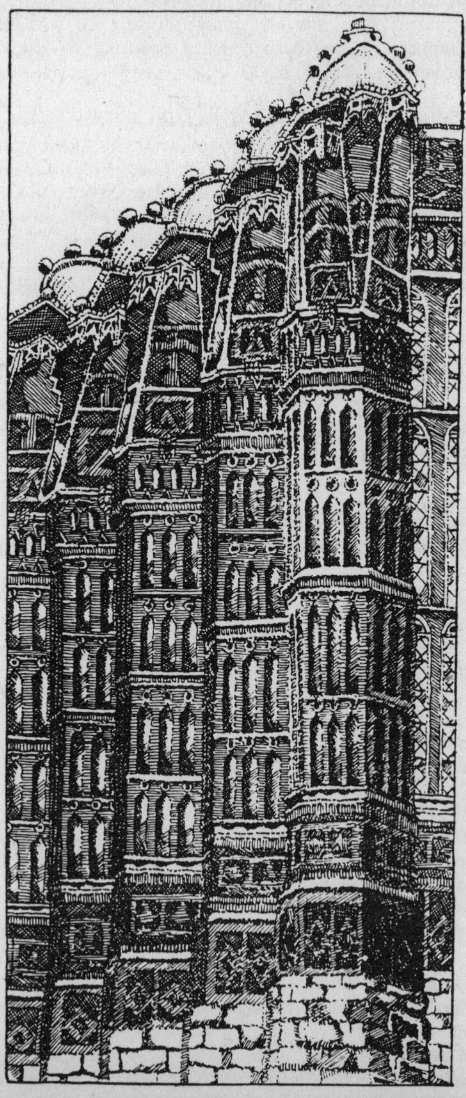

"A sense of history, or conversely, a sense of fantasy and romance" was the message Melinda Giordano of Los Angeles, California wanted to convey in this illustration, published in Western Humanities Review. *The quarterly literary magazine, which Giordano found in the* Artist's Market, *paid $50 for reprint rights.*

ists should look at some of the recent issues." Send finished cartoons to Jack Garlington, editor. SASE. Reports in 1 week if "uninterested; longer if interested." Pays $50 on acceptance. Buys first North American serial rights.
Illustrations: Buys 2 illustrations/issue; buys all from freelancers. Receives 4 submissions/week from freelancers. Send query letter with samples. Prefers to see finished art. SASE. Reports in 1 week if "uninterested; longer if interested." To show a portfolio, mail appropriate materials. Buys first North American serial rights. Payment varies for cover art; pays $50 b&w, inside; on acceptance.
Tips: "We don't use cartoon gags. The best idea would be to check out a copy of the magazine—which should be in most university libraries—before submitting materials."

WESTERN OUTDOORS,3197-E Airport Loop Dr., Costa Mesa CA 92626. (714)546-4370. Art Director: Gayle Radestock. Emphasizes hunting and fishing and related activities in the western states; directed to men and women interested in pursuing these activities in the 11 contiguous western states plus Alaska, Hawaii, British Columbia and western Mexico. Published 10 times/year. Circ. 150,000. Returns original artwork after publication.
Illustrations: Works on assignment only. Send query letter with samples to be kept on file. Accepts photocopies as samples. Samples not filed are returned by SASE. Reports within 30 days. Write for appointment to show portfolio. Buys first rights. Pays on acceptance.

THE WESTERN PRODUCER, Box 2500, Saskatoon, Saskatchewan S7K 2C4 Canada. (306)665-3500. For farm families in western Canada. Weekly. Circ. 140,000.
Cartoons: Receives 12/week from freelance artists. Uses only cartoons about rural life. SASE (nonresidents include IRC). Reports in 3 weeks. Buys first Canadian rights. Pays $15, b&w line drawings; on acceptance. No illustrations.

***WESTERN RV TRAVELER**, (formerly California Traveler), 2019 Clement AVe., Alameda CA 94501. (415)865-0159. Creative Director: David Hebenstreit. "RV magazine of the West" for RV-owners and travel-oriented readers. Monthly. Circ. 100,000. Accepts previously published material. Original artwork returned after publication. Sample copy available.
Cartoons: Buys 1-5 cartoons/issue from freelancers. Prefers single panel with or without gagline; b&w line drawings or b&w washes. Send query letter with finished cartoons. Write to schedule an appointment to show a portfolio. Material not kept on file is returned by SASE. Reports only if interested. Buys one-time rights. Pays $5, b&w.
Illustrations: Buys 5-10 illustrations/issue from freelancers. Prefers line drawings for newsprint publication. Send query letter with resume, tear sheets, photostats, photocopies and photographs. Samples not filed are returned by SASE. Reports only if interested. Write to schedule an appointment to show a portfolio, which should include original/final art, final reproduction/product, tear sheets, photostats, photographs and three-dimensional work. Buys one-time rights. Pays $100, color, cover; $5, b&w, inside; on publication.

WESTERN SPORTSMAN, Box 737, Regina, Saskatchewan S4P 3A8 Canada. (306)352-8384. Editor-in-Chief: Rick Bates. For fishermen, hunters, campers and outdoorsmen. Bimonthly. Circ. 28,000. Original artwork returned after publication. Sample copy $3; artist's guidelines for SASE (nonresidents include IRC).
Cartoons: Buys 90 cartoons/year on the outdoors; single, double and multiple panel with gaglines. Send art or query with samples. SASE (nonresidents include IRC). Reports in 3 weeks. Buys first North American serial rights. Pays $20, b&w line drawings; on acceptance.
Illustrations: Buys 8 illustrations/year on the outdoors. Mail art or query with samples. SASE (nonresidents include IRC). Reports in 3 weeks. Buys first North American serial rights. Pays $50-200, b&w line drawings, inside; on acceptance.

WESTERN'S WORLD, East-West Network, Inc., Suite 800, 5900 Wilshire Blvd., Los Angeles CA 90036. (213)937-5810. Editor: Ed Dwyer. Art Director: Jim Kiehle. For airline passengers. Monthly. Original work returned after publication. Sample copy $2.
Illustrations: Buys 1 illustration every 3-4 months. Works on assignment only. Send query letter with brochure showing art style and tear sheets. Reports in 1 month. Buys first rights. Negotiates payment; pays on acceptance.

WESTWAYS, Terminal Annex, Box 2890, Los Angeles CA 90051. (213)741-4760. Editor: Mary Ann Fisher. Production Manager: Vincent J. Corso. For the people of the Western US. Emphasizes current and historical events, culture, art, travel and recreation. Monthly. Circ. 478,000.
Illustrations: Buys assigned themes on travel, history, and arts in the West. Send resume to be kept on file. Do not call. Buys first rights, based on decision of the editor. Cover: Pays $400. Inside: Pays $50-150, drawings; $150, 4-color illustrations; on publication.

WHISKEY ISLAND MAGAZINE, University Center 7, Cleveland State University, Cleveland OH 44115. Editor: Leah Borovich. For all writers; poetry, short fiction and drama. Published 2-3 times annually. Circ. 2,000. Photocopied and simultaneous submissions OK.
Illustrations: All photos and other graphics accepted; no limitation by theme; b&w. Send query letter with photocopies, photographs and b&w drawings. SASE. Reports in 12 weeks. To show a portfolio, mail thumbnails, roughs, original/final art, photographs and b&w. Payment is two contributor's copies; on publication.
Tips: "Have good lines and drawings done in black and white."

WHISPERS, 70 Highland Ave., Binghamton NY 13905. Editor-in-Chief/Art Director: Stuart David Schiff. For college-educated adults interested in literate fantasy, horror, art and fiction. Published 1-2 times/year. Circ. 3,000. Original artwork returned after publication. Sample copy $3.50.
Illustrations: Uses 10-20 illustrations/issue; buys 2-3/issue from freelancers. Receives 5-10 submissions/week from freelancers. Interested in fantasy and horror. Send photocopied samples of finished art. SASE. Send flyer and tear sheets to be kept on file for future assignments. Reports in 30-60 days. Buys first North American serial rights. Pays $100-200, color, cover; $10-25, b&w, inside. Pays by arrangement to retain artwork after use.
Tips: Especially looks for "clean lines, originality and non-comic book appearance of humans" in artwork.

WILSON LIBRARY BULLETIN, 950 University Ave., Bronx NY 10452. (212)588-8400. Editor: Milo Nelson. Emphasizes the issues and the practice of library science. Published 10 times/year. Circ. 25,000. Free sample copy.
Cartoons: Buys 2-3 cartoons/issue on education and library science; single panel with gagline. Mail finished art. SASE. Reports back only if interested. Buys first rights. Pays $100, b&w line drawings and washes; on acceptance.
Illustrations: Uses 1-2 illustrations/issue; buys all from freelancers. Works on assignment only. Send query letter, business card and samples to be kept on file. Reports back only if interested. Call for appointment to show portfolio. Buys first rights. Cover: Pays $300, color washes. Inside: Pays $100-200, b&w line drawings and washes; $20, spot drawings; on publication.

WINDSOR THIS MONTH MAGAZINE, Box 1029, Station A, Windsor, Ontario N9A 6P4 Canada. (519)966-7411. Publisher: J.S. Woloschuk. Editor: Laura Rosenthal. Features Windsor-oriented issues, interviews, opinion, answers. Published 12 times/year. Circ. 22,000.
Illustrations: Buys 3/issue on assigned themes. Send query letter with samples. Include SASE (nonresidents include IRC). Reports in 1 week. Buys first North American serial rights. Negotiates pay, color and b&w; on publication.
Tips: "Send sample of published work."

WINES & VINES, 1800 Lincoln Ave., San Rafael CA 94901. (415)453-9700. Editor: Philip E. Hiaring. Emphasizes the grape and wine industry in North America for the trade—growers, winemakers, merchants. Monthly. Circ. 5,800. Accepts previously published material. Original artwork not returned after publication.
Cartoons: Buys approximately 3 cartoons/year. Prefers single panel with gagline; b&w line drawings. Send query letter with roughs to be kept on file. Material not kept on file is not returned. Reports within 1 month. Buys first rights. Pays $10.
Illustrations: Send query letter to be kept on file. Reports within 1 month. Buys first rights. Pays $50-100, color, cover; $15, b&w, inside. Pays on acceptance.

***WINNING**, 15115 S. 76 E. Ave., Bixby OK 74008. (918)366-4441. Graphics Manager: J.D. Gibson. Newspaper emphasizing contests, sweepstakes and lottery. Monthly. Circ. 250,000. Accepts previously published material after publication. Sample copy available.
Cartoons: Buys 2-3 cartoons/issue from freelancers. Prefers contests, sweepstakes and lottery as themes. Prefers single, double or multiple panel, with or without gagline; b&w line drawings. Send samples of style to be kept on file. Material not kept on file is returned by SASE. Reports only if interested. Negotiates rights purchased.
Illustrations: Buys 2-3 illustrations/issue from freelancers. Send query letter with tear sheets. Samples not filed are returned by SASE. Does not report back.

WISCONSIN RESTAURATEUR, 122 W. Washington, Madison WI 53703. (608)251-3663. Editor: Jan LaRue. Emphasizes the restaurant industry. Readers are "restaurateurs, hospitals, schools, institutions, cafeterias, food service students, chefs, etc." Monthly. Circ. 3,600, except convention issue (March), 13,000. Original artwork returned after publication. Free sample copy; art guidelines for SASE. Especially needs cover material.

Cartoons: Buys 1 cartoon/issue from freelancer. Receives 5 cartoons/week from freelancers. "Uses much material pertaining to conventions, food shows, etc. Sanitation issue good. Cartoons about employees. No off-color material." Prefers b&w line drawings with gaglines. Send finished cartoons. SASE. Reports in 2 weeks. Buys first North American serial rights. Pays $8 on publication.

Illustrations: Uses 5 illustrations/issue; buys 1/issue from freelancer. Receives 1 illustration/week from freelance artists. Freelancers chosen "at random, depending on theme and articles featured for the month." Looks for "the unusual, pertaining to the food service industry. No offbeat or questionable material." Prefers b&w line drawings and washes for covers. Send brochure showing art style or resume to be kept on file for future assignments. Buys first North American serial rights. To show a portfolio, mail appropriate materials, which should include roughs, original/final art and b&w. Pays $25, b&w and $50, color, cover; $15, b&w, $20, color, inside; on acceptance.

Tips: Trends within the field include "seafood, low-calorie beverages and more convenience foods." Changes within the magazine include "new cover design, and the use of more freelance material—pictures and illustrations. Study back issues."

WISCONSIN TRAILS, Box 5650, Madison WI 53705. (608)231-2444. Production Manager: Nancy Mead. Concerns travel, recreation, history, industry and personalities in Wisconsin. Published 6 times/year. Circ. 25,000. Previously published and photocopied submissions OK. Artists' guidelines for SASE.

Illustrations: Buys 6 illustrations/issue from freelancers. Receives less than 1 submission/week from freelancers. "Art work is done on assignment, to illustrate specific articles. All articles deal with Wisconsin. We allow artists considerable stylistic latitude." Send samples (photocopies OK) of style; indication of artist's favorite topics; name, address and phone number to be kept on file for future assignments. SASE. Reporting time varies. Buys one-time rights on a work-for-hire basis. Pays $25-300, inside; on publication.

THE WITTENBURG DOOR, 1224 Greenfield Dr., El Cajon CA 92021. (619)440-2333, (916)842-1301. Editor: Mike Yaconelli. For men and women, usually connected with the church. Bimonthly. Circ. 20,000.

Cartoons: Buys 2-3 cartoons/issue on assignment. Purchases 2-3 cartoons/month from freelance artists. "Very selective." Uses satire/humor on religious themes geared to evangelicals. Send query letter with original art. SASE. Reports in 3 months. Pays $50, b&w; on publication.

Tips: "Submit original art by mail—please don't send only a query letter. Humor should be biting, satirical, daring, subtle, "off-the-wall," or any combination of above."

WOMAN BEAUTIFUL, Allied Publications, 1776 Lake Worth Rd., Lake Worth FL 33460. Editor: Mark Adams. For students at beauty schools and people who patronize beauty salons. Bimonthly. Circ. 12,000.

Cartoons: Buys 2 cartoons/issue on any subject. Send finished art. SASE. Reports in 2 months. Pays $10 for b&w; on publication.

WONDER TIME, 6401 The Paseo, Kansas City MO 64131. (816)333-7000. Editor: Evelyn Beals. "Story paper" emphasizing inspiration and character building material for first and second graders, 6-8 years old. Weekly. Circ. 40,000. Does not accept previously published material. Original artwork not returned to the artist after publication. Sample copy free for SASE with 44¢ postage. Art guidelines available.

Illustrations: Buys 1/issue. Works on assignment only. Send query letter with tear sheets or photocopies to be kept on file. Reports only if interested. Buys all rights. Pays $30-40, b&w, cover; on acceptance.

WOODENBOAT, Box 78, Brooklin ME 04616. Editor: Jonathan A. Wilson. Executive Editor: Billy R. Sims; Senior Editor: Peter H. Spectre. Managing Editor: Jennifer Buckley. Concerns designing, building, repairing, using and maintaining wooden boats. Bimonthly. Circ. 100,000. Previously published work OK. Sample copy $3.50.

Illustrations: Buys 48/year on wooden boats or related items. Send query letter with samples. SASE for return of material. Reports in 1-2 months. "We are always in need of high quality technical drawings. Rates vary, but usually $25-300. Buys first North American serial rights. Pays on publication.

Tips: "We work with several professionals on an assignment basis, but most of the illustrative material that we use in the magazine is submitted with a feature article. When we need additional material, however, we will try to contact a good freelancer in the appropriate geographic area."

WOODMEN OF THE WORLD, 1700 Farnam St., Omaha NE 68102. (402)342-1890. Editor-in-Chief: Leland A. Larson. For members of the Woodmen of the World Life Insurance Society and their families.

Emphasizes Society activities, children's and women's interests and humor. Monthly. Circ. 470,000. Previously published work OK. Original artwork returned after publication, if arrangements are made. Free sample copy.

Cartoons: Buys 1-6 cartoons/issue from freelancers. Receives 10-50 submissions/week from freelancers. Especially needs cartoons. Interested in general interest subjects; single panel. Send finished cartoons. SASE. Reports in 2 weeks. Buys various rights. Pays $10, b&w line drawings, washes and halftones; on acceptance.

Illustrations: Uses 5-10 illustrations/year; buys 3-4/year from freelancers. Interested in lodge activities, seasonal, humorous and human interest themes. Works on assignment only. Send brochure showing art style or flyers to be kept on file. Prefers to see finished art. SASE. Reports in 2 weeks. Buys one-time rights. Payment varies according to job.

Tips: Especially looks for creative thinking, technique and quality when reviewing samples. Artists should avoid "one-track stylization; vary the media used and techniques, if possible."

WORDS, 1015 N. York Rd, Willow Grove PA 19090. (215)657-3220. Art Director: Nancy Okuniewski. Emphasizes information systems and word processing for word processing professionals, consultants, educators and manufacturers; male and female; 20-50 years of age. Bimonthly. Circ. over 18,000. Original artwork returned after publication. Free sample copy for SASE.

Illustrations: Buys 1 illustration/issue from freelancers. Interested in "all styles" and "themes on editorial features of office automation." Works on assignment only. Send brochure with samples of style. Samples returned by SASE. Provide resume, business card and/or brochure to be kept on file for possible future assignments. Reports in 3 weeks. Call for appointment. Pays $50-300 inside, b&w line or wash; $300-500 for 4-color cover art; on publication.

Tips: "We're interested in a variety of styles and treatments. We're looking for clean, competent, modern and hi-tech looking graphics; simple, yet sophisticated. Present what you feel represents your best work (quality vs. quantity)."

***THE WORK BOAT**, Box 2400, Covington LA 70434. (504)893-2930. Editor: H.L. Peace. Managing Editor: Chip Edgar. Emphasizes news of the work boat industry for those involved with towboats, barges, oil rigs, dredges, crew boats and tugboats. Monthly. Circ. 13,600.

Illustrations: Suitable subjects are tow boats, pushboats, tug boats, offshore crew/supply boats, dredges; photos for cover. "Must evoke feeling of working in our industry. Action required. Allow 3 months lead for seasonal covers." Send query letter with color prints or slides. SASE. Reports in 4 weeks. Pays on acceptance.

WORKBENCH, Modern Handcraft, Inc., 4251 Pennsylvania, Kansas City MO 64111. Editor-in-Chief: Jay W. Hedden. For woodworkers and do-it-yourself persons. Bimonthly. Circ. 870,000. "Art accepted only as part of a package of copy, photos and drawings." Free sample copy and artists' guidelines.

Cartoons: Buys 15 cartoons/year. Interested in woodworking and do-it-yourself themes; single panel with gagline. Submit art. SASE. Reports in 1 month. Buys all rights, but may reassign rights to artist after publication. Pays on acceptance. Pays $20 minimum, b&w line drawings.

***WRENCH AND BENCH MAGAZINE**, 100 Seneca Ave., Rochester NY 14621. (716)338-1522. Editor: Donald Wood. For metalworking technical management. Readers are management and engineering personnel. Monthly. Circ. 16,000. Purchased artwork not returned.

Cartoons: Uses 3-4 cartoons/issue, all from freelancers. Receives 1 submission/week from freelancers. Interested in engineering and metalworking. Prefers single panel, b&w line drawings with gag lines. Prefers finished cartoons. SASE. Reports in 1 week. Buys one-time rights. Pays $5-10; on acceptance.

Tips: "There is a trend toward 'use of computers and numerical control' in our field. Artists should get a copy of our magazine before making submissions."

WRITER'S DIGEST, 9933 Alliance Rd., Cincinnati OH 45242. Art Director: Carol Buchanan. Assistant Editor: Sharon Rudd (for cartoons). Emphasizes freelance writing for freelance writers. Monthly. Circ. 200,000. Original artwork returned after publication. Sample copy $2.

Cartoons: Buys 3 cartoons/issue from freelancers. Theme: the writing life—cartoons that deal with writers and the trials of writing and selling their work. Also, writing from a historical standpoint (past works), language use and other literary themes. Prefers single panel with or without gagline. Send finished cartoons. Material returned by SASE. Reports within 1 month. Buys first rights or one-time rights. Pays $50-85, b&w; on acceptance.

Illustrations: Buys 4 illustrations/month from freelancers. Theme: the writing life (b&w line art primarily). Works on assignment only. Send brochure and samples to be kept on file; slides will be returned. Accepts photocopies as samples. Samples returned by SASE. Reports only if interested. Write for appointment to show portfolio. Buys one-time rights. Pays $400, color, cover; $50-200, inside, b&w. Pays on acceptance.

***WRITER'S INFO**, Box 2377, Coeur d'Alene ID 83814. (208)667-7511. Editor: Linda Hutton. Estab. 1985. Newsletter emphasizing freelancing for beginning freelance writers and poets. Monthly. Circ. 100. Accepts previously published material. Sample copy free for SASE with 39¢ postage. Art guidelines free for SASE with 22¢ postage.
Illustrations: Buys 3-5 illustrations/issue from freelancers. Prefers writing and seasonal themes. Send query letter with resume, tear sheets and photocopies. Samples not filed are returned by SASE. Reports within 4 weeks. To show a portfolio, mail tear sheets and photostats. Buys one-time rights. Pays $1-10, b&w; inside; on acceptance.

WRITER'S YEARBOOK, 9933 Alliance Rd., Cincinnati OH 45242. Submissions Editor: Sharon Rudd. Emphasizes writing and marketing techniques, business topics for writers and writing opportunities for freelance writers and people trying to get started in writing. Annually. Original artwork returned with one copy of the issue in which it appears. Sample copy $3.95. Affiliated with *Writer's Digest*. Cartoons admitted to either publication are considered for both.
Cartoons: Uses 6-10 freelance cartoons/issue. "All cartoons must pertain to writing—its joys, agonies, quirks. All styles accepted, but high-quality art is a must." Prefers single panel, with or without gagline, b&w line drawings or washes. "Verticals are always considered, but horizontals—especially severe horizontals—are hard to come by." Send finished cartoons. Samples returned by SASE. Reports within 3 weeks. Buys first North American serial rights, one-time use. Pays $50 minimum, b&w. Pays on acceptance.
Tips: "A cluttery style does not appeal to us. Send finished, not rough art, with clearly typed gaglines. Cartoons without gaglines must be particularly well executed."

X-IT MAGAZINE, Box 102, Station C, St. John's, Newfoundland A1C 5H5 Canada. (709)753-8802. Editor: Ken J. Harvey. Emphasizes arts and entertainment for those interested in the visual and literary arts. Triannually. Circ. 3,000. Accepts previously published material. Original artwork returned after publication. Sample copy $3.
Cartoons: Buys 3-6 cartoons/issue from freelancers. Prefers contemporary, but open to wide area of styles. Accepts single, double or multiple panel with or without gagline; b&w line drawings or washes. Send b&w samples of style or finished cartoons. Material returned by SASE (nonresidents include IRCs) only if requested. Reports within 3 weeks. Buys first rights or one-time rights. Write for appointment to show portfolio. Pays $15-150, b&w; on publication.
Illustrations: Buys 7-12 illustrations/issue from freelancers. Prefers contemporary, but open to many styles. Send query letter with brochure and tear sheets or photocopies. Samples returned by SASE (nonresidents include IRCs) only if requested. Reports within 3 weeks. Buys first rights or one-time rights. Write for appointment to show portfolio. Pays $15-150, b&w, inside; on publication.

YACHT RACING & CRUISING, 111 E Ave., Norwalk CT 06851. (203)853-9921. Managing Editor: Douglas O. Logan. Emphasizes performance sailboat events and instructional articles for "performance-oriented sailors." Published 12 times/year. Circ. 45,000. Original artwork returned after publication. Sample copy $1.75.
Illustrations: Works on assignment only. Send query letter with roughs. Samples returned by SASE. Buys first rights. Pays on publication.

YACHTING, 5 River Rd., Box 1200, Cos Cob CT 06807. (203)629-8300. Associate Editor: Deborah Meisels. For top-level participants in boating in all its forms, power and sail. Monthly. Circ. 150,000. Art guidelines for SASE.
Illustrations: Buys 10 spot illustrations/year. Query. SASE. Reports in 2-3 weeks. Buys all rights. Pays $50, b&w, inside.

***YACHTSMAN MAGAZINE**, 2019 Clement Ave., Alameda CA 94501. (415)865-7500. Creative Director: David Hebenstreit. Tabloid emphasizing yachting and boating. Monthly. Circ. 50,000. Accepts previously published material. Original artwork returned after publication. Sample copy free for SASE with 75¢ postage.
Cartoons: Buys 1-5 cartoons/issue from freelancers. Prefers boating or yachting themes. Prefers single, double or multiple panel with or without gagline; b&w line drawings or b&w washes. Send query letter with finished cartoons to be kept on file. Material not kept on file is returned by SASE. Does not report back. Write to schedule an appointment to show a portfolio. Buys one-time rights. Pays $5, b&w.
Illustrations: Buys 1-10 illustrations/issue from freelancers. Prefers yachting or boating themes. Send query letter with samples. Samples not filed are returned by SASE. Reports only if interested. Write to

schedule an appointment to show a portfolio, which should include final reproductional/product. Buys one-time rights. Pays $100, b&w and $100, color, cover; $10, b&w, inside; on publication.

YANKEE MAGAZINE, Main St., Dublin NH 03444. (603)563-8111. Design Editor: J. Porter. Regional magazine about New England. Monthly. Circ. 1 million. Accepts previously published material. Returns original artwork after publication. Sample copy $1.50.
Cartoons: Buys 4 cartoons/issue from freelancers. Cartoons must be "very funny and relative to New England lifestyle." Send query letter with samples of style to be kept on file. Material not filed is returned by SASE. Reports only if interested. Buys one-time rights. Pays $50 second rights, $100 first rights, b&w.
Illustrations: Buys 30 illustrations/issue from freelancers. Send query letter with tear sheets, slides or photographs to be kept on file. Samples not filed are returned by SASE. Reports only if interested. Buys one-time rights. Pays $200-650, color, cover; $100-550 for b&w and $150-750 for color, inside; on acceptance.

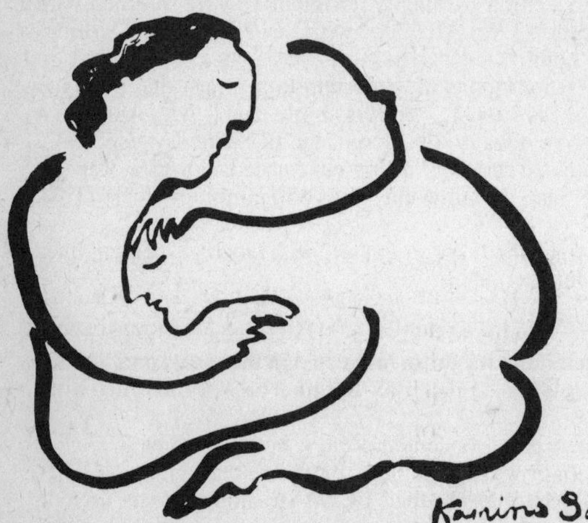

Freelance artist Jeannie Kamins sold her brush and ink rendering as fine art as well as an illustration in Yellow Silk. *Lily Pond, editor of the erotic journal, purchased reprint rights to the piece which Kamins wanted to convey "tenderness."*

YELLOW SILK: Journal of Erotic Arts, Box 6374, Albany CA 94706. (415)841-6500. Publisher: Lily Pond. Emphasizes erotic literature and arts for well educated, highly literate readership, generally personally involved in arts field. Quarterly. Circ. 10,000. Does not accept previously published material. Returns original artwork after publication. Sample copy $3.50.
Cartoons: Uses 0-3/issue. Prefers themes involving sexuality and/or human relationships. " 'All persuasions, no brutality' is editoral policy. Nothing tasteless." Accepts any cartoon format except color. Send query letter with finished cartoons or photocopies to be kept on file. Include phone number, name and address on each sample. Material not filed is returned by SASE with correct stamps, no meters. Reports only if SASE included. Buys first rights or reprint rights. Pays $15/page (4 panels) plus 3 copies; on publication.
Illustrations: Uses 9-12/issue by one artist if possible. Considers "anything in the widest definitions of eroticism except brutality, bondage or S&M. Nothing tasteless. No pornography. All sexual persuasions represented." Send photocopies, slides, photostats, photographs or originals, "all sent at artist's risk." to be kept on file. Color is OK. Include name, address and telephone number on all samples. Samples not filed returned by SASE. Reports within 8 weeks. To show a portfolio, mail original/final art, color, photostats, photographs, b&w and slides. Buys first rights or reprint rights. Pays $50 plus copies; on publication.
Tips: "Read the magazine first."

YOUNG AMBASSADOR, Box 82808, Lincoln NE 68501. (402)474-4567. Art Director: Win Mumma. "Our purpose is to help Christian teens live consistently for Christ, and to help them grow in their knowledge of the Bible and its principles for living." Monthly. Circ. 80,000. Original artwork not returned after publication. Free sample copy.
Cartoons: Managing Editor: Nancy Brumbaugh Bayne. Buys 2-3 cartoons/issue from freelancers. Receives 4 submissions/week from freelancers. Interested in wholesome humor for teens; single panel. Prefers to see finished cartoons. Reports in 3 weeks. Buys all rights on a work-for-hire basis.
Illustrations: Some illustrations purchased on assignment only. Submit slides or tear sheets with query letter. Humorous and cartoon-style illustrations mostly done in-house; a few assigned. Pays $50 b&w, $100, color.

The diversity of the publications included here means there's something for everyone, whether you're gearing your work to specialized inhouse newsletters, regional newspapers or national tabloids. Dailies, weeklies, newspaper magazine supplements—they're all found in this section.

Since many of the publications have specialized audiences, either by area of interest or geographic region, your ability to understand the slant of a publication will be your greatest asset in making sales to these markets. The major needs of these publications are cartoons and illustrations, but if you reside nearby, don't overlook those that indicate they use freelance artists for advertising, layout, production work and peripheral services. Strong black-and-white work is most desirable here since few of these publications work in color. An understanding of reduction and the absorption quality of newsprint can help to produce work that will be useful to these markets.

The large, national newspapers have been the ones most affected by today's economic status—giving rise to mergers, sales and cessation of publication. Weeklies and smaller publications have been affected in the same ways, but to a lesser degree since they are functioning on much smaller budgets. Inhouse publications are affected only where company cost-cutting has resulted in a reduction of page count or paper quality.

Larger newspapers were the frontrunners for using computerized typesetting, and now they are using the computer for production duties. Smaller publications are now able to invest in modern typesetting equipment but still rely on artists for graphics.

For further information and other names and addresses, consult *Writer's Market*, *The Newspaper and Allied Services Directory*, *Ayer Directory of Publications* and *Editor & Publisher*.

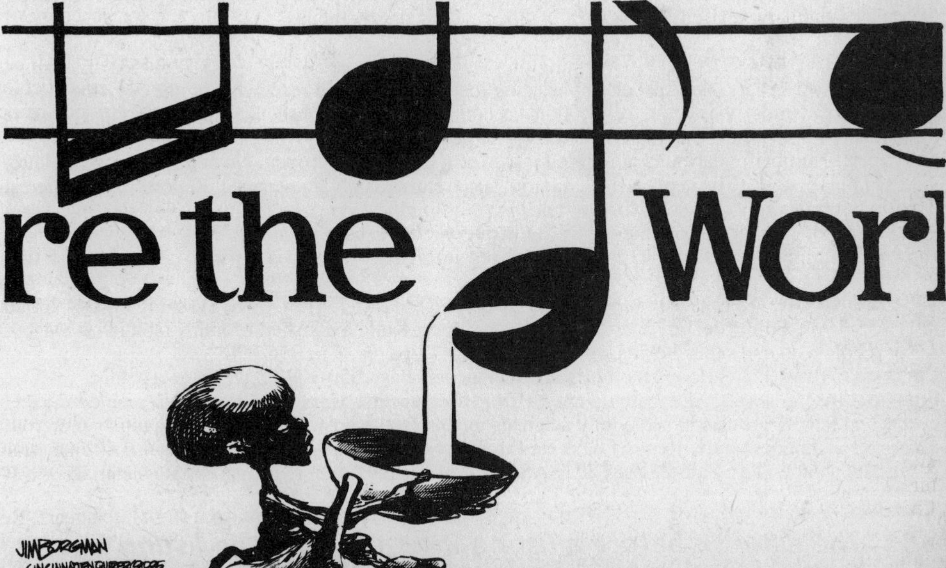

Jim Borgman, editorial cartoonist of the Cincinnati Enquirer, can summarize the entire U.S.A. for Africa pledge in one graphic image; it's the special gift of an editorial cartoonist.

AMERICAN MEDICAL NEWS, 535 N. Dearborn St., Chicago IL 60610. (312)645-4441. Editor: Dick Walt. Emphasizes news and opinions on developments, legislation and business in medicine. For physicians. Weekly newspaper. Circ. 315,000. Photocopied and simultaneous submissions OK. Original artwork not returned after publication. Free sample copy.
Cartoons: Contact: Sher Watts, assistant executive editor. Uses 1 cartoon/issue, all from freelancers. Receives "dozens" of submissions/week from freelancers. Interested in medical themes; single panel. Prefers to see finished cartoons. SASE. Reports in 4 weeks. Usually buys first North American rights. Pays up to $100, b&w; on acceptance.
Illustrations: Contact: Sher Watts, assistant executive editor. Number illustrations used/issue varies; number bought/issue from freelancers varies. Works on assignment only. Send query letter with brochure showing art style. Samples returned by SASE. "We don't look at many portfolios, but portfolio should include original/final art, color and tear sheets." Usually buys first North American rights. Payment varies; "we have paid as much as $600 for single illustration." Pays on acceptance.
Tips: "I will look at any cartoons. I usually work with artists only from the Chicago area, because we need to see them in person."

THE AMERICAN NEWSPAPER CARRIER, Box 15300, Winston-Salem NC 27113. Editor: Marilyn H. Rollins. A monthly inspirational newsletter for pre-teen and teenage newspaper carriers. Original artwork not returned after publication. Sample copy and art guidelines free for SASE.
Cartoons: Uses freelance and staff cartoons. Publishes 2-3 single panel and 1 multiple panel per issue. Prefers original b&w line drawings. Usually buys all rights. Pays $10-45 on acceptance.
Illustrations: Buys 1-2 per issue, all freelance. Works on assignment only. Send query letter with tear sheets and photocopies to be kept on file. Samples not returned. To show a portfolio, mail b&w and photocopies. Usually buys all rights. Pays $10-30 on acceptance.

***AMERICANS FOR LEGAL REFORM AND CITIZENS LEGAL MANUAL SERIES**, Suite 300, Halt, 1319 F St. NW, Washington DC 20004. Creative Manager: Bob Schmitt. Tabloid emphasizing self help law, consumer education, and legal reform issues. Circ. 115,000. Accepts previously published material. Original artwork returned after publication.
Cartoons: Buys 1-2 cartoons/issue from freelancers. Prefers current legal reform issues as themes. Prefers single, double or multiple panel with or without gagline; b&w line drawings or b&w washes. Send query letter with samples of style to be kept on file. Write to schedule an appointment to show a portfolio. Samples not filed are not returned. Reports only if interested. Buys one-time rights, reprint rights or negotiates rights purchased. Negotiates payment.
Illustrations: Prefers legal reform issues as themes. Send query letter with resume, photocopies, halftones and photos. Samples not filed are not returned. Write to schedule an appointment to show a portfolio, which should include thumbnails, roughs, original/final art, final reproduction/product and b&w. Negotiates rights purchased. Negotiates payment. Pays on acceptance.

ANCHOR BAY BEACON, 51170 Washington, New Baltimore MI 48047. (313)725-4531. Executive Editor: Michael Eckert. Newspaper emphasizing local news for paid readership in one city, one village and three townships. Weekly. Circ. 8,000. Accepts previously published material. Original work returned after publication. Sample copy free for large manilla SASE with 50¢ postage.
Cartoons: Number of cartoons purchased/issue from freelancers is open. No color. Send query letter with samples of style to be kept on file. Material filed returned only if requested. Reports only if interested. Buys reprint rights. Negotiates pay rate; pays on publication.
Illustrations: Works on assignment only. Send query letter to be kept on file. Write for appointment to show portfolio. Reports only if interested. Buys reprint rights. Negotiates pay rate; pays on publication.

APA MONITOR, American Psychological Association, 1200 17th St. NW, Washington DC 20036. (202)955-7690. Editor: Jeffrey Mervis. Associate Editor: Kathleen Fisher. Monthly tabloid newspaper for psychologists and other behavioral scientists. 64-72 pages. Circ. 75,000.
Cartoons: Buys 1-2 cartoons/month from freelancers. Pays $50-100 b&w; on acceptance.
Illustrations: Buys 2-5 illustrations/month from freelancers. Uses 30 illustrations/year on current events and feature articles in behavioral sciences/mental health area. Washington area artists preferred. Works on assignment only. Reports back on future assignment possibilities. Query with resume, tear sheets and photocopies. Sample copy $3. SASE. To show a portfolio, mail appropriate materials or call

The asterisk before a listing indicates that the listing is new in this edition. New markets are often the most receptive to freelance contributions.

to schedule an appointment; portfolio should include original/final art, final reproduction/product, photographs and b&w. Original artwork returned after publication, if requested. Buys first North American serial rights. Pays $175, b&w cover and inside; on publication.
Tips: "Be creative, think about topics relevant to psychology, and be willing to work at below-market rates in exchange for artistic freedom."

BALLS AND STRIKES NEWSPAPER, 2801 N.E. 50th St., Oklahoma City OK 73111. (405)424-5266. Communications Director: Bill Plummer III. Official publication of the amateur softball association. Emphasizes amateur softball for "the more than 30 million people who play amateur softball; they come from all walks of life and hold varied jobs." Published 8 times/year. Circ. 250,000. Previously published material OK. Original work returned after publication. Free sample copy available.
Illustrations: Uses 2-4 illustrations/issue. No drug or alcohol themes. Works on assignment only. Send query letter with resume and business card to be kept on file. Samples returned. Reports in 3 days. Buys all rights. Pays on publication.

BALTIMORE SUN MAGAZINE, 501 N. Calvert St., Baltimore MD 21278. (301)332-6600. Editor: Susan Baer. Emphasizes general interest topics to the Maryland area; audience is families, educated. Weekly. Circ. 400,000. Accepts previously published material. Returns original art after publication. Sample copy free for SASE.
Illustrations: Uses 2 illustrations/issue; buys both from freelancers. Considers all styles. Works on assignment only. Send query letter with samples to be kept on file. Call or write for appointment to show portfolio. Prefers slides or tear sheets as samples. Material not filed is returned. Reports in 2-3 weeks. Negotiates rights purchased. Pays $200-300, color cover; $100, b&w, and $200, color, inside; on publication.

BARTER COMMUNIQUE, Box 2527, Sarasota FL 33578. (813)349-3300. Art Director: Robert J. Murley. Concerns bartering; for radio, TV stations, newspapers, magazines, travel and ad agencies. Quarterly tabloid. Circ. 50,000.
Cartoons: Buys 5/issue on barter situations. Send roughs. Pays $5, b&w; on publication.
Illustrations: Query with samples. SASE. Reports in 2 weeks. Pays $5, b&w; on publication.
Tips: Looks for "uniqueness" in reviewing samples.

BLACK VOICE NEWS, Box 1581, Riverside CA 92502. (714)889-0506 or 682-6070. Contact: Hardy Brown, Jr. Newspaper emphasizing general topics for "the black community with various backgrounds, and Hispanics and whites who are in tune with that community." Weekly. Circ. 5,000. Sample copy free for SASE.
Cartoons: Prefers political, historic and topical themes. Accepts single, double or multiple panel with or without gagline; b&w line drawings. Send query letter with samples of style to be kept on file; write for appointment to show portfolio. Material not filed is returned by SASE. Reports back only if interested. Buys one-time or reprint rights; pays on publication.
Illustrations: Send query letter with samples to be kept on file; write for appointment to show portfolio. Samples not filed are returned by SASE. Reports back only if interested. Buys one-time or reprint rights; pays on publication.

BOOKPLATES IN THE NEWS, Apt. F, 605 N. Stoneman Ave., Alhambra CA 91801. (213)283-1936 (evenings and weekends). Director: Audrey Spencer Arellanes. Emphasizes bookplates for those who use bookplates whether individuals or institutions, those who collect them, artists who design them, art historians, genealogists, historians, antiquarian booktrade and others for tracing provenance of a volume; also publishes yearbook annually. Quarterly. Circ. 200. Original work returned after publication. Previously published material OK "on occasion, usually from foreign publications." Sample copy $4; art guidelines for SASE.
Illustrations: Illustrations are bookplates. "Appearance of work in our publications should produce requests for bookplate commissions." Send query letter and finished art. Reports in 3 weeks. No payment.

THE BOSTON PHOENIX, 100 Massachusetts Ave., Boston MA 02115. (617)536-5390. Design Director: Cleo Leontis. Weekly. Circ. 150,000. Original work returned after publication by SASE. Sample copy $3.50.
Illustrations: Uses 2-8 b&w illustrations/issue, occasional color; buys all from freelancers. Uses 1-2 humorous and cartoon-style illustrations/week on assignment. Send samples of style (no originals) and resume to be kept on file for possible future assignments. Call for appointment. Reports in 6 weeks. Buys one-time rights. Pays on publication.

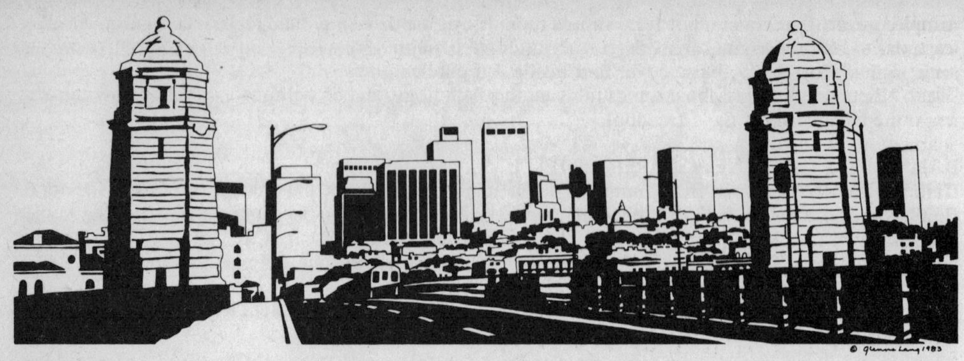

Matthew Gilbert, managing editor of Boston Review, *asked Glenna Lang of Cambridge, Massachusetts, to create a logo for the newspaper's "Around Town" column. "I wanted a feeling of old and new Boston," says Lang, "and of entering the city of Boston. My own artwork has been primarily about cities, and this was a chance to do an illustration about the city in which I live." Gilbert bought first North American serial rights to the artwork.*

THE BOSTON REVIEW, 33 Harrison Ave., Boston MA 02111. (617)350-5353. Editor: Mark Silk. Tabloid. Emphasizes arts and culture for persons of college age and older interested/involved in the arts, literature and related cultural and political topics. Bimonthly. Circ. 10,000. Accepts simultaneous submissions. Original artwork returned after publication. Sample copy $3.
Cartoons: Has not previously used cartoons, but will consider. "Must be b&w work, anything original, creative, inspiring." Send photocopies. Prefers single panel, b&w line drawings. Material not kept on file is returned by SASE. Reports only if interested. Negotiates rights purchased. Negotiates payment. Pays $60-100 b&w, inside; on publication.
Illustrations: Buys 2-4 illustrations/issue from freelancers. Themes and styles are open; b&w work only. Send query letter with resume and samples to be kept on file. Open to any type of sample. Samples not kept on file are returned by SASE. Reports only if interested. To show a portfolio, mail original/final art, final reproduction/product and tear sheets. Negotiates rights purchased. Negotiates pay for inside art. Pays on publication.

THE BREAD RAPPER, 2103 Noyes, Evanston IL 60201. Editor-in-Chief: Laurie Lawlor. Concerns banking services and involvement of bank with community; received with checking account statement. Photocopied submissions OK. Sample copy and artist's guidelines with SASE.
Cartoons: Buys 1 cartoon/issue on banking; single panel with gagline. No negative bank slants (bank robberies, etc.), please. Mail art. SASE. Reports within 8 weeks. Buys all rights. Pays $20 minimum, b&w line drawings and washes; on publication.

***BRUM BEAT**, 190 Monument Rd., Birmingham B16 800 England. (021)454-7020. Editor: Jim Simpson. Newspaper emphasizing music and entertainment for ages 16 to 35 interested in music and music-related activities. Monthly. Circ. 40,000. Accepts previously published material. Original artwork returned after publication. Sample copy free for SASE with 31 pence postage.
Cartoons: Currently buys no cartoons but will consider music-related ones. Send samples of style to be kept on file. Material not kept on file is returned by SASE. Reports only if interested. Buys one-time rights. Payment varied.
Illustrations: Buys few illustrations. Prefers music-related themes. Send samples. Samples not filed are returned by SASE. Reports only if interested. Pays on publication.

BUILDING BRIEFS, Dan Burch Associates, 2338 Frankfort Ave., Louisville KY 40206. (502)895-4881. Program Manager: Sharon Hildenbrandt. Newsletter. Emphasizes design/build and conventional methods of construction for commercial and industrial buildings, plus other topics such as landscaping, security, and energy-saving ideas. Directed to potential clients of a building contractor in the nonresidential market, company presidents, board members and managerial personnel who will construct or renovate their buildings. Bimonthly. Circ. 25,000 + . Original artwork returned after publication. Sample copy available.
Cartoons: Buys 1 cartoon/issue from freelancers. Prefers themes related to construction; light humor,

simple line art. Prefers single panel with gagline; b&w line drawings. Send query letter with finished cartoons to be kept on file. Material not kept on file is returned. Reports only if interested. Buys one-time rights. Pays $50, b&w; on publication.
Tips: "Spend a little time researching the design/build industry. Talk to a design/build contractor to learn the basics—what the concept of design/build is. Two industry publications where more can be learned are *Metal Construction News* and *Metal Building Review*."

THE BURLINGTON LOOK, Burlington Industries, Box 21207, Greensboro NC 27420. (919)379-2339. Publications Editor: Tlontina Miller. Tabloid. Emphasizes textiles and home furnishings for all domestic employees of Burlington Industries plus opinion leaders in the plant communities. Published 8 times/year. Circ. 50,000. Accepts previously published material and simultaneous submissions. Original artwork not returned after publication unless requested. Sample copy free for SASE.
Cartoons: Uses 1-2 cartoons/issue; buys all from freelancers. Prefers single, double or multiple panel without gagline; b&w line drawings. Send query letter with samples of style to be kept on file. Call for appointment to show portfolio; "if local artists are interested, we will view portfolios." Material not kept on file is returned only if requested. Reports within 10 days. Negotiates rights purchased and payment; pays on acceptance.
Illustrations: Currently uses 1-2 illustrations/issue—"works with local artists mostly"; buys all from freelancers. Themes/styles vary depending on subject matter. Works on assignment only. Send query letter with resume, business card, samples and tear sheets to be kept on file. Prefers photostats or photographs as samples; "I'd rather not have original work for fear it may be damaged or get lost." Samples not kept on file are returned only if requested. Reports within 2 weeks. Negotiates rights purchased. Payment varies according to size and complexity; pays on acceptance.
Tips: "Looking for illustrators with the creativity to be able to illustrate and visually communicate various story concepts."

BY-LINES, Box 48, Ft. Smith AR 72902. Director Public Relations & Advertising: John T. Greer. Tabloid. Emphasizes business (trucking related) for employees of ABF Freight System, Inc. Monthly. Circ. 7,000. Accepts previously published material and simultaneous submissions. Original artwork returned after publication. Sends art guidelines only if specifically interested in artist's work.
Cartoons: Uses 1-2 cartoons/issue. Prefers single panel; b&w line drawings, b&w washes. Send query letter with samples of style to be kept on file; write for appointment to show portfolio. Material not kept on file is returned only if requested. Reports only if interested. Buys reprint rights. Payment varies; pays on acceptance.
Illustrations: Number of illustrations used/issue varies. Works on assignment only. Send query letter with samples to be kept on file; write for appointment to show portfolio. Samples not kept on file are returned only if requested. Reports only if interested. Buys reprint rights. Payment varies; pays on acceptance.

CALIFORNIA APPAREL NEWS, 945 S. Wall St., Los Angeles CA 90015. (213)626-0411. Art Director: John Miller. Emphasizes fashion for the trade. Weekly. Circ. 25,000. Returns originals after publication.
Illustrations: Buys 10 illustrations/issue from freelancers. Considers fashion illustration. Works on assignment only. Send query letter with brochure, resume, business card and samples to be kept on file. Call for appointment to show portfolio. Accepts photostats, tear sheets, photocopies, slides or photographs as samples. Samples not filed returned only if requested. Reports only if interested. Negotiates rights purchased. Pays on publication.

THE CALIFORNIA STATE EMPLOYEE, 1108 O St., Sacramento CA 95814. (916)444-8134. Editor: Robert C. Striegel. Emphasizes public employee labor news for 130,000 civil service and university employees. Newspaper published 6 times/year by California State Employees Association. Circ. 131,000. Previously published material OK "depending on where published." Original work not returned after publication. Free sample copy for SASE.
Cartoons: Uses 1 cartoon/issue; buys all from freelancers. Interested in themes related to job or union, any style; single, double or multi-panel with or without gagline, b&w line drawings and washes. Usually buys from work submitted on speculation. Occasionally works on assignment. Send query letter with samples of style. Samples returned by SASE. Reports in 2 weeks. Buys reprint rights. Pays $20 for single panel on spec, $50 on assignment. Negotiates on other sizes. Pays on acceptance.
Illustrations: Uses 1 illustration/issue; buys some from freelancers. Interested in any style, labor theme. Works on assignment only. Send query letter with samples of style. Provide business card, samples and tear sheets to be kept on file. Samples not kept on file are returned by SASE. Reports in 2 weeks. Buys reprint rights. Pays $30-90 inside, b&w line drawings and washes; on acceptance.

***THE CAPITAL**, 213 West St., Annapolis MD 21401. (301)268-5000, ext. 211. Managing Director: Tom Marquardt. Daily. Circ. 40,000. Original artwork returned on request.
Cartoons: Buys 50 cartoons/year from NEA. Prefers editorial cartoons. Prefers single panel; b&w washes. Send query letter with samples of style to be kept on file. Reports only if interested. Write for appointment to show portfolio. Buys one-time rights. Pays on publication.
Illustrations: Buys 25 illustrations/year from freelancers. Works on assignment only. Send query letter with brochure showing art style or resume and photocopies. Samples not filed are returned only if requested. Reports only if interested. Write to schedule an appointment to show a portfolio, which should include original/final art. Buys one-time rights. Pays $25 for b&w, cover; $15 for b&w, inside. Pays on publication.

***CARTOON WORLD**, Box 30367, Lincoln NE 68503. (112)435-3191. Editor/Publisher: George Hartman. Newsletter "slanted to amateur and professional freelance cartoonists." Monthly. Circ. 300. Accepts previously published material. Returns original artwork after publication. Sample copy $4; art guidelines available.
Cartoons: Does not want individual cartoons; seeks articles on cartooning, illustrated with cartoons, that will benefit other cartoonists. Topics as how to cartoon, how to create ideas, cartoon business plans, hints and markets. Send query letter with originals only. Reports within 10 days. Material will not be returned nor considered for publication without return postage. To show a portfolio, mail appropriate materials, which should include final reproduction/product. Buys reprint rights. Pays $5/8½x11" page, on acceptance.
Tips: "I only use stuff that helps in some way any pro or amateur cartoonist or artist."

CENTRAL MASS MEDIA INC., Worcester Magazine, Business Worcester, Ocean State Business, Centrumguide, Box 1000, Worcester MA 01614. (617)799-0511. Art Director: Mark Minter. Concerns central Massachusetts and Rhode Island. Weekly and monthly newspapers. Circ. 50,000.
Cartoons: Buys 2 cartoons/week from freelancers. Pays $15-50, b&w; on publication.
Illustrations: Buys on assigned themes. Send query letter with photocopies. To show a portfolio, mail final reproduction/product and tear sheets. Buys one-time rights. Cover: Pays $75-100, gray opaques, b&w line drawings and washes; $100, color. Inside: Pays $15-50, gray opaques, b&w line drawings and washes; on publication.

THE CHARLOTTE OBSERVER/THE CHARLOTTE NEWS, 600 S. Tryon St., Charlotte NC 28202. Promotion Manager: Coco Killian. Art Director for Advertising: Chuck Cole. Daily newspapers; "largest in the Carolinas." Circ. 250,000 + .
Illustrations: Call for appointment to show portfolio. Especially looks for "quality, neatness, creativity and imagination. It doesn't have to bowl me over—sometimes it can be just a spark."

CHICAGO READER, Box 11101, Chicago IL 60611. (312)828-0350. Editor-in-Chief: Robert A. Roth. Cartoon/Illustration Editor: Robert E. McCamant. For young adults in lakefront neighborhoods interested in things to do in Chicago and feature stories on city life. Weekly. Circ. 120,000. Sample copy $2.
Cartoons: Buys 9 cartoons/issue on any topic; single, double and multi-panel. Pays $10 and up. "At present, we carry eight regular cartoon features, plus one or more irregularly-appearing ones. While we are not actively looking for more, we will consider anything, and find the space if the material warrants it." Send photocopies (no originals). Buys one-time rights; pays by 15th of month following publication.
Illustrations: Buys 3 illustrations/issue on assigned themes. Send photocopies or arrange interview to show portfolio. SASE. Buys one-time rights. Pays by 15th of month following publication. Cover and inside: Pays $110-200, b&w line drawings and washes.

THE CHRISTIAN SCIENCE MONITOR, 1 Norway St., Boston MA 02115. (617)262-2300. Design Director: Susan Ballenger Zyner. Newspaper emphasizing analytical reporting of current events; diverse features and news features for well-educated, well-informed readers in all fields—specifically politicians, educators, business people. Daily. Circ. 160,000. Original artwork returned after publication. Sample copy and art guidelines available.
Illustrations: Buys 1-2 illustrations/week from freelancers. Prefers editorial ("op-ed') conceptual themes; line, wash or scratchboard. Works on assignment only. Send samples to be filed. Samples should be 8½x11" photocopies; no originals. Samples not returned. Reports only if interested. Buys first rights. Pays $100-150, b&w; on publication.

THE CHRONICLE OF HIGHER EDUCATION, Suite 700, 1255 23rd St. NW, Washington DC 20037. (202)466-1035. Art Director: Peter Stafford. Emphasizes all aspects of higher education for college and university administrators, professors, students and staff. Weekly. Circ. 75,000. Sample copy available.

Cartoons: Uses approximately 10 cartoons/year. Prefers higher education related themes, i.e., sports, high cost of tuition, student loans, energy conservation on campus. Prefers single panel, with gagline; b&w line drawings or b&w washes. Send query letter with samples of style to be kept on file. Material not kept on file is returned only if requested. Reports only if interested. Buys one-time rights. Pays on publication.
Illustrations: Buys 1 illustration/week from freelancers. Uses 1 illustration/issue; buys all from freelancers. Uses a variety of styles, depending on the tone of the story. Works on assignment only. Send query letter with photostats or good quality photocopy for line work; photographs or slides for halftone work, business card and tear sheets to be kept on file. Samples are returned only if requested. Reports only if interested. Buys one-time rights. Pays $100 and up depending on size, b&w, inside. Pays on publication.

CLEVELAND PLAIN DEALER, 1801 Superior Ave., Cleveland OH 44114. (216)344-4447. Graphics Editor: Bill Osterdorf. Newspaper. Emphasizes current events, features for metropolitan daily readership. Circ. 500,000. Accepts previously published material. Original artwork returned after publication if requested.
Illustrations: Buys 6 illustrations/week from freelancers. Preferred themes are any dealing with current affairs. Works on assignment only. Send query letter with resume, tear sheets, photostats, photocopies, slides and photographs to be kept on file. Samples not filed are returned only if requested. Reports only interested. To show a portfolio, mail tear sheets, photostats and b&w. Buys one-time rights. Pays $150, b&w, cover; $50, b&w, inside; on publication.
Tips: Likes to see *newspaper* or other editorial illustrations as samples. Has strong need for local, technical illustrator and graphic artists who can produce interesting charts and maps.

***COMMON FUTURES**, Future Studies Centre, Birmingham Settlement, 318 Summer Ln., Birmingham UK B19 3RL. (021)359-3562. Editor: Christian Kunz. Newsletter emphasizing social and environmental trends and future studies for international audiences. Quarterly. Circ. 500. Accepts previously published material. Original artwork returned after publication. Sample copy free for SASE.
Cartoons: Buys 2-3 cartoons/issue from freelancers. Prefers social comment; "alternative interpretations of current issues." Prefers single panel with and without gagline; b&w line drawings. Send query letter with samples of style to be kept on file. Samples not filed returned by SASE. Reports only if interested. Negotiates rights purchased. Pays $5-10, b&w. Buys 1-2 illustrations/issue from freelancers. Prefers ecological and social comment as themes. Send query letter with resume and photocopies. Samples not filed returned by SASE. Reports only if interested. To show a portfolio, mail appropriate material, which should include roughs and b&w. Negotiates rights purchased. Pays $8-10, b&w, cover, $5-8, b&w inside; on publication.

COMPUTERWORLD FOCUS, 375 Cochituate Rd., Framingham MA 01701. Art Director: Tom Monahan. Tabloid. Emphasizes news and products relating to the computer field. Monthly. Returns original artwork after publication. Sample copy free for SASE.
Illustrations: Buys 2 illustrations/week. Themes depend on the storyline. Works on assignment only. Send query letter with brochure and photocopies or photostats to be kept on file. Reports back only if interested. Buys first rights. To show portfolio, mail appropriate materials or call to schedule an appointment; portfolio should include original/final art, final reproduction/product, color, photostats and b&w. Pays $175, b&w and $225 + color, inside; on acceptance.

CONNECTICUT TRAVELER, 2276 Whitney Ave., Hamden CT 06518. (203)281-7505. Managing Director of Publications: Elke P. Martin. Newspaper. Estab. 1983. Emphasizes automobile travel, safety and maintenance, national and international travel and regional events (New England) for AAA members. Monthly. Circ. 155,000. Accepts previously published material. Returns original artwork after publication. Sample copy free for SASE; art guidelines available.
Cartoons: Buys 1 cartoon/issue from freelancers. Prefers single panel with gagline; b&w line drawings; b&w washes. Send query letter with samples of style to be kept on file. Reports within 2 weeks. Buys reprint rights or negotiates rights purchased. Pays on publication.

THE CONSTANTIAN, 123 Orr Rd., Pittsburgh PA 15241. (412)831-8750. Editor: Randall J. Dicks. "We (Constantian Society) are monarchists and royalists, interested in monarchy as a political system and royalty as persons and personalities." Bimonthly newsletter. Circ. 400. Previously published work OK. Sample copy for 39¢ and SASE; free artist's guidelines.
Cartoons: "We have used a cartoon only once, but would certainly consider using them. It is best to write us about the idea first and send samples." Send query letter with resume and samples. To show a portfolio, mail appropriate materials. SASE. Reports within 1 week. Buys various rights. Pays $5-10, b&w line drawings; on acceptance or publication.

Illustrations: "We use a lot of decorative drawings and work which relate to our subject matter (heraldic items of different nationalities, coats of arms, monograms, etc.)." SASE. Reports within 1 week. Buys various rights. Pays $10 and up, b&w line drawings; on acceptance or publication.
Tips: "Now we are using a MacIntosh Computer for our journal—it has new look and changes in format. Artists should have some understanding of our subject—monarchy and royalty."

CONSTRUCTION SUPERVISION & SAFETY LETTER, 24 Rope Ferry Rd., Waterford CT 06386. (203)442-4365. Editor: DeLoris Lidestri. Emphasizes construction supervision for supervisors who work with their crews. Covers bricklayers, carpenters, electricians, painters, plasterers, plumbers and building laborers. Semimonthly. Circ. 3,700. Original artwork not returned after publication. Free sample copy.
Cartoons: Uses 1 cartoon/issue which is done by a freelancer. Receives 5-7 submissions/week from freelancers. Uses "situations that deal with supervision in construction. Cartoons that depict both men and women as workers and/or supervisors needed. No sexist material, please." Format: single panel, b&w line drawings with gagline. Prefers to see finished cartoons. SASE. Reports in 2 weeks. Buys all rights. Pays $10 on acceptance.

THE CRANSTON MIRROR, 250 Auburn St., Cranston RI 02910. Contact: Malcolm L. Daniels. Weekly newspaper. Circ. 10,000. Original artwork returned after publication. Prefers local artists. Also uses artists for layout, illustration, technical art, paste-up, lettering and retouching. Pays $175, booklet; $15-75, illustrations.
Cartoons: Uses 2 cartoons/issue; buys 1 or none/issue from freelancers. Receives 3-4 submissions/week from freelancers. Interested in local editorial subjects. Call for interview to show portfolio (except July and August). Prefers to see finished cartoons. Reports in 1 week. Pays $20, b&w.
Illustrations: Uses 2-4 illustrations/issue; buys 1-2/issue from freelancers. Send resume and photocopies to be kept on file for future assignments. Reports in 1 week. Call or write to schedule an appointment to show a portfolio, which should include original/final art and photostats. Pays $30-50, b&w, cover; $25, b&w, inside; on publication.
Tips: Especially looks for "unique idea, quality workmanship and regard to detail. Ideas, however, are paramount. Be neat. Have material ready and know what you want to say for a portfolio review."

CYCLE NEWS, Box 498, Long Beach CA 90801. (213)427-7433. Editor: John Ulrich. For the motorcycle enthusiast. Weekly newspaper. Circ. 88,000. Previously published work OK. Returns originals to artist after publication. Sample copy available. Art guidelines not available.
Cartoons: Buys 0-2 cartoons/issue. Send query letter with finished cartoons and SASE. Reports back only if interested. Negotiates payment and rights purchased. Pays on publication.
Illustrations: Buys varying number of illustrations/issue. Works on assignment only. Send query letter with samples and SASE. Prefers photocopies as samples. Reports only if interested. Negotiates payment and rights purchased. Pays on publication.

***DIRECT MARKETING**, 224 Seventh St., Garden City NY 11530. (516)746-6700. Art Directors: Barbara Marcinka or Kathy Conway. Emphasizes direct marketing for direct marketers. Monthly. Circ. 18,000. Accepts previously published art. Original artwork returned after publication. Sample copy and art guidelines available.
Cartoons: Prefers b&w line drawings and b&w washes. Material not filed returned only if requested. Write or call to schedule an appointment to show a portfolio.
Illustrations: Buys 1-2 illustrations/issue from freelancers. Prefers conceptual illustrations—b&w. Send query letter with resume, tear sheets, photostats, slides and photographs. Reports only if interested. Write to schedule an appointment to show a portfolio, which should include roughs, original/final art, final reproduction/product, color and b&w.
Tips: "Artist should have some work experience—preferably b&w line drawings."

DOLLARS & SENSE, 325 Pennsylvania Ave. SE, Washington DC 20003. (202)543-1300. Editor: Tom Palmer. For people interested in reducing taxes and government spending. 10 issues/year. Circ. 140,000. Previously published material and simultaneous submissions OK. Especially needs federal budget information. Original work not returned after publication. Free sample copy for SASE.
Cartoons: Uses 3 cartoons/issue; number bought from freelancers varies. Interested in political/taxation themes. Send finished cartoons. Samples returned by SASE. Reports within 2 weeks. Negotiates one-time and first rights. Payment varies; on publication.
Illustrations: Uses 4 illustrations/issue. Interested in political themes. Send finished art or samples of style. Samples returned by SASE. Reports within 2 weeks. Negotiates rights. Pays $60-150 cover, color washes; inside, payment varies; on publication.
Tips: "Either make the graphics very general in nature or send in very specific cartoons."

THE EVENING SUN, 501 N. Calvert St., Baltimore MD 21278. (301)332-6529. Art Director: Chuck Lankford. Daily newspaper for general audience. Circ. 145,000. Accepts previously published material. Original artwork sometimes returned after publication. Art guidelines available.
Cartoons: Buys 2-3 cartoons/issue from freelancers. Theme and style vary according to story content. Prefers multiple panel without gagline; b&w line drawings or color washes. Send samples of style to be kept on file; write for appointment to show portfolio. Material not filed is returned by SASE only if requested. Reports only if interested. Buys all rights or negotiates rights purchased. Pays variable rate, b&w and color, on publication.
Illustrations: Theme and style vary according to story content. Send query letter with samples to be kept on file; write for appointment to show portfolio. Photocopies acceptable as samples. Samples not filed are returned only if requested. Reports only if interested. Negotiates rights purchased. Pays variable rate, b&w and color: on publication.

***THE FOREMAN'S LETTER**, 24 Rope Ferry Rd., Waterford CT 06386. Editor: Carl Thunberg. For industrial supervisors.
Cartoons: Usually uses 1 cartoon/issue; may buy up to 2/issue from freelancers. Receives 20 submissions/week from freelancers. Interested in "supervisor-worker relations; avoid sexism and other discriminatory situations." Prefers single panel, finished cartoons. Send query letter with brochure showing art style. SASE. Reports in 1 week. To show a portfolio, mail photostats. Buys all rights. Pays $10-15; on acceptance.

***FREEWAY**, Box 632, Glen Ellyn IL 60138. (312)668-6000. Designer: Mardelle Ayers. Sunday School paper emphasizing Christian living for teenagers from a conservative, evangical Christian upbringing. Published 4 quarters a year, 13 issues per quarter. Circ. 60,000. Accepts previously published material. Returns original artwork after publication. Sample copy free for SASE with 22¢ postage.
Cartoons: Buys 4-5 cartoons/quarter. Prefers any style or theme that appeals to teens. Prefers single, double or multiple panel with gagline; b&w line drawings or b&w washes. Send query letter with finished cartoons. Material not kept on file is returned by SASE. Reports within 4 weeks. Buys first rights. Pays $15, b&w.
Illustrations; Buys 1-3 illustrations/issue from freelancers. Works on assignment only. Prefers any theme or style appealing to teens. Send query letter with resume, photostats and photocopies. Samples not filed are returned by SASE if requested. Reports only if interested. To show a portfolio, mail photostats and b&w photos. Payment is variable on acceptance.

FRUITION, Box 872-WM, Santa Cruz CA 95061. (408)458-3365. Editor: C.L. Olson. Newsletter. Emphasizes planting of public access food trees; establishing community food tree nurseries; achieving superior health through simple natural means. Biannually. Circ. 300. Accepts previously published material and simultaneous submissions. Originals returned to artist after publication if stamped, artist-supplied packaging is provided. Sample copy for $2; art guidelines free for SASE.
Cartoons: Uses 1 cartoon/issue. Prefers single panel; b&w line drawings, b&w washes. Send query letter with finished cartoons. Material is returned by SASE. Reports within 3 weeks if interested. Negotiates rights purchased and pay rate; pays on acceptance.
Illustrations: Uses 4 illustrations/issue; buys 1/issue from freelancers. Send query letter with brochure showing or resume, tear sheets, photostats, photographs or slides and photographs. Samples not filed are returned by SASE. Reports within 3 weeks. Write to schedule an appointment to show a portfolio, which should include original/final art. Negotiates pay rate; pays on acceptance.
Tips: Especially looks for "good line work and overall balance relating to fruit and nut trees."

GAY NEWS, 254 S. 11th St., Philadelphia PA 19107. (215)625-8501. Design Director: Gary L. Day. Newspaper. Emphasizes news and feature articles for gay men and lesbians. Weekly. Readership estimate, 15-20,000. Accepts previously published material and simultaneous submissions. Original artwork returned after publication. Sample copy and art guidelines free for SASE.
Illustrations: Buys occasional illustrations/issue from freelancers. Themes and styles depend on accompanying article. Works on assignment only. Send query letter with business card, photocopies and tear sheets to be returned. "We prefer not to be sent original art as a sample." Samples not kept on file returned by SASE. Reports within 2 weeks. To show a portfolio, mail photostats and b&w. Negotiates rights purchased. Pays $20 for b&w, inside; on publication.

THE GERMANTOWN COURIER, 156 W. Chelten Ave., Philadelphia PA 19144. (215)848-4300. Editor: Debbie Flood. Newspaper emphasizing neighborhood news in northwest Philadelphia; low to middle income. Weekly. Circ. 25,000. Original work returned after publication. Sample copy and art guidelines available.

Cartoons: Prefers themes on Philadelphia news/general news and events; political-cultural relevance. Single, double or multi-panel with gagline OK; b&w line drawings. Send query letter with finished cartoons to be kept on file. Material not filed returned only if requested. Reports only if interested. Buys first rights or reprint rights. Pays $5, b&w; on publication.
Illustrations: Occasionally buys illustrations from freelancers. Uses illustrations to accompany news stories. Works on assignment only. Send query letter with resume and samples to be kept on file. Prefers good quality photocopies as samples. Samples not filed returned by SASE only if requested. Reports only if interested. Buys first rights or reprint rights. Pays $5 on publication.

THE GOODY MIRROR, 1000 W. Main St., Manchester GA 31816. (404)846-8481. Editor: Ward Garrett. Emphasizes employee communications for employees, production, supervision, management, stock holders. Quarterly. Circ. 5,000. Accepts previously published material and simultaneous submissions. Original artwork returned after publication. Sample copy for SASE.
Cartoons: Uses 1-2 cartoons/issue; buys all from freelancers. Prefers single panel with gagline; b&w line drawings. Send query letter with samples of style and roughs to be kept on file. Material not kept on file is returned only if requested. Reports within 3 weeks. Buys one-time rights. Pays $10, b&w. Pays on acceptance.
Illustrations: Uses 2 illustrations/issue; buys all from freelancers. Prefers themes illustrative of editorial thrusts—dollar breakdown, specific situations. Works on assignment only. Send query letter with samples to be kept on file. Prefers photostats as samples. Samples are returned by SASE if not kept on file. Reports within 3 weeks. Buys one-time rights. Payment depends on assignment. Pays on acceptance.

GUARDIAN,33 W. 17th ST., New York NY 10011. Photo/Graphics Editor: Jeff Jones. Independent radical newspaper with national and international news and cultural reviews for nonsectarian leftists and activists. Weekly. Circ. 20,000. Accepts previously published material. Original artwork returned by SASE after publication. Sample copy available; art guidelines free for SASE.
Cartoons: Buys 7 cartoons/issue from freelancers. Prefers b&w, pen & ink, scratch board; progressive themes. Prefers single, double or multiple panel; b&w line drawings. Send query letter with sample of style not larger than 8½x11" to be kept on file; write for appointment to show portfolio. Material not filed is returned by SASE. Reports only if interested. Negotiates rights purchased. Pays $15, b&w; on publication.
Illustrations: Buys 3 illustrations/issue from freelancers. Themes: progressive politics, issues. Send query letter and photocopies not larger than 8½x11" to be kept on file. Samples not filed are returned by SASE. Reports only if interested. To show a portfolio, mail appropriate materials, which should include original/final art, tear sheets, photostats, photographs and b&w. Negotiates rights purchased. Pays $15, b&w, cover, inside; on publication.

HIGH COUNTRY NEWS, Box 1090, Paonia CO 81428. (303)527-4898. Editor: Betsy Marston. Emphasizes energy, economic and environmental issues, Rocky Mountain regional pieces for national audience, all ages, occupations. Biweekly. Circ. 4,500. Accepts previously published material and simultaneous submissions. Original artwork returned after publication if accompanied by postage.
Illustrations: Uses 5 illustrations/issue; buys 3 illustrations/issue from freelancers. Send query letter with samples and/or tear sheets to be kept on file. Prefers photocopies as samples. Samples not kept on file are returned by SASE. Reports within 1 month. Buys one-time rights. Pays after publication.

HIGH-TECH MANAGER'S BULLETIN, 24 Rope Ferry Rd., Waterford CT 06386. (203)442-4365. Contact: Editor. Emphasis is on the supervision of technicians in high technology industry. Semimonthly. Free sample copy.
Cartoons: Uses 1 cartoon/issue; buys from freelancer. Interested in non-sexist material which pokes fun at aspects of high technology production and supervision. "Send material after reading guidelines." Prefers single panel b&w line drawings with or without the gagline. SASE. Reports in 3-6 weeks. To show a portfolio, mail appropriate materials, which should include roughs. Buys all rights. Pays $10 for b&w; on acceptances.
Tips: "Read guidelines, know the field and study sample before submission."

HOSPITAL SUPERVISOR'S BULLETIN, 24 Rope Ferry Rd., Waterford CT 06386. (203)442-4365. Editor: Janice Endresen. Emphasizes management methods for hospital supervisors of nonmedical departments. Bimonthly newsletter. Circ. 7,000. Original artwork not returned after publication. Free sample copy and artist's guidelines.
Cartoons: Buys 1/issue on any aspect of hospital environment; single panel with gagline. "We prefer cartoons that emphasize the natural humor in life, life's foibles, rather than humor at the expense of others." Pays $10, b&w line drawings. Mail roughs. SASE. Reports within 2 weeks. Pays on acceptance. Buys all rights.

Tips: "We see more professionalism and more dignity in our field. Stay away from sexist humor and de-moralizing humor—poking fun at people. Laugh with them not at them."

***JAPAN ECONOMIC SURVEY**, Suite 211, 1000 Connecticut Ave. NW, Washington DC 20036. Editor: Michael Chinworth. Newsletter emphasizing US-Japan economic and political issues/developments for opinionmakers in government, business and academic. Monthly. Circ. 3,500. Accepts previously published material. Original artwork usually returned after publication. Sample copy available.
Cartoons: Buys 3-4 cartoons/year from freelancers. Prefers single panel without gagline; b&w line drawings. Send query letter with samples of style to be kept on file. Reports only if interested. Buys one-time rights. Payment varies.
Illustrations: Buys 3-4 illustrations/year from freelancers. Works on assignment only. Send query letter with samples. Samples not filed are not returned. Reports only if interested. Write to schedule an appointment to show a portfolio. Buys one-time rights. Pays on acceptance.

***JEWISH CURRENT EVENTS**, 430 Keller Ave., Elmont NY 11003. Editor-in-Chief: Samuel Deutsch. Art Director: S. Askenazi. For Jewish audience. Biweekly. Previously published and simultaneous submissions OK.
Cartoons: Buys camera-ready art with Jewish content or flavor or adaptable for such; single, double and multiple panel. Submit art. SASE. Reports in 1 week. Pays $15-100 plus, b&w line drawings; on publication.

THE JOURNAL, Addiction Research Foundation, 33 Russell St., Toronto, Ontario M5S 2S1 Canada. (416)595-6053. Editor: Anne MacLennan. Concerns drug and alcohol research, treatment, prevention and education. Monthly. Circ. 26,000. Free sample copy and guidelines.
Cartoons: Uses cartoons occasionally; buys 1/month from freelancers. Receives 1 submission/month from freelancers. Interested in "themes relating to alcohol and other drug use." Prefers finished cartoons. Pays from $30, 3x5 minimum cartoons; on publication.
Illustrations: Buys 1 illustration/month from freelancers. Send photocopies. Write to schedule an appointment to show a portfolio, which should include roughs and b&w. Pays $200 b&w, cover and inside; on publication.

THE JOURNAL, INC., 106 W. Main St., Box 369, Williamston SC 29697. (803)847-7361. Publisher: William C. Meade. Newspaper. Audience is rural and urban—mill town, agricultural and industrial. Weekly. Circ. 5,700. Accepts previously published material. Sample copy available.
Cartoons: Buys 1 cartoon/issue. Prefers political, humorous and family themes. Prefers double-panel with gagline; b&w line drawings. Send finished cartoons to be kept on file. Material not filed not returned. Reports only if interested. To show a portfolio, mail appropriate materials, which should include final reproduction/product and b&w. Pays on publication.

***THE JOURNAL NEWSPAPERS**, The Journal, Springfield VA 22159. (703)750-8779. Entertainment Editor: Buzz McClain. Emphasizes daily news and features. Daily. Circ. 150,000. Accepts previously published material. Original artwork returned after publication.
Illustrations: Buys a few illustrations from freelancers. Works on assignment only. Send query letter with resume and tear sheets. Samples not filed are returned only if requested. Reports only if interested. Call to schedule an appointment to show a portfolio, which should include original/final art and tear sheets. Buys first rights. Pays on publication.

JOURNAL PUBLISHING CO. INC., 7 Main St., Box 68, Adams NY 13605. (315)232-2141. Editor: Robert S. Rhodes. Newspapers for farm and recreation audience. *Empire State Farmer*; bimonthly; circ. 9,000; and *Jefferson County Journal*; weekly; circ. 3,500. Accepts previously published material. Original work returned after publication, Sample copy free for SASE. Art guidelines available.
Cartoons: Buys 2-3 cartoons/issue from freelancers. Prefers single panel with or without gagline; b&w line drawings. Send query letter with samples of style or finished cartoons to be kept on file. Material not filed returned by SASE. Pays on acceptance.
Illustrations: Send query letter with samples to be kept on file. Prefers tear sheets as samples.

THE KERSHAW NEWS-ERA, 202 East Marion, Box 398, Kershaw SC 29067. (803)475-6095. Co-owner/Editor: Jim McKeown Jr. Newspaper emphasizing general news including textile industry and agriculture; music, theatre and drama; hunting; and creative crafts. "We have a special edition TMC, Total Market Coverage, circ. 5,100." Weekly 2,200. Accepts previously published material. Original work returned after publication. Sample copy free for SASE with 50¢ postage. Art guidelines free for SASE with 50¢ postage or postage required for return mailing.
Cartoons: Buys 2 cartoons/issue from freelancers. Prefers political and humorous themes appropriate

for small town. Prefers multi-panel with gagline; b&w line drawings. Send query letter with samples of style to be kept on file. Material not filed returned by SASE. Reports only if interested. Buys reprint rights. Negotiates payment. Pays on publication.

LAURENS COUNTY ADVERTISER, Box 490, Laurens SC 29360. (803)984-2586. Editor: Grant Vosburgh. Newspaper emphasizing local news for a "strictly county audience looking for strictly county news." Biweekly. Circ. 9,000. Accepts previously published material. Sample copy available.
Cartoons: "We may need cartoons on occasion to accompany specific stories." Send query letter with samples of style. Reports within 1 week. Pay rate negotiable on publication.
Illustrations: "We need illustrations on occasion with specific stories." Works on assignment only. Send query letter with samples. Reports within 1 week. Negotiates payment.

LIGHTWAVE, the Journal of Fiber Optics, 235 Bear Hill Rd., Waltham MA 02154. (617)890-2700. Editor: John Ryan. Estab. 1984. Newspaper. Emphasizes fiber optics for communication and sensing for engineers. Monthly. Circ. 12,000. Sometimes accepts previously published material. Returns original artwork after publication on request. Sample copy $3.50 for paid subscribers; $4 nonsubscribers.
Cartoons: Considers b&w line drawings with or without gaglines. Send query letter with samples of style or roughs to be kept on file. Write for appointment to show portfolio. Material not filed returned by SASE. Reports only if interested. Buys first rights. Pays $100 for b&w; on acceptance.
Illustrations: Buys 2 illustrations/issue from freelancers. Prefers sketches of real people or objects. Send query letter with samples to be kept on file. Write for appointment to show portfolio. Prefers tear sheets or photocopies as samples. Samples not filed returned by SASE. Reports only if interested. Buys first rights. Pays $50-100 for b&w; on acceptance.

THE LOCAL NEWS, Box 466, Windermere FL 32786. (305)298-2401. Associate Editor: Darrell R. Julian. News magazine with emphasis on local events; general interest. Audience: 60% ages 25-40 years, upper middle-class, educated and sophisticated; 40% ages over 55, middle-class retirees reflecting all areas of US. Prefers original material, but previously published material considered if publications disclosed. Sample copy $1.40.
Cartoons: Buys 1-2 cartoons/issue from freelancers. Interested in "witty and comic development that reveals the absurdities of everyday life; off-the-wall styles in the Gary Larson "The Far Side" vein; and political cartoons tailored for a very conservative (politically) audience." Prefers single, double or multiple panel with or without gagline; b&w line drawings or washes. Send nonreturnable copy only. Reports within 2 months. Buys first rights, one-time rights or reprint rights. Pays $10, b&w; on accpetance.
Illustrations: Theme and style depend on requirements of piece. Works on assignment only. Buys first rights, one-time or reprint rights. Pays $10, b&w, inside.

THE MANITOBA TEACHER, 191 Harcourt St., Winnipeg, Manitoba R3J 3H2 Canada. (204)888-7961. Editor: Mrs. Miep van Raalte. Emphasizes education for teachers and others in Manitoba. 4 issues/year between September and June. Circ. 16,900. Free sample copy and art guidelines.
Cartoons: Uses less than 2 cartoons/year relating to education in Manitoba. Prefers single panel, b&w line drawing with gagline. Send roughs and samples of style. SAE (nonresidents include IRC). Reports in 1 month.
Illustrations: Interested in b&w line drawings for inside. Send roughs and samples of style. SAE (nonresidents include IRC). Reports in 1 month.
Tips: Especially needs cartoons and illustrations related directly to the Manitoba scene. "Inquire before sending work."

MASS HIGH TECH, 755 Mt. Auburn St., Watertown MA 02172. (617)924-2422. Editor-in-Chief: Alan R. Earls. Newspaper. Emphasizes high technology businesses, schools, etc., in greater Boston (Eastern Massachusetts) and New England area for programmers, engineers, managers and other technical professionals. Bimonthly. Circ. 36,000. Original artwork returned after publication. Sample copy with $2 postage or money order.
Cartoons: Buys 1-2 cartoons/issue from freelancers. Prefers single panel. Send actual work or samples. Reports in 1 month. Buys first North American serial rights. Pays $25 + on publication.
Illustrations: Works on assignment only. Send query letter with brochure to be kept on file. Prefers photostats as samples. Samples not kept on file are returned only if requested. Reports only if interested. Material not copyrighted. Pays $25 + on publication.

***THE MIAMI HERALD**, One Herald Plaza, Miami FL 33101. (305)376-3431. Director of Editorial Art: Randy Stano. Daily newspaper for "a large Cuban population plus a near-even Anglo mix and Hai-

tian influence—a young vs. elderly population." Circ. 475,000 daily, over 500,000 on Sunday. Accepts previously published material. Original artwork returned after publication. Sample copy available; plus job descriptions/specs are available.
Cartoons: Occasionally buys cartoons from freelancers. Material not filed is returned. Reports only if interested. Write or call for appointment to show portfolio. Buys one-time rights. Pays on acceptance.
Illustrations: Buys 1-6 illustrations/week from freelancers. Works on assignment only. Send resume, tear sheets and slides. Samples not filed are returned if requested. Reports only if interested. Call or write to schedule an appointment to show a portfolio, which should include final reproduction/product and tear sheets. Buys one-time or reprint rights. Pays $150-300 for b&w and $300-450 for color, cover. Pays on acceptance.
Tips: "Keep an open mind."

***MILKWEED CHRONICLE**, Box 24303, Minneapolis MN 55424. (612)332-3192. Art Director: Rand Scholes. Emphasizes poetry and graphics with the conversation between the two for readers and writers of poetry, artists, and those interested in visuals. Consumer tabloid published 3 times/year. Circ. 5,000. Receives 3 cartoons and 2 illustrations/week from freelance artists. Previously published material OK but prefers original work. Original work returned after publication. Sample copy $4.
Cartoons: Number used varies—"if enough of quality, could run 30%." Buys about 10/issue from freelancers. Interested in quality based on theme of issue or based on play of poetics and visuals; single, double or multiple panel without gagline. Send finished cartoons or samples of style. Samples returned by SASE. "We try to answer queries and make decision at due times for each issue—every 4 months." Buys one-time rights. Pays $10-25, b&w; on publication.
Illustrations: Uses 25-40 illustrations/issue; buys 10-30 from freelancers. Style is open, quality, theme of page (poetry, essay, etc.) and issue. Provide finished art, samples of style and tear sheets to be kept onfile for possible future assignments. Samples returned by SAE. "We try to answer queries and make decision at due times for each issue—every 4 months." Write for appointment or submit portfolio. Pays $20-100 cover, $10-50 inside, b&w line drawings and washes; on publication.

MILWAUKEE JOURNAL, Box 661, Milwaukee WI 53201. Managing Editor/News: Steve Hammah. Daily. Circ. 310,000.
Cartoons: Managing Editor/Features: George Lockwood. Buys themes acceptable to family readership; single panel. Query with samples. SASE. Reports in 2 weeks. Buys one-time rights. Pays $15 minimum, washes.
Illustrations: Art Director: Vincent Catteruccia. Buys themes acceptable to family readership. Query with samples. SASE. Reports in 2 weeks. Buys all rights. Inside: Pays $10 minimum.
Tips: There is a trend toward "more graphics to accompany news stories."

NATIONAL ENQUIRER, Lantana FL 33464. Cartoon Editor: Michele L. Cooke. Weekly tabloid. Circ. 6,000,000. Previously published work OK if cartoonist owns rights.
Cartoons: Buys 450 cartoons/year on "all subjects the family reader can relate to, especially animal and husband-wife situations. Captionless cartoons have a better chance of selling here." Receives 2,000 cartoons/week from freelance artists, buys 8/week from freelancers. Especially needs Christmas cartoon spread (submit by August). Send query letter with original cartoons. Mail 8½x11" art. SASE. Reports in 2 weeks. "No portfolios, please." Buys first rights. Pays $300 maximum, b&w single panel; $40 every panel thereafter; pays on acceptance.
Tips: "Study 5-6 issues before submitting. Check captions for spelling. New submitters should send introductory letter. All cartoonists should include phone and social security number. Know your market. We have no use for political or off-color gags. Neatness counts and sloppy, stained artwork registers a negative reaction. Besides neatness, we also look for "correct spelling and punctuation on captions and in the body of the cartoon, accurate rendering of the subject (if the subject is a duck, make it look like a duck and not a goose, swan or chicken), and *most important* is visual impact! Prefers 8½x11" instead of 'halfs.' If submitting reprints, know *who* owns the rights."

THE NATIONAL LAW JOURNAL, Suite 900, 111 8th Ave., New York NY 10011. (212)741-8300. Art Director: Cynthia Currie. Tabloid emphasizing law for attorneys. Weekly. Circ. 38,000. Original artwork returned after publication. Sample copy $2.
Cartoons: Buys 1 cartoon/issue from freelancers. Prefers single panel; b&w line drawings. Send query letter with samples of style or finished cartoons. Material not filed is returned. Reports within 2 weeks. Buys all rights. Pays $100, b&w; on acceptance.
Illustrations: Buys 2 illustrations/month from freelancers. Works on assignment only. Send query letter with brochure to be kept on file. Samples returned only if requested. Reports within 2 weeks. Buys all rights. Pays $125, b&w, cover, inside; on acceptance.

***NATIONAL LIBRARIAN**, Box 586, Alma MI 48801. (517)463-7227. Editor: Peter Dollard. Emphasizes professional issues related to librarianship. Quarterly. Circ. 500. Original work returned after publication. Free sample copy and publication guidelines for SASE.
Cartoons: Uses single panel b&w line drawings with gagline. Send query letter with finished cartoons. Samples returned. Reports in 2-4 weeks. Material not copyrighted. Pays $25, b&w; on acceptance.
Illustrations: Uses 1-2 illustrations/issue. Send query letter with finished art. Reports in 2 weeks. Material not copyrighted. Pays $25; on acceptance.

NETWORK WORLD, (formerly *Computerworld on Communications*), 375 Cochituate Rd., Framingham MA 01701. (617)879-0700. Art Director: Dianne Gronberg. Tabloid. Emphasizes news and products relating to the communications field. Weekly. Returns original artwork after publication. Sample copy free for SASE.
Illustrations: Number purchased/issue varies. Themes depend on the storyline. Works on assignment only. Send query letter with brochure and photocopies to be kept on file. Write for appointment to show portfolio. Reports only if interested. Buys first rights. Pays $175-200 for b&w and $225-400 for color, inside; on acceptance.

NEW ALASKAN, Rt. 1, Box 677, Ketchikan AK 99901. (907)247-2490. Editor: Bob Pickrell. Emphasizes Southeastern Alaska lifestyle, history and politics for general public in this area. Monthly. Circ. 6,000. Previously published material and simultaneous submissions OK. Original work returned after publication by SASE. Sample copy $1.50; art guidelines for SASE.
Cartoons: Uses 1 cartoon/issue; buys 1 from freelancers. Interested only in art with a Southeastern Alaska tie-in; single panel with or without gagline, b&w line drawings. Send roughs or samples of style. Samples returned by SASE. Reports in 3 months. Negotiates rights purchased. Pays $25 up, b&w; on publication.
Illustrations: Uses 2 illustrations/issue; buys 1 from freelancers. Interested only in art with a Southeastern tie-in. "We prefer manuscripts with illustrations except for cover art which can stand by itself." Works on assignment only. Provide business card and samples to be kept on file for possible future assignments. Samples returned by SASE. Reports in 3 months. Negotiates rights purchased and payment; on publication.

NEW ENGLAND RUNNING, Box 658, Brattleboro VT 05301. Contact: Editorial Department. Tabloid. Emphasizes New England running, primarily competitive. Monthly. Circ. 4,000. Original artwork returned after publication. Sample copy $2.
Cartoons: Uses 1 cartoon/issue; buys from freelancer. Prefers single panel, with gagline; b&w line drawings. Send query letter with samples of style to be kept on file. Material not kept on file is returned by SASE. Reports in 1 month. Buys one-time rights. Pays $10, b&w; on publication.
Illustrations: Uses 2 illustrations/year; buys all from freelancers. Send query letter with clippings and photocopies and tear sheets to be kept on file. Prefers clippings or photocopies as samples. Samples not kept on file are returned by SASE. Reports within 1 month. Buys one-time rights. Pays $10-20, b&w; on publication.
Tips: "We need simple cartoons done in bold, black lines for best reproduction."

THE NEW SOUTHERN LITERARY MESSENGER, 400 S. Laurel St., Richmond VA 23220. (804)780-1244. Editor: Charles Lohmann. Tabloid. Emphasizes poetry and short stories. Quarterly. Circ. 400. Accepts previously published material. Returns original artwork after publication. Sample copy $1. Art guidelines free for SASE with 32¢ postage.
Cartoons: Buys 3 or 4/issue. Prefers single, double or multiple panel with or without gagline; b&w line drawings. Send query letter to be kept on file. Write for appointment to show portfolio. Reports within 3 weeks. Purchases one-time reprint rights. Pays $5; on publication.
Tips: "Don't call or write unless you live in Richmond, VA. I only work personally, face-to-face with artists."

NEW YORK ANTIQUE ALMANAC, Box 335, Lawrence NY 11559. (516)371-3300. Editor: Carol Nadel. For art, antiques and nostalgia collectors/investors. Monthly tabloid. Circ. 52,000. Reports within 4-6 weeks. Previously published work OK. Original artwork returned after publication, if requested. Free sample copy.
Cartoons: Uses 1 cartoon/issue; buys 1/issue from freelancers. Receives 1 submission/week from freelancers. Interested in antiques, nostalgia and money. Prefers finished cartoons. SASE. Reports in 4 weeks. Buys all rights, but may reassign rights to artist after publication. Pays $5-20, b&w; on publication.
Illustrations: Buys 24/year on collecting and investing. Buys all rights, but may reassign rights to artist after publication. Pays $5 minimum, b&w; on publication.

THE NEWS OF SOUTHERN BERKS, 124 N. Chestnut St., Boyertown PA 19512. (215)689-9558. General Manager. Editor: Sherry Herrlinger. Weekly family newspaper (weddings, births, editorials, sports, school coverage, local government for all ages and income. Circ. 4,000. Accepts previously published material. Original work returned after publication with SASE. Sample copy free for SASE with 75¢ postage.
Cartoons: Prefers local themes (Southeastern Berks County, Pennsylvania). Send samples of style. Write for appointment to show portfolio. Material not filed returned by SASE. Negotiates rights purchased. Pays on acceptance.
Illustrations: Send samples. Write for appointment to show portfolio. Prefers photocopies as samples. Samples not filed returned by SASE. Negotiates rights purchased. Pays on acceptance.

***NEWSDAY**, 235 Pinelawn Rd., Melville NY 11050. (516)454-2303. Art Director: Warren Weilbacher. Daily newspaper. Circ. 50,000. Original artwork returned after publication. Sample copy and art guidelines available.
Illustrations: Buys 4-5 illustrations/week from freelancers. Send query letter with brochure showing art style. Samples not filed are returned. Reports only if interested. Call to schedule an appointment to show a portfolio, which should include original/final art, final reproduction/product, color, tear sheets, photostats and b&w photos. Buys one-time rights. Pays $350 for b&w and $400 for color, cover; $100-250 for b&w; $150-300 for color, inside. Pays on publication.
Tips: "Let your portfolio talk for you."

***NEW YORK TODAY**, 78-11 Kew Forest Ln., Forest Hills NY 11375. (718)544-1254 or 544-1254. Editor: Ray Wilson.
Needs: Weekly newspaper. Buys from 35 freelance artists/year. Works mostly on assignment only. Considers b&w samples. Also needs freelance artists for advertising and publicity.
First Contact & Terms: Send query letter with brochure showing art style or resume, tear sheets and photographs "if on assignment." Samples not filed are returned by SASE. Reports back within 20 days. Pays a "minimum fee—must quote artist lowest rate; on publication. Considers skill and experience of artist and saleability of artwork when establishing payment. Buys all rights.
Tips: "Write to the publisher or editor asking and suggesting an article on a certain subject. Wait for reply and state your fee with suggested article."

NORTH MYRTLE BEACH TIMES, Box 725, North Myrtle Beach SC 29597. (803)249-1122 or 249-3525. Publisher and General Manager: Pauline L. Lowman. Semiweekly. Circ. 9,500. Simultaneous submissions OK. Original work returned after publication if requested. Free sample copy and art guidelines.
Cartoons: Uses 2 cartoons/issue. Interested in editorial themes; double panel b&w line drawings with gagline. Send query letter with resume and samples of style. Samples returned by SASE. Reports in 2 weeks. To show a portfolio, mail appropriate materials or call to schedule an appointment. Material not copyrighted. Pays on acceptance.
Illustrations: Uses editorial themes. Send query letter with samples of style. Samples returned by SASE. Reports in 2 weeks. Material not copyrighted. Pays on publication.
Tips: "Be original and able to express ideas well. Be neat with work and have interesting samples to show."

NURSINGWORLD JOURNAL, 470 Boston Post Rd., Weston MA 02193. (617)899-2702. Editor: Bernard Smith. Readers are "student and experienced nurses interested in keeping their skills current and seeking employment, trends in nursing, relocation or area hiring trends in nursing, reviews of nursing articles, feature stories." Specialty is health care publications. Monthly. Circ. 40,000. Sample copy $2.

> **❝** *Cleaner, simpler designs are being used for greeting cards. There is more contemporary calligraphy, including multi-colored work. Computerized graphics are just beginning to impact.* **❞**
>
> *Rev. Norbert Schappler, The Printing House of Conception Abbey*

Cartoons: Uses 1-3 cartoons/issue. Receives 25 submissions/month from freelancers. Interested in hospital or nursing themes. Prefers b&w line drawing with gagline. Send finished cartoons. SASE. Reports within 6 months. Buys one-time rights. Pays $5-10 for b&w; on publication.
Illustrations: Uses 3 illustrations/issue. Receives 10 submissions/month from freelancers. Interested in general illustrations that go along with editorial; usually people or nature. Works on assignment. "Freelancers call, send us samples, and we make a decision at that time if their style fits our paper. If it does, we keep their names on file, then contact them for assignments." Send roughs. SASE. Reports within 6 months. Prefers b&w line drawings. Buys all rights on a work-for-hire basis. Pays $50-100 for b&w or color cover, $50 for inside b&w. Pays on publication.
Tips: Interested in seeing "any articles you're interested in. Submissions from editor's point of view."

NUTRITION HEALTH REVIEW, 171 Madison Ave., New York NY 10016. Features Editor: F.R. Rifkin. Tabloid. Emphasizes physical health, mental health, nutrition, food preparation and medicine. For a general audience. Quarterly. Circ. 165,000 paid. Accepts simultaneous submissions. Sample copy $1.25.
Cartoons: Uses 10 cartoons/issue. Prefers single panel with or without gagline; b&w line drawings. Send finished cartoons to be kept on file; samples returned by SASE if not purchased. Reports within 30 days. Buys first rights or all rights. Pays $15 + , b&w; on acceptance.
Illustrations: Number illustrations varies/issue. Send samples to be kept on file; write for appointment to show portfolio. If samples are requested, prefers to see photostats. Samples returned by SASE. Reports back. Buys first rights or all rights. Pays $200, b&w, cover and $25 for b&w inside; on acceptance.

THE OFFICIAL COMDEX SHOW DAILY, 300 1st Ave., Needham MA 02194. (617)449-6600. Production Manager/Art Director: Linda Peterson. Tabloid. Emphasizes computers and computer-related products for attendees and exhibitors at the U.S. Comdex Shows. Seasonal: Fall, Winter, Spring. Circ. 35,000. Accepts previously published material. Original artwork returned after publication if requested. Sample copy free for SASE; art guidelines available.
Cartoons: Buys 50-100 cartoons/issue from freelancers; buys 300-400/year from freelancers. "Computer graphics used in cartoon illustration. Application ties in well as our newspaper is read by people in the computer industry." Wants anything related to computers, trade shows, Las Vegas, Los Angeles or Atlanta. Prefers single panel with or without gagline; b&w line drawings. Send query letter with roughs or finished cartoons to be kept on file. Material not filed is returned by SASE only if requested. Reports within several weeks. Buys one-time rights. Pays $18; on acceptance.
Illustrations: Themes: computers/trade shows/computer related products. Humorous and cartoon-style illustrations used once a year. Works on assignment only. Send query letter with tear sheets, photostats, photocopies, slides and photographs to be kept on file. Samples returned by SASE only if requested. Reports within several weeks only if interested. Call or write to schedule an appointment to show a portfolio, which should include final reproduction/product, tear sheets and photostats. Buys one-time rights. Pays $50-100, b&w; on acceptance.

OFFSHORE, New England's Boating Magazine, 1981 Chestnut St., Newton MA 02164. (617)244-7520. Art Director: Dave Daver. Tabloid emphasizing boating for New England boat owners. Monthly. Circ. 18,000. Accepts previously published material. Original artwork returned after publication. Sample copy for SASE with $1.15 postage.
Cartoons: Buys 2 cartoons/issue from freelancers. Prefers single panel; b&w line drawings. Send query letter with samples of style to be kept on file. Material not filed is returned by SASE. Reports within 1 week. Buys first rights. Pays $10-25, b&w; on acceptance.
Ilustrations: Buys 2 illustrations/issue from freelancers. Prefers hard line. Works on assignment only. Send samples to be kept on file. Prefers photostats or tear sheets as samples. Samples not filed are returned by SASE. Reports within 1 week. Buys first rights. Pays $100-175, color, cover; $20-50, b&w, inside; on acceptance.

OUR GANG, One Children's Plaza, Dayton OH 45404. (513)226-8332. Editor/Communications Specialist: Susan A. Brockman. Magapaper. Emphasizes hospital (CMC) programs, employees, volunteers, health topics. Monthly. Circ. 2,200. Accepts previously published material and simultaneous submissions. Original artwork returned after publication. Sample copy and art guidelines free for SASE.
Cartoons: Buys 6 cartoons/year from freelancers. Prefers offbeat, funny-looking people (i.e., Phil Frank). Prefers single panel, without gagline; b&w line drawings. Send query letter with samples of style to be kept on file. Material not kept on file is returned by SASE if requested. Reports only if interested. Write for appointment to show portfolio. Negotiates rights purchased and pay rate; pays on publication.
Illustrations: Uses illustrations 12 times/year; buys all from freelancers. Prefers "cartoonish" style.

Works on assignment only. Send query letter with tear sheets and photostats to be kept on file. Samples not kept on file are returned by SASE if requested. Reports only if interested. Call or write for appointment to show portfolio. Negotiates rights purchased and pay rate; pays on publication.

THE PAPERWORKER, Box 1475, Nashville TN 37202. (615)834-8590. Editor/Director of Publications: Monte L. Byers. Emphasizes labor subjects for membership of industrial union. Monthly tabloid. Circ. 250,000. Accepts previously published material. Original artwork not returned after publication. Sample copy free for SASE with 20¢ postage.
Cartoons: Buys 1-5 cartoons/issue from freelancers. Considers labor and national issue themes. Prefers single panel with gagline; b&w line drawings. Send query letter with finished cartoons to be kept on file. Material not filed is returned by SASE only if requested. Reports within several weeks. Buys one-time rights. Pays variable rates for b&w and color; on publication.
Illustrations: Buys 1-3 illustrations/issue from freelancers. Themes/styles vary to accompany text. Works on assignment only. Send query letter with samples to be kept on file. Prefers tear sheets as samples. Samples returned only if requested. Reports within several weeks. Buys one-time rights. Pays variable rates for b&w and color, inside; on publication.

PAWPRINTS, FONZ Publications, National Zoological Park, Washington DC 20008. (202)673-4993. Publications Director: Bettina Conner. Newsletter emphasizing zoo animals, conservation and preservation of endangered species for children, 6-16. Bimonthly. Circ. 8,000. Accepts previously published material. Returns original artwork after publication. Sample copy for $1.
Illustrations: Buys 1-2/issue from freelance artists. Prefers educational games and puzzles depicting exotic animals. Send photostats or tear sheets. Samples are returned by SASE. Reports within 6 weeks. Send query letter with tear sheets and photostats. Call to schedule an appointment to show a portfolio, which should include original/final art, final reproduction/product and tear sheets. Buys first rights. Pays $100 for b&w, cover; $50 for b&w, inside; on publication.
Tips: "Originality of puzzle or game idea especially important."

PERSONNEL ADVISORY BULLETIN, Bureau of Business Practice, 24 Rope Ferry Rd., Waterford CT 06386. Editor: Laura Gardner. For personnel managers and practitioners in smaller companies—white collar and industrial. Features interviewing and hiring, training, benefits, career development, promotion practices, counseling, record keeping, etc. Bimonthly newsletter. Original artwork not returned after publication. No previously published material or simultaneous submissions. Free sample copy.
Cartoons: Uses 1 cartoon/issue; buys 1/issue from freelancers. Receives 15-20 submissions/week from freelancers. Buys 30/year on "personnel-oriented situations. Please, no sexist situations and male boss/dumb female secretary jokes." Prefers single panel. Mail finished art. SASE. Reports in 2 weeks. Buys all rights. Pays $10 for b&w line drawings. Pays on acceptance.
Tips: "We're trying to be more selective in choosing strictly personnel-oriented subject matter. Avoid anything smacking of sexism or other discriminatory attitudes. Don't overdo hiring-firing situations. Make captions *literate* and *funny*."

THE PLAIN DEALER MAGAZINE, 1801 Superior Ave., Cleveland OH 44114. (216)344-4578. Design Director: Gerard Sealy. Sunday color roto magazine supplement to *The Plain Dealer* newspaper. Broad-based, general audience. Weekly. Circ. 500,000. Original artwork returned after publication. Sample copy free for SASE.
Cartoons: Uses 2-3 cartoons/issue; buys 1-2/issue from freelancers. Prefers single panel with or without gagline; b&w line drawings. Send finished cartoons. Material is returned by SASE. Reports only if interested. Buys one-time rights. Pays $50, b&w; on publication.
Illustrations: Buys 4-5 illustrations/issue; buys all from freelancers. All styles considered. Works on assignment basis only. Send query letter with brochure, business card and samples to be kept on file; call for appointment to show portfolio. No original art; all other types of samples considered. Reports only if interested. Buys first rights. Pays $400 maximum, color, cover; $300 maximum, b&w, and $400 maximum, color, inside; on publication.

PRESS-ENTERPRISE, Box 792, Riverside CA 92502. (714)684-1200. Assistant Managing Editor/Features & Art: Sally Ann Mass. Daily newspaper in Southern California emphasizing general subjects. Circ. 140,000. Original artwork returned after publication.
Illustrations: Buys 1 editorial illustration/week from freelancers. Uses various themes and styles. Works on assignment only. Send query letter, resume and samples to be kept on file. Samples not filed are returned only if requested. Reports within 2 weeks. Negotiates rights purchased. Write for appointment to show portfolio. Pays variable rates; on acceptance.
Tips: "Resume and samples absolute necessity."

***PUBLICATIONS CO.**, 1220 Maple Ave., Los Angeles CA 90015. Editor: Lucie Dubovik. Emphasizes general business for companies, service organizations, etc. and journalism in schools. Monthly. Accepts previously published material. Sample copy and art guidelines free for SASE.
Cartoons: Buys several cartoons/issue from freelancers. Prefers business, industry, factory, schools, and teen situations, plus seasonal material as themes. Prefers single panel with gagline; b&w line drawings. Send query letter with samples of style or finished cartoons. Material not filed is returned by SASE. Reports within 1 month. Buys reprint rights. Pays on acceptance.
Illustrations: Buys several illustrations/issue from freelancers. Prefers business, industry, factory, school and teen situations plus seasonal material as themes. Send query letter with original art. Samples not filed are returned by SASE. Reports within 1 month. Buys reprint rights. Pays on acceptance.

PUBLISHING CONCEPTS CORPORATION, Main St., Luttrell TN 37779. For a general audience with middle to upper incomes. Weekly. Circ. 60,190. Previously published material OK. Original artwork returned after publication. Free sample copy for SASE; art guidelines available. Receives 8 cartoons and 3 illustrations/week from freelance artists.
Cartoons: Uses 10 cartoons/issue; buys all from freelancers. Interested in general, national themes; single panel, b&w line drawings. Send finished cartoons. Samples returned by SASE. Reports in 1 week. Negotiates rights purchased. Pays $10-50, b&w; on acceptance.
Illustrations: Number of illustrations/issue varies. Will review all themes and styles for interest. Provide business card and samples to be kept on file for possible future assignments. Send samples of style. Samples returned by SASE. Reports in 1 week. Buys one-time rights. Pays $10-40 cover, b&w line drawings; on acceptance.
Tips: "We publish several publications and work submitted on a freelance basis may be considered for any one of several publications. Prices paid vary with quality of work, degree of interest at the time received or readership interest for the next two weeks."

ROLLING STONE, 745 5th Ave., New York NY 10151. (212)758-3800. Art Director: Derek W. Ungless. Coverage includes music, film, social issues, investigative reporting, books and new life styles. Biweekly tabloid. Original artwork returned after publication.
Illustrations: Buys 1-2 illustrations/issue. Illustrations are assigned to particular editorial needs. Works on assignment only. Submit samples of style or portfolio. Samples returned by SASE. Provide business card to be kept on file for future assignments. Reports as soon as possible. Buys one-time publication rights.

SALESMANSHIP AND FOREMANSHIP AND EFFECTIVE EXECUTIVE, Dartnell Corporation, 4660 N. Ravenswood Ave., Chicago IL 60640. Art Director: G.C. Gormaly, Jr. Emphasizes salesmanship. Monthly. Previously published material OK.
Cartoons: Uses 1 cartoon/issue. Prefers single panel with or without gagline, b&w line drawings or b&w washes. Send query letter and samples of style. Samples returned. Reports in 1 month. Negotiates rights purchased. Pays $20-50, b&w; on acceptance.
Illustrations: Uses illustrations occasionally; seldom buys from freelancers. Send query letter and samples of style to be kept on file for possible future assignments. Samples not kept on file are returned. Reports in 2 months. Buys reprint rights. Pays $100-300 cover, $100-150 inside, b&w line or tone drawings; on acceptance.

***SANTA CRUZ SENTINEL**, 207 Church St., Santa Cruz CA 95060. (408)423-4242. Entertainment Editor: Greg Beebe. Daily newspaper. Published Monday through Friday and Sunday. Circ. 35,000. Original artwork returned after publication. Sample copy and art guidelines available.
Cartoons: Buys 1 cartoon/week from freelancers. Material not filed is returned by SASE. Reports only if interested. Write for appointment to show portfolio. Buys one-time rights. Pays on publication.
Illustrations: Buys 2 illustrations/month from freelancers. Works on assignment only. Send query letter with brochure showing art style or resume and tear sheets. Samples not filed are returned by SASE. Reports only if interested. To show a portfolio, mail appropriate materials or write to schedule an appointment; portfolio should include original/final art, final reproduction/product, color and tear sheets. Buys one-time rights. Pays $75 for b&w and $175 for color, cover; $50 for b&w, inside; on publication.
Tips: "Artists seem to be able to work quicker, without sacrificing quality. Keep trying."

SHOW BUSINESS, 29th Fl., 1501 Broadway, New York NY 10036. (212)354-7600, ext. 20. Assistant Publisher: Paul O'Connor. Casting newspaper for investors, producers, directors, press people, agents, photographers, performing artists and models. Weekly. Circ. 36,000. Accepts previously published material. Original artwork returned after publication. Art guidelines free for SASE with $1.37 postage.
Cartoons: Considers theatre or film themes. Prefers double panel. Send samples of style. Call for appointment to show portfolio. Material returned by SASE. Reports within 2 weeks. Negotiates rights purchased. Pays on publication.

Illustrations: Buys 4 illustrations/issue from freelancers. Prefers theatre or film themes. Send query letter with samples. Call for appointment to show portfolio. Prefers photostats as samples. Samples are returned by SASE. Reports within 2 weeks. Negotiates rights purchased. Pays on publication.

SKYDIVING, Box 1520, Deland FL 32721. (904)736-9779. Editor: Michael Truffer. Emphasizes skydiving for sport parachutists, worldwide dealers and equipment manufacturers. Monthly. Circ. 7,200.
Cartoons: Uses 1-2 cartoons/issue; buys 0-1 from freelancers. Receives 1-2 submissions/week from freelancers. Interested in themes relating to skydiving or aviation. Prefers single panel b&w line drawings with gagline. Send finished cartoons or samples of style. SASE. Reports in 1 week. Buys one-time rights. Pays $10 minimum for b&w; on publication.
Tips: Artists "must *know* parachuting; cartoons must be funny."

SOUTHERN JEWISH WEEKLY, Box 3297, Jacksonville FL 32206. (904)634-1812. Editor: R. Miller. Emphasizes human interest material and short stories. "The only Jewish newspaper covering all of Florida and the Southeast." Weekly. Circ. 28,500.
Illustrations: Buys 2 illustrations/year on Jewish themes that pertain to newspaper's articles. Send query letter with resume and samples. Seasonal themes must arrive 2 weeks in advance of holiday. SASE. Reports in 1 week. Pays $10 minimum, b&w; on publication.
Tips: "Send samples of work along with resume to us one month or more in advance of Jewish holiday being featured."

SOUTHWEST DIGEST, 510 E. 23rd St., Lubbock TX 79404. (806)762-3612. Co-Publisher-Managing Editor: Eddie P. Richardson. Newspaper emphasizing positive black images, and community building and rebuilding "primarily oriented to the black community and basically reflective of the black community, but serving all people." Weekly. Accepts previously published material. Original work returned after publication.
Cartoons: Number of cartoons purchased/issue from freelancers varies. Prefers economic development, community development, community pride and awareness, and black uplifting themes. Single, double or multi-panel with gagline; b&w line drawings. Send query letter with samples of style, roughs or finished cartoons to be kept on file. Write or call for appointment to show portfolio. Material not filed returned by SASE only if requested. Buys first, one-time, reprint, or all rights; or negotiates rights purchased. Pays on publication.
Illustrations: Send query letter with brochure or samples to be kept on file. Write or call for appointment to show portfolio. Prefers photostats, tear sheets, photocopies, photographs, etc. as samples. Samples not filed returned by SASE only if requested. Reports only if interested. Negotiates rights purchased. Pays on publication.

***SPARKS JOURNAL**, Society of Wireless Pioneers, Box 530, Santa Rosa CA 95402. Editor: William A. Breniman. For radio-telegraph men who handle(d) communications with ships and at-shore stations; included are military, commercial, aeronautical and governmental communications personnel. "Since many have earned their living aboard ships as 'Sparks,' we like to bring a nautical flavor to our pages." Quarterly tabloid newspaper. Circ. 5,000 (members) plus some libraries and museums. Accepts previously published material "if it fits."
Cartoons: Buys 15-20 cartoons/issue. Send query letter with samples. To show a portfolio, mail appropriate materials, which should include b&w drawings. Pays $2-30 for b&w; on acceptance.
Illustrations: Uses illustrative headings for various articles. Buys 4-10 illustrations/issue. Send query letter with brochure showing art style or tear sheets and photocopies. Uses b&w only; no color. Include SASE. Buys reprint rights. Pays $25-100 for b&w, cover; $10-25 for b&w, inside; on acceptance.
Tips: "Those who have a love of the sea and things nautical, and are also versed in wireless telegraph or transmission via Hertzian waves (communications), would probably be able to furnish the type of material we use. We are a professional, nonprofit organization; we do not cater to the amateur radio (including CB) field. We also publish *The Skipper's Log* (quarterly tabloid, members only), *Port's O'Call* (biennial), *Sparks* (in series, annual), and a book-format almanac."

THE STATE JOURNAL-REGISTER, 1 Copley Plaza, Box 219, Springfield IL 62705. (217)788-1475. Photography Editor: Barry Locher. Emphasizes news and features for the town and surrounding area. Daily. Circ. 75,000. Accepts previously published material and simultaneous submissions. Original artwork returned after publication. Sample copy and art guidelines free for SASE.
Illustrations: "Uses approximately 6-7 photographs/issue and occasionally graphs, charts, maps, artwork. We buy only some illustrations from freelancers, not all. Staff does some work." Works on assignment only. Send query letter with samples to be kept on file. Samples are returned if not kept on file. Negotiates rights purchased. Pays $100-200, b&w and color, cover. Pays $50-150, b&w and color, inside; on publication.

THE SUPERVISOR, Kemper Group, Long Grove IL 60049. (312)540-2094. Editor: Mary Puccinelli. Newsletter. Emphasizes industrial and fleet safety for supervisors responsible for industrial safety and/ or fleet safety. Bimonthly. Circ. 50,000. Accepts simultaneous submissions. Original artwork not returned after publication. Sample copy free for SASE.
Cartoons: Uses 2 cartoons/issue; buys all from freelancers. Seeks "very funny cartoons;" can be "off-beat" but not offensive. Topics for the year are sent to prospective artists in June. Prefers single panel, with gagline; b&w line drawings. Send query letter with samples of style to be kept on file. Material not kept on file is returned by SASE. Reports within 1 month. Buys all rights. Payment varies; on acceptance.

SUPERVISOR'S BULLETIN, 24 Rope Ferry Rd., Waterford CT 06386. (203)739-0286. Editor: Steve Finn. Emphasizes "manufacturing supervision for front-line supervision in the shop. Not office and non-union." Semimonthly. Free sample copy.
Cartoons: Uses 1-2 cartoons/issue; buys all from freelancers. Receives "a dozen or so/month." Interested in nonsexist material that represents the real world, women and minorities, and pokes fun at aspects of shop supervision: safety, productivity, motivation, discipline, etc. Prefers single panel b&w line drawings with or without gagline. Send roughs. SASE. Reports in 2 weeks. Buys all rights. Pays $10 for b&w; on acceptance.

***TEENS TODAY**, 6401 The Paseo, Kansas City MO 64131. (816)333-7000. Editor: Gary Siverwright. For junior and senior high school students who attend Church of the Nazarene. Weekly. Circ. 60,000. Original work not returned after publication. Free sample copy with SASE.
Illustrations: Uses 1-2 illustrations/issue; buys 1-2/issue from freelancers; all illustrations go with stories. Works on assignment only. Prefers to see resume, flyer and tear sheets to be kept on file. SASE. Reports in 6-8 weeks.

TELEBRIEFS, Illinois Bell Telephone Co., 225 W. Randolph, Chicago IL 60606. Contact: Editor. Monthly newsletter for telephone customers. Circ. 3,500,000. Mail art. SASE. Reports in 2 weeks. Photocopies OK. Original artwork not returned after publication. Free sample copy.
Cartoons: Uses 2 cartoons/issue, all from freelancers. Receives 8 submissions/month from freelancers. Cartoons "must be telephone company or telecommunications related." Single panel. "No ethnic humor. We reduce cartoons to 1¾x1¾ so we need few elements, drawn very boldly. Prefer strong visual with captions of 10 or fewer words." Prefers finished cartoons. SASE. Reports in 2 weeks. Buys all rights on a work-for-hire basis. Pays $40, line drawings with shading; on acceptance.
Illustrations: Buys 1 illustration/week from freelancers. Send photocopies. To show a portfolio, mail appropriate materials, which should include roughs, original/final art and photostats.
Tips: "Since break up of Bell System, Illinois Bell is no longer in the business of learning, selling, or installing telephone equipment. Cartoons should mainly imply telephone usage, such as speaking on phone."

***TELEWOMAN NEWSLETTER**, Box 2306, Pleasant Hill CA 94523. Editor: Anne J. D'Arcey. Newsletter emphasizing lesbian resources—art, literature and spiritual orientations for lesbians and woman—identified. Monthly. Circ. 1,500. Accepts previously published material. Original artwork returned after publication. Sample copy free for SASE with 56¢ postage. Art guidelines free for SASE with 56¢ postage.
Cartoons: Accepts 1 cartoon/issue. Prefers lesbian humor as themes. Prefers single panel; b&w line drawings. Send query letter with samples of style or finished cartoons. Material not filed is returned by SASE. Reports within 2 weeks. Buys one-time rights. "We trade art for subscriptions."
Illustrations: Accepts 1-2 illustrations/issue from freelancers. Prefers women subjects. Send query letter with samples. Prefers photocopies. Samples not filed are returned by SASE. Reports within 2 weeks. Buys one-time rights.

TOWERS CLUB, USA, Box 2038, Vancouver WA 98668. (206)574-3084. Chief Executive Officer: Jerry Buchanan. Emphasizes "anything that offers a new entrepreneurial opportunity, especially through mail order. The newsletter for 'Find a Need and Fill It' people." Readers are 80% male with average age of 48 and income of $35,000. Monthly except August and December. Circ. 4,000. Previously published material and simultaneous submissions OK. Original work returned after publication by SASE. Sample copy $3.
Cartoons: Uses 1 cartoon/issue; buys all from freelancers. Interested in themes of selling how-to-do-it information, showing it as a profitable and honorable profession; single panel with gagline, b&w line drawings. Send finished cartoons. Samples returned by SASE. Reports in 1 week. Buys one-time rights. Pays $15-25, b&w; on publication.
Illustrations: Uses 5-7 illustrations/issue. Interested in realistic, illustrative art of typists, computers,

small print shop operations, mail order, etc.; no comical themes. Especially needs line drawings of typists/writers/office workers, money, mail delivery, affluent people, intelligent and successful faces, etc. Send brochure showing art style. Provide samples to be kept on file for possible future assignments. Samples not kept on file are returned by SASE. Reports in 1 week. Buys one-time rights. Makes some permanent purchases. Negotiates payment depending on rights purchased; on acceptance.

Tips: "Newsletters are going more to using typesetting and artwork to brighten pages. Subscribe to our *Towers Club, USA* newsletter and study content and artwork used. Normally $60 per year, we will give discount to artists who show us a portfolio of their work. Our theme will lead them to much other business, as we are about creative self-publishing/marketing exclusively. Most cartoonists have little or no genuine sense of humor. I suggest they tie in with someone who does and split the fee. Illustrators should see several copies of the publication they hope to draw for before submitting their samples. It could save a lot of postage."

TRI-STATE MAGAZINE, (formerly *Cincinnati Enquirer Sunday Magazine*), 617 Vine St., Cincinnati OH 45202. (513)721-2700. Editor: Bill Thompson. Art Director: Marty Eggerding. Weekly. Circ. 300,000.

Illustrations: Uses 1-2 illustrations/issue on assigned themes. "We rarely, if ever, use unsolicited freelance art. The usual procedure is for the artist to show a portfolio. If we like the work, we'll give the artist a manuscript to illustrate." Works on assignment only. Samples returned by SASE. Reports back on future assignment possibilities. Provide business card to be kept on file for future assignments. Prefers to see portfolio. SASE. Reporting time varies. Buys all rights on a work-for-hire basis. Pays $50-200 maximum, b&w line drawings and washes; $150-350 maximum, color illustrations and cover.

***UNION ELECTRIC NEWS**, Box 149, St. Louis MO 63166. Supervisor, Public Information: D.J. Walther. For employees and retirees. Semimonthly. Circ. 10,200. Previously published material and simultaneous submissions OK. Original work not returned after publication. Free sample copy and art guidelines for SASE.

Cartoons: Uses less than 1 cartoon/issue; buys all from freelancers. Interested in cartoons illustrative for article embellishment; b&w line drawings or washes. Send query letter with samples of style and resume. Samples returned by SASE. Reports in 2 weeks.

Illustrations: Uses 1 illustration/issue; buys all from freelancers. Works on assignment only. Interested in clean, current styles. Send query letter with resume and samples of style, prices and turn-around times. Provide resume, brochure, samples and tear sheets to be kept on file for possible future assignments. Samples not kept on file are returned by SASE. Reports in 2 weeks. Pays on acceptance.

UTILITY SUPERVISION, 24 Rope Ferry Rd., Waterford CT 06386. (203)442-4365. Editor: DeLoris Lidestri. Emphasizes utility system installation, maintenance and repair for front-line supervisors in the field (not plant or office). Semimonthly. Circ. 4,000. Free sample copy.

Cartoons: Uses 1 cartoon/issue; buys all from freelancers. Interested in non-sexist material which pokes fun at some of the problems of utility supervision and/or utility field work. Prefers single panel b&w line drawings with or without gagline. Send finished cartoons. SASE. Reports in 2 weeks. Buys all rights. Pays $10 for b&w on acceptance.

VELO-NEWS, Box 1257, Brattleboro VT 05301. Associate Editor: Geoff Drake. Tabloid. Emphasizes bicycle racing for competitors, coaches, officials, enthusiasts. Published 18 times/year. Circ. 14,000. Accepts previously published material and simultaneous submissions. Original artwork returned after publication. Sample copy $2.

Cartoons: Uses cartoons irregularly; buys from freelancers. Prefers single panel, with gagline; b&w line drawings. Send query letter with samples of style to be kept on file. Material not kept on file is returned by SASE. Reports within 2 weeks. Buys one-time rights. Pays $15, b&w; on publication.

WAREHOUSING SUPERVISOR'S BULLETIN, 24 Rope Ferry Rd., Waterford CT 06386. (203)442-4365. Contact: Isabel Will-Becker. Emphasizes warehouse, shipping, traffic, material handling for front-line supervision. Semimonthly. Free sample copy.

Cartoons: Uses 1 cartoon/issue; buys from freelancer. Interested in non-sexist material which pokes fun at aspects of warehouse operations and supervision. Prefers single panel b&w line drawings with or without gagline. Send roughs. SASE. Reports in 3-6 weeks. To show a portfolio, mail appropriate materials, which should include b&w. Buys all rights. Pays $10 for b&w on acceptance.

Tips: "Study samples, and don't use sexist stereotypes."

WDS FORUM, 9933 Alliance Rd., Cincinnati OH 45242. (513)984-0717. Editor: Ms. Kirk Polking. Sixteen-page bimonthly newsletter emphasizing writing techniques and marketing for Writer's Digest School students. Circ. 10,000.

Close-up

Jim Borgman
Cartoonist
The Cincinnati Enquirer
Cincinnati, Ohio

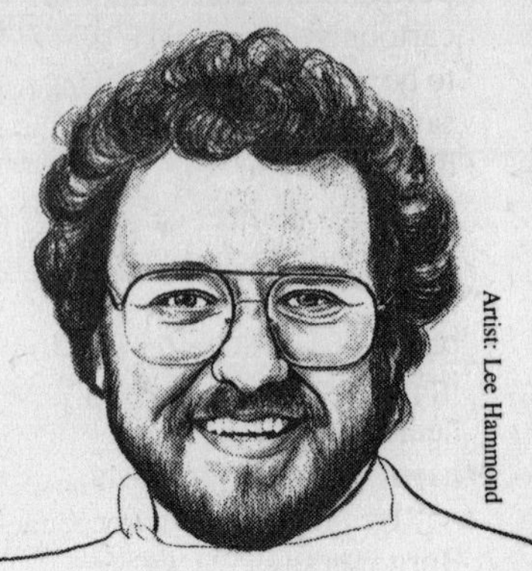

Twelve years ago, he was just a talented notebook doo-
dler who got a fine arts degree in college and lucked into the editorial cartoonist's slot on the major newspaper in his home city. Now, he's an internationally
syndicated political cartoonist.

Not a bad decade for Jim Borgman, *The Cincinnati Enquirer*'s own pictorial funny bone since 1976. Though his
name may not be a household word, millions of people have chuckled over his detailed caricatures of President Reagan, The Superbowl, U.S.A. For Africa and anything else in today's
headlines. Created with brush and ink on a drawing board in his office at *The Cincinnati Enquirer*, they've been reprinted in *Time, Newsweek, The New York Times "Week in Review,"
The Chicago Tribune, The Washington Post* and 200 other international publications.

Despite this high-gear career, Borgman says he never really had a master plan for success.
"I was not born an angry young man with causes to promote in print," he confesses. "I didn't
even read the paper that much when I was younger." In fact, it wasn't until his senior year at
Kenyon College when he joined the staff of the school paper, that he realized he could turn his
love for caricatures into a viable career goal.

Just before his graduation in 1976, young Borgman peddled his portfolio into the offices of
The Cincinnati Enquirer and more or less walked out with the job of editorial cartoonist. "My
timing was right," he explains. "The previous editorial cartoonist there had just retired and
the paper happened to be looking for a young person with a newer drawing style and an understanding of the local scene."

After being well-received by the local audience, Borgman set his sights to national syndication, and eventually was picked up by King Features in 1980. Other auspices followed,
among them three Best of Gannett awards, a nomination for the Pulitzer Prize in 1985 and two
books of his published works, *Smorgasborgman* (1982) and *The Great Communicator*
(1985).

Now for the punchline. A success story like Borgman's only occurs once in a blue moon.
"There are about 250 newspapers in this country that have their own editorial cartoonist," he
says. "And just in a city the size of Cincinnati, there are probably between 200 and 300 people wanting to get such a position.

"Because of this, cartooning is not a field open to the mediocre," Borgman continues.
"You have to exhibit a desire to be published, to be drawing every day. In other words, you
have to be pretty single-minded about pursuing your goal."

Though Borgman may have started out a little tentative about what he wanted to do with his
life, he soon found that success would only come to him if he lived his profession. He has
spent the last 10 years waking up to *National Public Radio*, reading every magazine and
newspaper at his disposal and generally keeping his eyes open for new ideas. "You never really put this job down," the cartoonist says. "Even when I'm walking down the street, I'm

constantly seeing images and making observations about the way people walk and talk.''

Once an artist decides he is willing to live and breathe cartooning, it's time to compile a portfolio and start pounding the pavement for employment. The specific job-hunting path a cartoonist should take depends on what type of cartooning he would like to do. ''If you want to be a political cartoonist, you should find the newspaper that will take a chance on you,'' he says. ''Once you're established locally, you can start sending your work around to all the syndicates. If you want to be a comic strip cartoonist, syndication is the first thing to try, since most newspapers get their strips from syndicates. If you want to do panel cartoons for magazines, you should start by freelancing and build from there.''

Borgman adds that on the way to success, all cartoonists have to learn to handle deadline pressure and develop a tough hide for editorial criticism and flack from readers. ''The most important thing, though, is to follow your own muse,'' he stresses. ''To a certain extent, it's healthy to fall in love with the cartoonists you really admire. But there comes a time when you have to turn all that off and try to find your own form of fun—your own voice.

''It is my nature to approach the news from an outsider, man-on-the-street point of view,'' Borgman says. ''I've found that I enjoy being the devil's advocate, or debater, rather than the preacher. I like to put my arm around the reader's shoulder and say, 'Isn't that bizarre?' ''

—*Betsy Schoellkopf*

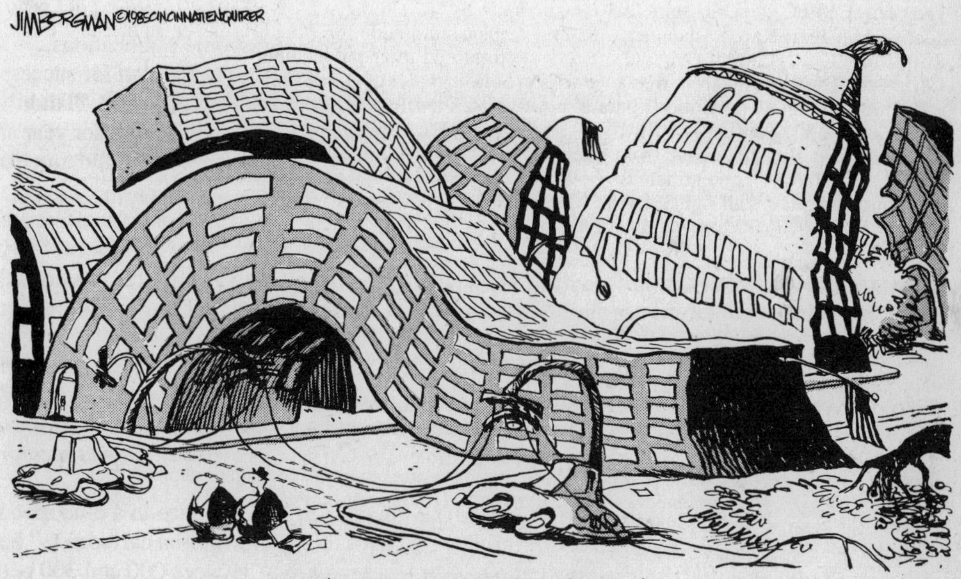

Borgman is able to capture the mood of his hometown as well as international events. Created with brush and ink, his editorial cartoons have been compiled in Smorgasborgman **and** The Great Communicator.

Cartoons: Needs work on "the joys and griefs of freelancing, that first check/rejection slip, trying to find time to write, postal problems, editor/author relations, etc." Send either finished art or roughs. SASE. Reports in 3 weeks. Pays $10, b&w.
Illustrations: "We might buy a few spot drawings, as fillers, of writer-related subject matter." SASE. Reports in 3 weeks. Send query letter with samples. Pays $5, each drawing; on acceptance. "Sorry our rates are so low but we carry no advertising and our newletter is primarily a service to our students."

WESTART, Box 6868, Auburn CA 95604. Editor: Martha Garcia. Emphasizes art for practicing artists, teachers, students, craftsmen, collectors and art patrons. Biweekly. Circ. 6,500. Previously published material OK. Original work returned after publication; SASE required. Free sample copy for SASE; art guidelines available. Photographs, cartoons and illustrations used as works of art in connection with current West Coast exhibition.

THE WETUMPKA HERALD, 300 Green St., Box 29, Wetumpka AL 36092. (205)567-7811. Editor & Publisher: Ellen T. Harris. Newspaper emphasizing local news, sports, etc. (small town) for family audience. Weekly. Circ. 3,600. Accepts previously published material. Sample copy free for SASE with 25¢ postage. Art guidelines free for SASE with 50¢ postage.
Cartoons: Single-panel with gagline; b&w line drawings. Send samples of style to be kept on file "except for material we do not consider using in the future." Write for appointment to show portfolio. Material not filed not returned. Reports only if interested.
Illustrations: Buys 1 illustration/issue from freelancers. Send query letter with samples to be kept on file "except for material we do not consider using in future." Write for appointment to show portfolio. Prefers photocopies or tearsheets as samples. Samples not filed not returned. Reports only if interested. Pays on publication.

THE WINE SPECTATOR, Suite 2040, 601 Van Ness, San Francisco CA 94102. (415)673-2040. Production Manager: Karen Magnuson. Tabloid emphasizing wine for wine lovers—consumer and trade. Bimonthly. Circ. 45,000. Original artwork not returned after publication.
Cartoons: Buys 1/issue from freelance artists. Send samples of style to be kept on file. Write or call for appointment to show portfolio. Material not filed is not returned. Reports only if interested. Buys all rights. Pays $50, b&w.
Illustrations: Buys 2-3/issue from freelance artists. Works on assignment only. Send samples to be kept on file. Call for appointment to show portfolio. Prefers photostats or tear sheets as samples. Does not report back. Buys all rights. Pays $100-200, b&w, or $200-250, color cover; and $50-150, b&w or $100-175, color, inside; on publication.

WOMEN ARTISTS NEWS, Box 3304, Grand Central Station, New York NY 10163. (212)666-6990. Editor: Rena Hansen. For women in all the arts with focus on the visual arts fields. Circ. 5,000. SASE. Reports in 2 weeks. Photocopied submissions OK. Original artwork returned after publication. Pays on publication "when funds available." SASE (57¢) for sample copy. Also uses artists for layout and brochures. Needs photographs.
Cartoons: Uses 0-2 cartoons/issue. Receives 1 submission/week from freelancers. Contact feature editor. Accepts cartoons on art and artists; double panel. Send finished art. Reports in 2 weeks. Pays $0-5, b&w washes.
Illustrations: Uses 20-30 illustrations (photographs)/issue; buys 4/issue from freelancers. Receives 10 submissions/week from freelancers. Provide samples (roughs) or published work to be kept on file for future assignments. Reports in 2 weeks. Buys all rights on a work-for-hire basis.

YOUNG AMERICAN, Box 12409, Portland OR 97212. (503)230-1895. Design Director: Richard Ferguson. Tabloid emphasizing fiction, fantasy, science, news and specialty subjects for children, 4-16 and family members. Monthly. Circ. 125,000. Accepts previously published material. Returns originals after publication. Sample copy SASE plus 50¢.
Cartoons: Buys 3-4/issue. "Themes should be relatable to children. We prefer realistic styles over free-style cartoons." Prefers single or multiple panel with gagline; b&w line drawings or b&w washes. Send finished cartoons to be kept on file. Material not filed returned by SASE. Reports only if interested. Buys reprint rights. Pays $5-10, b&w; on publication.
Illustrations: Buys 3-4/issue. Works on assignment only. Send brochure, business card, photostats, tear sheets, color slides or printed material to be kept on file. Call for appointment to show portfolio. Samples not filed are returned by SASE. Reports only if interested. Buys one-time rights. Pays $20-50, b&w, inside; $100 maximum, color, inside; on publication.

Performing arts groups, those involved in music, theatre and dance, rely on artists to provide their lifeblood—visual projection. Not only do artists literally set the stage for these groups, but they also provide visual exposure through promotional materials such as programs, brochures, flyers and invitations.

The needs of these groups vary according to their particular medium. Musical groups such as symphonies require artwork mainly for posters, programs and brochures. Likewise, ballet, opera and theatre companies require the talents of artists for promotional materials, but they also need scene designers and painters, costume designers and lighting specialists for their productions.

With all promotional material, especially programs, freelance artists must exhibit the ability to complement print with eye-catching illustrations. If your interest is lighting, set or costume design, you will need technical knowledge of the subject as well as an artistic background; include samples of your drafting and model-making abilities in your portfolios, plus a few sketches to demonstrate your drawing ability.

As with any market area, research performing arts groups as much as possible before approaching them with your work. If you find that you have an empathy for one category over another, perhaps a preference for dance rather than theatre, then focus your efforts in your area of preference. You'll need a familiarity with the particular 'feel' of a milieu to visually translate it to others.

The listings provide descriptions of a variety of groups. Some have only seasonal needs such as summer theatres; we've tried to indicate when a group's needs are heaviest. We also indicate if a listing offers artists short-term residencies.

For further names and information about performing arts groups, consult the *American Dance Directory*, *Dance Magazine*, the *Summer Theatre Directory*, *American Theatre Association Directory*, *Theatre Profiles*, the *Music Industry Directory*, *Musical America*, and the Central Opera Theatre's *Opera/Musical Theatre Companies and Workshops in the United States and Canada*.

AFRICA I DANCE THEATRE, 1194 Nostrand Ave., Brooklyn NY 11225. (212)493-4500. Administrator: Roger Francis. African dance company and theatre, repertory, 23 members.
Needs: Works with 5-10 freelance artists/year. Prefers local artists with performing arts experience. Uses artists for advertising and brochure design and illustration; program and set design, posters, lighting and scenery.
First Contact & Terms: Send query letter with brochure, resume, business card, photostats, photographs and tear sheets to be kept on file. Reports within 2 weeks. Payment dependent upon extensiveness of project. Considers complexity of project, available budget, skill and experience of artist, how work will be used, turnaround time and rights purchased when establishing payment.

***ALASKA REPERTORY THEATRE**, Suite 201, 705 W. 6th Ave., Anchorage AK 99501. (907)276-2327. General Manager: Bennett E. Taber. A LORT "B" House, producing 4 mainstage productions and a summer production every year.
Needs: Works with 10-20 freelance designers and crafts people/year; needs heaviest September-April. Uses designers for costume design, lighting and scenery design.
First Contact & Terms: Send resume to be kept on file. Samples not returned. Reporting time "depends on show." Pays by the project, $700-2,200 average, for design.

***ALLIANCE THEATRE COMPANY/ATLANTA CHILDREN'S THEATRE**, 1280 Peachtree St. NE, Atlanta GA 30309. (404)898-1132. Marketing Director: Kim Resnik. Regional theatre company producing for adults and children.

Close-up

Gary Halcott
Business Manager, AMAS Repertory Theatre, Inc.
New York, New York

A great poster captures an audience long before the curtain goes up. That's true for small theatres as well as for large ones in a city crammed full of entertainment.

That's why AMAS Repertory Theatre, Inc., seeks out artists who can convey in visual terms the special excitement of a production.

AMAS is a 17-year-old nonprofit theatre in New York. Directed by its founder Rosetta La-Noire, AMAS is dedicated to the production of original musicals and is committed to works with a multi-racial focus. Its success can be seen in shows like the hit *Bubbling Brown Sugar*, which was showcased at AMAS and went on to critical acclaim.

AMAS uses designers to create posters, illustrations and brochures as well as scenic, lighting and costume designers for work on its productions at East 104th Street. Business manager Gary Halcott explains that AMAS is an Off-Off-Broadway theatre, a classification that depends on limited seating and income and has little to do with location.

As an Off-Off-Broadway theatre, AMAS is able to work with non-union scenic designers. Because of this, Halcott says, the theatre places special emphasis on creativity, rather than credentials. "All artists are judged on an individual basis here. What's really important to us when we hire a designer is what he or she can do, and how well that fits our needs for a particular production."

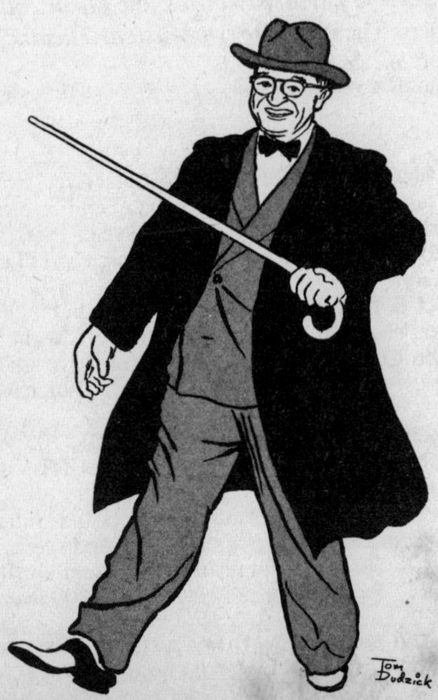

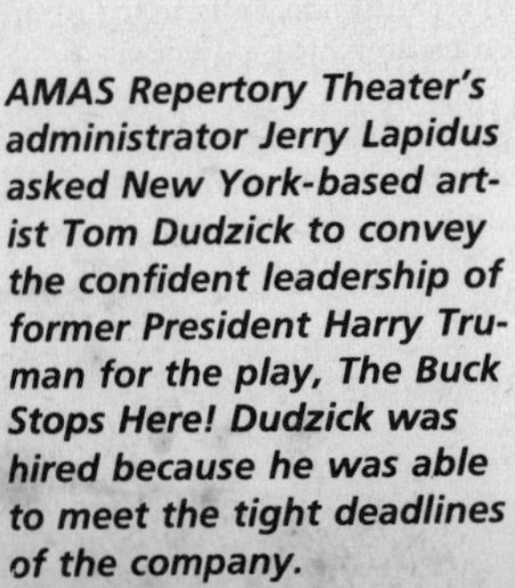

AMAS Repertory Theater's administrator Jerry Lapidus asked New York-based artist Tom Dudzick to convey the confident leadership of former President Harry Truman for the play, The Buck Stops Here! Dudzick was hired because he was able to meet the tight deadlines of the company.

Use an up-to-date Market Directory!

Don't let your <u>Artist's Market</u> turn old on you.

You may be reluctant to give up this copy of <u>Artist's Market.</u> After all, you would never discard an old friend.

But resist the urge to hold onto an old <u>Artist's Market</u>! Like your first portfolio or your favorite pair of jeans, the time will come when this copy of <u>Artist's Market</u> will have to be replaced.

In fact, if you're still using this <u>1987 Artist's Market</u> when the calendar reads 1988, your old friend isn't your best friend anymore. Many of the buyers listed here have moved or been promoted. Many of the addresses are now incorrect. Rates of pay have certainly changed, and even each buyer's art needs are changed from last year.

You can't afford to use an out-of-date book to plan your marketing efforts. But there's an easy way for you to stay current—order the <u>1988 Artist's Market</u>. All you have to do is complete the attached post card and return it with your payment or charge card information. Best of all, we'll send you the 1988 edition at the 1987 price—just $16.95. The <u>1988 Artist's Market</u> will be published and ready for shipment in October 1987.

Make sure you have the most current marketing information—order the new edition of <u>Artist's Market</u> now.

To order, drop this postpaid card in the mail.

☐ YES! I want the most current edition of <u>Artist's Market</u>. Please send me the <u>1988 Artist's Market</u> at the 1987 price—$16.95. I have included $2.00 for postage and handling. (Ohio residents add 5½% sales tax.) NOTE: <u>1988 Artist's Market</u> will be ready for shipment in October 1987.

☐ Payment enclosed (Slip this card and your payment into an envelope.)

☐ Charge my:　　☐ Visa　　☐ MasterCard

Account #_______________________ Exp. Date_____________________

Signature____

Name____

Address____

City______________________ State_______________ Zip______________

(This offer expires August 1, 1988. Please allow 30 days for delivery.)

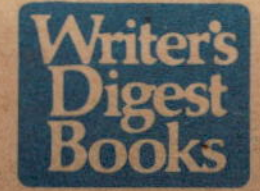

9933 Alliance Road
Cincinnati, Ohio 45242

2156

Theatre companies such as AMAS also require on-site production work. "You do have to be in New York to work with a theatre like this. We can't do it by phone."

There are special benefits in working with a small theatre showcasing new productions, since a "little" show may move on to the big time. "Our designers hold contracts with the show's originators—the writers and composers—and have a first refusal option if the show is chosen to go on to commercial production," Halcott explains.

Halcott says that the process of developing sharp graphics to promote a production through posters and print material is an interesting mix of collaboration and artistic independence. "A lot depends on whatever feeling an artist gets from reading the script and listening to the music. But there is always an exchange between the graphic artist and the scenic artists.

"Sometimes the result is totally unrelated, sometimes very close. I've seen graphic artists and scenic designers come up with the same idea totally independently after studying the script."

—Linda Pender

Needs: Works with 2-3 freelance artists/year. Prefers experienced local artists. Uses artists for the design, illustration and layout of advertising and brochures plus poster design and illustration. Prefers "clean, modern, free strokes. But mostly, work that is appropriate to particular use."
First Contact & Terms: Send query letter with brochure showing art style or resume and tear sheets, photocopies and actual pieces. Samples not filed are returned by SASE. Reports only if interested. Write to schedule an appointment to show a portfolio, which should include thumbnails, roughs, final reproduction/product and photographs. Pays for design by the project, $50 minimum. Pays for illustration by the project, $50 minimum. Considers complexity of project, client's budget and skill and experience of artist.
Tips: "Do your home work on the pieces we do now. Know something of our company and design needs."

AMAS REPERTORY THEATRE, INC., 1 E. 104th St., New York NY 10029. (212)369-8000. Founder and Artistic Director: Rosetta LeNoire. Administrator & Business Manager: Gary Halcott. Administrator: Jerry Lapidus. A professional theatre. Programs include the creation of original musical theatre, classes for young people and adults, a senior citizens tour, workshops, etc.
Needs: Works with 8-12 freelance artists/year. Needs heaviest in fall, winter and spring (Sept.-June). Works on assignment only. Uses artists for brochure design, illustration and layout; poster design and illustration; program, set and costume design; lighting; and scenery.
First Contact & Terms: Send query letter with brochure showing art style or resume and samples to be kept on file. Reports back within 1 month. Call to schedule an appointment to show a portfolio. Pays for design by the project, $50-350 average. Considers how work will be used when establishing payment.

ARIZONA OPERA COMPANY, 3501 N. Mountain Ave., Tucson AZ 85719. (602)293-4336. General Director: Glynn Ross. "The only state-wide opera company in the United States, and the only opera company in Arizona, performing in both Tucson and Phoenix. It presents Grand Opera with professional artists, nationally recognized directors, full staging with elaborate costumes, lighting and so forth."

Market conditions are constantly changing! If this is 1988 or later, buy the newest edition of Artist's Market at your favorite bookstore or order directly from Writer's Digest Books.

Needs: Works with 3-4 freelance artists/year. Experience is required. Works on assignments only. Needs heaviest October-March. Uses artists for advertising design, illustration and layout; poster design and illustration; brochure, set and costume design; lighting and scenery.
First Contact & Terms: Send query letter with resume to be kept on file. Material not filed returned by SASE. Considers complexity of project and how work will be used when establishing payment.

***BACK ALLEY THEATRE**, 15231 Burbank Blvd., Van Nuys CA 91411. (818)780-2240. Producer: Laura Zucker. Theatre company producing live theatre.
Needs: Prefers local artists. Uses artists for advertising and brochure design, illustration and layout; posters and set design.
First Contact & Terms: Send query letter with resume, tear sheets, slides and photographs. Samples not filed are returned by SASE. Reports only if interested. Write to schedule an appointment to show a portfolio, which should inlcude roughs, tear sheets and photographs. Pays for design by the project, $100 minimum. Considers complexity of project and turnaround time when establishing payment.

BALLETACOMA, 508 6th Ave., Tacoma WA 98402. (206)272-9631. Administrative Director: Carlene Garner. Nonprofit regional ballet company composed of 30 dancers; performance season includes "The Nutcracker Ballet" and two other major productions.
Needs: Works with 3 freelance artists/year; needs heaviest in August-September, January, March. Uses artists for advertising, brochure and program design, illustration and layout; set and costume design; posters, lighting and scenery.
First Contact & Terms: Send query letter with brochure showing art style or resume and photostats and photographs to be kept on file. Reports within 2 weeks. Call for appointment to show portfolio, which should include original/final art and photostats. Pays for design and illustration by the project, $25-500 average. Considers complexity of project, available budget, skill and experience of artist and how work will be used when establishing payment.
Tips: "Art is usually the first impression one sees of an upcoming performance. Therefore the style and quality are vital to the production."

BALTIMORE OPERA COMPANY, 527 N. Charles St., Baltimore MD 21201. (301)727-0592. Public Relations Director: Kathleen Laughery. Producer of grand opera and a touring opera company presenting 3 main productions annually. Freelance art needs heaviest in the summer for fall/winter season.
Needs: Uses artists for the design, illustration and layout of advertising and brochures and also for poster design and illustration, set design, costume design, lighting and scenery.
First Contact & Terms: Works on assignment only. Send query letter with brochure showing art style or resume and samples to be kept on file. Reports back only if interested. Write for appointment to show portfolio. Considers project's budget, and skill and experience of the artist when establishing payment.

THE BATON ROUGE SYMPHONY ORCHESTRA, Box 103, Baton Rouge LA 70821. (504)387-6166. Publicist: Ruth Laney. Eighty-member professional symphony orchestra with fulltime resident music director/conductor. Fourteen regular-season concerts/year (October-May), an outdoor concert series, ensemble appearances, etc.; 2,500 subscribers.
Needs: Works with 1-2 freelance artists/year; needs heaviest in spring: design and produce brochure promoting fall season - 25,000 copies. Summer: design and produce 2 season program covers. Uses artists for advertising, brochure and program design, illustration and layout; posters, t-shirt and billboard design. "We look for extremely high quality, a certain level of sophistication, dramatic impact and an artist who can work well with our staff and who can project the image we want."
First Contact & Terms: Send query letter with brochure, resume, business card, photostats and tear sheets to be kept on file. Call for appointment to show portfolio. Reports only if interested. Considers complexity of project, available budget, skill and experience of artist, how work will be used, turnaround time and rights purchased when establishing payment. "We prefer to establish a fee for the project at hand. Our status as a nonprofit institution means we have a rather small budget, but we are willing to pay competitive prices for good work."
Tips: "We look for originality in design and concept and require technical accuracy. When submitting, submit treatments only and research thoroughly before including designs depicting musical instruments, instrumentation, period, etc."

BERKSHIRE PUBLIC THEATRE, INC., Box 860, 30 Union St., Pittsfield MA 01202. (413)445-4631. Director: Frank Bessell. Regional repertory theatre with an artistic and technical company of 100, an administrative staff of 15 and an audience of 30,000 yearly. "A year-round company performing classical and contemporary drama, musicals and cabarets, original works and children's theatre. Company of about 100—is ever exapanding."
Needs: Works with 10 freelance artists/year. Needs are heaviest with the beginning of each production,

an average of one/month. Uses artists for the design, illustration and layout of advertising and brochures, for poster design and illustration; set and costume design; lighting and scenery.
First Contact & Terms: Send query letter with resume and samples to be kept on file. Call or write to schedule an appointment to show a portfolio, which should include thumbnails, roughs, original/final art, final reproduction/product, color, tear sheets, photostats, photographs, b&w or "anything that best represents you." Pays by the project for design and illustration; negotiates payment. "Sometimes barters exchanges in lieu of dollars."
Tips: Art must have "clean and sharp, meticulous detail, new and exciting, *not canned*." There is more use of warmer "pantone colors, more creative use of layout—as a result, there is more direct collaboration to fill our needs."

***THE BETHUNE BALLET**, 3096 Lake Hollywood Dr., Hollywood CA 90068. (213)874-0481. Artistic Director: Zina Bethune. Ten member multi-media ballet company "incorporating visual technology (film, video, laser, animation and special effects) to enhance and expand the traditional theater of dance."
Needs: Works on assignment only. Uses artists for advertising, brochure, poster, program, set and costume design; lighting; scenery; film and video; special effects, i.e., lasers, image transference, etc.
First Contact & Terms: Send query letter with brochure, resume, business card and samples to be kept on file. Write for appointment to show portfolio. Prefers good representation of artist's work as samples. Samples not returned. Reports only if interested. Pays by the project. Negotiates pay considering complexity of project, available budget, and skill and experience of artist.
Tips: Artists should use "the movement and sweep of dance to express a variety of concepts and images. As a dance company whose concept is a futuristic one, this helps us capture who and what we are." Research the company's needs before you attempt to sell to them.

BINGHAMTON SYMPHONY ORCHESTRA, 334 N Press Bldg., 19 Chenango St., Binghamton NY 13901. (607)723-8242. Contact: Publicity Director or Executive Director. Classical and popular orchestral music entertainment; also, chamber music.
Needs: Works with 2-4 freelance artists/year. Needs are seasonal, especially in the spring. Uses artists for advertising and brochure design, illustration and layout; and set design.
First Contact & Terms: Interested in quality, inexpensive work. Send query letter with brochure, resume and samples to be kept on file. Samples not filed are returned only if requested. To show a portfolio, mail appropriate materials or call or write to schedule an appointment. Pays $50-500 average.

***BUFFALO PHILARMONIC ORCHESTRA**, 71 Symphony Circle, Buffalo NY 14222. (716)885-0331. Marketing Director: Maggie Schmid. Symphony orchestra presenting 150 musical concerts throughout western New York annually plus a state tour.
Needs: Works with 10 or more freelance artists/year. Uses artists for the design, illustration and layout of advertising and brochures plus window design, pack design, P-O-P displays, mechanicals, posters and direct mail.
First Contact & Terms: Phone first, then send query letter with brochure showing art style. Samples not filed are returned only if requested. Reports back within 2 weeks. Call to schedule an appointment to show a portfolio, which should include original/final art and final reproduction/product. Pays for design by the project, $100-2,000. Considers complexity of project, skill and experience of artist and turnaround time when establishing payment.

CASA MANANA MUSICALS INC., Box 9054, Ft. Worth TX 76107. (817)332-9319. General Manager/Producer: Bud Franks. Director of Playhouse/Assistant Manager: Charles Ballinger. Theatrical company performing summer stock, children's theater and classics.
Needs: Assigns 8 jobs/year. Uses artists for costumes, promotional materials, sets and theatrical lighting.
First Contact & Terms: Query with resume. SASE. Reports within 2 weeks. Pay varies.

THE CHARLESTON SYMPHONY ORCHESTRA, Box 2292, Charleston WV 25328. (304)342-0151. Director of Communications: Michael Fanning. Symphony orchestra "whose patrons represent a broad socio-economic spectrum of music lovers—from classical to pops."
Needs: Works with 1-2 freelance artists/year. Needs heaviest in January-February. Works on assignment only. Uses artists for advertising and brochure design and illustration; and poster illustration. Prefers "clean, contemporary lines with slight feel of elegance; however, not overstated."
First Contact & Terms: Send query letter with brochure, resume, business card and samples to be kept on file. Call for appointment to show portfolio. Samples not filed are returned. Reports only if interested. Payment negotiated; usually on a bidding process. Considers project's budget, skill and experience of the artist, and turnaround time when establishing payment.

CHEN & DANCERS/HTDC, 2nd Fl., 70 Mulberry St., New York NY 10013. (212)349-0126. Artistic Director: Chen Hsueh-Tung. Chen & Dancers is a modern dance company performing theatrical, humorous and poetic works rooted in Asian themes. The company presents regular NY seasons and tours the U.S. and abroad.

Needs: Works with 10 freelance artists/year. Needs heaviest in fall and spring. Uses freelance artists for advertising, brochure, catalog, poster, program, set and costume design; lighting and scenery. "As an Asian-American modern dance company, we need designs that are contemporary expressions of our traditional heritage."

First Contact & Terms: "Artists must be able to produce theatrical designs with an oriental aesthetic sensibility—simple, not ornate or garish. Send query letter with brochure, resume, business card, photostats, slides, photographs, photocopies or tear sheets to be kept on file. Call or write for appointment to show portfolio. Reports back only if interested. Pays by the project up to $500 for design. Considers complexity of project, project's budget, skill and experience of the artist and how work will be used when estabilishing payment.

CHICAGO CITY THEATRE COMPANY, 3340 N. Clark St., Chicago IL 60657. (312)880-1002. Co-director: Joseph Ehrenberg. Performing arts organization including dance, training.

Needs: Works with 4-6 freelance artists/year; needs heaviest in late summer through spring. Uses artists for advertising, brochure and program design; set and costume design; posters and lighting. "We have logo and basic approach to advertising designs."

First Contact & Terms: Send brochure, resume and samples usually to be kept on file. "Samples might be thrown after observing" or returned by SASE if requested. Accepts any type of samples. Reports only if interested. Call or write for appointment to show portfolio. Pays for design by the project, $50-500 average. Considers complexity of project, available budget and rights purchased when establishing payment.

***CHICAGO REPERTORY DANCE ENSEMBLE**, 1016 N. Dearborn, Chicago IL 60610. (312)869-3149. Public Relations Director: Alice George. Repertory dance company performing modern, ballet and jazz styles.

Needs: Works with 30-50 freelance artists/year. Uses artists for the design, illustration and layout of advertising and brochure plus paste-up, posters, direct mail, postcards and newsletters. Prefers an innovative style with an artistic rather than businesslike tone.

First Contact & Terms: Send query letter with brochure showing art style or resume and samples. Samples not filed are returned if accompanied by SASE. Reports only if interested. Call or write to schedule an appointment to show a portfolio. Payment is negotiable.

Tips: "Please call or write to establish our current schedule and needs. We are especially interested in artists who are eager to donate themselves (not materials) in return for enjoyable work. We are looking for stunning visual and theatrical effects."

CITI ARTS/THEATRE CONCORD, 1950 Parkside Dr., Concord CA 94519. (415)671-3065. Contact: Jim Jester. Visual Arts Department for public art competitions and display areas. Produces musicals, comedy, drama and ballet year round, primarily between September through May. Assigns 3-10 jobs/year.

Needs: Works with up to 4 illustrators and 4 designers/year. Works on assignment only. Uses artists for costume design, flyers, graphic/set design, posters, programs, theatrical lighting, Art in Public Places projects, and advertising and brochure design, illustration and layout.

First Contact & Terms: Query, then mail slides or photos. Samples returned by SASE. Reports back on future assignment possibilities. Call or write to schedule an appointment to show a portfolio, which should include thumbnails, roughs, original/final art, photographs and b&w.

THE CLEVELAND INSTITUTE OF MUSIC, 11021 East Blvd., Cleveland OH 44106. (216)791-5165. Public Relations Director: Jean Caldwell. Performing arts center and conservatory of music.

Needs: Assigns 15 jobs and buys 20 illustrations/year. Local artists only. Uses artists for illustration, layout and graphics for advertising, annual reports, bumper stickers, costumes, direct mail brochures, exhibits, flyers, graphics, posters, programs, stages, record jackets and catalogs.

First Contact & Terms: Send query letter with brochure showing art style or tear sheets, photostats and photocopies. SASE. Reports within 1 day. Call or write to schedule an appointment to show a portfolio, which should include thumbnails, roughs, original/final art, final reproduction/product, tear sheets and photostats. Payment varies; on acceptance.

COCTEAU REPERTORY CO., 330 Bowery, New York NY 10012. (212)677-0060. Artistic Director: Eve Adamson. Performs 6 plays in rotating repertory with a resident company each year.

Needs: Works with 6-10 freelance artists/year. "We prefer classical repertory and/or European experi-

ence." Works on assignment only. Needs heaviest August-March. Uses artists for brochure, set and costume design; and lighting and scenery. "We prefer non-realistic designs, strong, central concepts."
First Contact & Terms: Send query letter with resume to be kept on file for 1 season. "We encourage artists to see our work before application." Samples accepted at interview only. Samples not filed are returned by SASE. Reports only if interested. Pays for design by the project, $200-300 average. Pays for illustration by the project, $150-650 average. Considers project's budget when establishing payment.

***CONCORD PAVILLION**, Box 6166, Concord CA 94524. (415)671-3373. Marketing Director: Jay Bedecarre. Performing arts center; presents dance, rock, pop music, jazz, symphonies, sports and boat shows. Assigns 3-5 jobs/year.
Needs: Works with 1-2 illustrators and 1-2 designers/year, spring and summer only. Uses artists for advertising design/layout, billboards, bumper stickers, direct mail brochures, flyers, graphic design posters, programs, set design, set/stage design painters, technical charts/illustrations and theatrical lighting design.
First Contact & Terms: Prefers local artists. Send photos, tear sheets or portfolio. SASE. Reports in 4 weeks. Works on assignment only. Samples returned by SASE. Provide resume, brochure and flyer to be kept on file for future assignments.

CONNECTICUT OPERA, 15 Lewis St., Hartford CT 06103. (203)241-0251. Director of Communications: Ginny Ludwig. Sixth oldest professional opera company in the US. Main season is 2 performances each of 4 major productions, some in original language and some in English performed in Bushnell Hall. Also operates a resident touring company, which performs fully staged and costumed productions throughout New England and the East Coast.
Needs: "We use freelance artists when we design our season brochure in the late winter and when we design brochures for single productions." Uses artists for advertising and brochure design, illustration and layout; program, set and costume design; and scenery.
First Contact & Terms: Send query letter with samples to be kept on file. "Send what is appropriate to designer style." Samples not kept on file are returned by SASE only if requested. Reports only if interested. Call or write for appointment to show portfolio. The fee depends on the project.
Tips: When reviewing an artist's work, looks for "originality and strong imagery whether it be graphic or illustrative; dynamic design rather than obscure. We are interested in strong graphic design that will help to market the product. Good design that doesn't translate into black-and-white newspaper ads is valueless."

CORTLAND REPERTORY THEATRE INC., Box 783, Cortland NY 13045. Resident summer theatre which produces 5 shows in summer. Assigns 5 jobs/summer.
Needs: Works with 5 designers/year; summers only. Uses designers for properties, sets, costume and lighting. Also uses artists for brochures (donation drive, subscription series) and flyer (early bird renewal).
First Contact & Terms: Query with resume in early winter. Works on assignment only. Pays $1,000-1,700 for 2 months work. Pays for design and illustrations by the project, $50-200 average. Considers available budget, skill and experience of artist and rights purchased when establishing payment.
Tips: "Do volunteer work in the area of your interest. This way you keep your skills sharp, you learn, and it places you in front of people who may someday be able to hire you. I also find trading services an excellent means to opening job situations. More and more industries and businesses are turning to professional artists for help in packaging, displays and advertising. This is very evident in the theatrical field."

DALLAS THEATER CENTER, 3636 Turtle Creek Blvd., Dallas TX 75219. Contact: Public Relations Director. A professional resident theatre with 3 performing spaces—Frank LW Theater, Arts District Theatre and In The Basement (experimental theater). Performs variety of plays from classic to contemporary. Yearly attendance of 100,000.
Needs: Prefers local artists as "we often need work rather quickly." Works on assignment basis only. Uses a varying number of freelance artists/year. Needs are heaviest in spring and fall although possibilities exist year-round for program and poster work. Uses freelance artists for advertising and brochure design, illustration and layout; poster and program design and illustration.
First Contact & Terms: Send query letter with business card and samples to be kept on file. Prefers photocopies as samples. Samples not kept on file are returned only with an SASE. Reports only if interested. Write for appointment to show portfolio. Pays by the project for design; by the hour or by the project, for illustration. Considers complexity of project, project's budget, skill and experience of the artist, how work will be used, turnaround time and rights purchased when establishing payment.

DANCE KALEIDOSCOPE, 429 E. Vermont, Indianapolis IN 46202. (317)634-8484. Artistic Director: Cherri Jaffee. Professional modern dance repertory company which tours Indiana. The repertory comes largely from guest choreographers out of New York City.
Needs: Works with several freelance artists/year; needs heaviest in October, March and May. Local artists only with previous experience in the arts "who enjoy the challenge of working within a limited budget. Artist must be willing to take direction from the board of directors." Uses artists for advertising, brochure, program, set and costume design; advertising, brochure and program layout; advertising illustration, posters, lighting and scenery. Prefers clean, bold style "that sells the product, not the graphics."
First Contact & Terms: Send query letter with brochure, resume, business card and tear sheets to be kept on file. Call for appointment to show portfolio. Samples not returned. Reports only if interested. Pays for design by the hour, $10-30 average; by the project, $50-100 average. Considers complexity of project, available budget, turnaround time and rights purchased when establishing payment.
Tips: "Artist must respect the company's need to use 'words' in some publications and not expect the art to carry the entire message."

DANCE 10, 334 Lakeview Ave., Clifton NJ 07011. (201)772-2120. Also: 2-4 Franklin Ave., Rutherford NJ 07070. (201)438-3628. Manager: Carl L. Presto. Service-related dance/theatre company providing jazz dance performances, lectures and demonstrations.
Needs: Works with 20 freelance artists/year. Uses artists for advertising, brochure, catalog and program design, illustration and layout; set and costume design, posters, lighting and scenery.
First Contact & Terms: Send query letter with resume and photography to be kept on file. Reports within 1 week. Write for appointment to show portfolio. Pays for design by the project. Considers complexity of project, available budget, how work will be used and rights purchased when establishing payment.

DAYTON BALLET, 140 N. Main St., Dayton OH 45402. (513)222-3661. Director/Choreographer: Stuart Sebastian. Ballet company of 17 professional dancers with a 22-member nonprofessional training company, board of trustees and Friends organization.
Needs: Works with 2-3 freelance artists/year. Uses artists for advertising, brochure, set and costume design; lighting and scenery.
First Contact & Terms: Send query letter with resume and samples. Samples returned. Reports within 3 weeks. Works on assignment only. Provide brochure/flyer and resume to be kept on file for possible future assignments. Pays by the project; negotiable.
Tips: "Line drawings are comic, romantic and flowing."

DENVER SYMPHONY ORCHESTRA, Suite 330, 910 Fifteenth St., Denver CO 80202.(303)572-1151. Contact: Marketing & Public Relations Director. Professional 88-member symphony orchestra performing classical and pops concerts.
Needs: Works with "numerous" freelance artists/year. Works on assignment only. Uses artists for advertising, brochure and catalog design, illustration and layout; poster and program design and illustration.
First Contact & Terms: Send query letter with brochure, resume, photostats, slides, photographs, photocopies or tear sheets to be kept on file. Samples not filed are returned only if requested. Reports within 3 weeks. Call or write for appointment to show portfolio. Payment varies. Considers complexity of project, project's budget, skill and experience of the artist, how work will be used and turnaround time when establishing payment.

*__*DULUTH BALLET__**, The Depot, 506 W. Michigan St., Duluth MN 55802. (218)722-2314. General Manager: Michael R. Garcia. Artistic Director: Gernot Petzold. Ballet company of 7 dancers with a repertoire ranging from modern/contemporary to classical dance styles.
Needs: Works with 3-4 freelance artists/year; needs heaviest approximately one month before fall, winter and spring concerts. Uses artists for advertising design, illustration and layout.
First Contact & Terms: Send query letter with brochure, resume, photostats and photography to be kept on file. Call or write for appointment to show portfolio. Samples returned by SASE if not kept on file. Pays for design by the project, $100-150 average. Pays for illustration by the project, $50-200 average. Considers complexity of project, available budget, skill and experience of artist, how work will be used, turnaround time and rights purchased when establishing payment.
Tips: "Make sure work is appropriate to our situation. Sometimes we receive material that has no application to what we are doing."

***JEFF DUNCAN IN SOLO CONCERT**, % J. Love, 916 Tyson St., Baltimore MD 21201. (301)685-3587. Director: Jeff Duncan. Mr. Jeff Duncan, as solo dancer.
Needs: Works with 1-3 freelance artists/year. Uses artists for brochure and costume design; brochure illustration and layout; posters and lighting.

First Contact & Terms: Previous performing arts art experience desirable. Send query letter with samples to be kept on file. Call for appointment to show portfolio. Prefers photographs as samples. Samples not kept on file are returned only if requested. Reports only if interested. Pays for design and illustration by the project, $300-850, average. Considers complexity of project and available budget when establishing payment.

EMPIRE STATE INSTITUTE FOR THE PERFORMING ARTS (ESIPA), Empire State Plaza, Albany NY 12223. (518)474-1199. Producing Director: Patricia B. Snyder. Professional resident theatre and performing arts center; 2 theatres 900, 450; usually 8 productions requiring designers each season.
Needs: Works with 30-40 artists/year. Works on assignment only. Uses artists for poster design and illustration, set and costume design, lighting and scenery.
First Contact & Terms: Send query letter and resume to be kept on file; do not send samples with first contact. Reports back only if interested. Write to schedule an appointment to show a portfolio. Pays for design; usually by the project, $1,000 average. Pays for illustration usually by the project, $500 average. Considers complexity of project, project's budget, skill and experience of the artist, and rights purchased when establishing payment.

FLAGSTAFF SYMPHONY ASSOCIATION, Box 122, Flagstaff AZ 86002. (602)774-4231. Manager: Harold Weller. The FSA is the "major musical arts organization in Northern Arizona, operating the Flagstaff Symphony Orchestra and sponsoring programs and concerts in addition to the orchestra's 15 concerts."
Needs: Works with 6 freelance artists/year. Needs heaviest in March and April. Local artists only. Works on assignment only. Uses artists for advertising, brochure and program design; newsletter layout and design (published quarterly).
First Contact & Terms: Send query letter with photocopies to be kept on file. Samples not filed are returned only if requested. Reports only if interested. Pays by individual arrangement. Considers project's budget when establishing payment.

***FLORIDA SYMPHONY ORCHESTRA**, Suite 3, 1900 N. Mills Ave., Orlando FL 32803. (305)896-0331. Director of Marketing: Sandra Kulmann. Symphony orchestra.
Needs: Uses 2 freelance artists/year. Prefers local artists. Uses artists for advertising and brochure design, illustration and layout plus paste-up, mechanicals and posters.
First Contact & Terms: Send query letter with brochure showing art style. Samples not filed are returned only if requested by artist. Reports only if interested. Call to schedule an appointment to show a portfolio, which should include roughs, original/final art, tear sheets and photographs. Considers complexity of project, skill and experience of artist and turnaround time.

***FMT**, Box 92127, Milwaukee WI 53202. Co-Director: Mike Moynihan. Theatre company.
Needs: Uses 2-4 freelance artists/year. Uses artists for advertising and brochure design, illustration and layout plus product design, costume design, textile design, calligraphy, paste-up, posters and direct mail.
First Contact & Terms: Send query letter with brochure showing art style or resume and tear sheets, photostats, photocopies, slides and photographs. Samples not filed are returned if accompanied by SASE. Reports only if interested. To show a portfolio, mail appropriate materials or write to schedule an appointment; portfolio should include original/final art, final reproduction/product, color, tear shets, photostats and photographs. Pays for design by the project, $25-500. Pays for illustrations by the project, $25-75. Considers complexity of project, client's budget and turnaround time.

GEVA THEATRE, 168 S. Clinton Ave., Rochester NY 14604. (716)232-1366. Director Marketing/Public Relations: Adele Fico-McCarthy. LORT C resident professional theatre with 8 plays/season, fall and winter; varied repetoire: classic, contemporary, premieres. Christmas and summer production.
Needs: Works with 6 freelance artists/year. Local artists only. Works on assignment only. Uses artists for advertising, and brochure and catalog design, illustration and layout; and poster design and illustration. Prefers "crisp, clean, slick" style.
First Contact & Terms: Send query letter with brochure, resume, business card, slides, photographs or photocopies to be kept on file; call or write for appointment to show portfolio. Samples not filed are returned by SASE only if requested. Reports only if interested. Pays for design and illustration by the project, $50-500 average; separate payment for layout and mechanicals. Considers complexity of the project, project's budget, skill and experience of the artist, how work will be used. Turnaround time and rights purchased when establishing payment.

GUS GIORDANO JAZZ DANCE CHICAGO, 614 Davis St., Evanston IL 60201. (312)866-9443. Coordinators: Peg and Nan Giordano. Jazz company consisting of 8-10 members.

Needs: Works with 2-3 freelance artists/year. Chicago area artists only. Works on assignment only. Uses artists for advertising and costume design, lighting and scenery.
First Contact & Terms: Call for appointment. Samples returned by SASE. Reports within weeks. Send resume to be kept on file for possible future assignments. Negotiates payment.

***GRAND RAPIDS SYMPHONY ORCHESTRA**, 415 Exhibitors Bldg., Grand Rapids MI 49503. (616)454-9451. Marketing and Public Relations Director: Susan M. Schwartz. General Manager: Peter W. Smith.
Needs: Uses artists for program covers, ads, fliers, bumper stickers and posters.
First Contact & Terms: Contact Public Relations Director initially by letter or phone. "We will respond to all inquiries for work if a call is made first to the PR Director by the artist." Pay based on quality and intended use of the work; negotiates.

GROUP MOTION MULTI-MEDIA DANCE THEATER, 624 S. 4th St., Philadelphia PA 19147. (215)928-1495. Co-Directors: Brigitta Herrmann, Manfred Fishbeck. Group motion multi-media dance theatre specializing in modern and innovative dance. "We have a local audience and offer performances, a variety of classes for children and adults, and workshops."
Needs: Works with 12 freelance artists/year. Works on assignment only. Needs heaviest fall through spring. Uses artists for advertising, brochure and poster design; and lighting.
First Contact & Terms: Send query letter with samples to be kept on file; call or write for appointment to show portfolio. Reports only if interested. Pays for design and illustration by the project, $25 minimum. Considers complexity of project, project's budget, skill and experience of artist, and how work will be used when establishing payment.

***THE GROUP THEATRE COMPANY**, 3940 Brooklyn Ave. NE, Seattle WA 98105. (206)545-4969. Marketing Director: Victory Searle. Professional theatre promoting a full theatrical season using flyers, brochures and posters. Other events generate invitations, etc.
Needs: Works with 6 freelance artists/year. Prefers local artists only. Uses artists for advertising illustration, brochure design, illustration and layout, posters and annual reports.
First Contact & Terms: Send query letter with brochure showing art style or resume, tear sheets and photocopies. Samples not filed are returned by SASE. Reports only if interested. Call or write to schedule an appointment to show portfolio, which should include thumbnails, roughs, final reproduction/product, color and tear sheets.
Tips: "We really negotiate each project. We are a non-profit organization. If you rigidly demand a top-of-the market fee, we're probably not for you."

***HAMPTON PLAYHOUSE**, Winnacunnet Rd., Hampton NJ 03842. (603)926-3073. Contact: General Manager. Summer theater running for 10-11 playing weeks each summer. "We also have a teen-aged workshop that runs for 8 weeks which employs a scenic artist and a technical director."
Needs: Works with 2 freelance artists/year; needs heaviest in summer. Works on assignment only. Uses artists for set design and costume design, lighting and scenery.
First Contact & Terms: Send query letter with brochure showing art style or resume, slides and photographs to be kept on file. Reports "as soon as possible, usually several months." Call or write to schedule an appointment to show a portfolio, which should include thumbnails, roughs, original/final art, final reproduction/product, color, tear sheets, photostats, photographs and b&w. Pays by the week; "although the designer has 2 weeks to design and execute each show, he gets paid each week for his work, $150-300 per week depending on experience."

HARLEQUIN DINNER THEATRE, 1330 Gude Dr., Rockville MD 20850. (301)340-6813. Assistant Producer: Bradford Watkins. Non-equity dinner theatre producing 6 shows a season plus mounting numerous original and touring productions.
Needs: Works with 20 freelance artists/year. East coast artists only; must be available for personal interview. Reporting time "2 weeks prior to opening." Works on assignment only. Uses artists for set and costume design; lighting and scenery.
First Contact & Terms: Send resume and submit portfolio for review. Samples returned upon request. Send resume to be kept on file. Negotiates payment by the project.

HARTFORD BALLET, 15 Lewis St., Hartford CT 06103. (203)549-0466. Director of Communications: Ginny Ludwig. Nationally-recognized company under the artistic direction of Michael Uthoff, with a repertory in classical and contemporary ballet; mainstage performances include twelve local performances of the annual holiday "Nutcracker" and other repertory productions featuring world premieres and revivals.
Needs: Freelance artists needed for brochure and advertising design, particularly in the spring and fall.

Designers also needed for costume, poster and scenic design, depending upon the needs of the current production.
First Contact & Terms: Send query letter and samples of work to be kept on file. Write for an appointment to show portfolio. If return of samples is requested, send SASE. Terms discussed before any work is contracted. Fees based upon project needs.
Tips: "We need a contemporary style with strong sales emphasis."

HARTFORD SYMPHONY ORCHESTRA, 609 Farmington Ave., Hartford CT 06105. (203)236-6101. Director of Marketing: David Suead. Full symphony orchestra averaging 40-50 concerts annually: outdoor summer concerts, presentation of chamber concerts, special festivals.
Needs: Works with 2-3 freelance artists/year; needs heaviest in January-April. Uses artists for advertising, brochure and program illustration; and posters. Style of artwork depends specifically on event to be promoted.
First Contact & Terms: Only concerned with quality of work, willingness to be flexible and overall cost. Send query letter with resume, business card and samples to be kept on file. Prefers samples of original work if possible, e.g., the printed piece for which work was done; slides also accepted. Samples returned by SASE if not kept on file. Reports within 1 month. Call for appointment to show portfolio. Pays for design by the project, $200-700 average. Pays for illustration by the project, $50-500 average. "We primarily work by project only; price agreed upon prior to any finished work commissioned/submitted." Considers available budget, skill and experience of artist, how work will be used and turnaround time when establishing payment.

***HOUSTON GRAND OPERA**, 615 Louisiana, Houston TX 77002. (713)546-0230. Contact: Elizabeth McMahon.
Needs: Works with 4-8 illustrators and 3-4 designers/year. Uses brochures, flyers, posters and newspapers.
First Contact & Terms: Send samples (designer: printed samples; illustrator: portfolio plus samples). Works on assignment only. Samples returned by SASE. Reports back on future assignment possibilities. Provide resume, business card, brochure, flyer, tear sheets and representative samples, if possible, to be kept on file for future assignments.
Tips: "As a nonprofit arts organization, we look for relationships with artists that can benefit the artists by associating with the Houston Grand Opera and can be economically feasible for us. Most of our artistic services are monetarily free, giving credit and a geat deal of exposure to artist."

HOUSTON SYMPHONY ORCHESTRA, 615 Louisiana, Houston TX 77025. Manager/Publications: Cynthia Lewis. Nonprofit organization.
Needs: Works with 10-20 freelance artists/year. Prefers artists that are inexpensive and willing to take direction. Uses artists for advertising and brochure design, illustration and layout; posters, direct mail and annual reports.
First Contact & Terms: Send query letter with samples. Samples not filed are returned by SASE. Reports only if interested. Considers complexity of project, client's budget, skill and experience of artist, how work will be used and turnaround time when establishing payment.
Tips: "Artist must be willing to take strategy direction and be flexible through approval process."

***INDIANAPOLIS BALLET THEATRE**, 411 E. Michigan, Indianapolis IN 46204. (317)637-8979. Director of Marketing: Mary Bashaw. Ballet company with tours and residencies.
Needs: Works with 5 freelance artists/year. Uses artists for the design, illustration and layout of advertising and brochure plus calligraphy, paste-up, posters and direct mail.
First Contact & Terms: Send query letter with resume and samples. Samples not filed are returned only on the nature of the job whether it's by the hour or by project. Considers complexity of project, client's budget, skill and experience of artist, how work will be used, turnaround time and rights purchased when establishing payment.
Tips: "Be flexible about deadlines, willingness to work with artistic staff and marketing on concept and final design."

INTAR-INTERNATIONAL ARTS RELATIONS, Box 788, New York NY 10109. (212)695-6134. Artistic Director: Max Ferra. Produces 1 stage reading/year and 2 playwriting labs/year.
Needs: Assigns 12-20 jobs/year; local artists only. Query with samples. Uses artists for set, costumes, light design. Also flyers and posters. Pays for design by the project, $100-500 average. Pays for illustrations by the project, $100-300. Considers complexity of project, available budget, skill and experience of artist, how work will be used and turnaround time when establishing payment.
Tips: "We prefer designers of Hispanic background or empathy with our culture, but it's not a prerequisite. We are trying to produce only new works, not the classics. Hispanic-Americans are our number one consideration."

ROBERT IVEY BALLET COMPANY, 1632 Ashley Hall Rd., Charleston SC 29407. (803)556-1343. Artistic Director: Robert C. Ivey. Consists of two companies: The Senior Company—classically trained men and women chosen in open auditions providing educational outreach in schools, lecture-demonstrations for community organizations and joint performances with area arts groups; and The Charleston Youth Ballet, offering training to dancers age 9-13.
Needs: Works with 12 freelance artists/year; needs heaviest in spring and fall. Uses artists for advertising, brochure, program, set and costume design; posters, lighting and scenery.
First Contact & Terms: Send query letter with brochure showing art style. To show a portfolio, mail appropriate materials, which should include roughs, final reproducion/product, photostats and photographs. Pays for design by the project, $300-500 average. Pays for illustration by the project, $500-800 average. "Poster illustrations and ad layouts change with each performance. Costume and set design pays considerably more." Considers complexity of project and available budget when establishing payment.
Tips: Artists fail to consider "the budget of the organization when presenting specs. Also that total budget must cover many phases. Artwork should be able to be recycled for several ventures."

JOHNSTOWN SYMPHONY ORCHESTRA, 244 Walnut St., Johnstown PA 15901. General Manager: Jeanne Gleason. Assigns 2-5 jobs/year.
Needs: Works with 1-2 illustrators/year in February. Needs design work in December and February. Uses artists for bumper stickers, direct mail brochures, flyers, graphics, posters, programs and record jackets. Pays $25-200/job for design.
First Contact & Terms: Send query letter with samples and resume. SASE. Reports within 1 week. Provide resume, brochure and flyer to be kept on file for future assignments.

***MELANIE LAJOIE AND THE PYRAMID DANCE COMPANY**, 199 Fairmont Ave., Worcester MA 01604. (617)756-3525 or 756-0110. Director/Featured Performer: Melanie Lajoie. Performs traditional ethnic dances of the Middle and Near East. Specializes in gypsy, peasant, religious ritual, tribal, harem, including dances of the sword, veils, and finger cymbals from a variety of countries.
Needs: Works with 1 freelance artist/year. Uses artists for advertising, brochure, catalog and set design; advertising brochure and catalog layout; catalog illustration; posters, lighting and scenery. Prefers Middle Eastern (Oriental, Persian) Old-World style.
First Contact & Terms: Local artists only; performing arts art experience necessary. Send query letter with brochure, resume, business card and photographs and photostats to be kept on file. Samples returned by SASE only if requested. Reports within 1 month if interested. Pays for design by the project, $25-300 average. Considers complexity of project, available budget, skill and experience of artist, how work will be used and rights purchased when establishing payment.

MATTI LASCOE DANCE THEATRE CO., 1014-A Cabrillo Park Dr., Santa Ana CA 92701. (714)542-1463. Artistic Director: Matti Lascoe. Sixteen member Caribbean dance and music ensemble with drummers and the Trinidad Steel Drum Band. Concert is called "Caribbean Splash."
Needs: Works with 2 freelance artists/year; needs heaviest in September-November, January-May. Uses artists for advertising, brochure, set and costume design; lighting and scenery.
First Contact & Terms: Experienced artists only. Send resume, photographs and tear sheets to be kept on file. Write for artists' guidelines. Samples returned by SASE only if requested. Reports only if interested. Pays for design and illustration by the project. Considers available budget when establishing payment.

LE GROUPE DE LA PLACE ROYALE, 130 Sparks St., Ottawa, Ontario K1P 5B6 Canada. (613)235-1493. Director of Development: Pamela Clegg. "Innovative, professional modern dance company with a 48-week season, 8 dancers, 1 artistic director, voice coach and an assistant artistic director. All choreography is original and there is voice and live musical accompaniment used in performance by the dancers. Use of original set and costume design by visual artists since 1966."
Needs: Works with 2-3 freelance artists/year. Uses artists for advertising, brochure and program design, illustration and layout; posters, lighting, holography, experimental video and film, photography and slide montage. Prefers to work with artists with at least a minimum exposure to modern dance. "Company normally has a very good idea of what it wants. It is then up to the artist to produce at least three variations on a given theme."
First Contact & Terms: Send query letter with brochure, resume and samples to be kept on file. "A letter will be sent if company is interested in artist's work. Will then ask about availability and request that an appointment be scheduled for an exchange with the artistic director and public relations officer." Prefers photographs, posters, flyers or slides if artwork is set or costume design, as samples. Samples returned by SASE only if requested. Reports within 2 weeks. Pays for design by the hour, $5-20 average; by the project, $750-2,500 average; by the day, $50-200 average. "Maximum payment varies with

scope of project and/or availability of funds." Considers complexity of project, available budget, skill and experience of artist, how work will be used and rights purchased when establishing payment.
Tips: "Approach should focus on movement and its visual expression."

LOOKING GLASS THEATRE, 175 Mathewson St., Providence RI 02903. (401)331-9080. Producing Director: Jeannie Walker. "Looking Glass Theatre is a children's theatre company that performs in New England. We do both mainstage and touring productions. We are particularly interested in touring sets."
Needs: Works with 5-7 freelance artists/year. Needs heaviest in September to June. Works on an assignment basis only. Uses freelance artists for advertising, set and costume design; lighting and scenery.
First Contact & Terms: Send query letter with resume to be kept on file. Call to schedule an appointment to show portfolio, which should include roughs, original/final art and photographs. Samples not kept on file are returned if accompanied by SASE. Reports back within 6 weeks. Call or write for appointment to show portfolio. Payment is negotiated depending upon project's budget and turnaround time.
Tips: "The difficulty of a durable and easily transported set that tours has limited the possibilities. However, we are searching for new and exciting sets. We would like sets that 'move' and include special effects."

***LYRIC OPERA COMPANY OF LONG ISLAND INC.**, Box 848, Bayport, Long Island NY 11705. Artistic Director: Michael Signorelli. Assigns 4 jobs/year "when active." Send resume.
Needs: Uses artists for costume design and scenic design. Submit estimated costs.

MARYLAND DANCE THEATER, Dance Dept., University of Maryland, College Park MD 20742. (301)454-3399. Artistic Director: Larry Warren. Incorporated, nonprofit, modern dance repertory company in residence at the University of Maryland consisting of approximately 15 students, faculty and area artists. Performances are given in the Washington/Baltimore area and throughout the mid-Atlantic states.
Needs: Works with 3-4 freelance artists/year; needs heaviest in November-May. Works primarily with local artists. Uses artists for advertising, brochure and program design and layout; costume design, posters and lighting.
First Contact & Terms: Send query letter with description of past work. Call or write for appointment to show portfolio. Pays for design by the project, $25-300 average, maybe higher depending on project. Considers complexity of project, available budget, skill and experience of artist, how work will be used and turnaround time when establishing payment.

MICHIGAN OPERA THEATRE, 6519 Second Ave., Detroit MI 48202. (313)874-7850. Director of Public Relations/Marketing: John Finck. Assigns 7-8 jobs/year.
Needs: Local artists only. Works on assignment only. Uses artists for ads, billboards, bumper stickers, direct mail pieces, brochures, flyers, posters, program books, costumes, set and theatrical lighting.
First Contact & Terms: Query with samples or portfolio. SASE. Reports within 1 month. Samples returned by SASE. Reports on future assignment possibilities. Provide resume and brochure to be kept on file for future assignments. Pays by the project. Considers complexity of project, available budget, skill and experience of artist, how work will be used and turnaround time when establishing payment.

MID-WILLAMETTE BALLET ENSEMBLE, Box 55, Salem OR 97308. (503)363-1403. Director, Salem Ballet School: Elfie Stevenin, DMA-DEA. Dance company of 15 ensemble students performing locally for community events and traditional concerts.
Needs: Works with 3 artists for poster designs, photography, brochure design; all fund-raising through parent organization only. Needs heaviest in fall and spring. Local artists only—"for the most part, they are artists who have children enrolled in classes." Uses artists for brochure design, posters and photography.
First Contact & Terms: Send business card to be kept on file. Pays for design by the project. Considers available budget when establishing payment.

***MILLBROOK PLAYHOUSE**, Mill Hall PA 17751. (717)748-8083. President: John W. Sheria. Summer stock theater.
Needs: Assigns 4 jobs/year. Works with 3 designers/year; June-August only. Uses artists for costumes, stages and theatrical lighting. Especially needs set designer and costume design.
First Contact & Terms: Query with resume. SASE. Reports in 2 weeks. Provide resume to be kept on file for future assignments. Pays room, board and spending money for design; payment varies.

MILWAUKEE SYMPHONY ORCHESTRA, 212 W. Wisconsin Ave., Milwaukee WI 53203. (414)291-6010. Public Relations: Polly Scott.

Needs: Local artists only. Uses artists for advertising, flyers, graphics and posters.
First Contact & Terms: Query or arrange interview. SASE. Reports in 2 weeks. Pays by the project according to complexity of project, available budget and turnaround time. Also considers trade of symphony tickets for artwork.

MINNESOTA JAZZ DANCE COMPANY, Zoe Sealy Dance Center, 1815 E. 38th St., Minneapolis MN 55407. (612)721-3031. Studio Manager: Edie Wright. Dance company which "creates and presents jazz dance in its concert art form; collaborates with visual artists; educates audiences through lecture demonstrations and workshops throughout the US."
Needs: Works with 6 freelance artists/year. Uses artists for advertising, brochure and program design, illustration and layout; set and costume design, posters and lighting.
First Contact & Terms: Send query letter with brochure, resume, business card, original work and tear sheets to be kept on file. Call or write for appointment to show portfolio. Samples returned by SASE only if requested. Reports within 6 weeks. Pays for design and illustration by the hour, $5-40 average; by the project, $50-100 average; by the day, $25-50 average. Considers available budget, and skill and experience of artist when establishing payment.

MJT DANCE CO., Box 108, Watertown MA 02172. (617)482-0351. Director: Margie J. Topf. Modern dance troupe.
Needs: Assigns 2-10 jobs/year. Local artists only. Uses artists for advertising, bumper stickers, direct mail brochures, flyers, graphics, posters, programs, tickets, exhibits and lighting. Especially needs brochure design, layout, paste-up.
First Contact & Terms: Send query letter with resume or arrange interview. SASE. Reports within 2 weeks. Pays $5-10/hour.
Tips: "Video is becoming a major consideration in the performing arts. Be well-versed in many different art forms."

MME. CADILLAC DANCERS & MUSICIANS-Dances of 17th Century French Settlers, Apt. 903, 15 E. Kirby, Detroit MI 48202. (313)967-4030 or 864-9067. Artistic Director: Harriet Berg.
Needs: Assigns 4 jobs/year. Uses artists for flyers, programs, announcements and ads.
First Contact & Terms: Send query letter. SASE. Negotiates pay.

***ELISA MONTE DANCE CO.**, 39 Great Jones St., New York NY 10012. (212)982-4264. Manager: Bernard Schmidt. Modern dance company.
Needs: Works with 2-3 freelance artists/year. Prefers local artists. Works on assignment only. Uses artists for advertising brochure and catalog design, illustration and layout plus mechanicals, posters and direct mail.
First Contact & Terms: Send query letter with brochure showing art style or resume, photocopies or photographs. Samples not filed are returned by SASE only if requested by artist. Reports only if interested. Call or write to schedule an appointment to show a portfolio, which should include roughs, final reproduction/product, color and photographs. Pays for design by the project, $500 minimum. Considers complexity of project, skill and experience of artist and how work will be used when establishing payment.

MUSIC SOCIETY OF THE MIDLAND CENTER FOR THE ARTS, 1801 W. St. Andrews, Midland MI 48640. (517)631-1072. Contact: Coordinator of Office and Marketing Services. A not-for-profit dance, theatre and music organization. "We produce our own events during the fall and winter season (mostly musical comedy and choral/dance concerts), and are presentors during our Summer Festival (June-August)."
Needs: Works with 3 freelance artists/year. Needs heaviest in spring and summer. Works on assignment only. Uses artists for advertising and brochure design and layout, and poster design and illustration. "We are open to any style."
First Contact & Terms: Send query letter with brochure, resume, and photocopies to be kept on file. Samples not filed are returned by SASE only if requested. Reports back only if interested. To show a portfolio, mail appropriate materials, which should include roughs, original/final art and final reproduction/product. Payment varies greatly. Considers project's budget, skill and experience of the artist and turnaround time when establishing payment.
Tips: Looking for "simply stated, colorful, 'fun,' eye-appealing style."

NASHVILLE SYMPHONY ORCHESTRA, 208 23rd Ave. N., Nashville TN 37203. (615)329-3033. Marketing and Public Relations Director: Debra Campagna. Regional symphony.
Needs: Works with 4 freelance artists/year. Works on assignment only. Uses artists for advertising and brochure design, illustration, and layout; poster and program design and illustration.

First Contact & Terms: Send query letter with brochure, business card and tear sheets to be kept on file. Call for appointment to show portfolio. Reports only if interested. "We determine a project estimate." Considers complexity of project, project's budget, how work will be used and turnaround time when establishing payment. Looks for a "clean, simple design that makes an immediate visual statement—copy aside."

NEW JERSEY SHAKESPEARE FESTIVAL, Drew University, Madison NJ 07940. Artistic Director: Paul Barry. Contemporary and classical theatrical troupe. Assigns 3-6 jobs/year.
Needs: Works with 1 or 2 illustrators and 3 designers/year. Design work for costumes, sets, props and lighting is seasonal, May-December. Uses artists for advertising, costumes, designer-in-residence, direct mail brochures, exhibits, flyers, graphics, posters, programs, sets and theatrical lighting.
First Contact & Terms: Query with resume or arrange interview to show portfolio. SASE. Reports within 1 week. Interviews for designers are held in March and April. Provide resume to be kept on file for future assignments. Pays $800-1,000/show for set and costume design (large shows).
Tips: "Our season has expanded to 27 playing weeks." An artist's work should display an "understanding of historical period, good use of color, practicality and fit of costumes. Sets should show an ease to build, and to change from one show to another."

NEW MEXICO SYMPHONY ORCHESTRA, Box 769, Albuquerque NM 87103. (505)843-7657. Executive Administrator: William Weinrod. Regional orchestra based in Albuquerque but serving state of New Mexico. Performs 50-60 concerts/year and 150 school programs. Basic concert series currently consists of 18 subscription concerts. In addition there are pops concerts and "specials" which require graphic promotional materials.
Needs: Works with 3-4 freelance artists/year; needs heaviest in spring/fall. Prefers local artists with performing arts art experience especially for layouts of ads and brochures. Uses artists for advertising, brochure and program design, illustration and layout; and posters.
First Contact & Terms: Send query letter with samples to be kept on file. Write for appointment to show portfolio. Prefers actual print samples. Samples returned only by request. Pays for design by the project, $100-2,500 average. Considers complexity of project and available budget when establishing payment.

***NEW ORLEANS OPERA GUILD INC. & CONCERT SERIES**, 570 Woodvine Ave., Metairie LA 70005. (504)525-7672 or 835-9583. Art Director: Mrs. E.B. Ludwig. Theatre.

***NEW ORLEANS SYMPHONY ORCHESTRA**, Suite 500, 212 Loyola Ave., New Orleans LA 70112. 524-0404. Marketing Director: Jeffrey W. Gettleman.
Needs: Works with 5 freelance artists/year. Uses artists for the design, illustration and layout of advertising, brochures and catalog plus window design, P-O-P displays, calligraphy, paste-up, mechanicals, posters and direct mail.
First Contact & Terms: Send query letter with resume and samples. Samples not filed are returned if requested. Reports back ASAP. Call to schedule an appointment to show a portfolio.

NEW PLAYWRIGHTS' THEATRE, 1742 Church St. NW, Washington DC 20036. (202)232-4527. Contact: Public Relations Director. New Playwrights' is an alternative theatre dedicated to the development of new American playwriting talent. It is an intimate theatre, seating only 125 people with over 1,000 season subscribers.
Needs: Works with 12 freelance artists/year. Works on assignment only. Needs heaviest September through June. Uses artists for brochure design, illustration and layout; poster design and illustration; set and costume design; lighting and scenery.
First Contact & Terms: Send query letter with slides, photographs, photocopies or tear sheets to be kept on file. Call or write for appointment to show portfolio. Samples are not returned. Reports only if interested. Pays by the project, $200-1,000 for design; $50-300 for illustration. Considers complexity of project, project's budget, skill and experience of artist, how work will be used and turnaround time when establishing payment.

NEW YORK CITY OPERA NATIONAL COMPANY, NY State Theater, Lincoln Center, New York NY 10023. (212)870-5635. Administrative Director: Nancy Kelly. Opera company founded in 1979 by Beverly Sills as a national touring company with the purpose of bringing opera to areas of the country without resident opera associations. Its primary function is to provide young singers an opportunity to gain performing experience; veteran singers use the tours to try new roles before singing them in New York.
Needs: Needs for freelance artists heaviest prior to tours in fall and winter. Uses artists for set and costume design. "Scenic and costume designers should be aware of the rigors of traveling productions and

should think about portability and economics." Artists also used for graphics for marketing the current production.

First Contact & Terms: Previous experience is advisable; union memberships are required for set and costume design. Send query letter with resume to be kept on file. Reports only if interested. Pays for design by the project; "varies according to design; follows union rates." Considers complexity of project and available budget when establishing payment.

Tips: "The use of artists is tied specifically to whatever opera we may be performing in a given year. We generally tour in the January-April time period and hire artists one year ahead of each tour."

NEW YORK HARP ENSEMBLE, 140 W. End Ave., New York NY 10023. Director: Dr. Aristid von Wurtzler. Concert group which tours the U.S., Europe, Africa, South America, Australia and the Near and Far East.

Needs: Works with 1 designer/year, summer only. Local artists only. Works on assignment only. Uses artists for direct mail brochures, posters, programs and record cover layouts. Especially needs work for brochures, posters and record cover.

First Contact & Terms: Submit samples (brochures, posters and record covers). Samples returned by SASE. Reports back on future assignment possibilities. Provide flyer to be kept on file for future assignments. Pays by the project for design and illustration. Considers available budget, and skill and experience of artist when establishing payment.

***THE ODC/SAN FRANCISCO**, 3153 17th St., San Francisco CA 94110. Dance company founded by Brenda Way in 1971 and based in San Francisco since 1976. Performs "a continuously evolving repertory of new dance works." Four choreographers draw from classical and modern dance technique theater, music.

Needs: Works with approximately 12 freelance artists/year. Needs artists all year round, but most heavily in early spring and fall. Artists "must possess skills of resourcefulness and flexibility. We work with restricted budgets and specific artistic considerations." Uses artists for advertising, brochure, catalog, program and costume design; advertising and brochure layout, posters, scenery and photography. Style must be "clean and clear; a strong image that effectively communicates something distinctive about the nature of the dance company."

First Contact & Terms: Send query letter with brochure showing art style or resume and samples to be kept on file; do not call. "Since we work with limited budgets, I like to work closely with the artist in the concept and the carry-through of a project." Original work not necessary as samples. Will look at anything that fairly represents the quality of the artist's work. Samples returned by SASE if not kept on file. Reports within 2 weeks. Write for appointment to show portfolio. Pays for design by the project. Considers complexity of project, available budget, and skill and experience of artist when establishing payment.

ODYSSEY THEATRE ENSEMBLE, 12111 Ohio Ave., West Los Angeles CA 90025. (213)826-1626. Production Manager: Lucy Pollak. Experimental theater troupe, specializing in live theatre in 3-theatre complex; equity waiver with 1,200 subscribers. Generally 20,000 audience members per year.

Needs: Uses artists for advertising and brochure design, illustration and layout; poster design and illustration, set and costume design, lighting, scenery, graphic and logo design for each play.

First Contact & Terms: Works with 20 artists. Send query letter with brochure showing art style or resume, tear sheets, photocopies, slides, photographs and "whatever is easy and inexpensive to send to indicate experience and style." SASE. Reports within 1 month. Call or write to schedule an appointment to show a portfolio, which should include roughs, final reproduction/product, photostats and photographs. Pays $25-300 for design and illustration; negotiates payment. Considers complexity of project, budget, skill and experience of the artist, and previous work done on a volunteer basis for the theatre.

Tips: "We have expanded our facility to three 99-seat Equity-waiver performing spaces."

***OKRA DANCE COMPANY**, 201 Warren St., Brooklyn NY 11201. (212)625-1740. Contact: Artistic Director. Professional modern dance repertory company consisting of 5 dancers and musicians. Styles range from modern, African, to character ballet. Works with other artists—musicians, poets, actors, visual artists—in interdisciplinary productions.

Needs: Works with 3 freelance artists/year. Uses artists for advertising, brochure, program, set and costume design; lighting, photography and video.

First Contact & Terms: Send query letter with brochure to be kept on file. Call or write for appointment to show portfolio. Reports only if interested. Pays for design and illustration by the project, $25-300 average. Considers complexity of project, available budget, skill and experience of artist and how work will be used when establishing payment.

OLYMPIC BALLET THEATRE, Anderson Cultural Center, 700 Main St., Edmonds WA 98020. (206)774-7570. Director: John and Helen Wilkins. Ballet company with 20 dancers, approximately 100 members and a Board of Trustees of 20 which does a full-length "Nutcracker" Spring Showcase and tour, lecture-demo's and mini-performances.
Needs: Works with 2 freelance artists/year. Needs heaviest in fall, winter and spring. Uses freelance artists for advertising, brochure, catalog, poster and program design and illustration, set and costume design.
First Contact & Terms: Works on assignment only. Call or write for appointment to show portfolio. Pays by the project, $25-500 for design; $25-100 for illustration. Considers complexity of project and project's budget when establishing payment.

***ONE ACT THEATRE COMPANY**, 430 Mason St., San Francisco CA 94102. (415)421-5355. Publicity Director: Randall Wilson. Nonprofit theatre focusing on professional productions and one-act plays.
Needs: Works with 10 freelance artists/year. Local artists only. Uses artists for advertising and brochure illustration and layout; paste-up, mechanicals, posters, direct mail, program and season subscription brochure.
First Contact & Terms: Send query letter with resume, tear sheets and photocopies. Samples not filed are returned by SASE. Call to schedule an appointment to show a portfolio, which should include thumbnails and roughs. Pays for design by the hour, $15-25. Pays for illustration by the project, $50-100. Considers client's budget and turnaround time when establishing payment.
Tips: "Excellent starting exposure for Bay area artists making initial contacts for larger firms."

OPERA/COLUMBUS, 50 W. Broad St. Mezz., Columbus OH 43215. (614)461-8101. Audience Development Director: Richard Wickersham. Opera company with 7 full-time staff members, 43-member board of trustees and 2,300 series ticket subscribers.
Needs: Works primarily with advertising and graphic design agency. Prefers local experienced artists. Works on assignment only. Occasional needs include brochure illustration and layout, poster design, advertising design.
First Contact & Terms: Send query letter with brochure, resume and samples to be kept on file; write for appointment to show portfolio. Prefers slides, photos, renderings or tear sheets as samples; slides are not filed. Samples not filed are returned only if requested. Reports only if interested. Pays by the project. Considers complexity of project, project's budget and turnaround time when establishing payment.

PARADISE SYMPHONY ORCHESTRA, 6686 Brook Way, Paradise CA 95969. (916)877-8360. Conductor: Thomas E. Wilson. June art festival by various mediums. SASE. Reports within 1 month.
Needs: Prefers local artists. Needs heaviest in June and December. Works on assignment only. Uses artists for brochure design, poster design and costume design. Prefers "a smart, clean, exciting style."
First Contact & Terms: Send query letter with brochure showing art style. To show a portfolio, mail appropriate materials, which should include final reproduction/product and photographs.
Tips: "First class promotional materials are necessary." Then is a "great need for excellent projection of the arts."

***PENNSYLVANIA BALLET**, 3 Parkway #922, Philadelphia PA 19102. (215)636-4400. Marketing Director: Nancy E. Depke.
Needs: Works with 10 freelance artists/year. Uses artists for advertising design and layout; brochure design, illustration and layout; paste-up, mechanicals, posters, direct mail and annual reports.
First Contact & Terms: Send resume, tear sheets, photostats and photocopies. Samples not filed are not returned. Reports only if interested. Call to schedule an appointment to show a portfolio, which should include thumbnails, roughs, original/final art, final reproduction/product, color, tear sheets, photostats and photographs. Pays for design by the hour, $35 maximum. Considers complexity of project, budget, and skill and experience of artist when establishing payment.

PENNSYLVANIA STAGE COMPANY, 837 Linden St., Allentown PA 18101. (215)434-6110. Producing Director: Gregory S. Hurst. "We are a LORT theatre, located 2 hours from New York City devoted to a diverse repertory of new and old works from Shakespeare to the world premiere production of a new musical. Our house seats 274 people, and we currently have 6,000 subscribers."
Needs: Works with 10 freelance artists/year; "We need freelance designers for our season which runs from October-July." "Artists must be able to come to Allentown for design consultation and construc-

" Theatre advertising must successfully combine dynamic, sensitive design and selling information. "

Barbara Kornick, Philadelphia Drama Guild

tion." Works on assignment only. Uses artists for set and costume design, lighting and scenery. "As a growing professional regional theatre, we have increased needs for graphic artists and photography for print materials (brochures, flyers), and particularly for our program magazine, *Callboard*, which is published eight times a year. "We would also be interested in theatre cartoons."
First Contact & Terms: Send query letter with resume. Prefers photostats, slides, b&w photos, color washes, roughs as samples. Samples returned by SASE. Reports back whether to expect possible future assignments. Provide resume to be kept on file for possible future assignments. Pays by the project, $500-1,500 average, for design; $25-125 for print material. Considers complexity of project, available budget, and skill and experience of artist when establishing payment.
Tips: "We prefer that designers have extensive experience designing for professional theater."

RUDY PEREZ PERFORMANCE ENSEMBLE, Box 36614, Los Angeles CA 90036. (213)931-3604. Artistic Director: Rudy Perez. Performance art and experimental dance company, also known as the Rudy Perez Dance Theater, is a nonprofit organization dependent on funding from National Endowment for the Arts and the California Arts Council; corporate and private fundings; box office and bookings currently in the LA area.
Needs: "The work is mainly collaborations with visual artists and composers." Uses artists for publicity before performances and updating press kits, brochures, etc.
First Contact & Terms: Send query letter with brochure and resume to be kept on file. Reports within 1 week. "Since we are a nonprofit organization we depend on in-kind services and/or negotiable fees."
Tips: Artists should have "an awareness of dance and theatre."

***THE STANZE PETERSON DANCE CENTER**, 7300 Scott St,. Houston TX 77021. (713)741-7534. Director: Stanze Peterson. Dance troupe.
Needs: Local artists only. Uses artists for direct mail brochures, programs and newspaper ads.
First Contact & Terms: Query and arrange interview to show portfolio. SASE. Call or write to schedule an appointment to show a portfolio, which should include original/final art or final reproduction/product. Pays by job.
Tips: "We use artists for our publicity materials to try to blend the two art forms."

***PHILADELPHIA DRAMA GUILD**, Suite 802, 112 S. 16th St., Philadelphia PA 19102. (215)563-7530. Marketing Director: Barbara Kornik. Professional theatre company producing 5 plays/season. "Philadelphia's largest and oldest resident professional theatre company, with 18,500 season ticket holders."
Needs: Works with 2 freelance artists/year. Prefers local artists with experience in arts/theatre design preferred. Works on assignment only. Uses artists for design, illustration and layout of advertising and brochure plus paste-up, mechanicals, posters, direct mail, annual reports and lobby displays.
First Contact & Terms: Send query letter with photocopies. Samples not filed are not returned. Reports back only if interested. Write to schedule an appointment to show a portfolio, which should include roughs, original/final art and color. Pays for design by the project, $50-2,000. Pays for illustration by the project, $25-200. Considers complexity of project, client's budget and turnaround time when establishing payment.
Tips: "Theatre advertising (particularly direct mail) has to reflect more the image of the company than strictly hard sell; it must successfully combine dynamic, sensitive design and selling information. We are looking for dynamically visual art, using lots of production shots."

PICCOLO OPERA COMPANY, Lee Jon Associates, #18662 Fairfield Ave., Detroit MI 48221. (313)861-6930. Contact: Lee Jon Associates. Opera company, performs in English, productions staged and in costume. Travels around the country. Performs for adults and for youngsters, with piano or orchestra.
Needs: Works on assignment only. Prefers artists with layout experience. Uses artists for advertising design, and brochure illustration and layout, poster design and set design. Pays by the project, $25-300; negotiable. Considers available budget, skill and experience of artist and creative talent of artist when establishing payment.
First Contact & Terms: Send query letter with resume and samples. SASE. Reports in 3-4 weeks.
Tips: When reviewing work, especially looks for "the impact of subject matter. Artists shouldn't overemphasize the design at the expense of the information; consider color in relation to legibility. We deal in emotions and the nostalgia aroused by music, so look for more 'romantic' design." Also interested in cartoon-style illustrations.

PIONEER PLAYHOUSE OF KENTUCKY, Danville KY 40422. (606)236-2747. Contact: Eben Henson. Regular summer stock theatre.
Needs: Works with 10 freelance artists/year; needs heaviest in summer. Uses artists for advertising,

poster, set and costume design; lighting and scenery. Prefers artists willing to work in the nature of apprenticeship. Works on assignment only. Uses artists for the design, illustration and layout by advertising and brochures, the illustration and layout of catalogs, set design, costume design, lighting and scenery.
First Contact & Terms: Send query letter and material to be kept on file. Reports within 4 weeks. Call to schedule an appointment to show a portfolio. No payment of salary; apprenticeships provide room and board.
Tips: "For persons breaking into any form of the theatre, apprenticeship is necessary. First one must establish himself with a reputable theater in order to advance in the theatrical profession."

POSEY SCHOOL OF DANCE, INC., Box 254, Northport NY 11768. (516)757-2700. President: Elsa Posey. Private school/professional training in performing arts.
Needs: Works with 4 or more freelance artists/year; needs heaviest in spring and fall. Prefers regional artists willing to work within nonprofit performing arts budget. Works on assignment only. Uses artists for advertising and brochure design, illustration and layout; poster and program design and illustration, set and costume design, lighting and scenery. Also uses artists for a newsletter and for advertising copy. Interested in (*appropriate* cartoons.)
First Contact & Terms: Send query letter with resume, tear sheets, photostats and photocopies. Samples returned by SASE. Reports within 4 weeks. To show a portfolio, mail tear sheets and photostats. Pays for design, $10-200 average; for illustration, $10-50 average. Negotiates payment. Considers complexity of project, available budget, skill and experience of artist, how work will be used and rights purchased when establishing payment.
Tips: Artist must have "illustrative ability with understanding of dance, dancer's body and movement. Looking for a more personal approach."

PROJECT OPERA, INC., 160 Main St., Northampton MA 01060. (413)584-8811. Artistic Director: Richard R. Rescia. Stated productions of opera.
Needs: Needs heaviest in fall and spring. Uses artists for set and costume design, and scenery.
First Contact & Terms: "We use regional artists where possible." Send query letter with resume and photocopies to be kept on file. Samples not filed are returned by SASE. Pays for design by the project. Considers complexity of project and project's budget when establishing payment.

***RAPID CITY SYMPHONY ORCHESTRA**, Box 8001, Rapid City SD 57709. (605)348-4676. Executive Director: Pat Lebrun. Nonprofit organization.
Needs: Works with 3-4 freelance artists/year. Uses artists for advertising design, brochure design, calligraphy and direct mail.
First Contact & Terms: Send query letter with brochure showing art style. Samples not filed are returned only if requested. Reports only if interested. To show a portfolio, mail appropriate materials. Pays for design by the hour, $20 maximum. Considers complexity of project, skill and experience of artist, and how work will be used when establishing payment.

ROCHESTER PHILHARMONIC ORCHESTRA, 108 East Ave., Rochester NY 14604. (716)454-2620. Director of Marketing: Nancy Calocerinos. Major orchestra performing 52 weeks/year, winter and summer seasons.
Needs: Works with 2 freelance artists/year. Needs heaviest between January and April. Local artists only, with at least three years' experience and a working knowledge of music. Works on assignment only. Uses artists for brochure, poster and program design.
First Contact & Terms: Send query letter with photocopies or tear sheets to be kept on file. Samples not filed are returned. Reports back only if interested. Pays for design by the project. Considers project's budget when establishing payment.

ROOSEVELT PARK AMPHITHEATRE, Middlesex County Department of Parks and Recreation, Box 661, New Brunswick NJ 08903. (201)548-2884. Producing Director: Ernest Albrecht. Musical theatre.
Needs: Works with 10 freelance artists/year; needs heaviest in spring through summer. Works on assignment only. Uses artists for set and costume design, lighting and scenery.
First Contact & Terms: Send query letter and resume. Prefers samples to be brought in person. Reports within 3 weeks. To show a portfolio, mail appropriate materials or write to schedule an appointment. Pays $600 average for design; salary.

SALT LAKE SYMPHONIC CHOIR, Box 45, Salt Lake City UT 84110. (801)466-8701. Contact: Manager. Assigns 5 jobs/year.
Needs: Works with 5 illustrators and 2 designers/year; fall only. Works on assignment. Uses artists for advertising, billboards, costumes, direct mail brochures, flyers, posters, programs, theatrical lighting and record jackets.

First Contact & Terms: Mail resume, brochure and flyer to be kept on file. SASE. Negotiates pay by the project.

SAN FRANCISCO OPERA CENTER, War Memorial Opera House, San Francisco Opera, San Francisco CA 94102. (415)565-6435. Manager: Christine Bullin. Assistant to the Manager: Susan Lamb. SFOC is the umbrella organization for the affiliates of the San Francisco Opera.
Needs: Works with 3-4 freelance artists/year; needs heaviest in summer preparing for fall and spring seasons. Uses artists for advertising, brochure and program design, illustration and layout; set and costume design, posters, lighting, scenery, and PR and educational packets.
First Contact & Terms: Send query letter with brochure, resume and business card, photostats, slides and photographs to be kept on file. Write for appointment to show portfolio. Reports only if interested. Pays for design and illustration by the project, $50-300 average. Considers available budget, how work will be used and rights purchased when establishing payment.

SAN JOSE SYMPHONY, Suite 200, 476 Park Ave., San Jose CA 95110. (408)287-7383. Director of Marketing/Public Relations: Pam Beran.
Needs: Assigns 10-15 jobs/year. Local artists only. Uses artists for advertising, direct mail/developmental brochures, ticket sales material, flyers, posters, programs and educational materials.
First Contact & Terms: Send query letter with resume and samples. SASE. Reports within 1 month. Pays for design or illustration by the hour, $25 minimum; by the project, $275-500 average. Considers complexity of project, available budget and how work will be used when establishing payment.

***SANTA BARBARA SYMPHONY**, 214 E. Victoria St., Stanta Barbara CA 93101. (805)965-6596. Contact: Managing Director. Professional symphony orchestra, 78 members. Presents 6 matinee and 7 evening performances, October-May. Travels to outlying areas for repeats of subscription concerts and youth concerts; regular subscription concerts at the Arlington Theatre; internationally renowned guest artists.
Needs: Works with 1-2 freelance artists/year; needs heaviest in early spring. Local artists only. Uses artists for advertising and brochure design, layout and illustration.
First Contact & Terms: Send query letter with brochure, resume and samples to be kept on file. Reports only if intereted. Call for appointment to show portfolio, which should include final reproduction/product. Artists submit fee schedule. Considers complexity of project, available budget, how work will be used and personality—"willingness to listen to our needs and comply with them"—when establishing payment.

SEATTLE OPERA ASSOCIATION, 305 Harrison, Seattle WA 98109. (206)443-4700. Press and Public Relations Director: Ernesto Alorda. Opera company.
Needs: Works with 5-7 freelance artists/year; needs heaviest in winter and spring. Uses artists for flyer/brochure design and layout, and season/festival posters.
First Contact & Terms: Send query letter with brochure, business card and photostats and photographs to be kept on file. Call for appointment to show portfolio. Samples returned by SASE if not kept on file. Pays $350/poster. Considers complexity of project, available budget and how work will be used when establishing payment.

SEATTLE SYMPHONY ORCHESTRA, 305 Harrison St., Seattle WA 98109. (206)447-4740. Director of Marketing and Public Relations: Marianne Lewis. Assigns approximately 4 jobs/year.
Needs: Works with 4 illustrators/year; September-June, only. Uses artists for advertising, direct mail brochures, flyers, graphics and posters. Especially needs design of season flyer, special flyers and posters.
First Contact & Terms: Local artists only. Query with samples. SASE. Reports within 2 weeks. Works on assignment only. No samples returned. Reports back on future assignment possibilities. Provide resume, brochure and flyer to be kept on file for future assignments. Pays market rate for design and illustration.
Tips: The trend is toward "excellent graphic design work—greater emphasis on business solicitation and businesslike look."

SHAWNEE SUMMER THEATRE OF GREENE COUNTY, INC., Box 22, Bloomfield IN 47424. Producer: Frank Hayashida. Resident production company offering 7 plays a year: serious, a musical, a mystery, comedies and 1 children's play.
Needs: Works with 25 freelance artists/year; only in late spring and summer. Uses artists for brochure illustrtion and layout, set and costume design, lighting and scenery.
First Contact & Terms: "Ours is a production company and all work is done by that company while in residence. All applicants must be willing to fill in as actors in large cast plays or musicals." Send query

letter with resume and color photos or slides of sample works; "We also insist on some kind of photograph of the applicant, even if only a Polaroid." Samples returned by SASE. Pays by the week. Write to schedule an appointment to show a portfolio, which should include thumbnails, original/final art, final reproduction/product, color, photographs and b&w.
Tips: "The theatre manages an art gallery and artist's work could be hung for one of the weeks during productions. Also, photos of work, articles concerning work and exhibits, and a good strong resume are helpful."

***SIGNORELLI BALLET**, Box 848, Bayport, Long Island NY 11705. Artistic Director and Choreographer: Pamela Signorelli. Produces 2-4 full or partial ballet per season using prominent artists and guest artists.
Needs: Uses artists for costume and scenic design.

SINGING BOYS OF PENNSYLVANIA, Box 110, State College, East Stroudsburg PA 18301, or Box 206, Wind Gap PA 18091. (717)421-6137 (business office) or (215)759-6002. Director: K. Bernard Schade. "Touring boychoir." Needs heaviest in fall and winter.
Needs: Local artists only. Works on assignment only. Uses artists for direct mail brochures, flyers, posters and record jackets, the design, illustration and layout of advertising and brochures; poster, set and costume design, lighting and scenery.
First Contact & Terms: Query.

SOUTHWEST JAZZ BALLET COMPANY, Box 38233, Houston TX 77088. (713)686-6299. Contact: President. Professional touring ballet company; producers of "America in Concert."
Needs: Works with 5 freelance artists/year. Works on assignment only. Uses artists for advertising illustration, brochure illustration and layout; poster illustration, costume design and scenery.
First Contact & Terms: Send query letter with resume and "end product" to be kept on file. Reports within 1 month. Call or write to schedule an appointment to show a portfolio, which should include final reproduction/product. Considers complexity of project when establishing payment.
Tips: Looking for '40s Americana style.

***SPRINGFIELD BALLET COMPANY**, Box 561, Springfield IL 62705. (217)789-4229. Company Manager: Marge Campane. "Forty-member dance organization that presents an autumn divertissement program, featuring jazz, modern and classical dance; an annual 'Nutcracker'; a spring full-length ballet."
Needs: Works with 4 freelance artists/year; needs heaviest in October, February and August. Illinois artists given preference; performing arts experience necessary. Uses artists for advertising, brochure, program, set and costume design; brochure and program illustration, program layout, posters, lighting and scenery.
First Contact & Terms: Send query letter with brochure, resume and photos to be kept on file. Prefers photographs or slides plus letters of endorsement; recent work resume as samples. Samples returned only by request. Reports only if interested or if requested. Write for appointment to show portfolio which should include original/final art. Pays for design by the project. Considers complexity of project, available budget, skill and experience of artist and rights purchased when establishing payment.

SPRINGFIELD SYMPHONY ORCHESTRA, Box 5191, Springfield IL 62705. (217)522-2838. General Manager: Catherine Wichterman. Metropolitan symphony orchestra performing 20 concerts.
Needs: Works with 1 freelance artist/year. Uses artist for brochure and program design. Contact in April.
First Contact & Terms: Send "original brochure work and program cover for symphony concerts" and cost estimate to be kept on file. Reports only if interested. Pays by the project. Considers available budget when establishing payment.

***STAGE #1**, Box 13607, Dallas TX 75231. (214)559-3754. Publicity Director: Phil Allen. Live theatre producing contemporary American plays.
Needs: Works with 3 freelance artists/year. Uses artists for advertising illustration, brochure design, posters and direct mail.
First Contact & Terms: Send query letter with brochure showing art style or resume, tear sheets and photocopies. Samples not filed returned by SASE. Reports only if interested. Call to schedule an appointment to show a portfolio, which should include final reproduction/product, tear sheets, photostats and photographs. Pays for design by the hour, $10-25; and illustration by the project, $25-100. "A good place for beginners. We will give credit on posters, programs, and brochures for any work contributed." Considers complexity of project, client's budget, skill and experience of artist, how work will be used, turnaround time and rights purchased when establishing payment.

Tips: "Expect very little pay from us or any other non-profit organization. We are always glad to give away tickets and publish names on goods completed."

"STRIKE AT THE WIND!" OUTDOOR DRAMA, Box 1059, Pembroke NC 28372. (919)521-2480 or 521-3112. General Manager: Carnell Locklear. Outdoor drama about Henry B. Lowery and the Indians of Robeson County during the Civil War. The company consists of 75 persons. Assigns 1 job/year.
Needs: Prefers local artists. Works on assignment only. Uses artists for billboards, bumper stickers, poster, animated TV spots, souvenir program cover, brochure illustration, poster illustrations and inside ads and editorials. Needs art that is "dramatic, historically accurate, entertainment-oriented with concepts illustrating Civil War era characters, places and things in southeastern North Carolina."
First Contact & Terms: Send brochure or resume with photographs to be kept on file. Reports in 4 weeks. Call for an appointment to show a portfolio. Provide resume, calling card, brochure, flyer and tear sheets to be kept on file for future assignments. Pays by the project. Considers complexity of the project when establishing payment.

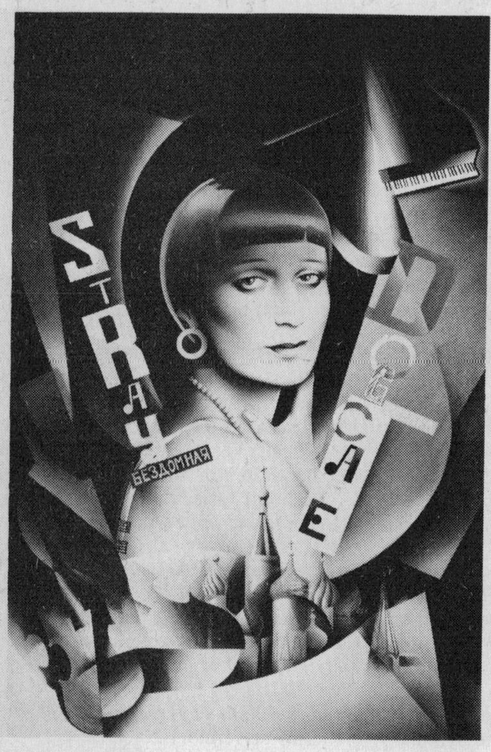

"The play this piece represents," says creative director Kathleen Robin-Lowry of the Mark Taper Forum in Los Angeles, "is a musical about the avant-garde poets of the Russian Revolution." Robin-Lowry purchased all rights and paid $1,000 to artist Richard Mahon. The artwork was used on the poster, the program and in newspaper advertisements.

***MARK TAPER FORUM**, 135 N. Grand Ave., Los Angeles CA 90012. (213)972-7259. Art Director: Kathleen Robin Lowry. In-house agency for the Mark Taper Forum of the Los Angeles Music Center. Provides advertising and posters for live theatre.
Needs: Works with 10 freelance artists/year. Prefers local artists only. Uses artists for the design and illustration of advertising, the illustration of brochures, paste-up and mechanicals. Prefers painterly styles, graphic b&w styles.
First Contact & Terms: Send brochure showing art style or tear sheets, photostats and slides. Samples not filed are returned by SASE. Reports only if interested. Call or write to schedule an appointment to show a portfolio, which should include original/final art, final reproduction/product, color, b&w and tear sheets. Pays for illustration by the project, $300-1,000. Considers client's budget; "this is non-profit theatre."

THEATRE OF YOUTH (TOY) CO. INC., Center Theatre, 681 Main St., Buffalo NY 14203. (716)856-4410. Artistic Director: Meg Pantera. "Buffalo's only professional resident theatre company, performing a full season of children and adult plays at their residence; while also touring schools with productions and workshops." Assigns 5 full-time and 4-10 professional service jobs per year. Write.

Needs: Professional actors, set and costume designers, and graphic artists. Uses artists for brochure designs, flyers, marquees, posters. Pays $250-500 costume and set designs and per show publicity design.
Tips: "Small companies such as TOY are seeking well-rounded practitioners, as opposed to rigid specialists, with an emphasis on ensemble. Submit inquiries early in the year, January through March, so we can arrange personal interviews.

THEATRE UNDER THE STARS, 4235 San Felipe, Houston TX 77027. (713)622-1626. Public Relations Director: Susie Works. Musical theatre production company producing 5 shows a year, one in Houston's outdoor theatre and 4 in the downtown music hall.
Needs: Works with 5-10 freelance artists/year. Works on assignment only. Uses artists for advertising and brochure design, illustration, and layout; and poster design and illustration.
First Contact & Terms: Send query letter with samples to be kept on file. Call for appointment to show portfolio. Samples not filed are returned by SASE. Reports within 2 weeks. Pays by the project; design, $50-5,000 average; illustration, $50-4,500 average. Considers complexity of the project, project's budget, skill and experience of the artist, how work will be used, turnaround time and rights purchased when establishing payment.

UNIVERSITY OF ROCHESTER SUMMER THEATER, River Station, Box 30185, Rochester NY 14627. (716)275-4088 (Monday-Wednesday-Friday). Managing Director: David Runzo. Semi-professional company offering 3 productions of classical and contemporary theatre each summer and a 4-hour college credit program.
Needs: Works with 6 freelance artists/year; needs heaviest in June, July, August. Artists must be able to teach area of concentration. Works on assignment only. Uses artists for set and costume design, lighting, scenery, as technical directors and stage manager. Also for brochures, programs and ads.
First Contact & Terms: Send query letter with resume, slides and b&w photos to be kept on file. Samples returned by SASE. Reports within 3 weeks. Call or write for appointment. Pays salary of $1,800-2,200 average for 11 weeks for design plus train transportation and half room—"paid through our budget of $2,500 by university artists."

VALOIS COMPANY OF DANCERS, HEC 214, University of Toledo, Toledo OH 43606. (419)537-2741. Art Director: Elaine Valois. Resident modern dance company active in public schools, workshops and mini-concerts plus an annual May show. Consists of 5-12 upperclasmen/graduates in dance.
Needs: Works with 6 freelance artist/year. Heaviest needs in spring. Prefers local artists. Uses artists for the design illustration and layout of advertising and brochures, poster design and illustration, costume design and lighting. "Student artists often help us, and we continue to support them and purchase from them when they go professional."
First Contact & Terms: Send query letter with brochure, business card and photostats to be kept on file. Samples not kept on file are returned only if requested. Reports within 2 weeks. To show a portfolio, mail appropriate materials or call to schedule an appointment; portfolio should include final reproduction "any representation." Pays by the project, $50-200 average, for design and illustration. Considers complexity of project, available budget and how work will be used when establishing payment.
Tips: "We have noticed more inventive use of photographic material blended in with graphics."

VICTORY GARDENS THEATER, 2257 N. Lincoln Ave., Chicago IL 60614. (312)549-5788. Managing Director: Marcelle McVay. "Subscriber-based not-for-profit professional theater, dedicated to the development of new works, and using Chicago talent."
Needs: Works with 10-20 freelance artists/year. Works with developing or experienced, local artists on assignment only. Uses artists for advertising, brochure, catalog and poster design and illustration; set, lighting and costume design.
First Contact & Terms: Send query letter with resume and tear sheets to be kept on file. Samples not filed are returned by SASE. Reports back only if interested. Pays for poster design by the project, $100-300 average; pays set, lighting and costume design according to U.S.A.A. Considers complexity of project, project's budget, skill and experience of the artist, and turnaround time when establishing payment.

***WALNUT STREET THEATRE COMPANY**, 9th and Walnut Sts., Philadelphia PA 19107. (215)574-3555. Promotions Manager: Leslie B. Goldstein. Theatre providing 5 major professional productions as part of a Subscription Series (19,000 + subscribers), a theatre school, a theatre camp for kids, co-productions, a Studio Theatre Season of four plays and a rental house.
Needs: Works with 2 freelance artists/year. Uses artists for brochure design, illustration and layout, posters, direct mail and annual reports.
First Contact & Terms: Send resume and samples. Samples not filed are returned by SASE. Reports within 6 weeks. Write to schedule an appointment to show a portfolio, which should include thumbnails, final reproduction/product, color and tear sheets. Considers complexity of project, client's budget, skill

and experience of artist, and how work will be used when establishing payment.
Tips: "We try to vary our style each season—something striking yet easily reproducible in many forms: brochures, posters, handbills and advertising."

***WICHITA SYMPHONY SOCIETY**, Suite 207, 225 W. Douglas, Wichita KS 67202. (316)267-5259. Public Relations Manager: Carolyn Kell. Symphony orchestra playing classical, pops and chamber music. "Theme for each season changes in classical series. Pops concerts all marketed separately with specific theme." Directed towards primarily: ages 50-65; secondarily; ages 30-50.
Needs: Works with 3 freelance artists/year. Uses artists for advertising and brochure design, illustration and layout; calligraphy, paste-up and direct mail. Needs heaviest in spring and fall. Works on assignment only. Uses artists for the design, illustration and layout of advertising, brochures and catalogs.
First Contact & Terms: Send query letter with brochure showing art style or resume and samples. Samples not filed are returned only if requested. Reports only if interested. Call to schedule an appointment to show a portfolio, which should include final reproduction/product and original/final art. Pays for design by the project, $200-1,000. Considers complexity of project, client's budget, how work wil be used and turnaround time when establishing payment.

***WISDOM BRIDGE THEATRE**, 1559 W. Howard St., Chicago IL 60626. (312)743-0486. Contact: Executive Director. "We are a 196 theatre on Chicago's north side. We have a subscriber base of 9,500 and present an eclectic season of work. Our work tends to be socially and politically conscientious." Assigns 28-62 jobs/year.
Needs: Works with 3 illustrators and 15 designers/year. Works on assignment only. Uses artists for advertising, costumes, direct mail brochures, exhibits, flyers, graphics, posters, programs, sets, composition, sound design, and audiovisuals, technical art and lighting. Pays $500-1,200/job design of sets, lights and costumes. Pays $300-600/job, brochure design.
First Contact & Terms: Send query letter with resume and tear sheets, photostats, photocopies, slides, photographs and technical drawings. Samples returned by SASE. Reports back on future assignment possibilities. Call or write to schedule an appointment to show a portfolio, which should include thumbnails, original/final art, final reproduction/product, color, tear sheets and photographs.
Tips: Prefers "a contemporary design embodying the latest in grahic trends."

ANNA WYMAN DANCE THEATRE, 1705 Marine Dr., West Vancouver, British Columbia V7V 1J5 Canada. (604)926-6041. 18 member modern dance company.
Needs: Works with several freelance artists/year. Uses artists for advertising, brochure and program design, illustration and layout; set and costume design; poster design and illustration; lighting and scenery.
First Contact & Terms: All commercial artists are subject to portfolio review and recommendation/approval by Artistic Director Anna Wyman. Send query letter with brochure, resume, business card, tear sheets, photostats, photocopies, slides and photographs to be kept on file. Samples not kept on file are returned only if requested. Reports within weeks. Portfolio should include thumbnails, roughs, original/final art, final reproduction/product, tear sheets, photostats, photographs and b&w. Call or write for appointment to show portfolio. Pays by the project. Considers complexity of project and available budget when establishing payment.

ZIVILI/TO LIFE! Celebrating Yugoslavia in Dance and Song, 12 Clover Ct., Granville OH 43023. (614)855-7805. Executive Director: Melissa Pintar Obenauf. Professional dance company performing exclusively the dances and songs of Yugoslavia. Consists of 40 dancers, singers and musicians.
Needs: Works with 10 freelance artists/year; needs heaviest in fall and spring. Uses artists for advertising, brochure, program design, illustration and layout; posters and lighting.
First Contact & Terms: Send query letter with resume, business card and samples to be kept on file. Accepts "any type" of samples. Reports within 2 weeks. Negotiates pay. Considers complexity of project, available budget, skill and experience of artist and how work will be used when establishing payment.

Album covers serve a dual purpose. They must communicate the concept of the sound inside, and they must catch the buyer's eye. A wide range of illustration and design is sought by record companies, since each album must project an individual message.

Artwork for album covers must be distinctive, provocative and appropriate to the performer and his music. Rock bands now have distinct visual styles, sharpened by their participation in videos. Gospel and country & western artists favor a more conservative image. Artwork for classical albums tends to be more abstract, capturing the images of noted composers of the past or of historical genres.

Technological advances have increased the artistic needs of record companies. Music is recorded on 12-inch albums, cassettes, compact disks and videos, all of which require different approaches. As music videos continue to grow in popularity, specialists will be needed for many facets of art direction in their production. Computer-enhanced art has revolutionized video artwork, adding the effect of overpainting and the graffiti look.

The industry continues to rely upon freelance artists to provide alternative and original approaches to record sleeve graphics. Successful recording artists often produce their own albums with an independent recording studio and then engage freelance designers to produce jackets. Independent labels are thus a most viable market for freelance artists because they seek fresh talent and experimental designs. Negotiate with the company for a credit line on the album jacket and then, later, a number of samples for your portfolio.

The packaging of albums changed after the industry's financial crisis of the last decade. Costly touches are gone, while marketing has emphasized point-of-purchase displays, posters and videos as collaterals to album art. Artists should study the current relationship of art and music in covers and promotional pieces by visiting record stores.

Creative directors at record companies are looking for a distinctive style that has a strong visual impact. A sample package should include examples that reflect a strong graphic image that literally beckons a viewer. Personal appointments are a good idea, since creative directors prefer to develop a rapport with artists they hire. Skills such as layout and paste-up are useful to fill many production jobs at record companies.

The names and addresses of hundreds of record companies and affiliated services, such as design, artwork and promotions, are listed in the *Songwriter's Market*, *Billboard International Buyer's Guide* and the *Music Industry Directory*.

***ALLEGIANCE RECORDS LTD. AND DISTRIBUTED LABELS**, 7525 Fountain Ave., Los Angeles CA 90046. (213)851-8852. Director Creative Services: Dee Westlund.
First Contact & Terms: Send query letter with brochure showing art style or resume, tear sheets, photostats and photographs. Samples not filed are returned by SASE, only if requested. Reports only if interested. Call to schedule an appointment to show a portfolio, which should include original/final art, final reproduction/product, color, tear sheets, photostats, photographs and b&w.

ART ATTACK RECORDS, INC., Box 31475, Fort Lowell Station, Tucson AZ 85751. (602)881-1212. President: William Cashman. Produces rock and roll, country/western, jazz, pop, and rhythm and blues, and solo artists.
Needs: Produces 4 records/year; works with 4 recording artists/year. Works with 5 visual artists/year. Uses artists for album cover design and illustration; catalog design and layout; advertising design, illustration and layout; and posters.
First Contact & Terms: Works on assignment only. Send query letter with brochure, business card, tear sheets or photographs to be kept on file. Samples not filed are returned by SASE only if requested. Reports only if interested. Write for appointment to show portfolio. Original artwork not returned to art-

ist. Pays by the hour, $10-25 average. Considers complexity of project and available budget when establishing payment. Purchases all rights.

ARZEE RECORD COMPANY and ARCADE RECORD COMPANY, 3010 N. Front St., Philadelphia Pa 19133. (215)426-5682. President: Rex Zario. Produces rock and roll, country/western, and rhythm and blues. Recent releases: "Rock Around the Clock," by James E. Myers; "World Apart," by Ray Whitley; "Why Do I Cry Over You," by Bill Haley.
Needs: Produces 25 records/year. Works with 150 visual artists/year. Uses artists for brochure and catalog design; posters.
First Contact & Terms: Send query letter with brochure and tear sheets to be kept on file. Samples not kept on file are returned by SASE if requested. Reports within 6 weeks. Originals not returned after job's completion. Call for appointment to show portfolio. Buys all rights.

AUDIOFIDELITY ENTERPRISES, INC., 519 Capobianco Plaza, Rahway NJ 07065. (201)388-5000. Art Director: Ron Warwell. Producers of movie and music videos, cinema classics, compact discs, cassettes and records. Music catagories are classical, soul, country western, jazz, pop, educational, rhythm and blues, salsa, ethnic, and specialty, plus more. Recent releases: Charlie Parker's "Bird Symbols," Willie Banks "The House of Prayer," Mantovani's "The Legend."
Needs: Produces 100 records and cassettes/year by 30 groups and 20 soloists. Works with 10 freelance artists/year. "Super pros" only. Uses artists for album cover, catalog and advertising illustration, and posters.
First Contact & Terms: Send query letter with brochure showing art style or resume, tear sheets, photostats, photocopies, slides, photographs and c-prints to be kept on file. Samples not kept on file are returned by SASE if requested. Reports only if interested. Call or write to schedule an appointment to show a portfolio, which should include original/final art, final reproduction/product, tear sheets, photostats and photographs. Pays by the project, $500 maximum. Considers complexity of project, available budget, skill and experience of artist, how work will be used and rights purchased when establishing payment. Negotiates rights purchased.
Tips: "Artists should have a knowledge of *Jazz*. We are specialists in producing the Great American Art form from the days of the Cotton Club to the present in audio and video formats. In the record industry CDs and videos are the hot items. Records are out—CDs in! Videos will service us in all areas of education, trade, sales and of course, entertainment. Designs changes will relate to high tech in the music and entertainment areas."

CLIFF AYERS PRODUCTIONS, 830 Glastonbury Rd. #614, Nashville TN 37217-1708. Producer: Chris Ostermeyer. Produces rock and roll, country/western and pop; group and solo artists. Recent releases: "Talk Back Tremblin' Lips," by Ernie Ashworth; "As Long As We're Together," by John Melnick; and "Nobody's Perfect," by Marilyn Jeffries.
Needs: Produces 75 records/year. Works with 40 visual artists/year. Works on assignment only. Uses artists for album cover design and illustration, brochure design and layout and direct mail packages.
First Contact & Terms: Send resume and tear sheets to be kept on file. Samples are not returned. Reports only if interested. Original art returned at job's completion. Write for appointment to show portfolio. Pays by the project. Considers available budget when establishing payment. Buys first rights.

BLUE ISLAND GRAPHICS, Box 171265, San Diego CA 92117-0975. (619)576-9666. President: Bob Gilbert. Produces rock and roll, country/western and pop. "We are a new company and will be signing new artists this year. Even though we are new, we always are looking for talent."
Needs: Produces 10-15 records/year. Works on assignment only. Uses 3 visual artists/year. Uses artists for album cover, brochure and advertising illustration; brochure, catalog and advertising layout; brochure and advertising design.
First Contact & Terms: Send query letter with resume, photostats, original work and tear sheets to be kept on file. SASE. Samples not kept on file are returned by SASE if requested. Reports within 1 month. Write for appointment to show portfolio. Originals not returned after job's completion. Pays by the hour, $10-15 average. Considers skill and experience of artist when establishing payment. Buys all rights.

BOLIVIA RECORDS CO., Box 1304, 1219 Kerlin Ave., Brewton AL 36427. (205)867-2228. Manager: Roy Edwards. Produces soul, country/western, pop, and rhythm and blues. Recent releases: "Was Young Love Born to Die," by Bobbie Roberson.

❝ *Modern technology is being applied to stagecraft—lasers, computers, etc.* **❞**

Jerry Lapidus, AMAS Repertory Theatre, Inc.

Needs: Produces 20 records/year; 40% of the album covers assigned to freelance designers and illustrators. Assigns 25 freelance jobs/year. Experienced artists only. Uses artists for album cover, brochure, poster, catalog and advertising design; album cover and catalog illustration; brochure and catalog layout; and direct mail packages. Prefers western scenes and color washes of landscapes as themes.
First Contact & Terms: Send query letter with brochure/flyer and samples or actual work. Samples returned by SASE. Works on assignment only. Reports back. Negotiates payment by the project. Buys all rights.
Tips: "Do good work and be dependable."

BOUQUET-ORCHID ENTERPRISES, Box 18284, Shreveport LA 71138. (318)686-7362. President: Bill Bohannon. Produces country, pop and contemporary gospel.
Needs: Produces 10 records/year; 5 of which have cover/jackets designed and illustrated by freelance artists. Uses artists for record album and brochure design.
First Contact & Terms: Send query letter with resume and samples. "I prefer a brief but concise overview of an artist's background and works showing the range of his talents." SASE. Reports within 2 weeks. Negotiates payment.

***BULLDOG RECORDS**, Suite 1301, 50 E. 42nd St., New York NY 10017. (212)687-2299. Contact in writing only: Howard Kruger, Vice President Creative Affairs. Produces rock and roll, classical, disco, soul, country/western, jazz, pop and rhythm and blues. Recent releases: Count Basie, Lena Horne, Vic Damone, Duke Ellington.
Needs: Produces 50 records/year; 100% of the album covers were assigned to freelance designers. Assigns 50 freelance jobs/year. Prefers artists with past work experience. Works on assignment only. Uses artists for album cover, poster, catalog and advertising design.
First Contact & Terms: Send resume, photostats and slides as samples. Samples not returned. Reports in 2 weeks. Original work not returned to artist after job's completion. Negotiates payment by the project. Negotiates rights purchased.

***CANDY RECORDS/HOLLI RECORDS/LIL' POSSUM RECORDS/SWEET TOOTH RECORDS**, 2716 Springlake Ct., Irving TX 75069. (214)790-5172. General Manager: Kenny Wayne. Produces rock and roll, soul, country/western, rhythm and blues, and blues: solo artists. Recent releases: "Bout A Broken Heart," by Michael Jeffrey; "Green Eyes," by Reign; and "Ain't It Good to Be a Winner," by Carter Holcomb; "Borned With The Blues and Raised on Rock N' Roll," by Kenny Wayne and special guest (LP).
Needs: Produces 4-5 records/year; works with 4-5 recording artists/year. Works on assignment only. Uses artists for album cover design and posters.
First Contact & Terms: Send query letter with resume and photographs to be kept on file. Call or write for appointment to show portfolio. Samples not filed are returned by SASE. Reports only if interested. Considers available budget when establishing payment. Purchases all rights.

CASTLE RECORDS, Box 1338, Merchantville NY 08109. President: Rob Russen. Produces rock and roll, disco, soul, country/western, and rhythm and blues. Recent releases: "Ain't No Thing" and "Be Happy," by Phoenix; "Luscious," by Heavy Weather.
Needs: Produces 6-12 records/year. Works with 3-6 freelance commercial artists/year. Uses artists for album cover design and posters.
First Contact & Terms: Send query letter with resume, business card and photographs to be kept on file. Samples not kept on file are returned by SASE if requested. Reports within 10 days. Originals not returned to artist after job's completion. Pay varies. Considers available budget, how work will be used and rights purchased when establishing payment. Buys all rights.

CDE, Box 41551, Atlanta GA 30331. President: Charles Edwards. Produces disco, soul, jazz, and rhythm and blues.
Needs: Produces 6-10 records/year; 100% of the album covers assigned to freelance designers, 100% to freelance illustrators. Assigns varying number of freelance jobs/year. Works on assignment only. Uses artists for album cover, poster, brochure and advertising design; album cover, poster and brochure illustration; and direct mail packages. No set style, "we are open-minded to any style."
First Contact & Terms: Send query letter with brochure showing art style, photostats and original work. Samples not returned. Reports within 2 months. Original work returned after job's completion "by request." Negotiates payment. Buys first rights or negotiates rights purchased.
Tips: "The business needs new and creative people."

CELESTIAL SOUND PRODUCTIONS, 28 South Villas, London NW1 England. 41-01-405-9883. Managing Director: Ron Warren Ganderton. Produces rock and roll, classical, soul, country/western,

jazz, pop, educational, and rhythm and blues; group and solo artists. Recent releases: "Starforce One," "Red Door," and "Once Bitten."
Needs: Works with "many" visual artists/year. Uses artists for album cover design and illustration; advertising and brochure design and illustrations, and posters.
First Contact & Terms: Send query letter with brochure showing art style or resume, business card and photographs to be kept on file "for a reasonable time." Samples not filed are returned by SASE only if requested. Reports within 5 days. Call to schedule an appointment to show a portfolio, which should include roughs, color, photographs and b&w. Original artwork returned after job's completion. Pays by the project. Considers available budget, how work will be used and rights purchased when establishing payment. Buys all rights, reprint rights or negotiates rights purchased.
Tips: "We are searching for revolutionary developments and those who have ideas and inspirations to express in creative progress."

CLARUS MUSIC LTD., 340 Bellevue Ave., Yonkers NY 10703. (914)591-7715. President: Selma Fass. Music publisher and children's record company. Assigns 2-3 jobs/year.
Needs: Produces 2-3 records/year; all of which have cover/jackets designed and illustrated by freelance artists. Works on assignment only. Uses artists for record covers, lettering and catalog design.
First Contact & Terms: Send query letter with resume, slides, tear sheets or photos of work. SASE. Reports within 2-4 weeks. Negotiates pay by the project. Buys all rights.

***CREOLE RECORDS LTD.**, 91-93 High St., Harlesden, London NW10 England. (01)965-9223. General Manager: Steve Tantum. Produces dance, disco, soul and pop; group artists and solo artists. Recent releases: "With You I Could Have It All," by Cissy Houston and Frankie Vaughn L.P.
Needs: Produces 45 records/year. Works with 15 visual artists/year. Uses artists for album cover design and illustration, brochure and catalog illustration, advertising design, illustration and layout, and posters.
First Contact & Terms: Send resume and samples to be kept on file. Accepts any samples. Samples not filed are returned by SAE (nonresidents include IRC). Reports within 2 weeks. Write to schedule an appointment to show a portfolio. Original art sometimes returned to artist. Payment varies. Considers complexity of project, available budget, skill and experience of commercial artist, how work will be used and rights purchased when establishing payment. Rights purchased varies.

CRYIN' IN THE STREETS RECORDS CORPORATION & AFFILIATES, Box 2544, Baton Rouge LA 70821. (504)924-6865. Director: Jimmy Angel/Ebb-Tide. Produces soul, country/western, jazz, pop, and rhythm and blues; group and solo artists. Recent releases: "Let 'Jesus' In," by The Mighty Serenades; "One More Lie," by Betsy Davidson; and "Ease My Mind," by George Perkins.
Needs: Produces fifteen 45's and 6 albums/year; works with 21-25 recording artists/year. Works with 100+ visual artists/year; averages 12 album covers/year. Uses artists for album cover design and illustration, brochure design and illustration, catalog layout, advertising illustration, direct mail packages, posters, video backdrops and production layouts. Acceptable art styles include cartoons and humorous and cartoon-style illustrations.
First Contact & Terms: Works with "professionals" only. Works on assignment only. Send query letter with resume and business card to be kept on file only if accepted. Prefers photocopies, photographs or tear sheets only when requested. Samples not filed are returned only by SASE. Reports within 30 days. Write for appointment to show portfolio. Original art returned to the artist. Pays by the project, $100-1,000 average. Considers complexity of project, available budget, skill and experience of commercial artist, how work will be used, turnaround time and rights purchased when establishing payment. Purchases all rights.

CURTISS UNIVERSAL RECORD MASTERS, Box 4740, Nashville TN 37216. (615)865-4740. Manager: S.D. Neal. Produces soul, country, jazz, folk, pop, rock and roll, and rhythm and blues. Recent releases by Dixie Dee & The Rhythm Rockers, and Ben Williams.
Needs: Produces 6 records/year; some of which have cover/jackets designed and illustrated by freelance artists. Works on assignment only. Uses artists for album cover and poster design.
First Contact & Terms: Send business card and samples to be kept on file. Submit portfolio for review. SASE. Reports within 3 weeks. Originals returned to artist after job's completion. Negotiates pay based on artist involved. Negotiates rights purchased.

***DAN THE MAN RECORDS AND PUBLISHING CO.**, Box 702, Cleveland OH 44107. President: Daniel L. Bischoff. Produces rock and roll, soul, country/western, pop, and rhythm and blues; group and solo artists. Recent releases: 2 singles by Johnny Wright; and 7 singles by Dan the Man.
Needs: Produces 10 records/year; works with 4-6 recording artists/year. Works with 4 visual artists/year. Uses artists for album cover design, direct mail packages and posters.

First Contact & Terms: Send query letter with resume, business card, photographs or photostats to be kept on file. Samples not filed are returned by SASE. Reports only if interested. Original art sometimes returned to the artist. Write for appointment to show portfolio, which should include photographs. Pays by the project. Considers how work will be used when establishing payment. Negotiates rights purchased.

DANCE-A-THON RECORDS, Box 13584, 26 17th St., Atlanta GA 30324. (404)872-6000. Director of Creative Services: P.B. Johnson. Produces rock, disco, bluegrass, country and spoken-word comedy records.
Needs: Buys 5 illustrations/year. Prefers artists with previous experience in the advertising/record medium. Uses artists for designing album jackets and accompanying advertising logos for labels and artists.
First Contact & Terms: Send query letter with resume and samples or previously published work. SASE. Reports within 6-8 weeks. Pays $100-350.

DAWN PRODUCTIONS, Joey Welz Music Complex, 2338 Fruitville Pike, Lancaster PA 17601. President: Joey Welz. Produces country/western, New Wave, rock and pop music albums. Recent releases: "American Made Country Roll," (LP) "No More Nightmares" (single), by Joey Welz (Caprice Records), "Heavy Metal Kids" and "Return of Haley's Comet" by Joey Weltz and the Great Train Robbery.
Needs: Produces 2 LPs and five 45s/year. Works with 3 groups and 3 soloists. Works with 2 visual artists/ year. Buys 1-3 illustrations/year. "Artists must be ready to go." Uses artists for album cover designs and illustrations. Especially needs stock jackets.
First Contact & Terms: Send brochure showing art style or tear sheets and photocopies. SASE. Reports only if interested. To show a portfolio, mail appropriate materials, which should include tear sheets, photostats and photographs. Considers available budget, rights purchased and how work will be used when establishing payment; "percentage paid by label releasing product."
Tips: "Be creative and easy to work with on terms. Four-color is too expensive. We are looking for more economical covers. In the field, we see a lot of picture discs and stock backgrounds with overlay of photos."

DELMARK RECORDS, 4243 N. Lincoln, Chicago IL 60618. (312)528-8834. Art Director: Bob Koester. Produces blues and jazz. Recent releases: "The Blues World of Little Walter";"North South" by Jimmy Johnson; and "Reality," by Frank Walton.
Needs: Chicago area artists only. Produces 5-10 records/year; all of which have cover/jackets designed and illustrated by freelance artists. Works on assignment only. "Our records do not sell like hits, but remain in our catalog and active in the market for many years. We are therefore more interested in clean designs that do not date rather than in flashy covers. Most of the artists who work for us are interested in the music we issue: jazz and blues. We are especially interested in artists who can arrive at interesting multicolor designs based on black and white photographs."
First Contact & Terms: Arrange interview to show portfolio (mixture of original and printed art). Samples returned by SASE. Reports back on future assignment possibilities. Send resume, tear sheet and samples to be kept on file for future assignments. Pays $50-250.

DESTINY RECORDS, Destiny Recording Studio, 31 Nassau Ave., Wilmington MA 01887. Contact: Larry Feeney. Produces rock and roll, disco, soul, country/western, jazz, folk, pop, and rhythm and blues; group and solo artists. Recent releases: "Decision," by Rude Awakening; "Prisoners," by Tinted Glass; "When You Thought I Had It," by True Desire; "Ritzi Anna," by Myron Skau.
Needs: Produces 6 records/year. Works with 3 visual artists/year. Uses artists for album cover design and illustration; brochure design, direct mail packages, advertising design and illustration and posters. "We're interested in futuristic forms." Especially needs "45 sleeves."
First Contact & Terms: Send query letter with nonreturnable color samples to be kept on file. Samples not filed are not returned. Write for appointment to show portfolio; do not call. Portfolio should include roughs, original/final art, color and photographs. Original art sometimes returned to the artist. Payment varies.

***DRIFTWOOD RECORDS**, Box 22988, Nashville TN 37202. Contact: Peter Kobal. Produces country/ western. Recent releases: "Careless Hands" by Margie L'Lane.
Needs: Produces 2 records/year. Works with 2 visual artists/year. Works on assignment only. Uses artists for album cover, brochure and advertising design and illustration; direct mail packages.
First Contact & Terms: Send query letter with brochure showing art style. Samples not filed are returned by SASE. Reports within 1 month. Write to schedule an appointment to show a portfolio, which should include original/final art. Pays for design by the project, $600-1,000 average. Considers available budget when establishing payment. Buys all rights.

***DUPUY RECORDS/PRODUCTIONS/PUBLISHING, INC.**, Suite 200, 10960 Ventura Blvd., Studio City CA 91604. Contact: Director. Produces rock and roll, soul, jazz, pop, rhythm and blues; group and solo artists. Recent releases: "Show Me Thy Way," "Livin' For Your Love," "Be There Tonight" and "She's My Lady," by Gordon Gilman.
Needs: Produces 3 or more records/year. Works with 6 visual artists/year. Local artists only with 5 years' experience or more. Works on assignment only. Uses artists for album cover, brochure, catalog and advertising design and illustration; posters.
First Contact & Terms: Send query letter with brochure showing art style. Samples not filed are returned by SASE. Reports only if interested. Call or write to schedule an appointment to show a portfolio, which should include roughs, original/final art, final reproduction/product, color, tear sheets, photostats, photographs and b&w. Pays by the project. Considers skill and experience of artist when establishing payment.

E.L.J. RECORD CO., 1344 Waldron, St. Louis MO 63130. (314)863-3605. President: Eddie Johnson. Produces rhythm and blues, rock and roll, jazz and pop music. Recent releases: "Morning Star," by Jimmy Jones; "Rock House Annie," by Ann Richardson; "Strange Feeling," by Eddie Johnson Trio; and "Wish I Was an Itty Bitty Girl," by the M&M Girls.
Needs: Produces 10 records/year by 4 groups and 4 soloists; all of which have cover/jackets designed and illustrated by freelance artists.
First Contact & Terms: Send query and samples. SASE. Reports within 6 weeks. To show a portfolio, mail appropriate materials, which should include photographs and tear sheets. Negotiates pay based on amount of creativity required and rights purchased.
Tips: "Send prices and sample designs of some of my material."

***EAGLE RECORDS**, Box 1027, Hermosa Beach CA 90254. President: Guthrie Thomas. Produces rock and roll, classical, country/western, jazz, folk, pop, rhythm and blues; group and solo artists. Recent releases include "Josh White" by Josh White; "John Nilsen" by John Nilsen; "Bully Boy" by Gene Atkins.
Needs: Produces 40 records/year; works with 20 groups and 20 soloists. Works with 6 visual artists/year. Uses artists for album cover design and illustration, and posters.
First Contact & Terms: Send query letter with brochure showing art style or tear sheets, slides and photographs. Samples not filed are not returned if by SASE. Reports within 60 days. To show a portfolio, mail appropriate materials, which should include original/final art, photographs and b&w. Pays by the project, $200 average. Considers how work will be used and rights purchased when establishing payment. Buys one-time rights or reprint rights.
Tips: "We only use absolute grade triple AAA quality color and b&w cover shots for album covers.

EPOCH UNIVERSAL PUBLICATIONS/NORTH AMERICAN LITURGY RESOURCES, 10802 N. 23rd Ave., Phoenix AZ 85029. (602)864-1980. Vice President: David Serey. Produces contemporary Christian inspirational, liturgical music. Recent releases: "The Steadfast Love" by St. Louis Jesuits; "O Joyful Light," by Fr. Michael Joncas.
Needs: Produces 10-20 records/year; 100% of the album covers were assigned to freelance designers. Works with 2-3 artists/year. Uses artists for album cover design and illustration; brochure, catalog and advertising design, illustration and layout; direct mail packages and posters. Prefers inspirational, symbolic themes, "in any medium that works." Prefers local artists with 3 or more years' experience, capable of quality work and willing to negotiate.
First Contact & Terms: Send query letter with brochure/flyer or resume and 10 photostats or slides to be kept on file. Samples not kept on file are returned by SASE. Reports only if interested. Original work not returned to artist after job's completion. Write for appointment to show portfolio. Negotiates payment by the project, $10-2,000 average. Rights purchased vary, depending on project; "we like to buy all rights."
Tips: "Phone calls are of little value. However, all mail is answered and all submissions are screened very carefully. Untried artists/designers or just beginning artists must be willing to do some work for the promotional aspect—giving exposure to their work."

EXECUTIVE RECORDS, 11 Shady Oak Trail, Charlotte NC 28210. (704)554-1162. Executive Director: Butch Kelly. Produces rock and roll, disco, soul, country/western, jazz, classical, gospel, pop, and rhythm and blues; group and solo artists. Recent releases include "Super Star" and "I Just Want Somebody to Love" by L.A. Star and "Show Me Love" by Jay Wylie.
Needs: Produces 9 records/year by 4 groups and 5 soloists. Works with 3 groups and 3 solo recording artists/year. Works with 2 visual artists/year. Seeks artists with 3 years' experience. Works on assignment only. Uses artists for album cover design, advertising design and layout, and direct mail packages.
First Contact & Terms: Send query letter with brochure, resume and photographs to be kept on file.

Samples not filed returned by SASE. Reports back only if interested. Original art sometimes returned to the artist. To show a portfolio, mail original/final art, color and photographs with SASE. Pays by the project, $25-100 average. Considers available budget, and skill and experience of commercial artist when establishing payment. Buys all rights.
Tips: "Just be original. We like to see more color. It's affected my use in a more positive way."

FACTORY BEAT RECORDS, INC., 521 5th Ave., New York NY 10175. Produces disco, pop, contemporary, and rhythm and blues. Recent releases: "Dance It Off" and "I Love Your Beat," by Rena; "Let's Slip Away" and "Everybody's Doin' It," by Charles T. Hudson.
Needs: Produces 2 albums/year.
First Contact & Terms: Send query letter with brochure and original work. to be kept on file. Samples not kept on file are returned by SASE. Reports only if interested. Originals not returned to artist after job's completion. Considers available budget when establishing payment. Negotiates rights purchased.

FAMOUS DOOR RECORDS, 141-10 Holly Ave., Flushing NY 11355. (718)463-6281. Contact: Harry Lim. Produces jazz. Recent releases: "More Miles, More Standards" by the Butch Miles Sextet; "L.A. After Dark" by the Ross Tompkins Quartet and "The Buenos Aires-New York Swing Connection" by the Jorge Anders All Star Septet.
Needs: Produces 8 records/year. Works with freelancers "only when regular artist is not available." Prefers local artists. Works on assignment only. Uses artists for album cover design.
First Contact & Terms: Send business card to be kept on file. Reports within 2 weeks. Originals not returned to artist after job's completion. Pays by the project, $150 minimum. Considers available budget when establishing payment. Buys all rights.

FARR MUSIC AND RECORDS, Box 1098, Somerville NJ 08876. Contact: Candace Campbell. Produces rock and roll, disco, soul, country/western, folk and pop; group and solo artists.
Needs: Produces 12 records/year by 8 groups and 4 soloists. Works with 40 visual artists/year. Uses artists for album cover design and illustration, brochure and catalog design, advertising design and illustration, and posters.
First Contact & Terms: Send query letter with resume, tear sheets, photostats, photocopies, slides and photographs to be kept on file. Samples not filed are returned by SASE. Reports within 3 weeks. To show a portfolio, mail appropriate materials, which should include roughs, final reproduction/product, color and photographs. Original art returned to the artist. Buys first rights or all rights.

GCS RECORDS, Suite 206, 1508 Harlem, Memphis TN 38114. (901)274-2726. Art Director: Reggie Ekridge. Produces disco, soul, pop, gospel, and rhythm and blues; group and solo artists. Recent releases: "Early Morning Man," by Cheryl Fox; "God is Coming Soon" by Stars of Nightingales.
Needs: Produces 20 records/year. Works with 3 visual artists/year. Prefers local artists. Uses artists for album cover design and illustration; brochure and advertising design and illustration; catalog design and layout; and direct mail packages. Especially needs album covers, catalog and brochure design.
First Contact & Terms: Send query letter with brochure showing art style, resume, tear sheets, photostats, photocopies and photographs to be kept on file. Samples not filed are returned by SASE only if requested. Reports only if interested. To show a portfolio, mail final reproduction/product, color, tear sheets, photostats and b&w. Payment negotiated/job. Considers complexity of project, available budget, how work will be used and rights purchased when establishing payment. Negotiates rights purchased.

***GRANDVILE RECORD CORP.**, Box 11960, Chicago IL 60611. Art Director: Danielle Render.
Needs: Works with 15 freelance visual artists/year. Uses visual artists for album jackets and original logo designs.
First Contact & Terms: Send query letter with resume, tear sheets, photostats and photocopies. Samples not filed are returned by SASE. Does not report back. To show a portfolio, mail roughs, original/final art, photostats, photographs and b&w. Pays for design by the project, $150-250. Pays for illustration by the project, $100-200. Considers complexity of project, client's budget and rights purchased when establishing payment. Negotiates rights purchased.

HARD HAT RECORDS AND CASSETTE TAPES, 519 N. Halifax Ave., Daytona Beach FL 32018. (904)252-0381. Vice President, Sales/Promotion: Bobby Lee. Produces rock and roll, country/western, folk and educational; group and solo artists. Publishes high school/college marching band arrangements. Recent releases: "Sand in my Shoes & V-A-C-A-T-I-O-N" by the Hard Hatters; "Just a Piece of Paper," Country Blues," Can't Get Over Lovin' You," and "Only Lies" by the Blue Bandana Country Band.
Needs: Produces 12-30 records/year. Works with 2-3 visual artists/year. Works on assignment only.

Uses artists for album cover design and illustration, advertising design and sheet music covers.
First Contact & Terms: Send query letter with brochure to be kept on file one year. Samples not filed are returned by SASE. Reports within 2 weeks. Write for appointment to show portfolio. Pays by the project. Considers complexity of project, available budget, skill and experience of artist, how work will be used, turnaround time and rights purchased when establishing payment. Purchases all rights.
Tips: "Video is playing a bigger part in the art market for record and tape companies. The market for this medium of musical entertainment has its own styles and needs."

HOLLYROCK RECORDS, Suite 170, 14116 E. Whittier Blvd., Whither CA 90602. A&R Directors: Dave Paton, Bob Brown. Produces country/western, rock, progressive rock, folk, pop, and rhythm and blues; group and solo artists, also comedy acts.
Needs: Produces 10 records/year. Works with 4 visual artists/year.
First Contact & Terms: Send slides, photostats, photographs, photocopies or tear sheets to be kept on file. Write for appointment to show portfolio. Reports within 4 weeks. Original art sometimes returned to the artist. Pay is negotiable. Considers complexity of project, available budget, skill and experience of artist, how work will be used, turnaround time and rights purchased when establishing payment. Buys first rights or all rights.

***INTERMODAL PRODUCTIONS**, Box 2199, Vancouver, British Columbia, V6B 3V7 Canada. (604)669-4399. President: John Rodney. Produces country/western, jazz, pop, and classical. Recent releases: "Can't Hear for Listening," by Elmer Gill and Lockjaw Davis; "Moonlight Sonata," by Robert Silverman.
Needs: Produces 6-8 records/year. Works with 2-3 freelance artists/year. Works on assignment only. Uses artists for album cover design and posters.
First Contact & Terms: Send query leter with photostats and photographs to be kept on file. Samples not kept on file returned by SASE. Reports only if interested. Originals not returned to artist after job's completion. Pays by the project, $150 minimum. Considers complexity of project, available budget and rights purchased when establishing payment. Buys all rights.

***J & J MUSICAL ENTERPRISES**, Suite 1103, 150 Fifth Ave., New York NY 10011. General Manager: Jeneane Claps.
Needs: Uses visual artists for record jackets/inserts.
First Contact & Terms: Send query letter with resume and tear sheets. Samples not filed are returned by SASE. Reports within 6 weeks. To show a portfolio, mail color, tear sheets and final reproduction/product. Pays for design by the project, $200 minimum. Pays for illustration by the project, $500 minimum. Considers complexity of project, how work will be used and rights purchased when establishing payment. Buys all rights.
Tips: "Be as neat and organized as possible."

***DICK JAMES ORGANIZATION**,1040 North Las Palmas Ave., Los Angeles CA 90038. (213)469-1940. General Manager: Arthur Braun. Produces rock and roll, country/western, pop and a latin motion picture. Recent releases: "Where I Belong," by The Beach Boys; music from the NBC-TV mini-series *Peter the Great*.

KIDERIAN RECORDS PRODUCTS, 4926 W. Gunnison, Chicago IL 60630. (312)764-1144. President: Raymond Peck. Produces rock and roll, classical, disco, soul, country/western, jazz, folk, pop, educational, rhythm and blues, and New Wave; group and solo artists. Recent releases: "Boyz," by Boy; "Creme Soda," by Creme Soda; and "Kiderian Sampler 2."
Needs: Produces 35-40 records/year; 100% of the album covers were assigned to freelance designers, 100% to freelance illustrators. Works with 8-14 visual artists/year. Half of all jobs/year require freelance artists. Works on assignment only. Uses artists for album cover design and illustration; posters; brochure design, illustration and layout; catalog design, illustration and layout; advertising design, illustration and layout; and direct mail packages. Accepts all styles.
First Contact & Terms: Send query letter with resume, photographs and slides to be kept on file. Samples not filed are returned by SASE. Original work returned to artist after job's completion. Pays by the project, $200-$450 average. Purchases all rights.

KIMBO EDUCATIONAL, 10 N. 3rd Ave., Long Branch NJ 07740. Production Coordinators: Amy Laufer and James Kimble. Educational record/cassette company. Produces 8 records and cassettes/year for schools, teacher supply stores and parents. Contents primarily early childhood physical fitness although other materials are produced for all ages.
Needs: Works with 3 freelance artists/year. Local artists only. Works on assignment only. Uses artists for ads, catalog design, album covers and flyer designs. Artist must have experience in the preparation of album jackets.

Close-up

Tom Nikosey
Typographer, album cover artist
Los Angeles, California

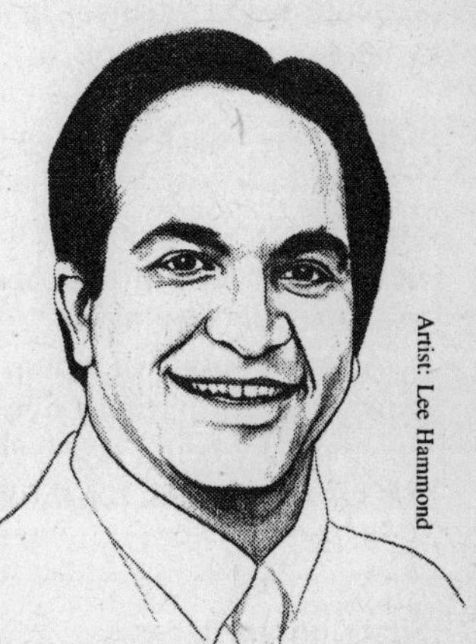

Tom Nikosey is a man who likes problems. "I like to be presented with a problem and solve it. I enjoy challenges."

That's one of the reasons Tom Nikosey is listed among America's top typographers. His hand-lettering talents have enabled him to meet the challenge of creating album covers for such a diversity of recording artists as Eric Clapton, Kenny Rogers, the Bee Gees, the Commodores and Cheech & Chong.

Nikosey focused on a love for lettering in art courses and specialized in typography at Pratt Institute in New York, his hometown. After graduation in 1972 he moved to California, where he produced paste-up and mechanicals for the *Los Angeles Free Press* and then served as assistant art director for an advertising agency. It was at this time that he began designing album covers. "Album art afforded me the chance to spread my wings, especially in logotype design. The parameters are wide."

After a decision to freelance, Tom learned that contacting record companies is similar to arranging appointments with advertising agencies; both want to see printed samples preceding an appointment. Black-and-white samples, even photocopies, are acceptable, but color creates a more professional package and is worth the investment.

"The idea of album art," Nikosey says, "is to create a basically two-dimensional design that reflects the sound inside." He suggests visiting record stores to study album covers and to cull the overall feeling projected by a record company. After choosing one or more companies whose styles mesh with yours, send five or ten printed pieces which reflect your current work. Follow up with a call to the creative director and establish a rapport with him. It is es-

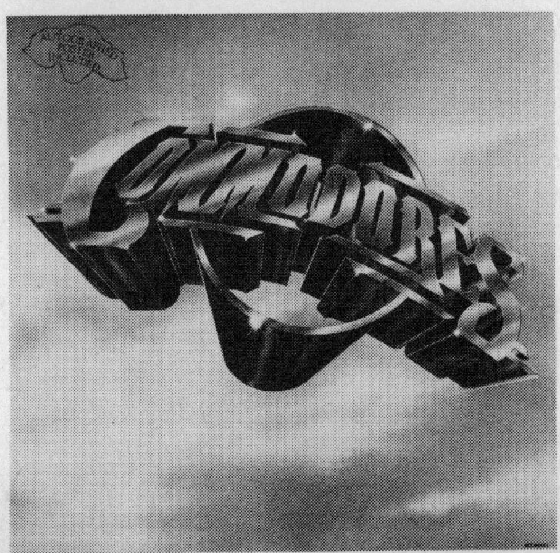

After establishing contacts throughout the record industry, Tom Nikosey has illustrated album covers for major stars, such as The Commodores, Eric Clapton, Kenny Rogers and the Bee Gees.

sential to know the needs of the company and, once you have an assignment, to clearly understand what each project entails.

To keep abreast of the industry, Nikosey subscribes not only to the magazines of the industry, such as *Billboard* and *Rolling Stone*, but also to an international array of publications in order to absorb nuances in lifestyle and aesthetics. "You have to stay fresh and excited. Keep your eyes and ears open."

In the advanced lettering courses that he teaches at the Art Center College of Design in Pasadena, the master typographer stresses there are no shortcuts in establishing a career. "There's no way around the right way." Fortified with solid drawing skills and an eye for design, the aspiring artist must "get it together emotionally, artistically and financially" in order to succeed. Through his years of experience he has learned a basic truth: "You have to be organized to stay alive. You have to treat it like a business."

As to the future of album art, Nikosey says, "The sky's the limit." He feels the industry is now "on the cutting edge of experiment," ripe for a revolutionary change. The energy generated by being involved in this artistic environment is reflected in Nikosey's enthusiasm for his profession. "I thrive on the challenges here. I love what I do."

First Contact & Terms: "It is very hard to do this type of material via mail." Write or call for appointment to show portfolio. Prefers photographs or actual samples of past work. Reports only if interested. Pays by the project. Album cover minimum $100; flyers, etc. lower minimum. Considers complexity of project and budget when establishing payment. Buys all rights.
Tips: "The jobs at Kimbo vary tremendously. We are an educational record company that produces material from infant level to senior citizen level. Sometimes we need cute 'kid-like' illustrations and sometimes graphic design will suffice. A person expereinced in preparing an album cover would certainly have an edge."

***KINGSWAY PUBLICATIONS LIMITED, Music Division**, Lottbridge Drove, Eastbourne, E. Sussex BN236NT England. 44-03-232-7454. Music Director: G. Shearn. Produces Christian music. Recent releases: "Songs of Fellowship" by Congregational Worship; "Waiting For Summer" by Phil & John; and "Make Way" by Graham Kendrick.
Needs: Produces 35 records by 12 groups and 12 soloists/year. Works with 3 freelance artists/year. Local artists only, "ideally with Christian background." Works on assignment only. Uses artists for album cover design and illustration.
First Contact & Terms: Send query letter with samples on request. Reports within 3 weeks. No originals returned to artist after job's completion. Pays by the project, $500 average. Considers complexity of project, available budget and how work will be used when establishing payment. Buys all rights.

SID KLEINER MUSIC ENTERPRISES, 3701 25th Ave. SW, Naples FL 33964. Managing Director: Sid Kleiner. Produces folk, rock, jazz, middle of the road and country recordings, and nutritional, organic gardening and health audiovisuals. Recent releases: "In A Country Mood" by Sid Kleiner. Query. SASE. Reports within 4 weeks. Material copyrighted.
Needs: Uses artists for album design, type specifying and audiovisuals. Pays $50 minimum/job.

LEMATT MUSIC LTD./Pogo Records Ltd./Swoop Records/Grenouille Records/Zarg Records-Check Records/Lee Music Ltd., ℅ Stewart House, Hill Bottom Rd., Sands, IND, EST, Highwycombe, Buckinghamshire, 0494-36301/36401 England. Manager: Director Ron Lee. Produces rock and roll, disco, country/western, pop, and rhythm and blues; group and solo artists. Recent releases "American Girl" by Hush; "Children Of The Night" by Nightmare; and "Phobias" by Orphan.
Needs: Produces 25 records/year; works with 12 groups and 6 soloists/year. Works with 1-2 visual artists/year. Works on assignment only. Uses a few cartoons and humorous and cartoon-style illustrations where applicable. Uses artists for album cover design and illustration; advertising design, illustration and layout; and posters.
First Contact & Terms: Send query letter with brochure, resume, business card, slides, photographs and videos to be kept on file. Samples not filed are returned by SASE (nonresidents send IRCs). Reports within 3 weeks. To show a portfolio, mail appropriate materials, which should include original/final art, final reproduction/product and photographs. Original artwork sometimes returned to artist. Considers complexity of project, available budget, skill and experience of artist, how work will be used and turnaround time when establishing payment.

LOCONTO PRODUCTIONS, 7766 N.W. 44th St., Sunrise FL 33321. (305)741-7766. Executive Vice President: Phyllis Finney Loconto. Produces rock and roll, classical, disco, soul, country/western, jazz, folk, pop, educational, and rhythm and blues; group and solo artists. Recent releases: "Barber Shop Quartet," by Suntones; "Drama/Keyboard," by Irving Fields; and "Jamming-Country," by Bascom "Bill" Dillon.
Needs: Works with 10 visual artists/year. Works on assignment only. Uses artists for album cover design and illustration; brochure, catalog and advertising design, illustration and layout; direct mail packages; and posters.
First Contact & Terms: Send business card. Pays by the project. Considers available budget when establishing payment. Negotiates rights purchased.

LONGHORN RECORDS, Box 1995, Studio City CA 91604. (213)656-0574. Contact: Harvey Appell. Produces country/western and folk records by solo and group artists. Recent releases: "Country Music High" by River Road Boy; "Sheets of Fire" by Bobby Bonchers; and "Take Me Home" by the Mulligans.
Needs: Produces 12 records/year. Works with 2-3 visual artists/year. Works on assignment only. Uses artists for album cover design and illustration, brochure illustration, catalog design, illustration and layout and posters.
First Contact & Terms: Send query letter with brochure showing art style or slides, photostats, photographs, photocopies or tear sheets. Call for appointment to show portfolio. Samples not filed are returned by SASE. Reports only if interested. To show a portfolio, mail appropriate materials or write to schedule an appointment; portfolio should include original/final art, final reproduction/product, photographs and b&w. Pays by the project. Considers available budget when establishing payment. Purchases all rights.

L'ORIENT PRODUCTIONS/WOULDN SHOE RECORDS, Box H, Harvard MA 01451. (617)456-8111. Art Director: Anne-Marie Alden. Chief Executive Officer: Stephen Bond Garvan. Produces rock and roll, soul, country/western and pop. Recent releases: "Time For Us," by Dean Adrien; "Inside the Storm," by New Moon; and "Your Time Too," by Linda Blaze; and "Lovers in Trouble" by Secrets.
Needs: Produces 3-6 records/year; works with 3-6 recording artists/year. Works with 3-4 visual artists/year. Works on assignment only. Uses artists for album cover design and illustration, advertising design and illustration, and posters.
First Contact & Terms: Send query letter with brochure, resume, slides, photostats, photographs or tear sheets. Samples not filed are returned by SASE. Reports only if interested. Original art sometimes returned to artist. Pays by the project, $50 minimum. Considers complexity of project, available budget, how work will be used, turnaround time and rights purchased when establishing payment. Buys all rights.

LUCIFER RECORDS, INC., Box 263, Brigantine NJ 08203. (609)266-2623. President: Ron Luciano. Produces pop, disco, and rock and roll.
Needs: Produces 2-12 records/year. Experienced artists only. Works on assignment only. Uses artists for album cover design and illustration; brochure design, illustration and layout; advertising layout; and posters.
First Contact & Terms: Send query letter with brochure, resume, business card, slides or photographs; SASE. Reports only if interested. Original art sometimes returned to artist. Considers budget, how work will be used, rights purchased and the assignment when establishing payment. Negotiates pay and rights purchased.

LEE MAGID, % GRASS ROOTS PRODUTIONS, Box 532, Malibu CA 90265. (213)858-7282. President: Lee Magid. Produces jazz, rock, country, blues, instrumental, gospel, classical, disco, folk, educational, pop and reggae; group and solo artists. Recent releases: "Hear Me Now," and "Again," by Ernie Andrews; "On The Streets Again," and "Live," by Rags Waldorf; and "Have Horns, Will Travel," by Russ Gary Big Band Express. Assigns 15 jobs/year.
Needs: Produces 15-20 records/year; works with 5 artists/year. Local artists only. Works on assignment only. Uses artists for album design and illustration; brochure design, illustration and layout; and advertising illustration. Sometimes uses cartoons and humorous and cartoon-style illustrations depending on project.
First Contact & Terms: Send query letter with resume, slides, photostats, photographs, photocopies or tear sheets to be kept on file. SASE. Samples not filed are returned by SASE. Reports only if interested. Write for appointment to show portfolio. Pays by the project. Considers available budget when establishing payment. Buys all rights.
Tips: "It's important for the artist to work closely with the producer, to coincide the feeling of the album, rather than throwing a piece of art against the wrong sound." Artists shouldn't "get overly progressive. 'Commercial' is the name of the game."

MAJEGA RECORDS/PRODUCTIONS, 240 E. Radcliffe Dr., Claremont CA 91711. (714)624-0677. President: Gary K. Buckley. Produces gospel, country and pop records, audiovisual presentations; i.e., filmstrips, slide/sound sync and multimedia programs. Recent releases: "Country Love," by Jerry Roark; "Steppin Out," by The Gospelmen; and "Sending a Copy Home," by Jody Barry.
Needs: Produces about 6 records/year; 4 of which have cover/jackets designed and illustrated by freelance artists. Works on assignment only. Uses artists for album covers, ad illustrations, logo designs, cartoons, charts & graphs and other promotional materials.
First Contact & Terms: Send query letter with resume, brochure, flyer and samples (2-3 tear sheets of varied styles if possible) to be kept on file for future assignments. "Samples provided should be relevant to type of work requested." Samples returned by SASE. Reports back on future assignment possibilities. Negotiates pay according to complexity of project and available budget.
Tips: "Look at existing covers and be conscious of the style of music inside. This will illustrate what the industry is accepting and give the artist a solid base to start creating from."

MESA RECORDS, 1204 Elmwood, Nashville TN 37212. (615)269-0593. General Manager: Taylor Sparks. Produces country/western. Recent releases: "Up On Your Love," and "Come In Planet Earth," by Karen Taylor-Good; "Honky Tonk Tonight" by Colt Daniels.
Needs: Produces 2 albums/year. Works with 2 visual artists/year. Uses artists for album cover design and illustration.
First Contact & Terms: Send query letter with resume to be kept on file. Reports only if interested. Original art not returned to artist. Negotiates payment. Considers complexity of project, available budget and rights purchased when establishing payment. Negotiates rights purchased.

MIRROR RECORDS INC; HOUSE OF GUITARS BLVD., 645 Titus Ave., Rochester NY 14617. (716)544-3500. Art Director: Armand Schaubroeck. Produces rock and roll, Heavy Metal, middle of the road and New Wave music. Recent releases: "Over the Rainbow," by Don Potter; "Here Are the Chesterfield Kings" and "I Shot My Guardian Angel," by Armand Schaubroeck Steals; "The Village Churchmice"; and "The Chesterfield'; "Stop," by the Kings.
Needs: Produces 4 records/year; all of which have cover/jackets designed and illustrated by freelance artists. Uses artists for catalogs, album covers, inner sleeves and advertising designs. "Always looking for new talent."
First Contact & Terms: Send query letter with brochure showing art style and samples. SASE. Reports within 1 month. Negotiates pay based on amount of creativity required, artist's previous experience, amount of time and artist expense.

***MONTICANA RECORDS**, Box 702, Snowdon Station, Montreal, Quebec H3X 3X8 Canada. General Manager: D. Leonard. Produces rock and roll, disco, soul, country/western, pop, educational and rhythm and blues.
Needs: Works with 4 freelance artists/year. Uses artists for album cover, brochure, catalog, advertising design; album cover, catalog, advertising illustration; brochure, catalog, advertising layout; and posters.
First Contact & Terms: Send query letter with brochure, resume, business card, photostats, slides, photographs and tear sheets. Samples not returned. Reports only if interested. Originals not returned to artist after job's completion. Pays by the hour, $5-20 average; by the project, $75-300 average. Considers complexity of project, available budget and skill and experience of artist when establishing payment. Buys all rights.

MOTOWN RECORD CORP., Graphics Dept., 16th Floor, 6255 Sunset Blvd., Los Angeles CA 90028. (213)468-3500. Art Director: Johnny Lee. Produces rock and roll, soul, pop, and rhythm and blues. Recent releases: "Say You, Say Me," by Lionel Richie; "In Square Circle," by Stevie Wonder; "Smoke Signal," by Smokey Robinson; and "Skin on Skin," by Vanity.
Needs: Produces 50 records/year. Works with 30 freelance artists/year. Works on assignment. Uses artists for album cover, catalog and advertising design and illustration; catalog and advertising layout and posters.
First Contact & Terms: Send brochure, slides, photographs and tear sheets to be kept on file; write for appointment to show portfolio. Samples not kept on file returned by SASE. Reports only if interested. Originals returned after job's completion. Pay depends on the project. Considers complexity of project, available budget and how work will be used when establishing payment. Buys one-time rights.

***MUSIC AND ARTS PROGRAMS OF AMERICA, INC.**, Box 771, Berkeley CA 94701. (415)525-4583. Associate Producer: Mark Freeman. Estab. 1985. Record publisher. Produces record jacket graphics, catalog design and layout for wholesale, retail and mail order purchasers.
First Contact & Terms: Send resume and photocopies. Samples not filed are returned by SASE. Re-

ports only if interested. Call or write to schedule an appointment to show a portfolio, which should include original/final art and final reproduction/product. Pays for design by the hour, $15 minimum. Pays for illustrations by the hour, $15 minimum. Considers complexity of project, client's budget and skill and experience of artist when establishing payment.
Tips: "This is a small nonprofit organization. We can offer national and international exposure plus an environment open to innovation and creativity. It is a good place for a talented but lesser-known artist to create published work."

MUSI-MATION, 135 E. Muller Rd., East Peoria IL 61611. (309)699-4000. General Manager: Martin Mitchell. Produces country/western, easy listening and religious; solo artists. Recent releases: "Day After Never" and "Happy Anniversary" by Wade Ray.
Needs: Produces 8-10 records/year; works with 8-10 recording artists/year. Works with 2 visual artists/year. Works on assignment only. Uses artists for album cover design and illustration, brochure illustration and posters.
First Contact & Terms: Send query letter with samples to be kept on file. Accepts any samples "which the artist feels displays his work best." Prefers to keep all samples. Reports within 2 weeks. Original art returned to artist. To show a portfolio, mail appropriate materials, which should include thumbnails, roughs, original/final art, final reproduction/product, color, tear sheets, photostats, photographs or b&w. Pay is negotiable. Artist submits proposal stating how he wants to work. Negotiates rights purchased.

MYSTIC OAK RECORDS, 1727 Elm St., Bethlehem PA 18017. (215)865-1083. Project Coordinator: Bill Byron. Produces rock and roll, classical, folk, pop, educational, New Wave and experimental. Recent releases: "Dreams," by Office Toys; "I Don't Lie," by the Polygraphs; and "Believe It Or Not," by the Trendsetters.
Needs: Produces 15-25 records/year by 4 groups and 3 soloists. Works with 6-12 freelance artists/year. Uses artists for album cover, brochure, and advertising design and illustration; and posters.
First Contact & Terms: Send query letter with resume, slides, photographs and tear sheets to be kept on file. Prefers original work as samples. Samples not kept on file are returned by SASE. Reports only if interested. Returns original artwork after job's completion if requested. To show a portfolio, mail appropriate materials, which should include final reproduction/product, color, tear sheets and photographs. Pays by the project, $100-1,200 average. Considers complexity of project, available budget and how work will be used when establishing payment. Negotiates rights purchased.
Tips: Especially looks for a "developed style that can be used throughout an artist's career to identify and separate his work from others. Present a professional package." In the field, there is "more use of freelancers to minimize costs. Art is becoming more experimental and animated."

NEAT RECORDS (D.W.E. LTD.), 71 High St. E, Wallsend NE28 7RJ England. A&R Director: Diane Davison. Produces rock and roll, and pop. Recent releases: "All For One," by Raven; and "At War with Satan," by Venom.
Needs: Produces 10 records/year. Works with 2-3 visual artists/year. Uses artists for album cover design and illustration, and posters.
First Contact & Terms: Send query letter with samples to be kept on file. Prefers examples of printed sleeves, not originals, as samples. Samples not kept on file are not returned. Reports only if interested. No originals returned to artist after job's completion. Negotiates fees. Considers complexity of project when establishing payment. Negotiates rights purchased.

NERVOUS RECORDS, 4/36 Dabbs Hill Ln., Northolt, Middlesex England. 44-01-422-3462. Contact: R. Williams. Produces rock and roll, and rockabilly. Recent releases: "Roll Over," by Ronnie & the Jitters; "At My Front Door," by Freddy Frogs; and "Do You Feel Restless," by Restless.
Needs: Produces 7 albums/year; works with 7 groups and soloists/year. Works with 3-4 visual artists/year. Uses artists for album cover design, brochure design, catalog design and advertising design.
First Contact & Terms: Send query letter with tear sheets; material may be kept on file. Write for appointment to show portfolio. Samples not filed are returned by SAE (nonresidents include IRC). Reports only if interested. Original art returned to the artist. Pays by the project, $50-200 average. Considers available budget and how work will be used when establishing payment. Buys first rights.
Tips: "We have noticed more use of imagery and caricatures in our field so fewer actual photographs used."

NEW ENGLAND ("HANK THE DRIFTER") HITS, Drawer 520, Stafford TX 77477. Produces country and western cassettes, albums, 45s and 8-track tapes.
Needs: Uses artists for record album and jacket design. Considers skill and experience of artist when establishing payment. Send postage for reply and return of material.

***NISE PRODUCTIONS INC.**, 413 Cooper St., Camden NJ 08102. (609)963-3190. General Manager: Sandy Perchetti. Head of A&R: Dan McKeown. Produces rock and roll, disco, soul, country/western, educational, and rhythm and blues; group and solo artists. A&R; also Production Offices for Power Up Records, (estab. 1985). Distributed nationally by Sutra, New York NY.
Needs: Produces 20 records/year; works with 4 recording artists/year. Works with 2 visual artists/year. Uses artists for album cover design and illustration, brochure design, illustration and layout.
First Contact & Terms: Works on assignment only. Send query letter with samples to be kept on file. Write for appointment to show portfolio. Samples not filed are returned by SASE. Reports within 2 weeks. Pays by job. Considers available budget when establishing payment. Purchases all rights.

NUCLEUS RECORDS, Box 111, Sea Bright NJ 07760. President: Robert Bowden. Produces country/ western, folk and pop. Recent releases: "Always" and "Make Believe" by Marco-Sison.
Needs: Produces 2 records/year. Artists with 3 years' experience only. Currently works with no freelance artists. Works on assignment only. Uses artists for album cover design.
First Contact & Terms: Send query letter with resume, original work and photographs. Write for appointment to show portfolio, which should include photographs. Samples are returned. Reports within 1 month. Originals returned to artist after job's completion. Considers skill and experience of artist when establishing payment. Buys all rights.

OHIO RECORDS, Box 655, Hudson OH 44236. (216)650-1330. A&R Director: Russ Delaney. Produces country/western; group and solo artists. Recent releases: "Taste of the Blues," (single) "Heeere's Ethel," by Ethel Delaney, and "A Penny for Your Dreams" by Bob Biers.
Needs: Produces 1 album, 2 singles/year. Uses artists for album cover design, brochure design and posters. Works on assignment only. Uses artists for album cover design and illustration and posters.
First Contact & Terms: Send samples to be kept on file. Accepts any samples. Samples not filed are returned by SASE. Reports only if interested. Pay is negotiable. Considers available budget when establishing payment.

POLKA TOWNE, 211 Post Ave., Westbury NY 11590. President: Teresa Zapolska. Produces polka records. Recent releases: "Dances of Poland," by Ted Maksymowicz Orchestra; "Jedzie Boat," by Frank Wojnarowski Orchestra; "Merry Christmas—Polish Carols," by Aria Choir; "I'm Proud To Be Polish" and "We're The Girls" by Teresa Zapolska Orchestra; newest: "Live, Love, Laugh" Teresa Zapolska All Girl Orch. Plus One.
Needs: Works on assignment only. Uses freelance artists for album cover design and illustration; uses 4-color covers.
First Contact & Terms: Send query letter with samples to be kept on file; "no photostats." Samples must apply to the polka area only. Reply and samples returned by SASE. Reports within 6 weeks. To show a portfolio, mail final reproduction/product. Original work not returned to artist after job's completion. Negotiates flat fee. Buys all rights.
I86

***PRAISE SOUND PRODUCTIONS LTD., (formerly Praise Industries Corp.)**, 7802 Express St., Burnaby, British Columbia V5A 1T4 Canada. (604)420-4227. Manager: Metro Yaroshuk. Produces gospel. Recent releases: "Servant," by Tunesmith; "Homespun," by New Born; and "Joan Cash," by Country Oak.
Needs: Produces 25 records/year. Works with 5 freelance artists/year. Works on assignment only. Artists with 3 years' experience only. Uses artists for album cover design.
First Contact & Terms: Send query letter with business card and samples to be kept on file. Write or call for appointment to show portfolio. Prefers original work as samples. Samples not kept on file are returned. Reports only if interested. Originals not returned to artist after job's completion. Pays by the project, $100-300 average. Considers rights purchased when establishing payment. Buys one-time rights.

***R.E.F. RECORDING CO./FRICK MUSIC PUBLISHING CO.**, 404 Bluegrass Ave., Madison TN 37115. (615)865-6380. Contact: Bob Frick. Produces country/western and gospel. Recent releases: "I Love You In Jesus" and "Headin For Heaven" by Bob Scott Frick; "Unworthy" by Bob Myers.
Needs: Produces 10 records/year; works with 3 groups artists/year. Works on assignment only.
First Contact & Terms: Send resume and photocopies to be kept on file. Write for appointment to show portfolio. Samples not filed are returned by SASE. Reports within 10 days only if interested.

***BRIAN RAINES MUSIC COMPANY**, Box 1376, Pickens SC 29671. (803)878-2953. President: Brian E. Raines. Estab. 1985. Produces country/western and Christian music with group and solo artists. Recent releases include "From the Heart," by Jim Hubbard; "He's Coming Back For Me," by Brian Raines and "Don't Step On My Family Name," by Heritage Quartet.

Needs: Produces 2 records/year. Uses artists for album cover design and illustration and advertising illustration.

First Contact & Terms: Send query letter with resume and photographs. Samples not filed are returned by SASE. Reports within 7 days. To show a portfolio, mail appropriate materials or write to schedule an appointment; portfolio should include photographs. Pays by the project, $5 minimum. Considers available budget and how work will be used when establishing payment. Buys all rights.

RANDALL PRODUCTIONS, Box 11960, Chicago IL 60611. (312)561-0027. President/Director: Mary Freeman. Produces rock and roll, disco, soul, country/western, jazz, pop, gospel, and rhythm and blues. Recent releases: "I Wanna Be With You," by Mickey Dee; "Why Do You Do Me Like You Do," by Emmett Beard (single), and "Someday You'll Be Runnin' To Me/Let Me Know, Let It Go," by Cabela/Schmitt.

Needs: Produces 10-12 records/year. Works with 5 freelance artists/year. Uses artists for album cover, brochure, catalog and advertising design; photography; video; and posters.

First Contact & Terms: Send query letter with brochure showing art style or original work and photographs to be kept on file. Samples not kept on file are returned by SASE if requested. Reports within 2 weeks. Pays by the project, $5-200 average. Considers complexity of project and available budget when establishing payment.

Tips: "We live in an age of identity, where the most liked are the least conservative."

RAVEN RECORDS, 1918 Wise Dr., Dothan AL 36303. (205)793-1329. President: Jerry Wise. Vice President: Steve Clayton. Produces rock and roll, soul, country/western, pop, and rhythm and blues. Recent releases: "Runner in the Night," by Frontrunner; and "Tell Me That You Love Me," by Heart to Heart.

Needs: Produces 5-10 records/year. Works with 2 freelance artists/year. "Most of our artists work on a speculation basis." Uses artists for album cover and brochure design.

First Contact & Terms: Send query letter with brochure and "a combination of original work and photographs" to be kept on file. Samples not kept on file returned by SASE. Reports within 30 days. Originals not returned to artist after job's completion. Call for appointment to show portfolio. Pays by the project, $25-500 average. Considers available budget, turnaround time and rights purchased when establishing payment. Buys all rights.

REVONAH RECORDS, Box 217, Ferndale NY 12734. (914)292-5965. Contact: Paul Gerry. Produces country/western and bluegrass.

Needs: Produces 6-10 records/year. Works with 3-4 freelance artists/year. "Work must be of a professional grade." Works on assignment only. Uses artists for album cover design.

First Contact & Terms: Send query letter with slides or actual work to be kept on file. Samples not filed are returned by SASE. Reports within 1 month. Call or write for appointment to show portfolio. Return of original artwork after job's completion "can be negotiated." Pays by the project, $75-250 average. Considers complexity of project, available budget, skill and experience of artist, how work will be used, turnaround time and rights purchased when establishing payment. Buys all rights.

RHYTHMS PRODUCTIONS, Whitney Bldg., Box 34485, Los Angeles CA 90034. (213)836-4678. President: R.S. White. Record and book publisher for children's market.

Needs: Works on assignment only. Prefers California artists. Produces 12 records and cassettes/year; all of which have cover/jackets designed and illustrated by freelance artists. Works with 3 visual artists/year. Uses artists for catalog covers/illustrations, direct mail brochures, layout, magazine ads, multimedia kits, paste-up, album design and book illustration. Artists must have a style that appeals to children.

First Contact & Terms: Buys 3-4 designs/year. Send query letter with brochure, resume and samples. Accepts any type sample. SASE. Reports within 3 weeks. Buys all rights on a work-for-hire basis.

ROBBINS RECORDS, HC80, Box 5B, Leesville LA 71446. National Representative: Sherree Stephens. Produces country/western and religious. Recent releases: "Jesus Amazes Me," "Wait Till You See My Miracle Home" and "Since I've Had A Change Of Heart" by Sherrie Stephens.

Needs: Produces various number of records/year. Works with various number of freelance artists/year. Works on assignment only. Uses artists for album cover design and posters.

First Contact and Terms: Send brochure to be kept on file. Reports only if interested. Originals not returned to artist after job's completion. Write for appointment to show portfolio. Pays by the project. Considers skill and experience of artist, how work will be used and rights purchased when establishing payment. Buys all rights.

ROB-LEE MUSIC/ALL STAR PROMOTIONS, Box 1338, Merchantville NJ 08109. (215)561-5822. President: Rob Russen. Produces rock and roll, disco, soul and country/western. Recent releases: "I

Came to Dance (I Came to Boogie)," by Phoenix; "Slow Down," by Philly Cream; and "Country Showdown," by Cross Country.

Needs: Produces 6 records/year. Works with 6 freelance artists/year. Uses artists for album cover, brochure and catalog design, and direct mail packages.

First Contact & Terms: Send query letter with brochure, resume, business card, samples and tear sheets, slides or photographs to be kept on file. Reports only if interested. Originals returned after job's completion. Pay varies. Considers complexity of project, available budget, how work will be used and rights purchased when establishing payment. Buy first, reprint or all rights; negotiates rights purchased.

ROSE HILL GROUP, 1326 Midland Ave., Syracuse NY 13205. (315)475-2936. Managing Director: Vincent Taft. Produces rock and roll, disco, pop and more. Recent releases: "Ocean Algae," by Taksim; "Lucky At Cards," by Kentucky; and "Skytrain," by Zarm.

Needs: Produces 5-10 records/year. Works with 5-10 freelance artists/year. Works on assignment only. Uses artists for album cover and advertising design, and posters.

First Contact & Terms: Send samples to be kept on file; write for appointment to show portfolio. Accepts "any legible format" as samples. Samples not filed returned by SASE. Reports only if interested. No originals returned after job's completion. Pays by the project, $50-500 average. Considers complexity of project and available budget when establishing payment. Negotiates rights purchased.

SCARAMOUCHE RECORDS, Drawer 1967, Warner Robins GA 31099. (912)953-2800. Director: Robert R. Kovach. Produces rock and roll, rhythm and blues, country/western, pop and gospel.

Needs: Produces 6 records/year; 50% of the album covers assigned to freelance designers. Works with 3 recording artists/year. Works with 2 visual artists/year. Assigns 5 freelance jobs/year. Works on assignment only. Uses artists for album cover design and illustration; brochure design, illustration and layout; advertising design, illustration and layout; and posters.

First Contact & Terms: Send query letter with photocopies or tear sheets and brochure to be kept on file. Samples returned by SASE. Reports within 3 months. Original art returned. Pays by the project, $100-800 average. Considers complexity of project, available budget, skill and experience of artist and rights purchased when establishing payment. Negotiates rights purchased.

SHANACHIE RECORDS CORP., Dalebrook Park, Ho-Ho-Kus NJ 07423. (201)445-5561. Art Director: Richard Nevins. Produces rock and roll, folk, pop, reggae and Irish music.

Needs: Produces 40 records/year. Works with 10 freelance artists/year. Uses artists for album cover design and illustration.

First Contact & Terms: Send query letter with photographs, printed samples and tear sheets to be kept on file. Reports within 21 days. Call or write for appointment to show portfolio. Artwork sometimes returned after job's completion. Pays by the project, $500 minimum. Considers complexity of project and available budget when establishing payment. Negotiates rights purchased.

SILVER BLUE PRODUCTIONS LTD., 220 Central Park S., New York NY 10019. (212)586-3535. President: Joel Diamond. Produces rock and roll, disco, country/western and pop. Recent releases: albums by Englebert Humperdinck, Helen Reddy, Sister Sledge, Gloria Gaynor.

Needs: Produces 20 records/year. All artwork is freelanced. Works on assignment only. Uses artists for album cover design and illustration, direct mail packages and posters.

First Contact & Terms: Send query letter with brochure, resume, business card, original work, photographs and tear sheets to be kept on file. Reports only if interested. Originals returned after job's completion. Negotiates pay. Considers complexity of project, available budget, skill and experience of artist, how work will be used, turnaround time and rights purchased when establishing payment. Negotiates rights purchased.

SINGSPIRATION MUSIC/RECORDS, Division of Zondervan Corp., 1415 Lake Dr. SE, Grand Rapids MI 49506. (616)698-3300. Contact: Phil Brower. Produces religious records.

Needs: Produces 20 records/year; all have cover/jackets designed and illustrated by freelance artists. Works on assignment only. Uses artists for design and illustration of albums and jackets.

First Contact & Terms: Send query letter with photocopied samples of previous art to be kept on file for future assignments. Reports within 2 weeks. SASE. Negotiates pay.

Tips: There is a trend toward "computer art and more airbrush; also more emphasis on lettering and type." When reviewing work looks for technique, style and up-to-date material—"no school assignment work if possible."

SONIC WAVE RECORDS, c/o Kiderian Records, 4926 W. Gunnison, Chicago IL 60630. (312)764-1144. President: Tom Petreli. Produces rock and roll, rhythm and blues, and New Wave. Recent releases: "New Wave Sampler," by Tom Petreli.

Needs: Produces 5-10 records/year. Assigns all jobs/year to freelance artists. Uses artists for album cover, poster, brochure, catalog and advertising design; and direct mail packages. Prefers "outrageous" covers.
First Contact & Terms: Send resume, tear sheets, photostats, slides. Reports within 1 month. Samples not kept on file are returned by SASE. Original work returned to artist after job's completion. Negotiates payment. Buys reprint rights.

***STARCREST PRODUCTIONS**, 209 Circle Hills Dr., Grand Forks ND 58201. (701)772-6831. President: George Hastings. Produces country, pop and gospel music. Recently released: Country gospel by Mary Joyce.
Needs: Produces 5 records/year; all of which have cover/jackets designed and illustrated by freelance artists. Uses artists for jacket and brochure design, and print ad illustrations.
First Contact & Terms: Send query letter and samples. SASE. Reports in 2 months. Negotiates pay based on amount of creativity required.

***STARGARD RECORDS**, Box 138, Boston MA 02101. (617)296-3327. Public Affairs: Neville Mason. Estab. 1984. Produces disco, soul, jazz, pop, rhythm and blues and reggae; group and solo artists. Recent releases: "Be Your Lover" and Midnight Magic" by Tow Zone; "She Changed," by B.K. Crew.
Needs: Produces 6 singles/year by 2 groups and 1 soloist. Works with 3 visual artists/year. Expects "reasonable rates and prompt service." Works on assignment only. Uses artists for album cover and advertising design and illustration.
First Contact & Terms: Send query letter with brochure showing art style or resume, photostats and photographs. Samples not filed are returned only if requested. Reports only if interested. To show a portfolio, mail thumbnails. Pays by the hour, $15 minimum; payment by project and day varies. Considers complexity of project and available budget when establishing payment. Negotiates rights purchased.

SUSAN RECORDS, Box 4740, Nashville TN 37216. (615)865-4740. Manager: Susan Neal. Produces rock and roll, disco, soul, country/western, rock-a-billy, jazz, pop, and rhythm and blues; group and solo artists. Recent release: "That's It Baby," by Dixie Dee.
Needs: Produces 15 records/year. Uses artists for album cover design and illustration; brochure design, illustration and layout; catalog design, illustration and layout; advertising design and layout.
First Contact & Terms: Send brochure, business card, SASE and photographs to be kept on file unless return requested. Samples not filed are returned by SASE. Reports within 15 days. Original art returned to the artist. Write for appointment to show portfolio. Considers available budget and rights purchased when establishing payment. Negotiates rights purchased.

3 G'S INDUSTRIES INC., 5500 Troost, Kansas City MO 64110. (816)361-8455. General Manager: Eugene Gold. Produces disco, soul, country/western, and rhythm and blues; group and solo artists. Recent releases: "Magic," and "Doin' It After Hours," by Suspension; and "Bootie Cutie," by Robert Newsome.
Needs: Produces 4 records/year. Works with 5 visual artists/year. Works on assignment only. Uses artists for album cover and advertising design, illustration and layout; and direct mail packages.
First Contact & Terms: Send photographs to be kept on file; call for appointment to show portfolio. Samples not filed are returned by SASE. Reports only if interested. Original artwork not returned to artist. Negotiates payment by the project. Considers skill and experience of artist when establishing payment. Negotiates rights purchased.

***TOP TEN MUSIC, INC.**, 130 W. 72 St., New York NY 10023. Produces rock and roll, disco, soul, country/western, jazz, folk, pop and rhythm and blues, records by group and solo artists. Recent release: "Happy at Home" by Bunny Valentine.
Needs: Produces 15 records/year by 10 groups and 5 soloists. Works with 5 visual artists/year. Uses artists for album cover design and illustration.
First Contact & Terms: Send query letter only. "Don't send samples." Payment and rights purchased are negotiated.

TOTAL SOUND RECORDS, Box 741, Lake Charles LA 70602. Branch offices: Box 1659, Beverly Hills CA 90213 and Box 1003, Milford PA 18337. Contact: Dr. Lawrence Herbst. (Beverly Hills Music, K-Larr Broadcasting Network, Larr Computer Corp., Lawrence Herbst Investment Trust, Inc. Lawrence Herbst Records.) Produces all types of record products.
Needs: Works on assignment only. Uses artists for album design and illustration, poster design, ad design and layout, brochure and catalog design, illustration and layout, and direct mail packages. Sometimes buys cartoons and humorous and cartoon-style illustrations.

First Contact & Terms: Send query letter with resume, tear sheets, photostats, photocopies and slides to be kept on file. Samples returned by SASE only. To show a portfolio, mail roughs, original/final art, final reproduction/product, color, tear sheets, photostats, photographs and b&w. Originals returned to artist at job's completion. Reports within 8 weeks. Pays $25 minimum; offers 14-20% royalties and advances. Buys all rights.
Tips: "Do good artwork, take your time and do a good job."

***TREND® RECORDS**, Box 201, Smyrna GA 30081. (404)432-2454. President: Tom Hodges. Produces soul, country, pop, rhythm and blues, middle of the road music, jazz; will consider custom releases. Recent release: "The Deer Hunter," by Dave Compton.
Needs: Produces 4 records/year by 2 groups and 2 soloists. Freelance artists design and illustrate 1 cover/jacket per year. "Working on 25th year anniversary album.
First Contact & Terms: Send query letter with samples. Send brochure or samples that can be kept on file for future reference. SASE. Reports in 1-3 weeks. Negotiates pay based on amount of creativity required.

***TURQUOISE RECORDS**, HC-84, Box 1358, Whitesburg KY 41858. (606)633-0485. Director: Pat Martin. Estab. 1985. Produces folk and bluegrass records. Recent releases include "Traditional Music of the Future" by No Strings Attached and "Thinking of Home" by Kentucky Ramblers.
Needs: Produces 4-6 records/year by 3-4 groups and 1-2 soloists. Works with 2-3 visual artists/year. Prefers regional artists. Works on assignment only. Uses artists for album cover, brochure, and catalog design and illustrations, and direct mail packages.
First Contact & Terms: Send query letter with tear sheets and photocopies. Samples not filed are returned by SASE. Reports within 3-4 weeks. To show a portfolio, mail roughs, final reproduction/product and tear sheets. Pays by the project, $50-250. Considers complexity of project, how work will be used and turnaround time when establishing payment. Buys all rights.

TYSCOT AND CIRCLE CITY RECORDS, 3532 N. Keystone Ave., Indianapolis IN 46218. (317)923-3343. President: Leonard Scott. Produces traditional and contemporary gospel. Recent releases: "Say You Believe," by Deliverance, "You Can Count On Me," by the Fords, "Everybody Don't Know Who Jesus Is," by The T.E.T.R.E.C. Choir.
Needs: Produces 10 records/year by 7 groups and 3 soloists. Works with 4 freelance artists/year. Works on assignment only. Uses artists for album cover, brochure, catalog and advertising design and illustration; direct mail packages and posters. Artists are used primarily for album cover design.
First Contact & Terms: Send query letter with brochure, resume, photostats, slides, original work or photographs to be kept on file. Samples not kept on file are returned by SASE. Reports only if interested. Originals returned to artist after job's completion. Call for appointment to show portfolio. Pays by the project. Considers available budget when establishing payment. Negotiates rights purchased.
Tips: "We are open to all artists. We look for uniqueness and quality in an artist's work, whether the art portrays what is currently in the marketplace—whether the art is marketable," says president Leonard Scott.

***ULTRAGROOVE/ORINDA RECORDS**, Box 838, Orinda CA 94563. (415)254-7600. Executive Vice President: C.J. Black. Produces classical, jazz and pop records, about 3-6 albums per month.
First Contact & Terms: Send samples and tear sheets. Samples not filed are returned only if requested. Reports only if interested. To show a portfolio, mail appropriate materials. Buys all rights.

***VELVET PRODUCTION CO.**, 517 W. 57th St., Los Angeles CA 90037. (213)753-7893. Manager: Aaron Johnson. Produces soul, and rhythm and blues. Recent releases: "Talking About Love," and "You Told Me to Stoop Down, Daddy," by Arlene Bell; "I Aint Jiving, Baby," by Chick Willis.
Needs: Produces 6 records/year. Works with 6 freelance artists/year. Experienced artists only. Works on assignment only. Uses artists for posters, album cover illustration, brochure design and catalog layout.
First Contact & Terms: Send query letter with brochure showing art style or resume, photostats and photocopies to be kept on file. Samples not kept on file are returned by SASE. Reports only if interested. Original artwork is returned after job's completion. Write for appointment to show portfolio. Pays by the project, $50-200 average. Negotiates rights purchased.

WILCOX ORGANIZATION LTD (ZODIAC RECORDS), Zodiac House, 1099A Finchley Rd., London NW11 England. 01-455-6620. Executive Director: Herb W. Wilcox. Produces rock and roll, soul, country/western, jazz, folk, and rhythm and blues. Recent releases: "Blues and All That Jazz," by Jeannie Lambe and U.K. All Stars; "Store It Up Til' Morning," by Kim Lesley & All Star U.K. Bands; and "After You've Gone," by Earl Hines-Mussy Spainer All Stars. Lists available.

Needs: Produces 12 albums/year. Works with 50 freelance artists/year. Uses artists for album cover, catalog and advertising design; catalog and advertising layout; catalog illustration; direct mail packages and posters.
First Contact & Terms: Send query letter with brochure, resume, business card, tear sheets, photostats or photographs to be kept on file. Samples not kept on file are returned by SAE (nonresidents include IRC). Reports within 7 days. Originals returned to artist after job's completion. Write for appointment to show portfolio. Contact only through artist's agent. Negotiates pay. Considers complexity of project and available budget when establishing payment. Negotiates rights purchased.

***YATAHEY RECORDS**, Box 31819, Dallas TX 75231. (214)750-0720. Art Director: C. Moran. Producer: Bart Barton. Produces country/western and gospel. Recent releases: "Catching Fire," by Angela Kaye; and "I Don't Want to Play the Cheatin' Game," by Brooks Brothers. Audio Henry *LP* "Gentleman", Audie Henry (singles) "Heaven Knows," "Sweet Salvation" (both top 10 Canada).
Needs: Produces 20 records/year. Uses artists for album cover and brochure design; advertising layout; and posters.
First Contact & Terms: Send query letter with business card, photographs and tear sheets to be kept on file. Samples not kept on file are returned by SASE. Reports only if interested. Original artwork is not returned after job's completion. Considers complexity of project, available budget, how work will be used and rights purchased when establishing payment. Buys all rights.

YAZOO RECORDS, INC., 245 Waverly Pl., New York NY 10014. (212)255-3698. Contact: Nick Perls. Produces jazz, folk, blues and ragtime. Recent releases: "Skip James's 1931 Session;" "Blind Lemon Jefferson" and "Ma Rainey's Black Bottom."
Needs: Produces 6 records/year. Works with 10 freelance artists/year. Desires "only artists who have good technique and can do portraiture if asked. Oil, gouache or watercolor OK. No colored pencils." Works on assignment only. Uses artists for album cover design and illustration.
First Contact & Terms: Send query letter with samples to be kept on file. Open to any form of sample. Samples not kept on file are returned by SASE only if requested. Reports only if interested. Originals returned to artist after job's completion. Call or write for appointment to show portfolio. Pays by the project. Considers complexity of project and rights purchased when establishing payment. Negotiates rights purchased.
Tips: "Have your technique together and don't be 'artsy'."

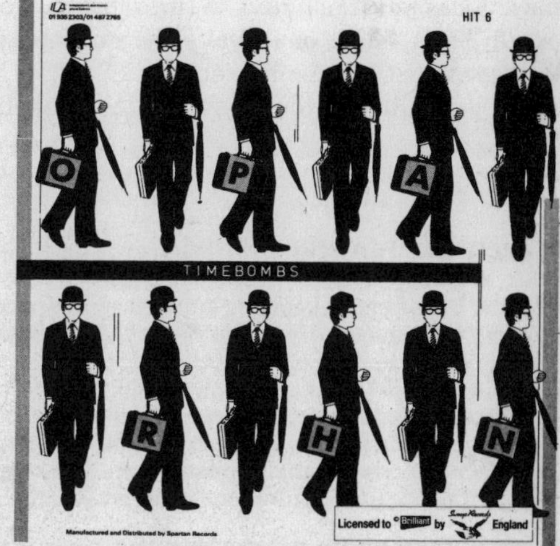

Ron Lee, creative director of Swoop Records in England (a division of Lematt Records), paid £150 for all rights for this single sleeve design. The pen-and-ink illustration conveys "the life of a typical English city business man."

Syndicates seem to be synonymous with publishing columns, but they also incorporate artwork. To graphic artists, syndicates are synonymous with cartoon panels, editorial cartoons and comic strips; they also provide puzzles and games to their newspaper clientele. Syndicates work with an individual artist on a continuing basis, usually the comic or editorial pages of newspapers.

The best way to approach a syndicate is to have ready a list of central characters and themes that will carry through your work. Create several weeks' worth of finished material drawn in a size two or three times larger than the standard size of a daily strip. Remember that lettering must be readable and illustration lines clear when the strip is reduced. Send quality photocopies or photostats. If a syndicate wishes to see originals, it will contact you.

Clip art firms provide their clients—individuals and businesses—with camera-ready illustrations, cartoons, spot drawings and decorative art in various sizes for use in newsletters, brochures, advertisements—wherever they wish to add visual interest to their printed materials. Clip art is becoming more and more imaginative and sophisticated in its subject matter, style and technique. Areas illustrated for today's market are diverse, ranging from animals and food to medicine and child care.

Artists interested in approaching clip art firms with their work should keep in mind that most firms are looking for work that appeals to a mass audience. A variety of styles might be accepted, but the overwhelming priority is that the artwork reproduce well in black and white. Your submissions should be a series of illustrations that lend themselves well to reproduction.

Clip art firms usually pay a flat fee per illustration and then send packets of camera-ready illustrations in various sizes to firms that pay for the service. Syndicates, on the other hand, usually pay a flat fee or a royalty, the amount depending on the number and the circulation of the papers that buy the artwork.

For more information on syndicates, consult *Editor & Publisher Syndicated Services*.

ADVENTURE FEATURE SYNDICATE, Suite 400, 329 Harvey Dr., Glendale CA 91206. (213)247-1721. Executive Editor: Orpha Harryman Barry. Syndicates to 200 newspaper and book publishers.
Needs: Buys from 20 freelance artists/year. Considers single, double and multi-panel cartoons. Prefers mystery, adventure and drama as themes. Also needs comic strips, and comic book and panel cartoonists. Works on assignment only.
First Contact & Terms: Send query letter with resume, samples and tear sheets to be kept on file; write for appointment to show portfolio. Prefers photostats as samples. Samples not kept on file are returned by SASE. Reports within 30 days. Pays 50% of gross income; on publication. Considers salability of artwork when establishing payment. Buys reprint rights; negotiates rights purchased.
Tips: "Comic strips need a four-week presentation package reduced to newspaper size."

***ARKIN MAGAZINE SYNDICATE INC.**, 761 NE 180 St., N. Miami Beach FL 33162. (305)651-5696. Managing Editor: Sarah N. Arkin. Syndicate serving 300-500 business and professional magazines and newspapers.
Needs: Buys from 1-2 freelance artists/year. Works on assignment only. Considers illustrations and b&w. Prefers line drawings. "All items we purchase must relate to our articles we already have at hand.

We need artists who can read our articles and prepare line drawings to illustrate the article and make it more salable.''
First Contact & Terms: Send query letter with samples. Samples not kept are returned if accompanied by a SASE. Reports within 2-3 weeks. Mail appropriate materials. Portfolio should include tearsheets and photostats. Pays $15-25/illustration; on acceptance. Considers salability of artwork when establishing payment. Buys all rights.
Tips: "Send samples of line drawings and advise availability of time, willingness to work within our pay schedule."

***ARTISTS AND WRITERS SYNDICATE**, 1034 National Press Building, Washington DC 20045. Associate Editor: David E. Steitz. Newspaper syndicate of comic features and news features serving daily and weekly publications worldwide. Buys from 2 freelance artists/year.
First Contact & Terms: Send query letter with resume and tear sheets, photocopies, and relevant newsprint background information. Samples not filed are returned by SASE. Reports within 15 days. To show a portfolio, mail appropriate materials such as tear sheets. Pays 50% of royalties or negotiates payment. Buys first rights.
Tips: "As a newspaper syndicate, we do not deal with one-time or occasional-use art. Keep submissions under six pages long and include SASE."

***B M ENTERPRISES**, Box 421, Farrell PA 16121. President: William (Bill) Murray. Syndicates to 400 weekly newspapers, schools and national and regional magazines.
Needs: Buys from 12 freelance artists/year. Considers single, double and multiple panel cartoons; line and spot drawings; b&w. Prefers humorous themes. Also uses artists for advertising.
First Contact & Terms: Prefers published artists only; however, others may submit. Send query letter with resume and tear sheets to be kept on file; write for appointment to show portfolio. Write for artists' guidelines. Samples not kept on file are returned by SASE. Reports within 30 days. Works on assignment only. Pays on acceptance. Considers skill and experience of artist when establishing payment. Buys all rights.
Tips: "Submit only best work."

CELEBRATION: A CREATIVE WORSHIP SERVICE, Box 281, Kansas City MO 64141. (816)531-0538. Editorial Office, 11211 Monticello Ave., Silver Spring MD 20902. (301)649-4937. Editor: Bill Freburger. Clients: Churches, clergy and worship committees.
Needs: Assigns 60/year. Uses artists for spot and line drawings on religious themes.
First Contact & Terms: Query; out-of-town artists only. Reports within 1 week. No originals returned to artist at job's completion. Pays $35/illustration.

***CITY NEWS SERVICE**, Box 39, Willow Springs MO 65793. (417)469-2423. President: Richard Weatherington. Editorial service providing editorial and graphic packages for magazines. Considers cartoons, caricature, tax and business subjects as themes; considers b&w line drawings and shading film.
Needs: Buys from 2 or more freelance artists/year.
First Contact & Terms: Send query letter with resume, tear sheets or photocopies. Samples should contain business subjects. Samples not filed are returned by SASE. Reports within 4-6 weeks. To show a portfolio, mail tear sheets or photostats. Pays for illustration by the project, $25 minimum. "We may buy art outright or split percentage of sales." Considers complexity of project, skill and experience of artist, how work will be used and rights purchased when establishing payment.
Tips: "We have the markets for multiple sales of editorial support art. We need talented artists to supply specific projects. We will work with beginning artists."

COMMUNITY AND SUBURBAN PRESS SERVICE, Box 639, Frankfort KY 40602. (502)223-1736. Editor/Publisher: Kennison Keene. Syndicates to 300 weekly, small daily and shopper publications throughout the USA, and 1,500 or more yearly.
Needs: Buys from 10 or more freelance artists/year. Considers double panel cartoons; illustrations and line drawings; b&w. Prefers humorous themes. Also uses artists for graduation and Christmas ads.
First Contact & Terms: Send samples. Write for artists' guidelines. Considers single panel cartoons. "Usually cartoon artists will submit 8 or 9 cartoons at a time, together with SASE." Samples not kept on file returned by SASE. Reports within 1 week. To show a portfolio, mail appropriate materials, which should include original/final art. "We pay $15/cartoon, if work is acceptable to us. Price to be negotiated on holiday greeting ads and graduation greeting ads." Pays on acceptance. Considers salability of artwork. Buys first rights.

COMMUNITY FEATURES, Dept. C, Box 1062, Berkeley CA 94701. Art Editor: B. Miller. Syndicates to 250 daily and weekly newspapers, shoppers, consumer magazines. Mails brochure of new syndicated

offerings to 500+ newspapers. Guidelines $1 and #10 SASE. Specify "artists' guidelines."
Needs: Interested in professional quality b&w illustrations, spot drawings, line art, square single, double and multiple panel cartoons; comic strips, illustrated educational panels, how-to, etc. Does not seek color. Looking for illustrators for regular weekly assignments, editorial cartoonists.
First Contact & Terms: Send samples (published and unpublished). Prefers tear sheets, veloxes, PMTs or excellent photocopies of art-boards. Reports within 2-6 weeks. Buys various rights. Purchases some one-shot. Will consider line-art on all topics listed in guidelines. Pays flat rate for one-shot and occasional work; 50% commission for regularly appearing features. Pays on publication.
Tips: "We look for a bold, modern look. Submit very clear copies with SASE if return is desired or leave samples of your work and we will contact you as the need arises."

COWLES SYNDICATE, INC., 715 Locust St., Des Moines IA 50304. (515)284-8244. President: Dennis R. Allen. Submission Editor: Tom Norquist. Syndicates to 2,000 newspapers and general magazines.
Needs: Buys several regular comic strips or panels/year. "We are looking for well-drawn, amusing/humorous comic strips (2 and 3 panel) to consider. Must have contemporary theme and apply to newspaper market; necessary to be consistently humorous. Continuity strips not marketable at this time. Submit strong representatives of versatility, art style, writing and humor abilities and background information of the concept as well as the background of creators of the comic."
First Contact & Terms: Send query letter with resume, samples, tear sheets and photocopies. Samples not kept are returned with SASE. Reports within 8 weeks. Buys all rights. Pays 50% of net proceeds. Pays on publication.
Tips: "Three areas of importance I consider when evaluating a comic are: 1) topic; 2) artwork; 3) humor and story line. Each area can be off slightly as a syndicate can work on with a creator, but copies of work submitted should best address those areas."

CRONIN FEATURE SYNDICATING INC., 7688 S.W. 105th Place, Miami FL 33173. (305)595-6050. Director of Marketing: Henry Carlton. Sales Manager: Ed Dresner. Syndicate serving 400 newspapers, newsletters, magazines and television.
Needs: Buys from a varying number of freelance artists/year. No cartoons.
First Contact & Terms: Send query letter with samples. Prefers photocopies as samples. Samples returned only if accompanied by an SASE. Payment is open and negotiable; on publication. Considers client's preferences when establishing payment. Negotiates rights purchased.
Tips: "Be as brief as possible with letters and samples."

DYNAMIC GRAPHICS INC., 6000 N. Forest Park Dr., Peoria IL 61614. (309)688-8800. Art Director: Frank Antal. Distributes to thousands of magazines, newspapers, agencies, industries and educational institutions.
Needs: Works with 15-20 artists/year. Illustrations, graphic design and elements; primarily b&w, but will consider some 2- and full-color. "We are currently seeking to contact established illustrators capable of handling b&w highly realistic illustration of contemporary people and situations."
First Contact & Terms: Submit portfolio. SASE. Reports within 1 month. Buys all rights. Negotiates payment. Pays on acceptance.
Tips: "Concentrate on mastering the basics in anatomy and figure illustration before settling into a 'personal' or 'interpretive' style!"

***EDITOR'S CHOICE CLIP ART QUARTERLY**, Box 529, Kitty Hawk NC 27979. (919)441-3141. President: William A. Ries. Clip art firm. Distributes quarterly to major corporations who publish employee newsletters or magazines.
Needs: Serious and humorous editorial illustrations, graphics, standing heads, etc. Works with 6-8 freelance artists/year. Prefers line illustrations in pen & ink, scratchboard, etc, or pencil illustration on textured board. Also buys graphic symbols. Work is related to business and industry, employee relations, health and wellness, physical fitness, family life, recreation, etc.
First Contact & Terms: Experienced illustrators and graphic designers only. Works on assignment only. Send query letter, resume and samples to be kept on file. Reports within 60 days. Prefers photocopies as samples. Samples returned by SASE if not kept on file. Original art not returned at job's completion. Buys all rights or negotiates limited use fee. Pays $30-100 for illustrations; negotiates payment amount, varies according to project. Pays on acceptance.
Tips: "Only accomplished illustrators will be considered. Amateurs need not apply. Send enough samples of variety of subjects and styles to show us what you can do."

***FILLERS FOR PUBLICATIONS**, 1220 Maple Ave., Los Angeles CA 90015. Editor-in-Chief: John Raydell. Managing Editor: Dean Bowie. Distributes to magazines and newspapers.

Needs: Buys 72 pieces/year. Considers single panel, current events, education, family life, retirement, factory and office themes.
First Contact & Terms: Mail art. SASE. Reports in 2 weeks. Previously published and simultaneous submissions OK. Buys all rights, but may reassign rights to artist after publication. Originals only returned upon request. Pays $5-10, line drawings, on acceptance.

***FOTO EXPRESSION**, Box 681, Station "A"., Downsview Ontario M3M 3A9 Canada. (416)736-0119. Director: M.J. Kubik. Serving 35 outlets.
Needs: Buys from 80 freelance artists/year. Considers single, double and multiple panel cartoons, illustrations, spot drawings, b&w and color.
First Contact & Terms: Send query letter with brochure showing art style or resume, tear sheets, slides and photographs. Samples not filed returned by SASE. Reports within 1 month. To show a portfolio, mail final reproduction/product, color, photographs and b&w. Artist receives percentage; on publication. Considers skill and experience of artist and rights purchased when establishing payment. Negotiates rights purchased.
Tips: "Quality and content are essential. Resume and samples must be accompanied by a SASE or, out of Canada, International Reply Coupon is required."

PAULA ROYCE GRAHAM, 2770 W. 5th St., Brooklyn NY 11224. (718)372-1920. Contact: Paula Royce Graham. Syndicates to newspapers and magazines.
Needs: Considers illustrations; b&w. Also uses artists for advertising and graphics.
First Contact & Terms: Send business card and tear sheets to be kept on file. Write for artists' guidelines. Samples not filed returned by SASE. Reports within days. Write for appointment to show portfolio. Pay is negotiable; on publication. Considers skill and experience of artist, client's preferences and rights purchased when establishing payment. Buys all rights.

GRAPHIC ARTS COMMUNICATIONS, Box 421, Farrell PA 16121. (412)962-2522. President: Bill Murray. Syndicates to 200 newspapers and magazines. Buys 400 pieces/year.
Needs: Humor through youth and family themes for single panel, strips and multi-panel cartoons. Needs ideas for anagrams, editorial cartoons and puzzles, and for new comic panel "Sugar & Spike."
First Contact & Terms: Query for guidelines. SASE. Reports within 4-6 weeks. No originals returned. Buys all rights. Pays 40% commission on acceptance.

GRAPHIC NEWS BUREAU, gabriel graphics. Box 38, Madison Square Station, New York NY 10010. (212)254-8863. Cable: NOLNOEL NY 5. Director: J.G. Bumberg. Custom syndications and promotions to customized lists, small dailies and selected weeklies.
Needs: Buys from 4-6 freelance artists/year. Prefers artists within easy access. No dogmatic, regional or pornographic themes. Uses single panel cartoons, illustration, halftones in line conversions and line drawings.
First Contact & Terms: Send query letter only. Reports within 4-6 weeks. Returns original art after reproduction on request with SASE. Provide 3x5 card to be kept on file for possible future assignments. Negotiates rights purchased; on publication.

HISPANIC LINK NEWS SERVICE, 1420 N St. NW, Washington DC 20005. (202)234-0737. General Manager: Hector Ericksen-Mendoza. Syndicated column service to 200 newspapers and a newsletter serving 750 private subscribers, "movers and shakers in the Hispanic community in U.S., plus others interested in Hispanics."
Needs: Buys from 20 freelance artists/year. Considers single panel cartoons; b&w, pen & ink line drawings. Work should have a Hispanic angle; "most are editorial cartoons, some straight humor."
First Contact & Terms: Send query letter with resume and photocopies to be kept on file. Samples not filed returned by SASE. Reports within 3 weeks. Call for appointment to show portfolio or contact through artist's agent. Pays flat fee of $25 average; on acceptance. Considers clients' preferences when establishing payment. Buys reprint rights and negotiates rights purchased; "while we ask for reprint rights, we also allow the artist to sell later."
Tips: "While we accept work from all artists, we are particularly interested in helping Hispanic artists showcase their work. Cartoons should offer a Hispanic perspective on current events or a Hispanic view of life."

HOSPITAL PR GRAPHICS, Box 529, Kitty Hawk NC 27949. (919)441-3141. President: William A. Ries. Clip art firm. Distributes monthly to hospitals and other health care organizations.
Needs: Works wih 4-5 freelance artists/year (at present). Uses illustrations, line drawings, spot drawings and graphic symbols related to health care for use in brochures, folders, newsletters, etc. Prefers sensitive line illustrations, spot drawings and graphics related to hospitals, nurses, doctors, patients,

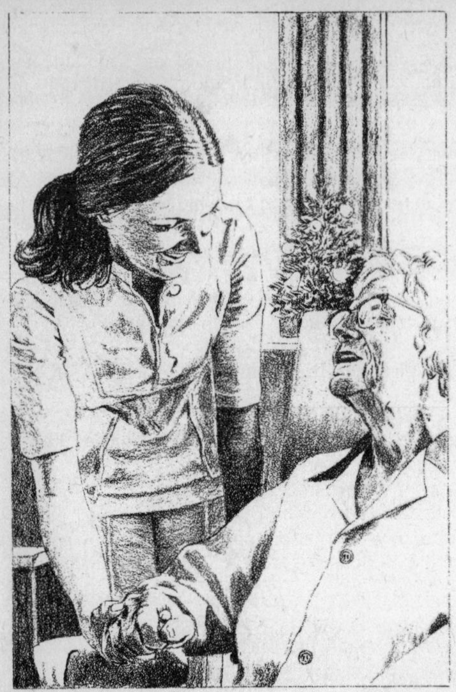

Joseph Stein of Bismark, North Dakota, was paid $100 for all rights to each illustration he completed for Hospital Graphics, a clip art division of William A. Ries & Associates in North Carolina. The works were commissioned for the monthly clip art service for hospitals "to provide Christmas-themed illustrations for use in community publications," according to publisher William Ries. "Stein was selected for this assignment," continues Ries, "because of his ability to handle sensitive subject matter and because he always meets our deadlines."

technicians, medical apparatus. Also buys 12 cartoons/year maximum.

First Contact & Terms: Experienced illustrators only, preferably having hospital exposure or access to resource material. Works on assignment only. Send query letter, resume, photostats or photocopies to be kept on file. Samples returned by SASE if not kept on file. Reports within 1 month. Original art not returned at job's completion. Buys all rights. Pays flat rate of $20-60 for illustrations; negotiates payment, varies according to project. Pays on acceptance.

Tips: "We are looking to establish a continuing relationship with at least 5-6 freelance graphic designers and illustrators. Illustration style should be serious, sensitive and somewhat idealized. Send enough samples to show the variety (if any) of styles you're capable of handling. Indicate the length of time it took to complete each illustration or graphic."

INTERNATIONAL ECO FEATURES SYNDICATE, Box 69193, West Hollywood CA 90069. (213)274-0954. Chief of Operations: Patrick C. Wall. Syndicate serving weekly newspapers, alternative newspapers, animal rights publications and alternative consciousness magazines.

Needs: Buys from 5-10 freelance artists/year. Considers single, double and multiple panel cartoons and illustrations; b&w, pen & ink drawings. Prefers ecology, the environment and animal rights as themes." Also uses artists for "possible works on behalf of environmental groups with which we are associated."

First Contact & Terms: Send query letter with samples to be kept on file unless not appropriate for stated themes. Write for appointment to show portfolio "if you are in Los Angeles area; don't make a special trip." Prefers photocopies as samples. Samples not filed returned by SASE. Reports back only if interested. Pays 50% of gross income; on publication "when we receive client's check." Considers salability of artwork when establishing payment. Buys one-time rights.

Tips: "If your artwork does not concern the environment, ecology or animal rights, don't bother to submit to us."

INTERPRESS OF LONDON AND NEW YORK, 400 Madison Ave., New York NY 10017. (212)832-2839. Editor/Publisher: Jeffrey Blyth. Syndicates to several dozen European magazines and newspapers.

Needs: Buys from 4-5 freelance artists/year. Prefers material which is universal in appeal; no "American only" material. Uses single and multi-panel cartoons.

First Contact & Terms: Send query letter and photographs; write for artists' guidelines. Samples not kept on file returned by SASE. Reports within 3 weeks. Purchases European rights. Pays 60% of net proceeds on publication.

***KING FEATURES SYNDICATE, INC.**, 235 E. 45 St. New York NY 10017. Art Director: Homer Lynn Jolly. Serves newspapers worldwide.
Needs: Buys from 15-20 freelance artists/year. Prefers local artists. Works on assignment only. Considers single, double and multiple panel cartoons, illustrations, spot drawings, b&w and color. Media and themes determined by project.
First Contact & Terms: Send query letter with brochure showing art style or resume, tear sheets, photostats and photocopies. Samples not filed are returned by SASE. Reports within 2 weeks. Write to schedule an appointment to show a portfolio, which should include original/final art, tearsheets and b&w. Pays flat fee $50 spot-1,000 for color promotion cover; on acceptance. Considers skill and experience of artist when establishing payment. Negotiates rights purchased.
Tips: "Write and send samples of work. If local, write for appointment. Please don't call."

LOS ANGELES TIMES SYNDICATE, 218 S. Spring St., Los Angeles CA 90012. (213)972-5198. Comics Editor: David Seidman.
Needs: Comic strips, panel cartoons and editorial cartoons. "We prefer humor to dramatic continuity (although humorous continuity is certainly acceptable). We need cartoons that run daily only—that is, Monday through Saturday—or daily-and-Sunday. We don't plan to buy cartoons that run on Sunday alone." Cartoons may be of any size as long as they're to scale with cartoons running in newspapers. (Strips usually run approximately 6⁷⁄₁₆x2", panel cartoons 3¹⁄₈x4"; editorial cartoons vary.)
First Contact & Terms: "Submit photocopies or photostats of 24 dailies. Submitting Sunday cartoons is optional; if you choose to submit them, send at least four of them. Coloring them is optional." Reports within 2 months. SASE. "We sign contracts with cartoonists to produce a set number of cartoons week after week. We send out about four contracts a year." Syndicate buys all rights. "We sell the cartoons to newspapers (if possible, we also sell merchandising rights and split the net profit with cartoonists."
Tips: "Don't imitate cartoons that are already in the paper. We prefer original features rather than strips that copy 'Garfield' or 'Doonesbury,' or editorial cartoonists who emulate Conrad or MacNelly. Since newspapers print cartoons very small and on newsprint, be careful with clutter, pattern screens or fine details. Avoid items that might bleed together, fade out or reproduce too small to see clearly. Keep sex, alcohol, violence and other potentially offensive subjects to a minimum. Politics is OK if you avoid being strident. (Mind you, don't censor yourself too much or become bland. We'd rather you be too wild than too boring.) We're very open to hearing from cartoonists. To confer with the comics editor, telephone between 8 a.m. and 6 p.m. Pacific time and ask for David Seidman (pronounced Seedman). We hardly ever match artists with writers or vice versa. Whether you yourself write or you work with a writer, we prefer people or teams who can do the entire job of creating a feature."

METRO ADVERTISING & MARKETING SERVICES, 33 W. 34th St., New York NY 10011. (800)223-1600. Contact: Andrew Shapiro. Clip art firm. Distributes to 4,500 daily and weekly paid and free circulation newspapers, schools, graphics and ad agencies and retail chains.
Needs: Buys from 50 freelance artists/year. Considers single panel cartoons; illustrations and line and spot drawings; b&w and color. Prefers all categories of themes associated with retail, classified, promotion and advertising. Also needs artists for special-interest tabloid section covers.
First Contact & Terms: Send query letter with brochure showing style or photostats, photocopies, slides, photographs and tear sheets to be kept on file. Samples not kept on file returned by SASE. Reports only if interested. To show a portfolio, mail appropriate materials or call to schedule an appointment. Works on assignment only. Pays flat fee of $50-1,000 average; on acceptance. Considers skill and experience of artist, salability of artwork and clients' preferences when establishing payment.
Tips: "Metro provides steady work, lead time and prompt payment. All applicants are seriously considered. Don't rely on 1-2 samples to create interest. Show a variety of styles and special ability to draw people in realistic situations. If specialty is graphic design, think how you would use samples in advertising."

MILLER SERVICES LIMITED, 45 Charles St. E., Toronto, Ontario M47 1S6 Canada. (416)925-4323. Features Editor: Valerie Carter. Syndicate serving approximately 200 daily and weekly newspapers and some magazines and text books.
Needs: Buys from 10 freelance artists/year. Considers single, double and multiple panel cartoons, editorial cartoons; b&w. Prefers pen & ink and pen & ink with washes.
First Contact & Terms: Send query letter with resume and tear sheets or photocopies. Samples returned only by SASE. Reports within a few weeks. Call or write for appointment to show portfolio, which should include photocopies. Artist receives 50% of gross income on publication. Considers skill and experience of artist, salability of artwork and client's preferences when establishing payment. Negotiates rights purchased.
Tips: "This is a very competitive market. Must gain exposure by being published in a directory of publications before submitting to syndicates."

MINORITY FEATURES SYNDICATE, Box 421, Farrell PA 16121. (412)962-2522. Chairman of the Board: Bill Murray. Clip art firm serving approximately 500 outlets.
Needs: Buys from 600 freelance artists/year. Considers single, double and multi-panel cartoons; illustrations and spot drawings. Prefers b&w pen & ink line drawings with family themes. Also uses artists for advertising art.
First Contact & Terms: Published artists only. Works on assignment only. Send query letter to be kept on file; write for artists' guidelines. Prefers photocopies as samples. Samples returned by SASE. Reports only if interested. Pay to artist is 50%; on acceptance. Considers rights purchased when establishing payment. Buys all rights.
Tips: "Submit only your best efforts."

NATIONAL NEWS BUREAU, 2019 Chancellor St., Philadelphia PA 19103. (215)569-0700. Editor: Harry Jay Katz. Syndicates to 1,000 outlets and publishes entertainment newspapers on a contract basis.
Needs: Buys from 500 freelance artists/year. Prefers entertainment themes. Uses single, double and multiple panel cartoons, illustrations, line and spot drawings.
First Contact & Terms: Send samples and resume. Samples returned by SASE. Reports within 2 weeks. Returns original art after reproduction. Send resume and samples to be kept on file for future assignments. Negotiates rights purchased. Pays flat rate; $5-100 for each piece; on publication.

NEWS AMERICA SYNDICATE, 1703 Kaiser Ave., Irvine CA 92714. President/CEO: Rick Newcombe. Syndicates to 2,500 daily and weekly newspapers around the world. Titles include "Andy Capp," "Mary Worth" and "Dennis the Menace."
Needs: Considers cartoon strips; single, double and multiple panel; illustrations, spot drawings, b&w and color. Must have strong main characters and theme. Prefers pen & ink and line drawings.
First Contact & Terms: Submit work (6-12 unpublished items) with cover letter. SASE. Reports within 2 months. Buys various rights. Write to schedule an appointment to show a portfolio, which should include original/final art and tear sheets. Pays royalties on publication. Free artists' guidelines.

NEWSPAPER ENTERPRISE ASSOCIATION INC./UNITED FEATURE SYNDICATE, 200 Park Ave., New York NY 10166. Director of Comic Art: Sarah Gillespie. Syndicates to more than 1,500 newspapers.
Needs: Comic strip ideas, editorial cartoons and comic panels. Prefers pen & ink. Contact via mail. Send copies, not originals, and SASE for return. All submissions answered. If used in NEA Daily Service, pays flat fee. If used in syndicate division, 50% commission.
Tips: "We are looking for innovative comic features with interesting characters. There should be an idea behind your feature that allows it to be open-ended. Whatever the 'staging,' you need an on-going narrative structure. The market is very, very tight. We take 3 new strips a year and get over 2,000 submissions. Concentrate on character more than subject matter."

***NORTHWIND STUDIOS INTERNATIONAL**, Box 295, Mobile Ave. #2, Camarillo CA 93010. (805)493-1661. Contact: John J. Tobin. Estab. 1984. Syndicates to 26 outlets of Christian magazines and Christian newsletters.
Needs: Buys from 8-10 freelance artists/year. Considers single panel cartoons. Prefers pen & ink line drawings with Christian themes only.
First Contact & Terms: Prefers experienced artists. Send resume or samples for consideration to be kept on file. Artists guidelines will be sent after review of resume and samples. Prefers photocopies as samples. Samples returned by SASE. Reports within 2 weeks. Pay artists $25-50; on acceptance. Considers skill and experience of artist, salability of artwork and rights purchased when establishing payment. Buys all rights.
Tips: "Northwind Studios International has a commitment of quality to all its subscribers, therefore we ask all artists who are applying for a position to be aware of these rules: 1) production of good wholesome, Christian cartoons; 2) no variations on our two characters; 3) maintain a 'Disney' style; 4) the ability to vary the widths of line; 5) willingness to rework. Because of this criteria it is necessary that we ask only qualified and talented artists apply. The right artists will find a long term and pleasant relationship with our studio."

OCEANIC PRESS SERVICE, Box 6538, Buena Park CA 90622-6538. (714)527-5651. Manager: Nat Carlton. Syndicates to 300 magazines, newspapers and subscribers in 30 countries. Titles include "What Every Woman Should Know About Men" and "How to Avoid Pressure."
Needs: Buys several hundred pieces/year. Considers cartoon strips (single, double and multiple panel) and illustrations. Prefers camera ready material (tear sheets or clippings). Themes include published sex cartoons, family cartoons, inflation, juvenile activities and jacket covers for paperbacks (color transparencies). Especially needs juvenile activity drawings and unusual sports cartoons; also sex cartoons.

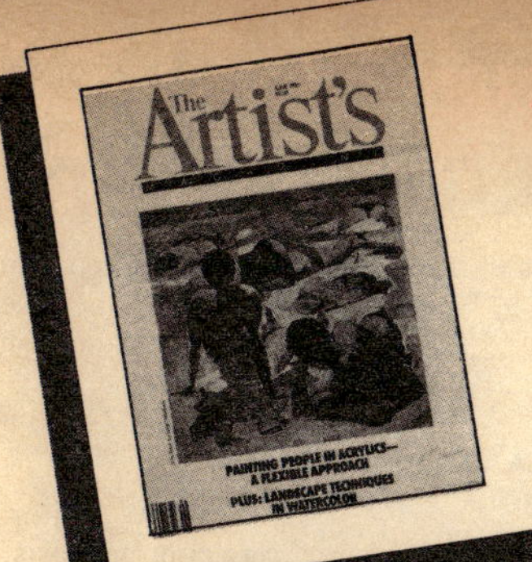

An invitation

to all artists: beginners . . . serious amateurs . . . professionals . . . art educators . . . art students . . .

to accept an examination copy of America's newest, most exciting how-to magazine for artists

with our compliments and without obligation.

See for yourself how THE ARTIST'S MAGAZINE can make you a better artist. Return the postage-paid card below and get a free introductory issue to read and use in your work.

With your free-examination copy we'll enter a 100% NO RISK Introductory Subscription for you . . . at a $9.00 savings off the regular price. If THE ARTIST'S MAGAZINE doesn't help you improve your skills, simply write "cancel" on our invoice, return it and keep the sample issue *with our compliments.*

In your introductory issue you'll see:

- Colorful, step-by-step instruction from America's top art professionals.
- Practical information on how and where to exhibit and sell your artwork.

- Regular columns on technique, questions and answers, new products and issues of interest both to amateurs and professionals
- The latest updates on books, seminars, tools and competitions for artists.

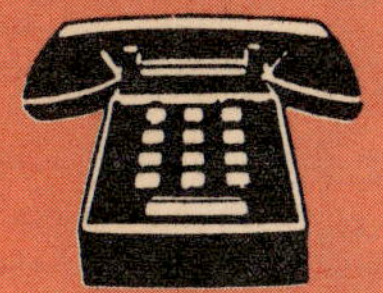

To accept this invitation

just phone our TOLL FREE number and charge your subscription to your credit card. Or tear off and mail this card today — no postage is needed.

1-800-341-1522
(in Maine call collect 236-2896)

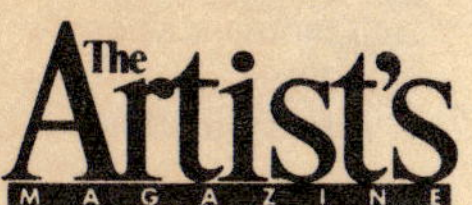

Free Issue Offer

YES! Send me a free-examination copy of THE ARTIST'S MAGAZINE. If the magazine doesn't help me improve my skills and show me how and where to exhibit and sell my work, I'll return your invoice marked "cancel" and owe nothing . . . or I'll honor it and pay just $15* for the next 11 issues (12 in all). That's a $9.00 savings off the regular subscription price!

Initial here: _______________________

NAME ____

ADDRESS ____

CITY   STATE   ZIP

Watch for your first issue to arrive in five weeks!

*Additional $4 postage billed for Canadian and foreign subscriptions.

VAM87-X

America's top artists show you how they create their work in practical step-by-step instruction

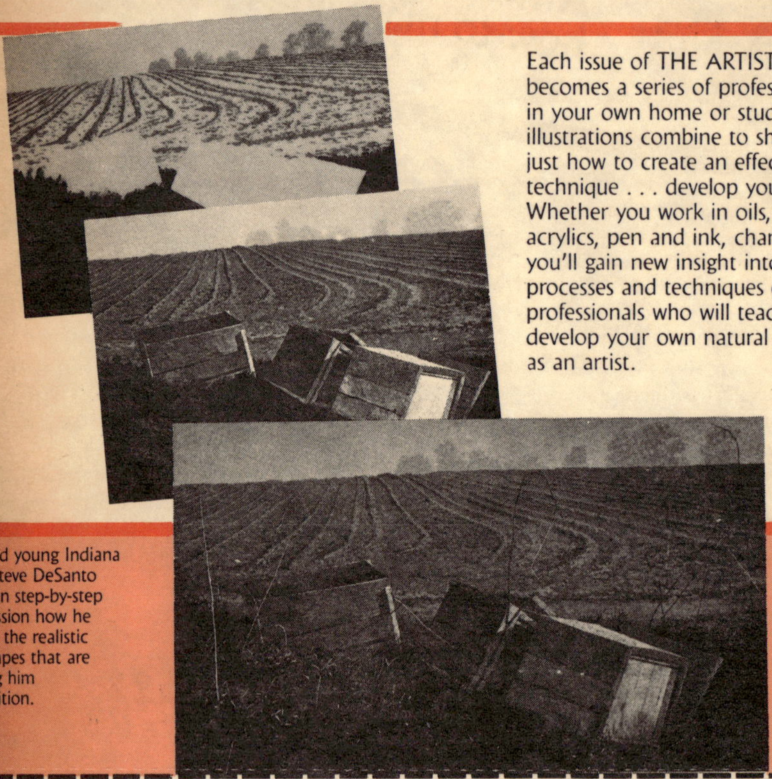

Each issue of THE ARTIST'S MAGAZINE becomes a series of professional art lessons in your own home or studio. Articles and illustrations combine to show you in detail just how to create an effect . . . master a technique . . . develop your own style. Whether you work in oils, watercolors, acrylics, pen and ink, charcoal or sculpture, you'll gain new insight into the creative processes and techniques of working professionals who will teach you how to develop your own natural talent and skills as an artist.

Talented young Indiana artist Steve DeSanto shows in step-by-step progression how he creates the realistic landscapes that are earning him recognition.

Don't miss a single issue. Use this card to start your no-risk subscription today.

NO POSTAGE NECESSARY IF MAILED IN THE UNITED STATES

BUSINESS REPLY MAIL

FIRST CLASS   PERMIT NO. 483 MARION, OHIO

POSTAGE WILL BE PAID BY ADDRESSEE

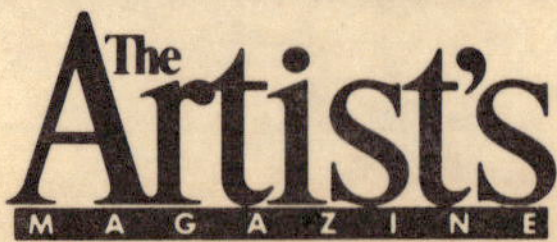

P.O. Box 1999
Marion, OH 43306-0001

Close-up

Joe Martin
Syndicated cartoonist
Sontana, Wisconsin

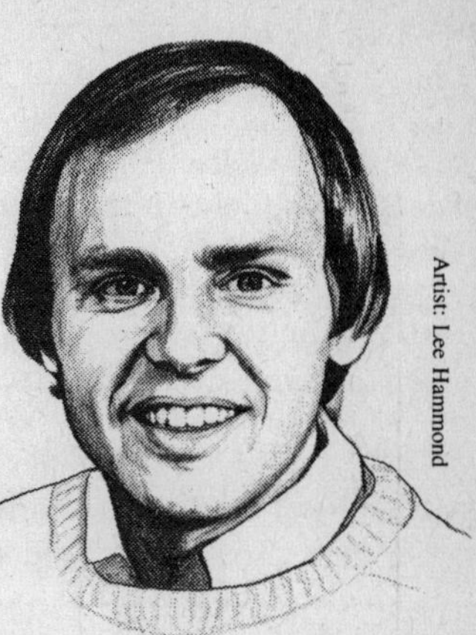

Syndicated cartoonist Joe Martin has an unmitigated passion for his work.

"If I had $50 million, I would do exactly what I'm doing now," says the Wisconsin resident. "I laugh at my own jokes and I have a lot of fun."

That sense of fun can now be found in three cartoon strips which Martin has in syndication—"Willie and Ethel," "Porterfield" and his latest, "Boffo," which went into syndication in June, '86. The latter cartoon strip makes the fourth one Martin has been able to place in syndication in the last ten years, his first being "Tucker," which was syndicated by News America and subsequently by Martin. Becoming syndicated was the realization of the cartoonist's dream for Martin, who says a number of the situations in "Tucker" and "Willie and Ethel" were auto biographical and taken from some of his experiences when he ran an employment agency.

"Write what you know about," says Martin. "I started writing about a guy who ran an employment agency. It was applying my own opinions to everyday situations I was familiar with. I think that if somebody wants to do a comic strip, he or she should pick something he can be familiar with and think funny about."

Unlike many successful cartoonists, Martin had no formal artistic training, explaining, however, that he used to do caricatures when he was in high school. The absence of any for-

PORTERFIELD   BY JOE MARTIN

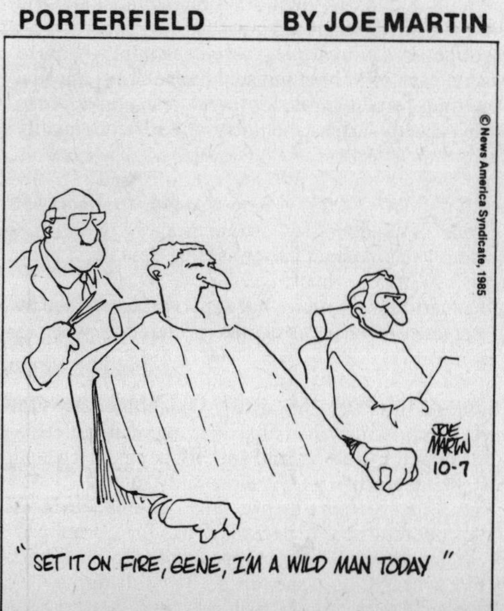

Joe Martin finds many humorous situations, such as in this Porterfield cartoon, by walking around town and jotting down ideas. He writes and draws 24 jokes a week, daily and Sunday, and sends out the work every two weeks.

mal training obviously has not had any adverse effect on Martin's success. For him, the actual drawing is a mechanical act, giving concrete form to his ideas. "I think ideas are the most important thing," he says.

Like most creative people, Martin feels that discipline is crucial to success. He gets up at 6 or 7 a.m., writes jokes until 3 p.m. and then he and his wife "have arguments over what we think is funny. Usually at night, I start drawing a little bit," he explains. He writes and draws 24 jokes a weeks, daily and Sunday, and sends the work out every two weeks. He is paid once a month and, of course, the amount is contingent on the number of papers in which his strips are syndicated.

Martin says he likes to deal on a 50-50 basis with his syndicate, meaning that he receives 50 per cent of the profits from his works. If there is a product marketed based on one of his creations, Martin would also receive 50 per cent of the sales generated.

For those working on a cartoon strip for submission to a syndicate, Martin advises elimination of a flowery cover letter because, he feels, the strip should stand on its own merits. The comic strip should explain itself through its jokes.

Martin also says aspiring strip cartoonists should have six weeks worth of strips prepared before they are sent off to a syndicate, and the strips should be done in color. "I I were going to start from scratch, I'd look over the newspapers. I'd think about what I didn't like about it (a strip) or what it needed."

The cartoonist says, "We need funny (in the newspapers). We need people who can write funny and have a clear art style. Even though *Nancy* was the corniest feature that ever hit, it was uncluttered . . . people read it to relax. After all, they're called the funny papers."

—*Bob Firestone, Jr.*

"God, sex and action is still a good formula. Poke fun at established TV shows. Bad economy means people must do their own home, car and other repairs. How-to articles with b&w line drawings are needed. Magazines will buy less and have more features staff-written. Quality is needed. People like to read more about celebrities, but it has to have a special angle, not the usual biographic run-of-the-mill profile. Much will be TV related. I'd like to see a good cartoon book on Sherlock Holmes, on Hollywood, on leading TV shows."
First Contact & Terms: Send query letter with photostats and samples of previously published work. Accepts tear sheets and clippings. SASE. Reports within 4 weeks. Buys all rights. To show a portfolio, mail appropriate materials, which should include final reproduction/product. Pays on publication. Originals returned to artist, or put on auction. Guidelines $1 with SASE.
Tips: "The trend is definitely toward women's market: money saving topics, service features—how to do home repair—anything to fight inflation; also unusual cartoons about unusual happenings; unusual sports; and cartoons with sophisticated international settings, credit cards, air travel. We would like to receive more clippings for foreign reprints. Competition is keen—artists should strive for better quality submissions."

PRESS ASSOCIATES INC., 806 15th St. NW, Washington DC 20005. (202)638-0444. Contact: Art Editor. News service serving "hundreds" of trade union newspapers and magazines.
Needs: Buys from 10-15 freelance artists/year. Considers single panel cartoons; line drawings; b&w. Prefers humorous and workplace themes—manufacturing, office, retail, etc.
First Contact & Terms: Send query letter with original cartoons. Samples not kept on file returned by SASE only if requested. Pays flat rate of $7.50; on acceptance. Considers clients' preferences when establishing payment. Buys first or reprint rights.

PROFESSIONAL ADVISORY COUNSEL, INC., Suite A-10, 7701 Broadway, Oklahoma City OK 73116. President: Larry W. Beavers. Syndicate serving approximately 1,000 international outlets.
Needs: Buys from over 30 freelance artists/year. Considers illustrations and spot drawings, b&w and color. Prefers camera-ready artwork. Also uses artists for advertising. Considers any media.
First Contact & Terms: Works on assignment only. Send query letter with brochure, resume, business card and samples to be kept on file if interested. Samples not returned. Especially looks for "simplicity and fast-relating/assimilating potential." Reports only if interested. Write for appointment to show portfolio and for artists' guidelines. Pays flat fee, $10-100 average; on acceptance. Buys all rights.
Tips: "Make your contact quick, concise and to-the-point."

***PUBLICATIONS CO.**, 1220 Maple Ave., Los Angeles CA 90015. (213)747-6541. Manager: John Raydell. Syndicates clip art to small newsletters. Buys 80 pages/year.
Needs: Buys full pages of 9-20 bits of art on the same subject, e.g., sports, office scenes, dancing, related objects, animals, cars, cowboys. Original can be on 8½x11" paper with 6x10" image area.
First Contact & Terms: Mail art. SASE. Reports in 3 weeks. Originals only returned to artist upon request. Pays $25-40/page.

SINGER COMMUNICATIONS, INC., 3164 Tyler Ave., Anaheim CA 92801. (714)527-5650. Executive Vice President: Natalie Carlton. Syndicates to 300 magazines, newspapers, book publishers and poster firms; strips include *They Changed History*, and *How It Began*. Artists' guidelines $1.
Needs: Buys several thousand pieces/year. Considers cartoon strips; single, double and multiple panel; family, children, sex, juvenile activities and games themes; universal material on current topics. Especially needs business, outerspace and credit card cartoons of 3-4 panels. Prefers to buy reprints or clips of previously published material.
First Contact & Terms: Send query letter with tear sheets. "Prefer to see tear sheets or camera ready copy or clippings." SASE. Reports within 2-3 weeks. Returns originals to artist at job's completion if requested at time of submission with SASE. To show a portfolio, mail appropriate materials, which should include final reproduction/product. Buys reprint or all rights; prefers foreign reprint rights. Pays 50% commission.
Tips: "Send us cartoons on subjects like inflation, taxes, sports or Christmas; we get thousands on sex. Everyone wants new ideas—not the same old characters, same old humor at the doctor or psychiatrist or at the bar. More sophistication is needed. Background is also needed—not just 2 people talking."

TRIBUNE MEDIA SERVICES, INC., 64 E. Concord St., Orlando FL 32801. (305)422-8181. Editor: Mike Argirion. Syndicate serving daily and Sunday newspapers.
Needs: Seeks comic strips and newspaper panels.
First Contact & Terms: Send query letter with resume and photocopies. Samples not filed are returned. Reports within 2-4 weeks.

***UNITED CARTOONIST SYNDICATE**, Box 7081, Corpus Christi TX 78415. (512)855-2480. President: Pedro R. Moreno. Syndicate serving South Africa outlets. Regular outlets vary from church newsletters to major newspapers or international comic syndicates.
Needs: Buys from 1-12 freelance artists/year. Consider single, double or multiple panel cartoons; b&w or color on Sundays. Prefers (medium) line drawings of pen & ink with zip-a-tone (no washes). Prefers family entertainment (clean) as themes.
First Contact & Terms: Send query letter with $5 for guidelines. Samples not filed returned by SASE. Reports within 7 days. To show a portfolio, mail tearsheets, b&w and reduced newspaper page size. Pays 40% of gross income on publication. Considers salability of artwork when establishing payment. Negotiates rights purchased.
Tips: "Before submitting your artwork, reduce your comic panel or comic strip in a newspaper page size. The amount of 2 to 48 comics are required for a good evaluation for possible syndication."

UNITED MEDIA, 200 Park Ave., New York NY 10166. (212)692-3819. Design Director: John Lane. Multimedia—United Feature Syndicate, NEA Feature Service, Pharos Books for 800-1,000 newspapers and bookstores.
Needs: Buys from 25-50 freelance artists/year. Themes vary according to assignment. Uses illustrations, line and spot drawings, book jacket and brochure designs.
First Contact & Terms: Send 6-12 tear sheets or photostats and resume or write for appointment. Samples returned by SASE. Reports within 3 weeks. Return of originals after reproduction is negotiable. Negotiates rights purchased and payment. Pays on acceptance.

UNIVERSAL PRESS SYNDICATE, 4400 Johnson Dr., Fairway KS 66205. Editorial Director: Lee Salem. Syndicate serving 2750 daily and weekly newspapers.
Needs: Comic strips and panels; text features. Considers single, double or multiple panel cartoons; b&w and color. Prefers photocopies of b&w, pen & ink, line drawings; other techniques are reviewed, but remember that this material will be published in newspapers.
First Contact & Terms: Reports within 4 weeks. To show a portfolio, mail photostats. Buys syndication rights. Send query letter with resume and photocopies.
Tips: "A well-conceived comic strip with strong characters, good humor and a contemporary feel will almost always get a good response. Be original."

Art Publishers and Distributors

The other sections of this book deal with commercial applications of art; this section provides outlets for a blend of fine art and graphic skills. Printed art reproductions offer the graphic artist creative freedom, repeat income and widespread exposure.

The services supplied by these firms vary. The publisher/printer handles only reproductions of works, leaving the actual distribution to the artist, while the publisher/distributor handles printing plus marketing. The distributor deals with the distribution and sales of works that have already been printed—either the artist already has available editions or he is willing to have prints made at his own expense.

The print and poster market provides collectible art at affordable prices. Publishers/distributors offer offset reproductions (prints reproduced by photomechanical means) which are issued as limited editions (printed in a limited amount with a higher retail price), unlimited editions (mass-produced at a lower price) and posters (artwork complemented by typography).

Art publishers/distributors seek artwork that retains a clarity of line and color when reproduced and contains clear, graphic images. Color plays a vital part, since print reproductions are often an integral factor in interior decoration. The subject matter must have a widespread appeal—wildlife, flowers, animals and landscapes being popular subjects. For continued sales, the subject or treatment should lend itself to a series.

Research the market by reading *Decor* and *Art Business News*. Select firms that specialize in your subject matter or style. Send for catalogs and request art guidelines when available. Discuss the market with owners or art buyers at interior decorating firms, frame shops or print galleries.

Most firms prefer artists to contact them through the mail. Send a cover letter on your letterhead, a resume or brochure, samples and an SASE. Samples should include photographs or slides that accurately represent your palette and tearsheets that demonstrate how your work appears in printed form.

Know what services the firm is furnishing and what is expected from you before you sign a contract. Reproduction rights and payment methods vary widely. The contract/agreement should include the names and addresses of both parties; a description of the work; payment and insurance terms; a copyright notice, guarantee of a credit line and the extent of promotion.

Names and addresses of art publishers/distributors can be found in *Decor's Sources Directory* and in the *Art Buyer's Index*.

***AA GRAPHICS, INC.**, 1200 N. 96th St., Seattle WA 98103. Art Director: Gail Gastfield. Publishes posters for a teenage market, minimum 5,000 run for department, record and poster stores, also discount drug stores. Artist's guidelines available. Send query letter with tear sheets, photostats, photocopies, slides and photographs; then submit sketch or photo of art. SASE. Reports in 2 weeks. Usually pays royalties of 10¢ per poster sold or an advance of $500 against future royalties.
Acceptable Work: Prefers 7x11" sketches; full-size posters are 23x35".
Tips: "Become familiar with popular posters by looking at designs in poster racks in stores."

AARDVARK ART, INC., 1100 Bryn Mawr, Bensenville IL 60106. (312)766-0400. President: Gerald McGlothlin. Produces limited and unlimited edition art reproductions for galleries. Publishes 4 artists/year. Experienced silk screen artists preferred. Negotiates ownership of original art. Send letter of inquiry and photos of art. SASE.

Acceptable Work: Photography and artwork of all kinds considered. Size to be proportional to 12x16", 18x24", or 24x36".

AARON ASHLEY INC., Room 1905, 230 5th Ave., New York NY 10001. (212)532-9227. Contact: Philip D. Ginsburg. Produces unlimited edition fine quality 4-color offset and hand-colored reproductions for distributors, manufacturers, jobbers, museums, schools and galleries. Publishes "many" new artists/year. Pays royalties or fee. Offers advance. Exclusive representation for unlimited editions. Written contract. Query, arrange interview or submit slides or photos. SASE. Reports immediately.
Needs: Unframed realistic and impressionistic paintings, especially marine, landscapes, sportings, florals, botanicals and Americana.

ALJON INTERNATIONAL, 1481 SW 32 Ave., Pompano Beach FL 33069. (305)971-0070. President: Ronald Dvoretz. Art distributor of watercolors, acrylic and oil paintings, enamels on copper and collages. Clients: galleries, furniture stores, home show people, interior designers and other wholesalers and jobbers. Distributes work for 18 domestic artists/year. Pays flat fee. Negotiates payment method; very often pays on weekly basis. Negotiates rights purchased. Requires exclusive representation. Provides insurance while work is at distributor, promotion and shipping to and from distributor. Send query letter with brochure and samples. Prefers slides or photos of originals as samples. Samples returned only if requested. Reports only if interested. Call or write for appointment to show portfolio.
Acceptable Work: Considers oil and acrylic paintings, watercolors, mixed media and enamels on copper. Especially likes large (4'x5' or larger) acrylic abstracts—can be college work.
Tips: "Disregard retail pricing and come equipped with adequate samples. We must know colors. Subject matter is not of utmost importance."

APPLE ARTS, LTD., Industrial Complex, Rt. 33 E, Freehold NJ 07728. (201)462-8686 or 1-800-dotless. President: M. Lav. Produces limited edition hand-pulled originals, positones and aluminum plate lithographs for own publishing and distribution, and custom work for the trade. Publishes 40-80 artists/year. Pays flat fee. Offers advance. Buys all rights. Provides promotion and shipping. Artist owns original art. Arrange interview. SASE. Reports in 2 weeks. Needs complete range of subject matter.

HERBERT ARNOT, INC., 250 W. 57th St., New York NY 10019. (212)245-8287. President: Peter Arnot. Art distributor of original oil paintings. Clients: galleries. Distributes work for 250 artists/year. Pays flat fee, $100-1,000 average. Provides promotion and shipping to and from distributor. Send query letter with brochure, resume, business card and samples to be kept on file. Prefers slides, photographs or original work as samples. Samples not filed are returned. Reports within 1 month. Call or write for appointment to show portfolio.
Acceptable Work: Considers oil and acrylic paintings. Has wide range of themes and styles—"mostly traditional/impressionistic, not modern."
Tips: "Professional quality, please."

ART BEATS, INC., 2435 S. Highland Dr., Salt Lake City UT 84106. (801)487-1588. President: Robert Gerrard. Vice President: Jill Gerrard. Art publisher and distributor of limited and unlimited editions and offset reproductions. Clients: gift shops, frame stores, department stores and galleries. Publishes 20 freelance artists/year. Distributes work for 50 artists/year. Pays royalty of 10%; negotiates payment method. Sometimes offers an advance. Prefers to buy all rights or first rights. Requires exclusive representation. Provides promotion, shipping from firm and written contract. Send query letter with brochure showing art style or tear sheets, slides and photographs to be kept on file. Samples not filed returned only if requested. Reports within 1 month. To show a portfolio, mail tear sheets, photostats and photographs.
Acceptable Work: Considers oil and acrylic paintings, pastels, watercolors and mixed media; no b&w. Especially likes children's, country and floral themes, "but always interested in new things."

***ARTCHOLOGY**, Box 1004, Redwood City CA 94064. (415)369-0126. President: Craig Stevens. Publisher/distributor of limited edition serigraphs and posters. Clients: art galleries, museums and interior designers.
Needs: Works with 5-7 artists/year. Pays $100-1,500; on acceptance. Buys all rights. Provides in-transit insurance and promotion.

 **The asterisk before a listing indicates that the listing is new in this edition. New markets are often the most receptive to freelance contributions.**

First Contact & Terms: Send query letter with slides. Samples not filed returned by SASE. Reports within 4-6 weeks. To show a portfolio, mail original/final art.
Acceptable Work: Considers line drawings and paintings no larger than 24"x48". Considers rights purchased when establishing payment.
Tips: "We will consider all work in realism."

ART IMAGE INC., 1577 Barry Ave., Los Angeles CA 90025. (213)826-9000. President: Allan Fierstein. Publishes and produces unlimited editions and limited editions that are pencil signed and numbered by the artist. Also distributes etchings, serigraphs, lithographs and water color paintings. "Other work we publish and distribute includes hand made paper, cast paper, paper weavings and paper construction." All work sold to galleries, frame shops, framed picture manufacturers, interior decorators and auctioneers. Publishes 12-16 artists per year; distributes the work of 24 artists. Negotiates payment. Requires exclusive representation. Provides shipping and a written contract. Send query letter with brochure showing art style, tear sheets, slides and photographs. SASE. Reports within 1 week. To show a portfolio, mail appropriate materials or write to schedule an appointment; portfolio should include photographs.
Acceptable Work: "All subject matter and all media in pairs or series of companion pieces."
Tips: "We are publishing and distributing more and more subject matter from offset limited editions to etchings, serigraphs, lithographs and original water color paintings."

ART 101 LTD., 1401 Chattahoochee Ave. NW, Atlanta GA 30318. (404)351-9146. Creative Director: Jules Stine. Art publisher of unlimited editions. Clients: gift and card shops and department stores. Publishes 2-4 artists/year. Pays flat fee of $500-1,500 average. All work is "work for hire," fees negotiated. Buys all rights. Provides shipping to and from firm and written contract. Send query letter with brochure, resume and samples to be kept on file. Samples not filed are returned. Reports within 10 days. Call or write for appointment to show portfolio.
Acceptable Work: Posters combine extensive copy and specially selected type with strong graphic design. Illustrations are secondary to the copy and design.

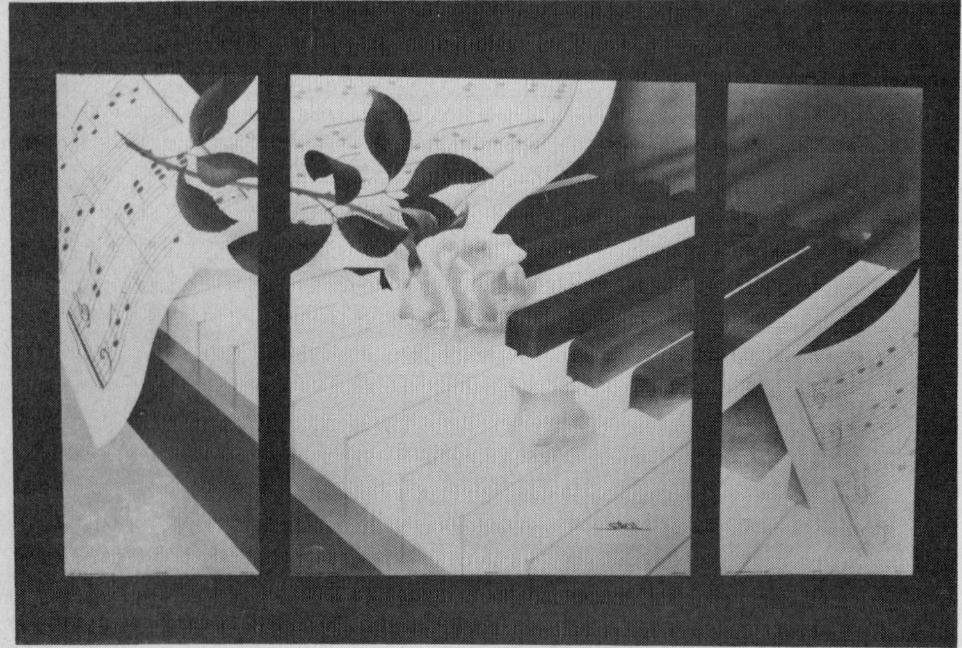

'Love Notes' is a triptych by artist Ken Shotwell of Stonington, Vermont, that was published by Art Resources International, Ltd. of Stamford, Connecticut. Robin Bonnist of Art Resources purchased reprint rights for unlimited prints. Shotwell used an airbrush to create the fine art print.

ART RESOURCES INTERNATIONAL, LTD., 98 Commerce St., Stamford CT 06902-4506. (203)967-4545, (800)228-2989. Vice President: Robin E. Bonnist. Art publisher. Publishes unlimited edition offset lithographs. Clients: galleries, department stores, distributors, framers throughout the world. Publishes 100 freelance artists/year. Distributes work of 200 artists/year. Also uses artists for advertising layout and brochure illustration. Pays by royalty 5-10%, or flat fee of $250-1,000. Offers advance in some cases. Requires exclusive representation of the artist for prints/posters during period of contract. Provides in-transit insurance, insurance while work is at publisher, shipping to and from firm, promotion and a written contract. Artist owns original work. Send query letter with brochure, tear sheets, slides and photographs to be kept on file or returned if requested; prefers to see slides or transparencies initially as samples, then reviews originals. Samples not kept on file returned by SASE. Reports within 1 month. Call or write for appointment to show portfolio, or mail appropriate materials, which should include transparencies, slides and photographs.
Acceptable Work: Considers oil and acrylic paintings, pastels, watercolors and mixed media. Prefers pairs or series, triptychs, diptychs.
Tips: "Please submit any and all ideas."

ART SOURCE, Unit 10, 70 Gibson Dr., Markham, Toronto, Ontario L3R 4C2 Canada. (416)475-8181. Art publisher and distributor. Produces posters, offset reproductions, art cards, handpulled originals, and prints using offset, lithograph, screen and etching for galleries and department stores. Publishes 20-30 freelance artists/year; distributes the works of 20-30 artists/year. Negotiates payment method. Negotiates rights purchased. Provides insurance while work is at publisher, promotion and a written contract. Negotiates ownership of original art. Send query letter with brochure, resume, and tear sheets, slides and photographs to be kept on file. To show a portfolio, mail thumbnails, tear sheets, photostats and photographs. Samples not kept on file returned by SASE if requested. Reports within 14 days.
Acceptable Work: Considers oil and acrylic paintings, pastels, watercolors, mixed media and photographs. Themes and styles open. Prefers pairs and series; unframed.
Tips: "Show us your work in its best possible way. We see you through what you show us." One of today's most popular mediums is the poster—"we publish many of them." Artists should be very sensitive to the needs of the markets where they are trying to sell their work.

ART SPECTRUM, division of Mitch Morse Gallery, Inc., 334 E. 59th St., New York NY 10022. (212)593-1812. President: Mitch Morse. Art publisher and distributor. Produces limited editions (maximum of 250 prints) and handpulled originals—all 'multi-original' editions of lithographs, etchings, collographs, serigraphs. Serves galleries, frame shops, hotels, interior designers, architects and corporate art specifiers. Publishes 8-10 freelance artists/year; distributes the works of 15-20 artists/year. Negotiates payment method. Offers advance. Negotiates rights purchased. Provides promotion and shipping. Artist owns original art. Send query letter with resume, slides and photographs to be kept on file. Call or write for appointment to show portfolio, which should include original/final art and photographs. Samples not kept on file are returned. Reports within 1 week.
Acceptable Work: Considers original fine art prints only. Offers "subjects primarily suitable for corporate offices. Not too literal; not too avant-garde." Prefers series; unframed (framed unacceptable); 30x40"maximum.
Tips: "Do not stop by without appointment. Do not come to an appointment with slides only—examples of actual work must be seen. No interest in reproductive (photo-mechanical) prints—originals only. Submit work that is "an improved version of an existing 'look' or something completely innovative." Actively seeking additional artists who do original paintings on paper. Trends show that the "current demand for contemporary has not yet peaked in many parts of the country. The leading indicators in the New York City design market point to a strong resurgence of Old English."

ARTHUR'S INTERNATIONAL, Box 10599, Honolulu HI 96816. President: Marvin C. Arthur. Art distributor handling original oil paintings primarily and also limited edition prints. Clients: galleries, collectors, etc. "Normally we purchase and pay for all art works handled. Exceptions have been made, though rarely, for other forms of representations." Negotiates payment determined by the talents of artist and his wants. "Artists may be represented on an exclusive basis for the Hawaiian Islands and to our own international gallery customers. May be on a selective per picture arrangement or encompass the taking on of all works produced." Provides agreement or contract. "We promote items purchased." Send brochure, slides or photographs to be kept on file if interested. No originals. Samples not filed returned by SASE. Reports back normally within 1 week.
Acceptable Work: Considers oil paintings, serigraphs, stone lithographs, plate lithographs, and gravures. "All paintings should be photographic in texture or have an eye appeal of the subject matter that is not a modern art puzzle."
Tips: "We are interested in fine quality work. Be realistic in compensation desired. Include information on artist's background, manner of painting and reason for art work subject matter selection; also any

track record on sales, wholesale or retail prices, type of outlets where sales made and what type of promotional work has been done. If you have no track record, that is fine also. Some of the highest paid started out with us when they were unknowns but they were very talented."

***ARTHURIAN ART GALLERY**, 5836 Lincoln Ave., Chicago IL 60053. Owner: Art Sahagian. Estab. 1985. Art distributor/gallery handling limited editions, handpulled originals, bronzes, watercolors, oil paintings and pastels. Works with 30-40 artists/year. Pays flat fee $50-1,000 average. Rights purchased varies with work. Provides insurance while work is at firm, promotion and a written contract. Send query letter with brochure showing art style or resume, photocopies and slides. Samples not filed returned by SASE. Reports within 30 days. To show a portfolio, mail appropriate materials or write to schedule an appointment. Portfolio should include original/final art, color, final reproduction/product and photographs. Considers complexity of project, client's budget, and skill and experience of artist when establishing payment.

ARTISTWORKS WHOLESALE INC., 2345 Olive St., Philadelphia PA 19130. (215)978-4700. Contact: Michael Markowicz. Art publisher and art distributor of offset reproductions and handpulled originals. Clients: distributors, galleries, decorators and other retailers. Works with 2-4 freelance artists/year. Negotiates payment method. Advance depends on payment method. Negotiates rights purchased. Requires exclusive representation. Provides in-transit insurance, insurance while work is at firm, promotion, shipping to and from firm and written contract. Send query letter with resume, slides and photographs to be kept on file. To show a portfolio, mail appropriate materials, which should include original/final art, final reproduction/product and photographs. "We only review original work after first seeing slides." Samples not filed returned by SASE.
Acceptable Work: Considers oil and acrylic paintings, pastels and watercolors; serigraphs. Especially likes still life/landscapes.
Tips: "We are looking for very well-executed still lifes and landscapes. We are not looking for traditional pieces but would rather work with a contemporary look. We have moved to Philadelphia. We have also received many more submissions than we can possibly publish. Artists should realize that we can only publish a few of the best works submitted. Submit only if you have producing high-quality, contemporary art."

ATLANTIC GALLERY, 1055 Thomas Jefferson St. NW, Washington DC 20007. (202)337-2299. Director: Virginia Smith. Art publisher/distributor. Publishes signed prints using offset lithography and hand-colored, handpulled restrike engravings. Clients: retail galleries, department stores, decorators, large commercial accounts. Publishes 3 freelance artists/year. Pays flat fee, $250-1,000 average. Offers advance. Buys one-time rights. Provides in-transit insurance, insurance while work is at publisher, promotion, shipping to and from publisher and a written contract. Negotiates ownership of original art. Send query letter with brochure, resume, slides, photographs and tear sheets to be kept on file. Samples not kept on file returned by SASE. Reports within 3 weeks. Call or write for appointment to show portfolio.
Acceptable Work: Considers oil and acrylic paintings, pastels and watercolors. Prefers traditional art.

***BECOME A POSTER**, (formerly Photo Environments), 2021 Vista del Man Ave., Los Angeles CA 90068. (213)465-9947. President: Joan Yarfitz. Works on assignment only. Uses freelance artists for marketing and advertising. Send query letter with brochure showing art style or samples. Samples not filed returned by SASE if requested. Call or write to schedule an appointment to show a portfolio. Negotiates payment. Considers clients' preferences when establishing payment. Negotiates rights purchased.
Acceptable Work: Considers illustraton, b&w, color and photograhy.

KATHLEEN BEHBEHANI FINE ART, INC., 5616 Royalton, Houston TX 77081. (713)661-8003. Owner: Kathleen Behbehani. Fine arts gallery representing works in oil, acrylic, watercolor, pastel, fiber, works on paper, original graphics and sculpture. Clients include private and corporate collectors, art consultants, other galleries and design trade. Negotiates payment method. Requires exclusive representation in immediate region. Provides insurance while work is in the gallery, and shipping to gallery. Written contracts are available. Work is given full-time, quality representation. Send query letter with resume and slides or photos. Contact Kathleen Behbehani or Melissa Rodwell by phone or mail. Prefers slides or photos for initial contact. All may be returned upon request.
Acceptable Work: Well-executed, quality fine art pieces in most any media, created by professional artists.

BERNARD PICTURE CO. INC., Box 4744, Stamford CT 06907. (203)357-7600. Vice President: Michael Katz. Designer: Rosemary Pellicone. Art publisher. Produces offset reproductions using offset

lithography for "manufacturers of product world-wide, i.e., framed pictures, plaques, etc." Publishes 300 freelance artists/year. Pays royalties to artist of 10%. Offers advance "depending on artist." Buys reprint rights. "Sometimes" requires exclusive representation of the artist. Provides in-transit insurance and insurance while work is at publisher. Artist owns original art. Send query letter with samples. Prefers slides, photos as samples—"then original work." Samples returned. Reports within 2 weeks. Call or write for appointment to show portfolio.
Acceptable Work: Considers all media, including, photography. Prefers series and sets; unframed.

***BROADWAY SHOW STOPPERS**, 345 E. 56th St., New York NY 10022. (212)593-2400. President: Sallie Kreda. Art publisher of offset reproductions. Clients: galleries and department stores. Works with 1 artist per year. Pays flat fee or royalty of 2-5%; negotiates method. Offers advance. Buys all rights or negotiates rights purchased. Provides promotion. Send query letter. Prefers to review slides. Material not filed is returned by SASE.
Acceptable Work: Considers mixed media.
Tips: "Write only."

C.R. FINE ARTS LTD., 249 A St., Boston MA 02210. (617)236-4225. President: Carol Robinson. Art publisher/distributor/gallery handling limited editions, sculptures and fine art posters. Clients: galleries, poster stores, department stores, decorators, art consultants. Publishes 5-6 artists/year; distributes work of 30 artists/year. Pays royalty (20%) or works on consignment (40% commission); payment method is negotiated. Offers advance. Negotiates rights purchased. Provides in-transit insurance, insurance while work is at firm, promotion, shipping to and from firm and a written contract. Send query letter with resume and slides to be kept on file. Samples not filed returned by SASE only if requested. Reports within 3 weeks. Write for appointment to show portfolio.
Acceptable Work: Considers pastels, watercolors and mixed media; serigraphs, and stone or plate lithographs. Especially likes flowers, seascapes, contemporary themes, beach scenes, animals, music themes, abstracts.

CANADIAN ART PRINTS INC., 736 Richards St., Vancouver, British Columbia V6B 3A4 Canada. (604)681-3485. President: J.H. Krieger. Publishes limited edition handpulled originals and offset reproductions for galleries, card and gift shops, department stores, framers and museum shops. Publishes 40-50 artists/year. Send slides or photos. Reports within 5 weeks. Provides promotion, shipping from publisher and written contract. Pays royalties.
Acceptable Work: Considers paintings, pastels, watercolors, intaglio, stone lithographs and serigraphs by Canadian artists; series.

***CARLA JEAN PUBLISHING**, Suite C519, 1237 Camino Del Mar, Del Mar CA 92014. Owner: Carla Bonny. Clients: galleries.
Needs: "Interested in artists that have potential for publishing limited editions." Send slides and photographs. Samples not filed are returned. Reports back within 2 weeks. To show a portfolio, mail appropriate materials, which should include photographs and slides. Considers saleability of artwork when establishing payment.
Acceptable Work: Prefers acrylics or oils. Presently publish an artist like Matisse . . . figurative.

CHINA ARTS INTERNATIONAL TRADING CO., INC., 54 Mott St., New York NY 10013. (212)226-5094. Assistant Manager: Hall P. Tam. Art distributor and gallery handling unlimited editions. Clients: galleries and wholesale distributors. Works with 20 freelance artists/year. Negotiates payment method. Buys reprint rights or negotiates rights purchased. Provides promotion and shipping from firm. Send brochure and business card to be kept on file. Prefers original work as samples. Samples not filed returned by SASE. Reports within 1 month. Write for appointment to show portfolio.
Acceptable Work: Considers watercolors. Especially likes lady, flower and bird, and landscape themes. Handles oriental paintings only.
Tips: Low prices are an important consideration.

CIRRUS EDITIONS, 542 S. Alameda St., Los Angeles CA 90013. President: Jean R. Milant. Produces limited edition hand-pulled originals for museums, galleries and private collectors. Publishes 3-4 artists/year. Send slides of work. Prefers slides as samples. Samples returned by SASE.
Acceptable Work: Contemporary paintings and sculpture.

DISCOVERY GALLERIES, 1260 Santa Monica Mall, Santa Monica CA 90401. (213)450-8989. Contact: Monroe Mendelsohn. Art publisher of gallery posters. Clients: frame shops and poster distributors, national and international. Pays flat fee for all poster rights. Provides insurance while work is at firm. Send query letter with brochure, colored photos or slides. "Never send us original artwork unsolicited."

Material is filed only at artist's request; "if artist is local, we like to look at portfolio." Samples not filed returned by SASE only. Reports within a week if interested; "otherwise, we simply mail back the samples within a couple of days after we receive them, provided postage has been provided. Call or write for appointment to show portfolio.

Acceptable Work: Considers acrylics and airbrush; offset and silkscreen posters.

Tips: "We are interested in publishing only 'decorative' work with a contemporary look aimed at a middle-brow audience; still lifes and highly stylized landscapes. No portraits. We look upon ourselves as publishers of wall decor. Colors are important and subject matter should be up-tempo and pleasant to look at. Remember, someone is choosing the work to decorate his living quarters. For hints and suggestions about color and moods, an artist does well to study some good contemporary wallpaper catalogs."

DODO GRAPHICS, INC., Box 585, 119 Cornelia St., Plattsburgh NY 12901. (518)561-7294. President: Frank How. Art publisher. Produces offset reproductions, art posters and handpulled originals for galleries, frame stores, manufacturers and distributors of prints and framed prints. Publishes 3-4 freelance artists/year. Buys copyright outright; also negotiates. Requires exclusive representation. Provides promotion, shipping to publisher and a written contract. Negotiates ownership of original art. Send brochure/flyer and slides or photographs. Samples returned. Reports within 3 months. Write for appointment to show a portfolio.

Acceptable Work: Considers pastels, watercolors and mixed media with floral, landscapes, still life in a contemporary style. Prefers unframed series; maximum size 28x22".

Tips: "Never send any original work. Slides or photographs, as many as possible, should be submitted." Sees a trend toward "more florals in the form of posters."

DONALD ART CO. INC., division Impress-Graphics, 30 Commerce Rd., Stamford CT 06904-2102. (203)348-9494. Art Coordinator: Bob Roberts. Produces unlimited edition offset reproductions for wholesale picture frame manufacturers, and manufacturers using art in their end products, for premiums and promotions. Send query letter with resume and photos or slides. Exclusive area representation required. Provides in-transit insurance, insurance while work is at publisher, shipping, promotion and written contract. Samples returned by SASE. Negotiates rights purchased.

Acceptable Work: Publishes 150 artists/year. Considers all types of paintings; oil, acrylic, watercolor, pastels, mixed media. Also needs work suitable for gallery posters.

Tips: "We have developed our division, Impress Graphics, for the publication and distribution of gallery posters. We will also be entering into the limited edition field, with some limited edition subjects already available. Look at the market to see what type of artwork is selling."

DRUCKER/VINCENT, INC., 45 Sheridan St., San Francisco CA 94103. (415)626-8610. Art Director: Richard Whittaker. Produces limited and unlimited editions, offset reproductions; fine art posters. Uses both offset lithography and silkscreen. Negotiates advances, payment and rights purchased. Provides insurance while work is at firm and a written contract. Send query letter with tear sheets, slides and photographs. Call or write for appointment to show portfolio, which should include slides and photographs. *No original work.* Samples returned by SASE if not kept on file.

Acceptable Work: All types of flat art, photographs, mechanicals, etc. Prefers work contemporary in style.

Tips: "Do not want surrealism or visionary art. Work must have strong aesthetic appeal to wide variety of people."

EDELMAN FINE ARTS, LTD., Suite 1503, 1140 Broadway, New York NY 10001. (212)683-4266. Vice President: H. Heather Edelman. Art distributor of original oil paintings. "We now handle watercolors, lithographs, serigraphs and "work on paper" as well as original oil paintings." Clients: galleries, interior designers and furniture stores. Distributers work for 150 artists/year. Negotiates payment method. Buys all rights. Provides in-transit insurance, insurance while work is at firm, promotion, shipping from firm and written contract. Send query letter with brochure, resume, tear sheets, photographs and "a sample of work on paper or canvas" to be kept on file. Call or write for appointment to show portfolio or mail original/final art and photographs. Reports within 1 week.

Acceptable Work: Considers oil and acrylic paintings, watercolors and mixed media. Especially likes Old World and Impressionist themes or styles.

Tips: Portfolio should include originals and only best work.

EMROSE ART CORPORATION OF FLORIDA, 5181 NE 12th Ave., Ft. Lauderdale FL 33334. (305)772-1386. President: Marvin Rosenbaum. Art publisher and dealer. Produces limited edition original lithographs for galleries, auctioneers and furniture stories. Pays flat fee. Negotiates rights purchased and ownership of original art. Send query letter. Prefers photos as samples. Samples not returned. Reports within 1 week. Provide material to be kept on file for possible future assignments.

Acceptable Work: Considers pen & ink line drawings, oil and acrylic paintings and watercolors. Accepts assorted styles and themes; prefers design oriented art. Prefers framed or unframed individual works of art.

***ATELIER ETTINGER INCORPORATED**, 155 Avenue of the Americas, New York NY 10013. (212)807-7607. President: Eleanor Ettinger. Flatbed limited edition lithographic studio. "All plates are hand drawn, hand proofed and printed on one of our 12-ton Voirin presses . . . classic flat bed lithographic presses hand built in France over 100 years ago" for galleries only. Provides insurance while work is at publisher, shipping from publisher and a written contract. Original art is returned to artist; plates are effaced. Send query letter with samples to be kept on file. Call for appointment to show portfolio. Prefers slides or photos as samples. Samples returned. Reports within 7 days.
Acceptable Work: Considers pen & ink drawings, oil and acrylic paintings, pastels, watercolors and mixed media. "Will consider any school of art for printing consideration."

***ELEANOR ETTINGER INCORPORATED**, 155 Avenue of the Americas, New York NY 10013. (212)807-7607. President: Eleanor Ettinger. Art publisher of limited edition prints. "All plates are hand drawn, hand proofed and printed on one of our 12-ton Voirin presses . . . classic flat bed lithographic presses hand built in France over 100 years ago" for galleries only. Publishes 6 freelance artists/year. Distributes work of 18 artists/year. Buys rights for limited edition prints. Provides insurance while work is at publisher, promotion and shipping from publisher. Original art is returned to artist; plates are effaced. Send query letter with brochure, tear sheets and slides to be kept on file. Samples returned. Reports within 7 days. Call for appointment to show portfolio.
Acceptable Work: Considers pen & ink drawings, oil and acrylic paintings, pastels, watercolors and mixed media. "Will consider any school of art for publishing consideration." Prefers series.
Tips: "The trend in realism has caused us to focus our attentions only in that area."

EXACTLY MY THOUGHTS, INC., 1819 Charlotte Dr., Charlotte NC 28203. (704)372-2747. President: Ronald D. Unger. Art publisher and distributor of limited and unlimited editions, offset reproductions and handpulled originals. Clients: galleries, specialty shops and hotel gift shops. Publishes 4 freelance artists/year. Distributes work for 8 artists/year. Pays in royalty of 25%. Buys first rights or reprint rights. Requires exclusive representation. Provides promotion and written contract. Send query letter with brochure, resume, slides or photographs to be kept on file. Samples not filed are returned. Reports within 1 month.
Acceptable Work: Considers pastels and watercolors; serigraphs, linocuts and woodcuts. Especially likes fantasy and dream-like themes or styles.

FAIRFAX PRINTS LTD., 4918 Delta River Dr., Lansing MI 48906. President: Gary Fairfax. General Manager: John Giuliani. Publishes limited and inexpensive unlimited edition offset reproductions for bookstores, gift shops, hobby shops, record stores, galleries and department stores. Publishes 1-2 artists/year. Send slides or 3x5 prints. SASE. Reports within 4-6 weeks. Provides insurance while work is at publisher, promotion, shipping from publisher and written contract. Send query letter with brochure, slides and photographs. To show a portfolio, mail original/final art, final reproduction/product and photographs. Buys poster rights only; sometimes negotiates rights; may also purchase originals. Pays royalties.
Acceptable Work: Subjects: wildlife and fantasy *only*. Realistic paintings (*no* photograpic work) and sculpture on wildlife (primarily "big cats" and predatory birds), or fantasy/science fiction themes (though work can be quite stylized); series. Pays advance against 5-10% royalties.
Tips: Especially needs "science fiction fantasy, realistic or stylized (but no "primitive" styles or amateurish work!) and wildlife, realistic styles only (esp. "Big Cats" or "Predatory Birds"). Please submit only finished, *professional calibre* work. Send slides or inexpensive 3x5 or 4x6 photos only—and include SASE if you wish work returned. *No* resumes/work experience needed."

FELIX ROSENSTIEL'S WIDOW & SON LTD., 33-35 Markham St., London SW3 England. 44-1-352-3551. Also New York office. Director: David A. Roe. Art publisher handling limited and unlimited editions, offset reproductions, hand coloured engravings and handpulled originals. Clients: galleries, department stores and wholesale picture manufactures. Publishes approximately 30-40 freelance artists/year. Negotiates payment method. Offers advance. Buys all rights or negotiates rights purchased. Provides in-transit insurance, insurance while work is at firm, promotion, shipping from firm and a written contract. Send query letter with slides and photographs. Samples returned by SASE (nonresidents include IRC). Reports within 30 days.
Acceptable Work: Considers pen & ink line drawings, oils, acrylics, pastels, watercolors and mixed media; serigraphs and stone or plate lithographs, woodcuts, linocuts, etchings and engravings.
Tips: "Posters are declining."

FINE ART RESOURCES, INC., 2179 Queensburg Lane, Palatine IL 60074. President: Gerard V. Perez. Art publisher. Publishes limited editions of handpulled original prints for galleries. *Does not* publish reproductions. Publishes 80 freelance artists/year. Pays flat fee, $500-5,000 average. Offers advance. Negotiates rights purchased. Requires exclusive representation of the artist. Provides insurance while work is at publisher, promotion and a written contract. Plates or screens destroyed after printing. Send query letter with original work, slides, photographs and tear sheets. Samples returned by SASE. Reports within 10 days.
Acceptable Work: Considers "strictly original prints." Publishes representational style. Prefers individual works of art; unframed; 30x40" maximum.

RUSSELL A. FINK GALLERY, Box 250, 9843 Gunston Rd., Lorton VA 22079. (703)550-9699. Contact: Russell A. Fink. Art publisher/dealer. Publishes offset reproductions using five-color offset lithography for galleries, individuals, framers. Publishes 3 freelance artists/year. Pays royalties to artist or negotiates payment method. Negotiates rights purchased. Provides insurance while work is at publisher, promotion and shipping from publisher. Negotiates ownership of original art. Send query letter with slides or photographs to be kept on file. Call or write for appointment to show portfolio. Samples returned if not kept on file.
Acceptable Work: Considers oil and acrylic paintings and watercolors. Prefers wildlife and sporting themes. Prefers individual works of art; unframed. "Submit photos or slides of at least near professional quality. Include size, price, media and other pertinent data regarding the artwork. Also send personal resume and be courteous enough to include SASE for return of any material sent to me."
Tips: "Looks for composition, style and technique in samples. Also how the artist views his own art. Mistakes artists make are arrogance, overpricing, explaining their art and underrating the dealer."

FIRST IMPRESSIONS, 3373 Wrightwood Dr., Studio City CA 91604. (213)656-1797. Marketing Director: Dana Axelrod. Art consultant and distributor. Original handpulled originals for galleries, designers and corporate clients. Work accepted on consignment basis only. Drawings, paintings, sculptures and tapestries accepted. Send brochure, photographs and slides of artwork with price. Slides returned by SASE. Reports within 1-2 weeks. Accepted slides kept on file for client presentation. Acceptance of work based on review of slides and resume. No personal interview without slide review. "No telephone appointments." To show a portfolio, mail appropriate materials, which should include photos of original/final art.
Acceptable Work: Considers landscape, florals, and abstract, illustrative and soft abstract styles. Prefers large individual works, series or pairs. Professional quality only.
Tips: "Colors and images today tend to be influenced by the interior design colors and styles. Large format 30x40 unique works on paper, contemporary imagery."

***FOXFIRE DIV., TOB, INC.**, 2730 N. Graham St., Charlotte NC 28206. Art Director: Larry O'Boyle. Series 500-750 outlets. "We sell lithographs, limited editions to frame shops, galleries and the like." Send query letter with resume and slides. Samples not filed are returned by SASE. Reports back within 10 days. To show a portfolio mail appropriate materials, which should include slides. Artist receives flat fee; on acceptance. Considers salability of artwork and rights purchased when establishing payment. Negotiates rights purchased.
Acceptable Work: Prefers watercolors/oils, with wildlife themes.

***FREELANCE VISUAL PRODUCTIONS INC.**, Box 843, Philadelphia PA 19105. (215)342-1492. President: Leonard Neil Friedman. Contact: Helen F. Weintraub, % Art Production and Design Dept. Query with samples (slides, and Photographic Prints) for our files. We will consider all submissions. Reports in 3 weeks. Negotiates rights purchased/royalty; depends on usage.
Acceptable Work: Considers pastels, oils, watercolors, acrylics, drawings, photographs, collage, art-deco, mixed media and inventive graphics (themes and styles open).
Tips: "We are dealing in a highly specialized production of paper products which include: greeting cards, calendars, posters and art decor products, limited and unlimited editions."

GALAXY OF GRAPHICS, LTD., 460 W. 34th St., New York NY 10001. (212)947-8989. President: Reid A. Fader. Art publisher of unlimited editions and offset reproductions. Clients: galleries and picture frame manufacturers. Publishes 25-50 freelance artists/year. Works with several hundred artists/year. Pays royalty of 10%. Offers advance. Buys all rights. Exclusive representation. Provides insurance while work is at firm, promotion, shipping from firm and written contract. Send photos or color slides or mail original/final art, final reproduction/product, color and photographs. Call or write for appointment to show portfolio. Samples are returned. Reports within a few days.
Acceptable Work: Considers pen & ink line drawings, oil and acrylic paintings, pastels, watercolors and mixed media; "any currently popular and generally accepted theme."

Tips: "Traditional imagery is becoming very strong; posters are fading; diptychs and triptychs are still very good sellers. Pastels are *out!*"

GALLERY ENTERPRISES, 1881 Abington Rd. or 310 Bethlehem Plaza Mall, Bethlehem PA 18018. (215)868-1139. Contact: David Michael Donnangelo. Art publisher/distributor/gallery agents. Publishes limited edition offset reproductions and handpulled originals using etching; lithography and offset methods. Clients: galleries and volume art buyers. Publishes 2 freelance artists/year. Pays flat fee, $3,000 minimum. Negotiates rights purchased. Provides a written contract. Publishes own original art. Send resume and samples to be kept on file. To show a portfolio, mail appropriate materials. Prefers actual sample print as a representation. Samples are kept on file. Reports within 3 months.
Acceptable Work: Considers pen & ink drawings and etchings. All works considered but prefers traditional and wildlife themes. Especially needs abstract, corporate art for large works. Prefers series; 20x30" maximum.
Tips: Artists "must be able to produce original images in volume. Only interested in commercially-minded artists."

GEME ART INC., 209 W. 6th St., Vancouver WA 98660. (206)693-7772. Art Director: Merilee Will. Publishes fine art prints and reproductions in unlimited editions. Clients: galleries, department stores— the general art market. Works with 40-80 artists/year. Publishes the works of 15-20 artists; distributes 23-40. Payment is negotiated on a royalty basis. Normally purchases all rights. Provides promotion, shipping from publisher and a contract. Query with color slides or photos. SASE. Reports only if interested. Call or write for appointment to show portfolio. Simultaneous submissions OK.
Acceptable Work: Considers oils, acrylics, pastels, watercolor and mixed media. Themework is open.

GESTATION PERIOD, 1946 N. Fourth St., Columbus OH 43201. Operations Manager: Bob Richman. Art distributor of offset reproductions. Clients: galleries, framers, college stores, gift stores, poster shops. Distributes 5-10 new artists/year "depending on what's available for our market." Payment method is negotiated. Generally offers an advance. Negotiates rights purchased. Generally does not require exclusive representation. Provides promotion packaging and shipping from firm. Send query letter with brochure and/or published samples to be kept on file. Samples not filed returned only if requested. Reports within 1 month.
Acceptable Work: Considers any medium including photography. Especially likes fine art/exhibition posters and humor.
Tips: "We only distribute published works. We do not publish at this time."

GRAPHIC ORIGINALS INC., 153 W. 27th St., New York NY 10001. (212)807-6180. President: Martin Levine. Art publisher and dealer. Produces limited editions of etchings and silkscreens for galleries. Negotiates payment and rights purchased. Publisher owns original art. Call for appointment. Send resume, photos or originals. Samples returned by SASE. Reports within 3 weeks.
Acceptable Work: Considers contemporary and realistic themes. Prefers unframed works; 24x30" maximum.

GRAPHICS INTERNATIONAL, Station E, Box 13292, Oakland CA 94661. (415)339-9310. Vice President: Rob R. Kral. Art publisher/distributor of limited and unlimited edition handpulled originals. Clients: galleries, frame shops, distributors and department stores. Number of artists worked with per year varies. Negotiates payment method. Buys all rights. Requires exclusive representation. Provides shipping from firm and a written contract. Send query letter with brochure, resume and samples to be kept on file. Accepts slides, photographs or original work as samples. Reports only if interested.
Acceptable Work: Considers pen & ink line drawings, watercolors and etchings. Especially likes traditional style.

GRAPHIQUE DE FRANCE, 46 Waltham St., Boston MA 02118. (617)482-5066. Contact: Scott Slater or Jean-Jacques Toulotte. Art publisher and distributor of fine art posters (offset and silkscreen). Clients: art galleries, poster shops, designers, architects, department stores, art consultants and framers. Publishes up to 50 images/year and always interested in working with artists, designers, illustrators and photographers. Distributes 1,200 different poster images. Pays 8-10% royalty of wholesale selling price and retain only the rights on the image for reproduction in poster form. Send query letter with "any available pictorial and literature." Send query letter and samples to be kept on file. Accepts "anything that is pictorial" as samples. Samples not filed are returned. Reports within 4-5 weeks. Call or write for appointment to show portfolio.
Acceptable Work: Considers all types of work suitable to be produced as posters. Especially likes realistic and decorate images.

GREEN RIVER TRADING CO., Boston Corners Rd., RD2, Box 130, Millerton NY 12546. (518)789-3311. President: Art Kerber. Art publisher. Produces limited edition, signed and numbered prints of Western and wildlife art for galleries, wholesale and retail. Works with 3 freelance artists/year. Also uses artists for advertising, brochure and catalog design, illustration and layout.
First Contact & Terms: Works on assignment only. Send query letter with brochure, resume, business card, and tear sheets, slides and photographs to be kept on file. Samples not kept on file returned only if requested. Reports within 2 weeks. Write for appointment to show portfolio. Pays by the hour, $65 maximum; by the project, $200-2,000 average. Considers complexity of project, skill and experience of artist, turnaround time and rights purchased when establishing payment.
Tips: Artists must be willing "to take advice."

HADDAD'S FINE ARTS INC., Box 3016 C, Anaheim CA 92803. President: James Haddad. Produces limited and unlimited edition originals and offset reproductions for galleries, art stores, schools and libraries. Publishes 40-70 artists/year. Buys reproduction rights. Provides insurance while work is at publisher, shipping from publisher and written contract. Submit slides. SASE. Reports within 60 days.
Acceptable Work: Unframed individual works and pairs; all media.

HOW & PEYER, LTD., Box 506, Laprairie, Quebec J5R 4X2 Canada. (518)561-7294. President: Frank How. Art publisher. Produces offset reproductions, art posters and handpulled originals for frame shops, art galleries, wholesale framers, department stores and distributors in over 20 countries. Publishes 2-4 freelance artists/year. Negotiates payment. Buys all rights. Requires exclusive representation. Provides promotion and a written contract. Negotiates ownership of original art. Send resume and photographs or slides, brochure, if available. Samples returned. Reports within 3 months. Provide resume, business card and brochure/flyer to be kept on file for possible future assignments.
Acceptable Work: Considers oil and acrylic paintings, pastels, watercolors and mixed media. Contemporary realistic styles and themes with broad appeal (no local scenes); landscapes, still-lifes, etc. Prefers unframed series; maximum 20x30" either horizontal or vertical.
Tips: "When submitting photographs, send as many different ones as possible. The artist should not make selection but should leave it up to the publisher. The more we can see, the better the chance that we are interested."

ICART VENDOR GRAPHICS, 8568 Pico Blvd., Los Angeles CA 90035. (213)653-3190. Director: Sandy Verin. Art publisher/distributor/gallery. Produces limited and unlimited editions of offset reproductions and handpulled original prints for galleries, decorators, corporations, collectors. Publishes 3-5 freelance artists/year. Distributes 30-40 artists/year. Pays flat fee, $250-1,000; royalties (5-10%) or negotiates payment method. "We also distribute." Offers advance. Buys all rights. Usually requires exclusive representation of the artist. Provides insurance while work is at publisher. Negotiates ownership of original art. Send brochure and samples. Prefers photographs, not slides, as samples. Samples returned by SASE. Reports within 1 month.
Acceptable Work: Considers oils, acrylics, watercolors and mixed media, also serigraphy and lithography. Likes airbrush. Prefers "turn-of-the-century through Art Deco period (1900s-1930s) styles." Prefers individual works of art, pairs, series; 30x40" maximum.
Tips: "Be original with your own ideas. Present clean, neat presentations in original or photographic form (no slides). Work should be done in the Art Deco style or Art Nouveau. Art Deco is preferred."

***IMPRESS GRAPHICS**, 30 Commerce Rd., Stamford CT 06904. (203)348-9494. National Sales Manager: Bob Roberts. Provides for magazines, trade shows and mailings. Send query letter with resume, slides and photographs. Samples not filed returned by SASE. Reports within 2 weeks. To show a portfolio, mail photographs and slides (duplicates).
Acceptable Work: Considers photographs, airbrush and paintings.

ARTHUR A. KAPLAN CO. INC.,, 460 W. 34th St., New York NY 10001. (212)947-8989. National Sales Manager: Reid Fader. Art publisher of unlimited editions, offset reproduction, prints and posters. Clients: galleries, department stores and picture frame manufacturers. Publishes approximately 40 freelance artists/year. Works with 300+ artists/year. Pays a royalty of 5-10%. Offers advance. Buys all rights. Requires exclusive representation. Provides insurance while work is at firm, promotion, shipping from firm and a written contract. Send resume, tear sheets, slides, photographs and original art to be kept on file. Material not filed is returned. Reports within 2-3 weeks. To show a portfolio, mail appropriate materials or call to schedule an appointment. Portfolio should include original/final art, final reproduction/product, color, tear sheets and photographs.
Acceptable Work: Considers pen & ink line drawings, oils, acrylics, pastels, watercolors, mixed media, photography.
Tips: "We cater to a mass market and require fine quality art with decorative and appealing subject matter. Don't be afraid to submit work—we'll consider anything and everything."

Close-up

Sandy Verin
Director, Icart Vendor Graphics
Los Angeles, California

It's important for artists to know what art styles and media an art publisher wants. "We like to publish art nouveau, art deco and very select contemporary images that we feel will fit into our line of posters," says Sandy Verin, director of the art publishing firm, Icart Vendor. "This is our identity, what we are sought out for in the marketplace, and we try to stay within these confines."

Verin works with a diverse group of artists at Icart, which has published the work of such artists as Muramasa Kudo (Japanese-westernized), Istvan Bernath (Hungarian Deco), Don Ahn (Korean oriental animals), Alberto Vargas (American pin-up girls), Louis Icart (Art Deco French) and Maxfield Parrish (Americana).

In preparing for her career, Verin studied fine art at UCLA Extension, Los Angeles City College, West Los Angeles City College and the Otis Art Institute (now Parsons & Otis School of Design), as well as with private instructors.

She prefers a clean style with a strong, well-defined, stylized look, preferably in the art deco style, but adds that strong, well-done contemporary images are certainly considered. "Colors should be well-integrated and popular in today's trends," adds Verin, and she favors airbrush because of its "velvety smoothness."

Themes are important to art publishers, too. "We prefer universal themes that appeal to the largest segment of the population," she says. She is not interested in portraiture or particular people. "I do not select 'trendy' images that are here today and gone tomorrow. I like to think of our line of images as timeless and always appropriate," she explains.

Strong, brightly colored posters executed in the latest decorating colors is a trend Verin sees in the art publishing field today. "Too often, though, when a successful poster sells on the market, there are many other 'knock-offs' or imitators," she says. "I have particular disdain for this practice and would never consider publishing anything not originally creative."

Because of the bulky size of original works, Verin prefers to review an artist's work in the form of color photographs. "I find slides very limiting unless viewed on a projector, which is inconvenient usually," she says.

One of the advantages freelance artists find in working for this Los Angeles art publisher is that Icart always incorporates the artist's name in the poster image, which helps to acquaint buyers with that artist and create a demand for his or her work. "We also do trade shows nationally and advertise heavily," says Verin. "All of this helps to expand the market, building a fine reputation for the artist." In turn, though, the artist must be willing to be guided whenever necessary and accept constructive criticism. "We both have a common goal of creating and selling a successful poster for mutual gain," she says.

—Pat Beusterien

***KEY WEST GRAPHICS, INC.**, 6 Portside Dr., Fort Lauderdale FL 33316. (305)463-1150. President: Jennifer Roberts. Estab. 1985. Clients: Trade magazines, galleries and trade shows. Uses artists for illustrations and color. Send query letter with brochure showing art style or resume, tear sheets, slides and photographs. Samples not filed returned by SASE. Reports within 5 weeks. To show a portfolio, mail appropriate materials or write to schedule an appointment. Portfolio should include original/final art, color and tear sheets.
Acceptable Work: Considers salability of artwork and rights purchased when establishing payment. Negotiates rights purchased. Considers pen & ink with washes and paintings and pastels. Prefers landscapes and dance scenes as themes. Prefers oils and acrylics.

KINGFISHER PRINTS LTD., 23A Horndon Industrial Park, West Horndon, Brentwood Essex CM13 3XD England. 44-0277-810111. Telex: 26048 Kingfisher. Cable: Kingfisher Brentwood. Art Director: John Stephenson. Publishes unlimited editions of offset lithographs for distribution to trade picture manufacturers such as department stores and wholesales. Publishes approximately 150 originals/year. Publishes 10 freelance artists/year. Send query letter with resume, slides or photographs with SASE (nonresidents include IRC). Samples are returned. Reports within 2 weeks. Buys all rights. Provides intransit insurance while work is at firm, shipping from your firm and a written contract. Send query letter with resume, slides and photographs. Write to schedule an appointment to show a portfolio, which should include original/final art, final reproduction/product, photographs and good color copies. Pays outright fee of $200-400; buys reproduction rights. Original art returned on completion of publication.
Acceptable Work: Considers all subjects suitable for sale to department stores, etc. Especially needs landscapes with a traditional approach and contemporary work on most subjects."
Tips: "Within the contemporary market we see a move towards stronger, brighter colours, punchy semi-photograhic imagery (illustration). Themes: Nostalgia, 50's, American imagery. We react to changes in fashion or trends in parallel fields, whether or not it be fashion design/colour, or architective/decoration, and we select our artwork and artists accordingly. Artists would now be working in conjunction with inhouse designers and illustrators for a more professional approach to achieving the desired results. If the artist has a portfolio to show, and he/she thinks it is suitable for our market, then he/she should not hesitate to call, as we are always on the look out for new artists."

DAVID LAWRENCE EDITIONS, Suite 38, 22541A Pacific Coast Hwy., Malibu CA 90265. (818)343-2293. President: David Lawrence. Art publisher/distributor handling limited and unlimited editions of offset reproductions. Clients: galleries and frame shops. Publishes 5-10 freelance artists and distributes work for 25 artists/year. Negotiates payment method and rights purchased. Requires exclusive representation. Provides promotion, shipping from firm and a written contract. Send a resume and "anything that gives a good representation of work" to be kept on file. Reports back only if interested. Call or write for appointment to show portfolio.
Acceptable Work: Considers all media for publication and distribution.

MARTIN LAWRENCE LIMITED EDITIONS, 7011 Hayvenhurst Ave., Van Nuys CA 91406. (818)988-0630. Art publisher. Publishes limited edition graphics, unlimited edition posters and originals by internationally known, up-an-coming and new artists.
First Contact & Terms: Contact by mail only. Send good quality slides or photographs, pertinent biographical information and SASE. Exclusive representation required.
Acceptable Work: Prefers oils, acrylics, watercolors, serigraphs, lithographs and etchings.

***LESLIE LEVY GALLERY**, 7141 Main St., Scottsdale AZ 85251. (602)947-0937. Associate Director: Lee Brotherton. Works with 20 freelance artists/year on consignment. Send query letter with resume and slides or photographs. Samples not filed returned by SASE. Reports within 3 weeks. Call or write to schedule an appointment to show a portfolio, which should include photographs or slides.

***BRUCE MCGAW GRAPHICS, INC.**, 230 Fifth Ave., New York NY 10001. (212)679-7823. Acquisitions: Paul Liptak. Send query letter with brochure showing art style or resume, tear sheets, photostats, photocopies, slides and photographs. Samples not filed returned by SASE. Reports within weeks. To show a portfolio mail color, tear sheets and photographs. Considers skill and experience of artist, salability of artwork, client's preferences and rights purchased when establishing payment.

MINOTAUR, 34 Bridgman Ave., Toronto, Ontario M54 1X3 Canada. (416)530-1454. Contact: J. Kevin Kelleher. Art publisher/distributor of fine art and photography posters. Clients: galleries, framers, wholesale framers and gift shops. Works with 18 artists/year. Pays flat fee, royalty or negotiates method; "a combination of purchase of rights plus royalty." Offers advance. Buys first rights. Provides a written contract. Send query letter with business card, slides, photographs or tear sheets to be kept on file. Material not filed is returned. Reports within days. Write for appointment to show portfolio.

Acceptable Work: Considers pen & ink line drawings, oils, acrylics, pastels and watercolors; serigraphs and stone or plate lithographs. Accepts "almost any contemporary theme."

MODERNART EDITIONS, INC., 80 5th Ave., New York NY 10011. (212)675-8505. Vice President: Elaine Lingwood. Art publisher. Publishes art posters using stone or plate lithography, silkscreen, lithographic offset. Publishes 15 freelance artists/year. Negotiates payment method. Negotiates rights purchased. Provides insurance while work is at publisher. Artist owns original art. Send slides. Call or write for appointment to show portfolio. "Include stamped, self-addressed envelope for return of materials."
Acceptable Work: Considers oil and acrylic paintings, pastels, watercolors and mixed media. Prefers soft abstracts, representational and graphic styles; interiors with flowers, land and cityscapes, beach scenes or gardens as themes. Prefers artwork unframed.

MITCH MORSE GALLERY INC., 334 E. 59th St., New York NY 10022. (212)593-1812. President: Mitch Morse. Art publisher and distributor. Produces limited edition handpulled originals for framers, galleries, interior designers, architects, hotels and better furniture stores. Publishes 8-10 artists/year distributes the work of 15-20 artists/year. Negotiates payment. Offers advance. Provides promotion and shipping. Send query letter with resume, and slides and photographs. SASE. Reports within 1 week.
Acceptable Work: Unframed realistic, impressionistic and romantic paintings, lithographs, serigraphs and etchings; individual works; 4x6' maximum.
Tips: "There is continued emphasis on color as a major ingredient in the selection of art and greater interest in more traditional subject matter. Actively seeking additional artists who do original paintings on paper."

NEW DECO, INC., 9328-D Sable Ridge Cr., Boca Raton FL 33428. (305)482-6295. President: Brad Morris. Art publisher/distributor. Produces limited editions using offset lithography for galleries, also publishes/distributes unlimited editions. Publishes 1 freelance artist/year. Needs new designs for reproduction. Pays flat fee. Offers advance. Negotiates rights purchased. Provides promotion, shipping and a written contract. Negotiates ownership of original art. Send brochure, resume, and tear sheets photostats or photographs to be kept on file. Samples not kept on file are returned. Reports only if interested. Call or write for appointment to show portflio, which should include tear sheets.
Acceptable Work: Prefers Art Deco, Art Nouveau themes and styles. Prefers individual works of art, pairs or series.

NEW YORK GRAPHIC SOCIETY, Box 1469, Greenwich CT 06836. (203)661-2400. Art & Production Manager: Caron Caswell. Art publisher/art distributor of offset reproductions, posters and handpulled originals. Clients: galleries, frame shops, museums and foreign trade. Publishes 10 new freelance artists/year. Distributes work for 10 new artists/year. Pays flat fee or royalty of 1.2%. Offers advance. Buys all print reproduction rights. Provides in-transit insurance from firm to artist, insurance while work is at firm, promotion, shipping from firm and a written contract; provide insurance for art requested. Send query letter with slides or photographs. Write for artist's guidelines. All submissions returned to artists by SASE after review. Reports within 2 months.
Acceptable Work: Considers oils, acrylics, pastels, watercolors and mixed media; pencil drawings (colored). Distributes posters only. Publishes/distributes serigraphs, stone lithographs, plate lithographs and woodcuts.
Tips: "We publish a broad variety of styles and themes. However, we do not publish experimental, hard-edge, sexually explicit or suggestive material. Work that is by definition fine art and easy to live with, that is, which would be considered decorative, is what we look for."

NOKES BERRY GRAPHICS, LTD., (formerly Gourmet Grafiks, Inc.), 300 Montgomery St., Alexandria VA 22314. (703)683-4686. President: Mary Nokes Berry. Art publisher of offset reproductions. Clients: galleries, department stores, interior designers and independent stores. "When publishing freelance artists, negotiates payment method and rights purchased." Provides promotion and written contract. Send query letter with brochure, resume, business card and slides to be kept on file. Samples not filed returned only if requested. Reports within 1 month. Samples not filed returned only if requested. Write for appointment to show portfolio.
Acceptable Work: Considers oils, acrylics, pastels, watercolors, mixed media and photography for publication and distribution.
Tips: Especially looks for timely pieces-new graphic approaches, current subjects, colors and themes. And, of course, the rare "timeless" art that is acceptable always. A mistake artists make is "ignoring the trends of the times and the suggestions which will make their work reflect what people want in their homes. There's a balance between accepting an artist's work exactly as is and using modifications (interpretation) to make the work timely."

NORTH BEACH STUDIOS, INC., 2565 Blackburn St., Clearwater FL 33575. President: James Cournoyer. Art publisher and art distributor handling limited editions of limited editions and handpulled originals. Clients: galleries, architects, interior designers and art consultants. Pays flat fee. Negotiates rights purchased. Offers an advance. Requires exclusive representation. Provides insurance when work is at firm, promotion, written contract and internationally distributed Fine Art catalogue (3 ring binder) containing expressly-select original hand-made editions of a small number of contemporary artists. Send query letter with brochure, resume, tear sheets, photostats, photocopies, slides and photographs to be kept on file. Accepts any sample showing reasonable reproduction. Samples returned by SASE only if requested. Reports within 1 month. To show a portfolio, mail original/final art, color, tear sheets, photostats, photographs and b&w.
Acceptable Work: Considers pen & ink line drawings and mixed media; serigraphs, stone lithographs, plate lithographs, woodcuts and linocuts. Especially likes contemporary, unusual and original themes or styles.
Tips: "No wildlife (eagles in particular!) More of the continued established growth of style throughout. Wants contemporary and original styles."

PAPER LIONS INC., 31320 Via Colinas #104 Westlake Village CA 91362-3907. (213)999-4100. President: Gordon Brown. Art publisher of unlimited editions. Clients: galleries, framers, department stores, mass market and auto specialty. Publishes 3-5 freelance artists/year. Payment method is negotiated. Buys all rights. Requires exclusive representation of artist. Provides a written contract. Send query letter with brochure, resume and samples to be kept on file. Reports within 3 weeks. Call for appointment to show portfolio.
Acceptable Work: "Any medium from which fine art posters can be made." Specializing in automotive art.

PARK SOUTH PRESENTATIONS LTD., 8D, 147 W. 27th St., New York NY 10011. (212)807-8989. President: Steven Danielpour. Publishes limited and unlimited edition reproductions and handpulled originals using genuine lithography (lithoverite), offset lithography, and silkscreen (seriography). Clients: retail, galleries, distributors, exporters, importers, collectors, interior designers, poster and frame shops. Publishes 4-5 freelance artists/year. Negotiates payment method; pays flat fee, royalties or on a consignment basis. Buys first rights, reprint rights or negotiates. Provides in-transit insurance, insurance while work is at publisher, promotion, shipping to and from publisher and written contract. Send query letter with resume, tear sheets, photostats and photocopies to be kept on file. Samples not kept on file returned by SASE. Reports within a few weeks. Write for appointment to show portfolio.
Acceptable Work: Considers oils, pen & ink drawings, acrylic paintings, pastels, watercolors and mixed media. Also serigraphs and plate litographs.
Tips: "Will need Art Deco, abstract, illustrative, landscape work. Likes to have as many samples as possible so we can get an in-depth view of the artist. Artists should understand that the mainstay of business is posters. Therefore, presentation of his artwork should be geared in this vein: art that would make good posters."

***PETERSEN PRINTS**, 6725 Sunset Blvd., Los Angeles CA 90028. Director: William L. Cooksey. Produces limited editions (maximum 800 prints) using offset lithography for galleries, department stores and publishes sporting merchandisers. Publishes 10-15 freelance artists/year. Buys all rights. Requires exclusive representation of the artist. Provides in-transit insurance, insurance while work is at publisher, promotion, shipping from publisher and a written contract. Artist owns original art. Send query letter with brochure, resume slides or photographs to be kept on file. Samples not kept on file are returned by SASE. Reports within 3 weeks. Write for appointment to show portfolio.
Acceptable Work: Considers oil and acrylic paintings and watercolors. Prefers paintings of sporting subjects: game birds, waterfowl and game animals. Prefers individual works of art.

JUDITH L. POSNER & ASSOCIATES, INC., 207 N. Milwaukee St., Milwaukee WI 53202. (414)352-3097. President: Judith L. Posner. Art publisher/distributor/gallery. Produces limited and unlimited editions of offset reproductions and original serigraphs and lithographs. Publishes 100 freelance artists/year. Pays royalty or works on consignment (50% commission). Buys one-time rights. Sometimes requires exclusive representation of artist. Provides a written contract. Send resume and photographs, slides or transparencies. Samples not kept on file are returned. Reports within 10 days.
Acceptable Work: Considers all media. Prefers series. Specializes in contemporary.
Tips: "Have something very exciting and unusual to show."

PRESTIGE ART GALLERIES, INC., 3909 W. Howard, Skokie IL 60076. (312)679-2555. President: Louis Schutz. Art publisher/dealer/gallery. Publishes limited editions and offset reproductions for retail

professionals and galleries. Publishes 4 freelance artists/year. Works on consignment basis; firm charges 33% commission. Buys all rights or negotiates rights purchased. Provides insurance while work is at publisher, promotion and a written contract. Publisher owns original art. Send query letter with brochure, resume and slides to be kept on file. Samples returned by SASE. Reports only if interested.
Acceptable Work: Considers oil and acrylic paintings. Prefers realism, and mother and child themes. Prefers individual works of art; unframed; 30x40" maximum.
Tips: "Be professional."

PRIMROSE PRESS, Box 302, New Hope PA 18938. (215)862-5518. President: George Knight. Art publisher. Publishes limited edition collotype reproductions for galleries. Publishes 3-5 freelance artists/year. Pays royalties to artist of 10-20%. Buys one-time rights. Provides in-transit insurance, insurance while work is at publisher, shipping from publisher and a written contract. Artist owns original art. Send query letter with tear sheets and slides to be kept on file. Prefers slides as samples. Samples returned by SASE if not kept on file. Reports within 10 days.
Acceptable Work: Considers pen & ink line drawings, oil and acrylic paintings, watercolors and mixed media. Publishes representational themes. Prefers individual works of art; 40x30" maximum.

THE PRINTMAKERS, 3373 Wrightwood Dr., Studio City CA 91604. (213)656-1797. President: Marcia Isaacs. Fine Art publishers and distributors. Handpulled original graphics for galleries, department stores, designers and corporate clients. Publishes 5 new artists/year; distributes the work of 15 artists/year. Pays on royalties based on retail price and production or consignment basis for original work. Send query letter with brochure showing art style or resume and non-returnable samples, such as slides or photographs. SASE. No personal interviews without staff slide review. To show a portfolio, mail photographs and SASE. Reports within 1-2 weeks. Provides printing and distribution.
Acceptable Work: Publishes etchings, purchases original lithographs and serigraphs. Prefers landscape and contemporary styles; "the artist must be able to produce the *original plate* from which the prints are pulled in our studio." Interested in landscape, still life, abstract, etc. Subjects must be suitable for gallery sales and office interiors. Minimum sizes: 18x24, 30x40". Written contract upon acceptance. Royalties paid quarterly or purchase.
Tips: To meet our requirements, artists need "good technical printmaking skill. We prefer B.A. degree and/or art school background. Professional artists/printmakers only."

***REECE GALLERIES INC.**, 24 West 57th St., New York NY 10019. (212)333-5830. Vice President: Leon Reece. Distributes to private corporations galleries. Works with many freelance artists/year. Send query letter with resume, slides and photographs. Samples not filed returned by SASE. Reports within 14 days. Call to schedule an appointment to show a portfolio, which should include original/final art. Pays 50% of net proceeds.
Acceptable Work: Considers skill and experience of artist, salability of artwork and clients' preferences when establishing payment. Prefers urban, abstract landscapes, prints and other media.
Tips: Artist should have "technical skill that must be obvious in the media worked overall quality; no offset work."

ROSEART/ROSENBAUM FINE ART INC., 5181 NE 12th Ave., Ft. Lauderdale FL 33334. (305)772-1387. President: Howard Rosenbaum. Produces limited edition handpulled original lithographs, etchings, monoprints and silkscreens for museums, auctioneers, designers and architects. Publishes 75 artists/year. Send slides or photos. SASE. Reports within 2 weeks. Provides insurance, promotion and written contract.
Acceptable Work: Drawings, paintings, pastels and watercolors; all styles and subjects; series. Maximum size: 30x40". Payment is negotiable.

ROSENBAUM FINE ART CORP., 5171 NE 12th Ave., Ft. Lauderdale FL 33334. (305)772-1386. Chairman: Marvin Rosenbaum. Art publisher of limited editions. Clients: galleries. Publishes 20 freelance artists/year. Distributes work for 50 artists/year. Pays flat fee. Buys all rights. Provides shipping to firm and written contract. Send query letter with slides to be kept on file. Samples returned. Write for appointment to show portfolio.
Acceptable Work: Considers pen & ink line drawings, oil and acrylic paintings, watercolors and mixed media; serigraphs and stone lithographs. Especially likes contemporary graphics.

***SCAFA-TORNABENE ART PUBLISHING CO. INC.**, 100 Snake Hill Rd., West Nyack NY 10994. (914)358-7600. Executive Vice President: Frank Tornabene. Produces unlimited edition offset reproductions for framers, galleries, museums, commercial art trade and manufacturers world-wide. Strong poster interest. Publishes 50-100 artists/year. Pays $200-350 flat fee for each accepted piece. Published artists (successful ones) can advance to royalty arrangements with advance against royalty. Buys only

reproduction rights (written contract). Artist maintains ownershp of original art. Requires exclusive publication rights to all accepted work. Send query letter first; with slides or photos and then arrange interview. SASE. Reports in about 2 weeks.
Acceptable Work: Unframed decorative paintings, watercolors, posters, photos and drawings; usually pairs and series.
Tips: Always looking for something new and different. "Study the market first. See and learn from what stores and galleries display and sell. Try to originate in a genre, rather than copycat. Trends begin with the artist."

***SOMERSET HOUSE PUBLISHING CORP.**, 10688 Haddington, Houston TX 77043. (713)465-0653. Contact: Lisa Ince. Clients: 5,000 retail art galleries. Publishes 30 freelance artists/year. Send query letter with slides. Samples not filed returned. Reports within months. To show a portfolio, mail final reproduction/product and photographs. Considers salability of artwork when establishing payment. Buys first rights.

***SOUNDWORKS GALLERY**, Box 70014, Eugene OR 97407. (503)933-2869. Director: Kitrick Short. Works with 5 freelance artists/year. Works on assignment only. Prefers etchings pen & ink and line drawings. Prefers religious and modern themes. Send query letter with brochure showing art style or resume and tear sheets, slides and photographs. Samples not filed are returned by SASE. Reports within 3 weeks. To show a portfolio an artist should mail original/final art, color and tear sheets. Artist receives 50% of net proceeds. Pays on publication. Considers skill and experience of artist, salability of artwork, client's preference and rights purchased when establishing payment. Buys all rights.
Acceptable Work: Prefers etchings; religious and modern themes.

SPORTSMAN'S COLLECTION, INC., Box 23, Grafton OH 44044. (216)458-8498. President: Donald W. Kaatz. Art publisher and of limited editions.Clients: galleries and corporations. Publishes 1 freelance artist/year. Works with 1 artist/year. Negotiates payment method. Sometimes offers advance. Negotiates rights purchased. Sometimes requires exclusive representation. Provides in-transit insurance, insurance while work is at firm, promotion, shipping to and from firm and written contract. Send query letter with resume and slides to be kept on file. Samples not filed returned by SASE only if requested. Reports within 2 weeks. Write for appointment to show portfolio, which should include photographs.
Acceptable Work: Considers oil and acrylic paintings and watercolors. Especially likes wildlife themes.
Tips: "There is a demand for high quality wildlife posters and limited edition prints—landscape with wildlife."

***STRICTLY LIMITED EDITIONS**, 3521 Pierce St., San Francisco CA 94123. Contact: Jacob F. Adler. Art publisher/distributor of limited edition handpulled originals. Clients: galleries. Works with 8-10 artists/year. Negotiates payment method and rights purchased. Provides promotion and a written contract. Send query letter with brochure and samples to be kept on file. Write for appointment to show portfolio. Prefers to review original work. Samples are returned only if requested. Reports back only if interested.
Acceptable Work: Considers original graphics; serigraphs and etchings. Especially likes a variety of styles in figurative art.
Tips: "Have patience!"

STUDIO HOUSE EDITONS, 415 W. Superior, Chicago IL 60610. (312)751-0974. Director: Bill Sosin. Art publisher of offset reproductions. Clients: galleries. Publishes 7 freelance artists/year. Distributes 15 artists/year. Negotiates payment method and rights purchased. Provides promotion. Send query letter with brochure and samples to be kept on file. Prefers slides as samples. Samples not filed returned only if requested. Reports only if interested.
Acceptable Work: Photographs; stone lithographs and plate lithographs. Especially likes decor themes or styles.
Tips: "Send only high quality transparent duplicates of best work."

JOHN SZOKE GRAPHICS INC., 164 Mercer St., New York NY 10012. Director: John Szoke. Produces limited edition handpulled originals for galleries, museums and private collectors. Publishes 10-25 artists/year. Charges commission or negotiates royalties. Offers advance. Provides promotion and written contract. Arrange interview or submit slides. SASE. Reports within 1 week.

***TELE GRAPHICS**, 607 E. Walnut St., Pasadena CA 91101. President: Ron Rybak. Estab. 1984. Art Publisher/art distributor handling limited editions, offset reproductions, unlimited editions and handpulled originals. Clients: galleries, picture framers, interior designers and regional distributors.

Publishes 1-4 freelance artists/year. Distributes work for 25 artists/ year. Works with 35-40 artists/year. Negotiates payment method. Offers advance. Negotiates rights purchased. Requires exclusive representation. Provide promotion, shipping from your firm and a written contract. Send query letter with resume and samples. Samples not filed returned only if requested. Reports within 30 days. Call or write to schedule an appointment to show a portfolio, which should include original/final art. Pays for design by the project. Considers skill and experience of artist, and rights purchased when establishing payment. **Tips:** "Be prepared to show as many varied examples of work as possible. We are not interested in seeing only 1 or 2 pieces."

THE WINN CORPORATION, Box 80096, Seattle WA 98108. (206)763-9544. President: Larry Winn. Art publisher and distributor of limited editions, offset reproductions and handpulled originals. Clients: interior designers, art galleries, frame shops, architects, art consultants, corporations, hotels, etc. Publishes 10 freelance artists/year (prints). Distributes work for 120 artists/year (posters). Negotiates payment method. Offers advance. Negotiates rights purchased. Requires exclusive representation. Provides in-transit insurance, insurance while work is at firm, promotion, shipping from firm and written contract. Send query letter with resume and slides. Slides returned by SASE. Reports within 1 month. **Acceptable Work:** Considers pen & ink line drawings, oil and acrylic paintings, pastels, watercolors and mixed media; serigraphs, stone lithographs, plate lithographs, woodcuts and linocuts. Especially interested in "good design and contemporary imagery."

WOODROSE FINE ARTS, 530 E. St., Eureka CA 95501. Contact: Business Manager. Art publisher/ distributor/gallery. Publishes offset lithographs for national and international distributors as well as galleries. Publishes 1-2 freelance artists/year. Negotiates payment method. Negotiates rights purchased. Requires exclusive representation of the artist. Provides insurance while work is at publisher, promotion and a written contract. Negotiates ownership of original art. Send query letter with brochure, slides or photographs to be kept on file. Samples not kept on file are returned only if requested. Reports only if interested. **Acceptable Work:** Considers acrylic paintings, watercolors, mixed media, silkscreens (serigraphs). Prefers graphic and floral themes. Prefers individual works of art. **Tips:** "Our work is published for the decorative poster art market; the greater the impact of the graphic design and composition the more likely we would be to consider the work. First consideration is given to California artists. We will also consider distributing works published by the artist."

California artist Muramasa Kudo is "a talented artist whose work is not so much oriental as westernized oriental," says Sandy Verin, director of Icart Vendor Graphics in Los Angeles. This piece, "Mermaid," was submitted in watercolor and published as an unlimited edition fine art poster. Kudo's work was selected by Verin because of its "creative imagery."

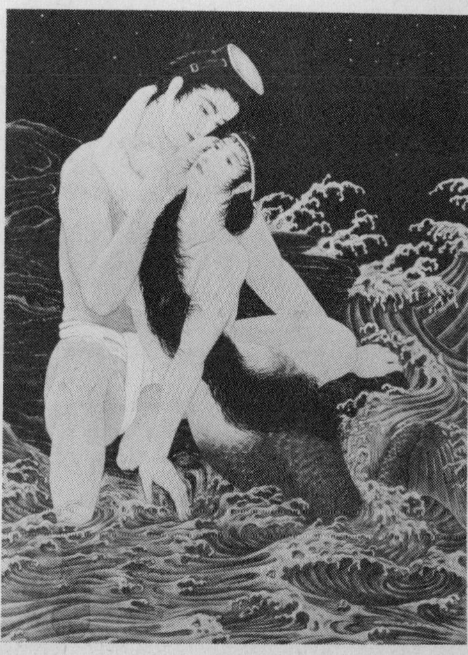

Appendix

The Business of Freelancing

For most artists striving to get ahead in the freelance graphic art market, desire—while necessary—is not enough. Talent and good art skills are requisites, as are consistency and flexibility in completing the various assignments you receive. Of almost equal importance to all these qualities is a sense of professionalism and knowledge of the business aspect of freelancing. The information that follows provides general guidelines covering basic areas of business. Use the information in this Appendix to handle your freelance business knowledgeably and professionally.

Pricing and negotiation

Pricing can be a stumbling block for a freelancer, and each job will present the artist with a new and different pricing situation. However, some basic considerations for establishing a price are: the rights sold; complexity of the project; the turnaround time or time needed for completion; how widely the project is being used (local, national or worldwide); the client's project budget; the ownership of the original art; use of an expense account; the going rate in that market area for similar projects; and the artist's reputation, skill and experience.

Negotiation is the art of reaching a mutual agreement so that both parties feel satisfied with the outcome. When a client details a project to you, you are hearing the client's needs and wants. He will never know (nor is it his responsibility to know) *your* needs and wants unless *you* speak up.

Experience is often the best teacher, but even in the beginning there are a few rules you can follow. First and foremost, *relax*. You're not out to win at all costs, but rather to work cooperatively *with* your client toward a common solution. Convey a positive attitude and listen carefully. Try to put yourself in your client's place so you "hear" what he is really saying. When you speak, do it slowly and distinctly which will force a rushed art buyer to slow down and listen to *you*. Most important, know your artist's rights and industry ethics thoroughly so you're a knowledgeable negotiator.

Contracts

In simplest terms, a contract is an agreement between two or more persons containing an offer, acceptance and consideration (each party giving something of value). Contracts may be written, oral or tacit, but to protect yourself most from misunderstanding and faulty memories, make it a practice to have a *written* contract *signed* and *dated* by you and the party you are dealing with.

Written contracts need not be extremely complicated forms—they can be as simple as a letter or note from you to your client listing the terms you have agreed upon verbally. The wisest move is to ask your client to sign the letter and return it to you; however, action taken on his part that is in accordance with the conditions of the agreement, such as sending you written instructions, etc., may also be interpreted as acceptance.

Read carefully any contract or purchase order you are asked to sign. If the terms are very complex or if you do not understand them, seek professional advice *before* signing. If it is a pre-printed or "standard" contract, look for terms within the copy which may not be agreeable to you such as "work-for-hire."

The items you want specified in your contract will vary according to the assignment and complexity of the project, but some basics are: your fee (basic fee and possibly kill fees, payment schedule, advances, expense compensation, etc.); service (an exact and specific description of what you are providing for the fee); usage (an exact and specific description of how the work may be used); and return of the original art. You may also wish to specify deadlines, how changes will be handled and/or compensated, etc.

Further information on contracts can be obtained from *Selling Your Graphic Design & Illustration* by Tad Crawford and Arie Kopelman.

Copyright

Copyright protection for works of art has been made less confusing by the copyright law of 1978. With this law, the copyright to a piece of art is automatic from the moment of creation—it belongs to the artist immediately.

Copyright protection prevents unauthorized copying, selling or other infringements on your work of art. You do not have to register your work with the U.S. Copyright Office until an infringement takes place. However, if you want to collect damages and attorney's fees, you have to register it within 3 months of publication. To protect yourself as much as possible and to avoid the risk of losing your copyright after publication, place a copyright notice on your work as soon as it is created.

The copyright notice is a c with a circle around it ©, followed by the year, date and your name or an abbreviation by which your name can be recognized. You can place the copyright notice on any accessible place, such as the back of a framed piece, but the front is preferable for commercial art. Definitely have your copyright notice on any work you are submitting to a noncopyrighted publication.

Your copyright can only be transferred in writing, and you or someone acting on your behalf must sign the transfer.

There are two exceptions to owning the copyright to a work from the moment of its creation. They are when you create work as part of your fulltime employment for someone else or when you agree to "work-for-hire," i.e., you're working for a client *as if* you are a fulltime employee. Then you own neither the copyright nor any of the reproduction rights to your work. Opposition by artists to work-for-hire is growing nationwide. Contact your state art council, national art organizations, and state and federal legislators to determine what legislation is being considered to change work-for-hire.

It is not difficult to register your work. Write to the U.S. Copyright Office, Library of Congress, Washington, DC 20559. You will be asked to complete the appropriate forms (Form VA is for material in the Visual Arts) and send them with the required fee ($10 per individual published piece or for a group of unpublished pieces) and copies or photos of your work. You will receive a certificate of registration which offers you more indepth protection if you anticipate legal problems than the copyright notice alone. You can also write and request the Copyright Information Kit, which explains copyright in more detail.

To receive a free guideline on copyright regulations and procedures for cartoons and comic strips, write for Circular R44, Information & Publication Section LM-455, U.S. Copyright Office, Library of Congress, Washington DC 20559.

An Artist's Handbook on Copyright is available for $6.95 (price includes postage and handling) from the Georgia Volunteer Lawyers for the Arts, Inc., Plaza Level 16, 42 Spring St. SW, Atlanta GA 30302.

Reproduction rights

When you sell "rights" to your work, you are selling the reproduction rights inherent in your ownership of the copyright. You are telling the art buyer how he can use your work, thus maintaining control over where and how it appears. The more rights you sell to one client, the more money you should receive. Negotiate this upfront with the art buyer *before* an agreement is signed.

If you sell first reproduction rights, you are giving the art buyer the right to reproduce your work once and to be the first to use it. You cannot sell first rights to two buyers—each cannot be "first." This differs from one-time rights, which mean the art buyer has the right to reproduce your work once, but he does not have to be first. Once the buyer has used the rights he purchased, he has no further claim to your work. If he wants to use it a second or third time, he must pay additional fees for that privilege.

Try to ascertain the use the buyer wishes to make of the artwork so that the rights sold can be worded accordingly. A publisher, for example, may ask for all rights but may actually only *need* first North American serial rights. Your immediate compensation may be less, but once he has published it you can sell the use of the artwork to other buyers which you could not do if the publisher owned all rights.

When you sell all reproduction rights, you are essentially allowing the buyer to reproduce the artwork as many times and in any way he wishes. You may still possess the original work, but the art buyer owns the reproduction rights to it and the financial compensation to you should reflect what you have sold.

Always know what rights you are selling. Contact and become involved in the Graphic Artists Guild (30 E. 20th St., New York NY 10003), which now includes the Cartoonists Guild, or other professional organizations for guidance in the areas of copyright and contracts. For further information consult *Legal Guide for the Visual Artist*, by Tad Crawford, (Madison Square Press), *Selling Your Graphic Design & Illustration* (St. Martin's Press), and *The Graphic Artists Guild Handbook: Pricing and Ethical Guidelines*, available from the Graphic Artists Guild.

Packaging

Your primary goal in packaging is to have your work or samples arrive undamaged. Before packaging original work make sure you have a copy (photograph, photostat, photocopy, slide or transparency) in your file at home. If changes are necessary on an assigned job, you can then see on your copy what the art director is discussing over the phone. Most important, if your work is lost you can make a duplicate.

If working on an assignment, allow mailing time in your production schedule. With today's overnight services, this will not necessarily have to be a great consideration, but one which must be kept in mind.

Flat work can be packaged between heavy cardboard or styrofoam. Cut the material slightly larger than the piece of flatwork and tape it closed. It is wise to include your business card or a piece of paper with your name and address on it on the outside of this packaging material in case the outer wrapper becomes separated from the inner packing. The work at least can then be returned to you.

The outer wrapping, depending on package size and quality of inner wrapping, may be a manila envelope, a foam padded envelope, a "bubble" envelope (one with plastic "bubbles" lining the inside), or brown wrapping paper. Use reinforced tape for closures. Make sure *one* side is clearly addressed.

Check the various types of envelopes and packaging material available at your local art supply, photography or stationery stores. Don't miss the opportunity to buy in bulk quantities if you are going to be doing a lot of mailing. The price is always lower.

Mailing

Become familiar with the types of mailing available. Your local post office has an information number for your questions and will be glad to provide you the information you need.

The U.S. Post Office mail classifications with which you will be most concerned are First Class and Fourth Class, more commonly called parcel post.

First Class mail is the type used every day for letters, etc. If the piece you are mailing is not the usual letter size, make sure to mark it First Class. Fourth Class is used for packages weighing 1-70 pounds and not more than 108 inches in length and girth combined.

The greatest disadvantage to using these classes of mail is that you cannot be guaranteed when the package/letter will arrive. If time is important to you, consider the special services the post office offers, such as, Priority Mail, Express Mail Next Day Service, and Special Delivery.

Certified mail includes a mailing receipt and provides a record of delivery at the addressee's post office. This type of mail is handled like ordinary mail, but you can request a return receipt on certain types of mail as your proof of delivery.

The post office offers insurance for a nominal cost.

United Parcel Service (UPS) will accept packages up to 70 pounds in weight and 108" length and girth combined. Cost is determined by weight, size and destination of the package and automatically includes insurance up to $100. You can purchase additional insurance.

UPS does have wrapping restrictions. Packages must be in heavy corrugated cardboard, with no string or paper on the outside, and be sealed with reinforced tape. UPS cannot guarantee how long it will take a package to arrive at its destination, but will track lost packages. It also offers Two-Day Blue Label Air Service to any destination in the U.S., and Next Day Service in specific zip code zones. Check locally to see if Next Day Service is available for your package. There is an additional charge for these services and for package pickup.

Today there is a growing number of airfreight services which make overnight delivery common. Check to see which ones are available in your area, but some of the more familiar names are Emery, Purolator and Federal Express. These firms offer varying rates according to weight of the package and urgency.

If you will be airfreighting large numbers of works or portfolios, it is advisable to set up an account. Most have priority service which offers overnight delivery direct to the client, or regular service which is delivery within two days. Some companies offer both an airfreight service and a ground courier service. The advantages of airfreight are the guaranteed delivery time and efficiency in tracking missing packages. The cost reflects these added services.

Greyhound Bus Lines and some commercial airlines also offer same-day or overnight package delivery. Check locally for rates and restrictions.

Record keeping

All your talent and art skills will mean nothing when it comes time to give an accounting of your business' profitability or when the IRS demands tax returns, if you haven't kept good business records.

It is usually the part least liked by artists, yet you have to realize that the freelancer is an independent businessperson and is held accountable as such.

The record keeping of daily expenses and income does not have to be an elaborate setup of ledgers. You can accomplish a satisfactory record by having two notebooks—one marked *accounts receivable* or money paid or owed you for work you have created, and the other marked *accounts payable*, or money you have spent on supplies, studio rent, fuel, etc.

The accounts receivable book should have areas for listing each project completed, the date it was completed, to whom it was delivered, the delivery date, the price of the job, the amount you received, the date you received it and any further remarks you think are necessary, such as rights sold.

The accounts payable book should include entries for work supplies purchased, the quantity, the cost, the date of the bill, the amount you paid, the date you paid it and any further remarks necessary. Save all bills and receipts.

This simple method of keeping track of your business will enable you to know how much you are bringing in versus your expenses. The most important thing is not to let a month's worth of statements and bills pile up—you will find yourself hopelessly lost and forgetting to enter information.

Begin to develop standard business practices. Ask for a receipt with every purchase. If possible, keep a separate checking account for business expenses alone. Cancelled checks not only help keep accurate records, but serve as evidence if a payment is challenged.

Don't forget to record driving expenses. A diary in the car helps you keep an accurate log of mileage, especially when on a local trip for supplies, etc. As long as your drive was business-related, you have a legitimate expenditure and tax deduction.

Are you entertaining a client at a business dinner? Keep a record of the date, place, cost, business relationship and the purpose of the meeting. Use your car diary to record these transactions immediately. Don't hesitate to ask the waiter or cashier for a receipt—it's a common business practice.

Even if you are not sure in some cases if a particular expense qualifies as a business-related tax deduction, obtain a receipt or bill. A tax advisor can clarify it for you later and it is always better to be safe than sorry.

If your business is very complex, you can have books set up for you by an accountant and continue the record keeping yourself. Retain your business records for at least four years.

Developing a file for each job is a good way to keep track of expenses. Drop in all related receipts and you can then determine if your fee was sufficient to cover these expenses and give you a profit. When preparing an invoice, you will have all pertinent material in one place. Place a copy of the invoice in the job file as well as records of payments and you can keep track of billing.

Sales tax

First you must convince the Internal Revenue Service (IRS) that you are conducting a business and not a hobby. This can be helped by keeping a separate business checking account, letterhead stationery and accurate bookkeeping. Then as a self-employed person, you are allowed business-related deductions which reduce the amount of taxable income you have to report, such as mileage for business trips, overnight lodging, depreciation on equipment, etc. You will be filing Schedule C of Form 1040, Profit (or Loss) from Business or Profession.

Depending on the complexity of your business and tax expertise, you may want to have a professional tax advisor to consult with or to complete your tax form. Skill levels vary among tax consultants so whom you choose depends on the amount of help you need and what you can afford. Those with the most training and skills will generally command the highest fees.

Most IRS offices have walk-in centers open year-round and offer over 90 free IRS publications containing tax information to help in preparation of your return. Be aware, however, that no matter what information you are given at an IRS office, it is still your responsibility to see that your return is correct.

The booklet that comes with your tax return forms contains names and addresses of Forms Distribution Centers by region where you can write for further information. Some post offices also carry a limited supply of forms.

The U.S. Small Business Administration can offer some assistance in supplying information on taxes. Contact your nearest SBA District Office. Many workshops are held by arts organizations around the country covering business management, often including detailed tax information. Inquire at your arts council, local arts organizations or a nearby college/university to see if a workshop is scheduled.

You will be asked to provide your Social Security number or your Employer Identification number (if you are a business) to the person/firm for whom you are doing a freelance project. This information is now necessary in order for payment to be made.

As this publication is going to press major tax reforms are being discussed. Anticipated changes may take effect sometime in 1987.

Sales Tax

Check regarding your state's regulations on sales tax. Some states claim that "creativity" and a service rendered cannot be taxed while others view it as a product you are selling and therefore taxable. Be certain you understand the sales tax laws to avoid being held liable for uncollected money at taxtime. Write to your state auditor for sales tax information.

Home office deduction

The Tax Reform Act of 1976 narrowed the opportunities for a taxpayer to be eligible for the home office deduction, restricting it to where the home office was the principal site of business and used on a regular, exclusive basis for the business. A taxpayer could claim only one principal place of business; thus anyone with a fulltime job, plus operating an art business out of his home, could not claim both as a principal place of business.

The rule has now been liberalized somewhat to permit taxpayers to claim the deduction if the space is used *exclusively* and *regularly* as a principal place of business "including a secondary trade or business." Thus, the taxpayer with more than one business can claim a principal place of business for each and claim a deduction for the studio at home. The factors taken into consideration by the IRS are the amount of income produced, the amount of time spent there and the nature of the facility. In some areas of the country, a studio can even share the same space with a nonbusiness use as long as a clearly defined area is used exclusively for business.

When a studio is a part of the principal residence, deductions are possible on an appropriate portion of mortgage interest, property taxes, rent, repair and utility bills, and depreciation.

When a studio is in a structure separate from the principal residence, requirements to obtain the deduction are less stringent.

However, check into the rule carefully to see if you *qualify* for the deduction. Consult a tax advisor to be certain you meet all of the requirements before attempting to take this deduction since its requirements and interpretations frequently change.

Acceptance (payment on). The artist is paid for his work as soon as the buyer decides to use it.

Airbrush. Small pencil-shaped pressure gun used to spray ink, paint or dyes to obtain graduated tonal effects.

Architectural delineator. An illustrator who sketches preliminary ideas for a presentation to a client.

ASAP. Abbreviation for as soon as possible.

Ben-day. An artificial process of shading line illustrations, named after its inventor.

Biennially. Once every two years.

Bimonthly. Once every two months.

Biweekly. Once every two weeks.

Bleed. Area of a plate or print that extends (bleeds off) beyond the edge of trimmed sheet.

Buy-out. The sale of all reproduction rights, and sometimes the original work, by the artist.

Calligraphy. The art of fine handwriting.

Camera-ready. Art that is completely prepared for copy camera platemaking.

Cel art. Artwork applied to plastic film, especially used in animation; also an abbreviation for artwork on celluloid.

Cibachrome. Trade name for a full color positive print made from a transparency.

Collaterals. Accompanying or auxiliary pieces, especially in advertising.

Collotype. A screenless, flat, printing process in which plates are coated with gelatin, exposed to continuous-tone negatives and printed on lithographic presses.

Color separation. Process of preparing artwork for the printer by separating one color from another by using overlays of transparent or translucent material for each color.

Commission. 1. Percentage of retail price taken by a sponsor/salesman on artwork sold. 2. Assignment given to an artist.

Compact disc. A small disc, about 4.7" in diameter, which contains digitized music that is incorporated as miscroscopic pits in the aluminum base. Also called digital audio discs.

Comprehensive. Complete sketch of layout showing how a finished illustration will look when printed; also called a comp.

Direct-mail package. Sales or promotional material that is distributed by mail. Usually consists of an outer envelope, a cover letter, brochure or flyer, SASE, and postpaid reply card, or order form with business reply envelope.

Edition. The total number of prints published of one piece of art.

Elhi. Abbreviation for elementary/high school.

Etching. A print made by the intaglio process, creating a design in the surface of a metal or other plate with a needle and using a mordant to bite out the design.

Gouache. Opaque watercolor with definite, appreciable film thickness and an actual paint layer.

Gagline. The words printed, usually directly beneath, a cartoon; also called a caption.

Halftone. Reproduction of a continuous tone illustration with the image formed by dots produced by a camera lens screen.

IRC. International Reply Coupon; purchased at the post office to enclose with artwork sent to a foreign buyer to cover his postage cost when replying.

Keyline. Identification, through signs and symbols, of the positions of illustrations and copy for the printer.

Kill fee. Portion of the agreed-upon price the artist receives for a job that was assigned, started, but then canceled.

Layout. Arrangement of photographs, illustrations, text and headlines for printed material.

Light table. Table with a light source beneath a glass top; especially useful in transferring art by tracing.

Line drawing. Illustration done with pencil or ink using no wash or other shading.

Lithography. Printing process based on a design made with a greasy substance on a limestone slab or metal plate and chemically treated so image areas take ink and non-image areas repel ink; during printing, non-image areas are kept wet with water.

Logotype. Name or design of a company or product used as a trademark on letterheads, direct mail packages, in advertising, etc., to establish visual identity; also called logo.

Mechanicals. Paste-up or preparation of work for printing.

Ms, mss. Abbreviation for manuscript(s).

Offset. Printing process in which a flat printing plate is treated to be ink-receptive in image areas and ink-repellent in non-image areas. Ink is transferred from the printing plate to a rubber plate, and then to the paper.

Overlay. Transparent cover over copy, where instructions, corrections or color location directions are given.

Panel. In cartooning, refers to the number of boxed-in illustrations, i.e. single panel, double panel or multi-panel.

Paste-up. Procedure involving coating the backside of art, type, photostats, etc., with rubber cement or wax and adhering them in their proper positions to the mechanical board. The boards are then used as finished art by the printer.

Perspective. The ability to see objects in relation to their relative positions and distance, and depict the volume and spatial relationships on paper.

Photostat. Black-and-white copies produced by an inexpensive photographic process using paper negatives; only line values are held with accuracy. Also called stat.

Pin registration. The use of highly accurate holes and special pins on copy, film, plates and presses to insure proper positioning and alignment of colors.

PMT. Photostat produced without a negative, somewhat like the Polaroid process.

P-O-P. Point-of-purchase; a display device or structure located with the product in or at the retail outlet to advertise or hold the product to increase sales.

Publication (payment on). The artist is paid for his work when it is published.

Query. Letter of inquiry to an editor or buyer eliciting his interest in a work you want to do or sell.

Rendering. A drawn representation of a building, interior, etc., in perspective.

Roughs. Preliminary sketches or drawings.

Royalty. An agreed percentage paid by the publisher to the artist for each copy of his work sold.

SASE. Abbreviation for self-addressed, stamped envelope.

Semiannual. Once every six months.

Semimonthly. Once every two weeks.

Semiweekly. Twice a week.

Serigraph. Silkscreen; stencil method of printing involving a stencil adhered to a fine mesh cloth and stretched tightly over a wooden frame. Paint is forced through the holes of the screen not blocked by the stencil.

Simultaneous submissions. Submission of the same artwork to more than one potential buyer at the same time.

Speculation. Creating artwork with no assurance that the buyer will purchase it or reimburse expenses in any way, as opposed to creating artwork on assignment.

Spot drawing. Small illustration used to decorate or enhance a page of type, or to serve as a column ending.

Storyboard. Series of panels which illustrates a progressive sequence of graphics and story copy for a TV commercial, film or filmstrip. Serves as a guide for the eventual finished product.

Tabloid. Publication where an ordinary newspaper page is turned sideways.

Tear sheet. Published page containing an artist's illustration, cartoon, design or photograph.

Template. Plastic stencil containing various sizes of commonly used shapes, symbols or letters which can be traced one at a time.

Thumbnail. A rough layout in miniature.

Transparency. A photographic positive film such as a color slide.

Type spec. Type specification; determination of the size and style of type to be used in a layout.

UPS. Universal Postal Union, a coupon for return of first-class surface letters.

Velox. Photoprint of a continuous tone subject that has been transformed into line art by means of a halftone screen.

Video. General category comprised of videocassettes and videotapes.

Wash. Thin application of transparent color, or watercolor black, for a pastel or gray tonal effect.

Index

Other Books of Interest

General Writing Books

Beginning Writer's Answer Book, edited by Polking and Bloss $14.95
Getting the Words Right: How to Revise, Edit and Rewrite, by Theodore A. Rees Cheney $13.95
How to Get Started in Writing, by Peggy Teeters (paper) $8.95
How to Write a Book Proposal, by Michael Larsen $9.95
How to Write & Sell Your Personal Experiences, by Lois Duncan (paper) $9.95
How to Write & Sell (Your Sense of) Humor, by Gene Perret (paper) $9.95
How to Write While You Sleep, by Elizabeth Ross $12.95
Law & the Writer, edited by Polking & Meranus (paper) $10.95
Knowing Where to Look: The Ultimate Guide to Research, by Lois Horowitz $16.95
Pinckert's Practical Grammar, by Robert C. Pinckert $12.95
The 29 Most Common Writing Mistakes & How to Avoid Them, by Judy Delton $9.95
Writer's Block & How to Use It, by Victoria Nelson $12.95
Writer's Guide to Research, by Lois Horowitz $9.95
Writer's Market, edited by Becky Williams $21.95
Writer's Resource Guide, edited by Bernadine Clark $16.95

Magazine/News Writing

Basic Magazine Writing, by Barbara Kevles $16.95
How to Sell Every Magazine Article You Write, by Lisa Collier Cool $14.95
How to Write & Sell the 8 Easiest Article Types, by Helene Schellenberg Barnhart $14.95
Writing Nonfiction that Sells, by Samm Sinclair Baker $14.95

Fiction Writing

Creating Short Fiction, by Damon Knight (paper) $8.95
Fiction Writer's Market, edited by Jean Fredette $18.95
Handbook of Short Story Writing, by Dickson and Smythe (paper) $8.95
How to Write & Sell Your First Novel, by Oscar Collier with Frances Spatz Leighton $14.95
Storycrafting, by Paul Darcy Boles $14.95
Writing Romance Fiction—For Love and Money, by Helene Schellenberg Barnhart $14.95
Writing the Modern Mystery, by Barbara Norville $15.95
Writing the Novel: From Plot to Print, by Lawrence Block (paper) $8.95

Special Interest Writing Books

The Craft of Comedy Writing, by Sol Saks $14.95
How to Make Money Writing About Fitness & Health, by Celia & Thomas Scully $16.95
How to Make Money Writing Fillers, by Connie Emerson (paper) $8.95
How to Write the Story of Your Life, by Frank P. Thomas $12.95
How You Can Make $50,000 a Year as a Nature Photojournalist, by Bill Thomas (paper) $17.95
Mystery Writer's Handbook, by The Mystery Writers of America (paper) $8.95
Nonfiction for Children: How to Write It, How to Sell It, by Ellen E.M. Roberts $16.95
On Being a Poet, by Judson Jerome $14.95
The Poet's Handbook, by Judson Jerome (paper) $8.95
Poet's Market, by Judson Jerome $16.95
Travel Writer's Handbook, by Louise Zobel (paper) $9.95
TV Scriptwriter's Handbook, by Alfred Brenner (paper) $9.95
Writing for Children & Teenagers, by Lee Wyndham (paper) $9.95

The Writing Business

Complete Guide to Self-Publishing, by Tom & Marilyn Ross $19.95
Editing for Print, by Geoffrey Rogers $14.95
How to Bulletproof Your Manuscript, by Bruce Henderson $9.95
How to Get Your Book Published, by Herbert W. Bell $15.95
How to Understand and Negotiate a Book Contract or Magazine Agreement, by Richard Balkin $11.95
Literary Agents: How to Get & Work with the Right One for You, by Michael Larsen $9.95
Professional Etiquette for Writers, by William Brohaugh $9.95

To order directly from the publisher, include $2.00 postage and handling for 1 book and 50¢ for each additional book. Allow 30 days for delivery.

Writer's Digest Books, Dept. B, 9933 Alliance Rd., Cincinnati OH 45242

Prices subject to change without notice.

Please Note:

The Artist's Market welcomes new listings. If you are a user of freelance design and illustration and would like to be considered for a listing in the next edition, contact the editor by March 1, 1987.
The *Artist's Market* also welcomes submissions of artwork for possible inclusion in the next edition. The policy for submissions is as follows:
(1) artwork must be submitted by a freelance artist or a market who uses freelance work;
(2) the artwork must have been published by one of the markets listed in the book.
If you have material to submit which fits these guidelines, send it to: Editor, Artist's Market, 9933 Alliance Rd., Cincinnati, OH 45242.

1987 Close-ups
Artist: Lee Hammond

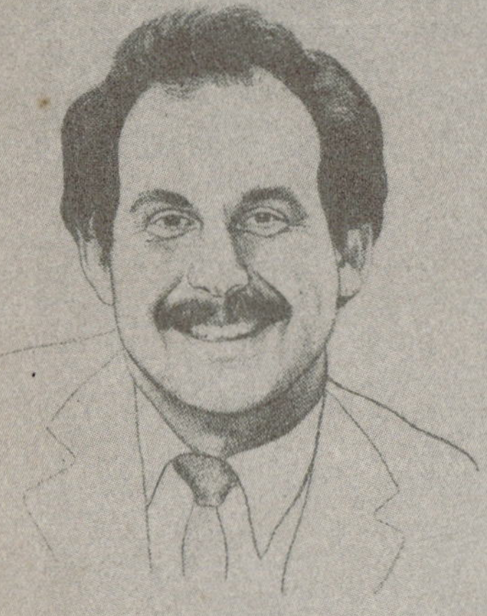

Jeff Berman
Art Designer
Page 129

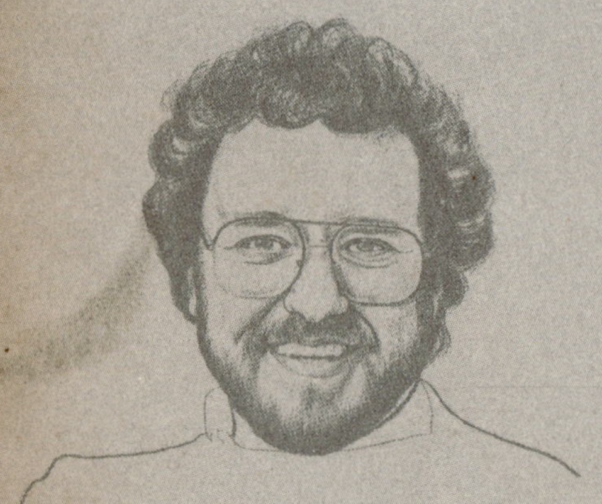

Jim Borgman
Editorial Cartoonist
Page 470

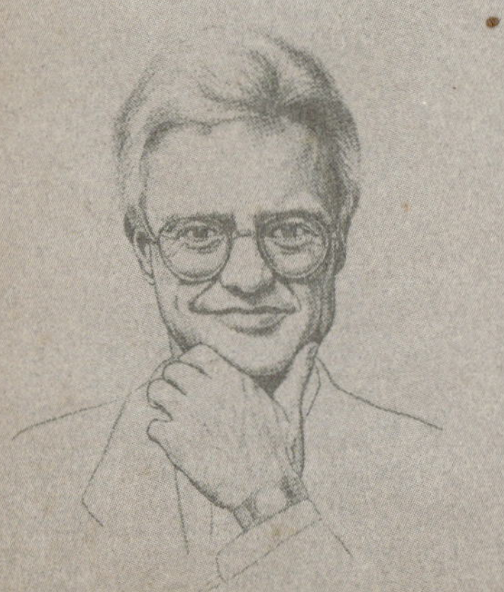

Martin Pedersen
Art Director/Designer
Page 148